Third Edition

UNDERSTANDING HUMAN DEVELOPMENT

Wendy L. Dunn
Coe College

Grace J. Craig
University of Massachusetts

PEARSON

Boston Columbus Indianapolis New York San Francisco Upper Saddle River
Amsterdam Cape Town Dubai London Madrid Milan Munich Paris Montréal Toronto
Delhi Mexico City São Paulo Sydney Hong Kong Seoul Singapore Taipei Tokyo

Editorial Director: *Craig Campanella*
Editor in Chief: *Jessica Mosher*
Executive Editor: *Erin Mitchell*
Senior Sponsoring Editor: *Amber Mackey*
Project Manager, Editorial: *Crystal McCarthy*
Director of Marketing: *Brandy Dawson*
Executive Marketing Manager: *Wendy Albert*
Managing Editor: *Denise Forlow*
Project Manager, Production: *Sherry Lewis*
Senior Operations Supervisor: *Diane Peirano*
Senior Operations Manager: *Mary Fischer*
Art Director: *Leslie Osher*
Text and Cover Designer: *Carmen DiBartolomeo, Red Kite Project*
Cover Photos: *(by order of appearance): Lisa F. Young/Fotolia, Pressmaster/Fotolia, Imagesource/GlowImages, Natalki/Fotolia, Corbis RF/GlowImages, Blend RF/GlowImages, Rubberball/GlowImages, Moodboard Premium/GlowImages, Darren Brode/Shutterstock.*
Senior Digital Media Editor: *Peter Sabatini*
Digital Media Editor: *Amy Trudell*
Media Project Manager: *Caitlin Smith*
Full-Service Project Management/Composition: *Cindy Sweeney, S4Carlisle Publishing Services*
Printer/Binder: *R.R. Donnelley, Willard*
Cover Printer: *Lehigh-Phoenix Color*
Text Font: *10/12 Palatino LT Std*

Credits and acknowledgments borrowed from other sources and reproduced, with permission, in this textbook appear on appropriate page within text (or on page 581).

Library of Congress Cataloging-in-Publication Data
Dunn, Wendy L.
Understanding human development / Wendy L. Dunn, Grace J. Craig. — 3rd ed.
p. cm.
Includes bibliographical references and index.
ISBN-13: 978-0-205-23365-6
ISBN-10: 0-205-23365-1
1. Developmental psychology. I. Dunn, Wendy. II. Title.
BF713.C714 2013
155—dc23

2012030939

10 9 8 7 6 5 4 3 2 1

PEARSON

Student Edition	ISBN 13:	978-0-205-23365-6
	ISBN 10:	0-205-23365-1
Books à la Carte	ISBN 13:	978-0-205-23387-8
	ISBN 10:	0-205-23387-2

BRIEF CONTENTS

PREFACE x

1 **INTRODUCTION TO HUMAN DEVELOPMENT** 1

2 **HEREDITY AND ENVIRONMENT** 34

3 **PRENATAL DEVELOPMENT AND CHILDBIRTH** 65

4 **INFANCY AND TODDLERHOOD: PHYSICAL, COGNITIVE, AND LANGUAGE DEVELOPMENT** 98

5 **INFANCY AND TODDLERHOOD: PERSONALITY AND SOCIOCULTURAL DEVELOPMENT** 130

6 **EARLY CHILDHOOD: PHYSICAL, COGNITIVE, AND LANGUAGE DEVELOPMENT** 157

7 **EARLY CHILDHOOD: PERSONALITY AND SOCIOCULTURAL DEVELOPMENT** 184

8 **MIDDLE CHILDHOOD: PHYSICAL AND COGNITIVE DEVELOPMENT** 218

9 **MIDDLE CHILDHOOD: PERSONALITY AND SOCIOCULTURAL DEVELOPMENT** 250

10 **ADOLESCENCE AND EMERGING ADULTHOOD: PHYSICAL AND COGNITIVE DEVELOPMENT** 274

11 **ADOLESCENCE AND EMERGING ADULTHOOD: PERSONALITY AND SOCIOCULTURAL DEVELOPMENT** 302

12 **YOUNG ADULTHOOD: PHYSICAL AND COGNITIVE DEVELOPMENT** 332

13 **YOUNG ADULTHOOD: PERSONALITY AND SOCIOCULTURAL DEVELOPMENT** 360

14 **MIDDLE ADULTHOOD: PHYSICAL AND COGNITIVE DEVELOPMENT** 391

15 **MIDDLE ADULTHOOD: PERSONALITY AND SOCIOCULTURAL DEVELOPMENT** 415

16 **OLDER ADULTHOOD: PHYSICAL AND COGNITIVE DEVELOPMENT** 441

17 **OLDER ADULTHOOD: PERSONALITY AND SOCIOCULTURAL DEVELOPMENT** 471

18 **DEATH AND DYING** 495

ANSWERS TO REVIEW THE FACTS 518 ■ *REFERENCES* 522 ■ *PHOTO CREDITS* 581 ■
NAME INDEX 582 ■ *SUBJECT INDEX* 599

CONTENTS

PREFACE x

CHAPTER 1 **INTRODUCTION TO HUMAN DEVELOPMENT** 1

Introduction to Development 2
- Lifespan Development 2
- Guiding Themes in Human Development 4

The Nature of Human Development 4
- Biology and Environment 4
- The Sociocultural Context 5
- TRY THIS! Exploring Attitudes About Child Rearing 6
- CHANGING PERSPECTIVES Children and War 7
- The Domains of Human Development 8

Theoretical Frameworks for Human Development 9
- The Role of Theory 9
- Biological Views of Human Development 10
- Psychodynamic Views of Human Development 11
- Behavioral Views of Human Development 13
- Cognitive Views of Human Development 16
- Integrating Theoretical Approaches 18

The Scientific Approach to the Study of Human Development 21
- Descriptive Methods 21
- Studying Development Across Time 23
- Correlation as a Descriptive Tool 24
- CURRENT ISSUES Fragile Families and Child Well-Being 25
- Experimental Approaches: The Study of Cause and Effect 26
- Summary of Research Methods 28
- Ethics in Developmental Research 29
- Development in Context 30

CHAPTER SUMMARY 31 ■ KEY TERMS 33

CHAPTER 2 **HEREDITY AND ENVIRONMENT** 34

Molecular Genetics 35
- Human Cells 35
- DNA 35
- Genes 38
- Protein Synthesis 38

Chromosomes, Genes, and Cell Division 39
- Cell Division and Reproduction 39
- From Genotype to Phenotype 40
- The Variation of Traits Among Individuals 41
- Gene–Environment Interactions: The Study of Epigenetics 43

Genetic Disorders 44
- Sex-Linked Disorders 44
- Autosomal Disorders 45
- Mitochondrial Disorders 47
- Genetic Counseling 48
- TRY THIS! Ethical Dilemmas in Gene Testing 49
- Advances in Genetic Research and Treatment 50

Behavior Genetics 50
- Twin and Adoption Studies 51
- CHANGING PERSPECTIVES Genetic Engineering and Cloning 52

Environmental Influences and Contexts 53
- Basic Processes That Affect Behavior 54
- Applied Behavior Analysis 55
- Social Learning and the Evolving Self-Concept 56

Environment in a Broader Context: Family and Culture 56
- Family Systems 56
- The Family as Transmitter of Culture 57
- CURRENT ISSUES The New Baby and the Extended Family System 58
- Sociocultural Influences on Development Across the Lifespan 58

CHAPTER SUMMARY 61 ■ KEY TERMS 64

CHAPTER 3 **PRENATAL DEVELOPMENT AND CHILDBIRTH** 65

Prenatal Growth and Development 66
- Trimesters and Periods 66
- Conception and the Germinal Period 66
- The Embryonic Period 68
- The Fetal Period 69
- Developmental Trends 71

Prenatal Environmental Influences 72
- Maternal Age 73
- Maternal Health and Nutrition 73
- Prenatal Health Care 74
- Critical Periods in Prenatal Development 74
- Teratogens and Their Effects 75

Childbirth 81
- Stages of Childbirth 81
- Approaches to Childbirth 82
- CHANGING PERSPECTIVES Nurse–Family Partnerships: An Early Intervention Program That Works 83
- Advances in Technology 84
- TRY THIS! Birthing Practices: Yesterday and Today 85
- Complications in Childbirth 87

The Evolving Family 89
- The Transition to Parenthood 89
- CURRENT ISSUES Kangaroo Care for Low-Birth-Weight Infants: An Experimental Approach Being Tried in Countries Around the World 90
- Pregnancy in a Changing World 91
- The Arrival of the Neonate 92

CHAPTER SUMMARY 95 ■ KEY TERMS 97

CHAPTER 4 **INFANCY AND TODDLERHOOD:** Physical, Cognitive, and Language Development 98

The Developing Brain 99
The Neonatal Period 100
States of Arousal 101
Learning and Habituation 101
Neonatal Assessment 102
Physical and Motor Development 103
Cultural Influences on Maturation 103
An Overview of Physical and Motor Development: The First 2 Years 104
CHANGING PERSPECTIVES Sudden Infant Death Syndrome and Shaken Baby Syndrome 106
Nutrition and Malnutrition 107
TRY THIS! Attitudes About Breastfeeding 111
Sensory and Perceptual Development 112
Vision and Visual Perception 112
Hearing and Auditory Perception 115
Taste, Smell, and Touch 115
Sensory Integration 116
Cognitive Development 116
Perceptual Organization and Categories 117
Piaget's Concept of Schemes 117
The Sensorimotor Period 117
Evaluating Piaget's View 120
Language Development 121
The Structure and Function of Language 121
Language Development in the First Year 121
Words and Sentences 123
The Language Explosion 123
Telegraphic Speech and Early Grammar 124
Theories of Language Development 124
CURRENT ISSUES Cats, Horses, and Tight Fits—Is Language Involved in Category Formation? 126
Cultural Aspects of Language Development 126
CHAPTER SUMMARY 127 ■ KEY TERMS 129

CHAPTER 5 **INFANCY AND TODDLERHOOD:** Personality and Sociocultural Development 130

The Foundations of Personality and Social Development 131
Emotional Development 131
Temperament 133
The Development of Trust 134
Feeding and Comforting 134
Cross-Cultural Comparisons on the Development of Trust 135
Attachment 136
Studying Infant and Toddler Attachment 136
TRY THIS! Replicating the Strange Situation 137
The Effects of Attachment 137
Explaining Attachment 138
The Relationship Between Attachment and Trust 140
The Role of Culture in Attachment 140
Separating from the Caregiver 141
Social Referencing and Culture 141
The Development of Autonomy 142
The Development of Prosocial Behavior 143
The Development of the Self 143
Attachment and Separation 144
The Family System: A Broader Context 145
Fathers 145
CHANGING PERSPECTIVES Fatherhood in the Changing American Family—What Matters? 146
Other Family Members as Caregivers 147
The Social Ecology of Child Care 148
CURRENT ISSUES Infant and Toddler Child Care 149
Infants and Toddlers with Special Needs 151
Infants and Toddlers with Visual Impairments 151
Infants and Toddlers with Hearing Impairments 152
Infants and Toddlers with Severe Disabilities 152
Infants and Toddlers Who Suffer from Abuse or Neglect 152
CHAPTER SUMMARY 154 ■ KEY TERMS 156

CHAPTER 6 **EARLY CHILDHOOD:** Physical, Cognitive, and Language Development 157

Physical Development 158
Changes in the Body 158
Brain Development 159
Human Development: An Interactive and Individual Approach 161
Motor Skills Development 161
Gross Motor Skills 161
Fine Motor Skills 162
Learning and Motor Skills 163
Cognitive Development 164
An Overview of Preoperational Thinking 164
Preoperational Substages and Thought 165
CURRENT ISSUES A Theory of Mind 166
Limitations of Preoperational Thinking 167
Conservation 168
Evaluating Piaget's Theory 169
Beyond Piaget: Social Perspectives 170
The Role of Memory 171
Language Development 173
Words and Concepts 173

Expanding Grammar 173
Mastering the Subtleties of Speech 174
The Influence of Parents' Language Use 175
Multicultural Aspects of Language Development 176

Play and Learning 177
Play and Cognitive Development 177
CHANGING PERSPECTIVES Bilingual Kindergarten and Play 179
TRY THIS! Watching Young Children Play 180

CHAPTER SUMMARY 181 ■ KEY TERMS 183

CHAPTER 7 **EARLY CHILDHOOD:** Personality and Sociocultural Development 184

Coping with Feelings and Emotions 186
Fear and Anxiety 186
Emotional Regulation 188
Shame and Guilt 189

Aggression and Prosocial Behavior 191
Aggression 191
CHANGING PERSPECTIVES Electronic Media: Is It Changing the Way That Children Grow Up? 194
Prosocial Behavior 194
TRY THIS! A Child's Choice in Media Programming 196

Developmental Conflicts 196
Initiative Versus Guilt 197

Peers, Play, and the Development of Social Competence 198
The Role of Imaginary Companions 198
Cultural Variations in Play 199
Social Competence and the Development of Social Skills 199
CURRENT ISSUES One Pathway to Social Competence 200

Understanding Self and Others 201
Social Concepts and Rules 201
Self-Concept 202
Self and Gender 203

Family Dynamics 205
Parenting Styles 205
Discipline and Self-Control 208
Sibling Dynamics 209
Child Maltreatment: Abuse and Neglect 210

CHAPTER SUMMARY 214 ■ KEY TERMS 217

CHAPTER 8 **MIDDLE CHILDHOOD:** Physical and Cognitive Development 218

Physical and Motor Development 219
Physical Growth and Change 219
Motor Skills Development 220
Brain Development 220
Health 222
CURRENT ISSUES Obesity in Childhood—An Outcome of Our Changing Lifestyle? 226

Cognitive Development 227
Piaget and Concrete Operational Thinking 227
Memory and Metacognition 229
Language and Literacy Development 230
Individual Differences in Intelligence 231
TRY THIS! Exploring Your Concept of Intelligence 235

Learning and Thinking in School 236
New Demands and Expectations 236
Developing Competent Learners and Critical Thinkers 237
Success in School 237

Intellectual and Developmental Disabilities 240
Intellectual Disabilities 240
Learning Disorders 242
CHANGING PERSPECTIVES Early Experience—Do Adverse Environments Cause Permanent Effects? 243
Attention Deficit Hyperactivity Disorder 244
Autism and Autism Spectrum Disorders 245

CHAPTER SUMMARY 247 ■ KEY TERMS 249

CHAPTER 9 **MIDDLE CHILDHOOD:** Personality and Sociocultural Development 250

Personality Development in an Expanding Social World 251
Three Perspectives on Middle Childhood 251
Self-Concept 252
Industry Versus Inferiority 252
Self-Esteem 252

Social Knowledge and Reasoning 253
The Development of Social Cognition 253
The Development of Morality 254

Peer Relationships 257
Functions of Friendship 257
Developmental Patterns in Friendship 257
Peer Groups 259
CURRENT ISSUES Friends and Enemies, Bullies and Victims—The Social Life of School 260
In-Groups, Out-Groups, and Prejudice 262

Family Influences in Middle Childhood 264
Parent–Child Interactions and Relationships 265
The Changing Nature of the Family 266
CHANGING PERSPECTIVES Families Coping in Difficult Circumstances 269
TRY THIS! The Impact of Divorce on Children 270

CHAPTER SUMMARY 271 ■ KEY TERMS 273

CHAPTER 10 ADOLESCENCE AND EMERGING ADULTHOOD: Physical and Cognitive Development 274

Adolescent Development in a Cultural and Historical Context 275
Adolescence and Emerging Adulthood in the United States Today 276
Physical Development and Adaptation 278
Physical Growth and Change 278
Puberty 279
Body Image and Adjustment 281
CURRENT ISSUES Diet and Exercise—Building a Healthy Lifestyle or an Eating Disorder? 282
Gender Identity and Sexual Practices 284
Six Decades of Changes in Sexual Practices 285
Factors That Influence Early Sexual Relationships 286
Consequences of Adolescent Sexual Behavior 286
Cognitive Changes in Adolescence 290
Brain Development in Adolescence 290
TRY THIS! Exploring the Effects of Early Parenting 291
Piaget's Period of Formal Operations 292
The Scope and Content of Adolescent Thought 294
CHANGING PERSPECTIVES How Adolescents Around the World Spend Their Time 295

CHAPTER SUMMARY 298 ■ KEY TERMS 301

CHAPTER 11 ADOLESCENCE AND EMERGING ADULTHOOD: Personality and Sociocultural Development 302

Developmental Tasks of Adolescence 304
Achieving Autonomy 304
Forming an Identity 305
Identity Formation, Culture, and Context 307
CURRENT ISSUES Ethnic Identity—A Key Component of Self-Definition 308
"Generation Me" 309
Family Dynamics 310
Intergenerational Communication 310
CHANGING PERSPECTIVES Family Obligation and Assistance During Adolescence 312
Peer Relationships During Adolescence 313
Social Comparison 313
Cliques and Crowds 315
Dating 316
Peers and Parents: A Clash of Cultures 317
Risk and Resilience in Adolescence 318
Risk Taking 318
The Use of Tobacco, Alcohol, Marijuana, and Other Drugs 318
Delinquency 322
Sexual Abuse of Adolescents 322
Stress, Depression, and Coping 323
Depression 324
Risk Factors for Psychological Problems 326
Protective Factors and Coping Responses 326
TRY THIS! Taking a Look at Adolescent Depression 327

CHAPTER SUMMARY 329 ■ KEY TERMS 331

CHAPTER 12 YOUNG ADULTHOOD: Physical and Cognitive Development 332

Perspectives on Adult Development 334
Age Clocks and Social Norms 334
Contextual Paradigms 335
General Physical Development 335
Strength and Stamina 335
CHANGING PERSPECTIVES History, Culture, and the Information Age 336
Fitness and Health 337
CURRENT ISSUES The Changing Face of HIV/AIDS 340
Sex and Sexuality 342
Fertility 342
Sexually Transmitted Diseases 342
Sexual Attitudes and Behavior 343
Sexual Identity and Sexual Orientation 344
Cognitive Development in Adulthood 348
Beyond Formal Operations 348
Postformal Thought 349
Emotional Intelligence 349
TRY THIS! Exploring Postformal Thought 350
Schaie's Stages of Adult Thinking 351
Frameworks for Understanding Adult Development 352
Stages and Contexts 352
Havighurst's Developmental Tasks 352
Erikson's Theory of Development 353
Levinson's Seasons of a Man's Life 353
The Limitations of Normative Models 354
Gould's Transformations in Early Adulthood 355
A Closing Comment 356

CHAPTER SUMMARY 357 ■ KEY TERMS 359

CHAPTER 13 YOUNG ADULTHOOD: Personality and Sociocultural Development 360

Self, Family, and Work 361
The Personal Self 361
Self as Family Member 363
Self as Worker 364

Forming Close Relationships 365
Adult Friendships 365
Couple Formation and Development 365
Marriage 368
Cohabitation 370
Gay and Lesbian Couples 370
Staying Single 371
CHANGING PERSPECTIVES Living Together or Living Alone 372

The Family Life Cycle and Adult Development 373
The Family Life Cycle 373
The Transition to Parenthood 373
Coping with Children's Developmental Stages 374
Single Parenthood 375

The Occupational Cycle 377
Stages of Occupational Life 377
Gaining a Place in the Workforce 378
Careers and Career Choices 379
Occupational Choice and Preparation 380

Work and Gender 381
Changes in Women's Work Patterns 381
The Many Meanings of Work 383
The Role of Women in Careers 383
The Dynamics of Dual-Earner Couples 383
TRY THIS! Exploring the Type of Career Best Matched to You 384
CURRENT ISSUES Juggling Work and Family Roles—The Special Challenge for Low-Income Dual-Career Couples 386

CHAPTER SUMMARY 388 ■ KEY TERMS 390

CHAPTER **14** **MIDDLE ADULTHOOD:** Physical and Cognitive Development 391

Development in Middle Adulthood 392
Prime Time or the Beginning of the End? 392
Midlife Crisis: Is It Real? 393
Perceptions and Realities at Midlife 394
TRY THIS! Just What *Is* Middle Age? 395

Physical Continuity and Change 395
Changes in Capabilities 396
The Climacteric 397
Sexuality in the Middle Years 400

Disease and Health 402
The Cumulative Effects of Health Habits 403
Stress and Health 405
Ethnicity, Poverty, and Health 406
CURRENT ISSUES Health and Social Issues—Why Are Some Groups at Risk? 407

Cognitive Continuity and Change 408
Fluid Versus Crystallized Intelligence 408
Experience and Expertise 410
Cognitive Skills in the Workplace 410
CHANGING PERSPECTIVES Retraining for Today's Technological Jobs 411

CHAPTER SUMMARY 412 ■ KEY TERMS 414

CHAPTER **15** **MIDDLE ADULTHOOD:** Personality and Sociocultural Development 415

Personality Continuity and Change 417
The Tasks of Middle Adulthood 417
Personal Reactions to Middle Adulthood 418

Family and Friends: Interpersonal Contexts 420
The Generation That Runs Things 420
Relationships with Adult Children 420
CURRENT ISSUES Studying Generativity in African-American and White U.S. Families 421
Relationships with Aging Parents 423
Becoming a Grandparent 425
Friendship: A Lifelong Perspective 426
TRY THIS! What Makes a Great Grandparent? 427

The Changing Family 427
Marriage, Divorce, and Remarriage 428
Blended Families 431
CHANGING PERSPECTIVES Blended Families—Themes and Variations 432

Occupational Continuity and Change 433
Job Change and Stress 434

Continuity and Change in the Structure of Personality 436
The Five-Factor Model 436
Stability or Change? 437

CHAPTER SUMMARY 438 ■ KEY TERMS 440

CHAPTER **16** **OLDER ADULTHOOD:** Physical and Cognitive Development 441

Aging Today 442
Ageism and Stereotypes 442
Four Decades of Later Life 445

The Physical Aspects of Aging 447
The Changing Body 448
Health, Disease, and Nutrition 452
CHANGING PERSPECTIVES Diabetes—Will Type 2 Diabetes Be the New Lifestyle Disease Epidemic? 454

The Causes of Aging 456
Theories of Aging 456

Cognitive Changes in Advanced Age 458
Understanding Various Aspects of Cognition 458
Cognitive Decline 462
CURRENT ISSUES Wisdom—Cross-Cultural or Culture Specific? 463

TRY THIS! Exploring Alzheimer's Disease 467
Compensating for an Aging Mind 467

CHAPTER SUMMARY 468 ■ KEY TERMS 470

CHAPTER 17 **OLDER ADULTHOOD:** Personality and Sociocultural Development 471

Personality and Aging 472
Developmental Tasks in Older Adulthood 472
Emotional Development in Older Adulthood 474
Continuity and Change in Older Adulthood 474
CURRENT ISSUES Psychological Well-Being in Later Adulthood 476
Successful Aging 477

Retirement: A Major Change in Status 478
Adjusting to Retirement 479
Retirement Options 480

Family and Friends: Interpersonal Contexts 482
When Parenting Is Over 482
Caring for an Ill Spouse 483
Widows and Widowers 483
TRY THIS! Exploring the Dimensions of Grandparenting 484

U.S. Social Policy and Older Adulthood 487
The Demographics of Aging 487
Lifestyle Options for Older Adults 489
Goals for the Care of Older Adults 490
CHANGING PERSPECTIVES Assisted Living—The In-Between Choice for Frail, Older Adults 491

CHAPTER SUMMARY 492 ■ KEY TERMS 494

CHAPTER 18 **DEATH AND DYING** 495

Thoughts and Fears of Death 496
Denial of Death 496
Reactions to Death 497
Managing the Anxiety Associated with One's Own Death 497
CURRENT ISSUES Searching for Meaning in Natural Disasters, Accidents, Terrorism, and Personal Tragedies 499

Confronting One's Own Death 499
Death as the Final Developmental Task 500
Stages of Adjustment 500
Coping with Terminal Illness 500
Alternative Trajectories 501

The Search for a Humane Death 503
Hospice 504
TRY THIS! Exploring the Dimensions of Hospice Care 505
The Right to Die 505

Grief and Bereavement 508
Grieving 509
Bereavement in Cross-Cultural Perspective 511
Rituals and Customs 511
The Death of a Child 512
CHANGING PERSPECTIVES Humane End-of-Life Care for Children Who Are Dying and for Their Families 513
Grieving When a Child Dies 513

Completing the Life Cycle 514

CHAPTER SUMMARY 515 ■ KEY TERMS 517

ANSWERS TO REVIEW THE FACTS 518 ■ *REFERENCES* 522 ■ *PHOTO CREDITS* 581 ■ *NAME INDEX* 582 ■ *SUBJECT INDEX* 599

PREFACE

Understanding Human Development, Third Edition, represents our belief that the story of each human life is a rich and compelling drama—one that deserves to be appreciated and understood. Our overarching goal in writing this book is to provide readers with a balance view for understanding human development as it unfolds across the lifespan a view that emphasizes the intricate, dynamic interactions among biological, psychological, and sociocultural forces. Indeed, we believe that a modern understanding of developmental processes must consider the biological and psychological changes that occur at various points in the lifespan, and must do so within relevant social and cultural contexts. Clearly, to ignore the important influences of family, society, and culture would leave us with explanations that not only are incomplete, but are flat and empty as well.

Reflecting the fact that developmental processes result from multiple interactions of many relevant variables across time, it is perhaps not surprising that our knowledge about human developmental processes and events has accumulated from a variety of perspectives. This book draws from many fields (psychology, biology, neuroscience, sociology, anthropology, history, nursing, medicine, and public health, to name a few) to provide an up-to-date presentation of key topics, issues, and controversies in the field of lifespan development. It has been our goal to prepare a text that reflects this comprehensive view of development across the lifespan.

We, of course, recognize that college students today are a diverse group—varying widely in age, ethnicity, personal experiences, and outlook, and in academic background and personal and career interests as well. Many students of human development will pursue a future in fields related to human services, including social work, education, nursing, counseling, various areas of psychology, and program administration. Some are already parents, and many will become parents in the near future; all have been children. Thus, although each student who reads this book has followed and will follow a unique developmental trajectory, all students have considerable firsthand experience with human development; each has been "doing" it for a number of years.

Because the study of human development is such a diverse enterprise, each of us "knows" the subject matter of human development from our own experience-based point of view. Thus, students come to their studies enriched by, but also embedded in, their attitudes, beliefs, biases, hopes, talents, language patterns, traumas, and more. We hope that as students study this book, they begin to not only see themselves more clearly but to see others in a wider context as well. We think that understanding development from a broader, more objective point of view is an important goal for students of human development.

We believe that most students have an irresistible curiosity about how humans "develop" and about how infancy, childhood, adolescence, and adulthood unfold, one into the other. This book encourages that curiosity through its emphasis on diversity. *Understanding Human Development* presents people as they are in the context of culture and subculture, both within the United States and beyond. The contemporary case studies and research efforts incorporated in the body of the text, as well as those highlighted in its special features, reflect this variety. It is our hope that every student will find himself or herself mirrored in the pages of this book, and that all will see the defining principles and ideas of human development as self-descriptive as well as pertaining to human nature in general.

Our approach incorporates applications and examples drawn from everyday life to illuminate the basic principles we describe. We encourage students to draw on their own experiences, and we hope students will weigh the evidence and ideas we present against these, and in the process, develop an informed, critical perspective on how we come to be who and what we are as human beings, on how our culture—broadly and narrowly defined—contributes to our development, and on what each of us can expect in our years to come.

—Wendy L. Dunn and Grace J. Craig

NEW TO THIS THIRD EDITION

The third edition of *Understanding Human Development* incorporates a substantive revision with a notable expansion and improvement in the quality of the learning and study tools that support the text:

- Expanded use of Learning Objectives, tied to Chapter Summary content and questions in the Test Item File
- Thorough integration of the newest research in developmental psychology, with over 80 to 90 new reference citations added per chapter to this edition
- Additional and up-to-date coverage of neurological development across the lifespan

We have added significant new content to every chapter. Of particular note are those additions covered in the following chapter-by-chapter list.

CHAPTER 1: INTRODUCTION TO HUMAN DEVELOPMENT

- Increased coverage of the subject matter and emphases on the "lifespan" approach to studying human development, including specific attention to the basic principles guiding lifespan developmental theory
- Updated coverage on the impact of war on children
- Better clarification of the basic tenets of Piaget's theory
- Clearer explanation of why replication of research is important to the progress of science
- Updated coverage of the Fragile Families and Child Well-Being studies

CHAPTER 2: HEREDITY AND ENVIRONMENT

- Improved explanation of the structure of the DNA molecule
- Clearer description of protein synthesis as the mechanism by which DNA instructions are conveyed
- New section on gene–environment interactions
- Expanded coverage of mutations and their effects
- New section on epigenetics and the epigenome
- Updated and expanded treatment of chromosomal and genetic disorders
- New section on mitochondrial disorders
- Updated section on cloning
- Improved coverage of twin and adoption studies

CHAPTER 3: PRENATAL DEVELOPMENT AND CHILDBIRTH

- Updated information about conception
- Additional information about causes for the increasing incidence of multiple births in developed economies
- Updated coverage about spontaneous abortion (miscarriage)
- Updated information on infant mortality rates around the world
- New section explaining the various ways in which teratogens work
- Updated coverage on the AIDS epidemic
- Updated and reorganized coverage of effects of drugs on prenatal development
- New section on environmental pollutants and radiation as teratogens
- Updated coverage of fetal alcohol spectrum disorder
- Updated discussion about the use of episiotomy as a common medical practice
- Improved and expanded coverage of prenatal diagnostic tests, including the quad screen and gestational diabetes testing
- New discussion of the ethical and health issues associated with elective use of ultrasound during pregnancy
- Updated coverage of the high rate of cesarean section births in developed economies
- New section on assistive reproductive technologies (ARTs), including the use of fertility drugs, artificial insemination, surrogacy, surgery, and *in vitro* fertilization
- Discussion of the practices of co-sleeping and babywearing as means to encourage healthy infant–caregiver attachment early in life

CHAPTER 4: INFANCY AND TODDLERHOOD: Physical, Cognitive, and Language Development

- Increased coverage of brain development in infancy, including myelination
- Expanded discussion of cultural factors that affect motor development
- Updated and expanded treatment of sudden infant death syndrome and shaken baby syndrome
- Updated coverage of breastfeeding around the world
- New section on the mirror neuron system and its role in imitation and empathy
- Updated discussion of early facial perception and the "other-race" effect
- Expanded coverage of Piaget's view of the sensorimotor period of development
- New information on early language development

CHAPTER 5: INFANCY AND TODDLERHOOD: Personality and Sociocultural Development

- Increased attention to the development of basic emotions
- Expanded coverage of temperament, including a comparison of the Thomas and Chess's and Rothbart's views, and an increased emphasis on epigenetic processes in its development
- Expanded coverage of cultural factors that influence the development of trust
- Expanded discussion of John Bowlby's work in conceptualizing infant–caregiver attachment
- Reorganization of the material on attachment
- Expanded coverage on disorganized/disoriented attachment
- New discussion of the "rouge test" as a method for studying attachment
- Updated coverage about the role fathers play in early development
- Updated discussion of child-care options and their use in the United States
- Improved documentation throughout the sections on the development of children with disabilities
- Updated coverage of content related to child maltreatment at early ages

CHAPTER 6: EARLY CHILDHOOD: Physical, Cognitive, and Language Development

- Increased coverage and discussion of brain lateralization, including sex differences
- New coverage of the link between motor development and school achievement
- New and expanded coverage about theory-of-mind problems and cross-cultural issues in the development of theory of mind
- New coverage on the development of gesturing as related to language development

- Expanded coverage of bilingual language development
- Expanded coverage of dramatic play, including links between play and academic achievement and literacy

CHAPTER 7: EARLY CHILDHOOD: Personality and Sociocultural Development

- Greater emphasis on the links between development of cognition and the ability to manage emotions
- New section on individual differences in temperament as they relate to fearfulness and anxiety
- Expanded coverage of cross-cultural variations in the way children experience positive and negative emotions
- Increased coverage of the gene × environment link concerning parental discipline and childhood aggression
- New research on the impact of violent video games on children's aggressiveness
- Updated coverage of the development of the young child's understanding of gender
- Inclusion of new work on cross-cultural differences in the advantages afforded by different parenting styles
- New information about positive advantages to being a later-born child in a large family
- Updated statistics on child maltreatment
- Increased attention to the various demographic factors linked to abuse and neglect

CHAPTER 8: MIDDLE CHILDHOOD: Physical and Cognitive Development

- Updated and expanded coverage of brain development during middle childhood
- Expanded coverage of the role of physical activity in health and weight control
- Additional information about government programs addressing the obesity epidemic
- Expanded and updated coverage of obesity, including genetic and epigenetic mechanisms that may be involved
- Inclusion of material on cultural forces that are involved in intelligence
- Updated discussion of gender differences and school success
- Expanded coverage on intellectual disabilities
- Updated discussion of how extreme deprivation in early life carries through developmentally in growth and cognition
- Expanded coverage of attention deficit hyperactivity disorder (ADHD), including work to incorporate cognitive symptoms in the diagnostic criteria
- New section on autism and autism spectrum disorders (ASD)

CHAPTER 9: MIDDLE CHILDHOOD: Personality and Sociocultural Development

- Updated discussion of self-esteem and self-concept development
- Updated coverage of the development of moral reasoning
- Updated content on the development of friendships during middle childhood
- New research presented on bullying
- Expanded discussion of children's popularity and its influences on development
- Updated coverage of ethnic identity development
- Reorganized section on peer relationships
- Updated coverage of changes in family structure in the United States, including those reflecting the economic downturn
- Revised treatment of single parenting and its impact on child development
- New research presented on the impact of parental divorce on child development

CHAPTER 10: ADOLESCENCE AND EMERGING ADULTHOOD: Physical and Cognitive Development

- Expanded discussion of different stages within the period of adolescence and emerging adulthood
- Updated and enhanced coverage of research on brain development during adolescence
- Updated and increased attention to the problem of adolescent obesity and eating disorders
- Updated statistics on the sexual behavior of U.S. adolescents
- Updated information about risks associated with early sexual activity
- New information presented about the disadvantages of teenage parenting
- New section on decision making in adolescence, explaining the development of "cold" versus "hot" decision-making processes

CHAPTER 11: ADOLESCENCE AND EMERGING ADULTHOOD: Personality and Sociocultural Development

- Updated discussion of identity formation for members of racial/ethnic minority groups and same-sex gender orientation
- New section on how sociocultural forces shape the identity development of members of "Generation Me"
- New section on friendship formation in the age of social media use
- Updated sections on the use of alcohol, cigarettes, marijuana, and other illicit drugs by adolescents and emerging adults
- New section on risk behavior associated with driving while under the influence of alcohol

- Expanded discussion of the impact of rape on teenagers
- Increased attention to the emergence of mental illnesses during adolescence and emerging adulthood
- Updated and expanded coverage of teenage suicides, including links to same-sex gendered youth and bullying

CHAPTER 12: YOUNG ADULTHOOD: Physical and Cognitive Development

- Updated section on physical fitness in young adulthood
- Updated discussion of the AIDS epidemic, both in the United States and around the world
- Expanded coverage of sexually transmitted diseases
- New section on sexual attitudes and behaviors expressed and held by U.S. adults today
- Updated discussion about the causal factors involved in sexual orientation
- Inclusion of new research on the diversity of sexuality in the United States
- Updated discussion of emotional intelligence

CHAPTER 13: YOUNG ADULTHOOD: Personality and Sociocultural Development

- Inclusion of a new section on "flow" as a modern perspective on the self
- New section on different traditions of marriage, including arranged marriages
- New section on marriage trends in the United States
- Expanded discussion of marriage traditions in non-Western cultures
- Expanded and updated coverage of single parenting
- Expanded and updated section on working women in the United States
- Incorporation of how the recent economic downturn is impacting working men and women in the United States
- Several new figures and tables to help clarify recent trends in marriage and work in the United States

CHAPTER 14: MIDDLE ADULTHOOD: Physical and Cognitive Development

- New section on the stages of menopause and what happens in each stage
- Updated information on hormone replacement therapy, including new recommendations from the North American Menopause Society
- New section on physical and emotional satisfaction with sex among men and women across adulthood
- New section on sexual behaviors among men and women across adulthood
- Updated statistics on health risks common to people during middle adulthood
- Updated information on Phase II and Phase III of the MIDUS (Midlife in the United States) study
- Inclusion of new information about the Affordable Care Act of 2010
- Updated information about brain changes during middle adulthood and their link to cognitive changes during this period

CHAPTER 15: MIDDLE ADULTHOOD: Personality and Sociocultural Development

- New discussion of the "boomerang generation"—those who return home to live with parents
- Revised discussion of the "empty nest," which emphasizes current research on the positive outcomes of launching children
- Updated statistics on marriage, divorce, and blended families in the United States today
- Attention to the impact of the current economic recession on family and career adjustments in the United States
- New information on friendships among adults in midlife
- Increased and updated coverage of personality adjustment during middle adulthood

CHAPTER 16: OLDER ADULTHOOD: Physical and Cognitive Development

- New section on cosmetic approaches to looking younger, in response to negative stereotypes about aging and attractiveness
- Updated information about age-related declines in attention and reaction time, especially as linked to driving
- Updated statistics throughout
- New section on the rise of prescription drug usage and costs in older adulthood
- Inclusion of more information about biological clock theories of aging, including description of the Hayflick limit
- Updated information about typical and nontypical cognitive decline in older adulthood
- Added and updated information on Alzheimer's disease, its causes, and its treatments

CHAPTER 17: OLDER ADULTHOOD: Personality and Sociocultural Development

- Updated coverage of emotional development in older adulthood
- Updated discussion of personality stability versus continuity in older adulthood
- Expanded coverage of social comparison theory as a means of coping with aging
- New section on the stages of adapting to retirement, as proposed by Robert Atchley

- Attention to how current economic factors are influencing retirement decisions and adjustment to older adulthood
- Updated coverage of population changes, the "graying" of America, and how those will impact social programs such as Social Security and Medicare
- Updated discussion of living arrangement options for frail older adults

CHAPTER 18: DEATH AND DYING

- Updated coverage of terror management theory
- Inclusion of criticism of Kübler-Ross's stages of death and dying
- Enhanced coverage of alternative trajectories of death
- New section on the "Five Wishes" approach to exercising some control over the process of dying
- New section describing Schoebe and Schut's dual-process model of stress and coping
- Clarification of bereavement as a process
- Updated coverage on child deaths

SPECIAL LEARNER-CENTERED FEATURES include...

CHANGING PERSPECTIVES explores controversies about human development, often within a specific cultural context, that encourage thought and discussion.

CURRENT ISSUES emphasizes the "doing" of developmental research and provides an opportunity for students to conceptualize how research projects help us better understand the processes involved in human development.

TRY THIS! challenges students to personally explore fundamental developmental issues and cultural controversies present in any discussion of human development. The suggested activities extend students' thinking and expertise in the field of human development.

LEARNING OBJECTIVES presented at the beginning of each chapter pose overarching themes, stimulating interest in the main topics and serving as a preview of the upcoming chapter. Learning Objectives also, are linked to the content of the Chapter Summaries and to all questions in the test item file.

CRITICAL THINKING QUESTIONS are incorporated into the chapter content, encouraging readers to consider the relevance of developmental concepts and events in the context of their own lives.

WATCH ON MYDEVELOPMENTLAB icons flag content throughout the chapters to indicate topic-related videos that are available to students. These videos provide students with greater detail on compelling topics, such as adolescent cliques, body image and eating disorders, making a career choice, genetic counseling, and much more.

REVIEW THE FACTS study aids follow each major section of the chapter; each includes a variety of questions posed in different formats that test the student's recall of important ideas. Answers to the Review the Facts questions can be found at the end of the book. A Practice on MyDevelopmentLab icon at the end of each Review the Facts box reminds the student that more questions can be found there.

TEACHING AND LEARNING PACKAGE

Test Item File (ISBN: 0-205-23368-6)
The Test Item File, written by Wendy Dunn, supports the assessment of student learning from the text and includes over 100 multiple-choice items per chapter. About 40% of these items assess student mastery of factual content. The remainder of the multiple-choice questions—more than 60 items per chapter—consists of conceptual and applied items that measure student comprehension on an even deeper level. All multiple-choice items are accompanied by an answer key listing the correct response and text reference where answers can be found; additionally, for conceptual and applied items, an analysis of why the correct response is the best choice among the alternatives is presented. All questions also are keyed to Learning Objectives, so instructors can ensure content coverage when constructing examinations.

For each chapter, the Test Item File additionally includes a selection of true-false questions, with explanations of why false items are incorrect, and sets of short-answer and essay questions. Available for download from **www.pearsonhighered.com/irc**.

Pearson MyTest (ISBN: 0-205-23367-8)
MyTest is a powerful assessment-generation program that helps instructors easily create and print quizzes and exams. Questions and tests can be authored online, allowing instructors ultimate flexibility and the tools to efficiently manage assessments anytime, anywhere! Instructors can easily access existing questions and edit, create, and store them using simple drag-and-drop and Word-like controls. Descriptors for each question indicate difficulty level, learning objective notation, and textbook page number for reference. In addition, each question maps to the text's major section and learning domains. For more information, go to **www.PearsonMyTest.com**.

PowerPoint Slides (ISBN: 0-205-23371-6)
These slides bring the book's powerful design right into the classroom, drawing students into the lecture and providing wonderful interactive activities and visuals. The slides are built around the text organization and offer multiple pathways or links between content areas. Available for download from **www.pearsonhighered.com/irc**.

Classroom Response System (CRS) PowerPoint Slides (ISBN: 0-205-23903-X)
These class lecture and discussion slides incorporate CRS "clicker" questions that process student responses and interpret them instantly. The slides are available for download at **www.pearsonhighered.com**.

Instructor's Resource Manual (ISBN: 020523366X)
This manual, compiled by Jayne Rose, offers an extensive collection of resources. Instructors will find activities, exercises, assignments, handouts, and demonstrations for in-class use. In addition, it includes guidelines on integrating the many Pearson media resources into the classroom and syllabus. This manual saves prep time and helps instructors maximize classroom time. Available for download from **www.pearsonhighered.com/irc**.

NEW to MyDevelopmentLab

MyDevelopmentLab delivers proven results in helping individual students succeed. Its automatically graded assessments, personalized study plan, and interactive eText provide engaging experiences that personalize, stimulate, and measure learning for each student. And, it comes from a trusted partner with educational expertise and a deep commitment to helping students, instructors, and departments achieve their goals. For more information, visit www.MyDevelopmentLab.com. MyDevelopmentLab features:

MyDevelopmentLab Video Series: This series of videos engages students and brings to life a wide range of topics spanning prenatal through the end of the lifespan. New international videos shot on location allow students to observe similarities and differences in human development across various cultures.

MyVirtualLife: Raise your child. Live your life. MyVirtualLife is two simulations in one. The first simulation allows students to raise a child from birth to age 18 and monitor the effects of their parenting decisions over time. In the second simulation, students make first-person decisions and see the impact of those decisions on their simulated future self over time. By incorporating physical, social, emotional, and cognitive development throughout the entire lifespan, MyVirtualLife helps students think critically as they apply their coursework to their own virtual lives.

ACKNOWLEDGMENTS

Understanding Human Development reflects the contributions of many individuals, although ultimately the responsibility for the content of the book rests with the authors. Foremost among the people we wish to acknowledge are the teachers, mentors, and colleagues who have encouraged and inspired us in our own study. We also wish to recognize the significance of the contributions of people of all ages we have learned from, including especially our students and research assistants, but also people with whom we have interacted across a wide variety of circumstances. We are grateful for the support of family and friends as well, and we wish to note that our closest personal relationships have perhaps taught us the most about the nuances and complexity of human development. Combined, the experiences, ideas, and insights of many people are reflected in this text.

Specifically, we would like to thank the professionals who contributed directly to the preparation and production of the third edition of this book. We owe considerable gratitude to the many instructors who generously agreed to review this text and make suggestions for improvements: Brady Phelps, *South Dakota State University*; Lauren Polvere, *Cazenovia College*; Amie Dunstan, *Lorain County Community College and Cuyahoga Community College*; Marvin Lee, *Tennessee State University*; Rob Weisskirch, *CSU Monterey Bay*; Bert Hayslip, *University of North Texas*; Sara Goldstein, *Montclair State University*; David Hurford *David Hurford*; Gaston Weisz, *Adelphi University*; Patricia Bellas, *Irvine Valley College*; Jennifer Vu, *University of Delaware*; Chelsea Hansen, *Midlands Technical College*; Jennifer Kampmann, *South Dakota State University*; Donna Mesler, *Seton Hall University*; Jyotsna Kalavar, *Penn State University*; Tresia Samani, *Rappahannock Community College*; Bette Beane, *UNCG/Randolph Community College*; Lisa Fozio-Thielk, *Waubonsee Community College*; Laura Pirazzi, *San Jose State University*; Wanda Clark, *South Plains College*; William Kimberlin, *Lorain County Community College*; Dianna Chiabotti, *Napa Valley College*; Erin Young, *Texas A&M University*; Sharon Carter, *Davidson County Community College*; Margaret Annunziata, *Davidson County Community College*; and Paul Kochmanski, *Erie Community College*. Along with the reviewers for the second edition, we owe many of the improvements in this edition to suggestions offered by these thoughtful and insightful people. We wish to thank all of these reviewers; we owe you a debt and want to recognize your efforts.

At Pearson, many, many people worked to bring the third edition of *Understanding Human Development* to life. These people are identified on the copyright page of the book; however several are deserving of special mention. Our sincere thanks and deep appreciation go to Jeff Marshall, Amber Mackey, and Erin Mitchell, who all played a role in planning the third edition and helped us bring it to fruition. Our editorial project manager, Crystal McCarthy, has been superb in providing us with the advice and assistance we needed to prepare this third edition. Although we have not collaborated directly with the design artists who developed the art plan for the book or with the production editors who made everything work, we are grateful to them for creating and producing an engaging, clear, and attractive layout and design for the third edition. Thanks also go to Cindy Sweeney at S4Carlisle Publishing Services, who translated our hand-written comments, arrows, instructions, and requests into the finished pages of this text. Lauren McFalls, also at S4Carlisle, worked tirelessly to find attractive images for the text and secure permissions so we could include the important work of others in this book. And finally, thanks to Rochelle Diogenes for suggesting our partnership on this book, which we believe has leveraged our specific skills, interests, and passions.

We also wish to thank other colleagues who helped us with various tasks. Most notably, thanks go to Dr. Jayne Rose at *Augustana College* in Illinois for her work in updating and expanding the content of the instructional materials that accompany the third edition of this text. We are grateful to Beth Valenta at *Coe College* for her assistance with the preparation of the manuscript. Finally, Wendy Dunn wishes to acknowledge the support of the ever-patient and always-encouraging Greg. He's the best.

Understanding Human Development

1

INTRODUCTION TO HUMAN DEVELOPMENT

LEARNING OBJECTIVES

- What is lifespan development and how universal are developmental periods, or stages?
- What guiding themes help us understand and organize our knowledge of human development?
- What does it mean to say that heredity and environment *interact* as they influence the course of development?
- How does a person's family and culture shape that person's developmental path?
- What kinds of changes occur within each of the major developmental domains: physical, cognitive, personality, and sociocultural?
- What contributions do theories of development make to our overall understanding of how human development unfolds?
- What important ideas are connected to each of the following theoretical perspectives: biological views, psychodynamic perspectives, behaviorism, cognitive-developmental theories, and systems approaches?
- Why is the study of human development considered from a scientific perspective?
- What types of research approaches do developmentalists commonly use in their study of human development?
- What ethical challenges do developmental researchers encounter as they attempt to understand the processes that guide human development?

CHAPTER OUTLINE

Introduction to Development
- Lifespan Development
- Guiding Themes in Human Development

The Nature of Human Development
- Biology and Environment
- The Sociocultural Context
- The Domains of Human Development

Theoretical Frameworks for Human Development
- The Role of Theory
- Biological Views of Human Development
- Psychodynamic Views of Human Development
- Behavioral Views of Human Development
- Cognitive Views of Human Development
- Integrating Theoretical Approaches

The Scientific Approach to the Study of Human Development
- Descriptive Methods
- Studying Development Across Time
- Correlation as a Descriptive Tool
- Experimental Approaches: The Study of Cause and Effect
- Summary of Research Methods
- Ethics in Developmental Research
- Development in Context

INTRODUCTION TO DEVELOPMENT

Complex and rich, full of quest and challenge, a human life is the product of many strands. Consider for a moment the person *you* are and the many influences that have combined to shape your life thus far. The genes you inherited from your parents; your relationships with your family and your friends; and your personal experiences, ideas, and dreams have all played an important role in shaping your unique self. The changes that these combined forces have produced in you comprise human development, which is the topic we explore throughout this book.

Lifespan Development

A Chronological Approach From a psychological perspective, **development** refers to the changes over time in a person's physical structure, thought, and behavior due both to biology and to experience. Thus, the subject matter of human lifespan development encompasses a person's entire life and all of the events that shape its direction (Baltes, Lindenberger, & Staudinger, 2006; Overton, 2010).

Developmental psychologists are psychologists whose primary interests center on understanding how development unfolds. Although as individuals we often focus on our uniqueness—what makes us different from other people—developmental psychologists generally focus their study on the common features that describe typical human development. Although there are exceptions, the broad and general changes that are associated with development typically occur in predictable patterns that are common to most individuals. For example, babies learn to sit up before they walk, children learn to talk before they read, and young adults tend to focus on different tasks and goals than do elderly adults.

To better understand the general patterns of developmental change, psychologists divide the lifespan into **developmental periods**, or **stages**, where each period corresponds to a segment of the lifespan during which predictable changes occur. Table 1-1 presents a common method of dividing the human lifespan into developmental periods. Although the developmental periods identified in Table 1-1 are typical for most people living in an industrialized society, there can be considerable variation in how individuals move through the periods in the lifespan. For example, children with mental disabilities or children with a background of physical or emotional

Do you think that the developmental periods that comprise typical lifespan development in the United States today will shift over the next few decades? Why or why not?

▼ Roby at age 7, in 1920, just after World War I.

▼ Roby in early adulthood, a stay-at-home mother, in 1947.

▲ Human development is the result of many intertwining, interacting forces, including those that reflect the cultural, historical, and social conditions within which each individual lives. Consider the world events that shaped the life of Roby Kesler, a friend of the second author.

development
The changes over time in the physical structure, thought, or behavior of a person as a result of both biological and environmental influences

developmental psychologists
Psychologists whose primary interests focus on the study of developmental processes and events

developmental period (or stage)
A discreet period of the lifespan during which predictable changes occur

Table 1-1 Developmental Periods in the Human Lifespan

Some developmental periods are defined primarily by biological events (e.g., the prenatal period), whereas others are defined more by societal expectations (e.g., adolescence).

Prenatal period:	Conception to birth
Infancy:	Birth to 12–15 months of age
Toddlerhood:	12–15 months to 2–3 years of age
Early childhood:	2–3 years to 5–6 years of age
Middle childhood:	5–6 years to approximately 12 years of age
Adolescence:	Approximately 12 years to 18–21 years of age
Young adulthood:	18–21 years to about 40 years of age
Middle adulthood:	About 40 years to about 60–65 years of age
Older adulthood:	About 60–65 years of age to death

abuse may be delayed in their development; therefore, they may move through these developmental periods at a slower pace than expected. Developmental periods also may be influenced by **culture**—the set of beliefs, values, and traditions shared by a particular group of people. For example, the transition from adolescence to adulthood varies considerably from culture to culture. Among some peoples of the world where lengthy educational opportunity is not available and economic life is demanding, adolescence may be a relatively short period, beginning at puberty and ending shortly thereafter when the person assumes full adult responsibilities. However, in the United States and in other economically developed societies, the period of adolescence is typically much longer. Some researchers are beginning to discuss the period between ages 18 and 25 as one of "emerging adulthood," noting that this period serves as a transition between adolescence and early adulthood (Arnett, 2009; Côté, 2006). Other developmental periods also can vary according to culture: In places where earning a livelihood is physically demanding and good nutrition and medical care are not readily available, older adulthood may begin as early as age 45. Despite the influence of particular circumstances on the pace at which a person proceeds through the developmental periods identified in Table 1-1, it is nonetheless the case that these periods typically are experienced by most people, and they are experienced in the order identified.

This division of the lifespan into developmental periods provides a good organizational framework to understand how human development unfolds. For this reason, we have adopted a **chronological**, or age-based, scheme as the basic organizing principle of this text. We will begin our study of developmental psychology with conception and proceed to explore, stage by stage, the sequence of developmental milestones associated with each subsequent period of development. Furthermore, each period of development is heavily dependent on the events that have come before; therefore, a chronological approach to the study of development provides the clearest map for understanding the changes in development that occur across the lifespan.

Can you think of an example of how physical development affects cognitive development or how cognitive development affects social development?

An Interactive Approach In order to understand human development during any period of the lifespan, consideration must be given to the significance of interacting events—biological and environmental, cultural and personal—because these are the factors that make each person's life unique and rich. Much of the exploration in this text centers on understanding the nature of these interacting forces and how they come together to shape each individual's development.

The text's focus on the interaction of developmental forces is reinforced by emphasizing an interdisciplinary perspective to examine developmental trends, principles, and processes. In upcoming chapters, you will learn about the biological, environmental, evolutionary, anthropological, sociological, and psychological forces that directly or indirectly influence the developing human organism. In particular, we give special attention to family ties and other important personal relationships because these relationships help define each person as an individual, and they serve as an important influence on a wide range of human behavior.

We also note that people are biological organisms. As such, all individuals inherit a set of unique genetic

▼ Roby, more than two decades later, reflecting the changes of the civil rights and women's movements.

▼ Roby in her 90s, at the beginning of the 21st century.

culture
The set of beliefs, values, and traditions shared by a particular group of people

chronological
Arranged according to age

Watch *The Features of Emerging Adulthood Across Cultures* on **MyDevelopmentLab** "instructions" that guides and shapes important aspects of how human development unfolds. However, development is not simply dictated by genes, and people do not simply react to changes in their environment; they interpret, think about, and react to the circumstances of their lives. Thus, it is important to recognize that people exist within a broader social culture, and the expectations of one's society can exert important influences in how human development proceeds.

In summary, this text examines the typical ways in which individuals change across the lifespan. Throughout, we emphasize the intricate *interaction*, or combination, of forces—both biological and environmental—that shapes each person's unique development. The text also emphasizes that human development is not simply a "program" that is set in place at birth and plays its way out as an individual moves through the lifespan. Rather, the development of an individual is best seen as a dynamic interplay of biological potentials, social and environmental forces, and the individual's own interpretation of and responses to these circumstances.

Guiding Themes in Human Development

The study of human development is fascinating; it is, after all, about *us*. However, it also is complex. Therefore, it is useful to lay out some general principles or *guiding themes* that can be used to organize the changes that are observed across the lifespan. Briefly stated, these general principles are:

- **Biological factors** and **environmental factors** influence the course of development throughout the lifespan, often through complex interactions.
- Development occurs within a **sociocultural context**. Influences from one's family, society, and culture shape each person's development and have important implications for understanding changes across the lifespan.
- For practical reasons, development is best understood by considering changes within particular *domains*, or categories, of human experience. Important domains to consider include physical growth and change, cognitive development, personality development, and sociocultural influences.
- Development is understood best when considered within a theoretical framework.
- Development is studied best by employing the methods of science.

The remainder of this chapter will explore more fully the implications of these five guiding principles.

REVIEW THE FACTS 1-1

1. To say that this text is arranged *chronologically* means that its arrangement is _________.
2. When we say that two events or forces *interact*, this means that they _________.
3. The two major forces that interact in human development are _________.
4. Influences from one's family, society, and culture are referred to as the _________.

Practice on MyDevelopmentLab

THE NATURE OF HUMAN DEVELOPMENT

Biology and Environment

Some developmental processes, such as growth during the prenatal period, the onset of puberty, and the arrival of gray hair, are primarily biological. Other aspects of development, such as learning calculus, navigating the Internet, or acquiring a taste for sushi, depend mainly on experience.

Most development throughout the lifespan, however, is a result of successive *interactions* between biology and experience. In general, it is not possible to categorize development as primarily biological or environmental; rather, it involves an ongoing, dynamic interplay between these two basic sets of causes. For example, every individual is born with a certain intellectual potential based on the specific nature of his or her central nervous system; that is, the biological makeup of a person's brain establishes a range within which that individual's intelligence will eventually fall. However, a person's intelligence also is a function of that person's childhood nutrition, home and school experiences, the values the person attaches to academic pursuits, and many additional environmental factors. As another example, perhaps a person was born with a certain personality tendency, such as shyness or extroversion. That person's present personality, however, is also a function of the person's lifelong interactions with other people, the sense of self that began to be acquired in infancy, the sociocultural context in which the person grew up, and much more. As you can see, both biological and environmental influences are involved in the process of human development.

The days are past when theorists argued over whether specific aspects of human development were *either* a function of biology *or* a function of experience, resulting from "nature" or "nurture," respectively. What theorists continue to debate (at

biological factors
Genetic, neurological, or physical conditions that affect the development of an individual

environmental factors
The specific situations that an individual experiences and that influence behavior and development

sociocultural context
A broad context that includes both social and cultural influences

times hotly) is *how much* and in *what way* a given characteristic or behavior is a result of biology or experience. Currently, several major research efforts are underway to enhance the understanding of the interactive nature of these two important determinants of development (Diamond, 2009; Kim-Cohen & Gold, 2009; Price & Jaffe, 2008; Rutter, 2008).

Maturation and Learning An issue related to the respective roles of biological and environmental influences involves the distinction between maturation and learning. **Maturation** is one term used when developmental changes are heavily influenced by biological processes. Therefore, we speak of the *maturing* nervous system or a more *mature* approach to problem solving as a means of noting the biological influence on these developmental processes. *Growth* and *aging* also are terms closely associated with biological changes over time.

On the other hand, the term **learning** infers that what is *learned* is the result of the person's interaction with the environment and is largely independent of biological influences. Thus, a child *learns* to ride a bike; however, the child's ability to achieve balance, which depends heavily on the development of physical strength and brain-based functions, is more a matter of *maturation.*

Distinctions between maturation and learning often are difficult because few, if any, developmental events are purely the result of either biology or environment. For example, menopause (the cessation of menstrual periods due to hormonal changes) in women is well understood to be a biologically influenced change. Yet recent research indicates that its timing and its symptoms may depend on life events as well, such as diet, obesity, and other aspects of lifestyle. To understand human development, it is important to focus on understanding the interactive nature of such forces and to consider how the individual responds to biological determinants and environmental opportunities throughout the lifespan (see Chapter 2).

The Sociocultural Context

Development is deeply embedded in **context**, the immediate and extended environmental settings in which it occurs. Sometimes context involves the role of the individual within the family, with the family being one of the most influential determinants of the path of developmental change. At other times the relevant context is broader, extending to the individual's society or even to the individual's culture. *Society* refers to the larger group of individuals within which an individual lives; *culture* refers not only to the people but also to the beliefs, the common practices, the language, and the norms associated with an individual's society. Society and culture are important determinants in human development, and they often are referred to collectively as the sociocultural context in which development unfolds (Cole, 2011).

▲ Learning continues throughout the lifespan, sometimes spurred on by the challenges of a changing historical context.

Historical Views of Childhood To understand the significance of the sociocultural context in human development, it is useful to consider how society and culture have influenced the definitions of developmental periods at various times. For example, conceptualizations of childhood and attitudes toward children have varied a great deal throughout history. Although relatively little is known about the attitudes of prehistoric civilizations toward children, the agriculture-based societies of today's Africa can provide some likely parallels. Such societies typically view children as coworkers and contributors (Georgas, Berry, van de Vijver, Kagitçibasi, & Poortinga, 2009; Kagitçibasi, 1996, 2007; Konner, 2010). Children are assigned household chores and errands at an early age, with their workload increasing as they grow older. As early as middle childhood, a substantial portion of a child's day is devoted to work, with children performing many of the same tasks as adults. Assuming that these present-day, agriculture-based African societies share important similarities with prehistoric

maturation
Developmental changes that are linked closely to biological processes

learning
Developmental changes that are dependent on a person's interactions with the environment

context
The particular setting or situation in which development occurs; the "backdrop" for development

TRY THIS!

Exploring Attitudes About Child Rearing

Even in a homogenous culture, there can be wide differences of opinion about child rearing. To explore some of these differences, identify a group of five or six people who you can interview individually for 10 minutes or more.

Once you have identified the people you will interview, construct a series of questions that you believe will demonstrate the differences in how they intend to raise, or are raising, their children. Some examples follow; however, you may wish to add to or replace some of these questions with questions of your own.

- What would you do if your 4-year-old son was masturbating in public?
- Do you think it is a good idea for babies to sleep in the same bed with their parents? If so, until what age?
- What would you do if you saw your 3-year-old child bite another child?
- What would you do if you caught your 6-year-old child shoplifting a candy bar from a convenience store?
- Would you ever spank your child? If yes, under what circumstances?
- What is the best advice you could give to the parents of a newborn?
- What would you do if the high school principal suspended your child for cheating on an important test?

Reflect on What You Observed

Did people give consistent or inconsistent responses to your questions? Were some questions more likely to elicit widely varying answers than others? Were you surprised by some of the answers you received? Do you think people responded honestly?

Consider the Issues

Do you think men and women might respond differently to these questions? To what extent do you think a person's own upbringing might influence his or her attitudes about child rearing? Were the people in your sample quite similar or different in background? How do you think your results might have differed if you had surveyed people of more widely varying backgrounds?

In paintings of the European nobility of the 16th, 17th, and even 18th centuries, children were regularly portrayed as miniature adults. It is hard to know if this was an art style or if it reflected the attitudes of the time.

SOURCE: Réunion des Musées Nationaux. Art Resource, NY.

societies, such a definition of childhood may have been common in early human cultures as well.

More is known about childhood in ancient Western civilizations, where children typically were viewed as material possessions and little more (de Mause, 1995; Fass, 2004). In parts of ancient Greece, strict obedience and harsh physical punishment were the norm; in ancient Rome, killing undesirable children or otherwise unwanted children, or selling them into servitude, was common. Parents were free to exploit their children in whatever ways they wished, child sexual abuse was rampant, and most children had no rights. Although child killing was finally outlawed in Christian Europe in the 12th century AD, it was not until the end of the Middle Ages (about 1500 AD) that general attitudes toward children began to change significantly. Although some researchers have argued that children still were considered to be "miniature adults" during the Middle Ages (see Ariès, 1962; Heywood, 2001), most researchers agree that beginning about 1500, childhood began to be considered as a period of innocence, much as it is seen today in many cultures, including that of the United States (see the box Try This! Exploring Attitudes About Child Rearing).

Do you think that culture-based expectations placed on children growing up in the United States today are becoming more relaxed or more strict? Why?

Nevertheless, even in modern times, some cultures continue to consider children as "economic assets" who are to be exploited, who are made to work, and who often are subjected to severe corporal (physical) punishment. In the United States, for example, it was not until the late 19th century that children gained special rights through the advent of child labor laws and compulsory schooling (Epstein & Lutjens, 2008). Laws defining child abuse and limiting the use of corporal punishment came even later. Even today, some forms of corporal punishment still are widely used: In the United States, some 80% of parents spank their children at least occasionally (Gershoff & Bitensky, 2007). Several nations, however, have outlawed *any* use of corporal punishment with children, and most industrialized nations have banned corporal punishment in the public schools. In the United States, 31 states have banned school-based corporal punishment, but the rest allow local school districts to decide if they will allow this type of punishment (Center for Effective Discipline, 2011).

Cultural Influences on Childhood At present, the historical shift continues toward more humane attitudes about children and child-rearing practices, with legal protection for children's

CHANGING PERSPECTIVES

Children and War

Today psychologists are focusing increasing attention on the effects of the broader context of historical events on human development and on how such events affect people at different points in the lifespan (Cole, 2011; Jensen, 2011). They are finding that traumatic events such as war often have profound and permanent effects on those involved, and children may be the most vulnerable of all, particularly young children who are just building the foundations for their later lives. According to a recent United Nations study, at the end of 2010 there were nearly 44 million people forcibly displaced worldwide, including 15.4 million refugees and 27.5 million people displaced within their own countries (United Nations High Commission for Refugees, 2011). Not surprisingly given the world political situation at the time, of the refugees, Afghans made up the largest group (30% of the refugee population) followed by Iraqis. Many of these refugees are children.

Although war has a devastating impact on all concerned, its effects on children are especially tragic. Many children are killed as innocent bystanders; others are orphaned and may wind up starving and sick, alone, or in ill-equipped refugee camps. Many also are subjected to sexual abuse. Before the first Persian Gulf War in 1991, Iraq had one of the lowest infant mortality rates in the developing world; by the mid-1990s the rate had more than doubled—increasing from 47 to 108 deaths per 1,000 live births, with many children dying of hunger, malnutrition, dysentery, and cancer. Fortunately, by 2011, the rate had declined to just under 42 deaths per 1,000 live births, reflecting the re-stabilization of the government and the emergence from war. A similar, although less dramatic, trend has also occurred in Afghanistan (Central Intelligence Agency, 2012).

What psychological effects does war bring to the children involved? Some of war's impact is immediate and obvious: demoralization, depression, and a chronic sense of fear and uncertainty. Numerous researchers also have found high rates of *posttraumatic stress disorder (PTSD)* in children who survive. For example, in a study of Palestinian children who had experienced war, it was found that almost three-fourths had at least mild PTSD symptoms, and over one-third had moderate to severe symptoms. These symptoms included high rates of sleep disturbances, complaints of physical pain or infirmity, the inability to feel normal emotions, problems in controlling their impulses, and difficulty concentrating (Thabet, Abed, & Vostanis, 2004). In addition, these children often suffered from depression, and their psychological symptoms were directly linked to the amount and severity of stress and traumatic events they had experienced. PTSD can emerge immediately or be delayed. It can persist for years, although fortunately for most children its effects subside once a more stable life is regained (Thabet & Vostanis, 2000). How parents respond to war trauma also affects the degree to which their children are traumatized (Thabet, Ibraheem, Shivram, Winter, & Vostanis, 2009). Children who fare best in times of war are those who have loving, well-educated, and healthy parents; who exhibit flexible and high-level thinking; who know and use multiple coping strategies; and who have good peer relationships and other means of social support (Massad, et al., 2009; Qouta, Punamäki, & El Sarraj, 2008). Siblings who provide intimacy and warmth also serve to reduce the damaging effects of the trauma that comes with war (Peltonen, Qouta, El Sarraj, & Punamäki, 2010).

Unfortunately, PTSD and other disorders are not the only effects of war. In many parts of the world children assume the role of soldier, either by forced conscription or simply for survival. In the 50 regions around the world that were at war during the 1990s, more than two-thirds of the conflicts involved the use of underage soldiers who sometimes were as young as age 5 and who often had not reached puberty (Boutwell & Klare, 2000). Today in 2011, it is estimated that 300,000 children are presently involved in armed conflicts around the world (UNICEF, 2011), taking place in as many as 86 different countries and territories worldwide (Coalition to Stop the Use of Child Soldiers, 2011). Perhaps it is not surprising that children may be left with bitterness and hatred toward the "enemy." For many such children in war zones around the world, hatred born of war may last for life, leading eventually to more wars.

When children grow up in dangerous, disrupted, and insecure environments, they face many challenges (Maton, 2003). Certainly, war leaves a mark on all those who are affected by it; for some, those scars are deep and permanent. Yet children are remarkably resilient and, even among those growing up in war-torn regions of the world, most are able to master the developmental tasks of childhood and adolescence and move on toward establishing meaningful adult lives.

---

rights now in place throughout most of the world. Even so, conceptualizations of childhood and what is appropriate in child rearing still vary considerably across cultures.

For example, Japanese children up to 3 years of age tend to sleep with their parents, grandparents, or siblings (Nugent, 1994; Shwalb, Nakazawa, & Shwalb, 2005). This sleeping arrangement appears to have evolved as part of a socialization process that attempts to foster a close relationship between children and their parents and others, reflecting a culture that values collective harmony. In such **collectivist cultures**, cooperation is stressed over competition. Group achievement is stressed over individual achievement, as is the good of the group over that of the individual, and self-sacrifice often is taken for granted. In all, collectivist cultures foster *interdependence,* which has strong implications for many aspects of personality development.

In contrast, by age 3, U.S. children are likely to be sleeping alone in a separate room, which is an arrangement that promotes individuality and helps children adapt to a society that values *independence* (Fass, 2004; Nugent, 1994; Shweder & Bidell, 2009). **Individualist cultures** such as the United States, which are predominantly Western, stress socialization that is noticeably different from that of collectivist cultures. Competition tends to predominate over cooperation, and personal achievement typically is valued more highly than group achievement. Overall, individual freedom and choice receive strong emphasis. Yet collectivist cultures and individualist cultures are not exactly "opposites;" rather, they emphasize different values to varying degrees. The ability to get along with others and to become a productive member of society are extremely important values in all cultures.

collectivist culture
A culture where the group takes precedence over the individual; cooperation and group achievement are stressed over competition and individual achievement

individualist culture
A culture where competition predominates over cooperation and personal achievement is typically valued more highly than group achievement; individual freedom and choice receive strong emphasis

Social and political factors also can affect attitudes toward childhood in different cultures. The forced conscription of hundreds of thousands of children to fight in the brutal ethnic wars that have raged in parts of Africa and many other regions of the world illustrates a view of childhood where children are not considered special nor are they protected (see the box Changing Perspectives: Children and War). As this example demonstrates, when the sociocultural context in which development occurs becomes torn, expectations about all members of the society change—and often not for the better.

Do you believe that collectivist or individualist cultures provide the better developmental environment for children? Why?

Economic factors, too, often influence attitudes about and treatment of children. For example, families that are more affluent tend to have fewer children. With fewer children, parents are under less pressure to provide for the basics; therefore, they have more time to enjoy and educate their children. In addition, children from affluent families have less need to undertake adult responsibilities, such as holding a job, at an early age.

It is important to note that humans are *social* beings, and the paths that human development take must be considered in light of the broadly defined sociocultural context in which each individual's life unfolds. We have provided a few examples of how a sociocultural context affects not only the interpretation of behavior within a particular developmental period (childhood), but also the expectations placed on, and the treatment of, individuals growing up in that environment. Of course, sociocultural context is important for development not only during childhood but also within each of the other developmental periods. In subsequent chapters, we will discuss how social and cultural conditions, as well as changes in economic conditions and family size and structure, impact development at other stages in the lifespan.

The Domains of Human Development

As we explore the process of human development, it is useful to consider the various types of abilities and developmental events that change as individuals move through the lifespan. For practical reasons, the human growth and change that occur within each developmental period are divided into four major *domains* or areas:

- Development in the **physical domain** involves changes in physical shape and size in addition to changes in brain structures, sensory capabilities, and motor skills.
- In the **cognitive domain**, development includes the acquisition of skills in perceiving, thinking, reasoning, and problem solving, as well as the intricate development and use of language.
- Development in the **personality domain** includes acquiring relatively stable and enduring personality traits, as well as a sense of self as an individual.
- The **sociocultural domain** includes both **socialization**, which occurs as we are deliberately taught and trained by parents and others about how to fit in and function in society (with or without formal schooling), and **enculturation**, which occurs as we learn about our culture more or less on our own, by observing and absorbing rather than being taught. Because much of what we learn involves the interaction of socialization and enculturation, we often use the term *sociocultural* in this text.

It is important to remember that domains are arbitrary segments of development used by researchers to better understand the incredibly complex interplay of forces that act on individuals. As you study the content of this text, keep in mind that real people are "whole" beings and not at all compartmentalized. Changes and continuities in each domain interact with other aspects of development in other domains. Babies who have learned to stand (a motor skill) see the world from a new angle (a perceptual skill); they may feel pleased with this new skill (an emotional event or personality accomplishment), and they may interact with others in new ways (social skills). Development is not piecemeal; it is *holistic,* involving the *whole* person.

REVIEW THE FACTS 1-2

1. Which of the following is more likely the result of maturation (as opposed to learning)?
   a. learning to walk
   b. learning to read
   c. learning to sing a folk song
   d. learning one's own name
2. In comparison to how children were treated in ancient Greece and Rome, today's children (at least in developing nations) are treated ________.
3. In a(n) ________ culture, cooperation is stressed over competition.
4. The United States would be considered a(n) ________ culture.
5. A discussion of how a child's problem-solving strategies change from age 3 to age 6 falls within which developmental domain?
6. The process by which we learn about our culture is called _____, whereas the specific instruction we receive about how to fit into society is called _____.

Practice on **MyDevelopmentLab**

Watch *Differences Between Collectivistic and Individualistic Cultures* on **MyDevelopmentLab**

personality domain
Those aspects of development that involve acquiring relatively stable and enduring traits, as well as a sense of self as an individual

enculturation
Learning about culture by observing and absorbing rather than being taught

physical domain
Those aspects of development that involve changes in physical shape and size, as well as changes in brain structure, sensory capabilities, and motor skills

sociocultural domain
Those aspects of development that focus on socialization and enculturation

cognitive domain
Those aspects of development that involve the acquisition of skills in perceiving, thinking, reasoning, and problem solving, as well as the intricate development and use of language

socialization
Teachings by parents and others about how to fit in and function in society

THEORETICAL FRAMEWORKS FOR HUMAN DEVELOPMENT

In a sense, all people are amateur developmental psychologists of sorts because everyone observes human behavior as it changes throughout the lifespan. In fact, conventional wisdom about development, which often is tied to cultural values and traditions, abounds. The influence of culture is clearly seen in examples of proverbs that provide advice about childhood and child rearing. As you can see by looking at examples of the proverbs that reflect various attitudes about childhood in Table 1-2, shared conceptualizations of children develop within a culture, and those views provide an explanation and a set of directions for the interpretation of developmental changes.

Can you suggest a proverb that your parents or caregivers repeated to you during your childhood? What lesson did that proverb reflect?

Developmental psychologists also have constructed common, shared explanations for how and why human development proceeds as it does. These explanations are called *theories,* and it is to the topic of theories of human development that we now turn.

Table 1-2 Selected Proverbs That Reflect Cultural Attitudes Toward Childhood and Child-Rearing Practices

"If you spare the rod, you spoil the child."
"Little pitchers have big ears."
"A child who isn't made to cry will make his mother cry."
"The creative adult is the child who survived."
"Excessive love spoils a child."
"A child who is given all that he demands won't succeed in life."
"A baby is God's opinion that life should go on."
"Out of the mouths of babes comes wisdom."
"A father with three children is thrice blessed."
"A bad child is sorrow to his father and bitterness to his mother."

The Role of Theory

As noted earlier, developmental psychology is not merely a collection of cultural wisdom; it is a *science.* As such, our understanding of human development is not based solely on our own experiences and beliefs, which, as we can see by examining the proverbs in Table 1-2, can vary dramatically from culture to culture. Rather, as scientists, we strive to construct a more comprehensive view of how development unfolds. Such organized, overarching views are called **theories**, which are defined as organized, coherent sets of ideas that help us to understand, to explain, and to make predictions. As such, theories are broad frameworks of understanding, and they include sets of interrelated assumptions and principles that help organize data and lead to predictions as well as to explanations. Ultimately, the goal of a theory is to help us understand a phenomenon.

Because human behavior is enormously complex, and because different views of development have been favored in different cultures and at various times in history, many theories describing human development have been proposed (Lerner, 2006; Lerner, Lewin-Bizan, & Warren, 2011; Miller, 2010).

Traditionally, theories about human development have been categorized into groups, based on the similarity of the assumptions upon which the theories are based. In the section that follows, we briefly describe the most influential theories in each of the following theoretical perspectives:

- Biologically based theories
- Psychodynamic theories
- Behavioral theories
- Cognitive theories

Before we begin our discussion about theory, however, perhaps we should enter a caution. As you study the theories presented in this text, it is easy to become confused because different theories may describe the same developmental event—for example, learning to talk or forming a gender identity—in quite different ways. Frequently, students see the different theoretical explanations as *competing* with each other, and they may wonder which view is correct and which view is wrong.

As you learn about the developmental theories presented in this text, it is important to keep in mind some basic ideas about theories. First, no theory is either right or wrong, although some theories that have not been supported with evidence have been discredited and are no longer seen as useful. Theories simply provide the best explanations that are currently available. This is true of all scientific theories, whether they describe the motion of atoms (in physics), the way the liver works (in biology), or the way a person develops (in psychology).

Can you think of a theory, from any scientific discipline, that was at one time useful but now is considered outdated? Why do you think this theory was abandoned?

Second, because there typically is more than one way to view a subject, there often are several theories that attempt to help us understand what we are studying. Therefore, different theories may seem to contradict each other at times. Rather than becoming frustrated by such inconsistencies, a better approach is to consider what each theory contributes and to use

theory
An organized, coherent set of ideas that helps us to understand, to explain, and to make predictions

that knowledge to better understand the phenomenon being studied.

Finally, it is important to understand that theories are based on **data**, which are the results of scientific study and investigation. Sometimes theories include explanations and ideas that seem strange or even wrong when considered today. For example, Sigmund Freud's theory suggests that even infants and young children feel sexual desires and they seek the pleasure associated with sexual gratification. Today, this seems like a bizarre idea to many people, and few, if any, scholars accept this explanation as a useful way to conceptualize moral development. Yet Freud's ideas were based on data—Freud's careful observation of human nature. Therefore, his ideas are worth considering with an open mind to see how they may be refined or modified to provide explanations or enhance the understanding of human development in today's world. All theories change over time as scientists discover new findings that help them better understand the topics they study.

Biological Views of Human Development

Humans, like all animals, are biological organisms. As such, biologically determined processes and events exert important influences on development. A recurring topic covered throughout this text is how developmental processes are shaped by biological forces.

Genetics The fundamental biological instructions for development are stored within each individual's genetic code. For over a century, researchers have been working to understand how the genes contained in this code are arranged and how they operate to guide the development of the human biological organism. Although there is still much to learn about genetic processes, a major breakthrough occurred when the **human genome**—the entire arrangement of all human genes—was successfully mapped through the joint effort of several research groups working on the Human Genome Project (Celera Genomics, 2000; see Chapter 2). Essentially, the mapping of the human genome has given scientists a way of understanding how specific locations in the genetic code are linked to the development of various traits and developmental events.

Although it will be many years before the incredibly complex functions of the genome are understood, the mapping of the genome has been heralded worldwide as one of the major scientific breakthroughs of human history, one with many consequences. Not only will our knowledge of the genome provide a basis for understanding diseases and finding cures, but it also will provide a platform for developmental psychologists to further their insights into the impact of biological mechanisms on human development. Of course, scientists recognize that genetically based traits are expressed through a particular environmental context. The person's experiences in the world shape and change how these biologically based processes ultimately unfold, and environmental conditions may actually alter the genes themselves via a process called *epigenetics* (Meaney, 2010; see Chapter 2). Developmental psychologists recognize that a better understanding of how genes work undoubtedly will lead to a clearer understanding of how developmental changes occur. As such, genetics is a topic of very special significance at present, and it is treated much more fully in Chapter 2, which focuses on heredity and environment.

Developmental Neuroscience The 1990s, labeled as "the decade of the brain" by President George H. W. Bush, saw an explosion of research in *neuroscience*, which is an area of study that attempts to understand the links between brain function, observable behavior, and mental experiences such as thought and emotion (Diamond & Amso, 2008; Johnson, 2011). In the past few years, researchers have made dramatic and exciting advances in their ability to study the brain in living organisms. Increasingly, studies that use harmless, noninvasive procedures such as brain scans (discussed further in Chapter 4) are being conducted with children and adolescents as well as with adults. Such research offers enormous promise for advancing the understanding of developmental processes.

Can you suggest a specific way in which a better understanding of brain processes will help us more clearly understand human lifespan development?

Much of this brain research has a developmental slant, giving rise to a subdiscipline appropriately called **developmental neuroscience**. A primary area of interest within this field is the development of our understanding of the brain structures and functions that are associated with different kinds of memory and problem-solving approaches (Bauer, 2009; Bunge, 2008), which are described in more detail in Chapters 4 and 6. Brain-scanning studies are helping psychologists understand the neurological mechanisms that underlie many types

---

data
The results from a scientific investigation (the singular of the word *data* is *datum*); data often are expressed as numbers, but data also may take other forms

Watch *How the Human Genome Map Affects You* on MyDevelopmentLab

Watch *Eddie Harmon Jones: Is there an increasing link between science and psychology?* on MyDevelopmentLab

developmental neuroscience
The study of the development of brain structures and the relationship between brain structures and functions and behavior and development

human genome
The entire arrangement of all human genes

of developmental changes, including the formation of early mother–infant relationships (Hofer, 2009), and the development of moral reasoning (Carpendale, Sokol, & Müller, 2010), self-regulation (Berger, 2011c), and basic personality styles. Recent studies, for example, have shown that adults who are naturally shy have different brain response patterns when they look at pictures of familiar versus unfamiliar faces as compared to "bold" adults (Beaton, et al., 2009). Brain-scanning techniques also are being used to better understand the brain changes that occur during periods of rapid cognitive development, such as infancy and childhood (Lewis & Carmody, 2008), adolescence (Casey, Getz, & Galvan, 2008; Giedd, 2008; Spear, 2010), and early adulthood (Groeschel, Vollmer, King, & Connelly, 2010).

Developmental neuroscience as a field of study is in its infancy. As such, there is much yet to be learned about how brain structures and functions influence behavior and developmental change. It is, however, one of the most rapidly growing areas in the study of human development, and we will explore these relationships between brain function and developmental change throughout the text, focusing on how brain structure and mental processing influence human development at all ages.

Evolution The process by which species change across generations is called **evolution**. Evolutionary theory is usually traced to ideas laid out by Charles Darwin (1809–1882) in his major work, *The Origin of Species* (1859/1958). Working in the mid-1800s, at a time before genetic mechanisms were well understood, Darwin outlined the theory of evolution, which remains today the most general theory in the life sciences (Valla & Williams, 2006). At the core of evolutionary theory is the concept of **natural selection**, which centers around a concept often referred to as "survival of the fittest."

The basic idea of natural selection rests on the fact that individuals within a species vary somewhat in physical and behavioral characteristics that are related to coping successfully with and adapting to their environment. Those members having characteristics that are better suited to their environment will be more likely to live long enough to reproduce, thereby passing the genes that determine these characteristics along to the next generation. Conversely, those individuals less well suited to the environment are less likely to live to reproductive age, and their genes drop out of the gene pool for the species. Natural selection, which typically operates over many successive generations, eventually produces shifts in the species' characteristics present in the population.

▲ Charles Darwin's theory of evolution helps us understand the biological basis of attachment—the emotional bond between infants and caregivers.

Few scientific ideas have generated more prolonged and heated controversy than the theory of evolution. Today explanations based on the mechanisms of evolution are widely embraced by developmental psychologists (LaFreniére, 2010). For example, one area of development that is especially important to understand is early childhood attachment, which describes how infants establish emotional relationships with important caregivers (Bell, 2010). Attachment lays the foundation for social and emotional development throughout the lifespan and it is oftentimes discussed from a biological or evolutionary perspective (see M. S. Ainsworth & Bowlby, 1991; Bowlby, 1969/1980). Of course, scientists increasingly understand that there are multiple causes—both biological and environmental—that continually interact to produce the complex array of thought and behavior associated with each individual. Nevertheless, a basic understanding of evolutionary processes helps developmental psychologists understand why human development proceeds as it does.

Psychodynamic Views of Human Development

Sigmund Freud (1856–1939), a physician practicing in Vienna in the early 1900s, founded what is now known as the **psychodynamic approach** (also referred to as the *psychoanalytic*

Watch *Developmental Cognitive Neuroscience: Adele Diamond* on **MyDevelopmentLab**

Watch *Joshua Aronson: What is the relationship between evolutionary theory and psychology today?* on **MyDevelopmentLab**

evolution
The process through which species change across generations

psychodynamic approach
The theory originated by Freud that emphasizes unconscious processes and the importance of early childhood development

natural selection
The theory originated by Darwin of survival of the fittest, where better-adapted individuals survive to reproduce, thereby transferring their genes to their offspring and into future generations

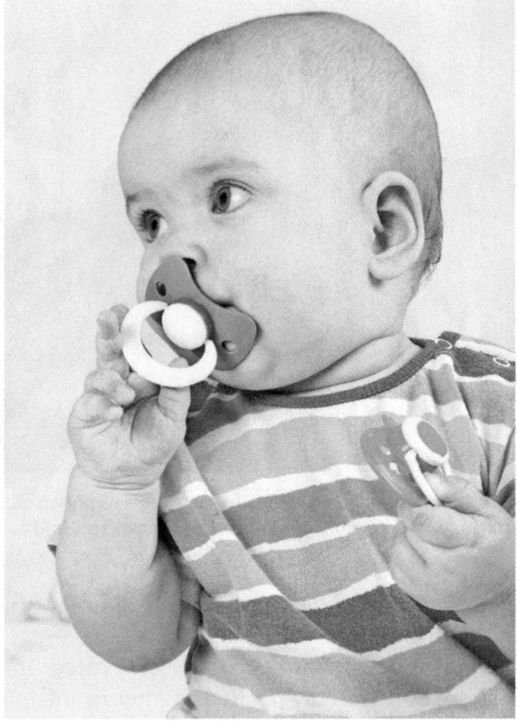

Sigmund Freud proposed that during the first year of life the child experiences sexual gratification by stimulation of the oral region—a developmental period he referred to as the oral stage.

Table 1-3 Freud's Psychosexual Stages

Age	Stage	Description
Birth to 18 months	Oral	The infant experiences pleasure from stimulation of the mouth, lips, and oral activities, especially sucking.
18 months to 3 years	Anal	The child's pleasure focuses on the anus and the elimination functions.
3 years to 6 years	Phallic	The child's pleasure focuses on the genitals, especially through masturbation.
6 years to 12 years	Latency	The child represses sexual interests and instead focuses on developing cognitive and interpersonal skills.
12 years and up	Genital	Adolescence triggers the reemergence of sexual impulses, with gratification dependent on finding a partner.

approach). This theoretical framework, developed largely through Freud's interpretations of the case studies of his patients (many of whom experienced psychiatric disorders), has had a profound effect on many areas within psychology, including human development. In many important ways, all psychodynamic theories trace their origins to the ideas first proposed by Freud.

Freud's Psychoanalytic Theory Although Freud's views are comprehensive and attempt to describe most of the important aspects of human behavior and cognition, it is within the domain of social and personality development that his ideas have exerted their greatest influence. Freud's perspective is important from a historical point of view and because it provides keen insights into the issues inherent in understanding human development. For this reason, Freudian concepts, or their modern equivalents, will be discussed at various points throughout the remainder of this text, and more detail about psychodynamic views will be provided as we explore the various stages of development.

For the present, the most important ideas that trace their origin to Freud are summarized in the following list:

- Freud believed that much of human development was determined by *unconscious* processes, which operated in parts of the mind (or psyche) of which we have no awareness.
- Much of our behavior and awareness is influenced by the interplay of three intrapsychic (mental) processes. Freud labeled these processes the id, the ego, and the superego. Freud believed that human behavior and development were heavily determined by how an individual dealt with conflicts involving *id* impulses, which motivate the individual to seek pleasure or to avoid pain, or those involving *superego* functions, which trigger an individual's conscience to feel guilty when social norms are violated. To mediate and resolve these conflicts, the *ego*—the rational and conscious part of our personality—attempts to reconcile *id* demands with *superego* prohibitions, while at the same time helping the individual function successfully in his or her social environment. Freud viewed these three processes of the id, the ego, and the superego not as regions of the brain but rather as metaphors for how the brain functioned.
- Freud saw development as proceeding through five *psychosexual stages* (see Table 1-3). In each stage, the person's sexual energies are channeled in different directions. Later development depends on how successfully the child is able to move through each stage. When a child experiences difficulty with development, a *fixation* may develop, which results in primitive behavior from that developmental stage being carried forward into adulthood. For example, an infant who is not well cared for may develop an *oral fixation,* which may reveal itself in adulthood as compulsive smoking, eating, or nail biting.
- Freud believed that the adult personality was heavily influenced by events that occurred in early childhood, especially in the first 5 or 6 years of life.

Today, our reaction to Freud's theory often is to note its limitations. Its heavy emphasis on sexual motivations; its focus on unconscious conflicts, especially during childhood; and its orientation toward abnormal behavior probably do reflect Freud's personal experiences with his patients and their sexually inhibited Victorian culture. However, many of Freud's central ideas continue to shape our understanding of human development, especially throughout childhood; for example, they are reflected in the work of modern ego psychologists, including Erik Erikson.

Erikson's Psychosocial Theory Erik Erikson (1902–1994) is called a *neo-Freudian* because his theory of personality development derives from Freud's, but Erikson's theory has a different emphasis. Instead of focusing most heavily on unconscious

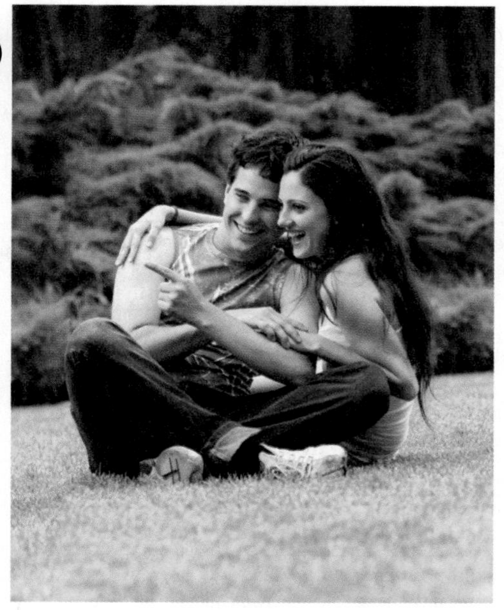

Erik Erikson proposed that individuals move through a series of psychosocial stages as they develop. He viewed the essential event in early adulthood as the need to establish meaningful, intimate relationships.

processes and psychosexual development, Erikson's view emphasizes conscious (or ego) forces. In terms of development, his view centers mainly on the effects of social interactions in shaping personality; his approach is therefore termed **psychosocial theory**.

The core concept of Erikson's theory is *ego identity*, which is defined as a basic sense of who we are as individuals in terms of self-concept and self-image. Erikson's theory emphasizes social interactions and argues that a major force in human development is the culture within which one is raised, especially with respect to the infant's early interactions with caregivers. According to Erikson, social forces continue to shape personality throughout the lifespan as the individual experiences relationships with others.

Based on case studies and thoughtful observations of people in various cultures, Erikson's theory also differs from Sigmund Freud's in that it includes developmental stages *throughout* the human lifespan instead of ending at the entrance into puberty (see Table 1-4). Underlying these developmental stages is what Erikson called the *epigenetic principle*, a biological concept that there is a "plan" built into all living organisms that determines, or at least sets the stage for, development throughout the organism's lifespan. (For his later ideas on epigenesis, see Erikson, 1984.)

Erikson, like Freud, believed that the ways in which an individual resolves the conflicts inherent in an earlier stage of development exert a strong influence on how later development unfolds. But Erikson acknowledged that the adjustments an individual makes at each stage can be altered or reversed later. For example, children who are denied affection and attention in infancy can make up for this deficiency if they are given extra attention at later stages. Erikson also believed that, although each developmental conflict is "critical" at only one stage, it is present throughout life. For example, autonomy needs are especially important to toddlers; however, throughout life, people must continually test the degree of autonomy they can express in each new relationship. We will return to each of Erikson's stages in later chapters. They provide an intuitively appealing description of some key concerns at each period of life.

Do you think Freud's or Erikson's views are more optimistic with respect to human lifespan development? Why?

Behavioral Views of Human Development

At about the same time that Freud was developing his ideas about the psychodynamic nature of personality, other scientists were working to understand human nature and development from a different perspective—one that emphasized understanding how individuals *behave*. Rather than focusing on thoughts or on the influence of underlying, unconscious process, these theorists—whose views became known collectively as **behaviorism**—defined the appropriate subject matter of psychology to be observable behavior. They argued that to focus attention on *unobservable* constructs, such as emotions, thoughts, or the unconscious, was an unscientific approach.

Over time, the behaviorist approach has softened somewhat, and modern behaviorists acknowledge that internal processes, such as cognition and emotion, do in fact play an important role in human experience. Nevertheless, even modern behaviorists focus their attention on how a person's environment affects behavior and development. Three general trends within the behaviorist tradition deserve special attention not only because they have historical significance but also because they provide useful concepts with which to understand human development. These are classical conditioning, operant conditioning, and social learning theory.

Classical Conditioning Classical conditioning is a form of learning in which a naturally occurring reflex becomes associated with an environmental cue. The basic principles of classical conditioning were first described by Ivan Pavlov (1849–1936), a Russian physiologist working to understand how the enzymes in saliva break down food in the digestive process. Using dogs as experimental subjects, Pavlov developed a technique in which he used dog food to stimulate their salivary response. He then collected their saliva to use in his chemical analysis.

psychosocial theory
Erikson's view that social interactions with others shape the development of personality

Watch *Erikson's Last Four Stages of Psychosocial Development* on MyDevelopmentLab

Watch *Classic Footage of Erik Erikson* on MyDevelopmentLab

behaviorism
The view that the appropriate focus of psychology should be on observable behavior

Watch *Erikson's First Four Stages of Psychosocial Development* on MyDevelopmentLab

Table 1-4 Erikson's Psychosocial Stages

Age	Stage	Description
Birth to 12 months	Trust versus mistrust	Infants learn about the basic trustworthiness of their environment from their caregivers. If their needs are consistently met and if they receive attention and affection, they form a global impression of the world as a safe place. However, if their world is inconsistent, painful, stressful, and threatening, they learn to expect more of the same and come to believe that life is unpredictable and untrustworthy.
12 months to 3 years	Autonomy versus shame and doubt	Toddlers discover their own body and how to control it. They explore feeding and dressing, toilet training, and new ways of moving about. When they begin to succeed in doing things for themselves, they gain a sense of self-confidence and self-control. However, if they continually fail and are punished or labeled as messy, sloppy, inadequate, or bad, they learn to feel shame and self-doubt.
3 years to 6 years	Initiative versus guilt	Children explore the world beyond themselves. They discover how the world works and how they can affect it. Their world consists of both real and imaginary people and things. If their explorations and activities are generally effective, they learn to deal with people and events in a constructive way and gain a sense of initiative. However, if they are severely criticized or frequently punished, they instead learn to feel guilty for many of their own actions.
6 years to 12 years	Industry versus inferiority	Children develop numerous skills and competencies in school, at home, and in the outside world. A sense of self is enriched by the realistic development of such competencies. Comparison with peers is increasingly significant. A negative evaluation of self as inferior compared to others is especially disruptive at this time.
12 years to 18 years or older	Ego identity versus ego diffusion	Before adolescence, children begin to learn a number of different roles: student, friend, older sibling, athlete, musician, and so forth. During adolescence, it becomes important to sort out and integrate those roles into a single, consistent identity. Adolescents seek basic values and attitudes that cut across their various roles. If they fail to form a central identity or if they cannot resolve a major conflict between two major roles with opposing value systems, the result is what Erikson called *ego diffusion*.
18 years or older to 40 years	Intimacy versus isolation	In late adolescence and young adulthood, the central developmental conflict is intimacy versus isolation. Intimacy involves more than sexual intimacy. It is the ability for an individual to share oneself with another person of either sex without fear of losing personal identity. Success in establishing intimacy is affected by the extent to which the five earlier conflicts have been resolved.
40 years to 65 years	Generativity versus self-absorption	In adulthood, after the earlier conflicts have been partly resolved, men and women are free to direct their attention more fully to the assistance of others. Often parents take satisfaction from helping their children. Individuals also can direct their energies associated with generativity to the solution of social issues. Failure to resolve earlier conflicts often leads to a preoccupation with self in terms of health, psychological needs, comfort, and so forth—a result referred to as self-absorption.
65 years and older	Integrity versus despair	In the last stages of life, it is typical for individuals to look back on their lives and to judge themselves. If people find that they are satisfied that their lives have had meaning and involvement, the result is a sense of integrity. However, if their lives seem to have consisted of a series of misdirected efforts and lost chances, the outcome is a sense of despair.

Pavlov noticed, though, that after a dog was subjected to the experimental treatment a few times, it began to salivate even *before* it was fed, in anticipation of its upcoming treat. (Perhaps you have noticed this same salivary response in yourself when you smelled a delicious food cooking in the kitchen.) Pavlov devoted the remainder of his career to studying this type of learning, now called **classical conditioning**, which is regarded as a major way in which human development and behavior, especially during childhood, are influenced by environmental events (see Figure 1-1). The principles of classical conditioning are described in Chapter 2.

Operant Conditioning Another means by which the environment influences human behavior and development is through **operant conditioning**, which describes how rewards and punishments exert an influence on our actions. Although many psychologists have contributed to our understanding of this phenomenon, B. F. Skinner (1904–1990) is perhaps most closely identified with this phenomenon.

Working mostly with rats and pigeons in a laboratory setting, Skinner devoted his career to understanding how behavior is influenced by the rewards or punishments that accompany it. Although considerable complexity is involved in

classical conditioning
A type of learning in which an association is learned between an environmental event and the stimulus–response reflex that follows (e.g., a salivary response when a person smells delicious food, even before the food enters the mouth)

operant conditioning
A type of learning that occurs when a behavior is followed by a reward (also called a reinforcement) or a punishment, which serves to make the future occurrence of the behavior more or less likely, respectively

▲ Pavlov's experiments on salivation in dogs led to his early description of what is now known as classical conditioning.

▲ B. F. Skinner, early in his career, is seen observing the operant behavior of a rat in one of his famous Skinner boxes.

a complete explanation of operant conditioning, its basic premise is very simple: We tend to repeat actions that are rewarded with positive consequences; we tend to discontinue behavior that is punished. It is not difficult to think of examples in our own lives in which reward and punishment have influenced, or operantly conditioned, our behavior and thereby influenced our development. Operant conditioning is further described in Chapter 2.

Can you think of an example in which your own behavior was changed due to reward or punishment? Can you cite an example in which reward or punishment did not produce its intended outcome?

Social Learning Theory Both classical conditioning and operant conditioning theories address how environmental circumstances affect the behavior of an organism. Yet, when the ways in which humans respond to and learn from their environments are considered, it is apparent that much of what people learn is not established via direct experience but rather is acquired from their observations of others. For example, if we see that everyone who sticks a hand in a bowl of water jerks it back yelling "hot," we do not need to place our own hand at risk to make a good guess that there is hot liquid in the bowl.

The fact that we can learn by observing the behavior of others forms the basis of **social learning theory**, which is a view that emphasizes the influence of the social behavior of others on our learning. Social learning theorists, such as Albert Bandura (whose work is described more fully later in this chapter), recognize that children and adults observe their own behavior and the behavior of others as well as the consequences of those behaviors. Even young children can anticipate consequences based on their observations of past situations and events. In turn, people form opinions about themselves and others and then behave in ways that are consistent with those opinions (Miller, 2011b). Along with classical conditioning and operant conditioning views, social learning theory contributes in important ways to the understanding of human behavior and development. These perspectives will be discussed more fully as we continue to explore development across the human lifespan.

social learning theory
A view that emphasizes the influence of the social behavior of others on our learning

Classical conditioning can be an important force in determining human behavior, especially behavior involving emotional responses. In a classic experiment performed in the early part of the 20th century, noted American behaviorist John B. Watson classically conditioned a fear response in a little boy named Albert. At the beginning of the experiment, Albert showed no fear whatsoever when he was presented with a furry white rat. However, in subsequent experimental sessions, whenever little Albert reached out to pet or play with the rat Watson frightened him by producing a loud, unpleasant noise behind his head, thereby distressing the boy and causing him to cry. After only a few pairings of the frightening noise and the rat little Albert came to fear the rat, and he cried at the sight of it. Thus, Albert's fear became classically conditioned (J. B. Watson & Raynor, 1920).

Although performing such an experiment would be considered unethical by today's standards, Watson's results do demonstrate the role that classical conditioning can play in the development of emotional responses, such as fear. Consider for a moment how you feel at the sight of a hypodermic needle when you walk into a dentist's or doctor's office, or your emotions when you think about kissing a romantic partner. Can you identify the original experiences that gave rise to your emotional responses?

FIGURE 1-1 An Early Example of Classical Conditioning The photo depicts Watson reminding Little Albert of the fear response previously associated with a white rat.

SOURCE: From "Conditioned emotional reactions," by J. B. Watson and R. Raynor, 1920, *Journal of Experimental Psychology*, (pp. 1–14).

Cognitive Views of Human Development

As strict behaviorist views began to give way to more *thought-centered perspectives* on human behavior, theories of human cognition—including views on cognitive development—became more mainstream. **Cognitive-developmental theories** focus on thinking, reasoning, and problem solving, with an emphasis on how such processes develop. Among the most important perspectives advanced in this view of human development are the cognitive-developmental theories formulated by Jean Piaget and Lev Vygotsky.

Piaget's Theory of Cognitive Development Jean Piaget (1896–1980) believed that the mind does not simply respond to stimuli and consequences but instead grows, changes, and adapts to the world (Piaget, 1950, 1970). Piaget's investigations grew out of his studies in biology and philosophy, and Darwin's theory of evolution had an especially important impact on his thinking. Piaget was particularly intrigued by the concept of **adaptation**, the process by which organisms change to be more successful in their environments.

Piaget's theory was based on his observations of his own children as well as other children that he studied, often in educational settings. Across these experiences, he noticed consistent patterns in how children solve problems and that these patterns differed in significant ways from those used by adults. Piaget concluded that children's thinking is *qualitatively* different from that of adults. In other words, differences in child and adult cognition are not confined to how

cognitive-developmental theory
An approach that focuses on the development of thinking, reasoning, and problem solving

adaptation
The process by which organisms change so that they will be more successful in a particular environment

▲ Jean Piaget believed that the mental schemes required to solve scientific reasoning problems do not develop until about age 11 or 12 years.

Table 1-5 Piaget's Stages of Cognitive Development

Age	Stage	Developmental milestones
Birth to approximately 2 years	Sensorimotor	Infants learn about the world through looking, grasping, mouthing, and other actions. Intelligence relies on the senses and bodily motion, beginning with simple reflexes that give rise to more complex, voluntary behaviors.
2 years to approximately 7 years	Preoperational	Children form concepts and use symbols, such as language, to help them communicate. Such concepts are limited to their personal, immediate experiences. Preoperational children possess very limited, and at times "magical," notions of cause and effect and have difficulty classifying objects or events. They do not hold broad, general theories, but instead they use their daily experiences to build specific knowledge. In addition, preoperational children neither make generalizations about classes of objects (e.g., all grandmothers) nor can they think through the consequences of a particular chain of events.
7 years to 11 or 12 years	Concrete operational	Children begin to think logically, to classify on more than one dimension at a time, and to understand mathematical concepts provided they can apply these operations to concrete or at least concretely imaginable objects or events. Concrete operational children begin to use logic in their thinking, but they may experience difficulty in understanding that a particular animal can be both a "dog" and a "terrier," and they can deal with only one classification at a time. Yet 7-year-olds understand that terriers are a smaller group within the larger group, dogs. They can also see other subgroups such as terriers and poodles as "small dogs" and golden retrievers and St. Bernards as "large dogs." This kind of thinking shows an understanding of *hierarchy* in classification.
11 or 12 years and beyond	Formal operational	Individuals can explore logical solutions to both concrete and abstract concepts. They can think systematically about all possibilities and come up with logical solutions. In addition, they can project into the future or recall the past when solving problems, and they can reason by analogy and metaphor. Formal operational thinking no longer needs to be tied to physical objects or events. This allows the individual to ask and answer "*what if*" questions (e.g., "What if I were to say this to that person?"). It also allows them to better understand the thoughts, motivations, and actions of others.

much children know, which naturally is less than adults know; there are also differences in the *ways* children and adults know and go about understanding things. Piaget identified four distinct stages of cognitive development that he felt described these qualitative changes in thinking and problem-solving abilities. Table 1-5 identifies these stages and notes the important developmental milestones that are associated with each stage.

Piaget believed that individuals are active participants in the learning process, seeking out new experiences by which to expand their knowledge. For Piaget, knowledge is organized into mental categories he called **schemas** or **schemes**, which become elaborated and refined through experiences. In some circumstances, new experiences fit very comfortably, with little effort, into an existing scheme; this type of learning is called **assimilation**. Consider the scheme for "driving a car." If a person already knows how to drive a Ford with an automatic transmission, learning to driving a Jeep automatic is a fairly easy learning task, as the Jeep "driving" actions—putting the car in Drive, manipulating the gas pedal and brake, and steering the car—are easily assimilated into the "Ford" scheme. However, if the Jeep has a manual transmission, which requires the driver to manually shift from one gear to another, the learning task is much more complex. Here, learning to drive the Jeep requires **accommodation**—the modification of the old "driving" scheme into something different than it was before. In Piaget's view, assimilation consists of interpreting new experiences in terms of existing schemes without changing them significantly; accommodation, in contrast, involves changing existing schemes to integrate new experiences. Most learning situations involve an interaction between both processes: People interpret what they experience in terms of what they already know, and because new experiences are rarely exactly like older ones, they notice and process differences as well (Piaget, 1950).

Piaget's views are not only helpful in understanding how children learn to manipulate their physical world but also in explaining such complex ideas as moral reasoning and how people acquire a sense of self. Although Piaget's theory has its critics and its shortcoming, as do all theories, it remains highly influential; we will investigate Piaget's views in detail in upcoming chapters of the text.

Vygotsky and Social-Cognitive Theory According to Piaget, the child is an "active scientist" who interacts with the physical environment and develops increasingly complex thought strategies.

Watch *Piaget's Stages of Cognitive Development* on **MyDevelopmentLab**

accommodation
Piaget's term for the process that requires schemes to change when a new object or event does not fit

schemes (or schemas)
Piaget's term for mental structures that process information, perceptions, and experiences; the schemes of individuals change as they grow

assimilation
In Piaget's theory, the process of incorporating new information into existing schemes

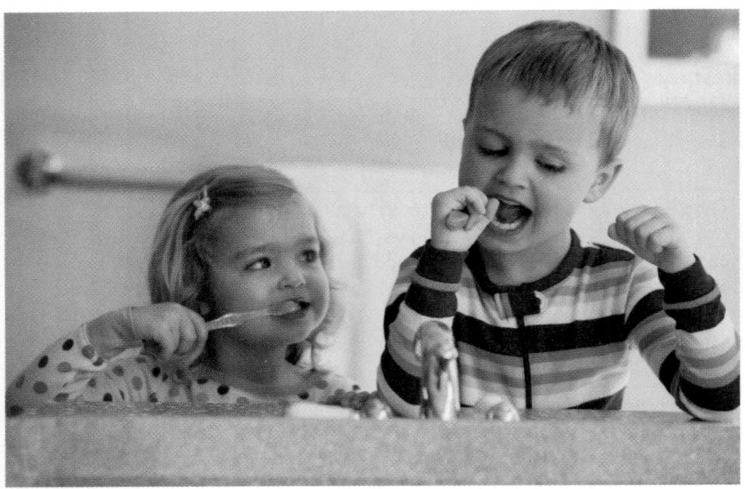

▲ Lev Vygotsky emphasized the important role that learning from other people plays in development. Older children or adults often serve as guides, helping younger children learn important cultural understandings, as well as other skills.

Today, however, developmental researchers also are emphasizing that children are *social* beings who play and talk with others and learn from these interactions as much or more than from discovering the answers to problems on their own (Crain, 2011). In a Piagetian lab, children typically work alone in solving the problems given to them by researchers. In real life, however, children have ongoing experiences in the company of adults and older peers who translate and help make sense of these experiences for them. Thus, children's cognitive development often is an "apprenticeship" in which more knowledgeable companions guide them in their understanding and skills (Rogoff, 1990; Wertsch, 2008).

Psychologist Lev Vygotsky (1896–1934), from the former Soviet Union, was among the first to emphasize the social context in which a large share of children's cognitive development takes place (e.g., see Vygotsky, 1935/1978). Vygotsky argued that what people learn is transmitted to them through the *shared meanings* of objects and events, which are passed from generation to generation through observation as well as through language (Daniels, 2011; Fernyhough, 2008). Simple activities such as cooking or somewhat more complex activities such as playing a particular sport are examples of concepts with such shared meanings. People develop their understanding and expertise of these culturally determined activities mainly through apprenticeship with learners who are more knowledgeable. This **guided participation** enables people to understand more and more about their world and to develop an increasing number of skills.

Vygotsky's emphasis on the role of "experts" in helping individuals learn provides a clear explanation not only of cognitive development but also of how people acquire their cultural traditions. As such, Vygotsky's view is an important perspective to consider and one to which we will return in subsequent chapters of text.

guided participation
Vygotsky's concept that people develop understanding and expertise mainly through apprenticeship with more knowledgeable learners

Integrating Theoretical Approaches

In the previous sections, we presented a quick overview of the major theories that psychologists use to explain development across the lifespan. A common response to a presentation of this sort is that there are "just too many theories" or "each theory seems totally different from all the others." In fact, one of the current challenges for developmental psychologists is to find a means of integrating this variety of perspectives into a single overarching theory—one that provides a more complete and comprehensive framework for understanding human development. One approach to this task involves the development of systems theories, or systems approaches.

Systems Approaches Gradually, over the last several decades, developmental research (and research in the social and behavioral sciences in general) has been shifting to a higher level of analysis that focuses on *systems* and how they change and evolve (Lerner, 2011; Thelen & Smith, 2006). Systems theories involve a broader focus—one that subsumes individual theories under a more general umbrella.

For example, the human body as a whole is a system: Its components include the head and brain, the sensory organs, the internal organs, the trunk, the musculature, and the limbs, all of which interact through processes such as blood circulation and neural transmission and serve many functions including simply keeping the body alive. At a somewhat finer level of analysis, the brain is a system: The various brain structures are components that interact in systematic ways to produce thought, emotion, and action. On a larger scale, a human family or other social group is also a system: Its components are the individuals it includes; it has a structure defined by society and its own rules; and it serves many functions ranging from surviving and remaining intact to accomplishing short- and long-term goals. As you can see, the term *system* can be applied to a broad range of issues and factors in human development and behavior at a microscopic level, at a macroscopic level, or anywhere in between. Interest in physiological systems and social groups as systems is not new; physiological systems research has been around for centuries, and social systems research has been around for several decades. What is relatively new is the application of systems models to complex *psychological* development and functioning (Fogel, King, & Shanker, 2008). Because systems theorists focus on the dynamic interplay between as many variables as possible and at as many levels as possible, systems theories hold considerable promise as a means of integrating views that center on biological, psychodynamic, behavioral, and cognitive perspectives (Johnston, 2010).

The Bioecological Model Perhaps the most influential systems model of human development originated with the work of Urie

Bronfenbrenner (1970, 1979), and this model continues to be refined and elaborated (Bronfenbrenner, 2005; Bronfenbrenner & Morris, 2006).

The **bioecological model** emphasizes that human development is a dynamic, interactive process that begins with an individual's genetic endowment and unfolds as a result of interactions with the immediate environment. Initially, this environment consists primarily of family members. As development proceeds, however, the child actively engages with the multiple environments in which she or he functions. Thus, the child is influenced not only by these particular settings but also by the interrelationships among them and the external influences from the larger environment. Bronfenbrenner and his colleagues picture the sociocultural environment as a nested arrangement of four concentric systems, as illustrated in Figure 1-2. Each expanding ring in the circle includes a broader array of social interactions in which the child participates as development unfolds. A key feature of the model is the fluid, back-and-forth interactions among the four systems across *time*, which results in an overarching system, or fifth level, referred to as the *chronosystem* (*chrono* means "time").

Newer versions of systems models increasingly focus on understanding how genetic mechanisms and biological processes interact with environmental experiences to shape the course of lifespan development (Johnston, 2010). As you can see, systems theories provide a broader focus for understanding human development. Thus, they offer the potential to help organize the more traditional theories described earlier in this chapter (Lerner, 2011).

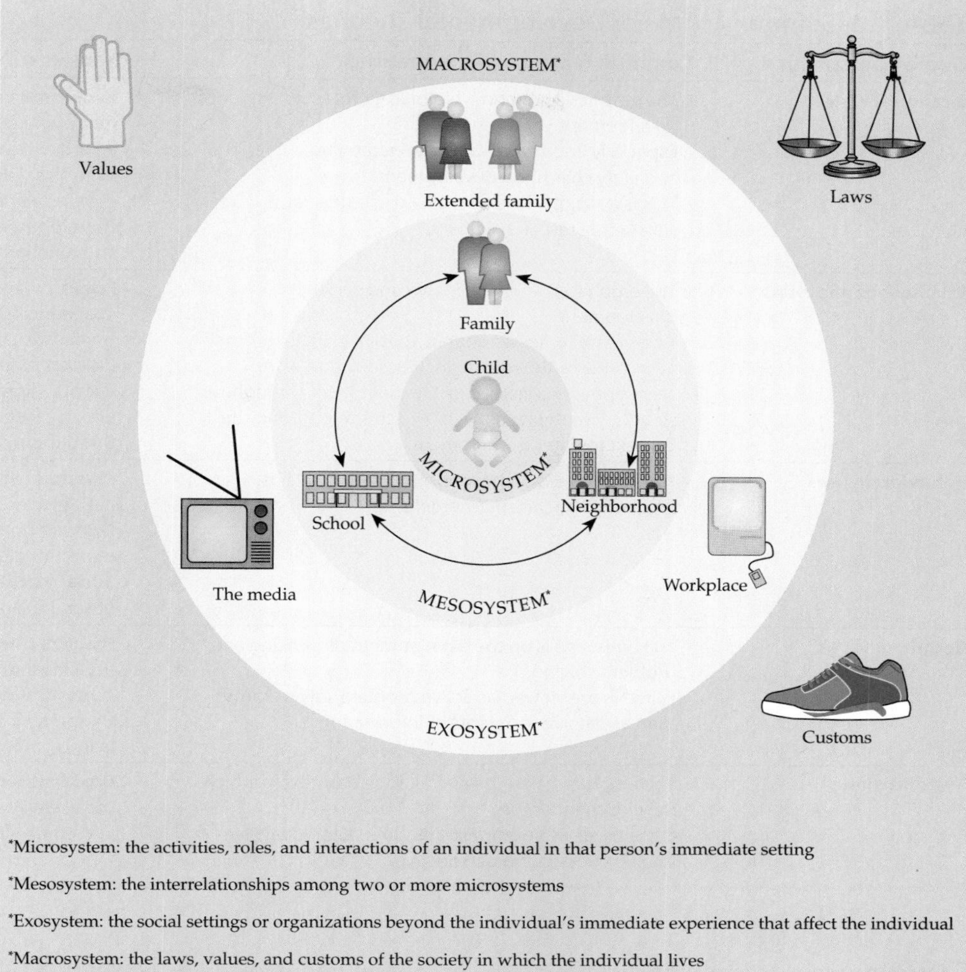

FIGURE 1-2 The Bioecological Model
The bioecological model emphasizes the idea that each person's development is influenced by a broad set of biological and environmental factors that continually interact as development unfolds across time. The influences of family and culture are especially important.

Toward a Theory of Lifespan Human Development Throughout the previous discussion of the influential theories of development, you may have noticed that each theoretical perspective emphasizes a somewhat different aspect of human development, whether that be the influence of biological forces, or of learning, cognition, social development, personality development, or the influence of culture and context (see Table 1-6). Indeed, each perspective has contributed much to our present-day understanding of human nature and development.

Considering your own development up to this point in your life, can you suggest a series of examples of how each level in the bioecological model has had an impact?

The study of human development, thus, includes the consideration of many different points of view. As we conclude this discussion of theories, we thought it useful to emphasize that human development also is defined by a set of core ideas—a set of concepts that apply to the study of constancy and change throughout the life course, from conception to death. We set forth the following six principles as a means of defining what lifespan human development involves (adapted from Baltes, 1987; Baltes, Lindenberger, & Staudinger, 2006):

bioecological model
A model that emphasizes that human development is a dynamic, interactive process that begins with an individual's genetic endowment and unfolds over time as a result of interactions with various levels of the environment

Table 1-6 Summary of Major Developmental Theories

Overall perspective	Common features of the theories	Theories of this type
Biological views	• The emphasis is on how biological processes influence development. • Especially important is the understanding of prenatal and early childhood development. • This is a rapidly developing field of study with substantial research activity.	• **Evolution:** Views development as the result of natural selection across many generations through which traits and behaviors that provide an adaptive advantage are passed on to future generations. • **Genetics:** Focuses on the role played by genes in shaping the developmental characteristics of the individual. • **Developmental neuroscience:** Emphasizes the role of brain structure and function as important determinants of human development.
Psychodynamic views	• The emphasis is on personality and social development. • To a greater or lesser degree, these theorists acknowledge the role of unconscious processes. • Development is viewed as the movement through stages, with the resolution of each stage setting the context for later development.	• **Freud's view:** Focuses on the importance of early childhood experiences, especially with the mother, and emphasizes the role of psychosexual conflicts and unconscious experience. • **Erikson's view:** Also focuses on social and personality development but adopts a lifespan framework that emphasizes the role of resolving basic developmental challenges, called *psychosocial conflicts,* which occur throughout the lifespan.
Behavioral views	• The emphasis is on how observable behavior is influenced by the environment.	• **Classical conditioning:** Describes learning of associations between neutral events and naturally occurring stimulus–response reflexes. • **Operant conditioning:** Describes the effect that rewards and punishments have on behavior. • **Social learning theory:** Emphasizes the importance of learning by observing and imitating the behavior of others.
Cognitive views	• The emphasis is on the development of thinking and problem solving. • Humans are viewed as active problem solvers rather than as passive recipients of information.	• **Piaget's theory of cognitive development:** Views the development of thinking and problem solving as moving through stages of increasing sophistication. • **Vygotsky's social-cognitive view:** Emphasizes the significance of learning from others who are more advanced in their knowledge.
Systems views	• The emphasis is on the overall social context in which development occurs. • Systems views attempt to combine theoretical ideas into an overarching perspective.	• **Bronfenbrenner's bioecological model:** Looks at development in social environments of varying degrees of closeness to the individual and emphasizes the interconnectedness of these environments.

- **Development is life long**, beginning at conception and ending at death. Throughout the entire lifespan, development continues.
- **Development is multidimensional**, consisting of interrelated systems, or domains. Among the most important of these to consider are physical development, cognitive development, and personality and sociocultural development.
- **Development is multidirectional and involves both losses and gains**. Some domains of development—language development, physical growth, social development—may show increases while at the same time other domains may remain static, or show decreases. Also, at some points in the lifespan, development proceeds toward greater competence, effectiveness, and growth; but at other points losses occur, skills decline, and effectiveness in coping with the environment may diminish.
- **Development is plastic**, meaning that it is flexible and can take many paths depending upon the particular circumstances within which individuals live their lives. The course of the lifespan is not set at conception, nor rigidly determined during childhood or at any other developmental period; rather development depends in many important ways on the various opportunities and choices an individual experiences and makes throughout the entire lifespan.
- **Development is context-dependent and historically and culturally embedded**. An individual's life can be best understood by considering the forces that act on other people who belong to the same age generation and who live within the same culture and historical period, as well as the unique experiences that only the individual experiences. Human development unfolds differently dependent on the sociocultural environment in which the individual lives, as well as on the specific and unique opportunities and challenges each individual faces.
- **The study of lifespan development is multidisciplinary**. The best understanding of lifespan development comes not from considering a single point of view or field of study, but rather by considering a variety of perspectives, including psychology, anthropology, biology, genetics, and sociology.

Throughout the remainder of this text, you will be reading about the developmental processes and milestones that occur as individuals move across the course of their lifespan. But before we begin that journey, let us pause to consider how developmental psychologists go about their work. In the final section of this chapter, we explore the methods that are commonly used to study the fascinating interplay of events that comprise human lifespan development.

REVIEW THE FACTS 1-3

1. Which of the following statements about a theory is *false*?
   a. Theories help us make predictions.
   b. Theories prove certain things to be true.
   c. Theories include sets of interrelated assumptions and principles.
   d. Theories help us to understand a phenomenon.
2. *Psychosocial theory* is the term used to describe __________'s view of development.
3. If you walked into a bakery and your mouth began watering at the smell of the delicious bread, this would best be explained by __________.
4. Suppose you are considering raising your hand in class to answer a question. However, the person just before you who did so was humiliated by the professor, even though her answer was quite good. You decide to keep quiet. The type of conditioning that best describes your response is called __________.
5. According to Piaget, if a child sees a picture of a kitten and says "doggie," but then is corrected so that he learns the difference between cats and dogs, he has engaged in which process?
   a. equilibration
   b. schematization
   c. assimilation
   d. accommodation
6. Vygotsky emphasized learning from a more knowledgeable person by serving as an apprentice. He called this process __________.
7. The broadest type of theory, and the one that attempts to incorporate other theories within its umbrella, is called __________.
8. Development is *plastic*. This means that __________.

Practice on **MyDevelopmentLab**

THE SCIENTIFIC APPROACH TO THE STUDY OF HUMAN DEVELOPMENT

As is true in other areas of scientific inquiry, investigation in the field of developmental psychology proceeds according to the methods of *science*. Scientific inquiry is conducted as objectively and systematically as possible, and it employs carefully defined methods for collecting data. Scientists also are held to strict ethical guidelines, which are especially important in the field of human development, because typically the focus of their study is on human beings.

In the last section of this chapter, we focus on how the methods of science are used to advance the understanding of human lifespan development. We begin with an examination of techniques that involve the observation of individuals in order to describe their development. Then we explore experimental approaches, which go beyond description and attempt to determine the causes of behavior and development. Finally, we comment on the ethical responsibilities that developmental researchers must accept as they conduct research that investigates human development.

Descriptive Methods

Case Studies One of the earliest methods used to study human development is an approach known as the **case study**, which involves compiling detailed information about an individual, a family, or a community. Case studies employ a variety of techniques—such as interviews, observations, and formal testing—to provide the researcher with as complete a picture as possible of an individual, a parent–child interaction, a patient–doctor interaction, a classroom climate, or even a cultural event.

The earliest case studies that took a developmental perspective were called **baby biographies**. Charles Darwin, for example, kept a daily record of his son's early development, as did Jean Piaget, two theorists whose work was described earlier in this chapter. Baby biographies typically focused on what might be called "mini-milestones," such as the ages at which infants first smiled, rolled over, sat upright, and so forth. However, there were several major problems with this approach. One problem was that it was never certain whether the "firsts" were accurate or merely the first time the biographer noticed the behaviors. In addition, especially with young infants, it often was hard to pinpoint exactly when a behavior became intentional and was not a developmental accident ("Was that a smile or a burp?"). Finally, there was always a question about whether the infants observed were "normal," or "typically developing," and therefore representative of all infants at their age.

Sometimes parents record significant events in their baby's life in a "baby book." How would such a book be similar to, and different from, a case study?

For these reasons, baby biographies were soon abandoned in favor of more thorough and systematic case studies. Sigmund Freud was an early and avid proponent of detailed case studies, as were a large number of early personality theorists. Case studies are still a preferred method of studying relatively rare mental and behavioral disorders; because of the small number of people who suffer from such disorders, other research approaches often are not feasible.

However, the case study method has some shortcomings. The task of sorting out details and making sense of the case study can be very time consuming. In addition, it is difficult to tell from the case study data alone what the relationships between events mean. For example, physical or sexual abuse or other emotional trauma during early childhood is almost always found in the case histories of adults with dissociative identity disorder, formerly known as multiple personality disorder

case study
The compilation of detailed information on an individual, a family, or a community through interviews, observations, and formal testing

baby biography
Recording mini-milestones of child development (e.g., the ages when the child discovers parts of the body, creeps, sits upright, or walks)

(e.g., see Cardeña & Gleaves, 2007; Ross, 2010). This does *not* necessarily mean that childhood sexual abuse *causes* later psychiatric illness, however, because many other explanations are possible. Although the case study method serves an important role in the clinical diagnosis and the treatment of individuals with specific problems, today this method is used less frequently by developmental psychologists who wish to understand the universal principles that guide human development.

Systematic Observation Another descriptive method used by developmental psychologists is referred to as *systematic observation*, which involves observing individuals or groups using carefully prescribed guidelines about the exact behaviors that are the focus of study as well as which situations are relevant. Sometimes the behavior of interest occurs in a natural setting, such as children playing a card game in school, and the researcher can observe such activity as it naturally occurs. One issue that concerns such **naturalistic observation** is that the researcher must not influence the behavior that is being studied; if the children are aware that they are being watched, their behavior may change, rendering the study invalid. Another consideration associated with naturalistic observation concerns an individual's right to privacy: Would you be comfortable if you found out that your behavior for the past 24 hours had been under the careful scrutiny of research psychologists? Finally, for behaviors that do not occur frequently, naturalistic observation often proves too inefficient to be useful.

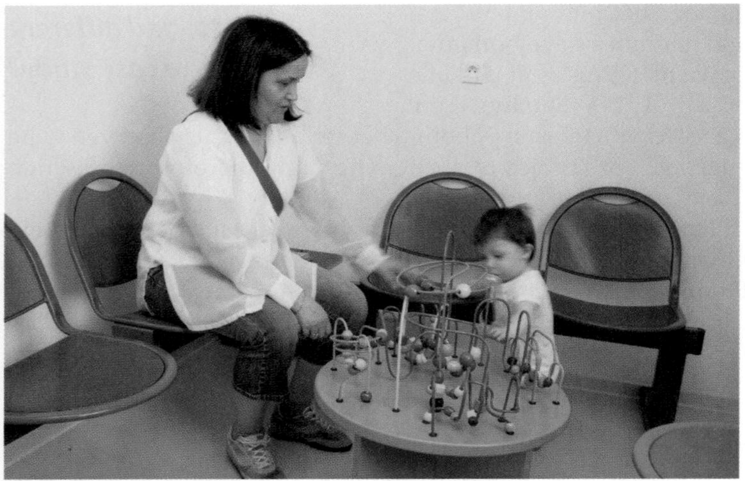

▲ Mary Ainsworth developed a research technique called the "strange situation" in which young children are observed when their mother leaves them alone or a stranger enters the room.

For these reasons, developmental researchers often prefer to conduct observational studies in a laboratory setting that is specifically set up to encourage the behaviors of interest. One example of such a **laboratory observation** is the "strange situation" developed by Mary Ainsworth and her colleagues (e.g., Ainsworth & Bell, 1970) to study the quality of infant–mother attachment. In "strange situation" studies, researchers watch from behind a one-way mirror as a mother and her infant enter a waiting room. Once the mother has engaged her child in play, a stranger enters the room and sits down. The mother then leaves. Ainsworth and her colleagues were particularly interested in how infants reacted to this mother separation: Did they cry and get upset? Did they act fearful of the stranger, or approach her to join in their play? What happened when the mother reentered the room? Did the infants express relief and joy or act angry over being deserted? Ainsworth argued that the infant's response to the mother in this strange situation was an indicator of the quality of the child's attachment—an important predictor of later social development (see Chapter 5).

Observational studies are useful to developmental researchers because they allow for the investigation of behavior as it naturally occurs. Even in laboratory observations, the emphasis is on creating a setting that encourages normal behavior. However, observational studies do have limitations. Some behaviors occur so infrequently that observational studies are impractical. In addition, there is always the possibility that the very process of observing a person's behavior changes it in some subtle yet important way. Ethical issues such as informed consent (described later in this section) must also be addressed. Nevertheless, the observational method has proven valuable in the investigation of many important developmental questions.

Questionnaires and Surveys The paper-and-pencil methods employed in **questionnaires** and **surveys** ask respondents to answer questions about past and present behavior, attitudes, preferences, opinions, feelings, and so forth. The distinction between these two approaches is one of scale: A questionnaire may be administered to one individual (typically as a part of a case study) or it may be administered to a large group of people—at which point it is usually called a survey. On occasion, questionnaires and surveys are administered verbally as well, either in person, by phone, or via the Internet, in which case they are referred to as **interviews**.

An obvious advantage of these methods of data collection is that a great deal of information can be collected on many individuals in an efficient and cost-effective manner. The central concerns associated with these methods center on whether the

naturalistic observation
The observational method in which researchers go into everyday settings and observe and record behavior while being as unobtrusive as possible

questionnaire
A paper-and-pencil method that asks respondents to answer questions about past or present behavior, attitudes, preferences, opinions, feelings, and so forth

Watch *Naturalistic Observation* on **MyDevelopmentLab**

survey
A questionnaire administered to a large group

laboratory observation
The observational method in which researchers set up controlled situations designed to elicit the behavior of interest

interview
A questionnaire that is administered verbally, usually in a one-on-one setting

respondents are answering truthfully and if the respondents are representative of the individuals about whom the researcher wishes to draw conclusions. Especially when surveys touch on issues that are of personal concern, such as sexual behavior or drug use, people may be reluctant to report their actual behavior or opinions. Also psychologists have long understood that people tend to remember their past actions in a more favorable light than was actually the case. Furthermore, people typically are not aware that their memories are flawed, making it impossible to know what actually did happen in the past.

Generally, the purpose of a survey or an interview is to understand the behavior or attitudes of a *population* of interest. Because it often is impractical (and sometimes impossible) to survey all members of that population, a *sample* of individuals in that population is selected and studied, and the results gathered from this sample are used to generalize to the population at large. Sampling always raises the question of whether the individuals in the sample fairly and accurately represent the larger population from which they are drawn. Whenever sampling is done, researchers must take care to ensure that **representative sampling** occurs; otherwise, their conclusion cannot validly apply to the population of interest. Most Internet surveys and those printed in magazines or conducted informally suffer from a lack of representative sampling because the people who choose to answer most likely are different in important ways from those who do not. Despite the obvious limitations associated with these methods, carefully constructed and well-administered surveys do provide researchers with important insights into human behavior and development.

Psychological Tests Sometimes it is important to understand how different levels of ability or different personality traits, dispositions, or levels of adjustment are related to human development. In order to explore such relationships, psychologists rely on psychological tests to measure the constructs of interest. Of course, such tests—which often involve the measurement of intelligence or personality traits such as extroversion or emotional stability—must be carefully constructed and administered so that accurate results are obtained. Although a discussion of what constitutes a good test lies beyond the coverage of this text, you should be aware that an entire field of psychological testing has developed in response to such concerns.

Studying Development Across Time

Because development is a dynamic and continuous process, developmental studies—in contrast to other types of research—often focus on changes that individuals experience as they grow

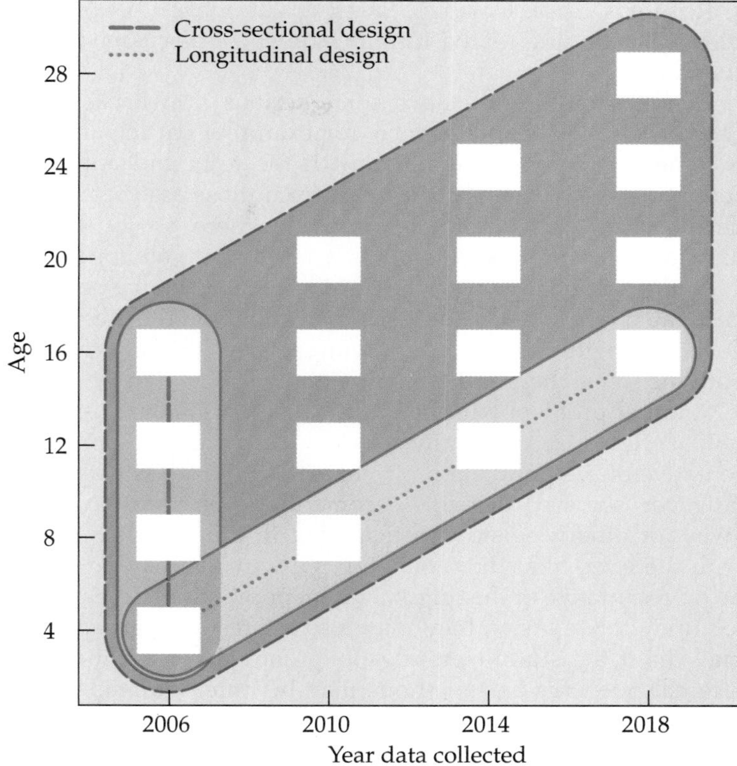

FIGURE 1-3 Developmental Research Designs Compared
The diagonal rows (e.g., the orange row) represent longitudinal studies, which follow a group of the same age across time. The vertical columns (e.g., the green column) represent cross-sectional studies, which look at different age cohort groups at the same time. The complete illustration is of the sequential-cohort design, which combines the other two approaches to study four different age cohort groups at four different points in time.

older. How do researchers gather data about developmental change? There are three general approaches, as illustrated in Figure 1-3.

The Longitudinal Design In a **longitudinal design**, a single group of individuals is studied repeatedly at different points in their lifespans. Sometimes researchers look at developmental processes very closely by studying individuals every week or even every day. For example, a group of 2-year-old children might be tested weekly to create a detailed picture of their language development. Longitudinal designs also have been applied to change across many years. A prominent example is the classic study of "gifted" children initiated in the early 1920s by Lewis Terman (1877–1956), a study that has followed a group of children into their older adult years (e.g., Friedman, Kern,

representative sampling
Selecting a sample from a larger population so that the sample represents, or mirrors, the population in every important way

longitudinal design
A study in which the same participants are studied at various points in time to see how they change as they age

& Reynolds, 2010; Holahan, Sears, & Chronbach, 1995; Kern, 2009). (The findings of the Terman studies are discussed in later chapters.)

Longitudinal studies have some serious drawbacks, however. In studies of intelligence, for example, participants can become practiced and familiar with the tests and appear to show progressive gains quite apart from those associated with development. Also, in practical terms, there obviously is a limit on how many such studies a researcher can conduct in a lifetime, especially when the developmental change being investigated is one that unfolds slowly throughout the lifespan. In general, longitudinal research requires a great deal of time from both the researchers and the participants.

Another problem with longitudinal studies is the possibility of bias. Researchers initially select participants who are representative of the population of interest. As the study continues, however, some participants become ill, go on vacation, move away, or otherwise stop participating in the research project, with the effect that the remaining participants may no longer be representative of the original target population. Researchers, too, may move away, they may lose interest, or perhaps they may die if the study continues long enough. In addition, the original purposes and methods may become outdated in any long-term longitudinal study. Often it becomes difficult to incorporate new approaches and still obtain data that can be compared to earlier findings.

Nevertheless, longitudinal studies yield detailed data about individual developmental change that other methods cannot obtain, and so they remain a popular research approach. As noted by Jeanne Brooks-Gunn and colleagues (e.g., Brooks-Gunn, Berlin, Leventhal, & Fuligni, 2000; Gardner, Roth, & Brooks-Gunn, 2008), several new and large-scale longitudinal projects are currently under way. They cover topics such as the effectiveness of early Head Start programs (Green, Furrer, & McAllister, 2011), how "fragile" families affect child well-being (see the box Current Issues: Fragile Families and Child Well-Being), how brain volumes decline with age (Taki, et al., 2011), how early life feeding practices affect illness rates at age 2 (Hetzner, Razza, Malone, & Brooks-Gunn, 2009), and many more areas.

The Cross-Sectional Design Like the longitudinal design, the cross-sectional method attempts to describe how individuals change across time. However, rather than following a group of individuals as they age, a **cross-sectional design** compares individuals of different ages *at one point in time.* Although cross-sectional research cannot assess individual development, it is quicker, cheaper, and more manageable than longitudinal research.

Cross-sectional designs require careful selection of their participants to ensure that the results are due to differences in development and not to other kinds of differences between the groups. For example, studies of adult intelligence, as well as many studies of changes associated with aging, have been plagued by problems of comparability: Is a sample of 70-year-olds, for example, as healthy, or as well educated, or from the same ethnic or sociocultural group as a sample of 30-year-olds? Such differences between groups that may exist are called **cohort effects**—we would say that the 30-year-old cohort may differ in important ways from the 70-year-old cohort. Cohort effects can therefore produce **confounding**: The researcher cannot be sure whether any obtained differences or trends are due to developmental factors or to historical factors that make different age groups unequal in some important way. Because of these cohort effects, early research on intellectual change across the adult lifespan indicated a greatly exaggerated decline in later adulthood (see Chapter 16); later research has shown such cognitive changes to be much less dramatic.

Why would researchers choose a cross-sectional approach over a longitudinal approach?

As you might have guessed, cross-sectional research across much shorter age ranges is less subject to cohort effects. Education and other historical factors tend to change relatively slowly so that, for example, a comparison of 4-year-olds, 6-year-olds, and 8-year-olds is not likely to be confounded with historical factors. Numerous examples of both longitudinal and cross-sectional research appear in later chapters.

The Sequential-Cohort Design Because problems exist with each of the approaches just described, researchers are now more inclined toward a mix of the two, which is called the **sequential-cohort design**. Thus, a researcher might start with a group of 4-year-olds, a group of 8-year-olds, and a group of 12-year-olds and study each cohort every 4 years for 12 years (see Figure 1-3), thereby allowing comparison from the ages of 4 to 24—the full range of ages from early childhood into early adulthood. Comparisons could then be made both longitudinally and cross-sectionally. Examples of this approach also appear in later chapters.

Correlation as a Descriptive Tool

Sometimes researchers wish to study the relationship that exists between two variables. For example, is the amount of violence watched on TV related to aggressive behavior displayed by children? The research technique employed to investigate such relationships is called **correlation**.

cross-sectional design
A study that compares individuals of different ages at one point in time (e.g., a group of 5-year-olds, a group of 8-year-olds, and a group of 11-year-olds)

sequential-cohort design
A research design where several overlapping cohorts of different ages are studied longitudinally

cohort effects
The sociocultural differences between people of different age groups

correlation
A research technique that describes the relationship, or correspondence, between two variables

confounding
The problem of not being sure whether any obtained differences or trends between cohorts are due to developmental factors or to historical factors associated with different cohort groups

CURRENT ISSUES

Fragile Families and Child Well-Being

Not all children grow up in families that promote healthy adjustment and development. Even in developed nations like the United States, significant numbers of children are growing up in less-than-optimal settings. The effects of environmental stress, such as poverty, abuse, poor child care, family conflict, and other tensions, typically occur over long periods, often throughout the entirety of a child's early life. Thus, these factors produce cumulative effects. Consequently, because early development is so important in establishing the foundation for development later in life, a number of studies have been initiated to investigate the impact that growing up in a fragile family has on the development of children raised in such settings (Evans & Kim, 2012; Waldfogel, Craigie, & Brooks-Gunn, 2010).

Of particular importance are the longitudinal studies that follow a group of individuals across time. Not only does this research method provide a snapshot view of how children are progressing at a given point in time, but it also provides researchers with a vehicle to observe the effects of improving or deteriorating environments and the impact of public policies or program changes that are aimed at improving the well-being of these at-risk children.

One such longitudinal study, called the Fragile Families and Child Well-Being Study, identified a cohort of 3,600 unmarried couples and 1,100 married couples who were recruited to participate upon the birth of their first child (Center for Research on Child Wellbeing, 2011). Begun in 1998, this sample, which was drawn from 20 different U.S. cities, represents a population that researchers know relatively little about; consequently, the findings are not always as expected. For example, more than one-half of the unwed couples in the study lived together and 30% of the remainder were romantically involved—a finding that contradicts a common stereotype about "unwed mothers." Furthermore, more than two-thirds of the unmarried participants expected to get married eventually, and the overwhelming majority of unwed mothers wanted the fathers to be involved in the child's life. Fathers were available for interviews in 75% of the unwed couples (Fuligni, McCabe, McLanahan, & Roth, 2003).

▲ Considerable misinformation and negative social stigma sometimes are associated with perceptions about the needs of those living in poor and highly stressed environments. Results from longitudinal studies are especially important in providing an accurate understanding of the actual circumstances that affect development in such contexts.

Other results from the Fragile Families study generally confirm expectations. Perhaps not surprisingly, most of the unmarried couples were not well equipped to provide financially for their children. Most fathers reported earnings of less than $20,000 per year, and the mother's annual earnings averaged $5,000. Over one-third of both the mothers and the fathers lacked a high school diploma. Most of the children were born healthy, but 10% were of low birth weight, and 20% of the mothers did not have prenatal care in the first 3 months of their pregnancy. The Fragile Families data has provided a much needed source of information about the impact that non-cohabiting parental relationships (Carlson & Högnäs, 2011; McLanahan & Beck, 2010) and nonresident fathers (Carlson & McLanahan, 2010) have on their children's development.

The original purpose of the Fragile Families study was to evaluate the impact of poverty and environmental stress on the development of young children. Thus, mothers and fathers were interviewed shortly after the child was born and again when the child was 12, 30, and 48 months old. Information on the child's health and well-being was collected from the mother each year. Independent in-home assessments of the child's development and well-being were made at 30 and 48 months, and shifts in each family's composition and circumstances also were assessed over the 4-year period. The Fragile Families study is still ongoing and has been expanded both in scope and length. The project now additionally includes studies of parental employment, child health, couple dynamics, and fathers' roles in child rearing. In 2007, the study launched a 9-year follow-up of participants that will include interviews with mothers, fathers, and the children themselves, along with in-home assessments of family interactions. Interviews are now complete and data from this phase of the study is expected to be published in 2012.

Although much cultural wisdom exists about how the needs of those living in poor and highly stressed environments can best be addressed, the views of policymakers about this population and the circumstances of their lives may well be colored by misinformation and negative social stigma. Thus, well-conceived and carefully conducted longitudinal research may reveal surprising results. Knowing more about the lives of the participants in this study and about how public policies and programs impact them may prompt researchers to find more effective ways to address their needs. In addition, this research may serve to inform public policy decisions so that programs are well tailored to provide relief and support (Fuligni, McCabe, McLanahan, & Roth, 2003; Waldfogel, Craigie, & Brooks-Gunn, 2010).

Watch *Single Mothers* on **MyDevelopmentLab**

The first step in a correlational study typically involves the measurement of the two variables of interest. In the previous example, we might measure how many hours a week the children in the study watch programming defined as violent and also measure how aggressive they are, perhaps by asking teachers to rate each child's aggressiveness on a scale of 1 to 10. Once the variables are measured, statistical techniques are applied to determine the numerical value, called the *correlation coefficient*, that describes their relationship to each other.

Correlation coefficients are expressed on a scale of 0 to 1.00 and can be either positive or negative. *Positive correlations* (from 0 to +1.00) describe relationships where as one variable increases the other variable increases as well. If the previously described study revealed that children who watch more hours of violent TV also express more violent play behavior, this would be a positive correlation. *Negative correlations* (from 0 to −1.00) result when as one variable increases the other variable decreases. If the study revealed that children who watched more hours of violent TV were actually less violent in their play, this would be reflected in a negative correlation.

Suppose a major research study found a large positive correlation between the amount of fat included in people's diets and the degree to which they are overweight. What are three possible causal explanations that might describe this correlational finding?

The strength of the relationship between the two variables is reflected in the *value* of the correlation coefficient. Weaker relationships result in correlations closer to zero. In fact, if there is no relationship at all, the correlation coefficient *is* zero. However, when the correspondence between variables is very clear and predictable, larger correlation coefficients result; and when there is a perfect relationship, the correlation coefficient takes on the value of +1.00 (if the correlation is positive) or −1.00 (if it is negative). Thus, the larger the value of the correlation coefficient is, the stronger the relationship between the variables.

It is important to note that correlation, by itself, is insufficient to reveal information about *causation* (what causes what). Although a large body of evidence from carefully controlled experiments has demonstrated that watching violence on television does in fact make many children more aggressive than they otherwise would be, it would be incorrect to draw this conclusion from the results of correlation studies alone. Correlation tells us that a relationship between variables exists, nothing more. If a positive correlation were obtained in the previously described study, several interpretations could be offered. For example, it *might* be true that watching TV violence increases aggressiveness. However, the reverse explanation might also be true: Maybe children who are inherently more aggressive prefer to watch violent TV programs. There are other possibilities as well: Maybe the more aggressive children are that way because their parents are violent and punish them harshly, which tends to make children more aggressive, and maybe the parents also select violent TV programs for the family to watch.

Although correlation is not an indicator of what causes what, it is an excellent research tool when used and interpreted appropriately. To investigate causal relationships, other research techniques have been developed. Foremost among these is the experiment.

Experimental Approaches: The Study of Cause and Effect

Basic to human nature is our curiosity about how things work. Early humans undoubtedly manipulated and poked and prodded things to see what would happen. Build a raft out of rocks; it sinks. Build a raft out of branches and limbs; it floats. Such simple tests, often driven by survival, would have been among the first experiments.

Today psychologists use the experimental method to explore such cause-and-effect relationships. Sometimes these methods involve the careful study of an individual, whose responses to changing conditions are the focus of research. For example, this method is often used in studies that involve *applied behavior analysis* (described in Chapter 2), where problem behaviors are systematically eliminated by using rewards and punishments. More often, however, developmental psychologists study the behavior of groups of individuals as they are exposed to different situations that are believed to affect behavior.

Experiments Focusing on Groups Experimental psychologists who study development are inclined to conduct group experiments in an attempt to arrive at general principles that might

▲ Albert Bandura studied aggression in children, making the point that children learn aggressive responses by watching adults.

random assignment
Placing participants in groups with the hope that the groups will be roughly equivalent (e.g., by drawing names from a container)

apply to all humans. Such experiments typically begin by identifying a group of volunteers who are willing to participate in the experiment. Next, these participants are divided into different groups, often using the technique of **random assignment**. Assigning participants *randomly* to groups enhances the probability that the groups will not differ from each other in significant ways. Therefore, any differences in the way the groups respond can be attributed to the different ways in which these various groups are treated.

Once the participants are assigned to different groups, these groups are then exposed to different *treatment conditions*. For example, if researchers are interested in studying the effect of viewing TV violence on aggressiveness in play behavior, they might divide a group of children randomly into two groups. One group would watch TV shows judged to be highly violent; the other group would watch nonviolent shows. These different treatment conditions in an experiment constitute the **independent variable**—the variable in an experiment that is manipulated by the experimenter in order to observe what effects it will have on behavior. As the final step in the experiment, the children's behavior on the **dependent variable**—the variable that the independent variable affects—is measured. In this example, the dependent variable would be some measure of the aggressiveness of children's play behavior.

As in Bandura's research, a child acts aggressively toward a Bobo doll in ways the child has seen an adult model act.

As you can see from this example, it is very important to assign children randomly to different independent variable groups. Suppose that instead of using random assignments, the children were allowed to choose which group they wanted to join. Such a procedure would likely produce two unequal groups: In the previous example, perhaps the "violent" group might include all the boys and the "nonviolent" group all the girls. If the results of such a study revealed that the group exposed to the violent programming played more aggressively, the researchers would not know whether that result was due to the type of TV programming the children watched or to the possibility that boys play more aggressively than girls. The random assignment of participants to groups allows experimenters to avoid confounding (described earlier in this chapter).

An actual example of developmental research on the influence of viewing violence on subsequent behavior is the now classic "Bobo doll" experiment performed by Albert Bandura (1965, 1969). In this experiment, three randomly assigned groups of preschool boys and girls watched a film in which an adult model "beat up" an inflated, adult-sized Bobo doll in specific ways. One group saw the adult model *rewarded* at the end of the film with praise from another adult. A second group saw the model *punished* by being scolded, and a third group saw the model experience *no consequences*. Thus, there were three different experimental treatments that constituted the *independent variable*, which in this case was defined as the consequences of aggression for the adult model depicted in the film. After viewing the film, each child was allowed to play with a Bobo doll of the child's size. Researchers counted the number of aggressive acts the children displayed in their play—this was the *dependent variable*—the behavior that is measured to determine if the independent variable had an effect. The results of this study clearly demonstrate that the consequences the model received had a marked impact on the children's imitation. Although the boys behaved more aggressively than the girls in all three independent variable groups, there was less aggression expressed by both boys and girls in the group that saw the adult model punished than was observed in the other two groups.

On the basis of a single experiment such as Bandura's, researchers would not make the sweeping generalization that watching adults being aggressive increases children's aggressiveness. Rather, they would want to repeat the experiment using different children, different kinds of filmed or televised violence, and differing measures of children's aggressiveness. If similar results were obtained, researchers then could conclude that these subsequent studies **replicated** the results of the original study. Replication of results is necessary for researchers to have confidence that their findings are reliable and that they apply to other situations similar to those tested in the studies conducted. Replication

independent variable
The variable in an experiment that is manipulated in order to observe its effects on the dependent variable

dependent variable
The variable in an experiment that changes as a result of manipulating the independent variable

replication (or replicate)
Systematic repetitions of an experiment or other research study to determine if the findings are reliable and if they can be generalized

Table 1-7 Descriptive and Experimental Research Methods and Their Advantages and Disadvantages

Method	Description	Advantages	Disadvantages
Case study	A case study provides a detailed picture of an individual based on interviews, observations, testing, and other information.	• Provides a detailed view of an individual, which is useful when the condition being studied is rare.	• May provide biased results if individuals do not represent their groups. • Case studies also are time and cost intensive.
Naturalistic observation	Naturalistic observation involves a systematic and unobtrusive observation of an individual (or group) in an everyday setting.	• Captures "real-world" behavior.	• May be difficult to unobtrusively observe the behavior of interest. • The behavior of interest also may be rare. • Naturalistic observation is time and cost intensive.
Laboratory observation	Laboratory observation involves a systematic observation of an individual (or group) in a setting designed to elicit the behavior of interest.	• Prompts the behavior under investigation to occur so that it can be observed. • The situation can be better controlled than in a naturalistic study.	• Behavior may change due to the participants' knowledge that they are being observed. • It may be difficult to prompt some types of behavior to occur.
Survey	The survey uses a set of questions that is intended to elicit responses from a sample of individuals, usually pertaining to attitudes, values, or behaviors.	• Large amounts of data can be collected with relative ease. • Sampling ensures that the data are representative of the population.	• Individuals may misrepresent themselves, either intentionally or due to bias. • Questions may be misleading or have multiple interpretations.
Psychological testing	Psychological testing uses a set of questions or problems that is designed to assess an individual's intelligence or personality.	• Important dimensions of human behavior can be measured. • Intelligence and personality have an important impact on development.	• Tests must be accurate. • Not all important variables are subject to testing.
Correlation	Correlation is the measurement of two variables and the statistical calculation that describes the relationship of the variables to each other.	• Correlational studies can identify important relationships among variables of interest.	• Correlation cannot be used to infer cause and effect.
Experiment	In an experiment, the experimenter manipulates the independent variable under study, with the results measured on the dependent variable.	• Experiments can be used to explore cause-and-effect relationships. • Experiments provide the experimenter with good control over experimental conditions.	• It sometimes is impossible to manipulate the independent variable of interest. In such cases, quasi-experiments sometimes can be designed and used. • Sometimes there are ethical limitations on what research questions can be investigated.

thus plays a central role in building a general understanding of the issue being studied. Indeed, subsequent research has shown that children readily learn how to copy aggressive acts when they watch violence in films or on TV; however, their display of aggressive behavior will likely depend on the consequences they associate with their actions (Bandura, 1965, 1969).

Why is replication such an important component of any program of scientific research?

The Quasi-Experimental Method Although the experimental method often is preferred because it gives the clearest picture of what caused the behavior that researchers wish to understand, in some situations it cannot be used. Researchers may wish to study an independent variable that cannot be randomly assigned to volunteers; for example, researchers cannot change the variable of sex (a person is either male or female); thus, sex cannot be assigned to people by the flip of a coin. In such cases, researchers often employ a **quasi-experimental method**, which is like an experiment but does not demand that all of the experiment's requirements (such as the random assignment of participants to treatment groups) be met. In choosing the most appropriate research method, developmentalists consider the questions they wish to answer, as well as the limitations imposed by both practical and ethical concerns. Thus, several different methods are used in lifespan development research, and evidence gathered from many different types of research projects will be presented in the chapters that follow.

quasi-experimental method
A research method, much like an experiment, that is used when an experiment is not possible (e.g., when volunteers cannot be randomly assigned to treatment groups)

Summary of Research Methods

In the previous section, we presented a brief overview of several commonly used research methods (see Table 1-7). Although each method has its limitations and weaknesses, each also has its strengths. Thus, all of these methods are used extensively by developmental researchers, depending on the particular issues that are being investigated.

Regardless of the particular research method chosen, however, researchers must always consider the ethical issues involved in their research. No one would argue that child abuse is not an important developmental topic and one that should be studied and better understood. Yet scientists would *never* suggest that abuse should be studied experimentally, where groups of children are intentionally abused just to see the effect. Even in nonexperimental studies of abuse, all kinds of ethical issues are raised, including an individual's (and a family's) rights of privacy and informed consent. Such ethical issues are the topic of the following—and final—section of this chapter.

Ethics in Developmental Research

Most people agree that experiments and studies using humans are necessary, especially if scientists are to understand and control the impact of potentially harmful events and situations. However, responsible scientists also understand that the individuals who participate in these studies should never be harmed as the result of their participation. Developmental psychologists in particular are in a difficult situation with respect to research ethics because many of the topics they study—child abuse, prejudice, aggression, tragedy, and grief—involve situations known to be harmful; yet, they affect human development in important ways.

To highlight the importance of conducting research so that no harm comes to individuals, several organizations have published strict ethical guidelines that cannot be violated, regardless of the significance of the topics under study. (There are similar guidelines that specify ethical requirements for research on animals.) For example, the American Psychological Association (APA) publishes a detailed set of ethical principles and a code of conduct with which all psychologists are expected to comply (APA, 2010). The APA also publishes books and manuals that describe in detail the distinctions between research practices that are acceptable and those that are not (e.g., Folkman & Sales, 2005; Nagy, 2011). The Society for Research in Child Development (SRCD, 2011) publishes similar guidelines oriented specifically toward research with children. These ethical guidelines are not merely recommendations; they are backed up by law, and developmental researchers are careful to comply with them (Folkman & Sales, 2005).

The guidelines that define acceptable standards for research with human participants embrace basic moral principles. These principles guide research decisions in many ways, including those described in the following paragraphs.

Protection from Harm No research should have the potential for serious or lasting physical or psychological harm. However, under certain carefully defined circumstances, psychologists may study humans under conditions that involve *minimal risk*. For example, suppose a researcher wants to demonstrate that 9-year-olds can understand a particular concept and solve certain problems that 5-year-olds cannot. If the researcher devises an experiment that gives the same set of difficult problems to groups of 5- and 9-year-olds, what is the ethical issue? Here the expectation might be that all of the 5-year-old children will experience repeated failure, most likely having been deceived about the solvability of the problems (otherwise they might simply give up too quickly). Is it ethical to have children (or anyone) go through the frustration of attempting unsolvable problems?

To answer questions such as these, all research organizations, including colleges and universities where research is conducted, are now required to have committees that review and evaluate research proposals. These screening committees are called **Institutional Review Boards (IRBs)**, and they carefully evaluate the risk to participants that likely may result from particular studies. The main task for such IRBs is to weigh the balance of potential risk to participants against the benefits to be derived from the research. Generally, IRBs will not allow research that involves more risk to participants than they might experience in everyday life. In the previous example, the IRB would likely reason that children do, at least occasionally, meet with failure on academic tasks in a regular school setting. Thus, this research probably would be granted approval with the stipulation that the participants be *debriefed* following the experiment; that is, they must be told what the purpose of the experiment was and that the problems were constructed in such a way so that no 5-year-old child could solve the problems.

Informed Consent In all cases, people should participate in research voluntarily, be fully informed of the nature and possible consequences of the research, and not be coerced in any way. Each of these requirements is an aspect of **informed consent**: ". . . [a] clear statement of the purposes, procedures, risks, and benefits . . . as well as the obligations and commitments of both the participants and the researchers" (Fischman, 2000, p. 35). Informed consent also requires that all participants must be free to discontinue their participation in the research at any point, for whatever reason, and without attempts being made to prevent them from doing so. This includes not withholding any payment or other compensation

Suppose a researcher proposes a study about how children react to criticism. The study involves having an adult teach a game to 4-, 6-, and 8-year-old children and then criticize the first instance when the child fails to remember one of the rules. Do you think an IRB would approve this study? What questions do you believe the board would expect the researchers to answer before approval would be given?

Institutional Review Boards (IRBs)
Screening committees at research institutions that evaluate all research projects relative to their potential harm to participants

informed consent
A clear statement of the procedures and risks, as well as the obligations of both the participants and the researchers

that has been offered: If a participant *begins* an experiment or other research project, he or she must be paid in full, regardless of whether the research study is completed.

As you may have noted, there is a potential conflict between informed consent and the deception that sometimes is necessary in research with humans. Deception is used because participants' behavior may change if they know the true purpose of an experiment: They may try to behave as they think the experimenter wants them to and be "good" participants or they may deliberately try to defeat the experimenter and be "bad" participants. How can a person give informed consent if the true purpose of the study is withheld? The generally accepted resolution of this conflict specifies that participants cannot be deceived in any way that might affect their decision to participate, although they can be deceived about the specific purposes of the research. Also participants must be thoroughly debriefed and told the true nature of the research as soon as possible following the conclusion of their participation in the study (Nagy, 2011). Because children, especially before age 10, do not fully understand the concept of informed consent (Vitiello, 2008), parents must be consulted and they must give their consent on behalf of their child.

Privacy and Confidentiality Information obtained in a research project must remain private and confidential. Privacy means, first, that personal information about the participant is not divulged without the person's consent and, second, that the participant is not given information that is unwanted, such as information derived from tests the person took or feedback about performance that might distress the person (Folkman & Sales, 2005).

Researchers can, of course, analyze general information about their participants, such as their age, sex, and other demographic characteristics; however, names and other identifying information about individual participants cannot be disclosed without their written permission. Privacy also means that information about participants is not shared with others: No agencies or individuals other than the researcher should have access to the participants' records, which may include information about their private lives, thoughts, fantasies, scores on intelligence or personality tests, or behavior during experiments.

Knowledge of Results Whether during debriefing or at a later time, such as when the research effort is completed, individuals have the right to be informed of the results of the study, and in terms that they can understand. Researchers must take special care to explain the results of their studies using vocabulary and explanations that any literate person can understand. When children are involved, these results are shared with their parents.

Beneficial Treatments Finally, each participant has the right to profit from any beneficial treatments provided to other participants in the study. For example, if a participant is assigned to a comparison or *control* group in an experiment on a new vaccine or on a psychological treatment and therefore does not receive the beneficial treatment during the experiment, that person is entitled to receive the treatment after the study concludes should it prove effective. In general, researchers must supply any positive benefits of research at no charge to all participants in return for their participation.

Development in Context

In this chapter, we have introduced you to the main issues that define the field of human lifespan development. In particular, we have focused on providing a brief summary of the major theoretical perspectives that have guided the thinking of researchers about human development and on describing the scientific methods that developmental psychologists commonly use today as they explore human behavior in a developmental context. The ideas presented in this chapter will be useful as you begin to study the changes that occur as individuals move through the lifespan.

However, before beginning this journey through the lifespan, we pause to consider the two major forces that guide these unfolding developmental events: the genetic instructions that are inherited from an individual's parents and the environmental influences that shape each person's development. We will investigate these topics—heredity and environment—in the next chapter.

REVIEW THE FACTS 1-4

1. Baby biographies are best considered to be examples of which scientific method?
2. Mary Ainsworth's "strange situation" is an example of the method called _________ that she used to study the developmental behavior called _________.
3. Suppose you identify a group of 4-year-olds and test them for extroversion at ages 4, 8, 12, and again when they are 16. This type of study is called
   a. a longitudinal design.
   b. a cross-sectional design.
   c. a cohort design.
   d. a sequential-cohort design.
4. When a researcher cannot determine whether a result in the data is due to the factor being studied or to another variable, this is called a problem of _________.
5. If researchers found that children who spent more hours playing computer games had slower reading speeds, they would have identified a _________ correlation.
6. Suppose that a researcher wanted to conduct an experiment to study the effectiveness of a phonics-based reading program compared to a whole-word program. The researcher divided a kindergarten randomly into two groups, gave each group different instruction for 2 months, and measured students' reading ability at the end of that time. In this experiment, what was the dependent variable?
7. In the experiment described in question 8, what was the independent variable?
8. Before a research study can be conducted, it must be evaluated for ethical issues by a group called a(n) _________.

Practice on MyDevelopmentLab

CHAPTER SUMMARY

Introduction to Development

What is lifespan development and how universal are developmental periods, or stages?

- *Development* refers to the changes over time in a person's physical structure, thought, and behavior due to biological and environmental influences. *Developmental psychologists* usually focus on the common features of development that most people experience, although they do acknowledge that each individual's development is unique to some extent.

What guiding themes help us understand and organize our knowledge of human development?

- To understand human development better, psychologists usually divide the lifespan into *developmental periods,* or *stages,* that are experienced in similar ways by most people in most cultures.
- Human development is the result of several interacting forces. These are both biological and environmental, with cultural and personal factors playing especially significant roles.
- Development occurs within a *social context,* and it is often understood best by considering the domains, or categories, of human experience.
- Development also is understood best when considered within a theoretical framework and when studied by employing the methods of science.

The Nature of Human Development

What does it mean to say that heredity and environment interact *as they influence the course of development?*

- Biological factors and environmental factors interact, or influence each other, as humans develop. Processes that are influenced more by biology, such as growth and aging, often are referred to as processes that involve *maturation.* Processes that change more due to environmental influences often are referred to as processes that involve *learning.* Yet most developmental events involve both biology and environment in interaction.
- An individual's society and culture can exert powerful influences on development. Generally, children are treated more kindly today, at least in developed nations, than in many earlier historical periods.

How does a person's family and culture shape that person's developmental path?

- *Collectivist cultures* stress interdependence and cooperation. *Individualist cultures* emphasize competition and personal achievement. The culture in which a person develops often has a significant impact on development.

What kinds of changes occur within each of the major developmental domains: physical, cognitive, personality, and sociocultural?

- For practical reasons, development is considered within four interacting domains: (1) *physical* growth and development; (2) *cognitive* growth, which includes language development; (3) *personality* development; and (4) *sociocultural* development. It is important to understand that development in one domain is influenced by, and in turn influences, development in other domains. Thus, development is interactive, and it also is holistic, meaning it involves the whole person.

Theoretical Frameworks for Human Development

What contributions do theories of development make to our overall understanding of how human development unfolds?

- Our understanding of development is based on science and is guided by theories. *Theories* are organized, coherent sets of ideas that help us to understand, to explain, and to make predictions. The goal of a theory is to aid in the understanding of a phenomenon.
- Theories change over time as they adjust to newly discovered information. Because there often is more than one way to interpret the *data* on which a theory is based, there are different theories that sometimes contradict each other, depending on the context in which the theory is applied.

What important ideas are connected to each of the following theoretical perspectives: biological views, psychodynamic perspectives, behaviorism, cognitive-developmental theories, and systems approaches?

- The genes each individual inherits play an important role in that person's development. The recent mapping of the *human genome* will contribute substantially to our understanding of biological influences on development.
- *Developmental neuroscience*, a field still in its infancy, attempts to understand how brain structures and function are linked to behavior and mental experience. New brain-imaging techniques are rapidly advancing work in this field.
- *Evolution*, which occurs through the process of *natural selection,* is an important explanation for fundamental aspects of human development, such as childhood attachment.
- Psychodynamic views, which generally trace their ideas back to the work of Sigmund Freud, emphasize the role of the unconscious mind and the interactions of the three psychic processes (the id, ego, and superego). Freud viewed development as proceeding through five psychosexual

stages, and he believed the adult personality was heavily influenced by events that occurred in childhood.

- Erik Erikson, a neo-Freudian, whose approach is termed *psychosocial theory,* emphasized ego forces and the influence of social interactions on development. He also believed that development occurs throughout the lifespan and that adjustments early in life set the stage for later development.
- Behaviorism emphasizes how individuals act. *Classical conditioning* (described by Ivan Pavlov) and *operant conditioning* (described by B. F. Skinner) are two important mechanisms that describe how environmental stimuli and rewards influence our behavior. *Social learning theory* (advocated by Albert Bandura) recognizes that people can learn by watching what happens to others and by remembering the consequences of past actions.
- Cognitive-developmental theories emphasize thinking, reasoning, and problem solving. Jean Piaget, a cognitive theorist, believed that the mind adapts to new ideas either by fitting new material in with what we already know *(assimilation)* or by changing our mental structures, called *schemes,* to *accommodate* the new information.
- Lev Vygotsky, another cognitive theorist, emphasized the importance of learning from other people, especially those who are more knowledgeable, through *guided participation.*
- Systems theories (or approaches) attempt to integrate theories by providing a broader focus. Urie Bronfenbrenner's *bioecological model* emphasizes that each person's genetic endowment unfolds in the context of narrower (e.g., one's family) and broader (e.g., society) social settings. Newer systems theories often focus on the interacting forces of genes and environment.
- Although developmental theories differ, they all attempt to describe and explain how humans change throughout the lifespan, as well as to describe and explain what events are most significant in guiding those changes.
- The lifespan developmental perspective emphasizes that development is life long, multidimensional, multidirectional (involving both losses and gains), plastic, context-dependent, and multidisciplinary.

The Scientific Approach to the Study of Human Development

Why is the study of human development considered from a scientific perspective?

- To ensure that conclusions are valid, the study of human development is conducted according to the rules of science, which specify a set of techniques, as well as ethical guidelines.

What types of research approaches do developmentalists commonly use in their study of human development?

- One scientific method is the *case study,* which involves compiling detailed information about an individual. Another descriptive method is *naturalistic observation,* where researchers carefully observe the behavior of a person as it naturally occurs. *Laboratory observations* are similar, but they are less natural because they take place under carefully constructed conditions.
- *Questionnaires, surveys,* and *interviews* are used to collect large amounts of data about people's attitudes and their descriptions of their behavior. Because often not all members of a population can be questioned, researchers select a *representative sample* to study and they use sample results to generalize to the population. *Psychological tests* also can be used to study traits such as intelligence or personality.
- Because development occurs across time, it is sometimes necessary to study how people change as they age. *Longitudinal studies* identify a cohort group and study the group at various times into the future. *Cross-sectional studies* identify groups of cohorts of different ages and study the groups at the same time. Both longitudinal and cross-sectional studies have limitations. They sometimes are combined into a *sequential-cohort design* that selects different age cohort groups and follows them longitudinally across time.
- Correlational studies involve the measurement of a group of people on two variables. If scores on one variable increase, and they increase on the other variable as well, a statistic called a *correlation coefficient* will have a positive value. If scores on the two variables are inversely related, a negative correlation coefficient is revealed. Correlational studies do not provide information about causation.
- If researchers wish to explore how variables cause a change in behavior, they generally use an experimental method of study. The procedure of an experiment is to *randomly assign* volunteers to different treatment conditions and to assign different levels of the *independent variable* to each group. Then the *dependent variable* is measured to see if the different treatments had different impacts.
- Each research method has strengths and weaknesses and each method is used appropriately under certain conditions. Sometimes methods are modified or combined, as in the *quasi-experimental method.* This method is sometimes used when conditions make conducting a true experiment impossible.
- Regardless of the method used to study development, it is important to *replicate* the studies to ensure that the results are reliable and can be generalized to similar conditions.

What ethical challenges do developmental researchers encounter as they attempt to understand the processes that guide human development?

- All scientific researchers must follow strict ethical guidelines to protect their study participants from potential harm. Research organizations require that all studies be reviewed and approved by *Institutional Review Boards (IRBs)* before the studies can be conducted.
- Among the most important ethical considerations are (a) that participants should not be harmed either physically or psychologically, (b) that they be informed about the nature and risks of the research, (c) that their responses are private and confidential, (d) that they are later informed of the results of the study, and (e) that they be able to receive any treatment that the study may have identified as beneficial to participants. When participants, such as children, cannot weigh experimental benefits and risks, parents or guardians can supply informed consent.

KEY TERMS

development (p. 2)
developmental psychologists (p. 2)
developmental period (or stage) (p. 2)
culture (p. 3)
chronological (p. 3)
biological factors (p. 4)
environmental factors (p. 4)
sociocultural context (p. 4)
maturation (p. 5)
learning (p. 5)
context (p. 5)
collectivist culture (p. 7)
individualist culture (p. 7)
physical domain (p. 8)
cognitive domain (p. 8)
personality domain (p. 8)
sociocultural domain (p. 8)
socialization (p. 8)
enculturation (p. 8)
theory (p. 9)
data (p. 10)
human genome (p. 10)
developmental neuroscience (p. 10)
evolution (p. 11)
natural selection (p. 11)
psychodynamic approach (p. 11)
psychosocial theory (p. 13)
behaviorism (p. 13)
classical conditioning (p. 14)
operant conditioning (p. 14)
social learning theory (p. 15)
cognitive-developmental theories (p. 16)
adaptation (p. 16)
schemes (p. 17)
assimilation (p. 17)
accommodation (p. 17)
guided participation (p. 18)
bioecological model (p. 19)
case study (p. 21)
baby biographies (p. 21)
naturalistic observation (p. 22)
laboratory observation (p. 22)
questionnaire (p. 22)
survey (p. 22)
interview (p. 22)
representative sampling (p. 23)
longitudinal design (p. 23)
cross-sectional design (p. 24)
cohort effects (p. 24)
confounding (p. 24)
sequential-cohort design (p. 24)
correlation (p. 24)
random assignment (p. 26)
independent variable (p. 27)
dependent variable (p. 27)
replication (or replicate) (p. 27)
quasi-experimental method (p. 28)
Institutional Review Boards (IRBs) (p. 29)
informed consent (p. 29)

MyVirtualLife

What decision would you make while raising a child? What would be the consequences of those decisions?

Find out by accessing **MyVirtualLife** at www.MyDevelopmentLab.com to raise a virtual child and live your own virtual life.

2 HEREDITY AND ENVIRONMENT

LEARNING OBJECTIVES

- Where in our cells are genetic instructions located, and how are these instructions encoded in our DNA?
- How do we inherit traits from our parents, and how are those traits expressed?
- How can environmental forces modify genetic instructions?
- What kinds of disorders are caused by problems in how genes are inherited and expressed?
- What techniques are available to help individuals deal with genetic disorders?
- Why is the study of behavior genetics important in helping us understand gene–environment interactions?
- Why are adopted children and twins of special interest to those who study behavior genetics?
- How do environmental events exert their influence on developmental processes?
- How do one's family and culture help shape the way that development unfolds?

CHAPTER OUTLINE

Molecular Genetics
- Human Cells
- DNA
- Genes
- Protein Synthesis

Chromosomes, Genes, and Cell Division
- Cell Division and Reproduction
- From Genotype to Phenotype
- The Variation of Traits Among Individuals
- Gene–Environment Interactions: The Study of Epigenetics

Genetic Disorders
- Sex-Linked Disorders
- Autosomal Disorders
- Mitochondrial Disorders
- Genetic Counseling
- Advances in Genetic Research and Treatment

Behavior Genetics
- Twin and Adoption Studies

Environmental Influences and Contexts
- Basic Processes That Affect Behavior
- Applied Behavior Analysis
- Social Learning and the Evolving Self-Concept

Environment in a Broader Context: Family and Culture
- Family Systems
- The Family as Transmitter of Culture
- Sociocultural Influences on Development Across the Lifespan

Heredity and environment—the two forces that interact to make each person a unique being, a person like no other who has ever lived or will ever live—are the subjects of this chapter. At the time of conception, when sperm and egg unite to form a new organism capable of life, the basic hereditary instructions are laid down in the form of the genes inherited from each person's mother and father. From that instant, the conditions in which the individual develops and lives—the environment—act to shape the path of growth and development. At every point along the path, the forces of heredity and environment *interact*; that is, they influence each other.

Our knowledge of how genetic mechanisms influence behavior is exploding at the present time, opening doors for new research that promises to revolutionize modern science. For example, DNA mapping has been of enormous help to anthropologists in tracing evolutionary history and understanding how human populations have migrated geographically throughout time, as well as to law enforcement investigators in solving crimes. New genetic techniques are revolutionizing medicine and opening exciting possibilities for the treatment of injury and disease. For example, scientists can now isolate cancer cells and copy, or "clone," them, thereby providing a new way of studying how cancer develops and how cancerous cells can effectively be turned "off" before they begin to grow (Brown, 2010). Work with stem cells offers the promise of genetically redirecting these cells to heal spinal cord injuries and brain diseases (Park, 2011). And, as we learn more about how hereditary and environmental forces interact, our concept of human development is sure to become more refined.

An understanding of the mechanisms by which hereditary and environmental forces interact is essential if we are to study how humans develop across the lifespan. Thus, we begin our exploration of human lifespan development with a discussion of how our genetic profile is established and how it unfolds within a particular environmental context.

MOLECULAR GENETICS

As noted in Chapter 1, in June 2000, scientists announced that the human genome—the location and sequence of genes on the human chromosomes—had successfully been mapped (Celera Genomics, 2000). By October 2004, the map was essentially complete (International Human Genome Sequencing Consortium, 2004). This achievement marked a significant breakthrough in our knowledge of how genetic processes guide our growth and development as we become unique human beings. To understand how genetic mechanisms work, we must first consider the structure of genes, which reside in the cells that make up the organisms.

Human Cells

The human body is composed of over 200 different kinds of **cells**, which are the smallest self-contained structures in our bodies. In spite of their diversity, virtually all of our somatic (bodily) cells have some essential things in common (see Figure 2-1). For example, each cell is surrounded by a *cell membrane*, which is porous to allow nutrients and other chemicals to enter and waste products to exit. Within the cell is the *cytoplasm*, which is composed of a fluid and a host of distinct and highly specialized structures that include the *mitochondria*, which are the "powerhouses" of the cell. Mitochondria process nutrients and provide the cell's energy. Other cell structures include the *endoplasmic reticulum*, the *Golgi apparatus*, and the *ribosomes*, which are involved in the production of the many kinds of *proteins* that are essential to the life and functioning of both the cell and the body as a whole. The cell's *nucleus*, which also is surrounded by a porous membrane, contains most of the **deoxyribonucleic acid (DNA)**, which contains the genetic instructions that direct growth and development.

DNA

The structure of DNA was first identified by James Watson and Francis Crick (1953), who received a Nobel Prize for this work.

cells
The smallest self-contained structures in the human body

deoxyribonucleic acid (DNA)
A large, complex molecule composed of carbon, hydrogen, oxygen, nitrogen, and phosphorus that contains the genetic code that regulates the functioning and development of an organism

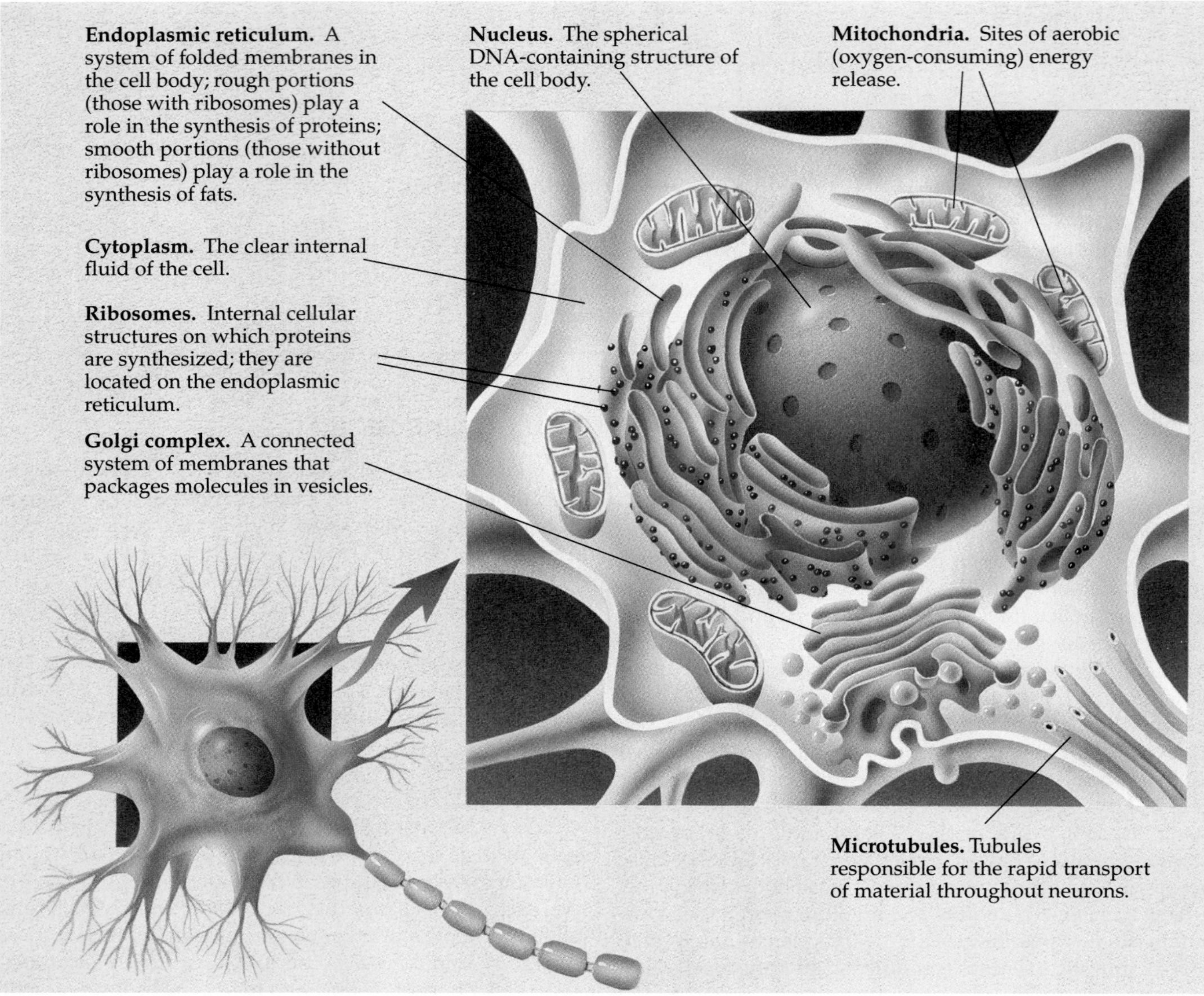

FIGURE 2-1 Major Features of a Typical Cell (Here, a Neuron or Nerve Cell)
Although there are many types of cells in the human body, they all share features in common.
SOURCE: Pinel, John P. J. (2011). Biopsychology, 8th edition. Pearson/Allyn and Bacon. Boston.

DNA is a highly complex *macromolecule:* It is made up of many smaller molecules that are arranged in the shape of a twisted ladder called a *double helix* (see Figure 2-2). If a segment of DNA is hypothetically "unwound," its building blocks, which are called **nucleotides**, can be seen. Each nucleotide consists of a phosphate molecule and a sugar molecule, which form the sides of the ladder, and one of four nitrogen–carbon–hydrogen **bases**: adenine (A), thymine (T), cytosine (C), and guanine (G), which are bound together into **base pairs** that form the rungs of the ladder. Figure 2-3 shows a segment of DNA visualized as a ladder, where the sides, or "backbone," are represented by "S" and "P" and the rungs by "C," "G," "T," and "A." Notice that the bases pair up in only two different patterns—because of their chemical nature, adenine can pair only with thymine (A-T and T-A) and cytosine can pair only with guanine (C-G and G-C).

The DNA molecule is elegant, indeed: Regardless of the species—orchid, oak tree, mouse, human—the genetic

nucleotides
The building blocks of DNA

base
A nitrogen–carbon–hydrogen component of nucleotides

base pair
A "rung" in the DNA ladder; the base adenine pairs only with the base thymine, and the base cytosine pairs only with the base guanine

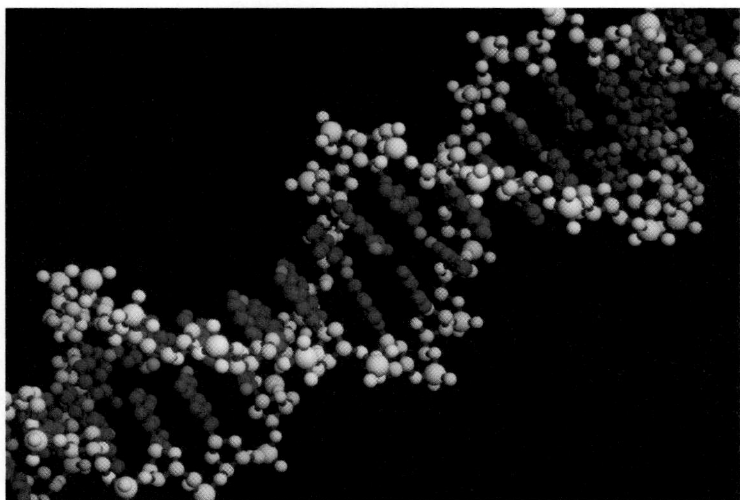

FIGURE 2-2 A Computer-Generated Simulation of a DNA Molecule
Note the twisted ladder-like structure, referred to as a double helix. Base pairs form the rungs on the DNA ladder, (here in blue and purple), and their sequence determines the genetic traits that are carried in the DNA of each individual.

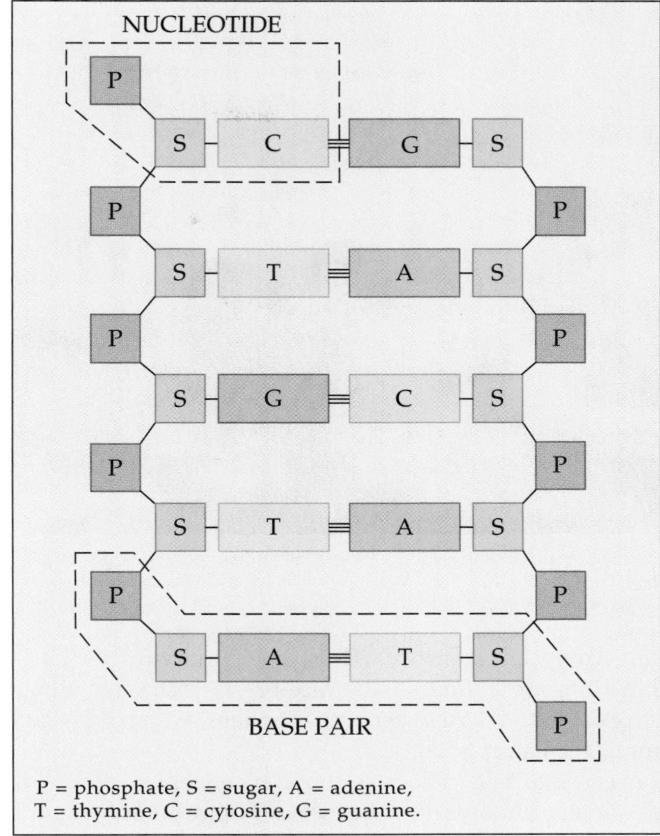

FIGURE 2-3 A Segment of DNA Visualized as a Ladder
Each nucleotide consists of a phosphate molecule and a sugar molecule that form the "sides" of the ladder and one of only four types of bases: adenine, thymine, cytosine, and guanine. Because of their chemical structures, adenine pairs only with thymine and cytosine pairs only with guanine. Genes are specific sections of the DNA molecule that provide instructions for the manufacture of a wide array of protein molecules.

instructions for life depend on the arrangement of only these four bases in the DNA molecule. How can such a simple system dictate how life unfolds? First, the number of base pairs in the DNA molecule is very large. In humans, for example, there are more than *3 billion* base pairs in the genome, allowing for an almost unlimited number of different sequences. Furthermore, any change in the order of base pairs in the genome can be significant, causing development to proceed in a different direction. Second, different species, and even different individuals within the same species, have different numbers of base pairs in their genome. For example, in contrast to the 3.2 billion base pairs in the human genome, the number in the genome of *E. coli* (the bacteria that is sometimes responsible for food poisoning) is 4.6 million pairs, whereas the number in the genome of the honey bee is 236 million pairs and in the black poplar tree is 480 million pairs. Finally, the order of the pairing is important: If adenine is on the left side of an A-T pair, this provides a different instruction than if adenine is on the right side of the T-A pair.

As noted, even small differences in the DNA code can have important genetic implications. For example, the DNA makeup of our closest genetic relative, the chimpanzee, is about 98% the same as ours; less than 2% of the DNA code accounts for the marked differences between chimpanzees and humans (Kehrer-Sawatzki & Cooper, 2007; Varki & Nelson, 2007). Moreover, the DNA of each normal human being is about 99.9% the same as that of every other normal human being (Oak Ridge National Laboratory, 2008); only 0.1% of the genome produces all the structural biological differences that exist between any two people.

Watch *DNA Molecules* on **MyDevelopmentLab**

One important implication of the fact that all humans share such a large proportion of their genes is that individuals have much more in common with other people than we sometimes assume. Even concepts such as race, which are sometimes used to classify people into disparate groups, become largely meaningless when considered from a genetic reference point. In fact, based on an examination of only a person's genome, identifying an individual's "race" is no simple matter (Dupré, 2008; Sternberg, Grigorenko, & Kidd, 2005).

When is the concept of "race" useful in describing a group of people? In what contexts is it meaningless?

Although genes do control the development of characteristics frequently associated with race (e.g., skin color, eye shape, hair color and texture), these traits do not occur as "either–or" features; rather, they are distributed continuously throughout the human population. For example, some White, blonde-haired people have curlier hair than some African Americans, even though curly hair is a physical characteristic more commonly associated with

According to the Human Genome Project, all humans are 99.9% genetically identical.

African-American ethnicity. Thus, each individual's base-pair combinations are so unique that race-based "markers" do not appear to exist in the human genome (Bonham, Warshauer-Baker, & Collins, 2005; Patrinos, 2004).

This is not to say, of course, that the concept of race is meaningless in a social or cultural context (Fujimura & Rajagopalan, 2011). However, the usage of the term *race* should be questioned if it suggests that an individual belongs to a genetically defined group. A more appropriate term in a context such as this is *ethnicity*, which avoids the genetic connotation that race often mistakenly implies and focuses instead on the shared cultural experiences of groups that define their members as similar (Fujimura, Rajagopalan, Ossorio, & Doksum, 2010).

Genes

The concept of **genes** as the basic units of heredity was around long before 1953 when Watson and Crick identified their biochemical nature. However, scientists now understand that a gene (which some prefer to call a *locus*) is a delineated segment of DNA that may be several hundred to several million base pairs long. The total number of genes in the human genome currently is unknown because different methods of gene identification yield slightly different numbers. However, a reasonable estimate would place the number at 20,000 to 25,000, which is far fewer than was originally thought (International Human Genome Sequencing Consortium, 2004; Pertea & Salzberg, 2010).

Protein Synthesis

The most significant role genes play is to build (or *synthesize*) **proteins**, which are molecules that perform a diverse array of crucial functions throughout the body (see Table 2-1). Protein synthesis occurs when the rungs in the DNA ladder break apart, separating the molecule into two pieces down the middle, where the bases are paired. This separation occurs much like "unzipping" a zipper, where the zipper teeth correspond to the bases. Once the DNA molecule is unzipped, leaving the open halves of each base pair exposed, unattached "free" bases in the cell ("A," "T," "C," and "G") are attracted to the open rungs of both sides of the base pair ladder. These free bases bind with the open sides of the unzipped molecule—A with T and C with G—and copies of the unzipped halves of the DNA molecule are thereby reproduced. These copies, then, are used as instructions for building the protein molecules needed for development. From various arrangements of these four different nucleotides on defined sections of the DNA molecule, hundreds of thousands of different proteins can be constructed; over 200,000 different proteins thus far have been identified in humans. The DNA that codes for these sequences of nucleotides thus serves as the instructions for life—a remarkably elegant system indeed. It is these DNA instructions that are transmitted from parent to child that we refer to when we speak of the *hereditary mechanism*.

Table 2-1 Common Proteins and Their Functions in the Human Body

Protein	Function
Enzymes (e.g., carbohydrases, lipases, nucleases)	Catalyze (speed up) the chemical reactions within cells and throughout the body
Collagen	Forms the basis for connective tissue in the body
DNA and RNA polymerase	Serve in DNA replication and gene expression
Hemoglobin	Transports oxygen in the blood
Insulin	Controls the glucose level in the blood
Contractile proteins (e.g., actin, myosin)	Form the muscles
Hormones	Regulate physical growth and development and adjust the body under stress
Antibodies, antigens	Protect the body from disease

SOURCE: Adapted from M. Hoefnagels, R. Lewis, D. Gaffin, and B. Parker, 2010, *Biology: Concepts and investigations*, New York: McGraw-Hill.

genes
The basic units of inheritance that are composed of sequences of base pairs within the DNA of an organism

proteins
Molecules that perform a diverse array of crucial functions in the human body (e.g., enzymes, hemoglobin, collagen, and hormones)

REVIEW THE FACTS 2-1

1. Approximately what percentage of their genes do two unrelated humans share?
   a. 50% b. 90%
   c. 98% d. 99.9%
2. In the DNA helix, which of the following is NOT one of the ways in which base pairs can vary on the nucleotide ladder?
   a. which bases pair with other bases
   b. which side of the ladder the base is on
   c. the order of the base pairs on the ladder
   d. the number of base pairs on the ladder
3. What is the major function that genes perform?
4. When scientists use the term *heredity mechanism,* they are referring to ___________________.

**Practice** on **MyDevelopmentLab**

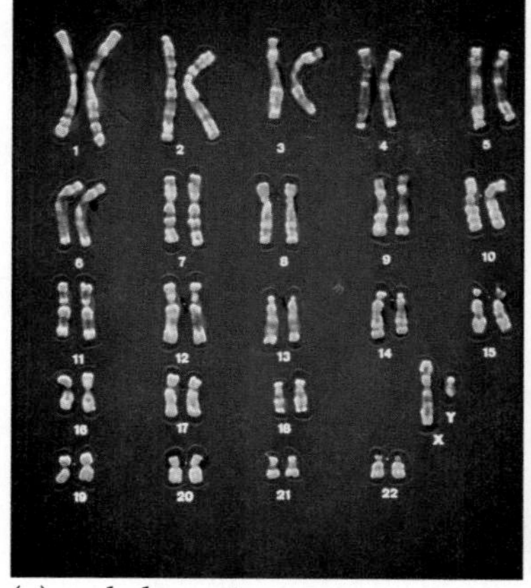

(a) male karyotype

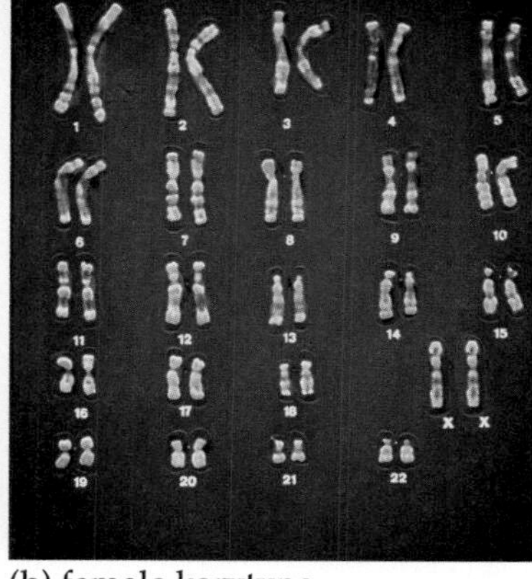

(b) female karytype

FIGURE 2-4 **Human Karyotypes**
Chromosomes, which contain our genes, can be photographed during cell division. For convenience, the photographs, called karyotypes or karyograms, are typically constructed so that the chromosomes are assembled into pairs. Each of the first 22 pairs is referred to by number, and the 23rd pair is labeled as either "X" or "Y." The X and Y chromosomes determine sex: XX is the normal configuration for females, XY for males. In the figure (a) shows the male karyotype and (b) the female karyotype. Note the much smaller Y chromosome in the male karyotype.

CHROMOSOMES, GENES, AND CELL DIVISION

For the most part, DNA is contained within the nuclei of the cells in the body, although some specialized DNA can also be found in the cells' mitochondria. For most of the time, DNA is spread out in the nucleus. However, when cells prepare to divide, the DNA thickens and assembles into "threads" called **chromosomes**, which contain segments of DNA and protein. In normal humans, all cells except sperm and eggs contain exactly 46 chromosomes arranged in 23 pairs. Twenty-two of the chromosome pairs are called **autosomes** and these are numbered, for the most part, from largest to smallest. The 23rd pair is composed of two **sex chromosomes**, so named because they determine the biological sex of the person. Sex chromosomes exist in two forms, "X" and "Y," named for their general shape. Females possess 2 "X" chromosomes (XX), whereas males possess 1 "X" and 1 "Y" chromosome (XY). Chromosomes are of varying sizes, and contain varying numbers of base pairs, and varying numbers of genes. In humans, for example, the smallest chromosomes contain about 50 million base pairs and a few hundred genes, whereas the largest contain about 250 million base pairs and a few thousand genes (National Center for Biotechnology Information, 2011a).

During cell division, chromosomes are visible under a microscope. In fact, some types of genetic defects can be identified by examining the visual appearance of the chromosomes that, when stained and rearranged, yield **karyotypes** (also called karyograms; see Figure 2-4). For example, Down syndrome (discussed later in this chapter) is seen in a karyotype as the presence of an extra chromosome, or of extra chromosome material, on the 21st chromosome pair.

Cell Division and Reproduction

All humans begin life as a single-celled organism created by the fertilization of an *ovum* (egg) by a sperm. Organisms grow and develop through cell division, which occurs throughout the lifespan. Cell division can follow two different paths. When the cells that divide are simply replicating themselves the process is called *mitosis;* however, when organisms produce ova or sperm, a different mechanism, which is called *meiosis,* is involved.

In **mitosis**, cell division involves the migration of chromosome material to the center of the cell's nucleus, where the DNA strands unwind and pull apart. In a process similar to protein synthesis, new base molecules ("A," "T," "C," and "G") attach to each half of the original "unzipped" chromosome, thereby creating *two* identical chromosomes from the original one. Cell division is completed when the new pairs of chromosomes separate, with each migrating to a different end of the cell's nucleus. The cell then divides and forms two separate cells; these two newly formed cells are identical to each other (see Figure 2-5) and, except in cases of mutation, they each contain an identical set of 46 chromosomes arranged in 23 pairs, just like those in the original cell.

chromosome
A chain of genes visible under a microscope; humans normally have 46 chromosomes

karyotype
A photograph of a cell's chromosomes arranged in pairs according to size

autosomes
In humans, consist of 22 of the 23 pairs of chromosomes, except those that determine sex

mitosis
The process of ordinary cell division that results in two cells identical to the parent cell

sex chromosomes
In humans, the 23rd chromosome pair, which determines sex

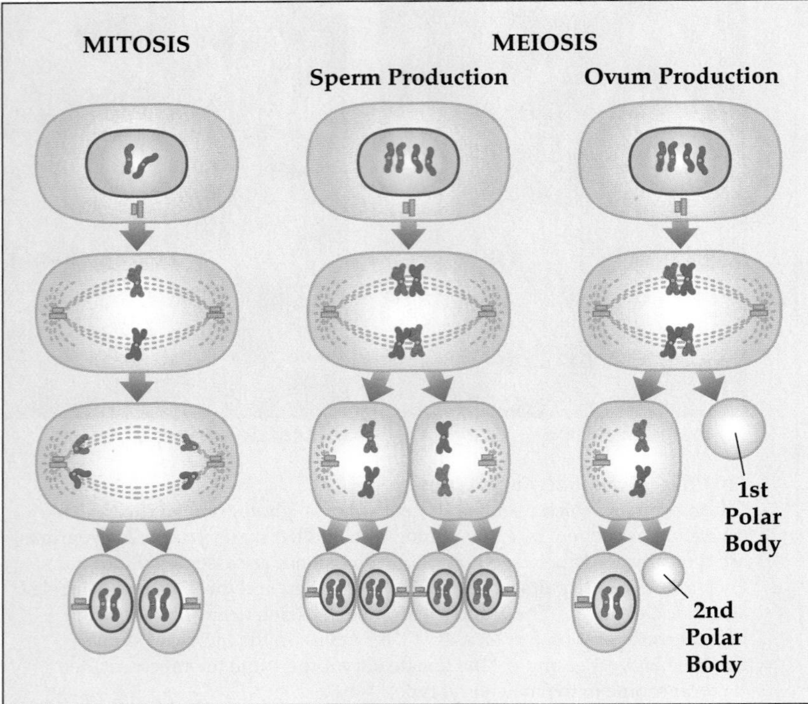

FIGURE 2-5 Comparison of Mitosis and Meiosis
Mitosis results in two cells that normally are identical to the original cell. In males, meiosis results in four sperm cells, each of which is genetically different. In females, meiosis results in only one relatively large ovum, plus two small polar bodies that are not capable of being fertilized. Sometimes the first polar body also divides, yielding a total of three nonfertilizable polar bodies.

Meiosis involves a somewhat different process. Recall that at conception, an ovum and a sperm combine to form an organism that has 23 *pairs* of chromosomes. Thus, both ovum and sperm contribute one half of each pair. Meiosis is the process by which reproductive cells (ova and sperm)—called **gametes**—are formed: This process results in cells that contain 23 chromosomes—one half of each pair, as shown in Figure 2-5.

In males, meiosis takes place in the testes and involves two rounds of division, resulting in four fertile *sperm cells.* On entrance into puberty (see Chapter 10), males normally begin producing many thousands of sperm cells on an ongoing basis, and they continue to do so throughout their lifespans. In contrast, meiosis in females begins in the ovaries well before birth, where all of the roughly 400,000 ova a woman will ever have begin their development. However, the final cell division that produces the fully formed ovum does not occur until the female enters puberty; then ova begin completing meiosis, or "ripening," approximately one ovum per month. In addition, the process of meiosis in women differs from that in men because most of the cellular material is concentrated in one of the three or four cells produced (the ovum), and the other, smaller cells (the *polar bodies*) are discarded by the body.

From Genotype to Phenotype

Just as chromosomes exist as pairs (one half from the mother, one half from the father), genes also exist in pairs. Alternate versions of a gene that perform the same function are called **alleles**; normally, one allele is inherited from the mother and the other from the father. Taken together, all of the pairs of alleles constitute the person's **genotype**, or genetic code.

On the 22 pairs of autosomes, every gene normally is paired and thus exists as two alleles. The sex chromosomes, however, are slightly different. In females, because the sex chromosomes are XX, genes exist as matched allele pairs here as well. In males (XY), however, there are many genes on the larger X chromosome for which there is no match on the smaller Y chromosome. These unpaired X-chromosome genes are important in determining sex-linked traits, which is a topic that we will return to later.

Simple Dominance and Recessiveness Some inherited traits, such as eye color, are primarily determined by a single gene pair (see Lewis, 2010). A child might inherit an allele for brown eyes *(B)* from the father and an allele for blue eyes *(b)* from the mother. The child's genotype for eye color would therefore be *Bb*. What actual eye color will the child display? As it happens, the allele for brown eyes *(B)* is **dominant**, and the allele for blue eyes *(b)* is **recessive**. When an allele is dominant, its presence in a gene pair has the tendency to cause that trait to be expressed as the **phenotype**, which is the displayed characteristic or trait. An individual with the genotype *BB* or *Bb* should therefore have the phenotype brown eyes.

If the two alleles for a simple dominant–recessive trait are the same, the individual is said to be **homozygous** for that trait; therefore, a homozygous individual's eye color could be either *BB* or *bb*. If the alleles differ, the individual is **heterozygous**—*bB* or *Bb*. For example, a recessive trait such as blue eyes can be displayed by a child of parents who both have brown eyes if *both* parents are heterozygous for that trait. What are the chances for heterozygous brown-eyed parents producing a blue-eyed child? Four combinations of allele pairs are possible: *BB, bB, Bb,* and *bb*. Because only *bb* can produce a child with blue eyes, the chance is one in four, or 25%. Note that if either brown-eyed parent is homozygous, there is no chance of having a blue-eyed child (see Figure 2-6).

Combinations of Genes It is important to note that relatively few human traits are controlled by only one gene pair. Combinations

meiosis
The process of cell division that yields sperm and ova, each including one half of a full set of chromosomes

genotype
The genetic code of a given individual

phenotype
In genetics, those traits that are expressed in the individual

gametes
Reproductive cells (ova and sperm) that are formed by the process of meiosis

dominant
In genetics, one gene of a gene pair that will cause a particular trait to be expressed

homozygous
Refers to the arrangement in which the two alleles for a simple dominant–recessive trait are the same

alleles
A pair of genes found on corresponding chromosomes that affect the same trait

recessive
In genetics, one gene of a gene pair that determines a trait in an individual only if the other member of that pair is also recessive

heterozygous
Refers to the arrangement in which the two alleles for a simple dominant–recessive trait differ

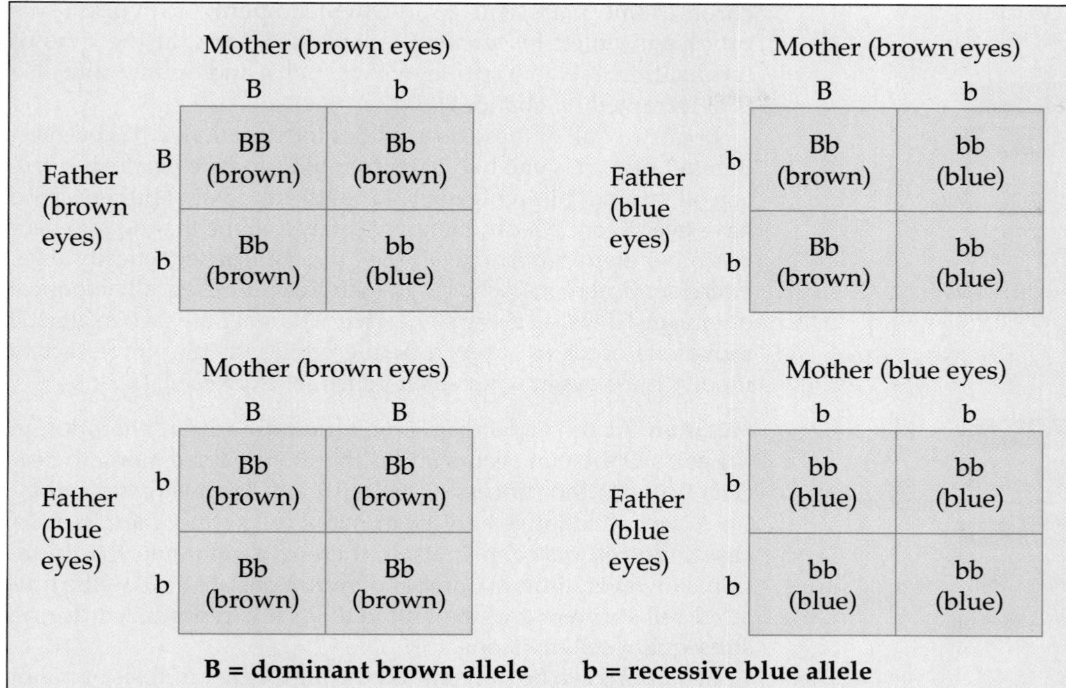

FIGURE 2-6 **Examples of Dominant–Recessive Gene Combinations: Genotype and Phenotype**

of many gene pairs determine most traits, such as those governing intelligence, height, and most forms of illness. When multiple genes are involved in determining how a trait is expressed, this is referred to as **polygenic inheritance**. Polygenic mechanisms typically give rise to offspring whose phenotypes differ markedly from those of either parent. Consider hair color: A brown-haired father and blonde-haired mother may have children whose hair varies in color from blonde, to brown, to even red. Polygenic mechanisms are exceedingly complex, and scientists are only now beginning to understand how they work (Omoto & Lurquin, 2004; Quackenbush, 2011).

Furthermore, even for those traits that are thought of as single-gene traits, such as eye color, numerous individual variations are possible (White & Rabago-Smith, 2011), in part because each gene contains hundreds or thousands of base pairs. Any alternation in base pairs may cause a gene to be expressed in a slightly different way, thus affecting the phenotype that is observed. Therefore, genetically determined traits are not simply "either–or" propositions. Rather, they lie on a continuum, and individuals may display any genetic characteristic to a greater or lesser degree. Thus, although it is unlikely that a homozygous brown-eyed parent *(BB)* would produce a blue-eyed child, it is possible.

The phenotypic expression of gene combinations is further complicated by the fact that some traits are coded by alleles that may be only partially dominant or partially recessive. *Sickle-cell anemia,* a medical condition in which *some* red blood cells are misshapen and therefore interfere with oxygen transport, is one example of such **incomplete dominance**. In other cases, alleles can be **codominant**, which means that neither allele is dominant over the other. When codominant traits are inherited, the result is a phenotype that is a blend. The A and B blood types are an example of codominance: If an individual inherits an A allele from one parent and a B allele from the other parent, the resulting blood type is a combination of the two: AB.

Sex-Linked Traits A particular set of genetic combinations occurs when traits are controlled by genes on the sex chromosomes; such traits are called **sex-linked traits**. Because the X chromosome contains many more genes than the Y chromosome, males are much more likely than females to display recessive phenotypes for sex-linked traits: If a recessive allele appears on the male's X chromosome, there often is no allele on the Y chromosome to offset it, and the recessive trait will be expressed as the individual's phenotype. In contrast, in females, the recessive trait will be expressed only if it occurs on both X chromosomes.

The Variation of Traits Among Individuals

All traits are inherited from only two sources—the mother and the father. How is it that offspring from the same parents are so completely unique?

Meiosis and Individual Variation Several different processes operate to ensure the uniqueness of each individual. For example, when the parents' chromosomes separate at the beginning of meiotic division, genetic material often randomly *crosses over* and is exchanged between the chromosomes, resulting in unique new *recombinant alleles* which carry a combination of both parents' genes (see Figure 2-7). Also, in the final stage of meiotic division, chance determines which half of the

polygenic inheritance
The inheritance of a trait that is determined by multiple genes

sex-linked traits
Traits that are determined by genes on the 23rd chromosome pair

incomplete dominance
The case in which a heterozygous genotype results in a phenotype that is intermediate between the phenotypes of dominant versus recessive homozygous genotypes (e.g., sickle-cell anemia)

codominance
The case in which both dominant and recessive alleles are expressed in the phenotype (e.g., the AB blood type)

Hair color genes

Eye color genes

Here, two chromosomes are shown, one having two recessive alleles for hair color (h) and eye color (e) and one having two dominant alleles for these traits (H and E).

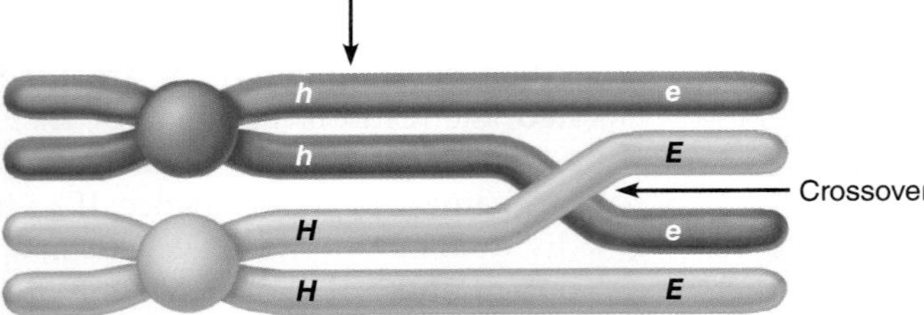

When crossing over occurs, genetic material is exchanged on alleles from the two chromosomes.

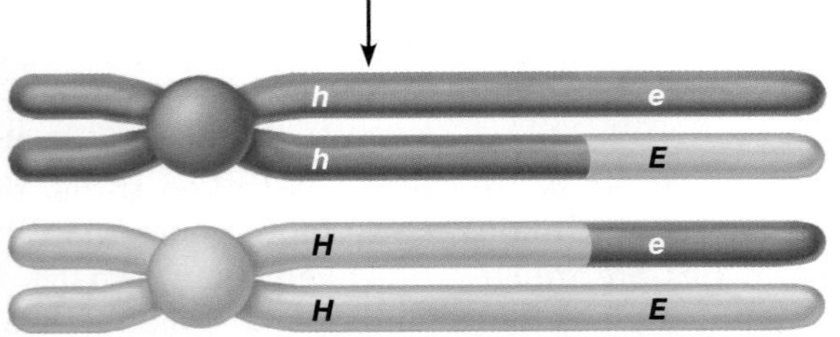

At the conclusion of the crossover, the genetic material on the crossed alleles becomes part of the new "recombinant" chromosomes.

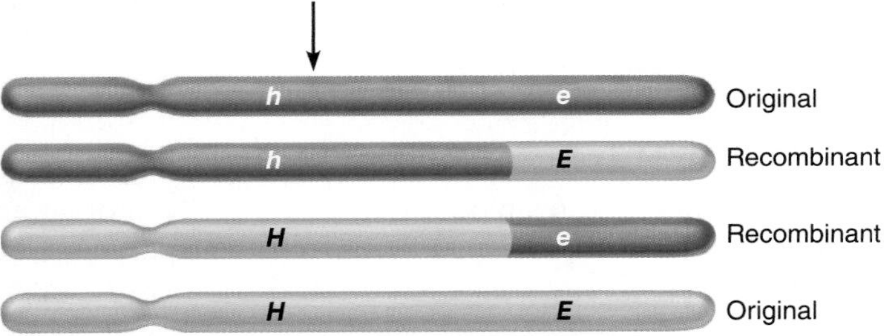

When chromosomes crossover, two original alleles remain, but two recombinant alleles have been formed.

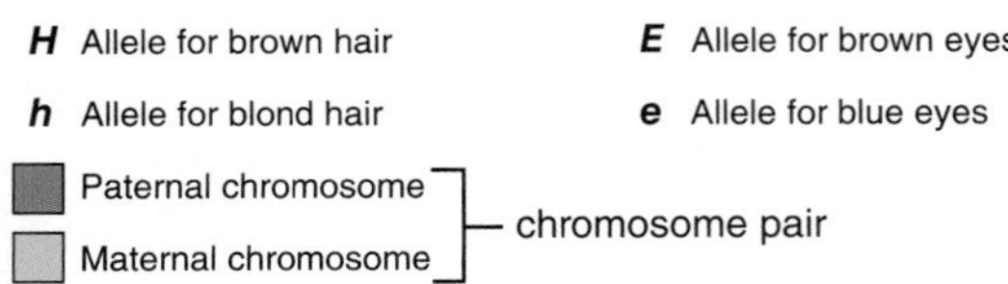

FIGURE 2-7 Crossing Over of Chromosomes
Sometimes during meiosis parts of chromosomes cross over, which creates new combinations of genes on a chromosome.

SOURCE: Derived from *Human Anatomy and Physiology* (9th ed.), by E.N. Marieb and K. Hoehn, 2013, Upper Saddle River, NJ: Pearson.

chromosome pairs will go into which sperm or ovum. (This process is called *independent assortment.*) Then, at the time of fertilization and conception, which sperm and ovum unite also is determined by chance.

Because of all of these possibilities for variation, it has been estimated that the same two parents could produce *hundreds of trillions* of unique children—many times the number of humans who have ever lived. We can therefore safely assume that no two people (other than identical twins; see Chapter 3) are genetically alike. Even identical twins, who begin their lives as genetically identical organisms, develop along somewhat different paths when genetic mutations occur or when differing environmental forces act to modify the ways in which their genes are expressed.

Mutation At the molecular level, a **mutation** is an alteration in the cell's DNA that occurs and is therefore passed along to new cells through the process of cell division. In most cases, mutations are maladaptive and the mutated cell simply dies; in other cases, the cell may repair itself, thereby eliminating the mutation. However, a small number of mutations are *viable*—the mutated cell survives and the mutated DNA is reproduced during subsequent cell divisions.

Mutations can be transmitted through either mitosis or meiosis (National Institutes of Health [NIH], 2011b). When mutation occurs during meiosis, the mutated DNA is contained in the sperm or ovum, and therefore is incorporated during fertilization into the offspring's DNA. Thus, the mutated genes are contained in all cells that subsequently develop from the fertilized ovum. In the case of mitotic cell division, the mutation occurs later in development, thus affecting only some of the cells in the organism. If the mutation occurs very early, perhaps when the organism consists of only a few cells, the mutation will be passed along to a large proportion of cells. However, if the mutation occurs later in life, it is passed only to subsequent divisions of that mutated cell, which may be quite few in number.

Thus, the effect a mutation has on development can vary significantly (Hartl, 2011). In many cases, viable mutations—even when they occur early in development—have little or no effect on development. In other cases, viable mutations can be beneficial, especially in an evolutionary sense, since they may improve the likelihood that the organism will survive and reproduce, thereby passing along the mutated genes to offspring. Mutations were once thought to be relatively rare, but molecular genetics research has shown that they actually occur quite frequently, supporting the idea that mutations may be important in the evolutionary process. Of course, mutations can be detrimental to development, even to the point of preventing the survival of the offspring. Regardless of their impact on development, mutations can result in genetically coded characteristics in offspring that were never present in the DNA of either parent.

Watch *Twins Separated at Birth, Reunited* on **MyDevelopmentLab**

mutation
An alteration in the DNA that typically occurs during mitosis or meiosis and is therefore transmitted to subsequent cells through cell division

Gene–Environment Interactions: The Study of Epigenetics

Individuals differ not only in their genes, of course, but also in the specific ways in which they experience their environments. Psychologists have long been aware that nongenetic forces play critically important roles in shaping human development: All sorts of environmental conditions affect development, including the family and culture one grows up within, the kind of education one experiences, and so forth. It is easy to make the mistake of considering the influence of genetic forces, or "nature," and those based in experience, or "nurture," as acting somewhat independently. Today, however, scientists understand that "nature" and "nurture" can never be considered separately; rather they are in constant dynamic interaction with each other. Just as it makes no sense to ask, "which contributes more to the area of a rectangle, its height or its width?" it also makes no sense to think of heredity and environment as separate forces that impact development independently (Meaney, 2010).

Psychologists have long understood that environmental forces can change the way in which genes express themselves. For example, the idea of genetic vulnerability rests on the assumption that the individual may develop in one direction if environmental conditions are favorable but in another way if conditions are harsh: A child may inherit a genetic tendency toward alcoholism, which will develop or not, depending in part on environmental factors, such as the religious tradition in which the child is raised or the way in which parents monitor the child's behavior (Dick et al., 2011). Genes also can act to modify the individual's environment. For example, a child who is genetically predisposed toward shyness likely will seek out different sorts of experiences than will a child who inherits genes that code for extraversion. Thus, the action of genes and of the environment can never be considered one independent of the other; rather, heredity and environment are entwined together, with each continually influencing the other. This is the core idea in the concept of "gene–environment interaction."

In fact, gene–environment interactions occur at many levels. For example, any discussion of development requires a consideration of not only genetic mechanisms but also of neural activity, behavior, and more global environmental circumstances such as one's physical, social, familial, and cultural surroundings (Gottlieb, 1998, 2007). Experiences at each of these levels are in constant interaction with those at all other levels throughout development. For example, one's culture affects parenting practices, which in turn affect brain development, which affects language development, which may affect social development and a myriad of other developmental phenomena. Furthermore, it is important to remember that the transmission of information from one generation to the next occurs at each level: Just as genes are transmitted from parent to offspring through the process of meiosis and fertilization, cultural practices are transmitted to members of the next generation through learning and shared experiences.

Although researchers have long understood that gene–environment interactions occur at many levels, it is only recently that the actual mechanisms through which genes and environmental forces interact are being identified. We now know, for example, that protein-coding genes make up only a small part of the DNA contained in cells; some segments of DNA—constituting as much as 98% of the DNA present—do not function as genes and therefore are not part of an individual's genotype. However, these "nongene" DNA segments can act to regulate the activity of genes, turning them "off" or "on." Thus, two individuals with identical genotypes might in fact have different phenotypes if their nongene DNA segments differ in ways that produce different patterns of gene expression. Furthermore, research suggests that environmental circumstances can affect the chemical structure of this nongene DNA, which in turn influences the activity of the genome itself. This may help explain why identical twins, with virtually identical genes, may experience different health outcomes: The twin who smokes cigarettes may develop lung cancer, whereas the nonsmoking twin does not. Here, the destructive impact of smoking may alter the structure of the nongene DNA, which then "turns on" the previously dormant cancer genes that can cause cells to develop abnormally. Additionally, we know that the DNA molecule is coiled around protein strands in the cell. Gene activation may vary depending on whether the DNA coils tightly or loosely, and the tightness of the coiling can be influenced by environmental factors, such as the presence of stress hormones that are released when the individual experiences stressful events in the environment. Geneticists use the term **epigenetics** (meaning "in addition to" or "on top of" genetics) to refer to this idea—that nongenetic factors influence how the genes behave, or express themselves (Meaney, 2010).

The significance of epigenetic forces on development is becoming more apparent as genetic research is becoming more sophisticated. Researchers are discovering, for instance, that environmental conditions can modify the expression of genes, and in a variety of ways. For example, maternal care, being raised in poverty, or variations in diet early in life, and perhaps later in life as well, can modify genetic expression through epigenetic processes (Kim & Evans, 2011). Because these modifications can become incorporated into the biological structure of the DNA molecule itself, they tend to remain active throughout the lifespan. Thus, experiences early in life can have a dramatic effect on later developmental outcomes—a topic we return to at many points in this text. Furthermore, epigenetic modifications may be transmitted to the next generation via the mechanism

Watch *The Big Picture: Genes, Evolution, and Human Behavior* on **MyDevelopmentLab**

Watch *Genetic Predisposition to Alcoholism* on **MyDevelopmentLab**

epigenetics
Literally translated as "in addition to" or "on top of" genetics; the ideas that non-genetic factors (factors not included in the genome) influence how the genes behave, or express themselves

of genetic inheritance (Diamond, 2009; Meaney, 2010). Thus, the significance of gene–environment interactions is quite important for researchers in the area of human development, as changes throughout the lifespan are heavily dependent on both genetic and environmental factors. Clearly, advances in genetics research are influencing the way in which psychologists and other researchers view the process of human development.

REVIEW THE FACTS 2-2

1. A stained, visible image of the chromosomes in a cell is called a(n) ______________.
2. If a cell with 46 chromosomes divides into two cells, each with a copy of the original 46 chromosomes, this process is called ______________.
3. Human females begin producing ova during the period of ______________ development and males begin producing sperm during the period of ______________ development.
4. Alternate versions of the same genes are called ______________.
5. The idea that chance determines which half of a chromosome pair is passed along to offspring is called ______________.
6. The term that refers to the nongenetic factors that influence how genes behave is ______________.

Practice on **MyDevelopmentLab**

GENETIC DISORDERS

Considering the complexity of the genetic mechanisms involved in inheritance, it sometimes seems nearly impossible that a healthy baby could *ever* be born. Yet, in the United States, most babies are born healthy and normal: Only about 3% (about 120,000 infants per year) are born with **congenital anomalies**, which many people still refer to as birth defects (Centers for Disease Control and Prevention, 2011a), and all but about 9,000 of these babies will survive past their first birthday.

Genetic anomalies typically involve problems with the instructions that govern the chains of biochemical reactions that occur in the body. Often these errors disrupt protein production. Because these reaction chains are complex and carefully sequenced, even a very simple error can damage the protein being synthesized or prevent it from having its normal effects. Considering the intricacy of protein synthesis and the huge number (3.2 billion) of base pairs involved, you might think that errors either through inheritance or mutation would be relatively common, and they are. However, as noted earlier, many mutations and other genetic errors are harmless, and many can be repaired within the cell. Furthermore, many are not passed along during cell division, since the mutated cell is not viable and simply dies. Nevertheless, anomalies do occur. Those that seriously disrupt the organism's development often result in prenatal death and spontaneous abortion (miscarriage). Those that are less serious may or may not affect later development.

Watch *Special Topics: Epigenetics – A Revolutionary Science* on **MyDevelopmentLab**

congenital anomalies
Also called birth defects; abnormalities that result from genetic and chromosomal problems as well as from exposure to toxins, disease, and other factors during the prenatal period

The term "genetic disorders" is a rather generic term that refers generally to the many different conditions that can result due to problems with an individual's DNA. In some cases, a disorder involves the faulty duplication of chromosome material, resulting in either too much, or too little, of one or more chromosomes being present in the cells. For example, one of the more common *chromosomal disorders* is Down syndrome, which, as you learned earlier, occurs as the result of having an extra chromosome, or piece of a chromosome, present on the 21st chromosome pair. In other cases, genetic problems are caused by the presence of specific genes that cause development to proceed in a nonnormal manner. An example of a *genetic disorder* is phenylketonuria (PKU), which occurs when a defective gene on chromosome 12 fails to direct the individual's cells to manufacture the enzyme that normally breaks down a chemical called phenylalanine that is contained in many foods. When phenylalanine levels build up, other essential chemicals are blocked from entering brain cells, and neurological damage results. Fortunately, simple blood tests can detect PKU, and most of the problems associated with this condition can be controlled through diet. Both chromosomal and genetic anomalies can occur on any of the 46 chromosomes. When the problems involve the X or Y chromosomes, the disorders often are described as being *sex-linked disorders*; when the problems occur on the autosomes, the disorders are referred to as *autosomal disorders*. Additionally, disorders also can result when the DNA contained in the cells' mitochondria is disrupted, either through inheritance or mutation.

Sex-Linked Disorders

Often, sex-linked genetic disorders occur via dominant–recessive genetic patterns. As noted previously, a recessive gene on the X chromosome is much more likely to be expressed as the phenotype in males than in females because the Y chromosome has no allele that might counteract the gene. Pattern baldness, which can include a receding hairline, loss of hair on the top of the head, or overall hair thinning, is a common example. Many men inherit the recessive allele and some display pattern baldness as early as in their teens. Many women carry the recessive allele as well, but a dominant allele on the other X chromosome prevents pattern baldness from being displayed. Unless a woman inherits a recessive allele from *both* parents, she is unlikely to display this genetic trait. Partial color blindness and hemophilia (a potentially serious blood-clotting disorder) are also much more common in males than females for the same reason (see Table 2-2).

Sex-linked disorders also can occur when the sex chromosomes do not replicate correctly. Extra or missing sex chromosomes

Table 2-2 Examples of Sex-Linked Disorders*

GENETIC

Color blindness

Color blindness is a recessive disorder that occurs in almost 1 of 12 males. Genetic, X-linked color blindness is usually partial; that is, the disorder affects the ability to distinguish certain colors but not others.

Hemophilia A and B

Hemophilia A and B are recessive disorders that occur in about 1 of 5,000 males. These interfere with normal blood clotting and occur at different loci on the X chromosome. Hemophilia A is usually accompanied by color blindness.

CHROMOSOMAL

Fragile X syndrome

Fragile X syndrome occurs in about 1 of 1,500 males and 1 of 2,500 females, and it results from a breakage of the tip of an X chromosome. The ratios for males and females are different because females have two X chromosomes whereas males have one, so a normal X chromosome in females may partially or completely offset a fragile one.

Klinefelter syndrome (XXY, XXXY, XXXXY)

Klinefelter syndrome occurs in about 1 of 1,000 males. The phenotype includes sterility, small external genitalia, undescended testicles, and breast enlargement. About 25% of men with Klinefelter syndrome have intellectual disabilities. Physical manifestations can be eased by hormone replacement therapy beginning in adolescence. The testosterone injections must be continued for life, however, to maintain male secondary sex characteristics.

Superfemale syndrome (XXX, XXXX, XXXXX)

Superfemale syndrome occurs in about 1 of 1,000 females. Although these women appear normally female and are fertile and capable of bearing children with normal sex chromosome counts, the women tend to score slightly below average in intelligence.

Supermale syndrome (XYY, XYYY, XYYYY)

Supermale syndrome occurs in about 1 of 1,000 males. These men tend to be taller than average, with a greater incidence of acne and minor skeletal abnormalities. It was once hypothesized that supermales are more aggressive and develop differently than males with a normal genotype. However, that conclusion turned out to be exaggerated. The National Academy of Sciences concluded that there is no evidence to support a relationship between an extra Y chromosome and aggressive, violent behavior.

Turner syndrome (XO)

Turner syndrome occurs in about 1 of 10,000 females. One of the X chromosomes is either missing or inactive. Individuals with Turner syndrome usually have an immature female appearance—they do not develop secondary sex characteristics. They also lack internal reproductive organs. These females may be abnormally short, and some have intellectual disabilities. The disorder is usually discovered at puberty, and hormone replacement therapy can help with a more normal appearance.

*Statistics for each of the disorders are based on U.S. live births. For the extra X and extra Y disorders, the symptoms usually are more severe the more Xs or Ys a person has.

SOURCES: J. Haydon, 2007, *Genetics in practice*, Hoboken, NJ: Wiley; and J. A. Knight, 2010, *Genetics and inherited condition*, Pasadena, CA: Salem Press.

occur in a variety of ways. For example, females may have extra X chromosomes, and males may have either extra X or Y chromosomes. Females may also have only one X chromosome, as noted in Table 2-2.

Chromosomal breakage also can occur, and this disorder is seen in both males and females. An example is the inherited genetic disorder called *fragile X syndrome*, which is a form of intellectual disability that affects about 1 in 1,500 males and 1 in 2,500 females (Hagerman, 2011; Lo-Castro, D'Agati, & Curatolo, 2011). Fragile X syndrome is caused by a gene replication error, which causes multiple copies of a gene sequence to be inserted into the tip of the X chromosome. As a result, the tip of the X chromosome is especially prone to breakage. This breakage produces the brain deficiencies that underlie intellectual disability, as well as several growth abnormalities such as a large and elongated head, large protruding ears, and a long face. Some babies with this condition also display atypical behavioral patterns such as hand clapping, hand biting, and hyperactivity. Fragile X syndrome is now the most common hereditary disorder associated with intellectual disability, which some people refer to as mental retardation (National Institutes of Health, 2011a).

Because fragile X syndrome involves a recessive gene on the X chromosome, males tend to be more severely affected than females because they lack a paired allele on the Y chromosome that might counteract the effects. However, almost 20% of males with a fragile X chromosome do not display the phenotype, and others display symptoms of varying degrees of severity depending on how many times the multiple copies of the gene have been inserted: The greater the number of multiple copies inserted, the more severe the symptoms (Hagerman, 2011; National Institutes of Health, 2011a). As the example of fragile X syndrome makes clear, a wide variety of outcomes is associated with genetic disorders of all types.

Autosomal Disorders

Like sex-linked disorders, disorders that involve the other 22 pairs of chromosomes can result either from defective genes or from extra (or missing) chromosomes. Table 2-3 summarizes selected autosomal disorders. *Down syndrome* is the most common autosomal anomaly, and it is the second leading inherited disorder associated with intellectual disability. The most

Table 2-3 Examples of Autosomal Disorders*

GENETIC

Angelman syndrome

Angelman syndrome is possibly a dominant disorder that occurs in about 1 of 10,000 to 15,000 people. It is determined by a set of mutated genes on chromosome 15, but only if they are the father's; several proteins that affect the functioning of the hypothalamus are not produced.

Cystic fibrosis

This recessive disorder occurs in about 1 of 2,500 people of White European ancestry; otherwise, the disorder is rare. Among the U.S. population of Whites, approximately 1,500 new cases occur each year. A mutated gene on the 7th chromosome fails to function properly, disrupting several metabolic pathways that lead to regulation of the exocrine glands in the pancreas. Excess mucus is produced throughout the body, including the lungs and digestive tract, and perspiration is altered so that the person is subject to salt depletion in hot weather. Death by early adulthood is common. Persons with cystic fibrosis must undergo extensive physical therapy to loosen the mucus several times a day—a fatiguing, time-consuming process. Most males and females also are infertile.

Huntington's disease

Huntington's disease, also called Huntington's chorea, is a dominant disorder that occurs in about 1 of 10,000 people. Huntington's disease is carried by a dominant gene on chromosome 4 that therefore can be inherited from only one parent. The faulty protein it synthesizes is called huntingtin, which is found in numerous cells, including the neurons of the brain. There it causes selective degeneration of neurons, in turn producing dementia, random jerking movements, and a lopsided, staggering walk. These symptoms get progressively worse until the person becomes mute and rigid and eventually dies. The deterioration can last as long as 30 years, although many people with the disease die much sooner of complications such as pneumonia or heart failure. The disease is insidious because no symptoms appear until about 35 years of age. Thus, people who eventually develop the disease may pass the gene along to their children long before they are aware that they are carrying it.

Phenylketonuria (PKU)

This recessive disorder occurs in about 1 of 10,000 people. A defective gene on chromosome 12 fails to synthesize the enzyme phenylalanine hydroxylase, which is responsible for converting the essential amino acid phenylalanine from dietary protein into tyrosine, another essential amino acid in a complex of metabolic pathways (but which also is available in food). After birth, when the mother's enzymes can no longer convert phenylalanine for the baby, the amino acid accumulates and blocks other essential amino acids from entering cells, including brain neurons. The result is brain and other neurological damage and severe-to-profound intellectual disability, in addition to symptoms such as uncontrollable muscle twitches and movements, hyperactivity, and convulsive seizures. All U.S. newborns now receive a PKU screen. Because phenylalanine is present in many foods, infants with PKU are immediately placed on a synthetic protein substitute that contains very low but necessary levels of phenylalanine. When treated, people with PKU have normal life expectancies and can reproduce. However, fertile women with PKU have a very high risk of miscarriage or birth disorders because the fetus grows in an abnormal uterine environment.

Prader–Willi syndrome

Prader–Willi syndrome is a recessive disorder that occurs in about 1 of 10,000 to 15,000 people. It is determined by a set of mutated genes on chromosome 15 but only if they are the mother's; several proteins that affect the functioning of the hypothalamus are not produced.

Sickle-cell trait and sickle-cell anemia

Sickle-cell trait occurs in about 1 of 12 U.S. African Americans; sickle-cell anemia occurs in about 1 of 500. Other groups whose ancestors lived in low-lying malarial wetlands show high rates as well. The defective gene on chromosome 11 produces mutated beta globin, a component of hemoglobin—the oxygen-transport protein in red blood cells. The resulting blood cells break easily and are sticky; breakage results in too few cells and anemia, and the broken cells clog blood vessels. Treatment typically takes the form of blood transfusions or bone-marrow transplants.

Tay–Sachs disease

This recessive disorder occurs in about 1 of 5,000 people of European Ashkenazi Jewish ancestry; otherwise it is very rare. Indirect evidence suggests a prior adaptation for heterozygote carriers in resisting tuberculosis. A defective gene on chromosome 15 fails to produce the enzyme hexosaminidase A, which catalyzes the fatty sphingolipids in brain neurons; lethal concentrations accumulate and neurons die. In its extreme form, the child appears normal at birth but begins to show signs of physical weakness and irritability within a few months. Death from brain degeneration or complications such as pneumonia usually occurs by age 3 to 5.

CHROMOSOMAL

Down syndrome

Down syndrome occurs in about 1 in 1,000 live births. Risk increases with maternal age: Pregnancies in women over age 35 (5 to 8% of all pregnancies) account for 20% of Down syndrome births.

*Statistics for each of the disorders are based on U.S. live births.

SOURCES: J. Haydon, 2007, *Genetics in practice*, Hoboken, NJ: Wiley; and J. A. Knight, 2010, *Genetics and inherited condition*, Pasadena, CA: Salem Press.

frequent type of Down syndrome is *trisomy-21,* in which an extra chromosome is attached to the 21st pair (Mijovic & Turk, 2008). Down syndrome occurs about once in every 1,000 live births for mothers under age 35, and the incidence steadily increases as the age of the mother increases (see Chapter 3). Individuals with Down syndrome usually have distinctive physical characteristics such as a round face and slanted eyes without eye folds; heart abnormalities, hearing problems, and respiratory problems also are common.

Individuals with Down syndrome, however, vary considerably in the degree of intellectual disability associated with the disorder. It is a myth, for example, that no one with Down syndrome can be a functional member in society. The notions that children with Down syndrome are happy and carefree and adults

▲ The extent of mental retardation varies widely in individuals with fragile X syndrome. Despite his limitations, this boy is learning to play the piano.

▲ Teenage girls dream and wonder about the future, and so does this girl with classic symptoms of Down syndrome.

with Down syndrome are stubborn and uncooperative are erroneous. Historically, researchers often painted a grim picture of the expected lifespan and adult functioning for individuals with Down syndrome, but those conclusions were based primarily on adults whose education and health had been neglected or who had spent many years "warehoused" in institutional environments. Today, special education can make a major difference in the lives of people with this syndrome, and some young adults with Down syndrome can achieve much in both work and independent living (Buckley & Johnson-Glenberg, 2008; Fidler & Nadel, 2007). The same is true, of course, for persons with other forms of mild to moderate intellectual disability.

Do you know a person who has Down syndrome? If so, how are the effects of this disorder manifested in this person?

Researchers recently have begun to understand many of the complexities involved in genetic inheritance. For example, it appears that which parent a gene comes from can have a profound impact on how that gene is expressed—a phenomenon called **gene imprinting** (e.g., see Dykens & Roof, 2008; Hogart, Patzel, & LaSalle, 2008; Paoloni-Giacobino & Chaillet, 2004). Examples include *Prader–Willi syndrome (PWS)* and *Angelman syndrome (AS*; see Table 2-3). In PWS, the infant's behavior appears essentially normal, although perhaps lethargic for the first year, but then relentless food seeking and overeating begin. An affected child (or later, adult) overeats to the point of obesity, and developmental delays and mild intellectual disability are typical. By contrast, in AS an affected infant's behavior again appears essentially normal for the first year, but the infant then begins to display frequent and inappropriate outbursts of laughing, uncontrollable movements, and severe intellectual disability. If the mother's genes are expressed, the result is PWS; if the father's genes are expressed, the result is AS.

Gene imprinting can result from several problems: In some cases, one parent's genes are defective; in other cases, the child receives both alleles from the same parent (e.g., Cummings, 2006). Gene imprinting also can result from epigenic processes that alter the activity of genes. For example, in some cases, the mother's copy of the gene is active and the father's is silenced; in other cases the opposite pattern may occur (Meaney, 2010). Thus, the specific symptoms that are produced depend on which genes—the mother's or the father's—are directing development.

Mitochondrial Disorders

Although most DNA is contained in the nuclei of cells, some DNA is contained in the mitochondria—small structures within each cell that convert food molecules into the energy that powers cell functions. When mitochondria possess DNA that is deficient in some way, various sorts of mitochondrial genetic disorders can result. Like other genetic disorders, mitochondrial disorders can affect the individual in a wide variety of ways. Sometimes the disorder is focused on only one organ

Watch *Down Syndrome* on **MyDevelopmentLab**

gene imprinting
A phenomenon in which gene expression and phenotype depend on which parent the genes come from (e.g., Prader–Willi syndrome [PWS] and Angelman syndrome [AS])

or part of the body—perhaps the eye or the brain. For example, in the case of mitochondrial encephalopathy, the problems are centered in the brain, and the disorder that results typically involves significant intellectual limitations.

Interestingly, mitochondrial disorders sometimes emerge only after a period of apparently normal development (Centers for Disease Control, 2011f). Scientists are working to understand what sorts of conditions appear to trigger the onset of the disease, and epigenetic processes are most likely involved (Dudek, 2010). In the case of mitochondrial encephalopathy, it appears that environmental circumstances—perhaps a high fever, malnutrition, or extreme dehydration—can turn on the mitochondrial genes that give rise to the disease process. Another interesting aspect of mitochondrial disorders is that the DNA in mitochondria are inherited only from the mother and therefore are transmitted only down the female side of the family; males who inherit defective mitochondrial DNA may have mitochondrial genetic disorders, but they cannot pass them along to their children. In fact, it appears that mitochondrial disorders are more likely to result from mutations than from inheritance, so oftentimes only one person in the family will experience the disorder (Chinnery, 2010). Also, if the mitochondrial disorder is the result of a mutation, usually only some of the mitochondria in the cells carry the mutated DNA, and others are normal. The degree to which a resulting disease process emerges appears to vary depending on the proportion of mitochondria that are affected, and there may be a minimum level that is necessary for any disease process to begin (Chinnery, 2010). Clearly, there is much left to be learned about mitochondrial genetic disorders, both in terms of causes and treatments, which at this point usually involve only managing the symptoms that occur.

Genetic Counseling

Because most recessive genes are not expressed, most people never know what kinds of defective genes they carry; yet most people probably harbor at least five to eight potentially lethal recessive genes in addition to many less harmful ones. For those individuals who wish to become parents, but who are thought to be at risk of bearing offspring with genetic problems, **genetic counseling** can be a valuable aid.

Genetic counseling is a widely available resource (although typically expensive) that can help potential parents evaluate genetic risk factors in childbearing and enable them to make informed decisions (see Table 2-4). Genetic counseling often includes the analysis of parental medical records and family histories to construct a genetic "pedigree," which identifies previous instances where congenital anomalies have occurred. Other techniques, such as parental blood analysis or prenatal screening (see Chapter 3), can detect many chromosomal or genetic anomalies—including the disorders listed in Table 2-2 and Table 2-3 and over several hundred others.

genetic counseling
A widely available resource that can help potential parents evaluate genetic risk factors in childbearing and enable them to make choices that reflect their values and circumstances

Table 2-4 Indications for Genetic Counseling

FAMILY HISTORY

- Neonatal deaths
- Children with multiple malformations or metabolic disorders
- Children with mental retardation, developmental delays, or failure to thrive
- Children with congenital anomalies, such as cleft palate, neural tube defects, clubfoot, congenital heart disease
- Children with unusual appearance, especially if accompanied by failure to thrive or suboptimal psychomotor development
- Any disease or disability that "runs in the family," especially hearing loss, blindness, neurodegenerative disorders, short stature, premature heart disease, immune deficiency, or abnormalities of the hair, skin, or bones

PARENTAL CONDITIONS

- Known genetic or chromosomal abnormality
- Amenorrhea (in women of childbearing age, absence or suppression of menstruation), aspermia (in men, a deficiency of seminal secretion or ejaculation), infertility, or abnormal sexual development
- Prior pregnancy loss or stillbirth
- Mother over age 35, father over age 55
- Father and mother biologically related to each other
- Ethnic background suggesting an increased risk for a specific disorder (see Table 2-3)
- Mother exposed to certain diseases, toxic agents, radiation, illegal drugs, or other potentially harmful agents prior to or during pregnancy (see Chapter 3)
- Genetic predisposition for cancer

SOURCE: Adapted from "Genetic evaluation/genetic counseling," by Mountain States Genetic Network, 2008, retrieved from http://www.mostgene.org/dir/indicate.htm.

If genetic counseling reveals the presence of a heritable genetic disorder in the parents, the counselor evaluates the couple's risk of having a baby with the disorder, puts the risk in perspective, and, if the couple decides that the risk is too great, suggests reproductive alternatives. Such alternatives may include adoption or artificial insemination of donor ovum or with donor sperm.

Genetic counseling is a highly specialized discipline that requires a technical knowledge of genetics and statistics and skill as a clinical therapist (Cassidy & Allanson, 2010; Peay & Austin, 2011). Decisions about risks are complex, and they often challenge the ethical value systems of parents who may not always agree. Genetic counselors increasingly pay special attention to the varying beliefs and cultural backgrounds of their clients, which are important factors that affect the decisions potential parents make as well as how they cope with any bad news they receive (Lewis, 2010).

Often the results of genetic tests are indeterminate. Even if a genetic defect is identified, the extent of the resulting disorder may be unknown. Consider the role of a genetic counselor who must advise the expectant parents that their child will have sickle-cell anemia. In its worst form, this disorder causes severe pain and perhaps early death. However, many sufferers

TRY THIS!

Ethical Dilemmas in Gene Testing

New technologies are quickly changing the landscape for genetic counseling. Until quite recently, the only method available to assess the risk for developing gene-linked illnesses was to study the medical histories of biologically related family members. Today, however, widely varying techniques are available to identify risk factors associated with many genetic disorders and diseases.

One set of diagnostic techniques involves examining the chromosomes an individual carries. Chromosomes are found in every cell in the body. Consequently, they can be obtained in a variety of ways—from swabs of skin cells in the mouth or nose; from blood, urine, or hair cells; or even from expected child's sloughed off cells that float in the amniotic fluid in the mother's uterus (see Chapter 3). Chromosome tests are used to detect genetic disorders that involve extra or missing chromosome material, such as Down and fragile X syndromes. However, most genetic disorders are more subtle than chromosome analysis can detect. Consequently, newer techniques have been developed that examine the DNA molecules contained in the chromosomes. These more refined tests allow scientists to look for specific gene sequences that are associated with particular disorders. DNA-based techniques—collectively called *gene testing*—involve finding specific segments on the DNA molecule that have undergone mutations associated with specific diseases. Gene testing holds considerable promise for diagnosing a broad array of genetically linked diseases and disorders, including cancer, some forms of mental illness, Alzheimer's disease, cystic fibrosis, diabetes, and many diseases affecting the brain and nervous system (National Human Genome Research Institute, 2011).

All genetic testing—whether it involves examining family medical histories or includes the study of chromosomes or DNA molecules—poses ethical considerations. Would you want to know, for example, if you will develop diabetes, cancer, or Alzheimer's disease? Or would you rather *not* know? (Public opinion polls suggest that people in the United States are about evenly split on such questions (NIH, 2011b).) Would you want to know if your expected child carried the extra chromosome linked to Down syndrome? Or if this child was a boy or a girl?

To investigate your own sense of the ethical dilemmas associated with genetic testing, try this: Consider the following scenarios and decide whether you *would* want to know, or *wouldn't* want to know, if your genes (or those of your expected child) contained markers linked to the following disorders. Then consider the reasons *why* you would want to know or not want to know. You also might ask a friend or family member these same questions. Do your judgments agree? If not, *why not*?

You (or your wife or sister) carry the BRCA genes that are associated with breast and ovarian cancer, raising risk factors significantly. (About 60% of women who carry these genes develop breast cancer and 15–40% develop ovarian cancer.)	________ I would want to know this ________ I would NOT want to know this
Your expected child has the genetic marker for fragile X syndrome (discussed in this chapter).	________ I would want to know this ________ I would NOT want to know this
Your genome includes the APOE gene, which puts you at significantly greater risk for developing late-onset Alzheimer's disease.	________ I would want to know this ________ I would NOT want to know this
Your expected child is a boy, carrying the normal XY chromosomes. (Assume the pregnancy is 2 months along.)	________ I would want to know this ________ I would NOT want to know this
You carry the gene for Huntington's disease, which onsets in midlife and involves progressive neurological disease resulting in severe mental and physical disability and eventual early death.	________ I would want to know this ________ I would NOT want to know this

There are many factors to consider as you think about the ethics concerning gene testing. On the positive side, gene testing can confirm a suspected diagnosis (such as Down syndrome) and help parents and others develop a plan of action for coping. It can help individuals understand the likelihood that an illness will develop later in life (such as breast cancer), so they can take early preventative action or be especially diligent in watching for early symptoms. Gene testing can be done prenatally, so parents can know early in the pregnancy if the expected child carries identifiable defective genes, and they can plan accordingly. However, gene testing does raise some serious ethical concerns. Oftentimes, genetic mutations raise the *probability* of developing a disorder, but do not guarantee a specific outcome. For example, about 60% of women who have either the BRCA1 or BRCA2 gene will develop breast cancer (a much higher percentage than women who do not have these genes), meaning that 40% will not (National Cancer Institute, 2012). Thus, even if a woman knows she carries these genes, it is difficult to know what actions are most appropriate. Also, some diseases or syndromes occur along a spectrum, meaning that some individuals who carry these genes are seriously affected but others have symptoms that are quite manageable. This raises the concern that some parents may choose to terminate a pregnancy if their expected child is not "perfect," even though developmental outcomes are unclear. Another concern is that children with "suspicious" genetic profiles will be regarded by parents and others as somehow abnormal, thereby destabilizing family interactions because the expectation is that illness or disability is just around the corner (Buchbinder & Timmermans, 2011).

As gene testing becomes more available—and more commonly used—many individuals will need to make ethical choices similar to those just discussed. More than 1,000 genetic tests currently are available, and gene testing technology is still in its infancy; new tests for many more disorders and diseases are in development (Oak Ridge National Laboratory, 2012). Furthermore, new methods of less invasive prenatal gene testing are rapidly being developed. For example, whereas only a few years ago it was necessary to perforate a mother's uterus to obtain a sample of amniotic fluid or placental tissue to get a DNA sample from her fetus, today noninvasive techniques can be performed using only a sample of the mother's blood (de Jong et al., 2011). Consequently the medical risks associated with gene testing are diminishing at the same time that many more genetic markers are being identified (Kelly & Farrimond, 2011). It seems clear that gene testing will become much more common in the near future. Consequently, ethical questions will become increasingly important to understand and grapple with as the options for gene testing increase.

can lead relatively normal lives with existing treatments, such as blood transfusions and bone-marrow transplants. Also, sickle-cell anemia currently is a target for gene therapy research (which will be explored further in the next section); therefore, a less invasive and less costly treatment could be on the horizon. These parents face a difficult decision indeed, as do many other parents whose developing children have a genetic anomaly for which a breakthrough cure could come at any time. Genetic counselors help parents to understand the risks and to clarify their values as they consider the options available.

Why do genetic counselors need to understand statistical probability to perform their job?

Advances in Genetic Research and Treatment

Both the technology of genetic research and our understanding of genetic determinants are advancing rapidly. The basis for many of these advances is **recombinant DNA technology**. Recombinant DNA techniques were first developed in the 1980s and have revolutionized the study of molecular genetics (Glick, Pasternak, & Patten, 2010; Khan, 2012). In brief, the term covers an assortment of highly sophisticated procedures in which DNA is extracted from cell nuclei and cleaved (cut) into segments by selected enzymes. Once the targeted genes have been sectioned, they can be inserted into host cells—usually from bacteria—where they can be replicated for use in a variety of ways.

Gene Therapy One way recombinant DNA techniques currently are being used is for the production of proteins that can be harvested from the bacteria in which they are grown. Once harvested, these proteins—such as human insulin for the treatment of diabetes, interferon for the treatment of a variety of immune-system diseases, and human growth hormones—can be given to patients whose own bodies do not produce them in sufficient quantities.

In addition, **gene therapies** are being developed that involve reinserting genetically altered cells into the person from whom they were harvested. The idea is that these "engineered" genes will then produce normal quantities of the missing or mutated protein. This approach has been tried with various genetic disorders but with limited success thus far, but research continues and offers the prospect of better results in the near future.

Another, more direct, experimental approach called *in vivo* gene therapy takes advantage of benign *retroviruses*, which are viruses capable of penetrating cells but without any adverse effects. In this approach, some viral genes are removed, a cloned human gene that is normal (lacking the genetic disorder) is inserted, the retrovirus is cultured in large numbers, and finally it is introduced into the patient. Here the idea is that the retrovirus will penetrate cells and deliver the normal gene. This approach also has experienced only limited success; however, it holds great promise for the future if certain technical obstacles can be overcome (e.g., see Cotrim & Baum, 2008; Friedmann, 2007; Kay, 2011). Another promising experimental approach is cloning, which is a controversial technique that is further explored in the box Changing Perspectives: Genetic Engineering and Cloning.

REVIEW THE FACTS 2-3

1. Approximately what percentage of babies born in the United States have congenital anomalies?
   a. less than 1% b. 1 to 2%
   c. 3% d. 7%
2. A person with a chromosome structure of XXX would be an example of which of the following?
   a. chromosomal breakage
   b. a dominant–recessive sex-linked trait
   c. fragile X syndrome
   d. a sex-linked congenital disorder
3. Down syndrome is caused by ______________.
4. The phenomenon of *gene imprinting* refers to which of the following?
   a. Dominant genes are more likely to be reflected in the phenotype.
   b. Which parent a gene comes from can have an impact.
   c. Tips of chromosomes are more likely to be replicated than center sections.
   d. Meiosis is more likely to involve mutations than mitosis.
5. A virus that is capable of penetrating cells without adverse effects, and therefore is useful in recombinant DNA applications, is called a(n) ______________.

Practice on MyDevelopmentLab

BEHAVIOR GENETICS

Although recent advances in genetic technology are impressive, the field of molecular genetics is in its infancy. Furthermore, even if we had complete knowledge of an individual's genome, this would provide only a partial explanation for how that person's traits would be expressed within an interactive environmental context. Understanding how genetic characteristics

Watch *Genetic Counseling* on MyDevelopmentLab

Watch *Human Cloning - The Ethics* on MyDevelopmentLab

recombinant DNA technology
An assortment of highly sophisticated procedures in which DNA is extracted from cell nuclei and cut into segments; the resulting fragments are then joined to self-replicating elements, in essence forming functional gene clones. These are then placed in host bacterial cells to be maintained and cultured

gene therapy
An approach to establishing cures for genetic disorders that can be applied at any point, from altering the molecular structure of DNA to altering the process of protein synthesis

operate within particular environmental settings is the focus of **behavior genetics**, an approach that assesses patterns of inheritance at the behavioral level—typically through the use of psychological tests, parental self-reports, or observations of children's behavior (Gottlieb, 1998; Gottlieb, Wahlsten, & Lickliter, 2006; Hood, 2010).

Modern behavior genetics incorporates the accepted view that complex traits are determined by heredity and environment in interaction. For the most part, the field also takes the view that what is inherited are *genetic predispositions*, or vulnerabilities, that are expressed in behavior to varying degree, or not at all, depending upon environmental influences. For example, a person might inherit a predisposition toward severe depression, but whether that person actually becomes severely depressed can depend upon a host of overlapping influences, ranging from family situation, to economic support, to particular traumatic experiences, and so forth. Thus, even if (or when) researchers know how all of the genetic information encoded in our DNA expresses itself, behavior genetics will still be important because it recognizes the epigenetic processes and interactive nature of heredity and environment.

Would the heritability of hair color be the same in a society in which hair dying was common as in a society in which hair dye was never used?

The primary tool of behavior genetics is the statistical technique of correlation, which measures *concordance:* the extent to which biologically related people show similar characteristics. Concordance rates form the basis of our estimates of **heritability**, which is the proportion of a trait, such as intelligence, that is thought to result from inherited, genetic factors. Heritability estimates must always be considered in the context in which these relationships are studied because environmental influences on behavior exert a more pronounced effect when such conditions vary widely from person to person. For example, when a trait is somewhat genetically based, related individuals will be more similar to each other if they are raised in the same, rather than widely different, environments. Because heritability estimates involve measuring the degree to which genetically related and unrelated individuals are similar on a trait, studies of twins and adopted children provide especially valuable data.

Twin and Adoption Studies

The logic behind the use of twin studies and adoption studies is similar: to investigate how individuals who are more, or less, alike genetically develop. In the case of twin studies, remember that identical (also called monozygotic) twins are identical genetically (except for mutations and epigenetic effects). If a trait has a high heritability, researchers expect that identical twins will be much more alike than will other individuals who share less genetic similarity. Adoption studies employ a similar logic: Adopted children have little genetic resemblance to their adoptive parents, but much more to their biological parents. If a trait is highly heritable, adopted children should resemble their biological parents more closely than their adoptive parents. There are many ongoing longitudinal studies of twins and adoptees, including the Minnesota Twin Study (Minnesota Center for Twin and Family Research, 2011) and the Colorado Adoption Project (Institute for Behavioral Genetics, 2011), and the results from research conducted on these and other similar populations have helped researchers understand more about the relative contribution of both genetic and environmental determinants of development (Segal, 2010).

Both adoption studies and twin studies suggest that heredity and environment both play important roles in the development of a wide range of human traits, including intelligence, personality, and susceptibility to mental as well as physical illness, even when the traits in question seem on the surface to be almost totally the result of environmental pressures (e.g., see Johnson, Terkheimer, Gottesman, & Bouchard, 2009; Malouff, Rooke, & Schutte, 2008; Sesardic, 2010). For example, we usually consider a person's use of tobacco and alcohol to be largely a matter of individual choice, perhaps reflecting the person's culture and upbringing; however, research suggests that genetic influences play a significant role in the development of these addictions (Young, Rhee, Stallings, Corley, & Hewitt, 2006; Young-Wolff, Enoch, & Prescott, 2011).

Although, as we argued earlier, hereditary forces and environmental influences are in continuous, dynamic interaction, adoption and twin studies do allow us some glimpse into the relative impact these variables have on how development unfolds (Visscher, Hill, & Wray, 2008). Most studies suggest, for example, that for individuals growing up in developed economies today, genes contribute about 50% of the variation in intelligence we observe among individuals (Davis, Arden, & Plomin, 2008; Lykken, 2007; Posthuma, de Geus, & Deary, 2009). Moreover, such findings have been replicated beyond the United States, for example in Japan (Lynn & Hattori, 1990), in India (Pal, Shyam, & Singh, 1997), and in Croatia (Bratko, Butkovic, & Chamorro-Premuzic, 2010). With respect to

How is it possible for an exceptionally intelligent person to have biological parents who have average IQs?

behavior genetics
The study of the relationship between behavior and genetic makeup

heritability
The extent to which a trait is inherited versus acquired, thus presuming a genetic basis; note that heritability estimates are influenced by the environments in which they are considered

Watch *The Basics: Genetic Mechanisms and Behavioral Genetics* on **MyDevelopmentLab**

CHANGING PERSPECTIVES

Genetic Engineering and Cloning

To clone something means to duplicate it exactly. In the context of genetic engineering, cloning can refer to the replication of DNA segments used to produce drugs such as insulin or to the exact duplication of an entire living organism. Both of these technologies have advanced dramatically in recent years. For example, in 1997, even the scientific community was stunned by the announcement of a successfully cloned sheep named "Dolly." Now, less than two decades later, cloning mammals has become rather routine. To date, scientists have successfully cloned 20 different species, including goats, pigs, deer, rabbits, mules, horses, and dogs. Incredibly, it is now well established that scientists most likely could successfully clone a complete human being from a single cell (American Medical Association, 2011). Certainly these new techniques in genetic engineering, and especially in cloning, raise serious ethical and moral concerns (Davis, 2010; Shamoo & Resnik, 2009).

To understand the ethical concerns, it is helpful to consider the issues involved. One thing to consider is that genetic engineering to modify the characteristics of an organism is not new; such techniques have been practiced for decades in agriculture in the form of selective breeding; the development of hybrid seeds and the breeding of race horses are but two examples. More recently, recombinant DNA techniques have been used to insert new genes into an organism's DNA, rendering the "improved" version better in some specific way. These techniques have been used to alter many of the foods we eat, for example, to produce rice or corn that is disease or mold resistant, or to produce vegetables that have more vitamins or a healthier composition, such as genetically engineered tomatoes with beta-carotene for good vision (Pasternak, 2003). Although at present the cost of cloning technology makes it unlikely that we will be eating cloned meat or produce any time soon, the U.S. Food and Drug Administration has declared that cloned foods would be safe to consume (U.S. Food and Drug Administration, 2011), so this may be a possibility in the future. Many scientists suggest that the new techniques in genetic engineering, and perhaps in cloning, might shorten the process of improving food production and help to feed the world's population, much of which is starving (Hodge, 2009; Solway, 2009).

Despite the promise for accomplishing humanitarian ends, there are ethical concerns connected with the use of genetic engineering techniques, and especially with cloning. In some cases, these concerns are at least somewhat unfounded. For example, those who fear that genetic engineering could produce a "runaway new breed" usually fail to consider that this same result—a modified DNA code—could occur through selective breeding techniques as well, and these have been used for many years to produce better strains of crops and animals. Even proponents, however, acknowledge that the speed with which organisms can be modified is greatly accelerated through genetic engineering, so some measure of concern may be appropriate. Cloning techniques raise special concerns. Even those applications that stop far short of human replication intrude into what some would consider the sanctity of life. For example, although most people consider the cloning of DNA segments in bacteria for the purpose of producing lifesaving drugs to be an acceptable use of genetic engineering technology, many people balk at the use of human embryo tissue for this purpose. Yet cloning techniques offer great promise not only for the production of drugs, but also for the production of organs for transplant. Given the severe shortage of donor organs, and the likely possibility that such organs could be "grown" from fetal tissue (Atala & Yoo, 2008; Koh & Atala, 2004), the ethical—and perhaps legal—questions surrounding this application of cloning techniques require serious consideration. At what point does life begin? Who "owns" fetal tissue (Davis, 2010; Häyry, 2010)? And, of course, the ethics of cloning a complete human being is especially controversial, prompting several nations, and the United Nations, to draft laws and recommendations that ban such an activity.

▲ This foal, born in February 2005, was the first horse cloned from a castrated endurance champion, Pieraz, winner of two world championships, one in 1994 in the Netherlands and another in 1996 in the United States. The procedure was done to preserve the genetic heritage of the champion.

A discussion of the ethics of genetic therapy and cloning technology is beyond the scope of this text. Good arguments can be made for all sides of the complex issues that exist (Davis, 2010; Steinbock, 2007). Perhaps at this point we might simply conclude that genetic technology is in its infancy; the next few years certainly will be filled with amazing advances and, along with these advances, continuing debate.

---

the development of personality, a similar, although more complex, pattern emerges: It appears that the genetic contribution to personality may be on the order of about 40%, with estimates ranging from 20 to 50%, depending on the situation in which individuals are studied (Ekehammer, et al., 2010; Rushton, Bons, & Hur, 2008; Segal, 2000).

One way of further examining the general contribution of heredity and environment to development is to consider the results of many studies, taken together. The technique of *meta-analysis* allows researchers to consider the results of several similar studies at the same time, weighing the quality of each as their results are averaged. One fairly recent

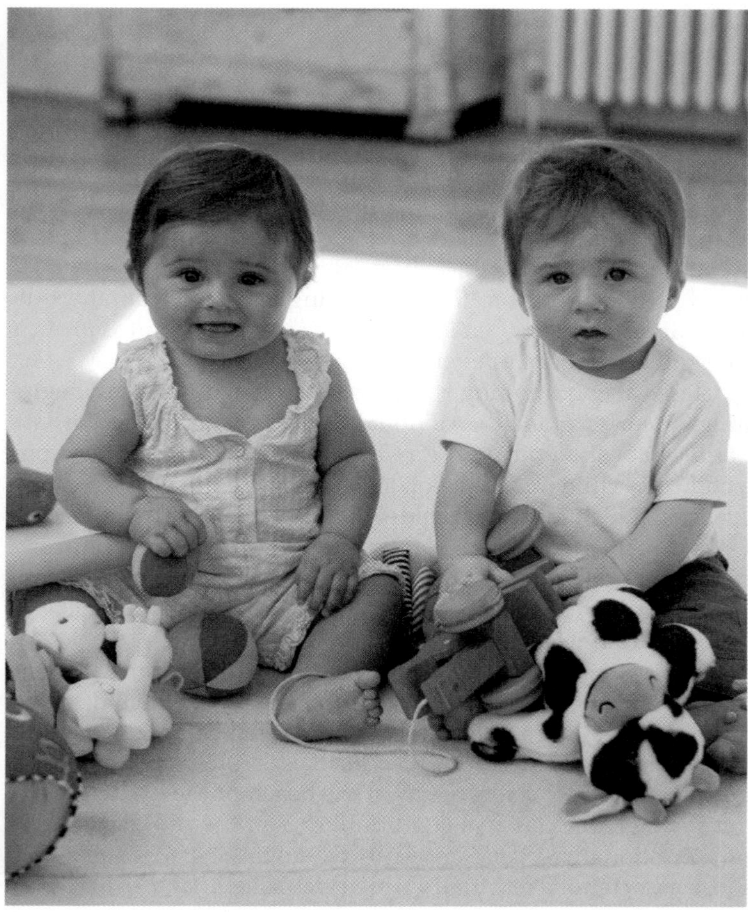

▲ Fraternal twins can be as similar or different genetically as siblings born at different times.

meta-analytic study of over 400 individual studies of the heritability of traits—including intelligence, language ability, psychiatric disorders including anxiety and depression, personality traits, and antisocial problems—suggests that 41% of human behavior is genetically influenced (Malouff, Rooke, & Schutte, 2008). However, results from twin studies and adoption studies are tricky to interpret because of the difficulty in determining the degree to which environments are alike or different for each individual. For example, even twins raised in the same home have different experiences, which begin in the womb. Such early environmental differences may have a profound effect on both intelligence and personality (Dickens & Flynn, 2001). In addition, children are not merely the passive recipients of their surroundings; the traits they possess *produce* an impact on the environment. Thus, although behavior genetics advances our ability to study the interaction of heredity and environment, it does not capture perfectly the complex interplay of these forces that are inextricably entwined throughout development across the lifespan. This subject is explored further in the box Try This! Exploring the Basis of Personality.

▲ Identical twins have the same genes and physical characteristics, including sex.

REVIEW THE FACTS 2-4

1. Why is the field of behavior genetics likely to continue to be important, even if (or when) scientists fully understand gene expression?
2. The proportion of a trait that is thought to result from genetic factors is referred to as ____________________.
3. When environmental conditions are stable, the heritability of a trait is likely to be (higher/lower) than when environmental conditions vary widely.
4. The heritability of intelligence in typical situations is approximately ____________________ and the heritability of personality characteristics is approximately ____________________.

   a. 10%; 50%
   b. 50%; 10%
   c. 10%; 10%
   d. 50%; 40%

Practice on **MyDevelopmentLab**

ENVIRONMENTAL INFLUENCES AND CONTEXTS

To gain a better understanding of how genetics and the environment interact, it is useful to consider how one's surroundings affect behavior. When psychologists use the word *environment*, generally they are referring to all of the factors, except for genes, that impact and influence an individual's behavior and course in life. As such, environmental influences range from the very narrow (being praised for sitting quietly) to the very broad (growing up in a culture of privilege or poverty). To understand the breadth of these forces on development, it is useful to consider them within the framework of an ecological system (see Chapter 1), which includes situations that directly impact

▲ Learning in a formal school environment involves both direct instruction and all the effects of peer, community, and cultural expectations.

specific behaviors (the microsystem) as well as those that are part of a much more general context in which development unfolds (the macrosystem).

Basic Processes That Affect Behavior

Every day, in ways great and small, our behavior is influenced by our prior experiences. Sometimes what is learned is very direct, involving simple learning mechanisms like habituation, classical conditioning, or operant conditioning.

Habituation One of the simplest yet most important kinds of learning is **habituation**, which involves learning to stop attending to a *stimulus*, or change, in the environment. For example, if you are reading this text, you probably are not attending to minor sounds occurring around you or to irrelevant images in your peripheral vision.

Normally, habituation helps "filter out" the repetitive and monotonous stimuli that often bombard us. Habituation, thus, enables us to stay focused and to attend to things that are important, although we can only attend to a limited amount of information at any given time. Research techniques based on habituation provide a very important method for studying infant capabilities (see Chapter 4).

Classical Conditioning Classical conditioning refers to the kind of learning that occurs when, through repeated trials, we learn to associate one stimulus with another naturally occurring stimulus–response sequence (refer to Chapter 1; see Figure 2-8). In everyday life, a cat learns that the sound of an electric can opener might be followed by a tasty treat; a dog learns that the sound of a car in the driveway might be followed by the arrival of its beloved owner; and a toddler learns that the word "No" might be followed by being removed from the situation. In each case, what is learned is that one stimulus *predicts* that some sequence of events will happen.

Can you think of a specific example in which your own behavior was controlled by classically conditioned stimuli?

Classical conditioning is a powerful force in our lives, beginning in early infancy. Emotional responses, in particular, are often established through classical conditioning. If a bee stings a child, the child may develop a fear of bees; and, if the fear generalizes, the child may even develop a fear of all flying insects. Unreasonable fears of objects or situations are called **phobias**; phobias—such as fear of the dark, fear of being in a closely confined space, and so forth—often are established through classical conditioning.

Positive emotional reactions can be conditioned in the same way as are negative responses. For example, feelings of relaxation or pleasure can be triggered by stimuli previously associated with enjoyable experiences, such as an old song that brings back memories of a sunny day at the beach or the excitement of a festival. Thus, classical conditioning is at the root of many of our emotional responses, even if we have long forgotten how those associations originally were established.

Operant Conditioning Many intentional behaviors, on the other hand, are more likely established via operant conditioning, which involves the application or removal of rewards (called *reinforcements*) and punishments to encourage or discourage us from acting in certain ways. When consequences—either positive or negative—follow behavior, they have the power to influence whether that behavior is more or less likely to be displayed again. **Reinforcers** increase the likelihood that a behavior will be repeated; **punishments** decrease that probability. For example, if you study hard and get an A, you are likely to study hard in the future; however, if you get an F, you may quit studying because, for most students, the F is a punishing grade. We should note that punishment, especially, is likely to produce some unexpected effects

Do you think parents should ever punish their children? If so, when? How?

habituation
Ceasing to attend or respond to repetitive stimulation; occurs at several levels, from sensation to perception to higher cognition

reinforcer
A stimulus that increases the likelihood that the behavior the reinforcer follows will recur

phobia
The unreasonable fear of an object or a situation

punishment
A stimulus that decreases the likelihood that the behavior the punishment follows will recur

Watch *Classic Footage of Little Albert* on **MyDevelopmentLab**

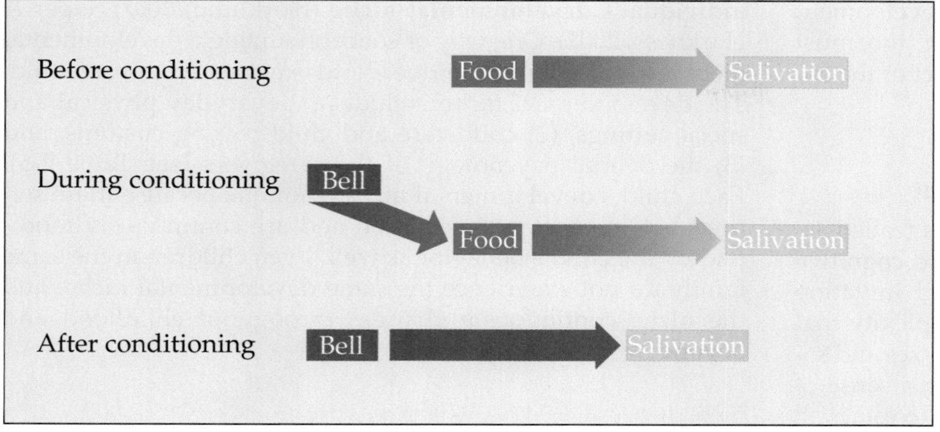

FIGURE 2-8 A Typical Classical Conditioning Procedure
In classical conditioning, a previously neutral stimulus (such as a ringing bell) is presented just before a biologically programmed stimulus–response occurs, such as putting food in the mouth (stimulus) that causes salivation (response). After repeated pairings of the neutral stimulus with the unconditioned S–R sequence, the neutral stimulus becomes associated, or *conditioned,* and it now produces a response like the original response (salivation), even when no food is presented.

because it often generalizes to the situation in which it occurs. For example, the student who gets an F may not only quit studying but also may develop a negative attitude about the teacher, the school, and classmates. We will return to a more detailed treatment of punishment later in the book.

Although reinforcement and punishment exert a powerful force on our behavior, not every action we take is followed directly by a positive or negative consequence. Instead, reinforcements and punishments occur only occasionally, according to what psychologists call **partial schedules**. For example, when children throw tantrums in stores, their parents *sometimes* give in and the children get what they want. Behaviors maintained by partial schedules can be very difficult to change, which is a conclusion to which any parent who has coped with tantrums in public can attest. Furthermore, reinforcers and punishments do not act only on behaviors that are complete or fully developed; rather, they often **shape** behavior through procedures called *successive approximations.* For example, if a parent wishes to use reinforcement to encourage a child with an anger management problem to behave more appropriately, the parent first may need to reinforce small improvements in behavioral control. As the child becomes more able to control the angry behavior, the parent can require better and better compliance before rewards are given. Shaping can also be used in toilet training a child: First praise the child for stating the need, then for sitting on the potty chair, and eventually for completing the entire act successfully.

Applied Behavior Analysis

Although human behavior is extraordinarily complex, simple learning processes, such as habituation and conditioning, underlie many habits and responses. In addition, we often rely, perhaps unwittingly, on conditioning principles when we try to modify our own behavior. For example, students may promise themselves a soda or a candy bar when they finish reading an assigned text chapter. The application of learning principles to change behavior is called **applied behavior analysis (ABA)**, or sometimes behavior modification. Practicing psychologists often use applied behavior analysis techniques as they help clients develop better coping mechanisms and behaviors.

Conditioning principles are important forces in establishing and maintaining behavior; however, to understand the richness of human development, we must also consider the *thinking* part of human nature. People do not merely *respond;* they reason, plan, interpret, and choose. Furthermore, human behavior is seldom the result of simple, clearly defined contingencies

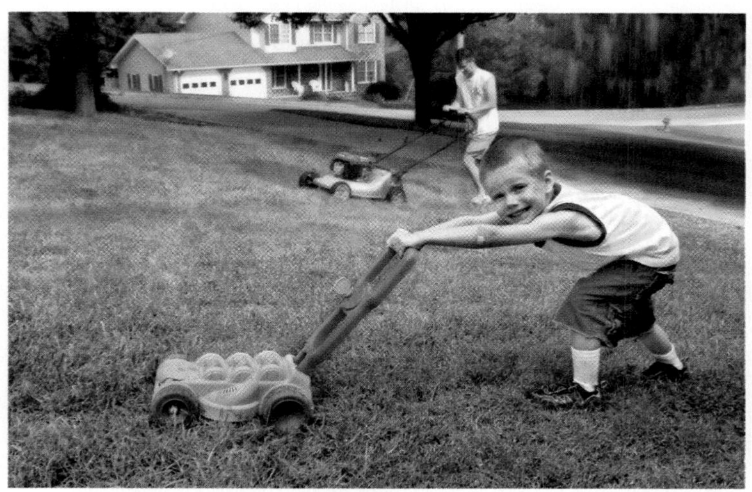

▲ Learning at home includes imitation of the important people in the child's life.

partial schedules
Occur when only some responses are reinforced or punished; produces much stronger habits than continuous reinforcement

shaping
Systematically reinforcing successive approximations to a desired behavior

applied behavior analysis (ABA)
A method that uses conditioning procedures—such as reinforcement, reward, and shaping—to change behavior (also called behavior modification)

among stimuli, responses, and rewards. Rather, development unfolds in a rich, broad, social context. These factors, too, must be considered when researchers reflect on the impact of the environment on human development.

Social Learning and the Evolving Self-Concept

The fact that people can learn by observing others (called *social learning;* see Chapter 1) and that they can use cognitive processes such as planning, problem solving, and imitation to direct their behavior is reflected in the vast complexity that characterizes human behavior. Both cognitive processes and social learning are intimately involved in developing a sense of self as distinct from others and eventually lead one to establish a **self-concept**—one's beliefs and feelings about oneself, which is what defines who an individual *is.*

An important concept in understanding the development of the self is **self-efficacy** (Bandura, 1997; Cervone, Mor, Orom, Shadel & Scott, 2011; Stack, Serbin, Enns, Ruttle, & Barrieau, 2010). In brief, self-efficacy refers to our beliefs about our own capabilities. When individuals have a strong sense of self-efficacy, for example, they believe they are capable and competent and can generally accomplish the tasks they set for themselves. Self-concept and self-efficacy are but two of the many dimensions that not only develop as the result of each individual's specific experiences but also depend on development within a broader context.

REVIEW THE FACTS 2-5

1. The kind of learning that involves ignoring a repetitive stimulus is called ______________.
2. The kind of learning that involves learning that the presence of a stimulus will *predict* some sequence of events is called ______________.
3. If an action is followed by a reinforcer, the action is more likely to be ______________.
4. Teaching a dog a complex set of behaviors by first teaching a simple behavior and then gradually increasing expectations before a reinforcement is given is called ______________.
5. One's beliefs and feelings about oneself are referred to as ______________.

Practice on **MyDevelopmentLab**

ENVIRONMENT IN A BROADER CONTEXT: FAMILY AND CULTURE

Each individual develops in an environment comprised of multiple settings. This unique world is referred to as that individual's **developmental niche** (Bjorklund, 2007; Super & Harkness, 2002). One way of conceptualizing a developmental niche is to consider the unique world experienced by each child. The developmental niche includes (1) everyday physical and social settings, (2) child-care and child-rearing customs, and (3) the overall psychology of the caregivers (see Table 2-5). Each child's developmental niche is unique because these settings are in constant interaction and are continuously modified by the child's behavior as well. Even children in the same family do not experience the same developmental niche, and the niche continuously changes throughout childhood and beyond.

Family Systems

At the heart of development is the family, especially when children are young. The family has a tremendous influence on the kind of person the child becomes and on the child's place in society. Indeed, the type of family into which a child is born can dramatically affect the expectations, roles, beliefs, and interrelationships the child later experiences throughout life (Hartup, 1995, 2006; Nugent, Petrauskas, & Brazelton, 2009), as well as the child's physical, cognitive, emotional, and social development.

Table 2-5 Components of a Child's Developmental Niche*

EVERYDAY PHYSICAL AND SOCIAL SETTINGS
Physical living conditions, such as size and type of the living space, sleep and eating schedules, and whether children sleep in the same area as the parents or other caregivers Social conditions, such as the size of the family, the presence or absence of siblings or extended family members, and others the child interacts within and around the home
CHILD-CARE AND CHILD-REARING CUSTOMS
Approaches to the specifics of caring for and rearing children that are normative for families and, in a larger sense, for cultures, such as the extent of formal versus informal schooling and training oriented toward independence from others versus dependence on others
OVERALL PSYCHOLOGY OF THE CAREGIVERS
Culturally based belief systems of the parents or other caregivers, including their expectations about their children's behavior and development and their feelings about what is "right" and what is "wrong," which they in turn impart to their children

*Note that all caregivers do not necessarily adhere to all culturally prescribed customs.

self-concept
One's beliefs and feelings about oneself; defines who an individual is

self-efficacy
What a person believes he or she is capable of doing in a given situation

developmental niche
The interaction of components—such as everyday physical and social settings, parenting and family customs, and the overall environmental context—that determines the unique world of each individual

▲ Neighborhoods as well as family systems help define our identity and our roles within a particular context and culture.

Often it is quite difficult to determine the degree to which members in a family share similar, versus dissimilar, environments. For example, siblings in the same family typically share many similar experiences, such as an overly strict parent or the values of the local neighborhood. Yet there also is a set of *nonshared* experiences and relationships that can be important determinants of the path development will take (Mullineaux, Deater-Deckard, Petrill, & Thompson, 2009). In one classic series of studies, the relationship between parents and their first-born child and the relationship between parents and their second-born child were compared over time (Dunn, 1986, 1993). As we might expect, mothers and first-born children often had a close and intense relationship, at least until the birth of the second child. With the birth of the second child, things became more complicated. If the first-born child had an affectionate relationship with the father, this affection tended to increase, as did the amount of conflict between the mother and the first-born child. In addition, if the mother gave a good deal of attention to the second child, the conflict between the mother and the first-born child escalated, and the more the mother played with the second child, the more the siblings quarreled with each other a year later. Clearly, members of the same family do not necessarily experience the same environment. Often these differences persist throughout childhood and adolescence, extending into adulthood, where they typically shape a person's own behavior as a parent.

Thus, each family member may play a specific role in interactions with other family members; for example, an older sibling may be responsible for younger siblings. Each family member may have alliances with some family members but not with others; for example, two sisters frequently may gang up against their brother. The network of interrelationships and expectations within the family is a unique and major influence on each child's social, emotional, and cognitive development. The relationships among family members are often seen most clearly when a new baby is born because this change brings about many transitions in how family members interact (see the box Current Issues: The New Baby and the Extended Family System).

ethnocentrism
The tendency to assume that our own beliefs, perceptions, customs, and values are correct or normal and that those of others are inferior or abnormal

The Family as Transmitter of Culture

Parents, too, play a major role in embedding their children into their society and its culture. For example, religious and ethnic traditions and moral values are conveyed to children from an early age, and parents typically play a key role. In some societies, this is a relatively easy task because parental values are highly consistent with clearly defined social expectations. In a cohesive, homogeneous society such as the Israeli *kibbutz,* people outside the family reinforce and expand parental teachings. There is little contradiction between the family's way of doing things and the customs of the community.

With respect to child rearing, what factors might be important in determining who the more influential members in a given family would be?

In a more complex multiethnic society, such as that of the United States, cultural traditions embraced by parents and those held by peers may oppose each other. For example, some minority parents struggle to instill the values of the minority culture so that their children will not become assimilated into the culture of the majority. Yet these cultural traditions and values may be in conflict with, or may just seem "odd," to members of the majority culture, and children are often caught in between. Clearly, in complex societies, the transmission of culture is not a simple matter. Usually, the more diverse the social fabric, the more pressure the family system experiences. It also becomes more difficult to transmit values when they are unfocused and in transition, and this is a challenge that families in the United States and in other transitional cultures face today.

Discussions of cultural diversity prompt the consideration of **ethnocentrism**, which is the tendency to assume that your culture's beliefs, perceptions, and values are true, correct, and factual, whereas those of other cultures are false, unusual, or bizarre. People often find it especially hard to suspend judgment on cultural differences that concern an aspect of life that they find personally important. For example, it often is assumed that single-parent families are less likely to instill "family values" than are families in which both parents are present. Yet a single mother who turns to her own mother for help with child care may transmit as clear a message about the value of family as does a more traditional two-parent family. Being a single parent oftentimes brings many hardships; however, it does not equate with being culturally impoverished or with providing low-quality child care. We will return to this issue at several points in later chapters.

Parental influences, of course, are just one element in the larger process of socialization. *Socialization* is a lifelong process through which individuals are taught to function as members of social

CURRENT ISSUES

The New Baby and the Extended Family System

Life is full of transitions that change the way we interact with others, including with members of our own family. One of the most significant of these transitions occurs with the birth of a baby. How a new baby affects family members' lives, of course, depends on circumstances specific to that family. When parents eagerly anticipate the arrival of a child, when social and economic resources are plentiful, and when the child is healthy, the transition for the family is usually quite manageable. However, such "ideal" circumstances do not always apply. Sometimes, the family unit is already stressed, and the new baby adds to pressures already present. Sometimes, too, the new baby has special needs that require more from caregivers than was anticipated.

Consider how the needs of a "low-birth-weight" baby can stress the family system. In a longitudinal study launched in the 1990s, researchers studied the impact of the birth of a new baby with special needs on mothers and on the extended family—including its structure and function—over a multiyear period (Martin, Brooks-Gunn, Klebanov, Buka, & McCormick, 2008). Results show that having a fragile or sick baby tests the ability, time, and energy resources not only of the mother and father but also often the entire extended family. Young parents, in particular, must often seek the aid of others to meet the demands of the infant and to also satisfy their own needs to finish their education or maintain a job to support the family (Goldrick-Rab & Sorensen, 2010; Leerkes & Burney, 2007).

In another 3-year longitudinal study of 985 premature, low-birth-weight babies and their families, similar results were found. In this study, families were recruited at eight major medical centers as part of the Infant Health and Development Program (IHDP; Martin, Brooks-Gunn, Klebanov, Buka, & McCormick, 2008). Of particular interest were the 554 families in which the mother was between the ages of 13 and 25; in these families, 54% of the mothers had not finished high school at the time the baby was born, and 45% of the families were below the poverty line at the time of the child's first birthday (Gordon, Chase-Lansdale, & Brooks-Gunn, 2004).

In this group of young mothers with premature infants, half lived in an extended household, usually with the newborn's maternal grandmother, but sometimes these young mothers lived with other family members as well. These living arrangements sometimes occurred because the young mother was going to high school and already living at home. In other cases, the young mother moved back in with family members to gain needed support and resources—both social and economic. Because day-care centers often are not available for premature infants, family members frequently provided a necessary support system for the new mother.

As might be expected, living in an extended family setting with an ill or premature infant provided family members with both benefits and challenges. Young mothers who resided with extended family members were more likely to continue their education and to seek and maintain jobs at a higher rate than were those who lived separately. It appears that residing with family helped them to attain greater success in continuing their education and in seeking and maintaining jobs, which was a conclusion drawn in earlier studies as well. However, young mothers who lived with their extended families tended to have less knowledge of child development, fewer parenting skills, and less self-confidence in their parenting role. Whether this was due to their lesser ability to parent in general or to the lowered responsibility they had to assume due to the support of their extended family is not entirely clear. The reasons why a mother chooses to live in an extended family situation are probably also important: When coresidence is the result of governmental laws or welfare policy rather than a free choice made by family members, outcomes appear to be far less positive (Gordon, Chase-Landsdale, & Brooks-Gunn, 2004).

It is important to note that although people in the United States tend to think of *traditional* families as composed of a mother, a father, and children, this *nuclear* family arrangement is not the only way that families are comprised. In fact, extended family living arrangements are common around the world, and people often forget that they also are common in the United States when there are needs that require the family's assistance. This is particularly true for families in poverty or for families from varied ethnic cultures and traditions: In the IHDP sample of young mothers, 63% of the mothers were African American, 11% were Hispanic, and 25% were White, Asian, or of some other ethnic background. It is also common when the child has special needs. Longitudinal studies are especially helpful in capturing the dynamics of how life transitions take place, as is the case when examining how the life course of young parents unfolds as they establish the family structures that will guide them through the next period of their lives (Waldfogel, Craigie, & Brooks-Gunn, 2010).

groups—families, communities, and work and friendship groups, among many others. Becoming socialized involves recognizing and dealing with the expectations of others, including family members, peers, teachers, and supervisors, to name just a few. Whether they are tense and anxiety producing or smooth and secure, an individual's relationships with others determine not only *what* the individual will learn but also *how well* the individual will learn.

What do you think the relationship between ethnocentrism and prejudice might be?

Socialization also forces individuals to deal with new situations. Infants are born into families; children go to school; families move to new neighborhoods; adolescents begin to date; people marry and raise their own families; older people retire from jobs; friends and relatives become ill or die. It is important to keep in mind that family units, social environments, and cultures are *not* fixed entities. An individual's social environment, which already is complex at birth, changes constantly and dynamically. In addition, each individual attends to and interprets the relevant aspects of the social and cultural environment in different ways; that is, individuals interact uniquely with their culture and context.

Sociocultural Influences on Development Across the Lifespan

An individual's experiences in life depend on a multitude of factors, including the sweeping events that characterize a particular historical period. Consider, for example, the U.S. generation that was born during the Great Depression and that experienced World War II as adolescents. These individuals entered college or the labor market during the postwar boom of the late 1940s and early 1950s, and many served in the armed forces during the Korean War, which was followed by a period of economic prosperity and relatively low unemployment. Thus, the period during which that generation entered adulthood was significantly marked by specific historical factors. Compare this **age cohort**—or age-defined group—to the "baby boomers" born in the post–World War II period of 1946 to 1960. That large group enjoyed the benefits of a growing economy in childhood and adolescence and experienced adolescence and adulthood in the turbulent 1960s. Or, perhaps more relevant to many readers of this text, consider the "millennials," that age cohort born during the two decades before the millennium (2000), whose experiences were shaped by the terrorist acts of September 11, 2001, and who have grown up always using information technology. Are members of these age cohorts similar? In some ways, yes, they are, but in other ways definitely not.

To gain a better understanding of the interaction between development and historical change, it is useful to consider cultural factors as being of three different types: *normative age-graded influences, normative history-graded influences,* and *nonnormative influences* (Baltes, 1987; Baltes & Smith, 2004). **Normative age-graded influences** are the biological and social changes that normally happen at predictable ages in a given society. Included in this category are puberty, menopause, and some physical aspects of aging, as well as predictable social events such as entering school, marrying, or retiring. Normative age-graded influences, especially when they reflect biologically programmed events, often occur at about the same age for most or all people in a particular society, although the ways in which these changes occur may vary from one society to the next. **Normative history-graded influences** are the historical events, such as wars, depressions, epidemics, and widespread technological advances, that affect large numbers of individuals in a given society at about the same time. **Nonnormative influences** are the individual environmental factors that do not occur at any predictable time in a person's life. Some examples of nonnormative influences include divorce, unemployment, illness, moving to a new community, sudden economic losses or gains, career changes, even a chance encounter with an influential individual. All of these influences are critical events that may define turning points in an individual's life (see Table 2-6).

Table 2-6 Factors That Affect the Development of an Individual

Factor	Definition	Examples
Normative age-graded influences	Biological and social changes that normally happen at a particular point in the lifespan	• Puberty • Menopause • Retirement • Marrying • Having children • Graduating from school
Normative history-graded influences	Historical events that affect large numbers of people in similar ways	• Wars • Economic boom or depression • Epidemics • Wide-spread technological innovation
Nonnormative influences	Factors that are specific to individuals and that do not occur at any predictable time in the lifespan	• Divorce • Illness • Unemployment • Career changes • Moving to a new community • Important personal changes

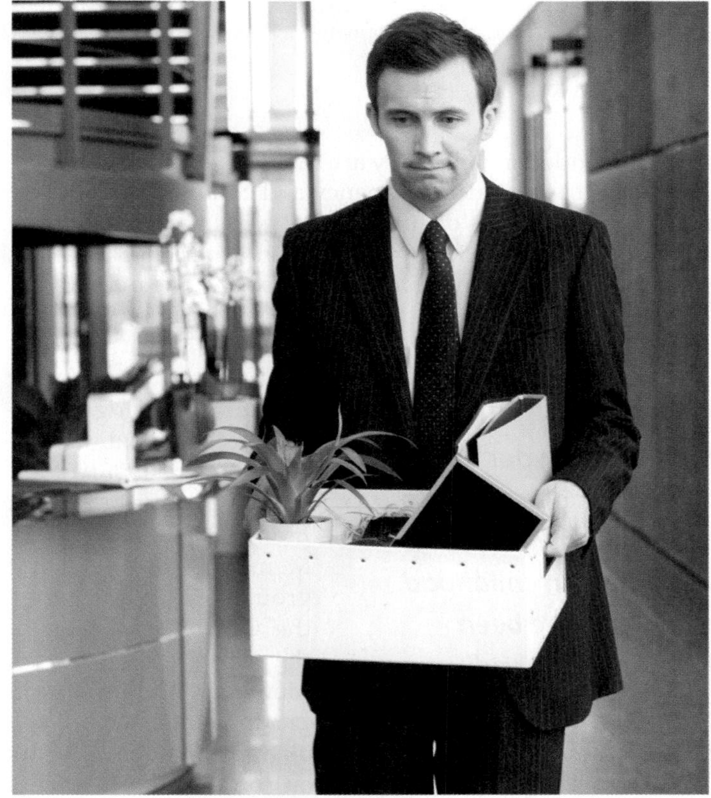

▲ Unexpected events such as job loss can have a profound impact on development.

Mediating Factors The impact of normative and nonnormative influences often varies according to age (see Figure 2-9). For example, children and older adults often are more strongly affected by age-graded influences; history-graded influences, such as economic depression and war, generally have their greatest impact during adolescence and early adulthood. Furthermore, normative and nonnormative influences do not affect every individual in exactly the same way; there are other factors that *mediate*—or affect—each individual's experience of these

age cohort
A group of individuals of similar ages

nonnormative influences
The individual environmental factors that do not occur at any predictable time in a person's life (e.g., divorce, unemployment, career changes)

normative age-graded influences
The biological and social changes that normally happen at predictable ages (e.g., puberty, menopause, entering school)

normative history-graded influences
The historical events that affect large numbers of individuals at the same time (e.g., wars, depressions, epidemics)

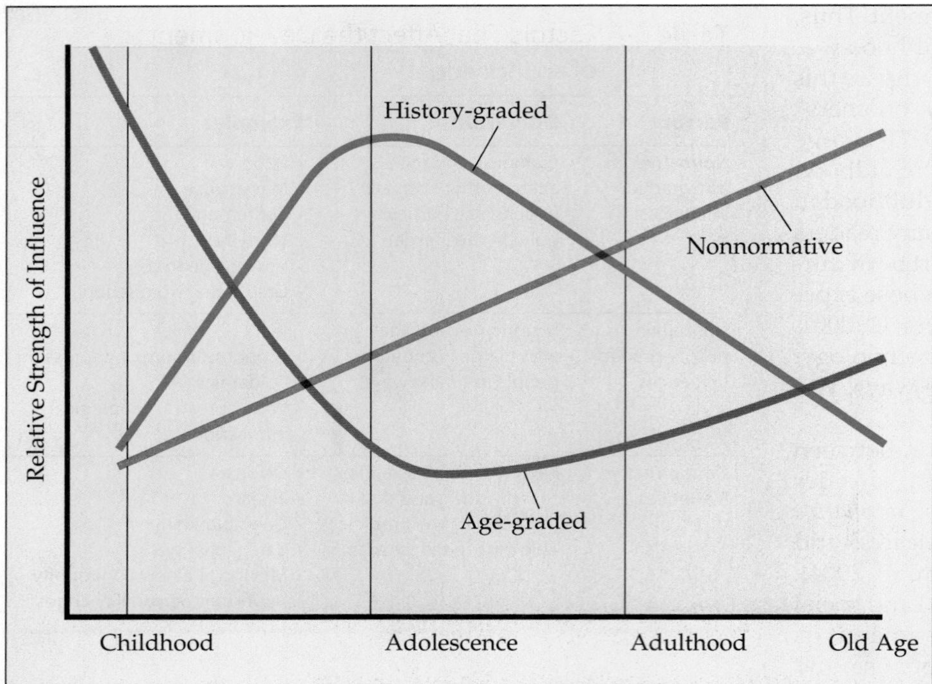

FIGURE 2-9 A Lifespan Profile on Influences
Age-graded, history-graded, and nonnormative influences affect people more directly at different times in their lifespans.

influences. Gender and ethnicity are two such examples. For example, women experience pregnancy and childbirth differently than do men, regardless of culture, and, within a given culture, members of ethnic minority groups often experience a variety of events in different ways than do members of the majority.

As you might guess, sociocultural factors often interact. Consider the following example of how history- and age-graded factors, mediated by sex, interact to produce different outcomes. Two groups of people were studied using an extensive longitudinal design (Elder, 1998; Elder, Caspi, & Burton, 1988; Elder & Johnson, 2002). Members of the first group were infants when the Great Depression of the early 1930s began. Members of the second group were of school age (about 10 years old) at the time. It took approximately 9 years for real recovery from the Depression to occur, so members of the first group were 1 to 10 years old during the period of greatest economic hardship, while members of the second group were 10 to 18 years old. Boys who were younger during those years showed more negative effects of the stress and the deprivation experienced by their families than did boys who were older at the time. Indeed, the older boys often worked to help the family survive, thereby further limiting their exposure to the family problems that frequently accompany unemployment and poverty. The girls in the study, however, showed a different pattern. The younger girls apparently formed an unusually strong mother–daughter bond while the family was suffering economic hardship. Consequently, as adults they actually were more goal oriented, competent, and assertive than were girls who were adolescents during the Depression years.

What has been your most challenging adjustment to college thus far? Has your development in childhood and adolescence been influential in your adjustment to college? If so, how?

In sum, development throughout the lifespan is best considered to be a complex interaction among several critically important factors. First, one's culture, including the impact of the historical period in which one lives, sets a general context for development. Second, various mediating factors—gender, ethnicity, socioeconomic background, and so on—are important determinants for how the broader cultural–historical forces will be experienced. Third, one's family and immediate environment will shape one's experiences in critically important ways. Finally, each person's unique personal characteristics, which result from the specific way in which genetic and environmental factors interact, will determine how that person will act on, and adapt to, the broader context in which life unfolds.

Human Development: An Interactive Process To reinforce the idea that development interacts within the full array of personal, family, cultural, and historical influences, consider the following case studies of two students:

> Elizabeth was born in an upper-middle-class suburb of Chicago, and was the older of two children. She attended a public high school that had won the National Blue Ribbon Award twice in the last 10 years. Elizabeth was a member of the women's soccer team, and she was nominated for homecoming queen, although she did not win. Elizabeth's parents, who have been married for 26 years, have set a high value on education for their two daughters and the girls were enrolled in several extracurricular activities, including ballet, voice lessons, and horseback riding. The family typically takes two trips together every year; this past year they traveled to London and Paris and the previous year to Cancun, Mexico, for a vacation on the beach. One of Elizabeth's bigger adjustments to college was learning to share a room because she always had not only her own bedroom, but her own private bath and TV room as well. For Elizabeth, the academic work at college is much like what she experienced in high school, and she has made friends easily. Yet, she feels considerable pressure to get into an occupation in which she will be "successful," a word that she defines in monetary terms. Elizabeth currently is thinking of majoring in premedicine because she thinks being a doctor would

accomplish her goal of helping others while at the same time provide her with a standard of living with which she would be comfortable.

Louanne grew up on a farm in southern Kansas, and she is the youngest of four children and the only girl. Her three brothers were expected to help their father on the family farm and eventually to take it over. Louanne's mother died from cancer when Louanne was 5, and her father never remarried. Louanne had never been very interested in the farm, although her father insisted that she fill her mother's role of preparing the food for the "men" and of taking care of the house. Despite these rather heavy household responsibilities, Louanne worked very hard in school and graduated at the top of her class, winning a scholarship to attend college tuition-free. Of particular importance to Louanne was a high school English teacher who encouraged her to continue her schooling. Although her father was not in favor of Louanne leaving home to attend college, he did allow her to go with the proviso that she get a job to pay for her living expenses and that she study something that would be "practical" and lead to a good job. He suggested that teaching or nursing would be good choices. Louanne's biggest adjustment to college has been trying to fit in socially with students who do not seem as serious about learning as she is. She resents the fact that her roommate stays up late at night and then comes in, sometimes quite drunk, and awakens her. Louanne works 30 hours a week as a cashier at a convenience store close to campus, and she has a work grant for 10 hours a week in the college cafeteria. Louanne has little time for friends or parties because her work schedule and studying keep her busy most of the time.

Perhaps you know people like Elizabeth or Louanne. In any case, as you consider their different backgrounds, different motivations, and different interests, perhaps you can gain a sense that development is not an easy process to understand. These two women's values and life experiences were strongly shaped by the families in which they were raised and by the opportunities they had as children and young adults. The differences in their stories and their development prompt researchers to take a closer look at the relationships among various developmental circumstances over the lifespan and at how the timing and influence of events affect each person differently.

As you read in upcoming chapters about the factors that impact development during the various periods of the lifespan, it is especially important to consider the ways in which hereditary and environmental factors interact to produce the uniqueness of each individual: No two people are ever the same. It is also important to look past the differences among individuals and to see the general patterns that describe the life courses of most individuals. To understand the full dimension of human lifespan development, we must consider not only the uniqueness of each person but also the developmental processes and milestones that set the common course of development that most people experience.

REVIEW THE FACTS 2-6

1. The unique world experienced by each individual is called the
   a. self-concept.
   b. developmental niche.
   c. nonnormative influence.
   d. cohort.
2. In comparison to single-ethnic societies, is socialization generally easier or harder in complex, multiethnic societies?
3. The tendency to assume that your culture's values, beliefs, and perceptions are correct or normal is called ______________.
4. The lifelong process through which individuals are taught to function as members of social groups is called ______________.
5. Which of the following is best considered a nonnormative influence?
   a. an economic depression affecting an entire country
   b. menopause
   c. retirement from work
   d. getting fired from your job at age 50
6. To say that heredity and environment *interact* means that
   a. heredity sets the stage on which environmental effects take place.
   b. heredity and environment are equally important.
   c. heredity and environment continually influence each other.
   d. environment determines how heredity will be expressed.

Practice on **MyDevelopmentLab**

CHAPTER SUMMARY

Molecular Genetics

Where in our cells are genetic instructions located, and how are these instructions encoded in our DNA?

- Rapid and dramatic advances in our understanding of genetic mechanisms have made the question of how heredity and environment interact a topic of great current interest. The mapping of the human genome, which first was announced in 2000, was a significant scientific event.
- Genetic instructions are contained in the *deoxyribonucleic acid (DNA)* molecules found mostly in the nucleus of each cell in a person's body. DNA is a complex molecule that consists of building blocks called *nucleotides* which contain four different types of *bases:* adenine, thymine, cytosine, and guanine.
- All DNA contains only these four bases. Furthermore, which two bases bond to form *base pairs* cannot vary: Adenine always pairs with thymine and cytosine always pairs with guanine. Human DNA includes about 3.2 billion base pairs. Genetic differences among individuals and among species are determined by which side of the ladder a base occupies, the order of the *base-pair* sequence, and the number of base pairs in the DNA molecule.
- There is much commonality in the DNA we share. Humans and chimpanzees share about 98% of the same DNA. Even

people with quite different appearances share nearly all (99.9%) of their DNA; thus, an individual's race cannot be determined only by examining that individual's DNA.

- The basic units of inheritance are called *genes,* which are delineated pieces of the DNA molecule. A reasonable estimate of the number of genes in the human genome is 20,000 to 25,000 genes. Genes work by directing the synthesis of over 200,000 different *proteins,* which are molecules that control the processes of life.

Chromosomes, Genes, and Cell Division

How do we inherit traits from our parents, and how are those traits expressed?

- When a cell prepares to divide, the DNA collects into *chromosomes,* which, in normal humans, are arranged into 23 pairs in all cells except the gametes (sperm and ova). These *gametes* (reproductive cells) contain one half of each pair—a total of 23 chromosomes.
- When cells divide to reproduce themselves the process is called *mitosis,* which creates two cells with identical sets of chromosomes (46 in humans). *Meiosis* is a cell division process that produces ova and sperm, each of which contains one half of the full set of chromosomes (23 in humans).
- The *genotype* refers to the genes that an individual inherits, half from the mother and half from the father. Genes, like chromosomes, exist as pairs, each half of which is an *allele.* Some alleles are *dominant* over others, and their characteristics will be expressed in the individual's *phenotype,* which is how that trait is seen or displayed.
- Nearly all human characteristics are *polygenic,* meaning they are determined by more than one gene pair. Thus, the expression of a phenotype is a very complex phenomenon. The complexity of gene expression is further complicated because some genes are *incompletely dominant* and some are *codominant.*
- Normal women inherit two X chromosomes; normal men inherit an X and a Y. Traits that are controlled by the *sex chromosomes* (X and Y) are called *sex-linked traits.* Because the males' Y chromosome is smaller than the females' second X, men are more likely to display *recessive* sex-linked traits in their phenotype.
- Many factors complicate how genes are passed from parents to offspring. Sometimes genetic material crosses over and is exchanged between chromosomes. In addition, which particular half of a chromosome pair is transmitted to a gamete is determined by chance—a process called *independent assortment.* Then, which sperm fertilizes which egg is also determined by chance. Thus, any two parents could hypothetically produce hundreds of trillions of unique offspring.

How can environmental forces modify genetic instructions?

- Genetic *mutations* occur when the DNA molecule is altered during cell division. When mutation occurs during meiosis, it is passed along to offspring in the sperm or ova. If it occurs during mitosis, it affects subsequent divisions of the mutated cell. Mutations can be beneficial or detrimental, even to the point of preventing survival of the offspring.
- Nongenetic, environmental forces (called "nature") also affect development, and are in constant, dynamic interaction with genetic forces (called "nuture"). Gene–environment interactions occur at many levels: genes, neural activity, behavior, culture. One way this interaction occurs involves *epigenetics,* where environmental forces produce changes in the nongene DNA that provides instructions to turn genes "on" or "off."

Genetic Disorders

What kinds of disorders are caused by problems in how genes are inherited and expressed?

- Congenital anomalies result from genetic errors, which often produce disruptions in protein synthesis.
- Sex-linked disorders can result when a recessive trait on the X chromosome of a male is not matched to an allele on the smaller Y chromosome. Common dominant–recessive sex-linked disorders include male pattern baldness, hemophilia, and color blindness. In addition, sex-linked disorders can occur when extra X or Y chromosome material is present or when one of these chromosomes is absent.
- Chromosomal breakage can occur; an example is the sex-linked genetic disorder fragile X syndrome, which is caused by a gene replication error affecting the tips of the X chromosome. Fragile X syndrome generally results in intellectual disability, along with certain growth anomalies. It is the most common hereditary disorder associated with intellectual disability. Because it affects the X chromosome, it is much more common among males.
- Chromosomal anomalies can also affect the other 22 pairs of autosomes. An example is Down syndrome, the risk of which increases as the mother's age at conception increases. Down syndrome is accompanied by intellectual disability and some distinctive physical characteristics, and it can include other health problems, such as heart abnormalities, hearing problems, and respiratory problems. In chromosomal anomalies that involve *gene imprinting,* the phenotype expressed depends on which parent the gene comes from.
- Some DNA is contained in the cells' mitochondria. When this DNA is deficient in some way, genetic mitochondrial disorders may result. Mitochondrial DNA is inherited only from the mother, so although males may have mitochondrial disorders, they cannot transmit them to offspring.

What techniques are available to help individuals deal with genetic disorders?

- Genetic inheritance is extremely complex. *Genetic counseling* helps prospective parents to determine the risks of having a baby affected by genetic anomalies and to make appropriate decisions based on these risks.

- Genetic research is advancing very rapidly. *Recombinant DNA technology* involves extracting DNA from cell nuclei and cutting it into sections with selected enzymes. These gene segments then can be inserted into host cells, usually in bacteria, where they can be reproduced. Recombinant DNA technology currently is used to produce a variety of proteins, such as insulin, and new techniques that involve "correcting" deficient genes by inserting new ones are on the horizon.

Behavior Genetics

Why is the study of behavior genetics important in helping us understand gene–environment interactions?

- Behavior genetics assesses patterns of inheritance at the behavioral level rather than at the molecular level. Behavior genetics is especially important because it recognizes that environmental effects can influence whether or how a genetic trait will be displayed.
- Behavior genetics examines the concordance, or correlation patterns, of a trait among people who share different degrees of genetic similarity.
- *Heritability,* an estimate of the degree to which genetics influences a trait, must always be considered in the context of how much environmental variation is involved.

Why adopted children and twins are of special interest to those who study behavior genetics?

- Adoption studies and twin studies provide useful data for heritability studies; when adopted children resemble their biological parents more than their adoptive parents, researchers can conclude that the trait in question has a high heritability.
- Twin studies also are useful because monozygotic (identical) twins share all of their genes. If a trait is highly heritable, researchers expect a higher concordance among monozygotic twins than among other siblings.
- Both adoption and twin studies are difficult to interpret because heredity and environment continually interact, making it very difficult to separate their impact.

Environmental Influences and Contexts

How do environmental events exert their influence on developmental processes?

- Environmental influences range from the very narrow, specific events in each person's life to the broad, cultural context in which development occurs.
- Three relatively simple forms of learning are habituation, classical conditioning, and operant conditioning. *Habituation* allows people to ignore irrelevant stimuli. *Classical conditioning* is especially important in acquiring emotional responses. *Operant conditioning* describes how rewards and punishments influence people's future behavior.
- When a *reinforcer* follows a behavior, that behavior is more likely to occur again in the future. When a *punishment* follows a behavior, that behavior is less likely to recur. Behaviors maintained by *partial schedules* of reinforcement or punishment are very difficult to change.
- Applied behavior analysis (ABA; also called behavior modification) involves the application of classical and operant conditioning principles to change, or modify, a pattern of behavior.
- Social learning refers to the fact that people can learn by observing others, using their cognitive processes. People who have a strong *self-concept* and see themselves as capable and competent have a strong sense of their *self-efficacy.*

Environment in a Broader Context: Family and Culture

How do one's family and culture help shape the way that development unfolds?

- Each individual experiences a different *developmental niche.* Even children in the same family often have quite different experiences, in part because their genetic differences act in different ways on that environment, producing different outcomes.
- Families play an especially important role in shaping their children's behavior and self-concept, as well as in embedding them into their society and culture. When families find themselves in situations where different cultural expectations are in conflict, this can cause family conflict and make cultural transmission more difficult.
- A group of individuals born during the same historical era is called an *age cohort.* Cultural factors can influence age cohorts in different ways: through biological and social changes that normally happen at the same age (*normative age-graded influences;* e.g., puberty), through major historical events that affect most people in a society (*normative history-graded influences;* e.g., war), and through factors that can affect an individual at any point (*nonnormative influences;* e.g., divorce or illness).
- Children and older adults usually are more strongly affected by age-graded influences; history-graded influences usually have their greatest impact on adolescents and young adults. Nonnormative influences can affect a person at any point in the lifespan. In addition, mediating factors, such as gender or ethnicity, can influence how all the factors affect development.
- Development throughout the lifespan is a complex interaction among an individual's culture, mediating factors, an individual's family and immediate environment, and each individual's unique characteristics. Hereditary and environmental forces continually interact as development unfolds. Although each individual is unique, from a developmental perspective the focus is on the common course of development that most people experience.

KEY TERMS

cells (p. 35)
deoxyribonucleic acid (DNA) (p. 35)
nucleotides (p. 36)
base (p. 36)
base pair (p. 36)
genes (p. 38)
proteins (p. 38)
chromosome (p. 39)
autosomes (p. 39)
sex chromosomes (p. 39)
karyotype (p. 39)
mitosis (p. 39)
meiosis (p. 40)
gametes (p. 40)
alleles (p. 40)
genotype (p. 40)
dominant (p. 40)
recessive (p. 40)
phenotype (p. 40)
homozygous (p. 40)
heterozygous (p. 40)
polygenic inheritance (p. 41)
incomplete dominance (p. 41)
codominance (p. 41)
sex-linked traits (p. 41)
mutation (p. 42)
epigenetics (p. 43)
congenital anomalies (p. 44)
gene imprinting (p. 47)
genetic counseling (p. 48)
recombinant DNA technology (p. 50)
gene therapy (p. 50)
behavior genetics (p. 51)
heritability (p. 51)
habituation (p. 54)
phobia (p. 54)
reinforcer (p. 54)
punishment (p. 54)
partial schedules (p. 55)
shaping (p. 55)
applied behavior analysis (p. 55)
self-concept (p. 56)
self-efficacy (p. 56)
developmental niche (p. 56)
ethnocentrism (p. 57)
age cohort (p. 59)
normative age-graded influences (p. 59)
normative history-graded influences (p. 59)
nonnormative influences (p. 59)

PRENATAL DEVELOPMENT AND CHILDBIRTH

3

LEARNING OBJECTIVES

- What major developmental events take place in each of the three prenatal periods of development?
- What are the major trends that guide human development during the prenatal period?
- How do maternal risk factors and protective factors affect the course of prenatal development?
- What is a "critical period" in development?
- How do teratogens interfere with normal prenatal development, and what are the effects associated with common teratogenic agents?
- What sequence of events unfolds during a normal childbirth?
- How have childbirth practices changed throughout the years?
- What technological advances have occurred with respect to pregnancy, and how have these changed the practice of childbirth?
- With the arrival of a new baby, how do mother and father adjust?
- In what ways is the newborn prepared to cope with the dramatic circumstance of birth?

CHAPTER OUTLINE

Prenatal Growth and Development
- Trimesters and Periods
- Conception and the Germinal Period
- The Embryonic Period
- The Fetal Period
- Developmental Trends

Prenatal Environmental Influences
- Maternal Age
- Maternal Health and Nutrition
- Prenatal Health Care
- Critical Periods in Prenatal Development
- Teratogens and Their Effects

Childbirth
- Stages of Childbirth
- Approaches to Childbirth
- Advances in Technology
- Complications in Childbirth

The Evolving Family
- The Transition to Parenthood
- Pregnancy in a Changing World
- The Arrival of the Neonate

When a human life is conceived, this event sets in motion both a genetically programmed sequence of developmental processes and a broad array of personal and interpersonal responses. For those who have been eagerly looking forward to having a baby, the news that conception has occurred is happy indeed, although most parents also have concerns about how their lives will change and how they will manage their new responsibilities. Presently, however, in the United States, about 50% of all pregnancies are unintended (Finer & Kost, 2011). For teens, the rate is even higher—about two-thirds of U.S. teen pregnancies are unplanned (Centers for Disease Control and Prevention [CDC], 2012d). For those who are not prepared, pregnancy is sometimes greeted with more trepidation than joy and often involves considerable adjustments.

Regardless of the circumstances by which a pregnancy occurs, development during the prenatal period follows an orderly sequence that reflects both the unfolding of genetically programmed processes and the particular environmental conditions experienced by the mother and, hence, the baby. We explore both of these influences in this chapter as we discuss the development that occurs in the first period of the lifespan—the prenatal period of development.

PRENATAL GROWTH AND DEVELOPMENT

The development of a unique human individual begins with fertilization. About the size of the period at the end of this sentence, a one-celled, fertilized egg carries all of the genetic information necessary to create an entire new organism.

Trimesters and Periods

Prenatal development is commonly described in terms of *trimesters,* which simply break the 9 months of the mother's pregnancy into three 3-month segments. However, from a developmental perspective, a more useful way of conceptualizing prenatal development is to divide it into three *periods*—the *germinal, embryonic,* and *fetal*—with each period corresponding to specific changes in the developing organism (see Table 3-1).

Conception and the Germinal Period

The **germinal period** begins with conception and ends about 2 weeks later when the fertilized egg is implanted in the wall of the uterus. Although conception can be simply defined as the union of a sperm and an ovum (egg), the process involved is actually quite complex (Gottlieb, Wahlsten, & Lickliter, 2006).

Table 3-1 Two Ways to Describe the Prenatal Period*

	Trimester	Developmental period
Day 1	First trimester (weeks 1 to 13)	Germinal period (conception through 2 weeks)
		Embryonic period (weeks 2 through 8)
		Fetal period (weeks 9 through 38)
	Second trimester (weeks 13 to 25)	
Day 266	Third trimester (weeks 25 to 38)	

*The prenatal period sometimes is described as beginning from the date of the mother's last menstrual period, where gestation is reported as 40 weeks. In this table, the prenatal period is considered to begin at conception; therefore, the gestation period is reported as 38 weeks (266 days).

germinal period
After conception, the period of very rapid cell division and initial cell differentiation lasting for approximately 2 weeks

OVULATION AND FERTILIZATION

FIGURE 3-1 Ovulation and Fertilization
In the first 2 weeks of prenatal development, the mature ovum emerges from the ovary and begins its journey to the uterus. Union of the sperm and the ovum normally occurs high in the fallopian tube. While this fertilized egg travels to the uterus, there are several cell divisions, called cleavages, that result in the formation of a blastula. Within a few days, the blastula becomes implanted in the uterine wall, where cell division continues.

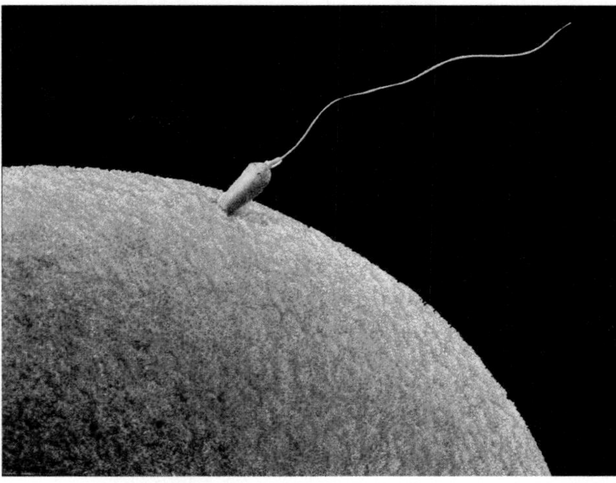

▲ A living human ovum and sperm at the moment of conception. Although several sperm cells may begin to penetrate the outer covering of the ovum, only one will actually fertilize it.

As discussed in the previous chapter, women are born with all the ova they will ever have, and these ova usually mature at a rate of one per month during a woman's reproductive years. About the 10th day after the start of a regular menstrual period, stimulated by hormones, an ovum enters the final stage of meiosis. By the end of the 13th or 14th day of this growth, the follicle (sac) surrounding the ovum breaks, releasing the mature ovum; this process is called **ovulation**. The mature ovum travels down one of the two **fallopian tubes** (see Figure 3-1), where it can survive for about 12 to 24 hours (American Pregnancy Association, 2012a). If the ovum is not fertilized by a sperm cell during this time, it continues to move down the fallopian tube, disintegrates in the **uterus**, and is sloughed off in the next menstrual flow.

In contrast to a woman's monthly production of a single egg, during a male's peak fertility in young adulthood, as many as a billion sperm cells can be produced in a day; some 200 million may be deposited each time ejaculation occurs. If sperm cells are not ejaculated, they degrade and are absorbed by the man's body.

Sperm cells, of course, are deposited in a women's vagina during sexual intercourse, where they can survive for about 5 days (Harms, 2010). Thus, there is a "window" of a week or so in each ovulatory cycle during which conception might occur.

For the tiny sperm cells, the trip to a potential rendezvous with an ovum in a fallopian tube is long and difficult, because the sperm must work their way upward through a 5-inch passageway that contains obstacles such as mucus, as well as acidic fluids that can be lethal. **Fertilization** occurs if one of these millions of sperm penetrates the cell membrane of the ovum. Over the next 24 hours, the genetic material of two individuals "fuses" and is translated into a new entity called a **zygote** (from the Greek root for "yoke or join together").

The germinal period is a time of extremely rapid cell division and organization. About 36 hours after conception, the 1-celled zygote divides, or *cleaves*, to produce 2 cells. Then a second division occurs in each cell, yielding 4 cells, and so on. The rate of cell division increases so that by the 6th day more than 100 cells (each one smaller, but containing exact copies of the original zygote's genetic material) have been produced (Marieb & Hoehn, 2012).

Differentiation and Implantation Toward the end of the first week, the dividing cells have developed into a **blastula**—a ball of cells around a fluid-filled center—that has made its way to the uterus. Once formed, the blastula starts to burrow into the lining of the uterus, breaking tiny blood vessels to obtain nutrients. Now the cells begin the process of *differentiation;* that is, they start separating into groups according to their future

ovulation
The release of an ovum into one of the two fallopian tubes; occurs approximately 14 days after menstruation

fertilization
The union of an ovum and a sperm; also called *conception*

fallopian tubes
Two passages that open out of the upper part of the uterus and carry ova from the ovary to the uterus

zygote
The first cell of a human being that occurs as a result of fertilization; a fertilized ovum

uterus
The structure that contains and nourishes the embryo and fetus

blastula
The hollow, fluid-filled sphere of cells that forms soon after conception

function. Some of the cells move to one side of the hollow sphere and form the *embryonic disk* from which the child itself will develop. Another group of cells begins to develop into the supportive structures that will nourish and protect the embryo. This is also the point at which home urine tests can assess pregnancy: The cells of the supportive structures begin secreting a detectable hormone called *human chorionic gonadotropin (hcg)*, which shuts down further ovulation and prevents the next menstrual period (Nilsson & Hamberger, 2009).

Within a few days, if all goes well, the blastula is implanted in the uterine wall. However, the crucial process of implantation is far from routine. An estimated two-thirds or more of all fertilized eggs are lost within the first 2 weeks, some because they are incompletely formed and others because the uterine environment is inhospitable (Marieb & Hoehn, 2012). An unsuccessful implantation may yield what resembles a heavy menstrual period that arrives a bit late, so the woman may not even realize that she was temporarily pregnant. In the United States, of those pregnancies that survive the first few weeks, 19% are aborted and 17% are lost through miscarriage later in the pregnancy; thus, 64% of these babies are successfully born (National Center for Health Statistics, 2008).

What Causes Twins? Sometimes in the first few divisions of the zygote, the two identical cells or small groups of cells separate and develop into two (or more) embryos. The result is **monozygotic (identical) twins**. Because they develop from the same fertilized zygote, they have the same genes: Identical twins are always the same sex and share the same physical traits (Reece et al., 2011). In other cases, two ova are released simultaneously and *each* unites with a different sperm, producing **dizygotic (fraternal) twins**. The genetic traits inherited by fraternal twins can be as similar or as different as those of any two siblings: Fraternal twins may be of the same sex or different sexes.

Up until about 1980, the percentage of pregnancies involving multiple births remained stable, at about 2%. However, since that time the rate of multiple births—including twins, triplets, and other higher-order births—has increased dramatically. For example, twin births increased 76% between 1980 and 2009, and triplet and other multiple births increased more than 400% (CDC, 2011g). Two factors appear to be involved. First, twinning and other multiple births are linked to maternal age, and more babies are born now to older mothers. This accounts for about one-third of the increase in the rate of multiple births experienced in the past three decades. The other two-thirds of this increase is accounted for by the increased use of fertility drugs and other reproductive therapies (Martin, Hamilton, & Osterman, 2012). Triplet births, for example, are 60 times more likely when fertility treatments are used (CDC, 2007b). Today, twins occur in about 1 in 30 pregnancies, and this rate appears to have stabilized. The rate of triplets and other nontwin multiple births has actually declined slightly, perhaps in response to guidelines from the American Society of Reproductive Medicine aimed at reducing the incidence of higher-order multiple births, and perhaps partly to the development of better assisted reproductive technologies (CDC, 2011g).

The Embryonic Period

The **embryonic period** starts when implantation is complete. It is a time of major structural development and growth that continues until 2 months after conception; the term **embryo** comes from the Greek word for "swell." During the embryonic period, both the supportive structures and the embryonic disk continue to develop.

The Supporting Structures During the embryonic period, the cells forming the supporting structures differentiate into the **placenta**, a disk-shaped mass of supporting tissue; the **umbilical cord**, a "rope" of tissue that contains two arteries and a vein that connect from the placenta to the developing child; and the **amniotic sac**, a membrane filled with watery **amniotic fluid** that helps cushion and protect the baby throughout the prenatal period. These structures serve primarily to nourish and sustain the developing baby.

The placenta is particularly important because it provides for the exchange of nutrients and waste products between mother and embryo. Interestingly, the mother and developing child do not share their blood; rather, the placenta permits the exchange of nutritive and waste materials by diffusion across cell membranes, normally without any exchange of blood cells. Thus, the placenta serves as a filter. Normally, smaller molecules—such as nutrients (including sugars, fats, and proteins), enzymes, vitamins, and antibodies to protect against disease—pass into the embryo, while the waste products carried by the embryo's blood pass out to the mother for elimination. Larger molecules, such as most bacteria and some salts, generally do not cross the placental barrier; however, many viruses contracted by the mother during pregnancy and potentially harmful drugs and other substances ingested by her unfortunately do cross the placental barrier. These are discussed at length later in the chapter.

monozygotic (identical) twins
Twins that result from the division of a single fertilized ovum, which then separates and forms two genetically identical individuals

embryo
From the Greek term for "swell"; refers to the developing baby from the period of implantation to the end of the second month—from 2 to 8 weeks

amniotic sac
A fluid-filled membrane that encloses the developing embryo or fetus

dizygotic (fraternal) twins
Twins that result from the fertilization of two separate ova by two separate sperm

placenta
A disk-shaped mass of tissue that forms along the wall of the uterus through which the embryo receives nutrients and discharges waste

amniotic fluid
Fluid contained in the amniotic sac that cushions and helps protect the embryo or fetus

embryonic period
The second prenatal period, which lasts from implantation to the end of the second month after conception; all the major structures and organs of the individual are formed at this time

umbilical cord
The "rope" of tissue that connects the placenta to the embryo; this rope contains two fetal arteries and one fetal vein

The Embryo The embryonic disk grows and develops rapidly during the embryonic period. Immediately after implantation, it develops into three distinct layers: The *ectoderm,* or outer layer, will become the skin, the sense organs, and the brain and nervous system; the *mesoderm,* or middle layer, will become muscles, blood, and the excretory system; and the *endoderm,* or inner layer, will become the digestive system, lungs, thyroid, thymus, and other organs. By the end of the 4th week after conception (and therefore only 2 weeks into the embryonic period), the heart is beating and the primitive nervous system, consisting of a *neural tube,* is functioning. Yet, at 4 weeks, the embryo is still only about one quarter of an inch (6 millimeters) long.

During the second month, all of the structures that we recognize as human develop rapidly. The arms and legs unfold from small buds on the sides of the trunk. Rudimentary eyes become visible, and the internal organs—the lungs, digestive system, and excretory system—are also forming, although they are not yet functional. By the end of the embryonic period, the embryo has developed arms, legs, fingers, toes, a face, a heart that beats, a brain, lungs, and all of the major organ systems (see Figure 3-2).

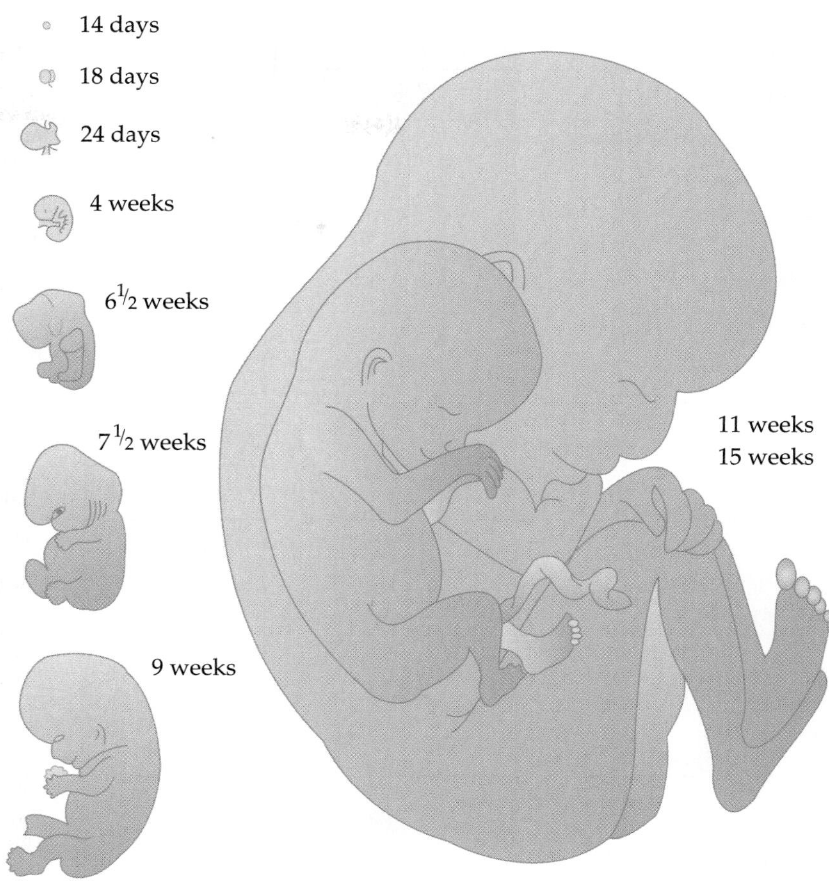

FIGURE 3-2 **Growth During the Embryonic Period**
This is a life-size illustration of the growth of the human embryo and fetus from 14 days to 15 weeks.

Spontaneous Abortions Miscarriages, technically called **spontaneous abortions**, occur primarily during the first trimester; almost 90% occur by 12 or 13 weeks, and miscarriages beyond 20 weeks are rare. Early miscarriages most often are caused by genetic defects that result in inadequate development of the placenta, the umbilical cord, or the embryo itself or in unsuccessful implantation (Vorvick & Storck, 2010). Maternal age is linked significantly to miscarriage risk. Mothers over the age of 30 are more likely to have pregnancies end in miscarriage, and risks continue to increase with advancing maternal age. For example, the risk of spontaneous abortion is four times higher for mothers age 45 than for mothers age 35 (Mayo Clinic, 2012). Paternal age, too, contributes to miscarriage risk, especially after age 35 (Iwayama et al., 2011); it appears that the miscarriage rate for pregnancies conceived by fathers over age 40 is nearly three times higher than that for fathers under age 25 (Kleinhaus, et al., 2006). Additionally, many maternal characteristics in addition to age are linked to an increased risk for miscarriage, including the mother's overall health; her use of drugs, alcohol, or cigarettes; as well as her exposure to environmental toxins, including radiation. Miscarriages also are more common when fathers have been exposed to toxic chemicals, radiation, or other environmental hazards (Friedler, 1996).

The rate of miscarriages is also linked to the sex of the embryo; male offspring are more likely than females to be spontaneously aborted. Although it is not possible to know exactly what the ratio of male-to-female conceptions is, it is clear that many more males than females are conceived. Some researchers suggest that as many as 170 males are conceived per 100 females (Pergament, Toydemir, & Fiddler, 2007), although more conservative estimates put the ratio closer to 125 to 100. This greater number of male conceptions reflects the greater likelihood for sperm containing the smaller Y chromosome to fertilize the egg. However, by the time of birth, the male-to-female sex ratio falls to about 105 to 100, showing the greater vulnerability of the male during the prenatal period (Cummings, 2011). Males continue to be more vulnerable, in fact, throughout childhood, and they are more likely than females to develop certain disorders, including some genetic disorders discussed in Chapter 2.

The Fetal Period

The **fetal period** lasts from the beginning of the third month until birth (or for about 7 months). During this period the organs and systems mature and become functional, although different systems develop at different points throughout this period (see

spontaneous abortion
Miscarriage; naturally triggered expulsion of the developing child before it is viable

fetal period
The final period of prenatal development, lasting from the end of the second month after conception until birth; during this period, organ systems mature and become functional

Table 3-2 Milestones of Development at Various Points During the Fetal Period

Week	Length	Weight	Developmental events
12	3 inches	1 ounce	• Arms, legs, fingers, and toes are developed and can be moved • Liver begins to function • Fingerprints are developed • Sexual organs are developed • Vocal cords and taste buds are formed • Eyes develop irises and nerves connecting eyes to brain are developed • Teeth begin to develop under gums
16	5½ inches	4 ounces	• Heartbeat is stronger and more regular, about 120 to 160 beats per minute • A soft hair (lanugo) develops that covers the body • Fingernails and toenails are developed
20	10 to 12 inches	8 ounces to 1 pound	• Senses of taste and smell are formed • Hair, eyelashes, and eyebrows are present • Movements can be detected by the mother • Fetus sucks its thumb
24	11 to 14 inches	1 pound to 1 pound 8 ounces	• Eyes are completely formed and open • Posture straightens and internal organs shift into proper positions • Brain development occurs, with first bursts of electrical activity present • Considered the age of viability in developed countries today
28	14 to 17 inches	2 pounds 8 ounces to 3 pounds	• Body fat is being accumulated • Body rhythms are developing (e.g., sleep, breathing) • Brain develops localized centers for various senses and motor activities • Fetus can now feel pain and touch • Fetus begins to respond to sound and vibration
32	16½ to 18 inches	4 to 5 pounds	• Fetus continues to develop fat and weight gain is rapid • Regulation of body systems becomes more refined • Most bones are formed, although they may be soft and flexible • Fetus is capable of surviving without intensive medical intervention
36 to 38	19 inches	6 pounds	• Daily rhythms of activity and sleep further develop • Hearing is complete • Fetus' position shifts to "head-down" • Protective coating called *vernix caseosa* begins to fall away • Lanugo dissolves • Antibodies are passed from the mother to protect the fetus from disease

Table 3-2). Particularly noteworthy is brain development. At about 24 weeks, the **fetus** (the French word for "pregnant" or "fruitful") begins to develop primitive brain waves, which have been virtually absent up until this time, although these early electrical patterns are similar to those that characterize brain death in adults. During the last trimester, the brain becomes more functional and therefore capable of regulating other body functions, such as breathing and sleeping.

Also, at 24 weeks, a healthy fetus reaches the **age of viability**, meaning it now has about a 50% chance of surviving outside the uterus if given high-quality intensive care, although currently over half of the surviving fetuses born at 24 weeks have serious anomalies. In contrast, at 25 weeks—only 1 week later—nearly 75% survive (and two-thirds of those with no major anomaly); at 28 weeks, over 90% survive with a good outcome, again provided that they receive quality intensive care (Nilsson & Hamberger, 2009). Despite modern medical advances and highly specialized care, however, infants who are born at earlier periods generally do not fare as well as those born closer to full term.

Infant health care, both for premature and full-term babies, has improved substantially, leading to significant improvement in infant mortality rates. In the United States, for example, infant mortality declined from 29.2 deaths per 1,000 live births in 1950 to just 6.14 in 2010, the most recent year for which data were available (National Center for Health Statistics, 2012). This dramatic decline in infant mortality has been accompanied by record high levels of U.S. women who received prenatal care. Today, more than 82% of U.S. women begin prenatal care in the first trimester, and only 3% receive no prenatal care

fetus
French term for "pregnant" or "fruitful"; refers to the developing baby from the end of the second month of gestation until birth

age of viability
The age (presently about 24 weeks) at which the fetus has a 50% chance of surviving outside the womb

Table 3-3 Infant Mortality Rates in Regions of the World: 1990 and 2011*

World region	Infant mortality rate: 1990	Infant mortality rate: 2011	Percent change
African Region	109	80	26.6%
Region of the Americas	33	15	54.5%
Southeast Asia Region	80	45	43.8%
European Region	28	12	57.1%
Eastern Mediterranean Region	77	54	29.9%
Western Pacific Region	36	18	50.0%

*Infant mortality is the probability of a child dying before the age of 1. Rates are expressed as the number dying per thousand live births.

SOURCE: From "Life expectancy and mortality," in *World Health Statistics 2011*. Retrieved from http://www.who.int/whosis/whostat/EN_WHS2011_Full,pdf. Reprinted by permission of World Health Organization.

(Reinold et al., 2011). Moreover, new medical treatments such as neonatal intensive care have allowed many babies born prematurely not simply to survive but also to lead healthy lives. Better access to health care, environmental interventions, improved nutrition, higher educational levels, and improved standards of living also have contributed to infant health, as well as to the dramatic drop in infant mortality, in many parts of the world, as shown in Table 3-3 (World Health Organization, 2012).

Things can sometimes go wrong, of course, but prenatal development normally occurs within a highly controlled and safe environment—the uterus—and follows an orderly, biologically programmed sequence. Thus, in about 9 months, the one-celled zygote normally has developed into perhaps 10 trillion cells organized into organs and systems. Figure 3-3 summarizes major milestones in prenatal development.

Developmental Trends

Changes and transitions in every aspect of development characterize prenatal development. To better understand how these developmental processes unfold, developmentalists look for common patterns, or themes, of development. Consistent with this goal, we see that during the prenatal period (and throughout childhood), physical growth and motor development exhibit three general trends.

First, development typically proceeds from the top of the body down, or from "head-to-tail"; this is termed the **cephalocaudal trend**. During the prenatal period, the head of the fetus is disproportionately larger than the rest of its body, and it will be years before the rest of the body catches up. (Incidentally, the cephalocaudal trend in physical growth is part of the reason that toddlers "toddle:" They are top-heavy.) A similar trend can be seen in motor development: Infants gain control over eye and head movements first, then arm and hand movements, and finally movements of their legs and feet.

Second, development usually proceeds from the middle of the body outward, or from "near-to-far"; this is the **proximodistal trend**. The upper arms and upper legs develop earlier than lower parts of these limbs, and infants reach and grab with the full hand long before they can pick up something small like peas and bits of carrot with their fingers and thumb.

Finally, there is the **gross-to-specific trend:** A fetus initially reacts to a poke on the skin with gross, generalized, whole-body movements, but as development proceeds, the movements become more localized and specific. For example, young children who are learning to write often move their whole bodies, perhaps including their tongues. Only later do they confine the action to the fingers, the hand, and wrist motions.

REVIEW THE FACTS 3-1

1. The germinal period ends when what event occurs?
2. About what percentage of zygotes become successfully implanted in the uterine wall?
3. Which of the following structures ultimately develops into the baby's brain?
   a. mesoderm b. neuroderm
   c. ectoderm d. endoderm
4. A more technical term for miscarriage is ___________.
5. The age of viability is defined as __________.
6. If we note that a baby first gains control over arm movements, then hand movements, and finally finger movements, this is best considered an example of what developmental trend?

Practice on **MyDevelopmentLab**

Watch *Fetal Development* on **MyDevelopmentLab**

gross-to-specific trend
The tendency to react to body stimuli with generalized, whole-body movements at first, with these responses becoming more local and specific later

cephalocaudal trend
The sequence of growth that occurs first in the head and progresses downward

proximodistal trend
The sequence of growth that occurs from the midline of the body outward

(a) First cleavage

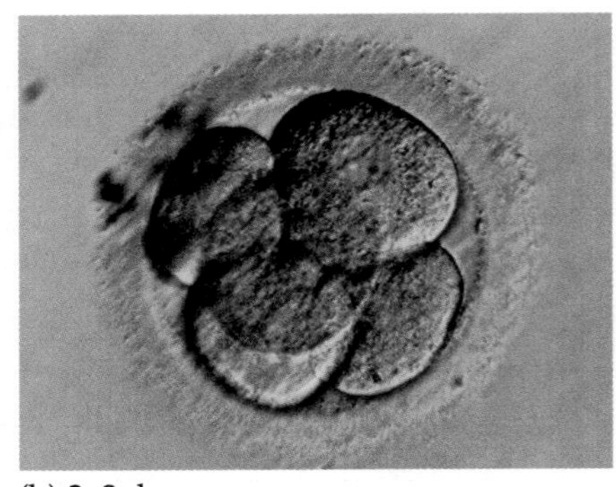

(b) 2–3 days

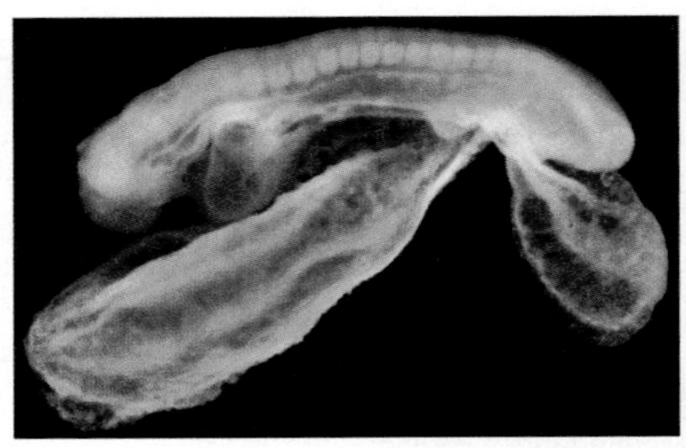

(c) 23 days

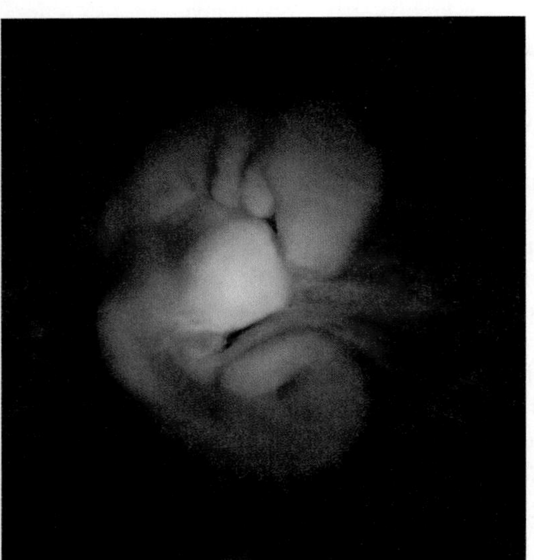

(d) 4 weeks

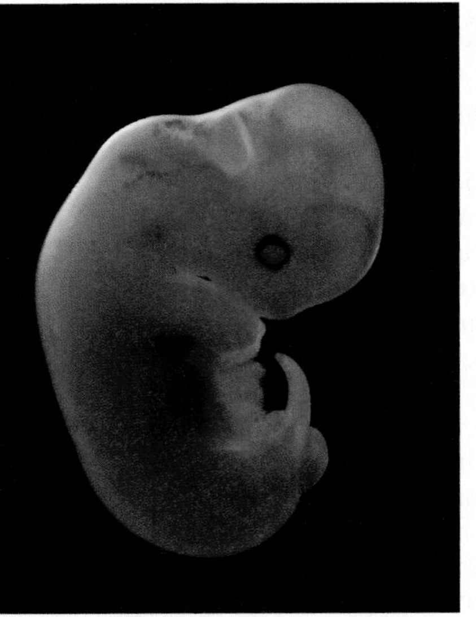

(e) 5 weeks

(f) 11 weeks

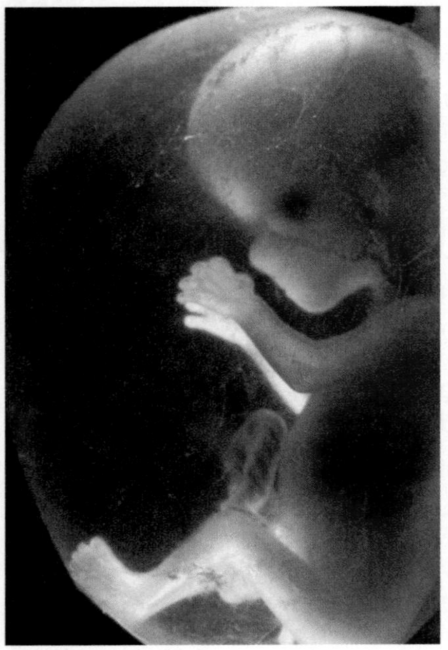

(g) 14 weeks

FIGURE 3-3 Ovulation and Fertilization
Major milestones in development: (a) A two-cell organism showing the first cleavage a few hours after fertilization. (b) The germinal period at 2 to 3 days—no cell differentiation exists yet. (c) An embryo at 23 days. Note the primitive spinal column in the developing embryo (at top). (d) A 4-week-old embryo. One can now distinguish the head (top), trunk, and tail. The heart and nervous system have started to function by this time. (e) A 5-week old embryo. The arms and the legs are beginning to unfold from the trunk. (f) An 11-week-old fetus showing the umbilical cord connection with the placenta. (g) A 14-week-old fetus showing the umbilical cord and the amniotic sac. All internal organs are formed but are not yet fully functional.

PRENATAL ENVIRONMENTAL INFLUENCES

Although much that happens during the prenatal period is biologically determined, environmental factors also operate during this stage, and both sets of factors can be involved when development goes awry. Although most live births in the United States are full-term healthy babies, every year some 12 to 13% are born preterm (before 37 weeks' gestation) and 3 to 4% are considered early preterm (before 34 weeks' gestation). Babies born early are at higher risk for a variety of health and developmental problems and often need special care (Federal Interagency Forum on Child and Family Statistics, U.S., 2011a). Additionally, about 2 to 3% of all live births are children with *congenital anomalies*—physical or mental conditions that used to be called birth defects. Such conditions range from minimal physical or mental anomalies, which may have little impact on the future development of the child, to gross anomalies that spell certain and almost immediate death.

Some people mistakenly assume that congenital anomalies happen only in families with defective genes; in reality, they can happen to anyone, and only a small proportion is the result of inherited factors. Environmental influences during the prenatal period or childbirth, such as the mother's age and health, as well as various environmental hazards, cause or contribute to the majority of congenital anomalies, as well as to the likelihood of preterm birth.

Maternal Age

The age of the mother interacts with the prenatal development of the child in ways that are not fully understood: Mothers in their 20s experience the lowest risk of miscarriages, stillbirths, and births of children with congenital anomalies (Liu, 2011; Martin, et al., 2011; Salihu, Wilson, Alio, & Kirby, 2008). For teenage mothers, the likeliest reason for the increased risk is that their bodies may not yet be mature enough to conceive and sustain a healthy developing child. Other risk factors for teens include socioeconomic factors, as well as immoderate use of alcohol and other drugs (Chedraui, 2008).

Do you think the availability of prenatal care and obstetrical advances are linked to the increase in the number of U.S. mothers who are choosing to delay having children into their 30s and 40s?

Older mothers are also at greater risk for miscarriage and for some congenital anomalies. One study of over 1.2 million pregnancies in Denmark indicated that the miscarriage rate was over 50% for women over age 40 and 75% for women over 45. The miscarriage rate for mothers age 20 to 24 was 9% by comparison (Andersen, Wohlfahrt, Christens, Olsen, & Melbye, 2000). With regard to congenital anomalies, the relationship between maternal age and Down syndrome has been studied extensively; generally accepted figures are that the incidence of Down syndrome increases from about 1 in 800 births for mothers under age 35 to about 1 in 25 for mothers age 45 or older.

Why are older women at greater risk? One factor may be that older mothers have older ova (remember that all of a woman's ova were formed before she was born). Whether due to aging alone or to damage that accrues over time, older ova might be defective in ways that affect development. Of course, older mothers' bodies also are older and hormone levels shift as women age; therefore, these factors also may contribute to increased risks.

Maternal Health and Nutrition

Regardless of age, mothers who begin pregnancy fit and in good health, eat a balanced diet rich in protein and calcium, and gain about 25 to 35 pounds (11 to 16 kilograms) are more likely to give birth to healthy babies. *Malnutrition* during pregnancy, whether caused by an insufficient amount of food or by eating food low in nutritional value, is linked to higher rates of spontaneous abortion, premature birth, and stillbirth. Malnourished mothers are also more likely to have babies with low birth weight, smaller head size, and smaller overall size.

One particularly problematic result of malnutrition is that it can cause reduced brain development not only in the late fetal period but also in early infancy. Furthermore, this effect is probably never completely overcome, even with good later nutrition (Chavez, Martinez, & Soberanes, 1995; de Souza, Fernandes, & doCarmo, 2011). Folic acid, which is found in liver, navy beans, and green leafy vegetables, may play an especially important role (Lucock, Xiaowei, Veysey, & Zoe, 2005; Marieb & Hoehn, 2012), although its mechanism is not well understood.

Malnutrition is especially problematic when it occurs over a long period of time. Research with animals has shown that the mother protects the fetus from the effects of short-term malnutrition by drawing on her own stored reserves. Therefore, if previously well-nourished mothers go through a temporary period of malnutrition during pregnancy, but the baby has a good diet and responsive caregivers after birth, there likely will be few long-lasting effects (Grantham-McGregor & Powell, 1994). However, when malnutrition is sustained over a long period of time, both baby and mother are at risk (Walker, Change, Powell, Simonoff, & Grantham-McGregor, 2007).

In regions that have been ravaged by famine or war, the effects of malnutrition on child development are especially clear: There are high rates of miscarriages and stillbirths, and children born to malnourished mothers may quickly develop diseases and fail to thrive unless immediate dietary adjustments are made. Fortunately, supplemental food programs begun at birth can have major benefits. For example, in a large long-term study in Guatemala, the health of children who received food supplements in infancy and in early childhood improved almost immediately. Even more striking were the long-term gains produced by a special program of protein-rich supplements: Years later, adolescents and young adults who had received the special supplements from birth performed significantly better in tests of knowledge, arithmetic,

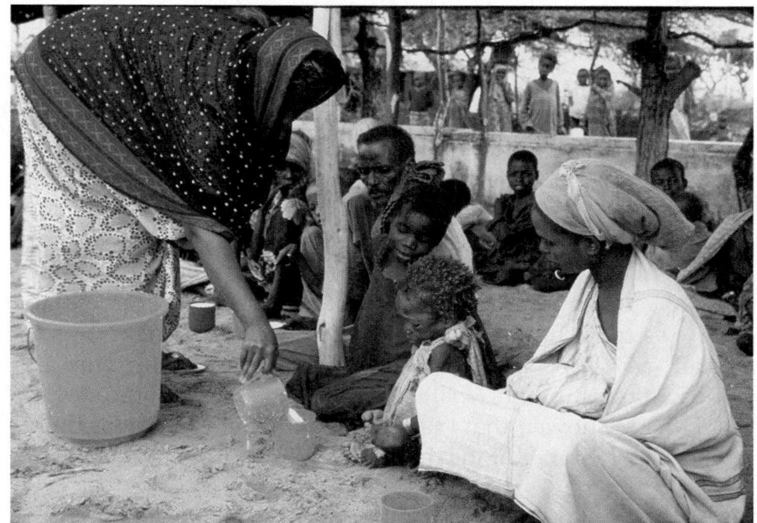

▲ The effects of malnutrition on child development are painfully apparent in countries ravaged by famine or war.

reading, vocabulary, and speed of information processing than did peers who had received no supplements before 2 years of age. The difference was particularly dramatic for individuals in below-poverty-level families and those with good primary education (Pollitt, Gorman, Engle, Martorell, & Rivera, 1993). Furthermore, the impact of early nutrition appears to be long lasting. As adults, the economic status of boys who had taken the supplements was higher, as reflected in higher wages, although this economic benefit was not seen among girls (Hoddinott, Maluccio, Behrman, Flores, & Martorell, 2008).

Prenatal Health Care

Along with good nutrition, adequate prenatal health care is associated with the delivery of healthy babies: One of the best predictors of delivering healthy, full-term babies is five or more visits to a doctor or health-care facility beginning in the first trimester of pregnancy. Good prenatal care usually includes a full medical examination, as well as advice about the value of exercise and good nutrition and the need to avoid the use of alcohol, tobacco, and illicit drugs (Edwards, 2006; Harms & Wick, 2011). The value of prenatal education is clear: Public-health outreach programs that provide prenatal health care to expectant mothers who might not otherwise receive it have been shown to be effective in reducing the rates of infant mortality and premature births. In addition, reduction in vaccine-preventable diseases such as measles, diphtheria, and type b meningitis have lowered infant mortality rates.

Critical Periods in Prenatal Development

The effects of many environmental influences, including those noted earlier, often depend on the point in the developmental sequence when the influence occurs. Figure 3-4 illustrates **critical periods** of prenatal development, which are periods during which the developing child is at greatest risk for different kinds of abnormalities as a result of exposure to **teratogens**—diseases, chemicals from air pollution or water contamination, radiation, or any other toxic agent that can harm the child. (The term comes from the ancient Greek word for "monster.")

Why is the effect of teratogens usually quite limited in the first 2 weeks after conception?

An extreme example of a teratogen that operates in a critical period of development involved thalidomide, a mild tranquilizer that was taken by many pregnant women in 1959 and 1960, primarily in Europe, to relieve nausea and other symptoms of morning sickness. Based on testing with animals, the drug was thought to be harmless, but within the next 2 years, as many as 10,000 babies were born with severe deformities as a result of their mothers' thalidomide use. A careful study of the pregnancies showed that the nature of the deformity was determined by the timing of the drug use. If the mother took the drug between the 34th and 38th days after her last menstrual period, the child had no ears. If she took the drug between the 38th and 47th days, the child had missing or stunted arms, and if she took the drug during the latter part of that time range, the child also had missing or stunted legs (McCredie, 2007). Although thalidomide was withdrawn from the market when its teratogenic effects became known, it has recently been reintroduced as a treatment for some types of cancer, including multiple myeloma (Mayo Clinic, 2010b). Consequently, physicians who prescribe this drug—or other drugs that might act as teratogens—must be especially careful when treating women of child-bearing age (see Table 3-5 for a list of some common teratogenic agents).

The action of teratogens is complex. Sometimes exposure to a specific teratogen inevitably causes miscarriage or damage to the embryo or fetus. Accidentally ingested poisons typically act in this way. More frequently, however, maternal exposure to a teratogen results in *increased risk* of damage, which may occur in varying degree or not at all, depending on a wide array of factors. For example, many teratogens have dose-specific effects, where limited exposure to small doses causes little or no damage, moderate exposure causes malformations, and large doses result in miscarriage. In part, these effects depend on the mother's ability to break down the teratogen and quickly eliminate it from her body, before it has much chance to accumulate in the immature embryonic or fetal tissue, where it causes significant damage (Ferreti, 2006; Hutchinson, 1991).

Teratogens generally are quite specific in how they affect development. For example, some substances have teratogenic effects in animals but not in humans; in other cases the reverse is true, as the example with thalidomide so tragically demonstrated. Also, teratogens sometimes exert their influence only during some periods of prenatal development and have no effect if present during noncritical periods. For example, the time between conception and implantation is sometimes referred to as the "all-or-none" period, because teratogens usually either kill the zygote, or have no effect on later development. Teratogens typically interfere most dramatically with development during the embryonic stage, as this is the period during which most organ systems and physical structures are formed. If a teratogen is introduced during the embryonic period, gross structural deformities may result. However, if the same teratogen is present during the later fetal period—when organ systems and structures are maturing—the result more often is to affect the size or function of the already-present structures. Thus, the effect of a short-acting teratogen is often tied directly to the specific systems that are developing at the time of exposure. For example, heart defects often result from teratogen exposure during the embryonic period, when this organ undergoes substantial formation and development. On the other hand, neurological impairments from teratogens can occur throughout most of the prenatal period and even into the early years after birth, because the brain and nervous system continue to develop throughout these periods.

Watch *Brain Development and Nutrition* on **MyDevelopmentLab**

critical period
The period of development during which the effect of a teratogen occurs

teratogen
Toxic agent of any kind that potentially causes abnormalities in the developing child

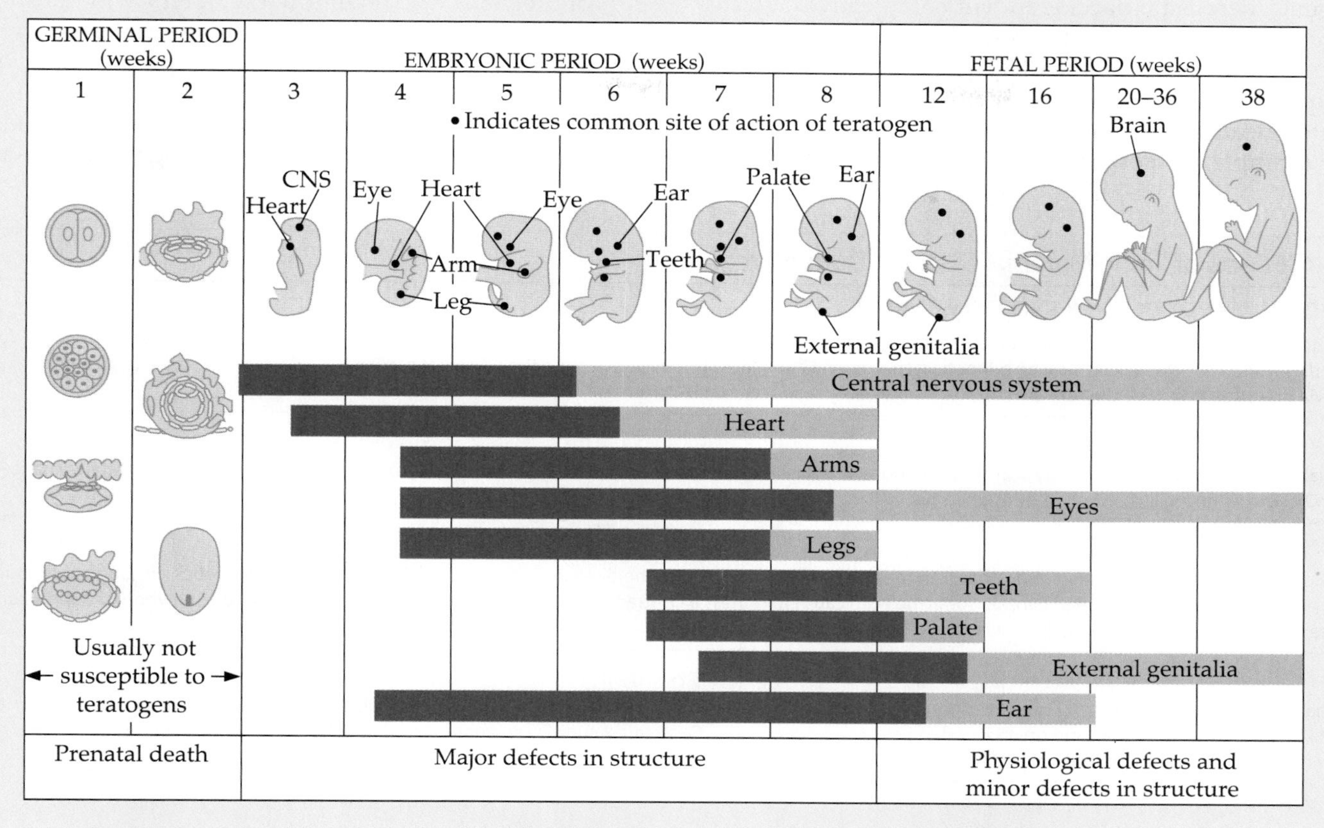

FIGURE 3-4 Critical Periods in Prenatal Development
Dark blue represents highly sensitive periods during which toxins may cause major structural damage; light blue represents less sensitive periods or times when minor or functional damage may occur.

Teratogens and Their Effects

The variety of environmental factors that have been shown to adversely affect prenatal development is staggering. Drugs, diseases, hormones, blood factors, radiation (including X-rays), exposure to toxins in the workplace, maternal age, nutrition, and inadequate prenatal care all have the potential to disrupt the normal development of the embryo or fetus (Ferretti, 2006; Sahin & Gungor, 2010) as do other factors that scientists have yet to identify.

Maternal Diseases Among the most devastating teratogens in terms of impact are diseases that are contracted by the mother and passed along to the developing embryo or fetus. In general, diseases may enter the child by several routes: through the placenta, as occurs with rubella (German measles) and human immunodeficiency virus (HIV); through the amniotic fluid, as sometimes occurs with syphilis and gonorrhea; and through the interchange of bodily fluids or blood, which can occur during labor and delivery or even through breastfeeding, as with HIV.

Not all diseases, of course, produce teratogenic effects. For example, most kinds of bacteria do not cross a normal placental barrier, so even a severe bacterial infection in the mother may have little or no effect on the fetus provided that she recovers quickly so that the infection does not markedly affect her overall health. However, smaller organisms, such as many viruses—including rubella, HIV, herpes simplex, and many varieties of cold and flu viruses—do cross the placental barrier and can inflict harm. Rubella, for example, can cause blindness, heart abnormalities, deafness, brain damage, or limb deformity in the embryo or fetus, depending on the specific period during which the mother contracts the virus. Some of the maternal diseases and other maternal conditions that can affect an embryo or fetus are summarized in Table 3-4.

One of the most devastating viruses that can be transmitted to the embryo or fetus is HIV which, if left untreated, eventually develops into AIDS (acquired immune deficiency disease) (AVERT, 2012). Although the number of babies with AIDS in the United States is relatively low, the situation is much worse elsewhere. In sub-Saharan Africa, for example, where the AIDS epidemic is particularly widespread, an estimated 22.9 million adults and children were living with HIV at the end of 2010—about 5% of the population of this region, and two-thirds of the global total (AVERT, 2012). Fortunately, the number of AIDS-related deaths worldwide has begun to decrease from the peak of 2.1 million people per year in 2004 to an estimated 1.8 million people in 2009—a decline of about 14% over 5 years (Joint United Nations Programme on HIV/AIDS, 2010). This decline is the result of both a decline in the number of new cases, which began in the late 1990s, and especially the increased availability of retroviral drug therapy and other forms of care and support to people living with AIDS.

At present, there is no vaccine to halt completely the transmission of the AIDS virus, but new therapies that involve combinations of drugs, called HAART (highly active antiretroviral therapies), or "drug cocktails," have dramatically reduced AIDS-related deaths and mother-to-infant transmission of the virus. For example, without treatment or breastfeeding, about 25% of pregnant women infected with HIV will transmit the virus to their babies (CDC, 2007a). However, if pregnant women take these antiretroviral drugs during pregnancy and during birth, the rate drops to less than 2 percent.

As retroviral drugs have become more widely available, the number of infected babies has dropped significantly—at least in

Table 3-4 Effects of Some Maternal Diseases During Pregnancy

ACQUIRED IMMUNE DEFICIENCY SYNDROME (AIDS)

AIDS is an incurable and often fatal, but sometimes treatable, disease caused by the human immunodeficiency virus (HIV) in which the immune system breaks down and the person dies from what would normally be minor bacterial or viral infections. This virus can cross the placental barrier, but infection also can occur during the birth process or via breastfeeding. (See the text discussion on how babies can contract HIV from their mothers.)

DIABETES

Maternal diabetes can cause numerous physical malformations; it also sometimes causes stillbirth. The fetus may grow larger than normal, increasing the chance of birth difficulties. Diabetes is normally controlled through a special diet.

GONORRHEA

Many people carry the bacterial infection gonorrhea, but they display no symptoms of the disease. Gonorrhea can be treated with antibiotics, although antibiotic-resistant strains of gonorrhea continue to evolve. Gonorrhea can cause blindness if contracted from the mother during delivery; therefore, newborns routinely are given silver nitrate eye drops immediately after birth as a preventive treatment.

HERPES SIMPLEX

The virus that causes genital herpes can cross the placental barrier, but infection is much more common during birth. Risks for the newborn include blindness, neurological problems, mental retardation, and death in a significant number of cases. Cesarean section is recommended if the mother has active herpes at the time that the baby is due to be born. Herpes simplex is currently incurable.

HIGH BLOOD PRESSURE

Chronic maternal high blood pressure can be treated with drugs; however, if it is not controlled during pregnancy, it can cause miscarriage.

INFLUENZA

The many strains of influenza virus can cross the placental barrier. The most common effects are spontaneous abortion early in pregnancy or premature labor later. Maternal fever, if uncontrolled, can also be fatal to the fetus.

RH FACTOR

Rh incompatibility between the mother and the developing child is a disease in the sense that a protein component of the mother's blood can cause severe congenital anomalies or death in the fetus. Most women are Rh positive, but some lack this blood component and are Rh negative. If an Rh-negative mother has an Rh-positive child and their blood comes into contact through placental seepage or during birth, the mother's bloodstream begins to build up antibodies that attack and destroy fetal red blood cells. Although there is usually no danger for a first-born child (and none for the mother), later-born children are highly at risk if they are Rh positive. Rh-negative mothers can be treated to prevent the buildup of the antibodies.

RUBELLA

If the rubella virus is contracted during the first 16 weeks of pregnancy (but after implantation) the risks of damage to the embryo or fetus are great, leading some parents to elect to terminate such pregnancies. Some children exposed prenatally to rubella are normal, but others are severely impaired.

SYPHILIS

Syphilis is a bacterial infection that normally does not pass the placental barrier during the first half of the pregnancy. It is most likely to be transmitted near or during birth. Syphilis can cause premature labor and miscarriage, deafness, and skin sores and lesions. Although syphilis can be treated with antibiotics, the drugs themselves can affect the embryo or fetus. Cesarean section delivery 1 to 2 weeks early is often recommended to prevent infection of the neonate.

TOXEMIA OF PREGNANCY

Two forms of maternal toxemia are *preeclampsia* and the more severe *eclampsia*. Typically, both forms develop during the third trimester, but the causes are unknown. Maternal symptoms of the disorders include elevated blood pressure, blurred vision, and puffy swelling of the face and hands. Eclampsia can cause fetal brain damage or death. However, both forms of toxemia usually can be controlled with bed rest and a special diet.

TOXOPLASMOSIS

Toxoplasmosis is a parasite that can be passed from mother to fetus. Usually undetected at birth, it can later cause serious problems, including blindness or intellectual disability. Toxaplasmosis is often shed in the feces of cats or kittens, so pregnant mothers should exercise great care in emptying cat litter boxes. The parasite also can be transmitted in food, so fruits and vegetables should be carefully washed and meat fully cooked. Medication is available as a treatment.

SOURCE: From *The introduction to public health,* by M. J. Schneider, 2011, Sudbury, MA: Jones and Bartlett Publishers; "Human tetratogens: A critical evaluation," by O. Diav-Citrin & G. Koren, retrieved from http://www.nvp-volumes.org/p2_4.htm.

those parts of the world where drugs are available and affordable. For example, in the United States, the number of babies born with HIV each year has declined from more than 2,000 two decades ago to fewer than 200 today (Elizabeth Glaser Pediatric AIDS Foundation, 2012). The good news is that by using a combination of HAART therapy to keep mothers' viral counts low and cesarean-section delivery methods when possible, it now appears that mother-infant HIV transmission can be reduced to near-zero (CDC, 2006; Suy, et al., 2008).

However, there still are challenges in reducing HIV infections during pregnancy and delivery. Only about 75% of pregnant women who are infected with HIV are aware of their health status, making prenatal screening an important component in reducing the number of HIV-infected babies born. Currently, the CDC is recommending that HIV testing be a part of prenatal health care for all pregnant women. And, it is still the case that until medical researchers develop a preventative method or cure, AIDS education and community-based outreach programs remain the main ways to stem the spread of this disease, especially in developing nations where HAART therapies and other AIDS drugs are largely unavailable.

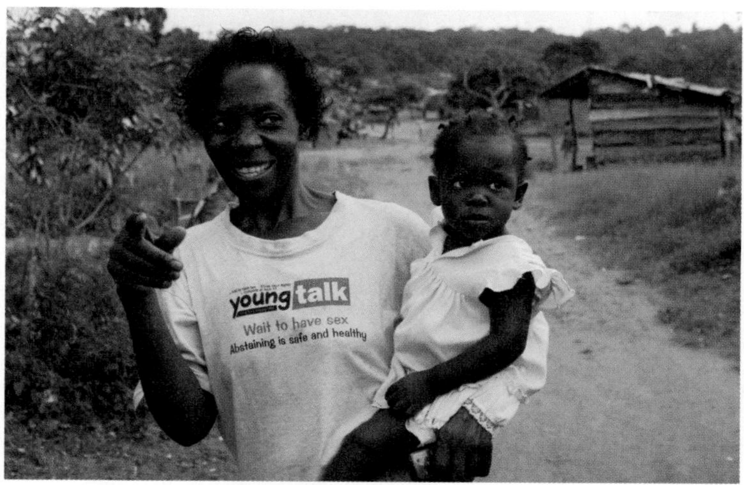

▲ Most mothers with HIV infection in the United States have access to treatment for themselves and their infants, unlike those in many parts of the world where stigma, misinformation, and poverty limit adequate treatment and prevention.

Prescription and Over-the-Counter Drugs Although it is difficult and sometimes impossible for pregnant women to prevent being exposed to teratogenic diseases, they usually can control their use of drugs. Yet, for a variety of reasons, many women do consume drugs during pregnancy (Hendry, 2009; SAMHSA, 2012). Sometimes, this is the result largely of ignorance: Many common drugs that pose virtually no risk for the mother may have a significant impact on the fetus. For example, tetracycline, a frequently prescribed antibiotic, has been shown to have adverse effects on fetal teeth and bones and can contribute to other congenital anomalies. Some anticonvulsant medications given to mothers with epilepsy can cause structural malformations, growth delays, heart abnormalities, mild mental retardation, or speech irregularities in babies. Accutane, a drug prescribed for the treatment of acne, is associated with high risk of miscarriage, along with increased risk of brain abnormality; mental retardation; ear, eye, and other facial abnormalities; and heart defects. Because many prescription drugs are associated with birth defects, it is imperative that women who may be pregnant consult with a knowledgeable physician before *any* medication is taken, including over-the-counter (OTC) medications, which also can harm the embryo or fetus (see Table 3-5). When monitored by a qualified physician, the use of some prescription drugs may be indicated: For example, there may be a greater risk to the unborn child if the mother's illness is not treated than the risk that the drug involved poses.

How can a drug that is harmless, or even beneficial, to the mother have a substantial negative effect on the developing embryo or fetus? One explanation is that the drug may arrest or interfere with developing organ systems but not have an effect once development is complete. In addition, some drugs and other chemicals can be turned into waste products and can be eliminated by the mother's mature body but not by the embryo or fetus. Thus, drugs that cross the placental barrier may be "trapped" and accumulate in the developing child to the degree that they cause severe damage. Recreational drugs, such as alcohol, nicotine, and other illegal substances, pose particular problems because women who use them often have a difficult time discontinuing their use.

Alcohol The most widely used "recreational" or "social" drug in the United States and in many other nations is alcohol, which has the potential to cause severe and permanent congenital anomalies, as well as to increase a women's risk of miscarriage (Jones & Streissguth, 2010). Recent findings show that one in seven women of childbearing age (18 to 44 years old) reported *risk drinking,* which is defined as seven or more drinks per week or five or more drinks on any one occasion (NCHS, 2011e). Because congenital anomalies associated with prenatal exposure to alcohol can readily occur in the first 3 to 8 weeks of pregnancy—often before a woman even knows that she is pregnant—accidental pregnancies can be problematic. In addition, 1 of every 30 women who knows that she is pregnant reports risk drinking.

Children of mothers who drink heavily during pregnancy may be born with a severe condition called **fetal alcohol syndrome (FAS)**, which occurs as often as 1 in 1,000 births and is the leading cause of intellectual disability in the United States (Warren, Hewitt, & Thomas, 2011). People with FAS

Watch *Teratogens and Their Effects* on **MyDevelopmentLab**

fetal alcohol syndrome (FAS)
A set of congenital abnormalities, including small size, low birth weight, certain facial characteristics, and mental retardation, that results from maternal alcohol consumption during pregnancy

Table 3-5 The Effects of Selected Drugs and Environmental Agents on Prenatal Development

Drugs
AMPHETAMINES Drugs in the amphetamine family were once widely prescribed as an aid to dieting because they very effectively suppress appetite. Today, they are prescribed only rarely, but forms such as *methamphetamine* are widely available on the illegal market. Amphetamine use during pregnancy can cause spontaneous abortion, stillbirth, or prematurity, as well as many of the same effects as those caused by cocaine.
COCAINE Cocaine ingestion during pregnancy, whether in powder or crack form, can have numerous lasting physical and psychological effects on the child.
MARIJUANA Smoking marijuana during pregnancy is linked to various congenital anomalies and to deficits in cognitive abilities.
NARCOTICS In general, narcotics such as codeine, morphine, heroin, dilaudid, and even methadone (a maintenance drug that suppresses narcotics withdrawal symptoms) depress fetal respiration and can cause behavioral disturbances in the infant. Babies born to women who use such drugs typically are smaller than normal, and they are less responsive as newborns. The babies show drug withdrawal symptoms—extreme irritability, shrill crying, vomiting, shaking, and poor temperature control. They tend to have low appetite and difficulty sucking, and their sleep patterns are disturbed, at least for the first several weeks. At 4 months, they are more tense and rigid and less coordinated than normal babies. Up to 12 months, they may have difficulty maintaining attention, and researchers suspect that attention and language deficits may persist well into childhood.
Legal Drugs
ALCOHOL Drinking can cause fetal alcohol syndrome (FAS) and the less severe fetal alcohol effects (FAE). The effects are the same regardless of which alcohol-containing beverage is consumed: beer, wine, liqueur, or liquor.
CAFFEINE The caffeine in coffee, tea, and soft drinks can retard prenatal growth and produces a slightly increased risk of miscarriage if consumed in amounts exceeding the equivalent of about six cups of coffee per day because the developing child lacks the enzymes that break down caffeine, allowing it to accumulate to potentially toxic levels.
OVER-THE-COUNTER DRUGS Many over-the-counter (OTC) medications such as analgesics, cough medicines, laxatives, and allergy pills are—at best—unsafe. Aspirin in large doses can lead to excessive bleeding and other problems. Large doses of antacid tablets or cough syrups, especially those that contain codeine, may not be entirely safe. Even vitamins are risky if taken in excess. Moreover, such substances do not clear from the fetus' system as easily as they do from the mother's system.
PRESCRIPTION MEDICATIONS Many prescription drugs have known teratogenic effects, which vary widely depending on the particular medication. All prescription drugs should be monitored carefully by a physician during pregnancy.
TOBACCO Smoking—whether cigarettes, cigars, or pipes—or the use of dipping or chewing tobacco can cause birth problems and congenital anomalies, as well as low birth weight and premature delivery.
TRANQUILIZERS AND SLEEPING PILLS Like alcohol, most tranquilizers and sleeping pills are central nervous system depressants. Although their effects generally are not thought to be severe (except in the case of thalidomide), if taken shortly before delivery they can cause the baby to be born sedated and they increase the risk of respiratory distress and anoxia.
Environmental Agents
AIR POLLUTANTS Increases in urban air pollutants, such as nitrogen dioxide, sulfur dioxide, and carbon monoxide, have been found to correlate with increases in miscarriages.
MERCURY, LEAD, AND OTHER POLLUTANTS Poisoning by mercury, lead, and other industrial by-products can occur through pollution of the water supply. The pollutants then find their way up the food chain into fish and other food sources. Dangerous chemicals also can be ingested through direct consumption of tainted water or air and can cause profound mental retardation and neurological impairment in the developing child.
PCBs PCBs (polychlorinated biphenyl compounds) were used in many manufacturing processes before the 1970s, when they were banned in the United States. Prenatal exposure to PCB compounds, which usually occurs through the food supply chain, has been associated with delayed growth and neurological impairments.
RADIATION Ionizing radiation, including X-rays, can cause microcephaly, intellectual disability, or skeletal malformations.

can usually be recognized by their distinctive facial characteristics. They tend to have a thin upper lip, a poorly developed indentation above the upper lip, a wide space between the margins of the eyelids, flat cheekbones, a small head, and a smaller-than-average stature throughout life. Low birth weight also is quite common. When the effects of prenatal exposure to alcohol are less severe, the condition is referred to as **fetal alcohol spectrum disorder (FASD)**. Usually children with FASD do not show the classic facial characteristics of FAS, but they do have mild growth retardation and various brain abnormalities, which may contribute to learning problems, mild intellectual disability, or behavioral difficulties.

How much alcohol can be safely consumed during pregnancy—if any—is still unclear. One study found that 14-year-old children whose mothers drank as little as one drink a week were significantly shorter and leaner and had a smaller head circumference than children of women who did not drink at all (Day, et al., 2002). Another study revealed that noticeable effects on the newborn were found for women who drank as little as three glasses of beer per week (Nugent, Greene, & Mazor, 1990). Other studies, however, failed to find such effects for mothers who consumed less than one drink per day (O'Callaghan, O'Callaghan, Najman, Williams, & Bor, 2007). Findings such as these led the U.S. surgeon general to issue a report in 2005, which states that "no amount of alcohol consumption can be considered safe during pregnancy" (U.S. Department of Health and Human Services, 2005). Typically, the advice given by physicians to pregnant women is to refrain entirely from consuming alcohol while pregnant.

Of course, the more alcohol that is consumed during pregnancy, the greater the risk of damage to the embryo or fetus. Studies generally have found that more than one-third of the infants born to mothers who drink heavily have congenital abnormalities. Even when alcohol is consumed in moderate amounts, such as 1 or 2 ounces daily, researchers have found higher-than-normal rates of respiratory and heart-rate abnormalities in the newborn, difficulty in adapting to normal sounds and lights, and lower mental development scores later in infancy (Jones & Streissguth, 2010; O'Callaghan, et al., 2007). Longer-term effects may include less attentiveness to adults and more trouble complying with instructions and rules. Children born to mothers who drink alcohol during pregnancy also are at greater risk for experiencing learning disabilities, attention problems, and hyperactivity (Pellegrino & Pellegrino, 2008), and these effects often persist into adolescence and beyond (Howell, Lynch, Platzman, Smith, & Coles, 2006). In addition, attachment during childhood, as well as a variety of social behaviors extending well into adulthood, may be disrupted by prenatal exposure to alcohol (Kelly, Day, & Streissguth, 2000).

Do you think more should be done to discourage pregnant women from drinking alcohol? If so, what?

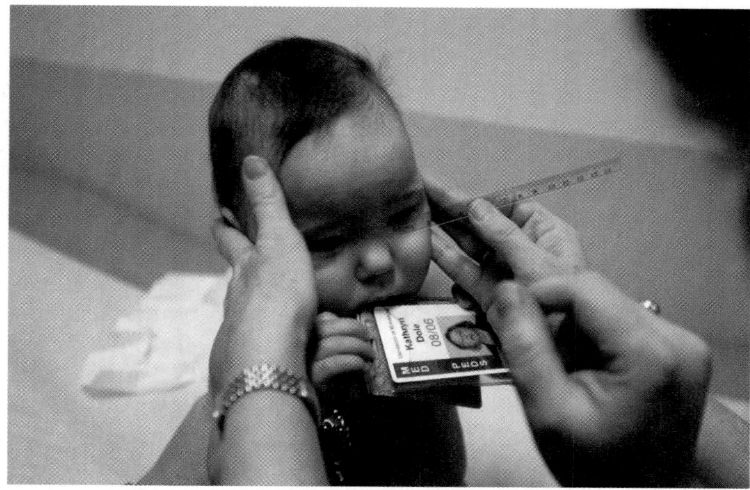

▲ *This young girl is being evaluated for the effects of fetal alcohol syndrome* (FAS).

The conclusion about alcohol is easy: *Any* level of drinking during pregnancy could be risky, and most women cut back or quit drinking once they know they are pregnant. Yet, 1 in 8 women report drinking alcohol while pregnant, and roughly 6% report that they are still drinking in the last 3 months of pregnancy; of these women, 2.9% are binge drinkers (CDC, 2011d; NCHS, 2007).

Tobacco Cigarette smoking has been clearly linked to fetal abnormalities, as well as to a variety of problems associated with growth and cognition: Among mothers who smoke heavily, rates of spontaneous abortion, stillbirth, and premature birth are significantly higher than among nonsmoking mothers (Bublitz & Stroud, 2012; Espy, et al., 2011), especially among adolescent mothers. Babies born to heavy smokers also tend to weigh less at birth than those born to nonsmokers, and they have delayed growth that can continue for years. Children of mothers who smoke regularly also display more cognitive and behavioral deficits and tend to do less well in school than do children of nonsmokers (Torpy, Lynm, & Glass, 2005), especially if mothers smoke more than a pack a day during pregnancy (Boutwell, Beaver, Gibson, & Ward, 2011). Some of these effects appear to also be linked to prenatal exposure to secondhand smoke (Genbacev, McMaster, Zdravkovic, & Fisher, 2003).

How does smoking damage or even kill fetuses? Most likely, epigenetic processes are involved: Smoking has a greater impact on some individuals than others (Wiebe et al., 2009). Research also points to the placenta and its role in nutrient exchange: Some forms of damage to the placenta that interfere with nutrient exchange occur only among women who smoke, and others occur more often among women who smoke than among those who do not (CDC, 2004; Ronco, Garrida, & Llanos, 2006). Smoking also

fetal alcohol spectrum disorder (FASD)
An umbrella term describing the range of effects, including physical, mental, and behavioral disabilities, associated with prenatal exposure to alcohol; similar to FAS, although with milder abnormalities

Watch *Fetal Alcohol Syndrome: Sidney* on **MyDevelopmentLab**

can constrict blood vessels in the uterus, reducing the flow of nutrients. Both problems can reduce the flow of oxygen and can cause **anoxia** as well, with potential damage to brain tissue.

Marijuana Smoking marijuana during pregnancy is also inadvisable (Bhavaneswar & Chang, 2009; Fried, 2008). Prenatal exposure to cannabis (marijuana) is linked to birth defects in the cardiovascular and gastrointestinal systems, as well as to structural defects such as cleft palate and limb deformities (Forrester & Mertz, 2007). Several studies also tie it to the presence of general cognitive deficiencies, including symptoms of increased impulsiveness and inability to pay attention as well as decreased general intellectual functioning and deficits in learning and memory (Goldschmidt , Richardson, Willford, Severtson, & Day, 2012; Huizink & Mulder, 2006). In one study, women who reported light to moderate marijuana use in their fourth to seventh months of pregnancy were found to have children with below-average intelligence as measured with standard intelligence tests (Goldschmidt, Richardson, Willford, & Day, 2008). Some research also suggests that prenatal exposure to marijuana may lead to a greater vulnerability to some mental disorders later in life (Sundram, 2006). The adverse effects associated with prenatal exposure to marijuana—as well as to other drugs—are especially significant for boys (Willford, Richardson, & Day, 2012). Although many factors are undoubtedly involved, research does suggest that marijuana exposure during pregnancy leads to disruptions in the development of the brain and other organ systems.

Cocaine and Other Amphetamine Drugs Although some studies of prenatal exposure to cocaine find no significant cocaine-related developmental impairments, many do reveal the link between cocaine exposure and both physical and cognitive impairments (Bennett, Bendersky, & Lewis, 2008; Brick, 2008). Some studies show that the risk of severe damage to the unborn child is considerable (Aneja, Iqbal, & Ahmed, 2006). Mothers who use cocaine experience more labor complications, and their infants have a higher risk of prematurity, growth retardation, mental retardation, and neuromotor dysfunction (Swanson, Streissguth, Sampson, & Olson, 1999). Although research thus far is inconclusive, it is also possible that cocaine increases the risk of spontaneous abortion (Mills, 1999; Ness, et al., 1999), as do other stimulants such as methamphetamine ("crank" or "ice") and even caffeine.

The majority of cocaine- or methamphetamine-exposed infants can be classified as "fragile." They are easily overloaded by normal environmental stimulation, have difficulty controlling the nervous system, and often cry frantically and seem unable to sleep. Even years later, after the most obvious symptoms have subsided, children of cocaine-using mothers have much higher rates of attention deficit disorder, language delays, and learning disabilities, and they also exhibit higher delinquent and aggressive behaviors. As is true for other substances, these effects seem especially apparent among boys (Carmody, Bennett, & Lewis, 2011; Lewis & Kestler, 2012). Studies also have found that prenatally exposed 4- to 6-year-olds experience higher rates of depression and anxiety and greater impulsivity and distractibility (Berger & Waldfogel, 2000; Chasnoff, et al., 1998; B. Lester, LaGrasse, & Bigsby, 1998). Clearly, mothers should avoid even the slightest cocaine or amphetamine use during pregnancy.

Fortunately, discontinuing cocaine or methamphetamine use early in the prenatal period often can limit the damage, and the delayed motor development present at birth may be mostly resolved by age 3 (Smith, et al., 2011). Also, at least for some children, negative effects may not be as severe if they receive good postnatal care. However, prenatal exposure to amphetamines is tied to negative outcomes for the baby, so pregnant women are usually advised to keep even caffeine consumption to a minimum in order to protect the health of their babies.

How might the environment of children whose mothers used illegal drugs while pregnant contribute to later behavioral difficulties?

Environmental Pollutants and Radiation Certain chemicals found in the environment can act as teratogens, as can exposure to radiation, including X-rays. Usually, an individual's exposure to the tiny amounts of these chemicals or radiation that naturally occur in the environment is not sufficient to cause any significant damage, even to an embryo or fetus. However, when an individual is subjected to a concentrated dose, or is continuously exposed over a long period of time, damage can result. When such exposure occurs during the prenatal period, these substances can act as teratogens.

Among the environmental pollutants most frequently identified as teratogens are mercury, lead, and polychlorinated biphenyl compounds (PBCs). Prenatal mercury exposure at a level sufficient to cause damage most often results from the mother's eating fish caught in polluted waters where the level of the methylmercury compound is high (Llop et al., 2012). The amount of mercury that accumulates from a high-fish diet usually is not sufficient to be toxic for an adult, but can act as a teratogen during pregnancy. Consequently, physicians usually recommend that pregnant women restrict the amount of fish they include in their diet, and in particular avoid eating swordfish, shark, and other larger fish caught in waters known to be polluted. Prenatal exposure to mercury is most likely to disrupt neurological development and cause intellectual disabilities.

Prenatal exposure to lead also is most likely to disrupt neurological development, but can lead to miscarriage or delayed physical and intellectual development (Jedrychowski et al., 2009; Lewis & Kestler, 2012). Recent research suggests that lead exposure may also be linked to the development of childhood allergies (Jedrychowski et al., 2011). Lead compounds are found in some industrial wastes and are used in some manufacturing processes, so women who work in such environments are usually reassigned to different jobs during their pregnancies. Lead is a chemical used in some forms of pottery glazes and paints,

anoxia
Lack of oxygen; can cause brain damage

so pregnant women should be especially careful to make sure they do not eat or drink from dishes or glassware that use lead in their manufacture. Lead used to be included in the formula for many types of house paint, so parents are warned to not let their young children suck on old painted toys or on paint chips from houses painted in earlier decades. Although lead has been banned as a paint additive in the United States since 1978, some other countries do not ban lead. Therefore, it is important for parents to be aware of lead exposure in items painted in other countries or before 1978 in the United States.

Like the use of lead in paints, the inclusion of PCB compounds was banned in the United States in 1979. PCBs were used in the manufacture of many products, especially plastics and florescent lamps, and they have a very long half-life, meaning that they break down very slowly. Prenatal PCB exposure is associated with delayed fetal growth, abnormal neural system development, and impaired behavioral and cognitive functions in a child. Recent work suggests that PCB exposure also may be linked to attention deficit hyperactivity disorder (Sagiv, et al., 2010; Yolton, 2011). Since PCBs were banned, the environmental level has been declining, but pregnant women usually are advised to reduce their consumption of fish, to wash and peel vegetables before eating them, and avoid handling old florescent lamps and cooling devices that may contain high levels of PCB compounds.

As we know from observing the effects of the nuclear bombing of Hiroshima and Nagasaki, Japan at the end of WW II, prenatal exposure to high doses of ionizing radiation is linked to abnormal brain development, intellectual disability, and various cancers in children. Fortunately, exposure to high doses of radiation is rare and most radiation exposure events will not be likely to cause health effects (CDC, 2011j). For example, medical diagnostic X-ray procedures involve very small doses of radiation and appear to be safe even when several are performed during pregnancy. However, the embryo and fetus are susceptible to the damaging effects of radiation, and therefore a cautious approach is in order. Women who may be pregnant and who work in settings where X-rays are used should be very careful to limit their exposure. Radiation effects are strongly tied to critical periods of development. For example, exposure during the first 2 weeks may interfere with implantation, but is unlikely to cause birth defects, whereas exposure during weeks 8 to 15 is especially significant in brain development (Donnelly, Smith, Farfan, & Ozcan, 2011).

With all of the admonitions about risk factors and teratogens, it may seem daunting to even consider having a baby. Yet, in any pregnancy, there is a balance between risk factors and protective factors. The diseases, drugs, and other toxins just discussed are indeed risk factors that can disrupt the normal development of the baby. However, it is important to note that the human body—both the mother's and the child's—seems to be able to filter out small amounts of toxins and provide protection against many teratogens. Additionally, when the mother is in good health, is reasonably fit physically, eats a nutritious diet, exercises moderation in lifestyle, and gets regular prenatal care, these provide protection for the unborn child.

Of course many young, economically poor, first-time mothers face daunting challenges as they ready themselves for the challenges of motherhood. However, when prenatal care is good and support is available, outcomes for mother and infant are usually favorable, as described in the Changing Perspectives: Nurse–Family Partnerships. It is important to note that, despite risks, the large majority of babies begin life ready to cope successfully.

REVIEW THE FACTS 3-2

1. Which of the following groups of mothers is associated with the lowest risk for congenital anomalies?
   a. women age 15 to 19 b. women age 20 to 29
   c. women age 30 to 39 d. women age 40 to 49
2. During which of the following periods is a teratogen *least* likely to have an effect?
   a. embryonic period b. fetal period
   c. germinal period d. first month after birth
3. What are three ways that teratogens can be passed from mother to baby?
4. Fetal alcohol syndrome is associated with all of the following consequences, *except*
   a. lip malformations.
   b. mental retardation.
   c. wider-than-normal space between the eyes.
   d. larger-than-average physical size.
5. Anoxia is a problem most often associated with prenatal exposure to which of the following drugs?
   a. tetracycline b. alcohol
   c. tobacco d. cocaine

Practice on **MyDevelopmentLab**

CHILDBIRTH

Regardless of a mother's experiences during the prenatal period, pregnancy results in the birth of a child—a developmental milestone subject to considerable cultural interpretation. However, although attitudes toward pregnancy and childbirth vary considerably from one culture to another, the birth process itself consists of a series of biologically programmed events.

Stages of Childbirth

The process of childbirth can be divided into three distinct stages: initial labor, labor and delivery, and afterbirth (American College of Obstetricians and Gynecologists, 2010; Fisanick, 2009).

Initial Labor In **initial labor**, the cervical opening of the uterus begins to dilate to allow for passage of the baby. Labor begins with mild uterine contractions, usually spaced 15 to 20 minutes apart. As labor progresses, the contractions increase in

initial labor
The first stage of labor, during which the cervical opening of the uterus begins to dilate to allow for passage of the baby

frequency and intensity until they occur only 3 to 5 minutes apart. Although initial labor can last from a few minutes to over 30 hours, the norms are 12 to 15 hours for the first child and 6 to 8 hours for later children. The muscular contractions of labor are involuntary, and it is best if the mother tries to relax during this period. Two other events may occur during initial labor. First, a mucus plug that covers the cervix is released. This is called *showing*, and it may include some bleeding. Second, the amniotic sac may break and amniotic fluid may rush forth, as when a mother's "water breaks."

Some mothers experience **false labor** (called *Braxton–Hicks contractions*), especially with the first child. False labor can be hard to distinguish from real labor, but one test that usually works is to have the expectant mother walk around: The pains of false labor tend to diminish, whereas those of real labor become more uncomfortable.

Labor and Delivery Once the cervix is fully dilated, the second stage of childbirth begins. At this stage, longer and more intense contractions occur every 2 to 3 minutes, and these contractions push the baby through the birth canal. If the mother is conscious, she can greatly assist in the delivery by controlling her breathing and "pushing," or bearing down, with her abdominal muscles during each contraction. Labor and delivery usually takes from 10 to 40 minutes and tends to be shorter with succeeding births.

Normally, the first part of the baby to emerge from the birth canal is the head. First it "crowns," or becomes visible, then it emerges farther with each contraction. Finally, in most normal births, the baby is born in a face-down position. Occasionally, obstetricians use steel or plastic *forceps* or a *vacuum extractor* (a cup placed on the baby's head and connected to a suction device) to grasp the head and hasten the birth, especially if complications arise.

During birth, the tissue of the mother's *perineum* (the region between the vagina and the rectum) must stretch considerably to allow the baby's head to emerge. In U.S. hospitals, the attending physician sometimes makes an incision called an **episiotomy** to enlarge the vaginal opening. It is believed that an incision will heal more neatly than the jagged tear that might otherwise occur. However, the practice of routine episiotomy has declined notably, with one study reporting the rate of 60.9% in 1979 versus a rate of 24.5% in 2004 (Frankman, Wang, Bunker, & Lowder, 2009). In part, this decline has been the result of the increasing use of cesarean delivery to address difficult births.

Afterbirth The expulsion of the placenta, the umbilical cord, and related tissues marks the third stage of childbirth, called **afterbirth**. This stage is virtually painless and typically occurs within 20 minutes after the delivery. Again, the mother can help by bearing down.

Approaches to Childbirth

Although the biology of childbirth is universal, the precise ways in which babies are delivered and cared for vary considerably across generations, across cultures, and from one family to another (McIntosh, 2012; Selin & Stone, 2009). For example, among the Cuna Indians of Panama, pregnant women traditionally visit the medicine man daily for drugs and are sedated throughout labor and delivery. Among the Kung-San, a tribal society in northwestern Botswana, women tell no one about their initial labor pains and go out into the bush alone to give

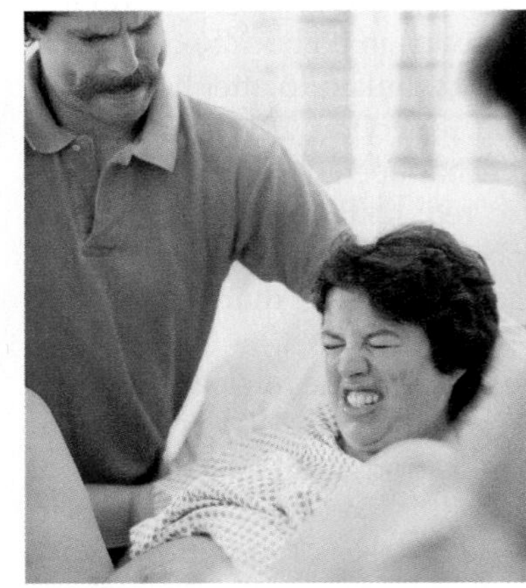

(a) Pushing

(b) Crowning

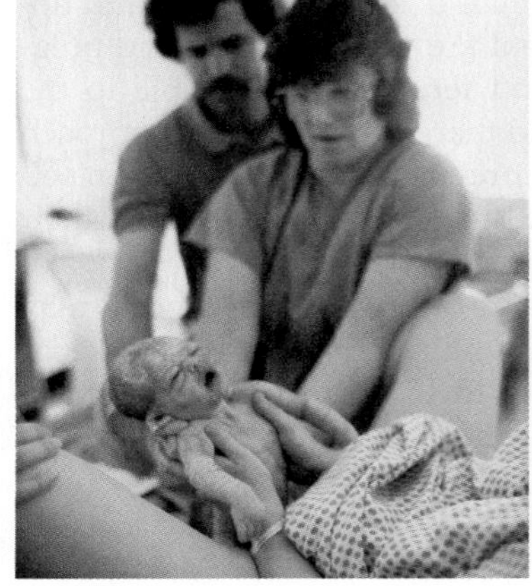

(c) Birth

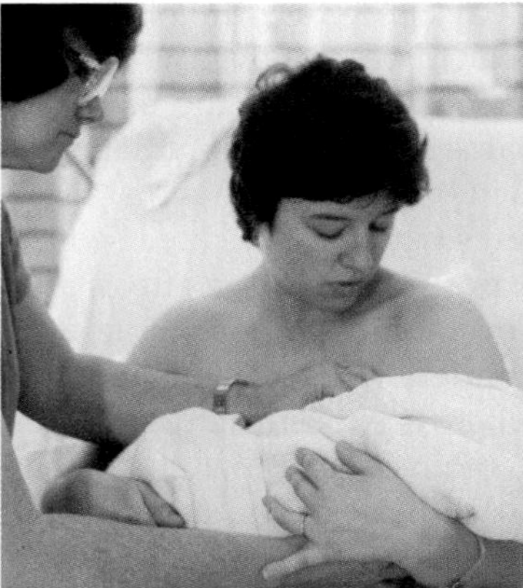

(d) Recovery

The sequence of childbirth.

false labor
Also called *Braxton–Hicks contractions*; contractions that generally diminish if the mother walks

afterbirth
The third and last stage of childbirth, typically occurs within 20 minutes after delivery, during which the placenta and the umbilical cord are expelled from the uterus

episiotomy
An incision to enlarge the vaginal opening

Watch *Labor* on MyDevelopmentLab

CHANGING PERSPECTIVES

Nurse–Family Partnerships: An Early Intervention Program That Works

During the prenatal period and the first 30 months of life, essential sensory, cognitive, and language systems are established that will guide later developmental processes. If development goes smoothly during this critical early period, the child is well positioned to handle later challenges successfully. However, not all children have a great start in life. Based on his early work in an inner-city day-care center, Dr. David Olds decided to tackle the problem of early-life intervention. Now, more than 30 years later, his "Nurse–Family Partnership" program has been implemented in 37 states and has improved the lives of hundreds of thousands of young families. What is the program, and how does it work to get life off to a positive start for the at-risk infants involved?

Essentially, the Nurse–Family Partnership is a public health program that focuses on helping mothers have healthier pregnancies, improving child health and early development, and increasing the self-sufficiency of mothers (Olds, 2010a). The program operates by providing first-time, low-income mothers, most of whom are unmarried teenagers, with home visitation services from public health nurses. The Nurse–Family Partnership begins when the mother is 20 to 28 weeks into her first pregnancy and focuses on addressing substance abuse issues and other behaviors that contribute to family poverty, subsequent pregnancies, poor maternal and infant outcomes, and poor child-care opportunities. Each mother enrolled in the program is matched with a highly trained public health nurse, who visits her every 1 to 2 weeks for the next 30 months, until the infant is about age 2. During these visits, the nurse talks with the mother and helps her anticipate and cope with the challenges associated with pregnancy and early child rearing (Nurse–Family Partnership, 2012). For example, during pregnancy, the nurse helps the mother find appropriate prenatal care, improve her diet, and reduce her use of cigarettes, alcohol, and illegal substances. She also helps the mother prepare for the arrival of her baby by educating her on the childbirth process and the immediate changes in lifestyle that having a newborn entails. Later, after the birth, the nurse provides coaching and education for the new mother, helping her understand the significance of good-quality care and encouraging her to use a nurturing and nonviolent child-rearing approach. Nurses in the program also work with the mother's existing support system, including family members, father, and friends, and assist in finding access to other health and human services the family may need. Here the focus may be on the mother's return to school, finding employment, and planning for future pregnancies.

How well does the program work? The Nurse–Family Partnership has attracted substantial support and funding because it is evidence based, and the results of the program show clearly that it works. For example, the following outcomes have been obtained (Council for Excellence in Government, 2008; Nurse–Family Partnership, 2012):

- 48% reduction in child abuse and neglect
- 56% reduction in emergency room visits for accidents and poisonings
- 59% reduction in arrests at age 15 for children raised in the program
- 67% reduction in behavioral and intellectual problems for children at age 6
- 72% fewer criminal convictions of mothers with children at age 15
- 20% less time spent on welfare
- 9 to 10% higher scores in reading and math for grade school children whose mothers were in the program

Additionally, infant health and development are improved, as reflected by better early language development, less difficulty at school entry, and better educational and occupational outcomes for children whose mothers are served.

The Nurse–Family Partnership program, of course, is not free. The total program costs are about $4,500 per family for each year of the 3-year program (Nurse–Family Partnership, 2012), with expenses borne by a variety of federal, state, and local agencies, as well as major nonprofit foundations. However, the benefit to society is about 5 times the dollars spent, realized mostly through a reduced need to access other government-based welfare programs (Nurse–Family Partnership, 2012). The investment of resources early in development has the potential to yield lifelong benefits to those involved, and the Nurse–Family Partnership looks to be an effective method for improving the opportunities of low-income mothers and their families (Olds, 2010b). By convincing young mothers that their new child is full of promise and is the most important person in their lives, visiting nurses are able to successfully encourage them to make major life changes that improve outcomes for their children and family members, as well as for themselves.

---

birth, where they deliver the baby, cut the cord, and stabilize the newborn—all without assistance (Barr, 2011; Cassidy, 2006).

In some cultures, home birthing is still the norm. However, today in most developed nations, the large majority of births take place in hospitals (Misago, Umenai, Noguchi, Mori, & Mori, 2000; Zander & Chamberlain, 1999). In the United States, for example, for each 1,000 babies born in a hospital, only about 6 are born at home (MacDorman, Menacker, & Declercq, 2010).

Watch *Pregnancy and Prenatal Care Across Cultures* on **MyDevelopmentLab**

midwife
A woman who is experienced in childbirth, with or without training, who assists with home delivery

traditional childbirth
Hospital labor and delivery, which treats childbirth as a medical procedure

What cultural factors might be involved in a woman's choices about childbirth options?

The Changing Views of Childbirth Childbirthing practices in the United States have changed rather dramatically over the past century (Wolf, 2009). One hundred years ago childbirth meant home delivery, often with the assistance of a family doctor or a **midwife**—a woman experienced in childbirth.

By the middle of the 20th century, as medicine improved and hospitals became more widely available, childbirth increasingly came to be viewed as a medical "procedure" rather than as a natural event. Correspondingly, in most Western nations, home births dropped from about 80% in 1930 to less than 1% in 2004 (MacDorman, Menacker, & Declercq, 2010). Other birthing practices also have changed. In the middle of the 20th century, for example, **traditional childbirth** was the norm. Traditional childbirth, the term used to describe hospital childbirth procedures performed by a medical team, usually meant that fathers were excluded from the labor and delivery rooms, and delivery often involved sedation or anesthesia for the mother, as would be the case for other surgical procedures (Fisanick, 2009; Wolf, 2009).

Contemporary Childbirth Practices Today, many women prefer a return to a more natural approach to childbirth, but with the ready availability of medical intervention if it is needed. This perspective, often called **"natural"** or **prepared childbirth**, is usually based on procedures developed by Fernand Lamaze (1958, 1970), although many variations of a relaxation-based approach to childbirth are available (Buckley, 2009; Camann & Alexander, 2006; Leboyer, 2009). In prepared childbirth, the expectant mother and her coach (father, family member, or friend) attend a short series of classes, where they learn about the biology of childbirth, and the mother practices relaxation exercises and control of her breathing with the coach serving as her assistant. (The relaxation exercises help reduce the pain of labor and delivery; the breathing and other techniques help distract the mother from any discomfort she may be feeling.) Fathers or partners can be more involved in the labor and delivery process as coaches and many new parents view this role as "partner" to be a significant one (Bradley, Hathaway, Hathaway, & Hathaway, 2008; Simkin, 2008). When the day arrives, the coach is present throughout childbirth to provide support and to help the mother stay as relaxed as possible. Medication is often kept to a minimum or perhaps not used at all, so the mother is conscious and alert and actively assists in the birthing process, thereby retaining a sense of control in the birth of the child. Because pain medications typically cross the placental barrier, babies also are more alert when medication is limited. However, a variety of anesthetics are available to mothers who need or request them (Wolf, 2009).

In many areas of the United States, hospitals are now providing delivery and recovery rooms that are more homelike or entire **birthing centers** or suites, either within or near the hospital (Kinnon, 1998). Birthing centers are designed to accommodate the entire childbirth process from labor through delivery and recovery; thus, they attempt to combine the privacy and intimacy of a home birth with the safety and backup of medical technology (Learner, 2005; Stoppard, 2012). Most birthing centers encourage prepared childbirth and an early return home, generally within 24 to 48 hours. They also encourage mothers to spend as much time as possible with their newborns to help promote early attachment, in contrast to earlier practices in which the baby was whisked away after birth and kept in a hospital nursery, perhaps for days. Most parents find birthing centers deeply satisfying. The centers keep the focus on the family and give the parents the maximum possible independence and control. Today, in most Western cultures childbirth is likely to be viewed as a natural, nonpathological event during which technological intervention should be kept to a minimum, unless needed to protect the well-being of the mother or child (see the accompanying box, Try This! Birthing Practices: Yesterday and Today).

Advances in Technology

Despite a return to the view that childbirth is a natural process rather than a medical event, technological innovations have improved both the safety associated with childbirth and the amount of information that parents and medical personnel can access before the birth actually begins.

Prenatal Screening Prenatal screening is sometimes used to determine whether a child will be "at risk" during childbirth, as well as whether or not congenital anomalies are present. Three popular assessment procedures—ultrasound, amniocentesis, and chorionic villus sampling (CVS)—are discussed here, with additional procedures presented in Table 3-6.

Ultrasound is the least invasive and most widely used method to provide information about the growth and health of the fetus. Harmless high-frequency sound waves are generated and recorded by a handheld device, much like a microphone, that is moved across the mother's abdomen; these then are used to produce a picture called a *sonogram*. Sonograms can detect structural problems such as body malformations, especially cranial anomalies such as *microcephaly* (extremely small upper head), which is associated with severe intellectual disability and perhaps death. Though it has traditionally been done around the 15th week, ultrasound with modern high-resolution scanning can now be done much earlier, usually in doctors' offices, clinics, and hospitals. For example, early ultrasound scanning is indicated if doctors suspect an *ectopic* (tubal) pregnancy, where implantation occurs in the fallopian tube rather than the uterus, a condition that is extremely hazardous for the mother (American Pregnancy Association, 2012b).

Because they appear to be safe and are noninvasive, many physicians use ultrasounds as a routine part of prenatal care (Medline Plus, 2012b; Siddique, Lauderdale, VanderWeele, & Lantos, 2009). However, these tests do add to the expense of prenatal care, and parents should know that ultrasounds are not required when the pregnancy is proceeding normally. Recently, commercial operations have begun to sell elective "nonmedical" ultrasounds to parents-to-be, advertising these pictures as "first portraits" of the baby. Is this a good idea? Most professionals

"natural" or prepared childbirth
Childbirth based on procedures developed by Fernand Lamaze, a French obstetrician who advocated treating childbirth as a natural, rather than a medical, process; usually emphasizes relaxation training and assistance from a "coach," who often is the father

birthing center
Place designed to accommodate the entire birth process, from labor through delivery and recovery; is set up to be more home-like, although it may reside in a hospital

Watch *Prenatal Ultrasound* on MyDevelopmentLab

ultrasound
A technique that uses sound waves to produce a picture of the fetus in the uterus

Watch *Conception, Pregnancy, and Childbirth: Dr. Holly Casele, Obstetrician* on MyDevelopmentLab

TRY THIS!

Birthing Practices: Yesterday and Today

Modern medical technology has advanced with incredible speed over the past several years, affecting the ways in which childbirth is routinely managed. How have birthing practices changed over time? To investigate this question, identify one or more friends or family members who have recently given birth, perhaps in the past 1 or 2 years. Next, interview some mothers of 1 or even 2 generations ago. Perhaps you might talk with your mother, your aunts, family friends, or your grandmother. Prepare a set of questions that will help you to understand what the birthing experience was like for these people. You might ask questions such as the following:

- What was the setting like where you gave birth?
- What medical practices were used?
- Did you receive any medications?
- How much did you know about your baby before he or she was born?
- Who was present when your baby was born?
- Did you experience critical moments in the birthing process?
- What advice did you receive from medical personnel or from family and friends about how to cope with the birth?
- How did you feel about the birth process?

Use your own judgment and interest to guide the questions you choose to explore.

Reflect on What You Observed

How have birthing practices changed over time, as reflected by the experiences of the people you interviewed? Do you think the experiences of the women you interviewed were typical, given the time when their babies were born?

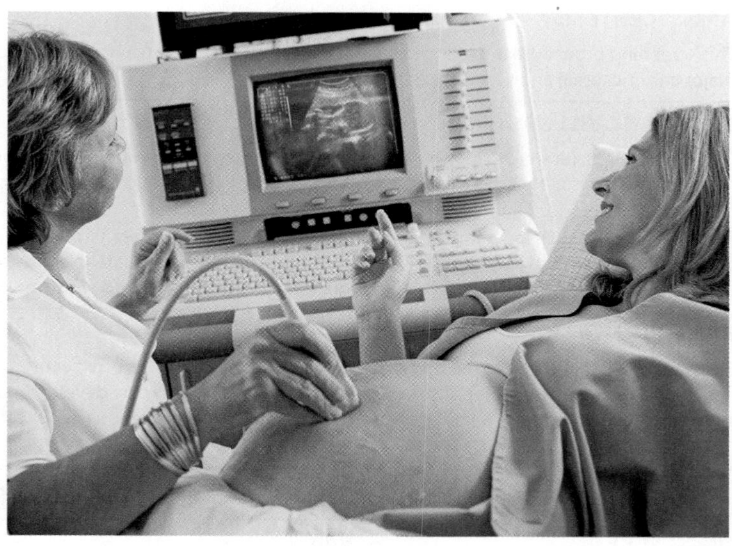

▲ The safety and reliability of ultrasound imagery used to inspect the fetus makes this technique popular among medical professionals.

Consider the Issues

What are some of the advantages and disadvantages of today's birthing practices in comparison to those of earlier decades? Do you think that birthing practices have advanced? In what ways? Are there ways in which modern practices detract from the experience of childbirth? If so, how? Across generations, were the mothers' experiences much the same or were they different? What were some of the family meanings of the birth event; for example, was the birth of a child considered to be more a medical–surgical event, a personal challenge, or a family milestone? Do you think these meanings have shifted from earlier times to today? If so, how?

---

conclude "probably not." Although ultrasound techniques appear to be safe, there are ethical issues involved, including the concern about what to do if the ultrasound reveals a problem with the fetus or the pregnancy (Leung & Pang, 2009). At present, ultrasound is best considered a medical procedure, to be performed when health care providers determine it would be useful in monitoring or protecting the health of the mother or her baby.

In **amniocentesis**, amniotic fluid is withdrawn from the amniotic sac with a syringe inserted through the mother's abdomen. The fluid contains discarded fetal cells, which can be karyotyped and analyzed for chromosomal or genetic anomalies (see Chapter 2). This procedure is usually done between the 14th and 20th weeks of pregnancy (*standard* amniocentesis), although it can be done as early as the 11th week (*early* amniocentesis) (American Pregnancy Association, 2012a). Either way, the results are not available for about 2 weeks because the fetal cells must be cultured. Obstetricians routinely recommend that women over age 35 consider amniocentesis because of age-related risks of genetic anomalies, especially Down syndrome. Amniocentesis usually is performed in conjunction with ultrasound so that the needle can be inserted into the amniotic sac without harming the fetus. The primary risk associated with amniocentesis is miscarriage, which occurs in about 1 of 400 procedures (American Pregnancy Association, 2006).

Why would a woman want to schedule an amniocentesis for earlier rather than later in her pregnancy?

Chorionic villus sampling (CVS) is a diagnostic procedure in which cells are drawn from the membranes that surround the fetus, either with a syringe or with a catheter. It is used to diagnose most of the same conditions as amniocentesis, but CVS can be conducted about 4 weeks earlier, usually at between 10 and 12 weeks after conception. However, the CVS procedure involves

amniocentesis
The withdrawal and analysis of amniotic fluid with a syringe to obtain discarded fetal cells for testing

chorionic villus sampling (CVS)
The withdrawal and analysis of cells from the membranes that surround the fetus, either with a syringe or with a catheter. Because more cells are collected in this procedure than in amniocentesis, the test can be completed more quickly

Table 3-6 Prenatal Assessment Methods

AMNIOCENTESIS
This screening procedure is used to obtain discarded fetal cells by using a syringe to withdraw a sample of amniotic fluid. The cells can be karyotyped and analyzed for major chromosomal and some genetic abnormalities.
CHORIONIC VILLUS SAMPLING (CVS)
In this procedure, fetal cells for karyotyping are drawn from the membranes that surround the fetus, either with a syringe or with a catheter.
FETOSCOPY
Fetoscopy is used to inspect the fetus for limb and facial abnormalities. In this method, a needle that contains a light source is inserted into the uterus to view the fetus directly and to withdraw a sample of fetal blood or tissue for the prenatal diagnosis of genetic disorders. Fetoscopy usually is not done until 15 to 18 weeks after conception. The risk of miscarriage and infection is greater than that associated with amniocentesis.
PREIMPLANTATION GENETIC DIAGNOSIS
Following *in vitro* (outside of the body) fertilization and culturing of a prospective mother's ovum, a single cell is microsurgically removed soon after cell division begins and analyzed for genetic defects. If the DNA is found to be healthy, the developing zygote will then be placed into the mother's body for implantation. Preimplantion screening is expensive, but it has been used successfully to detect serious genetic disorders, such as cystic fibrosis, hemophilia, sickle-cell anemia, and Tay–Sachs disease.
ULTRASOUND
In this screening procedure, high-frequency sound waves produce a picture of the fetus, which is called a *sonogram*. Sonograms can detect structural problems.
QUAD SCREEN
A quad screen is a prenatal test that measures four substances in a pregnant woman's blood, which is collected by a routine blood draw. Typically, the test is done between weeks 15 and 20 of pregnancy, and it is used, along with other factors such as the mother's age and her health status, to assess the risk that the baby has certain developmental or chromosomal conditions, such as spina bifida (a disorder of the spine and spinal cord) or Down syndrome. If the test indicates that a high risk for one of these conditions is present, then the mother can decide whether or not to pursue more invasive diagnostic testing, such as amniocentesis, for confirmation.
GESTATIONAL DIABETES TESTING
Some women develop a form of pregnancy-specific diabetes, called gestational diabetes, that can compromise their own, and their baby's, health. The test, which normally is done between the 24th and 28th week of pregnancy, consists of drinking a syrupy glucose (sugar) solution, followed an hour later by a blood test to determine if the mother is metabolizing the sugar normally. If the blood sugar level is higher than normal, other tests are likely to be performed and the mother's health status will be carefully monitored.
OTHER MATERNAL BLOOD ANALYSES
Because some fetal byproducts enter the maternal bloodstream early in pregnancy, maternal blood analysis can be a helpful diagnostic tool around 8 weeks after conception. One common maternal blood analysis tests for alpha fetoprotein, which is elevated if the fetus has kidney disease, an abnormal esophageal closure, or severe central nervous system abnormalities.

slightly more risk than standard amniocentesis (MedlinePlus, 2012a), so those who choose CVS often do so because there is a high probability that they are carrying a baby with a serious genetic abnormality. Should they choose it, abortion is safer early in the pregnancy (before 12 weeks) and also tends to have less serious psychological effects on the parents than abortion later in pregnancy. Early studies sometimes linked CVS to defects in a baby's finger or toes; however, this risk appears to be a concern only if the procedure is done before the ninth week of pregnancy (Mayo Clinic, 2010a).

High Technology for High-Risk Pregnancies In the past 30 years, obstetrical medicine has progressed dramatically. Infants who would not have survived in the 1970s are now thriving in record numbers. For example, over 75% of premature infants born today who weigh 750 to 1,000 grams (1.6 to 2.2 pounds) will survive in a well-equipped intensive care unit for newborns; in 1972, only 20% survived.

Improved survival rates are the result of many types of medical advances. One common technique involves the use of **fetal monitors**, which can be applied either externally or internally. An *external* monitor records the intensity of uterine contractions and the baby's heartbeat by means of two belts placed around the mother's abdomen. Continuous external monitoring from the beginning of labor typically is used in births where potential complications, such as bleeding during labor, a very long or fast labor, or maternal high blood pressure, occur.

Internal monitoring is a more invasive procedure that records contractions, the baby's heartbeat, and other critical functioning more directly. An internal monitor consists of a plastic tube containing electrodes that are inserted into the vagina and attached to the baby's head. It can assess uterine pressure, fetal

Watch *Chorionic Villus Testing* on **MyDevelopmentLab**

fetal monitor
The external monitor records the intensity of uterine contractions and the baby's heartbeat by means of two belts placed around the mother's abdomen. The internal monitor consists of a plastic tube containing electrodes that is inserted through the vagina and attached to the baby's head

breathing, head compression, umbilical compression, and poor fetal oxygen intake. Typically, internal monitoring is indicated only in high-risk situations, because its use is linked to an increase in otherwise unnecessary cesarean sections.

Complications in Childbirth

A variety of circumstances can give rise to complications in childbirth, in addition to the risk factors previously noted. For example, the amniotic sac may rupture prematurely, leaving the fetus unprotected and vulnerable to infections. Sometimes labor may be delayed or it may be so prolonged that the fetus is placed at risk. In addition, when the baby is positioned in **breech presentation** (buttocks first; see Figure 3-5) or *posterior presentation* (facing the mother's abdomen rather than her back), a more difficult birth process often results.

Cesarean Section When complications arise or when the fetus experiences distress during labor, the childbirth team may resort to **cesarean section** surgery, in which the baby is removed through the mother's abdominal wall. This procedure, which is also called C-section, frequently is performed under regional anesthesia so that the mother is awake and aware. Because the procedure is quick, very little of the anesthesia reaches the infant, and the outcome for both mother and infant is excellent in most cases.

Do you think the percentage of births in the United States by cesarean section will continue to rise in the next decade, or will it level off or decline? What factors might be involved?

Nevertheless, many researchers believe that the rate of cesarean births—which in the United States was more than 32% in 2009 (Martin, et al., 2011)—is far too high (Yamamoto, 2011): C-sections continue to be the most common form of major surgery; some hospitals perform over 40% of childbirths by this method. Some consumer advocates suggest that the high rate of cesarean births is a result of increased, but unnecessary, technology in the delivery room, which often includes the use of invasive prenatal screening, fetal monitoring, and routine use of drugs to induce labor. Supporting this position, in 1999 the American Academy of Pediatrics (AAP, 1999) took the position that electronic fetal monitoring should be abandoned in low-risk pregnancies because "... this technology hurts women by increasing operative delivery rates" (p. 1037).

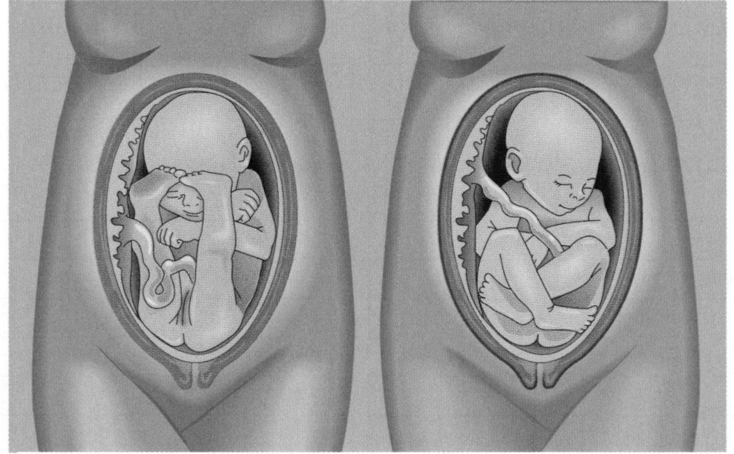

FIGURE 3-5 Two Types of Breech Presentation
Delivery in breech presentation is difficult for both the mother and the infant.

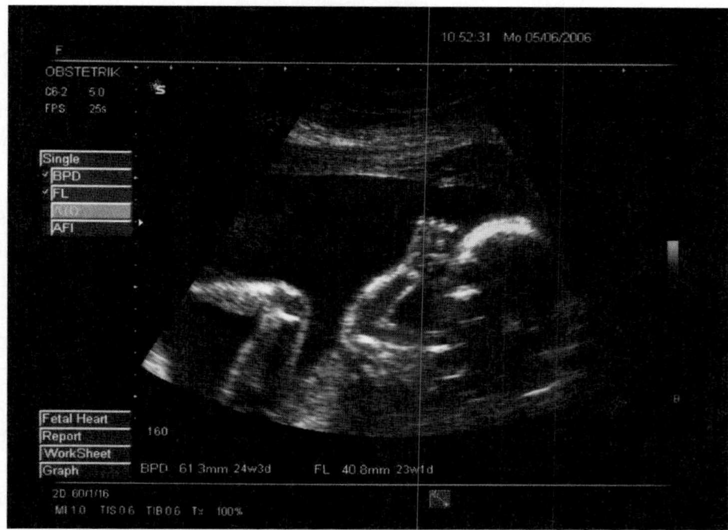

▲ Sonograms such as this one at 5 months can be an important medical tool to help assess the health and developmental progress of the fetus. In addition, proud parents may begin to "bond" with this unique image and bring the print home as the expected child's first portrait.

Why is the high rate of C-sections a problem, given that the procedure is relatively safe? One reason is that it is major abdominal surgery that requires a much longer recovery period than normal childbirth. Also, it is expensive and puts a greater financial strain on parents and their health insurance providers, although in cases of difficult birth the cost of a C-section is usually comparable to that of vaginal delivery (Palencia, et al., 2006). In some of the cases in which it is used, it may not improve outcomes: For example, in the case of breech presentation, vaginal delivery usually results in an equally good outcome for mother and baby (Hannah, et al., 2002). Also, many doctors continue to recommend C-sections for all subsequent deliveries, once one has been performed. However, new surgical techniques render that recommendation questionable. Today between 60–80% of women who have previously undergone cesarean birth can have a normal vaginal delivery (American Pregnancy Association, 2012c; Mayo Clinic, 2011). Finally and perhaps most important, some mothers' psychological reactions to cesarean childbirth can be quite negative (Waldenstroem, 1999), especially if they had

breech presentation
The baby's position in the uterus where the head will emerge last; assistance is sometimes needed in such cases to prevent injury to the infant, including anoxia

cesarean section
Surgical procedure used to remove the baby and the mother's placenta from the uterus by cutting through the mother's abdominal wall

general instead of regional anesthesia and "missed the event." However, psychological responses to childbirth are complex, and cultural factors in many instances play an important role. Nevertheless, although mothers are informed of the risks of C-sections, as well as of the benefits, the percentage of births by C-section has increased over the past two decades.

The Apgar Scale Regardless of *how* they are born, not all newborns are equally well equipped to adjust to the changes that occur at birth, and it is essential to detect any problems or weaknesses as early as possible. In 1953, Virginia Apgar devised a standard scoring system that allows hospitals to evaluate a newborn's condition quickly and objectively. The **Apgar Scoring System** is presented in Table 3-7. At 1 minute and again at 5 minutes after birth, the scorer observes the newborn's pulse, breathing, muscle tone, general reflex response, and general skin tone, giving a rating of 0, 1, or 2 to each factor. A perfect Apgar score is 10 points, with a score of 7 or more considered normal. Scores below 7 indicate that some bodily processes are not functioning fully and may require special procedures. Babies with a score of 4 or less require immediate emergency measures. Particularly when the Apgar scores are low, a newborn may also be assessed on the more detailed Brazelton Neonatal Behavioral Assessment Scale (see Chapter 4), and early development will be tracked very closely to determine if any long-term consequences are likely.

Premature Birth A relatively common risk factor is *prematurity,* a general term used to describe babies who are born too early or are too small. Prematurity can occur for a number of reasons, the most common of which is a multiple birth, in which two or more infants are born at the same time. Other causes include disabilities of the fetus, maternal diseases, maternal smoking or other drug use, and malnutrition; prematurity can result from many of the same causes as miscarriage.

The most common indicator of prematurity is *low birth weight* (LBW), defined by the World Health Organization (WHO) as weighing less than 5 pounds 8 ounces (2.5 kilograms) at birth (WHO, 2011). LBW most often results from one of two situations, which are sometimes confused. The first is **preterm status**. An infant born before a gestation period of 35 weeks (or 37 weeks from the mother's last menstrual period) is preterm, and most preterm infants have LBW. The second indicator is **small-for-date**. A *full-term* newborn who is LBW is considered small-for-date. Fetal malnutrition is one cause of small-for-date babies.

What kinds of emotional responses do you think would be typical for parents whose baby is born prematurely?

Regardless of whether an infant is preterm or small-for-date, premature infants usually have greater difficulty adjusting to the external world than do healthy, full-term babies. For example, immediately after birth, temperature control is a common problem: Premature infants have even fewer fat cells than full-term infants, and they have a harder time maintaining body heat. For this reason, newborns with LBW are usually placed in incubators immediately after birth. Another common problem with premature infants involves providing appropriate nutrition: In their first few months, most premature infants are unable to catch up to full-term infants in weight and height.

Some premature infants experience difficulties that can lead to problems later in development. For example, learning disabilities and hyperactivity are more common among premature than full-term, normal-birth-weight babies (e.g., Claas, et al., 2011; Groen-Blokhuis, van Beijsterveldt, & Boomsma, 2011; Shum, Neulinger, O'Callaghan, & Mohay, 2008; Taylor & Espy, 2009), although the possible means by which such problems may develop is unclear. The relationship between prematurity and later problems is undoubtedly complex. For example, prenatal conditions such as malnutrition, faulty development of the placenta, or crowding in the uterus may result in a number of symptoms, only one of which is prematurity.

Table 3-7 The Apgar Scoring System for Newborns

	Scores		
	0	**1**	**2**
Pulse	Absent	Less than 100	More than 100
Breathing	Absent	Slow, irregular	Strong cry
Muscle tone	Limp	Some flexion of extremities	Active motion
Reflex response	No response	Grimace	Vigorous cry
Color*	Blue, pale	Body pink	Completely pink

*For non-Whites, alternative tests of mucous membranes, palms, and soles are used.

SOURCE: From "Proposal for a new method of evaluating the newborn infant," by V. Apgar, 1953, *Anesthesia and Analgesia, 32,* p. 260. Copyright 1953. Reprinted by permission of Lippincott, Williams & Wilkins.

Apgar Scoring System
A standard scoring system that allows physicians to evaluate an infant's health status quickly and objectively

small-for-date
A full-term newborn who weighs less than 5 pounds 8 ounces

Watch *Premature Birth and the Neonatal Intensive Care Unit* on **MyDevelopmentLab**

preterm status
An infant born before a gestation period of 35 weeks

Thus, prematurity is often a *symptom* of an abnormality rather than a cause.

Because of their fragile health, premature babies typically receive special medical care, often with the result that they have less caregiver contact. Because studies have demonstrated that early care and attention are instrumental in forming the base for later attachment and development, hospitals now encourage parents and other caregivers of premature infants to interact by holding, calming, and stroking them; by breastfeeding; and by participating in their care (Nilsson & Hamberger, 2009). A new technique called *kangaroo care* emphasizes the role that close physical contact and a quiet, calm environment can play in helping premature babies through their first challenging weeks (see Current Issues: Kangaroo Care for Low-Birth-Weight Infants—An Experimental Approach Being Tried in Countries Around the World). Early contact and attention seem to contribute to higher social and intellectual competence throughout childhood, thereby setting the stage for successful development later in life.

REVIEW THE FACTS 3-3

1. During labor and delivery, contractions occur about every
   a. 5 to 10 minutes. b. 2 to 3 minutes.
   c. minute. d. 15 to 30 seconds.
2. Why would physicians perform an episiotomy?
3. Which period of labor is associated with the most discomfort for the mother?
4. At about what prenatal age is ultrasound usually first performed?
   a. 2nd week b. 15th week
   c. 24th week d. 32nd week
5. The use of internal fetal monitors is linked to which of the following?
   a. increase in unnecessary cesarean sections
   b. increase in brain damage to the unborn baby
   c. increase in development of learning disabilities in childhood
   d. decrease in medications given to the mother
6. Over the past two decades, the rate of C-section births has
   a. increased. b. decreased.
   c. stayed the same. d. fluctuated dramatically.
7. If a baby is born at 38 weeks and weighs 4 pounds, this condition would be called ______________.

Practice on **MyDevelopmentLab**

THE EVOLVING FAMILY

Regardless of how a baby enters the world, he or she is born into a particular environment that will have a profound impact of how development proceeds. For nearly all infants the most important context in which early development takes place is the family.

The Transition to Parenthood

As we have seen, childbirth is not just a medical event; it also is a psychological and a social milestone full of meaning for the family. Especially when the pregnancy is planned, parents usually are elated and eager to experience the joys of parenting. However, the months before a baby's birth can be stressful as well, as mothers and fathers plan and adjust in anticipation of their baby's birth (Boyce, Condon, Barton, & Corkindale, 2007).

The transition to becoming a parent begins well before a child is born and continues well afterward. It is conditioned both by culture and by the biological changes that occur in a mother's body as pregnancy progresses. For example, motivations for childbearing vary considerably from one culture to another (Raphael-Leff, 2010). In some cultures, children are valued as financial assets or as providers for the parents in their old age. In others, children represent those who will maintain family traditions or fulfill parents' personal needs and goals. Sometimes children are regarded simply as a duty or a necessary burden. Children are accepted as inevitable in other cultures and as a natural part of life for which conscious decision making is not necessary. In India, for example, traditional Hindu women want to have children to guarantee themselves a good life and afterlife (LeVine, 1989).

Adjustments for the Mother In all cultures, pregnant women must adjust to the physical, psychological, and social changes that come with motherhood (Fisanick, 2009; LeVay & Baldwin, 2009). Even before the fetus is large enough to cause alterations in a woman's appearance, she may feel nauseated or experience fullness or a tingling sensation in her breasts. Often she may suffer fatigue and emotional hypersensitivity during the early weeks of pregnancy—with direct effects on other family members. In contrast, in the middle stage of pregnancy, a woman may experience a sense of heightened well-being. In fact, some of her bodily systems, such as the circulatory system, may show increased capacity and functioning. Finally, in the last stages of pregnancy, some physical discomfort is usual, along with, at times, a feeling of emotional burden. Increased weight, reduced mobility, altered balance, pressure on internal organs from the growing fetus, and hormonal fluctuations are among the changes experienced by all pregnant women. Other symptoms, such as varicose veins, heartburn, frequent urination, and shortness of breath, contribute to the discomfort some women feel. There are wide individual differences in the *amount* of discomfort, fatigue, or emotional concern women experience during the last few weeks; and some women find the last stages of pregnancy to be much easier than do others.

What do you think are the most typical concerns prospective parents experience today? How might these vary among individuals of different social, cultural, or gender groups?

Not surprisingly, pregnancy usually affects the mother's psychological state as well; it is often accompanied by considerable uncertainty about the future. In particular, the mother may be unsure about her career plans following childbirth, and she may be anxious about her ability to care for a child, fearful of the possibility of congenital anomalies, concerned about finances,

CURRENT ISSUES

Kangaroo Care for Low-Birth-Weight Infants: An Experimental Approach Being Tried in Countries Around the World

The developing countries of the world have made major medical advances in the last several decades in caring for very small premature infants. With good postnatal care, many small infants today not only survive their precarious start but also develop with few, if any, physical disabilities. However, just a decade ago, as many as one half of the children born prematurely—at 27 to 30 weeks or at a weight less than 1,000 grams—grew up with learning disabilities, which often became apparent in middle childhood and adolescence. Researchers noticed that oftentimes such children experienced difficulty with focusing their attention, planning, and organizing their tasks.

Given the important developments that take place in the nervous system during the last months of the prenatal period, top neonatal experts began to wonder if the highly stimulating, noisy environment of typical neonatal intensive care units (NICUs) might be contributing to some low-birth-weight infants' later problems. At 27 to 34 weeks, the fetal brain is fully engaged in important "wiring," establishing connections that will later determine important aspects of learning and behavior. For full-term infants, this period is spent in the quiet, warm, protected uterine environment, where noises are muffled and the primary stimulation is the rhythmic sounds of the mother's body. However, for those infants who are born too early, or are in some other way delayed in development, these final important weeks can be full of commotion, confusion, and unpredictability (Vandenberg, 2007).

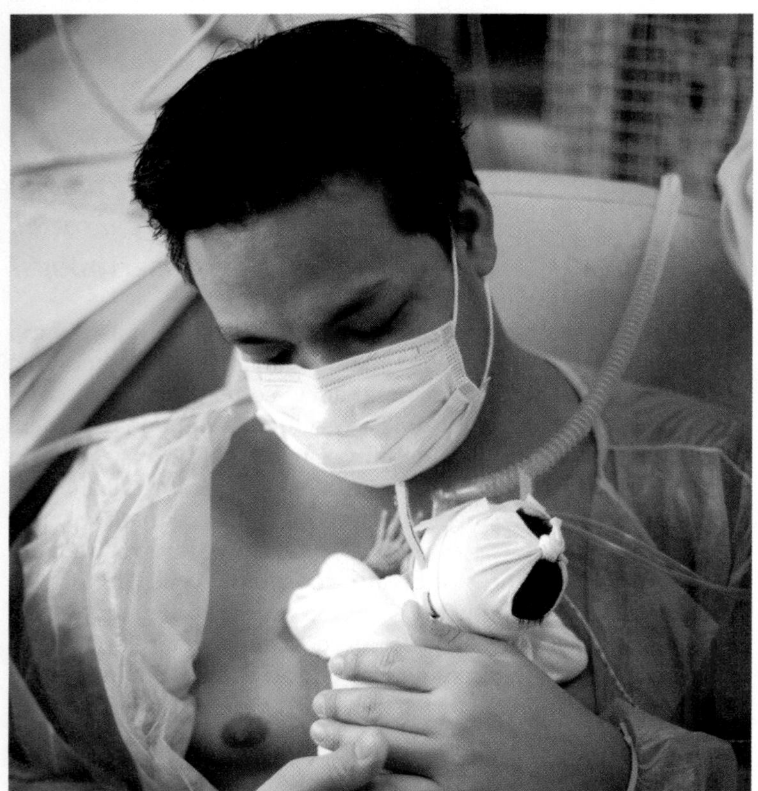

▲ Even fathers can do "kangaroo care."

Of course, a noisy and commotion-filled environment during birth is usually necessary to medically treat the fragile preemie. However, once the birth process was complete, experts wondered if something different could be done to help the infant cope with an environment that might be overwhelming. Some NICUs began to create infant-care settings that tried to mimic the calm, comforting womb experience in an attempt to assist these fragile babies in organizing their world. Quiet, semidark nooks were created in the hospital, where babies were placed directly on their mothers' (or fathers') chests, skin to skin, for several hours a day to help calm and stabilize the fragile baby. Small studies seemed to indicate that babies did well with the procedure: They slept longer, breastfed more effectively, and gained weight.

There is now a name for this procedure—*kangaroo care*—and it is being tried in several countries around the world to address the needs of the large numbers of children, especially in developing nations, who are born too soon or who are too small (March of Dimes, 2011; WHO, 2003). In a nutshell, kangaroo care—named after the way a kangaroo mother carries her young in a protected pouch after birth—involves early, continuous, and prolonged skin-to-skin contact between the infant and the mother (or other caregiver). It is initiated in the hospital, where parents can be coached in various techniques about positioning and carrying the infant, and mothers are usually encouraged to breastfeed, which provides another important way that mother–infant contact is established. It is a gentle method that avoids the agitation, commotion, and noise that usually exist in an NICU. It also involves providing support and guidance for mothers and caregivers of premature babies who are challenging to care for due to their special needs and fragile condition (Charpak, 2006).

Research on the effectiveness of kangaroo care in supporting normal development for premature babies is promising (Feldman, 2011). For example, in one longitudinal study conducted in Columbia (Tessier, et al., 2003), where kangaroo care is practiced widely, researchers examined the outcomes for 431 low-birth-weight and premature infants who were randomly assigned to receive either traditional care or kangaroo care. At 12 months of age, those who received kangaroo care were assessed to have higher IQs, and this positive impact was most pronounced for those infants who were more premature, who required more intensive care at birth, and who had a diagnosis of possible neurological problems at age 6 months. Furthermore, a follow-up study found that kangaroo care contributed to a better care-giving environment and greater father involvement, especially for baby boys (Tessier, et al., 2009). Importantly, evidence also suggests that kangaroo care promotes not only healthier parent–infant relationships but also faster brain maturation in healthy preterm infants (Scher et al., 2009), leading the World Health Organization to advocate for this practice throughout the world (The Partnership for Maternal, Newborn, and Child Health, 2011).

The techniques of kangaroo care are easily learned and generally are quickly and popularly adopted (Quasem, Sloan, Chawdhury, Ahmed, & Winikoff, 2003). They also help build confidence in parents of fragile babies. As one new mother of a premature baby commented, "I used to be worried by what I would see or hear in the (hospital) nursery, but as I learned to feel my baby get stronger in the K (Kangaroo) position, I started to visit the baby more often because it was not a scary place anymore" (Robles & McCoshen, 2008). It seems both mothers and babies may benefit from using kangaroo care techniques. This early intensive, skin-to-skin contact has no negative implications for development, and it may give some fragile babies—especially those born in parts of the world where technological advances in medicine are not widely available—a better start in life.

or uncomfortable with the idea of being a mother. Ambivalence is common: A woman may be eager to have a child, yet disappointed when she must share her time, energy, and husband with that child. Many women also wonder whether they will be able to fulfill the expectations of everyone who will need them, including the new baby, any older children, the husband, aging parents, close friends, and perhaps job supervisors and coworkers as well. Pregnancy is a time when prospective mothers experience many emotions.

The Father's Changing Role At first glance, the father's role seems easy compared to the major physical and emotional changes that the mother undergoes. Yet that usually isn't the case (Boyce, Condon, Barton, & Corkindale, 2007; Chin & Hall, 2011). Most fathers report feeling excited and proud, but some also feel "left out" by the mother's attention to the developing child. Most men also report an increased sense of responsibility that can seem overwhelming at times (Genesoni & Tallandini, 2009): Fathers worry about the future as much as mothers do. Many feel concern about their ability to support the new family and about their role as a parent. Fathers also tend to be concerned about whether the child will like and respect them and whether they will be able to meet the child's emotional needs. Some fathers take the opportunity to learn more about children and parenting; and some make new financial arrangements. Many attempt to give their wife more emotional support. When fathers are involved in their partner's pregnancy, the mothers are more likely to get first-trimester prenatal care, and, among mothers who smoked at conception, cigarette consumption has been shown to be significantly reduced (Martin, et al., 2007). Thus, the father's involvement during pregnancy and delivery can have a beneficial effect on not only his partner's health but also on his baby's and his own (Plantin, Olukoya, & Ny, 2011). When there are other children in the family, fathers often spend more time with them and help them prepare for the new arrival.

Expectant fathers also may go through a phase in which they identify with their wife and actually display symptoms of their wife's pregnancy. A somewhat extreme example occurs among the natives of the Yucatan in Mexico, where pregnancy is "confirmed" when the woman's *mate* experiences nausea, diarrhea, vomiting, or cramps (Pruett, 1987).

Pregnancy in a Changing World

Not all couples who wish to have children are able to do so. In the United States, about 10% of women have difficulty getting pregnant or staying pregnant, and fertility problems are about equally common in men and women (CDC, 2011e). Altogether, difficulty in conceiving a child is an issue for about 12% of U.S. couples (Asch & Marmor, 2008). However, thanks to the development of many forms of *reproductive technologies*, many couples who experience fertility problems are able to conceive a child (see Table 3-8). Today in the United States, about 4% of women who seek to become pregnant use one or more types of fertility treatments (Duwe, Reefhuis, Honein, Schieve, & Rasmussen, 2010).

One of the more intriguing fertility technologies involves the removal of ova from the woman's body, fertilization in the laboratory by introducing sperm to the dish where the eggs are kept, and then, after about 3 to 5 days, implantation of fertilized ova into the woman's uterus. Originally called the "test-tube babies" technique when it was introduced in 1981, these methods now are referred to as **assisted reproductive technologies**, or **ART**. ART, although time-consuming and expensive, has made it possible for many couples who could not conceive to become pregnant. Today, ART accounts for about 1% of the pregnancies conceived in the United States. Costs for ART vary widely among countries, with the United States standing out as the most expensive (Connolly, Hoorens, & Chambers, 2010). U.S. couples seeking ART treatment might expect to pay somewhere between $12,000 and $15,000 for one cycle of therapy, which, if unsuccessful, would need to be repeated (Asch & Marmor, 2008; MedlinePlus, 2010). Success is not guaranteed: The chances of giving birth to a live baby following a single trial of ART vary by maternal age, but range from about 42% for healthy women under age 35 to about 25% for those nearing age 40, and drop to about 15% for women over age 41 (MedlinePlus, 2010). In some cases health insurance plans cover the costs for ART, but in other cases these expenses must be paid by the parents. In estimating costs, it also is appropriate to consider the expenses of caring for multiple-birth pregnancies, which are more common with ART than in traditionally conceived pregnancies; about 11% of ART pregnancies involve multiple births. Finally, there is some question about whether or not ART-conceived children may be at slightly greater risk for developmental or medical problems (MedlinePlus, 2010).

ART, as well as the other reproductive technologies noted in Table 3-8, involve ethical and moral issues as well (Asch & Marmor, 2008; Horowitz, Galst, & Elster, 2010). There is, of course, the concern about any extra fertilized eggs that are not chosen for implantation. Especially for those who believe that life begins at conception, this is a serious consideration. Also, several types of ART allow gay and lesbian couples to have children, for example through the artificial insemination of a woman using a donor's sperm or through the use of a surrogate impregnated with sperm from a man. For those who view homosexuality as a moral issue, these practices are troubling. Costs are also an issue: Should access to ART be restricted to only those who can afford it? Other concerns center around surrogacy: Is it ethically acceptable to pay someone to carry a child? And, what if a contracted surrogate decides she wants to keep the child and not follow through with allowing the child to be adopted? Certainly difficult questions abound, leading the American Medical Association to convene a task force in 1996 to study the ethical issues associated with the use of reproductive technologies and practices and make recommendations. Irrespective of the challenges associated with fertility treatments of all sorts, it is important to keep in mind that many individuals and couples have found that the result—having a child of their own—is well worth the costs.

assisted reproductive technologies (ART)
Fertility treatments that involve extracting ova from the mother, fertilizing these ova with sperm in the laboratory, and implanting the fertilized eggs back into the mother's, or a surrogate's, uterus

Table 3-8 Common Approaches to Treating Infertility

ASSISTED REPRODUCTIVE TECHNOLOGIES (ART)

ART refers to a group of different methods by which ova are removed from the mother's body, are mixed with sperm from the father, and then fertilized zygotes are implanted in the mother's uterus. ART is expensive and time-consuming, but it does allow couples who could not conceive using other approaches to become pregnant. ART can involve the use of donor eggs or donor sperm, and also can be used in situations in which a surrogate is involved.

HORMONE THERAPY (ALSO CALLED FERTILITY DRUGS)

If the infertility problems are the result of ovulation problems, these can sometimes be corrected medically with the use of specific drugs that address a various types of hormonal problems. Infertility medicines can act on the pituitary gland, the ovaries, or other hormonal systems in the woman's body that may require re-regulation. One problem associated with the use of infertility drugs is that they sometimes work too well, stimulating the release of several ova, which can result in multiple-birth pregnancies. These multiple-birth pregnancies are accompanied by higher risks.

INTRAUTERINE INSEMINATION (IUI) (ALSO CALLED ARTIFICIAL INSEMINATION)

IUI involves collecting sperm, either from the father or a sperm donor, preparing it, and injecting it into the woman's body. IUI is used most often when the father has an inadequate supply of sperm, the mother has cervical mucus problems, or when the fertility problems are unexplained.

SURROGACY

When the mother cannot produce her own ova, or when she cannot carry a pregnancy to term, surrogacy can be an option. A surrogate is a woman who agrees to become pregnant using the father's sperm, or who agrees to carry the mother's fertilized egg in her uterus. The surrogate agrees to give up the baby for adoption to the parents following birth.

SURGERY

Sometimes infertility problems can be corrected with surgery, either for the mother or father.

The Arrival of the Neonate

It is easy to see that *both* parents' attitudes toward pregnancy and childbirth are shaped by their culture. Regardless of culture, however, the birth of a baby sets in play important transitions, both for the **neonate**—a term given to newborns up to about 1 month of age—and for their families.

The Trauma of Being Born "Birth trauma" is often addressed by personality theorists, like Freud, who view the changes associated with birth to be foundational for later personality development. Regardless of how one interprets such views, birth *is* a radical transition from the protected, supporting environment of the uterus to a much less certain, even harsh external environment. No longer will oxygen and nutrients be provided as needed. Newborns must breathe for themselves and learn to communicate their needs and wants in a social world that may or may not be responsive to them.

Childbirth is remarkably stressful for the newborn. However, a normal full-term baby is well prepared to cope. For example, in the last few moments before birth, infants experience a major surge of adrenaline and noradrenaline, the hormones that counter stress. The adrenaline also helps to counteract any initial oxygen deficiency and prepares babies for breathing through their lungs. The first breaths may be difficult because the amniotic fluid that was in the lungs must be expelled and millions of tiny sacs in the lungs must be filled with air; yet, within minutes, most infants are breathing regularly. Newborns also have relatively high levels of a natural painkiller called *beta-endorphin* circulating in their blood, and most infants are alert and receptive shortly after birth. Many experts have suggested that this period of extended alertness, which may last for an hour or more, is an ideal time for the parents and the infant to start getting acquainted (Fisanick, 2009; Nilsson & Hamberger, 2009).

Size and Appearance At birth, unprepared first-time parents are often surprised at the physical appearance of their newborn. If the birth is vaginal, the neonate's head probably looks misshapen and elongated because of a process called *molding*. At the time of birth, the soft, bony plates of the skull—called **fontanels**—are connected only by cartilage areas, which are squeezed together in the birth canal to allow the baby's head to pass through, giving the newborn a "cone-head" appearance. Fontanels do not fully harden and fuse until late in infancy, which is why an infant's or young toddler's head must be protected from bumps; otherwise, there is a risk of concussion. In addition, a neonate's external genitalia may appear enlarged because of the presence of hormones that passed to the baby prior to birth, and the body may be covered with remnants of the *vernix caseosa*, a cheesy-looking protective coating, or *lanugo* hair, which should disappear during the first month (Towle, 2009). Thus, the average full-term infant, who will weigh between 5 pounds 8 ounces and 9 pounds 8 ounces (2.5 to 4.3 kilograms) and is between 19 and 22 inches (48 to 56 centimeters) long, may not look like the smooth, plump infant shown on TV and in magazine ads.

The First Few Days: A Period of Adjustment Despite their helpless appearance, full-term newborns are sturdy little beings who are already making profound adaptations to their new lives (Nugent, Petrauskas, & Brazelton, 2009; Simkin, 2010). Over the first few days after birth, babies must make significant

neonate
Baby in the first month of life

fontanels
The soft, bony plates of the skull, connected by cartilage

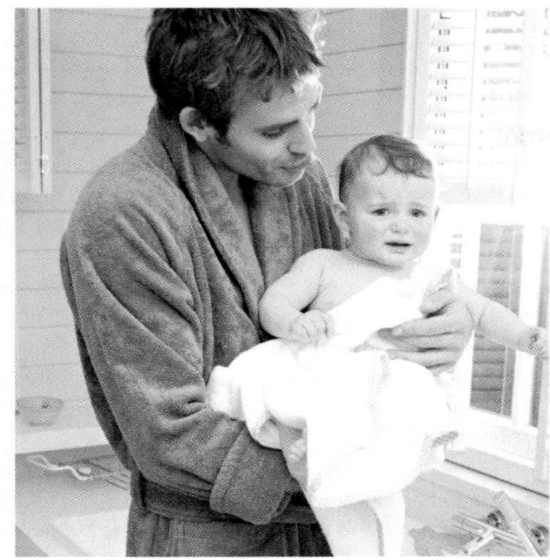

Both mothers and fathers must make major adjustments to their new roles and the pull and tug of family and job life. Fathers can play a very important role in helping their families adjust.

adjustments in respiration, blood circulation, digestion, and temperature regulation.

For example, with the first breaths of air, the lungs inflate and begin to work as the basic organ of the neonate's own respiratory system. During the first few days after birth, neonates usually experience periods of coughing and sneezing. These often alarm new parents, but they are a natural way to clear mucus and amniotic fluid from the infant's air passages. The onset of breathing also marks a significant change in the neonate's circulatory system. The baby's heart no longer needs to pump blood to the placenta for oxygen: Instead, a valve in the baby's heart closes and redirects the flow of blood to the lungs. Such changes begin immediately after birth but are not completed for several days.

Digestion also changes radically after birth: Before birth, nourishment was provided via the placenta; after birth, the infant's own digestive system must begin to function, although digestive adjustments usually occur more slowly than those associated with respiration and circulation. The neonate's temperature regulation system also adjusts gradually to its new environment: Within the uterus, the baby's skin was maintained at a constant temperature; after birth, the baby's own metabolism must protect it from even minor changes in external temperature. This is why, unless they are placed in incubators, babies must be carefully covered to keep them warm during the first few days and weeks of life. Gradually, they become able to maintain a constant body temperature, aided by the layer of fat that continues to accumulate during the early weeks.

Reflexes To help them make the transition to life outside the womb, infants enter the world with biologically based behaviors that can be classified as *survival reflexes* and *primitive reflexes* (see Table 3-9). **Survival reflexes** are just that reflexes necessary for adaptation and survival, especially during the first days or weeks before the higher brain centers begin to take control. Breathing, for example, is reflexive, although it becomes somewhat subject to voluntary control after the first few months. Likewise, rooting and sucking, which are highly adaptive reflexes for finding a nipple and obtaining milk, are reflexive at first but become voluntary and, therefore, under the infant's control after a few months. Other survival reflexes—such as coughing, sneezing, gagging, hiccupping, and yawning—also are present at birth, but they remain reflexive throughout life.

A typical part of a newborn's physical involves testing to see if reflexes are present. What kinds of conditions might a physician be investigating by measuring these reflexes?

Although not directly linked to present-day survival, **primitive reflexes** may have been important at some point in our evolutionary history (Bartlett, 1997; Goddard, 2009). The *Moro reflex,* for example, is the newborn's startle reaction. When newborns are startled by a loud sound or by the sensation of being dropped, they react first by extending both arms to the side, with fingers outstretched as if to catch onto someone or something. The arms then gradually come back to the midline. Thus, the Moro reflex might have had survival value in the distant past: In case of a fall, neonates who grasped their mother's body hair would be most likely to survive. A related reflex is the *palmar* grasp. When the palm of a neonate's hand is stimulated by an object such as a finger or a pencil, the infant's fingers will close tightly in a grasp. Indeed, some neonates can grasp with enough strength to support their full weight for up to a minute. Because many primitive reflexes normally disappear during the first several months of life, they have diagnostic value: If they do not disappear more or less on schedule, it may be a sign of neurological problems.

The Beginnings of Attachment As we have seen, babies come into the world with competent physiological and behavioral systems in place that allow them to adjust to their new, semi-independent existence. However, social and emotional processes also play a key role in early development. Perhaps the most significant of these is referred to as **attachment**, the emotional bond between parents and children that includes elements such as feeling close and loving.

Can you think of another example that demonstrates the reciprocal nature of early infant–caregiver attachment?

An important aspect of attachment is that it is *reciprocal;* that is, it extends from infant to caregiver, as well as from caregiver to infant. Many early attachment-related behaviors demonstrate

survival reflexes
Biologically programmed behaviors, such as breathing, rooting, and sucking, that are related to the neonate's ability to survive

attachment
The reciprocal emotional bond that develops between a child and caregivers

primitive reflexes
Biologically programmed behaviors without immediate survival value but that may have been associated with survival in our evolutionary past

Watch *The Newborn's Reflexes* on **MyDevelopmentLab**

Table 3-9 Infant Reflexes

Survival Reflexes	Primitive Reflexes
Breathing Infants reflexively inhale to obtain oxygen and exhale to expel carbon dioxide. Breathing is permanently reflexive in that it does not require conscious effort, although after the first few months of life we can voluntarily control our breathing—up to a point.	**Moro (startle)** When infants are startled by loud sounds or by suddenly being dropped a few inches, they will first spread their arms and stretch out their fingers, then bring their arms back to their body and clench their fingers. This reflex disappears after about 4 months.
Rooting If you touch an infant's cheek, the infant will turn its head toward the stimulus and open its mouth as if expecting a nipple. This reflex normally disappears after 3 or 4 months.	**Palmar** When an infant's palm is stimulated, the infant will grasp tightly and increase the strength of the grasp if the stimulus is pulled away. This reflex disappears after about 5 months.
Sucking If you touch or otherwise stimulate an infant's mouth, the infant will respond by sucking and making rhythmic movements with the mouth and tongue. This reflex gradually becomes voluntary over the first few months.	**Plantar** When an object or a finger is placed on the sole of an infant's foot near the toes, the infant responds by trying to flex the foot. This reflex is similar to the palmar reflex, but it disappears after about 9 months.
Pupillary The pupils of infants' eyes narrow in bright light and when going to sleep and widen in dim light and when waking up. This is a permanent reflex.	**Babinski** If you stroke the sole of an infant's foot from heel to toes, the infant will spread the small toes and raise the large one. This reflex disappears after about 6 months.
Eye blink Infants blink in response to an object moving quickly toward their eyes or to a puff of air. This is a permanent reflex.	**Stepping** When infants are held upright with their feet against a flat surface and are moved forward, they appear to walk in a coordinated way. This reflex disappears after 2 or 3 months.
	Swimming Infants will *attempt to* swim in a coordinated way if placed in water in a prone position. This reflex disappears after about 6 months.
	Tonic neck When infants' heads are turned to one side, they will extend the arm and leg on that side and flex the arm and leg on the opposite side, as in a fencing position. This reflex disappears after about 4 months.

SOURCE: Adapted in part from *Lifelong motor development* (4th ed.), by C. P. Gabbard, 2004, San Francisco: Benjamin Cummings; and *Attention, balance and coordination: The A.B.C.s of learning success*, by S. Goddard, 2009, Oxford, England: Wiley-Blackwell.

this reciprocity. Consider, for example, early feeding: Almost immediately after birth, breastfed infants find the breast and start to nurse as mothers hold them close, establish eye contact, and talk to them. In turn, a baby's responses trigger physical processes within the mother's body. When babies lick or suck on the mother's nipples, the secretion of *prolactin* (a hormone important in nursing) and *oxytocin* (a hormone that causes the uterus to contract and reduces bleeding) increase. The infant also benefits from early breastfeeding: Although milk often is not yet available, the mother produces a substance called *colostrum* that appears to help clear the infant's digestive system and can confer many of the mother's immunities to the newborn. (The choice of breast- versus bottle-feeding is discussed in Chapter 4.)

The critical feature of early attachment is not who the caregiver is, but rather that someone fills the caregiver's role. Parents who adopt children before their first birthday typically develop parent–child attachment relationships that are comparable to those that begin in the moments immediately following birth (van der Dries, Juffer, van IJzendoorn, & Bakermans-Kranenburg, 2009). Even when children are adopted after age 1, normal, secure attachment relationships develop in a large majority of cases (Pace, Zavattini, D'Alessio, &

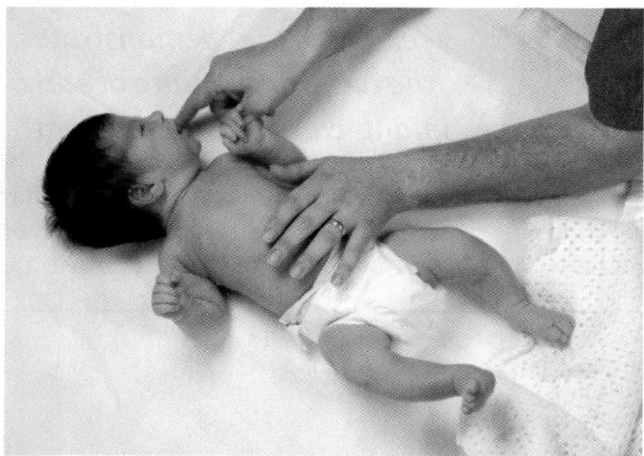

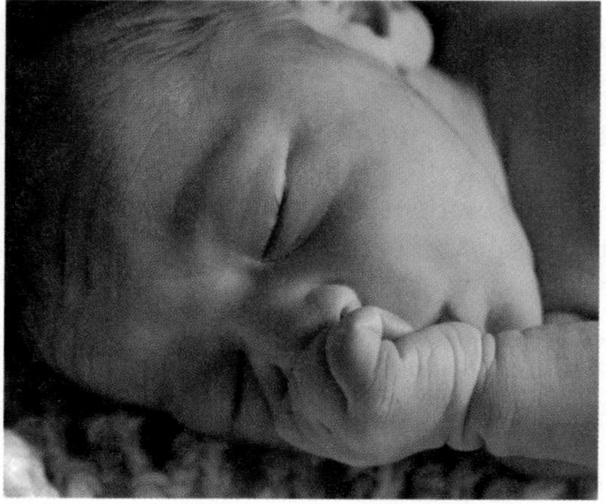

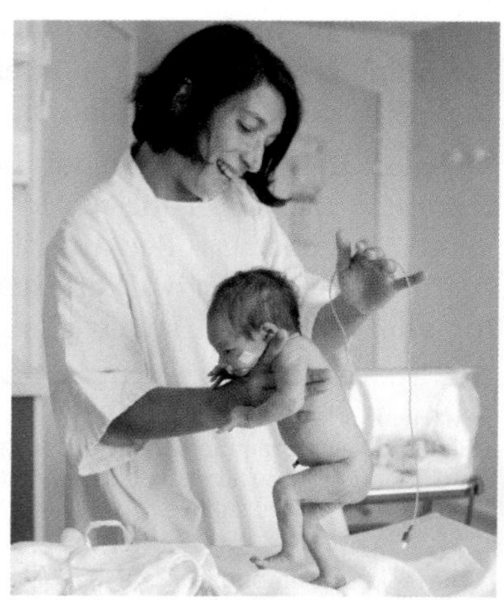

▲ Some reflexes of the newborn: (left) rooting reflex, (middle) sucking reflex, and (right) stepping reflex.

Zavattini, 2012). However, regardless of the particular circumstances surrounding birth, it is important to nurture early infant–caregiver interactions (whether with parents or other caregivers) because these establish the foundation for the attachment relationships that continue to develop throughout life (Feeney, Passmore, & Peterson, 2007; Roberson, 2006). Many of the things that most parents do with their newborns serve to strengthen the caregiver–infant attachment relationship, such as holding and rocking, or singing to, the new baby. The development of early attachment relationships is the goal of many intentional parenting practices, also, including *co-sleeping* (allowing the infant to sleep beside one or both parents), and *baby-wearing* (carrying the baby in a sling or carrier throughout the day). It also is an important part of kangaroo care (see Current Issues: Kangaroo Care for Low Birth-Weight Infants). Thus, the dynamic interplay between neonate and parents or other caregivers displays the nature of this most important foundation for later social and personality development. Again and again in later chapters, we will see evidence for the significance of early attachment of caregivers and infants. We also will see the continuing significance of the family environment on development as we consider how development unfolds across the lifespan.

REVIEW THE FACTS 3-4

1. During which of the following phases of pregnancy does the mother typically feel the best?
   a. early weeks b. middle weeks c. later weeks
2. The term used to describe a newborn baby is __________.
3. In the last few moments before birth, infants experience a surge of __________ in their system.
   a. dopamine b. potassium
   c. adrenaline d. calcium
4. Why does a baby born through vaginal delivery usually have a cone-shaped head?
5. Vernix caseosa is __________.
6. The first "milk" produced by the mother is called __________.

Practice on **MyDevelopmentLab**

CHAPTER SUMMARY

Prenatal Growth and Development

What major developmental events take place in each of the three prenatal periods of development?

- Prenatal development can be divided into three 3-month trimesters; however, a more useful way of conceptualizing the developmental changes taking place is to consider three periods: the *germinal* (0 to 2 weeks), the *embryonic* (2 through 8 weeks), and the *fetal* (from 9 through 38 weeks).
- *Ovulation* usually occurs about 2 weeks after the start of a menstrual period. The ovum (egg) travels through the *fallopian tube,* where *fertilization* may take place if sperm are present, thus creating a *zygote.*
- By the end of the first week, cells have organized into a *blastula,* which then implants into the uterine wall; then cells begin the process of differentiation.
- *Monozygotic (identical) twins* are formed when a single zygote divides, forming two embryos that have the same genes. *Dizygotic (fraternal) twins* result when two ova are fertilized by two different sperm. Multiple births are becoming more common, due to older average maternal age and to increased use of reproductive therapies.
- During the *embryonic period,* the supportive structures differentiate into the *placenta,* the *umbilical cord,* and the *amniotic sac.* The *embryonic disk,* which will become the baby, develops into three distinct layers: the *ectoderm* (which will become the skin, sense organs, and brain and nervous system), the *mesoderm* (which will become muscles, blood, and the excretory system), and the *endoderm* (which will become the digestive system, lungs, thyroid, thymus, and other organs).
- During the second month, most body structures develop. The major exception is the brain.
- More males than females are conceived, but more males are also miscarried.
- During the *fetal period,* organs and systems mature and develop, especially the brain and nervous system.
- Infant health care has improved substantially, with infant mortality rates in developed nations dropping to new lows. In addition, new medical treatments have lowered the *age of viability* to about 24 weeks.

What are the major trends that guide human development during the prenatal period?

- Three general trends characterize early developmental processes: the *cephalocaudal trend* (development advances from the head to the feet), the *proximodistal trend* (development proceeds from the middle of the body outward), and the *gross-to-specific trend* (responses become more specific as development advances).

Prenatal Environmental Influences

How do maternal risk factors and protective factors affect the course of prenatal development?

- Both genetic defects and environmental influences during the prenatal period and complications during childbirth can result in congenital anomalies.
- Maternal age is linked to an increased incidence of congenital anomalies, with women in their 20s being in the lowest risk category.
- Malnutrition during pregnancy is linked to higher rates of spontaneous abortion, premature birth, and stillbirth, as well as to later difficulties in the baby's development. Malnutrition is especially problematic when it occurs over a

long period of time; however, intervention programs often can be successful.

- Early and good prenatal care is associated with having healthy babies.

What is a "critical period" in development?

- *Teratogens* can include maternal illness or exposure to harmful chemicals, drugs, or radiation. Teratogens often operate during a *critical period,* during which their presence can significantly disrupt normal developmental processes.

How do teratogens interfere with normal prenatal development, and what are the effects associated with common teratogenic agents?

- Because the placenta keeps the mother's and baby's blood supplies separate, it can screen some larger disease molecules and keep them from being passed from mother to baby. Viruses (such as rubella, HIV, and the flu), which are smaller organisms, often cross the placental barrier and may affect the baby.
- Left untreated, HIV is transmitted by infected mothers to their unborn children in about one-fourth of cases. Treatment with newer drugs has reduced this rate to less than 2%, although these drugs are largely unavailable in many parts of the developing world where the AIDS epidemic is raging.
- Certain prescription drugs can have teratogenic effects, as can alcohol, which can result in *fetal alcohol syndrome (FAS),* now the leading cause of intellectual disability in the United States. Less severe cases may result in *fetal alcohol spectrum disorder (FASD).* The more alcohol that the mother consumes, the greater is the risk of congenital anomalies. Any level of drinking during pregnancy is considered risky.
- Women who smoke during pregnancy are at higher risk for stillbirth, prematurity, and spontaneous abortion, as well as for having low-birth-weight children and children who display cognitive and behavioral deficits. Smoking may cause *anoxia,* and it may interfere with nutrient exchange across the placenta. The mother's marijuana use may also place the newborn at similar risk.
- Prenatal exposure to amphetamine drugs (such as cocaine and methamphetamine) is associated with an array of problems, many of which involve the functioning of the nervous system. When the exposure is limited to early in the prenatal period, good postnatal care may help to limit the damage such drugs cause.
- Exposure to environmental pollutants such as mercury, lead, and PCB compounds can have serious consequences for prenatal development. Also, ionizing radiation, including X-rays, can interfere with normal prenatal development. Fortunately, exposure to these teratogens typically occurs at low levels that are unlikely to cause significant impairment.

Childbirth

What sequence of events unfolds during a normal childbirth?

- Childbirth is divided into three stages: *initial labor,* during which the cervix dilates; *labor and delivery,* when the baby is pushed through the birth canal; and *afterbirth,* when the placenta is expelled.

How have childbirth practices changed throughout the years?

- Childbirth practices vary widely from culture to culture and in the United States from generation to generation.
- Today, many women prefer a *natural* or *prepared childbirth,* although most also want medical assistance to be available if needed. Natural childbirth emphasizes preparation, relaxation techniques, the presence of a coach to assist with relaxation, and minimal use of medication.
- *Birthing centers,* which are designed to accommodate the entire childbirth process, are becoming more common and popular.

What technological advances have occurred with respect to pregnancy, and how have these changed the practice of childbirth?

- Technological advances have improved physicians' abilities to detect problems earlier in pregnancy. *Ultrasound,* the most widely used and minimally invasive technique, uses sound waves to create an image of the unborn baby. In *amniocentesis,* amniotic fluid is withdrawn with a syringe so that chromosomal anomalies can be detected. *Chorionic villus sampling (CVS)* can be conducted earlier than amniocentesis, but it poses a slightly greater risk. *Fetal monitors* also can be used during the birth process to monitor the baby's physiological functions.
- *Cesarean section* involves a surgical procedure in which the baby is removed through the mother's abdominal wall. Today C-sections are performed in more than 30% of U.S. births, a higher rate than some experts believe is medically warranted. C-sections often are used when birth complications, such as *breech presentation,* arise.
- At birth, the baby's general health can be evaluated on a 10-point scale called the *Apgar Scoring System.*
- Prematurity is associated with low birth weight, which can result from being born too soon (*preterm status*) or from being too small (*small-for-date*). Premature infants have more difficulty adjusting after birth, and sometimes these problems lead to learning or behavioral problems in childhood, although the mechanisms involved are complex. Early physical contact and attention from caregivers seems to contribute to better outcomes for premature babies.

The Evolving Family

With the arrival of a new baby, how do mother and father adjust?

- Childbirth is a medical event, but it also is a psychological and social milestone for the family. Childbearing customs, expectations, and adjustments vary widely from culture to culture.

- Often mothers feel ambivalence about the upcoming birth, with some feelings of excitement and happiness mixed with some feelings of uncertainty and worry. Fathers also experience a range of emotions and concerns.
- New fertility treatments, including *assisted reproductive technologies* (ART), make it possible for some couples with fertility problems to become parents. These therapies raise ethical concerns.

In what ways is the newborn prepared to cope with the dramatic circumstance of birth?

- Birth marks a dramatic transition for newborns, whose bodies prepare for the stress of being born by circulating more hormones, such as adrenaline and noradrenaline, as well as beta-endorphins. Consequently, most newborns are quite alert for an hour or more after birth.
- The *fontanels* of the skull are not fully hardened at birth, allowing more flexibility during the birth processes. Consequently, care must be taken to not bump a baby's head, because the soft spots in the skull leave the brain vulnerable to injury.
- The average full-term newborn weighs between 5 pounds 8 ounces and 9 pounds 8 ounces, is between 19 and 22 inches long, may have enlarged genitalia (due to hormones), and may be covered with vernix caseosa and lanugo hair.
- Upon birth, newborns must make major adjustments in their respiration, circulation, digestion, and temperature regulation systems.
- Babies are born with *survival reflexes* that are necessary for their survival; examples include breathing, sucking, rooting, sneezing, and gagging. Other *primitive reflexes* are also present, which may have had survival value in our evolutionary past. Most primitive reflexes disappear in the first months of life; if they do not, there may be underlying neurological problems.
- *Attachment* describes the emotional bond that forms between infant and caregiver. Attachment is reciprocal, with both infants and caregivers participating in its formation. Attachment establishes the foundation for later social and personality development.

KEY TERMS

germinal period (p. 66)
ovulation (p. 67)
fallopian tubes (p. 67)
uterus (p. 67)
fertilization (p. 67)
zygote (p. 67)
blastula (p. 67)
monozygotic (identical) twins (p. 68)
dizygotic (fraternal) twins (p. 68)
embryonic period (p. 68)
embryo (p. 68)
placenta (p. 68)
umbilical cord (p. 68)
amniotic sac (p. 68)
amniotic fluid (p. 68)
spontaneous abortion (p. 69)
fetal period (p. 69)
fetus (p. 70)
age of viability (p. 70)
cephalocaudal trend (p. 71)
proximodistal trend (p. 71)
gross-to-specific trend (p. 71)
critical period (p. 74)
teratogen (p. 74)
fetal alcohol syndrome (FAS) (p. 77)
fetal alcohol spectrum disorder (FASD) (p. 79)
anoxia (p. 80)
initial labor (p. 81)
false labor (p. 82)
episiotomy (p. 82)
afterbirth (p. 82)
midwife (p. 83)
traditional childbirth (p. 83)
"natural" or prepared childbirth (p. 84)
birthing center (p. 84)
ultrasound (p. 84)
amniocentesis (p. 85)
chorionic villus sampling (CVS) (p. 85)
fetal monitor (p. 86)
breech presentation (p. 87)
cesarean section (p. 87)
Apgar Scoring System (p. 88)
preterm status (p. 88)
small-for-date (p. 88)
assisted reproductive technologies (ARTs) (p. 91)
neonate (p. 92)
fontanels (p. 92)
survival reflexes (p. 93)
primitive reflexes (p. 93)
attachment (p. 93)

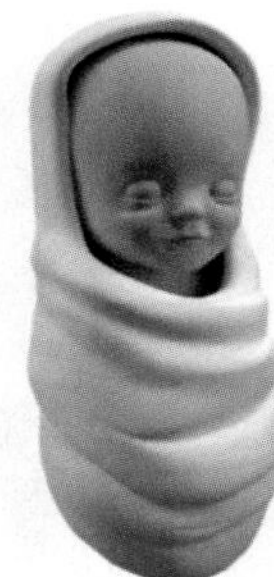

MyVirtualLife

What decision would you make while raising a child? What would be the consequences of those decisions?

Find out by accessing **MyVirtualLife** at www.MyDevelopmentLab.com to raise a virtual child and live your own virtual life.

4 INFANCY AND TODDLERHOOD
Physical, Cognitive, and Language Development

LEARNING OBJECTIVES

- What changes take place in the infant's brain that allow for the dramatic developments of the first 2 years of life?
- What changes in an infant's general behavior and arousal typically occur during the first month of life?
- How does the simple form of learning called *habituation* provide a means to study how infants think?
- How do physical development and motor abilities advance during infancy and toddlerhood?
- What role does nutrition play in early development?
- What sensory and perceptual abilities is the newborn equipped with, and how do these change during the period of infancy and toddlerhood?
- What mechanisms appear to explain the infant's ability to imitate and learn through observation?
- According to the view of Jean Piaget, how does the infant learn to *think*?
- What major milestones occur in language learning during the first 2 years of life?
- How can we best explain how children learn to speak and understand language?

CHAPTER OUTLINE

The Developing Brain

The Neonatal Period
- States of Arousal
- Learning and Habituation
- Neonatal Assessment

Physical and Motor Development
- Cultural Influences on Maturation
- An Overview of Physical and Motor Development: The First 2 Years
- Nutrition and Malnutrition

Sensory and Perceptual Development
- Vision and Visual Perception
- Hearing and Auditory Perception
- Taste, Smell, and Touch
- Sensory Integration

Cognitive Development
- Perceptual Organization and Categories
- Piaget's Concept of Schemes
- The Sensorimotor Period
- Evaluating Piaget's View

Language Development
- The Structure and Function of Language
- Language Development in the First Year
- Words and Sentences
- The Language Explosion
- Telegraphic Speech and Early Grammar
- Theories of Language Development
- Cultural Aspects of Language Development

Newborn infants enter the world quite capable of sensing and responding to their environment. They can see and hear, taste and smell, and feel pressure and pain. They're selective in what they look at, preferring some visual forms to others. They learn, although their abilities are limited, and they communicate largely through crying and gesture. Although neonates are born with certain competencies, they have no real knowledge of life: day and night, self and others, mine and yours, boy and girl. Yet just 2 short years later, children are thinking, wondering, and expressing their thoughts and feelings through language. During the first 2 years of life—the developmental period we refer to as **infancy** and **toddlerhood**—change is more rapid and more dramatic than during any other 2-year period. It is an amazing transformation.

In this chapter, we begin with a look at the competencies of the neonate and then discuss what is known about physical, motor, sensory, and perceptual development during the first 2 years of life. We then turn our attention to cognitive development and to the development of language—a key aspect of cognitive development. Before we turn to these topics, however, we provide a brief look at the infant brain because neurological functioning underlies much of human development in infancy.

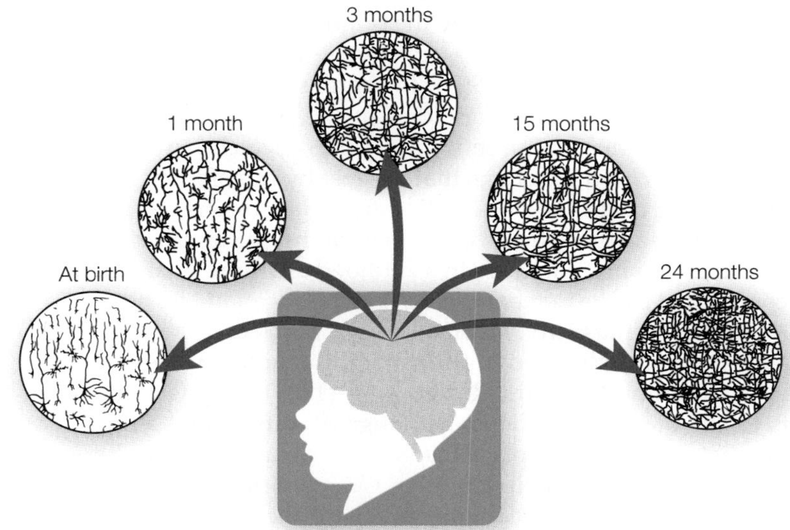

FIGURE 4-1 Development of Neurons
The growth of neural fibers and synapses takes place at an astonishing pace over the infant's first 2 years as shown in these slides of the visual cortex. Note especially the development of branches that allow neurons to communicate with each other.

THE DEVELOPING BRAIN

As we all know, the brain is the organ that governs our actions, emotions, sensations, and abilities. It allows us to think, remember, solve problems, communicate, and maintain our sense of who we are. As we have seen in previous chapters, the brain is composed of about 100 billion *neurons*, which communicate with each other through networked connections called *synapses*, and *glial cells* that support and nourish the neurons and also enhance the efficiency of communication in the nervous system. Although most of the neurons we will ever have in our lifetimes are developed during the prenatal period and are thus present at birth, they do undergo much growth and differentiation during early childhood, developing more branches and, therefore, more elaborate connection pathways (see Figure 4-1).

In addition, the number of glial cells continues to increase rapidly throughout the first 2 years and even on into childhood and adolescence (Cicchetti & Cohen, 2006; Gazzaniga, Ivry, & Mangun, 2009; Keating, 2011). Glial cells, which nurture and support the neurons, are also important because they produce a fatty substance called *myelin*. Myelin is deposited around neurons and improves the efficiency with which they communicate. The production of myelin—called *myelination*—begins at about

infancy
The period from about age 4 weeks to about 1 year

toddlerhood
The period from about age 1, when the infant begins walking, until about age 2

the 14th week of the prenatal period, although little myelin is present at birth. Rather, myelination of the nervous system is most rapid during infancy, although it continues throughout childhood and into adolescence.

The rapid growth in the size of neurons, the complexity of neural branching, the number of glial cells, and the production of myelin produce a **brain growth spurt** during infancy and toddlerhood. Although at birth the brain weighs only about 25% of its adult weight, by age 1, it has grown to 70% of its adult weight; by age 3, the brain has grown to 90% of its adult weight. This growth spurt continues, although more slowly, throughout childhood and accounts for the young brain's considerable **plasticity**—the degree to which the brain can be modified through experience. The early plasticity of the brain allows the brain to interact with the environment (Fox, Levitt, & Nelson, 2010). Thus, experiences change the brain, which in turn allows for different responses to the environment (Gazzaniga, Ivry, & Mangun, 2009; Nelson, 1999). Brain plasticity also makes it more possible to reassign functions in the case of brain damage or injury. Thus, children who experience such injuries are often able to *relearn* functions that are lost by transferring them to a different part of the brain. Because adult brains have lost much of this early plasticity, often they cannot accomplish such relearning, and brain injuries in adulthood are more likely to be accompanied by permanent disabilities.

The brain's plasticity in infancy and early childhood also makes it susceptible to environmental influences. In a series of classic experiments, Mark Rosenzweig (1969) assigned infant rats to one of two conditions. Although all rats received nutritious diets, some were placed in standard cages where there were few options for their activities. Others, however, were assigned to "enriched" environments where there were running wheels, levers to press, steps to climb, and other "rat toys" to play with. Although the predominant view at the time was that brain development was heavily controlled by genetic factors (and thus environmental factors were insignificant), Rosenzweig's results demonstrated quite the contrary. Rats raised in the enriched environments developed brains that were not only heavier but also had thicker layers of cortex cells and more neurochemical activity at synapses.

We often learn to do very well those things we practice. Describe how neural pruning might explain this statement.

Similar results to those found in the rat studies also appear to be the case when we look at children who were raised in socially impoverished conditions, particularly if the conditions were severe (Cicchetti, 2002; Cicchetti & Curtis, 2006). However, it does appear that at least some of the negative effects of such deprivation may be reversible if intervention occurs (see Chapter 6). One explanation for our ability to later compensate for earlier trauma is that brain development during infancy is not simply a matter of increasing the number of connections among neurons. Rather, what occurs is both growth and "pruning" where, as the result of each child's unique experiences, some synaptic connections develop and others are eliminated, or pruned away. According to Alison Gopnik and her colleagues (Gopnik, Meltzoff, & Kuhl, 1999, 2008), neurons in the brain of a newborn average about 2,500 synapses, increasing to a peak of about 15,000 synapses by age 2 or 3—many more than are present in an adult brain. Many of these early connections are not maintained, presumably because they are not used. Through this elimination of weak connections, the brain fine-tunes itself in response to the environment in which the infant develops. Findings such as these are very exciting and indicate that experiences early in life can have profound consequences for development—a topic to which we will return later in the text.

REVIEW THE FACTS 4-1

1. The connections between nerve cells are called
   a. neurons. b. glia.
   c. transmitters. d. synapses.
2. If the same brain injury occurred in a 2-year-old and a 40-year-old, who would have a better chance of recovering lost functions?
3. In experiments with rats, those raised in an enriched environment developed
   a. heavier and more active brain structures.
   b. a greater need for sexual activity.
   c. obesity.
   d. more serious diseases, such as cancer.
4. All other things being equal, which of the following individuals will have the most synapses present in the brain?
   a. a newborn b. a 2-year-old
   c. a 40-year-old d. an 80-year-old

Practice on **MyDevelopmentLab**

THE NEONATAL PERIOD

The first month of life is a very special period because the baby—who is referred to during this time as a *neonate*—must adjust to life outside the protected environment of the mother's womb. Thus, the neonatal period is a time of recovery from the birth process and of fine-tuning of vital functions, such as respiration, circulation, digestion, and regulation of body temperature. It is also a time for learning to cope with changes and challenges in the physical and social environment. How well equipped is a typical neonate for such tasks?

Watch *The Basics: How the Brain Works?* on **MyDevelopmentLab**

brain growth spurt Rapid growth during infancy in the size of neurons, the number of glial cells, and the complexity of neural connections

plasticity The degree to which the brain can be modified through experience; plasticity is greater at early ages

Until the 1960s, it was thought that neonates were largely incapable of organized, self-directed behavior. In fact, it was not uncommon to view the infant's world as a "blooming, buzzing confusion," as William James (1842–1910) described it (James, 1890/1950). However, later research has shown that newborns' capabilities had been grossly underestimated. We now know that neonates are capable of organized, predictable responses and of more complex cognitive activity than was once thought. The key to a more accurate understanding of infants is in the development of more effective ways to study their behavior. Early studies often used observational methods developed for older children, with the result that infants, who typically were laid on their backs, seemed incapable of many interesting responses. However, as research techniques have become better attuned to the capabilities of babies, we have developed a clearer understanding of the many skills and abilities they do possess.

States of Arousal

If you watch sleeping newborns, you will notice that they sometimes lie calmly and quietly and at other times they twitch and grimace. Similarly, when they are awake, babies may be calm or they may thrash about wildly and cry. In a now-classic observational study of infants' activity, Peter Wolff (1966) identified six newborn behavioral states: waking activity, crying, alert inactivity, drowsiness, regular sleep, and irregular sleep (see Table 4-1).

As newborns adjust to their environment, the daily pattern of these states becomes more regular and predictable. In addition, the amount of time spent in each state changes. For example, newborns initially spend most of the day in either regular or irregular sleep and wake frequently during the night. By 4 months, however, most infants spend several hours in alert activity and are usually sleeping through the night. In addition, an infant's responsiveness to others and to the environment often depends on his or her behavioral state. For example, in a state of alert inactivity, infants are easily stimulated and react to sounds or sights with increased activity, whereas infants who are already in an active state tend to calm down when stimulated. Behavioral states are thus linked to one of the most important tasks for the newborn—learning to understand the environment.

Learning and Habituation

As all parents know, learning is readily observable from birth on. For example, neonates quiet down in response to familiar sounds, songs, or lullabies, demonstrating that they remember and recognize sounds that have been comforting in the past. Classic research studies also have demonstrated the neonate's capabilities to learn. For example, newborns were classically conditioned to turn their head to the right at the sound of a bell but to the left at the sound of a buzzer to obtain milk. This research demonstrated not only their ability to learn but also their ability to discriminate between similar stimuli—a bell versus a

Table 4-1 Six States of Arousal in Infants

Arousal state	Activity
Waking activity	• The baby frequently engages in motor activity that involves the entire body • The eyes are open • Breathing is highly irregular
Crying	• The baby cries and engages in vigorous, disorganized motor activity • Crying may take different forms (e.g., hunger cries, anger cries, and pain or discomfort cries)
Alert inactivity	• The eyes are open, bright, and shining • The eyes follow moving objects • The baby is fairly inactive, with a relaxed face
Drowsiness	• The baby is fairly inactive • The eyes open and close • Breathing is regular but faster than in regular sleep • The eyes may have a dull, glazed quality when open
Regular sleep	• The eyes are closed • The body is completely relaxed • Breathing is slow and regular • The face looks relaxed • The eyelids are still
Irregular sleep	• The eyes are closed • Gentle limb movements occur (e.g., writhing, stirring, and stretching) • Grimaces and other facial expressions occur • Breathing is irregular and faster than in regular sleep • Rapid eye movements (REMs) occasionally occur; these may indicate dreaming

SOURCE: Adapted from "The natural history of crying and other vocalizations in early infancy," by P. H. Wolff, 1966, 1969, in B. M. Foss (Ed.), *Determinants of infant behavior (Vol. 4): Based on the proceedings of the fourth Tavistock Study Group on Mother–Infant Interaction*. London: Methuen.

buzzer (Papousek, 1961). A neonate's early ability to imitate facial expressions also demonstrates learning, as we will discuss later in this chapter.

Newborns also exhibit a simple form of learning called *habituation,* which allows them to ignore meaningless, repetitive stimuli in the environment. In fact, habituation is a very important, although somewhat basic, adaptive mechanism. For example, this ability to ignore repetitive stimuli enables the newborn to sleep despite the sound of a TV or a noisy fan. Yet when a new sound does occur—perhaps the mother's voice—the baby's attention is recaptured.

Habituation also provides developmentalists with an effective research technique (see Oakes, 2010). In the **habituation method**, researchers habituate infants to certain stimuli to study their perceptual capabilities. For example, a newborn's response at the onset of a moderately loud tone is a faster heartbeat, a change in breathing, and sometimes crying or generally increased activity. As the tone continues, however, the infant soon habituates and stops responding. Then the frequency of the tone is changed slightly. If responding resumes, it is clear that the infant perceived the difference between the two stimuli. The habituation method continues to be used extensively to study infant capabilities (e.g., see Hoff, 2011; Kavšek & Yonas, 2012). Because sucking comes under voluntary control early, it has been used extensively in habituation studies of neonatal learning and visual preferences (e.g., see Field, Diego, Hernandez-Reif, & Fernandez, 2007; Floccia, Christophe, & Bertoncini, 1997).

Infants often stop sucking when they notice a change in their environment. Can you suggest how the sucking response might be combined with the habituation method to study infants' ability to discriminate among different colors or shapes?

Neonatal Assessment

By observing neonatal reflexive actions (see Chapter 3), arousal states, and early learning capabilities, we can build an understanding of the competence of the newborn. These same behaviors can be used as a basis for determining the general health of an individual neonate as well. If we add an assessment of the newborn's responsiveness, self-regulation, and activity level, we know a good deal about how well a particular infant will fare in the coming months.

Often during the first few days of a baby's life, hospitals perform evaluations that may include a neurological examination and a behavioral assessment (see Chapter 3). One such evaluation method is the **Newborn Behavioral Observation (NBO)**, system a new and more streamlined version of the original Neonatal Behavioral Assessment Scale (NBAS) developed by Kevin Nugent, Barry Brazelton, and their colleagues (Brazelton Institute, 2012). The NBO and its precursor, the NBAS, have been used by many hospitals to assess neonatal health and have also been employed in hundreds of research efforts aimed at better understanding how early responses contribute to later personality and social development (Lester & Sparrow, 2010; Nugent, Keefer, Minear, Johnson, & Blanchard,, 2007). The NBO consists of 18 items that assess the infant in the following areas (Brazelton Institute, 2012):

- capacity to habituate to external light and sound stimuli
- quality of motor tone and activity level
- capacity for self-regulation (including crying and consolability)
- response to stress
- visual, auditory, and social-interactive capacities (degree of alertness and response to both human and nonhuman stimuli)

The NBO emphasizes the unique profile of a neonate's competencies and patterns of responding. Thus, it is not surprising that parents who observe a physician administer the NBO become much more sensitive to the capabilities and individuality of their newborn. Parents who seem unsure about what to expect or how to cope with their baby's behavior during the first several months of life also can receive training, which is

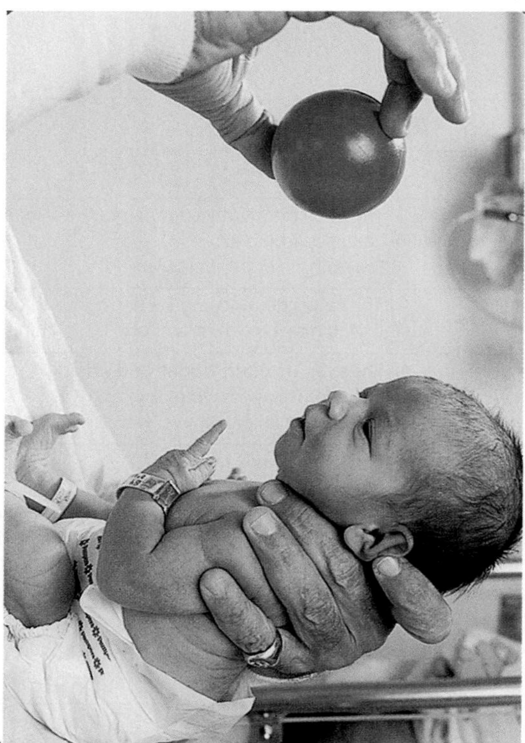

Notice how this 2-day-old infant vigorously struggles to visually follow the red ball in the NBO test. This alert orientation to visual and auditory stimuli is a sign of healthy competence. Already, the infant is learning to organize the visual world.

Watch *Habituation* on **MyDevelopmentLab**

habituation method
To study infant perceptual capabilities, researchers habituate infants to certain stimuli, and then change the stimuli and observe the infant's response

Newborn Behavioral Observation (NBO)
A scale used to assess neurological functioning, behavioral capabilities, and social responsiveness of newborns

especially helpful when their baby is difficult or requires special care (Brazelton Institute, 2012; Brazelton & Nugent, 2011; Nugent, Petrauskas, & Brazelton, 2009).

The neonatal period is characterized by substantial adjustments for both newborns and their caregivers. These adjustments, of course, set the stage for development throughout infancy—a period of rapid and dramatic changes. Foremost among these are developments we observe with respect to physical growth and motor capabilities, which are the topics we explore in the next section of this chapter.

REVIEW THE FACTS 4-2

1. As neonates adjust to their environment, does their pattern of activity become more predictable or less predictable?
2. At about what age do most babies begin sleeping through the night?
3. Suppose you showed newborns a series of pictures of different human faces, recording how long they looked at each face. If habituation occurs, which face in the series would you expect them to look at for the shortest time?
   a. the first face in the series
   b. the second face in the series
   c. the middle face in the series
   d. the last face in the series
4. Which of the following is *not* evaluated on the Newborn Behavioral Observation scale?
   a. ability to habituate to a new stimulus
   b. ability to habituate to light
   c. ability to be soothed
   d. ability to sleep through the night

PHYSICAL AND MOTOR DEVELOPMENT

Any observer of human development is sure to notice that physical and motor development proceeds in a particular, prescribed pattern and that normal infants reach developmental milestones, such as rolling over and walking, at similar ages. Arnold Gesell (1880–1961), a pioneer in the field, observed hundreds of infants and children (e.g., see Gesell, 1940), recording the details of when and how certain behaviors emerged, such as crawling, walking, running, picking up a small pellet, cutting with scissors, managing a pencil, or drawing human figures. On the basis of the resulting data, he compiled the first detailed reports of the capabilities of *average* children at different ages—the Gesell Scales.

Cultural Influences on Maturation

In the healthy, well-nourished children Gesell observed, the behaviors under study emerged in an orderly and predictable sequence and with remarkable consistency. By knowing the age of a child, Gesell could predict not only the child's approximate height and weight but also what the child knew or could do. Consequently, Gesell concluded that most of a child's achievements result from an internal biological timetable. Behavior, thus, emerges as a function of *maturation.*

Gesell's view, however, underestimated the impact of the infant's environment. We now know that children raised in widely different social or historical contexts develop somewhat differently than those described in Gesell's schedules who all came from the same socioeconomic class and community. For example, today infants in the United States normally begin "free" walking between 11 and 13 months of age instead of at 15 months as Gesell observed, presumably because baby care customs have changed: In the 1930s, infants spent more time resting and lying flat on their backs than they do now, so they did not get as much early practice with the skills leading up to walking.

Regardless of culture, healthy infants sit up before they creep or crawl, they creep or crawl before they walk, and they walk before they run. What does this statement imply about the relationship between biological and environmental influences that affect development?

Also, there are cultural differences in the onset of walking. For example, West Indian infants, whether living in Jamaica or East London, normally walk about a month earlier than other London infants, probably because their mothers use massage and encourage vigorous exercise (Hopkins, 1991). Historically, infants raised in some Guatemalan villages—where they spent their first year confined to a small and dark hut, were not played with, were rarely spoken to, and were poorly nourished—walked months later (Kagan, 1978). Even today, cultural differences have an impact on the rate at which different types of skills develop in early life (Karasik, Adolph, Tamis-LeMonda, & Bornstein, 2010). For example, in comparing infants raised in Cameroon to those raised in Germany, researchers noted that mothers in these countries treated their babies somewhat differently. These different maternal practices led Cameroon babies to develop more advanced gross motor development, but German infants to show earlier development of fine motor development and cognitive skills (Lohaus et al., 2011). Thus, different patterns of socialization and infant care can influence the rate at which early motor development proceeds.

Studies such as these demonstrate that early motor development can be somewhat subject to acceleration or deceleration due to how infants are raised. However, these differences are small and also are inconsequential over the longer term because early differences typically disappear over time (Roze, et al., 2010). Thus, although children develop at their own pace and in the context of their sociocultural environment, there are common patterns of growth and development we expect normal infants to attain.

Before we turn to discuss these typical patterns of growth, we believe it is especially important to emphasize that physical growth and motor development are intricately linked to brain development and to cognitive and social development.

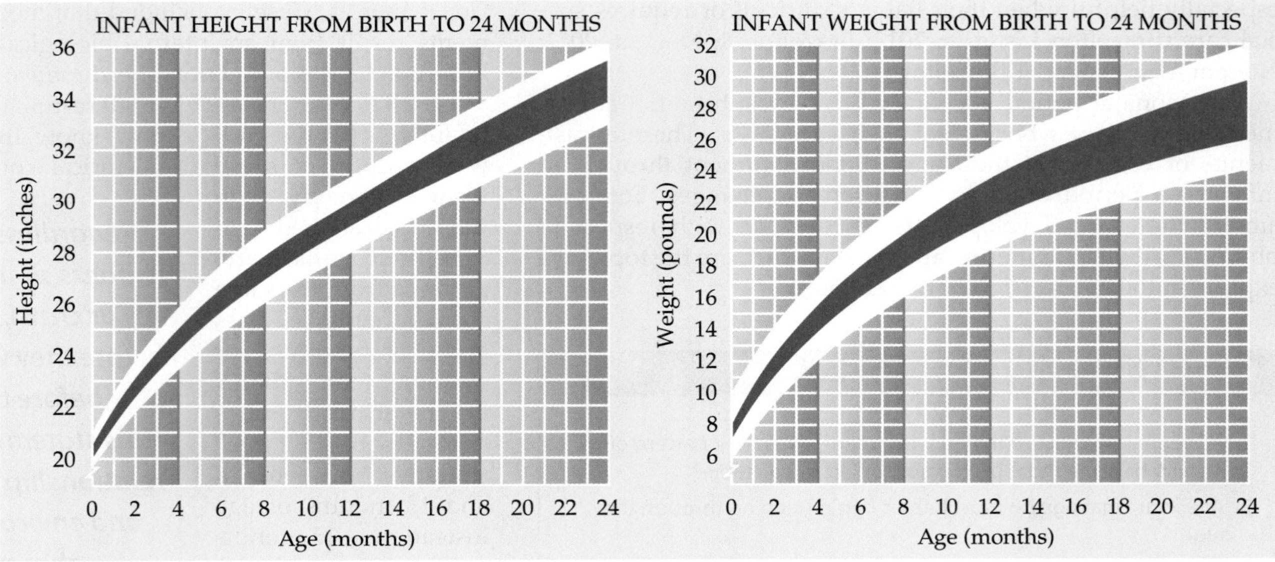

FIGURE 4-2 Growth Rates for Height and Weight
The weight and height of about 50% of full-term infants at a given age will fall within the purple band; about 15% will fall within each of the white regions. Thus, on average, 80% of infants will have weights and heights somewhere within these regions. Note that the band widens for older infants.

Motor milestones, such as crawling, walking, and learning to use the hands to grasp, increase enormously the infants' opportunities for social interactions and new learning situations and these, in turn, propel physical development. Body, brain, and experience influence each other: Physical and motor developments occur not simply through biologically programmed maturation but are part of an interacting, dynamic system (Meltzoff, Waismeyer, & Gopnik, 2012; Rakison & Woodward, 2008). Therefore, before we begin the discussion of other aspects of development, it is useful to note the basic developmental parameters for physical growth and motor development (Adolph & Berger, 2006; Payne & Isaacs, 2012).

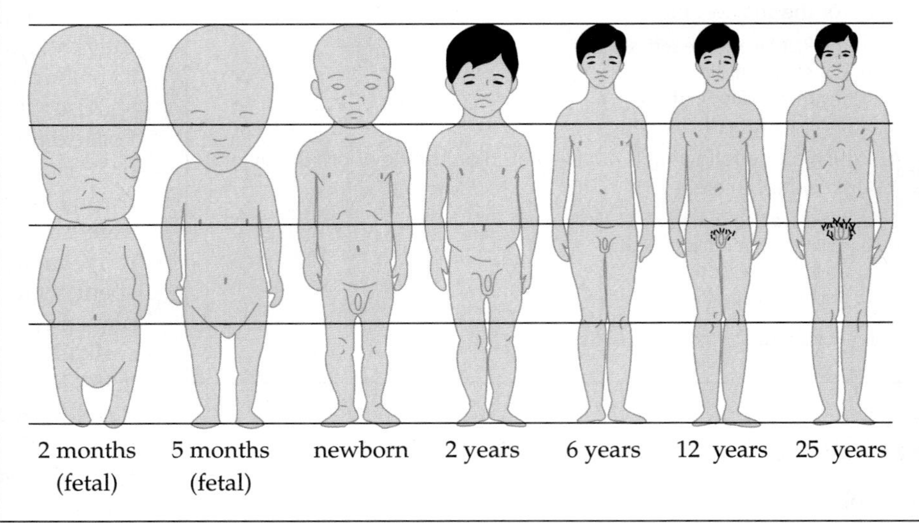

FIGURE 4-3 Growth Trends
The cephalocaudal (head to tail) and the proximodistal (central trunk to extremities) developmental trends continue after birth. The proportions of the child's body change dramatically in infancy and early childhood.

An Overview of Physical and Motor Development: The First 2 Years

The First 4 Months Many important developmental changes occur during the first 4 months of life as the newborn acclimates to life outside the womb. By the end of this time, for example, most infants have nearly doubled in weight (see Figure 4-2), and their bodies have started to lengthen. Body growth throughout childhood involves a shift in head-to-body proportion as well: At birth, the size of the baby's head is about one-quarter of its total body length, whereas the size of an adult's head is about one-tenth of the adult's total body length (see Figure 4-3).

Can you provide an example of a reflex that is involuntary in infancy but under our conscious control as adults?

At 4 months, babies' skin has lost the newborn look, and their fine birth hair is being replaced by permanent hair. Their eyes now focus rather well. When awake, they may coo contentedly and smile in response to pleasant stimuli. Vision and hearing have improved rapidly as well, as we'll see in the next section of this chapter. The infant's teeth and bones are also changing. In some children, the first tooth erupts at 4 or 5 months. Many bones are still soft cartilage; they tend to be pliable under stress and rarely break. Muscles, however, may pull easily and be injured, for example, if young infants are hoisted by the arms and swung about in play. Sometimes, too, parents attempt to stop a baby's crying by vigorously shaking him or her, without understanding that this practice may be quite dangerous. Because the young infant has not yet developed much strength or good muscle control, being shaken can result in brain damage, sometimes called *shaken baby syndrome* (see the box Changing Perspectives: Sudden Infant Death Syndrome and Shaken Baby Syndrome).

Self-discovery also usually begins at about 4 months. Infants discover their own hands and fingers and spend minutes at a time watching them, studying their movements, bringing them together, and grasping one hand with the other, as they practice and refine their motor control. In addition, many of the newborn's reflexes normally disappear in the second and third months and gradually are replaced by voluntary actions as the higher brain centers take control.

From 5 to 8 Months In terms of overall physical appearance, the 8-month-old baby does not differ dramatically from the 4-month-old. Although heavier and usually with thicker and longer hair, the 8-month-old still looks like a baby despite some developmental shifts, such as the reorientation of the feet from inward turning to a downward orientation that sets the stage for walking.

One important transition during this period is the development of **fine motor skills**, which primarily involve the use of the hands and fingers to perform tasks that require considerable coordination and dexterity, such as grasping an attractive object like a baby's rattle. If a 1-month-old is presented with such an object, the infant most likely will react by opening and closing his hands, waving his arms, and perhaps opening his mouth. However, at 1 month of age, the infant will not be able to coordinate these movements into a complete, intentional act. During the next 4 to 5 months, infants begin to develop the rudiments of hand–eye coordination, using visual input to direct their exploration with their hands.

Successful reaching and grasping is complex and requires not only accurate depth perception and voluntary control of the arms and hands but also the ability to organize these behaviors into a smooth sequence. It is not until about 5 to 6 months of age that infants can combine reaching, grasping, mouthing, and perceiving into a smooth sequence—a developmental milestone called the *visually guided reach* (Foroud & Whishaw, 2012; Phillips & Wellman, 2005; Rochat, Goubet, & Senders, 1999). This newfound ability to engage in a more systematic exploration of objects—with the hands, the eyes, and the mouth used individually or in combination—also sets the stage for later development. For example, most 6-month-old babies can pass objects from hand to hand, some can use their hands to grasp, and they usually can bang two objects together—often joyfully and endlessly.

▲ Infants' ability to use their hands progresses over the first year from a global full-hand swipe to the use of a pincer grasp of just the thumb and forefinger.

Gross motor skills, which involve the use of the larger muscles or the whole body, show progressive refinements as well. In fact, learning to move from one place to another is one of the greatest achievements in infancy (Adolph, 2008). During this period, most babies learn to crawl on the floor or to creep on their hands and knees, although some infants develop alternative methods of moving such as "bear walking," which employs both hands and feet, or "scooting" while in a sitting position. Most 8-month-olds can get themselves into a sitting position, and nearly all can sit without support if placed in a sitting position. If they are placed on their feet, many 8-month-olds can stand while holding on to a support. Many 8-month-olds begin to play social games, such as peek-a-boo, bye-bye, and patty-cake, and most enjoy handing an item back and forth with an adult. Another quickly learned game is dropping an object and watching someone pick it up and hand it back—a source of endless pleasure for some infants.

Can you describe a particular activity that includes the visually guided reach?

From 9 to 12 Months By 12 months most infants are about three times heavier than they were at birth, although girls tend to weigh slightly less than boys. On average, about half of 12-month-old infants in the United States are standing alone and taking their first tentative steps toward becoming *toddlers*. As noted earlier, however, the age at which walking begins varies widely, depending both on individual development and on sociocultural factors. The ability to stand and walk gives the toddler a new visual perspective, and locomotion allows for more active exploration. Infants can now get into, over, and under things. Motor development is spurred on by new and exciting things to approach and see. Exploring at new levels and with new skills promotes cognitive and perceptual development although at times the coordination of motor ability with judgment may be problematic. For example, Karen Adolph and her colleagues (e.g., Karasik, Tamis-LeMonda, & Adolf, 2011) have observed the capabilities of infants as they learned to walk. In one study, researchers observed infants of different ages as they crawled or walked up and down "slopes" at varying angles

fine motor skills
Those skills that involve the use of the hands and fingers to perform intricate movements

Watch *Development of the Grasp Reflex* on **MyDevelopmentLab**

gross motor skills
Those skills that involve the larger muscles or the whole body to perform more general movements

CHANGING PERSPECTIVES

Sudden Infant Death Syndrome and Shaken Baby Syndrome

In the Western world, infant mortality has been reduced dramatically in the last several decades, due for the most part to good nutrition, regular medical care, and a reasonably safe environment. In Europe and the United States, for example, the rate of infant mortality (deaths in the first year of life) has dropped to about 7 deaths per 1,000 live births, and it continues to decline (NCHS, 2011c). Today, most infant deaths occur shortly after birth, as the result of the two leading causes of infant death—congenital malformations and low birth weight (or premature delivery). But two types of infant death that can happen to seemingly normal and healthy full-term infants are still very troubling—*sudden infant death syndrome*, or SIDS, and *shaken baby syndrome*.

Today in the United States, SIDS is the first leading cause of death in infants between 1 month and 1 year of age, with the most deaths occurring between months 2 and 4 (NCHS, 2011b). Although the rate of SIDS has declined more than 50% since 1990—mostly as the result of the American Academy of Pediatrics' recommendation to place babies on their backs, rather than their stomachs, to sleep—SIDS still accounts for about 30% of all infant deaths after 1 month of age. What causes SIDS, and what can be done to prevent it from happening?

First, it is important to note that death resulting from SIDS, which is sometimes referred to by its older name "crib death," usually occurs at night when the infant and the family are asleep. Mounting evidence suggests that babies born with certain kinds of brain abnormalities or vulnerabilities might be especially susceptible to SIDS. Several mechanisms might be involved. For example, SIDS is most common during the period of brain development during which a changeover takes place from more reflexive to more voluntary control by the brain. It is possible that in susceptible babies there is a gap in brain control of respiration during which breathing reflexes are not maintained and death occurs because breathing stops. Support for the view that respiration mechanisms are involved comes from studies that show that babies who sleep on their stomach (in the prone position) are at greater risk for SIDS and also have lower levels of oxygen in their blood, as well as greater difficulty in being awakened (Wong et al., 2011). Infections also may play a role: A disproportionately large number of SIDS babies have infections just prior to their deaths (Singh Joy, 2008). Also, more SIDS deaths are reported in the winter months when infections are more common. General health most likely is also involved: SIDS is more common among babies born to very young mothers, or mothers who have only late prenatal care or no prenatal care at all. Premature babies and low-birth-weight babies also are at higher risk. It is also possible that some cases of SIDS reflect a genetic defect or vulnerability. For example, boys are more susceptible to SIDS than are girls, as they are to many other childhood disorders.

Culture also seems to play a role. In comparison to non-Hispanic White babies, infants who are African American are at two to three times the risk, and Native American babies are about three times more susceptible. Babies of Asian-American or Hispanic decent are less likely to die as the result of SIDS (NCHS, 2011b). These cultural patterns suggest that some risk factors may be preventable. Recently, the American Academy of Pediatrics (AAP, 2011b) has issued a revised set of recommendations aimed at reducing the occurrence of SIDS. These recommendations include the following:

- Place babies on their backs to sleep for every sleep period, including naps.
- Provide a firm sleep surface.
- Room sharing, but without bed sharing, is recommended.
- Keep soft objects, including stuffed animals, and loose bedding out of the crib.
- Consider offering a pacifier at nap time and bedtime.
- Don't overheat the room.

In addition, the AAP recommends that all pregnant women receive good prenatal care and that they avoid smoking, alcohol, and illicit drugs during pregnancy and after birth. The AAP also recommends breastfeeding, if possible.

A different kind of problem causes shaken baby syndrome, which is the leading cause of death in child abuse cases in the United States (Wheeler, 2001, 2003). Death or, in less severe cases, brain injury results when an infant is shaken with enough force that the baby's brain bounces against the skull, causing it to swell, bruise, and bleed. Shaking also can damage nerve fibers in the neck that control breathing, causing the baby to suffer oxygen deprivation. Shaken baby syndrome does *not* result from the gentle playing that normally occurs between infant and caregiver; it is the result of violent shaking. This distinction has led the American Academy of Pediatrics to recommend that pediatricians use the term "abusive head trauma" when referring to cases involving head trauma as the result of shaking (AAP, 2011a). Most often, the shaking occurs when caregivers experience uncontrolled frustration, often when the infant is crying inconsolably. When the brain injury is severe, death is often the result. However, many babies suffer milder but accumulated injuries from being shaken repeatedly, which can include vision problems resulting from retinal damage; hearing loss; cerebral palsy; various types of intellectual disability; or problems with learning, memory, physical coordination, or speech (National Institute of Neurological Disorders and Stroke, 2010).

Parents or others accused of causing injuries to a child are, of course, subject to legal prosecution for child abuse or perhaps even murder. However, courts must take care when prosecuting suspected cases, as the same symptoms as those associated with shaken baby syndrome can be caused by factors other than abuse, such as rare diseases or even accidents (Wheeler, 2001). Also, most infants diagnosed with shaken baby syndrome do not have obvious, observable signs of abuse, such as bruises or broken bones. Rather, the brain injury problems that result are harder to observe, and diagnosis is difficult. In the absence of eyewitness testimony, physicians are called on to describe what the specific injuries entail, and how they most likely could have come about. Certainly, the courts must weigh evidence very carefully in suspected cases (Geddes & Plunkett, 2004). What can be done to reduce the incidence of abusive head trauma cases? One approach that shows promise is to administer a comprehensive, hospital-based parent education program that is delivered at the time a baby is born. In one such program, all hospitals in an eight-county region of western New York State required new parents to participate in an education program that described the results of violent infant shaking. When the impact of this program was evaluated 6 years later, the results were impressive: During the 6-year period in which babies were followed, there was a 47% decrease in cases of abusive head trauma. Furthermore, no such decline occurred among babies in a Pennsylvania control group in which no head-injury education programming was provided (Dias, et al., 2005). Thus, parental education seems to be one important key in reducing the tragedy that results when infants are abused in this way.

Watch *SIDS* on MyDevelopmentLab

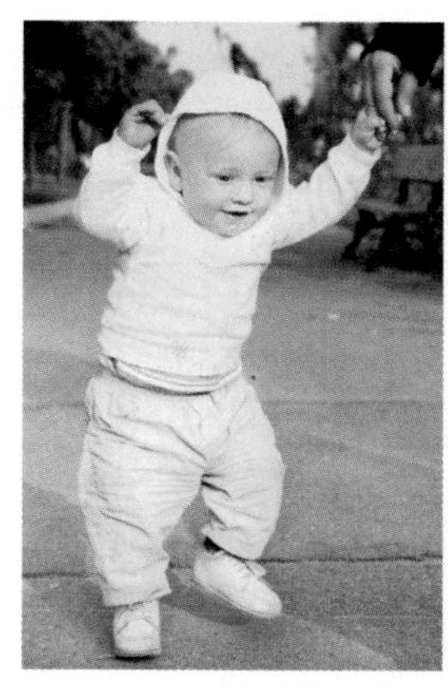

▲ An infant's gross motor skills leading to walking may show considerable individuality. When walking finally occurs, infants need to relearn some of what they previously knew, based on how things look from their new perspective and by incorporating their increasing knowledge about what is safe or dangerous.

(Adolph, 2008). They found that at age 8½ months, infants typically charged up steep slopes, crawling without hesitation. Then, perhaps after surveying the downward side, they continued on headfirst, where most got into trouble and needed to be rescued by the experimenters. In contrast, 14-month-old "walkers" were better judges of risk; after walking up the steep slope, they changed strategies and carefully and safely slid down.

Babies usually learn motor skills in a particular order. For example, children master stair ascent at about 11 months of age but do not learn how to descend stairs until about 2 months later (Berger, Theuring, & Adolph, 2007). Interestingly, children with stairs in their home learn to ascend at an earlier age, but all infants learn to descend at the same age, demonstrating the powerful role of biological maturation.

By 9 to 12 months, babies are learning to play social games, and they "hide" by covering their eyes. They can roll a ball back and forth with an adult and throw small objects, making up in persistence for what they lack in skill. Many children begin to feed themselves at this age, using a spoon and holding their own drinking cup. It is not yet the neatest behavior, but it is a beginning of independent self-care.

Twelve-month-olds actively manipulate their environment. They undo latches, open cabinets, pull toys, and twist lamp cords. Their newly developed *pincer grasp*—a fine motor skill that involves using the thumb and forefinger to "pinch" a small object—allows them to pick up grass, hairs, matches, dead insects, you name it. They can turn on the TV, open windows, and poke things into electrical outlets, which is why relatively constant supervision and a childproofed house become necessary.

From 13 to 18 Months At 18 months of age, children weigh up to four times their birth weight; however, by this age, the rate of increase in weight gain has slowed. Almost all children are walking alone at this age. Some are not yet able to climb stairs, however, and most have considerable difficulty kicking a ball because they cannot free one foot. They also find pedaling tricycles or jumping nearly impossible.

At 18 months, children may be stacking two to four cubes or blocks to build a tower, and they often manage to scribble with a crayon or a pencil. Their ability to feed themselves has improved considerably, and they may be able to partly undress themselves. Many of their actions imitate what they see others doing—"reading" a book, "sweeping" the floor, or where applicable, "chatting" on a toy telephone.

From 19 to 24 Months By their second birthday, toddlers typically weigh just over four times as much as they did at birth, and their rate of growth is continuing to taper off.

Two-year-olds can usually pedal a tricycle, jump in place on both feet, balance briefly on one foot, and throw a ball. They climb up steps. They crawl into, under, and over objects and furniture; they manipulate, carry, handle, push, or pull anything within reach. They pour water, mold clay, stretch the stretchable, bend the bendable. They transport items in carts and wagons. In every way imaginable they explore, test, and probe their physical world. Two-year-olds can also dress and undress, although they often need assistance.

If they are given a crayon or pencil, 2-year-olds may scribble and be fascinated with the magical marks that appear. They may stack six to eight blocks or cubes to build towers, and they can construct a three-block "bridge." Their spontaneous block play shows matching of shapes and symmetry, the beginning of categorization.

As these examples demonstrate, physical and motor development during the first 2 years is a complex, dynamic process (see Table 4-2 for an overview). Each developing system—perceptual, motor, cognitive, and social—supports the others and depends on parallel advances as development proceeds. Brain development, too, not only limits development but also depends on information the child receives from sensing, exploring, and acting on the environment (Cohen & Cashon, 2003; Goswami, 2008a; Wu, Gopnik, Richardson, & Kirkham, 2011). Thus, *all* of these interacting systems are helped or hindered by the social context in which the infant develops. One especially critical aspect of the environment that affects early growth and physical development is nutrition.

Nutrition and Malnutrition

The United States may be one of the best-fed and most obese nations in the world, but many of its people still suffer from

Watch *Motor Development in Infants and Toddlers: Karen Adolph* on **MyDevelopmentLab**

Table 4-2 An Overview of the First 2 Years

Age	Weight	Activities	Developmental milestones
0 to 4 months	2 x birth weight	• Eyes can focus • Reflexes taken over by voluntary control	• "Discovery" of the hands and fingers • Beginning of social smiling
5 to 8 months		• First tooth (4 to 5 months) • Development of fine motor skills • Development of gross motor skills • Simple social games, like peek-a-boo	• Development of the "visually guided reach" • Sitting upright without support • Some creeping and/or crawling
9 to 12 months	3 x birth weight	• Self-feeding and drinking from a cup • More complex social games	• Standing and walking • Development of the "pincer grasp"
13 to 18 months	4 x birth weight	• Can stack blocks • Can partially dress self • Uses crayons to "draw" in scribbles • Interest in "imitation" games and activities	• Can walk without support • May be able to climb stairs
19 to 24 months	Growth rate begins to slow	• Can pedal a tricycle • Can jump (on both feet, not on one) • Can throw a ball	• High interest in exploring the environment

SOURCE: From *Bayley scales of infant and toddler development* (3rd ed.) (Bayley-III). Copyright © 2005 by NCS Pearson, Inc. Reproduced with permission. All rights reserved. "Bayley Scales of Infant and Toddler Development" is a trademark, in the U.S. and/or other countries, of Pearson Education, Inc. or its affiliate(s).

nutritional deficiencies, especially deficiencies of iron and protein (Black & Hurley, 2010). For example, one study of low-income families reported that 20 to 24% of their infants suffered from iron deficiency anemia (Pollitt, 1994). Similar figures have been reported for other nutritional deficiencies, and it is likely that cuts in food-stamp programs and related services have increased the levels of malnutrition in U.S. low-income families in the years since Pollitt's study. Even people who can afford a good diet often consume too many *empty calories* in the form of foods that are high in carbohydrates but low in protein, vitamins, and minerals. A current population-wide estimate of the percent of U.S. infants with iron deficiency would be about 10% (Mahoney, Motil, Drutz, & Hoppin, 2012).

Why are nutritional deficiencies that affect brain development especially problematic?

Around the world in many developing nations, the situation is worse. The World Health Organization (WHO) has estimated that, in 2010, nearly 30% of children under 5 years of age suffer moderate to severe **stunting** as a result of malnutrition (WHO, 2012a), and nearly 30% of people of all ages suffer from one or more forms of malnutrition. In turn, almost half of the annual 10 million deaths of children under age 5 in developing nations are associated with malnutrition; malnutrition contributes to one-third of all child deaths worldwide (UNICEF, 2012b).

Malnutrition during infancy and early childhood is especially problematic because serious deficiencies in the first 30 months of life have effects that are rarely eliminated later (Grantham-McGregor, et al., 2007). Physical growth may be permanently stunted, and there may be delays in maturation and learning (UNICEF, 2012b). Long-term deficits in brain size, together with deficits in attention and information processing, can also occur.

There are two basic types of malnutrition: insufficient total quantity of food and inadequate quantities of foods that contain essential ingredients, such as proteins, vitamins, and minerals. With regard to the former, starvation or the severe lack of food produces deficiencies in protein and in total calorie intake and results in a condition called **marasmus**, in which muscles waste away and stored fat is depleted. Fortunately, if the period of starvation is relatively short, there appear to be few or no long-term negative effects.

A more common type of malnutrition found especially in developing nations occurs when sufficient calories are available but food sources are deficient in one or more necessary nutrients. One such deficiency results in **kwashiorkor**, a condition caused by insufficient protein intake. In famine-plagued Africa, kwashiorkor often results from the customary African practice of placing a nursing child in the home of relatives for weaning if the mother becomes pregnant again. Once removed from the mother's protein-rich breast milk, such children often suffer protein deficiency. The effects of kwashiorkor in the first 3 years of life can be highly damaging in the long run because brain development is directly affected. These and other nutrient deficiencies, along with their effects on children, are summarized in Table 4-3.

stunting
Failure to achieve full adult height due to malnutrition in childhood

marasmus
Type of malnutrition caused by an insufficient total quantity of food where muscles waste away and stored fat is depleted; if the duration is short, no long-term negative effects result

kwashiorkor
Type of severe malnutrition caused by insufficient protein; in the first 3 years of life, the effects of kwashiorkor can be highly damaging because brain development is directly affected

Table 4-3 Some Important Nutrient Deficiencies and How They Affect Children

Nutrient deficiency	Possible effects
Iodine deficiency	• Impaired brain development and associated mental function • Inability to hear or speak • Goiter (an enlargement of the thyroid gland, resulting in either hypothyroidism or hyperthyroidism, with effects on growth)
Iron deficiency	• Anemia • Impaired psychomotor development and coordination • Decreased activity level
Protein deficiency	• Kwashiorkor (affects brain development, may lead to deficits in attention and information processing) • Stunting (failure to achieve full adult height)
Protein and calorie deficiency	• Marasmus (muscles waste away and stored fat is depleted, affects brain development, may lead to deficits in attention and information processing) • Stunting
Vitamin A deficiency	• Severe visual impairment • Possible blindness • A markedly increased susceptibility to common childhood diseases

SOURCE: From "Some important nutritional deficiencies," by World Health Organization, 2000, in *Malnutrition: The global picture*. Retrieved from http://www.who.int/nut/documents/nhd_mip_2000.pdf. Reprinted by permission of World Health Organization.

For many children, lack of sufficient protein in infancy starts a downward cycle that seriously limits their potential. In one study, children in Barbados who were healthy at birth but malnourished during the first year of life were followed until age 11. As the result of a vigorous public health and nutrition program, the children eventually caught up in most aspects of physical growth, but in academic tests at age 11 they showed, on average, a substantial 12-point deficit compared to matched pairs who did not experience malnutrition (Galler, 1984). What went wrong? In a careful follow-up study that used parent interviews, teacher reports, and observation of the children, two findings emerged. First, the malnourished children's behavior was characterized by impulsiveness and attention deficit, making it harder for them to succeed in academic tasks. Second, their parents, most of whom had also been through periods of protein malnutrition, had low energy and symptoms of depression and therefore could not provide a stimulating, focused, or consistent environment for their children (Galler, et al., 2006). In fact, parental depression and hopelessness, together with impulsive and inattentive children, are commonly found in studies of protein malnutrition (Carter, 2010; Galler et al., 2010; Lozoff, et al., 2007). Subsequent follow-up suggests that the depressive symptoms that are seen in adolescents who experience malnutrition during early childhood are not solely the result of being raised in an unstimulating environment. Rather, early malnutrition appears to independently set the stage for the development of depression later in life (Galler et al., 2010). Because well-nourished children have a better chance of becoming productive adults, investment in providing adequate nutrition for children in the developing world is a good economic—as well as humanitarian—investment (Hoddinott, Maluccio, Behrman, Flores, & Martorell, 2008).

Fortunately, even in cases of severe malnutrition during infancy, food supplement programs combined with education can produce dramatic results. In a study in Bogota, Colombia, poverty-level children who were given food supplements for the first 3 years of life showed much less growth retardation and all-around better functioning than comparison groups that did not participate in the program. Furthermore, the improvement was still evident 3 years after the supplements were discontinued (Super, Herrera, & Mora, 1990). For over a decade now, establishing and maintaining programs that get enough food and the right kind of food to the children of the world have been top priorities for both WHO and UNICEF.

Breastfeeding Versus Bottle-Feeding Throughout the world, a mother's milk (or a manufactured substitute) is the major source of nutrition for infants. Although some variations in feeding practices exists, for the first 6 months of life, milk is generally the only food, or at least the primary food, that infants consume. Whether a mother's milk is superior to commercial milk formulas produced as substitutes is a question that generates substantial discourse and sometimes hotly divided opinions. In the past, arguments favored bottle-feeding, often citing that formula was nutritionally superior or more sanitary. However, today most health-care professionals urge mothers who are able to breastfeed their babies. Globally, the percentage of women who choose to breastfeed is increasing, although only about 40% of children in the developing world are exclusively breastfed during the first 6 months of their lives (UNICEF, 2012b). In the United States, the percent of mothers who breastfeed their newborns is about 75%, but this rate falls off to about 40% by age 6 months, and less than a fourth of U.S. babies are still receiving breast milk at 1 year of age (CDC, 2011b; March of Dimes, 2012).

Breastfeeding is strongly encouraged by many organizations interested in promoting children's health, including WHO, UNICEF, the March of Dimes, the American Academy of Pediatrics, and the Surgeon General of the United States. This unified front favors breastfeeding because the breast milk of a well-fed mother contains a remarkably well-balanced combination of nutrients and other beneficial substances. In many parts of the

▲ Experts agree that, when possible, breastfeeding is usually preferable to bottlefeeding.

Table 4-4 Percentage of Babies Being Breastfed in Developing Nations, by Regions of the World

Region	Exclusively breastfed 0–6 months (%)	Still breastfeeding at age 2 (%)
Sub-Saharan Africa	33	46
Middle East and North Africa	34	31
South Asia	45	76
East Asia and the Pacific	29	44
Latin America and Caribbean	42	33
Developing Countries, Average	37	56

SOURCE: From *The state of the world's children, UNICEF, 2012,* New York: Author, Table 2, "Nutrition."

world, it is also much more sanitary than is formula, which may be mixed with contaminated water. As noted by UNICEF:

> [Breast milk] has profound impact on a child's survival, health, nutrition and development. Breast milk provides all of the nutrients, vitamins, and minerals an infant needs for growth for the first six months, and no other liquids or food are needed. In addition, breast milk carries antibodies from the mother that help combat disease. . . . Breastfeeding also lowers the risk of chronic conditions later in life, such as obesity, high cholesterol, high blood pressure, diabetes, childhood asthma and childhood leukaemias. Studies have shown that breastfed infants do better on intelligence and behavior tests into adulthood than formula-fed babies. (UNICEF, 2012a)

Breast milk suits most babies. In addition, breast milk is always fresh and ready at the right temperature, does not need refrigeration, and is normally sterile, making it an especially good choice for third-world infants. Unless the mother is very ill, has an inadequate diet, or uses alcohol or other drugs, breast milk is generally better for a baby's health. Even a malnourished mother's milk can provide adequate nutrients, although often at a cost to her own health.

Despite these advantages, many mothers still choose to bottle-feed their infants. Bottle-feeding causes no hardship or nutritional problems for the great majority of infants in developed nations, but the shift to commercial infant formula has resulted in widespread malnutrition in developing nations (UNICEF, 2012a). Because people in developing nations often lack the money to buy sufficient quantities of, what are for them, extremely expensive breast-milk substitutes, they sometimes water down formulas to stretch them, thereby depriving their babies of adequate nutrition. In addition, many babies become ill and die when commercial formula is diluted with contaminated water, thereby transmitting bacterial diseases to the infant. WHO (2012) estimates that in developing nations where infant mortality rates are high, optimal breastfeeding has the potential to prevent 1.4 million deaths in children under age 5. Even in developed countries, breastfeeding is associated with better mortality. In the United States, non-breastfed infants had a 25% higher mortality rate; in the United Kingdom, 6 months of exclusive breastfeeding was associated with a 53% decrease in hospital admissions for diarrhea and a 27% decrease in respiratory tract infections (UNICEF, 2008a).

weaning
The process of shifting the infant's diet from breast- or bottle-feeding to eating and drinking a wider variety of foods

Why do some mothers breastfeed and others bottle-feed? It appears that good nutrition is only one of many factors influencing their choice (see the box Try This! Attitudes About Breastfeeding). Obviously, cultural factors; personal factors, such as social obligations and the availability of a peer group that accepts breastfeeding; and even national policies may have an effect (see Table 4-4). For example, the United States lacked a family leave policy until 1993, making it difficult for most working mothers to stay at home for any extended period following the birth of the baby. Also, because many employers did not readily accommodate the family-related needs of employees, many women who returned to work a few weeks after the birth of their child found it difficult to combine full-time employment with breastfeeding. However, due in part to a more family-centered focus embraced today by many employers, an increasing number of companies now provide rooms with lactation equipment and refrigeration to allow mothers to collect their breast milk during each workday, which then can be fed to their baby the following day.

Weaning and the Introduction of Solid Foods **Weaning**—the process of shifting an infant's diet from exclusively breast- or bottle-feeding to eating and drinking a wider variety of foods—is largely dependent on culture, as well as on individual preference. Some mothers in industrialized nations begin weaning their babies from the breast or bottle at 3 to 4 months or even earlier; others continue breastfeeding for as long as 2 to 3 years. Although extended breastfeeding is rare among middle- and upper-class mothers in the United States, 2 to 3 years is not unusual in many cultures around the world.

Are you aware of organizational policies in your college or place of employment that either encourage or discourage new mothers to breastfeed their babies?

Normally in most Western industrialized settings, at about 4 months infants gradually start accepting strained foods. Usually they begin with simple cereals such as rice, and their diet expands to include a variety of cereals and pureed fruits, followed later by strained vegetables and meats. By 8 months, most infants are eating a broad range of specially prepared foods, and milk consumption is usually reduced.

Weaning is a crucial time because of the possibility of malnutrition, as we noted earlier. Particularly vulnerable are 1-year-olds who have already been weaned from the breast in families that cannot afford nutritious foods. These children may survive on diets composed of potato chips, dry cereals, and cookies—foods that typically provide calories but few nutrients. Even if enough milk or a variety of nutritious foods are available, 1-year-olds may be unwilling to drink a sufficient amount of milk from a cup or to eat protein-rich foods, especially if tastier but less nutritious foods are readily available.

Nutrition sets the stage for much of an individual's later physical development, and we will revisit this topic in upcoming chapters. In the next section of this chapter, however, we explore how infants' sensory and perceptual abilities develop during the first 2 years—a period filled with exciting changes with respect to these capabilities.

REVIEW THE FACTS 4-3

1. When development is thought to be heavily influenced by the unfolding of a biologically determined timetable, it is referred to as
   a. adaptation. b. accommodation.
   c. maturation. d. habituated.
2. From birth to age 4 months, a typical baby's weight
   a. increases by 25%. b. increases by 50%.
   c. doubles. d. triples.
3. Picking up a piece of cereal with the thumb and forefinger is an example of what kind of motor skill?
4. At about what age do babies begin to play games like peek-a-boo?
   a. 4 months b. 8 months
   c. 12 months d. 15 months
5. Studies of children with protein deficiency often find that children's behaviors are characterized by __________ and their parents exhibit __________.
6. Today, health-care professionals generally recommend
   a. breastfeeding.
   b. bottle-feeding.
   c. a combination of breastfeeding and bottle-feeding.

Practice on **MyDevelopmentLab**

TRY THIS!

Attitudes About Breastfeeding

Parents make a significant decision when they decide whether their newborn will be breastfed or bottle-fed. In most situations, there are many advantages associated with breastfeeding; however, there are inconveniences as well, including social and cultural expectations about what is *proper* and *desirable.*

To explore these attitudes about breastfeeding, first select a group of people to whom you might ask questions about their opinions on this topic. Following is a set of questions that can serve as a guide, but feel free to modify these or add your own questions to get at issues that are of interest to you:

- What do you see as the major advantages associated with breastfeeding a baby? With bottle-feeding a baby?
- What are the major disadvantages associated with breastfeeding? With bottle-feeding?
- *For women:* Have you, or would you, choose to breastfeed or bottle-feed? Why?
- *For men:* Would you prefer the mother of your baby to breastfeed or to bottle-feed? Why?
- In comparison to women who bottle-feed, do you think women who breastfeed their babies are more feminine or less feminine? Do you think they are more attentive to their babies than women who bottle-feed? Do you think women who breastfeed are more or less likely to be politically liberal? Do you think they are more self-confident than women who bottle-feed their babies?

Reflect on What You Observed

In general, how did people respond to the topic of breastfeeding versus bottle-feeding? What advantages and disadvantages did people cite? Were their responses consistent with information presented in the text? Did men and women hold similar views, or did gender make a difference in the responses you got? Did you discern any general attitudes about how breastfeeding mothers were described? If so, what were they? Do you think mothers should be able to breastfeed their infants in public places like restaurants? Why or why not?

Consider the Issues

Many people have strong emotional reactions when they consider the issue of breastfeeding versus bottle-feeding: Some see breastfeeding as completely natural; others are repelled by the practice, especially if it is done in public. Did you feel that people responded to your questions in an emotional way? Do you think that age, gender, social class, or ethnicity might make a difference in the kind of responses that people give? What do *you* think about breastfeeding? How would you answer the questions in your survey?

SENSORY AND PERCEPTUAL DEVELOPMENT

Can newborn babies see patterns and the details of objects? Can they see color and depth? Can they hear a low whisper? How sensitive are they to touch? Research indicates that all of the senses are operating at birth. Thus, **sensation**—the translation of external stimulation into neural impulses—is highly developed. In contrast, **perception**—the active process of interpreting information from the senses—is limited and selective at birth. Perception is a cognitive process that gives organization and meaning to sensory information. It develops rapidly over the first 6 months, followed by fine-tuning over the first several years of life.

Several methods of study have been developed that enhance researchers' understanding of the sensory and perceptual capabilities of infants (see Table 4-5). In particular, carefully developed research questions, cameras and recording devices that capture attention and gaze, and innovative ways to surprise the baby have advanced our ability to understand how even very young infants experience the world. Great progress has also been made with the use of brain scanning and recording technologies, especially with noninvasive functional magnetic resonance imaging (fMRI). These various methods have been employed to understand, among other things, how newborns and infants see and process visual information.

Vision and Visual Perception

Neonates are born with a functioning set of visual structures and a visual perception system that, although immature, is well organized and coherent (de Haan, 2008; Shipley & Zacks, 2008; Slater & Johnson, 1998). For example, from birth, newborns' eyes are sensitive to brightness, their pupils contract and dilate according to the amount of light present, and they have some control over eye movements, as evidenced by their ability to visually track (follow) an object such as a doctor's face or a penlight as it moves across their field of vision.

The Early Development of Visual Perception Infants' vision is not, however, completely developed at birth (Slater et al., 2011; Slater & Johnson, 1998). It has long been known that newborns focus optimally on objects at a range of 7 to 10 inches (17.8 to 25.4 centimeters), with objects closer or farther away appearing blurred. Until about the end of the second month, newborns also lack fine convergence of the eyes, which means that they cannot focus both eyes on a single point. Focusing ability, however, improves rapidly; 3- to 4-month-olds focus almost as well as adults (Aslin, 1987). Visual acuity also sharpens dramatically in the first 6 months.

Older infants also are better able to control their eye movements; they can track moving objects more consistently and for longer periods. They also spend more time scanning and surveying their environment. By 3 or 4 months, infants can use motion, shape, and spatial positioning to help define the objects in their world (Braddock & Atkinson, 2011; Gwiazda & Birch, 2001). Color discrimination improves steadily during the first year (Okamura, So Kanazawa, & Yamaguchi, 2007). Although newborns can discriminate some bright colors, by 2 months, they can discriminate among most colors (Adams & Courage, 1995), and by 6 months their color perception nearly equals

Table 4-5 Methods of Studying Infant Sensation, Perception, and Cognition

Physiology-based methods	
Anatomical investigation	Scientific and medical examination of sensory structures and brain development
Physiological recordings	Measurement of physiological responses such as heart rate, blood pressure, and skin temperature to detect changes in arousal and infants' reactions to various stimuli
Brain imaging	Various techniques used (especially positron emission tomography [PET] scans and functional MRIs) to observe ongoing activity in sensory regions in the brain while infants engage in various tasks
Event-related potential and evoked potential techniques	Like an electroencephalogram (EEG); these techniques use electrodes pasted to the head to record general patterns of electrical activity in the brain
Learning/Habituation-based methods	
Novelty paradigm	Based on habituation, this method records the length of time an infant attends to a situation and the degree to which a change in the situation attracts the infant's attention
Preference paradigm	Presents two stimuli and records the amount of time the infant attends to each; can be modified so that an infant can produce a preferred outcome (e.g., hearing the mother's voice) by engaging in a specific behavior (e.g., sucking on a pacifier)
Surprise paradigm	Measures the infant's reaction (both behavioral and physiological changes) when an unexpected situation is encountered

sensation
The translation of stimulus energy, such as light waves, into a neural impulse by a sense organ

perception
The complex process by which the brain interprets and gives meaning to sensory information

that of adults (Adams & Courage, 1995; Franklin, Bevis, Ling, & Hurlbert, 2010; Teller, 1998).

Selective Attention in Visual Development Despite their visual limitations, it is clear that newborns can visually perceive their environment because they are selective about what they look at. For example, classic research indicates that newborns prefer to look at patterns of *moderate* complexity, focusing most attention at the edges and contours of objects, especially curves (Bushnell, 2001, 2003; Cohen & Cashon, 2003). Newborn babies also are highly responsive to the human face (Cashon, 2011; Macchi, Valenza, Simion, & Leo, 2008; Pascalis & Kelly, 2009; Turati, Cassia, Simion, & Leo, 2006; Turati, Macchi, Cassia, Simion, & Leo, 2006). When presented with pictures of their mother and an unfamiliar woman, even infants as young as 2 weeks of age preferred to look at their mother's photo, and they sometimes turned completely away from the image of the stranger (MacFarlane, 1978). This ability to discriminate their mother may have had significant survival value in our evolutionary past, and it is still highly adaptive in forming a secure infant–caregiver attachment (see Chapter 5). Also, when newborns only a few days old were presented with pictures of a happy face and a fearful face, they looked longer at the happy face (Farroni, Menon, Rigato, & Johnson, 2007), again suggesting that infants are well prepared to engage in early attachment interactions with their mothers. Clearly, infants are born with an impressive set of visual competencies, which become better developed and more complete as the result of their experiences (Bhatt & Quinn, 2011).

Infants are especially attentive to images of the human face, although the focus of their attention shifts somewhat as they develop. At 2 months, infants look at internal features of the face, such as the eyes. By 5 months, they more often look at the mouth of a person who is talking. By 6 to 7 months, they respond to whole facial expressions and can discriminate differing expressions, such as "happy" versus "fearful" (Lewkowitz & Hansen-Tift, 2012; Nelson & de Haan, 1996). Interestingly, research also indicates that 6-month-olds' brain activity consistently differs in response to faces compared to objects—as does that of adults (de Haan & Nelson, 1999; Southgate, Csibra, Kaufman, & Johnson, 2008). Facial perception is a complex phenomenon, as research on the "other-race" effect demonstrates. Like adults, infants as young as 6 months of age have more trouble distinguishing between faces of people belonging to a racial group to which they have little exposure (Balas, Westerlund, Hung, & Nelson, 2011). It is tempting to think that this "other-race" effect is the result of obvious cues, such as skin color, but research suggests that this is not the case. For example, one study presented babies with photographs of same-race versus other-race faces that were modified in such a way that skin color cues were minimized by using gray-scale images of equal intensity. Even when skin color was eliminated as a cue for race, babies still had more trouble recognizing faces of "other-race" adults (Anzures, Pascalis, Quinn, Slater, & Lee, 2011). Thus, facial recognition seems to be based on a complex assessment of shape-based and feature-based cues, and not merely on obvious color differences among faces. Of course, learning plays a role—infants have an easier time distinguishing among faces whose features are similar to those of their mothers, and thus are more familiar. Yet, it does seem as if *what* the infants attend to—the shape and configuration of the facial features—is prewired and emerges very early in life (Pascalis, Kelly, & Schwarzer, 2009).

One of the more remarkable examples of a neonate's visual perception of faces is the early ability to seemingly imitate facial expressions. When infants only 2 or 3 days old are exposed to an adult model who displays a series of expressions—such as pursing the lips, sticking out the tongue, and opening the mouth—they oftentimes match their own expression to that of the model (Meltzoff & Moore, 1977, 2002; see Figure 4-4). Although it has been argued that newborns perform such behaviors in response to a variety of stimuli—or perhaps even reflexively—and therefore might not strictly be imitating (e.g., see Jones, 1996; Jones & Herbert, 2006), it does appear that they see the stimuli and respond in a selective way that at least resembles imitation.

Mirror Neurons and Imitation Imitation is, of course, an extremely important ability—we learn much of what we know by watching others, by observing cause-and-effect events in our environment, and by copying the actions that we see as leading to the outcomes we desire (Meltzoff & Williamson, 2010). Recently, neuroscience researchers have identified a system of neurons in the brains of humans and some other animals that may explain how imitation works. The cells in this neural system—called **mirror neurons**—are active both when an individual performs a specific action and when the person observes the action being performed by another. Thus, the mirror neuron system provides information about how individuals are able to connect what they observe in their environment to their own actions. As such, the system provides a means of explaining how imitation learning occurs (Iacoboni, 2012).

The original research that led to the discovery of mirror neurons involved the study of hand movement in macaque monkeys (e.g., Gallese, Fadiga, Fogassi, & Rizzolatti, 1996; Rizzolatti & Craighero, 2004; Rizzolatti, Fogassi, & Gallese, 2006). To study the neural mechanisms involved in hand movement, very small microelectrodes were surgically implanted into the monkeys' brains in such a way that the activity of only a single neuron would be recorded. The researchers noticed that, as predicted, these individual neurons fired when the monkeys picked up a piece of food, indicating that this neural system in the brain was involved in hand movements. However, what was surprising

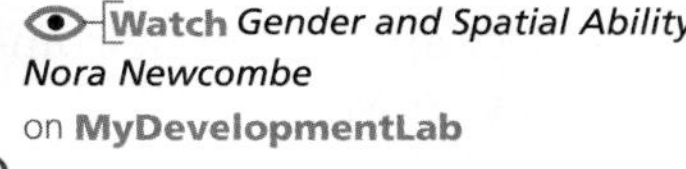
Gender and Spatial Ability: Nora Newcombe on **MyDevelopmentLab**

mirror neurons
Neurons in the brains of humans and some other animals that fire both when an individual performs a specific action and when the individual watches this action being performed by another

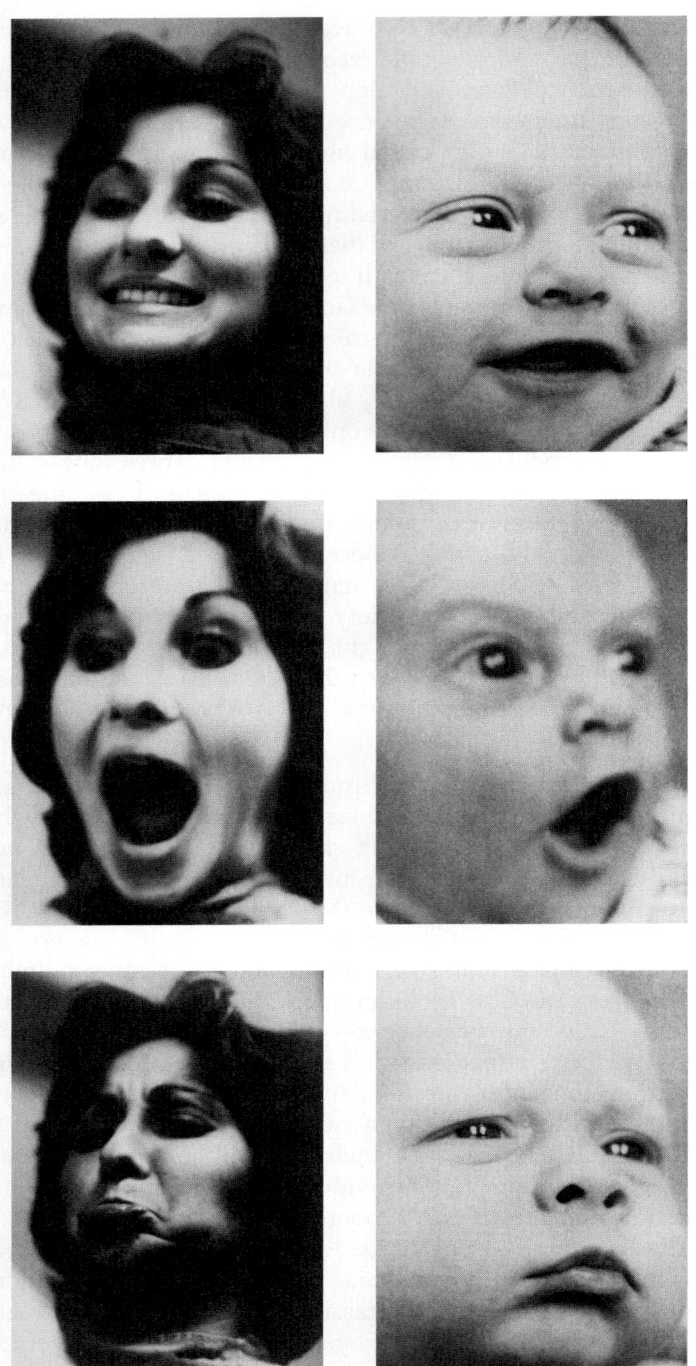

FIGURE 4-4 Imitations by Newborns
Although some theorists disagree, it seems clear that very young neonates are capable of behaviors that closely resemble imitation.

was that these same neurons fired when the monkeys *watched* a person pick up the food—no action was required. Thus, these "mirror neurons," as they came to be called, appeared to work in the same way regardless of whether an action was *performed* or *observed* (Rizzolatti, Sinigaglia, & Anderson, 2008).

Subsequent work using both functional magnetic resonance imaging (fMRI) and the same single-neuron recording techniques as used in the original monkey studies has confirmed that human brains, like those of the macaque monkeys, also contain a mirror neuron system (e.g., Molenberghs, Cunnington, & Mattingley, 2009; Rizzolatti & Sinigaglia, 2010). Researchers are now studying how mirror neurons may provide a neurological explanation for how individuals connect their actions and thought. In particular, the discovery of mirror neurons has been a very exciting development in understanding the basis of imitation and social learning—how we learn by watching others (Glenberg, 2011a,b). It also has led to considerable speculation that mirror neurons may help explain many other important human abilities, ranging from our ability to understand speech to our ability to comprehend how others think about problems (Corballis, 2010). It may also serve as the basis for *empathy*—the ability to understand how another person feels (Gallese, Gernsbacher, Heyes, Hickok, & Iacoboni, 2011; Preston & de Waal, 2002). Recently, scientists have begun to speculate about the possibility that malfunctions in the mirror neuron system may be implicated in *autism*, a disorder that involves—among other features—social withdrawal and abnormal and uncontrolled social behavior. (Autism is discussed more fully in Chapter 8.) Some researchers are speculating that autism may be the result of a "broken" mirror neuron system. Although there is debate about how mirror neuron systems may be involved (e.g., Schroeder, Desrocher, Bebko, & Cappadocia, 2010; Southgate, Gergely, & Csibra, 2009), research is under way that should help researchers better understand the relationship between brain activity and this and many other important topics in human development. Clearly, the discovery of mirror neuron systems in the brain is an exciting new path for understanding the development of many important human abilities (Casile, Caggiano, & Ferrari, 2011; Rizzolatti, Sinigaglia & Anderson, 2008).

Depth and Distance Perception A key aspect of visual perception is the ability to see that some things are closer and others are farther away. Even with one eye closed (monocular vision), we can determine the approximate distance of objects by relying on a variety of environmental cues. Depth perception is even better when we use both eyes (binocular vision) because each eye sees objects from a slightly different angle and the brain is able to process this visual disparity as a means of determining depth and distance.

Why is the development of depth perception an important accomplishment for the infant?

Researchers have studied infants to determine how they develop depth perception. Although the inability to accurately focus the eyes probably limits the newborn's perception of distance or depth, there is some evidence that the rudiments of depth perception are present from a very early age (Braddick & Atkinson, 2011). Even as early as 6 weeks, infants use spatial cues to react defensively—by dodging, blinking, or showing other forms of avoidance—when an object appears to be coming directly at them (Dodwell, Humphrey, & Muir, 1987). Binocular vision emerges at about 4 months (Aslin & Smith, 1988); at this age, infants can swipe with reasonable accuracy at a toy

FIGURE 4-5 A Visual Cliff Apparatus
Even when coaxed by their mothers, infants 6 months or older will not crawl over the edge of the visual cliff.

that is dangled in front of them. By 5 to 6 months, they also have a well-controlled, visually guided reach, as noted earlier.

A classic approach to assessing infants' depth perception uses the "visual cliff" created by Eleanor Gibson and her colleagues (e.g., Gibson & Walk, 1960) to simulate depth (see Figure 4-5). On one side of the horizontal surface, a heavy piece of glass covers a solid surface. On the other side, the glass is well above the floor, simulating a cliff. Infants 6 months or older typically refuse to crawl across the cliff, indicating they perceive the drop-off.

Data from a variety of sources indicate that perception of distance or depth develops within the first few weeks (Cohen & Cashon, 2003), although it continues to develop throughout at least the first 7 months (Yonas & Granrud, 2006). The *meaning* of distance or depth is learned more gradually, however, as the child begins to move about in the environment. For example, in the visual-cliff experiments, if the mother is encouraging, the baby can often be coaxed to cross the deep side if the depth is relatively shallow (Kermoian & Campos, 1988). However, the same baby will refuse to cross if the mother signals that it is dangerous by speaking anxiously or by otherwise expressing fear. Thus, we see that perceptual development relies not only on the maturation of biological mechanisms but also on our understanding of cognitive and social events as well.

Hearing and Auditory Perception

It is obvious that newborn infants can hear: They are startled by loud sounds; they are soothed by low-pitched sounds, such as lullabies; and they fuss when they hear high-pitched squeaks and whistles. How refined is neonatal hearing, or *audition?*

The anatomical structures for hearing are well developed in the newborn (Aslin, Clayards, & Bardhan, 2008). For the first few weeks, however, there is excess fluid and tissue in the middle ear, and hearing is believed to be muffled—similar to the way you hear if you have a head cold. Acuity of hearing improves considerably over the first few months, and infants have fairly well-developed auditory perception within the first 6 months of life.

Infants also can localize the sources of sounds. Even in their first few days of life, they will turn their head toward a sound or a voice. Later, somewhat after they develop visually guided reach, they can use sound cues to localize objects in the dark (Clifton, Rochat, Robin, & Berthier, 1994; LaGasse, Van Vorst, Brunner, & Zucker, 1999), which is an impressive display of their auditory abilities. However, the brain structures that transmit and interpret auditory information are not fully developed at birth but rather continue to develop well into adulthood (Poulsen, Picton, & Paus, 2007). Nevertheless, even newborns can respond to a wide range of sounds.

The Early Development of Auditory Perception In general, infants are especially attentive to human speech (Burnham & Mattock, 2011; Mattock, Amitay, & Moore, 2010). Neonates prefer human voices and their mother's voice in particular. This is likely because of the regular exposure to their mother's voice prior to birth. Moreover, in studies where researchers had mothers read certain passages aloud prior to the birth of their child, it was found that neonates later preferred those passages over novel ones—indicating an early capability for relatively complex speech discrimination (DeCasper, Lecanuet, Busnel, & Granier-Deferre, 1994). This early preference for the sounds of human speech, along with the significance infants attach to it, sets the stage for the development of language, which is discussed more fully at the end of this chapter (Lecanuet, Granier-Deferre, & DeCasper, 2005).

Are there other behaviors and abilities that appear to be linked to the baby's propensity to learn language? What might these be?

Taste, Smell, and Touch

The senses of taste and smell are fully operational at birth. Newborns discriminate among sweet, salty, sour, and bitter tastes, as evidenced by facial expressions (Rosenstein & Oster, 1988). They also can discriminate between odors (Goubet, et al., 2002) and react negatively to strong odors. They also are

Watch *Classic Footage of Eleanor Gibson, Richard Walk, and the visual cliff* on **MyDevelopmentLab**

Watch *Tracking Technologies and Infant Perception: Scott Johnson* on **MyDevelopmentLab**

selectively attracted to positive odors, such as those of a lactating mother (Makin & Porter, 1989). As early as 4 days of age, infants can distinguish the smell of their mother from that of another woman, and they prefer her familiar scent (Porter & Winberg, 1999).

The sense of touch is well developed even in preterm newborns, and soft, regular touch can provide comfort (Stack, 2010). For example, regular stroking of tiny preterm infants in their incubators helps regulate their breathing and other bodily processes, and simply holding newborns' arms or legs is often enough to soothe them. Swaddling—the practice of wrapping a baby tightly in a cloth or a blanket—has a similar effect (Nugent & Brazelton, 2000). Newborns also feel pain, causing some parents and physicians to question the wisdom of pain-inducing practices such as circumcision, thereby calling into question certain cultural traditions.

Sensory Integration

Infants possess good sensory and perceptual abilities at birth, and these abilities are quickly expanded and refined in the first few months of life. How adept are newborns at *integrating*, or combining, the information gathered from different sensory channels—such as vision and touch—into coordinated perceptions?

Research generally indicates that sensory integration occurs early and rapidly and may be present at birth (Hollich & Prince, 2009; Meltzoff, 2007). In one classic study, infants were allowed to suck on one of two different pacifiers, one covered with bumps and the other smooth. When the pacifier was removed and the infants were simply shown each pacifier, they looked longer at the one that they had just felt in their mouth, which indicates they were integrating its visual appearance with its feel in the mouth (Meltzoff & Borton, 1979). In another study, 4-month-olds were shown two novel films with a soundtrack that matched only one film. The infants preferred to look at the film that matched the sound (Kuhl & Meltzoff, 1988), indicating visual–auditory integration. Comparable results have been obtained with 6-month-olds matching male and female faces with voices (Walker-Andrews, Bahrick, Raglioni, & Diaz, 1991), with 7-month-olds using matched versus mismatched facial expressions and vocalizations (Soken & Pick, 1999), and in similar studies conducted by numerous other researchers (see Lickliter & Bahrick, 2000). It has even been found that newborns only a few *hours* old can readily learn arbitrary pairings of sights and sounds (Morrongiello, Fenwick, & Chance, 1998).

Of course, sensory integration becomes better refined as development proceeds; older infants are better at it than are younger infants (Neil, Chee-Ruiter, Scheier, Lewkowicz, & Shimojo, 2006; Robinson & Sloutsky, 2007). As infants develop, their experiences with the environment become incorporated with sensory and perceptual information as well (Scott, Pascalis, & Nelson, 2007). For example, younger infants placed on the visual cliff recognize depth, but they do not appear to recognize it as unsafe. Older infants, who possess more experience with depth—and with what happens if they crawl off a step—see the danger and refuse to crawl onto the glass over the "deep" side. Furthermore, infants retain these experiences as they continue to develop. For example, infants who have learned to avoid crawling over the "deep" side of the visual cliff are likely to maintain their avoidance when they begin walking (Withering et al., 2005).

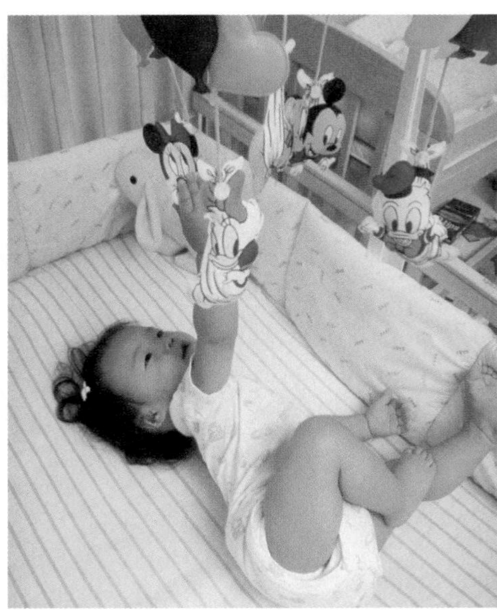

The coordinating of vision with reaching—the visually guided reach—is one of the milestones in development.

In general, as infants develop, their abilities increasingly begin to take on a cognitive focus. Thinking and gaining knowledge about our world are critically important aspects of human development. In the next section of the chapter, we explore the development of these cognitive abilities.

REVIEW THE FACTS 4-4

1. The process of converting external stimuli into neural impulses is __________; the process of interpreting the meaning of those impulses is __________.
2. The neurons in the brain that fire both when an action is performed and when it is observed are called __________ neurons.
3. When we perceive depth with one eye closed, we are using cues associated with __________ vision.
4. Infants seem especially attentive to what kinds of sounds?
5. If an infant were placed on a visual cliff, which of the following abilities would develop first?
   a. the ability to recognize depth
   b. the ability to judge the situation as unsafe

Practice on **MyDevelopmentLab**

COGNITIVE DEVELOPMENT

Cognition is a set of interrelated processes through which we gain and use knowledge about our world. It includes thinking, learning, perceiving, remembering, and understanding—all processes central to our understanding of human nature. *Cognitive development* refers to the growth and refinement of these intellectual processes. In infancy, cognitive development is closely linked to the development of sensation and perception because these capabilities provide the foundations for early thought. In fact, some of the earliest events in cognitive development involve the categorization of objects into groups based on how we perceive such objects to be alike and different from each other.

Perceptual Organization and Categories

Some researchers believe that infants may be born with the ability to "carve up" the physical world into **categories** (Gelman, 1998, 2003; Rakison, 2010) well before they can express them in words or solve problems that involve placing objects into groups with similar members. For example, by 3 months of age, infants can distinguish between male and female faces and voices almost as well as adults can, and they can tell the difference when they look at two versus three objects. This does not mean that infants have conceptual knowledge about men and women or that they understand the concept of number, but it does indicate that they can, and do, organize their perceptions of objects and events into groups, or categories (Balas, Westerlund, Hung, & Nelson, 2011; Mandler, 1992; Quinn, 2002). At 7 or 8 months, for example, infants have at least a global concept of animals versus vehicles; at 9 months, with practice, they can differentiate between birds and airplanes. Thus, it appears that perceptual analysis is working even in very young infants; they are sorting, organizing, and noticing differences and similarities early on, and these early attempts at categorization continue as development proceeds (Cohen & Cashon, 2003). Although we do not yet fully understand how infants form categories (Gliga, Mareschal, & Johnson, 2008; Oakes & Madole, 2000), we do know that, from very early in development, infants organize the world they experience according to the similarities and differences they perceive.

Piaget's Concept of Schemes

The idea that infants organize their world into categories plays an important role in many theories of cognitive development. Several of these perspectives are discussed at various points throughout this text. In this chapter, we focus on the work of Jean Piaget, one of the most influential developmental theorists of the 20th century (see Chapter 1). Piaget believed that infants are active, alert, creative beings who possess mental structures called *schemes* (or *schemas*). Schemes are much like mental categories because they provide the structure according to which the world is organized.

The Sensorimotor Period

According to Piaget, the infant's first schemes are built around the basic reflexes present at birth (see Chapter 3), and they are elaborated through the infant's sensory and perceptual experiences. Innate, instinctive behavioral schemes, such as looking, visually following, sucking, grasping, and crying, are thus the building blocks for cognitive development. Over the next 24 months—a stage Piaget called the **sensorimotor period**—these reflexive schemes are transformed into early concepts of objects, people, and self. Thus, sensorimotor behavior is where intelligence begins.

Adaptation The process by which simple, inborn reflexes are gradually transformed into our understanding of ourselves and our world is called **adaptation**. According to Piaget's theory, adaptation occurs when we experience new events in our environment and adjust our mental schemes to include the new information. Adaptation can occur in two ways: through *assimilation*, in which a new event is simply incorporated into an already present scheme, and through *accommodation*, which requires us to modify a scheme in order to incorporate the new information. For example, an early scheme is the sucking reflex. If a caretaker introduces a nipple-shaped pacifier to a 2-week-old infant, chances are that the baby will *assimilate* this new experience, thereby requiring no adjustment to the original sucking scheme. Imagine, however, the first time the baby attempts to drink from a cup; here the sucking reflex must *accommodate* (change) in order to adjust to the new method of delivering milk. It is through a balance of assimilation and accommodation that our intellect develops in response to our experiences.

Sensorimotor Stages Piaget viewed the sensorimotor period as comprised of six fairly discreet stages (see Table 4-6). Each stage involves significant advances over the previous stage, as schemes become better adapted to the infant's environment and to the infant's developing skills and abilities. Although a thorough discussion of each of these six stages is beyond the scope of this text, there are a few major accomplishments that occur during the sensorimotor period.

Can you think of games or activities that involve the process of categorization?

Object Play Right from birth, infants are interested in the world around them. At about 5 months, when they acquire the ability to reach out and grasp, babies begin to engage in *object play*, in which the manipulation of objects provides pleasure. Object play develops through identifiable stages, starting with simple explorations at about 5 months. As infants gain greater motor control, they begin to wave objects around, put them in their mouths, and test them by hitting them against other objects, although they are not yet aware of their use or function. By 12 months, infants examine objects closely before putting them in their mouths. By 15 to 18 months, they try to use objects appropriately. For example, they may pretend to drink from a toy cup or brush their hair with a toy brush. By 21 months, they use many objects appropriately: They try to feed a doll with a spoon, place a doll in the driver's seat of a toy truck, or use keys to unlock an imaginary door. Play becomes even more realistic by 24 months.

category
A grouping of different things that have some feature in common

sensorimotor period
Piaget's first period of cognitive development (from birth to about 2 years)

adaptation
In Piaget's theory, the process by which infant schemes are elaborated, modified, and developed; adaptation typically involves assimilation and accommodation

Table 4-6 Six Stages of Sensorimotor Development

Stage	Age	Description	Example
Stage 1: The Use of Reflexes	0 to 1 month	Early reflexes (such as sucking, grasping, looking, and hearing) stabilize and are used in a variety of situations in which they are appropriate.	Neonates suck whenever their mouths are stimulated, whether that be by breast, nipple, pacifier, or parent's finger.
Stage 2: Adaptation of Early Reflexes	1 to 4 months	Reflexes become more intentional, and can be repeated when desired.	Infants can intentionally put their thumbs in their mouth and suck for comfort; infants can focus their gaze and intentionally *look* at something.
Stage 3: The Beginning of Intention	4 to 8 months	Infants now experience "desire" in advance of gratification; they also begin to develop the concept of object permanence.	Infants can look at a rattle held in their hand, and intentionally shake it to produce noise; infants can search for a partially hidden object, indicating that they can conceptualize the whole object even if it is not completely in view.
Stage 4: Goal-Directed Activities and Object Search	8 to 12 months	Infants can apply old behaviors to new situations; they also now understand that objects exist even when completely out of view.	Infants can intentionally imitate an already-learned action, such as hand clapping or vocalizing; they also will search for an object hidden under a pillow, although they become confused if the object is moved to a second location.
Stage 5: The Invention of New Behaviors	12 to 18 months	Toddlers can invent new behaviors they have never before performed; they begin to explore using trial-and-error methods.	Toddlers can "play" drums by banging on toys or pots, and by using different "sticks" such as hands, rattles, or spoons. They also can now imitate actions they have never performed before, such as dialing a toy telephone.
Stage 6: Internal Representation of the External World	18 to 24 months	Toddlers can picture events mentally and can to some extent "think" about them. This allows toddlers to solve some novel problems and to imitate actions after the model has disappeared (deferred imitation).	Toddlers can engage in "pretend" play, for example, pretending to have a tea party for dolls. They also can now understand that objects can be represented mentally, which sets the stage for language acquisition.

Toddlers take dolls out for walks and line up trucks and trailers in the right order. Realistic play is a precursor to later imaginary play, where *pretend* becomes the most interesting game.

Object Permanence According to Piaget, **object permanence** is a major accomplishment of the sensorimotor period. Object permanence is the awareness that objects exist in time and space, whether or not they are present and in view. With regard to objects in general, "out of sight, out of mind" seems to be literally true throughout much of early infancy. If a young infant cannot see something, then that something does not exist. Thus, a covered toy holds no interest, even if the infant continues to hold onto it under the cover.

The development of object permanence involves a series of cognitive accomplishments. First, infants as young as 2 months old are able to recognize familiar objects. For example, they become excited at the sight of a bottle or their caregivers. In addition, at about 2 months, infants may watch a moving object disappear behind one side of a screen and then shift their eyes to the other side to see if the object reappears. Their visual tracking is excellent and well timed, and they are surprised if something does not reappear. However, they do not seem to mind when a completely different object appears from behind the screen. In fact, infants up to 5 months old will accept a variety of changes in disappearing objects with no distress or surprise.

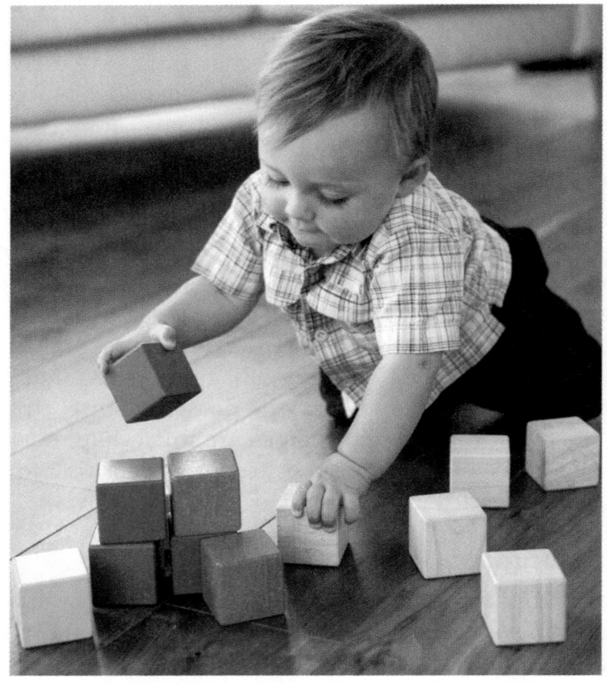

▲ Even before the end of the first year, infants are sorting, organizing, and discovering perceptual categories. Later, as 2- and 3-year-olds, they can learn the words that go with their perceptual categories.

Watch *The Sensorimotor Stage* on **MyDevelopmentLab**

object permanence
According to Piaget, the realization by infants beginning at about 8 months that objects continue to exist when they are out of sight

Watch *Hidden Elephant (Object Permanance)* on **MyDevelopmentLab**

Infants more than 5 months old are more discriminating trackers. They are disturbed if a different object appears or if the same object reappears but moves faster or more slowly than before. However, even these older infants can be fooled, and most infants do not develop a mature sense of object permanence as measured on tasks such as these until near the end of the sensorimotor period.

Although Piaget's view of the development of object permanence provides a good description for how this scheme develops, many researchers still disagree about the specific roles that infant cognition may play (Baillargeon, Li, Gertner, & Wu, 2011; L. B. Cohen & Cashon, 2003, 2006). For example, when 6-month-old infants were shown either a disk-shaped or triangle-shaped object that was then hidden from their view, they were not surprised if the object changed shape while hidden, but they were surprised if it disappeared (Kibbe & Leslie, 2011). Thus, it appears that object permanence develops sequentially, much as Piaget described. However, researchers also note that object permanence may develop earlier than Piaget proposed. For example, infants often are capable of more adultlike behavior when the tasks are more obvious than those used by Piaget (Baillargeon, 2004; Song & Baillargeon, 2008). For example, infants develop a sense of object permanence about their mothers as early as 8 months, much sooner than Piaget's view predicts. In addition, research suggests that an infant's failure to track an object moving behind a screen may be more a problem with *integrating* the tasks of looking, reaching, and remembering rather than a lack of the development of object permanence (Smith, Thelen, Titzer, & McLin, 1999).

Sensory integration may also be involved, as demonstrated by an experiment in which 6½-month-old infants were presented with audible or silent objects that remained visible, became hidden by darkness, or became hidden by being covered up (Shinskey, 2008). Auditory cues helped the babies search when objects were covered by darkness but not when they were hidden by being covered up. Results suggest that auditory information becomes more integrated into infants' object representation with experience over time and that object permanence develops gradually throughout infancy as babies accumulate experience in the world, learning more about the objects in it (Moore & Meltzoff, 2008).

Imitation Imitation, like object play and object permanence, develops in complexity throughout infancy. Although it is difficult to determine whether early actions are imitations or are merely coincidence or reflexive behavior, by 3 to 4 months, infants and their mothers often begin to engage in imitative talking, in which the infant appears to be trying to match the sounds of the mother's voice. Typically, however, the mother begins the game by imitating the infant, and it can be hard to tell who is imitating whom. By 6 or 7 months, infants can imitate simple gestures and actions fairly accurately, and by 9 months, infants can imitate more complex gestures, such as banging two objects together. During the second year, as other cognitive skills develop, infants begin to imitate entire series of actions or gestures. Although early on infants imitate only actions that they choose themselves, later they are able to imitate actions requested of them, such as brushing their teeth. Some toddlers even toilet train themselves by imitating an older child or a caregiver.

Can you describe how mother–infant "dialogue" demonstrates the concept of reciprocal interaction between infants and caregivers?

Does imitation require a mental representation of the action being imitated? Is it thinking? Piaget believed that even simple imitation requires complex thought; therefore, he predicted that infants would not be capable of imitating unfamiliar, novel actions until they were at least 9 months old. He also believed that **deferred imitation**—imitating something that happened hours or even days before—requires cognitive skills, such as memory, that are not sufficiently developed in the first 18 months.

However, subsequent research shows that infants can imitate unfamiliar actions considerably earlier than Piaget predicted. For example, children of parents who are deaf begin to learn and use sign language as early as 6 or 7 months (Mandler, 1988) and nearly all children appear to have developed a conceptual system complex enough to allow for language to begin by at least 9 months of age (Mandler, 2004b, 2007), which is much earlier than Piaget noted. Research studies also demonstrate that infants are capable of deferred imitation well before 18 months. For example, one study (Meltzoff, 1988a, 1988b) used novel toys, such as a box with a hidden button that would sound a beep. Infants were shown how to operate the toys but were not given the opportunity to

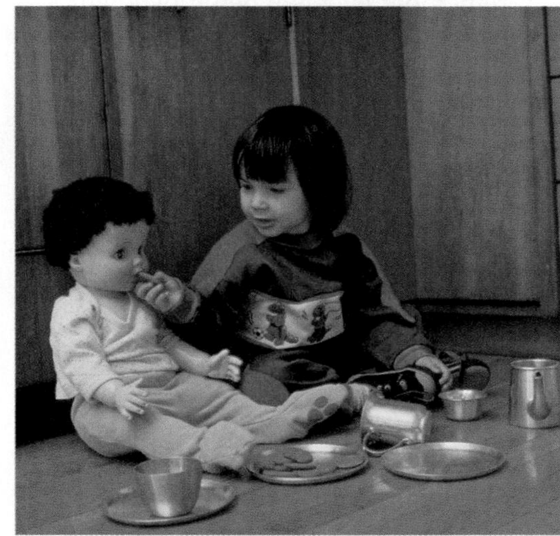

Children generally start pretending between 6 and 12 months—particularly if they have the help of an older sibling. Here, pretend play on the part of an older child is well-developed.

Watch *The Role of Gesture in Thinking: Susan Goldwin-Meadow* on **MyDevelopmentLab**

deferred imitation
Imitating something that happened hours or even days earlier

perform these actions right away. The researchers found that 11-month-olds could reproduce the actions up to 24 hours later, and 14-month-olds could reproduce them as much as a week later. Subsequent research has demonstrated deferred imitation after a 24-hour delay with infants as young as 6 months of age (Barr, Dowden, & Hayne, 1996; Collie & Hayne, 1999), although these young infants require more exposure to the target behaviors than older infants do. It is also worth noting that young infants display apparently stable individual differences in the capability for deferred imitation (Heimann & Meltzoff, 1996); some are consistently better than others, independent of age, and these early differences carry through into childhood. For example, one study showed that low performance on deferred imitation tasks at 9 and 14 months was associated with lower scores on tests of cognitive abilities at age 4 (Strid, Tjus, Smith, Melzoff, & Heimann, 2006).

Memory and Symbolic Representation The sensorimotor abilities discussed thus far generally require some form of memory. Clearly, by the end of infancy, memory processes are reliable and well developed (Bauer, 2004, 2007). We noted earlier that 4-month-old infants prefer to look at novel objects, which shows that they have already established memory for the familiar. An infant who imitates must remember the sounds and actions of another person, at least briefly. Infants who search for a toy where they have seen it hidden are remembering the location of that toy.

Very young infants appear to have especially powerful memory for *visual* events (Daman-Wasserman, Brennan, Radcliffe, Prigot, & Fagen, 2006). Habituation studies have shown that infants as young as 2 months of age store visual patterns (Cohen & Cashon, 2003), and 5-month-olds can recognize patterns 48 hours later and photographs of human faces 2 weeks later (Pascalis, de Haan, Nelson, & de Schonen, 1998). Memories of dramatic events may be remembered even longer. Infants also are more likely to remember events when movement and motion are involved (Hayne & Rovee-Collier, 1995) or when music is associated with the events (Fagen, et al., 1997). Infants as young as 6 months can form associations between objects that were not physically present and had never occurred together, indicating that memory processes are present and active very early in infancy—earlier than previously thought (Cuevas, Rovee-Collier, & Learmonth, 2006).

Memory in early infancy is often tied to actions—a finding consistent with recent work on the mirror neuron system (D'Angiulli & Schibli, 2011). For example, infants smack their lips before food or a bottle reaches their mouth. They may drop a rattle, yet continue to shake the hand that held it. Such actions are early indicators that the baby is acquiring **symbolic representation**—the ability to visualize or otherwise think about something that isn't physically present. Pretending, which typically begins between 6 and 12 months of age, also relies on the infant's capacity for symbolic representation because it requires the use of actions to represent objects, events, or ideas.

As is true of other sensorimotor abilities, pretending behavior develops in a predictable sequence (Berk, Mann, & Ogan, 2006; Cohen, 2006b; Kavanaugh, 2006). The first stage occurs by about 11 or 12 months; most children of this age pretend to eat, drink, or sleep—all familiar actions. In the next few months, the range and amount of pretend activity increase dramatically, and, as children grow older, toys and other objects are incorporated into pretend play. By 15 to 18 months, for example, children "feed" their brothers, sisters, dolls, and adults with cups, spoons, and forks. By 20 to 26 months, children develop the ability to pretend that an object is something other than what it is; a broom may become a horse or a paper sack may become a hat. Such pretending represents a further step in cognitive development. By noting the rough similarities between a horse and a broom, children combine a distant concept (horse) with an available one (broom) and thus establish a symbolic relationship between the two. Table 4-7 presents a summary of sensorimotor developments.

Language, of course, is the ultimate system of symbolic representation, where words are used to represent not only things but also actions, events, and, ultimately, ideas. We will explore infants' language development in the closing section of the chapter; however, before we do, it is important to summarize how Piaget's theory of cognitive development during infancy is viewed today.

Evaluating Piaget's View

Piaget's theory of infant cognitive development has fueled decades of research and debate. His careful, naturalistic observations of infants have challenged others to look more closely and have led to the development of new experimental techniques and a proliferation of interest in infant research (Cohen & Cashon, 2003, 2006; Oakes, Cashon, Casasola, & Rakison, 2011; Zigler & Gilman, 1998). His emphasis on the interaction between maturation and experience and on infants' active, adaptive, and constructive role in their own learning brought a new respect to infant research, as well as a clearer perspective to the interplay between heredity and environment.

However, in some respects, Piaget's view of sensorimotor development has been challenged by subsequent research. As we have seen, some developmental processes, such as object permanence and deferred imitation, occur earlier than Piaget proposed. Most theorists today view infants as more competent than Piaget believed (Gopnik, 2010; Mandler, 2007; Meltzoff, 2000). Also, Piaget probably overemphasized motor development and did not sufficiently recognize the significance of early perceptual advances (Gibson, 2000; Mandler, 2004a). Nevertheless, because of its historical significance and comprehensive scope, Piaget's description of the sensorimotor period continues to serve as a general foundation for understanding cognitive development in infancy.

Watch *Learning and Memory in Infants: Kimberley Cuevas* on **MyDevelopmentLab**

symbolic representation
The use of a word, picture, gesture, or other sign to represent past and present events, experiences, and concepts

Watch *Neurological Basis of Memory: Howard Eichenbaum* on **MyDevelopmentLab**

Table 4-7 An Overview of Sensorimotor Development

	0 to 6 months	**6 to 12 months**	**12 to 18 months**	**18 to 24 months**
Play with objects	Very simple exploration of objects (put things in the mouth)	More sophisticated exploration (bang things; spin or shake rattles)	Begins to use objects appropriately (drink from a cup; comb hair)	Extends use of objects to novel situations ("feed" a doll; "drive" toy truck)
Object permanence	Early: recognize familiar objects Later: track the movement of an object behind a screen	Becomes curious when objects *change* while behind a screen	→	Capable of searching for objects from location to location
Imitation	Some limited imitation of simple actions	Imitation of simple gestures (banging two objects together; dropping a ball)	Imitation of self-chosen actions (putting on a cap; playing)	Imitation of even complex actions on command (Can you touch your . . .?)
Memory and symbolic representation	Some limited memory; prefers mother, for example, indicating a memory for her	Begin to engage in common behavior: pretending (pretend to eat, nap)	Can pretend to perform simple symbolic activities ("feed" a doll; "drive" a car)	Can pretend that one object is actually something else (pretend a broom is a horse; a curtain is a dress)

REVIEW THE FACTS 4-5

1. Infants' earliest categories are usually based on
   a. language-based labels.
   b. quantity or number.
   c. how words sound.
   d. perceptions of how objects are similar and different.
2. If an infant incorporates a new event into an existing scheme, this is called __________; if the scheme must be changed, then the process is one of __________.
3. Suppose a baby is looking at a rattle that is then placed under a blanket. The baby now acts as if there never was a rattle. This inability to understand that the rattle still exists is called a lack of __________.
4. When an infant observes an action and repeats the action at a later time, this is referred to as __________.
5. Symbolic representation refers to the idea that
   a. infants remember visual events better than auditory events.
   b. infants can think about things that are not physically present.
   c. language develops after thought.
   d. infants habituate more quickly as they get older.

Practice on MyDevelopmentLab

LANGUAGE DEVELOPMENT

The Structure and Function of Language

In order to understand how language develops, it is useful to first consider its structure and uses. All human languages consist of words, which are strung together according to each language's specific rules of grammar into phrases or sentences that convey complex meaning. (See Table 4-8 for a summary and a brief description of the terms used to describe the more specific aspects of the structure of language.) Words, in turn, are constructed by combining basic sounds—called *phonemes*—which usually vary somewhat from language to language. Language development involves learning to speak or produce oral language, learning the meaning of words, learning rules for combining words into sentences, and—in most cultures—eventually learning to read and write. Language development takes two forms. **Receptive language** refers to understanding spoken or written words and sentences. **Productive language** refers to producing language through speaking or writing. Receptive and productive language develop simultaneously, although receptive language typically leads productive language. For example, a parent may ask her 14-month-old, "Will you go into the kitchen and bring back the cookies?" The child may be incapable of producing such a sentence but will return with the cookies. Throughout the life span, receptive vocabulary tends to be larger than productive vocabulary; that is, we can understand more words than we can use.

Based on your experiences with people who learn a second language, does receptive language seem to lead to productive language? What might this signify about the general nature of language learning?

Language Development in the First Year

The development of language production begins with undifferentiated cries at birth, which soon adapt so that they convey different meanings, such as "I'm hungry!" or "I'm tired," to their

receptive language
The repertoire of words and commands that a child understands, even though she or he may not be able to use them

productive language
Spoken or written language or communication

Watch *Language Learning* on MyDevelopmentLab

Table 4-8 Linguistic Terminology

Phonemes	The basic units of sound in a language. English, for example, has about 45 phonemes. These include the sounds indicated by the letters of the alphabet plus the variations in those sounds for vowels and some consonants. Distinct combinations, such as *-th* in words like *the* or *that* and *-ng* in *talking* or *thinking* are also phonemes.
Morphemes	The basic units of meaning in a language. A word can be a single morpheme, or it can include additional morphemes such as *-s* for plural, *-'s* for possessive, and *-ed* for past tense.
Semantics	How meaning is assigned to morphemes or morpheme combinations. Semantics includes connotation and context (i.e., how word meanings change according to the situation).
Syntax	Governs how words are combined into meaningful statements such as sentences.
Grammar	Grammar is a comprehensive term that includes all of the previously mentioned terms (i.e., phonemes, morphemes, semantics, and the syntax of a language).

Table 4-9 Milestones in Language Development

Average age*	Language behavior demonstrated by the child
by 12 weeks	Smiles when talked to; makes cooing sounds
16 weeks	Turns head in response to the human voice
20 weeks	Makes vowel and consonant sounds while cooing
6 months	Cooing changes to babbling, which contains all the sounds of human speech
8 months	Certain syllables repeated (e.g., "Ma-ma")
12 months	Understands some words; may say a few
18 months	Can produce up to 50 words
24 months	Has a vocabulary of more than 50 words; uses some two-word phrases
30 months	Vocabulary increases to several hundred words; uses phrases of three to five words
36 months	Vocabulary of about 1,000 words
48 months	Most basic aspects of language are well established

*The ages given are strictly averages. Individual infants can differ by weeks at the younger milestones and by months at the older ones.

SOURCE: From "Language development: Some milestones," by R. A. Baron, 1995, in *Psychology* (3rd ed., Table 7-3, p. 285). Copyright © 1995 by Pearson Education. Reprinted by permission of Pearson Education, Inc.

caregivers (Zukow-Goldring, 2012; Meadows, Elias, & Bain, 2000). Receptive language also develops very early: Even in the third trimester of prenatal development, premature infants are able to discriminate some speech sounds from others, leading researchers to suggest that these may be the first discriminatory responses of any kind to be made by the brain (Cheour-Luhtanen, Alho, Sainio, Rinne, & Reinikainen, 1996). Even before birth, it appears that infants are prepared to respond to and learn language (Gillam, Bedore, & Davis, 2011; Hollich, 2010).

Can you suggest phonemes that are used in other languages that are not found in English?

Language learning commences very early in development (Gervain & Mehler, 2010; Kuhl & Rivera-Gaxiola, 2008). By 12 weeks, and sometimes sooner, infants begin to coo, and by about the third month, infants can distinguish between very similar sounds such as *b* and *p* or *d* and *t*. Young infants also can detect regional accents. For example, one study demonstrated that 5-month old infants in England could distinguish between their own South-West English accent and an unfamiliar Welsh English accent (Butler, Floccia, Goslin, & Panneton, 2011). Interestingly, during the first year, infants can sometimes detect differences in speech sounds that older children and adults cannot detect. For example, in one study, it was observed that 7-month-old infants in Japan had the same accuracy distinguishing between the *r* and *l* sounds as did infants in the United States. However, by 10 months of age, the Japanese infants had lost the ability to make this distinction (e.g., see Kuhl & Iverson, 1995). This is interesting because although English speakers hear a clear difference between the *r* and *l* phonemes, Japanese speakers generally do not. Thus, it seems we are born with the flexibility to learn any language, and it is our experience that shapes the particular language we learn (Iverson, et al., 2003).

Although babies usually do not begin using words until near the end of their first year, they are nonetheless acquiring a knowledge of language during these earliest months (see Table 4-9 for milestones in language development). The cooing that began as early as 12 weeks becomes more varied and complex, and by around 6 months, these early vocalizations take on the characteristics of *babbling,* which involves the repetition of syllables that sound very much like speech, such as *ma-ma* or *bah-bah.* How important is babbling? How does it prepare a baby for speaking?

A baby's babbling is an irresistible form of verbal communication, and caregivers throughout the world delight in imitating and encouraging it. Thus, babbling serves a social function, and the interaction between baby and caregiver encourages not only the development of language but also emotional and interpersonal development as well (Goldstein & Schwade, 2008; C. A. Nelson & de Haan, 1996). Babbling is also a problem-solving activity. Babies babble as a way of figuring out how to make the specific sounds needed to say words, and babbling appears to help babies learn the sounds of their language. For example, although the babbling of babies who hear and babies who are deaf is the same at first, over time only the babbling of the infants who hear moves closer to the sounds used in their language (Nathani, Oller, & Neal, 2007). Moreover, the babbling of babies who are deaf appears to lessen significantly after about 6 months. This indicates that babbling plays a key role in learning the specific sounds needed to speak the language of one's culture. Babies with chronic or frequent ear infections also may be less attentive to speech sounds because the ear infections interfere with their ability to hear (Brandone, Salkind, Golinkoff, & Hirsh-Pasek, 2006; Rvachew, Slawinski, Williams, & Green, 1999). Infants who experience such difficulties, however, can benefit from speech–language therapy (Rvachew, Nowak, &

Cloutier, 2004) and research suggests that early deficits generally disappear by age 5 (Roberts, Rosenfeld, & Zeisel, 2004).

Receptive vocabulary also develops quickly during the first year as the infant learns to identify individual words from the string of sounds that make up spoken language (Gervain & Mehler, 2010). This is not an easy task; consider how difficult it is for adults to identify individual words when someone speaks in an unfamiliar language. Nevertheless, usually around 3 months of age, infants are beginning to perceive single syllables (Eimas, 1999), and toward the end of the first year, infants can follow simple directions from adults. Although babies depend on social cues as well as language to help them perform these tasks correctly, their ability to *hear* individual words sets the stage for the production of spoken language (Swingley, 2008; Vihman, 2013).

Words and Sentences

Most children utter their first words around the end of the first year. Their vocabulary grows slowly at first, then much more rapidly. However, there is wide individual variation in the rate at which language learning progresses. Toddlers who seem to progress rather slowly are not necessarily developmentally delayed; they may be preoccupied with other tasks, such as learning to walk. Regardless of the pace of language learning, however, language development follows a regular and predictable *sequence* in every language (Hirsh-Pasek & Golinkoff, 1996; Imai, et al., 2008).

Early Words and Meanings Around the world, infants' first utterances are single words. These first words are most often nouns (usually names of people and things in their immediate environment) (Bornstein, et al., 2004), although some early words represent actions, such as "no-no," "bye-bye," and "up!" There is considerable consistency across cultures in the first words that infants utter, as shown in Table 4-10. Of the first 20 words spoken by infants in the United States, Hong Kong, and Beijing, 6 were the same (*Daddy, Mommy, Bye, Hi, UhOh,* and *WoofWoof*), and several others were quite similar (Tardif, et al., 2008). At first, children do not have the ability to use words in combination. Instead they engage in **holophrastic speech**—one-word utterances that convey complex ideas. Thus, in different contexts and with different intonations and gestures, "mama" may mean "I want my mama" or "Mama, I'm hungry" or "There she is, my mama."

A child's first words are often **overextensions**. Although first words typically refer to a *specific* person, object, or action, the child overgeneralizes these first words to include broader categories. For example, a child may use the name of the family's pet dog, Sugar Pie, to refer to all dogs and perhaps even all furry, four-legged mammals (see Table 4-11 for additional examples of overextensions). As children learn more about defining categories (e.g., these are dogs; those are cats), they also learn words appropriate to each category. Learning a new word often assists the child in making a finer categorical distinction. For example, when a child learns the word *truck,* the child must then learn how to differentiate between trucks and other vehicles. Thus, learning words appears both to lead and to follow the development of thinking, which reflects the overarching, interactive nature of human development (see the box Current Issues: Cats, Horses, and Tight Fits).

Table 4-10 The 20 Most Common First Words Among Children from the United States, Hong Kong, and Beijing*

Order of appearance	United States	Hong Kong	Beijing
1	**Daddy**	**Daddy**	**Mommy**
2	**Mommy**	Aah	**Daddy**
3	BaaBaa	**Mommy**	Grandma (paternal)
4	**Bye**	Yum Yum	Grandpa (paternal)
5	**Hi**	Sister	**Hello**
6	**UhOh**	**UhOh**	Hit
7	Grr	Hit	Uncle
8	Bottle	**Hello**	Grab
9	YumYum	Milk	Auntie
10	Dog	Naughty	**Bye**
11	No	Brother	**UhOh**
12	**WoofWoof**	Grandma (maternal)	Wow
13	Vroom	Grandma (paternal)	Sister
14	Kitty	**Bye**	**WoofWoof**
15	Ball	Bread	Brother
16	Baby	Auntie	Hug/Hold
17	Duck	Ball	Light
18	Cat	Grandpa	Grandma (maternal)
19	Ouch	Car	Egg
20	Banana	**WoofWoof**	Vroom

*Words in boldface were among the 20 most common first words among children in all three cultures; words are translated into their English equivalents.

SOURCE: Adapted from "Baby's first 10 words," by T. Tardif, P. Fletcher, W. Liang, Z. Zhang, N. Kacirot, and V. A. Marchman, 2008, *Developmental Psychology, 44*(4), pp. 929–938.

The Language Explosion

At an average age of about 21 months, regardless of language or culture, there occurs a "language explosion" in which children begin to acquire new vocabulary at a much faster rate (Gillam,

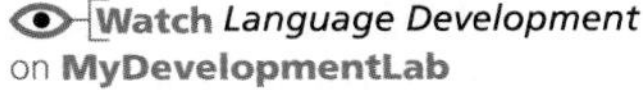
Watch *Language Development* on **MyDevelopmentLab**

holophrastic speech
In the early stages of language acquisition, the young child's use of single words to convey complete thoughts

overextensions
The young child's tendency to overgeneralize specific words, as when a child uses "Lassie" as the term for all dogs

Table 4-11 Examples of Overextensions of First Words

Child's first word	First word is used to represent	Possible common extensions	Extending property of the first word
Birdie	Robins that are flying in the sky	Crows, dragonflies, airplanes in the air—anything that flies in the sky	Movement
Ball	Beach ball that is a favorite plaything	Cupcake, marshmallow, ping pong ball, small round pillow, circle drawn on a page—anything that looks round	Shape
Bug	Ant	All small insects, spiders, crumbs, pebbles—anything that is small	Size
Doggie	The family's pet Cocker Spaniel	All dogs, cats, and other small animals that have fur, a pair of fuzzy slippers, a fur hat, a soft blanket—anything with a soft, furry texture	Texture

SOURCE: Adapted from "Language development," by J. G. De Villiers and P. A. De Villiers, 1992, in M. H. Bornstein & M. Lamb (Eds.), *Developmental psychology: An advanced textbook* (3rd ed., pp. 337–419). Hillsdale, NJ: Erlbaum; and *Early language*, by J. G. De Villiers and P. A. De Villiers, 1979, Cambridge, MA: Harvard University.

Bedore, Davis, & Marquardt, 2011; Golinkoff & Hirsh-Pasek, 2000), often learning more new words per week than they have acquired in all of the months since they began to talk. This explosion appears to be linked to toddlers' increasing skills in categorization, as well as to their increasing attention to the relationship between social cues and words. Prior to the language explosion, children pay little attention to cues from parents and others as to whether a new word is *meant* for them to learn. When the explosion starts, children become extremely sensitive to such cues and use them in their rapid acquisition of words; however, their reading of social cues is not perfect. As most caregivers know firsthand, children at this age are also quite capable and willing to learn certain words that definitely are not meant for them (Golinkoff & Hirsh-Pasek, 2000) and subsequently blurt them out at exactly the wrong time—perhaps causing considerable embarrassment for the parents.

Telegraphic Speech and Early Grammar

Just before the language explosion begins, children usually begin to put words together. The first attempts typically are two words that represent two ideas: "Daddy see," "Sock off," "More juice." Implicit rules of syntax soon appear, and children use two-word sentences in consistent ways. They may say "See dog" or "See truck" as they point at things. They do not say "Truck see."

Do you think that the concept of telegraphic speech also pertains to a person's early attempts to learn a second language? Can you give an example?

What kinds of linguistic rules do children use at this stage? When children start to put words together, their sentences are sharply limited by the number of words they can use. The result is what Roger Brown (1973) called **telegraphic speech**, in which only the most informative words are retained.

telegraphic speech
The utterances of 18-month-olds to 2-year-olds that omit the less significant words and include only the words that carry the most meaning

Telegraphic speech is, necessarily, limited in terms of how much information can be conveyed. However, by combining even a few words with gestures, tone, and context, toddlers can communicate quite effectively. Furthermore, like nearly all other aspects of early language development, the kinds of concepts communicated via two-word utterances appear to be similar across cultures (Marchman & Thal, 2005; Slobin, 1997), supporting the view that early language development is biologically prewired in the human organism (see Table 4-12). Yet, individual and cultural styles emerge quickly. For example, when Chinese, Japanese, and Korean adults speak, they often omit nouns from their sentences and they stress verbs. Consequently, Asian toddlers use more verbs than do U.S. toddlers (Tardif, Gelman, & Xu, 1999). The question of the interaction of biological and environmental factors in language development is one that has long generated considerable interest.

Theories of Language Development

Over the years, a great deal of research and theorizing has been devoted to understanding how we progress from crying to babbling to speaking an adult language. Although there has been considerable controversy as to precisely how language development works, two general positions are usually advanced.

Imitation and Reinforcement Views Imitation plays a large role in many aspects of human learning, and language learning is no exception (Moerk, 2000). Children's first words are obviously learned by hearing and imitating: Children cannot make themselves understood with words they invent. Parents do encourage language learning and they reinforce their children for language production in both general and specific ways.

However, although reinforcement does play a role in language learning, it does not explain many important aspects of language development. For example, much of children's speech is original; therefore, it could never have been reinforced. When a child says "amn't I?" or "me go" or "I have two feets," these phases are the result of processes that do not rely on imitation

Table 4-12 Meanings Conveyed by Two-Word Utterances Across Cultures

Meaning	Two-word utterance example
Identification	See truck.
Location	Baby there.
Nonexistence	Allgone candy.
Negation	Not naughty.
Possession	My book.
Attribution	Big doggie.
Agent: action	Me run!
Action: location	Go bed.
Action: direct object	Kiss daddy.
Action: indirect object	Give mama.
Action: instrument	Fill bottle.
Question	Where kitty?

SOURCE: Table adapted from "They learn the same way all around the world," by D. I. Slobin, 1972, *Psychology Today*, 6(2), pp. 71–74, 82. Copyright © 1972 by Sussex Publishers, Inc. Reprinted by permission of *Psychology Today magazine.*

and reinforcement. In addition, when parents *do* reinforce early language, they are likely to reinforce or punish according to the truth or accuracy of what is said or the desirability of the child's behavior, rather than on grammatical correctness. For example, if a child proudly says, "I eated my peas!" the parents will probably praise the child—unless, of course, the statement is not true.

Biologically Based Views Because imitation and reinforcement do not appear to explain certain aspects of language development and because humans learn language quickly and universally despite wide variations in their cultures, most theorists today acknowledge that biology plays an important role in language acquisition. Noam Chomsky advanced one early view of language development that emphasized the universal nature of language learning.

According to Chomsky (1959), children are preprogrammed to learn language because they are born with a cognitive structure specially developed for this task. This **language acquisition device (LAD)** enables children to process linguistic information and "extract" rules with which they create language; that is, when children hear people talk, their brains are *prewired* to acquire the words and rules of the language to which they are exposed.

Although the literal existence of a "language center" in the brain is an idea no longer embraced, research does suggest that brain development does shape language development (Christiansen & Chater, 2008). For example, deaf children

language acquisition device (LAD)
Chomsky's term for an innate set of mental structures that aids children in language learning

Parents who talk and read to their toddlers in a mutually enjoyable way have children who talk more and have larger vocabularies at age 3.

who are exposed to neither spoken language nor a formal sign language sometimes make up their own sign language system (Goldin-Meadow & Mylander, 1998). Their developing brains appear to naturally accommodate the production of language. In addition, in early development, deaf babies babble just like hearing babies do, indicating that babbling is not the result of imitation or reinforcement but rather is biologically programmed. Further support comes from work that demonstrates that human languages share common features (Chomsky, 1995) and that all humans learn language in much the same way and at the same time in their development (Tomasello, 2011).

The view that language development is closely tied to the maturation of the brain has helped us focus on the importance of brain development. Considering the universal presence of language in all human cultures and the commonalities of language development despite large variations in environment, it is difficult to argue that genetic mechanisms do *not* play an important role in directing the brain's development with respect to language functions. In fact, some researchers believe they have identified a gene that may trigger other genes involved in language development to "turn on" (Lai, Fisher, Hurst, Vargha-Khadem & Monaco, 2001). Also, a gene mutation (FOXP2) has been identified as a cause of developmental speech and language disorders in humans (Spiteri, et al., 2007), and two other genes have been implicated in the development of the facility to learn "tonal" languages, such as Chinese, that convey meaning according to speech tones (Choi, 2007). However, much more research will be required before we understand the genetic mechanisms involved in this intricate system. As more research accumulates about both genetics and brain structures and

CURRENT ISSUES

Cats, Horses, and Tight Fits—Is Language Involved in Category Formation?

▲ Even in the everyday world, infants and toddlers who have several examples of a category like "horse"—in a book, for example—are noticing similarities and differences. There is a lot of perceptual learning that occurs before preschool.

How is it infants form the categories we use to organize the world around us? How does a baby learn that a German shepherd is a dog but not a cat, or that a person fits into a different category than a truck? Does language play a role?

Peter Eimas and Paul Quinn (1994) studied the formation of perceptually based categories in infants as young as 3 months of age in order to answer questions such as these. In their experiments, Eimas and Quinn placed a viewing box around each infant as the infant sat comfortably on mother's lap. Using a habituation technique, the researchers presented the infants with two colored pictures of different horses to look at, repeating this procedure six times, each time with different horses displayed. On the seventh trial, however, each infant was presented with two new pictures, one of a different horse and one of another animal (a zebra, a cat, or a giraffe). The question was, would the infant spend more time looking at the horse or the "new" animal? In other words, did infants form a category of *horses?* If the infants had formed the horse category, the researchers reasoned that habituation would have occurred through the six previous trials; therefore, the infants' attention would be drawn to the *new* kind of animal. What happened?

Eimas and Quinn found that most infants looked longer at the new kind of animal. These same results were found when infants were shown pictures of cats six times in a row and then were shown a pair consisting of a cat and a new animal (either a dog or a horse). Although some infants continued to show a preference to look at the familiar animal, most infants habituated to the repeated presentations of the familiar animal. When the new animal was presented, their attention was drawn to it, thereby indicating that they had made a category-based distinction (Eimas & Quinn, 1994; Quinn, Eimas, & Tarr, 2001; Quinn & Oates, 2004).

Taking the idea of how infants form perceptual categories a bit further, we might ask, do infants around the world learn the same categories? One way to determine this is to look for situations in which there are cultural differences in the languages that describe such categories. If category formation is universal, then different language labels for categories should not make a difference in how infants form categories.

A test of this idea was designed by Susan Hespos and Elizabeth Spelke (2004), who noted that in Korean there are commonly used words for actions that are "tight fitting" versus "loose fitting." For example, if a small cylinder is placed in a larger cylinder and there is a lot of space between the two, this is loose fitting; if the cylinders barely fit together, this is tight fitting. In English, this concept is not easily coded into a single word. Instead, placing objects *in* and *on* are more common distinctions. Hespos and Spelke had 5-month-old infants who were sitting on their mothers' lap watch one of four different scenarios. Using cylinders that were either solid or hollow, infants saw a smaller cylinder placed either in or on another cylinder in either a tight-fitting or loose-fitting arrangement. Both English and Korean babies quickly learned to habituate to the tight-fit or loose-fit displays, and then, on the test trial, picked out the novel, or different, "fitting" situation. Thus, babies from both cultures learned the loose-fit–tight-fit distinction with comparable ease. However, when the same task was performed by Korean- and English-speaking adults, the English-speaking adults had more difficulty learning the concept than did the Korean-speaking adults. One possible conclusion from research such as this is that infants are busy finding the regularities in their perceptual world and forming concepts long before they learn the labels that language provides to describe these concepts (Hespos & Spelke, 2007). What do you think? To what extent does our language shape the way we think about the world? To what extent does the world we live in determine the structure of our language?

functions, we hope to gain a clearer understanding of how language is processed by the brain, as well as how these processes develop.

Cultural Aspects of Language Development

Today, developmental psychologists acknowledge that language development, like the development of so many human capabilities, is linked to the biological maturation of the brain. Language development also is influenced by environmental experiences, including culture (Chan, et al., 2011). Supporting the idea that culture matters is research that investigates the influence of social class on language development. When compared to children from middle-income professional families, children from families on welfare were found to develop basic language skills and structures in much the same way and at the same time. However, children from middle-income homes had much larger vocabularies as the result of their parents spending almost twice as much time talking to them (Hart & Risley, 1995; Horton-Ikard & Weismer, 2007). In addition, the vocabularies of 2-year-old toddlers were shown to be directly tied to the mother's use of a wide vocabulary, as well as to the amount of time she spent talking to the child (Huttenlocher, Haight, Bruk, Seltzer, & Lyons, 1991), again demonstrating the impact of culture. For example, when mothers were instructed to verbally respond to their 9½-month-old infants' babbling, the infants rapidly restructured their babbling, incorporating the mother's speech patterns into their own (Goldstein & Schwade, 2008). Psychologists today believe that infants actively seek out information about language and they learn from it (Polka, Rvachew, & Mattock, 2007).

Thus, as we have seen throughout early development, it is the *interplay* of biological maturation and social context that sets the course of an individual's development. Language development is linked to cognitive development that, in turn, depends on the development of the brain, on physical and perceptual abilities, and on experiences (Iverson, 2010). Biological and social factors also jointly influence the early development of emotion and personality, which are the topics we explore in the next chapter.

REVIEW THE FACTS 4-6

1. The basic sounds of language are called __________.
2. In an experiment with infants in Japan and infants in the United States, which group was less able to make the distinction between the *l* and the *r* sound?
   a. 7-month-old infants in Japan
   b. 7-month-old infants in the United States
   c. 10-month-old infants in Japan
   d. 10-month-old infants in the United States
3. When a 1-year-old uses a few words to express a complex idea (for example, "bye-bye"), this is called __________.
4. If a child uses the word *truck* to refer to all vehicles that have wheels (including cars, motorcycles, and trucks), this is best thought of as an example of
   a. holophrastic speech.
   b. telegraphic speech.
   c. receptive language.
   d. an overextension.
5. Chomsky's description of the language acquisition device suggests the most significant factor in learning language is
   a. imitation.
   b. reinforcement.
   c. biological prewiring of the brain.
   d. culture.

CHAPTER SUMMARY

The Developing Brain

What changes take place in the infant's brain that allow for the dramatic developments of the first 2 years of life?

- During the first 2 years of life—called *infancy* and *toddlerhood*—developmental change is more rapid and more dramatic than in any other 2-year period.
- The brain is composed of about 100 billion neurons, along with glial cells that support and nourish the neurons and produce myelin. During the first 2 years, the brain undergoes a *brain growth spurt,* increasing in size and in the number of connections among neurons.
- The *plasticity* of the young brain allows it to be modified as it adapts to the environment and also makes it possible to reassign functions should injury occur in a particular part of the brain.
- The brain develops both by adding new connections among neurons and by pruning away connections that are not needed. In this way, the brain is fine-tuned in response to the person's environment. Early experiences in life can have important consequences for later development.

The Neonatal Period

What changes in an infant's general behavior and arousal typically occur during the first month of life?

- Neonates exhibit several states of arousal, which become more regular and more predictable with time. Neonates also are capable of learning.
- The first month of life—called the *neonatal period*—is a time of recovery from the birth process and a period of adjustment as the newborn's organ systems begin to function.

How does the simple form of learning called habituation provide a means to study how infants think?

- The neonate's ability to habituate helps reduce the confusion present in the environment and also provides a useful research method by which infant behavior can be studied.
- Newborns are often given a neurological and a behavioral assessment to determine their health. The *Newborn Behavioral Observation system* (NBO) is one such evaluation method. Parents who observe such an assessment often develop a better understanding of their infant's sensitivities and capabilities.
- The neonatal period sets the stage for development throughout infancy.

Physical and Motor Development

How do physical development and motor abilities advance during infancy and toddlerhood?

- The Gesell Scales summarize the physical and motor capabilities of average children at different ages. These capabilities emerge in a predictable sequence. Although physical and motor development are heavily influenced by biological events, or maturation, they can also be influenced by the environment. As always, heredity and environment interact, or influence each other.
- In the first 4 months, physical growth is rapid. Self-discovery begins to occur at the end of this period, and many reflexes disappear as more intentional cognitive processes begin to control behavior.
- *Fine motor skills* begin to develop at 5 to 8 months of age, as does hand–eye coordination. The visually guided reach also develops during this period. *Gross motor skills* also become more refined; by the end of this period, most babies are crawling and sitting without support. By 8 months of age, they also are beginning to play simple social games.
- At 12 months of age, about 50% of infants are standing and taking their first steps. Their ability to move around provides many new opportunities to engage with and to experience their environment. At about 12 months of age, they also develop the pincer grasp, and many begin to feed themselves and play social games.
- At 18 months, toddlers may be scribbling with a crayon or pencil, stacking blocks, feeding themselves, and imitating the actions of adults.

- Two-year-olds can peddle a tricycle and throw a ball, climb steps, dress themselves, and begin to categorize objects.
- Each developing system—perceptual, motor, cognitive, and social—supports the other systems and depends on parallel advances as development proceeds. These developments are linked to and interact with the developing brain.

What role does nutrition play in early development?

- Most people in the United States have sufficient quantities of food, but many have poor diets that are deficient in some essential nutrients, especially iron, protein, vitamins, and minerals. Around the world, malnutrition results in *stunting* for about 30% of children under age 5. Early malnutrition is especially serious because it results in delays in learning and maturation, and may limit brain development, thereby producing deficits that are difficult or impossible to remediate later.
- One type of malnutrition, called *marasmus,* occurs from an insufficient total quantity of food. If the period of starvation is for a short time, it probably will not cause permanent damage. Another kind of malnutrition results when calorie intake is sufficient but the food sources are deficient in one or more essential nutrients. *Kwashiorkor,* a condition caused by protein deficiency, is especially common in developing nations and often occurs when children are weaned from breast milk. Although food supplement programs, such as those sponsored by WHO and UNICEF, can have positive effects, often extended early malnourishment has permanent effects.
- Most infants consume primarily or only milk up to age 6 months. Today, health-care providers encourage mothers to breastfeed rather than bottle-feed because breast milk provides the proper blend of nutrients, provides better immunity, and is sterile—a very important consideration in settings where water may be contaminated.
- Culture often influences when *weaning* occurs, which is sometimes as early as 3 or 4 months of age or as late as 2 to 3 years of age. The primary risk to children is getting a diet with sufficient nutrients, either because such foods are unavailable or because less nutritious but better-tasting foods are available.

Sensory and Perceptual Development

What sensory and perceptual abilities is the newborn equipped with, and how do these change during the period of infancy and toddlerhood?

- Although infants can see immediately after birth, their vision for objects farther away than about 7 to 10 inches is blurry. Focusing ability develops rapidly, so that by 3 to 4 months of age, infants focus as well as adults. They also improve their ability to track moving objects and to discriminate among colors.
- Newborns prefer to look at stimuli of moderate complexity and are highly responsive to the human face. It appears that much of the infant's facial perception ability is biologically programmed.

What mechanisms appear to explain the infant's ability to imitate and learn through observation?

- The *mirror neuron* system in the brain is activated in the same way when an action is performed as when it is observed. Thus, this system may provide a biological explanation for imitation, as well as empathy—the ability to understand how another person feels or thinks. Defects in the mirror neuron system may be involved in autism.
- The infant's ability to perceive depth begins to develop at a very early age, even as early as 6 weeks after birth. Binocular vision emerges at about 4 months. Experiments using the visual-cliff apparatus indicate that infants' perception of depth is learned before they understand the meaning of depth. Perceptual development involves an interaction of the maturation of biological systems and the understanding of social and cognitive events.
- At birth, infants can hear, and their hearing acuity improves over the first few months. They also are especially attentive to the sounds of human speech, which sets the stage for language development. The senses of taste, smell, and touch are also well developed at birth.
- Newborns are capable of sensory integration, an ability that continues to improve as development proceeds.

Cognitive Development

According to the view of Jean Piaget, how does the infant learn to think?

- Cognitive development in infancy is closely linked to the development of sensation and perception. For example, it appears that infants form perception-based categories, even before they acquire a full understanding of what such categories represent.
- Jean Piaget believed that infants possess mental structures called *schemes* (or *schemas*), which function like categories for thought. In the *sensorimotor period* (from birth to about 2 years), basic reflexes are transformed into concepts through *adaptation*—the process by which we adjust our schemes according to the experiences we have. Adaptation occurs through assimilation and accommodation.
- Schemes become more elaborate as infants develop through the sensorimotor period, as can be seen in how they play with objects. *Object permanence* is a major accomplishment in this developmental period, which means that the infant understands that objects exist even if they are hidden from view.
- Imitation of others' actions also develops during the sensorimotor period. Piaget believed that imitation requires cognitive skills that develop late in this period. However, research indicates that infants are capable of imitation, even when it is deferred, much earlier than Piaget proposed.
- Infants have an especially good memory for visual events, especially if they are dramatic. Memories are also often tied to actions. As the infant's memory abilities develop, the infant becomes capable of *symbolic representation,* which is a precursor to language development.

- Although Piaget's view of child development has been exceptionally influential, recent perspectives suggest that at least some developmental processes occur earlier than he proposed. In addition, Piaget probably overemphasized the significance of motor development and underemphasized the role that perceptual development plays in cognitive development in infancy.

Language Development

What major milestones occur in language learning during the first 2 years of life?

- Although they develop simultaneously, *receptive language*—the ability to understand spoken or written words or sentences—is typically more advanced than *productive language*—the ability to speak or write.
- Receptive and productive language begin to develop very early, suggesting that infants are biologically prepared to learn language. We are born with the capacity to learn any language, and our environment determines which language we learn.
- Babbling serves a social function and also helps infants learn the sounds of their language. Deaf babies babble, indicating that this activity is biologically prewired, but they do not continue to refine their speech sounds, as hearing babies do. By age 3 to 4 months, infants begin to perceive single syllables, and by age 1 can follow simple directions.
- Most babies say their first words around the end of their first year, although the ages vary considerably among children. The sequence of language learning is consistent: single words (usually nouns), then two-word "sentences," then more complex speech. Early words are often *overextensions*, or overgeneralizations. Language both leads and follows the child's ability to make categorical distinctions.
- The language explosion begins at about age 21 months and involves the rapid expansion of the child's vocabulary. At about age 2½, children begin to string words together, at first using only the most informative words that convey the most meaning. This *telegraphic speech* is influenced by the particular language the child is learning and quickly becomes elaborated into more adultlike speech.

How can we best explain how children learn to speak and understand language?

- Two general views have been advanced to explain how language develops. Imitation and reinforcement are undoubtedly involved, but this view does not explain all aspects of language development. Most experts acknowledge that biology plays a large role in language acquisition.
- Noam Chomsky proposed that children are biologically programmed to learn language because they are born with a cognitive structure called a *language acquisition device (LAD).* Although there is no known neurological evidence that such a device actually exists in the brain, many sources of evidence support a biologically based view. Certainly, brain development and language development are closely tied.
- Cultural factors, however, can also influence language development. For example, children who grow up in language-rich homes have larger vocabularies. Biological and environmental factors—including brain development; cognitive, motor, and perceptual development; and environmental and cultural factors—all interact to jointly influence the development of language.

KEY TERMS

infancy (p. 99)
toddlerhood (p. 99)
brain growth spurt (p. 100)
plasticity (p. 100)
habituation method (p. 102)
Newborn Behavioral Observation (NBO) (p. 102)
fine motor skills (p. 105)
gross motor skills (p. 105)
stunting (p. 108)
marasmus (p. 108)
kwashiorkor (p. 108)
weaning (p. 110)
sensation (p. 112)
perception (p. 112)
mirror neurons (p. 113)
category (p. 117)
sensorimotor period (p. 117)
adaptation (p. 117)
object permanence (p. 118)
deferred imitation (p. 119)
symbolic representation (p. 120)
receptive language (p. 121)
productive language (p. 121)
holophrastic speech (p. 123)
overextensions (p. 123)
telegraphic speech (p. 124)
language acquisition device (LAD) (p. 125)

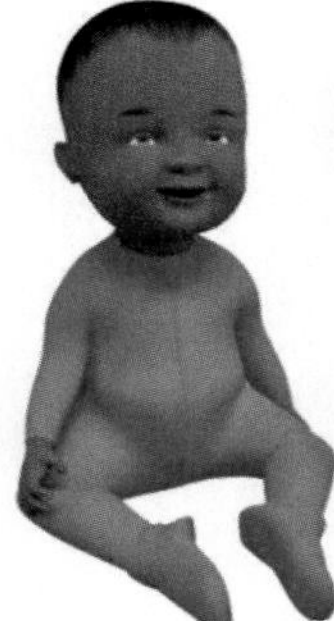

5 INFANCY AND TODDLERHOOD
Personality and Sociocultural Development

LEARNING OBJECTIVES

- What role does temperament play in the emotional development of infants and toddlers?
- What can parents do to ensure that their infant develops a trusting orientation to the world and a strong attachment to them?
- To what does the term *attachment* refer, and how does the development of early infant attachment influence later development throughout childhood?
- How do infants and toddlers develop a sense of their own autonomy without losing their attachment to their caregivers?
- How do infants' understanding of others and their concept of the "self" develop during the first 2 years of life?
- Can fathers be good "mothers" for their children?
- How do other caregivers, including family members other than the parents as well as child-care workers, influence development in infancy and toddlerhood?
- What special challenges are faced by the caregivers of infants and toddlers with special needs?
- How does child maltreatment influence development and autonomy?

CHAPTER OUTLINE

The Foundations of Personality and Social Development
Emotional Development
Temperament

The Development of Trust
Feeding and Comforting
Cross-Cultural Comparisons on the Development of Trust

Attachment
Studying Infant and Toddler Attachment
The Effects of Attachment
Explaining Attachment
The Relationship Between Attachment and Trust
The Role of Culture in Attachment

Separating from the Caregiver
Social Referencing and Culture
The Development of Autonomy
The Development of Prosocial Behavior
The Development of the Self
Attachment and Separation

The Family System: A Broader Context
Fathers
Other Family Members as Caregivers
The Social Ecology of Child Care

Infants and Toddlers with Special Needs
Infants and Toddlers with Visual Impairments
Infants and Toddlers with Hearing Impairments
Infants and Toddlers with Severe Disabilities
Infants and Toddlers Who Suffer from Abuse or Neglect

Infants are born into an environment that is rich with expectations, norms, values, and traditions. All of these factors and more will help shape their **personality**, which can be defined as one's characteristic beliefs, attitudes, and ways of interacting with others. Perhaps no period of development is more critical than this first one—the period we refer to as infancy and toddlerhood.

THE FOUNDATIONS OF PERSONALITY AND SOCIAL DEVELOPMENT

Dramatic changes of all kinds occur during the first 2 years of life. As we learned in the previous chapter, physical growth and brain maturation set the stage for cognitive development, including the emergence of language. Social development also proceeds during this period, as babies learn about the responsiveness or unresponsiveness of the people who care for them. They develop emotional control and establish critically important relationships with their caregivers, first developing healthy attachments, and later learning to separate and develop a secure sense of self. Throughout this period, the impact that caregivers have on an infant's development is especially important. In this chapter, we focus on the emotional and social development that occurs in the first 2 years—a period that establishes the base on which later development rests. It is to these topics that we now turn.

Emotional Development

At birth, the emotional repertoire of infants is limited, although neonates do convey different emotional states by crying in different ways, by changing their level of activity, and by attending to things that interest them for short periods. As infants develop, their emotional states become more complex. Babies focus first on managing distress and comfort. Then they begin the process of exchanging signals, sounds, and smiles with a responsive caregiver. Gradually, over the first year, universal, biologically based **basic emotions** emerge, such as sadness, anger, disgust, fear, and pleasure (Ekman, 1992; Ekman & Cordaro, 2011). Later, primarily in the second year, socially oriented emotions emerge—such as pride, shame, embarrassment, guilt, and empathy—as the toddler gains an increasingly greater understanding of self and others. Such emotional development proceeds in stages as the infant gains experience with others and develops the cognitive skills necessary for more complex thought (see Table 5-1).

Can you describe an example of how infants' emotional development becomes more complex as they grow older?

The Reciprocal Nature of Emotional Development The development of emotion—and emotional self-control—depends in large part on the interactions that occur between infants and their caregivers (Greenspan, 2007a; Witherington, Campos, Harringer, Bryan, & Margett, 2010). For example, parents can encourage the development of emotionally healthy children through playful intimacy, games, fantasy, and verbal and nonverbal conversation, as well as by learning to understand their baby's communications (Greenspan, 2007b).

To learn more about the two-way *affective,* or emotional, communication system that defines the infant's interaction with the primary caregiver during the first 6 months of life, Edward Tronick (1989) devised a now-classic laboratory experiment that focused on the mutual expectations of parents and infants. In this *still-face experiment,* parents were first asked to sit and play with their 3-month-old infants in their usual manner. After 3 minutes, the experimenter asked the parents to stop communicating with their babies. The parents were instructed

personality
The characteristic beliefs, attitudes, and ways of interacting with others

Watch *Social and Personality Development* on **MyDevelopmentLab**

basic emotions
Emotional states that emerge very early in development, occur in infants in all cultures, and are to some extent biologically based

Table 5-1 Milestones in Early Emotional Development

Age	Developmental milestone	Description
By 3 months	Becoming calm, attentive, and interested in the world	• Infants seek to feel regulated and calm in the early weeks and try to use all of their senses to experience the world around them • They seek a balance between over- and under-stimulation • They become increasingly responsive socially, using signaling and orienting behavior—such as crying, vocalizing, and visual following—to establish contact • Infants do not discriminate between their primary caregivers and other people and react to everyone in much the same way
By 5 months	Falling in love	• Self-regulated infants become more alert to the world around them • Infants recognize familiar figures and increasingly direct their attention toward significant caregivers rather than toward strangers • They find the human world pleasurable and exciting now and show it • Infants smile eagerly and respond with the whole body
By 9 months	Becoming a two-way communicator	• Infants begin to engage in dialogues with others • Mother and infant initiate their own playful sequences of communication, including looking at each other, playing short games, and taking rests; fathers and siblings do the same
By 14 to 18 months	Solving problems and forming an organized sense of self	• Toddlers can now do more things for themselves • They take a more active role in the emotional partnership with their mothers and fathers • They can signal their needs more effectively and precisely than before • Toddlers begin using words to communicate • Emotions, including anger, sadness, and happiness, have emerged • Toddlers delight in solving problems that expand their cognitive abilities • Toddlers have a well-developed sense of self by the end of this period
By 24 to 30 months	Discovering a world of ideas	• Toddlers can now symbolize, pretend, and form mental images of people and things • They can learn about the social world through pretend play • Toddlers can feel the ambivalent needs of autonomy and dependency because of an acquired sense of self • Their emotional repertoire expands during this period to include social emotions, such as empathy, embarrassment, and gradually shame, pride, and guilt, coinciding with the new sense of self and a growing knowledge of social rules
By 36 to 48 months	Building bridges between ideas	• Young children have settled into a kind of partnership with the give-and-take of close relationships with significant others • Young children can discern what the caregiver expects of them and they try to modify their behavior to meet those expectations and to achieve their own goals

SOURCE: Adapted from S. I. Greenspan and N. T. Greenspan, 1985, *First feelings: Milestones in the emotional development of your baby and child*, New York: Viking; and S. I. Greenspan and N. T. Greenspan, 1999, *Building healthy minds: The six experiences that create intelligence and emotional growth in babies and young children*, Cambridge, MA: Perseus.

to continue looking at their infants but to put on a blank, still face. The infants typically responded with surprise and tried to engage the parent with smiles, coos, and general activity, but the parent maintained the blank expression. How did the infants respond?

Within a few minutes, the infants' behavior began to deteriorate. They looked away, sucked their thumbs, and looked pained. Some began to whimper and cry, whereas others had involuntary responses, such as drooling or hiccupping. Thus, although the parents still were present and attending, they suddenly and unexpectedly were unavailable emotionally, and the infants had difficulty coping with the change.

Experiments such as this provide a clear demonstration of the strength and importance of emotional communication between caregivers and even very young infants. For example, one study using the still-face procedure showed that, just hours after birth, newborns adjusted their behavior by decreasing eye contact and exhibiting signs of distress when an adult interaction partner became nonresponsive (Nagy, 2008). Thus, even newborns sensitively monitor the behavior of others, and when an adult disconnects from the infant, the infant's behavior becomes less organized as a result. As Tronick and others have found (e.g., Tronick, 2005, 2007), emotional *communication* is a major determinant of children's emotional development, especially when that communication is with the mother (Melinder, Forbes, Tronick, Fikke, & Gredeback, 2010). When parent–child communication is strong and predictable, infants show greater emotional stability and recover from being upset more easily (Conradt & Ablow, 2010). When the reciprocal two-way communication system fails—as it does, for example, when the primary caregiver is chronically depressed or ill—the emotional development of the infant may be at risk.

Table 5-2 Styles of Temperament

Temperament style	Percentage of children	Characteristics
Easy	40%	• Moods usually are positive and seldom explosive • Regular in basic routines, such as sleeping and eating • Adapts easily to new people and situations
Difficult	10%	• Cries often, with intensity, and expresses other negative moods • Irregular in basic routines • Reacts to change with difficulty and slowness
Slow to warm up	15%	• Has both positive and negative moods, which are usually mild • Moderately regular in basic routines • Reacts negatively to new people and situations initially but successfully adjusts over a period of time
Not categorized	35%	• Unable to categorize because child displays a combination of easy, difficult, and slow-to-warm-up temperament characteristics

SOURCE: Adapted from "Styles of temperament," by A. Thomas and S. Chess, 2007, in *Temperament & development* (p. 70), Routledge/Taylor & Francis Group.

Temperament

Of course, emotional responses vary considerably from one child to another, reflecting differences in basic **temperament**, which is the inborn, characteristic way that infants interact with the world around them (Buss, 2012a, 2012b; Thompson, Winer, & Goodvin, 2011; Wachs & Bates, 2010). For example, some neonates are more sensitive to light or sudden loud sounds than are others. Some react more quickly and dramatically to discomfort. Some are more fussy, some are more calm, and some are active and vigorous. Temperament does have an emotional basis, whereas emotions come and go rather quickly. But as situations change and needs are met, temperament is a more stable and characteristic aspect of an individual's basic response to life (Wachs & Bates, 2010).

Pioneering research into the basic styles of temperament was conducted by Alexander Thomas and Stella Chess (1977; Chess & Thomas, 1996). In their New York Longitudinal Study, Thomas and Chess followed 133 infants into adulthood, studying such characteristics as the regularity of their habits, their reactions to changes in their routines, their responses to caregivers and strangers, what kind of moods generally described their disposition, and so forth. Based on their observations, Thomas and Chess concluded that most children could be categorized into one of three temperamental styles: *easy* (often in a good mood and predictable), *difficult* (often irritable and unpredictable), and *slow to warm up* (moody and resistant to attention; see Table 5-2).

Based on what you know about your own period of infancy, do you think you would have been categorized as a child who was easy, difficult, or slow to warm up?

Mary Rothbart (2007) conceptualized temperament using a slightly different focus—one that applies to older children as well as to infants. There are three broad dimensions of temperament in Rothbart's scale, as presented in Table 5-3, which are biologically based and linked to the individual's genetic endowment (Posner, Rothbart, & Sheese, 2007). Although Rothbart's dimensions differ in some ways from the styles identified decades earlier by Thomas and Chess, there are important commonalities as well. For example, easy children can be described as those high in effortful control, low in negative affectivity, and moderate in extroversion. Difficult children are low in effortful control, high in negative affectivity, and may also be high in extroversion. Slow-to-warm-up children are low in extroversion. Other researchers have conceptualized temperament using different labels, but most recognize that temperament describes how individuals differ in their emotionality, their activity level, their impulsiveness, and their sociability (Buss, 2012a).

For most people, the basic temperamental patterns present early in life persist throughout development, which is an indicator that temperament is biologically based (Degnan, et al., 2011; McAdams & Olson, 2010). For others, how, the degree or intensity of temperament style shifts, as infants, toddlers, and young children grow and change in daily encounters with family and other caregivers (Rothbart & Bates, 2006). Today, most researchers think of temperament as an epigenetic system in which environmental experiences modify the underlying genetic basis of this predisposition to respond in particular ways (Berger, 2011b).

Indeed, the "match" between a caregiver's expectations for behavior and an infant's temperamental style is an important determinant of caregiver–infant interactions and, in turn, the child's adjustment. When there is a "bad fit," such as when a highly active, emotionally volatile child is raised in a strict environment where quiet behavior is expected and inflexible rules are applied, the child is more likely to have a difficult adjustment. Parents, to the extent that they are able, should try to create an environment that works with, rather than against, the basic temperamental style of the infant.

temperament
The inborn characteristic way that infants interact with the world around them

Table 5-3 Rothbart's Broad Dimensions of Temperament

Dimension of temperament	Characteristics on which infants differ from each other
Effortful control	• The capacity to focus attention and shift attention when desired • The capacity to plan future actions and inhibit inappropriate responses • The ability to perceive small amounts of stimulation in the environment • The ability to derive pleasure from low-intensity activities or stimuli
Negative affectivity	• The degree of frustration experienced when goals are blocked or tasks are interrupted • Amount of fear felt when distress is anticipated • Amount of discomfort experienced when sensory overstimulation occurs • Amount of sadness felt when disappointment, loss, or suffering is experienced • The ability to be soothed or comforted when distressed, overexcited, or aroused
Extroversion (also called surgency)	• The level of motor activity exhibited • Shyness • Pleasure derived from high intensity or novelty • Smiling and laughing in response to changes in the environment • Impulsivity and the speed with which responses are initiated • Positive excitement and anticipation for expected pleasurable activities • Desire for warmth and closeness with others

SOURCE: Adapted from, M. K. Rothbart, 2007, "Temperament, development, and personality, *Current Directions in Psychological Science*, *16*(4), 207–212.

REVIEW THE FACTS 5-1

1. Which of the following emotional developments is the last to emerge in infants?
   a. feeling socially oriented emotions such as shame or pride
   b. managing distress
   c. managing comfort
   d. exchanging signals and signs with the caregiver
2. Suppose little Andre becomes quite upset whenever things in his environment change; however, he generally responds passively without becoming agitated. According to Thomas and Chess, his temperament style would best be considered
   a. cold.
   b. easy.
   c. soothable.
   d. slow to warm up.
3. If Rothbart described a child as low in effortful control, high in negative affectivity, and high in extroversion, that child's temperament would fit best into which of the following styles?
   a. slow to warm up
   b. difficult
   c. easy
   d. not categorized
4. Give an example of a bad fit between an infant's temperament and a caregiver's style of child rearing.

Practice on **MyDevelopmentLab**

THE DEVELOPMENT OF TRUST

Regardless of the emotional and temperamental style that characterizes an individual infant, a common hallmark of social development that occurs in the first year of life involves the development of trust. The development of trust marks the first stage of Erikson's theory of psychosocial development (see Chapter 1), and it is during this stage that infants learn whether they can depend on the people around them and whether their social environment is consistent and predictable.

Feeding and Comforting

A basic sense of trust is conveyed to the infant through the mother's (or other primary caregiver's) nurturing behavior; that is, trust is conveyed through the caregiver's responsiveness to the infant's needs. Mothers and other caregivers convey their values and attitudes in a variety of ways to the infant, but particularly important are the mother's behaviors when feeding her baby and also how she provides comfort when the infant experiences distress. From their caregivers' reactions, children learn when to feel anxious or guilty, when to feel comfortable and secure, and whether they are valued or are perceived as a nuisance. All of these feelings contribute—for better or for worse—to the child's developing sense of trust.

Researchers who study the development of trust often focus on how feeding fits into the overall pattern of nurturant care. Feeding, whether by breast or bottle, allows for a special closeness between mother and child, reflecting the mother's sensitivity and responsiveness. All theories of human development acknowledge the important early socialization associated with feeding. Foremost among these is Sigmund Freud's view, which argued that the first year of life is characterized by a focus on oral stimulation that is associated most closely with the feeding rituals established by the mother. According to Freud, much of later personality development depends on how the child's oral needs are gratified in this first year of life (see Chapter 1). Other theorists also see the caregiver's approach to feeding as setting the stage for later development. For example, Erik Erikson also believed that the manner in which the mother attends to the hunger needs of the infant is critically important in the development of trust. When infants learn that their hunger needs will be met promptly and lovingly, they develop a sense of trust. If they are not fed when hungry, they instead learn that they cannot depend on their caregivers, and a sense of mistrust is more likely to develop. Of course, feeding is not the only important way in which caregivers interact with their babies. Trusting relationships also are encouraged when parents interact lovingly and in positive ways with their infants—holding them gently, speaking to them in soft tones, singing to them, and so forth. When infants learn they can depend on their caregivers to calm them when they are distressed, attend to them when they are anxious, and interact with them in positive ways, they are more likely to develop a secure sense of basic trust.

Cross-Cultural Comparisons on the Development of Trust

Culture—broadly defined as the behavior and beliefs of a particular group—plays a very important role in shaping how early development unfolds (Weisner, 2011). Cultures vary widely in child-rearing practices. For example, in some cultures infants and toddlers are seldom separated from their mothers; they are carried around during most of the first year, are usually breast-fed on demand until perhaps the age of 3, sleep in the same bed as the parents, and accompany their mother nearly wherever she goes (Mistry & Saraswathi, 2003). In other cultures—and especially in the United States—infants are treated in a much more independent manner. For example, most U.S. infants sleep in cribs, oftentimes in a separate room from parents. They are fed on a regular schedule that conforms to their parents' schedules, rather than whenever they are hungry. They spend less time in physical contact with the mother and more time in infant seats, car seats, and in child-care facilities where multiple caregivers are the norm.

Cultures also vary in the ways that the infant is comforted in times of distress. In some cultures, the mother assumes a calming, nurturing role and performs nearly all of the child care. In other cultures, many other people are involved in the care of the infant. In Italy, for example, nurturance of the infant is a social affair (Hsu & Lavelli, 2005; New, 1989, 2008). Although researchers found that Italian mothers do most of the feeding, dressing, and cleaning of their infants in an indulgent and caring fashion, family members, friends, and neighbors also contribute to their care, often in a robust manner. Especially surprising was the amount of teasing that occurred in the Italian family culture, even when the infant became upset and cried. Pacifiers were held just out of reach; adults said, "Here comes Daddy!" only to laugh and declare "He isn't here anymore!"; and infants were jiggled and pinched to awaken them when the adults wanted to play with them.

What impact do these varying cultural practices have on the development of trust? Interestingly, regardless of cultural practices, infants who are able to establish consistent and positive emotional relationships with their caregivers generally fare very well (Bornstein, Putnick, Suwalsky, Venuti, & Gini, 2012). Part of the explanation has to do with the fact that healthy emotional development requires a balance in the development of *trust* (which allows infants to form secure relationships with others) and *mistrust* (which teaches them to protect themselves when conditions are threatening). Thus, cultural variations in the particular ways in which an infant is cared for probably include some mix of trust-building and mistrust-building experiences. So long as trust predominates, healthy development is likely to occur. Part of the explanation, too, rests on the fact that healthy mother–infant relationships in all cultures contribute mostly to the development of trust, which leads to positive developmental outcomes (Halberstadt & Lozada, 2011). Of course, when unhealthy, neglectful, or abusive infant–caregiver relationships exist, the development of mistrust

▲ An infant's trust and security come from learning what to expect in a particular mother–infant relationship. Each relationship is rich with personal, family, and cultural styles of care and communication.

predominates. This is a serious developmental problem because these earliest relationships oftentimes set the stage for later difficulties in forming positive and healthy relationships throughout life. One of the first and most important of these relationships is the emotional bond that forms between infants and their mothers or caregivers—*attachment*—the topic to which we turn in the next section of this chapter.

REVIEW THE FACTS 5-2

1. If infants learn that their needs will be met and that their environment is predictable, Erikson would say that these factors contribute to the development of __________.
2. Especially important to the development of trust is the task of __________.
3. In Freud's view, the first year of life is characterized by __________ stimulation.
4. To encourage healthy development, what should be the relationship between the development of trust and mistrust?
5. Does the development of trust in infancy vary widely as the result of culture?

✓ Practice on **MyDevelopmentLab**

ATTACHMENT

Along with developing the confidence that their basic needs will be attended to, in their first year infants also begin to form relationships with their caregivers. The first such relationship—and undoubtedly the most influential—occurs between infants and their mothers or other primary caregivers, and this emotional bond is referred to as *attachment* (Posada & Kaloustian, 2010). As we will see, attachment is *synchronous:* It involves sharing experiences back and forth between the caregiver and the infant in a cooperative manner, which involves them in a process that is ongoing and interactive.

John Bowlby, an early pioneer in the study of attachment, was among the first to describe these early infant–caregiver emotional bonds and to comment on their significant role in later development (e.g., Bowlby, 1988, 1989; Roisman & Grohl, 2011; Shaver & Fraley, 2010). Because attachment is so crucial to an infant's overall psychosocial development, it is important to examine the mechanisms through which it occurs. Working with Bowlby, Mary Ainsworth, a psychologist who devoted the majority of her professional career to understanding infants' early social relationships, defined attachment behaviors as those that primarily promote nearness to a *specific* person (Ainsworth, 1983; Ainsworth & Bowlby, 1991). Such behaviors include signaling (crying, smiling, or vocalizing), orienting (looking), displaying movements relating to another person (following or approaching), and making active attempts at physical contact (clambering up, embracing, or clinging).

Studying Infant and Toddler Attachment

Much of what we presently understand about attachment traces back to the early research of Mary Ainsworth and her colleagues (Ainsworth, 1979, 1985, 1995; Ainsworth, Blehar, Waters, & Wall, 1978). For example, Ainsworth's *strange-situation test* (which also is described in Chapter 1) is often used to assess the quality of infant attachment to the primary caregiver. The general procedure involves the mother leaving a 12- to 18-month-old baby with a stranger in a room full of toys. The behaviors of interest are how the child responds when the mother leaves and then when she returns. Table 5-4 summarizes the eight steps in the strange situation procedure .

Using the strange-situation test, Ainsworth found two basic types of attachment. Between 60 and 70% of U.S. middle-class babies displayed the first type of attachment, which is called **secure attachment**, where a strong emotional bond between a child and a caregiver develops because of responsive caregiving. These toddlers can separate themselves somewhat easily from their mother and explore toys even when the stranger is present. Although they may become upset when their mother leaves, they greet her warmly and become calm quickly when she returns. The mother thus serves as a *secure base* around which her infant can explore, and can return to if the environment seems threatening.

Why would securely attached infants show less distress than insecurely attached infants when their mothers leave them?

The remaining babies—about 30 to 40%—displayed **insecure attachment**, which often results from inconsistent or unresponsive caregiving. Insecure attachment takes three distinct forms. In one form, called **resistant attachment**, the child becomes angry when the mother leaves and avoids her when she returns. In another form of insecure attachment, called **avoidant attachment**, the child responds to the mother ambivalently, simultaneously seeking and rejecting affection and not becoming upset when the mother leaves the room (Ainsworth, 1985). Ainsworth later recognized a third form of insecure attachment (Ainsworth, 1995, 2010; Main & Solomon, 1986): In **disorganized/disoriented attachment**, the child behaves in contradictory and confused ways—such as avoiding the mother's gaze while being held or coming to her

secure attachment
A strong emotional bond between a child and a caregiver that develops because of responsive caregiving

avoidant attachment
Insecure attachment that is characterized by ambivalence toward the mother

insecure attachment
A fragile emotional bond between a child and a caregiver that often is the result of inconsistent or unresponsive caregiving

disorganized/disoriented attachment
Insecure attachment that is characterized by contradictory behavior and confusion toward the mother

resistant attachment
Insecure attachment that is characterized by anger and avoidance of the mother

TRY THIS!

Replicating the Strange Situation

To study infant attachment, Mary Ainsworth devised a method called the *strange situation*, which is described in detail in Table 5-4. To better understand how infants respond in such a setting, try to replicate Ainsworth's situation. If you or a friend occasionally babysit for a toddler about 12 to 18 months old, perhaps you could ask the parent to create a strange environment as he or she gets ready to leave. Another option is to visit a child-care center that accepts 12- to 18-month-old children and ask to observe the toddlers' reactions when their caregivers leave. You also may be able to set up a strange situation in a child-care setting if a child is attached to a particular caregiver. Be creative and try to replicate Ainsworth's procedure as well as you can.

Reflect on What You Observed

Did the children you observed exhibit distress when their caregivers left the room? How could you tell? Was the distress mild or extreme? How did the children react when their caregivers reentered the room? What kind of attachment do you think best described each child's reaction? What evidence did you see of secure versus insecure attachment?

Consider the Issues

Do you think the setting you observed was a good replication of Ainsworth's original strange situation? How did your setting differ? Do you think such differences were influential in what you were able to observe? If you can interview the caregivers you observed, ask them what their child's typical behavior is like when they separate. Based on this information and your own observation, how would you describe each child's attachment style—secure or insecure? What evidence would you cite to support your conclusion?

Table 5-4 The "Strange Situation" Paradigm Developed by Mary Ainsworth

Step 1	Parent and infant are escorted into a waiting room filled with chairs, and which has a one-way mirror through which the investigator can unobtrusively watch the infant
Step 2	Parent takes a seat and places the infant on the floor to play with toys
Step 3	Stranger enters the room, takes a seat, and talks briefly to the parent
Step 4	Once the infant gets settled, parent leaves the room, and stranger interacts with the baby, offering comfort if the baby becomes upset
Step 5	Parent returns to the room and interacts with the infant; the stranger leaves
Step 6	Once the infant is settled again, parent again leaves the room, leaving the infant alone
Step 7	Stranger re-enters the room and interacts with the infant
Step 8	Parent re-enters the room, interacts with the baby, and encourages the baby to play with the toys

▲ Mary Ainsworth created the "strange situation" procedure in order to observe how infants respond when their mothers leave them and later return. Here, this infant appears secure and confident as he interacts with Ainsworth.

with no visible emotionality. (See the box Try This! Replicating the Strange Situation.) Many practitioners view disorganized/disoriented attachment as the most perilous, as children who are confused about whom they can trust—or those who feel they can trust no one—have no way of organizing their emotional experiences (Liotti, 2012; Solomon & George, 2011).

The Effects of Attachment

Longitudinal studies that compare infants who have secure versus insecure attachment often have found dramatic differences in personality and social development as early as 18 months of age (e.g., Fearon, Bakersmans-Kranenburg, van IJzendoorn, Lapsley, & Roisman, 2010; Greenman & Tardif, 2010; Priddis & Howieson, 2012). Most studies indicate that securely attached children are more curious, sociable, independent, and competent than their insecurely attached peers at ages 2, 3, 4, and 5. In addition, securely attached infants generally are more enthusiastic, persistent, and less cooperative. By age 2, they are more effective in coping with their peers, and they spontaneously invent more imaginative and symbolic play. Later, in elementary school, children who have experienced secure attachment during infancy persist in their work longer, they are more eager to learn new skills, and they exhibit more highly developed social skills in interacting with adults and peers (Berlin, Cassidy, & Appleyard, 2010; Cassidy & Shaver, 2008; Sroufe, 2005).

Thus, it appears that securely attached children do even simple things better than children who are insecurely attached and are, in general, better prepared to undertake later developmental tasks of all types. Not surprisingly, securely attached 3-year-olds also tend to be better liked by their peers (Cassidy & Shaver, 2008).

In contrast, infants who fail to form secure attachments often experience a variety of problems, ranging from difficulty in adjustment to problems with social behavior (e.g., Fearon, 2010). Research shows that insecurely attached 2-year-olds often exhibit hyperactivity or chronic stress reactions, and there is some evidence that such responses may interfere with brain development. For example, research shows that chronic stress in rats disturbs the development of the parts of the brain that involve fearfulness, vigilance, learning, memory, and attention. Generalizing to humans, it may be that secure attachment provides a kind of buffer against these disturbances, whereas insecure attachment leaves the brain open to insults that lead to long-term anxiety, timidity, and learning difficulties (Fonagy & Target, 2005; Wright, 1997).

Behavioral problems in childhood also may be linked to insecure attachment. For example, the children of depressed caregivers—who generally are less responsive to their children—have been found to have more difficulty with emotional control at age 4 and have lower self-confidence at age 5 (Maughan, Cicchetti, Toth, & Rogosch, 2007). Insecure attachment may also intensify feeding problems, possibly leading to malnutrition (Chatoor, et al., 2004): Research on a young, low-income urban population in Chile suggested that a significant association may exist between maternal insensitivity, insecure attachment, and chronic malnutrition among young children (Valenzuela, 1997). Furthermore, problems with attachment can disrupt other important social relationships, including those involving the child's peers (Lewis, 2005; Schneider, Atkinson, & Tardif, 2001; Verissimo, et al., 2011).

Explaining Attachment

Studies of attachment often demonstrate that the quality of the relationship between a caregiver and an infant provides the basis of attachment and also is closely linked to many other key aspects of development. Why, and how, does this important relationship develop?

Some evidence for explaining attachment can be gathered by observing the behavior of mothers and infants. Typically, infants who develop secure attachments have caregivers who provide consistent attention to the infants' needs and who interact with the baby with sensitivity and a warm, caring attitude (Main, 2000). On the other hand, babies who develop an insecure attachment often have caregivers who are inattentive or emotionally rejecting (Berlin & Cassidy, 1999; Cassidy & Shaver, 2008). Physical abuse and neglect can also play a negative role in the development of attachment (Chaffin, et al., 2006), as can parental depression (Levy, 2007; Trapolini, Ungerer, & McMahon, 2007), as these issues often interfere with the establishment of reliable, loving, and *synchronous* (two-way) interactions between the caregiver and the infant.

Research clearly indicates that environmental circumstances and learning can have a powerful effect on how attachment bonds are established. Earlier in the 20th century, especially, behaviorists explained attachment as the result of conditioning, in which infants learn to associate the presence of the caregiver with the pleasure associated with the satisfaction of biological needs, such as being fed when hungry or having their diaper changed when soiled. Psychoanalytic theorists, most notably Sigmund Freud, viewed attachment in much the same way as the behaviorists. They explained attachment as developing out of early mother–infant contact and the satisfaction of the infant's needs, especially during feeding—hence the significance associated with oral stimulation during the first year.

Other scientists, however, have advanced more biologically based views (e.g., Simpson & Belsky, 2010). Arguing that attachment-type behavior is often seen in animals, they view attachment more as an instinct that has survival value because it serves to keep newborns close to their mothers, where they can be protected and where they can observe and imitate her effective behaviors. For example, **imprinting**, which is the formation of a bond between some newborn animals (especially birds) and their mothers, appears to be present at birth and therefore the result of biological programming rather than learning. In now-classic research, Konrad Lorenz noted that newly hatched goslings, which normally imprint on their mothers, would imprint on any moving object—the family dog or even Lorenz himself—if that object, rather than the mother goose, were present when the goslings hatched (Hess, 1973).

What is it about this earliest relationship that forms the basis for attachment? In another now-classic study, Harry Harlow (1959) noted that when monkeys in his lab were raised without their mothers, they often developed maladapted behaviors. They were easily frightened, irritable, and reluctant to eat or play, despite the fact that they had a nutritious diet and were otherwise well cared for. Some monkeys even died. Obviously, these baby monkeys needed something more than regular feeding to thrive and develop.

To investigate, Harlow and his colleagues placed two artificial surrogate "mothers" in each infant monkey's cage. One surrogate mother was made of metal that was equipped with a milk source to feed the infant, and the other was made of a soft terrycloth fabric that was not equipped for feeding (Harlow & Harlow, 1962). The results of the study were striking: The infant monkeys

▲ Orphaned goslings nurtured by Konrad Lorenz during the critical imprinting period follow him as if he were their real mother.

imprinting
The formation of a bond between some newborn animals (especially birds) and their mothers, which appears to be present at birth

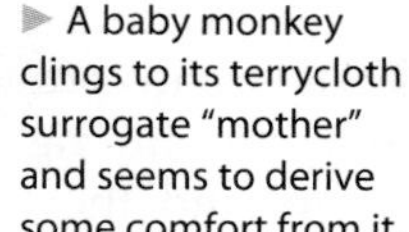

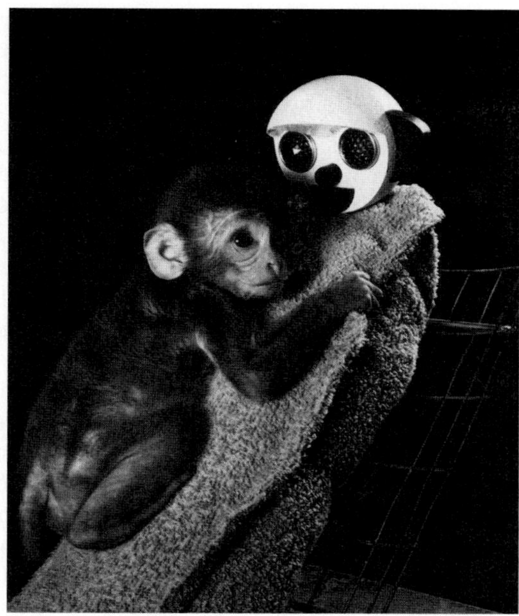

A baby monkey clings to its terrycloth surrogate "mother" and seems to derive some comfort from it.

showed a distinct preference for the surrogate made of terrycloth. They spent more time clinging and vocalizing to it, and they ran to it when they were frightened. Apparently, attachment requires more from the mother than mere physical presence or the provision of food (Suomi, 2010). As theorists now know, it is the *quality* of the mother–infant bond that is critically important, and both biological and environmental forces play a role.

The Reciprocal Nature of Attachment A view that acknowledges the *interactive* nature of biologically based and social forces in the development of attachment has been proposed by John Bowlby (1999a, 1999b; Shaver & Fraby, 2010). Taking an evolutionary perspective, Bowlby argued that biologically preprogrammed behaviors that enhance infant survival and normal development occur in *both* the infant and the caregiver. For example, mothers talk to, cuddle, and take pleasure in gently attending to their infants, and infants respond by engaging their mothers in eye contact, and later with smiling and cooing. These reciprocal behaviors become elaborated and continue to develop during the first few years in a series of stages that reflect the growing competencies of the newborn (Ainsworth & Bowlby, 1991). See Table 5-5 for Bowlby's stages of attachment.

The development of **synchrony**, which is defined as the back-and-forth interactions between caregiver and infant, is especially important in the development of attachment, although it is also a characteristic of many other developmental processes (Bornstein & Tamis-LeMonda, 2010). For example, contrary to what reinforcement theory would predict, mothers who quickly and consistently respond to their infants' crying over the first few months are more likely to have infants who cry *less* by the end of the first year (Bell & Ainsworth, 1972; Bornstein, Tamis-Lemonda, Chun-Shin, & Haynes, 2008). When mothers fail to respond, perhaps in the mistaken belief that picking up a crying child will only reinforce the crying and thereby make it more frequent, infants learn to persist until they are attended to or until they wear themselves out, learning instead that their needs are not always met. Infants who do not establish good synchrony with their caregivers also have a more difficult time establishing

Do you think the results of Harlow's study of infant monkeys generalize to human relationships? What evidence can you provide that supports your answer?

Table 5-5 Bowlby's Stages of Attachment

Stage	Age	Description
1	Birth to 2 months	• Newborns exhibit attachment behaviors that are directed toward any person, including but not limited to familiar people • Attachment behaviors are instinctive, and very general in nature
2	2 to 7 months	• Infants become attached to a primary caregiver—usually the mother—or to only a very small number of primary caregivers • Separation anxiety develops toward the end of this period; here, the infant experiences emotional distress when the primary caregiver leaves, or separates from, the infant
3	7 to 24 months	• Attachment extends to other significant caregivers—day-care workers, older siblings, and so forth • Infants begin to engage with significant caregivers to draw them into synchronous attachment-related behaviors, thereby laying the groundwork for language and social development
4	24 months on	• Attachments extend to peers, as well as to caregivers • Toddlers and young children begin to develop more refined social and cognitive skills, allowing them to take others' feelings into consideration and develop empathy

Watch *Classic Footage of Harlow's Monkeys: Contact Comfort* on **MyDevelopmentLab**

synchrony
The back-and-forth interactions between an infant and a caregiver

the kind of give-and-take required for the development of more advanced communication. It is not surprising that synchrony between infant and caregiver during the first few months is a good predictor of secure attachment at age 1, as well as more sophisticated patterns of mutual communication at that age (Bowlby, 2007).

The nature of the parent–child interaction that emerges from the development of attachment in the first 2 years of life forms an important basis for all future relationships, not only in childhood but throughout adulthood as well (Magai, 2010). Many theorists focus on the significance of early attachment. One such view is that of Erik Erikson, who describes this early attachment relationship with caregivers as the development of trust.

The Relationship Between Attachment and Trust

As discussed earlier, Erikson (1993) saw the critical developmental issue of the first year to be the establishment of **trust versus mistrust**. When attachments are secure, infants are able to depend on their caregivers to provide not only for their basic needs, such as food and safety, but also for their psychological needs, which Harlow's research demonstrates are also of fundamental importance. Thus, securely attached infants are likely to develop *trust*, the belief that the world is a safe place and that they will be secure and taken care of. When attachment goes awry, however, *mistrust* is likely to develop. Here the infant may experience deprivation, which can be social, emotional, or physical, if caregiving is absent or abusive. As mentioned earlier, normal development involves a balance between learning to trust as well as to mistrust situations where danger may lie. Developing the ability to trust is a key to healthy social and emotional adjustment. As you can see, the early relationship formed between a caregiver and an infant is critically important to the healthy development of the child.

The Role of Culture in Attachment

Regardless of culture, infants all over the world normally establish attachment relationships with their primary caregivers by around 8 or 9 months of age. However, although the sequence of development of these first relationships is fairly consistent across cultures, the details can vary dramatically, depending on the personality of the parents, their specific child-rearing practices, and the temperament and personality of the baby (Karen, 2008).

Can you think of examples of specific behavior that would contribute to the development of an individualist orientation? To a collectivist orientation?

Cultural values play a particularly important role in attachment (Super & Harkness, 2010; van IJzendoorn & Sagi-Schwartz, 2010). For example, a study of mother–infant interactions among middle-class U.S. Anglo and Puerto Rican mothers and their first-born infants during feeding, social play, teaching, and free play showed that Anglo mothers emphasized socialization goals that fostered individualism. Puerto Rican mothers, on the other hand, fostered goals more consistent with a family unity orientation (Carlson & Harwood, 2003; Harwood, Schoelmerich, Schulze, & Gonzalez, 1999). Thus, parents' behaviors reflect general cultural values, which are transmitted to children through early socialization.

There also are cross-cultural variations in *whom* the infant attaches to. In the United States and much of Western Europe, child development experts have assumed that a single primary relationship—usually with the mother—is ideal for healthy infant development. However, in other cultures, a primary mother–infant relationship is supplemented by many other relationships. Grandmothers, aunts, fathers, siblings, and neighbors take turns caring for the infant. To the extent that these relationships are reasonably consistent, healthy attachment with these caregivers, as well as with the mother, emerges (Howes & Spieker, 2010).

Attachment relationships also vary from culture to culture according to the type of interactions infants have with their caregivers (Metzger, Erdman, & Ng, 2010; Rothbaum, Morelli, &

▲ At about 7 months, infants become wary of strangers. This stranger anxiety is a landmark in the infant's social development.

Watch *Attachment in Infants* on **MyDevelopmentLab**

trust versus mistrust
According to Erikson, the first critical developmental issue that is resolved in the first year of life

Rusk, 2011). In most Western cultures, a typical mother–infant relationship is primarily *social* and is characterized by game playing and interactive dialogues. In other cultures, however, infants have close *physical* contact with caregivers—including being carried in a back sling and co-sleeping with a parent or another adult—but do not have frequent face-to-face interactions.

Thus, although the quality of relationships is important, many cultural and subcultural variations can foster healthy attachment. Regardless of culture, however, attachment plays a critically important role in development, and it has been the subject of one of the largest and most important research efforts in the field of lifespan development.

REVIEW THE FACTS 5-3

1. If a child in a strange-situation test acts angry when the mother leaves and avoids her when she returns, this is best described as what kind of attachment?
2. Which of the following does *not* appear to disrupt attachment?
   a. parents who are depressed
   b. neglectful parents
   c. having multiple caregivers
   d. parents who are abusive
3. If a duckling is hatched by a mother cat, it will follow the cat around. This phenomenon is called ___________.
4. The back-and-forth interactions between infant and caregiver are called ___________, to accentuate their reciprocal nature.
5. Which of the following, over the long term, will more likely result in an infant who cries less?
   a. ignoring early crying, so the infant learns that crying will not lead to reinforcement
   b. responding promptly to an infant's crying and giving comfort
6. In comparison to more collectivist cultures, in cultures like the United States, infant attachment is usually
   a. social.
   b. with several family members.
   c. physical.
   d. less well developed.

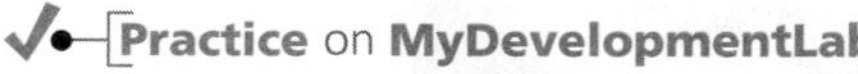
Practice on MyDevelopmentLab

SEPARATING FROM THE CAREGIVER

As Bowlby and others acknowledge, when babies are born, they make little distinction among caregivers and others. As we saw in the previous chapter, although even neonates can distinguish their own mothers from other caregivers, they exhibit little preference for one caregiver over another or even over a stranger. By about 7 months of age, however, this changes. Babies who have been smiling, welcoming, friendly, and accepting toward strangers suddenly become shy and wary of them. At the same time, some infants become extremely upset when they are left alone in a strange place even for a moment. This universal response is called **stranger anxiety** or **separation anxiety**, and it signals a shift in the infant's ability to process information about the world (Lamb, 1988; Nelson & Bennett, 2008). Although many babies do not experience intense stranger and separation anxiety, for those who do, such reactions often continue throughout the remainder of the first year and through much of the second year.

Most developmental psychologists see stranger and separation anxiety as being closely tied to the infant's cognitive development. As cognitive processes mature, infants develop schemes for what is familiar, and they notice anything that is new and strange. Once such schemes develop, infants can distinguish caregivers from strangers, and they often become keenly aware when the primary caregiver is absent. Thus, according to the **discrepancy hypothesis**, separation anxiety results when infants become capable of detecting departures from the known or the expected. Because the caregiver's presence typically coincides with safety, things seem secure when familiar caregivers are present but uncertain when they are absent.

Do you think the temperament of an infant might affect the way that stranger and separation anxiety are experienced? If so, what might the relationship be?

By 9 months the separation-anxiety reaction is further complicated by social learning. When mothers or other caregivers react to strangers with concern, infants are more likely to also respond with anxiety. When such signaling, called **social referencing**, is positive, and when parents monitor and control their own emotional reactions, they help their infants and toddlers adjust positively to strangers and strange situations.

Social Referencing and Culture

When infants and toddlers are unsure whether a situation is safe or unsafe, good or bad, they often seek information by looking to adults for emotional signals (Stenberg, 2009; Vaillant-Molina & Bahrick, 2012). Infants look for emotional signals in many circumstances, including how far to wander away from the caregiver and whether or not to explore a strange object. Perhaps you have observed a child who falls and scrapes a knee

Watch *Parent-Child Attachments: Ross Thompson* on MyDevelopmentLab

discrepancy hypothesis
A cognitive theory stating that at around 7 months, infants acquire schemes for familiar objects; when a new image or object is presented that differs from the old one, the child experiences uncertainty and anxiety

stranger and separation anxiety
An infant's fear of strangers or of being separated from the caregiver; both occur in the second half of the first year and indicate, in part, a new cognitive ability to respond to differences in the environment

social referencing
The subtle emotional signals, usually from the parent, that influence the infant's behavior

Watch *Separation Anxiety* on MyDevelopmentLab

Watch *Social Referencing* on MyDevelopmentLab

and then looks at the mother to gauge her reactions before becoming upset. Of course, infants reference fathers as well as mothers. Although they typically look more at mothers than at fathers when both parents are present, the father's signals appear to be equally effective in regulating behavior (Thompson, Easterbrooks, & Padilla-Walker, 2003).

Through social referencing, parents teach infants as young as 1 year of age the values of their culture. For example, the transmission of cultural values through social referencing has been demonstrated in a series of studies of the Kung San, a hunter–gatherer culture in Botswana (Bakeman, Adamson, Konner, & Barr, 1990, 1997; Barr, 2011; Kruger & Konner, 2010). For the Kung San, sharing is highly valued. When cultural anthropologists looked at mothers and their 10- to 12-month-old infants, they were surprised to find that, in contrast to many U.S. parents, the Kung San parents seemed to pay no attention to the infant's exploration of objects. They did not smile or talk about the objects, nor did they punish their children as they picked up twigs, grass, parts of food, nut shells, bones, and the like. Their attitude was reflected in statements translated as, "He's teaching himself." Instead of focusing on the child's exploration, the adults paid close attention to the *sharing* of objects, with commands like "Give it to me" or "Here, take this," thereby imparting values central to sharing over those more focused on the development of the individual.

Parents also use social referencing to convey cultural meaning to older infants and toddlers by including them in social interactions, even though children of this age are often peripheral to the ongoing social life of the family and community. For example, Barbara Rogoff and colleagues (Rogoff, Mistry, Goncu, & Mosier, 1993) visited four communities—a Mayan Indian town in Guatemala, a middle-class urban community in the United States, a tribal village in India, and a middle-class urban neighborhood in Turkey—to study how adults help toddlers learn appropriate social behavior. Sometimes toddlers were given direct instruction and help, but often they learned through their own keen observation, imitation, and participation in adult activities. For example, toddlers usually ate with the family at dinnertime (finger foods instead of adult foods) and therefore learned to imitate the conversation and gestures of adults and older siblings. By being included, they also could enjoy good feelings and laughter and were encouraged to take small adultlike actions, such as lifting a cup for a toast. In these ways, the values of the culture are incorporated into children's understanding of their world, and children learn to separate themselves from their caregivers, thereby becoming more independent.

The Development of Autonomy

Regardless of culture, during the second year, toddlers become more comfortable in exploring on their own. Although they continue to rely on their caregivers for emotional support, they begin to reach out on their own in their quest for *autonomy*—their need to be independent and separate from their caregivers. The significance of this developmental milestone was recognized by Erik Erikson, who saw the patterns of separating from the caregiver as a conflict between **autonomy versus shame and doubt**, which is resolved in the second and third years of a child's life (Erikson, 1993). How toddlers approach this task is determined largely by their previous experiences. Children who have developed a trusting relationship with their caregivers during the first year of life, thereby developing a healthy autonomy from their caregivers, are better prepared to take the first steps toward independence than are those who are insecurely attached. Toddlers who have failed to form secure attachments, however, are likely to have a more difficult time. Parents also play an important role. When parents are both sensitive to their toddler's emotions and also encourage independence and exploration, a healthy sense of autonomy is likely to develop (Bernier, Carlson, & Whipple, 2010; Holden, 2010; Whipple, Bernier, & Mageau, 2011).

However, even toddlers with secure attachments have difficulty forming a separate, autonomous identity. They often seem torn between a desire to stay close to their mother or caregiver and a desire to be independent. Their new sense of separateness appears to frighten them. Indeed, toddlers experience a wide range of emotions and eventually develop new ways to deal with those emotions, such as suppressing their crying. The way parents deal with the conflict between autonomy and dependence typically is expressed in their approach to discipline.

Discipline What limits should a parent or caregiver set on a child's behavior? Some parents, afraid that any kind of control over their children's behavior will interfere with creative exploration and independence, passively stand by while their 2-year-olds do whatever they please—in *your* home as well as their

For a toddler, the psychological pulls and tugs of autonomy and dependency needs can be direct and undisguised.

autonomy versus shame and doubt
According to Erikson, the second critical developmental issue that is resolved in the second and third years

own. When they do discipline, it is often harsh, reflecting the adults' sense of frustration. Other parents, determined not to spoil their children and convinced that 2-year-olds should act like responsible little adults, set so many limits on behavior that their children literally cannot do anything right. Although it is easy to see the errors in these extremes, it is not easy to provide guidelines that work for every situation.

Parental feedback helps children see how their actions affect others. In fact, children need feedback if they are to become sensitive to the needs of others. Feedback might consist of praise for good behavior, such as "What a good helper you are" or it might take the form of mild scolding, such as "Don't do that, it hurts your brother." The key to feedback is that it should focus on the *behavior*—not the child—as the object of criticism.

Children who have a strong attachment relationship and whose needs are met through loving interaction with an adult are neither spoiled by attention nor frightened or threatened by reasonable limits. They are stronger and more confident because they have a secure base from which to venture forth into independent activities. The secure-base phenomenon is robust indeed and, despite the fact that different cultures have somewhat different definitions of how the *ideal* child should behave, it is observed in many cultures in addition to the United States, including China, Germany, Korea, Japan, and Israel (Jin, Jacobvitz, Hazen, & Jung, 2012; Posada, et al., 1995).

Toilet training One form of discipline that historically has received substantial attention from psychologists is toilet training. Freud's view in particular emphasized the significance of how the child copes with this first major conflict between self-control and parental control. Accordingly, Freud believed that toilet training that was begun too early or that was too strict could produce an *anal fixation* that would be carried forward in development, interfering with normal development later in life. Similarly, a too lax approach to toilet training could cause other problems to develop.

Researchers today take a broader view of toilet training, seeing it as but one aspect of development that is part of a cluster of child-rearing issues. By itself, toilet training is no longer considered a major issue in social and personality development. For example, parents who are severe and harsh in toilet training are usually just as strict about other behaviors that require self-mastery and independence, such as feeding, dressing, and general exploration. This strict parental control can have pronounced effects on personality development, creating a child who is inhibited and fearful of anything new or, conversely, a rebellious child.

The Development of Prosocial Behavior

During the second year, as toddlers continue the separation process and become more autonomous, they begin to cooperate, share, help, and respond empathetically to emotional distress in others. Many studies have focused on the development of these **prosocial behaviors**, which are intended to benefit others. Like other aspects of behavior, prosocial behaviors develop sequentially (Hutman & Dapretto, 2009; Roth-Hanania, Davidov, & Zahn-Waxler, 2011). For example, in studies of cooperation in simple tasks, very few 12-month-old infants cooperate with each other. At 18 months, cooperation is infrequent and appears accidental. At 24 months, with a little coaching, nearly all toddlers can cooperate (Brownell, Romani, & Zerwas, 2007; Thompson, Easterbrooks, & Padilla-Walker, 2003).

How do you think the development of trust might be related to the development of prosocial behavior?

Likewise, concern for others emerges during the second year. In one series of studies (Radke-Yarrow, Zahn-Waxler, & Chapman, 1983; Zahn-Waxler & Radke-Yarrow, 1992), mothers were asked to pretend that they had just hurt themselves. At 21 months, toddlers were confused and anxious about the mother's distress. However, 3 months later, some of the toddlers had learned soothing, comforting behaviors by observing the behavior of their mothers, who regularly responded with empathy when the child was in distress.

The development of **empathy**—the ability to understand another's feelings and perspective—is closely linked to secure attachments and to how children themselves are treated when hurt or in need of help (Farrant, Devine, Maybery, & Fletcher, 2012). For example, when mothers are warm and loving, their children exhibit more empathy during their second year of life. In contrast, children of mothers who control with anger tend to show less empathy (Azar, 1997; Spinrad & Stifter, 2006). The development of empathy also is linked to cognitive development and to the toddler's developing sense of *self* versus *other*. Indeed, the development of *self-concept*—one's perception of personal identity—is among the more important outcomes of the developmental events in infancy and toddlerhood.

The Development of the Self

At birth, infants cannot differentiate between themselves and the world around them. Gradually, however, they begin to realize that they are separate and unique beings (Rochat, 2010). For example, by about 7 months of age, stranger anxiety emerges, which indicates that babies are beginning to develop a sense of the separate identities of various people, including themselves. Later in their first year, infants begin to realize that they can *cause* things to happen: They clearly enjoy throwing their Cheerios, one by one, onto the floor, and they understand that it was they who spilled the milk. By 18 months, toddlers clearly can recognize themselves in pictures and in the mirror (see Table 5-6).

Researchers often study the development of self by observing the reaction of infants when they look at themselves in a mirror. One interesting variation of this technique is the *rouge test*. In this

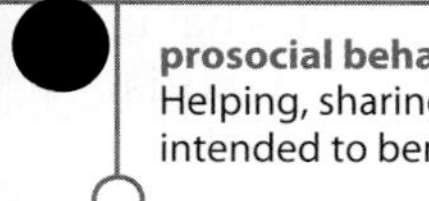

prosocial behavior
Helping, sharing, or cooperative actions that are intended to benefit others

empathy
The ability to understand another's feelings and perspective

Table 5-6 Who Is That Baby in the Mirror?

At 16 months, an infant studies "that baby" in the mirror.

During the first 2 years of life, infants and toddlers make giant leaps in self-knowledge. From experiments that involve infants and toddlers of various ages looking at themselves in the mirror, it appears that self-knowledge develops in stages, as follows.

BEFORE 8 MONTHS OF AGE

Infants appear to be attracted to the image of an infant in the mirror, but it is unclear whether they recognize the image as their own. Sometimes infants 6 to 8 months old will recognize that their own movements correspond with the movements they observe in the mirror.

BETWEEN 8 AND 16 MONTHS OF AGE

Infants and toddlers can tell the difference between their own image and the images of others who are clearly different from themselves, such as an older child. During this period, they begin to associate specific features with their sense of self. Nevertheless, they will sometimes crawl around the mirror to try to find the *other* baby. If a researcher puts a dot of red rouge on the baby's nose, the baby notices it but points to the nose in the mirror and not to his or her own nose.

AT ABOUT 18 MONTHS OF AGE

Toddlers no longer need environmental clues to make the connection between the baby in the mirror and themselves; that is, they recognize the image they see in the mirror is their own image. If the researcher now puts a dot of red rouge on the toddler's nose, there is a classic reaction. The toddler points to her own nose, turns her head away from the mirror, drops her eyes, smiles, and looks embarrassed.

BY 2 YEARS OF AGE

Self-knowledge expands to include awareness of activities as well as appearance. A 2-year-old who preens in front of a mirror is engaging in a self-admiring activity.

SOURCE: Adapted from *Social cognition and the acquisition of self*, by M. Lewis and J. Brooks-Gunn, 1979, New York: Plenum Press.

procedure, a dab of rouge (colored makeup) is applied to the end of the infant's or toddler's nose. Observers then watch to see what these "marked" babies do when they look at themselves in a mirror. If the babies reach out to touch the nose of the "baby in the mirror," this is interpreted to mean that they have not yet developed an understanding that the image they see is actually a representation of themselves. Once self-concept becomes better developed, however, babies in the rouge test look in the mirror and touch their *own* noses, indicating they understand that the image they see is not another baby but rather is a reflection of their own image.

Early research on the rouge test, and other mirror tests of self-concept, suggested that toddlers first show signs of self-recognition at about 18 to 24 months of age. However, this research looked at only children raised in Western societies, such as the United States and Canada. More recent research has used these mirror-based techniques to explore self-concept development in non-Western societies, and with quite different results. Interestingly, toddlers raised in non-Western cultures, such as Fiji, Saint Lucia, Granada, Peru, and India, show delayed self-concept development when measured using this test (Broesch, Callaghan, Henrich, Murphy, & Rochat, 2011; Kärtner, Keller, & Chahry, 2010). Furthermore, the development of self-concept was closely related to the emergence of prosocial behavior only in Western cultures, further supporting the idea that there are cross-cultural differences in how the development of self-concept occurs. Despite these cross-cultural variations, however, it is true that toddlers acquire the understanding that they are separate beings sometime near the middle of their second year. For example, toddlers' awareness of sex roles begins to develop at about 21 months of age (Lewis, Haviland-Jones, & Barrett, 2008) as girls and boys begin to exhibit gender-specific behaviors that are reflective of their culture.

Watch *Self-Awareness* on **MyDevelopmentLab**

Predictably, the toddler's growing sense of self frequently produces emotional reactions to others, sometimes in the form of temper tantrums. As toddlers become more aware of their own feelings, they react more strongly to frustration and hurt and may respond with intense emotion. Their developing self-awareness also is reflected in their language. By the end of the second year, children's speech is filled with references to themselves. The words *me* and *mine* take on new significance, and the concept of ownership is clearly and strongly acted out. Even in families and cultures that emphasize sharing and minimize ownership, toddlers are often extremely possessive. It may be that they develop the concept of ownership to round out their understanding of self.

Attachment and Separation

Much of the discussion in this chapter centers around the two fundamental tasks of infancy and toddlerhood: forming a secure attachment to the primary caregiver and then, beginning in about the second year, separating from that caregiver and establishing an independent, autonomous self. Although newborns come into the world as unique human beings—each with a particular temperament, set of abilities, preferences, and so forth—these two fundamental tasks provide a consistent focus for development in the first 2 years (see Table 5-7 for a summary).

Consistency in early development is also a function of environmental factors. Most children are raised in early environments that are quite similar. For example, in most cultures and during most historical periods, the large majority of babies have a single primary caregiver—most often their mother—who is primarily responsible for meeting their needs and guiding their development. Most infants also are raised in situations where

Table 5-7 Important Factors in Personality Development During Infancy and Toddlerhood

Factor	Developmental outcome
Temperament	• At birth, infants display behavioral styles that can influence how their parents react to and care for them, in turn reciprocally influencing the infants' personality development. • Some infants are easy, some are difficult, and some are slow to warm up. Infants differ in their degree of effortful control, negative affectivity, and extroversion.
Attachment	• Responsive caregiving fosters securely attached infants who later are likely to develop into curious, sociable, independent, and competent individuals during early childhood. • Unresponsive or indifferent caregiving fosters insecurely attached infants who later are less enthusiastic, less persistent, and less cooperative compared to securely attached infants.
Social referencing	• Personality development and behavior are strongly influenced by emotional signals, as well as other signals that parents provide for their infants in social situations. • Cultural values and meanings are also conveyed through social referencing.
Parental discipline	• Especially during toddlerhood, the way parents balance their children's attempts at autonomy with necessary discipline and limits is important. • Either extreme—placing too few or too many limits—can interfere with healthy personality development.
Self-concept	• Personality revolves around a sense of self or personal identity. • Children and adults tend to behave in ways that are consistent with their self-concept, which is based in part on gender, physical abilities, and physical appearance. In turn, even young children reflect on matters such as whether they are good or bad, how others view them, and whether they are acceptable, competent human beings when forming their self-concept.

they are loved and well cared for, at least with respect to the available resources. In addition, most babies come into the world with a full set of sensory and intellectual capabilities that, as we saw in Chapter 4, develops quickly as the neonate gains experience with the environment.

There are, however, deviations from these standard patterns. In the last sections of this chapter, we explore some of these special circumstances and their impact on the development of attachment and autonomy. In the next section, we look at the family system.

REVIEW THE FACTS 5-4

1. Children often learn cultural values by observing how their caregivers respond, which is a phenomenon called
   a. attachment. b. social referencing.
   c. synchrony. d. the discrepancy hypothesis.
2. According to Erikson, the conflict during toddlerhood is one of __________ versus __________.
3. Behaviors that are intended to benefit others are called __________ behaviors.
4. The ability to understand another person's feelings and perspective is called
   a. prosocial behavior. b. synchrony.
   c. self-concept. d. empathy.
5. Children begin to become aware of culturally determined sex roles at about what age?
6. The two most fundamental tasks in the first 2 years are __________ and __________.

Practice on **MyDevelopmentLab**

THE FAMILY SYSTEM: A BROADER CONTEXT

Fathers

Historically, at least in Western cultures, fathers have played a relatively small role in infant care. However, especially since the mid-20th century, fathers' roles in child care have been expanding (Saracho & Spodek, 2008; Shwalb, Shwalb, & Lamb, 2013). (See the box Changing Perspectives: Fatherhood in the Changing American Family—What Matters? to learn more about the changing role of fathers.) As research clearly shows, fathers can be as responsive to their infant's cues as can mothers (Parke, 1996; Shears & Robinson, 2005); they can successfully provide routine child care; and they can bathe, diaper, feed, and rock as skillfully as mothers. Infants can become as attached to their fathers as to their mothers, and infants can also experience the same level of separation anxiety as with their mothers (Bretherton, 2010; Hock & Lutz, 1998; Tamis-Lemonda & Cabrera, 2002). Moreover, as might be expected, fathers who spend more time taking care of their young children form stronger attachments to them, and their children benefit (Lamb, 2004; Newland, Coyl, & Freeman, 2008). Despite these shared capabilities, however, most fathers still do not take *primary* responsibility for infant care. Therefore, the father's relationship with the infant often is different from the mother's.

Fathering Styles In many developed countries, including the United States, the father's role in child rearing continues to evolve as more and more mothers work outside the home. However, some traditional differences in how fathers and mothers interact with their infants persist (Freeman, Newland, & Coyl, 2010; Lamb & Lewis, 2010). In two-parent homes, for example, mothers are likely to hold infants for caretaking purposes; fathers are more likely to hold infants during play (Parke,

CHANGING PERSPECTIVES

Fatherhood in the Changing American Family—What Matters?

The storybook images of families of young children, with Dad returning home after work to his stay-at-home wife and briefly playing with the children while dinner is prepared, are not the portraits of most U.S. families in the 21st century. Nothing has changed this scene quite as much as the economic reality of women's necessary participation in the workforce outside the home (Cabrera, Tamis-Lemonda, Bradley, Hofferth, & Lamb, 2000). Women have always worked; however, in the early 20th century, much of that work was in the family business or on the farm, so women retained their ability to also watch over their children. In 1950, only 12% of U.S. mothers of children under age 6 worked outside the home; in 2011, about 64% of U.S. mothers of young children did. Today more than half of mothers with young babies work outside the home: About 56% of mothers with infants under 1 year of age were in the workforce in 2011—a percentage that varied little between mothers who were married and those who were not (U.S. Department of Labor, 2007).

Clearly, family roles have changed—we now have many patterns of how individual families share the responsibilities of work and child care, including a fairly new category of stay-at-home dads. Although there now are more options for parents to work flexible hours or to work in home-based jobs, for most families with young children, the reality of the work/family juggle often is a struggle and a source of stress. The norm, if there is one, is a two-income family, with both mom and dad juggling child care and work, usually with the help of relatives, friends, a child-care center, or a family child-care provider. What changes do these shifts imply for the roles and responsibilities for parents?

One way families are adjusting, particularly over the past three decades, is that many fathers are becoming more involved in the lives of their children (Lamb, 2004, 2010; Pleck, 1997). On average, fathers in two-parent households used to spend only 30 to 45% as much time with their children as did mothers. They now spend 67% as much time on weekdays and 87% as much time on weekends (Yeung, Duncan, & Hill, 2000; Yeung, Sandberg, Davis-Kean, & Hofferth, 2001). In addition, the more money that mothers earn, the more likely it is that fathers spend increased time with the children. Although mothers continue to do the bulk of the feeding and the diapering for their infants, in most homes the increasing role of fathers makes child rearing a more fully shared responsibility. Fathers, of course, like mothers, need to learn these parenting roles, yet fathers sometimes have little experience from their own childhoods on which to model their fathering behaviors.

What is the most important element of effective fatherhood? Is it the time spent with the child, the skillfulness of the father's parenting, or perhaps his attitude toward this new role? Although all of these are important, recent studies suggest that the following items comprise the "big three" elements of effective fatherhood (Lamb, 2010b; Leerkes & Burney, 2007; Shears & Robinson, 2005).

- **Accessibility:** The father needs to be present and available to the child.
- **Engagement:** The father needs to be in direct contact with the child, providing care and interacting in a close, warm, and consistent manner.
- **Responsibility:** The father needs to participate fully in making decisions about child care, which includes arranging for child care, meals, doctors' visits, and other activities.

The period of infancy is an especially important time of growth and change for babies and parents alike, as each teaches the other about successful parenting. Fortunately, infants and toddlers come biologically equipped with engaging smiles, direct emotions, and the clear need to become emotionally attached to their caregivers. They also are quite good at letting their needs be known. Fathers who are accessible, engaged, and responsible generally have little difficulty in developing an effective parenting style. In fact, parents who master these skills during their child's infancy and toddlerhood find that their children listen to them and respond more positively in other periods of life, for example, in adolescence (Lamb, 2010b).

Thus, the development of effective parenting skills—whether for the mother or the father or for both parents—is a good investment of time and energy. Effective parenting skills set the stage, in so many important ways, for accomplishing positive transitions in the developmental periods that will follow.

Why might older fathers be more likely than younger fathers to adopt a role more similar to the traditional "mother" role?

1996). Fathers also generally are more physical and spontaneous, tending toward unusual, vigorous, and unpredictable games, which infants find highly exciting (Lamb, 2004). In contrast, mothers typically engage their infants in subtle, shifting, gradual play, or they initiate conventional games such as pat-a-cake.

When the father is the primary or sole caregiver of the infant or toddler, his behavior changes, and he acts more like a traditional mother (Parke, 1996). Surprisingly, some research also suggests that older fathers are more likely to behave like traditional mothers when playing with their children, whereas younger fathers are more likely to conform to the traditional *father* role (Neville & Parke, 1997). As infants grow older and require less direct care, father–infant interaction is likely to increase (Lamb, 2004).

Fathers who frequently interact with their infants, who are responsive to their signals, and who become significant figures in their children's world are likely to develop into forceful—and positive—agents of socialization. This is particularly the case when the parents' marriage is of high quality (Barnett, Min, Mills-Koonce, Willonghby, & Cox, 2008). In contrast, fathers who are inaccessible to their infants may have difficulty establishing strong emotional ties later on, although even fathers who do not live with their families can remain involved with their children, visiting and playing with them and providing emotional support (Amato & Dorius, 2010). Fathers who adopt a control-oriented, authoritarian approach are less likely to become involved in their infants' care, shifting child-care responsibilities to the mother (Gaertner, Spinrad, Eisenberg, & Greving, 2007). It is also

Watch *Co-parenting, Relationships, and Socioemotional Development: Sarah Schoppe-Sullivan* on **MyDevelopmentLab**

possible, of course, for fathers to have a negative influence on infant development. For example, a father's alcoholism has been associated with negative father–infant interaction, as characterized by diminished paternal sensitivity and responsiveness. In such situations, the risks for later maladjustment among children can be seen as early as infancy (Elden, Edwards, & Leonard, 2007).

Fathers and the Family System Many U.S. fathers currently are broadening their parenting role, even during the period of their child's infancy (Garbarino, 2000; Lamb, 2010a). However, there are economic and social reasons why fathers usually are not equal partners in infant care. If one parent works while the other stays at home to care for the infant, the parent who works is typically the father, although there certainly are exceptions, and these exceptions are becoming more common.

Most couples work through their differing responses to infant care by selecting complementary roles for the father and the mother. However, whether the father takes a role as a partner or as a helper, his influence on the infant (and the family) is considerable, and is generally positive. One study, for example, demonstrated that fathers contributed positively to their children's cognitive and language development when measured at ages 24 and 36 months and to their social and emotional development when measured at 24 months, 36 months, and just before they began kindergarten (Cabrera, Shannon, & Tamis-LeMonda, 2007). These effects were most positive for fathers who were well educated and who were involved with the children's mothers in supportive relationships. This result is typical: In a review of 24 studies that examined the impact that fathers had on their young children, 22 showed that fathers' involvement resulted in positive effects (Sarkadi, Kristiansson, Oberklaid, & Bremberg, 2008). In particular, father involvement seems to reduce the occurrence of behavioral problems in boys and of psychological problems in young women, while enhancing the cognitive development for children of both genders. The positive impact of fathering seems to be the result of being involved in fathering: Those fathers who are more involved with their children have the most positive impact on their development (Combs-Orme & Renkert, 2009; Leerkes & Burney, 2007).

Other Family Members as Caregivers

In collectivist cultures particularly, the care of the infant extends beyond the parents to other members of the family and sometimes into the wider community. Even in Western cultures, older siblings often serve as important social models. Children learn how to share, cooperate, help, and empathize by watching their older brothers or sisters and, as they grow older, by interacting with them (Brody, 2004; Reynolds, Dorner, & Orellana, 2011). In important ways, older siblings provide information about appropriate gender roles and family customs and values. Also, in some cultures, the older sibling is the principal caretaker of the younger child and therefore plays an even larger role in the child's development.

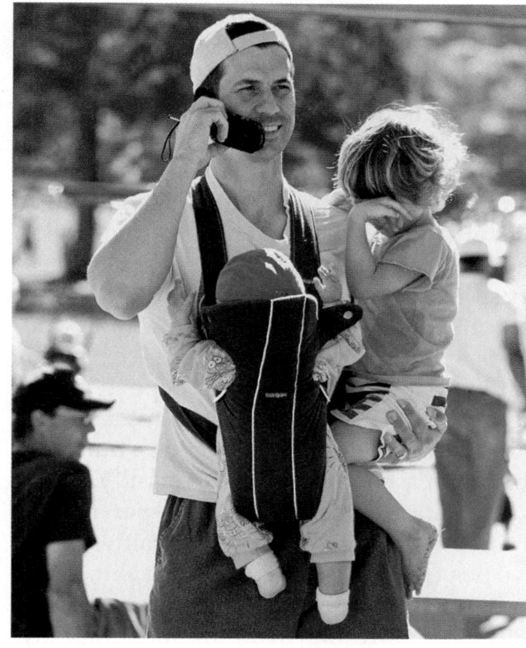

Fathers, as well as mothers, may find it difficult to juggle the many tasks of work and parenting.

There can, of course, be trouble when a second child is born (Cuspi, 2012; Whiteman, Bernard, & Jensen, 2011). One of the authors of this text remembers all too well her 3-year-old daughter's request to "Please pull over and dump 'him' out of here" on the way home from the hospital after her brother's birth. Such **sibling rivalry** is natural when a new baby is born because parents often pay less attention to and have less time and energy for the first-born child.

Were there people other than your mother or father who played an especially important role in your early development? What effect did they have?

The way that parents handle these changes, however, can influence the degree of strife, competition, and rivalry that develops between siblings (Milevsky, 2011). For example, if parents attempt to enlist the older sibling in the care of the newborn, an alliance is often created both between the siblings and between the older sibling and the parents. The mother and father and the older child may refer to the newborn as "our baby." In general, if parents set aside special time for the first child after the birth of a second child, it is more likely that the firstborn child will feel special rather than disregarded.

Grandparents In many cultures, including the United States, grandparents see their adult children and grandchildren at least weekly and therefore have an important role in socialization.

sibling rivalry
Strife and competition between siblings, such as for parental attention

Watch *Sibling Rivalry* on **MyDevelopmentLab**

In families where both parents work, grandparents sometimes are the primary caregivers; they also often serve as babysitters (Williams, 2011). Grandparents can be particularly important to the stability of single-parent households, where about one-third of U.S. children under age 18 now live (U.S. Census Bureau, 2012a), and to the 56% of all families with infants under age 1 whose mothers are in the labor force (U.S. Department of Labor, 2012).

Grandparents' roles are usually different from parents' roles, however, and different attachment relationships are formed. Toddlers can have a secure attachment with a parent and an insecure attachment with a grandparent or quite the opposite. Sometimes there is a strain between the generations. This is particularly stressful when the parents must depend on the grandparents for their children's primary care. In other cases, children's relationships with a grandparent provide a buffer for a difficult relationship with a parent (Berlin & Cassidy, 1999). Grandparents play an important role in single-parent and blended families, but their impact is even more positive when there are also positive ties to parents (Ruiz & Silverstein, 2007). When grandparents do not assume primary child-care responsibilities, they typically offer more approval, support, empathy, and sympathy, and they use less discipline; such relationships tend to be more playful and relaxed (Lewis, Haviland-Jones, & Barrett, 2008). Grandparents also tend to have more time to tell the child stories about "way-back-when," which can help create a sense of family identity and tradition.

U.S. Labor Force Participation Rates for Women with Children Under Age 3

Year	Percentage in labor force
1975	34.3
1980	41.9
1985	49.5
1990	53.6
1995	58.7
2000	61.0
2005	58.9
2009	61.1

FIGURE 5-1 Percentage of Mothers with Children 0 to 3 Years Who Participate in the Labor Force, 1975–2009

Today, about 60% of U.S. women with children under age 3 work outside the home, a percentage nearly double that of 30 years ago.

Note: The highest labor force participation rate for women is for mothers with children age 6–17; in 2009 this rate was 78%.

SOURCE: From Bureau of Labor Statistics, 2010, *Women in the labor force: A databook*, retrieved from http://www.bls.gov/cps/wlf-databook-2010.htm.

The Social Ecology of Child Care

Family members and others can provide effective support in raising a child; however, as noted previously, the primary responsibility for infant care in most societies historically has fallen to the mother. The reasons for this are closely linked to biological necessity, especially for feeding. In modern times, however, and especially in industrialized societies, alternative methods of nurturance have become commonplace. Refrigeration is almost universally available, allowing mothers who breastfeed to store their milk, which can then be fed to the infant by any available caregiver. In addition, a host of infant formulas, or milk substitutes, is widely available.

These changes in modernization have been accompanied by sweeping social changes as well. Even compared to just a generation ago, many more women with young children now work outside the home (see Figure 5-1), and the divorce rate has risen to the point where about 40% of all first marriages now end in divorce. Increasingly, caregivers other than the mother are assuming the primary responsibility for raising children. One major impact these changes have produced concerns the **social ecology of child care**, which is the overall environment in which child care takes place, both within and beyond the home.

Cross-Cultural Perspectives of Child Care When we talk about the social ecology of child care, we are referring to a whole complex of programs, as well as social values; these programs and values include government policy and support, community approval or disapproval, and the costs associated with various child-care options. As you might suspect, the social ecology of child care differs from one country to another. In Sweden, for example, a large-scale study found that 85% of mothers with children under school age work part-time or full-time outside the home. In such a situation, there is an enormous need for

social ecology of child care
The overall environment in which child care occurs, both within and beyond the home

▲ Today over 60% of mothers of infants and toddlers work outside the home and they rely on a wide variety of child care options. Here, a toddler is cared for by her grandmother while her mother works—a good child care option for this family.

CURRENT ISSUES

Infant and Toddler Child Care

Caring for young children poses challenges–especially for parents who work outside the home. Here, a father struggles with getting himself ready for work, while he also prepares his child for the day ahead.

Decisions about child care are among the most difficult that many parents must make. Currently in the United States just over three-fourths (76%) of infants and toddlers receive care from someone other than their parents (U.S. Census Bureau, 2011d). This percentage increases as children approach school age, and especially if the mother is employed: Over 87% of working mothers with children under age 5 rely on some form of child care to help them raise their children. On what options do they depend? More than three-fourths of working mothers with children under age 5 regularly rely on family members to provide care for their young children, and nearly two-thirds turn to day-care centers, nursery schools and preschools, Head Start programs, or home-based care given by a paid child-care worker (see Figure 5-2). Over one-fourth of parents (28.7%) use multiple child-care arrangements, often combining the care given by family members with that provided by nonfamily organizations and agencies (U.S. Census Bureau, 2011d).

Choosing the type of child care that best fits a family's needs is hard, and child care is expensive. In 2010, the average weekly expenditure for child care in the United States was $138, a figure that represented 7.3% of an above-poverty-level family's total income and 40.0% of a below-poverty-level family's total income. For families with children under age 5, the average child-care cost jumped to $171 per week, and this cost, as well as the percentage of family income devoted to child-care expenses, continues to rise (U.S. Census Bureau, 2012b).

How should families choose which child-care options will be best for them and their children? What impact do the various child-care arrangements have on the development of young children? To answer such questions, several large-scale studies have been initiated, both in the United States and in other countries.

Perhaps the largest longitudinal study currently going on in the United States is sponsored by the National Institute of Child Health and Human Development (NICHD). Begun in 1991, the NICHD study identified 1,364 infants and their families shortly after birth to investigate the role that both the home environment and child-care arrangements of various types have on the development of children (NICHD, 2006, 2012). This study is especially important because participants were selected to represent the country's socioeconomic and ethnic diversity from 10 different sites around the United States. The NICHD study includes families that use child care as well as those that do not, thereby allowing comparisons between children whose mothers stayed at home and those whose mothers returned to work. The child-care arrangements studied included not only children who were cared for by relatives in their own homes by family members but also all other forms of child care. The NICHD study, formally titled the Study of Early Child Care and Youth Development (SECCYD), seeks to understand the impact of various forms of child care on four key developmental outcomes: cognitive and language development, social behavior, emotional development and attachment, and health and physical growth. The most recent results have followed the children in the study into elementary school up through the ninth grade (NICHD, 2012). Although the funding for the SECCYD ended in 2009, researchers continue to mine this valuable source of data as they try to better understand how child-care experiences shape the outcomes of children's lives.

What do the results of the NICHD study suggest? Is child care good or bad for children's development? Perhaps the results of the study suggest both conclusions. First, it seems that children who spend time in child care gain some advantage in developing their cognitive and language skills during the first 3 years of life. Furthermore, higher-quality child care, in which caregivers interact closely with the children in their care,

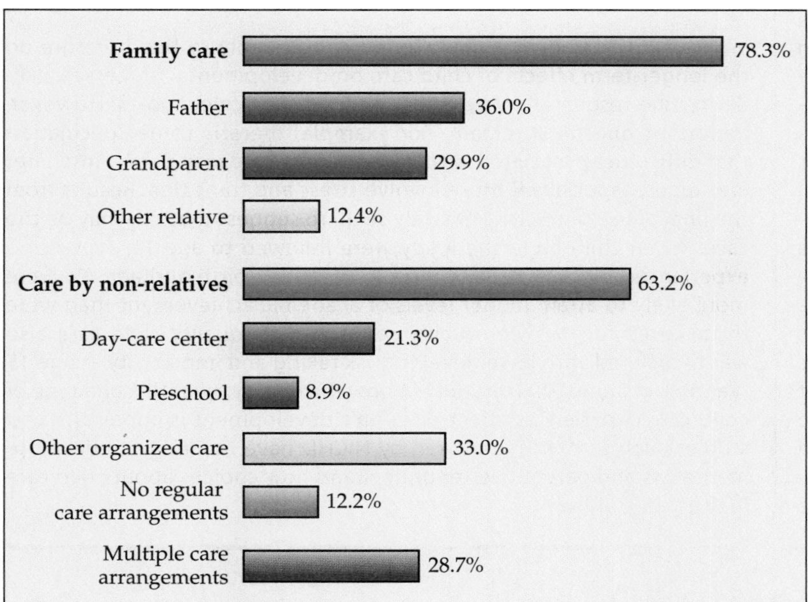

FIGURE 5-2 Varieties of Child-Care Arrangements Used by Working Mothers with Children Under Age 5

*NOTE: Totals do not add to 100% because several methods often are employed.

SOURCE: "Who's minding the kids? Child care arrangements: Spring 2010," U.S. Census Bureau, 2011, retrieved from http://www.census.gov/hhes/childcare/data/sipp/2010/tables.html.

(continued)

Table 5-8 Choosing a High-Quality Child-Care Facility

High-quality child care can result from many different arrangements. The key to evaluating the quality of a child-care arrangement is to assess the child's safety, the warmth and attentiveness of the caregivers to the needs and interests of the child, and the way in which caregivers and parents can communicate.

A good way to evaluate the features of high-quality child care is to ask a series of questions, such as these:

- Do the adult caregivers enjoy spending time with children?
- Are there enough caregivers? (See the table that follows this list for the recommended caregiver-to-child ratios.)
- Do the children interact with the same caregivers each day so that they can develop a feeling of consistency and security?
- Is the facility licensed? Is it clean? Is it safe?
- Are the food and snacks healthy and attractive to children?
- Does the facility have an adequate number and variety of toys, games, and educational materials?
- Do the caregivers promote curiosity, self-confidence, and healthy lifestyles?
- Do the caregivers promote self-discipline, respect for others, and the development of self-esteem?
- Does the facility encourage parental involvement?
- Is there an open-door policy that allows parents to visit unannounced?
- Is there sufficient opportunity for parents' ideas and opinions to be considered and responded to?

What additional questions would you ask if you wanted to make a decision on whether to place a child into a child-care setting? Which of the previous questions do you think are most important in making a decision about child care?

predicted greater school readiness at age 4½ as reflected in standardized tests of number skills and language skills. It was also linked to more positive interactions with other children at age 3 (see Table 5-8). However, child care also is associated with some apparent disadvantages. Most notably, children who spent significant time in child care generally demonstrated more "externalizing problems," such as disobedience and aggressiveness to other children, when they entered school. Not unexpectedly, these social difficulties were more apparent among children enrolled in lower-quality care options and those who spent a larger proportion of their time in child care.

Do these early advantages and disadvantages last over time? Children in the NICHD study were followed into the fifth and sixth grades to see if the early care-related behaviors continued once children were in school. In general, results suggest that they do (Belsky, et al., 2007). For example, children who experienced higher-quality child care maintained their cognitive and language advantages into the fifth grade, as reflected by better vocabulary scores. Vocabulary ability is important early in life because it is so closely linked to reading ability. The key here seems to be the quality of the verbal interactions between children and caregivers. In terms of social and behavioral development, early relationships were partially retained, but behavior problems apparent in the sixth grade seemed to be associated only with child care provided in an institutional setting. Children who were cared for by relatives or in home-based settings appeared to experience no greater aggressiveness or social problems than did children cared for by their mothers. Furthermore, aggressiveness was higher only among children cared for in low-quality facilities where the number of children in the groups was large. Thus, the negative outcomes associated with day care seem to be localized to settings where quality is lacking (McCartney, et al., 2010).

One other conclusion from the NICHD study is important to note: Parenting is a stronger and more consistent predictor of child outcomes than is the child-care setting. Perhaps this is not surprising, considering that most children experience a range of care arrangements in their early years: Children in the NICHD study averaged five different child-care settings between ages 3 months and 4½ years (see Figure 5-2), and six different classroom settings in their first 6 years of school. Parenting arrangements and interaction styles, on the hand, were relatively stable in the first 10 years of life.

Age of children	Caregiver-to-child ratio*
Birth to 1 year	1:3
1 to 2 years	1:4
2 to 3 years	1:5
3 to 4 years	1:8
4 to 5 years	1:9

*These ratios were suggested from guidelines provided by the National Association for the Education of Young Children (2008). These recommendations are consistent with those of the National Network for Child Care (Bosche & Jacobs, 2005).

The NICHD study has contributed considerably to the literature on the longer-term effects of child care on developmental processes, validating the results of many earlier and smaller-scale studies. However, important questions remain. For example, there is some speculation that difficulties associated with lower-quality care may persist into later life stages, especially if those involve stress and transition. Results from the final phase of the NICHD study seem to suggest that this may be the case. When children in the study were followed to age 15, those who experienced higher-quality child care between birth and age 4½ were more likely to attain higher levels of academic achievement than were those cared for in lower-quality settings. High-quality child care also was associated with lower levels of risk taking and impulsivity at age 15 (Vandell, et al., 2010). The study of how the quality, quantity, and type of child care experiences affect children's development is important, and studies such as that undertaken by NICHD have helped both developmentalists and parents better understand how choices about child care may affect children.

Watch *Lisa: Adjusting to Day Care* on **MyDevelopmentLab**

child care, which is met by a publicly funded child-care system in which every child is guaranteed a place in preschool at age 18 months (Alexandroni, 2007; Andersson, 1989; Sweden.se, 2012). There are day-care centers, as well as family-based day-care providers who are called *day mothers.* Both the day-care centers and the day mothers are licensed and regulated. There is also a system of open preschools where mothers or day mothers may take children to play with other children and receive advice and support.

By comparison, parents in the United States receive little public support. They are financially responsible for providing whatever supplemental child care they need and are assisted in this responsibility only if their income is low. Because over 61% of U.S. mothers of children under age 3 and nearly 64% of mothers with children under age 6 work outside the home (U.S. Department of Labor, 2010), many families face the difficult task of finding suitable child care at an affordable price. This topic is explored more fully in the box Current Issues: Infant and Toddler Child Care. In the next section, we explore the challenges for caregivers of infants and toddlers with special needs.

REVIEW THE FACTS 5-5

1. The primary reason that fathers are assuming more significant roles in child care is ___________.
2. When the father is the sole caregiver, he acts more like a
   a. playmate. b. teacher.
   c. mother. d. disciplinarian.
3. In comparison to individualist societies, is infant care in collectivist societies more likely or less likely to extend to other members of the extended family?
4. What percentage of U.S. mothers with children under age 3 are now in the labor force?
   a. 25% b. 41%
   c. 61% d. 78%
5. The social ecology of child care refers to
   a. the interaction between infant and mother.
   b. the environment in which child care takes place.
   c. the degree to which discipline is used to control behavior.
   d. imprinting.

Practice on **MyDevelopmentLab**

INFANTS AND TODDLERS WITH SPECIAL NEEDS

As studies of the impact of day care remind us, it is important to remember that development proceeds best when the child is loved and cared for but also is allowed sufficient room to explore. In this way, the child develops a trusting orientation toward the environment, as well as an independent, autonomous self. Providing a normal, positive environment for development is a challenge for all caregivers, but it is especially challenging for parents of children with special needs.

Watch *Mathematical Knowledge and Problem Solving: Martha Alibali* on **MyDevelopmentLab**

Infants and Toddlers with Visual Impairments

Visual communication between a caregiver and child is normally a key factor in the establishment of attachment. Infants depend on visual signals from their caregivers to learn about their world. Caregivers, too, depend heavily on subtle responses from their infants, such as returning their glance, smiling, and visually following their caregiver, to maintain and support their own behavior. In cases where the infant is blind, it is essential that the parents and the unseeing child establish a synchronous communication system that compensates for the child's disability (Bigelow, 2005).

An obvious challenge for a blind infant is to find effective ways to learn about the world. As we have seen, in early life, one of a healthy infant's best-developed resources for acquiring information is through the visual–perceptual system. Babies look at and visually follow everything new, and they have distinct visual preferences. As noted, they especially like looking at human faces. However, infants who are blind cannot observe the subtle changes in their caregivers' facial expressions or follow their movements. Thus, they fail to receive the kinds of information that infants who can see use in formulating their own responses. Consequently, blind infants who are competent except for their lack of sight typically do not develop signals for "I want that" or "Pick me up" until near the end of the first year.

Another problem that can develop with an infant with visual impairments is that the caregiver may feel the infant is unresponsive. Despite the fact that the lack of sight is usually apparent at birth or very shortly after birth, it is still very difficult for caregivers to acknowledge the impact that this disability has on their feelings of being involved in their baby's world. Thus, the first few months of life often are extremely difficult for both the caregiver and the infant who is blind. These infants do not develop a selective, responsive smile as early as sighted children, they do not smile as often or as ecstatically, and they have fewer facial expressions (Troester & Brambring, 1992). Infants who are blind also experience some delay in learning language skills (Brambring, 2007) and significant delays in learning motor skills (Brambring, 2006). The infant's seeming lack of responsiveness and developmental delays can be emotionally devastating for the caregiver. Thus, there is a danger that communication and mutuality will break down and that the caregiver will tend to avoid the child.

To address this issue, mothers and other caregivers of babies who are blind are encouraged to talk to or to sing to their infant as much as possible. Also, studies have shown that infants who are blind develop their skills for reaching for objects sooner if the objects make sounds than if they are simply placed in the baby's hand (Ihsen, Troester, & Bambring, 2010), suggesting that parents may find the use of "noisy" toys to be especially helpful to development. This, and a variety of other interventions, can help families adjust more successfully (Holbrook, 2006).

Infants and Toddlers with Hearing Impairments

The developmental difficulties of infants who are deaf follow a different pattern than that of infants who are blind, although these children, too, can proceed through development with positive outcomes. In the first few months of life, their well-developed visual sense generally makes up for the problems imposed by their hearing impairments. After the first 6 months, however, communication between the parent and the infant can begin to deteriorate because the infant's responses might not meet the parents' expectations.

To make matters worse, the discovery that the child cannot hear sometimes does not occur until the second year, by which time the child has already missed a great deal of communication via language. Although newborn hearing screening tests are becoming the norm in many developed countries, the diagnosis of a child's deafness still may come as a shock to parents who have not recognized the disability (Young, 2010). Oftentimes, the first indications of hearing impairment in 1-year-olds appear to be their lack of "startle" reactions when people approach; the child simply does not hear them coming. In 2-year-olds, there also may be temper tantrums and frequent disobedience owing to failure to hear what the parents want. This may be accompanied by the toddler's overall failure to develop normal expectations about the world. In particular, the presence of a severe hearing impairment may threaten the development of healthy attachment between parents and child (Thomson, Kennedy, & Kuebli, 2011).

Like parents of children who are blind, parents of children who are deaf need special training and counseling (Spencer & Marschark, 2006). Without careful attention during infancy, hearing impairment can result in poor communication during the early childhood years and beyond, which can lead to severe social, intellectual, and psychological problems later. However, when caregivers use appropriate techniques and react to their infants and toddlers with love and assistance, these children can, and generally do, develop normal social responses and relationships. For example, infants and toddlers who cannot hear often develop a large, expressive vocabulary of hand signals. Training parents and caregivers to watch for and interpret hand signals of children who cannot hear greatly enhances parent–child interaction, attachment formation, and subsequent socialization, as do other home-based interventions with parents and caregivers (Beelman & Bambring, 1998). Early intervention also improves outcomes substantially (White, 2006), making early diagnosis an important goal.

Infants and Toddlers with Severe Disabilities

When an infant is born with a severe disability, such as cerebral palsy or severe mental retardation, there is a high risk of parental rejection, withdrawal, and depression. An infant with a severe disability can strain family finances as well as marital ties and may trigger a variety of disturbances in other children

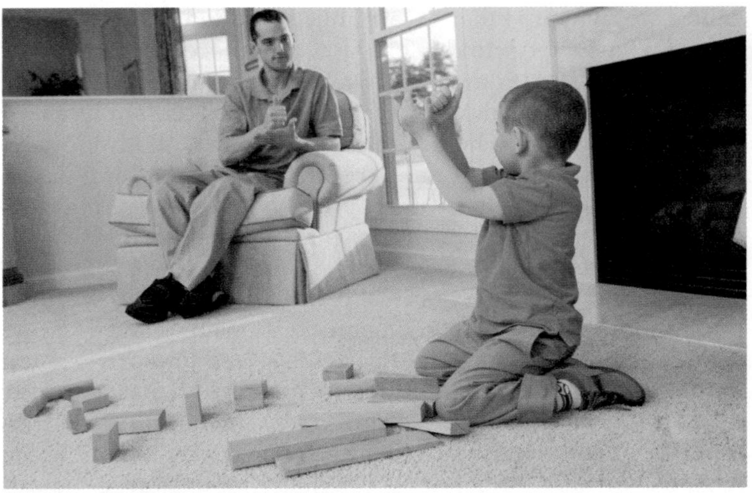

▲ Communication with a hearing-impaired child needs to begin early and become a part of natural family routines. Here, his father has learned sign language in order to "talk" with his hearing-impaired son.

in the family (Whitman, 2008). Child-care workers and other health care providers can help with a family's early adjustment problems, and they should be consulted from birth (Blasco, Johnson, & Palomo-Gonzalez, 2008). Early success or failure in coping with initial traumas can greatly affect parents' ability to make wise decisions about child care and education (Gavidia-Payne & Stoneman, 2004; Turnbull & Turnbull, 2001).

Children with severe disabilities also can pose adjustment problems for siblings, grandparents, and others involved in their care (Keilty & Galvin, 2006). As you might expect, families with close emotional ties usually cope more effectively with a child's disability. For example, when grandparents have closer ties with their children and grandchildren, they are more supportive and involved. In addition, grandparents with higher educational levels interact more positively with grandchildren with severe disabilities (Fingerman, 1998), indicating that educational programs can assist caregivers in providing effective and positive support for a child with severe disabilities.

What advice would you give to a friend who is the parent of a child who is blind or deaf?

Whereas coping with a child with disabilities poses special challenges for their caregivers, caring for *any* baby, regardless of how sweet its disposition, can be tiring and taxing. Attending to the needs of a newborn or infant requires a significant amount of time, energy, and money. It is not surprising that sometimes parenting breaks down, especially when resources are scarce, resulting in child neglect or abuse.

Infants and Toddlers Who Suffer from Abuse or Neglect

Child abuse refers to physical or psychological injuries that are *intentionally* inflicted by an adult. **Child neglect**, which is more often unintentional, involves the failure of a caregiver to respond to or to care for a child. Taken together, these topics are often referred to as **child maltreatment**—any form of domestic violence that affects the lives of children. Although both child abuse and neglect are more fully discussed in Chapter 7, a few comments are appropriate in this chapter on infancy and toddlerhood as well.

As noted throughout our treatment of infancy and toddlerhood, early infant–caregiver attachment is critical to later development. Child abuse and neglect interfere with attachment (Baer & Martinez, 2006; Cevezo, Pons-Salvador, & Trenado, 2008). When abuse or neglect begins in infancy, the nurturant relationship on which the infant depends is threatened; therefore, early abuse and neglect can have devastating effects that last throughout life (Gil, 2010). Of course, abuse that begins later in infancy also can threaten development. Studies have shown that toddlers who have suffered physical maltreatment experience distortions and delays in the development of their sense of self and in their language and cognitive development. Abuse is regrettable regardless of when it occurs, but when infants are securely attached during the first year, abuse during the second year, especially when its source is someone other than the primary caregiver, generally is less damaging (Beeghly & Cicchetti, 1994; Connell-Carrick, 2010).

Sometimes the effects of abuse or neglect are obvious, involving bruises, burns, and broken bones. At other times, and especially when the issue is neglect, the problem is harder to detect. Child neglect can sometimes be subtle and even unintentional, as when an intrusive, interfering style of caregiving—one that ignores the baby's wishes and disrupts the baby's activities—is imposed. For example, studies suggest that when a mother's style of interaction with her 6-month-old infant is highly intrusive and persistent, the child may later demonstrate poor academic, social, emotional, and behavioral skills (Egelund, Pianta, & O'Brien, 1993; Leiter, 2007). In addition, some infants are more resilient to abuse and neglect than others. The worst case occurs when an abusive situation develops with a biologically or temperamentally vulnerable infant. Here the result is often an infant who shows insecure attachment and experiences frequent distress and episodes of angry behavior, as well as later maladjustment (Cassidy & Berlin, 1994).

Physicians, teachers, and some other professionals are required by law to report cases in which they suspect child abuse or neglect. Are these laws a good thing? Why or why not?

Physicians and others who are responsible for children need to be particularly aware of the link between neglect and the **failure-to-thrive syndrome**, in which infants are small for their age and emaciated, they appear sick, and they are unable to digest food properly (Kaneshiro, 2011). Failure to thrive can occur as a result of malnutrition, which can be associated with other health concerns. In many cases, however, it appears to be linked to a lack of affection and attention, including poor-quality or nonexistent attachment. Sometimes, of course, both factors are involved.

By definition, infants with failure-to-thrive syndrome weigh in the lower 3% of the normal weight range for their age group and show no evidence of specific disease or abnormality that would explain their failure to grow. They often are listless and withdrawn, perhaps even immobile, and they oftentimes exhibit developmental disabilities. Such infants typically avoid eye contact by staring in a wide-eyed gaze, turning away, or covering their face or eyes. Although diagnosis of the cause of failure to thrive is difficult, one key that should be explored is whether there is a disruption in the home or the social environment. When the failure to thrive is the result of child neglect, it often can be reversed with proper nutrition and attention (Black, Dubowitz, Krishnakumar, & Starr, 2007).

Why would anyone abuse or neglect a baby? In some cases, mothers of failure-to-thrive, abused, or neglected infants are themselves physically ill, depressed, or otherwise mentally disordered (Hay et al., 2011). In other cases, the caregivers are alcoholics or addicted to drugs. Studies show that many abusive or neglectful parents had negative early childhood experiences themselves; that is, they too were abused or neglected (e.g., Cicchetti, Rogosch, & Toth, 2006; Taft et al., 2008). Certainly, not all people who were abused as children grow up to abuse their own children, but too often the cycle is repeated.

Responding to Abuse and Neglect In summary, abused and neglected babies are at risk for physical, cognitive, and emotional impairments. Furthermore, because these traumas threaten the social and emotional development of the young child, they are likely to interfere with social relationships at many future points in development, including healthy parent–child attachments in infancy, satisfying peer relationships in childhood, and fulfilling romantic and sexual relationships in adolescence and emerging adulthood (Trickett & Negriff, 2011). What can we do to reverse the effects of abuse and neglect?

One approach, of course, is to remove the baby from the abusive situation and assign care to grandparents, other relatives, or foster or adoptive parents who can offer the baby the safe and secure nurturing that is necessary for them to begin to recover. Another option, if the abuse is not as severe, is to have the parents attend parenting skills programs or counseling, which appears to be helpful in not only correcting the abuse but also in reducing overall family stress and pathology. For example, a National Clinical Evaluation study examined the outcomes of 19 separate

child abuse
The intentional physical or psychological injuries inflicted on a child by an adult

child neglect
The failure of a caregiver to respond to or care for a child; child neglect is often unintentional

child maltreatment
Any form of domestic violence that affects the lives of children; includes both child abuse and child neglect

Watch *Child Abuse Mandatory Reporting* on **MyDevelopmentLab**

failure-to-thrive syndrome
A condition that may result from malnutrition or unresponsive caregiving in which infants are small for their age, often appear emaciated or sick, and typically are unable to digest food properly

projects that trained teachers to use therapeutic techniques with maltreated children between the ages of 18 months and 8 years. The study found that about 70% of these children improved in their social, emotional, adaptive, and cognitive skills (Daro, 1993; Daro & McCurdy, 2007). Programs that provide training and therapy for both abusive caregivers and the abused child seem to be particularly effective (VanFleet & Topham, 2011).

Another solution is to encourage parents to seek support from others. Most parents rely to some extent on informal support networks, which can consist of family members, neighbors, and friends, to help them cope with the stress of parenting. In cases of abuse and neglect, parents can be encouraged to seek out such networks and to depend on them for support. Also, more formal networks can be provided, such as peer support groups or community resource centers. These networks also can help a vulnerable parent get through difficult times. Both informal and formal social support interventions can help dysfunctional families end the cycle of abuse or neglect that adversely affects the baby, as well as the other children in the family (Barnett, 1997, 2007). Finally, social intervention programs can be provided to target the sources of some of the underlying causes of abuse, such as poverty, drug abuse, and mental illness. Such programs and their effectiveness in remediating a wide array of developmental issues will be addressed at various points in the upcoming chapters of this text (Cicchetti & Toth, 2010; Toth & Cicchetti, 2006).

In this chapter, we have explored a variety of factors that contribute to the infant's ability to develop a healthy and secure attachment to the caregiver and then begin to separate from that caregiver as the baby begins to establish an independent and autonomous sense of self. We will continue to explore how these earliest experiences contribute to development as we investigate the next period in lifespan development, which is called early childhood.

REVIEW THE FACTS 5-6

1. What two significant challenges do parents of infants with visual impairments typically face?
2. What advice is often given to caregivers of infants who are visually impaired?
3. Which is generally discovered earlier in life, a visual impairment or a hearing impairment?
4. Which of the following involves the intentional harm of a child?
   a. child neglect
   b. child abuse
   c. both a and b
   d. neither a nor b
5. Which of the following is *not* one of the characteristics commonly associated with failure-to-thrive syndrome?
   a. extreme aggressiveness
   b. listlessness
   c. low body weight
   d. general sickliness and digestive problems

CHAPTER SUMMARY

The Foundations of Personality and Social Development

What role does temperament play in the emotional development of infants and toddlers?

- In infancy and toddlerhood—the first 2 years—babies develop attachments to their caregivers and then learn to separate as they gain a secure sense of themselves.
- In the still-face experiment, when parents stopped being emotionally responsive, their infants typically exhibited distress. Emotional communication between parents and their infants is a major determinant of children's emotional development.
- *Temperament* refers to the inborn, characteristic way a person reacts to the world. Most children can be categorized as easy, difficult, or slow to warm up. Temperament also is linked to the degree to which individuals are characterized by effortful control, negative affectivity, and extroversion.
- Although temperament is often stable across development, basic temperament patterns can shift in response to environmental conditions. One especially important aspect of early development is the degree of fit between the temperament of the baby and the caregiver's style of interacting.

The Development of Trust

What can parents do to ensure that their infant develops a trusting orientation to the world and a strong attachment to them?

- Erikson's first developmental task is the development of *trust versus mistrust*.
- Trust develops when infants learn that the environment is predictable and stable and that they can depend on their caregivers to meet their needs. Feeding and comforting are two important components of establishing trust.
- Cultural differences exist in feeding and comforting practices.
- Healthy adjustment requires a balance between developing trust (which allows infants to form secure attachments) and mistrust (which teaches them to protect themselves from threat). Developing trust, however, should prevail.

Attachment

To what does the term attachment *refer, and how does the development of early infant attachment influence later development throughout childhood?*

- Becoming attached to caregivers, which usually occurs by age 8 or 9 months, is the most influential social relationship that infants establish.
- In Mary Ainsworth's strange-situation test, mothers left their 12- to 18-month-old toddlers in a room with toys and a stranger. Of the U.S. infants studied, 60 to 70% displayed *secure attachment;* that is, they had a strong emotional bond with their caregiver because of responsive caregiving. The

remainder of the toddlers displayed *insecure attachment,* which is the result of inconsistent or unresponsive caregiving.

- Insecure attachment can take three distinct forms: *resistant attachment,* characterized by anger and avoidance of the mother or caregiver; *avoidant attachment,* characterized by ambivalence toward the mother or caregiver; or *disorganized/disoriented attachment,* characterized by contradictory behavior and confusion toward the mother or primary caregiver. Of these, disorganized/disoriented attachment generally is associated with the poorest developmental outcomes.
- Securely attached infants are generally more curious, sociable, independent, and competent than their insecurely attached peers. These positive characteristics are associated with many other advantages throughout childhood. Infants who fail to develop secure attachments often experience a variety of adjustment and behavioral problems.
- Behaviorists and psychoanalytic theorists usually stress the role of conditioning, reinforcement, and the reduction of needs in the development of attachment. Other theorists note that attachment in humans in some ways resembles *imprinting* in animals. Imprinting involves the formation of a bond between some newborn animals and their mothers that appears to be present a birth, suggesting that it is a biologically programmed rather than a learned behavior.
- Harlow's research with infant monkeys showed that healthy attachment requires more than food and physical presence: It is a social bond.
- In Bowlby's evolutionary view, attachment depends on the development of *synchrony,* which is the continuous back-and-forth interaction between infants and their caregivers. When caregivers are responsive, stronger attachment results.
- Erikson saw the critical developmental issue of the first year to be the establishment of *trust versus mistrust.* Securely attached infants are more likely to develop trust.
- Although culture can influence the specific ways in which attachment develops, regardless of culture, infants and caregivers in healthy relationships will form these social bonds.

Separating from the Caregiver

How do infants and toddlers develop a sense of their own autonomy without losing their attachment to their caregivers?

- At about 7 months of age, babies universally develop *stranger anxiety,* also called *separation anxiety*, which is a fear of strangers or of being separated from their caregiver. The development of stranger and separation anxiety indicates that sufficient cognitive development has occurred that the infant now recognizes when the caregiver is absent or when a new object is presented that differs from the old one. The *discrepancy hypothesis* suggests that this new awareness gives rise to uncertainty and anxiety.
- *Social referencing* refers to the idea that infants look to caregivers for information in ambiguous situations. By gauging the mother's subtle emotional signals, the infant learns how to respond. Social referencing plays a large role in conveying cultural understandings to children.
- During their second year, children establish a sense of their own autonomy, which is their need to be separate and independent from their caregivers. Erikson viewed these patterns of separating from the caregiver as a conflict between *autonomy versus shame and doubt,* which usually is resolved in the second or third years of a life. Autonomy is facilitated when trust has been well established in infancy.
- Children generally develop best when they have a strong attachment relationship, when their needs are met by a loving caregiver, and when they must conform to reasonable limits. Although early theories like Freud's often emphasized the significance of toilet training, today this event is generally considered to be only one of several important determinants of parent–child interactions.

How do infants' understanding of others and their concept of the "self" develop during the first 2 years of life?

- Behavior that benefits others, called *prosocial behavior,* develops sequentially and begins to emerge in the second year. The development of *empathy,* which is the ability to understand another's feelings and perspective, is linked to secure attachment and is also related to the toddler's development of self-concept.
- Infants gradually develop an understanding that they are separate from the world around them and that their actions can be intentional. As they become more autonomous, they exhibit emotional responses more often, especially when their wishes are thwarted. Toddlers often are extremely possessive, indicating they understand the difference between "self" and "others."

The Family System: A Broader Context

Can fathers be good "mothers" for their children?

- Since the mid-20th century, fathers in the United States have played an increasingly important role in child rearing. However, most fathers do not assume the primary responsibility for child care, although they are equally competent as are mothers.
- In comparison to mothers, fathers are more likely to engage in play and exciting activities and to be more physical. However, older fathers are more likely to adopt a role more similar to that of traditional mothers. Fathers usually interact more frequently as their infants get older.
- Although, in general, fathers are assuming larger child-care roles, they seldom assume the primary caregiver role unless the mother is absent. When the father is absent, considerable stress is generally placed on the family.

How do other caregivers, including family members other than the parents as well as child-care workers, influence development in infancy and toddlerhood?

- Other family or community members can assist in child care, and shared child care is more common in collectivist cultures. Although siblings can play a major role in child care and socialization, *sibling rivalry* also can develop as older siblings compete for parental attention.

- Grandparents often fill an important role in child care, especially in single-parent families or when mothers work. Although a variety of relationships among children and grandparents can exist, in general, grandparents are more approving and use less discipline than parents.
- The *social ecology of child care* includes the arrangements, programs, and values that are associated with various child-care options. There are large cultural differences among various countries and social groups with respect to how children are cared for.
- A major consideration for many U.S. families is high-quality child care for their children, particularly considering that 61% of mothers of children under age 3 and 64% of mothers with children under age 6 work outside the home.

Infants and Toddlers with Special Needs

What special challenges are faced by the caregivers of infants and toddlers with special needs?

- Providing a normal, positive environment often poses special challenges for parents and caregivers of infants with special needs.
- A key challenge for parents whose infants are visually impaired is to establish synchronous communication. A typical problem is that parents often feel that visually impaired infants are unresponsive.
- Parents often are at first unaware that their infant has a hearing impairment; sometimes it is not until the second year that such an impairment is discovered. Consequently, the infant has missed some opportunity for early language development and parent–infant interactions may have become strained due to the parents' perceived unresponsiveness of the infant. The use of hand signals is an effective technique of communication, and infants and toddlers with hearing impairments, like those with visual impairments, generally develop normal social responses and relationships.
- When an infant has a severe disability, this often strains marital ties and may trigger a variety of disturbances in other children in the family. When family members have close emotional ties, they typically cope more effectively with a child with a severe disability.

How does child maltreatment influence development and autonomy?

- *Child abuse* involves intentional physical or psychological injuries to a child inflicted by an adult. *Child neglect*, which more often is unintentional, involves the failure of a caregiver to respond to or care for a child. Child abuse and neglect interfere with attachment, especially when they occur in the first year or when the abuse or neglect is inflicted by the primary caregiver.
- Although malnutrition and other conditions can contribute to the *failure-to-thrive syndrome*, child neglect is sometimes the cause. Children who fail to thrive are small for their age and often appear sick.
- Abused and neglected infants and toddlers are at risk for physical, cognitive, and emotional impairments. To remedy abuse, children can be removed from the abusive home or parents can be counseled to stop their abusive behavior. Parents also can seek support from others, either through formal or informal channels. Finally, programs can address the underlying social triggers of abuse, such as poverty, drug abuse, and mental illness.

KEY TERMS

personality (p. 131)
basic emotions (p. 131)
temperament (p. 133)
secure attachment (p. 136)
insecure attachment (p. 136)
resistant attachment (p. 136)
avoidant attachment (p. 136)
disorganized/disoriented attachment (p. 136)
imprinting (p. 138)
synchrony (p. 139)
trust versus mistrust (p. 140)
stranger and separation anxiety (p. 141)
discrepancy hypothesis (p. 141)
social referencing (p. 141)
autonomy versus shame and doubt (p. 142)
prosocial behavior (p. 143)
empathy (p. 143)
sibling rivalry (p. 147)
social ecology of child care (p. 148)
child abuse (p. 153)
child neglect (p. 153)
child maltreatment (p. 153)
failure-to-thrive syndrome (p. 153)

MyVirtualLife

What decision would you make while raising a child? What would be the consequences of those decisions?

Find out by accessing **MyVirtualLife** at www.MyDevelopmentLab.com to raise a virtual child and live your own virtual life.

EARLY CHILDHOOD
Physical, Cognitive, and Language Development

6

LEARNING OBJECTIVES

- What does it mean to say that human development is integrated, interactive, and dynamic?
- What role do physical development and brain maturation play in the major developmental events that characterize early childhood?
- What distinguishes gross motor from fine motor skills, and how does each develop during early childhood?
- What are the main cognitive achievements of early childhood, according to Piaget?
- How do Vygotsky's view of cognitive development and the view embraced by information-processing theorists differ from that proposed by Piaget?
- In what ways does a child's memory develop during the preschool years?
- What predictable changes occur in language development during the period of early childhood?
- What does it mean to say that play both mirrors and encourages cognitive development?

CHAPTER OUTLINE

Physical Development
- Changes in the Body
- Brain Development
- Human Development: An Interactive and Individual Approach

Motor Skills Development
- Gross Motor Skills
- Fine Motor Skills
- Learning and Motor Skills

Cognitive Development
- An Overview of Preoperational Thinking
- Preoperational Substages and Thought
- Limitations of Preoperational Thinking
- Conservation
- Evaluating Piaget's Theory
- Beyond Piaget: Social Perspectives
- The Role of Memory

Language Development
- Words and Concepts
- Expanding Grammar
- Mastering the Subtleties of Speech
- The Influence of Parents' Language Use
- Multicultural Aspects of Language Development

Play and Learning
- Play and Cognitive Development

Early childhood—the span of years from roughly age 2 to age 6—is a time of remarkable growth and achievement in every realm of development. Chubby toddlers with large heads and short limbs become slimmer 6-year-olds with smoother coördination and increased strength. Motor skills develop as well: Children learn to run, skip, and throw a ball, and they develop and refine the fine motor skills they need to write the alphabet, dress themselves, or place puzzle pieces in the correct place.

Accompanying such physical development are rapid and dramatic changes in children's ability to think. Cognitively, at age 2, toddlers can form simple categories and react to their environments; by age 6, children's thinking is much more rich and complex. In many ways, their thinking is like the logical thought that characterizes adult cognition. Along with this cognitive development, and reflective of it, comes the development of language. At age 2, most toddlers are speaking in two- or three-word "sentences," using only a few hundred vocabulary words and limited grammatical rules; however, by age 6, they are speaking in complete sentences and with essentially correct grammatical structure. Play, too, becomes increasingly elaborate, which reflects these significant cognitive advances.

Changes in physical and cognitive development depend, of course, on many factors. However, the development of the brain is of particular importance. In fact, neurological development underlies much of the developmental pattern of early childhood; it guides advancements in thinking, memory, problem solving, language, physical coordination, and social and emotional development.

At age 3, the child ventures forth without the wide stance of the toddler. At age 5, there is not just added size but also greater balance, refinement, control, and self-confidence in movement.

Thus, the ways in which children behave and think—and the ways in which their brains develop—form an integrated, interactive, and dynamic system (Diamond, 2007, 2009; Huston & Bentley, 2010; Thelen, 2008; Thelen & Smith, 2006; Thomas & Johnson, 2008). Each developmental milestone reached triggers others, and to understand how development proceeds, we must consider changes within each domain in the context of other changes that are taking place. For example, as children become physically stronger and more capable, they use their newfound abilities to explore and experience a wider range of situations, which enhances their opportunities for cognitive development. Think for a moment about the possibilities that open up for infants the moment they learn to crawl or walk! Indeed, children *do* explore. They are highly motivated to seek new environments, to experiment with new abilities, and to learn about the world around them.

In this chapter, we begin with a brief discussion of physical growth, emphasizing the changes that take place in the brain. We then examine cognitive development, paying particular attention to language development, as it—perhaps more than any other single characteristic of this period—emblemizes the transition out of infancy into childhood. We end the chapter by examining the role of play, which is a universal and important aspect of development in early childhood.

PHYSICAL DEVELOPMENT

Between the ages of 2 and 6, a child's body loses the look of infancy as it changes in size, proportions, and shape. At the same time, rapid brain development leads to more sophisticated and complex learning abilities and the refinement of gross and fine motor skills.

Changes in the Body

From age 2 to 6, children's rate of growth slows when compared to the growth that occurred during the first 2 years of life. Healthy children may grow in spurts during early childhood, and there is considerable variation in the growth rates and patterns experienced by individual children. During early childhood, young children typically gain an average of about 4 pounds 12 ounces (2 kilograms), and they grow about 3 inches (7.6 centimeters) taller, each year. Early childhood is also a period when substantial skeletal maturation occurs. Throughout this period, bones develop and harden through *ossification,* in which soft tissue or cartilage is transformed into bone (see Figure 6-1).

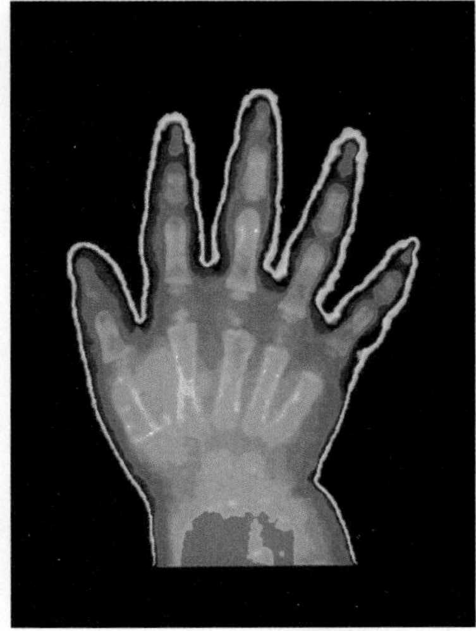
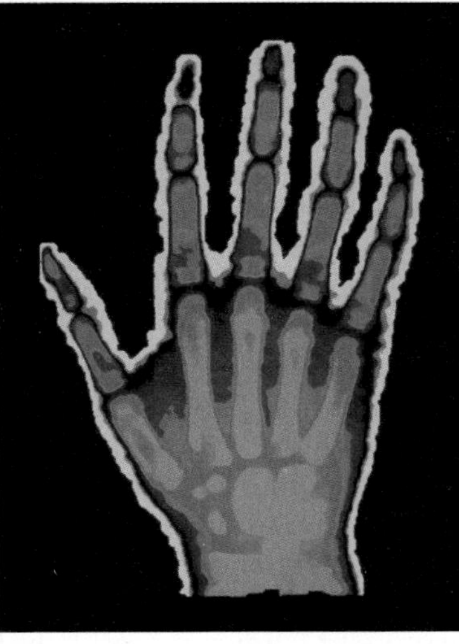

FIGURE 6-1 X-Ray of a 2-Year-Old's (left) and a 6-Year-Old's (right) Hand and Wrist

Note the greater degree of ossification in the older child's bones; especially in the wrist.

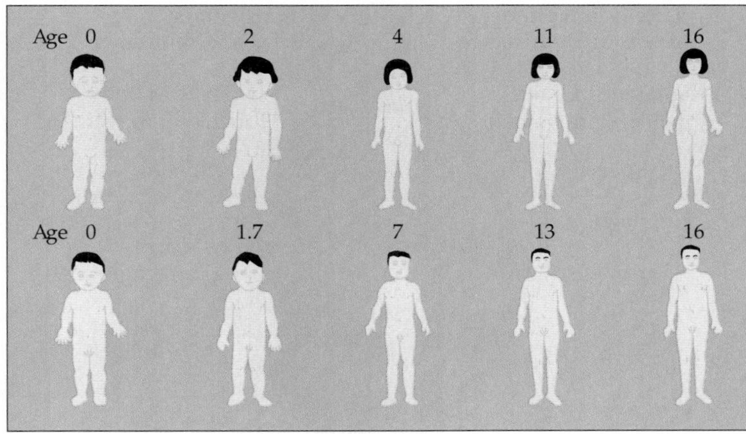

FIGURE 6-2 Changing Body Proportions in Girls and Boys from Birth to Maturity

SOURCE: From B. Nichols, 1994, *Moving and learning: The elementary school physical education experience* (3rd ed.), copyright © 1994. Reprinted by permission of the McGraw-Hill Companies, Inc.

Body Proportions In addition to getting bigger, body proportions also change dramatically throughout childhood, as shown in Figure 6-2. For example, at birth the head comprises one-quarter of overall body length. By age 16, although the head has doubled in size, it now accounts for only one-eighth of body length. Elongation of the lower body and legs accelerates and children begin to lose the baby fat associated with infancy and toddlerhood. Consequently, young children carry a greater proportion of their weight in their upper body than do adults, which gives them a higher center of gravity. Being top-heavy makes it more difficult to control body movements. In early childhood, children lose their balance more easily and have difficulty coming to a quick stop without tipping forward. They also have difficulty catching a large ball without falling backward. As children's body proportions continue to change throughout childhood, their center of gravity gradually descends to the pelvic area, which enhances their ability to perform movements that are more athletic.

Brain Development

Rapid changes in body size and proportion are obvious signs of growth, but unseen changes also are taking place in the brain. Despite the fact that by age 5 the child's brain is nearly the size of an adult's, much neural development occurs in early childhood and beyond, continuing processes begun in earlier periods (Bransford, Brown, & Cocking, 2008; Coch, Fischer, & Dawson, 2010; Johnson & De Haan, 2011). For example, the *brain growth spurt* (see Chapter 4), which involves both the rapid development of interconnections among neurons and the pruning away of connections that are not needed, continues throughout early childhood and even extends somewhat into adulthood (Groeschel, Vollmer, King, & Connelly, 2010; Johnson & De Haan, 2011; Johnson, Munakata, & Gilmore, 2008). Thus, the *plasticity* (flexibility) of the brain to adapt is high during early childhood.

Maturation of the brain and the central nervous system also includes **myelination**, which is the formation of sheathing cells that insulate the neurons and make transmission of neural impulses much more efficient. Myelination of the neurons for motor reflexes and vision begins in early infancy, followed by myelination of the neurons for more complex motor activities, and then those controlling eye–hand coordination, attention span, memory, and self-control (Capone & Kaufman, 2008). Thus, myelination of the central nervous system closely parallels the development of cognitive and motor abilities during the early childhood years and beyond.

Lateralization Another way in which the brain develops during early childhood is that it becomes increasingly *lateralized*. The brain's cerebral cortex is divided into two hemispheres—the left and the right. In processing information and controlling behavior, the hemispheres sometimes specialize. **Lateralization** is the process where specific skills and competencies become localized in a particular cerebral hemisphere.

Most motor functions—such as hand control, foot control, and so forth—are heavily lateralized, with the left hemisphere controlling the right side of the body, and vice versa. The same is true for sensations felt throughout the body (see Figure 6-3). Language is another function that is controlled in large part in one hemisphere of the brain. For most people, and for nearly

Watch *Special Topics: The Plastic Brain* on **MyDevelopmentLab**

myelination
The formation of the myelin sheath that surrounds and insulates neurons in the nervous system pathways; this sheath increases the speed of transmission and the precision of communication within the nervous system

lateralization
The process whereby specific skills and competencies become localized in either the left or right cerebral hemisphere

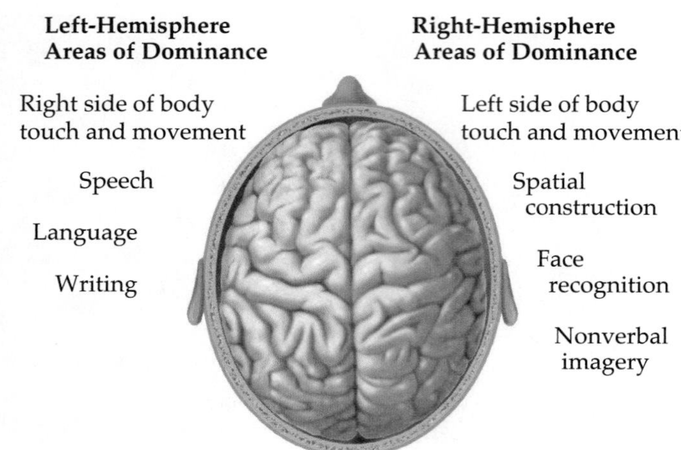

FIGURE 6-3 Functions Typically Associated with the Right and Left Cerebral Hemispheres

In most people, the left hemisphere of the brain processes information about touch and movement for the right side of the body; the right hemisphere processes such information for the left side of the body. The left hemisphere is usually dominant in verbal tasks, whereas the right hemisphere is typically more involved in nonverbal, visual, and spatial tasks.

SOURCE: Adapted from C. G. Morris, A. A. Maisto, & W. L. Dunn, 2007, *Psychology: Concepts and applications*, copyright © 2007. Reprinted by permission of Pearson Education, Inc., Upper Saddle River, NJ.

all right-handed people, language is heavily lateralized in the left hemisphere. Consequently, damage to this region of the brain often results in a severe and sometimes complete inability to speak or understand language, especially if the damage occurs in adulthood, when the brain has lost most of its plasticity.

Many other cognitive functions, to a greater or a lesser degree, are lateralized more in one hemisphere than the other (Kinsbourne, 2009). Although the popular press has overstated the significance of this lateralization, the left hemisphere generally is lateralized for skills that involve logical and sequential operations, such as writing, scientific reasoning, and quantitative logic. For most people, the right hemisphere is lateralized for spatial processing and for the more artistic and creative kinds of thought, as shown in Figure 6-3. Interestingly, new research suggests that there may be sex differences in brain lateralization. In particular, the language regions in female brains may be more deeply lateralized. If this proves to be the case, this finding may help explain why language development generally occurs faster and language abilities are more advanced in girls than in boys (Sommer, 2010).

It is tempting to oversimplify the significance of brain lateralization. Perhaps you have heard artistic people described as *right-brained* and those who prefer a logical, scientific approach as *left-brained.* Although many cognitive functions are lateralized, it is of paramount importance to recognize that the *entire* brain is involved in nearly all functioning. Lateralized (or otherwise specialized) functions simply focus a greater degree of control and activity in one area of the brain than in others. It is important to remember that the various parts of the brain are in constant networked communication.

Handedness Another function that is lateralized is *handedness*—our preference for using one hand over the other. Throughout the world, about 90% of people are right-handed, and an interesting sex difference occurs: Women are more likely to be right-handed than men (Papadatou-Pastou, Martin, Munafo, & Jones, 2008). Although people at any age can learn to use their nonpreferred hand, it appears that handedness develops very early in life; by 5 months of age, most children demonstrate a clear preference for using one hand over the other (Marschik, Einspieler, Strohmeier, Garzarolli, & Prechtl, 2008). Research has shown that handedness may develop much earlier: Using ultrasound, fetuses were observed sucking their thumbs, and they were eight times more likely to be sucking the thumb on the *right* hand (Hepper, Wells, & Lynch, 2005). When these fetuses were followed to ages 10 to 12 years, all 60 of the "right-thumb" fetuses were right-handed, but of the 15 "left-thumb" fetuses, 5 had become right-handed. Thus, early hand preferences seem more predictive for later development among right-handers.

Accumulating evidence suggests that handedness may have a genetic basis; therefore, it may be prewired (Gutwinski, et al., 2011; Linke & Kersebaum, 2005). So, too, may be *footedness,* our preference for relying more on one foot than the other, a tendency that is further refined during middle childhood. Researchers suggest that because footedness is less socially influenced than handedness—as parents may force left-handed children to use the right hand but allow footedness to develop without correction—the development of foot preference may actually be a more sensitive indicator of the pace of brain lateralization (Nelson, DeHaan, & Thomas, 2006).

Handedness is of special interest to developmentalists because it is intimately linked to language lateralization in the brain (Papadatou-Pastou, Martin, Munafo, & Jones, 2008; Szaflarski et al., 2012). As mentioned previously, for the large majority of right-handed people, language is highly localized in areas of the left hemisphere. For the remaining 10% or so of the population who are left-handed, language is often shared by the two sides of the brain. This finding suggests that the brains of left-handed people may be less lateralized, in general, than the brains of right-handed people (Springer & Deutsch, 2003; Stemmer & Whitaker, 2008).

Brain Development and Early Intervention Early brain development sets the stage for later maturation, as well as for growth in all areas of development—cognitive, language, social, and emotional. Thus, many theorists believe that intervention aimed at remedying developmental problems should begin as early as possible, so that brain development is influenced early on, when plasticity is high. Research supports this view: Other things being equal, those educational programs and intervention projects that enroll high-risk children in early infancy generally have a much greater impact than those that are begun later in life (Walker, 2011). Of course, the quality of the program also matters. Day-care programs that emphasize a comprehensive approach and therefore address broad issues—such as nutritional needs, other health needs, social development, cognitive development, family functioning, as well as child functioning—are more likely to produce positive results (NICHD, 2009).

Although the first 3 years of life constitute a critical period for brain development, this does not mean that the window of opportunity for later development of cognitive functions somehow closes after that. Quality interventions begun after age 3 still help. As various theorists have noted (e.g., Baltes, Reuter-Lorenz, & Rösler, 2006; Johnson & De Haan, 2011), learning and its corresponding brain development continue throughout the lifespan. However, our rapidly increasing understanding of early brain development highlights the importance of the first few years for establishing patterns that will continue throughout the lifespan.

Human Development: An Interactive and Individual Approach

It is important to emphasize that brain development and other aspects of development *interact;* that is, they influence each other and, in turn, are influenced by each other. For example, consider the impact of malnutrition. As we saw in Chapter 3, prolonged deprivation of essential nutrients can have pronounced effects on children's physical and motor development. Sustained periods of malnutrition during early childhood also limit children's cognitive development both directly and indirectly. The situation is much more complex than a simple scenario of "malnutrition causes brain damage, which causes delayed cognitive development." Malnutrition can directly produce brain damage that is sometimes reversible, but sometimes not. At the same time, however, it sets off a dynamic and reciprocal process in which, for example, the child becomes lethargic and only minimally explores and learns from the environment, thus interfering with cognitive development. Malnutrition also produces delayed physical growth and development of motor skills that likely will lower parental expectations and, in turn, delay cognitive development. In addition, environments that involve malnutrition are often impoverished in other ways as well: Parents may be stressed, health care may be substandard, and opportunities for learning and other positive interactions may be limited. As you can see, a single aspect of development can never be separated from the development of the whole child.

Can you suggest how a child's development of skill in a sport such as soccer or basketball can be thought of as the result of the* interaction *of brain development, motor development, and social and environmental factors?

Finally, it is important to note that generalized statements about growth may or may not apply to individual children. Each child's physical growth is the result of a myriad of factors, including genetics, nutrition, parental encouragement, and opportunities to play and exercise. Each of these factors presents itself in multiple ways throughout development. Hence, a child who may appear delayed at one point in childhood may compensate and spurt ahead, making up ground and perhaps even advancing beyond what is considered normal at a future point. Indeed, each child is unique. Although it is useful to consider general trends, typical expectations, and the average ages at which children attain particular developmental milestones in an attempt to forge an overarching theory of human development, we should not lose sight of each individual's uniqueness. Keeping these two principles in mind—that development is interactive and that individuals experience development in unique ways—we extend our study of the period of early childhood with a discussion of the development of motor skills.

REVIEW THE FACTS 6-1

1. In comparison to 2-year-olds, the center of gravity for 6-year-olds is ____________.
2. The myelination of the nervous system serves to make the transmission of neural impulses ____________.
3. To say that a brain function is lateralized means that it ____________.
4. For people who are right-handed, language is usually localized in the ____________ of the brain.
5. Intervention programs for at-risk children are generally more effective when they
   a. are begun after age 3 rather than in infancy.
   b. emphasize cognitive functions and do not address social needs.
   c. do not attempt to do too much, such as addressing both nutritional and health needs.
   d. address overall family functioning, not just the needs of the child.

Practice on **MyDevelopmentLab**

MOTOR SKILLS DEVELOPMENT

As children's brains develop and their bodies grow in size and strength during early childhood, their motor skills also improve markedly (Elliott, Hayes, & Bennett, 2012). The most dramatic changes in motor development involve gross motor skills, such as running, hopping, and throwing. In contrast, fine motor skills, such as writing and handling eating utensils, develop more slowly.

Gross Motor Skills

Compared to infants, 2-year-olds are amazingly competent, but they still have a long way to go. They can walk and run, but they are still relatively short and round. They walk with a wide stance and a swaying gait. Toddlers also tend to use both arms (or legs) when only one is necessary. When handed

Table 6-1 Motor Development During Early Childhood

2-year-olds	3-year-olds	4-year-olds	5-year-olds
Walk with a wide stance and body sway	Keep legs closer together when walking and running	Can vary rhythm of running	Can walk a balance beam
Can climb, push, pull, run, and hang by both hands	Can run and move more smoothly	Skip awkwardly; jump	Skip smoothly; stand on one foot
Have little endurance	Reach for objects with their preferred hand	Have greater strength, endurance, and coordination	Can manage buttons and zippers; may tie shoelaces
Reach for objects with two hands	Smear and daub paint; stack blocks	Draw shapes and simple figures; make paintings; use blocks for building	Use utensils and tools correctly

Can you suggest a few motor behaviors that you perform that demonstrate the principle of automaticity?

a cookie, for example, a 2-year-old is likely to extend both hands.

By age 3, children's legs stay closer together when walking and running, and they no longer need to pay attention to what their legs and feet are doing. Thus, their gross motor behavior is showing signs of **automaticity**, which is the ability to perform motor behaviors without consciously thinking about them. Three-year-olds run, turn, and stop more smoothly than 2-year-olds do, although their ankles and wrists are not as flexible as they will be by age 4 or 5. They are also more likely to extend only the preferred hand to receive an object such as a cookie.

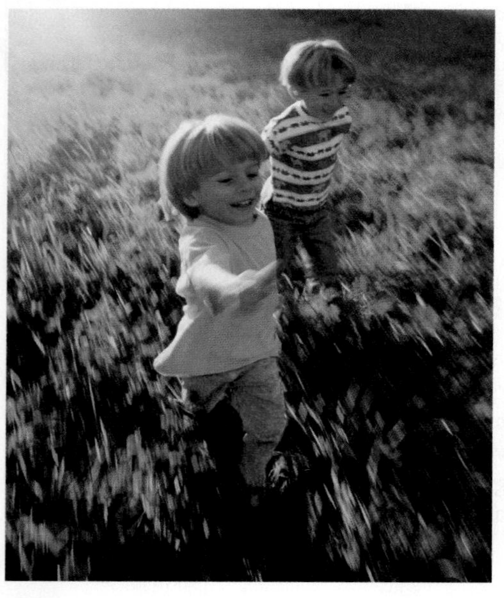

A sister, less than 2 years older, is way ahead of her 2-year-old brother in gross motor skills, even skills such as running in tall grass.

By age 4, children can vary the rhythm of their running. Many 4-year-olds can skip, although awkwardly, and they can execute a running jump or a standing broad jump. By age 5, they can skip smoothly, walk along a balance beam confidently, stand on one foot for several seconds, and imitate dance steps. Many 5-year-olds can throw a ball overhand and catch a large ball thrown to them, although such skills continue to be refined over the next several years. For a brief summary of motor development across early childhood, see Table 6-1.

Children's overall activity level generally peaks between the ages of 2 and 3, and gradually declines throughout the remaining years of early childhood. The decline in activity occurs earlier for girls than for boys, which may explain why boys may have more trouble sitting still in kindergarten than girls do (Buchmann, DiPrete, & McDaniel, 2008). Motor activities also become functionally subordinated during early childhood. **Functional subordination** is the integration of a number of separate, simple actions or schemes into a more complex pattern of behavior. Actions that are initially performed for their own sake later become integrated into more complex, purposeful skills. For example, when a child first learns to hop, hopping is an end in itself; later, hopping becomes part of a dance or game as it is functionally subordinated to more complex sports skills.

Fine Motor Skills

Fine motor skills often require the coordinated and dexterous use of hand, fingers, and thumb. By age 2, children have refined earlier grasping schemes (see Chapter 4), and by the end of the third year, these simple responses become better integrated and coordinated with other motor, perceptual, and verbal behaviors. Fine motor skills also begin to display automaticity. For example, 4-year-olds can carry on a dinner conversation while manipulating a fork or other eating utensil. Despite their increasing competence, however, young children still have difficulty with precise fine motor movements. This difficulty is linked to the immaturity of the child's central nervous system,

Watch *Gross Motor Skills* on **MyDevelopmentLab**

functional subordination
The integration of a number of separate, simple actions or schemes into a more complex pattern of behavior

automaticity
The ability to perform motor behaviors without consciously thinking about them

Watch *The Growing Child* on **MyDevelopmentLab**

Table 6-2 Conditions Involved in Learning Motor Skills

Condition	Definition	Example
Readiness	Acquiring or developing the necessary prerequisite skills to perform an action	Alice must develop a certain amount of physical strength, hand–eye coordination, foot–eye coordination, attention, and concentration before she can climb a ladder.
Practice	Repeating a skill in order to perfect it	Bobby kicks a ball over and over to improve his kicking skill.
Attention	Developing the ability to maintain focus on the skill at hand	Latoya must be able to concentrate in order to stack six blocks on top of each other.
Feedback	Gathering information about how well a skill is being performed to refine the skill and internalizing pleasure when an action is completed successfully.	Abdul is pleased with himself when he is able to pour milk from a pitcher to a glass without spilling.

where the pruning of synapses and myelination are still in progress, as well as to the child's limited patience and relatively short attention span.

As children gain fine motor skills, they become increasingly competent in taking care of themselves and in carrying out their daily activities. Usually at 2 to 3 years of age, for example, children can put on and remove simple items of clothing. They can handle large zippers and use chopsticks or a spoon somewhat effectively.

A 3- to 4-year-old child can fasten and unfasten items of clothing and independently serve food, although children of this age sometimes make a mess while doing so. By the time children are 4 to 5 years old, they can dress and undress themselves without assistance and use eating utensils well. Children who are 5 to 6 years of age can typically tie a simple knot, and 6-year-olds who wear shoes with laces usually can tie them, although many still find it difficult and may ask for help instead.

Learning and Motor Skills

The motor skills that young children learn first are usually actions involved in everyday life. Young children are highly motivated to develop their motor abilities because these skills increase their ability to move around, perform self-care, and be creative. Some young children also learn more highly skilled activities, such as gymnastics, playing the piano, or even riding horses or other animals. Regardless of whether motor abilities are acquired naturally in the developmental process or because the child is encouraged to learn a particular skill, a number of conditions are important in determining the limits of motor learning (see Table 6-2 and figure 6-4).

Learning any new skill—whether motor or cognitive—is easiest if the child is *ready* to learn. *Readiness* implies that a certain level of maturation has been achieved and that the necessary prerequisite skills are in place so that the child can profit from training. Readiness is especially important during periods of transition, such as when children enter school. Usually, children entering kindergarten are assessed for their readiness to benefit from formal education. Research shows that children who possess entry-level skills in math and reading and who are able to focus their attention are more likely to do well in school settings, both in kindergarten and in later grades (Duncan et al., 2007). Additionally, fine-motor skills also seem to be important predictors of school success: Children who have better developed fine motor skills when they enter kindergarten show higher levels of school achievement later in grade school (Grissmer, Grimm, Aiyer, Murrah, & Steele, 2010).

For a child to be ready to learn, the necessary neural pathways must be developed, and the child also must be able to link his or her perception of the new action with the performance of the action (Blythe, 2000; Thomas & Johnson, 2008). Although it can be difficult to know when a child is ready to learn a new skill, classic studies in Russia and the United States have indicated that children who are introduced to new motor learning at the optimal point of readiness learn quickly and with little training or effort because new skills are built on skills that were acquired earlier (Bertenthal & Clifton, 1998). Children frequently give clues when

At about what age did you learn to read? Do you remember whether you learned easily or with difficulty? What might your early experience with reading suggest about the concept of readiness?

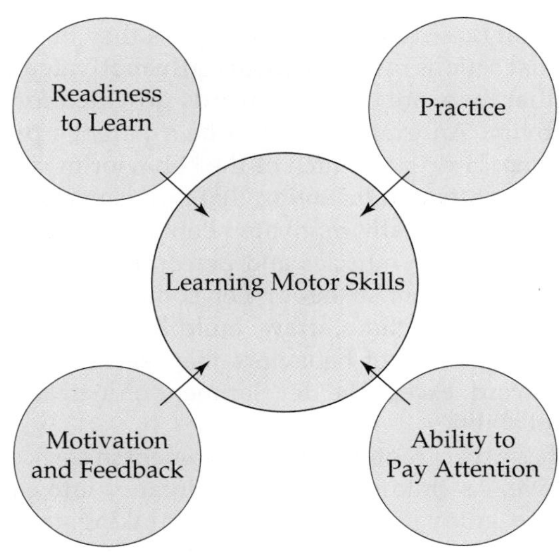

FIGURE 6-4 Four Factors That Promote Motor Learning

they have reached the optimal readiness for a given skill: Watch for them to begin imitating the behavior on their own.

Practice is also essential to motor development. For example, children cannot master climbing if they have not actually practiced climbing. When children live in limited, restricted environments, their development of motor skills typically lags. Children who lack objects to play with, places to explore, tools to use, or people to imitate usually have trouble developing motor skills. On the other hand, given a rich, active environment, children tend to pace their own learning appropriately. They imitate behaviors, often repeating them endlessly. They do things like repeatedly pouring water from one container to another to explore the concepts of full and empty or fast and slow. Such self-designed and self-paced schedules of learning are often more efficient than are lessons programmed by adults.

Motor learning is also enhanced by *attention*, which requires an alert and engaged state of mind. How can children's attention be improved? Young children cannot simply be told what to do and how to do it. Instead, 2- and 3-year-old children learn new motor skills most efficiently by discovering and expanding their own actions or by being led through activities. Exercises and games can be used to teach young children to move their arms and legs in special ways. Between the ages of 3 and 5, children continue to learn best through active imitation. Only when children have reached age 6 or 7 can they begin to attend to verbal instructions and follow them reasonably well.

Finally, the ongoing *feedback* children receive for their efforts helps them acquire and refine their motor skills. On the one hand, parents and peers notice their accomplishments and encourage them to do more. More importantly, feedback also comes from successfully performing the behavior itself, from the feel of running faster or pouring juice into a glass without spilling. In fact, the feedback we receive from our muscles, eyes, ears, and other senses provides us with the information we need to monitor, control, and modify our actions. Successful actions bring their own reward as children learn through trial and error what behaviors are most effective.

The concept of feedback relates to classic work on *motivation*—on what *causes* children to behave as they do. Sometimes it is clear that actions involve **extrinsically motivated behavior**, meaning that there are explicit rewards provided for performing an activity. An example would be a parent's praise for a job well done. However, much of the behavior in childhood is **intrinsically motivated behavior**; that is, it is performed for its own sake. In intrinsically motivated behavior, feedback comes from the child's own muscles and perceptions, it involves the child's self-assessment of his or her competence or mastery. Children run, jump, climb, draw, build block towers, and engage in a wide array of behaviors that lead to no particular extrinsic reward, except the development of increasingly complex, useful abilities.

As we have seen, motor skill development in early childhood is impressive. As children move from infancy into early childhood, their cognitive abilities—such as thinking, memory, and problem solving—advance rapidly as well. We explore cognitive development in the next section.

REVIEW THE FACTS 6-2

1. Throughout early childhood, __________ motor skills develop sooner than __________ motor skills.
2. Children's overall activity level peaks between what ages?
   a. 1 to 2 years
   b. 2 to 3 years
   c. 3 to 4 years
   d. 5 to 6 years
3. At age 3, Jamal stacks blocks for the pure pleasure of doing so. By age 5, he stacks blocks in order to build a house. We would describe this change in his motor skills as an example of __________.
4. The development of fine motor skills is closely linked to the maturation of __________.
5. Which of the following is the best example of extrinsic motivation?
   a. building a block tower with four blocks that does not fall down
   b. having the child's father say "Great shot" when the child rolls a ball into a tray
   c. being able to hop three times on one foot without falling over

Practice on MyDevelopmentLab

COGNITIVE DEVELOPMENT

When we look at all the developmental changes that occur during early childhood, it is often difficult to disentangle the contributions of increasing physical competence from those of cognitive development, because these systems interact in such intricate and important ways. For example, children often use their bodies as a means of testing their developing knowledge and understanding: A child who throws stones of varying sizes into the river is learning some basics about weight, force, angles, and trajectories.

Despite the complexity of cognitive development, several important perspectives have emerged to explain how it proceeds. Because of its importance, both historically and in terms of the explanatory power of its ideas, our discussion begins with an examination of Jean Piaget's viewpoint about how cognitive development unfolds in early childhood.

An Overview of Preoperational Thinking

Recall from Chapter 1 that Piaget described cognitive development in terms of discrete stages through which children progress on their way to understanding the world. According to Piaget, children actively construct a personal view of their world. They build their own reality through experimentation; they are like little scientists working diligently to figure out

extrinsically motivated behavior
Behavior performed to obtain explicit rewards or to avoid explicit adverse events

intrinsically motivated behavior
Behavior performed for its own sake, with no particular goal or explicit reward

how the world works. They explore their surroundings and comprehend new information based on their current level and ways of understanding. When they encounter something familiar, they *assimilate* it. When they encounter something new and different, they *accommodate* their thinking to incorporate it. Indeed, the process of organizing knowledge and experiences into conceptual schemes, or "theories," about the world—and then accommodating them as more information becomes available to the child—provides a good explanation for how children learn about the world (Kuhn, 2011).

Can you think of examples that demonstrate Piaget's conclusion that young children are "little scientists"? Do you think this phrase accurately describes how young children learn?

Piaget referred to early childhood as the **preoperational period**. This period in cognitive development builds on schemes that were developed in the *sensorimotor period* (see Chapter 4), and it will form the basis on which middle childhood's stage of *concrete operations* will be based (see Chapter 8). In Piaget's view, children enter the preoperational stage with only rudimentary language and thinking abilities and leave it asking sophisticated questions, such as "Where did Grandma go when she died?"

What is preoperational thinking like? Let's consider the question in conjunction with the dramatic cognitive advances children make during this stage.

Preoperational Substages and Thought

Piaget's preoperational period lasts from about age 2 to age 7 (Miller, 2011a). It usually is divided into two parts—the early preoperational or **preconceptual period** (about age 2 to age 4 or 5) and the **intuitive (or transitional) period** (about age 4 or 5 to age 7).

The preconceptual period is highlighted by the increasingly complex use of symbols and symbolic (pretend) play. Previously, a child's thinking was limited to the immediate physical environment. Now symbols—and especially language—enable the child to think about things that are not immediately present. Not only is the child's thinking more flexible than before, but also words now have the power to communicate, even when the things they name are absent.

Piaget observed that preconceptual children, however, still have difficulty with major categories of reality. For example, their thinking displays *animism:* They may think that anything that moves is alive—the sun, the moon, clouds, an automobile, or a train. They also display *reification:* Objects and people in their thoughts and dreams are very real to them. For preconceptual children, even imaginary objects are thought of as being as real as those that actually are present in the child's environment. It is no wonder that preconceptual children enjoy stories about trains, animals, or imaginary characters that act like real people.

▲ Children in Piaget's preoperational period are often bound by their perceptual egocentrism, which makes it impossible for them to imagine what an object looks like to another person seated in a different position. Here we would expect the young boy to have a very difficult time understanding that the people staying in the lodge at the base of the mountain could not see the trees on his side of the mountain.

Such approaches to thinking stem partly from another characteristic of young children's thinking, which is called **egocentrism**. This term refers to children's tendency to see and understand things in terms of their personal point of view; theirs is a self-centered view of the world (Kesselring, 2011). Egocentrism is often demonstrated with the *mountain problem,* which uses a three-dimensional model of a set of mountains that rests on a table at which the child is seated (see photo). Even young children can accurately describe how the mountains look from their own point of view, but the preoperational child typically is unable to imagine how the mountains would appear from another perspective, for example, to a person sitting across the table. Thus, young children's egocentrism limits their ability to understand perspectives other than their own, including different spatial, social, and emotional perspectives (see the box Current Issues: A Theory of Mind).

In the intuitive (or transitional) period of the preoperational stage of development, children begin to separate mental from physical reality, which allows them to understand that thinking about something is not the same as experiencing it. For example, children of this age can imagine what a flying cow would look like, but they also know that flying cows do not exist. At this age, children also begin to understand causation, or

---

preoperational period
According to Piaget, the developmental stage associated with early childhood

intuitive (or transitional) period
For Piaget, the second part of the preoperational period (about age 4 or 5 to age 7), during which children begin to understand causation, as well as to undertake simple mental operations and form a more realistic view of their world

Watch *Concrete Operational Thinking* on **MyDevelopmentLab**

egocentrism
A self-centered view of the world where children tend to see things in terms of their personal point of view and fail to take others' perspectives

preconceptual period
For Piaget, the first part of the preoperational period (about age 2 to age 4 or 5), which is highlighted by the increasingly complex use of symbols and symbolic play

A Theory of Mind

To what extent does egocentrism limit a young child's thinking? We know that a child can mistakenly assume that Daddy knows what happened at day care, although he was not there, or that his grandmother, who is on the other end of the telephone, knows or can see what the child is doing. However, that same child can play a trick on Daddy and hide his razor when he is out of the room, fully understanding that Daddy does not know where the razor is hidden.

What do young children understand about the thoughts, feelings, and intentions of others? When and how do they develop these understandings? In the last few decades, numerous researchers have studied the development of young children's base of knowledge, and they often refer to it as the child's developing *theory of mind* (Apperly, 2010; Doherty, 2009; Wellman, 2011). We do not know all of the answers, but the following list presents some of the pieces:

- Perception: Even 3-year-old children sometimes behave differently when their parents are out of the room. They can hide things and then giggle when Mom or Dad has trouble finding them. However, 3-year-olds also can talk on the phone to Grandpa and think he knows what toy the child is holding. In an experiment, preschoolers were shown two identical objects—one red and one blue. Out of the child's view, one of these was placed in a tube, which was then presented to the child in such a way that the child could feel it but could not see it. When asked what color the object was, children under 5 named a color emphatically, although they could not possibly have known the object's color. Not until about age 5 did they realize that they could not know the object's color by feeling it (Lillard & Curenton, 1999).
- Emotions: Toddlers usually understand anger or fear in another person and many can empathize when someone is hurt. However, they do not understand emotions that do not represent true feelings until age 5 or 6. For example, toddlers do not understand the polite smile that an older sister gives when she receives a present she does not like.
- Beliefs: Preschoolers generally assume that others know what they know. For example, if a preschooler knows that Scooter is her dog's name, she assumes the teacher knows his name as well. *False belief* tasks are often used to study the limits of children's thinking. In one version of such a task, children are shown a familiar candy box and asked what they think is inside. They typically say "candy," but when the box is opened, it is full of pencils. When asked to remember what they thought was in the box when they first came in the room, they typically say "pencils," indicating that they do not understand how their earlier and present realities differ. Next, they are told that a friend is coming into the room and are asked what the friend will think is in the box. Again, young children most often say "pencils" because they know the box contains pencils, and they incorrectly infer that the friend will also know this. It takes a while for children to understand that we have beliefs based on our experiences, and that sometimes those beliefs are false because we do not have enough evidence.

Understanding the feelings, thoughts, intentions, and viewpoints of others is crucial for forming close friendships, for working cooperatively with others, and for functioning effectively in society. Do children around the world develop the ability to understand another's thoughts in the same way? Research suggests the answer is a qualified yes. In a study that examined how 3-, 4-, and 5-year-old children from Peru, India, Samoa, Thailand, and Canada solved theory-of-mind problems, children from all the different cultures performed much the same way (Callaghan, et al., 2005). In the basic experiment, the experimenter first showed the child a small toy that was placed under one of three bowls. The experimenter then left the room and a second experimenter entered and instructed the child to move the toy from under the original bowl and place it under a different bowl. The child was then asked where the first experimenter would look for the toy when he or she returned to the room. Could children understand that the absent experimenter would not know the toy had been moved? Results of the study showed that, in every culture, 3-year-old children had difficulty in correctly anticipating the experimenter's lack of knowledge, whereas 5-year-old children could easily solve this problem correctly. Thus, there appears to be a universal milestone in the development of "mind" that occurs between the ages of 3 and 5, regardless of cultural background.

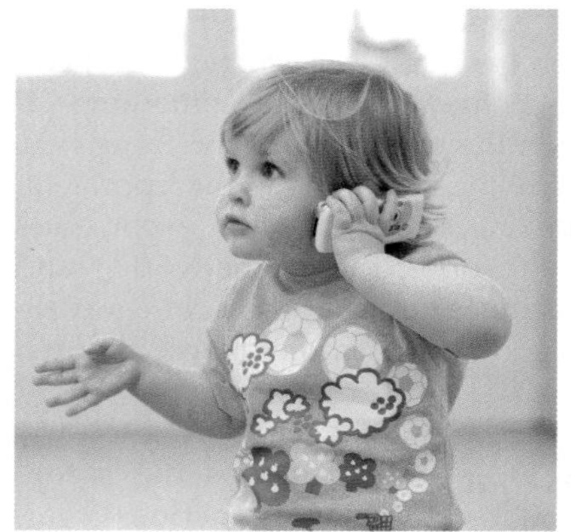

◄ Preschoolers usually assume that others must know whatever they know. Talking on the phone can be a challenge for both the young child and for Grandma on the other end of the conversation because the child assumes that Grandma also sees what the child sees.

However, culture *does* seem to matter when it comes to the order in which young children master the steps that lead to a mature theory of mind. Studies have shown, for example, that when preschool children are asked to solve five different types of "theory of mind" tasks (see Table 6-3), those raised in the United States—a Western culture in which independence is valued and emotions are typically displayed—the tasks are mastered in the order presented in the table. Specifically, U.S. preschoolers were first able to correctly solve tasks involving diverse desires, followed by diverse beliefs, then knowledge access, then false beliefs, and finally hidden emotions (Wellman, et al., 2006). The same pattern of development also was seen among preschool children in Australia (Peterson & Wellman, 2009) and in Germany (Kristen, Thoermer, Hofer, Aschersleben, & Sodian, 2006, cited in Shahaeian, Peterson, Slaughter, & Wellman, 2011)—two other Western, individualist cultures. However, when Chinese preschoolers were tested with these same five tasks, a different developmental pattern emerged: Although Chinese children solved the *same total number* of tasks correctly as did the children in the Western cultures, they solved some tasks more easily and had more difficulty with others. In particular, Chinese children were more advanced when asked the "knowledge access" questions, but had more difficulty with the "diverse beliefs" tasks—a pattern consistent with their own country's standards and values (Liu, Wellman, Tardif, & Sabbagh, 2008; Wellman, et al., 2006). Thus, in cultures that emphasize filial respect of elders, conformity to cultural traditions and rules, and reliance on well-established knowledge, the pattern in which the "mind" develops reflects these values, perhaps as the result of child-rearing practices that model and emphasize these traditions. Similar results recently have been replicated in a study of children in Iran and Australia; here Australian preschoolers were found to master the theory-of-mind tasks in typical Western order, and preschoolers in Iran—a collectivist culture much like China—followed the Chinese pattern of mastery (Shahaeian, Peterson, Slaughter, & Wellman, 2011). Thus, it seems that the development of "mind"—like so many other developmental processes—is based in a deep conceptual structure that guides cognitive development, yet at the same time is shaped by cultural practices as well (Perner, Mauer, & Hildenbrand, 2011).

Table 6-3 Different Tasks Used to Study the Development of a Theory of Mind

Task	Example
Diverse desires	Robert is given the choice between playing with a truck and some building blocks. He chooses the truck. When asked what another child would like to play with, Robert emphatically says, "truck!" indicating he does not understand that the other child may have different preferences.
Diverse beliefs	Sasha believes that Mommy is in the bedroom and is told that another child believes that Mommy is in the kitchen. When asked where the other child will search for Mommy, Sasha says, "in the bedroom," indicating that she does not understand the other child's beliefs differ from her own.
Knowledge access	Mark watches as a small car toy is put into a box. Then another child enters the room. When asked if the second child knows what is in the box, Mark says, "yes, a toy car." This indicates that Mark does not differentiate between what he knows and what someone else knows.
False beliefs	Kia is shown three boxes of different colors and is instructed to place a ring into the yellow box. She then is asked to predict which box her brother will think the ring is in, and she says, "the yellow one," indicating that she falsely believes that the other person knows what she knows.
Hidden emotions	Laura is shown a picture of a parent yelling at a child and is told that the child does not want the parent to know how scared he is. Laura is shown two pictures of the child's face—one showing the child is scared and the other showing the child as brave—and she is asked to point to the picture that shows how the child really feels and then the one that shows how he is making his face look. If Laura has a mature theory of mind, she can correctly point to the appropriate faces.

SOURCE: From "Culture and the sequence of steps in theory of mind development," by A. Shahaeian, C. C. Peterson, V. Slaughter, & H. M. Wellman, 2011, *Developmental Psychology, 47*(5), 1239–1247; and *Theory of mind: How children understand others' thoughts and feelings*, by M. J. Doherty, 2009, New York: Psychology Press.

what causes what. Egocentrism eases somewhat, and intuitive children often can understand multiple points of view and how things relate to each other, although sometimes in an inconsistent and incomplete way. Although rational thinking increases during this period, children are still often willing to use magical thinking to explain things. Thus, they are fascinated by stories of people or animals with magical powers, and their thinking is not completely bounded by reality. For example, although 4- to 6-year-olds basically understand that an adult cannot be transformed into a child and that people cannot pass through solid objects, the majority will change their opinion if an adult relates a fairy tale as if it were true (Subbotsky, 1994). Thus, although thinking advances dramatically during the intuitive period, and in many ways the young child's reasoning is quite well developed by age 6, in other ways it is still limited, as we will see.

Symbolic Representation The most dramatic cognitive difference between infants and 2-year-olds is in their use of **symbolic representation**, which is the use of actions, images, words, or other signs to represent past and present events, experiences, and concepts. The development of symbolic representation marks the transition from the sensorimotor period to the preoperational period. This transition can be seen most clearly in language development and in symbolic play (DeLoache, 2011; Flavell, Miller, & Miller, 2002; Walker & Murachver, 2012). At about 2 years of age, children begin to imitate past events, roles, and actions. For example, a 2-year-old might use gestures to act out an extensive sequence of events, such as a car ride or a story from a favorite book or folktale. The ability to employ numbers to represent quantity is another use of symbolic representation. Still another is the acquisition of skills in drawing and artistic representation, which begins during the preoperational stage (Jolley, 2010). Table 6-4 presents an overview of the characteristics of preoperational thought.

Although symbolic representation starts at the end of the sensorimotor period, it continues to be refined; a child is much better at symbolization at age 4 than at age 2, and better at age 6 than at age 4. For example, in one experiment, researchers found that the younger children—2½-year-olds—needed props similar to real objects for their pretend games. In contrast, 3½-year-olds could represent objects with quite different props or act out a situation without props (Marzolf & DeLoache, 1994), as they had developed the ability to think symbolically about the objects (Troseth, Bloom, DeLoache, 2007). Symbolic representation also builds on early experiences, although children sometimes experience breakthroughs in which their understanding of some symbolic relationships occurs fairly suddenly.

The development of symbolic thinking advances cognitive development in a variety of ways. For example, it can help children in social interactions by allowing them to become more sensitive to the feelings and viewpoints of others. This sensitivity, in turn, helps them make the transition to less egocentric and more *sociocentric* thinking.

Limitations of Preoperational Thinking

In spite of the development of symbolic representation, preoperational children have a long way to go before they are logical thinkers. Their thought processes are limited in many ways, as evidenced by observations of their behavior and by experiments designed to test the limits of their thinking. The limitations on

Watch *Theory of Mind* on **MyDevelopmentLab**

symbolic representation
The use of actions, images, words, or other signs to represent past and present events, experiences, and concepts; marks the emergence of the preoperational period

Table 6-4 Characteristics of Preoperational Thought

Characteristic	Description	Example
Animism	Assuming that all things that move are alive and have human characteristics	"That car must feel sad when it gets left alone in the rain."
Reification	Believing that people and objects in stories and dreams are real	"Don't let that purple three-headed monster ever come in our house!"
Egocentrism	Viewing everything from a personal point of view rather than objectively	"I'm hungry, so you should eat, too."
Symbolic representation	Using actions, images, or words to represent past or present events, experiences, and concepts	"Look at me drive this car to the store." (when pretending to drive)

Table 6-5 Limitations of Preoperational Thinking

Limitation	Description	Example
Concreteness	Tendency to think in terms of what can be directly experienced	A child is asked, "How big is an ocean?" The child replies, "It's so big you can't walk across it."
Irreversibility	Inability to think backward, or to see how an event can be reversed	A 3-year-old girl is asked, "Do you have a sister?" She replies, "Yes." The child is then asked, "What's her name?" "Jessica," she replies. "Does Jessica have a sister?" She says, "No."
Egocentrism	Inability to take another person's point of view	When looking at an object from the side, the child cannot envision what it would look like from an overhead perspective.
Centration	Inability to focus on more than one aspect of a situation at a time	A young boy is presented with a collection of red and yellow wooden beads and asked, "Are there more wooden beads or red beads?" The child replies, "I don't know."
Time, space, and sequence	Inability to consider the correct ordering of events; for example, making distinctions between past, present, and future; confusion about cause-and-effect and time-linked events	Upon starting a 100-mile car trip, a child asks, "How long will it take?" The father replies, "About 2 hours." Just 5 minutes later the child asks, "Are we halfway there yet?"

children's thinking include concreteness; irreversibility; egocentrism; centration; and difficulties with concepts of time, space, and sequence. Table 6-5 provides descriptions and examples of these limitations. In Piaget's terms, the preoperational child still cannot perform many of the *mental operations* (thought processes) that characterize mature thinking. Many of these limitations can be observed by examining how children approach the classic Piagetian problems of conservation.

Conservation

Piaget's **conservation** problems have been offered as evidence for the limitations of preoperational thinking. The term *conservation* refers to understanding that changing the shape or appearance of objects and materials does not change their mass, volume, number, and so forth.

Conservation of Mass Figure 6-5 shows one test for conservation of mass. Here a child is presented with two identical balls of clay. As the child watches, one ball is transformed into various shapes while the other ball remains untouched. Consider

conservation
The understanding that changing the shape or appearance of objects does not change their mass, volume, or number

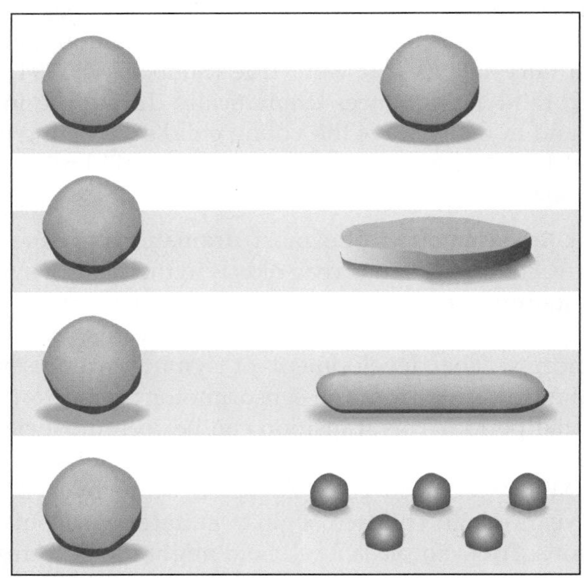

FIGURE 6-5 Conservation of Mass Problems
In this conservation experiment, a child is shown two identical balls of clay. One ball remains the same,while the other is transformed into various shapes.

the case in which one of the balls is rolled into a long sausage shape. Now the child is asked, "Which ball contains more clay?" Although this problem is exceedingly easy for older children or adults, the preoperational child most likely will say either that the sausage shape contains more clay or that it contains less, depending on whether the child attends to length or height. The preoperational child, thus, fails to *conserve*—to understand that changing the shape of an object does not alter its mass.

Conservation of Number The development of numerical abilities is an especially intriguing area—both because of the amount of formal education that is invested in teaching children to use numbers and the many essential applications of numbers in everyday life. A number-conservation task is shown in Figure 6-6. The researcher first places six candies in each of two rows, one above the other and spaced in the same way. After the child agrees that the two rows contain the same number of candies, the researcher removes one of the candies from one row and spreads out the remaining candies. To conserve number, the child must recognize that the longer row actually contains one less candy despite its *wider* appearance. Children younger than age 5 or 6 are often fooled and judge that the longer row contains more candies.

Conservation of Volume Piaget observed that preoperational children typically do not conserve volume, as indicated by his classic liquid–beakers problem (see Figure 6-7). Here the child is first presented with two identical beakers containing the same amount of liquid. When asked, "Are they the same?" the child readily says, "Yes." Then, *as the child watches*, the contents of one of the original beakers is poured into a tall, slender beaker. Now the child is asked, "Are they the same, or are they different?" Preoperational children tend to say that the amount of the liquid

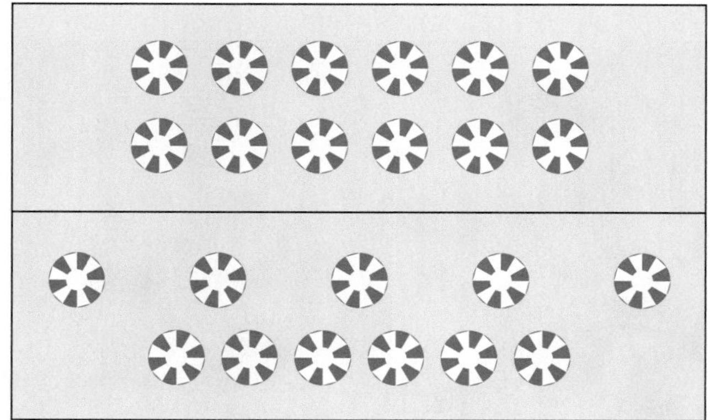

FIGURE 6-6 A Conservation of Number Problem
When shown the arrangement of candies represented by the top two rows in the figure above and asked whether one line has more or both lines are the same, the typical 4- or 5-year-old will count the candies and correctly answer that both lines contain the same number. Now,while the child watches, one candy is removed from the upper row and the remaining candies are spread farther apart, and the candies in the lower row are pushed closer together. Even when they are told they may eat the candies in the line that contains more, preoperational children, who have already correctly counted the number of candies in each line, generally insist that the longer line has more candies.Thus, they demonstrate the inability to conserve number when objects are spaced apart in different ways.

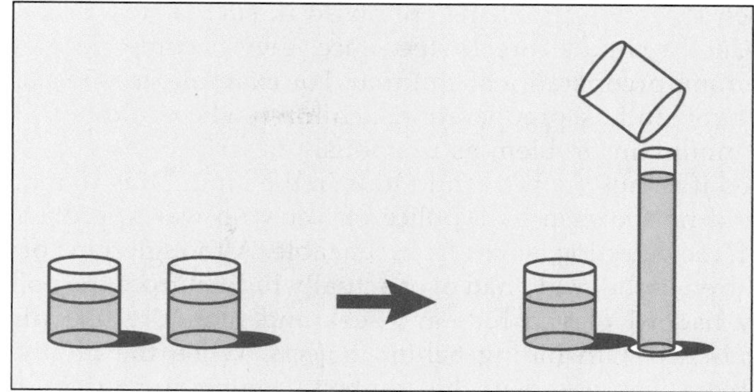

FIGURE 6-7 Preoperational children typically judge there to be more water in the taller beaker, even though they have watched the water from the shorter beaker be poured directly into it.

in the beakers is different, perhaps even adding that the taller beaker contains more liquid.

Why are preoperational children unable to solve conservation problems that, for adults, seem easy and obvious? First, *centration* apparently gets in the way: The child attends to only one dimension, such as height or length, and does not realize that a compensating change occurs in the beaker's width or in the number of candies in a row. It is also important to recognize that, for the preoperational child, these are *perceptual* problems and not *logical* ones. The child simply focuses on the here-and-now. For preoperational children, the state of the liquids before the pouring is a completely different and separate circumstance than the state of the liquids afterward. Similarly, children's perception of the shape of the ball of clay before it is rolled into a sausage shape and their perception of it after being rolled are two unconnected images. In other words, from the child's point of view, the pouring or rolling are irrelevant. *Irreversibility* also is a factor: It does not occur to the child that the liquid in the taller beaker could be poured back into the original one or that the clay can be rerolled into a ball and therefore must be the same. Again, the child lacks the necessary logical approach.

Using the ideas that underlie Piaget's conservation problems, can you suggest why even adults find magic tricks so interesting to consider?

Evaluating Piaget's Theory

Piaget's view of cognitive development has served as a basis for thinking about the preoperational child, and it has generated a substantial body of research (Beins, 2012). Although his general views have been supported, subsequent research has pointed out that children are probably more competent and their thinking is not as limited as Piaget's view suggests (Bibok, Müller, & Carpendale, 2009; Miller, 2011a).

For example, although preoperational children do tend to be egocentric and preoccupied with their own perspective on things, in some situations they *can* take another person's point of view. Thus, the young child's egocentrism is not absolute but rather reflects a preferred approach to solving most problems.

When Piagetian problems are posed in such a way that they tap into a child's direct experience, they become clear even to young preoperational children. For example, in one classic series of studies, preoperational children who could not solve the mountain problem as previously described were instead asked if a naughty boy could hide in the mountains so that he would not be seen by a police officer who was approaching from the direction across from the table. Although none of the children in the study had ever actually hidden from the police, they had all played hide-and-seek and therefore had direct experience with hiding behind objects. When the mountain problem was posed in this context, preoperational children generally had no difficulty taking the police officer's point of view. Even 3-year-olds were successful at the task when it was described with realistic terms (Hughes & Donaldson, 1979). Young children are also better than Piaget thought at taking other's perspectives in the context of understanding their feelings and intentions (Lillard, 2007; Lillard & Curenton, 1999). Conversely, when Piaget's tasks are described in strictly formal or hypothetical ways, even adults can be easily led to wrong conclusions (McDonald & Stuart-Hamilton, 2003; Winer, Craig, & Weinbaum, 1992).

Why might young children be able to explain how to get from their homes to their schools but not be able to explain how to get from the schools to their homes?

Numerous studies also have shown that preoperational children occasionally *can* attend to more than one dimension at a time and think in terms of how things change rather than only of the beginning and end states—thus, in effect, displaying elements of conservation (Siegler & Ellis, 1996; Sternberg, 2006b). These more complex approaches are not dominant modes of thought for the preoperational child. However, it appears the child's ability to perform complex mental operations is not as strictly limited as Piaget thought. Perhaps not surprisingly, preoperational children also have been shown to be more competent in using numbers than Piaget believed (Baroody, Lai, & Mix, 2006; Flavell, Miller, & Miller, 2002). For example, when asked to solve problems about six or fewer cookies, 3- to 5-year-olds displayed an array of premathematical abilities and concepts (Baroody, 2000). However, young children must gain more advanced reasoning abilities before they can learn to perform the numerical operations required to add, subtract, multiply, and divide (Becker, 1993).

Beyond Piaget: Social Perspectives

Another limitation of Piaget's perspective is its rather narrow focus on the problem-solving aspects of cognitive development. Many contemporary theorists view cognitive developmental processes as also being *social* in nature, and they emphasize the important ways in which others in the child's environment influence the development of the child's thought processes. Rather than seeing children as little scientists, these theorists take a broader perspective in understanding cognitive development. Although they acknowledge that, as Piaget described, children do engage in solitary exploration aimed at making sense of their world, they emphasize that children also develop their cognitive abilities through interactions with more experienced people, such as parents, teachers, and older children.

According to this more social perspective, the ways in which adults demonstrate how to solve problems help children learn to think. In the course of these social interactions, parents and others also pass on society's rules and expectations. When young children help tidy up the home or join in singing folk songs, specific aspects of culture are transmitted from the more experienced members (adults) to the less experienced members (children). Thus, children's participation in routine daily activities provides material both for the development of their cognitive abilities and their social and cultural understanding.

Most theorists today believe that the child's understanding of the world is embedded in cultural knowledge. All cultures initiate children into activities through guided participation, and such interactions with others provide important information and guidance for children as they develop their cognitive abilities. How does this happen?

Vygotsky's Zone of Proximal Development According to Lev Vygotsky (see Chapter 1), children's thinking and social skills develop by participating in activities that are slightly beyond their competence, provided they are given the assistance of others who are more skilled and knowledgeable (Daniels, 2011). As you may recall, Vygotsky emphasized that much of children's cognitive growth takes place through guided participation, in what he called the **zone of proximal development**. The

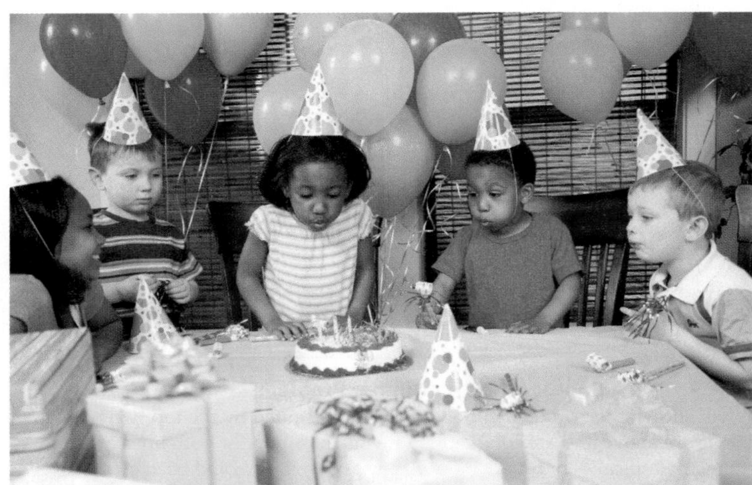

▲ These children have learned birthday rituals through guided participation.

zone of proximal development
Vygotsky's concept that children's cognitive growth develops through participation in activities slightly beyond their competence with the help of adults or older children

Who were the people that served as your most important "guides" during your early childhood years? How did they help you learn?

lower limit of this zone is determined by the child's competence when solving problems alone. However, children often receive help or guidance from adults or children who are further advanced in their thinking. Through coaching, modeling, and instruction, a child can often solve problems that would otherwise be too difficult. The child's ability to solve problems with such assistance establishes the upper limit of the zone. In this way, social forces advance the child's cognitive development.

The way in which adults and others structure learning tasks for children can contribute greatly to the child's understanding if the tasks are presented along with the proper amount of guidance. However, if adults provide too little support, the child cannot develop a correct solution and learning is not advanced. If there is too much help, the children just accept the solution without discovering it themselves or without learning how the problem was solved. The most effective instruction involves **scaffolding**, which is the progressive structuring of tasks by parents or others so that the level of task difficulty is appropriate. The level of support that the child receives changes as the child becomes more competent. The goal of scaffolding is to provide the proper amount of guidance—enough so the child will be able to solve the problem, but not so much that self-discovery is limited.

Do you think that Vygotsky's description of scaffolding also applies in describing how well adults learn difficult material or skills?

Cognitive development unfolds as children experiment with the world around them, learning from others how to structure and solve problems. A particularly important activity for children is social play, which moves them toward more advanced levels of social and cognitive skills (Cohen, 2006; Duncan & Tarulli, 2003), a topic we address later in this chapter. Collaboration with others seems to foster both short-term and long-term learning (Sommerville & Hammond, 2007), both of which help the young child develop more advanced memory strategies.

The Role of Memory

Memory is central to cognitive development. Memory processes, which change rapidly over the first years of life, reach nearly adult capabilities by about age 7 (Gathercole, 1998, 2007), thereby establishing a base on which subsequent cognitive development can be built. To understand how memory processes develop in early childhood, it is useful to consider the structure of memory.

Memory Processes: A Brief Overview The *information-processing perspective* provides a useful way to understand how memory works (Atkinson & Shiffrin, 1971; Bjorklund, 2004; Halford & Andrews, 2011; Mayer, 2012; Schneider, 2011). According to this view, human memory is conceptualized as operating much like a computer, with information being brought into the memory system, processed, and then stored for later retrieval and use. As information enters the memory system, it is *encoded* (categorized) in a meaningful way. Much of this encoding takes place in *working memory,* which is an important component of *short-term memory*. When we are actively thinking about something, we are using this working part of our memory system. Information that is important enough to be retained is stored in *long-term memory,* which involves creating structural changes in the brain that most likely involve the creation of new *synapses,* which are the connections among neurons (Gazzaniga, 2009). Failure to remember can result from disruptions at any point in the information-processing system: The information may never have been attended to or encoded; it may not have been stored in long-term memory; or it may be in storage but we are unable to locate and retrieve it, perhaps owing to inefficient strategies for remembering. The development of memory in childhood requires learning effective strategies for encoding new information into usable formats and for retrieving the stored information.

Recognition and Recall Studies of children's memory skills in early childhood have often focused on two different types of information retrieval: recognition and recall. **Recognition** refers to the ability to correctly identify objects or situations previously experienced when they appear again. For example, children may recognize a picture or a person they have seen before, although they may not be able to tell us much about the memory. **Recall** refers to the ability to retrieve stored information and memories with or without cues or prompts. For example, a child might be asked to tell a story from memory.

Assuming that the information to be remembered has been stored in long-term memory, there still can be difficulties in retrieval. Recall tasks generally are much harder than are recognition tasks, both for children and for adults (Moulin, 2011; Radvansky, 2011). For example, in one classic study that compared recall versus recognition performance of younger and older children, children were given two different types of problems to solve. In the recognition task where many objects were shown only once to children between the ages of 2 and 5, even the youngest children could correctly point to 81% of the objects as having been seen before; the older children recognized 92% of the objects. However, when children between the ages of 2 and 4 were asked to recall objects by naming them, 3-year-olds could name only 22% of the items and 4-year-olds only 40% (Schneider & Bjorklund, 1998). Memory does improve in early childhood, however. For example, subsequent research also has shown that, compared to older children, younger

scaffolding
The progressive structuring of tasks by parents or others so that the level of task difficulty is appropriate

recognition
The ability to correctly identify objects or situations previously experienced when they appear again

recall
The ability to retrieve stored information and memories with or without cues or prompts

children can be more easily lured away from correct recognitions by misleading questions (Myers, et al., 2003; Principe, Guilliano, & Root, 2008). Age-related differences in memory continues to be a topic of considerable research interest (e.g., Moulin & Gathercole, 2008; Schneider, 2011).

Developing Memory Strategies It generally has been assumed that young children's difficulties with recall are attributable to poor *strategies* for encoding and retrieval (Schneider, 2011; Shing, Werkle-Bergner, Li, & Lindenberger, 2008). In early childhood, children do not spontaneously organize or mentally rehearse information in the way that older children and adults do; therefore, their encoding is not as effective. For example, if you ask an adult to memorize a list of words, such as *cat, chair, airplane, dog, desk,* and *car,* the adult automatically classifies the items as *animals, furniture,* and *vehicles* and rehearses the items within each category; young children do not.

Infants and young children do, however, use some memory strategies (DeLoache, 2011). In one study, 18- to 24-month-old toddlers watched an experimenter hide a Big Bird doll under a pillow, and they were told to remember where Big Bird had been hidden because they would later be asked where it was. The experimenter then distracted the children with other toys for several minutes. During the delay, the children frequently interrupted their play to talk about Big Bird, point at the hiding place, stand near it, or even attempt to retrieve Big Bird, clearly indicating that they were trying to remember its location (DeLoache, Cassidy, & Brown, 1985). Indeed, in a longitudinal study of memory conducted in Germany, the two critical elements that determined children's memory development were their memory capacity and their ability to use multiple strategies to help them remember (Kron-Sperl, Schneider, & Hasselhorn, 2008).

Can children be taught more efficient strategies for remembering information? Overall, studies demonstrate that young children *can* learn cognitive skills beyond their current repertoire, but many of these prescribed learning strategies do not produce long-term results. Those learning strategies that *do* appear to enhance children's ability to remember often involve organizing information according to spatial, rather than concept-related, cues (Hund & Naroleski, 2008; Schneider & Bjorklund, 1998). Thus, a task that involves recalling items according to where they are stored in the home (things in my toy box or things in the kitchen) would likely be more effective than one based on categorical information (items of clothing or kitchen appliances). In addition, when children are actively involved in a memory task, they remember better. When researchers compared a group of children who were asked to *remember* toys to another group who were asked to *play with* the toys, the children involved in active play demonstrated better memory (Newman, 1990). Verbalizing thoughts also improves memory. In a study of problem solving, 4- and 5-year-olds were asked to solve classification problems and were prompted to either explain their correct solutions to their mothers or to themselves, or to repeat the solutions. Results showed that explaining the solutions improved children's ability to remember them and apply them again when solving problems later, and explaining to Mom was the most effective memory strategy (Rittle-Johnson, Saylor, & Swygert, 2008). Memory strategies improve steadily during the preschool years (Bjorklund, Dukes, & Brown, 2009), and memory abilities are closely related to language ability, a topic we discuss later in this chapter.

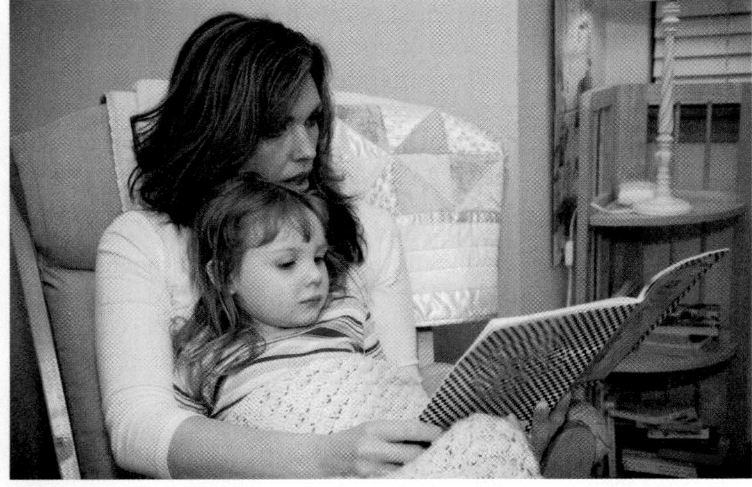

▲ Young children develop scripts for routine events. Here, reading a story is part of this child's nap time ritual.

Memory for Scripts Memories organized according to the sequence in which events occur are also easier for children to remember. In fact, even young children can remember information that is ordered *temporally*—that is, in a time-based sequence (Atance & Hanson, 2011). For example, young children in one study were asked to describe how they had made objects from clay 2 weeks earlier (Smith, Ratner, & Hobart, 1987). When the children were given the opportunity to make the same objects again, they could describe how they had worked step by step. Apparently, young children can organize and remember sequences of actions even after a single experience with them. However, younger children remember events only in the order in which they actually occurred: Only when young children become extremely familiar with an event can they reverse the order of steps.

What kind of strategy do children use in forming time-sequenced memories? It appears that children develop *scripts* for routine events, such as what happens at dinner time, what happens when they go to preschool, and so forth (Hudson & Mayhew, 2009). These scripts, which serve as lists for what happens first, second, and so forth, provide a useful scheme for remembering time-sequenced events. Indeed, scripts may be the young child's most powerful mental tool for understanding the world (Flavell, Miller, & Miller, 2002). Scripts for routine activities can be quite rigid at first, for example, a child's bedtime ritual. They are learned as a complex whole, and they can only be modified gradually so that variations or omitted items in the ritual do not cause distress. These scripts become "stories about me in my world" and are full of the rules and roles of one's family, religion, and culture.

In general, early childhood is a period during which cognitive skills—such as memory, problem solving, and thinking—develop rapidly. Considering the differences between a 2-year-old who is still in diapers and speaking in two- or three-word sentences, and a 6-year-old who is perhaps in kindergarten and responding to a variety of social and cognitive demands, it becomes clear how much intellectual growth takes place in these few years. The development of cognitive skills is reflected in the development of language, which is the topic we explore in the next section of this chapter.

REVIEW THE FACTS 6-3

1. Absorbing new knowledge into an already formed cognitive structure is called ___________; adjusting the structure in order to incorporate the new information is called ___________.
2. When a child is unable to understand another person's point of view, we refer to this as __________.
3. If a child uses a bucket as a hat, this behavior demonstrates the idea of _____________.
4. Suppose a 4-year-old watches you roll two pieces of clay into equal-size balls. You ask him if the balls have the same amount of clay. He says they do. Now you ask him to flatten one ball, and again ask him if the balls have the same amount of clay. What answer would you expect? Why?
5. For Vygotsky, the difference between a child's ability to solve a task without assistance and the child's ability to solve it with some mentoring is called ___________.
6. When we are actively thinking about something, the part of our memory we are using is
   a. encoding memory. b. long-term memory.
   c. implicit memory. d. short-term memory.

Practice on **MyDevelopmentLab**

LANGUAGE DEVELOPMENT

By the age of 2, children have already developed a small but useful vocabulary, which they employ by using systematic linguistic rules to communicate (see Chapter 4). In early childhood, the use of language explodes, as children rapidly expand their vocabularies, their use of grammatical forms, and their understanding of language as a sociocultural activity (Tomasello, 2011).

Words and Concepts

As you may recall (see Chapter 4), the first words learned in infancy usually are names for common objects *(daddy* and *doggie)* and actions *(Uh-oh* and *bye).* Throughout early childhood, children's vocabulary explodes. By age 3, most children can use 900 to 1,000 words; by age 6, most children have a productive vocabulary of 2,600 words and can understand more than 20,000 (Owens, 2008). Beginning at about 18 months of age, children learn an average of about nine new words a day; the variety of the different types of words learned expands as well (Hoover, Sterling, & Storkel, 2011).

In particular, early childhood is the period in which children acquire the idea that words can be used to express *concepts,* or ideas, and their vocabularies develop accordingly. However, young children's understanding of concepts is often incomplete. For example, they often understand one concept, such as *more,* much earlier than they know the word or the concept that contrasts with it, such as *less.* A 3-year-old may easily be able to tell you which dish has more candy but not which dish has less.

Oftentimes, young children want to say things but do not know the right word, so they invent a word. They use nouns in place of verbs, as in "Mommy, pencil it" for "Mommy, write it." At least through age 3, children also have difficulty with pronouns. For example, a child might say, "Us need to take a nap." Even when corrected, such errors persist until age 4 or 5, and sometimes longer.

Expanding Grammar

As young children expand their vocabularies and learn to use words to express concepts, they also become much more proficient in combining words into sentences, so that by the end of early childhood their speech is nearly indistinguishable from that of an adult. As we saw in Chapter 4, much of early language development is universal across cultures, and this consistency extends through early childhood as well. For example, regardless of their specific language, children learn the rules of grammar in an orderly sequence (see Table 6-6), and they

Table 6-6 Stages of Grammar Acquisition

Stage	Description
1	• Young children speak in two-word utterances, referred to as *telegraphic speech.* • Children's use of words conforms to simple rules. • For example, if the child uses the word order, "Mommy! Up!" the child will not reverse the order of the words and say "Up! Mommy!"
2	• Sentences become somewhat longer. • Children begin to learn the *rules* of speech (e.g., past tense conveyed by adding *-ed* and plural conveyed by adding an *-s*).
3	• Sentences become more elaborate. • Grammar becomes more correct, as exceptions to rules are learned *(went,* not *goed* or *mice,* not *mouses).* • Young children do not understand the passive voice and become confused by sentences such as "The boy is helped by the girl," failing to see that the girl is the actor.
4 and 5	• Language use continues to develop and becomes more sophisticated, employing clauses and conveying complex and multiple ideas. • By age 4 1/2, children have a good grasp of most syntax, although refinement continues.

SOURCE: Based on *A first language: The early stages*, by R. Brown, 1973, Cambridge, MA: Harvard University Press.

◀ Often young children talk out loud while they work or play. Sometimes the talk is pretend dialogue, but more often it fulfills other functions.

master certain skills and rules before others (Bloom, 1998; Harley, 2008).

In fact, it appears that children extract the rules of grammar through an active process by listening to the speech of others rather than by being explicitly taught. Evidence for this conclusion comes from studies that examine how children's speech patterns change in early childhood. Although early on children correctly imitate the sentence patterns they hear in their language, at about age 3 or 4, they begin to **overregularize** their use of certain language rules and apply the rules they are learning to cases that should be treated as exceptions. For example, in English, most verbs are expressed in past tense by adding an *-ed* (e.g., play/played), and most nouns are made plural by adding an *-s* to the end of words (e.g., bug/bugs). As children begin to learn these grammatical patterns, they often overregularize grammar rules to all cases, and only later in their language development do they learn the exceptions. Thus, although their earliest usage of such words is correct, as they learn rules, they begin to use words like *goed* instead of *went*, *breaked* instead of *broke*, or *foots* instead of *feet*. As any parent knows, this tendency to overregularize is quite resistant to correction by parents and teachers. Later, as children become more skilled with language, these incorrect constructions are replaced with their correct forms (Jaswal, McKercher, & Vanderborght, 2008; Marcus, 1996).

Mastering the Subtleties of Speech

Of course, there is much more to communication than putting words together correctly into sentences. Language mirrors cognitive development, and vice versa. Thus, as children learn to talk, they also learn how to think about themselves and their world. One way in which this two-way interaction of language and cognition can be seen is by examining what psychologists call **private speech**, which is the language we use when we talk to ourselves.

Private Speech All people, young and old, talk to themselves. However, young children engage in private speech often, aloud, and in public settings. In fact, private speech comprises a large amount of their talking: Children between the ages of 4 and 8 have been observed talking to themselves about 20% of the time in schools that allow it (Berk, 1994b). Private speech can help children solve problems more effectively; children skilled in private speech generally have better social skills and less negative behavior (Winsler, et al., 2003) and are more creative (Daugherty & White, 2008).

Do you think the private speech of adults serves the same purposes as the private speech of children? Why or why not?

Consider Jamal's private speech when putting a puzzle together while alone in his room: "This piece doesn't fit. Where's a round one? No, it doesn't. It's too big. This one is small. . . ." What purpose does private speech serve? Vygotsky (1934/1987) observed that private speech may help develop inner thought and self-direction. As such, it provides a means by which the child can make the transition from early speech, which often involves responding to adult commands, to inner speech, and the ability to think symbolically using words. Words come to represent objects, actions, and ideas; and private speech is a means of practicing how words and the things they represent are linked, as symbolic thinking develops. Private speech thus corresponds to the developing thought processes in a child's mind (Femyhough, 2009; Feigenbaum, 2009).

Public Speech and Pragmatics Language, of course, serves a public function as well; it is the primary means by which people communicate. The use of language as a system of communication also develops during early childhood. If you listen to younger children's conversations with one another, for instance, one of the first things you will notice is that their conversations do not run smoothly. Very young children's conversations are often **collective monologues**—two children appear to take turns speaking to each other, but they may be talking about entirely different, unrelated subjects. Consider the following example:

Molly: Look at my dolly. She's pretty.

Gina: I think peanut butter sandwiches are yummy.

Molly: I think she needs a hat.

Gina: I like jelly on my sandwiches, too.

Molly: Let's go over there and play house.

Collective monologues represent children's attempts to learn how to speak to others, and learning to take turns is an

overregularize
To incorrectly generalize language rules to cases that are exceptions; typically done by preschool children who are rapidly expanding their vocabularies

private speech
Talking aloud to oneself

collective monologues
Children's conversations that include taking turns talking but not necessarily about the same topic

important aspect of **pragmatics**, the social and cultural aspects of language.

Pragmatics involves much more than taking turns, of course. Children must also learn to adjust their conversations to reduce social friction, conflict, and embarrassment. Adjustment means using courtesy markers, such as *please* and *thank you*, paying attention, and selecting suitable topics and the proper forms of address and phrasing. It also means being aware of the social status of the other person. For example, children learn to talk in one way to younger children, in another way to their peers, and in still another way to older children or adults.

Cross-Cultural Perspectives of the Pragmatics of Speech Cross-cultural research has shown that the pragmatics of speech differs throughout the world in accord with the cultural values that parents communicate to their children. For example, researchers studying differences between child-rearing practices in Germany and the United States noted that German parents tended to speak to their children in more authoritative, dominating ways than did the U.S. parents. The U.S. parents focused more on satisfying their children's desires and intentions. The societal values that underlie these tendencies were communicated, in part, with modal verbs. Verbs such as *must, may, might, can, could,* and *should* express cultural concepts such as necessity, possibility, obligation, and permission. Thus, German mothers focused more on necessity ("You will have to tell me what you want") and obligation ("You must pick up your toys"). In contrast, the U.S. mothers emphasized intention ("I'm going to take you to the movies") and possibility ("That might happen"). Young children then adopt such tendencies in their own speech (Shatz, 1991).

Language, of course, includes more than just words; much of what we communicate to others is the result of the intonation patterns we create with the sound of our voice and the nonverbal gestures we use as we speak. Gestures, for example, are especially important in conveying information about spatial relationships among objects. Gestures also appear to be linked to language development in general ways. For example, children who are born deaf develop a system of communication that relies on gestures, even if there is no sign language system taught to them (Goldin-Meadow, 2011). Thus, gesturing seems to be a biologically programmed form of language development, as is the development of spoken language. Even very young children learn to use gestures to communicate with their parents—often before they learn the words they need to communicate ideas (Goldin-Meadow, 2009). For example, a hungry 10-month old may point at her bottle, saying "Ah-Ah-Ah!" to communicate that she wants to eat.

Cross-cultural variations exist in how children learn these nonword components of language, just as they do in speech. Compare, for example, Turkish and English: To describe the path of two moving objects, English speakers use a single word and a single gesture; Turkish speakers use two separate words and two separate gestures. To investigate how children acquire nonverbal gestures, a study compared children ages 3, 5, and 9 who were raised in English-speaking environments with children of the same ages raised in Turkish-speaking environments (Özyürek, et al., 2008). Each child was shown a brief video clip of two moving objects and then was asked to describe the motion of the objects in words while being videotaped. When researchers analyzed results, an interesting pattern emerged: At all ages tested, children's speech followed that of adults in their culture, indicating that grammatical rules had been learned correctly by age 3. However, children at ages 3 and 5 used the same single gesture, despite differences in adult gesturing in these two cultures. Culture-specific patterns of gesturing appeared only later in development at age 9. Results such as these suggest that language development is a complex process that occurs sequentially throughout childhood and that speech shapes other aspects of development, such as the use of gestures (Tomasello, 2011).

The Influence of Parents' Language Use

Every culture transmits language to its children, and, as the studies cited previously make apparent, parents typically provide the earliest and most important guidance in a young child's development of language. When parents speak with their children, they communicate far more than words, sentences, and syntax. They demonstrate how thoughts are expressed and how ideas are exchanged. They teach the child about categories and symbols, about how to translate the complexities of the world into ideas and words, and about how their cultural standards are interpreted and applied.

These conceptual tools serve as a scaffold for the child to use in understanding the world. For example, studies have shown that reading picture books to children can facilitate language learning (Hood, Conlon, & Andrews, 2008). This is especially true when parents ask open-ended questions that encourage the child to expand the story and when they respond appropriately to the child's attempts to answer the questions, thereby facilitating conceptual understanding (Bracken & Fischel, 2008; Lonigan, 2006).

Language and Gender Parents also use language as a tool to help their children develop a sense of self and a conception of how they should relate to other people. Gender is a case in point. Assumptions about gender are often culturally embedded in parents' thinking, which causes them to talk differently to male and female children (Hoff, 2009). Why might this be?

In a now-classic study (O'Brien & Nagle, 1987), researchers analyzed the language used by mothers and fathers while playing

Can you think of toys that either encourage or discourage language practice? Do you think that language-encouraging toys are more commonly preferred by girls than boys?

pragmatics
The social and cultural aspects of language use

Watch *Music Is/Is Not A Universal Language: Steven Demorest and Steven Morrison* on **MyDevelopmentLab**

with their toddlers, using toys such as vehicles or dolls. Playing with dolls elicited more verbal interaction, whereas playing with vehicles involved little talking—regardless of whether the parents were playing with their daughters or their sons. Thus, children who play with dolls may have more opportunities to learn and practice language than do children who play with other toys. Play with gender-stereotyped toys emerges at about age 2, which is the same time that language learning accelerates. Thus, girls may experience early language environments that are more sophisticated, and this may partly explain why girls develop verbal skills somewhat ahead of boys.

Multicultural Aspects of Language Development

As we have seen, social forces exert a strong influence on language development. Although many children grow up within a single, more-or-less homogeneous cultural tradition, others are raised in multicultural environments, which often include exposure to more than one language system. What effect does being raised in such a multicultural setting have on language development? How do children raised in bilingual environments—where they must learn two languages—progress?

Bilingualism Language is not only a means of communication; it is also a symbol of social or group identity. As such, individuals who learn two or more languages are regarded differently, depending on the values their cultures attach to bilingualism. As you would guess, the status of bilingualism in different nations is strongly affected by issues of social class and political power. In Europe, for example, bilingualism is associated with being an educated, cultured citizen of the world. In the United States, bilingualism is more often associated with first- or second-generation immigrant status, which is not always viewed positively by the majority. Although cultural diversity in the United States has become more widely accepted, the millions of U.S. children growing up in bilingual environments still experience difficulty in being integrated into English-only settings, such as in the school classroom. How do children manage when they learn two languages rather than one?

Learning two languages during infancy and early childhood would appear to be a complex task: two systems of rules, two sets of vocabulary, and different pronunciations. However, most children who are bilingual in their earliest years show little confusion between the rules of the two languages by age 3 (e.g., Nicoladis, 1999, 2008; García & Náñez, 2011b), although they sometimes use words from the two languages interchangeably. It is also noteworthy that speaking a native language at home and a second language at school apparently does not interfere with either language—if anything, it improves a child's usage and grasp of both (Kovelman, Baker, & Petitto, 2008; Winsler, Díaz, Espinosa, & Rodriguez, 1999). Thus, the cognitive demand of learning two languages appears manageable for most young children, and this is especially true if each language is used in a different context and by different speakers.

Does learning two languages during early childhood interfere with other aspects of a child's cognitive development? Early studies in the United States and the United Kingdom suggested that learning two languages at too young an age could be detrimental to cognitive development. In this older research, bilingual children generally scored lower on standardized tests than did monolingual English-speaking children. However, most of these studies did not take into account the socioeconomic level of either the children or their parents. In other words, the scores of the bilingual children were likely lower due to other reasons, such as poverty, poor schooling, or a lack of familiarity with their new culture. Early studies also tended to focus on language outcomes in middle childhood, often ignoring the way in which early language development proceeded in monolingual versus bilingual environments.

Taking a lifespan view, a more complete explanation of language development in bilingual environments comes into focus. Using modern brain-scanning techniques, research shows that young babies do not differentiate between words spoken in one versus another language. For example, at age 6 to 9 months, bilingual infants responded to both Spanish and English words with the same pattern of brain responses. However, by 10 to 12 months of age, these same babies were able to distinguish between Spanish versus English words, exhibiting different neurological response patterns for words according to language (Garcia-Sierra, et al., 2011). Thus, it does appear that the brains of bilingual infants are programmed somewhat differently than are those of infants exposed to only one language.

Perhaps the important question is this: Is being raised in a bilingual environment an advantage or disadvantage when it comes to early language learning? The answer depends on how one looks at this question. For example, at about age 1, when babies begin to use words, it appears that bilingual babies develop language more slowly than monolingual babies, and use fewer words. This is, in fact, the case if one looks only at the number of words acquired within a particular language, for example, in English. However, when one combines the number of English and non-English words together, it is clear that the *total*

▲ Children from two or more different heritage languages often start elementary school together in the same class.The challenge is to find a mode of instruction that maximizes each child's oral and written language development, self-respect, and academic progress.

vocabulary of these bilingual children matches that of monolingual children (Hoff, et al., 2012). Later in childhood, a wide variety of findings is obtained, with some studies showing definite advantages in language development associated with bilingualism (e.g., Barac & Bialystok, 2012; Bialysok, Luk, Peets, & Yang, 2010; Okanda, Moriguchi, & Itakura, 2010) and others showing a more mixed pattern of results (e.g., Mancilla-Marinez & Lesaux, 2011). In part, these different results probably reflect different approaches to the education of children for whom the language taught in school (or spoken by the majority culture) is not their first language.

Today, most research supports the conclusion that linguistically, culturally, and probably cognitively, it is often an advantage to grow up bilingual (Bialystok, 2007, 2011). On each count, children are exposed to different ways of thinking about and doing things that may later make them more flexible and therefore more adaptive to our changing world. In addition, with the globalization of our world, the ability to speak more than one language can be a powerful asset later in life, opening doors not only to new ways of thinking but also to jobs and other cultural opportunities (García & Núñez, 2011a). Given the dramatically increasing numbers of non-English-speaking children entering schools in the United States, considerable attention at the national level is being directed at developing effective programs to help these children successfully assimilate (e.g., de Groot, 2011; García, 2011; García & Náñez, 2011c). Indeed, a wide variety of educational approaches to accommodate nonnative language speakers exists, and research is helping policy makers better understand which approaches are most successful in meeting the needs of bilingual children (see the box Changing Perspective: Bilingual Kindergarten and Play for information about one such program).

REVIEW THE FACTS 6-4

1. At age 4, LaNae begins to say she "goed to the store," although at age 3 she used the correct verb, *went*. This is an example of __________.
2. The social and cultural aspects of language are called __________.
3. *Jackie*: I like to comb my dolly's hair.

   Julia: I think baking cookies is best.

   Jackie: My dolly's hair is black.

   Julia: Chocolate chips are yummy.

   This exchange is best described as an example of

   a. overregularization.
   b. pragmatics.
   c. a script.
   d. a collective monologue.
4. According to the text, why might girls develop verbal skills earlier than boys?
5. When a child learns two languages rather than one, we refer to the child as ___________.

Practice on **MyDevelopmentLab**

Watch *Bilingual Family* on **MyDevelopmentLab**

PLAY AND LEARNING

Play, according to Piaget, is the child's work. Every aspect of development during early childhood is enhanced through play. Play is children's unique way of experiencing the world and of practicing and improving their skills, and it is found in all cultures.

Do you think adults, like children, learn important skills through activities we would define as play? What might these skills and activities be?

Play is the work of childhood because it occupies such a central role in the young child's development. It promotes the growth of sensory–perceptual capabilities and physical skills while providing endless opportunities to exercise and expand intellectual skills. Furthermore, play is different from any other kind of activity. By its very nature, it is not directed toward goals; rather, it is intrinsically rewarding. Play is defined as behavior that is engaged in simply for pleasure, has no purpose other than itself, is chosen by the player or players, requires players to be actively engaged, and is related to other areas of life. Play promotes social development and enhances creativity. In other words, play truly is developmental business.

Play and Cognitive Development

Play takes many forms (see Table 6-7) and promotes cognitive development in many ways. One way preoperational children use play is to learn about their physical surroundings. Children

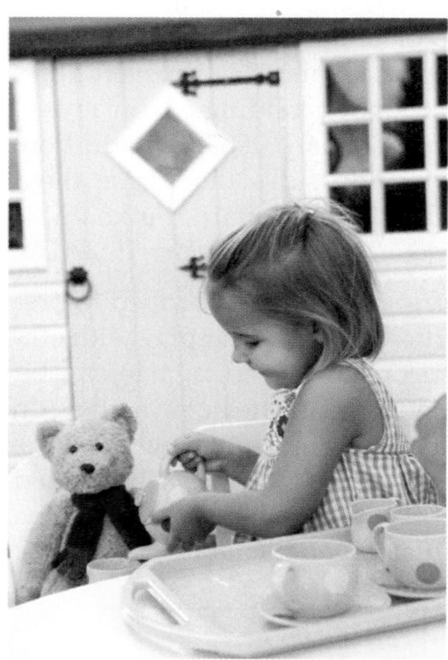

This girl is playing pretend; here, she is pouring pretend tea for her favorite stuffed bear. Through play, children can practice many skills such as turn-taking, social courtesy, and appropriate conversation.

Table 6-7 Kinds of Play

Type of play	Description	Examples
Sensory pleasure	Sensory experience in and of itself without another goal, which teaches children essential facts about their bodies and the environment	• Early: splashing water, banging pots • Later: plucking flower petals to experience their form and smell
Play with motion	Motor activity enjoyed for its own sake, which is often exciting and also provides practice in body coordination	• Early: rocking, blowing bubbles with saliva • Later: running, jumping, twirling, and spinning
Rough-and-tumble play	Play provides exercise and release of energy, also helps children learn how to handle their feelings, control impulses, and distinguish between pretend and real; more common in boys than girls	• Wrestling, pushing, and mock fighting that is done for fun with no intent for injury
Play with language	Manipulation of sounds, patterns, and the meanings of language without the intent to communicate; aim may be to entertain others; sometimes used to create rituals and thereby control experiences	• Early: repeating sounds, such as "ba-ba-ba-ba-ba" • Later: rhyming, creating words
Dramatic play and modeling	Imitation of whole patterns of behavior; includes fantasy and new ways of interacting and use of fantasy and imagination	• Pretending, or acting out or imitating different roles (e.g., playing teacher or truck driver)
Games, rituals, and competitive play	Play involves cooperation with others and with following rules that define appropriate behavior; contributes to the development of learning rules, understanding cause-and-effect and consequences of various actions, and learning about winning and losing	• Playing simple games with others, such as hide-and-seek or duck, duck, goose

also use dramatic play to master symbolic representation and increase their social knowledge, thereby reducing their self-centered orientation. In many other ways as well, play relates to cognitive abilities, both reflecting a child's current state of development and preparing the child for new and more advanced capabilities to come.

Exploring Physical Objects When young children play with physical objects—sand, stones, and water, for example—they learn the properties and physical laws that govern these objects. When playing in sand, a child learns that different objects leave different marks. When bouncing a ball, a child learns that throwing the ball harder will make it bounce higher. By engaging in constructive play, children acquire bits of information that they use to build their knowledge. Greater knowledge, in turn, gives them increasingly higher levels of understanding and competence. Gradually, they learn to compare and classify events and objects, and they develop a better understanding of concepts—such as size, shape, and texture (Gelman, 2007). In addition, through active play, children develop skills that make them feel physically confident and self-assured (Lillard, Pinkham, & Smith, 2011; Mathieson & Banerjee, 2010; Sluss & Jarrett, 2007).

Play and Egocentrism The *egocentrism* that Piaget ascribed to preoperational children is particularly evident in their play with others. Two-year-olds will watch other children and seem interested in them, but they usually will not approach them. If they do approach, the interaction typically centers on playing with the same toy or object—not with the other child. Children 2 years old and younger may appear to be playing together, but most often they are playing out separate fantasies independently, engaging in what some people call **parallel play**, to indicate that there is little social interaction between participants, although they are in proximity to each other. As we saw earlier, even their conversations often track on quite separate topics.

Between their second and third year, however, children's play begins to reflect greater social maturity (Ensor & Hughes, 2008). The play of 3-year-olds, for example, shows a better understanding of others' views than is seen at age 2; this, in turn, allows children to be better at role-playing games. By age 3 or 4, as children become less egocentric, they are better able to cooperate in play, and they begin to understand how to relate to others. For example, in one early study (Shatz & Gelman, 1973), researchers asked 4-year-olds to describe to 2-year-olds how a specific toy worked. Even 4-year-olds understood the need to address younger children in simpler terms. The researchers found that 4-year-olds spoke slowly; they used short sentences; they employed many attention-getting words, such as *look* and *here;* and they frequently repeated the child's name. Four-year-olds did not speak to older children or adults in the same manner, indicating that they were able to understand the differing perspectives of others.

How is the decline in children's egocentrism related to their increasing capacity for social play?

As with all behaviors, however, social maturity is relative. At the age of 3, or even at the age of 4, children can still be very stubborn and negative, and their general framework of understanding remains quite egocentric. However, other people are more important to 3-year-olds than they were a year earlier; therefore,

Watch *Play in Early Childhood* on **MyDevelopmentLab**

parallel play
The play typically engaged in by 2-year-olds, which is characterized by each child playing independently, although in proximity to each other

CHANGING PERSPECTIVES

Bilingual Kindergarten and Play

It is not easy to attend a school where everyone speaks another language. Spanish-speaking children in a U.S. school, where English is the dominant language, face a somewhat foreign environment. Furthermore, their knowledge, as mediated through another language, is not always valued by teachers or by peers. There is much debate in the field of education as to how best to help children learn English as a second language quickly and effectively, but in a fashion that enhances the child's identity and sense of competence. Several *bilingual education* models currently are being used (García & Núñez, 2011c). One, which often is called an *inclusion* or *immersion* model, involves classes taught exclusively in English. In this model, non-English-speaking children are immersed in the majority language, with the idea that they will eventually learn it out of necessity. Another model involves teaching most course content in the children's native language, but includes one class period a day of *English as a Second Language* instruction. This approach preserves much of the native language and original culture of the students while they learn the new language of the majority culture.

A new model that may offer an even more successful approach takes a different view: Teach children in their own language but create ample opportunities for different language groups to *interact,* which requires all members of the class to learn a second language (Alanis & Rodriguez, 2008; DePalma, 2010; Garcia, 2009). Let's take a closer look at how such a *two-way bilingual education* approach has worked in a kindergarten classroom comprised of roughly equal numbers of Spanish- and English-speaking children (Norbis, 2004).

An important aspect of two-way bilingual education is that classes are taught in both languages. In this particular class, one teacher taught in English and another in Spanish, although translations to the other language frequently were provided. As children became more fluent in their second language, they were encouraged to sit with that group, thereby strengthening their second-language skills. Another important feature was that although units were taught in both languages, all students learned vocabulary for each unit in *both* languages, and special events—such as films, class guests, field trips, and other activities—required some knowledge of both languages.

Especially important was the opportunity for Spanish- and English-speaking children to play together, which was encouraged through the creation of a popular *dramatic play center*, where each child was assigned to a mixed-language, mixed-culture group of five to six children for 20 to 30 minutes each day. In this center, children could informally develop scenarios using their new vocabulary, act out roles, and construct their group stories. The center had costumes, furniture, and props that changed depending on the current unit of study. In addition, the children made many of the props. Although most of the dramatic play took place in English, which was the dominant language in the school and community, no teacher mandated this rule.

An example of how these mixed-language, mixed-culture play groups evolved is instructive. In April, during the transportation unit, the children in the class made a giant airplane and named it Rainbow Airlines. They made tickets, sold them, and collected them. Their dramatic play with the airplane lasted nearly 3 weeks, allowing a lot of time for informal language practice and for changing roles and events. Usually this plane traveled back and forth to Puerto Rico, a destination that many of these children knew something about. Children, of course, learned more than a second language in their make-believe play—they also brought what they knew from their experiences in the broader culture to the play scene. Consider the transcript from Flight 002, where Carlos, Sam, and Ty jockey for the powerful roles of pilot and copilot and try to exclude Yandra from a position in the cockpit.

Carlos: Hurry up, the plane is going up!

Carlos: Bring a chair. (looks at Sam; Sam does not move, but Yandra brings a chair.)

Carlos: No, you can't. (to Yandra)

Carlos: But you can't, you can't! (to Yandra)

Carlos: This is three persons! (Carlos now is physically pushing Yandra from the cockpit area.)

Ty: We are taking off. We are blasting off, without you. (to Yandra)

Yandra: YOU DON'T MAKE THE RULES! (shouting) GET OUT OF HERE!

Ty: I make the rules.

Carlos: I make the rules and say this plane CRASHED.

Carlos has learned enough English to compete quite successfully in this drama and wins the support of Ty, an English-dominant child who often has the leading role in a scene. Yandra, however, is not to be denied. She attempts to be a copilot by taking some headphones, a realistic prop. Later, she takes some money and makes an announcement.

Yandra: I AM A POLICEMAN. I AM A POLICEWOMAN. (and then, as a policewoman, she orders) Drop your stuff.

From this example, we see that the children have learned to interact in English, which is a notable accomplishment in any bilingual kindergarten classroom. Children here learn language in order to use it for effective communication to achieve their goals. We also see that children connect play, language, culture, and their own desires and bring all of these together at the same time. Learning, thus, occurs in a rich and complex context. Since play provides such critically important experiences during development in early childhood, educational programs such as the one described here benefit when learning goals are incorporated with children's natural affinity for play.

---

beginning at about age 3, children seek out more social interaction (see the box Try This! Watching Young Children Play).

Dramatic Play and Social Knowledge Older preoperational children test their social knowledge in **dramatic play**, which develops at about age 3 or 4 but begins in earnest at about age 4. Through imitation, pretending, and role playing, dramatic play promotes the growth of symbolic representation. It also enables children to project themselves into other personalities, experiment with different roles, and experience a broader range of thought and feeling, all of which contribute to expanding the child's knowledge and cognitive abilities (Lillard, Pinkham, & Smith, 2011).

As you might expect, there appears to be a relationship between children's sophistication with dramatic play and their

dramatic play
Play that develops at about age 3 or 4 that is characterized by meaningful interactions among children, often including imitation, pretending, and role playing

TRY THIS!

Watching Young Children Play

Between the ages of 2 and 6, the way that young children play together changes dramatically. To observe how children's cognitive and social skills develop through play, try this activity. Go to a place where young children play. This might be a preschool playground, the play section of a shopping mall, or a play group at a parent's house. Depending on the setting, you might want to let the adults in charge know that you are a college student working on a research activity, so they don't become concerned about a stranger watching their children play.

Observe the play of children you judge to be 2 or 3 years old. Record how many times they speak to another child around them. How many times do they talk to no one in particular? How many times do they share or interact with another child of a similar age?

Repeat your observations for children 4 or 5 years old.

Reflect on What You Observed

Did the younger children engage in parallel play, as defined in the text? What aspects of their play would be considered parallel rather than truly social? Did they engage in social play? If so, how? Did the older children engage in parallel play? Did they interact in more social ways with other children? If they did, in what kinds of activities did they interact? Did they communicate more? If so, about what? Did you observe any dramatic play? What kinds of behaviors did you see that fit the description of dramatic play outlined in the text?

Consider the Issues

In thinking about how younger and older children play, in what ways do you think their language skills might have limited their ability to play together? Did you see evidence of egocentrism? Do you think their play was limited by the cognitive development or by their motor skills? What evidence did you see in the play activities you observed that supports the idea that different developmental systems interact with each other in the process of playing?

---

ability to make distinctions between appearance and reality. Children who have had lots of practice with dramatic play at ages 3 and 4 are better able to understand that objects can look like something else. They also are better able to understand someone else's perspective or feelings (Flavell, Flavell, & Green, 2001; Kavanaugh, 2006; refer to the box Current Issues: A Theory of Mind earlier in the chapter).

In general, children who engage in higher levels of dramatic play are more socially competent and more popular with their peers. In contrast, children who spend more time in parallel play are not only less socially competent, but also more likely to engage in overall problem behaviors (Newton & Jenvey, 2011). The value of dramatic play is substantial, both in terms of personal development and also in school achievement. In particular, social play has been positively linked to reading ability and other literacy skills (Fleer, 2011; Roskos, Christie, Widman, & Holding, 2010), indicating that socially skilled children also do better in school. Of course, it is difficult to interpret the meaning of such results, as so many different factors are involved. Nevertheless, results such as these suggest a variety of approaches. For example, preschools can help young children prepare for the educational demands of grade school by helping them develop the prerequisite skills that are needed for successful social interactions, such as sharing, listening, not interrupting, identifying feelings and emotions, following directions, and so forth (Reddy, 2012). Many of these lessons can occur during supervised but relatively unstructured play. Additionally, as pressure increases for "outcomes-based" learning results in science, math, and reading, it may be wise to consider the value of play in developing the prerequisite skills that enhance cognitive learning in a classroom setting (Roskos & Christie, 2007b). Rather than reducing the opportunities for unstructured play in preschool classrooms, a better course may be to build in time for social, dramatic play.

As noted, dramatic play allows children to experiment with a large variety of behaviors and to experience the consequences of those behaviors and the emotions associated with them. For example, children who play hospital with dolls, friends, or even alone will play many different roles, such as patient, doctor, nurse, or visitor. In acting out these roles, they can experience fears and anxieties about illness and about their dependence on others in a play setting that is safe and non-threatening. One of the most valuable aspects of dramatic play is that it allows children to express intense feelings, such as anger or fear. Play helps children to resolve conflicts, such as those between themselves and their parents or siblings, and it helps them to resolve those feelings and conflicts in ways that they can cope with and understand. As the result, dramatic play leads to a better understanding of others, as well as to a clearer definition of self (Kavanaugh, 2006; Lillard, 2011; Newton & Jenvey, 2011).

The Role of Peers Playing with other children is a highly valued activity for young children. Given the opportunity, children typically spend more time interacting directly with each other than with adults. Children play with siblings and other children at home, in the neighborhood, and at school. In many cultures, the significance of children's interactions with other children is even greater than it is in U.S. middle-class culture (Fleer, 2010; Rogoff, 2003; Rogoff, Correa-Chávez, & Silva, 2011). For example, younger children in some societies are cared for largely by 5- to 10-year-old children (Beckman, Aksu-Koç & Kâgitçibasi, 2009; Rogoff, 2003).

Especially important to development are groups that include children of various ages. Mixed-age peer groups can offer older children the opportunity to practice teaching and child care with younger children, and younger children can imitate and practice role relations with older children. Our earlier discussions of scaffolding and of the zone of proximal development make clear the significance of having older children as role models for those who are younger. In addition, when older children play with children who are younger, they can gain practice with more supervisory, mature roles in an emotionally safe and nonthreatening setting. Thus, for both younger and older children, play activities in mixed-age groups can encourage the development of new ways of thinking and problem solving (Smith & Gosso, 2010).

In so many ways, play both mirrors and encourages cognitive development, as well as the refinement of physical and motor skills that rapidly advance during the period of early childhood. Play also reflects and promotes personality and sociocultural development in early childhood, which are the topics we explore in the next chapter.

REVIEW THE FACTS 6-5

1. Who said that play is the work of children?
   a. Vygotsky b. Freud
   c. Skinner d. Piaget
2. Two-year-olds often appear to be playing together, but, in fact, they are more likely to be engaging in separate activities. This kind of play is called __________.
3. Generally speaking, are children who engage in more frequent dramatic play likely to be more egocentric or less egocentric?
4. Generally speaking, it is probably best for young children to play with
   a. children of various ages.
   b. children of their own age.
   c. adults, especially parents and teachers.
   d. themselves, so they learn more about themselves.
5. Vygotsky's concept of the zone of proximal development suggests that play is especially valuable when it includes
   a. younger children.
   b. children of the same age.
   c. older children.
   d. lots of toys.

Practice on MyDevelopmentLab

CHAPTER SUMMARY

Physical Development

What does it mean to say that human development is integrated, interactive, and dynamic?

- Development is integrated, interactive, and dynamic. This means that the different systems—such as thinking, behavior, brain development, and physical changes—continuously influence each other and are constantly changing.

What role do physical development and brain maturation play in the major developmental events that characterize early childhood?

- Early childhood is a time of rapid physical growth and development; children's bodies become longer, more slender, and less top-heavy. Bones also ossify, or harden.
- The brain growth spurt, which involves the rapid development of interconnections among neurons and the pruning away of unused connections, continues throughout early childhood, allowing for considerable neural plasticity during this period.
- Myelination and lateralization also occur. *Myelination* is the formation of sheathing cells that insulate the neurons and make transmission of neural impulses much more efficient. *Lateralization* is the process where specific skills and competencies become localized in a particular cerebral hemisphere. Many functions are lateralized, including the control of body movements, some cognitive functions, language, and handedness.
- Although learning and its corresponding brain development occur throughout life, early brain development sets the stage for later development and therefore is very important.
- An individual's development is the result of genetics, experiences, nutrition and care, and the opportunity to play and exercise. Furthermore, these factors interact in dynamic and intricate ways, which further enhances the uniqueness of every individual.

Motor Skills Development

What distinguishes gross motor from fine motor skills, and how does each develop during early childhood?

- As they move through early childhood, young children develop *automaticity*, which is the ability to perform increasingly complex motor activities without consciously thinking about what they are doing.
- Gross motor skills include whole-body movements, such as running, skipping, or throwing a ball. Fine motor skills require more coordinated and dexterous use of the hands, fingers, and thumbs, as when writing or picking up a small object.
- As children grow older, their motor skills show *functional subordination*, meaning that simple motor skills become integrated into more complex, purposeful skills.
- Children learn new skills more easily when they are ready—that is, when the necessary prerequisite skills are in place. Readiness involves the maturation of the brain and of the physical systems on which the skill is based.

- Motor development also requires practice, and the ability to direct attention toward the skill to be learned. Feedback informs children about the success of their actions. Feedback may involve *extrinsically motivated behavior*, such as when actions are rewarded or encouraged, or *intrinsically motivated behavior*, in which rewards come from our internalized feelings of competence and success.

Cognitive Development

What are the main cognitive achievements of early childhood, according to Piaget?

- Jean Piaget viewed cognitive development as consisting of a series of four periods: sensorimotor, preoperational, concrete operational, and formal operational. In early childhood, children are in the *preoperational period*, and they begin this period with rudimentary language and thinking abilities.
- The preoperational period is divided into two parts. The first part, the *preconceptual period* (about ages 2 to 4 or 5), is highlighted by the increasingly complex use of symbols and symbolic play. The second part, the *intuitive* (or *transitional*) *period* (about ages 4 or 5 to 7), is highlighted by children's increasing understanding of causation, as well as their undertaking of simple mental operations and more realistic views of the world.
- Piaget believed children actively construct their view of the world by assimilating and accommodating new experiences.
- Characteristics of the preoperational period include the increased use of symbolic play (including language), animistic thinking, reification, magical thinking, and especially egocentrism. *Egocentrism* involves a self-centered view of the world, where children tend to see things in terms of their personal point of view.
- The use of actions, images, or words to represent past and present events, experiences, and concepts is called *symbolic representation*, and it marks the emergence of the preoperational period. The development of language is an especially important elaboration of symbolic representation.
- Young children have difficulty performing many mental operations, which is Piaget's term for thought processes. For example, they have problems with *conservation*, which is the understanding that changing the shape or appearance of an object does not change its mass, volume, or number. Young children's difficulty with conservation occurs partly because they cannot attend to more than one dimension of a problem at a time. They also tend to see problems as involving perception rather than logic, and they have difficulty thinking backward from an end state to the situations that produced it.
- Critics of Piaget's view of cognitive development argue that children's thinking is not as limited as he described. When given problems that are framed in contexts that are more familiar, children can sometimes solve problems using more advanced logic than they typically employ. Piaget also underemphasized the role of social aspects in learning, which were emphasized by Lev Vygotsky.

How do Vygotsky's view of cognitive development and the view embraced by information-processing theorists differ from that proposed by Piaget?

- Vygotsky found that children can often be encouraged to solve problems that originally were too difficult for them if they are shown how by a more knowledgeable person. The *zone of proximal development* is Vygotsky's concept that children's cognitive growth develops through guided participation in activities slightly beyond their competence—with the help of adults or older children. Learning occurs best when the proper amount of guidance through the progressive structuring of tasks, called *scaffolding*, is provided—enough so that the child can solve the problem but not so much that self-discovery is limited.
- Information-processing theory views memory much like a computer: Information enters memory where it is encoded; we hold it in short-term memory when we are actively using the information; and we file it for future use in long-term memory.
- Two different types of information retrieval are recognition and recall. *Recognition* is the ability to correctly identify objects or situations previously experienced when they appear again. *Recall* is the ability to retrieve stored information and memories with or without cues or prompts. Recall generally is more difficult than recognition.
- Memory is improved when we use effective strategies for encoding and retrieval. More effective strategies are learned as children develop. An especially effective strategy for children involves learning scripts, or sequences of routine events that take place, such as "how I go to bed."

Language Development

What predictable changes occur in language development during the period of early childhood?

- In early childhood, the use of language explodes, as evidenced by the stunningly rapid growth of vocabulary, the use of words to express concepts, the increasing length and complexity of children's expressions, and more complex grammar.
- Children do not learn language simply by imitation; rather, they also learn rules and sometimes apply them inappropriately, as when they *overregularize*.
- According to Vygotsky, *private speech*, the language we use when we talk to ourselves, may help us develop our inner

thought and self-direction; in addition, it may give us a means to make a transition from symbolic thinking to using words.

- As children learn to speak, they often engage in *collective monologues*, in which they appear to take turns speaking to each other; but, in fact, they are probably talking about quite different things. Collective monologues point out the important role of *pragmatics* in learning to use language. Pragmatics, the social and cultural aspects of language use, often vary across cultures, which reflects the important role played by social expectations and conventions. Gestures, for example, often play an important role in communication and these, like other pragmatics, vary from culture to culture.
- In early childhood, girls' verbal skills usually are more advanced than boys' language skills. This may be partly the result of gender-stereotyped play experiences.
- Although language learning is an incredibly complex task, young children typically have little difficulty learning two languages, especially if they are used by different speakers and in different contexts. Although knowing a second language may be regarded differently in various cultures, in our increasingly diverse world, it is usually considered to be an advantage.

Play and Learning

What does it mean to say that play both mirrors and encourages cognitive development?

- Play is intrinsically motivated behavior that promotes cognitive development in many ways. It allows children to explore their physical surroundings, to master symbolic representation, to reduce their egocentrism, and to gain self-confidence.
- Children become more social and interactive in their play as they grow older. Two-year-olds typically engage in *parallel play*, which is characterized by each child playing independently, although in proximity to each other. By age 4, most children engage in *dramatic play*, in which they pretend, imitate, role play, and learn to interact.
- Children who have more experience with dramatic play are better able to understand another's perspective, to consider others' feelings, and to have a clearer definition of self. Dramatic play also seems to be linked to academic performance, and especially to the development of literacy skills.
- Dramatic play also allows children to experiment with different roles, cope with fears and anxieties, and express their emotions. Play with other children is especially important, as it reflects and promotes social and personality development, as well as the development of cognitive and motor skills.

KEY TERMS

myelination (p. 159)
lateralization (p. 159)
automaticity (p. 162)
functional subordination (p. 162)
extrinsically motivated behavior (p. 164)
intrinsically motivated behavior (p. 164)
preoperational period (p. 165)
preconceptual period (p. 165)
intuitive (or transitional) period (p. 165)
egocentrism (p. 165)
symbolic representation (p. 167)
conservation (p. 168)
zone of proximal development (p. 170)
scaffolding (p. 171)
recognition (p. 171)
recall (p. 171)
overregularize (p. 174)
private speech (p. 174)
collective monologues (p. 174)
pragmatics (p. 175)
parallel play (p. 178)
dramatic play (p. 179)

MyVirtualLife

What decision would you make while raising a child? What would be the consequences of those decisions?

Find out by accessing **MyVirtualLife** at www.MyDevelopmentLab.com to raise a virtual child and live your own virtual life.

7 EARLY CHILDHOOD
Personality and Sociocultural Development

LEARNING OBJECTIVES

- What distinguishes anxiety from fear, and how do young children learn to manage these emotions?
- Why is learning to control emotions such an important developmental event in early childhood?
- What factors give rise to aggression in early childhood, and what factors help children control their aggressive tendencies?
- Does viewing violent content presented on TV and via other media have an impact on how young children learn to manage their aggressive tendencies?
- How does the child develop increasingly more sophisticated prosocial behavior during the period of early childhood?
- How do young children resolve the developmental conflict between initiative and guilt?
- What developmental functions does play serve during early childhood, and how does a child's interactions with peers assist in the development of social competence?
- How do preschool children acquire their understanding of rules and social concepts?
- How do children come to understand the concept of gender?
- What kinds of parenting styles and family dynamics lead to the healthiest adjustment for children?
- What demographic features describe child maltreatment patterns in the United States today, and what impact does maltreatment have on the children who are victimized?

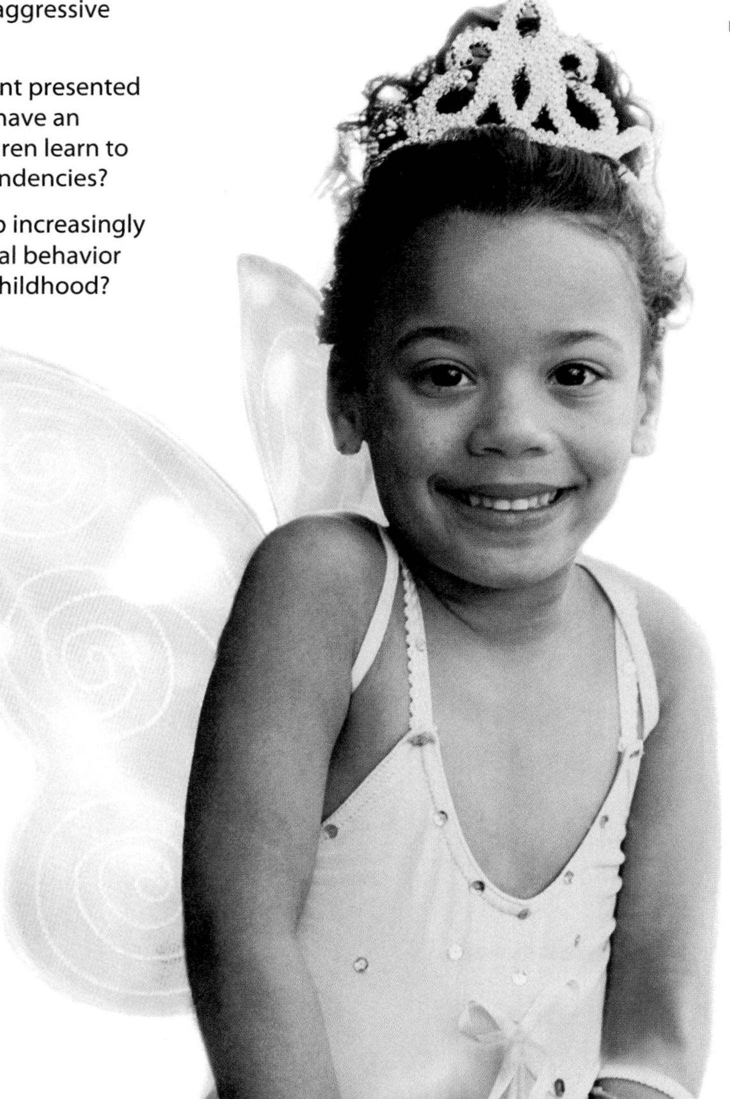

CHAPTER OUTLINE

Coping with Feelings and Emotions
- Fear and Anxiety
- Emotional Regulation
- Shame and Guilt

Aggression and Prosocial Behavior
- Aggression
- Prosocial Behavior

Developmental Conflicts
- Initiative Versus Guilt

Peers, Play, and the Development of Social Competence
- The Role of Imaginary Companions
- Cultural Variations in Play
- Social Competence and the Development of Social Skills

Understanding Self and Others
- Social Concepts and Rules
- Self-Concept
- Self and Gender

Family Dynamics
- Parenting Styles
- Discipline and Self-Control
- Sibling Dynamics
- Child Maltreatment: Abuse and Neglect

Early childhood—the period spanning roughly from ages 2 to 6—is a time of rapid developmental change. Not only do children grow and mature physically, but also their cognitive abilities, including their understanding of themselves, others, and their culture, accelerate during this period. During this preschool period, young children increasingly gain an understanding of themselves and their place in a particular social world, as well as who they are within the social context of their community. They learn what is expected of them in their family and their community—what is good and bad behavior for boys and girls like them. They learn how to handle their feelings in socially appropriate ways. In other words, young children learn the norms, rules, and cultural meanings of their society, and they develop a self-concept that may persist throughout their lives.

Early childhood is also a period during which emotional and social development unfolds, establishing an important foundation for later development. As we saw in Chapter 1, several theoretical traditions have arisen to explain these changes. Table 7-1 presents a review of three major theoretical perspectives, which will assist your understanding of social and personality development.

As you will see, there is dramatic growth in children's self-control and social competence during the four important years that span from age 2 to age 6. Although 2-year-olds have all the basic emotions of 6-year-olds (or for that matter, of adults), their expression of these emotions is immediate, impulsive, and direct. They cannot wait to have their desires satisfied. In contrast, 6-year-olds are much more verbal and thoughtful; they are a little less quick to anger, and they often can censor or control their behavior. Their coping patterns are far more diverse than are those of 2-year-olds. In short, most 6-year-olds have become quite refined in their abilities to cope and have developed their own distinctive styles based on a developing self-image. The personal style that a child develops in these years may be the foundation of a lifelong pattern of behavior.

In this chapter, we weave the ideas from the three major theoretical perspectives described in Table 7-1 into the descriptions of the many major changes that take place in early childhood.

Table 7-1 Brief Review of Three Major Theoretical Perspectives

Theoretical Perspective	Description of Significant Developmental Events in Early Childhood	Historically Important Theorists
Psychoanalytic (also called psychodynamic) view	• The emphasis is on the child's feelings, drives, and developmental conflicts. • Young children must learn to cope with powerful emotions, such as anxiety, in socially acceptable ways. • Erikson emphasized the growth of autonomy and the need to balance it with children's dependence on parents during this period.	Sigmund Freud Erik Erikson
Social-learning view	• The emphasis is on the links between cognition, behavior, and the environment. • The child's behavior is shaped by external rewards and punishments, as well as by role models. • Rewards also can be internal; that is, children may behave in ways that augment self-esteem, pride, and a sense of accomplishment.	Albert Bandura
Cognitive-developmental view	• The emphasis is on children's thoughts and concepts as the organizers of their social behavior. • Young children develop increasingly complex concepts; they learn what it means to be a girl or a boy, a friend or a leader. • Children learn about culturally appropriate gender schemas and judge what behaviors are appropriate for boys and for girls, and they choose to either accept or reject these schemas.	Jean Piaget Lev Vygotsky

In early childhood, personality development is forged in the context of relationships.

We explore how young children learn to manage their feelings and emotions, as well as how they develop their abilities to relate to others—both peers and adults—by looking at aggression, prosocial behavior, and developmental conflicts. We also examine how young children form important aspects of their self-concepts. Finally, because parents play such an important role in the development of young children, we close the chapter with an examination of how family dynamics influence developmental processes and outcomes.

COPING WITH FEELINGS AND EMOTIONS

One of the earliest tasks that young children must cope with is to learn to manage the wide range of feelings and emotions they experience. Some of these are positive—such as joy, affection, and pride. Others—such as anger, fear, anxiety, jealousy, frustration, and pain—obviously are not. Whether the feelings are positive or negative, however, young children must acquire some means of regulating their feelings and expressing them in socially acceptable ways.

Fear and Anxiety

One of the most important forces that children must learn to handle is the stress caused by fear and anxiety. Although people sometimes use these words interchangeably, these two emotions are not synonymous. **Fear** is a state of arousal, tension, or apprehension caused by a specific, identifiable stimulus or situation. For example, a child may fear the dark, or lightning and thunder, or the child may have a *phobia* (an irrational fear) of big dogs or high places. In contrast, **anxiety** is a more *generalized* emotional state that produces a feeling of uneasiness, apprehension, or fear that stems from a vague or unknown source.

Although some children may become anxious in specific situations, those who are characterized as *anxious* experience regular and continuing feelings of apprehension and unease, often without knowing why. A move to a new neighborhood or a sudden change in parental expectations, such as the beginning of toilet training, may induce anxiety that seems to come from nowhere. Many psychologists believe that some anxiety inevitably accompanies the socialization process as children attempt to avoid the pain of parental displeasure and discipline (Muris, 2007; Wenar, 1990). The development of fear and anxiety is also linked to cognitive development. As children get older and become more competent in symbolic thought and hypothetical reasoning, they also become capable of imagining situations that provoke anxiety—for example, who will take care of me if Mother dies (Broeren & Muris, 2009; Muris, 2010)?

Causes of Fear and Anxiety Fear and anxiety can have many causes. The sources of some fears are easily identified, such as fear of the nurse who gives inoculations or the dread inspired by the sight of a neighborhood bully. Other fears are harder to understand. For example, even well-adjusted young children may express irrational fears that their parents will leave them or stop loving them. Although most parents usually act in a loving and accepting manner, sometimes even good parents may appear to withdraw their love, attention, and protection when children misbehave. Young children may overreact and develop anxieties well out of proportion to the parent's behavior.

Can you suggest a way in which anxiety may contribute in a positive way to the social development of young children?

Another source of anxiety for young children is the anticipation of other types of punishment, especially physical punishment. Children who are 2 years old may not have a realistic idea of how far their parents will go when punishing them. Unfortunately, some parents do use physical punishment, which is a topic we return to later in this chapter. Under these circumstances, fear and anxiety are normal and rational responses.

Fear and anxiety also may be increased or even created by the child's imagination. For example, children often imagine that the birth of a new baby will cause their parents to reject them. Sometimes anxiety results from children's awareness of their own unacceptable feelings—anger at a parent or other caregiver, jealousy of a sibling or a friend, or a recurrent desire to be held or treated like a baby.

Individual Differences in Fearfulness and Anxiety Of course, fearfulness and anxiety are experienced differently by different people, and individual differences appears very early in life, leading

fear
A state of arousal, tension, or apprehension caused by a specific and identifiable stimulus or situation

anxiety
A feeling of uneasiness, apprehension, or fear that has a vague or unknown source

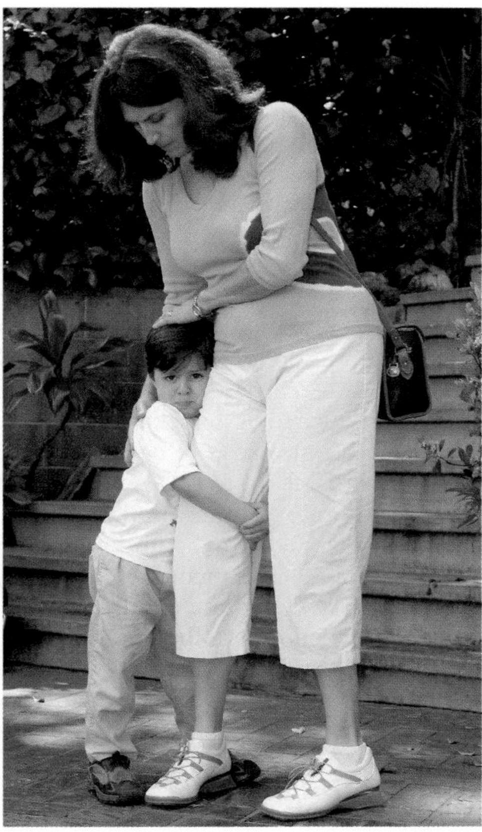

▶ Young children experience strong emotions but have yet to learn strategies for coping with those feelings.

some researchers to suggest that biological forces underlie at least some aspects of fear and anxiety (e.g., Buss, 2011; Kagan, 2000). For example, one way of categorizing children is on the basis of *temperament*—the stable differences in behavior and responsiveness that appear in infancy and involve genetic and biological, as well as environmental and cultural, forces. In classic research, Jerome Kagan and his colleagues identified two different temperamental types based on the degree to which children exhibited *behavioral inhibition*—how children respond to social situations that they have not previously experienced (e.g., Kagan, Reznick, & Gibbons, 1989). According to Kagan, about 10 to 20% of children can be classified as "behaviorally inhibited," meaning that that they are typically shy and withdrawn in unfamiliar situations. Such children also experience higher levels of anxiety when they attempt new tasks or are faced with new challenges. Some researchers refer to such children as "shy," and these children typically experience higher levels of fear and anxiety than do behaviorally uninhibited children.

Currently, researchers are trying to understand if these early temperamental dispositions remain stable throughout life, and if they are linked to developmental problems later in life (Detweiler, Comer, & Albano, 2010; Schmidt & Buss, 2010). Some research suggests that the answer to this second question is yes. For example, researchers generally find that children who are socially skilled are more confident in their interactions with peers, and thus are better able to develop meaningful friendships, to perform better in school, and to ultimately develop an emotionally healthy self-concept (Rubin, Bowker, & Gazelle, 2010). Children who are socially unskilled, in comparison, are more likely to suffer rejection by their peers and to experience other social and academic problems. They also are at greater risk for all kinds of negative adjustment problems, including excessive anxiety (Rubin, Coplan, & Bowker, 2009). Of course, environmental context can make a difference, both for the better and the worse. When a temperamentally vulnerable child is raised in a challenging environment—where uncertainty is high and poor parenting predominates—then outcomes are generally poorer. However, when parents are supportive and are able to help their shy children learn to adapt to new situations and interact successfully with unfamiliar children, then development generally proceeds along a more positive course (Buss, 2011; Hasting, Nuselovici, Rubin, & Cheah, 2010).

Historical, Cultural, and Developmental Influences As a result of differences in cultural and family backgrounds, children experience fear and anxiety about different things. A hundred years ago, children were afraid of wolves and bears. Fifty years ago, they worried more about goblins and bogeymen. In recent times, their nightmares are more often populated with extraterrestrial creatures and killer robots (Draper & James, 1985). It is not inappropriate to speculate that television and other media have an impact on the specific form these early fears take.

There also are striking cultural differences in the way children express their fears or whether they express their fears at all (e.g., Taimalu & Lahikainen, 2007; Zvolensky, McNeil, Porter, & Stewart, 2001). In contemporary Western culture, showing fear is generally frowned upon. Children are supposed to be brave; most parents worry about a child who is unusually fearful. In contrast, traditional Navajo parents believe that it is healthy and normal for a child to be afraid; they consider a fearless child foolhardy. In one study, Navajo parents reported an average of 22 fears in their children, including fears of supernatural beings; in contrast, a group of White parents from rural Montana reported an average of only 4 fears in their children (Tikalsky & Wallace, 1988).

A child's fears also reflect the child's level of cognitive development, which becomes more abstract as the older child gains greater cognitive sophistication and develops the ability to represent objects symbolically (Broeren & Muris, 2009; Sayfan, 2008). For example, a classic study of children's fears (Jersild & Holmes, 1935) found that younger children were most likely to be afraid of specific objects or situations, such as strangers, unfamiliar things, the dark, loud noises, or falling. In contrast, children age 5 or 6 were more likely to fear imaginary or abstract things, such as monsters, robbers, death, being alone, or being ridiculed. Fifty years later, researchers found most of the same fears in young children, except that fear of the dark, of being alone, and of unfamiliar things now appear at earlier ages (Draper & James, 1985). Today, researchers view the specific fears that children have as being closely linked to their cognitive abilities. Preschool children generally are afraid of imaginary creatures, animals, natural environmental events (e.g., thunder), and of being separated from their caregivers. These fears subside as children enter grade school, but are replaced with

How might children's increasing skills in symbolic representation be linked to the specific objects or situations that children of different ages fear?

fears more closely linked to bodily injury, physical danger, and school performance. In adolescence, fears tend to center on more abstract issues, such as death, social affairs, or becoming terminally ill. Interestingly, this "sequence of fears" is seen across cultures, but tends to be more pronounced among boys than girls (Broeren & Muris, 2009; Zhao & Wang, 2009).

Of course, in today's world, there are many sources of fear, anxiety, and stress. Some are a normal part of growing up, such as being yelled at for accidentally breaking something or being teased by an older sibling. Other conditions can be more serious or involve chronic and long-term stresses, such as growing up in unfavorable living environments that may include poverty, parental conflict or drug use, or in dangerous neighborhoods. Even more extreme conditions occur when children must cope with major disasters or terrors, such as earthquakes, floods, and wars (Belsky, 2008; Osofsky, 2011). Severe or long-term stressful situations can drain the psychological resources of even the most resilient child (Warren & Sroufe, 2004).

Coping with Fear and Anxiety Fear and anxiety are normal emotions that, at times, are felt by everyone; they often serve a useful purpose, and it is important to keep this in mind. Learning to avoid dangerous situations and learning to develop strategies for maintaining emotional control are important to healthy development at any age. How can we help young children cope with fear and anxiety?

Ignoring children's fears will not always make them go away, and using force or ridicule is likely to have negative results. Instead, at least when their fears are mild, children can be gently and sympathetically encouraged to confront and overcome them. Parents can help by demonstrating that there is little to fear. For example, to help a child who is afraid of nighttime robbers, parents can have the child watch while they check the locks on all the doors and verify the home's security. If a child's fears seem unusually intense or extremely resistant, parents also can turn to a psychologist for professional help (Last, 2006).

Often the best way to help children cope with anxiety is to reduce unnecessary stress in their lives. When children show unusually high levels of tension or have frequent temper tantrums, it is often helpful to simplify their lives by maintaining daily routines; specifying clearly what is expected of them; and helping them anticipate special events, such as visits from friends and relatives. Other helpful strategies include reducing their exposure to parental fighting or violent television programs and protecting them from being teased or tormented by siblings or neighborhood bullies or gangs.

Parents also should thoughtfully consider the cause of seemingly irrational or naughty behavior. In response to feelings of anxiety, children (like adults) sometimes may employ **defense mechanisms**, which are psychodynamic "tricks" (behaviors) that individuals use to disguise or reduce tensions that lead anxiety. For example, a commonly used defense mechanism is **rationalization**, which involves deluding oneself by creating reasonable, but false, explanations for events: A child who was not invited to a party might rationalize that he would not have had a good time at the party anyway. Common defense mechanisms, which play an especially important role in the psychoanalytic tradition, are listed in Table 7-2. By age 5 or 6, most children have learned to use some of these ways of coping in order to reduce their anxiety.

Not all life stresses can be avoided or minimized, of course. Children must learn to cope with the birth of a sibling, moving to a new home, or entering day care as well as perhaps with their parents' divorce, the untimely death of a parent, or natural disasters. Under such circumstances, parents and teachers can often ease the young child's fears and keep anxieties under control by attending to the underlying issues with concern and sensitivity (see Table 7-3). Also, talking about fears and anxieties can help a child cope, and several good books are available to guide such conversations between parents and children (e.g., Annunziata & Nemiroff, 2009).

Children also develop their own means of coping with fear and anxiety. For example, quite normal 2- to 4-year-olds often display highly repetitive, ritualized behaviors that would be deemed obsessive–compulsive in adults. A child who is afraid of the dark, for example, might develop a highly specific ritual for saying good night to parents in a certain order and with an exact number of kisses or hugs, thus reducing anxiety about going to bed. Parents who react favorably to their child's attempt at coping enable the child to progress toward healthy emotional development.

Emotional Regulation

Emotional development requires that children learn to deal with a wide range of emotions, not just fear and anxiety, in socially acceptable ways—a process called *emotion regulation* (Eisenberg, Smith, & Spinrad, 2011; Eisenberg & Sulik, 2012). Emotions, and the child's ability to manage them, are of course closely linked to brain development (Berger, 2011a). As the brain wires itself during early childhood, centers of emotional control appear to shift so that by age 3 or 4 years, the "executive control" centers in the frontal lobes of the brain are now involved in the regulation of emotion (Rothbart, Sheese, Rueda, & Posner, 2011). As the brain continues to mature, developing children continue to gain greater control of their emotions. Thus, the development of emotional regulation is a normal part of children's development, especially during the first 8 years of life (Brownell & Kopp, 2007; Eisenberg, Spinrad, & Eggum, 2010). Particularly important to

defense mechanisms
The psychodynamic "tricks" (behaviors) that individuals use to disguise or reduce tensions that lead to anxiety

rationalization
Deluding oneself by creating reasonable, but false, explanations for events

Table 7-2 Selected Defense Mechanisms Used by Children

Defense Mechanism	Description
Identification	Incorporating the values, attitudes, and beliefs of others; children adopt the attitudes of powerful figures, such as parents, in order to become more like these figures—more lovable, powerful, and accepted—which helps reduce the anxiety they often feel about their own relative helplessness.
Denial	Refusing to admit that a situation exists or that an event happened; for example, children may react to an upsetting situation such as the death of a pet by pretending that the pet is still living in the house and sleeping with them at night.
Displacement	Substituting something or someone else for the real source of anger or fear; for example, a child may be angry with his baby sister, but he cannot hit her. Perhaps he cannot even admit to himself that he wants to hit her, so he torments the family dog or cat instead.
Projection	Attributing undesirable thoughts or actions to someone else and, in the process, distorting reality; "She did it, not me" is a projective statement. "He wants to hurt me" may seem more acceptable than "I want to hurt him." Projection thus sets the stage for a distorted form of self-defense; for example, "If he wants to hurt me, I'd better do it to him first."
Rationalization	Persuading oneself that one does not want what one cannot have; even relatively young children are capable of talking themselves out of things. A child who does not get invited to a party might decide, "Oh, well. I wouldn't have had a good time anyway." Rationalization is a common defense mechanism that continues to develop and be refined well into adulthood.
Reaction formation	Behaving in ways opposite to one's inclinations; when children have thoughts or desires that make them anxious, they may react by behaving in a contradictory way. For example, they might like to cling to their parents, but instead they push them away and behave with exaggerated independence and assertiveness.
Regression	Returning to an earlier or more infantile form of behavior as a way of coping with a stressful situation; for example, a frustrated 8-year-old suddenly reverts to sucking her thumb and carrying around her blanket, regressing to behaviors that were given up years before.
Repression	An extreme form of denial in which the person unconsciously erases a frightening event or circumstance from awareness; there is no need to rely on fantasy because the child literally does not consciously remember that the event ever occurred.
Withdrawal	Removing oneself from an unpleasant situation; this is a very common defense mechanism in young children. It is the most direct defense possible. If a situation seems too difficult, the child withdraws from it either physically or mentally.

this process is the children's ability to manage feelings of shame and guilt, which generally develop during the second and third years of life (Lagattuta & Thompson, 2007).

Shame and Guilt

Although shame and guilt are similar, contemporary developmentalists view shame as a more painful and intense emotion than guilt because shame goes to the core the child's sense of identity (Stuewig et al., 2010). Whereas guilt is usually associated with a particular action or behavior, shame is more likely to be viewed as a characteristic of the child, rather than the child's behavior. As such, shame reflects negatively on one's identity and is associated with the desire to undo aspects of the *self*. Children who are ashamed of themselves are usually motivated by the desire to change for the better—for example, to be kinder or more honest. However, shame also can be linked to aggression if the child's behavior does not measure up to expectations. When children are ashamed of themselves, they sometimes lash out, hurting others as a consequence of their frustration. Guilt, on the other hand, involves acknowledging that one has been involved in a morally wrong *outcome*. Thus, guilt is more likely than shame to be associated with a particular behavior, and guilt can be satisfied—at least in part—by undoing the action or making reparation for it. As such, guilt is not so closely related to one's self-concept and therefore generally does not affect the person's core identity. Guilty children wish to change their bad behavior but typically do not experience the threat to self-concept that feelings of shame involve.

Table 7-3 Guidelines for Parents to Help Young Children Cope with Stress

When a young child is experiencing an especially stressful situation, parents and other caregivers can often help their child cope with stress by following some basic guidelines.

- Learn to recognize and interpret stress reactions in children.
- Provide a warm, secure base to help children regain confidence.
- Allow opportunities for children to discuss their feelings; shared trauma is easier to handle.
- Temporarily allow immature behavior, such as thumb sucking, cuddling a blanket, fussing, or sitting on laps.
- Help children give meaning to the event or circumstance by providing explanations appropriate to their age level.

SOURCE: Adapted from A. S. Honig, 1986, "Stress and coping in young children," *Young Children, 41*(5), 50–63; and by A. Wilde, 2008, "Helping children cope with stress," retrieved, from http://www.abc.net.au/health/features/stories/2008/01/29/2148045.htm.

Watch *Emotion Regulation: James Coan* on **MyDevelopmentLab**

Interestingly, there appear to be cultural forces at work in the degree to which children experience the negative emotions of shame and guilt, as well as the positive emotion of pride. In a recent study, for example, researchers studied how children living in Japan, Korea, and the United States experienced each of these three emotions—shame, guilt, and pride. Although all children experienced all of these emotions, Japanese children were most likely to report feeling shame, Korean children scored highest on guilt, and children living in the United States scored highest in pride (Furukawa & Tangney, 2012). Researchers also noted that among all children, shame was more closely associated with aggression, whereas guilt was likely to be associated with a tendency to take responsibility for one's actions, results consistent with other research.

As the previous study suggests, shame and guilt (and pride) are universal emotions that all children experience to some degree. Healthy development is characterized by experiencing these emotions when circumstances are appropriate. For example, if children intentionally misbehave, they *should* experience guilt; if they cheat on a game, they *should* experience shame. In fact, if children do *not* feel guilty when their behavior violates social norms, or feel ashamed of themselves when they fail to live up to reasonable expectations, they also are more likely to experience a variety of emotional problems, such as disruptive behaviors, personality disorders, and autism (Tangney, Stuewig, & Mashek, 2007). Shame and guilt, thus, are directly related to the child's ability to develop appropriate emotion regulation (Rothbart & Scheese, 2007).

Learning to Restrain Emotions Children learn very early that open displays of negative feelings are usually unacceptable in public places—including nursery schools and day-care centers. Also, as children grow older, their parents' expectations for emotional regulation increase: It's okay for babies to cry when they are hungry, but it is not okay for 6-year-olds to do so. Children who do not learn such lessons at home are at risk of being socially rejected outside the home. In particular, children who cry a lot or who express other negative emotions are likely to be unpopular with their peers (Denham, et al., 2003; Dougherty, 2006).

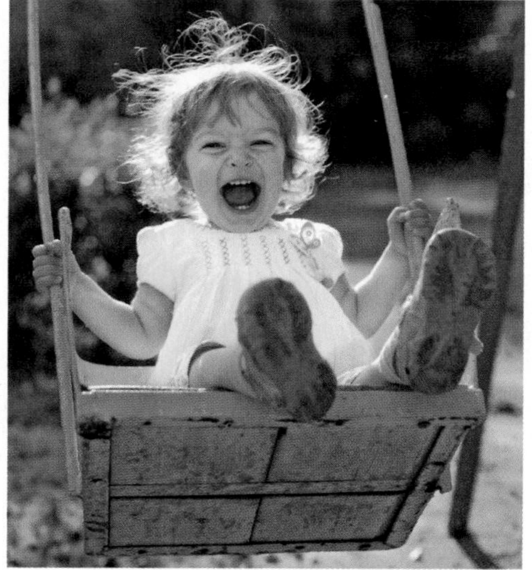

Young children freely express positive emotions like pleasure and joy, but by age 6 they often begin to restrain even these emotions.

Learning to manage negative emotions, of course, is not the same as not having them—negative emotions are an inevitable part of life. Learning to manage anger is especially important. In one longitudinal study, children who were still having temper tantrums at age 10 were tracked into adulthood (Caspi, 1998). The researchers found that these children tended to be unsuccessful as adults as a result of their continuing outbursts of anger. They had difficulty holding jobs, and their marriages often ended in divorce. Similar results have been obtained in studies conducted in Germany that follow aggressive children into adulthood (Asendorph, Denissen, & van Aken, 2008). In fact, one of the goals of emotional regulation is reached when children can come to accept their angry feelings as a normal part of themselves while at the same time learning to control or redirect their reactions to such feelings. When redirected appropriately, anger can even be a motivating force—a way of overcoming obstacles—and can help children stand up for themselves or others they see wronged. Thus, learning to control negative feelings, not eliminate them, is the aim of healthy emotional regulation.

Can you think of an episode in your life in which anger was a positive motivating force?

In many cultures, children must also learn to restrain their positive emotions, which they do as they grow older. Children who are 2 years old deal with spontaneous feelings—such as joy, affection, excitement, and playfulness—quite differently than children who are 6 years old. Just as 2-year-olds are direct in expressing distress, they also are likely to openly display positive feelings; they freely jump up and down or clap their hands when they are excited. As early socialization continues, children may be required to learn to subdue such open expressiveness or to limit their spontaneity to acceptable occasions, such as parties and games.

Sensuality and Sexual Curiosity In most cultures, children are expected to restrain their curiosity about their own bodies. Two-year-olds, however, are very sensual creatures. Consistent with psychoanalytic theory, such sensuality is primarily oral during infancy; however, a fascination with the genital regions usually develops at about age 3 or 4. Masturbation and sexual play are quite common during early childhood, although children in most traditional Western cultures quickly learn not to display such behaviors when adults are present. As children discover that self-stimulation is pleasurable, most develop an active curiosity about their bodies and ask many sex-related questions.

There are many variations in how different cultures—and even different families within the same culture—respond to children's developing sensuality and sexual curiosity. Whether openly or in private, however, sensual exploration is a natural and vital part of development that begins in early childhood and continues into adolescence and adulthood. As is true with

Watch *Positive Emotions: Michael Cohn* on **MyDevelopmentLab**

the development of other emotions, children must find socially appropriate ways to express their sexuality.

Children must also learn to manage conflict and achieve a balance between protecting themselves and asserting their interests without harming others. Young children must learn to control their aggressive tendencies and engage in positive prosocial behaviors, such as helping and sharing. How they develop these abilities is the topic we explore in the next section.

REVIEW THE FACTS 7-1

1. An irrational fear, such as a fear of clowns, is called a(n) __________.
2. Sometimes children cope with fear and anxiety by redirecting these emotions, engaging in the use of what are called __________.
3. The emotion that goes to the core of the child's identity and is linked to the desire to change aspects of the self is called
   a. guilt. b. rationalization.
   c. anxiety. d. shame.
4. Difficulty in learning to regulate anger is associated with all of the following, *except*
   a. later marriage difficulties.
   b. reduced reliance on defense mechanisms.
   c. unpopularity in childhood.
   d. trouble holding a job.
5. Around age 3 or 4, children develop a fascination with
   a. their genitals. b. their oral region.
   c. animals. d. younger children.

Practice on **MyDevelopmentLab**

AGGRESSION AND PROSOCIAL BEHAVIOR

It is impossible to look at current world events and argue that the topic of aggression is of limited significance. Psychologists have long been interested in various aspects of human aggression. They have researched how it develops, what factors influence its display, and how to encourage people toward more peaceful and cooperative approaches to conflict resolution.

Animals, like humans, engage in both aggressive and prosocial behaviors. How might the aggressive and prosocial behaviors of humans differ from those displayed by animals?

From a developmental perspective, aggression is generally viewed as a natural response, one that is universally displayed across all cultures and historical periods. Yet, we do know that not all people are equally aggressive and that circumstances can exert a powerful influence on how children learn to manage their aggressive impulses. Children also display prosocial, helpful behaviors, which also develop in an environmental context. Just as children must learn to regulate their emotions, such as fear and anxiety, they also must develop appropriate methods of managing their aggression and learn to further develop their prosocial behavior.

Aggression

Aggression consists of a broad category of responses (see Table 7-4). In young children, it is a common response to anger and hostility. Not surprisingly, when parents or others criticize the young child's attempts at developing competence, often the child's response is physical aggression—such as hitting or destroying property. *Frustration*, which occurs when goals are blocked, can also give rise to physically aggressive responses. Consider the child who unsuccessfully works and works at stacking a set of blocks and finally responds to his failure by kicking the blocks across the room.

Whatever its causes, physical aggression typically increases at the beginning of early childhood and then declines as verbal aggression begins to replace it (Côté, Vailancourt, Barker, Nagin, & Tremblay, 2007; Underwood, 2011). The decline in physical aggression is associated with children's growing ability to resolve conflicts in nonaggressive ways—through negotiation, for example—and with their improving experience in *how* to play (Dodge, Coie, & Lynam, 2006). In addition, by the age of 6 or 7, children are less egocentric and better able to understand another child's point of view. This helps in two ways: Children are less likely to misinterpret another child's behavior as aggression, which might invite retaliation, and they are better able to empathize with how another child feels when harmed.

Punishment and Modeling Social forces, such as punishment and modeling, also influence aggression. The urge to behave aggressively can be triggered by settings that produce anger, hostility, or frustration. For example, *punishment* can create a tendency to behave aggressively—especially if the punishment is harsh and frequent. If children are punished for aggressive acts, they usually avoid those behaviors that lead to punishment—at least in the presence of the person who has punished them. Ironically, however, children who are frequently punished typically become more aggressive. For example, their aggression at home

Table 7-4 Types of Aggression

Type	Definition	Example
Hostile aggression	Behavior intended to harm another person	A child intentionally hits another child.
Instrumental aggression	Behavior not intended to hurt another but does so accidentally	A child runs to get a toy and accidentally knocks another child down.
Assertiveness	Standing up for one's rights	A child tells his teacher that another child has taken one of his possessions.

Watch *In the Real World: Learning Aggression* on **MyDevelopmentLab**

may decrease, but they may become more aggressive at school. They also may express aggression in different ways, such as tattling or name-calling.

Adults who use physical punishment to curb a child's aggression also are *modeling* aggressive behavior. As noted earlier (see Chapter 1), observing aggressive models can strongly influence antisocial behavior, both because such exposure teaches the child *how* to display aggression and because it seems to sanction the use of force as an acceptable reaction. For example, one study found that young children who received spankings at home were more aggressive and exhibited more negative behavioral adjustment at age 3 and in first grade than children who did not (Mulvaney & Mebert, 2007). In another especially well-controlled study, increased spanking at age 3 corresponded to higher levels of aggressive behavior at age 5 (Taylor, Manganello, Lee, & Rice, 2010). The link between harsh physical punishment and childhood aggression is well established and it also is reciprocal: high levels of physical discipline escalate children's aggressiveness, which in turn is likely to result in even more physical discipline (Lansford, et al., 2011).

However, the relationship between punishment and aggressive behavior and between observing aggressive models and children's own later aggression are far from simple (Tremblay, 2012). Much depends on the context in which the punishment or modeling occurs. For example, children will react differently to watching a cartoon character on TV punch a villain than they will to watching their father hit an older sibling. Similarly, if the aggressor is a respected role model, the effect is different than if the aggressor is a disliked neighborhood bully. In addition, when a child is able to empathize with the person receiving the aggression, a very different lesson is learned than if the child identifies with the aggressor. Parents and teachers can help children develop more mature and appropriate ways of understanding why aggression occurs by explaining how individuals can deal more effectively with their own aggressive impulses (Tremblay, 2011).

The relationships among factors that influence childhood aggression are undoubtedly far-reaching and complex. Yet, understanding these relationships are important. Indeed, childhood aggression can be viewed as a major public health issue, in that it is linked to dropping out of high school, smoking, risky sexual behavior, dangerous driving, early and single parenting, and living in poverty (Temcheff, et al., 2011). What causes some children to behave aggressively, and what can be done to prevent this behavior? As noted above, parenting behaviors are undoubtedly involved. Yet, not all children who experience harsh physical punishment develop aggressive behaviors as the result. This leads researchers to suggest that other factors are in play as well. One explanation that has been proposed recently is that genes and environment interact in producing aggressive behavior in children (Huesmann, Dubow, & Boxer, 2011; Tremblay, 2012). For example, results of a recent study of monozygotic and dizygotic twins clearly showed that both physical punishment and genetic risk factors contributed to children's development of aggression-related behaviors (Boutwell, Franklin, Barnes, & Beaver, 2011). Furthermore, this explanation seems to apply especially to boys, who generally are found to exhibit more aggression than girls throughout the lifespan (Côté, 2009). Thus, a gene-environment model seems to provide a more complete explanation for the development of aggressive tendencies in children than does a view based solely on environmental factors, such as parenting. It appears that some children inherit a predisposition toward aggressive behavior, and that challenging environmental circumstances are particularly influential in the development of these children.

Watch Classic Footage of Bandura's *Bobo Doll Experiment* on MyDevelopmentLab

Media and Violence Regardless of the specific ways in which genetics and environmental forces interact in the development of aggression, it is clear that children learn appropriate ways of responding by watching others and copying their behavior. Not all models of aggression come from children's immediate environment, of course. Powerful models also are presented via media, such as radio, video games, the Internet, and TV, the last of which is the most pervasive of all. In recent decades, TV viewing has become a powerful influence on children's development. Although in 1950, only 1 family in 10 had a TV set, today virtually every home in the United States, Western Europe, and Japan has at least one TV; many homes have several; and more than half of all U.S. children have a TV in their bedrooms (Beresin, 2010). Figure 7-1 shows the average number of hours per day young children in the United States spend on various activities. On average, American children spend about 28 hours

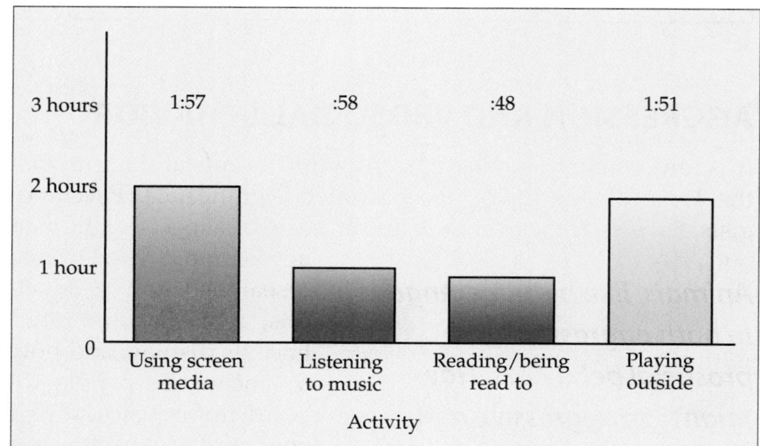

FIGURE 7-1 Average Amount of Time Spent by U.S. Children Age 0–6 in Various Activities

In the United States, young children aged 0 to 6 spend, on average, about the same amount of time per day using screen media as playing outside, and they spend more time listening to music than reading or being read to (Rideout, Hamel, & Kalser Family Foundation, 2006).

SOURCE: From *The Media Family: Electronic Media in the Lives of Infants, Toddlers, Preschoolers and Their Families"* (#7500), by the Henry J. Kaiser Family Foundation, May 2006. This information was reprinted with permission of the Henry J. Kaiser Family Foundation. The Kaiser Family Foundation is a nonprofit private operating foundation, based in Menlo Park, California, dedicated to producing and communicating the best possible analysis and information on health issues.

a week watching television—more time than they spend in any other activity, except sleep (Rideout & Hamel, 2006). Before entering formal schooling, U.S. children are likely to have watched about 4,000 hours of television. For better or worse, television programming has become a major socializing force in the United States, in other industrialized nations, and throughout much of the world (see the box Changing Perspectives: Electronic Media: Is It Changing the Way That Children Grow Up?).

The wide-ranging influence of television—and the increasing influence of music videos, video games, and the Internet—continues to be a major focus of developmental research (Kirsh, 2012; Singer & Singer, 2000). Much of this research continues to assess the effects of media violence. Cartoons, which are targeted specifically at children, typically are very violent, as are many of the video games that children play. Moreover, TV news programs expose children to violence in the real world—and more than two-thirds of U.S. households have the TV on when news programs are televised, such as during the evening meal (Levin, 1998). Many researchers have concluded that exposing children to large doses of casual violence on the TV screen teaches them to think of aggression as a commonplace and acceptable way of dealing with frustration and anger. Not surprisingly, many studies have shown that exposure to televised violence produces a significant increase in the actual aggressiveness of viewers (Murray, 2008). In addition, TV programming changes attitudes: Children become desensitized to the effects of violence and learn to justify their violent behavior when they believe they are right (Ostrov, Gentile, & Crick, 2006).

Why do you think violence is such a predominant theme in TV, movies, music, and video games?

Despite the prevalence of research validating the link between media violence and childhood aggressive behavior, some researchers question the degree to which a *causal* relationship exists (e.g., Kutner, Olson, Grimes, Anderson, & Bergen, 2008). In particular, researchers are questioning the degree to which the violence depicted in popular video games contributes to aggressive tendencies in children. In a recent meta-analysis on the topic, researchers concluded that the impact of media violence in general, and media violence as portrayed on video games in particular, had but a small impact on aggressiveness in children (Ferguson & Kilburn, 2010). Perhaps the conclusion at this point in time is that viewing violence may impact different children in different ways. For children who are susceptible to these messages, perhaps because of their own personality, cognitive functioning, and environmental situation, it probably makes sense to limit the exposure to violent programming that is available (Wilson, 2008). Certainly no harm comes to children who do not see violent images depicted on TV and other media.

Watch *Television Violence* on **MyDevelopmentLab**

For some children, the habitual viewing of aggressive programs may be combined with an environment in which many role models, such as parents, siblings, or friends, are also aggressive or antisocial. This combination seems to increase aggressive behavior, especially in children with behavioral or emotional problems (Huesmann & Miller, 1994). And TV is not the only media source presenting violent, stereotyped messages, although the visual power of television does make it especially salient to young children. Consider the lyrics of songs played on teen radio, the culture of violence that surrounds some popular singers, and the violent acts and themes depicted in many video games (Anderson & Bushman, 2001).

Furthermore, violence is not the only problematic behavior that is modeled on TV. Another media-related issue of concern is that some groups of people are frequently portrayed in a stereotyped fashion: Members of minority groups may be depicted in unfavorable ways; women may be shown in passive, subordinate roles; and older people may be made to appear senile or burdensome. Although some programming aims to correct these unfair stereotypes, children (and others) are still exposed to plenty of examples where prejudice plays a role (Martin, 2008; Morgan, 2007). If unsupervised, young children also may be exposed to considerable and increasingly graphic sexual content (Cantor, et al., 2001).

Parents, of course, can control, at least to some extent, the type of programming their children watch. Since 1996, the TV industry has voluntarily published parental guideline ratings that indicate the degree of violence and sexually explicit content that the programming includes. In addition, TVs built since 1998 are required to be equipped with a V-chip, which allows parents to block out shows they do not want their children to watch.

Even when parents monitor and censor their children's TV viewing, however, many so-called family shows and commercials display engaging images that may be inappropriate for young children. Media also bombards children outside their homes. Eliminating all images of violence and other undesirable behavior from children's experience may be an unattainable goal.

Of course, television can also have a positive influence on children's thoughts and actions (Brown, Lamb, & Tappan, 2009). Positive behaviors can be modeled and taught, rather than negative behaviors. Carefully designed children's programs interweave positive themes, such as cooperation, sharing, affection, friendship, persistence at tasks, control of aggression, and coping with frustration. Research suggests that children who watch such programs, even for relatively short periods, become more cooperative, sympathetic, and nurturing (Greitemeyer, 2011; Mares, Palmer, & Sullivan, 2008). Although children who watch more TV read less

Do you think racial, ethnic, age, and gender stereotypes portrayed in media are generally favorable or unfavorable? What impact do you think such portrayals have on children's attitudes and behaviors?

CHANGING PERSPECTIVES

Electronic Media: Is It Changing the Way That Children Grow Up?

In the developed world, today's infants and young children are growing up immersed in media—TVs, DVD players, computers, iPods, and video games are part of most children's lives. Nearly all U.S. children—99%—have TVs in their homes; a third (33%) of children age 6 and younger and half of all children have TVs in their bedrooms (Beresin, 2010; Rideout & Hamel, 2006). Nearly all of these children have a VCR or DVD player in the home, and almost one in five has a DVD player in the family car. Half also have a video game player in the home, and nearly a third have their own handheld video game player. More than three-fourths of young children live in a household with a computer, and the large majority of these are connected to the Internet.

And children—even very young children—use these media. In a typical day, 83% of children ages 6 months to 6 years use some form of screen media (TV, DVD, video games, or computers): 75% watch TV, 32% watch videos, 16% use a computer, and 11% play with video games. The heavy use of media by children has prompted the American Academy of Pediatrics (AAP) to issue a statement cautioning parents about the effects of media use (AAP, 2008).

The concerns associated with heavy media use by young children are many. Children are great imitators of what they observe, for better or worse. Although many characters viewed by children display positive behaviors, other characters behave in ways that represent gender or racial stereotypes. Especially troubling is the amount of violent behavior present in programs seen by children. One study estimated that by the time children are 18 years old, they will have seen 200,000 acts of violence on TV, including 40,000 murders (Beresin, 2010). Parents report that their children sometimes imitate the aggressive behaviors they see (Rideout, Vandewater, & Wartella, 2003), a finding that is especially troubling because childhood exposure to media violence predicts aggressive behavior in adulthood for men and women, especially among children who identify with aggressive or violent media characters (Huesmann, Moise-Titus, Podolski, & Eron, 2003).

The development of aggressive behavior and stereotyped thinking is not the only concern associated with heavy TV viewing. More attention is being focused on the possible link between childhood obesity and time spent in front of media. TV viewing, of course, displaces time available for physical activity; children who watch the most TV play outside less than children who don't watch as much TV (Vandewater, et al., 2005). It also presents children with a plethora of advertisements for high-calorie foods of poor nutritional quality (Jenvey, 2007). The combination of less physical play and unhealthy food preferences may well be an important contributor to the rapidly increasing incidence of childhood obesity in the United States and other developed nations (Philipsen & Brooks-Gunn, 2008).

Yet another concern is that the time spent with media may actually lead to a shift in the way young children's brains are becoming wired (Ritter, 2008; Small, 2008). Brain development is rapid in early childhood and plasticity is high (see Chapter 3), meaning that the brain wires itself partly in response to environmental experiences. If young children spend more time on technology-related tasks and less time interacting with other people in playtime and through other social activities, this may shift the way the brain develops in early childhood, creating what neuroscientist Gary Small calls the "iBrain." This view may seem far-fetched, but scientists do know that experience is reflected in brain development. One study, for example, examined the brains of right-handed violists: When compared to brains of nonmusicians, the violinists' brains showed considerably greater development in the motor and somatosensory areas that control fine motor movements of the left hand (the hand that plays the strings; Schwenkreis, et al., 2007). Is it possible that heavy use of media might have similar effects on the development of the brain in early childhood?

We have much to learn about the impact technology will have on future generations of children. For example, does the fast-paced nature of most programming and technology affect children's attention spans, making it more difficult for them to stay on task in activities that require sustained attention? Is early computer use linked to later educational achievement? Has the media culture contributed to problems with reading or with the development of language? Has media use affected the socialization patterns of young children interacting in preschool? Do children develop a somewhat different approach to peer relationships as the result of the images they see on TV? These and other questions are of great interest to those studying early development, and research will continue to address such issues.

In the majority of homes the TV is on more than half of the child's waking hours. During some of those hours, children pay close attention to this form of "socialization."

(Vandewater, et al., 2005), those who watch programs with educational content may actually benefit in terms of reading skill development (Moses, 2008). Thus, the choice of programming is important (see the box Try This! A Child's Choice in Media Programming). Accordingly, television can encourage various forms of *prosocial* behavior.

Prosocial Behavior

Prosocial behaviors are actions intended to benefit others (Eisenburg & Fabes, 1998; Spinrad & Eisenberg, 2009). These actions include comforting, sympathizing, assisting, sharing, cooperating, rescuing, protecting, and defending. Prosocial behavior is not just a set of social skills, however. When fully developed, it is accompanied by feelings of friendship, caring, and warmth—including *empathy*, which is the ability to understand the feelings and perspectives of others. For example, if a child watches a person who is sad and the child consequently also feels sad, the child is experiencing empathy. Signs of empathy—such as facial, behavioral, and physiological reactions to seeing others in need or distress—have been linked to

▲ Empathy, caring, and sharing emerge in early childhood but these prosocial feelings and behaviors need some support from adults in order to flourish. Boys, particularly, are sometimes not supported in the development of caring.

prosocial behavior (Eisenberg, Eggum, & Edwards, 2010), indicating that we are more likely to act generously to others when we understand their feelings and needs.

Prosocial behavior begins to develop in early childhood and may be displayed by children as young as age 2. Parents exert a powerful influence on the development of prosocial behaviors in young children, as do siblings. For example, young children who have secure attachment relationships with their caregivers are more likely to be successful in a wide range of peer interactions at age 3 (Moss, Bureau, Cyr, Mongeau, & St-Laurent, 2004). Also, children who can regulate their emotional responses and behavior, who are more sympathetic to others, and who are more "mindful" or aware of others' needs and interests generally exhibit more prosocial behavior (Eisenberg, 2010). Thus, personal characteristics of the child seem to be involved as well.

The Roots of Prosocial Behavior Like aggression, prosocial behavior is seen in every society and culture, suggesting the involvement of an innate, biological mechanism. However, as you might expect, the ways in which prosocial behaviors are defined and the degree to which they develop depend somewhat on the situation and the standards of the family and the culture. For example, in the United States, competitiveness is highly valued, and U.S. children typically become less cooperative and more competitive as they grow older. When playing a game that can be won only if the two players cooperate, one study found that 4- and 5-year-olds often cooperated. Older children, however, tended to compete with each other; as a result, neither player won (Madsen, 1971). In studies of Mexican children and children raised in Israeli kibbutzim, however, researchers found that older children were more likely to cooperate, presumably because their cultures emphasize group goals more than individual achievement (Eisenberg & Fabes, 1998). Such cultural influences also were found in a study in which small groups of 6- to 10-year-old children worked together to learn how to fold origami paper figures (Mejía-Arauz, Rogoff, Dexter, & Najafi, 2007). Children raised in an indigenous Mexican culture, whose mothers averaged only seven grades of schooling, were more likely to coordinate their work, whereas U.S. children of European heritage were more likely to work alone. When U.S. children did work together, their work often involved chatting rather than nonverbal communication about folding. Interaction patterns of U.S. children of Mexican heritage whose mothers had extensive schooling showed an intermediate interaction pattern or resembled U.S. children of European heritage. The existence of culture-specific patters of prosocial behavior raises a question: What factors influence the development of prosocial behaviors?

Because reward, punishment, and modeling affect aggression, it is natural to assume that they also affect helping and sharing behaviors. Although research on prosocial behavior is often technically difficult and may even raise ethical concerns, many studies have, in fact, demonstrated the influence of modeling on prosocial behavior. In a typical study, a group of children observe a person performing a prosocial act, such as putting toys or money into a box designated for needy children. After watching the generous model, each child is given an opportunity to donate something. Researchers usually find that children who witness another person's generosity become more generous themselves (Eisenberg, Fabes, & Spinrad, 2006). In addition, prosocial models generally are more effective when the model is perceived as nurturing or has a special relationship with the child; empathy may be involved as well. Prosocial behavior, thus, appears to be a complex issue that involves not only the child's willingness and ability to make an appropriate response but also the child's appreciation of another person's feelings and needs. How can we encourage young children to develop more prosocial behavior?

Suggest a specific way in which parents can model prosocial behavior for their children. What lesson might this modeling teach?

One approach is to encourage children to *role play*, or act out, how another person might behave. Role playing serves to help children gain a better understanding of another person's point of view and feelings, thereby encouraging empathy (Eggum et al., 2011). Another approach is to explain to children the consequences that their actions will have for others; however, to be effective, the explanations must be appropriate to the age level of the child. When possible, children can be praised or rewarded in other ways for behaving prosocially. Finally, a particularly powerful means of encouraging prosocial behavior is to model it, both by demonstrating helpfulness, cooperation, and other positive responses in our own actions—especially with the child—and by exposing the child

Watch *Competition in Friendships* on **MyDevelopmentLab**

TRY THIS!

A Child's Choice in Media Programming

Television and movies are an ever-present influence in the lives of many preschoolers, and young children often have strong preferences in the kinds of programs they prefer to watch. Each generation has programs that become part of the common culture—*Howdy Doody* in the 1950s, *Sesame Street* and *Star Wars* in the 1970s, and now Sponge Bob and his friends (among others) command attention in many households with young children. What do children learn from these programs? How are they influenced by the messages they see and hear? What do they understand about the events on the screen?

To investigate how children think about what they watch on TV, try observing a young child who is watching a TV show or DVD. Note especially what aspects of the show hold the child's attention and when the child's attention seems to wander. Try talking to the child while the show is playing about the themes of the show. Be flexible as you ask about what is happening, what happened before, and what the child thinks will happen next. Try observing two children, one older (about age 5 or 6) and one younger (about age 2½ to 4). If possible, talk to the child (or children) after the program is over, asking questions such as the following:

- What are your favorite TV shows?
- Who is your favorite character?
- Why do you like this character best?
- What is your favorite movie?
- What did you like best about your favorite movie?
- How many times have you seen it?

Use your imagination so that your conversation provides an impression of what kinds of programs the child prefers and what aspects of the show or media are most influential in shaping the child's thinking. You may need to ask several simple questions about each character—their actions, feelings, intentions, and the consequences of their actions, such as "What did Sponge Bob do? Why did he do that? Then what happened? Is Sponge Bob a good guy or a bad guy? How do you know?"

Reflect on What You Observed

Children, and especially young children, often are able to focus their attention on some aspects of programming; however, they become distracted during other periods. What parts of the show or movie seemed the most attention grabbing for the child or children you observed? Was the child able to follow the story line? Was the child able to verbally express what was happening? Which characters did the child most closely identify with? How much did the child understand about the action and themes of the show?

Consider the Issues

Was it clear whether the child's favorite programs attempted to model positive behavior, or did negative themes run through these shows? How much violence was present in the action or language? How did the child explain what was happening? If you observed children of different ages, how did age seem to affect the child's attention and viewing preferences? What kinds of moral issues were present in the programming that the children watched? Do you think these values are appropriate for young children? Why or why not?

to other positive role models, whether through the TV, school, or other settings (Spinrad, & Eisenberg, 2009). Learning to get along with others is an important task of early childhood and we will continue to learn about this task throughout the remainder of this chapter. In the next section, we explore early childhood developmental conflicts and the development of initiative versus guilt.

REVIEW THE FACTS 7-2

1. When a child's goals are blocked, this gives rise to ___________, which can produce aggression.
2. The child's decreasing egocentrism is related to aggression in what two ways?
3. How does punishment typically affect aggressive urges?
4. What is the relationship between children's heavy viewing of violence on TV and the amount of aggressive behavior they display?
5. Positive behaviors such as helping and sharing are termed _________.
6. When children are able to understand and experience the emotions another person is feeling, this is called _________.
7. Is prosocial behavior the result of heredity, environment, or both?

Practice on **MyDevelopmentLab**

DEVELOPMENTAL CONFLICTS

Trying to express their feelings in socially acceptable ways and learning to behave appropriately are not the only tasks that children face during early childhood. Developmental conflicts also arise as children adjust to their own changing needs. As we saw in Chapter 5, young children are pulled in one direction by their desire for independence and in another direction by their continuing reliance on their parents to provide for their needs. They must also deal with issues of mastery and competence.

As you may recall, according to Erik Erikson, the challenge for the 2-year-old is to develop a sense of autonomy without triggering feelings of shame and doubt. If children are generally successful in doing things for themselves, they become self-confident. If, however, their efforts at autonomy are frustrated by criticism or punishment, they are more likely to think they have failed and feel ashamed and doubtful about themselves (Erikson, 1993).

This conflict between opposing needs (independence versus reliance on caregivers) typically peaks at about age 2. Children at this age, which frequently is called *the terrible twos*, often become uncooperative and defiant, and temper tantrums become common. About age 3, however, children tend to become more compliant and cooperative again, especially if they have had a healthy adjustment to their newly developed sense of autonomy. Once they have learned that they *can* be independent from their parents or caregivers, they begin to focus on developing feelings of competence, which involves the development of *initiative versus guilt*.

It is important to note that development is continuous: There is not a particular day that separates when a child achieves autonomy and therefore is able to move forward to focus on attaining competence. Rather, the development of autonomy and initiative are intertwined: As children learn to be more independent from their caregivers, they are then able to begin to develop their own feelings of achievement. Thus, the transition from Erikson's stage of autonomy to his next stage of initiative is a gradual one that extends throughout early childhood. It is characterized by children's increasing independence from their caregivers and their greater attention to developing their own abilities.

Initiative Versus Guilt

According to Erikson's theory, in the third stage of development, which he termed **initiative versus guilt**, the primary developmental conflict for 3- to 6-year-old children focuses on mastery and competence. Initiative refers to the purposefulness of young children as they ambitiously explore their surroundings (Erikson, 1964, 1989). Young children eagerly learn new skills, interact with their peers, and seek the guidance of parents in their social interactions. For most children, some feelings of guilt also are inevitable, such as when they choose to violate their parents' wishes as they explore their world. Guilt is triggered by the child's newly emerging *conscience*, which is an internal guide that matches the child's behavior to accepted moral standards. Thus, when children violate rules that apply to them, their conscience makes them feel guilty, and they thereby are reminded to reconsider their actions in the future.

The key to healthy development in young children is to achieve a balance between initiative and guilt. As Erikson pointed out, excessive guilt can dampen the child's initiative, especially if parents harshly suppress or criticize their children's natural curiosity. In such cases, children's self-confidence and initiative break down, resulting in timidity and fearfulness that can remain a part of their personality for life. Conversely, parents who do not correct their children's bad behavior or set clear expectations for what is appropriate may encourage them to set unrealistic expectations, which also can be problematic for later development.

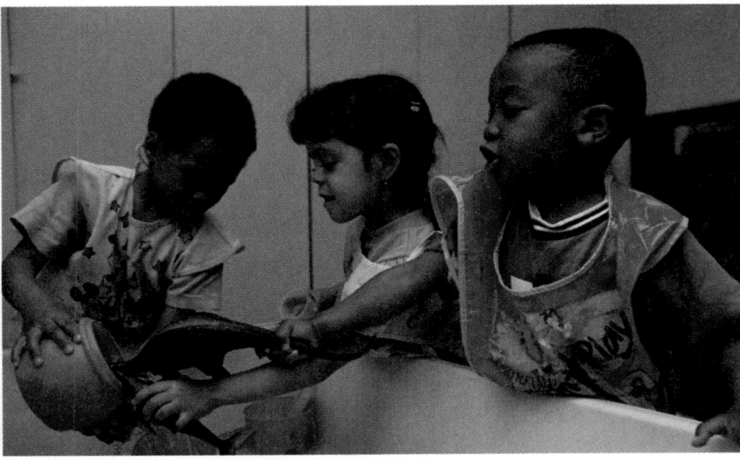

▲ Many preschool activities can serve as a backdrop for lessons in initiative, social influence, and mastery within ongoing peer relationships.

Most children, fortunately, take minor setbacks in stride, and they use them as instructions for approaching developmental tasks in the future. A different outcome, however, can result when children's attempts at mastery or autonomy meet with constant failure or frustration. What happens when children have little or no opportunity to try things on their own? What happens when their environment is so chaotic that they cannot see the consequences of their acts?

When conditions exist that prevent children from becoming independent, they often respond by becoming overly passive or anxious. Children who are chronically ill or have physical disabilities may have limited opportunity to become independent and test their skills. Also, children who grow up in dangerous surroundings may need to be restrained for their own safety or have their activities closely supervised. Circumstances such as these inhibit the development of independence, thereby limiting the child's ability to separate from caregivers and establish a sense of personal initiative and self-reliance.

Children need to master their environment to feel competent and successful. If they do not develop a sense of initiative, they may stop trying to learn and instead become passive in their interactions with the world. Many studies have shown that children who cannot become independent also fail to develop an active, exploratory, self-confident approach to learning. When they enter school, these children often fail to engage with the process of learning (Denham, et al., 2003; Denham, et al., 2012). Their earlier failures at developing a secure sense of their own competence often translate into an attitude that any attempts they make to learn in an academic setting will be met with failure as well. Young children who fail to develop a sense of confidence in their abilities may also develop more disruptive or even aggressive behavior. They may learn to deny, minimize, or disguise their needs instead. Finally, the child who fails to develop a secure self-concept will likely have difficulty establishing successful relationships with peers. As we discuss in the next sections, peer relationships are central to the development of both social skills and self-concept—developmental tasks that are extremely important for young children.

In thinking about your own experiences in elementary school, were the most disruptive children the more academically talented? How might disruptiveness and academic success be linked?

initiative versus guilt
According to Erikson's theory, 3- to 6-year-old children's primary developmental conflict, which focuses on the development of mastery and competence

REVIEW THE FACTS 7-3

1. For Erikson, the developmental conflict for 2-year-olds centers on developing __________.
2. The internal guide that children develop that lets them know when their behavior violates moral standards is called
   a. the empathetic self.
   b. a defense mechanism.
   c. the conscience.
   d. rationalization.
3. When parents set expectations that are too high to attain, their children often develop all of the following, *except*
   a. passive behavior.
   b. aggressive behavior.
   c. anxiety.
   d. empathy.

Practice on **MyDevelopmentLab**

PEERS, PLAY, AND THE DEVELOPMENT OF SOCIAL COMPETENCE

Children influence one another in many ways. They provide emotional support in a variety of situations, they serve as models, and they engage in and encourage complex imaginative play.

As we saw in Chapter 6, play is the work of children. It not only provides an outlet for their considerable energy, but it also provides a context in which they explore, create, and develop their social and intellectual skills. For very young children, play is primarily a solitary activity, as they experiment with and learn about their own bodies and simple objects. Later, play becomes more social, involving caregivers and, eventually, other children (see Table 7-5). Because it involves the development of both social skills and self-regulation, play sets the stage for the development of successful peer relationships. It also involves increasingly complex cognitive skills, and it is not surprising that play is linked to educational achievement as well (Newton & Jenvey, 2011; Whitebread, Coltman, Jameson, & Lander, 2009).

Beginning about age 4, children begin to engage in a particular form of dramatic play referred to as *social pretend play*, which involves imagination and the sharing of fantasies in accordance with agreed-upon rules. Pretend play offers children many opportunities for discussion, reflective thought, and joint problem solving (Roskos & Christie, 2007a; Spivak & Howes, 2011; Xu, 2010). Together, children negotiate mutually acceptable activities and construct the play framework. For example, if two 5-year-olds pretend that they are astronauts, both children share their limited knowledge and develop play sequences in a cooperative fashion.

The Role of Imaginary Companions

As a part of their play, many young children create **imaginary companions**—invisible characters who may seem quite real to the child—who become a regular part of their daily routines (Klausen & Passman, 2006). Children give these characters names, they mention them in their conversations, and they

The development of play in childhood has long been of interest to developmental researchers, as shown by this table from an article published in 1932. Today, children's play is considered to be an important developmental activity, and social play emerges early in childhood.

Table 7-5 The Development of Play

Age: 2	3	4	5	6	7
solitary play children play with toys but do not interact with others					
	onlooker play children observe others as they play				
		parallel play children play alongside each other but do not interact			
			associative play children share materials but do not coordinate their activities		
				cooperative play children engage in a single activity together	

SOURCE: Adapted from "Social participation among pre-school children," by M. B. Parten, 1932, *Journal of Abnormal and Social Psychology, 27*, 243–269.

imaginary companions
Invisible companions that children create and treat as if they are very real

play with them. Imaginary companions help children deal with fears, provide companionship during periods of loneliness, and provide reassurance.

Research indicates that as many as 65% of young children have imaginary companions, and, normally, having imaginary friends is associated with positive personality characteristics. For example, compared with children who do not have imaginary companions, those who do have been found to be more sociable and less shy, as well as to have more friends, be more creative, and participate more in family activities (Gleason , Sebanc, & Hartup, 2000; Hoff, 2005; Trionfi & Reese, 2009). Imaginary companions also seem to help children learn social skills and practice conversations. Children who have imaginary companions are more likely to be cooperative and friendly with both peers and adults and have a better developed understanding of emotion (Davis, Meins, & Ferryhough, 2011; Gleason, 2000; Taylor, Carlson, Maring, Gerow, & Charley, 2004). Children who have active imaginations also have an easier time mastering symbolic representation, which is the key to understanding abstract concepts and complex relationships and ideas.

Cultural Variations in Play

There are, of course, cultural aspects embedded in play. In fact, play is a primary vehicle for practicing the values, behaviors, and roles of society. Through play, for example, children act out themes, stories, or episodes that express their understanding of their culture (Fleer, 2010; Nicolopoulou, 2006; Smith, 2010).

When children pretend, the roles they imitate channel and direct their behavior. For example, a child playing father or mother imitates the parent's behavior as the child understands it. Because major social roles and values differ from one culture to another, we would expect to find that the specifics of play also vary across cultures. This appears to be true, although play itself is found in all cultures (e.g., see Edwards, 2005; Xu, 2010).

Even in cultures where there is little time for play, children frequently create play situations by integrating chores and fun. For example, Kipsigis children in Kenya play tag while tending herds or climb trees while watching younger siblings. Work songs are common among Amish children as they collectively wash potatoes or shuck peas. Children in countries that are at war often play war games.

What types of play were predominant in your own childhood? Do you think these forms of play reflected important aspects of your culture?

There are, however, vast differences in the amount and type of play observed both across and within cultures (Tudge, 2008). In some cultures, children's games are simple; in others, they are complex and elaborate. In some cultures, competitive games are virtually nonexistent and cooperative games are the rule. For example, the day nurseries of the former Soviet Union typically emphasized collective play in the form of group games and provided complex toys that required more than one child to make them work, thereby reflecting and teaching the communal emphasis of the society. In cultures where daily survival depends on motor skills, games of physical skill usually are emphasized. For example, in hunter–gather societies where machetes are used to cut through dense undergrowth, playful competition in the speed of machete use is the norm. In other societies, foot races, competitive tracking, and spear-throwing contests are the main types of play.

▲ Pretend play offers the opportunity for children to share their knowledge, negotiate appropriate activities, and jointly construct the play sequence.

social competence
The ability to initiate and maintain satisfying reciprocal relationships with peers

Social Competence and the Development of Social Skills

Regardless of how a culture defines play, there are always some children who get along better with their peers than do others. For example, when we observe children in nursery schools, day-care centers, or kindergartens, it is apparent that some children are socially competent with their peers and others are not. For better or worse, some children are more popular and make friends more easily. By age 5 or 6 years, social competence usually is well established and, for many children, popularity is remarkably stable over the years. Children who are rejected by their peers in kindergarten are likely to be rejected in middle childhood as well and are also more likely to have adjustment problems in adolescence and adulthood (Gooren, van Lier, Stegge, Terwogt, & Koot, 2011).

Social competence is the ability to initiate and maintain satisfying reciprocal relationships with peers. Socially competent children are more popular with their peers, can make and maintain friendships more easily, and can have satisfying relationships with adults. Through these interactions, children develop the skills and social knowledge that leads them to greater social competence. Researchers have identified various components of social competence, including emotional regulation, social

CURRENT ISSUES

One Pathway to Social Competence

Social competence is an important accomplishment of development in early childhood. Children who are more socially competent adjust better to their peers and to the regimen that the classroom requires (Denham, Bassett, & Wyatt, 2007; Rose-Krasnor & Denham, 2009). Even as early as kindergarten, there is a wide range of social competence among children in the classroom. Several studies found that children who are more socially competent in kindergarten adjust better to elementary school, and they perform better academically. How do young children become socially competent? What are the developmental pathways involved?

Social competence involves several components (Denham, et al., 2012; Katz & McClellan, 1997; Rubin, Bukowski, & Parker, 2006). For example, the *dispositions* of some children, which are relatively enduring ways of responding, contribute to social competence: Socially competent children are more likely to be cooperative, responsive, and empathetic to others. Socially competent children also have better *social skills,* such as the ability to take turns and to participate in conversations. Socially competent children have a better understanding of *social knowledge*: They are aware of the behaviors that are considered appropriate and inappropriate. In addition, socially competent children have a sufficient mastery of the language and knowledge shared by other children, such as the characters' names on popular TV shows, and this knowledge allows them to interact with their peers effectively. Finally, *emotional regulation* seems to be particularly important in the development of social competence (Denham, et al., 2003, 2012; Calkins & Mackler, 2011).

To further explore the relationship between emotional control and the development of social competence, Susan Denham and her colleagues (2003) studied the development of 143 preschoolers longitudinally over a period of 2 years. The researchers were particularly interested in the children's emotional competence, which includes their emotional expressiveness, emotional knowledge, and emotional regulation. Young children express joy and fear, pride and guilt, anger and empathy, and loneliness and anxiety often in ways that are spontaneous and not controlled well. However, children gradually learn to manage these feelings so that they are not overwhelming. Would children who better controlled their emotions develop better social competence? If so, why? Denham and her colleagues reasoned that, to the extent that children are able to control and cope with these feelings, they are more likely to have successful social interactions. When children interact successfully, they also develop additional social skills and knowledge and become more socially competent. What results did this study reveal?

Based on interviews and observations of children and questionnaires completed by parents and teachers, social and emotional behaviors were assessed twice: The first assessment occurred at age 3 to 4 and the second in kindergarten. Using complex statistical techniques to analyze their findings, the researchers found that children who were socially competent at age 3 were also more competent at age 5. These children, who were well on their way to coping effectively with a range of emotions, just kept getting better and better at emotional control. Furthermore, emotional competence at age 3 was a better predictor of later social competence than were social skills or dispositions. Thus, the development of emotional competence may be a critically important developmental task for young children, much like the development of attachment is in the first year of life. When children gain better emotional control and act in less impulsive ways, they can have more successful interactions with their peers, which provides an advantage in learning social knowledge and skills (Gomes & Livesey, 2008).

Studies such as this demonstrate the dynamic process of the interaction of nature and nurture. It is not just temperament or training that predicts social competence, although these factors are important (Eisenberg, 2010; Gaertner, Spinrad, & Eisenberg, 2008). Rather, it is the gradual interactive process of coping in the everyday world of school and home with responsive adults and peers that shapes key abilities such as emotional competence. Early success in developmental tasks also lays the foundation for later development and contributes to positive adjustment, such as the development of social competence. In this way, children learn to integrate new and more challenging experiences with the competencies they have already developed.

---

knowledge, social skills, and social disposition (Calkins & Mackler, 2011; Katz & McClellan, 1997). Of these, emotional regulation, which is the ability to respond to situations with appropriately controlled, yet flexible emotions, seems especially important (see the box Current Issues: One Pathway to Social Competence).

Social competence is often reflected in popularity among peers. Popular children are more cooperative and interactive and generally display more prosocial behaviors during play with their peers; some of these behaviors are summarized in Table 7-6 (Asher, Rose, & Gabriel, 2001; Cillessen, 2011; Rubin, Copian, Bowker, & McDonald, 2011). Popular children also score higher on theory-of-mind tasks, indicating they are better able to understand another child's feelings and perspectives (Newton & Jenvey, 2011; Slaughter, Dennis, & Pritchard, 2002; Rose-Krasnor & Denham, 2009). In contrast, unpopular, rejected children often are either more aggressive or more withdrawn. They may also simply be "out of sync" with their peers' activities and social interactions (Sturaro,

◀ Children who lack social competence are often ignored or actively rejected from group play. If this isolation persists, such children will miss out on later social learning of the group.

Table 7-6 Some Characteristics of Popular Children in Kindergarten

Young children who are popular display certain behaviors in their interactions with their peers. They:

- Join in with other children by moving into the group slowly, making relevant comments, and sharing information
- Are sensitive to the needs and activities of others
- Do not force themselves on other children
- Are content to play alongside other children
- Use good self-control
- Are not aggressive
- Possess strategies for maintaining friendships
- Show helpful behavior
- Are good at maintaining communication
- Are good at sharing information
- Are responsive to other children's suggestions
- Possess strategies for conflict resolution
- Are less likely to use aggressive or physical solutions when faced with conflict

van Lier, Cuijpers, & Koot, 2011). Why do some children lack the social skills that make others popular?

Abuse or neglect during early childhood can be a factor. Research indicates that young children who are physically maltreated by their caregivers are more likely to be rejected by their peers. Because they often have difficulty forming effective peer relationships, abused children are often more disliked, less popular, and more socially withdrawn than children who are not abused (Anthonysamy & Zimmer-Gembeck, 2007); the extent to which they are rejected by peers also increases with age (Dodge, Pettit, & Bates, 1994). Less dramatic but nonetheless potentially important contributors to unpopularity include being *sheltered* by parents and allowed little interaction with peers, being singled out as *different* by peers, or simply getting off to a bad start when first entering a group-care setting. In addition, as you might imagine, highly aggressive children are likely to be unpopular.

There are, of course, some cultural variations in peer acceptance and rejection. For example, in studies of European Canadian and Chinese Canadian children, shyness and quiet behavior were linked to positive responses among children raised in the Chinese culture but not among those raised in the European tradition (Chen, DeSouza, Chen, & Wang, 2006; Chen & Tse, 2008). Thus, popularity seems to be related to conforming to cultural standards. Children who are "different," however defined, are less likely to be regarded positively by peers.

Because peer relations are important to healthy social development, it is important to help children establish positive social skills as early as possible (Anthonysamy & Zimmer-Gembeck, 2007). Adults can help in several ways. First, they can teach social skills directly through modeling and encouragement. Second, they can support opportunities for successful social experiences with peers by drawing unpopular children into group activities and helping them learn how to get along with others. Third, they can provide opportunities to play with other children, as well as the appropriate space and play materials. For example, dolls, clothes for dress-up activities, toy cars and trucks, blocks, and puppets promote cooperative play and offer opportunities for interaction. Finally, and especially with young children, adult caregivers can be available to help initiate activities, negotiate conflicts, and provide social information (Katz & McClellan, 1997).

REVIEW THE FACTS 7-4

1. Approximately what percentage of young children have imaginary companions?
   a. 5% b. 20%
   c. 65% d. 95%
2. The ability to initiate and maintain satisfying reciprocal relationships with others is the definition of
   a. empathy. b. autonomy.
   c. initiative. d. social competence.
3. Social competence usually is well established by age ________ and is relatively ________ throughout life.
   a. 6; stable b. 3; stable
   c. 6; unstable d. 3; unstable
4. Socially competent children are especially good at regulating their ________.
5. What is the relationship between popularity and aggression?

Practice on **MyDevelopmentLab**

UNDERSTANDING SELF AND OTHERS

In this chapter, our focus thus far has concentrated on specific types of behavior, such as how children learn to handle feelings, behave appropriately, and establish social relationships. However, children also act in a more comprehensive way. They put together various specific behaviors to create overall *patterns* of behavior that are appropriate for their gender, family, and culture. As their cognitive abilities develop, children are also able to think in more complex and integrated ways. As we have seen, one aspect of this development is their expanding ability to interact successfully with others, as in when they play. Another way that development proceeds is reflected in how young children begin to understand social concepts—those dimensions of their world that relate to how people behave and interact (Dunn, 2008).

Social Concepts and Rules

Young children busily sort things out, classify behaviors as good or bad, and attempt to find meaning in the *social* world—just as they do in the physical world. Central to the development of social concepts and rules is **internalization**, where children learn to incorporate the values and moral standards of their society into their understanding of themselves.

internalization
The process of incorporating the values and moral standards of one's society into one's self-concept, or understanding of oneself

How do children internalize values and rules? Initially, they may simply imitate verbal patterns: A 2-year-old says "No, no, no!" as she marks on the wall with crayons. She continues doing what she wants to do; however, at the same time, she shows the beginnings of self-restraint by telling herself that she should not be doing it. As development proceeds, children begin to incorporate *social concepts* into their thinking, which often involve understanding how they, as well as other people, think and act. Although many of these concepts are far too abstract for young children, they struggle to understand them in the context of their own level of cognitive sophistication.

Young children who are learning about social concepts often ask, "Why did he or she do that?" The answers often involve attributions about personality and character. For example, the question "Why did Alvon give me his cookie?" may be answered with "Because Alvon is a nice boy." As children grow older, they progressively become more likely to see other people, as well as themselves, as having stable character attributes. In this way, children begin to build positive *self-concepts*, which define how they think about themselves.

What do you think are the most important character attributes that define your personality? Do you think these have changed much since your childhood?

At the same time, young children must learn to understand how *others* think—what they intend, what they feel, and what they want. In fact, the development of social understanding is so important to human development and it begins so early that many psychologists consider it to be an innate potential, much like the ability to learn language (Lillard & Curenton, 1999). Understanding what others are thinking and feeling is particularly relevant to forming early friendships and minimizing disputes. (Refer to the box Current Issues: A Theory of Mind in Chapter 6 for more information.)

Social Concepts in Friendships Social concepts and rules surrounding children's friendships have been studied extensively (Buysse, Goldman, West, & Hollingsworth, 2008; Hughes & Dunn, 2007; Howes, 2009; Majors, 2012). Despite the fact that even young children enjoy the company of other children, they do not acquire a clear understanding of friendship until middle childhood, when their cognitive and social development has progressed to the point where relationships built on mutual trust are possible.

However, young children do behave differently with friends than with strangers, and some 4- and 5-year-olds can maintain close, caring relationships over an extended period. In one study, for example, young children who watched puppet scenarios that involved either a friend or an acquaintance in trouble reacted differently, depending on which character was involved. They responded with more empathy to the friend and showed a greater willingness to help the friend (Costin & Jones, 1992).

Children also demonstrate their growing awareness of social concepts when they engage in arguments or disputes with others. Even children as young as 3 years of age can justify their behavior in terms of social rules with expressions like "Now it's my turn!" or the consequences of an action with expressions like "Stop, you'll break it if you do that!" As children move through early childhood, their understanding of social concepts expands, allowing them to develop closer, more personal relationships with their peers and with others (Hughes & Dunn, 2007; Rubin, Coplan, Chen, Bowker, & McDonald, 2011). Their ability to develop friendships also indicates a growing understanding of *themselves* as their self-concepts form and become better developed.

Self-Concept

Even 2-year-old children have some understanding of self. As we saw in Chapter 5, by 21 months, children can recognize themselves in the mirror; if they see a red mark on their nose, they typically show embarrassment. In addition, the language of 2-year-olds contains many assertions of possession, which imply me versus you: Examples include expressions such as "My shoe," "My doll," or "My car." This assertiveness can be viewed as a cognitive achievement and not as selfishness: Children are increasing their understanding of self and others as separate beings.

Self-understanding, in fact, is closely linked to the child's understanding of the social world. Understanding how one appears to others is an essential step in the development of self-knowledge and self-concept. As children develop, they increasingly define themselves in the context of their relationships with others. Not surprisingly, children who are most social also have more fully developed self-concepts (Harter, 2006).

The self-understanding that children construct helps them regulate their behavior. For example, as they learn who and what they are, children create a cognitive theory, or *personal script*, about themselves that provides guidelines for appropriate behavior, such as "I am a good girl—I don't hit."

As children bring their behavior and their self-concept into alignment, they develop certain generalized attitudes about themselves—a sense of well-being, for example, or a feeling that they are "slow" or "bratty." Many of these ideas begin to emerge very early and at a nonverbal level. Children also begin to develop ideals, and they begin measuring themselves against who they think they ought to be. Often children's self-evaluations are a direct reflection of what other people think of them—for better or for worse. Imagine a lovable 2-year-old with a talent for getting into mischief, whose older siblings call him "Loser" whenever he gets into trouble. By the age of 7, this child might be making a conscious effort to maintain his reputation for being bad. The early influence of others, thus, can have a powerful effect on the development of the basic elements of a person's self-concept.

How might the development of autonomy contribute to children's increasing sense of self?

Watch *Motivation: Carol Dweck* on **MyDevelopmentLab**

Self and Gender

A particularly important dimension of our self-concept is how we think about our **gender identity**, which is our conceptualization of what it means to be male or female. Of course, genetics determines an individual's **sex**, which is a biological description. The environment, or culture, however, provides a conceptual understanding of being male or female, which is more closely related to the concept of **gender**. Therefore, biology and environment both play important parts in determining our **gender roles**, which reflect cultural definitions and expectations about being male or female.

It may be tempting to view gender-related behavior as having a single or simple cause, for example, "It's in the genes." However, this is not the case. Rather, the development of gender identity results from an interweaving of a wide variety of forces, both biological and environmental, which combine together to form the child's unique sense of being male or female.

How do children acquire their sense of gender identity? For perspective, let's look first at some differences between the sexes that set the stage for this process.

Male–Female Differences During Early Childhood Many differences between boys and girls exist, including those that are biologically programmed as well as those that result from sociocultural contexts and learning (Wood & Eagly, 2010). For example, male babies, on average, are born slightly longer and heavier than female babies. Newborn girls, on the other hand, have slightly more mature skeletons and are a bit more responsive to touch. As toddlers, again strictly on average, boys are somewhat more aggressive and girls have a slight edge in verbal abilities. Throughout childhood, girls develop slightly faster than boys. By age 12, the average girl is well into adolescence, whereas physically the average boy is still a preadolescent (see Chapter 10).

It is easy, however, to overemphasize the differences between boys and girls, as both cultural expectations and portrayals in the mass media often present gender-stereotyped images. For example, girls are frequently portrayed as being more social and less achievement oriented than boys. However, research demonstrates that most such gender differences do not exist (Eagly & Wood, 2012; Spelke, 2005). For example, there appear to be no consistent gender differences in sociability, self-esteem, motivation to achieve, or even rote learning and certain analytical skills. In addition, when gender differences are found, it is important to note that the actual differences between boys and girls are small, and there is considerable overlap between the sexes. For example, many girls are more aggressive than many boys, and many boys are not as good at math as many girls.

Perhaps not surprisingly, some gender differences identified in earlier U.S. studies appear to be shrinking, as the roles previously ascribed to women and men become more flexible. For example, although boys continue to outperform girls on tests of mathematical ability, the gap in average scores is narrowing and gender differences in performance in grades 2 to 11 are now trivial (Hyde, Lindberg, Linn, Ellis, & Williams, 2008). For example, in 2011, male high school seniors taking the SAT scored 5 points higher on the Critical Reading test and 31 points higher on the Mathematics test compared to female students. Forty years early, these same score disparities were larger: 12 points and 43 points, respectively (The College Board, 2011). These findings suggest that cultural changes—specifically, changed views of gender-appropriate behavior—have influenced the social roles open to girls and boys, and to women and men (Halpern, 2012).

Androgyny One cultural shift currently taking place in the United States is a growing acceptance of *androgyny*—the view that all people, whether male or female, are capable of developing a wide range of traits. This view suggests that feminine and masculine are not opposite ends of a single dimension; instead, they are viewed as two separate dimensions, which means that it is possible for a person to be high or low on either or both. Stated differently, desirable masculine and feminine traits can easily exist in the same person regardless of gender. Both men and women are capable of being ambitious, self-reliant, and of having assertive traits, which traditionally have been associated with masculine roles. Both men and women can also be affectionate, gentle, sensitive, and nurturing, which are traits consistent with traditional feminine roles. Such a blend of traits in either a woman or a man is referred to as an **androgynous personality**.

Although there is a cultural shift toward a more androgynous view of gender in the United States, there continue to be considerable variations in the gender expectations placed on children in different families. In fact, most children in the United States today hold fairly traditional concepts about gender. Perhaps this is not surprising, as children's gender schemes are developed from their experience, and many aspects of contemporary U.S. culture continue to be quite traditional (e.g., Bronstein, 2006; Leaper & Bigler, 2011).

If parents wish to encourage their children to develop a more androgynous gender identity, they can do so by modeling and accepting such behavior (Bronstein, 2006). For example, the child's father could vacuum the rug, clean bathrooms, and mend clothing, and the child's mother could mow the lawn, repair appliances, and take out the trash. In addition, when both parents approve of these shared roles in the family, a more androgynous view of gender roles is encouraged.

The Development of Gender Identity Regardless of the particular way in which a specific culture or family defines gender-specific behavior, gender identity develops in predictable ways. For

---

gender identity
The knowledge of who we are as male or female

gender roles
Roles we adopt that correspond to cultural definitions and expectations about being female or male

sex
The genetic and biological determination of whether we are male or female

Watch *The Basics: Sex and Gender Differences* on **MyDevelopmentLab**

gender
A conceptual understanding of being male or female, which is largely defined by culture

androgynous personality
Personality type that includes characteristics that are both masculine and feminine traits

By the end of early childhood, most children have a well-established gender role and gender identity. What aspects associated with the male gender role can you observe in this photo of a young boy?

example, by about age 2½, most children can readily label people as boys or girls or as men or women, and they can accurately answer the question "Are you a boy or a girl?"

Although young children easily can discriminate between females and males, they may be confused about what this distinction means. For example, many 3-year-olds believe that if a boy puts on a dress he becomes a girl, and they may not realize that only boys can become fathers and only girls can become mothers. In addition, young children's thinking is concrete and inflexible, and they often exaggerate gender-specific behaviors and rigidly conform to **gender-role stereotypes**, which are fixed ideas about appropriate male and female behavior (Arthur, Bigler, Liben, Gelman, & Ruble, 2008). For example, a 3-year-old girl might say, "You can't play with that *doll*; you're a BOY!" Even when children are exposed to an androgynous view of gender, they typically see *feminine* and *masculine* as two distinct and mutually exclusive categories (Wood & Eagly, 2010). This belief appears in nearly every culture, although different cultures and sometimes groups within those cultures vary considerably in the specific attributes that they ascribe to males and females.

Regardless of the specific traits associated with males or females, most experts agree that the development of **gender schemes**, which are the child's concepts of gender, depends in part on the child's level of cognitive development. This development proceeds along with the child's increasingly complex understanding of the world (Leaper & Bigler, 2011; Ruble, Martin & Berenbaum, 2006). For example, it is not until about age 5 that children begin to understand that their gender is stable and stays the same despite changes in superficial appearance; this is a concept referred to as **gender constancy** (see Table 7-7). It is only after the development of gender constancy that children understand that girls invariably become women, that boys invariably become men, and that gender is consistent over time.

Younger children also view gender more as an absolute characteristic of an individual, rather than a quality that is modifiable. For example, in a study of 5- and 10-year-old children, researchers found that younger children categorize "boys" and "girls" in the same way they view "cows" and "pigs" (Taylor, Rhodes, & Gelman, 2009). Only at age 10 did children begin to understand that gender-stereotyped behaviors (such as "likes to play with trucks") could be applied to both boys and girls. Thus, younger children tend to see gender as an absolute; only later in childhood do they come to understand that environmental factors can modify their concepts of what it seems to be a "boy" or a "girl," and that the stereotype associated with one gender can also be applied in some cases to the other.

Many cognitive-developmental psychologists believe that children are intrinsically motivated to acquire values, interests, and behaviors consistent with their gender, which is a process called **self-socialization**. Children typically develop rigid concepts of what boys do and what girls do. For example, boys play with cars and do not cry; girls play with dolls and like to dress up. Usually, children are more interested in the details of behaviors that are gender appropriate and less so in gender-inappropriate behaviors (Ruble & Martin, 1998), and they will better attend to and remember information that is consistent with their gender schemes. As children progressively become more capable of understanding

Table 7-7 The Development of Gender Schemes Across Early Childhood

Level of Scheme	Approximate Age	Characteristics of Behavior
Gender identity	2 to 5 years	• Can label people as boys or girls by age 2½ • Are confused about the meaning of being a boy or girl • Believe gender is changed by surface appearance; for example, changing clothes changes gender
Gender constancy	5 to 7 years	• Understand that gender is stable and permanent • Understand that boys grow up to become daddies or men and girls grow up to become mommies or women • Understand that gender is consistent over time and situations

gender-role stereotypes
Rigid and fixed ideas about what is appropriate male or female behavior

self-socialization
The process by which children are intrinsically motivated to acquire values, interests, and behaviors consistent with their gender and culture

gender schemes
The concepts (including stereotypes) that define how a person thinks about the behaviors and attitudes that are appropriate for males and females

gender constancy
The older child's understanding that a person's gender is stable and stays the same despite changes in superficial appearance

what it means to be a girl or a boy, their ideas about culturally appropriate behavior for females and males become clearer.

How are gender attributes learned? Over the years, several theoretical viewpoints have been suggested. All such theories, though, view early learning as particularly important. Rewards, punishment, and modeling behaviors that are related to the child's gender begin early. In one classic study (Smith & Lloyd, 1978), female college students were observed interacting with a 6-month-old infant who was not their own. The baby was sometimes dressed as a girl and sometimes as a boy. When the college students thought the infant was a boy, they were more likely to encourage "him" to walk, crawl, and engage in physical play. When they thought the baby was a girl, "she" was handled more gently and was encouraged to talk.

Developing a gender role and a gender identity, however, is not just a result of models and rewards. In fact, indirect messages conveyed by caregivers shape children's self-perceptions and gender identity, sometimes in ways neither children nor parents recognize (Bronstein, 2006). For example, Susan Gelman and her colleagues (Gelman, Taylor, & Nguyen, 2004) observed mothers' conversations about gender with their 2½-, 4½-, and 6½-year-old children as they were looking at picture books and drawings of men and women and boys and girls who were exhibiting typical and atypical gender behavior. As mothers conversed with their children, they did a lot of simple labeling, such as "The mother is cooking" or "The woman is mowing the lawn." Although most of the mothers stated that they did not want to foster gender-based stereotypes, and most said they valued a gender-egalitarian view, their children—especially those in the youngest group—did a lot of gender labeling, sometimes in a very stereotypical fashion. For example, younger children often made rules, such as "Daddies drive trucks." In addition, mothers frequently did not contradict the rules. It appears that young children often insist on clear gender rules, and not until they reach age 5 or 6 can they become comfortable with more flexible gender categories. This type of concrete thinking characterizes cognitive development during early childhood.

When you were a child, what popular toys were usually preferred by boys? Which were preferred by girls? Do you think today's toys are designed with gender issues in mind?

Parents affect their children's ideas of gender directly and indirectly in many ways (Ruble, Martin, & Berenbaum, 2006). Fathers' influence seems particularly important and becomes more influential as children grow older (Lamb, 2010b; Lamb & Lewis, 2011). Fathers, more frequently than mothers, teach specific gender roles by reinforcing femininity in daughters and masculinity in sons. However, both parents and other family members exert a powerful influence on the development of gender identity, as well as on each of the other specific behaviors we have discussed in this chapter, such as regulating emotions, learning to control aggression, promoting prosocial behaviors, and developing competence. In the final section of this chapter, we explore the general dynamics of family life, as well as the role the family plays in the development of the young child.

▲ Children's developing understanding of gender-appropriate behavior and gender schemes often involves modeling and dramatic play.

REVIEW THE FACTS 7-5

1. Our sense of who we are is called our ___________.
2. At about what age do children become able to recognize themselves when they look into a mirror?
   a. 8 months b. 15 months
   c. 21 months d. 36 months
3. How does our use of the terms *sex* versus *gender* reflect the relative importance of heredity and environment?
4. Which of the following gender differences is most clearly documented by research findings?
   a. Boys have higher self-esteem.
   b. Girls are more sociable.
   c. Girls are less achievement oriented.
   d. Boys are more aggressive.
5. Is the view that *male* and *female* are opposite ends of a gender continuum consistent or inconsistent with the concept of androgyny?
6. A child's understanding of gender is referred to as a
   a. gender scheme. b. gender stereotype.
   c. gender role. d. gender constant.

Practice on **MyDevelopmentLab**

FAMILY DYNAMICS

Many family dynamics—parenting styles, number and spacing of children, interactions among siblings, discipline techniques—affect development during early childhood. Because young children are heavily dependent on their parents, parents play a particularly important role in early development.

Parenting Styles

Just as each individual is unique, each family is unique. However, parents do exhibit particular styles when interacting with their children. Two dimensions of parenting that are especially important in characterizing parenting styles are control and warmth.

Parental control refers to how restrictive the parents are. Restrictive parents limit their children's freedom; they actively enforce compliance with rules and see that children fulfill their responsibilities. In contrast, nonrestrictive parents are minimally controlling, make fewer demands, and place fewer restraints on their children's behavior and expression of emotions. *Parental warmth* refers to the amount of affection and approval the parents display. Warm, nurturing parents smile at their children frequently and give praise and encouragement. They limit criticism, punishment, and signs of disapproval. In contrast, hostile parents criticize, punish, and ignore their children, rarely expressing affection or approval.

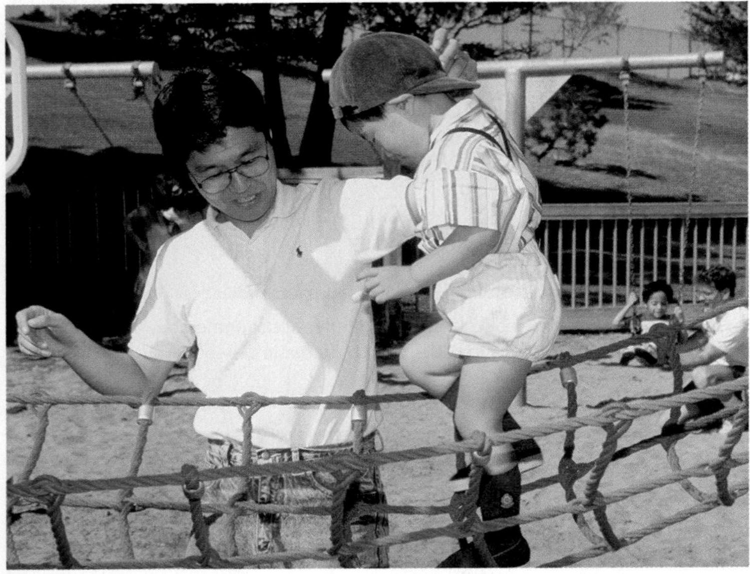

▲ Authoritative parents encourage the developing autonomy of their children while at the same time setting reasonable limits.

Four Parenting Styles By focusing on these dimensions of parental control and warmth, Diana Baumrind (1975, 1980) was able to classify parenting styles into three distinct patterns: *authoritative, authoritarian*, and *permissive*. Subsequent research suggests a fourth style as well—*indifferent* parenting (Maccoby & Martin, 1983). These are summarized in Table 7-8. Each parenting style is associated with different outcomes for children's development.

Authoritative parents combine a moderately high degree of control with warmth, acceptance, and encouragement of autonomy. Although they set limits on behavior, the limits are reasonable, and authoritative parents provide explanations appropriate to the child's level of comprehension. Their actions do not seem arbitrary or unfair; as a result, their children more willingly accept restrictions. Authoritative parents also listen to their children's objections and are flexible when it is appropriate. For example, if a young girl wants to visit at a friend's house beyond the hour when she is normally expected

Table 7-8 Parenting Styles Based on Warmth and Control

Parenting style	Level of Control and Warmth	Description
Authoritative	Moderately high control High warmth	• Parents accept and encourage the growing autonomy of their children • Parents have open communication with their children • Parents set flexible rules • Children found to be the best adjusted—most self-reliant, self-controlled, and socially competent • Children have better school performance and higher self-esteem
Authoritarian	High control Low warmth	• Parents issue commands and expect them to be obeyed • Parents have little communication with their children • Parents set inflexible rules • Parents allow children to gain little independence from them • Children found to be withdrawn, fearful, moody, unassertive, and irritable • Girls tend to remain passive and dependent during adolescence; boys may become rebellious and aggressive
Permissive	Low control High warmth	• Parents allow much freedom and have few or no restraints on their children • Children receive unconditional love by parents • There is communication from children to parents but parents provide little guidance for children • Some children tend to be aggressive and rebellious • Some children tend to be socially inept, self-indulgent, and impulsive • Some children may be active, outgoing, and creative
Indifferent	Low control Low warmth	• Parents focus on stress in their own lives; have no energy left for their children • Parents lack affection for their children • Parents set no limits for their children • If indifferent parents also show hostility (as neglectful parents do), children tend to show a high expression of destructive impulses and delinquent behavior

Watch *Parenting Styles* on **MyDevelopmentLab**

authoritative parents
Parents who combine a high degree of warmth, acceptance, and encouragement of autonomy with firm but flexible control; they encourage communication and negotiation in rule setting within the family

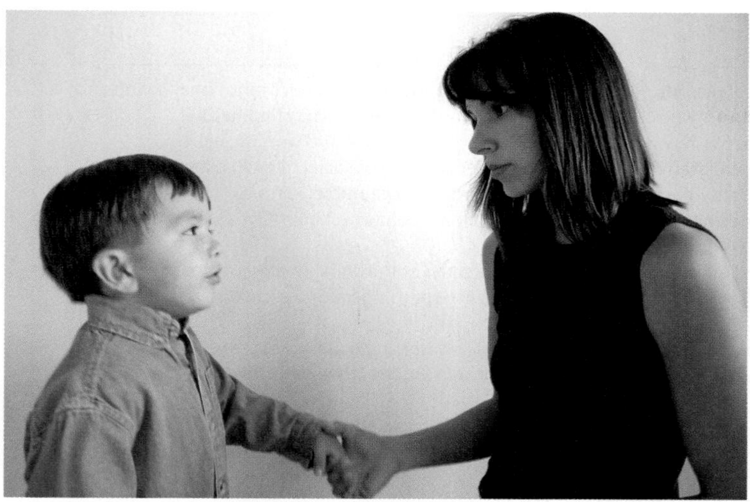

▲ What happens next after a child's transgression in this moment of parental disappointment and child guilt? What will this child learn about power and authority, or about himself as a moral child?

to be home, authoritative parents might ask her why; what the circumstances will be, such as whether the friend's parents will be there; and whether it will interfere with her responsibilities, such as homework or chores. If there are no problems, the parents might allow the small deviation from the rules.

Authoritarian parents are highly controlling and tend to show little warmth toward their children. They adhere rigidly to rules. In the situation just described, their response to their daughter's request would probably be refusal accompanied by statements like "A rule is a rule" or "Because I said so!" If the child argues or resists, the parents might become angry and impose punishment, which often is physical. Authoritarian parents issue commands and expect them to be obeyed; they avoid lengthy verbal exchanges with their children. They behave as if their rules are set in concrete and cannot be changed, which can make the child's attempts at autonomy highly frustrating.

Permissive parents show a great deal of warmth and exercise little control, placing few or no restraints on their children's behavior. The issue of staying out later than usual would probably not even arise because there would be few curfews in the first place, along with no fixed times for going to bed and no rule that the child must always keep her parents informed of her whereabouts. Rather than asking her parents if she can stay out later than usual, the young girl might simply tell her parents what she plans to do or perhaps just let them find out about it afterward. When permissive parents are annoyed or impatient with their children, they often suppress these feelings. According to Baumrind (1975), many permissive parents are so intent on showing their children unconditional love that they fail to perform other important parental functions—in particular, setting necessary limits on their children's behavior.

Indifferent parents neither set limits nor display much affection or approval—perhaps because they are coping with their own addiction problems or mental health issues, or because their own lives are so stressful that they do not have enough energy left over to provide guidance and support for their children.

Effects of Different Parenting Styles What kinds of outcomes do the various parenting styles produce? Generally, children of authoritative parents have been found to fare well in most respects. They are most likely to be self-reliant, self-controlled, and socially competent. These children typically develop higher self-esteem and do better in school than children reared with the other parenting styles (DeHart, Pelham, & Tennen, 2006; Rinaldi & Howe, 2012). Children with difficult temperaments especially benefit from authoritative parenting (Paulussen-Hoogeboom, Stams, Hermanns, Peetsma, & Van Den Wittenboer, 2008).

What positive benefits and negative consequences can result when parents provide unconditional love? Why should parents both love their children and also establish rules and expectations?

Other parenting styles are often associated with difficulties, at least in mainstream American culture. As you might guess, authoritarian parents tend to produce withdrawn, fearful children who are dependent, moody, unassertive, and irritable. As adolescents, these children—especially boys—may overreact to the restrictive, punishing environment in which they were reared and become rebellious and aggressive (Baumrind, 1989; Fletcher, Walls, Cook, Madison, & Bridges, 2008).

Although permissiveness in parenting is the opposite of restrictiveness, it does not necessarily produce the opposite results. Children of permissive parents also may be rebellious and aggressive. In addition, they tend to be self-indulgent, impulsive, and socially inept, although some may be active, outgoing, and creative (Baumrind, 1989). In particular, permissive parenting by mothers has been associated with behavioral problems in childhood, whereas authoritative parenting generally predicts more positive behavioral outcomes (Rinaldi & Howe, 2012).

The worst outcome, however, is often found in children of indifferent parents. When hostility and lack of warmth accompany permissiveness, children tend to show high expression of destructive impulses as well as delinquent behavior.

Although Baumrind's now-classic research forms the basis for much of our understanding of parenting behavior, we must acknowledge that families, like individuals, are unique and that no parenting style is good or bad in every situation. Furthermore, parenting styles can vary considerably across cultures and subcultures, and no one style is universally considered best

authoritarian parents
Parents who are highly controlling, show little warmth, and adhere to rigid rules; in families headed by authoritarian parents, children contribute little to the family's decision-making process

permissive parents
Parents who exercise little control over their children but are high in warmth

indifferent parents
Parents who neither set limits nor display much affection or approval

Table 7-9 Advice to Parents for Establishing Discipline

Discipline practices vary from culture to culture, from family to family, and across historical periods. However, research suggests that children's emotional health and development are fostered when parents adopt a warm and consistent environment. Following are some general principles that parents may find helpful.

- **Provide the child with a safe and loving environment.** Children flourish in environments in which parents provide both guidance and warmth.
- **Provide explanations, not just rules.** By explaining why certain behavior is expected, children develop a better understanding of social rules. Explanations that emphasize how the child's actions affect others encourage the development of an empathy-based understanding of what is acceptable.
- **Be consistent.** It is normal for children to test their limits, and if parents are inconsistent, children are encouraged to try misbehaving again. Consistency also helps children develop a clearer expectation for how they should behave.
- **Provide realistic feedback about the child's behavior.** Avoid being overly critical and make sure that criticism is directed at the child's behavior, not at his or her sense of self-worth. Although appropriate praise fosters the development of a healthy self-concept, don't overpraise. Overpraising leads the child to a false sense of accomplishment and may lead to confusion when others provide more realistic feedback.
- **Eliminate the use of bribes.** Rewards are positive outcomes that follow good behavior, and they are effective. Social rewards, such as praise, are especially effective because they encourage the development of a positive self-concept and a warm and loving parent–child relationship. Bribes are rewards given before the good behavior occurs and should be avoided.
- **Stay calm and avoid physical punishment.** Physical punishment may be effective in the short term but will likely lead to more aggressive behavior that may generalize to other situations. Avoid yelling and screaming; if parents feel they may lose control, they should take a break until they can regain their composure.
- **Be a good role model.** Demonstrate through the parents' own actions the kind of behavior desired in the child.

SOURCE: Several sources for parenting advice are available online. One good source is the website for the American Academy of Pediatrics (www.aap.org). Although the advice noted in this table comes from a variety of sources, one source that focuses on specific behavioral approaches is the "Discipline guide for children," available at keepkidshealthy.com, a pediatrician's guide to children's health and safety, http://www.keepkidshealthy.com/parenting_tips/discipline/index.html.

(Chen & Rubin, 2011; Rudy & Grasec, 2006). Traditional Chinese parents, for example, are often described as authoritarian and highly controlling, yet the "training" approach they use in child rearing fosters high academic achievement (Chao, 2001), as well as other positive outcomes. In Brazil, children raised in indulgent, permissive families fared even better than those with authoritative parents (Martínez, García, & Yubero, 2007). The advantages associated with permissive parenting were also found in a study conducted in Spain (Garcia & Garcia, 2009), suggesting that parent–child relationships in Spanish-based cultures may be structured somewhat differently than those found in U.S. majority-culture families. However, studies conducted in Pakistan (Akter, Hanif, Tariq, & Atta, 2011) and in Iran (Ejei, Lavasani, Malahmadi, & Khezri, 2011) show similar outcomes as do those conducted in the United States—that authoritative parenting is most closely linked to positive developmental outcomes for children. Therefore, it is critically important to recognize, as these examples demonstrate, that researchers who study family dynamics must also be familiar with the cultures in which the families are embedded. What is interpreted as moderate warmth or moderate control in one culture may not have the same meaning in others. Thus, researchers must take care to understand the cultural context of the relationships they study.

Discipline and Self-Control

Regardless of the general style that parents use when interacting with their children, there are bound to be conflicts as parents set limits and children assert their growing need to be independent. Thus, establishing the rules of discipline is an especially important task for parents.

Common methods of disciplining children—setting rules and limits and enforcing them—have varied across historical periods and different cultures. Also, different styles of discipline are adopted within different families. Regardless of culture, though, the most productive disciplinary technique usually involves setting reasonable rules that are enforced fairly; establishing a warm, caring, and consistent environment; and keeping two-way communication as open as possible—a recipe for creating an authoritative style of parenting (see Table 7-9).

Parents, of course, are in a better position than children to control the home environment, and this is particularly true when children are very young. However, the goal of discipline goes beyond simply controlling children's behavior. The goal is for children to establish their own self-control, not only of their behavior but of their emotions as well. How can parents encourage their children to develop emotional self-control?

Although children's emotional responses are often difficult to deal with, parents who help their children think about their emotions and express them constructively have the most positive effect. The key is for parents to make an *emotional connection* with their children rather than ignoring, disapproving, or just accepting the child's emotional responses. One father, for example, tried to distract his daughter by putting her in front of the TV when she was upset and sad. Although the father was concerned, he was not actively helping his daughter understand and control her feelings of sadness. A more effective approach would have been to ask the child why she was sad and to have talked with her about what she could do to make herself feel better.

Helping children achieve emotional self-control is an important aspect of directing their behavior in positive and productive directions. Being able to control emotions contributes not only to children's emotional development, but it also has implications for their success (Diamond & Lee, 2011; Eisenberg, Smith, & Spinrad, 2011). For example, regardless of their IQs, children whose parents had taught them how to cope emotionally had longer attention spans, scored higher on reading and math achievement tests, exhibited fewer behavioral problems, and had slower heart rates. In addition, urine samples from these children contained smaller amounts of hormones associated with stress (Gottman & Katz, 2002; Gottman, Katz, & Hooven, 1996).

The Negotiation of Shared Goals When children learn to develop their own self-control, they are able to take part in relationships within the family more fully (Junn & Boyatzis, 2011). For example, when children can control their emotions, parents and children often can reach an agreement on **shared goals**, which involves a common understanding of how family interactions will be conducted and what their outcomes will be. The result is a harmonious atmosphere in which decisions are reached without much struggle for control. Families that achieve such a balance have a fairly high degree of intimacy, and their interactions are stable and mutually rewarding.

Families that are unable to achieve shared goals must negotiate everything—from what to have for supper to where to go on vacation. When either the parents or the children dominate the situation, negotiation is difficult and the family atmosphere may become unstable. Such a situation often weakens the socialization process during middle childhood and adolescence, making it more difficult for children to effect a smooth transition from dependence on the family to independence and close peer friendships.

Sibling Dynamics

For most children, parents are not the only members of their family. Siblings also are involved, and their roles in the family can play an important part in the development of the young child.

Children's relationships with their siblings can vary widely on a variety of dimensions. Siblings can be devotedly loyal to each other, despise each other, or form an ambivalent love–hate relationship that may continue for life. Attachment to siblings may be as strong as child–parent attachment; in contrast, siblings may have little to do with each other and lead separate emotional lives. Regardless of the degree of interpersonal closeness, siblings can play an important role in helping each other identify and learn social concepts and establish appropriate social roles (Hughes & Dunn, 2007; Whiteman, Bernard, & Jensen, 2011).

If you have one or more siblings, how would you describe your relationships? Can you think of people you know who have especially close relationships with siblings?

Questions often arise about siblings and the similarities of their personalities. Because siblings are produced from the same gene pool and are raised in the same home environment, people frequently perceive that all children in a family will be similar in personality. Actually, research shows quite the opposite; siblings raised in the same family are likely to have very different personalities, often as different as those of unrelated children (Kerr, 2008; Plomin, Asbury, & Dunn, 2001; Plomin & Daniels, 1987).

One reason for personality differences is that children *need* to establish distinct identities for themselves. Thus, if an older sibling is serious and studious, a younger one may choose to be boisterous as a means of establishing a separate role; a girl who has four sisters and no brothers may carve out her own niche in the family by taking on a tomboy role. Although siblings in the same family share many experiences, including living in the same home with the same set of parents, they also have many unshared experiences and relationships. In fact, environmental effects are largely specific to each child, rather than being common to the entire family (Dunn, 2007; Plomin, 1990; Turkheimer & Waldron, 2000).

Birth Order What effect does birth order have on children's personality? Although personality theorists frequently have speculated about the effects that being the oldest, youngest, or middle sibling plays on the development of personality, it appears that few, if any, important and consistent personality differences result solely from birth order. The one exception is that being the oldest child is often associated with some advantages, especially in the area of intellectual skills. On average, first-borns have slightly higher IQs and achieve more in school and in their careers.

Any effects in intellectual ability or achievement associated with being a first-born child are most likely associated with the child's role in the family. Simply put, the first-born child benefits from *all* of the parent's attention, whereas subsequent children must share. This explanation is supported by cross-cultural research (Murray, Brody, Simons, Cutrona, & Gibbons, 2008). The first-born child in a U.S. family usually is at least temporarily the only child in the home and has his or her own room and possessions, with liberal access to parents for conversation and games. In contrast, first-born children in agriculture-based cultures, such as those studied in Kenya (LeVine, 1990), often involve communal living quarters, with the child living with older children from other families who function much like older siblings. As a result, the benefits associated with being first-born are markedly less. Interestingly, "only" children also tend to be high achievers, although their IQs are slightly lower on average than that of the oldest child in a family of two or three children. Although they benefit from their parents' full attention, they also lack the opportunity to serve as teachers for their younger siblings, which can enhance their intellectual development.

As you might expect, there are some advantages associated with being a "younger" sibling as well. For example, younger siblings often show an advantage in physical performance compared to first-born or only children, perhaps because older children in a family "push" a younger sibling to keep up with them in their play. In one such study of 3½- to 7-year-old children, those with older brothers or sisters performed better than first-born or only children on measures of physical fitness, body coordination, and manual dexterity (Krombholz, 2006). Also, some research suggests that having older siblings is a factor associated with relatively good mental health. In a study of large families, having older siblings was linked to better overall mental health, whereas having younger siblings was linked to relatively poorer mental health (Lawson & Mace, 2010). It is unclear how such an effect might be best explained, but it is interesting to speculate about how having older siblings to talk

shared goals
A common understanding between parents and children about how family interactions will be conducted and what their outcomes will be

to, to learn from, and to model might encourage healthy development in many general ways.

Of course, average differences based on birth order tend to be small, and—as with gender differences—they tell us nothing about individual children. We can all think of families in which the youngest child has the highest IQ, and the oldest is the star athlete. However, larger and more consistent differences appear when researchers look at family size and measures of intellectual achievement. For example, the more children there are in a family, the lower their IQs tend to be and the less likely they are to graduate from high school. In thinking about these differences, though, it is important to keep in mind that family size is correlated with a wide array of socioeconomic variables, including family structure (whether there are two parents or one) and income. These variables, too, are significantly correlated with IQ and school achievement in children, making the interpretation of family size correlations very difficult. Cross-cultural studies can shed some light on this issue. For example, in a study of family size and academic achievement among 15-year-olds living in 20 different countries, researchers found that the link between large family size and low achievement was much weaker in societies with stronger public support for child care, universal child benefits, and larger public expenditures on education and the family (Park, 2008). Results such as these suggest that it is not so much family size, per se, that determines outcomes, but rather more general societal factors such as poverty and access to quality education.

Children around the world are raised in a variety of environments, and they develop accordingly. However, despite these differences in their situations, young children experience many of the same conflicts as they work to develop autonomy and competence. Children who develop a warm and loving yet independent relationship with their caregivers and a confident sense of their own abilities are prepared to enter middle childhood and cope successfully with new demands and challenges.

Not all children, however, emerge from their early years having mastered these basic competencies. Particularly troubling in American culture is the effect of child abuse on the development of young children.

Child Maltreatment: Abuse and Neglect

The U.S. Child Abuse Prevention and Treatment Act (CAPTA), first passed by Congress in 1974 and reauthorized most recently in 2010, defines **child maltreatment** as any act, or failure to act, on the part of a caretaker or parent that results in death, serious physical or emotional harm, or sexual abuse or exploitation of a child, as well as situations that present an imminent risk of serious harm. As such, child maltreatment includes both *child abuse*, which involves an action against a child, and *child neglect*, which involves the failure to adequately care for a child. Both child abuse and child neglect have devastating consequences for the children who are subjected to them. Regardless of the child's age, an abusing parent or caregiver destroys the expectations of love, trust, and dependence that are so essential to healthy personality and social development. Not surprisingly, severe developmental problems frequently result.

Do you think that spanking is an acceptable form of punishment for children ages 2 to 6? Why or why not?

It can sometimes be difficult, however, to draw the line between child abuse and acceptable punishment, partly because the distinction varies according to community and cultural standards and partly because governments are not inclined to intrude into the arena of family dynamics. Historically, as discussed in Chapter 1, many cultures condoned and even encouraged physical mistreatment that is now considered shocking and brutal. In Western cultures, for example, harsh physical punishment was viewed as necessary to discipline and educate children. Other cultures sanctioned acts that would now be defined as forms of physical cruelty—such as foot binding, skull shaping, or ritual scarring—and sometimes associated them with deep symbolic meaning and reverence.

Despite some existing cultural and community variations in the definition of acceptable levels of child discipline, today in the United States any action that results in harm to a child is considered child maltreatment. Laws are in place to punish offenders and, in compliance with CAPTA, individuals who have responsibility for caring for children are legally required to report suspected cases of child maltreatment. These "mandatory reporters" include physicians, child-care workers, teachers, social workers, law enforcement officers, and others who are responsible for children's welfare. Indeed, of the child abuse referrals reported in 2010, 57% were made by mandatory reporters; the remaining 43% were made by parents, relatives, friends, neighbors, and anonymous sources (U.S. Department of Health and Human Services [DHHS], 2011).

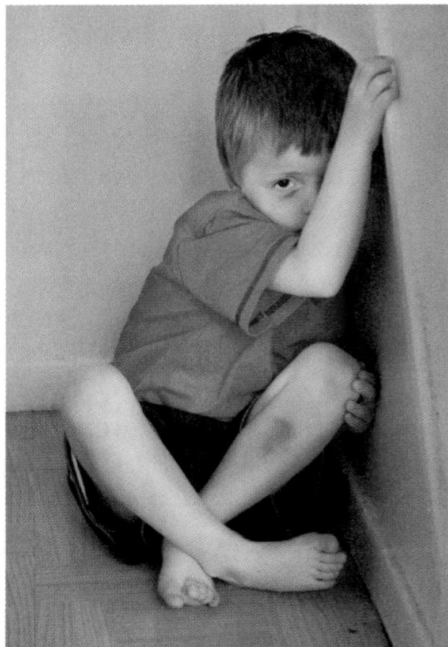

Young children live in the frightening "land of the giants." They are dependent on the benevolent wisdom, guidance, and restraint of the adults around them.

child maltreatment
Any form of child abuse, child neglect, or other domestic violence that affects the lives of children

Physical Abuse and Neglect Sadly, child maltreatment is not uncommon, in the United States and elsewhere in the world. In the United States, state and local child protective services investigate about 3.3 million reports of suspected child abuse or neglect each year, which involve about 5.9 million children (DHHS, 2011). Once a report of suspected abuse is filed, a series of steps will be followed to determine if abuse has actually occurred. Following the filing of a report, a caseworker is assigned to investigate the circumstances and determine if a formal response is appropriate. Of the 3.3 million reports made in 2010, 1.5 million were dismissed because no evidence of abuse or neglect was apparent, and 1.8 million were judged to be serious enough that a response was warranted—and these involved 3 million children. When a response is called for, caseworkers then conduct a thorough investigation of the circumstances of the suspected maltreatment. Because child maltreatment is a serious crime with serious consequences not only for the family but also for the child—who may be removed from the home if abuse seems apparent—these investigations are quite thorough. In most investigations, charges of abuse are not filed. In 2010, 19% of investigated cases ended in charges of criminal abuse. These cases involved 695,000 children—a national rate of maltreatment of about 9.2 victims per 1,000 children, or about 1% of the population of children in the United States (Samuels, 2011). Although an abuse rate of 1% is far too high, this estimate may in fact be deceptively low. Other authors suggest that a more valid rate of child abuse today in the United States may be more in the range 4 to 5%, noting that many cases of actual abuse are not reported, and of those that are, the actual circumstances of abuse might not be adequately documented so that legal action can be taken (Finkelhor, Ormrod, Turner, & Hamby, 2005). Clearly, child maltreatment is a major societal issue in the United States today.

Although these figures may be appalling, they are not unique to the United States: Similar rates are found in many developed countries around the world, and rates in underdeveloped parts of the world often are considerably higher, even when cultural notions of child treatment are taken into account (World Health Organization, 2010). Although reliable data are scarce, many of the same patterns of child maltreatment seen in the United States are present in societies around the globe. For example, abuse is much more common among children under age 4; also, parents are by far the most likely abusers. Risk factors for abuse are similar: being raised by a single parent or young parents without extended family support, household overcrowding, presence of violent relationships in the home, having unrealistic expectations about child development, and poverty. In most places around the world, boys are more often the victims of physical beatings and punishment than are girls, but girls are more likely to be victims of infanticide, sexual abuse, neglect, or forced prostitution.

More is known about child abuse in the United States than elsewhere, although even here reporting issues make accurate estimates difficult to obtain. According to government statistics of substantiated cases of child maltreatment (DHHS, 2011), by far the most common type of abuse was child neglect, which accounted for 78% of the cases documented (see Figure 7-2). In terms of age, it is the youngest children who are most likely to be abused.

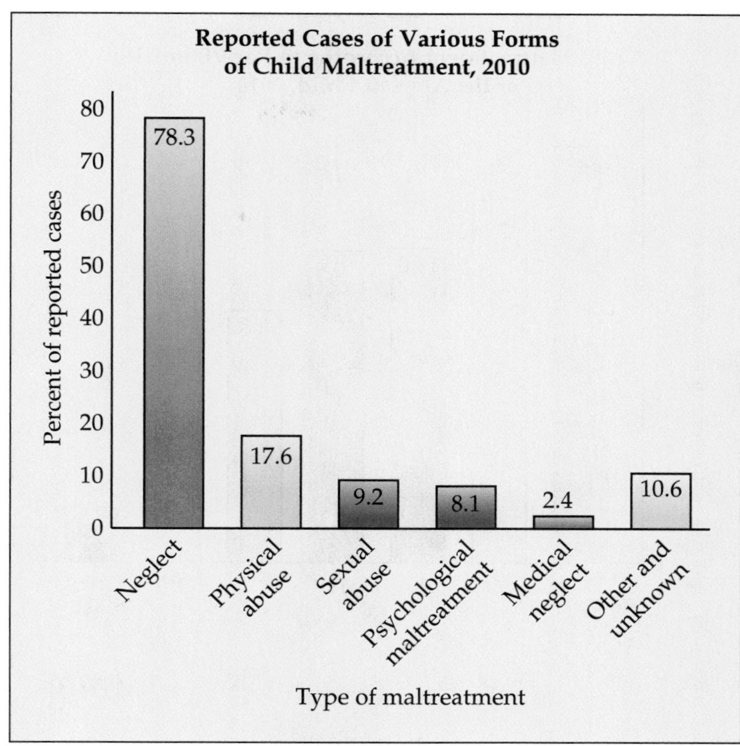

FIGURE 7-2 **Reported Cases of Various Forms of Child Maltreatment, 2010**

NOTE: Percentages exceed 100% because some cases involve multiple types of maltreatment.

SOURCE: *Child maltreatment, 2010,* U.S. Department of Health and Human Services, Administration for Children and Families, Administration on Children, Youth and Families, and Children's Bureau.

Children under the age of 1 year were victimized at the rate of 20.6 cases per 1,000 children in 2010—a rate of just over 2% of the population in this age group. Rates of maltreatment drop to a little more than 1% of the population among 2-, 3-, and 4-year-olds, and rates fall even further as children grow older. Girls and boys are about equally likely to be victimized. In 2010, 48.5% of documented cases of abuse were perpetrated against boys, and 51.5% against girls. With respect to race and ethnicity, African-American children experienced the highest levels of abuse reflecting the unequal socioeconomic circumstances associated with race and ethnicity in the U.S. today (see Figure 7-3).

Parents are by far the most likely perpetrators of child maltreatment: In 2010, 81% of victims were abused by a parent, either acting alone or with another person (DHHS, 2011). Mothers are more likely than fathers to maltreat their children, in part because they spend more time with them. In 2010, about two-fifths (37.2%) of victims were maltreated by their mother acting alone, about one-fifth (19.1%) by their father acting alone, and one-fifth (18.5%) by both parents (DHHS, 2011). In particular, when child maltreatment involves neglect, mothers are much more likely to be involved. Often neglect involves the failure to provide for the child's basic needs of food, shelter, and comfort, but it can also result when medical or educational needs are unmet. Not surprisingly, neglect is often associated with poverty: Although neglect can be intentional, it also can result from lack of resources or knowledge about appropriate child care. Regardless of the

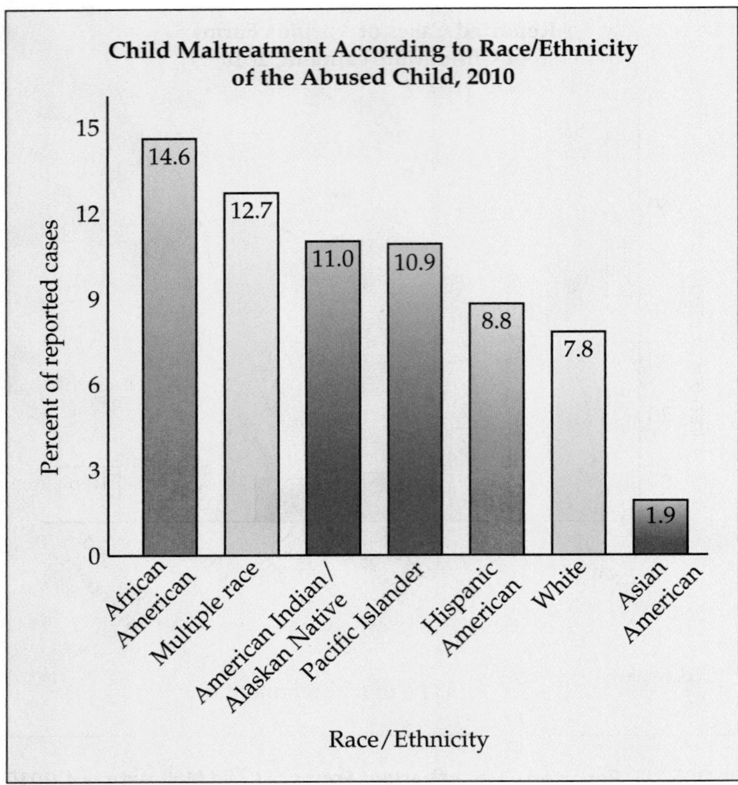

FIGURE 7-3 Child Maltreatment According to Race/Ethnicity of the Abused Child, 2010
Race and ethnicity are associated with many variables that also are linked to child maltreatment, including poverty, employment, access to child care , and immigrant status. Programs that address these social problems, where they exist, can have a positive impact and provide stressed families with valuable assistance.

SOURCE: *Child maltreatment, 2010*, U.S. Department of Health and Human Services, Administration for Children and Families, Administration on Children, Youth and Families, and Children's Bureau.

cause, even subtle forms of child neglect can have severe long-term consequences (Erickson & Egeland, 2002).

In terms of physical abuse, in 2010 more than 1,500 children died as the result of child maltreatment, with nearly 80% of these deaths occurring among children younger than age 4 (DHHS, 2011). Statistically, younger children also sustain more serious injuries than older ones; of those who survive, many suffer traumatic brain injuries that can have permanent, detrimental effects on potentially any aspect of development and functioning—especially if the trauma occurs during infancy or toddlerhood (Lowenthal, 1998). When abuse is physical, fathers are more likely than mothers to be involved. Sexual abuse presents a somewhat more complex picture: Although 95% of sexual abuse is committed by men, when little girls are involved, the child's biological father usually does not commit the abuse: Stepfathers are five times more likely to abuse female children than are biological fathers (Wolfe, Wolfe, & Best, 1988), and sexual abuse is frequently committed by other males in the family. Despite common myths, homosexual men are not more likely to sexually abuse children than heterosexual men, and sexual abuse by strangers is relatively uncommon (Mannarino, 2001).

Psychological Abuse Physical abuse is always accompanied by psychological components that may be more damaging than the physical abuse itself, and psychological abuse can have devastating effects on development, even in the absence of physical abuse. Psychological abuse can take multiple forms (Hart, Brassard, Binggeli, & Davidson, 2002), especially when cultural diversity is considered (Fontes & O'Neill-Arana, 2008). It can range from mild, unkind treatment that virtually all children experience to outrageous, demeaning, and emotionally damaging abuse (see Table 7-10). Psychological maltreatment damages the parenting relationship that should be nurturing and trustworthy. When this relationship is eroded, normal development of almost every aspect of psychological development can be negatively affected. Fortunately, the psychological trauma experienced by most children is not intense or frequent enough to cause serious, permanent damage (Hart, Brassard, Binggeli, & Davidson, 2002).

Effects of Child Abuse All types of child abuse can have long-term effects on children's emotional well-being (Mannarino, 2011; Toth, Manly, & Hathaway, 2011). Children's self-esteem can be irreparably damaged, and maltreated children may find it difficult to trust anyone because of the fear of exploitation and pain. Thus, abused children tend to isolate themselves and may experience more stress and display highly aggressive behaviors when approached than do children who have not been subjected to such abuse (Alink, Cicchetti, Kim, & Rogosch, 2012; Murray-Close, Han, Cicchetti, Crick, & Rogosch, 2008). In addition, abused children tend to have more school-related problems than children raised in nonabusive homes (Cicchetti & Toth, 2000, 2005). Adolescents and adults who were abused as children are at

Why might child neglect be especially difficult for health-care workers or teachers to detect?

Table 7-10 Forms of Psychological Child Maltreatment

Form of abuse	Description
Rejection	Actively refusing the requests or needs of a child in a way that implies a strong dislike of the child
Denial of emotional responsiveness	Passive withholding of affection that involves behaviors such as coldness or failing to respond to the child's attempts to communicate
Degradation	Humiliating children in public or calling them names like "Dummy;" children's self-esteem is lowered by frequent assaults on their dignity or intelligence
Terrorization	Being forced to witness the abuse of a loved one or being threatened with personal abuse, for example, a child who suffers regular beatings or is told "I'll break every bone in your body;" a more subtle form of terrorism occurs when the parent abandons a misbehaving child on the street or in a store
Isolation	Refusing to allow a child to play with friends or take part in family activities; some forms of isolation may also be terrorization; for example, locking a child in a closet
Exploitation	Taking advantage of a child's innocence or weakness; for example, sexual abuse—the most obvious form

greater risk of psychological problems, including depression, alcoholism, and drug abuse; their incidence of suicide attempts is also higher than average (Miller-Perrin & Perrin, 2007; Toth, Rogosch, Caplan, & Cicchetti, 2011).

Abused children also are more likely to have trouble controlling their emotions and behavior, and they tend to be less socially competent than children who are not abused (Curtis & Cicchetti, 2007; O'Dougherty Wright, 2007; Toth, Harris, Goodman, & Cicchetti, 2011). When researchers conducted a longitudinal study of a sample of physically abused 5-year-olds, they found that these children were less popular and more socially withdrawn than their nonabused peers and that these peer-related problems increased during each year of the 5-year study (Dodge, Pettit, & Bates, 1994).

Researchers also speculate that a history of family conflict that involves verbal and physical abuse may have a cumulative impact on children's socialization. Abused children are caught in damaged relationships and are not socialized in positive, supportive ways. They may learn defiance, manipulation, and other problem behaviors as ways of escaping maltreatment; they also may learn to exploit, degrade, or terrorize. For example, when followed to age 21, children who were physically abused in their first 5 years were at greater risk for arrest, juvenile delinquency, and dropping out of school and were more likely to become a teenage parent and have difficulty holding a job (Lansford, et al., 2007). These findings pertain to both abused boys and abused girls. Sadly, abused children may come to *expect* interpersonal relationships to be painful—with pervasive, long-term consequences.

Causes of Child Maltreatment What causes adults to abuse young children? Various explanations have been proposed, and each contributes somewhat to our understanding of the risk factors for abuse. One theoretical framework that has been especially helpful is the ecological perspective, as discussed in Chapter 1. Normally, there are several interacting factors that contribute to child maltreatment; there is no one type of parent who abuses their children. Ecological models are helpful in explaining child maltreatment because they recognize the complex multifaceted issues involved (see Table 7-11 and Figure 7-4). For example, we know that many child abusers were abused as children. Perhaps abused children pattern their own parenting behaviors after their parents, thus perpetuating patterns of abuse. However, more than half of abusive parents were not abused as children. Another possibility is that the abusive parent has unrealistic views of the kinds of behavior that are appropriate in a child and has not learned appropriate parenting skills to cope. Supporting this view is evidence that abusive parents usually single out one child for mistreatment, and that infants and very young children are the most frequent targets (Miller-Perrin & Perrin, 2007). In addition, children with physical disabilities, mental disorders, or difficult temperaments are at especially high risk (DHHS, 2011).

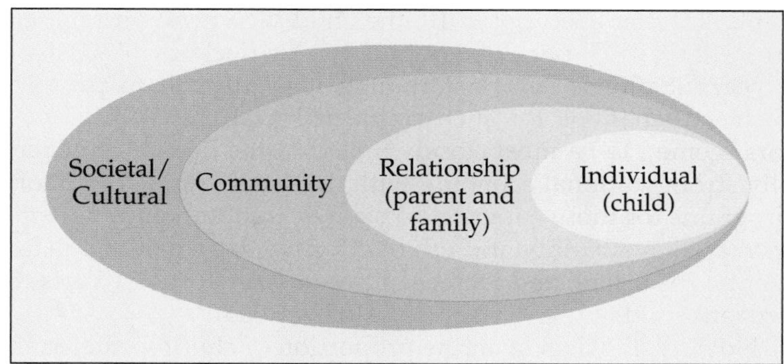

FIGURE 7-4 **Ecological Model for Understanding Child Maltreatment**

SOURCE: From *World report on violence and health: Summary*, World Health Organization, 2002, Geneva: Author.

We also know that although physical abuse of children is found at all socioeconomic levels, it is more likely to occur in poverty-stricken homes. This may be partly because abuse in middle-class homes is less likely to come to the attention of authorities. It is also true, however, that general family stresses, such as those associated with poverty, increase the risk of child abuse. Unemployment, for example, is another risk factor. In addition to creating financial problems, unemployment lowers the parent's social status and self-esteem. An unemployed parent may try to compensate by wielding authority at home through physical domination. Social isolation is another common characteristic of families in which child abuse occurs: When parents have no one to ask for help when they need it, they may take out their frustrations on their children.

In recent years, various forms of child maltreatment have shown a dramatic decline in the United States. Compared to the peak in 1993, by 2004 there were 20% fewer cases of abuse and neglect reported; during the same period, statistics suggest a 40 to 70% decline in cases of physical and sexual abuse (Finkelhor & Jones, 2006; Jones, Finkelhor, & Halter, 2006). This decline has continued during the past 5 years as

Table 7-11 Ecological Levels of Influence in Child Maltreatment (see also Figure 7-4)

Child Characteristics	Premature, sickly, difficult temperament, high activity level
Parent characteristics	Belief in harsh physical punishment, unreasonable expectations for child behavior, drug or alcohol abuse, history of abuse as a child, faulty assumptions about the motivation of the child's behavior, mental illness
Family factors	Poverty, high stress, social isolation, domestic violence, frequent unemployment, overcrowded household, frequent moves, distance from extended family
Community factors	High-crime neighborhood, social crowding or isolation, few family supports, few recreational opportunities, limited day-care availability
Cultural factors	Approval of physical force and violence to solve problems, in reality or in the drama, music, or storytelling of the culture

well. Between 2006 and 2010, the child victimization rate fell from 12.0 to 10.0 per 1,000 population—a decline of 20% over 5 years (Samuels, 2011). Although it is difficult to provide clear explanations for such complex social shifts, three factors seemed to be most closely linked to the decline: a generally strong national economy with nationally funded support programs for those experiencing poverty and unemployment, increased availability and use of effective drug treatments for mental disorders, and increased and more effective efforts to prevent child abuse (Finkelhor & Jones, 2006).

Notably, the decline in the proportion of children subjected to maltreatment was accompanied by a dramatic increase in the number of suspected abuse cases reported. Thus, as the visibility of child maltreatment has been raised in public awareness, the incidence has decreased. Such improvements suggest that social programs and policies can have a dramatic effect on reducing child maltreatment. Child abuse prevention programs typically focus on two goals: providing social support to parents and teaching them better methods of discipline. Programs that focus on teaching high-risk parents new and more realistic ways of understanding their young children's behavior are usually effective, especially if they are begun early in infancy or toddlerhood and are intensive and long term (e.g., Klevens & Whitaker, 2007; Waterhouse, 2008). As noted earlier, abuse can contribute to developmental problems at later stages life. Consequently, we will continue to examine the effects of abuse as we explore development in subsequent periods of the lifespan, such as in middle childhood, which is the focus of the next two chapters.

REVIEW THE FACTS 7-6

1. Which style of parenting generally produces the best outcomes for children? What characterizes this style of parenting?
2. State three things that parents can do to establish a positive context for disciplining their children.
3. When families continually argue about rules of conduct and relationships are strained, this is an example of the failure to establish __________ goals.
4. Among siblings, environmental factors (are/are not) mostly the same for each child.
5. In general, children in which of the following groups are most likely to show an advantage in intellectual skills?
   a. a first-born child in a small family
   b. a first-born child in a large family
   c. a middle child in a large family
   d. the youngest child in a large family
6. Parents who were abused as children are __________ to become abusive parents, compared to parents who were not abused.
   a. less likely b. more likely c. equally likely

Practice on **MyDevelopmentLab**

CHAPTER SUMMARY

Coping with Feelings and Emotions

What distinguishes anxiety from fear, and how do young children learn to manage these emotions?

- One of the fundamental tasks of young childhood is learning to regulate emotions.
- Especially important to emotional development is the child's ability to cope with fear and anxiety. *Fear* is a state of arousal, tension, or apprehension caused by a specific and identifiable stimulus or situation. *Anxiety* is a feeling of uneasiness, apprehension, or fear that has a vague or unknown source.
- Children's specific fears and anxieties are influenced in part by their culture, and some cultures are more accepting of these emotions than others. In addition, fears and anxieties become more abstract as children's cognitive development unfolds.
- Fear and anxiety are normal emotions that often serve a useful purpose, although some children have temperaments that make them especially vulnerable to anxiety. Parents can help children learn to cope with anxiety-producing situations by reducing stress and by serving as positive role models.
- Parents also should understand that children sometimes rely on *defense mechanisms,* which are the psychodynamic tricks and behaviors used by individuals to disguise or reduce tensions that lead to fear or anxiety; these can be useful to the child, especially if parents react favorably. A commonly used defense mechanism is *rationalization,* which involves deluding oneself by creating reasonable but false explanations for events.

Why is learning to control emotions such an important developmental event in early childhood?

- Emotional regulation—learning to deal with emotions in acceptable ways—is a normal part of children's development. For example, children must learn to deal with feelings of guilt when their behavior violates social norms. Shame occurs when children desire to change aspects of their *self,* and it is therefore a more intense and painful emotion than guilt.
- Negative emotions are a part of life, and young children must learn to manage them. Children who have difficulty dealing with anger tend to have more difficulty in school, with peers, and as adults in their jobs and in their personal relationships.
- At about age 3 or 4, children usually develop a curiosity about their genital region, and they commonly engage in sexual play and masturbation. Cultural expectations often limit the expression of such behaviors, so children must learn to adapt their behavior in socially appropriate ways.

Aggression and Prosocial Behavior

What factors give rise to aggression in early childhood, and what factors help children control their aggressive tendencies?

- Aggression is a universal and natural response, but circumstances can exert a powerful influence on the display of aggressive behavior. For example, frustration at having one's goals blocked can give rise to aggression.
- Physical aggression typically increases in early childhood, but then it declines as children learn to resolve conflicts or when verbal aggression takes its place. As egocentrism decreases, so does aggression.
- Children can learn to be aggressive by observing aggressive models, although the context is important in determining how children will respond. When children learn to empathize with a victim, their aggression usually is diminished.
- Punishment, especially if it is harsh and frequent, tends to increase aggressive behavior because punishment often causes frustration. In addition, the person delivering the punishment serves as an aggressive model.

Does viewing violent content presented on TV and via other media have an impact on how young children learn to manage their aggressive tendencies?

- TV and other media have become a pervasive influence in U.S. children's lives. The prevalence of violence and aggression in programming, even for young children, is of special concern. Exposure to media violence is often linked to aggressive behavior because it leads children to see violence as commonplace. They become desensitized to its effects, and they associate aggression with attractive role models.
- TV programming may also be problematic when it depicts groups of people in unfavorable stereotypic ways, thereby encouraging prejudice. Because media presence is so broad, it is difficult for parents to control their children's exposure to negative messages.
- Children's programming can teach positive behaviors when the themes are prosocial.

How does the child develop increasingly more sophisticated prosocial behavior during the period of early childhood?

- Prosocial behaviors, which include positive social skills and a sense of empathy, begin to develop at about age 2. The development of prosocial behaviors is supported when children have secure relationships with parents. Cultural values and expectations also play a role in the development of prosocial behaviors.
- Prosocial behavior can be encouraged by exposing children to models who demonstrate positive behaviors, especially if empathy is involved and the model has a special relationship with the child. Encouraging children to role play can help them understand another person's feelings, thereby increasing empathy. Prosocial behavior also can be encouraged by rewarding the child's prosocial behaviors and by explaining the consequences that their actions will have for others.

Developmental Conflicts

How do young children resolve the developmental conflict between initiative and guilt?

- Young children experience conflict between their need to rely on their parents and their desire for independence. Beginning about age 3, they also must deal with issues of mastery and competence, which Erikson identified as the conflict between *initiative versus guilt.*
- The key to healthy development in early childhood is to achieve a balance between initiative and guilt, the latter of which is aroused by the child's *conscience* when his or her behavior violates social or moral standards.
- Parents who discourage children's curiosity and exploration or who set unrealistically high expectations contribute to feelings of guilt, thereby discouraging the development of initiative. In such cases, children often become passive or anxious, and they may exhibit aggressive behavior as well.

Peers, Play, and the Development of Social Competence

What developmental functions does play serve during early childhood, and how does a child's interactions with peers assist in the development of social competence?

- As children develop, their play becomes more social. At about age 4, children begin to engage in social pretend play, which involves the use of imagination, the sharing of fantasies, and the inclusion of agreed-upon rules. Play is found in all cultures, although its specific forms can vary.
- Many children invent *imaginary companions*—invisible companions that children create and pretend are very real. Children who have imaginary companions tend to be less shy, they are more creative, and they have more friends.
- Some children are more socially competent, and therefore more popular, than others. Children who have developed *social competence* have the ability to initiate and maintain satisfying reciprocal relationships with others. By age 5 or 6, social competence is well established, and it typically is stable throughout life. Thus, it is important to encourage young children to develop social competence. The ability to regulate emotions is especially important in the development of social competence.
- Unpopular children often are more aggressive or, conversely, more withdrawn than others. Factors that can lead to unpopularity include abuse or neglect, being overly sheltered by parents, being different from peers, or just getting off to a bad start with peers.
- Parents can assist children in social development by modeling and encouraging social skills, by creating opportunities for positive group activities, and by helping children play successfully with others.

Understanding Self and Others

How do preschool children acquire their understanding of rules and social concepts?

- Children learn to incorporate the values and morals of their society into their understanding of themselves through a process called *internalization.* As young children develop, they begin to incorporate social concepts—understanding how people think and act—into their thinking.
- As children grow older, they begin to develop their self-concept, which defines how they think of themselves. They also become more likely to see themselves and others as having stable character attributes, or traits.
- Self-understanding is linked to cognitive development, as is the child's understanding of the social world. Children who are more social generally have more fully developed self-concepts.
- As children bring their self-concept and their behavior into alignment, they develop general attitudes about themselves. These self-conclusions often reflect what others think of them. In young childhood, children also begin to measure themselves against their ideals—what they think they ought to be.

How do children come to understand the concept of gender?

- The term *sex*, when used by psychologists, refers to the genetic and biological determinations of being male and female.
- *Gender* is a person's conceptual understanding of being male or female, which is largely defined by culture. People's knowledge of who they are as male or female is called *gender identity.* Gender identity results from the interaction of biological and environmental forces.
- Some differences between boys and girls exist from birth; however, these differences frequently are overemphasized because cultural roles often exaggerate *gender-stereotyped* behaviors. Many gender differences are diminishing as U.S. culture becomes more flexible in defining gender-appropriate behavior. *Gender roles* are the roles that correspond to cultural definitions and expectations about psychologically male or female, and these roles serve to define appropriate male and female behaviors.
- An *androgynous personality* is one in which stereotypically male and female traits are blended together. Although U.S. culture is shifting toward an androgynous view—that both sexes are capable of traditional male and female roles—there is still considerable variation in how individual families and social groups define appropriate gender-related behavior.
- Gender identity develops in predictable ways. First children learn to label people as either boys or girls. Then they develop definitions of what traits are associated with gender. The development of *gender schemes*—the child's understanding of gender—depends on cognitive development. *Gender constancy,* which is a child's understanding that gender is stable and permanent despite changes in superficial appearance, usually does not develop until about age 5.
- The process of *self-socialization* implies that children are intrinsically motivated to acquire the values, interests, and behaviors associated with their gender. Early learning is very important: From a very early age, adults treat boys and girls differently, often in subtle ways. Fathers' influence may be particularly important in establishing gender roles in children. Yet, consistent with the level of their cognitive development, children also construct rules that define gender categories, even when parents do not intentionally teach such gender-stereotyped definitions.

Family Dynamics

What kinds of parenting styles and family dynamics lead to the healthiest adjustment for children?

- Parents play an especially important role in the development of young children, particularly with respect to how parents exert control and express warmth.
- Parenting styles fall into four distinct styles: authoritative, authoritarian, permissive, and indifferent. Authoritative parenting usually produces the best outcomes for children. However, cultural factors must be taken into consideration when evaluating parenting styles.
- *Authoritative parents* combine a high degree of warmth, acceptance, and encouragement of autonomy with firm but flexible control. This style of parenting is associated with the best outcomes for children. *Authoritarian parents* are highly controlling, show little warmth, and adhere to rigid rules, which often results in rebellious or aggressive behavior in children. Children raised by *permissive parents* who exercise little control but provide a lot of warmth tend to be aggressive, self-indulgent and socially inept, or creative. *Indifferent parents* neither set limits nor display much affection or approval, which leads to perhaps the worst outcomes, including destructive impulses.
- How parents manage discipline is an important aspect of the effect that parents have on their children's development. The aim of discipline is not only to control children's behavior but also to help them develop emotional self-control.
- Parental discipline generally produces the best outcomes when parents set reasonable limits and enforce them, are warm, communicate, and establish an emotional connection with their children.
- When families can agree on *shared goals* that represent the common understanding for how family interactions will occur, there is less struggle for control, more rewarding interactions, and more intimacy in the family.
- Sibling relationships vary widely, and siblings often have very different personalities.

- Although birth order is generally unimportant, some small advantages, especially in intellectual skills, are associated with being a first-born child, an only child, and with coming from a small family. These advantages are most likely the result of extra parental attention, and they are subject to cultural forces.

What demographic features describe child maltreatment patterns in the United States today, and what impact does maltreatment have on the children who are victimized?

- Although there are cultural differences in the degree of physical punishment that is considered acceptable, when children are injured either physically or psychologically, this is defined as child maltreatment in most cultures.
- Child maltreatment can include physical abuse, sexual abuse, psychological abuse, neglect, and other forms of domestic violence. Physical abuse most often involves parents, and serious injuries and death are more likely to occur when children are very young. Neglect, which can be unintentional, involves the parents' failure to provide for the child's needs. Sexual abuse is much more likely to be committed by men than women, and girls are at greater risk than boys.
- Psychological maltreatment is always an aspect of physical abuse but may occur in the absence of physical harm. Psychological maltreatment disrupts healthy parent–child relationships, thereby affecting almost every aspect of psychological development. All types of child abuse can have many long-term negative effects, especially with respect to emotional control.
- Child maltreatment is associated with several factors. Parents who abuse their children may have learned abusive behavior from their own parents, they may have unrealistic expectations for their children's behavior, they may be experiencing stress from their life situation, they may be socially isolated, or they may have children who pose special challenges. Ecological models emphasize multiple interacting forces on development and they are especially helpful in understanding the causes of child maltreatment.
- The number of child abuse cases in the United States has been declining since 1993 due to better use of psychiatric medications, a relatively strong economy and better social support programs, and more effective prevention efforts. Child abuse can be addressed through parent-education programs that provide social support and teach nonabusive methods of discipline. However, children sometimes must be removed from their homes to prevent continued abuse.

KEY TERMS

fear (p. 186)
anxiety (p. 186)
defense mechanisms (p. 188)
rationalization (p. 188)
initiative versus guilt (p. 197)
imaginary companions (p. 198)
social competence (p. 199)
internalization (p. 201)
gender identity (p. 203)
sex (p. 203)
gender (p. 203)
gender roles (p. 203)
androgynous personality (p. 203)
gender-role stereotypes (p. 204)
gender schemes (p. 204)
gender constancy (p. 204)
self-socialization (p. 204)
authoritative parents (p. 206)
authoritarian parents (p. 207)
permissive parents (p. 207)
indifferent parents (p. 207)
shared goals (p. 209)
child maltreatment (p. 210)

MyVirtualLife

What decision would you make while raising a child? What would be the consequences of those decisions?

Find out by accessing **MyVirtualLife** at
www.MyDevelopmentLab.com
to raise a virtual child and live your own virtual life.

8 MIDDLE CHILDHOOD
Physical and Cognitive Development

LEARNING OBJECTIVES

- How does a typical child's body change during the period of middle childhood?
- What health-related risk factors pertain especially to children during the grade school years?
- How did Piaget conceptualize the thought processes that take shape during middle childhood?
- In what ways does a child's memory develop during the period of middle childhood?
- How do the typical child's language and literacy skills develop between the ages of 6 and 12?
- How is intelligence defined by researchers working in the field today?
- What are the most important adjustments faced by children when they begin school?
- What factors are associated with academic success during the period of middle childhood?
- How are intellectual disabilities defined, and what philosophy guides the education of children with disabilities in the United States today?
- What symptoms typically are associated with attention-deficit/hyperactivity disorder (ADHD) and with autism spectrum disorders, what are the likely causes of these disorders, and what treatments are appropriate?

CHAPTER OUTLINE

Physical and Motor Development
- Physical Growth and Change
- Motor Skills Development
- Brain Development Health

Cognitive Development
- Piaget and Concrete Operational Thinking
- Memory and Metacognition
- Language and Literacy Development
- Individual Differences in Intelligence

Learning and Thinking in School
- New Demands and Expectations
- Developing Competent Learners and Critical Thinkers
- Success in School

Intellectual and Developmental Disabilities
- Intellectual Disabilities
- Learning Disorders
- Attention-Deficit/Hyperactivity Disorder
- Autism and Autism Spectrum Disorder

Middle childhood—in Western nations, the span of years from about ages 6 to 12—is an exciting time for learning and refining skills. During these years, children focus on testing themselves and on meeting challenges—their own as well as those imposed by their world (Campbell, 2011). Erik Erikson called middle childhood the period of *industry,* which nicely captures the spirit of this stage—the word is derived from the Latin for "to build."

In this chapter, we look at the ways that children build both physical and cognitive competencies. We also look at schooling and at developmental problems encountered in middle childhood, including how academic and intellectual development is measured. Finally, we explore some of the more common developmental disorders that can influence development in middle childhood, including intellectual disability, learning disorders, and attention-deficit/hyperactivity disorder.

Throughout this chapter, we will return to three ideas about development. First, development is *continuous:* The changes we observe in middle childhood build on the development that has already occurred in earlier years. Second, physical, cognitive, and psychosocial factors *interact,* thereby influencing each other as they weave together in each child's life. Third, development in middle childhood occurs in a broader *social context* of school, peers, and the neighborhood. We begin our discussion of middle childhood by examining the physical and motor development that occurs during this period.

PHYSICAL AND MOTOR DEVELOPMENT

During the elementary school years, children refine their motor abilities and become more independent (Payne & Isaacs, 2012; Zembar & Blume, 2009). Given the appropriate opportunities or training, children can learn to ride a bicycle, jump rope, swim, dance, write, or play a musical instrument. Group sports—such as baseball, basketball, and soccer—become important as children's coordination and physical abilities improve, and their social and cognitive competence increases. In addition, middle childhood is a period during which eating and exercise patterns often become established, setting the stage for a variety of health-related issues later in development.

What sports and games are the most popular during middle childhood where you live? Why do you think these activities are the ones most children at this age prefer?

Physical Growth and Change

Growth Growth is slower and steadier during middle childhood than during the first 2 years of life. The average 6-year-old weighs 45 pounds (20.4 kilograms) and is about 3½ feet (just over a meter) tall (Centers for Disease Control and Prevention [CDC], 2000). Gradual, regular growth continues until about age 9 for girls and age 11 for boys; at that point, the *adolescent growth spurt* begins (see Chapter 10). The changes in body size and proportion that are typical of middle childhood are illustrated in Figure 8-1.

There is wide variability in the timing of growth, however; not all children mature at the same rate. For example, girls tend to be slightly shorter and lighter than boys until age 9, after which their growth accelerates because their growth spurt begins earlier. Although, on average, boys and girls are equally strong during middle childhood, there are substantial individual differences in body size and proportion. Such differences may affect the child's body image and self-concept, which is yet another way that physical, social, and cognitive development interacts.

Skeletal Maturation Just as many observable physical changes occur during the years of middle childhood, there also are changes that are internal. During middle childhood, bones grow longer as the body lengthens and broadens. Sometimes these periods of rapid bone growth produce *growing pains,* which are episodes of stiffness and aching that are particularly common at night. These pains are quite common in adolescence but can occur as early as age 4. Parents can help children cope with growing pains by massaging the area, providing a heating pad, and offering assurance that they are a normal response to growth (Dowshen, 2007).

Parents should also be aware that because the skeleton and ligaments of the school-age child are not mature, overly stringent physical training may cause injuries. In the United States, for example, it is common for Little League pitchers to injure their shoulders and elbows. Wrist, ankle, and knee injuries are also associated with vigorous sports when they are undertaken at too young an age.

Another skeletal change in middle childhood occurs when children start to lose their primary (baby) teeth, which begins

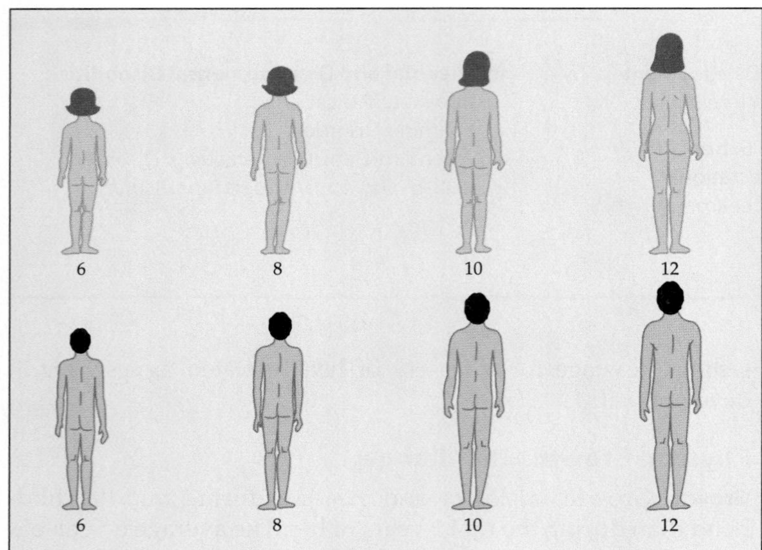

FIGURE 8-1 **Changes in Body Size and Proportion During Middle Childhood**
Broad variations in growth patterns occur during middle childhood. The illustrated changes are typical.

at about age 6 or 7. Soon thereafter, their first permanent teeth emerge, which usually appear too big for the child's mouth until facial growth catches up. Two noticeable landmarks of middle childhood are the toothless smile of a 6-year-old and the beaver-toothed grin of an 8-year-old.

Motor Skills Development

Gross Motor Skills By the time children enter kindergarten at about age 5, locomotor skills—such as running, jumping, and hopping—are well in place. However, during middle childhood, these skills are expanded and children grow stronger and more capable (Haywood & Getchell, 2009). For example, at age 7, a boy can typically throw a ball about 34 feet. By age 10, he can probably throw it twice as far; by age 12, three times as far. Accuracy improves as well, and middle childhood is a time when interest in sports and daredevil stunts is very high.

Although studies often find that boys are more athletic than girls during middle childhood, such gender differences in motor skills before puberty are more a function of opportunity and cultural expectations than of differences attributable to sex (Nichols, 1994; Nurse, 2009). In fact, differences in skill levels are closely linked to the amount of time children spend practicing. For example, girls who participate in Little League develop longer, more accurate throws than girls who sit on the sidelines. Boys and girls who play soccer and other sports that are played equally often by both genders typically develop skills at a similar pace during middle childhood.

Are there sports, games, or other physical activities that are more encouraged for boys than girls in the neighborhood in which you live? Are there activities that are encouraged more for girls than boys? If so, do these reflect commonly held gender stereotypes?

Fine Motor Skills Fine motor skills also develop rapidly during middle childhood, especially when practice is encouraged. When children draw, paint, cut, and mold with clay, they are developing their abilities for more complex skills such as writing. Hand–eye coordination improves with practice. This allows children to draw increasingly complex shapes—first circles, then squares, then triangles—which leads to the ability to form letters or other symbols. Most of the fine motor skills required for writing develop between the ages of 6 and 7, although some quite normal children cannot draw a diamond or master many letter shapes until age 8.

Ideally, children develop mastery over their bodies and at the same time gain feelings of competence and self-worth that are essential to good mental health. Controlling their bodies also helps them win the acceptance of peers. Awkward, poorly coordinated children sometimes are left out of group activities and may continue to feel rejected long after their awkwardness disappears. Table 8-1 summarizes the physical development that takes place during middle childhood.

Brain Development

Brain development in middle childhood continues along paths set in earlier years, and neural plasticity remains high (Giedd et al., 2011; Johnson, 2011; Raznahan et al., 2011). To a considerable degree, brain growth and development is tied to genetic influences (Giedd et al., 2010), although early life experiences do exert influence on how the brain develops, especially in infancy and early childhood (Lenroot et al., 2009).

Brain Growth Most of the growth in the overall size of the human brain occurs early in life: By age 6, the human brain has reached approximately 95% of its maximum size. The overall mass or size of the brain peaks at age 10½ for girls and age 14½ for boys (Giedd, 2008). These findings may seem somewhat surprising, given the frequently held but mistaken belief that brain size corresponds to intellect and problem-solving abilities, which continue to develop throughout adolescence and adulthood. In fact, brain volumes vary considerably among healthy individuals: Children of the same age may have as much as a 50% difference in total brain volume, even though their intellectual and social skills may not differ appreciably. Sex differences are present as well: In childhood, as in adulthood, total brain size is about 10% larger, on average, in boys than girls (Groeschel, Vollmer, King, & Connelly, 2010). As we will see in Chapter 10, the number of cells in the brain diminishes throughout later childhood, adolescence, and adulthood, as neural pruning takes place and unused or unimportant neural circuits are discarded (Casey, Giedd, & Thomas, 2000). Thus, brain development in childhood and adolescence involves a balance of growth, as well as the pruning away, of neural cells.

Table 8-1 Physical Development During Middle Childhood

Age	Major Developmental Changes
5 to 6 years	• Steady increases in height and weight • Steady growth in strength for both boys and girls • Growing awareness of the placement and actions of large body parts • Increased use of all body parts • Improvement in gross motor skills • Improvement in fine motor skills
7 to 8 years	• Steady increase in height and weight • Steady increase in strength for both boys and girls • Increased use of all body parts • Refinement of gross motor skills • Improvement in fine motor skills • Increasing individual variation in level of specific motor skills based on experience
9 to 10 years	• Beginning of growth spurt for girls • Increase in strength for girls accompanied by loss of flexibility • Awareness and development of all body parts and systems • Ability to combine motor skills more fluidly • Balance improvement
11 years	• Girls generally taller and heavier than boys • Beginning of growth spurt for boys • Accurate judgment in intercepting moving objects • Continued combination of more fluid motor skills • Continued improvement of fine motor skills • Continued increasing variability in motor skill performance

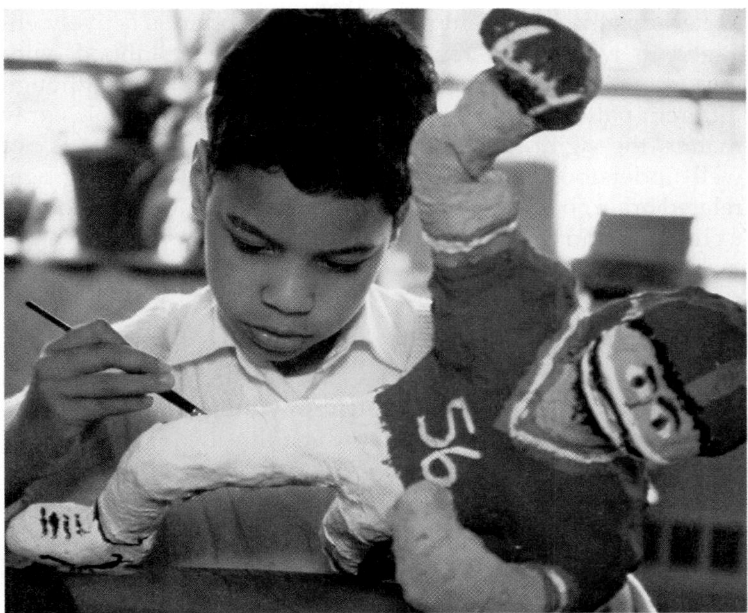

▲ By middle childhood children are developing the fine motor skills required to draw, write, paint, cut, and shape materials like clay and papier-mâché.

Other changes in the brain take place during childhood as well. For example, changes in the part of the brain called the cerebellum follow much the same developmental trajectory as do those in the cerebral cortex; the size of the cerebellum increases in childhood to a peak around the time children enter adolescence, and then its volume begins to decline (Tiemeier, et al., 2010). Also, cerebellar size is about 10 to 13% larger in boys than girls—a difference similar to that found in the cerebral hemispheres. Because the cerebellum appears to play a role in both autism and attention-deficit/hyperactivity disorder—which typically are both associated with childhood onset—further study of cerebellar development is especially important (Tiemeier, et al., 2010).

White Matter and Gray Matter During childhood, the brain continues to better organize itself, assigning certain tasks to certain of its regions. For example, *brain lateralization*—the process of assigning specific functions to defined regions in the left and right hemispheres of the brain—becomes more pronounced during the school years (Thatcher, Walker, & Guidice, 1987). Brain lateralization is accommodated, in part, by development of the corpus callosum, the bundle of neurons that connects the left and right hemispheres of the brain. During childhood and adolescence, the corpus callosum continues to increase in size, allowing for greater coordination between activities controlled by each hemisphere, including sensory processing, memory storage and retrieval, attention and arousal, and language and hearing functions (Giedd, 2008).

The corpus callosum consists of brain tissue often referred to as "white matter." The term *white matter* is descriptive in that it refers to brain tissue that contains many axons surrounded by white, fatty myelin. White matter, which is present throughout the brain but is concentrated mostly under the brain's surface, or cortex, serves to insulate the neurons, increasing the speed with which they can convey messages. Myelin also serves to synchronize the timing of neural messages, so that messages from different parts of the brain arrive at their destination in a coordinated fashion (Fields & Stevens-Graham, 2002). White matter increases throughout childhood and adolescence, as thought processes become more efficient (Giedd, 2008; Giedd et al., 2011).

Other regions of the brain are referred to as "gray matter," reflecting the relative lack of myelin in these regions. Gray matter, which is composed mostly of cell bodies, comprises most of the mass of the brain itself and is associated with higher-level cognitive functions such as attention, emotion, language, and memory. Most of the brain's cortex, or surface area, is gray matter. Gray matter follows a different developmental path than does white matter, peaking in volume in middle childhood—at age 9½ in girls and 10½ in boys—and then declining in adolescence (Giedd, 2008). Correspondingly, the cognitive functions associated with gray matter activity undergo rapid development during these childhood years, although the relationship between the development of cognitive abilities and the development of neural structures is poorly understood. The pruning away of gray matter that occurs following childhood, as neural connections become more streamlined and efficient, appears to underlie the development of more subtle cognitive functions, such as judgment and complex reasoning (see Chapter 10).

Perhaps the important point is that the brain is actively engaged in wiring and rewiring itself during childhood, with important implications for cognitive development. Although different patterns of growth occur in white matter versus gray matter, the significance of these differences at present is not well understood. However, research aimed at studying age-related brain changes is presently of very high interest, and new techniques and findings are emerging rapidly.

Health

Middle childhood is typically one of the healthiest periods in life. Although minor illnesses—such as ear infections, colds, and upset stomachs—are prevalent in younger children, most 6- to 12-year-olds experience few such illnesses. This is partly the result of greater immunity due to previous exposure and partly because most school-age children have somewhat better nutrition, health, and safety habits than younger children (Land, 2008). Minor illnesses do occur, however, and these may have the desirable side effect of helping children learn to cope with stress. In addition, vision problems begin to emerge during middle childhood: By the sixth grade, 25% of White middle-class children in the United States have been fitted with glasses or contact lenses.

Physical Fitness Health is often measured in terms of the absence of illness. A better measure of health, however, is *physical fitness*, that is, the optimal functioning of the heart, lungs, muscles, and blood vessels. Physical fitness does not require that children become star athletes. It simply requires that they engage in regular exercise that involves four aspects of conditioning: flexibility, muscle endurance, muscle strength, and cardiovascular efficiency.

Because of the increasingly poor level of physical fitness in the U.S. population, in 2008, the U.S. government issued its first ever "Physical Activity Guidelines for Americans" program. Guidelines for children and teenagers recommend that all U.S. children and teens engage in 60 minutes or more of aerobic, muscle-strengthening, or physical activity every day (CDC, 2012f). As a way of determining compliance, the CDC is launching a national survey—called "The National Youth Fitness Survey "(NYFS)"—to evaluate the health and fitness of U.S. children ages 3 to 15. Children who volunteer to participate will travel to mobile centers, where their height, weight, strength, and fitness will be measured and they will be interviewed about their eating and exercise habits and drug, tobacco, and alcohol use (National Health and Nutrition Examination Survey [NHAMES], 2012f).

The NYFS project is not the only intervention supported by the U.S. government. In 2011, First Lady Michelle Obama launched the "Let's Move" campaign to encourage children to get more exercise (Let's Move, 2012). Also, federal guidelines for physical education have been suggested for elementary schools. These guidelines advise that classes should not only aim to increase children's skill and overall level of physical activity but also aim to establish healthy, active patterns of behavior that will carry through into adulthood. Thus, national health objectives call not only for physical education classes to meet every day but also that these classes engage students in active physical exercise—preferably lifelong activities such as jogging and swimming—for at least 50% of the time devoted to physical education (CDC, 1997, 2012e). The U.S. Department of Education has urged all schools to adopt the new guidelines, but only some schools have implemented them thus far and it remains to be seen how fully the recommendations will be embraced, especially in schools facing budget shortfalls and other financial strains.

Despite the emphasis that many elementary schools place on physical education, physical activity and exercise have been on the decline among U.S. children. Given the number of hours that school-age children spend watching TV and playing video games, it is not surprising that many live sedentary lives. In addition, some children may not be allowed to play outside for safety reasons, which creates a situation that reduces their activity level still further. Not surprisingly, obesity is becoming a problem for an increasing number of children, especially in the United States and in other industrialized nations.

Obesity Currently, nearly 19% of U.S. children ages 6 to 11 are considered to be *obese*, which represents a huge increase from the early 1970s when the incidence was only 4% (National Center for Health Statistics [NCHS], 2012). (See the box Current Issues: Obesity in Childhood—An Outcome of Our Changing Lifestyle?) In particular, African-American and Mexican-American children are especially at risk: In the years 2007 through 2010, the percentage of children in these groups who were obese was nearly 24%—nearly one-fourth of these populations. Childhood obesity clearly is a growing problem (see Figure 8-2).

Nearly 70% of the children who are obese at ages 10 to 13 will continue to be seriously overweight as adults (Worobey, 2008), which places them at a heightened risk for developing heart disease, high blood pressure, diabetes, and numerous other medical problems. Childhood obesity is also associated with serious social and psychological consequences, which can be as damaging as the physical health consequences associated with obesity (Goble, 2008). Peers may reject or stereotype overweight children and call them names (DeAngelis, 2004). The result can be a negative self-image that may make overweight children even more reluctant to play with peers and engage in physical activities and sports that might help them lose weight—thus creating a vicious circle that helps maintain high weight levels.

What types of things can parents and teachers do to encourage children who are not physically active to engage in more fitness-oriented activities?

What qualifies a child as being obese? Although earlier definitions often used simple weight-based comparisons among children of the same age, researchers now define obesity by a child's weight-to-height ratio with an index called the *body mass index*, or *BMI* (Nihiser, et al., 2007). The BMI is computed by

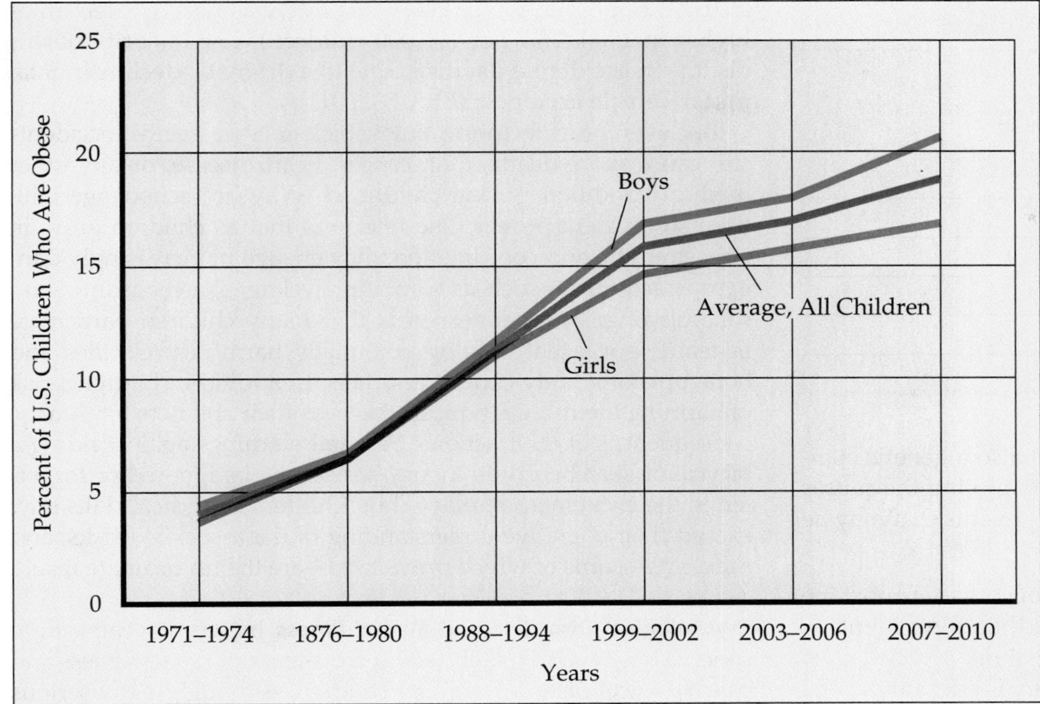

FIGURE 8-2 Trends in U.S. Childhood Obesity Ages 6 to 11 years, 1971–1974 to 2007–2010.

SOURCE: National Center for Health Statistics. (2012). Obesity among children and adolescents 6 to 11 years of age, by selected characteristics: United States, selected years 1971–1974 through 2007–2010. Health, United States, 2011: With Special Feature on Socioeconomic Status and Health. Author: Hyattsville, MD.

dividing a person's weight in pounds by the square of his or her height in inches; that ratio is then multiplied by a constant of 703. The BMI can then be compared to a simple chart that estimates the degree to which an individual is underweight or overweight. Table 8-2 shows the BMI computation, as well as a chart to evaluate BMI. Although BMI ratios have become the standard method of determining weight categories, the BMI ratio is not a perfect means of estimating obesity, especially because it does not consider to what degree a person's weight results from fat versus muscle tissue. In fact, some highly muscular athletes show up on the BMI table as being obese, despite the fact that they are in excellent physical condition. This is because muscle tissue is much heavier than fat, and athletes' bodies are very high in muscle mass. Nevertheless, the BMI provides a good means for individuals of any age to quickly estimate the degree to which their body weight falls inside or outside of the range considered normal.

Asthma Increasingly, children in many Westernized developed countries are developing asthma—a chronic inflammatory disorder of the airways. Today, asthma is the most prevalent chronic disease in children in the United States: In 2010, 14% of U.S. children under the age of 18 had been diagnosed with this disorder (NCHS, 2011a). Children with asthma at times have difficulty breathing and this can cause serious problems. In fact, a small percentage of children actually suffer asthma attacks sufficiently severe to completely prevent their breathing and cause death. Children with asthma are more likely to develop other diseases as well. In addition, asthma may contribute to children's inability to engage in sports and active play as well as to their number of school absences.

What do we know about this disorder? First, as noted previously, it is becoming more prevalent: The percentage of children under age 18 with asthma has increased from 12% to 14% in just the past 10 years (NCHS, 2011a). This increase in incidence has been especially pronounced among Black children: Nearly 50% more African-American children were diagnosed with asthma in 2011 than only 10 years earlier in 2001 (CDC, 2011a). Second, it affects more boys than girls, it affects more African-American children than Hispanic or White children, and it affects more children in the South and Midwest than in other regions of the United States (NCHS, 2011a). It also is more common in urban areas than in rural areas, and it is more prevalent among children who are raised in poverty (see Figure 8-3). As for its cause, researchers are still investigating. Some research suggests that pollution may be partly responsible, especially indoor pollution (American Lung Association, 2011; R. Doyle, 2000). Children who spend more time indoors have greater exposure to household allergens including pets and dust mites. They may also fail to develop immune responses when their outdoor activities are limited, in part because they are not exposed to environmental agents and infections that help them build healthy immune systems (National Heart, Lung,

▲ Patterns of unhealthy diet and exercise, established during childhood, are difficult to change.

Table 8-2 Assessing Obesity

What is your BMI? What is your status?

Computing body mass index (BMI): $\frac{\text{weight in pounds}}{(\text{height in inches})^2} \times 703 = \text{BMI}$

BMI	Status
Below 18.5	Underweight
18.5–24.9	Normal
25.0–29.9	Overweight
30.0–39.9	Obese
40 and above	Morbidly obese

and Blood Institute [NHLBI], 2012). There is also a genetic component to this disease. Ongoing research is exploring the causes of asthma, as well as working to develop treatments that may be more effective.

Accidents and Injuries Obesity and asthma, of course, are not the only health risks associated with middle childhood. Accidents—especially motor vehicle accidents—cause more child deaths than the six other major causes of death combined: pneumonia or influenza, heart disease, birth defects, cancer, suicide, and homicide—and accidents also are the leading cause of physical disability in childhood (see Figure 8-4). Overall, nearly one-half of all childhood deaths result from injuries and accidents. Fortunately, deaths due to accidents in childhood have declined dramatically over the past three decades. Whereas accidental deaths occurred at a rate of 5.7 children per 100,000 children in the U.S. population in 2009, this rate was nearly three times higher in 1980 (16.7 per 100,000 children). The majority of this decline in accidental deaths is due to a dramatic decline in fatal motor vehicle accidents (FIFCFS, 2011b).

But even after factoring out vehicle-related deaths, accidents still cause more deaths than cancer, heart disease, or any other medical condition during childhood. Why are school-age children so accident-prone? One reason is that as children grow in size, strength, and coordination, they engage in increasingly dangerous activities—such as climbing, cycling, skateboarding, and rollerblading. Another reason is that many children participate in team sports that employ potentially harmful projectiles and bone-breaking body contact and falls. In addition, children's risk of harming themselves typically exceeds their ability to foresee the consequences of their actions. Parental warnings against riding a bicycle or skateboard on a busy street may be ignored or forgotten in the excitement of play. Thus, children's physical skills may exceed their cognitive understanding of the associated risks, and accidents—some of which prove fatal—are the unfortunate result.

Psychological Disorders and Mental Illness In recent years, more concern has been raised about the prevalence of mental illness and psychological disorders among children. Although many serious mental disorders, such as schizophrenia and bipolar disorder, typically begin in late adolescence or early adulthood, therapists increasingly are diagnosing cases among grade-school-age children as well. According to estimates provided by the U.S. surgeon general, about 20% of children and adolescents ages 9 to 17 are estimated to have mental disorders with at least mild functional impairment, with about 5 to 9% of these cases being identified as

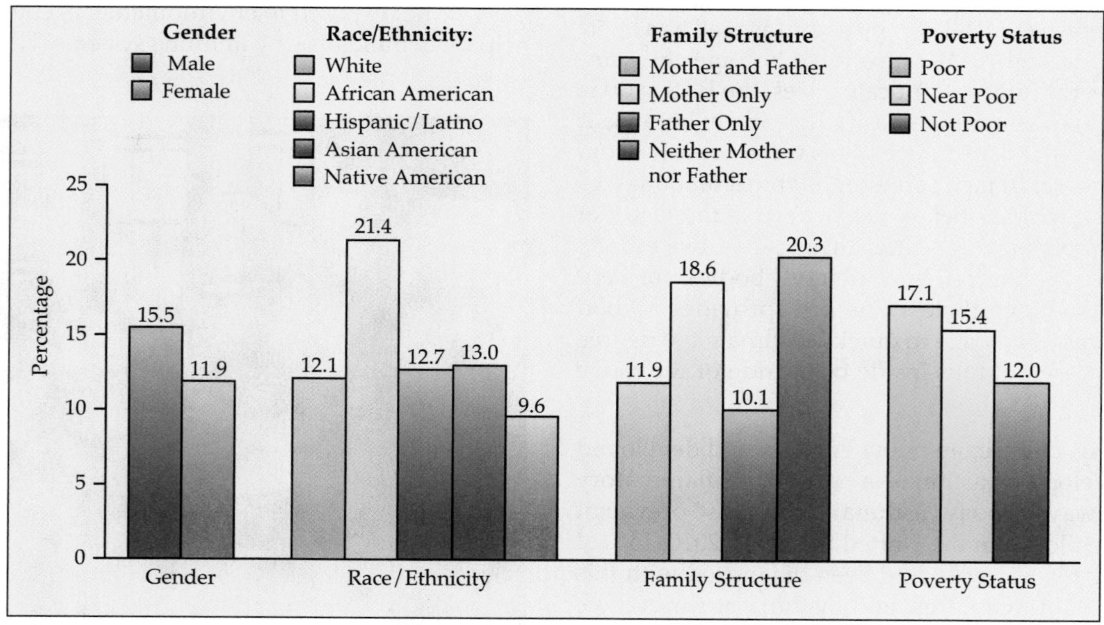

FIGURE 8-3 Percentage of U.S. Children Under Age 18 Who Have Asthma, by Gender, Race/Ethnicity, Family Structure, and Poverty Status, 2010

Asthma is a complex disease that is influenced by a host of demographic factors.

SOURCE: "Summary health statistics for U.S. children: National Health Interview Survey, 2010," by B. Bloom, R. A. Cohen, & G. Freeman, 2011, National Center for Health Statistics, retrieved from http://www.cdc.gov/nchs/data/series/sr_10/sr_10_250.pdf.

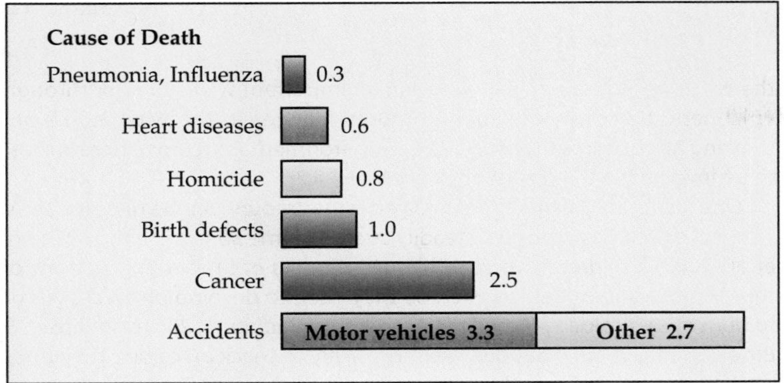

FIGURE 8-4 **Major Causes of Deaths for U.S. Children Ages 5–14 (per 100,000 children in 2009)**

SOURCE: From *America's Children: Key national indicators of well being, 2011,* by the Federal Interagency Forum on Child and Family Statistics, 2011, Washington, DC: U.S. Government Printing Office.

"serious emotional disturbances" (National Alliance on Mental Illness [NAMI], 2012c; USDHHS, 2008). (See Table 8-3 for a listing of some common disorders that can emerge during childhood.)

Although most disorders become more common as children enter adolescence and young adulthood, some disorders are most often diagnosed in childhood, including autism (and autism spectrum disorders) and attention-deficit/hyperactivity disorder (ADHD). Both of these disorders are discussed in more detail later in this chapter.

Although the causes of autism and ADHD are not well understood, most practitioners today are aware of their symptoms, and accurate diagnosis is generally made. However, other disorders—especially those involving child-onset mental illness—are not as likely to be accurately diagnosed. Of serious concern is the general underrecognition of mental illness as a major problem of childhood: Only about one in five children with such disorders receives treatment (NAMI, 2012a). Often, parents, teachers, and health-care providers are not familiar with the symptoms associated with childhood onset of mental illnesses and psychological disorders, which can differ somewhat from those associated with adult forms of these conditions (Barry & Pickard, 2008). When disorders are not identified early and treated effectively, they often lead to a downward spiral of functioning that plays out over many years and often includes school failure, followed by poor employment opportunities, and poverty in adulthood.

Once diagnosis is made, treatment decisions also can be difficult: Many treatments are available, ranging from family therapy to individual counseling to drug therapies, and each can be effective depending on the characteristics of the child, the family, and the situation (Hersen & Reitman, 2008; NAMI, 2012b). However, gaps in the scientific knowledge concerning which treatments work best for which disorders and in which specific family circumstances still limit the safety and effectiveness of options. In particular, prescribing medications for children raises serious questions. Even

Table 8-3 Psychological Disorders and Mental Illnesses Sometimes Diagnosed in Childhood

Disorder	Prevalence in the U.S. Child Population	Brief Description of the Disorder
Attention-deficit/hyperactivity disorder (ADHD)	3–5% of children	A disorder of childhood characterized by difficulty in maintaining task-oriented activity, including impulsivity, excessive motor activity, and/or difficulty in sustaining attention
Autism spectrum disorder (ASD)	3–4% of children	A variety of disorders of childhood, including autism, that all involve a wide range of problematic behaviors, including deficits in language, perception, and motor development, along with social withdrawal
Conduct disorder	10% (ages 9–17); more common in adolescence than in middle childhood	A behavioral disorder, sometimes diagnosed in childhood, that is characterized by antisocial behaviors that violate social rules and/or the rights of others
Depression	10–15% (of children and adolescents)	Psychological disorder characterized by sad mood, reduced energy, cognitive impairment, irritability (in children), and feeling of hopelessness; adult prevalence is comparable to child and adolescent rate
Bipolar disorder	2% of adult population; sometimes diagnosed in childhood	Also known as manic–depression; disorder characterized by mood shifts including periods of depression and of mania (heightened mood and energy)
Schizophrenia, childhood onset	1 in 40,000 children under age 12	Mental disorder characterized by significant disturbances of cognition, perception, behavior, and mood; adult prevalence is about 1%
Posttraumatic stress disorder (PTSD)	Varies significantly according to degree of stress experienced	Anxiety disorder that results from exposure to extremely stressful events, such as child abuse, parental homicide, sexual abuse, or community violence

SOURCE: Adapted from *Abnormal psychology: Core concepts*, by J. N. Butcher, S. Mineka, and J. M. Hooley, 2009, Harlow: Pearson Education; *Mental health: A report of the surgeon general*, U.S. Department of Health and Human Services (USDHHS), 2008, retrieved from http://www.surgeongeneral.gov/library/mentalhealth/chapter2/sec2_1.html; and *Child and adolescent mental illness and drug use Statistics*, American Academy of Child and Adolescent Psychiatry (AACAP), 2009, retrieved from http://www.aacap.org/cs/root/resources_for_families/child_and_adolescent_mental_illness.

CURRENT ISSUES

Obesity in Childhood—An Outcome of Our Changing Lifestyle?

The prevalence of obesity among children is dramatically on the rise, both in the United States and in many other developed and developing nations around the world: How can we explain this troubling increase in the numbers of children who are seriously overweight? As is the case for most complex behaviors, both biological and environmental factors are almost certainly involved.

From a biological perspective, the tendency toward obesity is partly determined by heredity, both narrowly defined according to the specific genes one inherits from one's parents, and more broadly defined as determined by evolutionary pressures. From an evolutionary perspective, we know that food was generally scarce for our early hunter–gatherer ancestors; when they were able to find food, they consumed it in massive quantities to protect against future scarcity. Our human gene pool may retain biological programming to eat as much food as we can consume whenever we can to build an energy reserve in the event that food is not available. In today's culture of abundance, where little physical activity is required for the majority of people, obesity may be the result. At the level of the individual, genetic factors undoubtedly play an influential role (Sanderson & Faith, 2010). A child with one obese parent has a 40% chance of becoming obese, and the probability increases to 80% if both parents are obese (Kinnunen, Pietiläinen, & Rissanen, 2006). In studies of adopted children, researchers generally find that children more closely resembled their biological parents in body weight than they do their adoptive parents (Rosenthal, 1990). This suggests that genetic, in contrast to environmental, determinants are heavily involved in body weight. Indeed, research summaries based on twin, adoption, and family studies lead to the conclusion that at least 50% of the causal factors linked to obesity are genetic in origin (Hebebrand & Hinney, 2009). Clearly, the genes one inherits from one's parents play an important role in determining one's body weight.

Genetics and evolutionary predispositions do not represent the entire story, however, and they should not be used as excuses for being overweight. Obesity is directly linked to the amount and types of food consumed—environment plays a critical role. In fact, it may be the case that obesity is best explained by a gene × environment interaction model, in which individuals who inherit certain genetic profiles are especially predisposed to overconsume foods, to prefer high-calorie foods, to burn excess calories less efficiently, and to prefer sedentary lifestyles that contribute to overweight. Individuals who inherit a "thin" genetic profile are more likely to adopt different eating and lifestyle habits, and are much less prone to weight gain and obesity (Farooqi, 2010). Epigenetic processes also may be involved (see Chapter 2). Specifically, a child's early eating and activity patterns may actually shape the way in which the genes controlling obesity act (Lillycrop & Burdge, 2011). According to this view, a calorie-rich and sedentary early environment sets the stage for the development of genetically driven biological and metabolic processes that lead to obesity.

In any case, it seems clear that both one's genes and one's environment are heavily involved in eating behaviors and obesity. Certainly, environmental factors must be considered in explaining the recent and dramatic increase in obesity among U.S. children, especially over the past 30 years. Gene pools do not shift quickly enough to explain this phenomenon and the environment must be involved in an important way, whether through epigenetic processes or simply through changes in the way people are thinking about and eating food. What environmental circumstances appear to be involved in the recent obesity epidemic?

One factor that seems to be involved is the amount of time devoted to TV viewing, which has increased steadily over the same 30-year period (O'Brien, et al., 2007). Children who spend large amounts of time sitting in front of the TV often do not get the exercise they need to develop physical skills or to burn excess calories (American Academy of Pediatrics, 2011b; Philipsen & Brooks-Gunn, 2008). They also are more likely to snack on calorie-rich foods as they relax in front of the screen (Brown, Nicholson, Broom, & Bittman, 2011; Kuhl, Clifford, & Stark, 2012). Video games, cell phones, and home computers have a similar impact. Many children spend inordinate amounts of time playing games, exchanging e-mail, texting their friends, visiting chat rooms, and surfing on the Internet.

Another important factor in the rise of obesity is that parents frequently encourage overeating. Beginning in infancy, some parents overfeed their children as a way of calming them or because they believe that a healthy baby should be round and plump. Later, parents may encourage their children to eat as a way of coping with frustration or anxiety or they may regularly offer them treats as a way to reinforce desired behaviors, thus fostering a habit of overeating. As noted previously, these early feeding practices may set in motion epigenetic processes that "set" the child's genes toward obesity. Food choice also is a factor in obesity. Perhaps as the result of aggressive advertising, but also because most children prefer the taste of high-fat, high-carbohydrate foods, children's diets are often unbalanced. This not only leads to the overconsumption of calories, but it also has an impact on the underconsumption of the vitamins and proteins needed for healthy growth and development.

What can be done to stop this increasing trend of obesity in children? One approach is to encourage children and parents to select a healthier diet. Schools can help by limiting children's access to nonnutritious foods and by providing educational programming that teaches children about healthier nutrition. One British study, for example, found that weight gains in 7- to 11-year-old children were limited when they were exposed to a school-based "ditch the fizz" campaign, which encouraged them to restrict their consumption of carbonated soft drinks (James, Thomas, Cavan, & Kerr, 2004). Other school-based programs also have been effective in helping children control their weight gain, especially when they include required physical activity, nutritious foods served during lunch, and involvement of parents (Katz, O'Connell, Njike, Yeh, & Nawaz, 2008; Safron & Cislak, 2011). These are approaches being picked up in the U.S. media, and also advocated by U.S. First Lady Michelle Obama's "Let's Move" program (see text discussion).

Indeed, public health efforts have shown to be effective in addressing other national health problems. Public health campaigns have led to the passage of seat-belt laws that save lives, to increasing taxes on cigarettes to discourage use and limiting where cigarettes can be smoked, and to treating city water supplies with fluoride to strengthen tooth enamel. What these successful examples have in common is that a body of research was advanced showing the need for change in health-related behavior, strong advocates took up these causes and lobbied for change, there was widespread media exposure, and eventually policies and laws were enacted to discourage unhealthy behaviors (Isaacs & Swartz, 2010). Perhaps a similar public policy approach can help curb the obesity epidemic in the United States as well.

On an individual level, overweight children also can be placed on modest diets, which generally include more healthy foods, such as fruits and vegetables, and less access to "junk" foods that are high in fat, sugar, and carbohydrates but low in nutritional value. Many sound programs are

Watch *The Problem of Childhood Obesity* on **MyDevelopmentLab**

available that help parents and children make healthier food selections and increase levels of physical activity that burn calories. Good programs usually advise that a first step is to get a medical evaluation to make sure the child is prepared to undertake a program of weight reduction. They also teach children how to make healthier food choices, to control portion size, and to start and maintain a reasonable exercise program. A key is that families are involved, both so the child is supported during the weight-loss program and also so that the healthier behaviors and habits learned during the program are maintained over a long period of time (American Academy of Pediatrics, 2012b; Young, Northern, Lister, Drummond, & O'Brien, 2007).

when drugs are effective in treating adults, children with the same diagnosis sometimes respond differently, and for some children drug side effects can be serious. Nevertheless, in the United States there has been a dramatic increase in the use of prescription drugs to treat behavioral and emotional problems in children and adolescents in recent years, due at least in part to the development of safer and more effective medications (American Psychological Association [APA], 2006). For example, in 2008, more than 8 million children and adolescents in the United States were taking medication to treat mental health issues—a rate higher than that of any other country in the world (APA, 2012). Decisions about the best treatment option should be guided by a consideration of the anticipated benefits of each treatment against its possible harms, and possibilities should include the absence of treatment as an option. An emphasis on this "evidence-based" approach to treatments is a sound recommendation made by a wide variety of public and private groups concerned with appropriate treatment for mental disorders in children (APA, 2006).

REVIEW THE FACTS 8-1

1. Compared to physical growth in early childhood, is physical growth in middle childhood faster or is it slower?
2. At age 8, the brain has grown to about __________ of its adult size.
   a. 40 to 45% b. 70 to 75%
   c. 80 to 85% d. 90 to 95%
3. Communication between the left and right brain hemispheres is improved in middle childhood as
   a. the corpus callosum becomes more mature.
   b. the frontal lobes become larger.
   c. lateralization takes place.
   d. neurons are added in large numbers.
4. About what percentage of U.S. children today are obese?
5. What is the leading cause of death during the middle childhood years?
6. About what percentage of U.S. children who have a mental disorder receive treatment?

Practice on **MyDevelopmentLab**

COGNITIVE DEVELOPMENT

Piaget and Concrete Operational Thinking

As we have seen in previous chapters, Jean Piaget characterized children's thinking as proceeding through a set of stages or periods. In adopting a stage approach, Piaget emphasized that the way children think about problems is transformed at particular defined times in development. As children move into middle childhood, they acquire not only more knowledge and skill, but, according to Piaget, they also solve problems and think about the world differently than they have before. Piaget referred to middle childhood as the **concrete operational period**. In Piaget's theory, the period of concrete operations is the third stage of cognitive development.

Comparing Preoperational and Concrete Operational Thinking According to Piaget's theory, children make the transition from preoperational thought (see Chapter 6) to concrete operational thought during the years from ages 5 to 7. As children approach this transition, thought becomes less intuitive and egocentric and more logical, as outlined in Table 8-4. Toward the end of the preoperational stage, the rigid, static, irreversible qualities of children's thought begin to "thaw out," as Piaget put it. Children's thinking becomes more reversible and

Table 8-4 Preoperational Versus Concrete Operational Thought in Children

Stage	Age	Thinking Style
Preoperational	From about 2 to 7 years	• Rigid and static • Irreversible • Focused on the here and now • Centered on one dimension • Egocentric • Focused on perceptual evidence
Concrete operational	From about 7 to 12 years	• Reversible • Flexible • Not limited to the here and now • Multidimensional • Less egocentric • Marked by the use of logical inferences • Marked by the search for cause-and-effect relationships

Watch *Autism: Dr. Kathy Pratt* on **MyDevelopmentLab**

concrete operational period
For Piaget, the third stage of cognitive development; begins at ages 5 to 7 and allows the child to perform mental operations, such as conservation, decentration, and reversibility, on objects that are concrete and that can be directly experienced

flexible and considerably more complex. Children now notice more than one aspect of an object and can use logic to solve problems. They can evaluate cause-and-effect relationships if they have the concrete object or situation in front of them, and they can see changes as they occur. When a piece of clay looks like a sausage, they no longer find it inconsistent that the clay was once a ball or that it can be molded back into that shape and be the same size.

An important difference between preoperational and concrete operational thought can be illustrated by school-age children's use of logical inference. Recall Piaget's liquid–beakers conservation problem (Chapter 6). After the liquid is poured from one beaker to another, preoperational children think of this situation as two different *perceptual* problems—one before the pouring and another one after. They usually judge that the tall, narrow glass holds more liquid than the short, wide one, although both quantities of liquid were shown to be identical at the start. In contrast, concrete operational children recognize that both containers must hold the same amount of liquid. For them, this is a single *logical* problem. Because they saw the liquid being poured from one beaker to another, they begin to think differently about states and transformations and can remember how the liquid appeared before it was poured into the tall, thin container. They can think about how its shape changed as it was poured from one glass into the other and can imagine the liquid being poured back. They also understand that changes in one dimension, such as height, can be compensated for by changes in another, such as width. Respectively, their thinking is both reversible and decentered.

In addition, concrete operational children begin to understand other problems involving conservation. For example, in Piaget's (1970) matchstick problem (see Figure 8-5), children are shown a zigzag row of six matchsticks and a straight row of five matchsticks placed end to end. When asked which row has more matchsticks, preoperational children generally center only on the distance between the end points of the rows and therefore pick the "longer" row with five matchsticks, even though they may have correctly counted the number of matchsticks in each row. Concrete operational children, however, can take into account what lies between the end points of the rows and therefore correctly choose the one with six matchsticks.

At about age 5½, children also become more skilled in verbal mediation—using words to help them understand and structure problems. This skill helps them to solve more complex problems, as well as to follow directions and to plan and complete a task, which are important skills required for school success.

Unlike preoperational children, concrete operational children can theorize about the world around them. They think about and anticipate what will happen; they make guesses about things and then test their hunches. They may estimate, for example, how many more breaths of air they can blow into a balloon before it pops, and they may keep blowing until they reach that goal. However, their ability to theorize is limited to objects and social relationships that they can see or concretely imagine. They do not develop theories about abstract concepts, thoughts, or relationships until they reach the stage of formal operations at about age 11 or 12 (see Chapter 10).

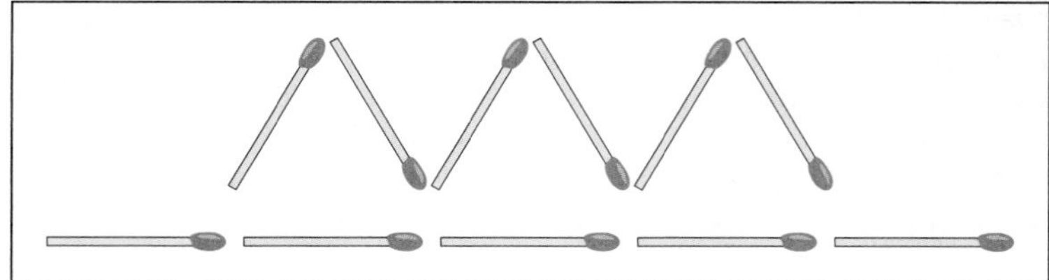

FIGURE 8-5 Piaget's Matchstick Problem
Concrete operational children realize that the six matchsticks in the zigzag top row will make a longer line than the five matchsticks in the straight bottom row. Younger children will say that the bottom row is the longest because they tend to center only on the end points of the two lines and not on what lies between them.

Of course, as noted earlier, development is continuous: The transition from preoperational to concrete operational thought does not happen overnight; rather, it requires experience in manipulating and learning about objects and materials in the environment. Nevertheless, cognitive development proceeds naturally, even without formal education or prompting. Children learn concrete operational thought largely on their own. As they actively explore their physical environment, asking themselves questions and finding the answers, they acquire the more complex and sophisticated forms of thinking that characterize middle childhood.

Piaget and Education Although cognitive development unfolds even in the absence of formal education, a question remains: Are there experiences that can accelerate thinking and problem solving? The response to this question is twofold. First, we should consider why we would want to speed up the development of a child's thinking. As long as children advance in their ways of thinking about their world, there seems to be little if any advantage that accrues to the accelerated child. Piaget himself discouraged parents from pushing their children: He felt cognitive development was more complete when children learned on their own—in their own way and at their own pace. The second response is that learning environments *can* be structured so that children receive the prerequisite experiences that lead to more rapid cognitive advances. Although educational programming does not dramatically transform children's cognitive development, educational experiences that guide children to see relationships in new ways can provide the foundation for cognitive

What kinds of activities can parents and teachers promote to help children gain experience that contributes to concrete operational thinking?

Watch *Development of Social Cognition* on **MyDevelopmentLab**

advances. For example, one such application involves the use of concrete objects to teach mathematical concepts to 5- to 7-year-olds. In introducing first- or second-grade children to the number concept of 16, a teacher might present several different spatial arrays of 16 cubes—grouped into two towers of 8, one row of 16, four rows of 4, and so on (see Figure 8-6). The teacher might then give verbal cues to help the children learn about the conservation of number—a critical concept in arithmetic—by pointing out that the number of cubes remains the same, although the length and width of the rows change.

There are many other applications of Piaget's concepts. For example, addition and subtraction involve an understanding of reversibility (e.g., 5 + 8 = 13; 13 – 5 = 8). Because children learn most readily when working with concrete examples, many educational curricula teach these arithmetic operations by having children manipulate objects, such as adding to one pile by subtracting from another. Piagetian concepts have been especially useful to teachers of math and science, but they have also been applied to social studies, music, and art.

Piaget's perspective views children as active learners who construct their own theories about how the world operates and who are self-motivated to change their theories when pieces of information do not fit (Bransford, Brown, & Cocking, 2008; Bruner, 2006). Thus, his perspective implies that educators should teach children to solve problems for their own sake, rather than work only for the teacher's praise (Dweck, 2007; Robins, 2012). According to Piaget, children's interest in learning depends on the intrinsic rewards they find in the encounter with the subject matter itself. Thus, children gain confidence from mastering problems and discovering principles, and they learn by *doing*—just as adults do.

Consequently, educators may fail if they fall into the trap of telling instead of showing. If teachers remove the real-life, concrete context of the subject they are teaching, children may be left with a body of arid facts and principles without the ability to apply them beyond the immediate situation. According to Piaget, children need to learn by actively exploring ideas and relationships and by solving problems in concrete, realistic contexts.

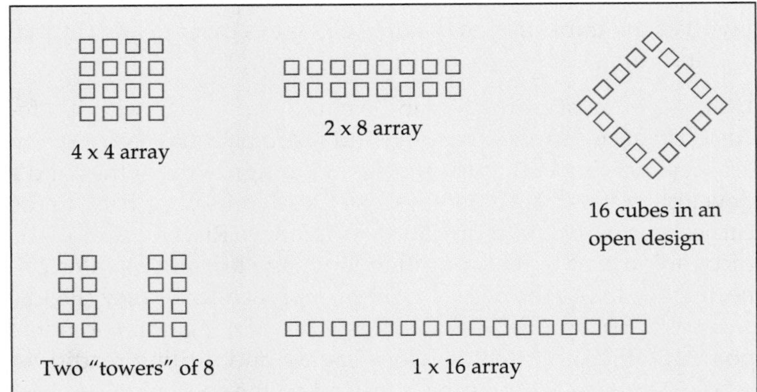

FIGURE 8-6 Spatial Arrays
Some possible spatial arrays of 16 cubes. By arranging the cubes in different ways, a teacher can help young schoolchildren understand the number concept of 16.

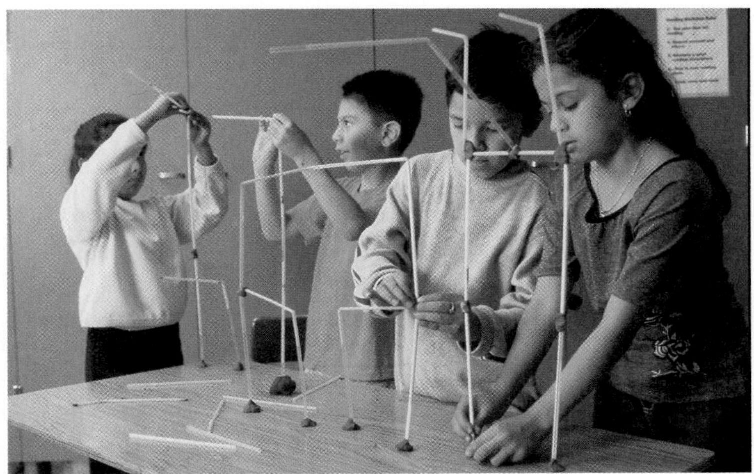

Classroom science projects and experiments done in small groups not only foster problem solving but also allow children to clarify their understanding through discussion and negotiation.

Memory and Metacognition

As the cognitive abilities of children advance in middle childhood, a number of significant developments occur in their memory abilities as well. Recall that preoperational children do well at recognition tasks but poorly at recall tasks; they also have trouble using memory strategies, such as rehearsal (see Chapter 6). Early in the period of concrete operations (between the ages of 5 and 7), children's ability to recall lists of items improves significantly, in part because they begin making conscious efforts to memorize information. They also begin to use more effective memory strategies. For example, in early childhood, children may look at material to be remembered and repeat it over and over. Later they typically learn to organize material into categories, and eventually they may create stories or visual images to help them remember particular items. The increasingly deliberate use of memory strategies makes an older child's recall more effective and efficient (Flavell, 2003, 2007).

To put it another way, elementary schoolchildren learn **control processes**—strategies and techniques that enhance memory. One such control process involves using *scripts,* which describe a standard sequence of events that comprise a familiar event, for example, getting ready for dinner. As you may recall, beginning around age 4 or 5, young children begin to construct scripts to help them remember. In middle childhood, these scripts become much more elaborate, and children develop other control processes as well, such as rehearsal, organization, semantic elaboration, mental imagery, and retrieval. These processes are described in Table 8-5.

Watch *The School-Age Child* on **MyDevelopmentLab**

control processes
Strategies and techniques that enhance memory

Table 8-5 Control Processes Used by Children in Middle Childhood

Control Process	Description of Developmental Changes
Rehearsal	• Younger children simply repeat items over and over. • Older children organize information into meaningful units that are easier to remember.
Organization	• Younger children use simple associations when thinking about relationships. • Older children organize information categorically, using more elaborate schemes.
Semantic elaboration	• Younger children recall events they experience. • Older children are able to infer things that logically would have occurred even if they did not experience them directly.
Mental imagery	• Younger children can imagine events if they receive careful instructions. • Older children are more likely to construct such mental images on their own and their images are more vivid.
Retrieval	• Younger children engage in simpler methods of remembering. • Older children use more flexible, creative, and efficient strategies to recall information.
Scripts	• Younger children construct scripts that include the typical events that occur in routine aspects of their lives, such as getting ready for bed. • Older children also rely on scripts, but their scripts are more elaborate and can be merged into broader categories.

Middle childhood is also a time when children develop more sophisticated intellectual processes that enable them to monitor their own thinking, memory, knowledge, goals, and actions—an ability called **metacognition.** Metacognition is *thinking about thinking,* and during middle childhood, children develop metacognitive abilities that they use in planning, making decisions, and solving problems. In a well-known description of metacognition, Flavell (1985) cited the following example: Preschool and elementary schoolchildren were asked to study a group of items until they were certain that they could remember them perfectly. When the elementary-aged children said that they were ready, they usually were. When tested, they remembered each item without error. In contrast, the younger children often said that they were ready when in fact they were not. Despite their good intentions, they did not have sufficient cognitive abilities to complete the task *and* to know when they had completed it; they could not monitor their own intellectual processes.

The ability to monitor thinking and memory begins at about age 6 and emerges more fully between the ages of 7 and 10. Even then, however, metacognition is better when the material to be learned is typical or familiar, and, like other aspects of cognitive ability, metacognitive skills continue to develop into adolescence. Just as a 9-year-old has greater metacognitive ability than a 4-year-old, a 15-year-old's self-monitoring skills far surpass those of a 9-year-old (Kuhn & Pease, 2006, 2010).

Language and Literacy Development

Language By the time children reach middle childhood, they are already competent speakers of their native language and are easily able to communicate even complex ideas through speech. Nevertheless, their language learning is not yet complete. In middle childhood, children's vocabulary continues to expand, and they master increasingly complex grammatical structures and more sophisticated language usage. For example, they begin to use and understand the passive voice, although their syntax may still be shaky: When asked to interpret the sentence, "The cat was chased by the dog," younger children oftentimes mistakenly infer that the cat is doing the chasing, whereas older children correctly understand that it is the dog that is chasing the cat. Older children can also infer that passive voice sentences like "John was watched as he walked along the beach" include participants who are not explicitly named.

metacognition
The intellectual process that enables people to monitor their thinking and memory; thinking about thinking

Schooling generally helps with language development, and in numerous ways. For some children, the language used at school is more formal, or in a different dialect, or is a different form of discourse than that practiced at home. By exposing children to more complex and elaborate forms of language, children's thought processes are refined and expanded. Because language and thought are closely interconnected, the frameworks of formal language also can contribute to how children structure a math or science problem at school. Likewise, these new ways of thinking carry over to how children observe nature, their neighborhood, their relationships at home, and perhaps even the art and music they encounter outside of school. Thus, language development involves the transmission of culture in ways that are both formal and informal (Gentner & Goldin-Meadow, 2003).

Literacy In most cultures, middle childhood brings with it a focus on *literacy*—skills in reading and writing. Today, most scholars view reading and writing as natural outgrowths of the child's developing language skills—skills whose roots trace back to the earliest forms of communication in infancy (Rhyner, 2009). The recognition that oral and written language learning is interconnected has led to the *whole-language* approach to literacy (Fields, Groth, & Spangler, 2008). Rather than looking for a distinct point at which children develop reading and writing readiness, whole-language theorists focus instead on the concept of *emergent literacy*—the view that skills associated with oral and written language acquisition begin to develop in infancy and gradually improve over a period of years (Israel & Duffy, 2008; Snow, 2006). Thus, the stories that an infant can only listen to, the "writing" that a toddler does with a crayon, and the preschooler's "reading" from memory that occurs in early childhood are all precursors to actual reading and writing. Parents and teachers

Literacy involves both reading and writing. Many factors are involved in developing literacy, ranging from formal instruction in an educational setting to the opportunity to interact and discuss ideas with parents, peers, and others.

Table 8-6 Conditions That Promote Literacy

1. **A print-rich environment**
   - Adults who read for their own purposes
   - Adults who write for their own purposes
   - Frequent story-time experiences
   - Information about letter names and sounds
   - Shared reading
   - Dictation and other shared writing experiences
   - High-quality literature is available
   - Answers to questions about written material
2. **A rich oral-language environment**
   - Adults who model good language use
   - Adults who listen to children
   - Free exploration of oral language
   - Peer conversation
   - Dramatic play roles
   - Experiences for vocabulary enrichment
   - Vocabulary information as requested
3. **Firsthand experiences of interest**
   - Opportunities for play
   - Rich daily living experiences
   - Field trips
   - Nature exploration
4. **Symbolic representation experiences**
   - Dramatic play
   - Opportunities for drawing and painting
   - Opportunities for music making and dancing
5. **Pressure-free experimentation with writing (independent writing)**
   - Drawing
   - Scribbling
   - Prealphabetic writing
   - Phonics-based spelling
6. **Pressure-free exploration of reading (independent reading)**
   - "Reading" from memory
   - Reading with contextual clues
   - Matching print to oral language
7. **Information about literacy skills**
   - Practice with left-to-right sequence of words on a page
   - Letter–sound relations (phonics)

can encourage the development of literacy by providing a rich home and school environment (see Table 8-6).

The development of reading and writing skills during middle childhood is a complex, multidimensional process. It rests on brain development, but also emerges out of a sociocultural context (Chiu & McBride-Chang, 2010; Kuhl, 2011). Children acquire the basics of literacy while interacting with their parents, siblings, teachers, and peers. Furthermore, these interactions differ. For example, children respond differently when they are actively engaged with their peers in learning to read than when they are working with a teacher (Daiute, Campbell, Griffin, Reddy, & Tivnan, 1993). Although teachers help children learn the knowledge and skills they need, peer interactions give them the opportunity to discuss ideas and problems spontaneously. Parents also make a major contribution to their children's literacy and are especially effective when they focus on discussing what is being read rather than on drilling and correcting specific reading skills (Hood, Conlon, & Andrews, 2008; Snow, Griffin, & Burns, 2005).

Taken together, children's social interactions lay the groundwork for the development of literacy, as well as for the specific, complex tasks involved in mastering written language. Although knowledge of phonics can be important, reading is more than simply decoding letters and words; writing is much more than knowing how to spell words and punctuate correctly. Just as communication or problem solving occurs within a social context, children learn to read and write in a social environment. When problems of literacy do occur, educators should—and usually do—take into consideration the family, peer, and teacher relationships that make up the child's social world. Of course, sometimes there are specific learning problems that make learning to read or write more difficult than would be expected: We discuss this topic in more detail later in this chapter. In addition, there are individual differences in children's intelligence that determine to some degree how easily they will learn. It is to this topic we next turn.

Individual Differences in Intelligence

Perhaps no issue in developmental psychology has been more controversial than intelligence and intelligence testing. The academic debate has often gone public because of the broad impact intelligence test scores can have on educational and social opportunities and because intelligence tests are administered widely and taken seriously in the United States and other industrialized nations. When young children are labeled on the basis of intelligence test

Watch *Literacy* on MyDevelopmentLab

Watch *Early Literacy Development: Frederick Morrison* on MyDevelopmentLab

How, in particular, are "smart" children treated differently in traditional academic settings? What can teachers do to create an environment in which children of all ability levels are equally valued?

scores, the results are often far reaching. "Smart" kids are treated differently and often have different—and better—opportunities than do those at the other end of the intelligence scale. Children's scores may affect the extent and quality of their education, determine the jobs they can obtain as adults, and have a lasting impact on their self-image.

Intelligence test scores also are involved in public policy decisions. Because intelligence is closely linked to academic performance, the evaluation of the success or failure of schools and social programs often depends on the intelligence of the enrolled students. Important decisions about how well programs succeed and which programs to fund often hinge on understanding the relationship between intelligence and academic success. How is intelligence measured?

Measuring Intelligence Alfred Binet, a psychologist who was commissioned by the French government to devise an objective method for identifying children who were not doing well in school, designed the first comprehensive intelligence test in the early 20th century. In 1916, Lewis Terman and his colleagues at Stanford University revised Binet's test for use in the United States. The resulting individually administered test gained wide acceptance during the 1940s and 1950s and—in its modern form, the **Stanford-Binet Intelligence Scale**, Fifth Edition (SB5)—is still widely used.

Binet's concept of intelligence focused on complex intellectual processes, such as judgment, reasoning, memory, and comprehension. Through extensive trial and error, he developed sets of test items involving problem solving, word definitions, and general knowledge that were appropriate for children of different ages. For example, if more than half of all 5-year-olds but fewer than half of all 4-year-olds could define the word *ball*, that might become an item on the test for 5-year-olds (Binet & Simon, 1905, 1916). Binet measured the intelligence of a given child by administering several sets of test items and determining the *mental age (MA)* that best described the child's level of ability. A 4-year-old who could answer questions at the level of the typical 5-year-old, thus, would have a mental age of 5.

Later test researchers developed a formula for expressing the child's intellectual level that made it possible to compare children of different *chronological ages (CAs)*, which are expressed as how old, in years and months, the children are. This measure, called the **intelligence quotient (IQ)**, was obtained as follows:

$$IQ = MA/CA \times 100$$

▲ In many developed nations, educational opportunities depend heavily on how well the child performs in school and on standardized tests.

Thus, an intellectually average 4-year-old would score an MA of 4 on the test; and this child's IQ would be 100 (4/4 × 100 = 100). An above-average 4-year-old with an MA of 5 would obtain an IQ of 125 (5/4 × 100 = 125); a below-average child with an MA of 3 would have an IQ of 75.

The computation of IQ made it possible to understand how a child's intellectual ability compared to that of peers of the same chronological age. However, there were problems with this *ratio approach* to IQ. For example, although the formula worked reasonably well with children and adolescents whose cognitive abilities were continuing to improve in predictable ways, it was difficult to assess adult intelligence by this means. What kinds of test items would uniformly and fairly assess the mental age of a 30-year-old versus that of a 40-year-old?

Primarily because of this drawback, IQ is now assessed using the **deviation IQ** approach, which assigns an IQ score by comparing an individual's test score with the scores of other people of the same age range. This technique was developed by David Wechsler and applied to a set of IQ tests that he and his colleagues developed (Wechsler, 1974). The test for early childhood is the Wechsler Preschool and Primary Scale of Intelligence, or WPPSI ("wippsie"); the test for childhood and adolescence is the Wechsler Intelligence Scale for Children, or WISC ("wisk"); and the test for adulthood is the Wechsler Adult Intelligence Scale, or WAIS ("wace"). An individual who takes any of these tests obtains a score that is compared statistically to the scores of other people of the same age.

Figure 8-7 illustrates the distribution of deviation IQ scores in the general population, based on the scoring system of the widely used Wechsler IQ tests. (The numbers for other intelligence tests are very similar.) Note the familiar *bell-shaped curve:* IQ is assumed to be normally distributed around an average

Watch *Successful Intelligence: Robert Sternberg* on **MyDevelopmentLab**

Stanford-Binet Intelligence Scale
The revised version of Binet's original intelligence test that is widely used in the United States today

intelligence quotient (IQ)
An individual's mental age divided by chronological age, which is multiplied by 100 to eliminate the decimal point; older version of how intelligence text scores were computed

deviation IQ
The approach used today that assigns an IQ score by comparing an individual's test score with the scores of other people in the same age range

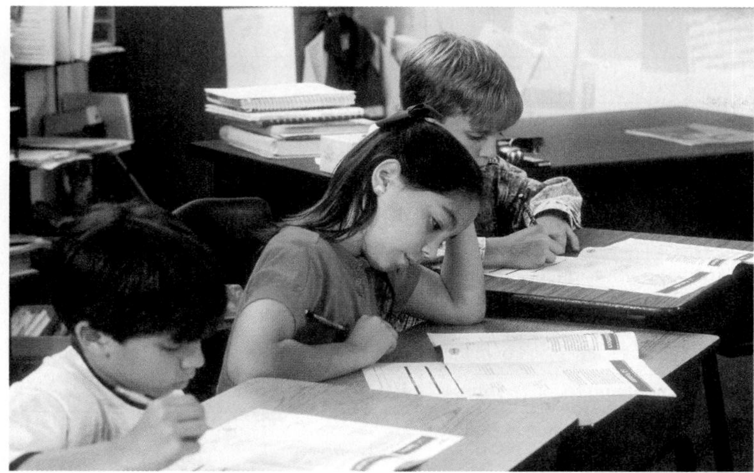

▲ Standardized tests can provide valuable information but sometimes measure a narrow range of abilities. A child's performance may reflect the child's anxiety level, test-taking skills, confidence, and several other factors, as well as the child's knowledge of the subject tested.

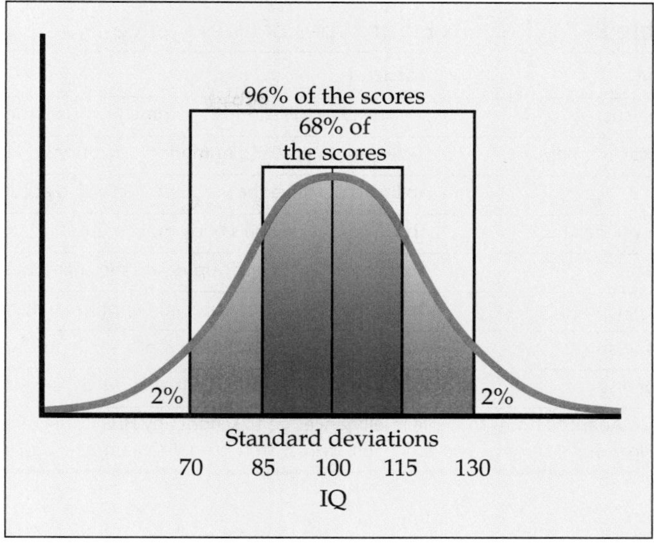

FIGURE 8-7 **Typical distribution of IQ in the General Population**

score of 100, with about two-thirds of the general population scoring between 85 and 115 and almost 96% of the population scoring between 70 and 130. That leaves roughly 2% scoring below 70, which is one criterion for defining intellectual disability—a characteristic also referred to by the older term "mental retardation." Roughly 2% score above 130, which is a popular cutoff point for defining giftedness.

It is important to keep in mind that test scores, however they are measured, are not perfect. First, there are measurement issues: No test is perfectly *reliable;* if a child were to take the same test a second time under the same circumstances, we would not expect the same exact score. Second, environmental factors can affect test scores; if the child feel threatened or is ill, anxious, or otherwise upset, the child's test score may suffer. Third, although intelligence tests are broad measures of intellectual ability, they do not measure every quality that contributes to—or works against—an individual's success. Fourth, intelligence tests are specific to the value of the culture in which they are developed. The skills that define intelligence in an upper-middle-class college-bound population are somewhat different than those that would be needed in an agrarian or hunter-gatherer society. Finally, tests measure an individual's intellectual abilities only at the time when they are administered; in other words, they measure *current* intellectual functioning. A popular misconception is that they assess intellectual *potential,* which is not the case. Thus, as noted earlier, labeling children as bright or dull based on IQ scores can be misleading and even detrimental to the child. IQ scores can change substantially over time as a function of schooling and other cognitive experiences; however, an early label may persist in spite of such change.

Watch Mother-Child IQ Correlation on **MyDevelopmentLab**

The Nature of Intelligence Perhaps the most important issue in the field of intelligence testing is also the most basic; that is, what exactly *is* intelligence? Because standard intelligence tests are used so pervasively, we often equate intelligence to the skills measured on tests like the Wechsler and the Stanford-Binet. However, tests differ in what and how they measure, and there are different, legitimate views about the most appropriate definition of intelligence.

Although some intelligence tests define intelligence as a single attribute, the majority of tests define it as a composite of abilities. For example, the current version of the WISC has separate subtests for information, comprehension, mathematics, vocabulary, digit span, picture arrangement, and other factors as well. These subtests yield a verbal IQ score, a performance IQ score, and a full-scale IQ score that combines the two. Other tests, including the Stanford-Binet, typically take a similar approach in breaking down general intelligence into separate components.

One multiple-component model of intelligence that recognizes a broad approach to understanding intellectual abilities has been proposed by Howard Gardner (Davis, Seider, & Gardner, 2011; Gardner, 2004, 2011). On the basis of studies of neurology, psychology, and human evolutionary history, Gardner identified seven distinct types of intelligence: *linguistic, logical–mathematical, spatial, bodily–kinesthetic, musical, interpersonal,* and *intrapersonal,* later adding *naturalist* for a total of eight (see Table 8-7). An important implication of Gardner's model is that different types of intelligence are important in different environments. In industrialized nations, linguistic and logical–mathematic

Can you suggest some occupations that would emphasize each of Gardner's eight different types of intellectual abilities?

Table 8-7 Gardner's Eight Types of Intelligence

Type	Definition
Linguistic	• Sensitivity to the sounds, rhythms, and meanings of words and the functions of language
Logical–mathematical	• Facility for logical and numerical operations and complex reasoning
Spatial	• Ability to perceive the visual–spatial world accurately and to manipulate those perceptions
Bodily–kinesthetic	• Ability to control one's body movements and to handle objects skillfully
Musical	• Ability to produce and appreciate the characteristics of music, such as rhythm, pitch, and timbre
Interpersonal	• Ability to correctly interpret and appropriately respond to the moods, temperament, and motivations of other people
Intrapersonal	• Ability to correctly understand one's own feelings and moods and to appreciate one's own strengths, weaknesses, desires, and intelligence
Naturalist	• Ability to classify plants, animals, and features of the natural environment and to make appropriate responses to each

SOURCE: Adapted from "Multiple intelligences go to school," by H. Gardner and T. Hatch, 1989, *Educational Researcher, 18*(8), 6; and *The essential Sternberg: Essays on intelligence, psychology, and education*, by R. J. Sternberg, J. C. Kaufman, and E. L. Grigorenko, 2009, New York: Springer.

intelligence are important for success; for an African bushman, spatial, bodily–kinesthetic, and naturalist intelligence are more likely to be of high significance (see the box Try This! Exploring Your Concept of Intelligence).

Another broad model of intelligence is Robert Sternberg's *triarchic (three-part) theory* of intelligence (Sternberg, 2011; Sternberg, Kaufman, & Grigorenko, 2009). According to the triarchic model, intelligence is comprised not only of those skills measured by commonly used intelligence tests, which Sternberg calls *componential intelligence*, but intelligence also includes *experiential intelligence*, the ability to cope with new tasks or situations that are unfamiliar, and *contextual intelligence*, the commonsense ability to adapt to the environment successfully. Sternberg's triarchic theory thus emphasizes the practical aspects of intelligence that are important in coping with real-world problems. Sternberg's view has been especially useful in helping researchers understand the relationship of intelligence to creativity (Sternberg, Jarvin, & Grigorenko, 2011) and in emphasizing the importance of common sense and the more practical aspects of intelligence that help people adapt successfully to their surroundings (Sternberg, Bonney, Gabora, & Merrifield, 2012). It also provides a useful perspective about how cultural forces shape our definition of intelligence (Sternberg, Grigorenko, Kidd, & Stemler, 2011).

Cultural Issues in Intelligence Testing As noted earlier, how intelligence is defined depends in part on the environment in which one lives. When the context is an industrialized setting—where formal education contributes in important ways to success—intelligence is commonly measured by tests such as the Wechsler and the Stanford-Binet.

However, using tests such as these to measure intelligence raises questions about cultural bias. Tests such as the Wechsler and Stanford-Binet assume wide exposure to the dominant culture. Not surprisingly, when average test scores of predominantly White, upper-middle-class children are compared to those of lower-class children, scores for the children in the economically advantaged group are typically higher. And, because in the United States today, economic privilege is more often associated with being White, and economic challenge with being a member of a group defined by its "non-White" race or ethnicity, these group average score differences are sometimes discussed as differences between racial groups (Cohen & Swerdlik, 2010; "Mainstream science," 1994).

Are their differences in intelligence among different racial groups that are not accounted for by differences in opportunities? Most research suggests the answer is no. For example, in one classic study, researchers investigated IQ profiles of Black and interracial children who had been adopted by White, middle-class parents. Although large-scale studies typically find lower average IQ scores for many U.S. minority groups (including Blacks, Hispanics, and Native Americans) when compared to Whites, the IQ scores and school achievements of these minority adopted children were well above average—and well above those of children with similar ethnic backgrounds but different cultural experiences (Weinberg, Scarr, & Waldman, 1992). In another study, African-American families in poor urban neighborhoods were given the opportunity to move to a better neighborhood, where their children transferred into better neighborhood schools. Three years later, the academic performance of these students was compared to that of children in a control group whose parents had moved to another poor neighborhood. In comparison to those who moved to poor neighborhoods, nearly all of the children who moved to better schools showed improvement in completing their homework, as well as in their attendance. Furthermore, the greatest improvement was among adolescent males, whose achievement test scores also were markedly better: The typical decline in test scores that often occurs for teenage boys in poor neighborhoods did not happen in the new environment (Leventhal & Brooks-Gunn, 2004).

TRY THIS!

Exploring Your Concept of Intelligence

Tests are a big part of academic life. Many colleges base part of their selection procedures on how well prospective students score on tests of intellectual abilities, which usually are measured by the SAT or ACT. Perhaps you took one or both of these tests for college admission, and maybe more than once. Many researchers today, however, believe that the concept of intelligence is considerably broader than the skills that tests like these measure. Although different views about intelligence exist, one way of looking at this concept is to use Howard Gardner's multi-factor model, which specifies that intelligence consists of eight different abilities.

To become more familiar with multiple-factor models of intelligence, try to rate yourself on each of Gardner's eight factors, which are presented in the following table. When you have completed rating yourself, talk to another person—maybe a good friend or family member—and ask that person to rate himself or herself. You may find the table that follows useful as you think about your strengths and weaknesses. In addition, refer to Table 8-7 for the definitions of Gardner's eight abilities, which are listed in the following table.

Reflect on What You Observed

How difficult was it to rate your own areas of strength and weakness? Do you have a clear understanding of the kinds of intelligence at which you excel? Are there areas where you think your abilities are much better than most other people or are not as good as those of most other people? Did you rate yourself about the same for all of the eight dimensions or do you think you are much better at some of these skills than others? How did your friend respond with regard to the various abilities represented in this exercise? Were you surprised at the responses he or she gave?

Consider the Issues

Which of the types of intelligence noted in the table do you think are most closely aligned with a *traditional* view of intelligence? Which do you think are most closely related to the skills needed to succeed in school? Which do you think are most important for success on the job? Which skills do you think are most important for success in life? Which are most highly valued in mainstream U.S. culture? Do you think this same set of priorities exists in other cultures as well? Why or why not? Do you think an exercise like this might change a person's view of intelligence? How might adopting a broader view of intelligence affect how we treat children in an educational setting?

Self-Rating on Gardner's Types of Intelligence

	Rate Yourself			Ask a Friend		
Type of Intelligence	Below Average	Average	Above Average	Below Average	Average	Above Average
Linguistic						
Logical–mathematical						
Spatial						
Bodily–kinesthetic						
Musical						
Interpersonal						
Intrapersonal						
Naturalist						

Research such as this suggests that race is not a factor in determining intelligence, although culture probably is. For example, researchers studied the academic achievement of 200 children of Southeast Asian "boat people" who had recently immigrated to the United States (Kaplan, Choy, & Whitmore, 1992). Despite harsh living conditions, economic challenges, and substandard educational opportunities, these children excelled in school and posted surprisingly high grade-point averages and high test scores, especially in math. Upon examination, researchers determined that this academic success resulted from a family environment that was dedicated to ensuring school success. For example, the entire family tackled evening homework. Parents set high standards and often completed their children's chores so that they could study, and older siblings assisted those who were younger.

Do you think your family emphasized school success? If so, how? If not, what other types of outcomes were emphasized in your home?

Perhaps the best way to understand the differences in average IQ scores that exist between minority and majority groups relates to the disparity in their social and economic circumstances. When factors such as these are considered, IQ score differences between groups all but disappear (Nisbett, et al., 2012; Ossorio, 2011; Suzuki, Short, & Lee, 2011). Thus, although genes and environment contribute to a particular child's measured IQ and both are important in determining intelligence, there is a dynamic interaction of these factors at play.

As noted earlier, intelligence tests originally were developed to predict a child's success in school. Along with several other factors, a child's intellectual ability is related to academic performance, which is the topic we investigate in the next section.

REVIEW THE FACTS 8-2

1. Did Piaget advocate trying to accelerate the pace of children's learning?
2. If a child constructs a memory for how events typically take place, such as what happens at bedtime, this memory for sequence is called __________.
3. Describe two ways in which children's ability to use language develops during middle childhood.
4. What is the *mental age* for a 7-year-old child who answers the same number of questions correctly as a typical 8-year-old?
5. When groups of children of different racial and ethnic backgrounds are raised in comparable environments, how do their average IQ scores generally compare?

Practice on **MyDevelopmentLab**

LEARNING AND THINKING IN SCHOOL

Where they exist, formal schools play a crucial role in children's development. When children begin school, they typically encounter demands and expectations that differ markedly from those at home. Not surprisingly, children show great variation in how well they adapt to these demands (Paris, Yeung, Wong, & Luo, 2012). Around the world, children also experience wide variations in their opportunities to attend school and the extent to which they take (or are allowed to take) advantage of it. In developed countries like the United States, virtually all children are literate. However, in the world's least-developed nations, a quarter of young men and a third of young women cannot read (UNICEF, 2012c; see Figure 8-8). Regardless of their individual situations, when children begin formal schooling there are adjustments that must occur.

New Demands and Expectations

Children entering school are separated from their parents, some for the first time, and they must learn to trust unfamiliar adults. At the same time, greater independence is expected of them. No longer can a little boy or girl yell to mother, "Put on my shoes!" Children must learn quickly to be more self-sufficient and, even in small classes, children must now compete for adult attention and assistance (Paris, Yeung, Wong, & Luo, 2012).

Watch *The Preschool Years: Egocentrism* on **MyDevelopmentLab**

Regardless of the school, there is always a gap between what is expected at home and what is expected in the classroom. The greater the gap, the more difficult the child's adjustment will be. Children who have just begun to internalize the rules of family life are suddenly expected to adapt to a new set of standards. Their success will depend on their family background, the school environment, and their own individuality. How well children have coped with dependency, autonomy, authority, aggression, and conscience will influence their adjustment to school. Although teachers usually recognize that the inner resources of children who have just started school may be shaky, they nonetheless must insist that the children adapt—and quickly.

How would you expect children's levels of egocentrism to influence how successfully they adapt to school?

From the first day of school, children are expected to learn the complex social rules that govern the social life of the classroom. Relations with classmates involve finding the right balance between cooperation and competition. Similarly, relations with teachers involve achieving a compromise between autonomy and obedience.

Most schools have elaborate codes of behavior: Children must listen when the teacher speaks, line up to go outside for recess, obtain permission to go to the bathroom, and raise

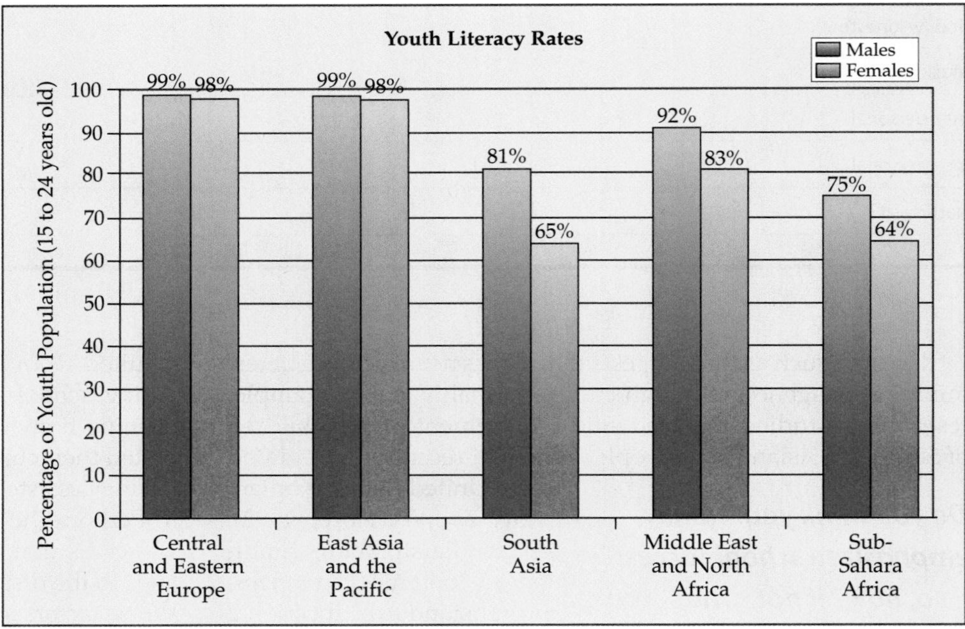

FIGURE 8-8 Youth Literacy Rates Around the World, 2005–2010
Youth literacy rate—the percentage of the population ages 15 to 24 who can read—varies significantly among different countries and regions of the world and between genders.

SOURCE: From Table 5, "Education," in *The state of the world's children* (p. 107), by UNICEF, 2012, New York: Author. Copyright © 2012 by UNICEF. Reprinted with permission of the publisher.

a hand before speaking. A great deal of class time may be spent on classroom management, which involves, among other things, organizing the classroom and teaching appropriate rules and expectations (Feeney, Moravcik, & Nolte, 2013; Korb, 2012; Marzano & Marzano, 2003). For example, in one classic study of public school classrooms, researchers recorded how much time teachers spent on the following activities: (a) teaching facts or concepts; (b) giving directions for a particular lesson; (c) stating general rules of behavior; (d) correcting, disciplining, and praising children; and (e) miscellaneous activities (Sieber & Gordon, 1981). The results were startling: In a 30-minute lesson, it was not unusual for a teacher to spend only 10 to 15% of the time on academic work—teaching facts and concepts or giving directions for a lesson. However, research indicates that children learn more in classes where the time spent on teaching and learning activities is maximized and the time spent on classroom management is minimized (Pressley, Gaskins, Solic, & Collins, 2006). Although organizing the classroom and teaching appropriate rules and expectations can be a good investment of time, especially early in the school year (Cameron, Connor, Morrison, & Jewkes, 2008), children learn most when teachers focus on academic content.

Developing Competent Learners and Critical Thinkers

In a rapidly changing world, there is much to learn and little time to learn it. With knowledge becoming obsolete literally overnight, people need to become lifelong learners who can integrate and organize a barrage of changing information. Thus, many educators are no longer focusing on memorization of facts and principles, but instead are helping the children become self-directed, competent learners and critical thinkers.

In recent years, many U.S. schools have placed a greater emphasis on teaching learning and thinking skills over facts. Many teachers also try to tailor instruction to each child's individual learning style and developmental level and to include activities that foster independent, self-regulated, self-paced learning. Educational psychologists generally recommend a range of teaching strategies to provide learning opportunities and develop thinking skills that emphasize not only remembering but also reasoning, reorganizing, relating, and reflecting (Costa, 2004; Ray & Smith, 2010).

Teaching students to develop critical thinking is more difficult than simply imparting facts and principles (A. Costa, 2004, 2008). One particularly effective way to encourage critical thinking is to assign students small-group projects and activities. Group activities are especially effective when they involve opportunities for in-depth inquiry and when children are encouraged to accurately monitor their progress (Bransford, Brown, Donovan, & Pellegrino, 2003; Delandtsheer, 2011). Group learning has been found to raise self-esteem, especially of female students, significantly more than when individual-centered teaching strategies are employed (Slavin, 2000). Also, when small-group projects are used effectively, children experience cooperative rather than competitive learning, and cooperative learning techniques have been found to increase overall performance (Johnson & Johnson, 2002, 2004).

achievement motivation
An internalized need to persist toward success and excellence

Success in School

Success in school, of course, is influenced by many factors. Children who are in poor health, who do not get enough to eat, who are preoccupied with problems at home, or who have low self-esteem do not fare as well compared to those raised in healthier settings. Self-perceived competence may also affect school performance. In one longitudinal study, for example, children from 10 elementary schools were tracked for 10 years: Perceived academic self-concept predicted educational attainment, even when family structure, socioeconomic status, and actual academic performance were factored in (Guay, Larose, & Boivin, 2004). Children's lack of scholarly self-confidence also is linked to a negative perception of social acceptance by other students: Students who were unpopular did not perceive themselves as competent learners (Larouche, Galand, & Bouffard, 2008).

According to David McClelland (1955), the reason that some children achieve more than others often stems from the values of the culture in which they are reared. After comparing several cultures during different periods of history, McClelland concluded that **achievement motivation**, which is defined as an internalized need to persist toward success and excellence, is an acquired and culturally based drive. In any given society at any

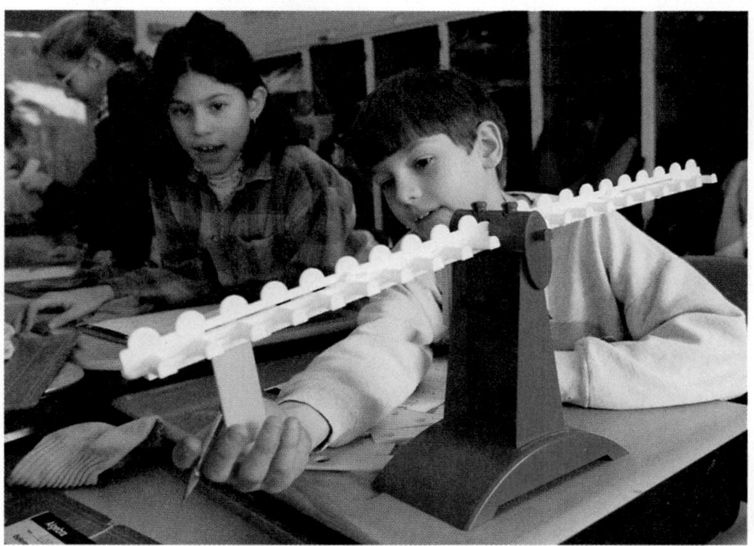

▲ Girls who do well in mathematics during middle childhood may put less effort into this subject when they become adolescents because of societal stereotypes that mathematical thinking is typically more "masculine" than "feminine."

time, some groups value achievement more highly than others. Different cultures or subcultures may also value different kinds of achievement; one group may stress educational goals while another may place more value on social success. Children whose parents stress values that are different from those of the school may bring less motivation to academic tasks.

Gender Differences and School Success Success in school is also influenced by gender differences (Gurian, 2011). A pioneering and now-classic review of the literature on gender differences (Maccoby & Jacklin, 1974) found that—on average—girls tended to outperform boys in verbal skills, and boys tended to do better in quantitative and spatial tasks. Although these gender differences have become smaller over the intervening 40-plus years, they still do exist (Halpern, 2012; Hyde & DeLamater, 2008).

There are many possible reasons for these gender differences. For example, there may be small sex differences in relevant brain development (Hines, 2004; Sommer, 2010); we know that girls' brains lateralize at a slightly faster pace, and this may have some impact on the development of certain academic abilities. Undoubtedly, different social expectations for boys and girls also profoundly influence their behavior (Leaper & Bigler, 2011; Wood & Eagly, 2010). In settings where traditional gender stereotypes are strong, somewhat different standards of academic achievement typically are held for boys versus girls. In the United States and most other countries around the world, these gender expectations usually favor boys. Thus, girls in such situations may experience a conflict between their desire to attain high levels of academic achievement but also be popular with peers in a classroom where high achievement is incompatible with the female gender role. For some girls, fitting in may become more important than academic achievement, and they may choose to underperform in order to conform to social expectations. To put it another way, some girls may find themselves "dumbing down" to be more popular in a traditionally defined, male-dominated culture. Fortunately, in most mainstream academic settings in the United States today, academic achievement is considered to be equally desirable for both boys and girls, and gender stereotyping has diminished from previous decades (Leaper & Bigler, 2011).

Even in settings that evenly encourage academic achievement for both boys and girls, however, some gender differences in instructional practices and expectations may exist. For example, mathematics and science traditionally have been defined as male-oriented subjects and literature and language as female-oriented disciplines. Parents and teachers may therefore assume that boys will do better in math and thus put greater effort into teaching math to boys than to girls (Raltan, Good, & Dweck, 2011). Correspondingly, teachers' expectations may influence their teaching of literacy tasks to the detriment of boys, perhaps by expecting less or by choosing reading that girls find more engaging. When readings are of less interest to boys than girls, boys' learning suffers (Graham, Tisher, Ainley, & Kennedy, 2008). Parents who are concerned about such gender-biased approaches to learning should visit their children's school and observe the behavior of both teachers and students (see Table 8-8). They might also consider placing their child into a single-sex school, although this decision should be made carefully, as research suggests that single-sex schools may actually increase gender stereotyping (Halpern et al., 2011).

Table 8-8 Questions Parents Should Ask When Evaluating Gender Bias in the Classroom

- Do teachers call on girls as much as they do on boys?
- Do they display the work of both sexes equally?
- Do they offer greater assistance to girls while allowing boys to solve problems on their own?
- Do they punish girls and boys for the same reasons?
- Do girls stand back while boys perform hands-on work in science labs?
- Are there girls-only and boys-only lines or teams?
- Do girls participate in sports at recess?
- Are any girls team captains?
- Can children of both sexes name 10 famous women in American history? (If not, the school may have a gender-biased curriculum.)

SOURCE: From "Helping teachers and schools to nip sex bias in the bud," by C. Rubenstein, *New York Times*, April 28, 1994, 143, p. C4.

Motivation for learning is influenced by many factors, including how parents and teachers encourage young children. In a now-classic article, Carol Dweck laid out a view of motivation and achievement that helps explain why gender differences exist in educational settings (Dweck, 1986). According to Dweck, boys and girls often are encouraged to develop somewhat different approaches to learning. Boys are more likely to adopt a "learning" orientation that emphasizes persistence even when tasks are difficult; girls, on the other hand, become focused more on "performance" expectations that emphasize success over persistence, thereby leading them to prefer easier tasks. Because mathematics often involves learning entirely new

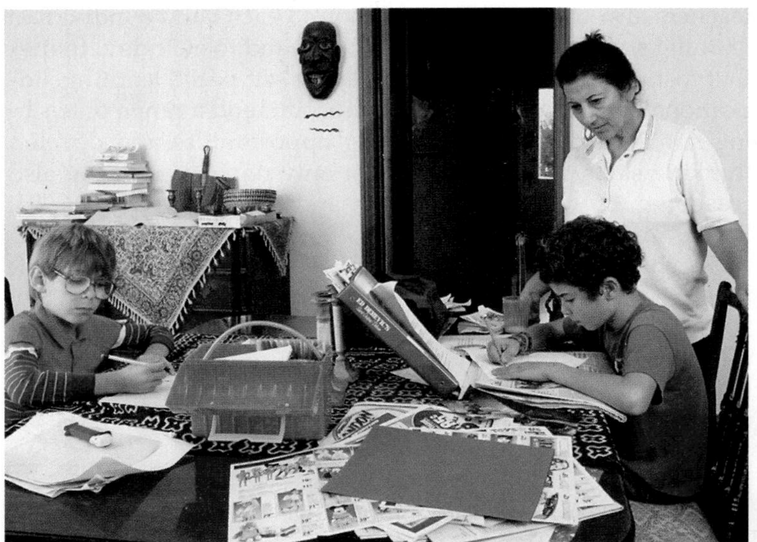

▲ Children who perform well in school tend to have parents who strongly value education and encourage their child's academic self-esteem.

Table 8-9 Examples of Ineffective and Effective Praise

Ineffective Praise	Effective Praise
"You are so intelligent, I'm really impressed with the quality of work you are able to do."	"You really studied for your social studies test. You read the material over several times, outlined it, and tested yourself on it. It really worked."
"You have real artistic talent. I think you are the most creative child in your class and have a bright future as an artist."	"You did a good job drawing. I like the detail you added to the people's faces."
"Just try your best, and if the work is too hard we'll figure out something else you can do."	"That was a hard math problem, but you stuck with it until you got it done. You stayed at your desk and kept your concentration. That's great!"

SOURCE: Adapted and quoted from "The secret to raising smart kids," by C. S. Dweck, 2008, *Scientific American Mind, 18*(6), 36–43.

Table 8-10 Advice to Parents for Raising Children Who Succeed Academically

- Parents of successful children have realistic beliefs about their children's current abilities, but they also have high expectations for the future. These parents help their children develop self-confidence by encouraging them to perform age-appropriate tasks both at school and at home.
- Parent–child relationships are warm and affectionate, and parents have discipline and control strategies that are authoritative rather than authoritarian (see Chapter 7). Parents place limits on their children's behavior, but the children feel safe and accepted.
- Perhaps most important of all, parents talk to their children. They read to them, listen to them, and have regular conversations with them. They support and enrich their children's exploration and inquiry, acting as role models in the process.

SOURCE: From *Failing at fairness: How America's schools cheat girls*, by M. Sadker and D. Sadker, 1994, Charles Scribner's Sons.

and often difficult skills, boys may be more likely to persist to mastery, whereas girls may be more likely to give up.

Dweck's view of the relationship between learning and motivation has received widespread support, in part because it leads toward more effective methods of teaching and parenting (Carr & Dweck, 2011; Elliot & Dweck, 2005). How can teachers and parents develop self-confidence and a greater sense of competence in their children? One critical goal is to encourage children to adopt a learning orientation rather than one based on performance alone. The child's perception of self-efficacy is critical. When children believe their failures are due to low ability, they often give up on difficult tasks because they incorrectly believe that there is nothing they can do to be successful. However, when parents and teachers emphasize a more flexible definition of intelligence—one that encourages the child to believe that effort will lead to success—the child develops a greater sense of competence and an improved self-concept. For example, in one study, children whose math grades were declining read and discussed an article entitled "You Can Grow Your Brain," which emphasized that the brain is like a muscle that gets stronger with use and that learning causes neurons to develop new connections. By the end of the term, these students' grades in math and overall school motivation had begun to improve compared to a similar student group that did not receive the "brainology" training (Dweck, 2008).

Praise also is critical in leading children to develop a strong and positive academic self-concept. However, praise must be carefully worded to emphasize learning goals (Dweck & Master, 2009). For instance, when praise is directed at children's level of a stable ability, such as superior intelligence, this can lead to feelings of failure when they encounter difficult tasks ("I'm just not smart enough") and to a fragile and defensive self-concept. However, when praise is directed toward the child's effort or toward specific accomplishments, it is a very valuable motivator, creating confidence and leading children to focus on the actions that lead to success (see Table 8-9).

Thus, teachers and parents play an important role in helping children of all levels of ability develop a sense of self-efficacy, self-confidence, and competence (Elliot & Dweck, 2007; Heckhausen & Dweck, 2009). Parents can do many things that contribute to their children's academic success (see Table 8-10). This is not to say, however, that all children are capable of experiencing the same kinds of success in school. We must acknowledge that school is just harder for some children than others: Children who possess lower levels of general intellectual ability will find the classroom a more challenging environment, as will children with certain types of developmental disorders, which we explore in the next section.

REVIEW THE FACTS 8-3

1. Children learn most when teachers emphasize which of the following?
   a. maintaining strict rules for appropriate behavior
   b. spending time on learning activities
   c. emphasizing differences in student's levels of ability
   d. assigning individual rather than group projects
2. Cooperative group-learning opportunities have been found to be especially important in enhancing the self-esteem of ____________.
3. A child's persistence toward success and excellence is called ____________.
4. In terms of intellectual skills, boys on average do better than girls in ____________ but poorer in ____________.
5. According to research by Carol Dweck, academic competence is highest when teachers and parents emphasize ____________ goals.
   a. performance b. self-inquiry
   c. learning d. group process

Practice on **MyDevelopmentLab**

INTELLECTUAL AND DEVELOPMENTAL DISABILITIES

The everyday life and future opportunities for children with special needs have changed radically over the last 30 years. These changes were propelled by the enactment of the 1975 landmark federal law Public Law 94-142 (PL 94-142), which originally was called the Education for All Handicapped Children's Act. In 1990, Public Law 94-142 was revised and renamed the Individuals with Disabilities Education Act (IDEA): It was realigned in 2004 to accommodate other legislative acts, including No Child Left Behind (U.S. Department of Education, 2012), and retitled as the *Individuals with Disabilities Education Improvement Act (IDEIA)*. Today, the scope of the IDEIA is broad, although its purpose is largely unchanged: To provide all children the right to a free and appropriate education (U.S. Department of Education, 2012).

Do you think that including children with special needs in regular classrooms and activities poses any potential problems for these children? If so, what might these be?

The IDEIA includes several key provisions with respect to education of children with intellectual and developmental disorders (Grigorenko, 2008). For example, it specifies that no longer should children with special needs be sent to special schools or hidden in the "special class" in the school building. Instead, all children are to be included in the life of the school, the playground, and the academic and cocurricular community to the maximum degree possible. Local schools have the responsibility to provide educational opportunities for children with special needs in the *least restrictive environment* possible. This means including children with special needs in regular classrooms and activities as much as is possible. The law also requires that an individual education plan (IEP) be prepared for each child identified as having special needs. IEPs identify the learning goals appropriate for each individual and note the support services that will be provided to help these children meet their goals. As children develop, their progress is evaluated, and their IEPs are adjusted as appropriate.

Although the policy of inclusion of individuals with special needs seems commonplace to us now, it was, in fact, a revolution at the time the federal law was first passed. One of the most significant changes has been a general shift in the public's attitude toward people with special needs. Rather than being defined by their disability, those with special needs are much more likely today to be seen and treated as individuals, with varying interests, strengths, personalities, along with a disability.

Today, about 12% of children in U.S. public schools receive some kind of special education service (Donovan & Cross, 2002), and there is a wide variety of physical, developmental, emotional, and intellectual disabilities that schools accommodate. Commonly provided services include those that assist children with speech and language impairments; emotional disorders, such as autism; and physical disabilities, such as hearing, visual, and orthopedic impairments. Schools also provide services that are appropriate for children with intellectual disabilities, which are discussed in the next section of the text.

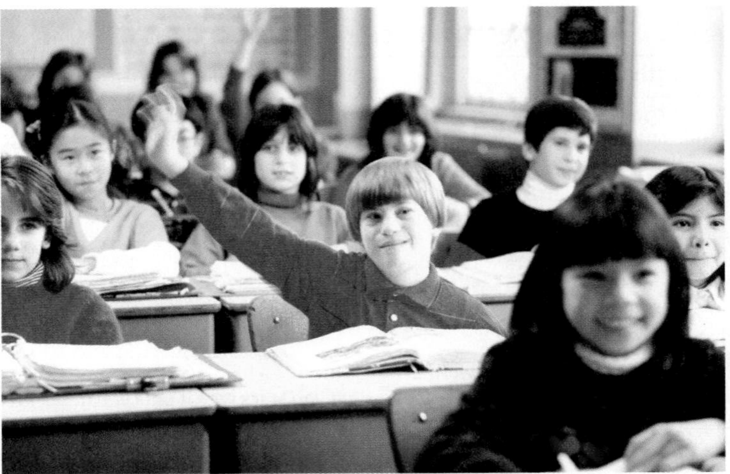

▲ In an "inclusion" classroom, students with disabilities participate along with others in all activities that are appropriate. Here, a child with Down syndrome is participating in a question-and-answer session, along with other members of the class.

Intellectual Disabilities

Intellectual disability is the term used today to refer to a condition characterized by significantly subaverage intellectual functioning and limited self-help skills. Although some people continue to refer to these learning-related problems using the older term *mental retardation*, most people today prefer the less pejorative term *intellectual disability*. Intellectual disabilities are often first noticed early in childhood, if a child is slow to develop age-appropriate motor, language, social, or self-help skills. However, unless the disability is very severe, formal diagnosis of intellectual disability usually occurs about the time a child begins school, when difficulty with learning new things becomes more apparent. Diagnosis involves an evaluation by a psychologist, who administers a standardized intelligence test and makes other assessments about the child's behavior. Intellectual disability affects about 2 to 3% of the population, and symptom profiles range from mild forms of this condition to profound impairment (see Table 8-12). Fortunately, about 85% of diagnosed cases of intellectual disability fall into the mild range (American Academy of Pediatrics, 2012a).

Intellectual disability can result from any of several hundred different causes, although the three most common of these are Down syndrome, fetal alcohol spectrum disorder (FASD), and fragile X syndrome. As we saw in Chapters 2 and 3, sometimes the cause of intellectual disability is biological, such as cases that result from hereditary disorders, such as phenylketonuria, or from genetic disorders, such as Down syndrome or fragile X syndrome. In other instances, the causes are environmentally induced, such as the disability that typically accompanies FASD. Intellectual disability can also result from trauma to the brain before, during, or after birth, as the result of either injury or oxygen deprivation.

intellectual disability
Disorder that is characterized by significantly subaverage intellectual functioning and limited self-help skills, with onset prior to age 18; formerly termed "mental retardation"

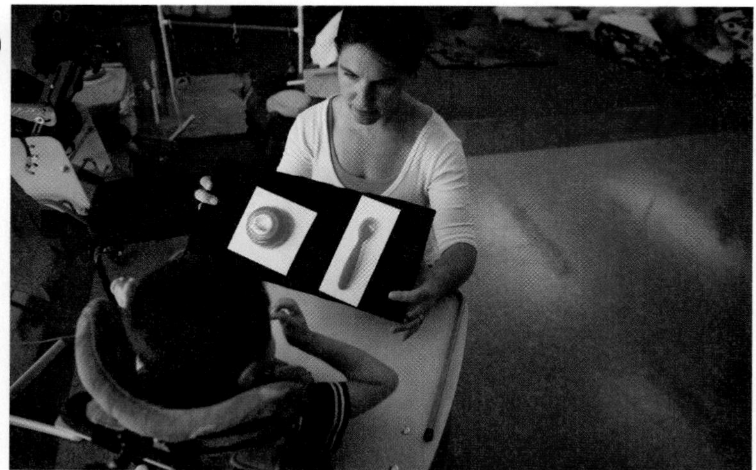

▲ Children who have disabilities are entitled to a free and appropriate education, under the provisions of the Individuals with Disabilities Education Improvement Act (IDEIA). Here, a young boy who cannot speak is choosing food or drink by using hand signals to point to a picture of a spoon or a sippy cup.

Table 8-11 Assumptions Guiding the Diagnosis of Intellectual Disability (Mental Retardation)

Diagnosis of intellectual disability depends on a complex clinical assessment of the individual, giving consideration to three central factors:

1. **IQ score** (usually around or below a score of 70 on standardized tests where average IQ is 100)
2. **Scores on tests of adaptive behavior,** including:
   - *conceptual skills*, such as language and literacy; understanding money, time, and numbering concepts; and self-direction
   - *social skills*, such as interpersonal skills, self-esteem, gullibility, social problem solving, and the ability to follow laws and rules and to avoid being victimized
   - *practical skills*, such as occupational skills, self-care skills, and abilities such as using money, traveling/transportation, protecting personal safety, and following good health-care practices
3. **Clinical assessment of cultural factors,** such as:
   - the community environment typical of the individual's peers and culture
   - linguistic diversity (do language skills hamper the person's ability to adapt?)
   - cultural differences in the way the individual communicates, moves, and behaves

SOURCE: From "FAQ on intellectual disability," American Association on Intellectual and Developmental Disabilities, 2008, retrieved from http://www.aaidd.org.

In rare circumstances, intellectual disability can result from social deprivation, although typically child maltreatment results in milder impairment than would warrant a diagnosis of disability. Also, in many cases, the cause of intellectual disability is unknown: In about one-third of the diagnosed cases, no particular cause or causes can be identified (The Arc, 2012).

According to the American Association on Intellectual and Development Disabilities (AAIDD, 2010), intellectual disabilities are disabilities that onset before age 18 and are characterized by significant limitation both in intellectual functioning and in adaptive behavior as expressed in conceptual, social, and practical adaptive skills. Furthermore, the AAIDD specifies that several assumptions must guide the diagnosis of an intellectual disability, which are outlined in Table 8-11.

As you can see from the table, these basic assumptions reflect a gradual evolution of attitudes about people with intellectual disabilities. Today, there is greater recognition that context is critically important. Although people with intellectual disabilities have some limitations, they may be better able to adapt to some contexts with minimal support but need much more support in other settings. Thus, each person must be recognized as an individual with specific abilities and challenges, and the task is to provide the necessary supports based on the adaptive needs of each person. As noted previously, federal laws require that school-age children with disorders be placed in the least restrictive environment, which usually means including children with intellectual disabilities in classes and activities with typically developing children, to the extent possible. As is true for children with other types of disabilities, individual education plans (IEPs) are developed for each child so that the child's opportunities are maximized.

Because the effects associated with intellectual disability vary widely from person to person, individuals are sometimes categorized according to the severity and extensiveness of their impairment (see Table 8-12). Most people with intellectual disability fall into the category of *mild retardation,* with IQs ranging between 55 and 70. Other categories of intellectual disability are *moderate* (IQs between 40 and 55), *severe* (IQs between 25 and 40), and *profound* (IQs below 25). It is important to note that many more people fall into the categories associated with higher levels of functioning rather than lower levels of functioning.

Although categories of disability are associated with specific IQ score ranges, we must emphasize the point that individuals are unique, and there are wide variations in what people lumped in the same category are capable of. The assignment of category labels to individuals tends to create an expectation that all people in a category will be very much alike. For these reasons, it is better to consider the characteristics and needs of the individual rather than to focus too much on the degree to which a person "fits" into a specific classification (see the box Changing Perspectives: Early Experience—Do Adverse Environments Cause Permanent Effects?).

As mentioned previously, intellectual disabilities, especially when mental impairment is mild, often are not diagnosed until several months after the child's birth and sometimes are diagnosed only when the child begins formal education. Regardless of when it is made, the diagnosis that a child has intellectual disabilities impacts the parents as well as other family members (Drew & Hardman, 2006). Parents may wonder what outcomes to expect and may worry about how they will take care of the special needs their child may have. Although a thorough discussion of options is beyond the scope of this text, there are many places where parents may receive guidance and assistance. For example, every large community has a chapter of the Arc (formerly the Association for Retarded Citizens), which can provide valuable support, information, and an array of services. Nearly all families learn to cope with the needs of a child with intellectual disabilities, and most families find the experience comparable to that associated with raising any child—full of challenge, but also of joy.

Table 8-12 Levels of Mental Retardation

Level	IQ Range	Percentage of Total Group	Required Level of Support	Characteristics of Children at this Level
Mild	55 to 70	85%	Intermittent	• Often not distinguishable from other children until they begin school • Able to develop social and language skills and can acquire academic skills up to about the sixth-grade level • Usually live in the community or in a supervised group home
Moderate	40 to 55	10%	Limited	• Can learn to communicate during preschool years but are not likely to proceed past second-grade-level academic skills • Usually go through vocational training and may work in sheltered workshops
Severe	25 to 40	3 to 4%	Extensive	• Poor motor development and poor communication skills • May learn to read "survival" words, such as *men, women,* and *stop* • Need a protective living situation, such as a group home
Profound	Below 25	1 to 2%	Pervasive	• Language and comprehension limited to simple requests and commands • Majority have some brain abnormality • Need constant supervision

SOURCE: Adapted from *Intellectual disability: Definition, classification, and systems of support,* 2010, American Association on Intellectual and Developmental Disabilities, Washington, DC: Author; and *Diagnostic and statistical manual of mental disorders* (DSM-IV, pp. 39–46), American Psychiatric Association, 1994, Washington, DC: Author.

Learning Disorders

Whereas intellectual disability implies a general intellectual deficit, **learning disorders,** also termed *learning disabilities,* involve difficulty in acquiring some specific academic skills but not others. Children with a learning disorder may have average or above-average general intellectual ability and no sensory or motor disabilities; however, they may struggle academically in a particular area, such as reading or math. Often, their overall academic achievement suffers: Difficulties in a major area of academic skill can generalize to other subjects, which is a problem that is particularly prevalent when the disorder involves reading.

The causes of learning disorders presently are not well understood, although it is known that they involve brain functioning in some way. For reasons that remain unclear, up to 80% of children with learning disorders are boys.

Although considerable attention is currently directed toward understanding the differences in how children learn, the traditional view, which is based on the American Psychiatric Association's *Diagnostic and Statistical Manual of Mental Disorders (DSM-IV-TR,* 2000), recognizes three main categories of learning disorders: *reading disorder; disorder of written expression,* which can involve anything from spelling and handwriting to syntax; and *mathematics disorder,* which can involve anything having to do with recognizing mathematical symbols and performing mathematical operations. Reading disorders in particular are quite common in children and they have a broad impact on academic performance. Although the broad topic of learning disorders is well beyond the scope of this text, we will offer a few brief comments about one particular type of reading disorder, *dyslexia,* in order to provide some exposure to the issues involved in understanding these complex phenomena.

learning disorders
Disorders that are associated with difficulty in acquiring some specific academic skills but not others despite normal intelligence and the absence of sensory or motor disabilities; may occur in areas such as reading, writing, or math

A Reading Disorder: Dyslexia Children with reading disorders can experience an array of problems, ranging from difficulties associated with hearing similar sounds as distinct to problems with comprehending and remembering written material. One common type of reading disorder is *dyslexia,* which involves incorrectly perceiving letters and words. Because children with dyslexia often confuse similar letters, such as *b* and *d,* or read *star* as *rats,* it is tempting to think of this problem as perceptual. However, only a small number of children diagnosed with dyslexia actually have anything wrong with their visual system and the large majority experience no perceptual problems (Handler & Fierson, 2011). For example, children with dyslexia may be exceptionally good at putting together puzzles. Why, then, do they make errors like confusing the letters *b* and *d?*

One observation is that reversal errors, like confusing *b* and *d* or *p* and *q,* are very common for beginning readers. Most children make errors of this type when they first learn to read, but most get through this stage quickly. Children with dyslexia somehow remain stuck in the early stages of reading (Lyytinen, Erskine, Aro, & Richardson, 2007). In addition, children with dyslexia often have broader language-based problems. For example, they may be delayed in learning to speak or their speech may be at a lower developmental level than that of their peers. Sometimes their difficulty in naming letters and written words is matched by their difficulty in naming objects or colors; it takes them longer than usual to recall an ordinary word like *key* or *blue.* They also may have trouble hearing the two separate syllables in a two-syllable word or recognizing that the spoken word *sat* starts with an *s* sound and ends with a *t* sound, suggesting that difficulties lie in the way speech sounds are processed in neural pathways (Brady, Braze, & Fowler, 2011; Catts & Adlof, 2011; Ramus & Szenkovits, 2008; Shaywitz, Morris, &

CHANGING PERSPECTIVES

Early Experience—Do Adverse Environments Cause Permanent Effects?

In today's world, not all children start life with the same set of advantages. When children's earliest environments are impoverished, there often are long-term negative effects on their psychosocial and intellectual development. Why might this be? One possibility is that the conditions present early in life tend to persist: When a child is born into an adverse environment—perhaps one involving poverty, abuse, or uncertainty—it often is difficult to change living circumstances dramatically for the better. Another possible explanation is that early experiences may shape the way children come to see the world, leading them to misinterpret their environments and act in maladaptive ways. A third possibility is that adverse environments may influence brain development, leading to permanent changes in the way children think about the world around them. Finally, epigenetic processes may be involved, through which environmental conditions modify the genetic code itself, altering developmental processes at the level of the gene. How do researchers attempt to understand how such complex developmental processes operate?

An opportunity to study issues such as these was presented when hundreds of children of various ages were rescued from the severely deprived, overcrowded environment of Romanian orphanages in the years between 1990 and 1992 and adopted by parents in the United Kingdom. In one long-itudinal study (Rutter, O'Conner, & the ERA Study Team, 2004), for example, a sample of these Romanian children was compared to a group of adopted children born in the United Kingdom. Four groups were studied: Romanian orphans were grouped according to the age at which they were removed from their impoverished environments: 45 were adopted by age 6 months, 54 were placed in adoptive homes between the ages of 6 and 24 months, and 54 were adopted between the ages of 24 and 42 months. The children born in the United Kingdom (U.K.) were all adopted by 6 months of age. How did these groups of children compare?

At the time of adoption, most Romanian children had experienced severe malnutrition, and over half were severely retarded in both intellectual and physical development. In addition, consistent with conditions of extreme deprivation, the head circumference of the Romanian children averaged more than two standard deviations below normal, placing them at about the third percentile. Cognitive deficits also were substantial, and the social and emotional functioning of these children in all age groups were generally disrupted.

By age 6, however, most of the Romanian adoptees were within the normal range for weight, although those who were adopted at older ages showed less recovery. There also was some recovery toward a normal head size by age 6, but this showed less improvement than was seen with weight. In addition, those who were older at the time of adoption and those who were the most malnourished at the time of adoption showed the least amount of recovery. In terms of cognitive deficits, over half of the Romanian children were severely retarded at the time of their adoption; however, by age 6, most of those in the younger group had shown remarkable recovery, and many of those in the older groups also showed striking improvements in intellectual abilities: Fewer than 3% of the children adopted by age 6 months had any serious cognitive deficits, although about one-third of the oldest group retained impairments at age 6, as shown in the table that follows. In terms of psychosocial adjustment, the Romanian adoptees generally showed improvement in their social and emotional functioning, although some of these children continued to show unusual or superficial attachment to their adoptive parents. Again, these adjustment problems were more predominant in children who were adopted at older ages.

More recently, the children in the original adoption study were followed up at age 11 (Rutter, et al., 2007) and again at age 15 (Rutter & Sonuga-Barke, 2010). For the most part, the patterns of deficiency present at age 6 were maintained, particularly in terms of cognitive abilities and school achievement. Even among the children who originally suffered the greatest degree of deprivation, cognitive growth continued through middle childhood and into adolescence. Furthermore, and surprisingly, among the most disadvantaged group of adoptees, cognitive gains actually *exceeded* those of children in the U.K. control groups. Thus, even a dozen years after severe deprivation, it appears that children continue to make modest progress in catching up in the development of their cognitive abilities (Beckett, Castle, Rutter, & Sonuga-Barke, 2010). However, a somewhat different pattern of recovery was found when looking at physical growth. Although cross-sectional studies generally show that early delays in physical development due to deprivation are temporary and that deprived children catch up in their growth trajectories over time (van Ijzendoorn, Bakermans-Kraenburg, & Juffer, 2007), that was not entirely the case in this sample of children. Instead, the catch-up in growth and physical development was seen at age 11, but then children in the most deprived group fell behind during the age period from age 11 to 15 (Sonuga-Barke, Schlotz, & Rutter, 2010). This rather surprising finding suggests that psychosocial deprivation has a long-term, pervasive effect that is not completely remediated over time. Instead, when children are taken out of a deprived setting and placed in a positive environment, what appears to happen is that there is a period of early, rapid catch-up in growth, but this catch-up may not be enough to send the child onto a normal trajectory that is maintained through adolescence.

Country of origin and age that children were adopted	Percentage of children with serious deficits at age 6	
	Cognitive impairment	Impairment in attachment behavior
U.K. children under 6 months	2.0%	3.8%
Romanian children under 6 months	2.3%	8.9%
Romanian children 6 to 24 months	12.0%	24.5%
Romanian children 25 to 42 months	32.6%	33.3%

SOURCE: From Rutter, M., O'Conner, T.C., & the English and Romanian Adoptees (ERA) Study Team. (2004). Are there biological programming effects for psychological development? Findings from a study of Romanian Adoptees. *Developmental Psychology,* 40, 81–94.

What do the results mean? What lessons should we take away from this set of studies, First, the effects of the adverse environment were more dramatic the longer the deprivation conditions lasted: Children who were adopted at younger ages did better than those who remained in the orphanages until they were older. Second, it also is apparent that not all children are alike: Some made remarkable recoveries, but others did not make such dramatic progress. Finally, the data from the Romanian adoption study suggest that a child's early environment sets in motion a pattern of growth and development that is in some ways modifiable through later experience, but in other ways is determined by factors experienced very early in life.

Thus, the results of studies such as this leave many questions unanswered. For example, is there a "critical period" during which certain experiences must occur for development to proceed normally? Is early brain development sculpted and shaped by early experiences? Why do some children appear to be hardier than others? What further recovery, if any, might we expect as these children grow older? Questions such as these continue to be addressed by developmental psychologists. Can you think of other issues that research studies such as these raise?

Shaywitz, 2008). Today, dyslexia is generally understood to be a disorder involving how basic speech sounds are processed in the language system in the brain (Fraser, Goswami, & Conti-Ramsden, 2010; Goswami, 2011). Neuroimaging studies point to its cause as being underactivation of the neural networks for reading, especially in the left hemisphere (Goswami, 2008a) and in the cerebellum (Stoodley & Stein, 2011). Genetic processes are also involved, and research suggests that epigenetic processes—through which environmental factors modify gene actions—are implicated as well (Smith, 2011). Because dyslexia is a disorder that qualifies affected individuals for accommodation under the Individuals with Disabilities Education Improvement Act, several approaches to intervention are being developed and used (Braaten, 2011; Richardson & Gilger 2005; Snowling & Hulme, 2011).

Helping Children with Learning Disorders Day after day, children with learning disorders are unable to do things that their classmates seem to accomplish effortlessly. With each failure, they may become increasingly insecure about their ability to perform well, and their self-esteem may suffer. Thus, children with learning disorders often have difficulty with social skills as well as with academic skills (Cowden, 2010; Yu, Buka, McCormick, Fitzmaurice, & Indurkhya, 2006). For example, classmates tend to interact less with a child who is not successful in school. Consequently, children with learning disorders may become increasingly isolated from their peers. This isolation also may be intensified by family members who find life with a child with a learning disorder to be highly stressful (Dyson, 2003). Some children with these disorders become shy and withdrawn, others become boastful, and others are prone to impulsive or angry outbursts. It can be difficult to help a child with a learning disorder develop confidence and experience success in other areas.

The treatment of any learning disability generally involves intensive remedial work including carefully sequenced tutorial instruction. Especially important are the approaches that emphasize the need to improve the child's confidence. When reading is hard, the majority of academic work is also difficult. However, having a learning disability should not be associated with failure: Thomas Edison, Nelson Rockefeller, and Hans Christian Andersen were all dyslexic as children.

The study of learning disorders is a challenging puzzle with a confusing array of expert opinions about their causes, symptoms, and treatments. A trip to any bookstore will yield scores of books that propose a variety of approaches about the best ways to cope with any learning disability (e.g., Braaten, 2011; Rayner, Pollatsek, Ashby & Clifton, 2012; Richards & Leafstedt, 2010). One common feature, however, is that experts agree that the earlier intervention begins, the better the child's chances for later success (e.g., Hulme & Snowling, 2011; Lehman, Salaway, Bagnato, Grom, & Willard, 2011).

Attention-Deficit/Hyperactivity Disorder

As is true for children with learning disorders, early intervention is also appropriate for children with **attention-deficit/hyperactivity disorder (ADHD)**, which includes symptoms of extreme inattentiveness, problems with impulse control, and high levels of activity (see Table 8-13). Although some children present only symptoms of attention deficit and others experience only hyperactivity, most children display at least some aspects of both; hence, this disorder is usually identified by the combined name, ADHD.

ADHD is difficult to diagnose, given the broad array of behaviors that are associated with the disorder and the degree of variability in the specific behaviors that individual children display. Although at present the disorder is diagnosed on the basis of symptoms involving either hyperactivity, or attention problems, or both, new research suggests that ADHD also involves impairment in certain types of cognitive functions (Gupta & Kar, 2010). Consequently, researchers are working to develop a more comprehensive and standardized means of identifying children who have this disorder, which will improve diagnostic accuracy and should lead to more effective treatment (Gupta, Kar, & Srinivasan, 2011).

Most researchers agree that ADHD involves irregularities in the way the brains of affected children process information. Some research suggests that the neurotransmitter dopamine may be involved, at least in some cases (e.g., Genro, Kieling, Rohde, & Hutz, 2010). The brains of children with ADHD also sometimes show structural differences in comparison to those of children without ADHD (e.g., Barkley, 2006; Klein, 2011; Qui, et al., 2011). Several possible causes of the brain irregularities have been suggested, including both hereditary and environmental factors. Studies of identical and fraternal twins suggest a strong genetic link in the disorder (Gillis, 1992; Greven, Rijsdijk, & Plomin, 2011; Wolraich, 2006). Among the environmental variables that serve as risk factors are early malnutrition, lead poisoning, problems during pregnancy or delivery, prenatal exposure to certain drugs of addiction such as nicotine and cocaine, and premature birth (Goldstein & DeVries, 2011; NIMH, 2012).

Treating Children with ADHD Regardless of its cause, there are several treatment options available to children diagnosed with ADHD. Many children who display symptoms of ADHD respond positively to amphetamine-type drugs, including the widely prescribed drugs Ritalin, Adderol, and Strattera (DuPaul & Kern, 2011a; Levrini & Prevatt, 2012), although these drugs are more likely to be prescribed for older, rather than younger, children. Although the typical response to stimulant drugs is to speed up central nervous system activity and, correspondingly, behavior, when children with ADHD take these

Watch *Dyslexia Detector* on **MyDevelopmentLab**

attention-deficit/hyperactivity disorder (ADHD) Disorder that involves symptoms of extreme inattentiveness, problems with impulse control, and high levels of activity; although some children present only symptoms of attention deficit and others experience only hyperactivity, usually both are in evidence

Watch *Attention Deficit Hyperactivity Disorder (ADHD): Dr. Raun Mel* on **MyDevelopmentLab**

Table 8-13 Common Characteristics of Children Diagnosed with Attention-Deficit/Hyperactivity Disorder (ADHD)

Three Types of Characteristics	Description
Inattention	• Has difficulty concentrating on a single topic or activity • Makes careless mistakes • Has unrelated thoughts that don't string together • Does not seem to be listening when spoken to • Has difficulty planning and organizing activities and completing them on time • Has some difficulty in learning new things, and performance depends somewhat on the type of task • Is easily distracted • Dislikes and has difficulty with tasks that require sustained mental effort • Has difficulty in completing tasks or following through with instructions • Is forgetful and frequently loses things
Hyperactivity	• Has difficulty in sitting still (squirms in seat, roams around the room) (Note: in adolescence, hyperactive behavior may be controlled but thoughts race) • Fidgets (taps things, wiggles feet, touches everything) • Talks a lot • Appears restless • Sometimes bounces from one activity to the next • Frequently tries to do more than one thing at the same time • Has difficulty playing quietly
Impulsivity	• Has difficulty thinking before acting (e.g., may hit or yell before thinking through the consequences) • Has problems in waiting to take a turn • Frequently interrupts others in conversation • In conversation, often blurts out responses before the other person is finished with speaking

SOURCE: *Attention deficit/hyperactivity disorder (ADHD)*, by the American Speech-Language-Hearing Association, 2012, retrieved from http://www.asha.org; and *Diagnostic and statistical manual of mental disorders* (4th ed., text rev.), by the American Psychiatric Association, 2000, Washington, DC: Author.

drugs, they become calmer and show improved concentration. These findings have led researchers to speculate that ADHD may result when the child's nervous system is chronically understimulated. According to this view, children with ADHD seek extra stimulation from their environment in order to raise the activity level in their brains. This stimulus-seeking behavior gives rise to their heightened activity level and their inability to concentrate. An alternative explanation suggests that Ritalin and similar drugs may act by boosting cognitive activity levels for control processes, thereby allowing these children to more effectively regulate other types of behavior.

Not all children with ADHD benefit from taking drugs, however, and there has been considerable controversy about drug side effects and possible overuse. However, for those children who respond favorably, Ritalin and similar drugs generally are linked to improvements in schoolwork and family and peer relationships (Barkley, 2006; DePaul, 2007).

For those children with ADHD who do not respond to drugs or whose parents choose to avoid using them, several alternate forms of treatment are available. Generally, the most effective programs are centered around contingency management—also referred to as applied behavioral analysis (Miller & Hinshaw, 2012; see Chapter 2). One example of such a program is educational management, which generally is implemented both at home and at school. Educational management restructures the child's environment by simplifying it, reducing distractions, making expectations more explicit, and generally reducing confusion. Effective programs of all types typically focus on specifying clear rules and expectations and providing rewards for controlled behavior (Fabiano, et al., 2007). Also, approaches that provide acceptable and constructive outlets for the boundless energy often associated with ADHD are likely to be especially useful (Armstrong, 1996).

Regardless of the approach used to manage conditions like ADHD or to remediate learning disorders, programs that are applied consistently by concerned and responsible caregivers are likely to have the best results. Also, as is true for many developmental disorders, early intervention seems to be important (DuPaul & Kern, 2011b). The same is true for another common disorder of childhood—autism—to which we now turn.

Autism and Autism Spectrum Disorder

Autism spectrum disorder (ASD) is a category of developmental brain disorders, the most severe form of which is termed **autism**. Autism spectrum disorders vary widely in the range of symptoms that are expressed, as well as in their severity. The

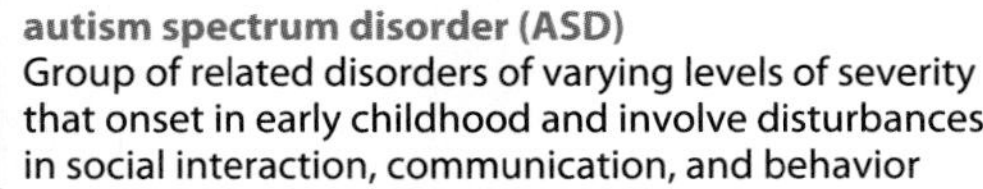

autism spectrum disorder (ASD)
Group of related disorders of varying levels of severity that onset in early childhood and involve disturbances in social interaction, communication, and behavior

autism
Most severe form of autism spectrum disorder; includes significant disturbances in social interaction, communication, and behavior

hallmark symptoms of these disorders involve disturbances in social interaction, communication, and behavior (see Table 8-14). In severe cases, disturbances involving social interaction are usually noticed in infancy, when the baby seems unresponsive to caregivers and seems to focus intently on one thing for long periods of time. In childhood, this impairment typically involves a preference for solitary activities, disinterest in having friends or the inability to interact appropriately with friends, and a diminished interest in other people in general. Children who have autism seldom show normal affection for caregivers, and seem distant and cold in their interactions with others. Communication skills, both verbal and nonverbal, may be absent entirely, or distorted. Children with severe forms of autism sometimes do not speak at all, or when they do, they speak in only single words or short sentences, and the pitch, tone, or rhythm of their speech is typically distorted. Usually, imaginative play is limited or involves a mechanical quality, or is absent entirely. Behavior of children diagnosed with autism is often repetitive, such as rocking back and forth or spinning objects over and over. Children with autism often focus on one small part of an object when they inspect it—for example, choosing to focus on the button on a jacket rather than the jacket itself. They typically prefer routine, highly stereotyped ways of doing things, and may become quite upset if any part of a ritual—for example, getting ready for bed—does not occur in the same way and in the same sequence every time it is performed. In severe cases, self-abuse, often in the form of head-banging or biting, is part of this disorder (APA, 2000).

Because the extreme forms of autism involve profound disturbances in social interactions, communication, and behavior, diagnosis usually occurs in infancy or early childhood, when parents notice that their baby is not developing a normal pattern of interactions with others. In order to make a diagnosis of ASD, symptoms must be present prior to the age of 3. However, in milder forms of this disorder, which include *Asperger's disorder*, parents may not have the child evaluated until later in childhood—perhaps when the child enters formal education and it becomes apparent to teachers and others that the child's development is delayed and inappropriate (CDC, 2012b). Regardless of when diagnosis is made, the period of middle childhood is often especially important when dealing with this disorder, as many of the typical advances made during these grade school years include the developmental of meaningful social relationships as well as academic skills—things that are difficult or impossible for children diagnosed with ASD.

Autism was first identified as a discreet mental disorder in the 1940s, although certainly there were children who had the symptom profile now called autism in earlier generations. It is clear that autism and autism spectrum disorders are being diagnosed much more frequently today than in the past, as physicians, teachers, and psychologists are becoming more familiar with the diagnosis. Today, researchers estimate that about 1 in 88 children in the United States will have some form of autism spectrum disorder by age 8, making ASD one of the most common forms of developmental disorders diagnosed today (CDC, 2012b). Scientists are not sure what causes autism, although it does seem apparent that genes play an important role. For example, if one identical twin has this disorder, there is about a 90% chance that the other twin will develop symptoms as well (National Institute of Neurological Disorders and Stroke [NINDS], 2012). Also, autism seems to run in families: If one child in a family is diagnosed with autism, the risk of a second child also being diagnosed is about 5%—about four to five times higher than in the population overall. For reasons that are unknown, boys are about five times more likely than girls to be diagnosed with autism—1 in 54 boys versus 1 in 252 girls (CDC, 2012b).

Table 8-14 Symptoms Typically Associated with Autism Spectrum Disorders

Symptom Category	Examples
Social interaction	• Impairment in using nonverbal gestures to initiate or maintain social interactions • No response when addressed by name • No smiling or social responsiveness • Impaired ability to make friends • Little or no interest in social or pretend play • Poor eye contact • Little or no engagement with others in reciprocal interactions
Communication	• No babbling or pointing by age 1; no single words by age 16 months; no two-word phrases by age 2 • Impairment in the ability to initiate or sustain conversations with others • Stereotyped or repetitive use of language
Behavior	• Excessive lining up of toys or objects • Focus on small parts of objects, rather than on the objects themselves • Preoccupation with stereotyped or restricted patterns of interest (e.g., focus on fiddling with buttons or zippers, a fascination with movement of objects) • Inflexibility in adjusting to new routines • Repetitive motion (e.g., spinning, rocking, hand-waving, whole-body movements)

SOURCE: Based on information in "The autism fact sheet," National Institute of Neurological Disorders and Stroke (NINDS), 2012, retrieved from http://www.ninds.gov/disorders/autism; and "Autistic disorder," in *Diagnostic and statistical manual of mental disorders* (4th ed., text rev.), American Psychiatric Association, 2000, Washington, DC: Author.

Autism spectrum disorders are thought to result from various problems associated with the brain. One theory currently receiving support is that these disorders involve a general lack of connectivity among the various regions of the brain (e.g., Just, Keller, Malave, Kana, & Varma, 2012; Schipul, Williams, Keller, Minshew, & Just, 2011). However, at present there is no cure for autism, although major research initiatives are under way to better understand the underlying causes and possible avenues of treatment. Today, treatment usually involves some form of applied behavioral analysis—this involves training the child to develop better social and language skills by using reinforcement, and then creating predictable environments in which these reinforcements are maintained. Sometimes medication also is given, especially if the child has seizures—which are fairly common among children diagnosed with ASD—or if the child has symptoms of other disorders, such as depression, anxiety, or obsessive–compulsive behavior (NINDS, 2012). Family counseling is also appropriate, so parents and other family members can better understand what to expect from the child and how to respond appropriately. Early intervention seems to be a key, and children who are nurtured in loving, supportive environments often have the most positive outcomes.

Indeed, all children benefit from growing up in environments that encourage their growth, support their emotional development, and help them learn the skills and competencies needed for successful lives. Children who are loved and well-cared for are afforded advantages in many areas of their lives. We discuss these topics in the next chapter, which focuses on personality and sociocultural development in middle childhood.

REVIEW THE FACTS 8-4

1. The purpose of PL 94-142, called the Education for All Handicapped Children Act, was to ensure that all children with special needs have access to ___________.
2. Since 1975, the percentage of children diagnosed with learning disabilities has __________. The percentage of children diagnosed with intellectual disabilities has __________.
3. Which of the following is *not* one of the *DSM-IV's* categories for diagnosis of learning disabilities?
   a. a mathematics disorder
   b. a disorder of written expression
   c. a reading disorder
   d. a disorder of scientific thinking
4. When children incorrectly perceive letters, for example, by confusing the letters *p* and *g*, this type of disorder is called ____________.
5. Does the evidence on ADHD suggest that this condition is the result of an understimulation or an overstimulation of the child's nervous system?
6. The disorder of childhood that involves problems with social interaction, communication skills, and behavior is termed ____________.

Practice on **MyDevelopmentLab**

CHAPTER SUMMARY

Physical and Motor Development

How does a typical child's body change during the period of middle childhood?

- Three themes run throughout development in middle childhood: Development is *continuous;* for each unique child, physical, cognitive, and psychosocial factors *interact;* and development occurs in a *broad social context.*
- Physical growth generally is gradual for boys and girls during middle childhood until they experience the adolescent growth spurt, which begins at about age 9 for girls and about age 11 for boys.
- Growing pains are common in adolescent children as their skeleton matures. During middle childhood, children's permanent teeth begin to come in.
- Brain development continues during middle childhood as some neurons continue to branch and others are pruned away. Lateralization becomes more pronounced, and the corpus callosum and other white-matter regions become more mature as myelination proceeds throughout the period of middle childhood. Gray-matter brain regions peak in size at about age 10.
- During middle childhood, gross motor skills continue to develop, along with increasing physical strength. Practice and cultural expectations most likely account for most gender differences in physical abilities during these years.
- Fine motor skills also develop, which leads to better handwriting, among other things.

What health-related risk factors pertain especially to children during the grade school years?

- Generally, middle childhood is one of the healthiest periods in life. However, vision problems begin to emerge during middle childhood: Approximately 25% of White children in the United States are fitted with glasses or contacts by sixth grade.
- Physical activity and fitness have been declining among U.S. children, perhaps in response to the increasing amount of time devoted to media, including TV and video games.
- Obesity is affecting an increasing number of children in the United States and other developed countries. Nearly 19% of U.S. grade-school-age children are obese, as measured by the body mass index (BMI). Obesity is linked to a heightened risk for health problems, as well as for social and psychological problems. Several factors contribute to childhood obesity.
- Asthma—a chronic inflammatory disorder of the airways—is becoming increasingly widespread among children in developing countries, and currently affects about 14% of U.S. children. Asthma is especially prevalent among boys, among African Americans, and among children living in poverty.

- The leading cause of death in middle childhood is accidents and their associated injuries, especially those involving motor vehicles. During middle childhood, children's physical skills may be more advanced than their understanding of risks, leading to dangerous behavior that causes accidents.
- Psychological disorders and mental illness can begin in middle childhood, raising concerns about accurate diagnosis and treatment.

Cognitive Development

How did Piaget conceptualize the thought processes that take shape during middle childhood?

- Piaget referred to middle childhood as the period of concrete operations. This third stage of cognitive development begins at about age 5 to 7. In the *concrete operational period,* children's thinking becomes more reversible, flexible, and complex. Children also begin to rely on language as an aid in problem solving and they gain the ability to conserve. However, their thinking is still bound to concrete examples; they have not yet mastered abstract ideas or relationships.
- Although the pace of children's learning can be modestly accelerated through instruction, Piaget believed that children are better off when they learn at their own pace. He also believed that learning is best when children are intrinsically motivated, rather than explicitly rewarded, for success.

In what ways does a child's memory develop during the period of middle childhood?

- Children's memory strategies and techniques, which are called *control processes,* improve with age. For example, scripts that children use to describe a typical sequence of events become more elaborate with age. During middle childhood, children also become better able to monitor their own thinking through a process called *metacognition.*

How do the typical child's language and literacy skills develop between the ages of 6 and 12?

- Vocabulary continues to expand in middle childhood, along with the development of more complex uses of language. Language use is important for transmitting culture to children.
- According to whole-language approaches, reading and writing are literacy skills that develop from earlier language abilities, and they are influenced by children's sociocultural context.

How is intelligence defined by researchers working in the field today?

- Children's scores on intelligence tests often have important implications for their educational and social opportunities. The first intelligence tests were designed to predict children's school success, and they emphasized judgment, reasoning, memory, and comprehension.
- Today, two commonly used intelligence tests are the *Stanford-Binet Intelligence Scale,* which is the revised version of Binet's original intelligence test, and the Wechsler tests (WPPSI, WISC, and WAIS). Both tests report scores on a scale where the average *intelligence quotient (IQ)* is 100. About two-thirds of the population scores between 85 and 115, and almost 96% scores between 70 and 130. Intelligence is now assessed using the *deviation IQ,* which assigns an IQ score by comparing an individual's test score with the scores of other people of the same age range.
- Test scores are not perfect measures of a child's underlying intelligence for a variety of reasons: intelligence tests are not perfectly reliable, environmental factors can affect scores, tests do not measure all aspects of intelligence, and tests are just one sample of behavior taken at a given point in time.
- Although we tend to think of intelligence as a single trait, many modern theorists view it as composed of several different abilities. Depending on the demands in a person's culture, certain types of abilities may be more important or they may be less important.
- Although members of some U.S. minority groups typically score lower (on average) on traditional intelligence tests than does the White majority, these lower scores are believed to result from cultural differences rather than from racial differences. When children move to environments with more opportunity and when families emphasize school success, children's academic performance generally improves.

Learning and Thinking in School

What are the most important adjustments faced by children when they begin school?

- Although children's opportunities to attend school vary widely around the world, when children do enter school, they face a variety of new expectations and adjustments.
- Many schools emphasize rules for appropriate behavior, although children learn more when teachers spend more time on teaching and learning and less time on maintaining order. A particularly useful approach is to assign students small-group projects and activities, which fosters the development of problem-solving skills and enhances self-esteem, especially among girls.
- School success is influenced by many factors, including students' *achievement motivation,* which is a learned drive that involves their persistence toward success and excellence. An individual's level of achievement motivation is influenced by culture, as well as by family values.
- There appear to be some gender differences in intellectual skills, although these differences are smaller now than they were 40 years ago. These differences could be due to sex differences in the brain, but gender-based social expectations undoubtedly play a role.
- Parents can encourage their children's academic success by creating a supportive environment, stressing the importance of education, and encouraging the development of self-esteem and self-efficacy. Children also benefit when parents emphasize effort, rather than ability, as the means to academic success.

Intellectual and Developmental Disabilities

What factors are associated with academic success during the period of middle childhood?

- Opportunities available to all children with intellectual or developmental disabilities and other special needs were radically expanded with the enactment of PL 94-142 in 1975, which originally was called the Education for All Handicapped Children Act. The current revision of this law is the Individuals with Disabilities Education Improvement Act (IDEIA). This law requires that all children with special needs be afforded educational opportunities in the least restrictive environment. Individual education plans (IEPs) must be prepared by educators for each child who is diagnosed with special needs. As the result of PL-142, students with special needs are less likely to be placed in special settings.

How are intellectual disabilities defined, and what philosophy guides the education of children with disabilities in the United States today?

- *Intellectual disabilities*, formerly called mental retardation, are characterized by significant limitations in both intellectual functioning and adaptive behavior that onsets before age 18. Individuals with intellectual disabilities vary widely in the specific limitations they experience.
- *Learning disorders* involve difficulty in acquiring some specific academic skills but not others. Typically, learning disorders fit into three main categories: reading disorder (including dyslexia), disorder of written expression, and mathematics disorder.
- Dyslexia, which is a particular kind of reading disorder, involves the confusion of letters. Dyslexia often involves other language-based problems.
- Children with learning disorders often have difficulties with social issues as well. Treatment for learning disorders is more effective when it begins early in life.

What symptoms typically are associated with attention-deficit/hyperactivity disorder (ADHD) and with autism spectrum disorder (ASD), what are the likely causes of these disorders, and what treatments are appropriate?

- *Attention-deficit/hyperactivity disorder (ADHD)* is characterized by extreme inattentiveness, problems with impulse control, and high levels of activity. ADHD may result from many different causes, both genetic and environmental.
- Many children diagnosed with ADHD respond positively to stimulant drugs, such as Ritalin, which suggests this disorder may involve understimulation of the child's nervous system. Those who do not respond positively to these drugs or whose parents prefer to not use drugs as treatment sometimes can be treated by modifying the environment to make it less confusing.
- *Autism* is the most severe form of the disorders referred to as *autism spectrum disorders (ASD)*. These disorders involve significant impairment in social interaction, communication, and behavior. Symptoms of ASD onset before age 3, but diagnosis of less severe forms often occurs during middle childhood. The number of children diagnosed with ASD is increasing. Today about 1 in 88 U.S. children have this disorder, which is much more common among boys than girls.
- Autism spectrum disorders involve problems with the brain, and genetic mechanisms are involved. At present there is no cure for ASD.

KEY TERMS

concrete operational period (p. 227)
control processes (p. 229)
metacognition (p. 230)
Stanford-Binet Intelligence Scale (p. 232)
intelligence quotient (IQ) (p. 232)
deviation IQ (p. 232)
achievement motivation (p. 237)
intellectual disability (p. 240)
learning disorders (p. 242)
attention-deficit/hyperactivity disorder (ADHD) (p. 244)
autism spectrum disorder (ASD) (p. 245)
autism (p. 245)

9 MIDDLE CHILDHOOD
Personality and Sociocultural Development

LEARNING OBJECTIVES

- What events in middle childhood enhance or detract from the child's developing self-concept?
- According to Erik Erikson, what is the central developmental conflict that must be resolved in middle childhood?
- How does self-esteem differ from self-concept, and what factors are linked to positive self-esteem in middle childhood?
- What are the three components of social cognition, and how does each help the child develop an understanding of the social world?
- How do children of different ages think about questions of right versus wrong?
- Why are friends important in middle childhood, and how do friendships change as children move through the period of middle childhood?
- What factors are linked to popularity during middle childhood?
- How does a child come to develop a sense of ethnic identity?
- How can parents help their children cope with stressful situations?
- When family structures change, such as when parents divorce or remarry, what developmental issues are posed for children?

CHAPTER OUTLINE

Personality Development in an Expanding Social World
- Three Perspectives on Middle Childhood
- Self-Concept
- Industry Versus Inferiority
- Self-Esteem

Social Knowledge and Reasoning
- The Development of Social Cognition
- The Development of Morality

Peer Relationships
- Functions of Friendship
- Developmental Patterns in Friendship
- Peer Groups
- In-Groups, Out-Groups, and Prejudice

Family Influences in Middle Childhood
- Parent–Child Interactions and Relationships
- The Changing Nature of the Family

If Shakespeare was right and all the world's a stage, then the stage on which children perform broadens dramatically during middle childhood—the period of development beginning at about age 6 and lasting until adolescence begins, around age 11 or 12. The emotional and social attachments of younger children centered primarily on the family; now children move into a broader world made up of peers, teachers, and other people in the wider community. Peers, in particular, are highly influential in shaping school-age children's behavior. Children's growing alliances with peers also influence how they come to see themselves and their place in the world.

Social cognition—the understanding of social relationships and events—is, in fact, of central importance in understanding how children of grade school age develop. In middle childhood, children's thoughts and social understandings increasingly mediate their behavior, although not perfectly. Children come to understand morality; the peer group; the circumstances of their families; and the future roles, relationships, and opportunities that are available to them. Some of these social concepts are directly taught, but many of them are learned by interpreting events and relationships as children attempt to understand their world.

As children's social worlds expand, so do their perspectives on the conflicts and stresses in their own families and living situations. Children who experience divorce must find ways of coping, as must children who are bullied by peers or are abused by parents or others. So, too, must children who have few friends, who struggle with school, or who live in environments that are uncertain, unsafe, or challenging in other ways. Children's methods of coping influence their patterns of social and emotional behavior, which help determine their personalities.

In this chapter, we explore the development of personality, as well as the development of social knowledge and reasoning in middle childhood. Then we look at the influence that peer relationships and family play in this developmental period. As we have done in earlier chapters, we again weave the ideas from major theoretical perspectives into the descriptions of the many major changes that take place in middle childhood. We begin our discussion by examining the development of children's personality that occurs during this period.

PERSONALITY DEVELOPMENT IN AN EXPANDING SOCIAL WORLD

Three Perspectives on Middle Childhood

How does a child's personality develop and change during middle childhood? Theorists within the field of human development have offered several points of view. Among these are perspectives within the social-learning, the psychodynamic, and the cognitive-developmental traditions (see Table 9-1). As was also true of their usefulness in explaining earlier periods of development, each of these views offers valuable insights for our understanding of personality development in middle childhood. Of particular importance in middle childhood is how these perspectives consider the development of *self*—children's views of their own personality and role in the larger environment. A central component of self is the child's self-concept.

Table 9-1 A Brief Review of Three Major Theoretical Perspectives on Middle Childhood

Theoretical Perspective	Description
Social-learning view	• Children develop habits and attitudes through observing and imitating models; in middle childhood these models are often peers. • Reinforcement is an important influence on how children behave, although parental control often weakens, being replaced by the need for social approval of peers, teachers, and coaches.
Psychodynamic view	• Family jealousies and turmoil typically are reduced during middle childhood, which Freud termed the period of *latency*. • Children turn their emotional energies toward peers, creative efforts, and learning the culturally prescribed tasks of the school and community. • Erikson described the central conflict of middle childhood as one of *industry versus inferiority*.
Cognitive-developmental view	• Children develop more mature thinking skills, which can be applied to solving social and intellectual problems. • Piaget described middle childhood as the period of concrete operations. • Emphasis is on the development of *self-concept*—how children think about themselves and how they establish their attitudes and values in the context of their society. • Self-esteem, which includes a self-evaluative component, also is an important concept, as is moral reasoning, which includes judgments about fairness, justice, and right and wrong.

Self-Concept

Studying the topic of *self-concept*—how children define who they are—helps us understand overall development during middle childhood, in that self-concept interweaves personality and social behavior. During this period, children form increasingly stable pictures of themselves, and their self-concepts become more realistic. Children also come to understand their skills and limitations more accurately, and their understanding of themselves organizes and orients their behavior (Rosen & Patterson, 2011).

In considering your own self-concept, how would you describe your best qualities and traits? Have these changed significantly since your childhood years?

Self-concepts are not always accurate, however, and this is especially the case at earlier ages. For example, children in the first grade tend to have more positive perceptions of their abilities and competencies than do older children (Archambault, Eccles, & Vida, 2010; Mantzicopoulos, 2006), which indicates that their perceptions of themselves are more idealistic and less realistic than they will be in later development. Self-concept becomes more accurate as children move through middle childhood. During the elementary school years, children continue to refine their understanding of others and, at the same time, they develop a greater flexibility in interacting with them. For example, gender identity and gender stereotypes emerge in children's thinking during these years as children begin to understand how to successfully relate to others (Blakemore, Berenbaum, & Liben, 2009; Halim & Ruble, 2010; Leaper & Bigler, 2011).

As children grow older, they also form more complex pictures of their own and other's physical, intellectual, and personality characteristics. For example, they attribute increasingly specific *traits*—stable personality characteristics—to themselves and others. Once children have established their view of the traits associated with a person, they try to behave consistently, and they expect consistency in the behavior of others. They also frequently compare themselves with their peers and draw conclusions such as, "I'm better than Susan at sports, but I'm not as popular as Tanya" or "My writing isn't as good as José's, but I'm better than he is at math." By making such comparisons, children begin to understand themselves in a more realistic way. Of course, how they perceive their own abilities compared to those of their peers forms an important foundation in their developing sense of self (Bagwell & Schmidt, 2011; Rubin, Coplan, Chen, & Bowker, 2011).

Industry Versus Inferiority

Erik Erikson recognized that how children come to define their skills relative to others is a critical aspect of development in middle childhood. You may recall that, for Erikson, the central task of middle childhood is to resolve the crisis of **industry versus inferiority**. Because success in middle childhood is heavily defined by educational attainment, especially in industrialized nations, much of children's time and energy is directed toward acquiring new knowledge and skills. When children succeed in school, they typically incorporate a sense of *industry* into their self-image—they learn that hard work produces results, and they continue to progress toward mastering their environment. In contrast, children who do not progress toward academic mastery often begin to feel inferior compared to their peers. This sense of *inferiority* can affect these children's personalities throughout life if it is not compensated by success in other activities that are valued, such as sports, music, or art. Thus, how children perform on tasks that are defined as important, and especially on those defined by success in the eyes of their peers, lays the groundwork for their self-esteem.

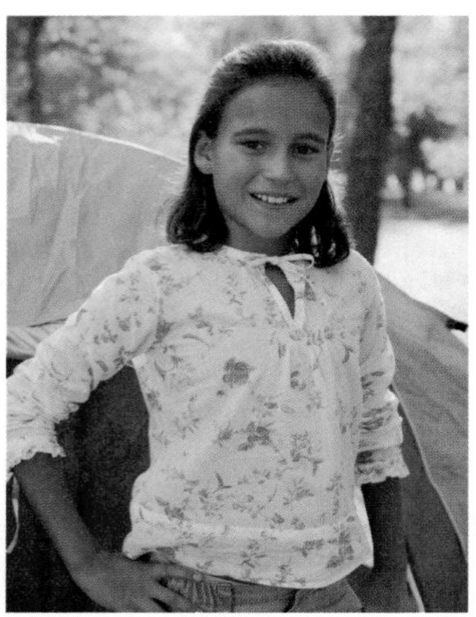

◄ Self-concepts in middle childhood are shaped by skills and roles in daily activities. Here, this girl expresses a positive self-concept, which is enhanced through successful interactions with others and mastery of new skills while at camp.

Self-Esteem

Whereas self-concept involves who you are and what you can do, **self-esteem** adds an evaluative component: Self-esteem refers to whether people see themselves positively (high self-esteem), negatively (low self-esteem), or somewhere in between. For example, when people have high self-esteem this means that they basically like themselves and typically feel competent in their social skills as well as in their other skills. When people have low self-esteem this means that they often dislike themselves, and they feel incompetent and inferior. Like self-concept, self-esteem has roots in early childhood and is influenced both by children's experiences with success and failure and by their interactions with parents and peers.

What factors do you believe have played the most significant role in the development of your own sense of self-esteem?

industry versus inferiority
In Erikson's theory, the third stage of development in which the child attempts to establish a sense of personal competence and mastery

self-esteem
One's attitude toward oneself, which can range from positive (high self-esteem) to negative (low self-esteem)

For children raised in cultures where formal education is expected, self-esteem is significantly correlated with academic achievement. Perhaps not surprisingly, children who do well in school typically have higher self-esteem than those who do poorly (Harter, 2006, 2012; Uszyriska-Jarmoc, 2007). The correlation between self-esteem and academic achievement is far from perfect, however: Many children who do poorly in school nonetheless manage to develop a healthy respect for themselves. Sometimes, these children excel in other activities, such as music or sports, which also are valued. In other cases, the subculture that is relevant to the child is one in which academic performance is disregarded or even seen as negative. Context is the critical variable: When family, peers, and the community view a child positively, high self-esteem is likely to result. This is how many ethnic minority children around the world manage to develop healthy self-esteem despite their continuing encounters with prejudice and bigotry (Sedikides & Spencer, 2007; Spencer-Rodgers & Collins, 2006).

For better or worse, development of self-esteem is a reciprocal process. Children tend to do well when they are confident in their own abilities; their success then bolsters and increases their self-esteem. In the same way, when children perform poorly, their confidence in their own ability decreases; their failures then tend to decrease their self-esteem still further. This low self-esteem limits their efforts, contributing to future poor performance, and so on. In all, personal successes or failures can lead children to see themselves as winners or losers, popular or unattractive. How can parents and others encourage the development of a child's positive self-esteem?

One thing parents can do to encourage the development of positive self-esteem is to seek out activities in which their children can be successful. If academic success is a challenge, parents can expose their children to other activities, such as sports, drama, painting, photography, or helping others, where their efforts are met with positive outcomes and appreciation. Another technique is to use praise to build self-esteem. Used in moderation, and given for legitimate accomplishments, praise can be quite effective.

Praise, however, also can be a double-edged sword. Too much praise or praise that does not reflect real accomplishments can prevent children from developing an accurate sense of their weaknesses as well as their strengths. They may begin to think, "I am great no matter what I do." This can create confusion and problems in peer and school relations (Aronson, 2002). Too much praise can lead children to develop unrealistic expectations in other ways as well (Dweck & Master, 2009; Kohn, 2006). The goal is to develop realistic self-representations that will help children guide their behavior (Harter, 2006, 2012). When excessive praise leads children to develop unrealistically high expectations, they often feel frustrated and even demoralized when they cannot attain the outcomes they have been led to expect. In addition, when praise is excessive, children may hear an implicit message that they are the center of the universe—which can hinder their developmental progress. For example, children who receive excessive praise often have difficulty overcoming an egocentric orientation, and they may be unable to understand the perspectives held by others. Further, children who receive excessive praise sometimes have difficulty acquiring a clear sense of right and wrong. For example, they may deny misdeeds even when caught red-handed because they are convinced of their own rightness (Damon, 1999; Hart, 2005). The development of positive self-esteem is an important aspect of healthy development during middle childhood, and it is tied to children's increasing skills in reasoning and social knowledge, which are topics explored in the next section.

social cognition
Thought, knowledge, and understanding that involve the social world

REVIEW THE FACTS 9-1

1. The theoretical view that emphasizes thinking, problem-solving skills, and the importance of people's self-concepts is the
   a. cognitive-developmental perspective.
   b. behavioral perspective.
   c. psychoanalytic perspective.
   d. social-learning perspective.
2. Erikson viewed middle childhood as centering on the development of ___________ versus ___________.
3. How children evaluate themselves, often with respect to their peers, is called
   a. industry. b. social cognition.
   c. self-esteem. d. self-concept.
4. The development of self-esteem is a *reciprocal* process. This means that ___________.
5. When a child is excessively praised, this often leads that child to all of the following, *except*
   a. the development of unrealistic expectations.
   b. frustration and demoralization.
   c. egocentrism.
   d. the development of a clear sense of right and wrong.

Practice on MyDevelopmentLab

SOCIAL KNOWLEDGE AND REASONING

Many factors contribute in important ways to children's developing sense of self. Of particular importance is the role played by *cognition,* as cognitive processes shape children's abilities to think about the world and their place in it. As we saw in Chapter 8, middle childhood is a period of important cognitive advances, as children move from the preoperational period into the period of concrete operations. The development of cognitive abilities is central to socialization during middle childhood.

The Development of Social Cognition

In early childhood, children's understanding of the world is limited by their egocentrism. During middle childhood, however, children gradually develop a less self-centered focus that takes into account what other people think and feel. **Social cognition,** which includes a person's knowledge and understanding of the social world, becomes an increasingly important determinant of behavior as children proceed through development (Frith & Frith, 2012). In middle childhood, children must learn how to deal with the complexities of friendship and justice, social rules and manners, gender-role conventions, obedience to authority, and moral law. Children begin to look at their social world and gradually come to understand the principles and rules that govern it, and they try to make sense of their experience as an organized whole.

One important aspect of social cognition is **social inference**, which involves guesses and assumptions about what another person is feeling, thinking, or intending. A child's ability to make correct social inferences develops significantly during middle childhood (Bengtson & Arvidsson, 2011; Uleman, Saribay, & Gonzalez, 2008). Younger children, for example, may see their mother smile and, regardless of context, assume that she is happy. Older children, on the other hand, are able to infer from other social cues that the smile is not a happy one, but instead an attempt to mask other emotions. When children develop the ability to make inferences about the thoughts and feelings of others, this is sometimes called *social perspective taking* (Elfers, Martin, & Sokol, 2008). A second component of social cognition is the child's understanding of **social responsibility**, which refers to the individual's obligations to family, friends, people in authority, and others. Children must learn to meet the social expectations of others if their social relationships are to flourish. Finally, social cognition also involves learning about **social regulations**, which are the customs and conventions that govern social interactions. Many social regulations are first learned by rote or imitation and applied rigidly. For example, a younger child learns that people must stand in line to use the drinking fountain, no exceptions. Later, children become more flexible and thoughtful about conforming to the customs of their gender, peer group, family, religion, ethnic group, school, or community authorities. Referring to the example just mentioned, the older child understands the concept of lining up, but also can grant an exception to an older adult, allowing out of courtesy this person to break the line and step in front of others. Figure 9-1 displays the three major aspects that comprise social cognition.

Why must egocentrism decline before social cognition can develop?

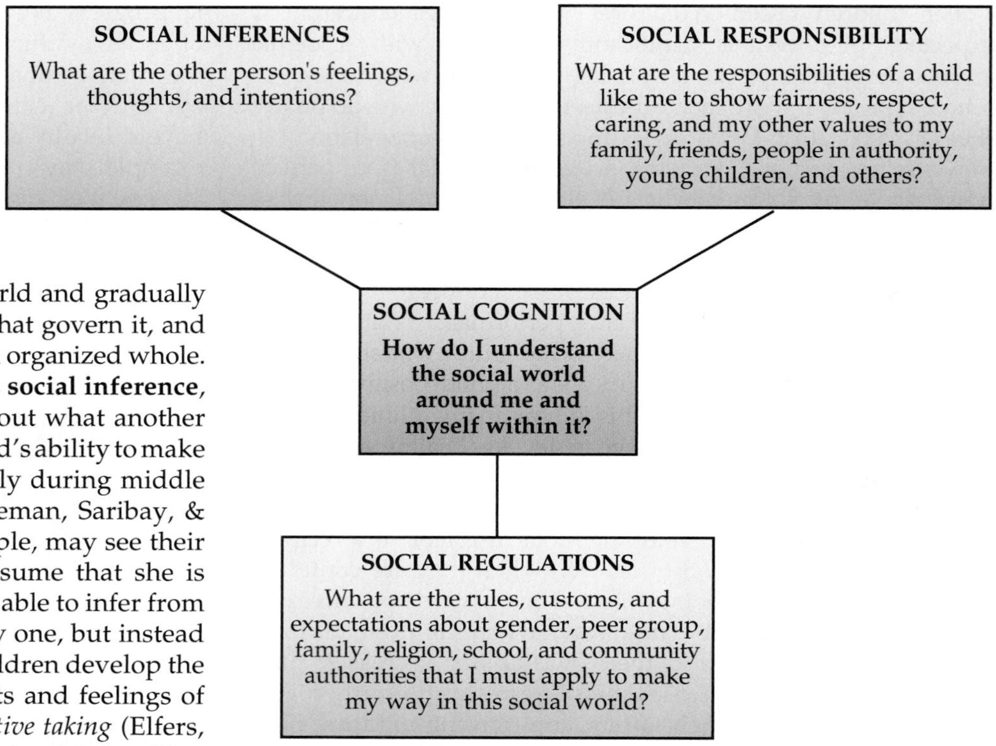

All three aspects of social cognition—inference, responsibility, and regulations—are involved in the child's developing ability to make moral judgments—to tell the difference between good and bad, kindness and cruelty, generosity and selfishness. Mature moral judgment is complex and involves much more than the rote learning of social rules and conventions. It involves making decisions about right and wrong, and learning to make these decisions is an important part of the personality development that takes place during middle childhood.

SOCIAL INFERENCES
What are the other person's feelings, thoughts, and intentions?

SOCIAL RESPONSIBILITY
What are the responsibilities of a child like me to show fairness, respect, caring, and my other values to my family, friends, people in authority, young children, and others?

SOCIAL COGNITION
How do I understand the social world around me and myself within it?

SOCIAL REGULATIONS
What are the rules, customs, and expectations about gender, peer group, family, religion, school, and community authorities that I must apply to make my way in this social world?

FIGURE 9-1 **Aspects of Social Cognition**
Social cognition is a complex concept that includes the child's understanding of social inferences, social responsibility, and social regulations.

The Development of Morality

There is considerable debate as to how children develop a sense of **morality** (Ferguson, 2010; Helwig & Turiel, 2010; Spinrad, Eisenberg, & Bernt, 2007), which is defined as a person's ideas about fairness and justice and right and wrong. Social-learning theorists emphasize the roles that conditioning and observational learning play. Modern psychodynamic theorists typically suggest that morality develops as we learn to cope with anxiety, guilt, and shame. Biologists are beginning to understand how early experiences shape the development of those brain regions that govern emotion, cognition, and morality (Narvaez,

social inference
An individual's guesses and assumptions about what another person is feeling, thinking, or intending

morality
A person's ideas about fairness and justice and right and wrong

social responsibility
An individual's obligations to family, friends, and society

social regulations
The customs and conventions that govern social interactions

Holter, & Vaydich, 2011). Cognitive-developmental theorists believe that, like intellectual development, morality develops in progressive, age-related stages. Although all of these views have contributed useful perspectives to the understanding of how children develop a sense of morality, it is the cognitive position that has provided the central context for our current understanding of moral development.

Moral Realism and Moral Relativism Jean Piaget was one of the earliest cognitive theorists to consider how moral development unfolds (Carpendale, 2009). According to Piaget (1932/1965), children's moral sense arises from the interaction between their developing cognitive structures and their gradually widening social experience. According to Piaget, moral development occurs across two stages. The first stage, called **moral realism**, emerges in early middle childhood; in this stage children think that all rules must be obeyed as if they were written in stone. To them, rules are real and indestructible, not abstract principles. Games, for example, must be played strictly according to the rules. A child at this stage also judges the morality of an act in terms of its consequences and is unable to judge intentions. For example, a young child will think that a child who accidentally breaks a stack of dishes while setting a table is much guiltier than a child who intentionally breaks one dish out of anger. Toward the end of middle childhood, children reach Piaget's second stage called **moral relativism**. Now they understand that rules are created and agreed upon cooperatively by individuals and that they can be changed if necessary. Correspondingly, children begin to realize that there is no absolute right or wrong and that morality depends not on consequences but on intentions.

Kohlberg's Preconventional, Conventional, and Postconventional Reasoning Piaget's two-stage theory of moral development was modified and expanded by Lawrence Kohlberg (1981, 1984; Kohlberg & Puka, 1994) (see Table 9-2). In developing his now-classic theory, Kohlberg (1969) asked individuals (children, adolescents, and adults) to read stories involving **moral dilemmas** and then asked them questions about whether a central character's behavior was moral or immoral. By evaluating their responses, Kohlberg was able to assess the kinds of moral reasoning each individual used. In each story, the leading character was faced with a moral dilemma, and the person being interviewed was asked to resolve the dilemma. Here is a classic example:

> In Europe, a woman was near death from a special kind of cancer. There was one drug that the doctors thought might save her. It was a form of radium that a druggist in the same town had recently discovered. The drug was expensive to make, but the druggist was charging 10 times what the drug cost him to make. He paid $200 for the radium and charged $2,000 for a small dose of the drug. The sick woman's husband, Heinz, went to everyone he knew to borrow the money, but he could only get together $1,000, which is half of what it cost. He told the druggist that his wife was dying and asked him to sell it cheaper or let him pay later. But the druggist said, "No, I discovered the drug, and I am going to make money from it." So Heinz got desperate and broke into the man's store to steal the drug for his wife. (Kohlberg, 1969, p. 379)

Should Heinz have stolen the drug? What do you think? Why? Was the druggist right to have charged so much more than it cost to make the drug? Why?

People's answers to questions such as these provided evidence that, as Piaget originally proposed, moral reasoning develops in an orderly fashion and in distinct stages. Kohlberg identified two ways in which moral reasoning develops in middle childhood. First, as development proceeds, moral decisions increasingly become based on internalized moral principles rather than on external consequences, such as getting

Table 9-2 Kohlberg's Six Stages of Moral Development

Level of Moral Reasoning	Stage of Moral Reasoning	Motivation for Moral Behavior
Level 1: Preconventional (based on punishments and rewards)	1	Obey rules in order to avoid punishment
	2	Obey rules to obtain rewards or to have favors returned
Level 2: Conventional (based on social conformity)	3	Conform to win the approval of others
	4	Conform to avoid disapproval or dislike of others
Level 3: Postconventional (based on moral principles)	5	Abide by laws of the land for the community's welfare
	6	Abide by universal ethical principles, which may or may not conform to society's laws or expectations.

SOURCE: Adapted from "The philosophy of moral development," by L. Kohlberg, 1981, in *Essays of moral development* (Vol. 1), New York: HarperCollins.

moral realism
Piaget's term for the first stage of moral development; children believe in rules as real, indestructible things, not as abstract principles

Watch *Kohlberg and the Heinz Dilemma* on **MyDevelopmentLab**

moral relativism
Piaget's term for the second stage of moral development; children realize rules are created and agreed upon cooperatively by individuals and can change if necessary

moral dilemmas
In Kohlberg's research, stories in which individuals are asked to judge whether a character's behavior was moral or immoral

caught. Second, moral judgments become less concrete and more abstract as children develop. Based on his observations, Kohlberg proposed that moral development unfolds through three broad levels: *preconventional, conventional,* and *postconventional,* each of which is subdivided into two stages (refer to Table 9-2). Thus, Kohlberg's theory specifies six distinct stages of moral development.

Critiques of Kohlberg's Theory Support for Kohlberg's theory was provided by studies showing that individuals generally progressed in moral development as this theory predicted. For example, in one 20-year longitudinal study that began with 48 boys, Kohlberg and his associates found remarkable support for the theory (Colby, Kohlberg, Gibbs, & Lieberman, 1994; Colby, Lawrence, Gibbs, & Lieberman, 1994). Today, most researchers acknowledge the significant contributions Kohlberg made to our understanding of moral development (Nucci & Gingo, 2011; Turiel, 2008). However, many objections have been raised about Kohlberg's theory and research. For example, from a methodological point of view, researchers have pointed out that it can be very difficult to follow Kohlberg's procedures exactly and to agree on how a child's responses to the moral dilemmas should be scored (Boom, 2010).

Another concern is that Kohlberg's research assesses moral *attitudes,* not moral *behavior;* there can be a substantial difference between thinking about moral questions and behaving morally. Consider the following example: Nearly all college students acknowledge that cheating is wrong, yet many students do in fact cheat when the stakes are high and the chances of being caught are low. The point is, moral decisions are not made in a vacuum. No matter how high our moral principles may be, when the time comes to act on them, our behavior may not reflect our thoughts or beliefs.

From a practical point of view, it is as important to teach children to *act* on their knowledge of right and wrong as it is to teach them right from wrong (Damon, 1999; Turiel & Killen, 2010). In turn, it is crucial that people incorporate their moral beliefs and attitudes as a central part of their moral identity—that is, the moral component of a person's self-concept. As noted earlier, self-concept organizes and orients behavior; thus, if moral beliefs are at the core, moral behavior becomes more likely.

Another criticism of Kohlberg's six-stage model is that it is too inflexible. Many factors go into moral judgments, ranging from the social customs of the culture in which individuals are reared to how they feel at a particular moment. For example, children and adults are capable of making moral judgments at a higher level one moment and at a lower level the next; they may even make judgments at a higher level for some issues, such as whether they would help someone who was injured, than they may make for others, such as whether they would invite someone they did not like to their home (Eisenberg, 1989a, 1989b). Thus, moral reasoning is not invariably tied to cognitive development, although people's cognitive sophistication—together with their capacity for empathy, opportunities for free choice, and knowledge of cultural expectations—frame the resulting moral judgments they make (Eisenberg & Eggum, 2008; Turiel, 2006, 2010). Among these factors, it appears that children's ability to understand and empathize with another's circumstances and to self-regulate their own behavior are especially important to the development of moral actions (Eisenberg, 2010; Eisenberg, Eggum, & Edwards, 2010).

moral absolutism
Any theory of morality that disregards cultural differences in moral beliefs

▲ Developing a sense of right and wrong involves understanding social rules and gaining experiences in social relationships.

Perhaps the most controversial challenge to Kohlberg's theory of morality is its stance of **moral absolutism:** Kohlberg's view suggests that all people develop moral reasoning in the same sequence according to the same general principles. As such, his view disregards significant cultural differences that determine what is or is not considered moral in a given culture (Nucci & Gingo, 2011; Sachdeva, Singh, & Medin, 2011). Kohlberg (1978) himself acknowledged that it is necessary to take into account the social and moral norms of the group to which a person belongs. In particular, he concluded that his sixth stage of moral development may not apply to all people in all cultures, but rather may reflect Western values.

Gender Differences in Moral Development One particular aspect of culture that has been shown to affect moral development in important ways is gender. Because Kohlberg based his theory on interviews with only boys and men, he did not address the possibility that moral development might proceed differently in females than in males. Carol Gilligan and her colleagues challenged Kohlberg's theory on the grounds of gender bias, noting that females' responses to Kohlberg's moral dilemmas often placed them at lower levels in his stage-based model (e.g., Gilligan, 1993, 1994). According to Gilligan, these gender differences arise because males and females use different criteria in making moral judgments. Based on her research of women's moral judgments, Gilligan proposed that there are two distinct types of moral reasoning, neither of which is superior to the other. One is based primarily on the concept of *justice*, the other primarily on human relationships and *caring*.

Gilligan also noted that in traditional U.S. culture, girls and boys are taught from early childhood to value different qualities. Boys are trained to strive for independence and to value abstract thinking. In contrast, girls are taught to be nurturing and caring and to value relationships with others. Thus, as a consequence of early gender-specific experiences, the justice perspective becomes characteristic of traditional masculine thinking; caring for others is more common in traditionally feminine thought. These gender-related differences in moral perspectives begin to emerge at about ages 9 to 12, at the same time that other aspects of self-concept are being defined.

Do you think there are culture-specific factors in addition to gender that might define how moral reasoning is structured? What might these be?

Regardless of when and exactly how moral reasoning develops, cultural forces play an important role in shaping how individuals form their value systems. Parents and other family members exert a strong influence in the development of moral reasoning, as well as in all other aspects of social and personality development. However, as children enter middle childhood, peers begin to assume a more important role in shaping attitudes and behavior, sometimes rivaling or even replacing parents as the most important forces in the child's socialization. How is it that peers exert this influence? Why are friends so important to school-age children? How do children cope when they feel rejected by their peers? These are just a few of the questions we consider in the next section of this chapter.

REVIEW THE FACTS 9-2

1. Dr. Perez is studying how children come to understand and think about their own behavior, as well as understand how others behave. Her area of interest would be called ___________.
2. Which of the following is *not* one of the three aspects of social cognition?
   a. social responsibility b. social egocentrism
   c. social inference d. social regulations
3. Piaget viewed moral development as a two-stage process, with the first stage being ___________ and the second being ___________.
4. According to Kohlberg, as moral reasoning develops, it becomes ___________ abstract and is based ___________ on the consequences that follow.
   a. more; more b. less; less
   c. more; less d. less; more
5. According to Carol Gilligan's view of moral reasoning, men are more likely to focus on concepts that involve ___________, whereas women are more likely to focus on concepts that involve ___________.

Practice on **MyDevelopmentLab**

PEER RELATIONSHIPS

Functions of Friendship

Children and adults alike benefit from close, trusting relationships. Friendships serve many functions during childhood, as they do throughout the remainder of life (Majors, 2012; Rubin, Bukowski, & Parker, 2006). With a friend, children can share their feelings, their fears, and every detail of their lives. Having a best friend to confide in teaches a child how to relate to others openly, without being self-conscious. Friendships also help children learn social concepts and social skills and to develop self-esteem. Friendship can provide the structure for activity; it reinforces and solidifies group norms, attitudes, and values; and it serves as a backdrop for individual and group competition. Friendship also can be a vehicle of self-expression. Although children who are friends may differ in some important ways, friendships that last usually are based on many shared values, attitudes, and expectations. Friendship interactions are centrally important in helping children define who they are (Bagwell & Schmidt, 2011; Zembar & Blume, 2009).

As you consider your own best friendships, on what factors would you judge these friendships to be based?

Children's concepts of friendship change as they develop. For example, as children grow older, they are more likely to keep secrets from adults (A. J. Watson & Valtin, 1997), whereas they share them with their friends. Friendships are also somewhat gender dependent. In middle childhood, most children have more friends of the same age and gender (Bagwell & Schmidt, 2011; Sebanc, Kearns, Hernandez, & Galvin, 2007). Also, close friendships are quite different among girls versus boys. At this age, girls tend to want to share intimate thoughts and secrets, whereas boys tend to reveal less of themselves to their friends (Maccoby, 1998; Rose, Glick, & Smith, 2011). Regardless of whether childhood friendships last for life or are short-lived, they are critically important to social and personality development in middle childhood. For example, children with stable, *satisfying* friendships have better attitudes toward school and achieve more and also are less likely to develop negative self-concepts and disruptive behavior patterns (Laursen, Bukowski, Aunola, & Nurmi, 2007; Rubin, Copian, Chen, Bowker, & McDonald, 2011).

Developmental Patterns in Friendship

In classic research on how children's friendships change as children mature, Robert Selman (1976, 1981) studied the friendships of children aged 7 to 12. Selman's approach was similar to the method used in Kohlberg's studies of moral development: Tell children stories involving a "relationship" dilemma, then ask them questions to assess their concepts of other people, their self-awareness and ability to reflect, their concepts of personality, and their ideas about friendship. Here is an example of the kind of stories Selman used:

▲ At age 6, friendships are with playmates who share activities; at age 11, friendships tend to involve both common interests and shared trust.

Kathy and Debbie have been best friends since they were 5. A new girl, Jeannette, moves into their neighborhood, but Debbie dislikes her because she considers Jeannette a show-off. Later, Jeannette invites Kathy to go to the circus on its one day in town. Kathy's problem is that she has promised to play with Debbie that same day. What will Kathy do?

Such stories raise questions about the nature of relationships and about more global issues such as loyalty and trust. They require children to think and talk about how friendships are formed and maintained and about what is important in a friendship. Based on patterns observed in children's responses, Selman (1981), identified four stages of friendship, which are summarized in Table 9-3. In the first stage (ages 6 and under), a friend is just a playmate—someone who lives nearby, goes to the same school, or has desirable toys. There is no understanding of the other person's perspective, so the typical response is that Kathy should simply go to the circus. At the second stage (ages 7 to 9), awareness of another person's feelings begins to appear. A child at this stage might say that Kathy could go to the circus with Jeannette and remain friends with Debbie only if Debbie did not object. At the third stage (ages 9 to 12), friends are seen as people who help each other, and the concept of *trust* appears. The child realizes that the friendship between Kathy and Debbie is different from the friendship between Kathy and Jeannette because the older friendship is based on long-standing trust. At the fourth stage, which was rare among the 11- and 12-year-olds studied, children are fully capable of looking at a relationship from another's perspective. A child at this level might say that Kathy and Debbie should be able to understand each other and work it out.

Do you think that Selman's view of friendship development is consistent with Piaget's description of the development of concrete operational thought? If so, in what ways?

Table 9-3 Selman's Stages of Friendship Development

Stage	Age	Characteristics
1	6 and under	• Friendship is based on physical or geographic factors. • Children are self-centered, with no understanding of the perspectives of other.
2	7 to 9	• Friendship begins to be based on reciprocity and awareness of others' feelings. • Friendship begins to be based on social actions and evaluation by each other's actions.
3	9 to 12	• Friendship is based on genuine give-and-take. • Friends are seen as people who help each other. • The mutual evaluation of each other's actions occurs. • The concept of trust appears.
4	11 to 12 and older	• Friendship is seen as a stable, continuing relationship based on trust. • Children can observe their friendship relationships from the perspective of a third party.

SOURCE: Adapted from "The child as a friendship philosopher," by R. L. Selman, 1981, in S. R. Asher and J. M. Gottman (Eds.), *The development of children's friendships* (pp. 242–272), Cambridge, England: Cambridge University Press.

Watch *Friendship During Middle Childhood* on **MyDevelopmentLab**

The stage model that Selman proposed provides a means for understanding how cognitive advances set the stage for social and personality development. In Selman's view, the primary force behind developmental changes in children's friendships is the ability to take another person's perspective (Elfers, Martin, & Sokol, 2008). Thus, for Selman, the quality of childhood friendships advances according to the pace of the child's decreasing egocentrism. Other researchers, however, view the development of friendships as a more complex process than Selman's model suggests, and they argue that real friendships are more complicated and involve more changes than Selman's model implies (Hartup, 2006; Rubin, Fredstrom, & Bowker, 2008; Rubin, et al., 2011). For example, many researchers note that peer relationships rely on self-regulatory and emotional development to a greater degree than Selman's cognitive-based model implies (Eisenberg, Smith, & Spinrad, 2011). Critics also note that Selman's model does not differentiate among different kinds of friendships. Although most children have one or more "best friends," these friendships shift at times, and children in unstable friendship patterns suffer in their popularity and prosocial relationships (Rubin, et al., 2011; Wojslawowitz-Bowker et al., 2006). Furthermore, many children lack reciprocal friendships, which are characterized by give-and-take (George & Hartmann, 1996), and some children are consistently unsuccessful at forming meaningful friendships. Finally, most researchers today agree that to understand the children's friendships fully, it is necessary to know something about *who* the children's friends are (see the box Current Issues: Friends and Enemies, Bullies and Victims—the Social Life of School). Thus, friendship is conceptualized today as a complex, multifaceted series of relationships, each with particular characteristics.

Peer Groups

Friendships in middle childhood often exist among several children, and groups of friends are referred to as peer groups. However, a **peer group** is more than just a group of kids. Rather, members of peer groups, who typically are of similar age, interact with one another regularly and share norms and goals. Group norms, which prescribe members' actions and values, govern interactions and influence each member, even though there usually are status differences within peer groups—some members are leaders, some are followers.

Developmental Trends Peer groups are important throughout middle childhood, but a developmental shift occurs in both their organization and their significance as children move through the middle childhood years from ages 6 to 12 (Brown & Dietz, 2009; Rubin, et al., 2011). In early middle childhood, peer groups are relatively informal. They are usually created by the children themselves, they have very few operating rules, and turnover in their membership is rapid. It is true that many of the group's activities, such as playing games or riding bikes, may be carried out according to precise rules, but the structure of the group itself is quite flexible.

The peer group takes on greater significance for its members when they reach the ages of 10 to 12, and peer groups typically develop a more formal structure during this period. Some groups may have special membership requirements, club meetings, and initiation rites, although the increasing practice of placing children in organized and supervised after-school activities tends to reduce the intensity of these group-defining rules. At this stage, separation of the sexes also becomes especially noticeable. Peer groups are now almost invariably composed of one sex, and boy groups and girl groups maintain different interests, activities, and styles of interaction (Maccoby, 1998; Rose, Glick, & Smith, 2011). In later middle childhood, peer pressure also becomes an important force, and conformity to group norms becomes extremely important. The strict attitudes about rules, conformity, and sex segregation that are characteristic of many peer groups composed of 10- to 12-year-olds usually do not diminish until midadolescence.

Peer Group Conformity As children move through middle childhood, they feel conflicting needs. Although they are strongly motivated toward independence, autonomy, mastery, and self-accomplishment, they also have a strong need to belong, to feel accepted, and to be part of a group. One means by which children at this age can become more emotionally independent from their parents is to transfer their needs for belonging and social support to the members of their peer group.

Some children, of course, become more dependent on their peer group than do others (Sandstrom, 2011). What factors influence the degree to which a particular child will conform? One general factor is age: Conformity to peer group norms becomes increasingly more important to children as they move through middle childhood, before it begins to decline in later adolescence. Also, children who conform the most often are especially sensitive to social cues for their behavior, and they tend to *self-monitor,* paying special attention to what they do and say and how their behavior affects others around them (Graziano, Leone, Musser, & Lautenschlager, 1987). Conforming children are especially concerned with how they appear to others, and they frequently compare themselves to their peers. Highly conforming children also are more likely to have feelings of inferiority, and they tend to be more dependent and anxious than other children.

Peer group conformity can have desirable effects. For example, studies have shown that peer group influence can encourage academic motivation. When peer group formation was studied in classes of fourth, fifth, and sixth graders, researchers found that peer groups tend to be composed of students with similar

peer group
A group of three or more people of similar age who interact with each other and who share norms and goals

Watch *Peer Acceptance* on **MyDevelopmentLab**

CURRENT ISSUES

Friends and Enemies, Bullies and Victims—the Social Life of School

▲ Some acts of bullying are aimed at personal or valued possessions as in this case where the victim is not present as his peers "trash his locker."

Children's concepts of their social selves—an important aspect of their self-identities—form in the context of their relationships with others. During middle childhood, many of these relationships are with peers of the same age. Friendships with other children provide a rich opportunity for learning because they involve social support; they teach the give-and-take nature of everyday activities; and they give the child practice in building and maintaining relationships, resolving conflicts, and learning skills that assist the child in becoming more socially competent. But not all of children's relationships with their peers are positive and productive. Sometimes friends behave badly, causing hurt, embarrassment, or emotional trauma to the person on whom they turn their negative behaviors. In addition, aggression, fear, anxiety, hatred, and a lack of support also may characterize some relationships. In recent years, attention has focused on better understanding, and preventing, one particular type of childhood relationship—bullying. Bullying is defined as repeated and intentional aggression directed by a bully against a less powerful victim (Guerra, Williams, & Sadek, 2011; Salmivalli & Peets, 2009).

Bullying is a particularly common form of negative relationship among both boys and girls, and it is present in every culture (Liu & Graves, 2011; Powell & Ladd, 2010; Rigby & Smith, 2011). For example, the tough kid who smashes his smaller peer's lunch every day or the popular girl who routinely embarrasses a homelier girl by calling public attention to her poor complexion or to her unattractive dress or hair is acting as a bully. Bullying generally peaks in middle childhood, diminishing as children move into adolescence (Bullock, 2002; Rigby, 2002). During childhood, girls and boys both report teasing, taunting, and other forms of physical abuse, although physical bullying is more common among boys (Murray-Close & Crick, 2006). Cyber-bullying—using computers to publish negative information about an individual—is a newer form that bullying can take. Perhaps not surprisingly, cyber-bullying appears to be on the rise (Rigby & Smith, 2011).

Unfortunately, bullying in childhood is fairly common: About one half of school-age children report that they have been teased or bullied in the past month. Some bullying is relatively mild and can be easily ignored or laughed off. Unfortunately, a significant number of children experience bullying on a regular basis, and it often impacts their social development, especially if they also are rejected by the wider peer group. Sometimes, these bullied children join with other victims or isolated children and form friendships that offer comfort. Such victim-based friendships, however, usually provide little positive experience in developing social skills related to peer acceptance. Children who are bullied repeatedly also sometimes turn to antisocial behavior as a means of coping.

Why do some children bully others? What qualities characterize children who are bullies, versus those who are victims? In one recent study, children were asked to provide reasons why they thought others acted as bullies, and they also commented on the characteristics that bullied children share (Guerra, Williams, & Sadek, 2011). The results of this study are provided in the table that follows.

Other studies generally show similar results. For example, in a meta-analysis that summarized the results of 153 studies of bullying, bullies were generally found to hold negative beliefs about others, have difficulty in both social competence and academic skills, have negative self-esteem, and have a history of being unable to resolve problems with other children in positive ways. Bullies also tended to come from families characterized by high conflict and poor parenting. Victims, on the other hand, tended to be those children who lack social skills, have difficulty relating to other children, have low self-esteem, and have a history of being isolated and rejected by peers (Cook, Williams, Guerra, Kim, & Sadek, 2010).

How can we best understand the need that some children feel to bully others or to treat some children as enemies? Several factors probably are

Qualities That Characterize Bullies and Victims

Reasons that children bully others		Characteristics of victims of bullying	
Reason	Example	Reason	Example
Emotional problems	• Bullies have low self-esteem • Bullies want attention	*Weak/Vulnerable*	• Victims are shy or weak; don't stand up for themselves
Youth culture	• Everyone does it	*Annoying*	• Victims say dumb things • Victims are "weird" kids
Fun	• Bullying is funny • There's nothing else to do	*Different*	• Victims stand out • Victims look strange or have different cultural backgrounds
Power	• Friends/gangs that encourage bullying give you power • Bullies are big/strong	*Gender*	• Boys are more likely than girls to be bullies • Girls seldom bully boys, but boys bully girls
Jealousy	• Bullies want what the victim has (e.g., money, high achievement)		
Popularity	• Bullies are "cool" • If I bully, I can be part of the gang/crowd		

SOURCE: "Understanding bullying and victimization during childhood and adolescence: A mixed methods study," by N. G. Guerra, K. R. Williams, & S. Sadek, 2011, *Child Development, 82*(1), 295–310.

(continued)

involved. For example, it is possible that having an enemy may be exciting and motivating, and bullying may allow children to draw their friends even closer to "deal" collectively with the enemy threat (Abecassis, 2004). Bullying also may be tied to children's need to develop an integrated sense of self: By focusing on the negative behaviors of another, it is possible for children to develop a contrasting set of positive self-attributes in response (Dixon & Smith, 2011). It also may provide a means for children to deal with their own unacceptable impulses by lashing out at others rather than directing their aggression at themselves (Hawley, Little, & Rodkin, 2007; Heilbron & Prinstein, 2008). Finally, if children believe that another child dislikes *them*, this may lead to a reciprocal response, especially if low self-esteem is involved.

Even if bullies derive some positive benefits from their actions, those who are bullied typically suffer. Consequently, most schools and parents work to reduce the amount of negative conflict among children in their care (Espelage & Holt, 2012; Rigby, 2012; Rigby & Bauman, 2010). For example, some elementary schools have developed programs to teach children to maintain a proper and respectful set of guidelines as they interact with each other. Many schools are beginning to adopt "social development" units into their curricula, and these units often include the topic of bullying. Many elementary schools also have incorporated more inclusive group projects into classroom assignments so that bullied and less popular children are included in supervised groups that provide all children a *safe* environment in which to work. However, such programs generally are effective only when they are maintained consistently over a long period of time and when they teach children a new set of guidelines for their behavior.

Have you experienced an instance of bullying? Were there children in your school who were bullies or children whom the bullies picked on? What was the school's response? How was the situation resolved? Do you think that there was long-term harm done to the child who was bullied? Did the bully grow up to be an aggressive, demeaning person? What do you think schools should do to encourage the development of more positive relationships among children?

---

motivations regarding school (Kindermann, 1993, 2007). Thus, because peer group members identify with each other, the peer group can foster learning and academic success, at least for children who identify with academically motivated groups. Fortunately, children are more likely to conform to peer pressure when it is positive than when it involves misbehavior, such as stealing, drinking, or using illegal drugs.

Peer groups, however, can sometimes encourage behavior that is destructive, either to group members or to individuals who are excluded from the group. In particular, aggressive behavior toward others can sometimes bring positive rewards. For example, although prosocial skills are linked to popularity and successful peer relations in childhood (Aikins & Litwack, 2011), so, too, is aggressiveness (Pellegrini, Roseth, Ryzin, & Solberg, 2011). Indeed, in middle childhood, favored status within the peer group is often linked to aggressive behavior (Mayeux, Houser, & Dyches, 2011). In one study of fourth to sixth graders, aggressive children were often nominated as the "coolest" members of their class by other aggressive children, and this was true for girls as well as boys (Rodkin, Farmer, Pearl, & Van Aker, 2006). Indeed, popularity within the peer group is a powerful motivating force for most children.

Popularity Within the Peer Group Especially in middle childhood, popularity is a particularly important dimension of group membership. Each peer group has some members who are more popular and some who are less popular. Furthermore, popularity is often a self-sustaining attribute: The adjustment of well-liked children is enhanced by their popularity; inept children become even less self-confident when rejected or ignored by the group (Aikins & Litwack, 2011).

What factors determine the popularity of a school-age child? As we saw in Chapter 7, children who have good emotional control and who can cooperate and share are most likely to be popular in early childhood. Once children enter school, other factors become involved as well (e.g., LaFontana & Cillessen, 2010; Rodkin & Roisman, 2010). Academic performance and athletic ability are particularly important in most settings. In general, popular children are brighter than average and do well in school; slow learners often are made fun of or ignored (Véronneau, Vitaro, Brendgen, Dishion, & Tremblay, 2010). Athletic ability is particularly important in settings like camps or playgrounds, where the peer group is involved in sports. Given the significance associated with athletics even in grade school, athletic ability is also associated with popularity in most schools, and this seems to be especially true during middle childhood and also for boys (Shakib, Veliz, Dunbar, & Sabo, 2011).

Extreme aggressiveness and extreme timidity also affect popularity. Few children like a bully, so the overly aggressive child often is shunned (Lansford, Malone, Dodge, Pettit, & Bates, 2010). Such a child may then become even more aggressive out of frustration or in an attempt to win by force what cannot be won by persuasion, perhaps becoming a social outcast in the process (Pedersen, Vitaro, Barker, & Borge, 2007). Similarly, a timid and anxious child is at risk of becoming a chronic victim who is picked on not only by bullies but also by nonaggressive children. Timid children, in particular, often suffer the most from peer rejection, at least in the U.S. majority culture: They tend to be lonelier and to worry more about their peer relationships than do aggressive children who are rejected by their peers (McHale, Dariotis, & Kauh, 2003; Parkhurst & Asher, 1992).

Interestingly, day-care experiences in early childhood may play an important role in how the link between popularity and aggressiveness develops in middle childhood. In one large-scale study using longitudinal data collected in the Study of Early Child Care and Youth Development, children in grades 3 through 6 were categorized into four groups according to their popularity with peers and their aggressiveness. Results suggest that an important factor linked to the "popular-aggressive" group of chil-

Watch *Bullying* on **MyDevelopmentLab**

Watch *Child and Adolescent Friendships: Brett Laursen* on **MyDevelopmentLab**

dren was having spent an extensive period of their early childhood in nonmaternal child care (Rodkin & Roisman, 2010). Why might this be the case? One explanation is that, in early child-care settings, those children who are more aggressive but still can get along with other children may gain desired social and material resources. Thus, their "situation-appropriate aggressiveness" may make them popular with their peers. Another explanation is that aggressive children who spend time in child care may be socialized to channel their aggressive energy in positive ways, as opposed to negative ways, making them more popular than aggressive children who do not receive this form of socialization. Not all studies of child care and aggressiveness find a clear link between these two factors, however (Côté, Geoffreoy, Borge, Rutter, & Tremblay, 2008), suggesting that appropriate social behavior is at least partly defined by culture and cultural expectations (Xinyin & French, 2008). For example, in cultures that value behavior that is more reserved, a timid child is more likely to fit comfortably into the peer group. Thus, it may be that popularity is not related so much to children's behavior as it is to traits that make them different from other members of the peer group. Obesity, a learning disorder, eyes of the "wrong" shape or skin of the "wrong" color, an unusual physical feature, a disability, or even an unusual name can set a child apart and lead to peer rejection and teasing.

Regardless of the cause of a child's popularity or unpopularity, status within the peer group affects the way children feel about themselves. In one study (Crick & Ladd, 1993) researchers assessed the feelings of loneliness, social anxiety, and social avoidance reported by groups of third and fifth graders. It was found that the way children feel about themselves and whether they blame themselves or others for what happens to them depends on their experiences with peers. Rejected children reported a higher degree of loneliness, and they had a greater tendency to blame unsatisfactory relationships on others than did children who were accepted members of the peer group. Children who are rejected by peers also show worse academic performance (Greenman, Schneider, & Tomada, 2009), making rejection more likely to recur in the future.

Peer acceptance, however, can be influenced by teacher feedback (Buysse, Goldman, West, & Hollingsworth, 2008). In one study (White & Kistner, 1992), a group of first and second graders viewed a video of a problem child (an actor) who was rejected by his peers. Following the film, the teacher made positive comments about the rejected child, which were effective in changing the students' negative perceptions. Another approach involves helping unpopular children learn behaviors that are more appropriate. Unpopular children can be taught to behave in ways that their peers appreciate (Ladd, Buhs, & Troop, 2002). When a child's unpopularity results from overly aggressive behavior, he or she can be encouraged to listen to others and take their direction rather than dominating the group. Similarly, shy children can be encouraged to interact with others in more positive ways. Instruction also can be directed at children in the peer group. For example, group members can be prompted to respond more favorably to less popular children and to include them in group activities and conversations.

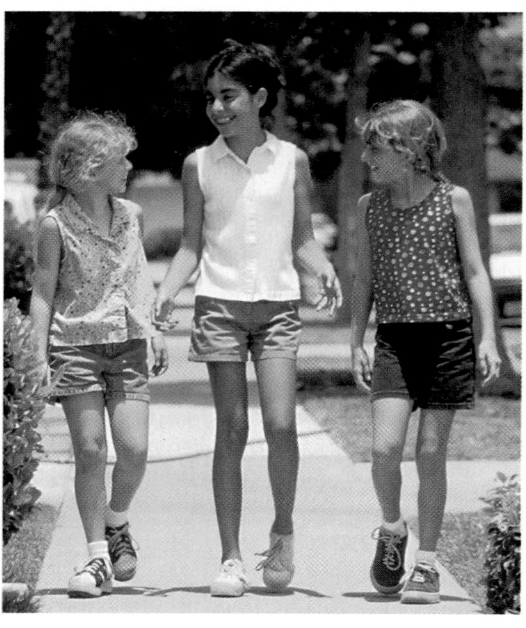

◀ Close friends often choose similar dress and hair styles, reflecting conformity pressures of their peer group.

Popularity is an important dimension of personal development, especially during the period of middle childhood, when peer relationships operate to define important dimensions of the individual's self-concept (LaFontana & Cillessen, 2010). Because popularity is often based on a child's ability to "fit in" with members of the peer group, pressure to conform to peer group expectations typically is high during this period of development. One particularly troubling aspect of peer group conformity manifests itself in prejudice against people who are different.

In-Groups, Out-Groups, and Prejudice

Prejudice is a negative attitude held without adequate reason toward people because of their membership in a certain group. Broad-based prejudice that exists within a society usually is defined on the basis of ethnicity, religion, race, social class, or some other noticeable set of attributes. Prejudice implies an *in-group*—people who believe they possess desirable characteristics—and an *out-group*—people who are perceived to be different and therefore undesirable. Often, prejudice leads to **discrimination**, which involves actions based on prejudice—for example, teasing or excluding members of a particular group.

Prejudice and discrimination may be directed at any individual, and for any reason. Sometimes it is a child's physical

prejudice
A negative attitude formed without adequate reason and usually directed toward people because of their membership in a certain group

discrimination
Treating others in a prejudiced manner

features that make him or her stand out as "different" and therefore become the subject of prejudice and the victim of discrimination; in other specific cases it may be a disability that generates teasing and exclusion from the group. However, within cultures there are general patterns of prejudice and discrimination, and these usually conform to class-related attributes, such as gender, religion, social class, race, or ethnicity.

In most cases, prejudice and discrimination are directed by the majority culture at members of less-powerful minority groups. In fact, ethnic prejudices are seen in every complex society in the world, as are gender prejudices. In the United States, many underrepresented racial/ethnic groups have experienced the negative effects of prejudice and discrimination at various periods in American culture, including African Americans, Irish Americans, Italian Americans, Asian Americans, Native Americans, and Hispanic Americans. In some cases, these prejudices have eased, as the members of the minority group have become more fully assimilated into mainstream culture. In other cases, prejudices remain, at least among some members of society.

Because child development is heavily influenced by culture, the various social groups to which the child belongs are powerful factors in determining how development unfolds (Hill & Witherspoon, 2011). How do children develop their sense of belonging to one group or another, and how does group membership contribute to the child's willingness to conform to group standards? In particular, how does one's membership in a majority or minority cultural group affect how development proceeds during middle childhood?

The Development of Ethnic Identity Ethnic awareness begins to develop during the early childhood years and reflects the culture within which the child is raised (Hudley & Irving, 2012). The first step in forming an ethnic identity involves learning which group one belongs to; the second step is learning what it means, in a cultural sense, to belong to that group (Rogers, et al., 2012).

Immigrant children often have a particularly challenging task in forging a realistic self-identity. Studies of ethnic identity formation often have focused on the experiences of children of migrant workers or refugees who have been uprooted from their familiar cultures and relocated to the United States early in their lives. These children's first challenge typically involves learning self-identifying labels, such as *Cambodian, daughter, Christian, pretty*, or *short*. Such labels almost always include those defining the child's ethnic identity. Family labels also are learned, such as *we are poor*, or *we are hardworking*, or *we are a musical family*. In one study of ethnic labeling, over 400 first-grade and fourth-grade immigrant children from a variety of ethnic groups were asked to select some labels that applied to them (Akiba, Szalacha, & Coll, 2004). Most children picked seven or more self-identifying labels, always including a gender label (boy or girl) and one or more ethnic labels. The majority of these children also picked a family role label, such as brother or daughter. In contrast, only one-third picked a color label, such as Black, and only one-fourth picked a religious label, such as Christian.

Do you think people's ethnic identity is a stronger force in their development if they are members of a minority or majority culture? Why do you hold this opinion?

However, first graders differed from fourth graders in the reasons and meanings of the labels they chose and in the priority they assigned to one label over another. Many of the first graders had little or no idea of the meaning of ethic labels: Some gave priority to the ethnic label, but many did not. Fourth graders not only knew more self-identifying labels—for example, Cambodian, Kymer, Cambodian American, Asian American—but they also had more complex and accurate meanings for these labels. Like the younger children, however, the importance they attached to their self-identifying ethnic label varied considerably from child to child. Although these older children knew they belonged to a smaller community associated with their ethnic status, the expectations and customs within their wider community were also important, and appeared to be more important for some children than for others.

Ethnic identity is a multifaceted, complex concept that is only gradually acquired, although the manner in which children come to incorporate a sense of their ethnicity is much the same from culture to culture (Quintana, 2008). Furthermore, these same principles hold for any child who is different from members of an otherwise homogeneous group that regards the child's differences as important. Thus, a Jewish child growing up in a Catholic neighborhood, a Saudi Arabian child in an Italian neighborhood, a White child in an African-American neighborhood, a Chinese child in a Japanese neighborhood, or an Irish Catholic child in an Irish Protestant neighborhood all go through this process.

Watch *Adolescence: Identity and Role Development and Ethnicity* on **MyDevelopmentLab**.

Is this child resting or is he excluded from the game due to race or, even, weight?

Understanding group differences and what it means to be a member of a group requires social cognition, which in turn depends on cognitive development (Park, 2011). Thus, a child whose thought is still egocentric and who can focus on only one dimension at a time assumes that people who are similar on one dimension, such as skin color, must be similar on other dimensions as well. As children grow older, they become more capable of seeing people as multidimensional (Rogers, et al., 2012; Verkuyten & De Wolf, 2007). In a study with English-speaking and French-speaking Canadian children (Doyle, Beaudet, & Aboud, 1988), for example, researchers found that older children had more flexible attitudes about members of the other language-speaking group.

However, the ability of older children to think with greater complexity does not always lead to a reduction in prejudice and discrimination (Apfelbaum, Pauker, Ambady, Sommers, & Norton, 2008). Conformity pressure from peer groups also can have a powerful effect (Yip & Douglass, 2011). For example, a study in a California town in which the schools were about half African American and half White found that older children actually were *less* likely than younger ones to have a friend of a different ethnicity: Interethnic friendships declined steadily from the fourth through the seventh grade. The researchers concluded that as children grow older, ethnic or racial similarity becomes an increasingly powerful basis for friendship (Ocampo, Knight, & Bernal, 1997).

There also may be explicit pressure from other members of an ethnically or racially based peer group to avoid forming friendships with members of a different group and this seems to be particularly the case in classrooms where most students are members of the majority culture (Rodkin, Wilson, & Ahn, 2007). For instance, African-American children who become friendly with White children may be pressured to give up these friendships because having friends who belong to the majority culture may connote disloyalty to their own ethnic culture, and vice versa. In extreme cases, this *out-group* effect may generalize: African-American children who succeed at school—regardless of the school's ethnic composition—may be perceived as being disloyal on grounds that school itself is a *White* institution.

Based on your own childhood experiences, what would you judge to be the most significant aspects of cultural identity? How was "privilege" defined: by money, by ethnicity, by talent, or by some other factor?

How can parents address these issues? The situation is really quite difficult for parents whose children are defined by their racial or ethnic status. During childhood, adjustment often is easier when the child is part of a group comprised of other members from the same ethnic group, all of whom come from similar backgrounds with common values and expectations. In fact, belonging to a group comprised only of members similar to oneself tends to improve self-esteem, at least in childhood. Yet the degree of acceptance that minority children find in the larger society often depends on their ability to conform to that society's norms. Parents are expected to teach their children the values of society, yet that very society may discriminate against them, necessarily implying a conflict of values.

Of course, ethnic or racial identity may not be the only, or even the most important, defining cultural force for a child. For example, a child growing up in a cultural setting characterized by poverty and a high crime rate experiences life in a very different way from a child growing up in an economically privileged environment, regardless of the child's race or ethnicity. When children are identified as belonging to a *disadvantaged* culture, and especially when that culture is identified according to these children's race or ethnicity, then they will inevitably face the problem of reconciling their own self-concepts with society's image of them. This clash of cultures can produce conflict, anxiety, or anger at any age, and peer pressure often aggravates the situation.

REVIEW THE FACTS 9-3

1. Define the key features in each of Selman's four stages of friendship development:
   - First stage ____________
   - Second stage ____________
   - Third stage ____________
   - Fourth stage ____________
2. Suggest two ways that peer groups change as children move through middle childhood.
3. Children who conform most to peer group expectations are also likely to
   a. be high achievers.
   b. be most popular.
   c. be less anxious.
   d. have more feelings of inferiority.
4. Which of the following is typically *not* associated with being popular?
   a. getting good grades in school
   b. being aggressive
   c. having good athletic ability
   d. being different or unique
5. Is prejudice an attitude or a behavior; is discrimination an attitude or a behavior?

Practice on **MyDevelopmentLab**

FAMILY INFLUENCES IN MIDDLE CHILDHOOD

Despite the time children spend with peers and in school, the family normally continues to be the most important socializing influence during middle childhood. Although children's march toward autonomy and independence places them in a much wider variety of groups and activities than are commonly found in the preschool years, school-age children continue to rely on their parents and other family members for support, guidance, and control. However, relationships within the family change as children mature, and parents must adjust to the child's developing abilities and preferences. Children also must adapt to pressures within the family.

▶ Parents teach the value of warmth and affection by their own behavior.

Parent–Child Interactions and Relationships

In middle childhood, the overall nature of parent–child interactions changes. Compared to when they were younger, children express less direct anger toward their parents and are less likely to whine, yell, or hit. As children begin their formal education, parents become less concerned with promoting autonomy and establishing daily routines and more concerned with their children's work habits and achievement (Lamb, Hwang, Ketterlinus, & Fracasso, 1999; Mowder, 2005). Although their role changes as their children grow older, parents continue to exert an especially important influence in middle childhood (Racz & McMahon, 2011). What factors contribute to optimal parenting during this period of development?

One important role for parents is to effectively monitor their children's activities and behavior. Monitoring means knowing where their children are, what they are doing, that their behavior is socially appropriate, and that they are attending to their schoolwork and other responsibilities. Although school-age children's behavior requires monitoring that is more subtle than when they were younger, parental monitoring continues to be very important. For example, researchers find that well-monitored children receive higher grades than those who are monitored less (Crouter, MacDermid, McHale, & Perry-Jenkins, 1990) and they are less likely to develop friendships with antisocial peers and delinquent patterns of behavior in early adolescence (Laird, Criss, Pettie, Dodge, & Bates, 2008). Perhaps not surprisingly, parental monitoring is more successful when earlier parent–child attachment is secure (Kerns, Aspelmeier, Gentzler, & Grabill, 2001; Richardson, 2005). In particular, fathers' relationships with their children seem to be important, especially in avoiding problem behavior in adolescence (Fosco, Stormshak, Dishion, & Winter, 2012).

Another important goal of parenting is to increase children's **self-regulated behavior**, which is their ability to control and direct their own behavior and to meet the requirements that parents and others impose upon them. Self-regulation is encouraged when parents use verbal reasoning and suggestion rather than strict approaches to discipline (Lamb, Ketterlinus, & Fracasso, 1992; Kochanska & Aksan, 2006). A reasoning-based parenting approach leads to more prosocial behavior and to better compliance with social rules. Also, parents who remind their children of the effects of their actions on others tend to have children who are more popular and whose moral standards are internalized more fully. In contrast, when parents simply assert their power over their children, as in authoritarian parenting, their children tend not to develop internalized standards and controls. Studies consistently find that parents who used power-assertive techniques are more likely to have children who comply with adults' demands when the adults are present but not when the adults are absent.

One way that parents can encourage self-regulated behavior is to gradually increase the child's involvement in family decisions. Children adjust best when their parents foster **coregulation**, which involves a sense of shared responsibility between parents and their children. By engaging in frequent discussions and negotiations with their children, parents can encourage greater independence while still providing support and guidance. In this context, the concept of *scaffolding* is especially useful in understanding optimal parenting. As you may recall, scaffolding involves the concept of presenting children with tasks just beyond their level of competence and then providing support and assistance that allows them to accomplish these tasks. As children become more competent, parents should adjust their expectations accordingly. When parents can match their expectations realistically to their children's expanding abilities and their need for independence, children blossom and the parent–child relationship flourishes (Bigner, 2010).

Can you suggest a specific example of how parents can use scaffolding to encourage coregulation?

Parenting, of course, is generally easier when parents are less stressed—economically, socially, emotionally, or in other ways (Ceballo & McLoyd, 2002; Jaffee, Hanscombe, Haworth, David, & Plomin, 2012; Solantaus, Leinonen, & Punamäki, 2004). When stress is lower, parents can be more responsive and supportive and can be better at providing appropriate discipline. Furthermore, healthy and positive parent–child relationships are important not only during childhood, when parents play a directing role, but also throughout the lifespan, and the quality of these long-term relationships is often established during middle childhood (Flouri, 2004; Maccoby, 1992).

Watch *Parental Control of Friendships in India* on **MyDevelopmentLab**

self-regulated behavior
Behavior that is controlled and directed by the child rather than by parents, teachers, or other external forces

coregulation
The development of a sense of shared responsibility between parents and their children

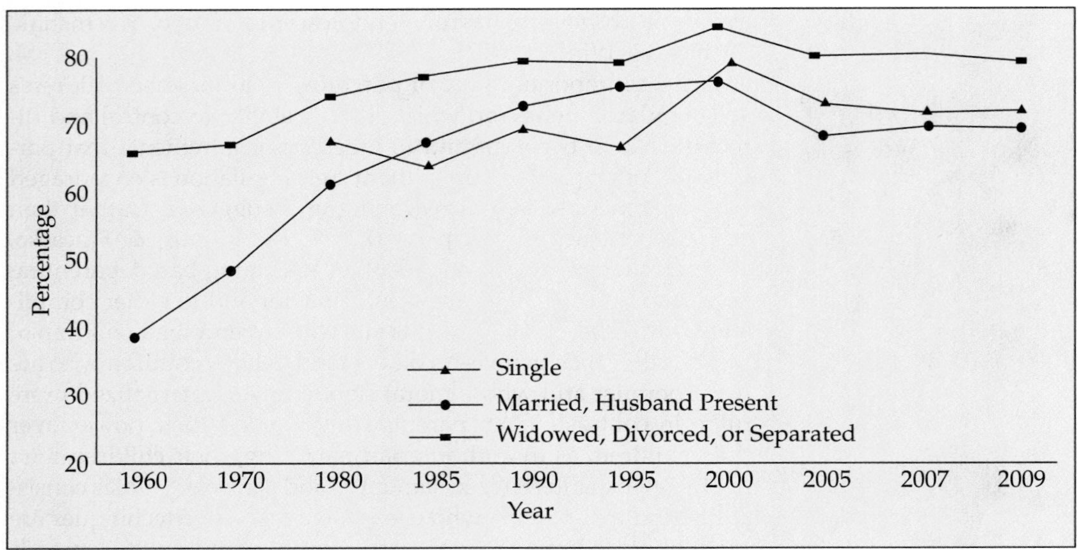

FIGURE 9-2 Percentages of Women in the U.S. Civilian Labor Force, 1960–2009
SOURCE: From "Table 599," *The statistical abstract of the United States, 2012,* by the U.S. Census Bureau, 2011, Washington, DC: U.S. Government Printing Office.

The Changing Nature of the Family

Parenting has changed appreciably over the past several decades, at least in industrialized nations. Whereas the "typical" family in the mid-20th century consisted of a mother, a father, and two or three children, contemporary U.S. families now incorporate many models of the family. Single parenthood, for example, has become commonplace: Today over 40% of U.S. births are to unmarried mothers—an increase of about 60% since 1985 (U.S. Census Bureau, 2012g).

Employment statistics also have changed, and married women are much more likely to be in the labor force now than was true in their grandmothers' time (see Figure 9-2). As you would expect, with the increase in the proportion of women who work, U.S. families have experienced rapid change. In 1948, only 26% of the mothers of school-age children ages 6 to 17 worked outside the home; in 1975, the figure was 51%; and in 2010, it was just over 77% (U.S. Department of Labor, 2011). Also, since the early 1950s, mothers of school-age children have been more likely to work than married women without children, which is partly due to the greater financial needs of families with children and partly due to the larger number of single-parent families led by women. According to the U.S. Census Bureau (2012c), 72% of single mothers; 70% of married mothers with husbands present; and 79% of divorced, separated, or widowed mothers are in the labor force. Indeed, in about two-thirds of two-parent U.S. families (66%), both parents work outside the home.

Despite the fact that parents are likely to work outside the home, many families face economic hardships. The number of single mothers who are unemployed and therefore likely to be living in poverty is high. Furthermore, the economic downturn that began in 2008 has had a worsening impact on families. For example, the unemployment rate for single mothers with children under age 18 was 27% in 2007; in 2011 it was 34.1% (see also Table 9-4). Clearly, our traditional definition of what constitutes a family is changing. What are the consequences of these changing patterns in family life?

The fact that most parents of school-age children now work outside the home has had an impact on social institutions, especially on those involving child care. In comparison to 20 or 30 years ago, there are many more after-school programs and arrangements available. Thus, the needs of children whose parents work are not simply neglected; rather, they are addressed in different ways through services provided by others.

Table 9-4 U.S. Single Parents Caring for Their Own Children and Their Employment Status, 2011 (in thousands)

	Employed	Unemployed	Percent Employed	
Children under age 6			2007	2011
Single mothers	2,047	1,448	64.7%	58.6%
Single fathers	845	222	85.7%	79.2%
Children ages 6 to 17				
Single mothers	3,575	1,468	77.9%	70.9%
Single fathers	1,063	267	84.9%	79.9%

SOURCE: From "Table 4," Department of Labor: Bureau of Labor Statistics, retrieved from http://www.bls.gov/news.release/famee.t04.htm.

Watch *A Family with Two Fathers* on **MyDevelopmentLab**

Children in closeknit adaptable families generally tend to be best equipped to cope with stressful situations. The trauma of a move is more easily handled by children whose families provide positive support.

Furthermore, having parents who work outside the home is likely to be viewed by children as the norm today, rather than as a family situation that is unusual or unwelcome. Perhaps as a result, children of working parents often seem remarkably insightful about and accepting of their busy parents' lifestyles. For example, in one study, children of working parents were interviewed one-on-one about how they felt their parents managed the balance of work and home responsibilities (Galinsky, 1999, 2005, Frontline, 2012). These children, who were in grades 3 to 12, generally thought that they were well supervised and that their parents often gave priority to family over work. They were often pleased and proud of their parents' accomplishments. Although parents who work often must juggle schedules, it appears that combining family and job responsibilities does work for most families.

Regardless of whether or not parents work, an important component for many of today's families is stress. Many life situations are inherently stressful for children and their families, including poverty, divorce, moving to a new town, suffering a serious illness or injury, and growing up in a dangerous environment. Even living in a well-functioning family in which both parents work provides a certain amount of stress for children. Indeed, in the interviews with children described in the preceding paragraph (Galinsky, 2005, Frontline, 2012), one of the surprising findings was that when children were asked what one thing they wished they could change about the way their parents' work affected their lives, their number one wish was that their parents would be less stressed and less tired.

Coping with Stress Although coping with stress is a normal part of every child's life, when stress is extreme and chronic and lasts over weeks, months, or years, it often takes a serious toll on children, as well as on adults. For example, research indicates that children who grow up in cultures of violence—such as in a war zone or in a dangerous inner-city neighborhood—often engage in aggressive play, have nightmares, and are troubled by sudden memories that intrude during school or other activities. Not surprisingly, chronic, ongoing violence produces a state of sustained stress (Dimitry, 2012; Kostelny & Garbarino, 2001; Werner, Frost, Macnee, McCabe, & Rice, 2012). Young children who live with constant violence tend to be fearful, depressed, and anxious. Many have trouble concentrating in school and suffer other school-related problems. Children may fear being abandoned and may become overly aggressive and insolent to disguise their fears. Many children develop blunted emotions—they are afraid to develop affection for people who may be killed or who may abandon them. In severe cases, their reaction is called *posttraumatic stress syndrome*. What determines a child's ability to cope constructively with stresses such as these?

Several factors appear to be involved (Betancourt & Khan, 2008; Grant, McMahon, Duffy, Taylor, & Compas, 2011). One is the sheer number of stressful situations in a child's life; a child (or adult) who can deal successfully with one stressful event may be overwhelmed if forced to deal with several at the same time (Hetherington & Blechman, 1996). A second factor is the child's perception or understanding of the event. For example, the first day of school can be a traumatic event in a child's life. A child who knows what to expect and who interprets this milestone as a sign of increasing maturity will experience less stress in making the transition than will a child who is not prepared or who associates school with negative outcomes. In addition, research clearly indicates that close-knit, adaptable families with open communication patterns and good problem-solving skills are better able to weather stressful events (Ortega, Beauchemin, & Kaniskan, 2008). Social support systems such as neighbors, relatives, friendship networks, or self-help groups also are valuable.

From a different perspective, temperament and early personality characteristics influence children's ability to cope with stressful environments (Gest & Davidson, 2011). For example, a 30-year study of Hawaiian children raised in family environments characterized by poverty, parental conflict or divorce, alcoholism, or mental illness revealed that most children developed into self-confident, successful, and emotionally stable adults despite these challenges (Werner, 1995). These **resilient children**, or children who overcome difficult environments to lead socially competent lives, shared certain characteristics. As babies, they had been temperamentally "easy" and had developed secure attachments to a parent or grandparent in the first year of life. Later, if that parent or grandparent was no longer available, these children had the ability to find someone else—another adult or even a sibling or a friend—who could provide the emotional support they needed. Thus, especially when conditions are stressful, positive self-esteem and good self-organization are strongly related to secure early attachments (see Chapter 5).

Do you consider yourself a resilient person? Why or why not?

resilient children
Children who are able to overcome difficult environments to lead socially competent lives

Table 9-5 Seven Guidelines for Single Parenting

1. Accept responsibilities and challenges. Maintain a positive attitude and the feeling that solutions are possible.
2. Give the parental role high priority. Successful single parents are willing to sacrifice time, money, and energy to meet their children's needs.
3. Use consistent, nonpunitive discipline.
4. Emphasize open communication. Encourage trust and the open expression of feelings.
5. Foster individuality within a supportive family unit.
6. Recognize the need for self-nurturance. Parents must understand the need to take care of themselves in order to be able to help their children.
7. Emphasize rituals and traditions, including bedtime routines, holiday celebrations, and special family activities.

SOURCE: Adapted from "Successful single parents," by M. R. Olson and J. A. Haynes, 1993, *Families in Society, 74*(5), 259–267; and *For better or for worse: Divorce reconsidered*, by E. M. Hetherington and J. Kelly, 2002, New York: W. W. Norton.

Stress and Single Parenting In 2010, about 70% of children in the United States were living in homes headed by two parents (or stepparents). Of the remaining 30%, 23% lived in homes headed by their mother, 3% in homes headed by their father, and 4% in homes headed by neither parent (Forum on Child and Family Statistics, 2011). Although most families headed by a single parent are well functioning, stress can be a concern associated particularly with single parenting because this family arrangement involves not only the lack of relief and support provided by a second caregiver, but it often is associated with economic challenges as well. In 2010, for example, 21% of all U.S. children were living in families whose income fell below the poverty line, but this percentage was nearly 40% for families headed by the mother, and nearly 50% when the mother was cohabiting with another adult. By contrast, only 10% of families headed by married parents had incomes below the poverty line (Forum on Child and Family Statistics, 2011).

Economic hardship is associated with an array of related problems, regardless of the family structure (Conger, & Donnellan, 2007; McLoyd, 2011; Votruba-Drzal, 2006). Housing is likely to be crowded; frequent moves are common. Meals may be skimpy and nutritionally poor and medical care may be lacking. One of the most troubling aspects about stressful situations such as these is the reciprocal nature of the problem. When maternal unemployment and work interruptions have a negative impact on mothers, there is often an indirect, negative impact on their children's well-being as well (McLoyd, 2011; Mistry, Vanderwater, Huston, & McLoyd, 2002). For example, in a study of 241 single U.S. African-American mothers and their children, researchers found that economic hardship took a toll on the mother's psychological functioning, in turn affecting her ability to be an effective parent and, therefore, negatively impacting the mother–child relationship. The mothers in the study showed symptoms of depression when they were unemployed; when depressed, they tended to punish their children more frequently. In turn, children who were punished frequently showed greater signs of cognitive distress and depression. Similar studies also emphasize the complex and interactive nature of economic hardship, parental distress, and parenting behaviors (Barnett, 2008; Mistry, Lowe, Benner, & Chien, 2008; Wadsworth & Santiago, 2008; see the box Changing Perspectives: Families Coping in Difficult Circumstances).

What solutions are available to families caught in a cycle of economic hardship, maternal depression, and poor parenting responses? Studies typically show that when single mothers perceive that tangible help is available they have fewer depressive symptoms; in addition, they feel better about their role as mothers, and they punish their children less. Assistance from other family members, such as a grandmother, an aunt, or even a generous friend, can provide much needed support, although such arrangements also can escalate conflict and thereby add to stress if the personal dynamics among caregivers are strained (Chase-Lansdale, Brooks-Gunn, & Zamsky, 1994; Taylor, Seaton, & Dominguez, 2008). Establishing clear rules and expectations for children also leads to better outcomes, as does adopting other parenting techniques that work in any type of family structure, such as those outlined in Table 9-5.

Clearly, most children who grow up in single-parent families are well adjusted and successful, and most single parents are able to manage the stresses in their lives, just as parents who are married do. In some cases, when mothers in single-parent families work at jobs that they like, their children have greater self-esteem and a greater sense of family organization and togetherness than do children whose mothers do not work or whose mothers work at jobs that they intensely dislike (Goldberg, Prause, Lucas-Thompson, & Himsel, 2008). Girls especially seem to benefit from having mothers who are employed. In fact, single-parent households sometimes represent less stressful living environments for children than do two-parent families in which parents argue and fight. When marriages end in divorce, for example, children and parents must cope with the psychological and emotional stresses associated with the breakup of the family, as well as the economic issues involved.

Watch *Being a Single Parent* on **MyDevelopmentLab**

Children of Divorce Today, over 40% of all U.S. marriages are expected to end in divorce. In 2010, just over 2 million people were married; just under 900,000 were divorced. Each year, over a million U.S. children experience the breakup of their families (U.S. Census Bureau, 2012o). Divorce affects everyone in the family unit, parents as well as children, and these effects are apparent in a number of ways. First, children feel a sense of loss because both parents strongly influence their children's development, and a divorce typically means that both parents will no longer be equally available to their children. Children

CHANGING PERSPECTIVES

Families Coping in Difficult Circumstances

Poverty alone does not cause negative outcomes for children. Everyone can think of people whose lives started out in impoverished circumstances and who have gone on to lead fulfilling, happy, and successful lives. However, the behavior of parents and their children is very much affected by the family's economic circumstances—sometimes for the better and sometimes for the worse. How do researchers study such complex interactions of broadly defined social variables?

One study identified 419 families in Milwaukee, Wisconsin, through their participation in a program for low-income families in which the parents worked a minimum of 30 hours a week. By evaluating teachers' and parents' ratings of children, as well as parents' reactions to child-rearing tasks, the results showed that when economic pressure mounted, parents became more distressed. Their stress then contributed to a more punishment-oriented style of discipline and to a less affectionate relationship with their children. Less-than-optimal parenting, in turn, was linked to lower teacher ratings of the children's prosocial behavior and to higher ratings of their behavioral problems (Mistry, Vandewater, Huston, & McLoyd, 2002).

Another study of broad social variables also emphasized an ecological framework (Ceballo & McLoyd, 2002; Ceballo, McLoyd, & Toyokawa, 2004). In a study of 262 poor African-American mothers of seventh- and eighth-grade children in Flint, Michigan, the conditions present in the family's neighborhood were found to help explain the relationship between mothers' ability to provide social support and their parenting behaviors. When neighborhood conditions worsened, the mother's emotional support and ability to take care of her children's needs weakened. When neighborhood quality was better, children's school performance improved due to increased academic effort.

In order to study such complex relationships, these studies used several different methods of measuring the variables of interest, such as parent and child interviews, teacher and parent ratings, as well as additional methods of determining the quality of neighborhoods and other economic circumstances. Studies such as these generally support the idea that difficult economic and social conditions contribute to parents' experience of distress (McLoyd, 2011). This stress reduces parents' effectiveness because it leads to a reduced ability to be a sensitive, responsive parent and to use effective supervision and monitoring. However, when heavy parental distress is absent, parents are better able to cope effectively. Apparently, when parents are worried, fatigued, or depressed, these conditions lead to less effective parenting behaviors. How do you think such complex issues can be addressed most effectively?

---

also may worry about what will happen to them if their parents divorce. Moreover, by the time a divorce occurs the family usually has already experienced a state of tension and stress for a long time. The children may have heard the word *divorce* spoken or shouted in their homes for months or even years, often accompanied by anger, fights, and crying. Even very young children usually know when their parents' relationship is disturbed.

Children react to divorce in a variety of ways, some of which reflect each individual child's temperament and emotional adjustment and some of which represent the particular features of how the divorce unfolds (Hetherington 2006; Lansford, 2009; see Table 9-6). In general, the consequences of divorce for children are more problematic when the level of hostility expressed between the parents is high, when the divorce involves major changes in the child's living arrangements and daily activities, and when one or both parents fail to maintain strong emotional attachments and stay involved in their children's lives.

Regardless of how the dynamics of a divorce unfold, there will be issues to address and adjustments to be made. For example, immediately after a divorce, children—especially those between the ages of 5 and 7—often appear confused. Divorce often involves some unpredictability. Consequently, children often test the rules to see if the world still works the way it did before. They may exhibit behavioral difficulties at home and at school, and their daily lives and their understanding of their social world may be disrupted.

Some children whose parents divorce experience considerable difficulty in adjustment (D'Onofrio, et al., 2006). For example, they may report higher incidences of anxiety and depression; they may have a greater number of academic problems; and they may be more likely to engage in "problem" behaviors, such as dropping out of school, using drugs, or be-

Table 9-6 Factors That Affect Children's Reactions to Divorce

- **The amount of hostility accompanying the divorce:** If there is a great deal of hostility and bitterness, it is much harder for children to adjust (Amato, 2001, 2006). Parental conflict lowers children's sense of well-being. When parents fight, children develop fear and anger. Children are especially vulnerable when they are forced to choose between their parents. Ongoing squabbles or legal battles over custody, division of property, child support, visitation, or child-care arrangements make the situation much more difficult for both children and parents.
- **The amount of actual change in the child's life:** If children continue to live in the same home, attend the same school, and have the same friends after a divorce, their adjustment problems are likely to be less severe. The more changes a child is forced to make, especially in the period immediately following the divorce, the more difficult the child's adjustment. Changes that disrupt daily routines, that require children to establish new friendships, and that require major dislocations and adjustments are more difficult (Hetherington, 2003).
- **The nature of the parent–child relationship:** Long-term involvement and emotional support from both parents help considerably (Bauserman, 2002), suggesting that the nature of ongoing parent–child interactions may be more important than whether both parents are present in the home. In fact, sometimes children of divorce are better off than they would have been had their parents stayed together and continued to argue and fight.

Watch *Pam: Divorced Mother of Nine-Year-Old* on **MyDevelopmentLab**

Try This!

The Impact of Divorce on Children

With more than 40% of today's marriages ending in divorce, most people have a good friend who has been affected by the dissolution of a marriage, and many people have coped with their own parents' divorce. When a divorce occurs during middle childhood, children often have difficulty adjusting to the changes that take place. Even when the divorce is amicable and comes as no surprise, the effect on grade school children is usually substantial. Not only must they adjust to the changes in their family's circumstances, but they also must adapt to adjustments in routines and social relationships. How do children think about the divorce of their parents?

To provide some real-world context for understanding these issues, try to identify a child between the ages of 6 and 12 whose parents have recently divorced. Perhaps the brothers or sisters of a friend or a member of your family might be in this circumstance. If you cannot find a child whose parents have recently divorced, identify a friend, family member, or colleague whose parents divorced. If possible, try to find a person who was in grade school at the time of the parents' divorce or a parent whose divorce occurred when his or her children were in grade school. The point is to identify a person who has firsthand experience with the effects of divorce on children. Formulate a set of questions to ask this person about how the divorce affected him or her. The following list provides some questions that you might ask:

- How old were you when your parents divorced?
- What was your family situation like before the divorce?
- What was it like after the divorce?
- What was the hardest thing to cope with?
- Did you blame your parents for the divorce?
- What is the hardest thing to cope with now?
- Were there any good things that resulted from the divorce?

You will need to choose your questions carefully so that you do not upset the person you are interviewing, especially if that person is a child.

Reflect on What You Observed

Interviewing children, especially about personal issues, is very challenging. Children frequently do not want to talk about things that trouble them, and you may need to discontinue the interview if you sense that your questions are upsetting the child. If you do complete an interview, either with a child or an adult, what general themes did you hear in the person's answers to your questions? Was the divorce a particularly difficult time in the person's life? What factors contributed to any hardships the person faced? Were there things that the parents did that made the child's adjustment either better or worse?

Consider the Issues

What advice would you give to a friend who was considering divorce if that friend had children in grade school? What things do you think make a child's adjustment harder? What things do you think make a child's adjustment easier? What external factors, such as money, extended family support, or social resources, might influence a child's adjustment? Do you think divorce is harder to cope with for some children than for others? What factors might help a child to be more resilient when the child's parents divorce?

---

coming sexually active at a young age. In addition, they may sometimes experience problems in establishing appropriate friendships, and they may have difficulty with low self-esteem as well. However, it is important to note that these same problems are found among children whose parents are happily married. Thus, it is important to recognize that, although a divorce almost always involves stress and adjustment, divorce in and of itself is not necessarily associated with negative consequences for child development (Lamb, 2012).

Parents can help their children adjust to a divorce in the same ways they would address other major changes in family life, for example, by setting clear limits and sticking to familiar routines as much as possible. For instance, when children question the need to go to bed, they may have to be told by their mother, "I know it's upsetting that Daddy's not coming home any more, but that doesn't mean you don't have to go to bed at 8:00. You still have to get up early in the morning and go to school, and you still need your rest." Teachers also can help by gently reminding the child of the school's rules and expectations and by being emotionally supportive.

How might a child's own egocentrism make adjustment to divorce more difficult?

reconstituted family
Also known as stepfamily; a family where a mother or a father with children has remarried to produce a new family

Another issue that sometimes arises following a divorce is the prospect of adding a new member or members to the family unit. Children, especially if they are younger, frequently hold onto the belief that somehow their parents will reconcile and that they may be able to bring this about if they are very good (Hetherington, 1992, 2003). If one or both parents enter into a new relationship, this hope is dashed. Consequently, the child may act out, often against the intruder, as a means of coping with the sense of loss and disillusionment. If a parent marries, thereby forming a **reconstituted family**, the issues may be further compounded (see also Chapter 15). Children, for example, may feel divided loyalties to their original parents and feel guilty about abandoning the noncustodial parent by giving affection to the stepparent. They may resent being disciplined by the new stepparent and may even resent the stepparent's attempts to win their affection. Children also may be unhappy about sharing their parent with their parent's new partner, and they may worry about being left out of the new family. Many children have an additional challenge because they must learn to live with stepsiblings, which may imply learning new rules about sharing as well as about many other family routines. (See the box Try This! The Impact of Divorce on Children.)

Despite the fact that a larger proportion of children from divorced families show adjustment difficulties than do children from families that have not experienced divorce, most

▲ Reconstituted families may be particularly difficult for older children, who may not accept a new mother due to loyalty to the first mother or who may resent an "adorable" new young sibling.

children do cope successfully with their parents' divorce. In fact, if family life is disruptive or abusive, the effect of divorce can be positive for the children in the family because the home environment after the divorce may be more stable and predictable. Of course, adjustment problems are not always obvious immediately. Sometimes difficulties emerge later, especially during adolescence and in response to the turmoil associated with attaining puberty (Amato, 2007; Amato & Dorius, 2010). Nevertheless, nearly all children cope—and most cope successfully—with the issues produced by their parents' divorce. Most children are quite resilient and adaptive, and most enter the next period of development—adolescence—ready for the challenges and opportunities this stage of the lifespan presents.

REVIEW THE FACTS 9-4

1. In middle childhood, which of the following is the major socializing force for most children?
   a. peers of both sexes b. peers of the same sex
   c. peers of the opposite sex d. family
2. The process by which children learn to control their own behavior is called ___________.
3. Currently, about what percentage of women with school-age children work outside the home?
   a. 39% b. 55%
   c. 71% d. 92%
4. Most single-parent families are headed by ___________.
5. When families are stressed, is it generally a good idea or a bad idea for parents to set clear rules and expectations for their children?
6. A reconstituted family refers to one in which ___________.

Practice on **MyDevelopmentLab**

CHAPTER SUMMARY

Personality Development in an Expanding Social World

What events in middle childhood enhance or detract from the child's developing self-concept?

- During middle childhood, the child's self-concept becomes more stable, more realistic, more complex, and more accurate.

According to Erik Erikson, what is the central developmental conflict that must be resolved in middle childhood?

- For Erikson, the central task of middle childhood focuses on resolving the crisis of *industry versus inferiority*. In industrialized nations that emphasize educational attainment, industry is often associated with the acquisition of new knowledge and skills.

How does self-esteem differ from self-concept, and what factors are linked to positive self-esteem in middle childhood?

- Children's *self-esteem* reflects their positive or negative evaluation of themselves. In cultures where formal education is expected, there is a significant correlation between self-esteem and academic achievement, as well as between self-esteem and achievement in other activities, such as sports or music. Positive self-esteem also is linked to being viewed positively by family, peers, and others.
- The development of self-esteem is a reciprocal process. Parents can positively influence their children's self-esteem by offering realistic praise and by encouraging them toward activities in which they can be successful. Excessive or unrealistic praise often leads to negative outcomes.

Social Knowledge and Reasoning

What are the three components of social cognition, and how does each help the child develop an understanding of the social world?

- During middle childhood, children make many advances in their cognitive abilities as they move from the preoperational stage to the stage that Piaget called concrete operations. Central to development is the child's expanding *social cognition*, which refers to an individual's thoughts, knowledge, and understanding about the social world.
- In middle childhood, children's thinking becomes less egocentric; therefore, they become better in dealing with complex social situations and in making correct *social inferences*, which are guesses and assumptions about another person's feelings, thoughts, and intentions. They also assume more *social responsibility*, which is their awareness of obligations to family, friends, and society. In addition, they learn *social regulations* that reflect the rules and conventions that govern their culture's social interactions.
- All three aspects of social cognition—inference, responsibility, and regulations—contribute to the child's ability to make moral judgments.

How do children of different ages think about questions of right versus wrong?

- Although many theoretical perspectives contribute to our understanding of moral development, theories that emphasize cognitive development are most central to our understanding of this concept. According to Piaget, children's sense of morality arises through the interaction of their developing cognitive structures and their widening social experience. In his first stage of moral development, termed *moral realism,* children view rules as real, indestructible things, not as abstract principles. Toward the end of middle childhood, Piaget's second stage of *moral relativism* develops, in which children realize that rules are created and agreed upon cooperatively by individuals and that they can be changed if necessary.
- Based on research that asked people to respond to stories involving *moral dilemmas,* Kohlberg noted that earlier in development, moral reasoning is based on external consequences and reasoning is concrete; later, it is based on internalized moral principles and becomes more abstract. Kohlberg developed a theory that specified three levels in the development of moral reasoning: the *preconventional, conventional,* and *postconventional* levels. Each level can be further broken into two stages, which results in a six-stage model.
- Criticisms of Kohlberg's view argue that his research investigates moral attitudes but not moral behavior and that moral development is not as neatly ordered and predictable as his six-stage model suggests. Perhaps the most controversial challenge is that Kohlberg's theory of morality disregards important differences among what different cultures view as moral, which is called *moral absolutism*. One such example involves gender differences: Kohlberg's view is challenged because his research defines advanced moral reasoning in terms of *justice,* which is a concept more characteristic of male enculturation. Women, however, may be as advanced in their moral development, although they are more likely to emphasize human relationships and *caring*.

Peer Relationships

Why are friends important in middle childhood, and how do friendships change as children move through the period of middle childhood?

- In middle childhood, most friends are of the same gender, and friendships during middle childhood serve many functions. Children's concept of friendship changes as they grow older. As children grow older, they increasingly depend on friends to keep secrets, although girls usually disclose more than do boys.
- Selman viewed friendships as developing through four stages: at first, friends are just playmates; then awareness of another's feelings emerges; in the third stage, trust develops and friends help each other; in the final stage, children can look at the relationship from another's perspective. Selman's model is sometimes criticized because it largely ignores the emotional aspects of friendship and does not attend sufficiently to the many types of friendships that children have.
- *Peer groups* are groups of three or more people of similar age who interact with each other and who share norms and goals. In early middle childhood, peer groups are relatively informal, and membership is usually quite flexible. At about ages 10 to 12, peer groups become more formal, have more rigid membership requirements, and usually are gender-segregated.
- Peers often conform—to greater or lesser degree—to the expectations of their peer group. They learn to self-monitor, paying attention to how others perceive them. Highly conforming children are especially concerned about how they are viewed and often are more dependent and anxious, and have feelings of inferiority. Peer group conformity can be good or bad, depending on the type of behavior advocated by the group.

What factors are linked to popularity during middle childhood?

- Popularity in one's peer group is an important dimension of group membership. Popular young children are likely to have good emotional control, and they can cooperate and share. As children grow older, high academic performance and athletic ability also become important in determining popularity and sometimes popular children are also aggressive. However, children who are overly aggressive, timid, or different in some way are usually less popular.
- Unpopular children sometimes can be encouraged to change the behavior that others object to, and teachers can play a large role in helping them improve their peer group status.

How does a child come to develop a sense of ethnic identity?

- Prejudice is a negative attitude formed without adequate reason, which is directed at a defined group of people; *discrimination* involves treating others in a prejudiced manner. Prejudice and discrimination often are directed at members of ethnic groups, and such *out-group* prejudice is seen in every society throughout the world.
- As children grow older, they become capable of thinking with greater complexity, although this does not always reduce prejudice because of increased pressure to conform. When ethnic or community cultural norms are different from those of the majority culture, children and their parents must reconcile these two sets of expectations.
- Developing an awareness on one's ethnic identity takes place largely in middle childhood, and follows a pattern dictated by the child's growing cognitive skills. Children who are members of a distinct minority group may encounter conflicts in maintaining their ethnic identity while also finding ways to fit into the majority culture.

Family Influences in Middle Childhood

How can parents help their children cope with stressful situations?

- Although peers become very important to children in middle childhood, the family normally continues to be children's most important socializing force. As children grow older, parents focus less on promoting autonomy and establishing daily routines and more on establishing work habits and achievement.

- Effective parenting in middle childhood involves subtle but effective monitoring of children's activities and behaviors. The goal is for children to achieve *self-regulated behavior,* where they control and direct their own personal behavior. Self-regulation is encouraged when parents reason with their children rather than make strict demands. Through *co-regulation,* parents and their children share responsibilities, which works well when parents use scaffolding techniques to lead children to develop increasing competence.
- Family structures have changed, with more mothers in the workforce and more families headed by a single parent, usually the mother.
- Many life situations are stressful for families and children. When stress is chronic and extreme, children and adults may develop symptoms, such as nightmares, fearfulness, depression, anxiety, trouble with concentration, aggressive behavior, or blunted emotions.
- Stress is better dealt with when stressful events do not pile up, when the child understands the event and knows what to expect, and when family and social support is available. Some children also are more resilient and are better able than others to deal with stress.
- Stress can be experienced in any family, but families headed by single parents are especially vulnerable because they often lack social support and economic resources. Furthermore, when parents are stressed, they often use less effective parenting techniques; therefore, the development of their children may be affected. Social support and setting clear rules and expectations for children can help parents deal more effectively with stress.

When family structures change, such as when parents divorce or remarry, what developmental issues are posed for children?

- Over 40% of all U.S. marriages are expected to end in divorce. Children respond to divorce in a variety of ways that reflect their own temperaments and emotional adjustment, as well as the circumstances of the divorce. Divorce is more traumatic for children when the parents' hostility is high, when it involves major changes for the child, and when parents fail to stay emotionally involved with and attached to their children.
- When parents divorce, children often experience adjustment problems, such as behavioral difficulties, anxiety, depression, and low self-esteem, and they often have more problems with school. However, most children are resilient and learn to cope with this stress. Parents can help by setting clear limits.
- When divorced parents remarry, thereby forming a *reconstituted family,* children are affected. For young children, the remarriage may dash their hopes for a reconciliation, however unrealistic. There also may be issues involving discipline from a stepparent or sharing with new family members. However, most children do cope, usually quite successfully.

KEY TERMS

industry versus inferiority (p. 252)
self-esteem (p. 252)
social cognition (p. 253)
social inference (p. 254)
social responsibility (p. 254)
social regulations (p. 254)
morality (p. 254)
moral realism (p. 255)
moral relativism (p. 255)
moral dilemmas (p. 255)
moral absolutism (p. 256)
peer group (p. 259)
prejudice (p. 262)
discrimination (p. 262)
self-regulated behavior (p. 265)
coregulation (p. 265)
resilient children (p. 267)
reconstituted family (p. 270)

MyVirtualLife

What decision would you make while raising a child? What would be the consequences of those decisions?

Find out by accessing **MyVirtualLife** at
www.MyDevelopmentLab.com
to raise a virtual child and live your own virtual life.

10 ADOLESCENCE AND EMERGING ADULTHOOD
Physical and Cognitive Development

LEARNING OBJECTIVES

- Do adolescents in cultures around the world, or who lived in different historical periods, experience the period of adolescence and emerging adulthood in much the same way?
- What features best characterize the developmental niche occupied by adolescents in the United States today?
- What physical changes occur as individuals move into adolescence, and what changes are specifically associated with puberty?
- Why do adolescents focus so intensely on issues of body image, and in what ways are their concerns about their appearance expressed?
- Is it better to sexually mature before or after most of one's peers?
- How have sexual practices and expectations changed in the United States over the past six decades?
- What brain changes are associated with development through the period of adolescence and emerging adulthood?
- What are "formal operations," and how does cognitive development change as the individual moves through adolescence?
- What is adolescent egocentrism, and how is it linked to the changes in cognitive development that teenagers and emerging adults typically experience?

CHAPTER OUTLINE

Adolescent Development in a Cultural and Historical Context
- Adolescence and Emerging Adulthood in the United States Today

Physical Development and Adaptation
- Physical Growth and Change
- Puberty
- Body Image and Adjustment

Gender Identity and Sexual Practices
- Six Decades of Changes in Sexual Practices
- Factors That Influence Early Sexual Relationships
- Consequences of Adolescent Sexual Behavior

Cognitive Changes in Adolescence
- Brain Development in Adolescence
- Piaget's Period of Formal Operations
- The Scope and Content of Adolescent Thought

Adolescence is the period of transition between childhood and adulthood, or, more formally, between puberty and maturity. In the United States and other industrialized nations, the span of life called *adolescence* often extends for a decade or more, and both the beginning and the end of this period of development are often ill-defined. Children frequently begin to act like adolescents considerably before their bodies reach sexual maturity—perhaps around age 10 or 11 for girls and around age 12 for boys—blurring their entry into this stage. Later, during the high school years and in the period—called *emerging adulthood*—between high school graduation and the person's full adoption of adult roles and responsibilities, social and cultural expectations play important roles in determining how and when entry into adulthood will take place. In this chapter, we first explore adolescent development within a cultural and an historical context. We next consider the physical development and adaptation that occur during this period, including the topics of physical growth and change, puberty, and adolescents' perceptions about body image. We then explore issues of gender identity and the changes in sexual practices that have occurred over the past 50 years, choosing to discuss these in the context of adolescence, as this is the first developmental period in which they exert considerable force. Finally, the chapter concludes with a look at the cognitive changes that occur during adolescence and the transition to adulthood. We now turn our attention to a central question: In today's culture, what defines the beginning and ending points of the period we call adolescence?

ADOLESCENT DEVELOPMENT IN A CULTURAL AND HISTORICAL CONTEXT

Historically, defining adolescence was not as complicated as it is today, and the period of the lifespan it occupied was much shorter (Lerner & Steinberg, 2009). Even today in many less industrialized countries, adolescence describes a relatively brief period of the lifespan. For example, adolescence in many agriculturally based cultures and hunter–gatherer societies begins when children enter their reproductive years. At this time, there is often a transition ritual called a **rite of passage**, which might include a ceremony, name change, or physical challenge. An apprenticeship of a year or two may follow and, by age 16 or 17, the young person achieves full, unqualified adulthood. Such a relatively rapid transformation is possible because the skills necessary for adult life in less industrialized societies can be mastered without a lengthy education. Still, the need for some period of transition is recognized everywhere; no society demands that a child become an adult overnight, and no society fails to recognize the attainment of adulthood. Regardless of culture, becoming an adult member of society is a universal milestone (Crockett & Silbereisen, 2011).

Adolescence is a transitional period in which individuals typically plan for their adult lives. Consequently, adolescents are particularly sensitive to the social world around them—its values, pressures, tensions, and unwritten rules. As they plan their own future, they oftentimes critique the social relationships and institutions around them. As social circumstances change, adolescents react and adapt. For example, in "hard times," such as during the Great Depression of the 1930s, many adolescents altered their plans, lost out on education, and did whatever was needed to help keep their families alive. Similarly, during the 1990s, adolescents in Eastern Europe experienced social upheaval as the Soviet Union disintegrated and the social system they knew was no longer available (Crockett & Silbereisen, 2011) and they were forced to adapt. Today in areas where terrorism is a constant worry, adolescents often adopt a different lifestyle and set of priorities than that of their older siblings who experienced adolescence just 5 years earlier.

Are there events in modern U.S. culture that serve as a rite of passage and signify a child's entry into adolescence?

Thus, any serious attempt to understand adolescence must be considered in the broader social context in which development occurs (Arnett, 2012). In contemporary U.S. culture, the developmental period between the end of childhood and the beginning of adulthood has become not only longer in years but also considerably more complex in terms of the choices and transitions adolescents experience. Consequently, scholars studying this period often break it into three distinct periods. The first of these is *early adolescence*, which begins at about age 10 or 11 when biological and physical changes associated with reproductive maturity start to occur. As you will learn later in this chapter, the age at which adolescence begins is somewhat earlier

rites of passage
Symbolic events or rituals to mark life transitions, such as from childhood to adult status

today than in previous historical periods, owing both to better nutrition and health care and to cultural forces that encourage children to adopt attitudes and behaviors typical of adolescents. Because nearly all young people in the United States attend high school, many scholars today mark the end of *early adolescence* at the entry into high school, which typically occurs at about age 14. *Later adolescence* comprises the high school years, roughly ages 14 to 18. Indeed, graduation from high school provides a convenient point at which to mark the entry into adulthood, yet few 18-year-olds are confident that they are truly "adults" (see Figure 10-1). For many young people, the years between ages 18 and 25 are filled with activities aimed at preparing for adulthood. Because these years are transitional between the high school experience and full immersion in adult responsibilities, many scholars today refer to this period as **emerging adulthood** (Arnett, 2000, 2011). Table 10-1 describes the three periods of adolescence and emerging adulthood.

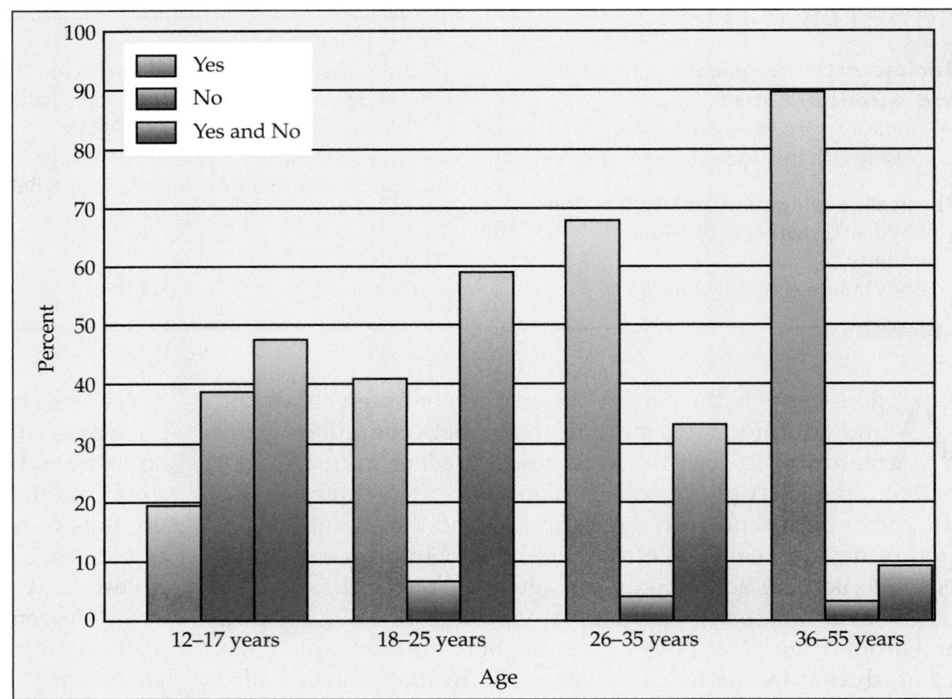

FIGURE 10-1 Age Differences in Response to the Question, "Do You Feel That You Have Reached Adulthood?"

SOURCE: From "Emerging adulthood: A theory of development from the late teens through the twenties," by J. J. Arnett, 2000, *American Psychologist, 55*, 469–480.

Thus, in economically developed countries today, the age at which the period of adolescence ends and the entry into adulthood occurs varies considerably from person to person. Some adolescents do in fact enter adulthood at around age 18, when they begin their life's work, marry, and begin to raise a family. Others delay their entry to adulthood, perhaps by continuing their academic preparation with several years of college study, by dating a variety of partners rather than establishing an exclusive romantic relationship, or by exploring a variety of jobs or careers before settling on their chosen work. For these young people, the period of emerging adulthood may be extended, lasting several years. For many of these young people, this transition through emerging adulthood is often gradual, involving a series of steps, each of which moves the individual closer to adopting full adult roles and responsibilities (Arnett, 2011). Regardless of the specific path each individual takes, however, adolescents eventually move into adulthood, and the period of adolescence is unique from both childhood and adulthood. Even in complex societies as in the United States, this developmental period for most young people is accompanied by fairly common expectations and events.

Adolescence and Emerging Adulthood in the United States Today

To understand adolescents and what adolescence and emerging adulthood is in contemporary U.S. culture, it helps to be aware of the special developmental niche in which adolescents live (Arnett, 2010a; Coleman, 2011). In the United States, adolescents and emerging adults are largely *age-segregated:* They interact mostly with other people of their same age and much less with younger children or adults. This is largely true because of the structure of the U.S. educational system, in which nearly all adolescents attend high schools organized by grades and most school activities involve only peers of the same age. Many colleges are mostly age-segregated as well. Adolescents often prefer the company of people of their own age, too, even when they have choices about with whom they wish to spend time. Except for the limited time they may spend babysitting or working in other jobs that bring them into contact with people either older or younger, adolescents typically spend their time with other adolescents.

emerging adulthood
In industrialized cultures, the transitional developmental period that bridges the end of adolescence and the beginning of adulthood, typically between ages 18 and 25

Table 10-1 Three Periods of Adolescence and Emerging Adulthood

Period	Age Range	Markers
Early adolescence	10 or 11 to about 14	Begins with the changes associated with puberty; ends when the adolescent enters high school
Later adolescence	About 14 to 18	Begins with entry into high school; ends with high school graduation
Emerging adulthood	About 18 to 25	Begins at high school graduation and may last a shorter or longer time, depending on how long it takes the adolescent to complete the tasks necessary for the transition to full adult status

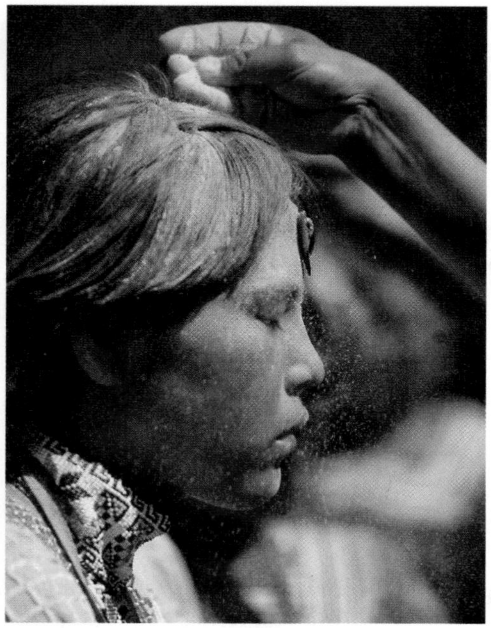

In this Apache coming-of-age ceremony in Arizona, this young woman is being blessed with pollen.

Age segregation can have negative effects. Being separated from younger children deprives younger adolescents of opportunities to guide and tutor those who are less knowledgeable than themselves. Separation from the adult world means that older adolescents miss opportunities to serve apprenticeships—to learn jobs by working alongside older, experienced people. They also are largely isolated from adult culture—the major activities, customs, and responsibilities of society—except for the limited time they may spend helping their parents with chores or working at after-school jobs.

Prolonged *economic dependence* is another characteristic of adolescence. In a society like the United States, adolescents typically depend on their parents for financial support while they acquire the extended education necessary for jobs that require technologically sophisticated skills. For those who do not obtain sufficient education, the low-level jobs available to them are usually neither interesting nor financially rewarding. Both situations typically lead adolescents to become frustrated and restless with their place in the world. Thus, adolescence is in many respects a time of restricted rights and opportunities and of prescribed roles. Although some theorists, such as Erikson (see Chapter 11), take a more positive view, seeing adolescence as a time when individuals are allowed to explore and experiment with various roles before taking on the responsibilities of the adult world, adolescents more often find their economic situation limiting and frustrating.

Adolescents also are often deeply affected by, and develop strong opinions about, the events of the time in which they live. Every era has its wars, religious movements, and economic ups and downs. Adolescents are especially vulnerable to such crises. They lose their jobs during economic downturns and are hired during economic booms. Adolescents and young adults fight in wars, participate in riots, and put their energies into movements for social reform. They often support radical political and religious movements with their idealism. Today's adolescents are affected not only by local and regional crises but also by crises in distant parts of the world. Adolescents are especially influenced by images projected by mass media—often more heavily than parents would like—which they have been absorbing throughout their childhood years (see Chapter 7). It appears that adolescents, with their rapidly developing physical and cognitive capacities, are particularly vulnerable to assuming the passive role of a mass-media consumer. They accept tragedy, sexuality, and brutality in a matter-of-fact way; perhaps, they develop a thirst for excessive stimulation, which is easily accessible through video games, loud music, the Internet, and TV. Perhaps they model their behavior on the trite or bizarre events they see portrayed or become absorbed with the often angry, socially deviant worlds portrayed by hip-hop, rap, and heavy metal music. Although positive images also are presented, adolescents—especially early in this period of the lifespan—tend to gravitate to the more grisly counterculture aspects of media programming. These images often form a part of the context in which their development takes place.

What do you think are the most popular TV shows, movies, and music among today's adolescents? How would you describe the themes these media portray?

For those individuals who experience an extended transition from adolescence to adulthood, the period of emerging adulthood is in many ways similar to the earlier years of adolescent development: Emerging adults are, for the most part, age-segregated, economically dependent on their parents, and deeply affected by social and political forces. However, this period also is characterized by common issues and challenges that are somewhat different from those experienced during middle and high school years, especially with respect to the choice of a career and a life partner (Arnett, 2010a, see Table 10-2). Nevertheless, the overall period of adolescence, whether it ends at age 18 or several years later, is generally characterized by instability, uncertainty, and challenge. In the next section, we explore the physical development and adaptation that take place as children enter and move through the period of adolescence.

REVIEW THE FACTS 10-1

1. A ceremony that is seen more often in less industrialized cultures to mark the beginning of a person's reproductive years is called a(n) ________.
2. In comparison to a less industrialized culture, is the period of adolescence in the United States longer or shorter?
3. In the United States, adolescents spend the most time with
   a. younger children.
   b. other adolescents.
   c. parents.
   d. adults other than parents.
4. The period of late adolescence, usually defined as between ages 18 and 25, is called ________.

Practice on **MyDevelopmentLab**

Table 10-2 Characteristics of Emerging Adulthood

Identity explorations	Emerging adults "try out" various possibilities about love and work, as they form an understanding of who they are, what they want in life, how they fit into society, and what their values, beliefs, and capabilities are.
Instability	Emerging adults move through various romantic relationships and friendships, try out various college majors or jobs, and also may make several geographic moves—out of their parents' home, to college, to a different town or state.
Self-focused perspective	Emerging adults learn to make decisions for themselves, and in so doing they adopt a focus on their own lives, wishes, preferences, and choices. This self-focus is healthy in that it allows them to better understand their identity.
Feelings of "in-between"	Emerging adults often feel that they are neither an adolescent nor an adult (see Figure 10-1). Often they adopt roles consistent with both earlier and later developmental periods.
Age of possibilities	Emerging adulthood often is a period of high hopes and expectations and of optimism about the future. Because they are in control of their choices, the possibilities of life seem open and positive.

SOURCE: From *Adolescence and emerging adulthood: A cultural approach* (4th ed., p. 15), by J. J. Arnett, copyright © 2010. Electronically reproduced by permission of Pearson Education, Inc., Upper Saddle River, NJ.

PHYSICAL DEVELOPMENT AND ADAPTATION

Physiologically, early adolescence ranks with the fetal period and infancy as a time of extremely rapid biological change. Unlike young children, however, adolescents anxiously monitor their development—or lack of it—typically basing their judgments on both knowledge and misinformation. They compare themselves with the prevailing ideals for their sex; in fact, trying to reconcile differences between the real and the ideal is a major problem for adolescents. Surprised, fascinated, embarrassed, or uncertain, they constantly compare themselves with others and revise their self-images. How parents react to their child's physical changes can also have a profound impact on the adolescent's adjustment.

Physical Growth and Change

The biological hallmarks of entry into adolescence are a marked increase in the rate of growth, rapid development of the reproductive organs, and the appearance of *secondary sex characteristics*—such as body hair, increased body fat and muscle, and enlargement and maturation of genitalia (Rosen, 2004; Tanner, 1962). Some developmental trends are the same for boys and girls—such as increased size, improved strength, and stamina; however, most changes are sex specific. One particularly noticeable change is an increase in body fat; some preadolescents become pudgy. In both males and females, fat is deposited in the breast area; this is permanent in females but temporary in males. As the growth spurt kicks in, boys generally lose most of the extra fat, whereas girls tend to keep it. Obesity, especially in industrialized countries like the United States, often becomes a problem beginning in preadolescence (see the box Current Issues: Obesity in Childhood—An Outcome of Our Changing Lifestyle? in Chapter 8).

The physical changes that occur upon entry into adolescence are controlled largely by **hormones,** which are biochemical substances that are secreted into the bloodstream in very tiny amounts by internal organs called *endocrine glands.* Hormones that eventually trigger adolescent growth and change are present in trace amounts from the fetal period onward, but their production greatly increases at about age 10 for girls and age 12 for boys—although there is considerable variability in the timing of these events for different children. This increase in hormone output is followed by the **adolescent growth spurt,** a period of rapid growth in physical size and strength, accompanied by changes in body proportions. Especially for girls, the growth spurt is a sign of entry into adolescence; the more noticeable changes associated with **puberty** (sexual maturity) follow the growth spurt by about a year (see Figure 10-2).

Clumsiness and awkwardness typically accompany the growth spurt as children learn to control their "new" bodies. Some of the clumsiness also occurs because the growth spurt is not always symmetrical; one leg may temporarily be longer than the other, one hand larger than the other. As you might imagine, the growth spurt is accompanied by an increase in appetite—especially for boys—as the body seeks the nutrients necessary for such rapid growth. Another change is an increase in the size and activity of *sebaceous* (oil-producing) glands in the skin, which can cause a teenager's face to break out in acne. Increased growth and activity of the sweat glands in the skin, especially in the armpit, result in a stronger body odor.

Male and Female Hormones Interestingly, both *male* and *female* hormones are present in members of both sexes. However, beginning in adolescence, males begin to produce considerably

hormones
Biochemical substances that are secreted into the bloodstream in very small amounts by the internal organs called endocrine glands; hormones exert an effect on particular target organs or tissues

adolescent growth spurt
A period of rapid growth in physical size and strength, accompanied by changes in body proportions, that occurs with the entrance into puberty

puberty
The attainment of sexual maturity in males and females

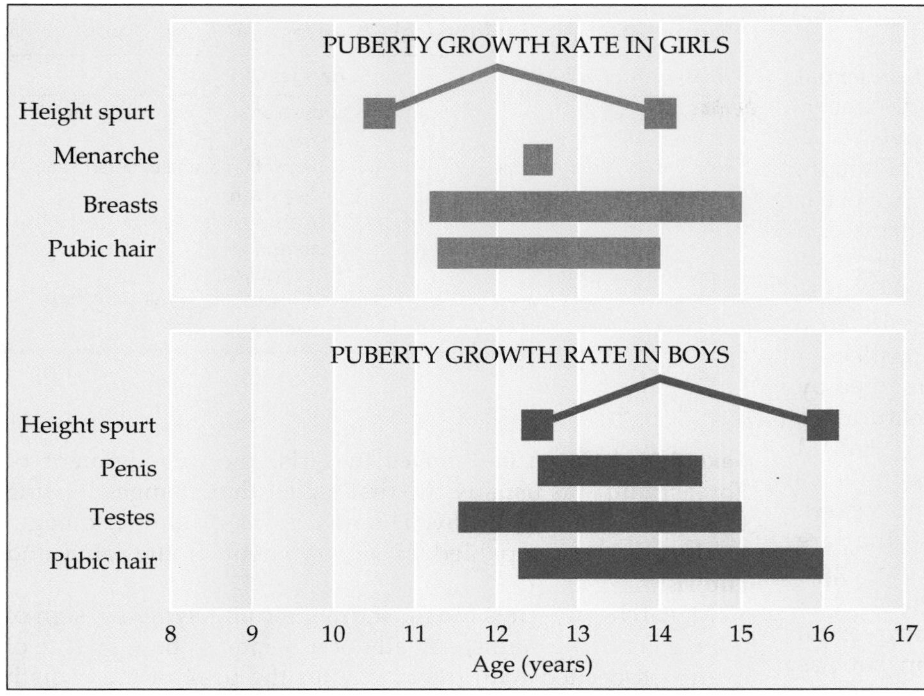

FIGURE 10-2 Growth Rates and Sexual Development During Puberty
The peak in the line labeled "height spurt" represents the point of most rapid growth. The bars below represent the average beginning and end of the events of puberty.

more of the hormones called **androgens**, of which the most important is **testosterone**, and females begin to produce more of the hormones **estrogen** and **progesterone**. These *sex* hormones act by influencing a specific set of targets or receptors. For example, the secretion of testosterone causes the penis to grow, the shoulders to broaden, and hair to grow in the genital area and on the face. Similarly, estrogen causes the uterus and breasts to grow and the hips to broaden.

Maintaining the balance in the production of hormones, including the sex hormones, is the job of two areas of the brain—the *hypothalamus* and the *pituitary gland.* The hypothalamus is the part of the brain that, among its other many functions, initiates growth and eventual reproductive capability during adolescence. The pituitary, located on the underside of the brain, is a "master gland" that produces several varieties of hormones. These include *growth hormone,* which controls the overall growth of the body, as well as some secondary *trophic* hormones. Trophic hormones stimulate and regulate the functioning of other glands, including the sex glands—the ovaries in females and the testes in males. In females, the sex glands secrete estrogens and regulate ovulation; in males, the sex glands secrete androgens and produce sperm.

Hormones also have a powerful effect on the brain and the nervous system. One way they act is through their early influence on brain development. Hormones present during the prenatal period can influence the growth and organization of the brain. We are only now beginning to understand the intricacies of how such processes unfold. Hormones also may activate specific behaviors at any point of development through their effects on the nervous system. Although conventional wisdom about adolescent behavior suggests that this is a period of "raging hormones" that instantly trigger radically changing moods and emotional outbursts, research suggests that such behavior, when it does occur, is the result of a complex set of factors. Among these factors are the adolescent's changing roles and responsibilities; social or cultural expectations that require difficult adjustments; or specific situations in home, school, or personal relationships that cause anxiety and other emotional responses (Guttman & Eccles, 2007). However, hormones do appear to trigger emotionality through their action on regions of the brain responsible for emotional control. The often volatile and risky behavior of adolescents may involve a complex interaction between the ongoing development in the adolescent brain and the specific way hormones influence its functioning, which we explore later in this chapter.

Puberty

Sexuality at any point during the lifespan is a complex affair, involving biological processes, social constraints and expectations, and emotional and intellectual responses. Because sexual maturation occurs during adolescence, this is also the time

▲ The onset of puberty requires considerable adaptation, whether to a suddenly crackly voice, longer legs, or unfamiliar passions or feelings.

androgens
Male sex hormones

progesterone
An important female sex hormone

testosterone
The primary male sex hormone

estrogen
An important female sex hormone

when all kinds of behaviors related to sexual attitudes and responsiveness emerge.

As noted earlier, puberty refers to the attainment of sexual maturity and the ability to have children (Archibald, Graber, & Brooks-Gunn, 2008). For girls, the approach of puberty is marked by the first menstrual period, or **menarche**; although, contrary to popular belief, the first ovulation may occur a year or more later. For boys, puberty is marked by the first emission of semen that contains viable sperm cells.

In many parts of the world, the onset of puberty is associated with major religious, cultural, or economic significance and may trigger elaborate rites and ceremonies. Regardless of its cultural importance, however, puberty is accompanied by several changes, including those related to sexual maturation (see Table 10-3). These changes frequently are dichotomized into those that are linked to the primary sex characteristics and those that trigger development of the secondary sex characteristics. *Primary sex characteristics* are those that are necessary for reproduction—production of mature *ova* (eggs) in women or of sperm in men. *Secondary sex characteristics* are the physical changes that are associated with sexual maturation but do not directly involve reproduction, such as the growth of pubic hair and changes in musculature and fat distribution.

Sexual Maturation in Males In boys, the first indication of puberty is accelerating growth of the testes and scrotum. The penis undergoes a similar acceleration in growth about 1 year later. In the meantime, pubic hair begins to appear but hair growth is not completed until after genital development is finished. During this period, there are also increases in the size of the heart and lungs. Because of the presence of testosterone, boys develop more red blood cells than girls. The extensive production of red blood cells may be one factor in the average superior strength and athletic ability of adolescent boys. The first emission of semen may take place as early as age 11 or as late as age 16. A boy's first ejaculation usually occurs during the growth spurt and may be a result of masturbation or it may occur during sleep in a "wet dream." These first emissions generally do not contain fertile sperm.

Which of the developing secondary sexual characteristics seem to generate a sense of pride among adolescent men? Are there some such changes that typically trigger embarrassment?

Characteristically, descriptions of adolescent boys include their awkwardly cracking voices. The actual voice change takes place relatively late in the sequence of pubertal changes; however, in many boys it occurs too gradually to constitute a developmental milestone.

Table 10-3 Typical Physical Changes in Adolescence

Changes in Girls	Changes in Boys
• Breast development	• Growth of testes and scrotal sac
• Growth of pubic hair	• Growth of pubic hair
• Growth of underarm hair	• Growth of facial and underarm hair
• Body growth	• Body growth
• Menarche	• Growth of penis
• Increased output of oil- and sweat-producing glands	• Change in voice
	• First ejaculation of semen
	• Increased output of oil- and sweat-producing glands

Sexual Maturation in Females In girls, the development of "breast buds" is usually the first signal that changes leading to puberty are under way. The uterus and vagina also begin to develop, accompanied by enlargement of the labia and clitoris.

Menarche, which is the most dramatic and symbolic sign of a girl's changing status, actually occurs late in the sequence of events associated with puberty, after the peak of the growth spurt. It may occur as early as age 9½ or as late as age 16½; in the United States, the average age at menarche currently is just under age 12½ (Vigil, Geary, & Byrd-Craven, 2005). In the United States, the age of menarche is continuing to decline, probably in part due to the increase in childhood obesity (McDowell, Brody, & Hughes, 2007). For example, from about 1990 to 2002, the decline was about a half month for White and Black girls, nearly 2 months for Mexican-American girls, but about 14 months—more than a year—for girls who were defined as being of an "other" racial ethnic group (Dershewitz, 2006). Clearly, cultural forces have an impact on the timing of sexual maturity.

Not surprisingly, given the impact of culture, in some parts of the world, menarche occurs considerably later than it does in the United States (Dosoky & Amoudi, 1997). For example, the average girl in the Czech Republic has her first period at age 14; among the Kikuyu of Kenya, the average age is 16; and for the Bindi of New Guinea, it is 18 (Powers, Hauser, & Kilner, 1989). Menarche typically occurs when a girl is nearing her adult height and has stored some body fat. For a girl of average height, menarche typically occurs when she weighs about 100 pounds (Frisch, 1988). Also, in earlier times, puberty generally occurred later than it does now (Tanner, 1998). In the 1840s, for example, the average age at puberty was 16½ for U.S. girls, and the social transition from youth to adulthood followed closely behind—in contrast to what happens today. This **secular trend**—the historical trend toward earlier sexual maturation—has occurred in many industrialized nations; however, it is not seen in all cultures.

menarche
The time of the first menstrual period

secular trend
The historical trend toward earlier sexual maturation

Watch *Adolescent Sexuality: Deborah L. Tolman* on MyDevelopmentLab

Watch *Development of Dating in Boys Versus Girls* on MyDevelopmentLab

Regardless of when they first occur, the first few menstrual cycles can vary greatly from one girl to another; they also tend to vary from one month to the next. In many cases, the early cycles are irregular and *anovulatory;* that is, a mature ovum is not produced. However, it is thoroughly unwise for a young teenage girl to assume that she is infertile. (We return to the subject of teenage pregnancy later in the chapter.)

Because the onset of menstruation provides such a clear marker for the beginning of sexual maturity in girls, there has been considerable research directed at understanding those factors that appear to advance or delay its onset. It is assumed that such influences also affect boys in comparable ways, although their sexual maturation is less obvious and therefore harder to study. One factor that affects the timing of the onset of menstruation is related to nutrition and general health, which are primary forces accounting for the secular trend. Girls from lower socioeconomic backgrounds, for instance, generally mature later (Dosoky & Amoudi, 1997). This is probably due to poorer nutrition and less access to health care. Age of menarche is linked to the level of body fat, although the precise nature of this relationship is not clear at the present time (Bau, 2009; Sherar, Baxter-Jones, & Mirwald, 2007). Genetics is most likely involved as well: Girls typically reach menarche at ages similar to those of their mothers (Segal & Stohs, 2007). Psychological issues may also be involved. For example, girls who grow up in supportive families tend to develop more slowly, especially if they have a warm, positive relationship with their fathers (Tither & Ellis, 2008). Undoubtedly, these—and most likely other—factors interact and most likely account for the variations observed in the average age at which menarche occurs across cultures, as well as within subcultures in the United States. Although the average age of menarche of White girls in the United States is presently 12½, African-American and Hispanic girls reach this developmental milestone 3 to 6 months earlier (Chumlea, et al., 2003; McDowell, Brody, & Hughes, 2007).

Although some girls view menarche as a positive event, many do not. One study found that only 23% of girls had positive attitudes about this event (Seiffge-Krenke, 1998). This may be because menstruation is accompanied by menstrual cramping in nearly half of all teenage girls. Premenstrual tension is also common and is often accompanied by irritability, depression, crying, bloating, and breast tenderness, although these symptoms usually can be reduced or eliminated with appropriate treatment (Goldman, 2007).

Body Image and Adjustment

As mentioned earlier, adolescents continually appraise their changing bodies. Are they the right shape and size? Are they coordinated or clumsy? How do they compare with the ideals portrayed by their culture?

Adolescents belong to what sociologists call a **marginal group**, a group between cultures or on the fringe of a dominant culture. Consequently, they typically exhibit an intensified need to conform. Adolescents can be intolerant of deviation from the expected norm, whether that be in body type (being too fat or too thin), extent of maturation (maturing late or early), or any number of traits they deem significant to their self-image. The mass media contribute to this intolerance by presenting stereotypical and idealized images of attractive, exuberant youths who glide through adolescence without pimples, braces, awkwardness, or weight problems. Because many adolescents are extremely sensitive about their appearance, discrepancies between their less-than-perfect self-image and the glowing ideals they see in the media often foster considerable anxiety and self-doubt (Birkeland, Melkevik, Holsen, & Wold, 2012).

Concerns About Body Image During middle childhood, children become keenly aware of different body types and ideals and gain a fairly clear idea of their own body type, proportions, and skills. In adolescence, social comparison with peers occurs almost continually and body type receives especially close scrutiny. Some young people subject themselves to intense dieting, whereas others engage in rigorous regimens of physical fitness and strength training. For boys, the primary concern is physical size and strength, and in particular their height and musculature are most important (Smolak & Stein, 2010). Girls, in contrast, more often worry about being too fat or too tall. (Ata, Ludden, & Lally, 2007). They focus on weight largely because of their concern with social acceptance. Thus, many normal weight and even lean adolescent girls consider themselves overweight. When carried to an extreme, such concerns can lead to obesity or to eating disorders, particularly **anorexia nervosa**, where a person is obsessed by thoughts of an unobtainable image of "perfect" thinness, and **bulimia nervosa**, which is characterized by bingeing and purging (see the box Current Issues: Diet and Exercise—Building a Healthy Lifestyle or an Eating Disorder?).

Who are the media personalities in today's culture that adolescents most aspire to be like? Do these people represent a particular desirable set of physical characteristics?

Although eating disorders are much less common among adolescent boys than girls, both groups are concerned about their size, shape, and physical appearance. Worries about skin are especially common: Almost half of all adolescents voice concerns about pimples and blackheads. Most also wish for one or more physical changes in themselves, although such self-consciousness diminishes in late adolescence and emerging adulthood. One longitudinal study found that satisfaction with body image is lowest for girls at age 13 and for boys at age 15; then it rises steadily. At every age from 11 to 18, however, it is

marginal group
A group between cultures or on the fringe of a dominant culture that typically exhibits an intensified need to conform

anorexia nervosa
An eating disorder in which a person is obsessed by thoughts of an unattainable image of "perfect" thinness; usually characterized by extreme thinness, which can result in death

bulimia nervosa
An eating disorder characterized by bingeing and purging

CURRENT ISSUES

Diet and Exercise—Building a Healthy Lifestyle or an Eating Disorder?

In contrast to toddlers and younger children, who for the most part are oblivious to how their bodies grow and change, adolescents are very aware of how their bodies look to themselves and to others. Even in cultural groups where preoccupation with one's appearance is frowned upon, most adolescents make note of how their bodies compare with those of their peers, as well as with the idealized images of what young people in their culture are *supposed* to look like. Adolescents in the United States certainly are bombarded by media images of young people with perfect hair, straight white teeth, beautiful complexions, and bodies that are perfectly sculpted and proportioned.

Body size and shape, of course, are influenced by heredity and by diet and exercise. During the adolescent years, young people sometimes become absorbed with issues of body image, and they try to adjust their eating habits and physical activities in an attempt to develop their bodies so that they conform more closely to their ideal image of what they should look like. When adolescents choose a healthy, balanced diet and undertake appropriate exercise programs, these efforts can be positive. However, a preoccupation with body image can become destructive for some adolescents, leading to unhealthy behavior that results in obesity or, conversely, in an eating disorder. What factors appear to be involved with obesity and eating disorders?

Obesity during the teenage years is an increasingly prevalent problem in the United States, as well as in many other industrialized countries. The 2007–2010 National Health and Nutrition Examination Survey (NHANES), compiled by the United States National Center for Health Statistics, revealed that over 18% of all U.S. teens were obese: In 1976 to 1980 this percentage was only 5%. Some ethnic groups are particularly at risk, as the NHANES data in the following table show. Lifestyle factors—such as reduced physical activity; the abundance of high-calorie, high-fat, and high-carbohydrate foods; and sedentary lifestyles—are major factors contributing to these societal shifts.

On the other end of the spectrum, chronic dieting may affect another 10 to 15% of U.S. adolescents, particularly (but not exclusively) girls (Polivy, Herman, Mills, & Wheeler, 2008). Surveys typically indicate that about half of adolescent girls and about one-fourth of adolescent boys report having been on some sort of diet during the previous year (Neumark-Sztainer, Wall, Larson, Eisenberg, & Loth, 2011). Just over 90% of women surveyed on one college campus reported that they have attempted to control their weight by dieting (National Association of Anorexia Nervosa, 2012), and this result is probably emblematic of students on many campuses in the United States.

▲ These teenage runway models are backstage awaiting the start of a fashion show. In the competition to meet the "ideal image," some will starve themselves and do serious damage to their bodies.

At the extreme, over 100,000 U.S. young people, most of them in their teens or early 20s, are quietly starving themselves into a self-monitored set of disease symptoms called *anorexia nervosa.* Others struggle with *bulimia nervosa,* another eating disorder that is characterized by eating "binges" that then trigger "purges," during which vomiting, laxatives, or sometimes extreme exercise regimens are used to eliminate the caloric intake of the just-eaten food. Still other teenagers engage in a third, broader, form of eating disorder, which typically involves chronic dieting, with its roller-coaster pattern of weight loss followed by relapse and weight gain (Eddy, Herzog, & Zucker, 2011).

Anorexia is a particularly serious problem because the obsession with food and thinness that characterize it can result in self-induced starvation. Anorexia affects about 1% of teenage girls, and about 20% of people diagnosed with this disorder will die from related complications, which include suicide and organ failure (National Association of Anorexia Nervosa, 2012). Bulimia also is a serious problem which, like anorexia, is about 10 times more common among women than men. Bulimia affects about 4% of U.S. women, and is sometimes difficult to detect, given that bulimics usually are

Prevalence of Obesity by Race/Ethnicity Among 12- to 19-Year-Olds

	Percent obese: 1988–1994	Percent obese: 2007–2010
Non-Hispanic White boys	11.6	17.1
Non-Hispanic White girls	7.4	14.6
Non-Hispanic Black boys	10.7	21.2
Non-Hispanic Black girls	13.2	27.1
Mexican-American boys	14.1	27.9%
Mexican-American girls	9.2	18.0

SOURCE: CDC (2011).

of normal body weight and often keep their bingeing and purging behavior a secret (Chavez & Insel, 2007).

Why do some young people develop disorders associated with eating? Both anorexia and bulimia are associated with body-image problems, meaning that typically these disorders involve both a distorted self-image, as well as an unrealistic view of an ideal body type: Those affected typically see themselves as fat, although, especially in the case of anorexia, they actually are overly thin, and perhaps even dangerously thin.

Many researchers have argued that the culture of female thinness widely portrayed as desirable in contemporary Western culture may be at the root of such problems for many genetically vulnerable young women. Personality factors also may be involved in the development of eating disorders. Young people who tend to be perfectionists, who are achievement oriented, and who are high in their need for control are those most likely to develop eating disorders and associated problems. Lifestyle choices may be implicated as well. Those who engage in strenuous exercise or who participate seriously in sports—especially gymnastics, wrestling, figure skating, diving, and ballet—also have been found to be at increased risk for eating disorders (National Association of Anorexia Nervosa, 2012). Those who diet repeatedly in an attempt to control their weight also are at greater risk for developing serious eating disorders (Goldschmidt, Wall, Loth, Le Grange, & Neumark-Sztainer, 2012).

Biology undoubtedly plays a role in the development of eating disorders (Racine, Root, Klump, & Bulik, 2011). Eating disorders tend to run in families, indicating a genetic component, which may be expressed through disturbances in neurotransmitter systems in the brain (Chavez & Insel, 2007; Polivy, Herman, & Boivin, 2008). The neurotransmitter serotonin is especially likely to be involved. Particularly among males, eating disorders are associated with depression, which is another disorder that likely involves serotonin pathways (Loth, Mond, Wall, & Neumark-Sztainer, 2011). Although the research on the link between eating disorders and mood disturbances largely is correlational, such evidence does suggest a biochemical factor may be implicated. Hormones also may play a role. Testosterone, which is present in a much higher proportion in adolescent boys than in adolescent girls, may serve as a protective factor against the development of these disorders.

Identifying the causes of an individual's eating disorder is a very difficult task. The factors noted previously affect individuals in different ways and to different degrees, and the pathways through which they interact are undoubtedly complex. Consequently, treatment must be tailored to the individual. In a culture that is bombarded with images of the perfect body, it is not hard to envision the pressures felt, especially by teenagers, to achieve such an idealized size and shape. Among those adolescents who are vulnerable, such cultural pressures may be sufficient to trigger the development of an eating disorder, with its associated symptoms and consequences.

▲ One reason girls often feel more mature than boys their own age is that the female growth spurt during puberty occurs about 2 years before the male growth spurt.

lower for girls than for boys (Rauste-von Wright, 1989; Vogt, 2010; Wertheim & Paxson, 2011), which may reflect a culture that is more critical of the physical appearance of girls. Mothers may play an especially important role in adolescent girls' body image. For girls, having a positive body image during adolescence is directly correlated with whether their mothers have a positive body image (Usmiani & Daniluk, 1997).

Early and Late Maturers As noted earlier, both sexes display wide variability in the timing of the hormone changes associated with entry into adolescence, causing some children to reach sexual maturity at considerably earlier ages than others. Although many teenagers have a fairly positive attitude toward their own rate of maturation (Pelletz, 1995), ill-timed maturation can be a problem. This is especially true for late-maturing boys.

Because girls mature on average 2 years earlier than boys, a late-maturing boy is the last of all adolescents to begin the growth spurt and reach puberty. Thus, he is smaller and less muscular than his male peers, which puts him at a disadvantage in most sports, as well as in many social situations. Other children and adults tend to treat a late-maturing boy as though he were a younger child, and the late maturer typically has a lower social status among his peers and often is perceived as less competent by adults (Brackbill & Nevill, 1981). Sometimes this perception becomes a self-fulfilling prophecy, and the boy reacts with childish dependence and immature behavior. In other cases, the boy may overcompensate by becoming highly aggressive. (Graber, Seeley, Brooks-Gunn, & Lewinsohn, 2004). In contrast, early-maturing boys tend to

If you could have chosen the age at which you reached puberty, what age would you have chosen? Why would you choose this age?

Watch *Anorexia Nervosa: Tamora* on **MyDevelopmentLab**

Watch *Body Image and Eating Disorders* on **MyDevelopmentLab**

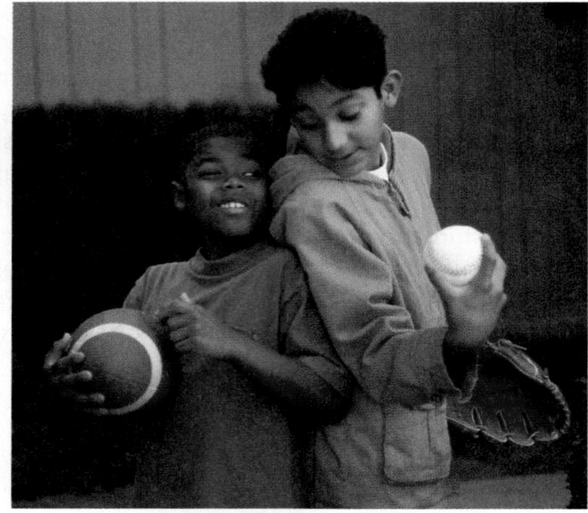

Two boys of the same age and grade can be at dramatically different points in their personal growth curve, a situation that can affect their self-image.

gain social and athletic advantages among their peers and enjoy a positive self-fulfilling prophecy. However, early maturation also can be a problem; valuable skills normally learned in childhood may be skipped, and expectations for adult behavior may become a confusing burden (Sussman, Dorn, & Schiefelbein, 2003). Early maturation, for example, is associated with alcohol abuse during adolescence, which sometimes persists into adulthood (Biehl, Natsuaki, & Ge, 2007). Overall, then, early maturation comes with both advantages and disadvantages for boys (Blumenthal, et al., 2011; Reardon, Leen-Feldner, & Hayward, 2009).

Early maturation is rarely a benefit for girls, at least not initially (Blumenthal, et al., 2011; DeRose, Shiyko, Foster, & Brooks-Gunn, 2011). Early-maturing girls are taller and more developed than all of their peers, both male and female. One effect is that they have fewer opportunities to discuss their physical and emotional changes with friends. Another is that they are significantly more likely to experience psychological distress over their maturity (Ge, Conger, & Elder, 1996) and be teased by peers. They also may be considered "easy" by older boys (Reynolds & Juvonen, 2011). All of these factors may contribute to the finding that early maturation in girls is correlated with lower self-esteem and other negative psychological issues, and this seems particularly true for White girls (DeRose, Shiyko, Foster, & Brooks-Gunn, 2011; Graber, Seeley, Brooks-Gunn, & Lewinsohn, 2004).

As is true for early-maturing boys, if girls' maturation is dramatically early—at ages 8 or 9—they also may miss valuable childhood psychological development. They also may be pressured into early sexual behavior: Both girls and boys who mature early are sexually active at younger ages on average. Like early-maturing boys, early-maturing girls typically experience higher psychological stress, and they exhibit higher rates of deviant behavior than their later-maturing age mates (Obeidallah, Brennan, Brooks-Gunn, & Earls, 2004; Sussman, Dorn, & Schiefelbein, 2003). After a difficult period of initial adjustment, however, some early-maturing girls eventually come to enjoy some benefits. For example, they may feel more attractive than their girlish-looking peers, they often are more popular with older boys, and they are more likely to date than their late-maturing peers. Late maturation for girls also can be advantageous because these girls mature at about the same time as most of their peers who are boys. They are therefore in a better position to share boy's interests and privileges. They also may be more popular with their age peers than are early-maturing girls.

Regardless of how individuals enter sexual maturity—early or late or with a positive or negative body image—they will bring certain attitudes and values to their experiences associated with becoming a sexual person. Although each person's experiences are unique, cultural expectations and norms play an important role in guiding adolescent attitudes and behaviors about sex. In the next section, we explore gender identity and sexual practices in adolescence.

REVIEW THE FACTS 10-2

1. During which of the following periods is biological change *least* rapid?
   a. the fetal period   b. infancy
   c. middle childhood   d. adolescence
2. Sexual maturation is called ________.
3. The primary male hormone is ________ and the two primary female hormones are ________ and ________.
4. The occurrence of a girl's first menstrual period is referred to as ________.
5. The finding that adolescents in many developed countries are reaching puberty at younger ages now than in the past is called the ________.
6. With respect to body image, teenage boys usually are most worried about being too ________, whereas girls are more concerned with being too ________.
   a. fat; tall   b. weak; fat
   c. tall; short   d. tall; fat
7. Is late maturation especially problematic for boys or for girls?

Practice on MyDevelopmentLab

GENDER IDENTITY AND SEXUAL PRACTICES

Some of the most interesting documentation of cross-cultural differences gathered by cultural anthropologists details how sexuality is displayed in various societies. As you are undoubtedly aware, wide variations exist, although sexuality is an important aspect of all cultures around the world. Elaborate rituals and strict social expectations have developed to govern sexual behavior, as well as attitudes about how, when, and with whom that behavior is to be revealed (Arnett, 2010a, 2012). Although a discussion of cross-cultural sexual norms and behavior is beyond the scope of this text, we will explore how social attitudes have changed—and rather dramatically—in the United States over the past 50 years and how these changes affect the sexual behavior and attitudes of contemporary American adolescents.

Six Decades of Changes in Sexual Practices

Expectations about appropriate adolescent sexual behavior in the 1950s and 1960s were quite different than what American teens encounter today. Before the mid-1960s, most young people felt that premarital sex was immoral, although peer pressure often impelled older adolescent boys to gain sexual experience before marriage. Girls, in contrast, were under pressure to remain chaste until marriage. By the late 1960s and early 1970s, sexual attitudes had changed considerably, partly because of the development and widespread distribution of birth control pills and partly because of the "free love" movement that accompanied protests against the Vietnam War and against "the establishment" in general. In a study of adolescent sexual attitudes during that era (Sorenson, 1973), for the first time, the majority of adolescents did not think of premarital sex as inherently right or wrong but instead judged it on the basis of the relationship between the participants—sexual relations before marriage were acceptable if the girl and boy were "in love." A majority also rejected the traditional **sexual double standard** that gave sexual freedom to boys but not to girls, reflecting themes of the women's movement and the crusade for civil rights. Almost 70% agreed that two people should not have to marry to have sex or live together. About 50% approved of **same-sex orientation**, which is defined by sexual attraction toward members of one's own sex. (A discussion of sexual orientation is presented in Chapter 12.) In all, beginning in the 1970s, the attitudes of teenagers in the United States generally were quite different from those of their much more conservative parents.

By the late 1970s, the *sexual revolution* was in full swing. Numerous studies reported an increasing trend toward sexual liberalization, reflected both by an increase in sexual activity among adolescents and by a change in societal attitudes. Society at large—not just young people—had become more accepting of a wide range of sexual behaviors, including masturbation, same-sex sexual activity, and unmarried couples having sex (Dreyer, 1982). In particular, the sexual revolution affected girls' behavior much more than it did boys' behavior. Although the percentage of adolescent boys who were sexually active remained constant from the 1940s through the 1970s, the proportion of 16-year-old girls who reported losing their virginity rose from 7% in the 1940s to 33% in 1971 and to 44% in 1982 (Brooks-Gunn & Furstenberg, 1986).

What factors do you think might have contributed to the dramatic increase that occurred between the 1940s and the 1980s in the percentage of girls who were sexually active?

However, by the 1980s, the sexual revolution was beginning to fade. Although there remained a wide variety of attitudes about sexuality, in general young people became more cautious about sexual activity, and monogamy—or at least serial monogamy—became fashionable again. For example, during the 1980s, when adolescents were asked what they thought of the sexual attitudes of the 1960s and 1970s, a sizable proportion viewed them as irresponsible. College students also were more likely to consider sexual promiscuity undesirable (Leo, 1984; Robinson & Jedlicka, 1982). The late 1980s saw a continuation of the trend toward more conservative attitudes about sexual matters (Murstein, Chalpin, Heard, & Vyse, 1989). Although young people still considered sex an essential part of romance, they were generally not in favor of casual sex (Abler & Sedlacek, 1989). Attitudes toward same-sex orientation and same-sex sexual activity also became more negative, reflecting a return to more conservative values (Williams & Jacoby, 1989).

Throughout the 1990s and into the first decade of the 21st century, cultural values in the United States regarding sexuality had largely stabilized, partly as the result of the aging of those who initiated the sexual revolution and who now find themselves squarely in middle age and partly because of increased attention to sexual education that resulted from the AIDS epidemic. In fact, youth today may be somewhat more conservative than their parents were. In 1991, for example, 37.5% of high school students reported being sexually active; in 2011 the comparable percentage was 33.7% (CDC, 2011k). Similar patterns occur when looking at the percent of high school students who report ever having had sexual intercourse: In 1991, this percentage was 54.1%; 20 years later it was 46% (National Center for Health Statistics [NCHS], 2011d). Although today there are wide variations in the expectations about what constitutes proper sexual behavior among both adolescents and adults, most people recognize that many adolescents will become sexually active at some point, most likely before they are married. The data bear this out: In 2009, about one-third of 9th graders had engaged in sexual intercourse, and almost two-thirds of 12th graders had engaged in it (NCHS, 2011d; see Figure 10-3).

Regardless of the specific generation in which a person comes of age, the emerging sexuality that is a biological feature of adolescence must be integrated into the adolescent's developing sense of self-concept. Adolescents must forge a new identity into which their masculinity or femininity is incorporated. Furthermore, this *gender identity* must not only be consistent with biological urges but also with relationships with friends, family, and community. It is important to remember that sexual behavior occurs in the context of relationships—romantic, casual, manipulative, teasing, or exploratory. Adolescents need to construct "gender scripts" that not only include the concepts of male and female but that also incorporate their own nature as sexual beings.

In the United States and in many industrialized countries, social attitudes about sex that are conveyed by parents, schools, and most religions are typically quite restrictive about the adolescent's practice of sexual behavior. Yet the media

sexual double standard
The view that sexual activity is more permissible for boys than for girls

same-sex orientation
Sexual attraction toward members of one's own sex

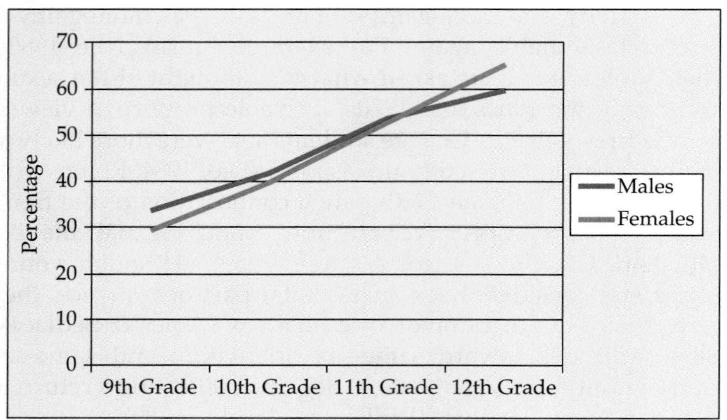

FIGURE 10-3 Percent of High School Students Who Ever Had Sexual Intercourse, by Gender and Year in School, 2009

SOURCE: Table 67, "Health risk behaviors among students in grades 9–12, by sex, grade level, race, and Hispanic origin: United States, selected years 1991–2009, in *Health, United States, 2011*, by the National Center for Health Statistics, Hyattsville, MD: Author.

often encourage permissive attitudes, and most adolescents are very aware of issues involving sexuality. These competing perspectives often produce psychological conflict as teenagers attempt to reconcile their feelings of sexual desire with the culture's expectations to exercise restraint (Crockett, Raffaelli, & Moilanen, 2003; Crockett & Silbereisen, 2000).

Factors That Influence Early Sexual Relationships

Although societal attitudes in the United States toward sexual behavior are somewhat more conservative now than they were in the 1970s, teenagers continue to be highly active sexually. The age at which they first have sex varies modestly by gender; it also varies considerably by ethnic group. In 2009, for example, 29% of female and 34% of male 9th graders reported being sexually active; however, this gender difference had reversed by 12th grade, with 65% of females and 60% of males reporting sexual activity (CDC, 2011m). Today, differences in sexual activity are more pronounced among ethnic groups than between genders. Sexual activity generally begins at a much earlier age for adolescent boys and girls who identify themselves as Black and also at a somewhat younger age for adolescent boys who identify themselves as Hispanic (see Figure 10-4).

Sexual activity also is associated with the adolescent's family situation. For example, adolescent boys and girls from two-parent families tend to have less and later sexual experience than those from single-parent families (Crockett, & Silbereisen, 2003; Zimmer-Gembeck & Helfand, 2008). Numerous studies have found that parent–child interactions also are involved. Adolescents who are sexually active are more likely to report poor communication with their parents. In contrast, high-quality parent–child communication has been correlated with adolescent sexual abstinence, as well as with safer sexual practices (Aspey et al., 2007; Deptula & Henry, 2010). Good parent–child relationships will not necessarily prevent young people from experimenting with sex, however. Attitudes of peers about sex are also very important. So, too, is the degree to which adolescents can rely on their peers for social support (Dishion, Ha, Nijmegen, & Veronneau, 2012; Hampton, McWatters, Jeffery, & Smith, 2005). If peers are engaging in risky sexual behavior, this often creates a situation in which conformity is expected and high status and popularity accrue to those who are sexually active (Moilanen, Crockett, Raffaelli, & Jones, 2010; Prinstein, Meade, & Cohen, 2003).

As noted earlier, the age at which sexual maturity occurs also plays a role in adolescent sexual activity. Individuals who mature early are likely to engage in sexual activity at a younger age than those who mature late (Miller, Norton, Fan, & Christopherson, 1998; Zimmer-Gembeck & Helfand, 2008). Additionally, regardless of when or why it occurs, early sexual activity, especially among boys, has been associated with other risky behaviors, such as drug use and delinquency (Bersamin, Walker, Fisher, & Grube, 2006; Lohman & Billings, 2008), which are topics we explore in more detail in the next chapter.

Consequences of Adolescent Sexual Behavior

The sexual revolution, and the increase in adolescent sexual activity it produced, has been accompanied by a variety of problems. Certainly one of the most serious of these is the spread of sexually transmitted diseases (STDs), often at epidemic proportions (see Chapter 12 for a discussion of STDs). About 19 million new cases of STDs are diagnosed each year in the United States, and nearly half of these are in adolescents. By age 24, it is estimated that about one-third of all sexually active young adults will have contracted one or more STDs (CDC, 2010). Although estimates are quite difficult to make, researchers generally believe that, at any given point in time, about 20% of sexually active U.S. teenagers will have an STD (DiClemente & Crosby, 2003). Among adolescents, the most common STDs are genital herpes and chlamydia, which both affect more women than men (CDC, 2011k). Both of these diseases can cause serious harm to a woman's reproductive system, increasing the risk of infertility and ectopic pregnancy. Fortunately, these diseases, and most other STDs, can be treated effectively, once an accurate diagnosis is made.

Why are educational programs that outline the risks associated with STDs not completely effective? What might be done to enhance their effectiveness among an adolescent population?

Watch *Adolescent Sexual Behavior* on **MyDevelopmentLab**

Watch *Dating in Adolescence* on **MyDevelopmentLab**

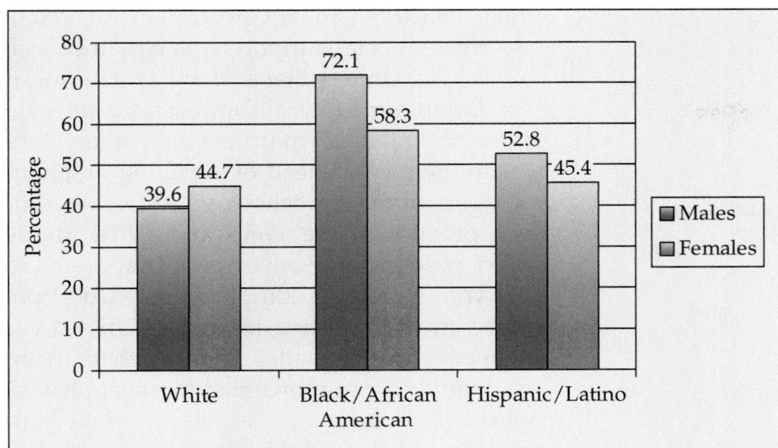

FIGURE 10-4 Percent of High School Students Who Ever Had Sexual Intercourse, by Gender and Racial/Ethnic Identity, 2009

SOURCE: Table 67, "Health risk behaviors among students in grades 9–12, by sex, grade level, race, and Hispanic origin: United States, selected years 1991–2009, in *Health, United States, 2011*, by the National Center for Health Statistics, Hyattsville, MD: Author.

The notable exception is, of course, AIDS, which is the disease that develops from infection with the human immunodeficiency virus, HIV. At present, HIV can be held in check for a while if powerful antiretroviral drugs are taken, but AIDS cannot be cured. Although most AIDS cases are diagnosed in adulthood, there are cases diagnosed in children and adolescents. Based on government estimates, about 5% of the people living with AIDS in the United States are between the ages of 13 and 24. However, it is reasonable to believe that this estimate is probably low, as the onset of disease symptoms often takes months or years to occur, and at least some adolescents who are infected are not aware that they are carrying the virus. Even so, in 2009, about 2,600 new cases of HIV were diagnosed among people in this age group, most of whom were male (CDC, 2011l). Unfortunately, although the rate of AIDS diagnosis declined between the years of 1993 and 1998, since that time the rate of diagnosis among adolescents has been increasing each year, and there is no leveling in sight. The increasing rate of HIV infection among adolescents appears not to be due to a lack of information about this disease. In fact, adolescents who are sexually active are generally aware of the risk of contracting AIDS. For example, in 2011, 12.9% of high school students were tested for the virus—a little more than a third of the number who reported being sexually active in that year (CDC, 2011l).

The risk of STD is high for adolescents and emerging adults, and so too is the risk of unplanned pregnancy. About 3.4% of girls between the ages of 15 and 19 gave birth in 2010, along with 9.0% of those age 20 to 24 (Hamilton, Martin, & Ventura, 2011), with a majority of these births being unplanned. Of course, the pregnancy rate is somewhat higher than these birth numbers describe, owing to miscarriage and abortion—the rates of both of which are somewhat higher for teens than they are for older mothers. Today, a little more half of teenagers who become pregnant give birth, about one-quarter of pregnancies (26%) are lost through abortion, and about one-fifth are lost due to miscarriage (20%) (Ventura, Curtin, & Abma, 2012). Taken together, these statistics suggest that the actual pregnancy rate is about 7 to 8% for girls of age 15 to 19, and about 16% for young women in the 20- to 24-year-old age group.

To understand teen pregnancy, it is important to consider cultural forces. Looking at births to teenagers age 15 to 17, two notable trends stand out (see Figure 10-5). First, there are large differences in fertility rates for girls in different racial/ethnic groups. For example, the fertility rate—the number of births per 1,000 women in the defined age group—is *much* higher for Black and Hispanic teenagers than it is for Asian-American adolescents. White Americans and Native Americans fall into the middle of this range. Second, the fertility rate for all groups has shifted dramatically over the past 30 years. The proportion of U.S. teens having babies reached a peak in about 1990, and since that time the fertility rate for women age 15 to 17 has declined steadily and dramatically, especially among Black and Hispanic teens. What factors influence the sexual behaviors of teenagers and emerging adults?

Why Teenagers Become Pregnant Although the rates of sexual activity among U.S. teenagers are comparable to those of most Western European nations, the pregnancy rates in those nations are generally much lower (Central Intelligence Agency, 2012). Why so many girls in the United States become pregnant is a major cause of concern. One factor seems to be that U.S. adolescents are less likely to use contraception.

Although today's teens are more likely to use contraception during intercourse than was the case in the early 1990s, there still are a sizeable number of adolescents who engage in sex without protection. Presently, about 22% of adolescent girls and 15% of adolescent boys do not use contraception at first intercourse (Martinez, Copen, & Abma, 2011). Most adolescents are not ignorant about the facts of reproduction. Rather, they are novices who are uncomfortable about making demands on a partner at times of high excitement. Some, too, are ambivalent about their own behavior; others take a passive attitude to the vagaries of desire. In addition, 7% of girls report that their first sexual intercourse was forced on them, that they were victims of rape. Another 11% report that their first sexual intercourse was voluntary but "unwanted," and almost half of adolescent girls report that they had "mixed feelings" about whether or not they wanted their first sexual encounter to happen (Marinez, Copen, & Abma, 2011). In these circumstances, birth control is generally not even considered (Crockett, et al., 2003). In all, about 41% of adolescent girls and 63% of adolescent boys wanted their first sexual experience to happen.

Watch *Sexually Transmissible Infections: Ken, STI Counselor* on **MyDevelopmentLab**

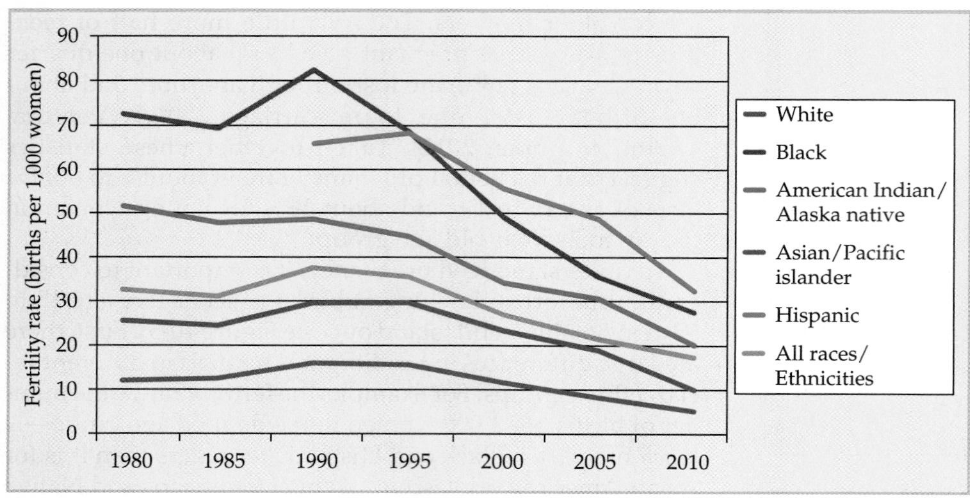

FIGURE 10-5 Ages 15 to 17, by Race/Ethnicity, for Four Decades, 1970–2010

SOURCE: "Births: Final data for 2009," by J. A. Martin, Brooks-Gunn, Klebanov, Buka, & McCormick, 2011, National-Vital Statistics Reports, 60(1); and "Births: Preliminary data for 2010," by B. E. Hamilton, J. A. Martin, & S. J. Ventura, *National Vital Statistics Reports, 60*(2). Both reports are published by the Centers for Disease Control and Prevention.

Thus, the sexual double standard continues to play a role in the way adolescents approach sexual encounters. At least among those adolescents who hold traditional values, both sexes tend to view the male as the sexual initiator and the female as the one who is responsible for setting limits on sexual activity. For example, boys are more likely to include contraception at first sex than are girls: Recall that only about 15% of adolescent boys failed to use contraception, compared to about 22% of girls (Martinez, Copen, & Abma, 2011).

As noted earlier, the rate of teen pregnancy and teen childbirth in the United States began a steady decline beginning in about 1992 (Martin, Brooks-Gunn, Klebanov, Buka, & McCormick, 2011). As can be seen in Figure 10-5, since 1992, births to adolescent mothers have dropped dramatically in all ethnic groups. This decline is likely the result of several factors. For example, teens today are more likely to use condoms, in part as the result of AIDS education and awareness. Also, broad-based educational programs have helped to redefine behavior and to encourage adolescents to think through the consequences of early parenting. Increased public attention also has prompted many changes that lead toward more responsible sexual behavior.

Culture, of course, is a very important determinant not only of what defines proper sexual behavior, but also how those who choose to engage in sexual activity are treated and supported. It should be noted that cultures around the world vary widely in their proportion of parents who are adolescents. For example, teen parenting is still the norm in sub-Saharan Africa, where over one-half of girls give birth before 18 years of age; however, in Japan and Korea, only 1% do (Central Intelligence Agency, 2012; Miller, Norton, Fan, & Christopherson, 2003). In terms of social support, it is certainly true that in the United States there is less social stigma and more formal support for teens who give birth outside of marriage today than there was in the past. Instead of expelling pregnant teenagers from high school, which was a common practice in the 1960s and 1970s, many school systems now have special programs to help young mothers complete their education. Government programs are in place that cover some expenses that adolescent mothers incur, and many young, unmarried mothers also receive support from their family, as well as from the father of their children. However, having a baby early in life does imply certain adjustments for the parents, regardless of whether or not the pregnancy was intended as well as the degree to which they are prepared to be parents.

Watch *Teen Pregnancy* on **MyDevelopmentLab**

The Effects of Early Parenthood What is the impact of early parenthood on a U.S. teenager's later development? Economically, the consequences are often damaging. Teenage mothers may be forced to drop out of school and therefore work at lower paying jobs, or they may become dependent on government support to help them meet expenses. Because of the pressures they feel to support their new family, many teenage fathers also leave school and take low-skilled, low-paying jobs. When teenage parents marry as a means of addressing an unplanned pregnancy, these marriages are more likely to involve conflict and to end in divorce. Although some early marriages are happy and long-lasting, many marriages under these circumstances do not involve positive outcomes, in part because early marriage often leads to dropping out of school.

In addition, a teenage pregnancy can be challenging because adolescent parents must deal with their own personal and social

It is generally difficult for teenage mothers to care for the needs of an infant while they also must attend to their own developmental needs.

development while trying to adapt to the needs of an infant or small child (Miller, Bayley, Christensen, Leavitt, & Coyl, 2003; Whiteley & Brown, 2010). Sometimes a teenage pregnancy is a response to the unmet need to feel loved, either because sexual activity was initiated as a means of forming a close relationship with another person or because one or both of the parents are expecting the dependent child to supply the love they feel is missing in their lives. In cases where teen parents have unrealistic ideas about the benefits they will receive through parenting, they likely will require help to achieve a realistic parenting relationship with their children. Table 10-4 summarizes some of the potential consequences of teen parenthood in the United States (Miller, et al., 2003).

If teenage parents do not marry, they may have no choice but to continue living at home in a dependent and perhaps disapproving situation during and after their pregnancy. Thus, some teenagers are motivated to get married in order to set up their own households. However, marriage is not necessarily the best solution to an adolescent mother's problems. Although early motherhood is often associated with previously noted challenges, in many cases it is preferable to early motherhood combined with early marriage. Adolescent marriage is more likely to lead to dropping out of high school than is adolescent pregnancy. Similarly, those who marry young are more likely to divorce than those who bear a child and marry later.

In some ways, children of teenage parents are at a disadvantage compared to children of older parents, as noted in Table 10-4 (Miller, et al., 2003). Young parents are more likely to neglect or abuse their children, most likely because these parents are often stressed and frustrated. Even if they are not abused, children may suffer from their teenage parents' lack of experience in handling adult responsibilities and caring for others. Children of teenage parents may be more likely to exhibit slow developmental and cognitive growth (Brooks-Gunn & Furstenberg, 1986; Dahinten, Shapka, & Willms, 2007), although some studies find that when adolescent parents have support, their children do not appear to be at a developmental disadvantage (Levine, Emery, & Pollack, 2007). If poverty, marital discord, and poor education exist simultaneously in the family for an extended period of time, the child's risk of developing emotional problems also increases (McLoyd, 1998; Scararnella, Neppl, Ontai, & Conger, 2008). Some teenage parents, however, do an excellent job of nurturing their children while continuing to grow toward adulthood themselves, especially if they receive assistance. Of course, much depends on the individual parents, on the resources available to them, on their resilience, and on the skills they bring to the tasks of parenting (see the box Try This! Exploring the Effects of Early Parenting).

How old were your parents when you were born? Do you think they would have been more effective parents if they had been older or younger? Why or why not?

Table 10-4 Summary of Teen Parenthood Consequences in the United States

People Affected	Consequences of Teen Parenthood (Compared to Older Parenthood)*
Adolescent mothers	• Less likely to marry the father of their first child • More likely to become divorced • More likely to spend twice as much time as a single parent prior to age 30 • More likely to drop out of school • Less likely to earn a high school diploma by age 30 • More likely to work more hours at a lower rate of pay
Adolescent fathers	• Less likely to earn a high school diploma • More likely to work in a blue-collar occupation • More likely to experience lower income levels • More likely to engage in delinquent and criminal behaviors
Children of adolescent parents	• More likely to be born premature and of low birth weight • More likely to experience serious or life-threatening medical conditions at birth • Less likely to receive quality medical care and nutrition • Less likely to receive necessary emotional support and cognitive stimulation • More likely to drop out of school • More likely to become involved in delinquent and criminal behaviors • More likely to bear children out of wedlock
Society	• Increased financial burden to taxpayers and extended families • Additional strain on the resources of governmental programs and systems

*The consequences for adolescent girls are in comparison to later-bearing mothers and the consequences for adolescent boys are in comparison to later-bearing fathers. The consequences for children of adolescent parents are in comparison to those raised by older parents.

SOURCE: From unnumbered table, "Adolescent pregnancy and childbirth," by Miller, et al., 2003, in G. R. Adams & M. D. Berzonsky (Eds.), *Blackwell handbook of adolescence* (p. 435). Copyright © 2003. Reprinted by permission of Blackwell Publishing, UK.

One challenge in addressing any problem associated with adolescent behavior concerns the level of understanding that teenagers are capable of. Although in many ways adolescents are more like adults than children, in other aspects of their life they have not yet developed mature adult capabilities. During the teenage years, the brain continues to develop, and it may not become capable of consistent and mature adult decision making until late in adolescence or even early adulthood. This raises questions such as: How do adolescent thought processes work? What changes occur in cognition as a 12-year-old child becomes an 18-year-old emerging adult? We address these and similar questions in the final section of this chapter.

REVIEW THE FACTS 10-3

1. During which of the following periods were sexual values and behaviors in the United States most liberal?
   a. early 1960s b. mid-1970s
   c. mid-1980s d. late 1990s to the present
2. The view that sexual activity is more permissible for boys than for girls is referred to as the ___________.
3. In the U.S. today, about __________ of 9th graders and __________ of 12th graders report having been sexually active:
   a. one-fourth; one-half b. one-third; two-thirds
   c. one-fourth; three-fourths d. one-half; three-fourths
4. Approximately what percentage of teenage girls who become pregnant have their babies?
5. Since 1991, the rate of teenage pregnancies in the United States has
   a. increased. b. decreased.
   c. remained steady.
6. Compared to people who marry later, the rate of divorce for teenage parents who marry is
   a. higher. b. lower.
   c. about the same.

✓ Practice on MyDevelopmentLab

COGNITIVE CHANGES IN ADOLESCENCE

Brain Development in Adolescence

Even into the mid-1990s, most researchers believed that brain development for the most part was complete by the time a person reached the teenage years. Now—largely as the result of advanced, noninvasive brain-imaging technologies—researchers are beginning to see that adolescence is a period of rather dramatic changes in the brain. Furthermore, these changes appear to play an important role in forming mature judgments and in making decisions (Spear, 2008; Van Leijenhorst, et al., 2010), which are two skills that develop throughout the period of adolescence.

Brain Imaging Recent studies that utilize advanced magnetic resonance imaging (MRI) technologies are providing researchers a much clearer look at how brain cells develop (Giedd et al., 2011). Because MRIs employ no radioactive tracers or X-rays that can be potentially harmful—a concern especially for children who are still growing—they can be used in longitudinal studies, which involve multiple scans of individuals taken across time. Thus, changes in the brain can be observed as an individual develops, leading to a clearer picture of how the brain changes across the lifespan.

In some cases, these new MRI studies—which most often involve functional magnetic resonance imaging (fMRI)—are documenting what researchers have previously known about brain development. For example, it has long been known that most brain growth occurs early in development: The human brain is about 95% of its adult size by age 6 and children's brain contain nearly *all* of the neurons that will ever develop. In other cases, the newer research methods have led to somewhat surprising conclusions. For example, we now know that children's brains actually contain *more* nerve cells than the adult brain will retain—a somewhat surprising result. Thus, much of brain development in early childhood results from not only the elaboration of the synaptic interconnections among the neurons—it also involves the pruning away of neurons that are not needed for functioning (see Chapter 4). Furthermore, fMRI studies have revealed that brain development is *not* largely complete by the end of childhood, as was previously thought. Rather, important changes continue to occur within the brain long past childhood, through adolescence, and perhaps even into early adulthood.

Changes in the Adolescent Brain What kinds of changes in the brain occur during middle childhood and adolescence? First, there appears to be a second wave of neural pruning and synapse development that occurs during middle childhood. In particular, neural branching occurs, which produces an increase in the brain's gray matter—that part of the brain comprised of neural tissue itself. FMRI studies show that the volume of gray matter increases in childhood, peaking in girls at about age 9½ and in boys at about age 10½ (Giedd, 2008; Giedd et al., 2011). After these peaks, the volume of gray matter decreases up to adulthood, leveling off at about age 25, indicating that adolescence is a period in which serious pruning away of neural tissue occurs (Durston, et al., 2001; Giorgio et al., 2010).

Another change that occurs during adolescence is that the volume of white matter increases, perhaps up to age 40 (Durston, et al., 2001; Giedd, 2008; Giorgio et al., 2010). White matter, as you may recall, is composed of the cells surrounded by fatty myelin that insulates nerve cells and fibers, allowing them to conduct information faster and more efficiently (see Chapter 4). Thus, throughout adolescence and well into adulthood, our ability to think and solve problems efficiently continues to expand.

The processes of pruning and increasing myelination do not, however, occur uniformly across the developing brain. Rather, they proceed first in the back of the brain in regions that are largely responsible for sensory functioning—vision, touch, hearing, and sensation. Next, pruning and myelination occur in the brain areas responsible for coordination. Finally, in late adolescence pruning and myelination proceed to the prefrontal cortex, where decision making, problem solving, and thought are believed to be centered (Casey, Getz, & Galvan, 2008; Ernst & Fudge, 2010; Hooper, Luciana, Conklin, & Yarger, 2004). Thus, complex mental functions that require coordinated thought and judgment are among the last to mature. Correspondingly, a person's ability to exercise mature problem solving, to appraise risk, and to make difficult decisions that involve multiple perspectives is most likely not fully elaborated until perhaps as late as early adulthood (Steinburg, 2011).

Brain development during adolescence, of course, underlies the changes in social cognition and social behavior typically associated with this developmental period. For example, specific

TRY THIS!

Exploring the Effects of Early Parenting

Being a parent at any age presents a variety of challenges, as well as delightful experiences. Adolescent parents often find themselves not only coping with the demands of raising a baby but with other issues as well. To explore your thinking about the issues involved in early parenting, try this.

First, think about how you were raised by your parents. If you have children of your own, you might instead think about how you are raising them. Then construct a list of the things that you consider especially critical for parents to do when raising a child. To get started, consider some of the following tasks associated with raising a healthy child:

- Provide enough income so that the child has adequate food and clothing
- Arrange for adequate day care or home care for the child
- Read to the child every day
- Arrange for the child to play with peers once the child is old enough to interact with other children
- Play with the child
- Teach moral lessons

Once you have made your list, think about the challenges faced by adolescents who become parents. What special difficulties might adolescent parents have in meeting a child's needs? Are there advantages that younger parents may have over older parents in any of the key parenting tasks? What do you think?

Reflect on What You Observed

What do you see as the major challenges faced by adolescents who become parents? Do the major challenges accrue from external constraints, such as money or child care, or are they more the result of personal demands on the parents' time and energy? Do you think single parents face a larger challenge? If so, in what ways? Do you wish your own parents were older or younger than they were when you were born? What advantages might children raised by older parents receive? What advantages might children raised by younger parents experience?

Consider the Issues

Many factors determine how a person adapts to the roles and responsibilities of being a parent. As you think about the special circumstances surrounding being a teenage parent, what personal characteristics do you think would predispose a person to be successful? What characteristics might make parenting especially hard? In terms of the support needed to raise a child, how can adolescents cope most successfully? What kinds of social and economic support are generally available? Do you think attitudes in one's culture about teenage parenting make a difference in how successful a teen parent likely will be? How so? Do you think there are programs that the United States should put in place to support the needs of adolescent parents? What might these be? How could these programs be structured to improve the welfare of children born to young parents? You might wish to discuss these issues with your friends or family. Are there generational differences among the people you know with respect to attitudes about teenage parenting? If so, what kinds of generational differences did you discover?

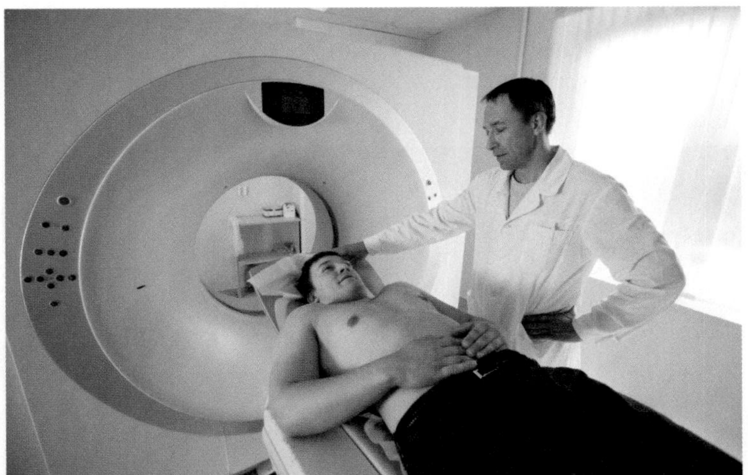

▲ This boy of 15 is being prepared for an MRI scan of his brain. MRIs are painless, although they require that the person remain motionless during the scan. This boy will listen to music to help him relax.

regions of the brain that are involved in self-awareness and self-concept undergo considerable remodeling during the teenage years. These brain changes correspond to behavioral characteristics commonly associated with adolescence, such as heightened self-consciousness and susceptibility to peer influence (Blakemore, 2008; Crone & Westenberg, 2009; Sebastian, Burnett, & Blakemore, 2008). The cerebellum—part of the lower brain that appears to be involved in coordinating movement and also in higher-level function—also continues to grow throughout adolescence and emerging adulthood (Strauch, 2008; Tiemeier, et al., 2010). Although it is unclear what significance should be associated with the developing cerebellum, it is clear that brain development in many regions is dramatic during the period of adolescence and early adulthood.

The Influence of Hormones on the Brain As we have seen, hormones that are produced in abundance during puberty have a dramatic effect on the development of physical characteristics associated with puberty. They also appear to target specific regions of the brain, particularly those related to emotional regulation and control, such as the amygdala. When the amygdala is triggered by the adolescent hormonal rush, emotions become volatile. Furthermore, activity in this region of the brain is associated with stimulus-seeking behavior, giving rise to the risky thrill-seeking tendencies that often characterize adolescent activities. The neurotransmitter dopamine also may be involved. It appears that adolescence is characterized by dopamine overactivity, and this, too, may be linked to the risk taking and heightened emotionality that is characteristic of adolescence (Wahlstrom, White, & Luciana, 2010). It seems clear that during adolescence, when risk-taking behavior is highly activated, the more control-oriented parts of the brain are still maturing. Thus, the behavior that results is likely to be risky and, perhaps even more important, lacking in the kind of judgment that allows a reasonable estimation of the risks involved (Asato, Terwilliger, Woo, & Luna, 2010; Casey, Getz, & Galvan, 2008).

This mismatch between emotion and cognitive control is evident in research that asks adults and children to look at photographs of people's faces and identify the emotions being displayed (Killgore, Oki, & Yurgelum-Todd, 2001; Killgore & Yurgelun-Todd, 2007; Moore, Pfeifer, Mazziotta, Iacoboni, 2012). By examining the activity level of various regions of the brain using functional MRI techniques, researchers were able to determine that children and young adolescents relied more heavily on the amygdala while solving these problems; older adolescents and adults showed greater activity in the frontal lobes, where more formulated, problem-solving activity is centered. The younger group made more errors in correctly identifying the emotions projected in the photos, and this was particularly true for boys. Thus, it may be that the emotional outbursts and overly emotional responses seen in teen behavior are largely the result of the pace with which different regions of the brain mature. Other risk-related behaviors, such as the use of alcohol and illegal drugs, may also be related to the ongoing development in the adolescent brain (Paus, 2010; Spear, 2002). Considering the influences that hormones have on brain development provides a more complete explanation for adolescent behavior than simpler explanations based solely on hormone activity would indicate.

Changes in the brain that occur as children mature into adulthood most likely underlie many important aspects of behavior. Foremost among these are changes is how adolescents experience emotion, make judgments about risky behavior, and actually *think.* During adolescence, there is normally an expansion in the capacity and style of thought that broadens the young person's awareness, imagination, judgment, and insight. These enhanced abilities lead to a rapid accumulation of knowledge that opens up a range of issues and problems that can both enrich and complicate adolescents' lives.

Can you think of instances in which adolescent judgment is different than the judgment of people just a few years older?

Cognitive development during adolescence is defined not only by increasingly abstract thinking but also by the increasing use of metacognition, thus enhancing teenagers' awareness of how they think and solve problems (see Chapter 8). Abstract thinking and metacognition exert a dramatic influence on the scope and content of an adolescent's memory and problem solving, as well on thinking in social contexts and on making moral judgments.

Piaget's Period of Formal Operations

As you may recall from earlier chapters, a particularly useful model of cognitive development was proposed by Jean Piaget, who viewed the development of thought as proceeding through four periods, or stages, of development (see Chapter 1). In infancy, thought is largely *sensorimotor;* in early childhood, it is characterized as *preoperational.* About the time children enter school, they become capable of performing what Piaget called *mental operations;* they become capable of thinking about objects from different perspectives and their problem-solving skills become much more logical. Despite the fact that preadolescent children are quite good thinkers who can solve most logical puzzles they encounter in day-to-day life, they generally do not, however, understand certain kinds of issues—those that require abstract reasoning or hypothetical constructs. These kinds of mental operations become available to them at about age 12, when they move into Piaget's final stage of cognitive development—a stage he called **formal operations**.

Formal Operational Thought In Piaget's view, formal operational thought involves a form of intellectual processing that is abstract, speculative, and independent of the immediate environment and circumstances (Moshman, 2009). It involves thinking about possibilities, as well as comparing reality with things that might or might not be. Whereas younger children are more comfortable with concrete, observable events, adolescents show a growing inclination to treat everything as a variation on what *could* be. Formal operational thought requires the ability to formulate, test, and evaluate hypotheses. Indeed, in Piaget's theory, logical and systematic hypothesis testing is the hallmark of the formal operational stage (see Figure 10-6). Formal operational thinking also involves the manipulation not only of known, verifiable events but also of the things that are contrary to fact (e.g., "Let's just suppose for the sake of discussion that . . .").

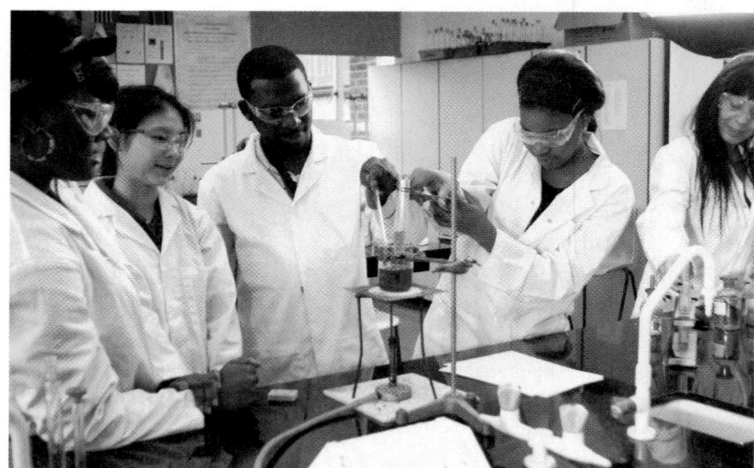

▲ In advanced science classes, students often need to make use of formal operational thought to systemically solve the problems posed.

Watch *Risk Taking and Delinquency* on **MyDevelopmentLab**

formal operations
For Piaget, the final stage of cognitive development, which begins at about age 12 and is characterized by the ability to reason hypothetically and think about abstract concepts

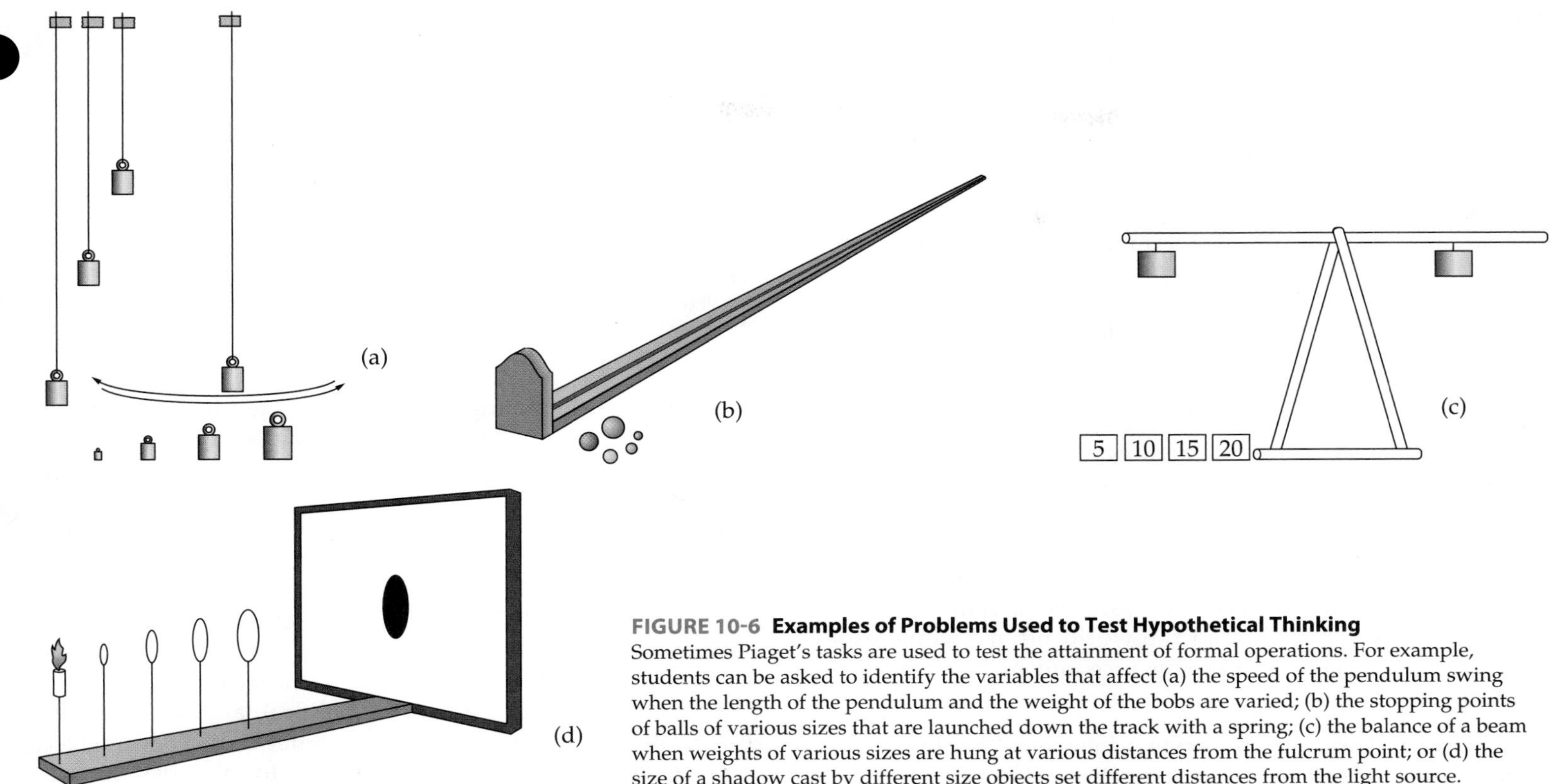

FIGURE 10-6 Examples of Problems Used to Test Hypothetical Thinking
Sometimes Piaget's tasks are used to test the attainment of formal operations. For example, students can be asked to identify the variables that affect (a) the speed of the pendulum swing when the length of the pendulum and the weight of the bobs are varied; (b) the stopping points of balls of various sizes that are launched down the track with a spring; (c) the balance of a beam when weights of various sizes are hung at various distances from the fulcrum point; or (d) the size of a shadow cast by different size objects set different distances from the light source.

In addition to their newfound abilities for abstract and hypothetical reasoning, adolescents also show an increasing ability to plan and to think ahead. In one study, 10th graders, 12th graders, college sophomores, and college seniors were asked to describe what they thought might happen to them in the future and to say how old they thought they would be when these events occurred (Greene, 1990). The older participants could look further into the future than the younger ones, and the narratives of the older students also were more specific. Formal operational thought thus can be characterized as a *second-order* process. Whereas first-order thinking involves discovering and examining relationships between objects, second-order thought involves thinking about one's thoughts, looking for links between relationships, and maneuvering between reality and possibility (Inhelder & Piaget, 1958).

Expanding Piaget's View Piaget's view of formal operations focused mostly on the development of thought processes that allow for more flexible and complex thinking and that involve abstract ideas and concepts (Miller, 2011a). Other changes in thinking also characterize adolescence, and these are frequently described as *information-processing functions* because they involve the development of increasingly effective *strategies* for thought, as well as the accumulation of *more* information and knowledge that can form the basis of thought.

In contrast to Piaget's view of defined stages in cognitive development, theorists who emphasize information-processing skills see the changes associated with the transition from childhood to adolescent thinking as much more gradual, with shifts back and forth between formal operational thought and earlier cognitive modes. They argue that the lines drawn between the thinking of children, adolescents, and adults are artificial; that cognitive development is a continuous process; and that even young children may have some formal operational abilities (Keating, 2004; Kuhn, 2009).

Piaget's four-stage view also suggests that all normal individuals attain the abilities associated with formal thought. However, it is generally agreed that not all individuals become capable of such thinking. A certain level of intelligence appears to be necessary for formal thought to exist. Cultural and socioeconomic factors, particularly educational level, also play a role; formal thought is more predominant among those with higher levels of education and who work in complex jobs, for example. Moreover, adolescents and adults who attain this level of cognitive development do not always use it consistently. For example, people who find themselves facing unfamiliar problems in unfamiliar situations are likely to fall back on more concrete reasoning.

Regardless of whether researchers and theorists subscribe to a more or less strict interpretation of Piaget's view of formal operational thought, they do acknowledge that cognitive advances typically are associated with entering adolescence (Moshman, 2011). Several of the hallmarks of these cognitive advances are noted in Table 10-5. Furthermore, cognitive capabilities are not the only aspects of thinking that change in adolescence.

The Scope and Content of Adolescent Thought

Because of new and improved cognitive skills, adolescents develop a much broader scope and richer complexity in the content of their thoughts than they were capable of in childhood (Galotti, 2011). Because the adolescent can now deal with contrary-to-fact situations, reading or viewing science fiction, fantasy, or horror is a popular pastime. For similar reasons, an interest in science or mathematics often develops at this age. Experimentation with different ways of thinking typically emerges during this period of development. For example, fascination with cults, with the occult, or with altered states of consciousness that can be caused by anything from meditation to drug-induced conditions becomes somewhat common during adolescence. Behavior also changes somewhat as children become adolescents. For example, teenagers choose to spend their leisure time in a variety of activities, many of which depend on their cultural context (see the box Changing Perspectives: How Adolescents Around the World Spend Their Time). Developing capabilities for abstract thinking also influences how adolescents examine the social world, and teenagers around the world often become especially concerned about social injustice and civil rights issues (Amsel, 2011).

Table 10-5 Hallmarks of Adolescent Cognition

- Ability to consider abstract ideas
- Hypothetical–deductive reasoning, where the adolescent can form and test alternative approaches to a problem
- Ability to think about several aspects of a problem, all at the same time
- Better memory and more knowledge
- Ability to use more complex and more efficient strategies for storing and retrieving information from memory
- More mature approach to planning and decision making, including the use of more elaborate scripts
- Ability to reflect on one's own thinking

Examining the World and the Family Adolescents' newfound ability to understand contrary-to-fact situations often affects parent–child relationships. Adolescents contrast their "ideal" parent with the real parent they see on a daily basis, and parents have a difficult time measuring up to their adolescents' expectations. Adolescents can be critical of all social institutions, including family and especially their parents; therefore, family bickering tends to escalate during early adolescence.

Many researchers believe, however, that the battles that rage over such daily activities as chores, dress, adornments (such as tattoos and jewelry that requires piercing), hairstyles, schoolwork, and family meals serve a useful purpose. These battles allow adolescents to test their independence over relatively minor issues and in the safety of their homes. Indeed, *negotiation* has become a popular word in the psychology of adolescence. Instead of talking about rebellion and the painful separation or alienation of teenagers from their families, many researchers prefer to describe adolescence as a time in which parents and teenagers negotiate new relationships with one another, much as they do with the negotiation of shared goals in the process of coregulation (see Chapter 9). Teenagers must gain more independence; parents must learn to see their child as more of an equal, with the right to differing opinions (Brown & Bakken, 2011). For most adolescents, the interplay between these competing needs is conducted within a caring, close relationship with their parents, which also serves healthy development. Research indicates, for example, that teenagers who had the strongest sense of themselves as individuals were more likely to have grown up in families where the parents offered guidance and warmth but also permitted their children to develop their own points of view (Wang, Dishion, Stormshak, & Willett, 2011; Zentner & Renaud, 2007).

What were some of the most important negotiations you entered into with your parents during your adolescence? Was negotiation a successful strategy for you and your family?

Another way that adolescent thinking shifts is that often, especially during middle and late adolescence, teenagers develop an increasing concern with social, political, and moral issues. Their understanding of the world becomes more sophisticated as they gain experience and can conceptualize theories and scenarios of greater complexity. As they begin to argue various sides of political and social issues, their concept of civil rights and civil liberties—including freedom of speech and religion—often changes (Helwig, 1995, 2006; Smetana & Villalobos, 2009). Adolescents also begin to see themselves in a broader context. Some of their swings and extremes of behavior occur when they start evaluating themselves intellectually. They now become more interested in what *they* think about issues—what *their* attitudes and values actually are. However, *knowledge of self* does not come easily nor does it occur overnight. In addition, adolescent self-discovery is sometimes limited, as any parent of a teenager can describe.

Adolescent Egocentrism Adolescents' self-absorption in understanding their own thoughts, attitudes, and values often leads them to a particular kind of egocentrism. One aspect of their *self*-centered view is that they often assume that other people are as fascinated with them as they are with themselves. Another is that they sometimes fail to distinguish between their own concerns and those of others. As a result, adolescents tend to jump to conclusions about the reactions of those around them and to assume that others will be as approving or as critical of them as they are of themselves. As a consequence, for example, adolescents are far more concerned than younger children about having their inadequacies revealed to others, and they often become extremely upset if they find that some aspect of their private life has been shared with others without their knowledge.

Watch *Adolescence: Social Changes* on **MyDevelopmentLab**

How Adolescents Around the World Spend Their Time

In every important respect, the development of young people—their minds, their attitudes, and even their bodies—is adapted to and transformed by the activities of their daily lives. Going to school, working at a job, participating in family responsibilities and events, playing sports, watching TV, and hanging out with friends all influence the developmental experiences of young people. During no other period of development are such activities more critical to the way in which lives are shaped than in adolescence, partly because adolescents have a greater choice in the activities they participate in than they did when they were younger. Especially interesting are the leisure activities preferred by adolescents. Although school and work absorb a large portion of the day's hours in many cultures, adolescents in every culture have at least some time for the activities they choose. How do adolescents in various cultures make these critically important choices?

Around the world, adolescence is a period of social learning and a period where adolescents restructure their roles in their societies (Arnett, 2012; Larson, Wilson, & Rickman, 2009). Leisure time represents an important perspective about how adolescents come to define themselves in the context of their culture. By participating in activities that they choose carefully, adolescents learn adult skills and expectations, gain control over their ability to make choices, and also become integrated into their communities. Because their free time is limited, adolescents must choose the activities in which they will participate.

How do researchers investigate the leisure time choices of teenagers? Generally, studies ask participants to keep time logs or daily diaries in which they record how they spend their time each day. Usually such studies require the participants to make several entries every day. In some studies researchers make periodic phone calls to participants and ask them about what they are doing at that very moment. In other studies, adolescents are asked to carry electronic pagers, perhaps for a week. If they miss a researcher's call, they can respond to a page by recording in a notebook what they are doing. By asking participants to note what they are doing at particular moments, researchers get a much more accurate picture of how activities spread across the day than if they were to depend on a person's recall of activities over perhaps a week or more. (Think for a moment how many minutes you spent watching TV, reading, and talking on the phone a week ago today.)

What results do such studies show? Compared to adolescents in other parts of the world, U.S. adolescents have more discretionary time (Larson, 2004; see the table that follows). They also spend less time on schoolwork than do teenagers in Europe or East Asia and generally work a little less. U.S. teenagers also spend more time talking with friends. Although friendships in adolescence serve many positive functions for teenagers, spending too much time with peers is—at least for some teens—a risk factor for developing problem behaviors such as alcohol, drug, and cigarette use; delinquency; and sexual activity (Barnes, Hoffman, Welte, Farrell, & Dintcheff, 2007). In comparison to more agricultural-based societies, both those in other parts of the world today and in the United States in generations past, U.S. adolescents spend considerably less time in household chores and income-generating labor for the family.

Culture is a highly defining force on how adolescents choose their leisure-time activities. For example, Korean and Japanese adolescents have much less free time and far more pressure for studying or for "discipline development" (Verma & Larson, 2003b). Japanese society is still somewhat suspicious of idle time, and young people are expected to be involved in activities, even if they do not enjoy them. There is little free time given to opportunities for creativity. Korean and Japanese teenagers spend large amounts of time working on homework, and when they do have the chance to elect their activities, they often choose free-time activities that are relatively passive. Indian adolescents' activities are still highly proscribed by class and gender lines. Even those Indian adolescents who live in urban areas, where opportunities for cultural and media entertainment are ample, often must spend considerable time on their studies because the educational system is highly competitive. In Italy, teens often spend time on such things as sports, hobbies, and reading—activities that are believed to provide a means of preparing for adulthood. By most of the world's standards, American youth have large amounts of free time, much of which is unregulated.

How adolescents use their leisure time undoubtedly reflects their individual interests and values and the specific demands made by their social and economic circumstances. However, culture also plays a strong role in shaping the types of choices that adolescents make, and these choices lead young people toward—or away from—certain types of activities. How did you spend your free time when you were 14 years old? How did you spend it when you were 16 years old? How do you spend your free time now? What activities do you value most? How do you think your choices of leisure activities have shaped, and are shaping, your life?

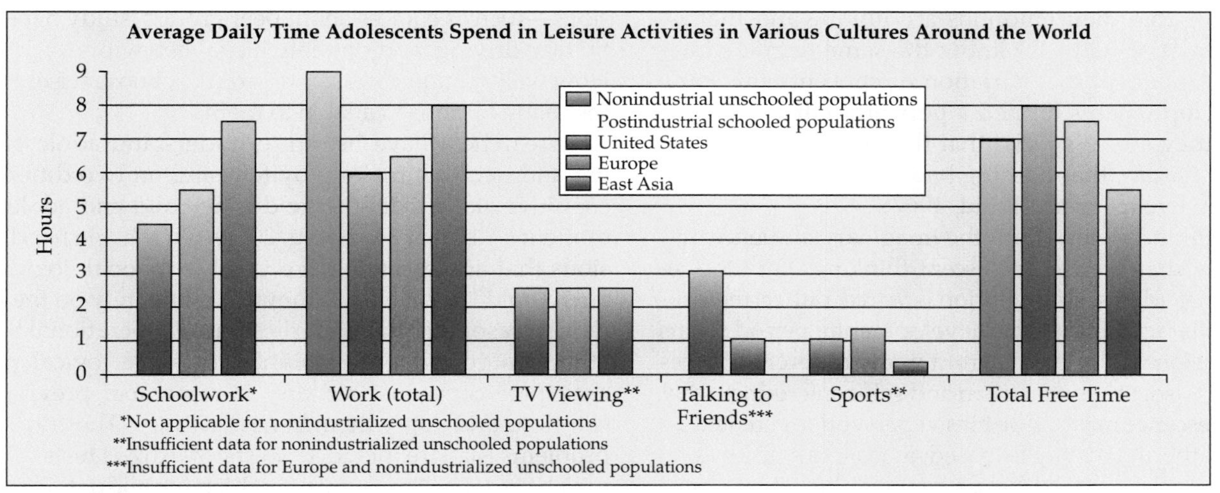

SOURCE: From "How U.S. Children and Adolescents Spend Their Time: What it does (and doesn't) tell us about their development," by R.W. Larson, 2004, in J. Lerner & A. Alberts (eds.), *Current Directions in Developmental Psychology*. (pp. 134–141). Upper Saddle River, NJ: Prentice Hall.

Watch *Adolescents' School Experiences* on **MyDevelopmentLab**

Watch *Western Influences on the World's Societies* on **MyDevelopmentLab**

◀ Not only do adolescents scrutinize their appearance, but also they may imagine in detail the possible reactions of their peers to each and every perceived imperfection. Intense self-scrutiny results from advances in thinking and from adolescent egocentrism.

According to David Elkind, the idea that adolescents see themselves as the center of everyone's scrutiny and attention has been referred to as the **imaginary audience** (Elkind, 1967). Adolescents often feel that everything they say and do is constantly on display. Small imperfections—a pimple, a stupid comment, or wearing the wrong shirt—often turn into a major *crisis,* in part because the adolescent believes everyone will notice and judge. The perception that they are constantly on stage also can lead adolescents to be very sensitive to criticism and to see even innocuous questions from parents as prying, critical, and overly personal.

Adolescents also are absorbed in their own feelings. They sometimes believe that their emotions are unique and that no one has ever known or will ever know the same degree of agony or ecstasy. As part of this variation of egocentrism, some adolescents develop what is termed a **personal fable**, which is their belief that they are so special that they should be exempt from the laws of nature, that nothing bad can happen to them, and that they will live forever (Elkind, 1967).

According to Elkind's view, both the imaginary audience and the personal fable characterize adolescent thinking. Yet little research suggests that adolescent cognition is *flawed*; rather, the risk-taking behavior characteristic of this developmental period seems to be multidimensional, originating from many different sources (Vartanian 2000). Also, the egocentrism and self-centeredness that characterize adolescence may not be biased perceptions created by the individual. Rather, they may be based, at least to some extent, in reality: During adolescence, the perceptions of others about one's self actually do have real and important consequences, as teenagers forge friendships, romantic relationships, and social structures with their peers (Bell & Bromnick, 2003). Finally, it is important to recognize that egocentric thinking is not purely confined to adolescence but rather continues on into emerging adulthood and perhaps, for some individuals, beyond. In one study that asked adolescents and adults to respond to questions that presented personal fable and imaginary audience themes, higher egocentrism scores were obtained for not only adolescents but also younger adults, ages 19 to 30, in comparison to adults in middle or older age groups (Frankenberger, 2000). Thus, egocentrism may be a powerful influence on behavior for emerging adults, especially when they enter into a new environment or life situation (Schwartz, Maynard, & Uzelac, 2008). The reemergence of adolescent egocentrism at later ages, in fact, can be an effective coping mechanism during such times of transition, for example, when entering college, beginning a new job or personal relationship, or leaving home. It may also explain why some especially risky behaviors—such as binge drinking, drug use, and sexual promiscuity—emerge as young people make the transition into college. We turn to a broader investigation of social behavior and its consequences in more detail in the chapter that follows.

How might the adolescent's developing capacity for abstract thought be related to the development of adolescent egocentrism?

Decision Making in Adolescence and Emerging Adulthood Risky behavior has long been identified as a characteristic that seems especially apparent among adolescents (Pharo, Sim, Graham, Gross, & Hayne, 2011). Yet, adolescence is also a time when young people are given more autonomy and responsibility for themselves. Increasingly throughout adolescence and emerging adulthood, young people are called on to make important decisions—such as choices about peer groups, study habits, sexual activities, driving, and possibly illegal behaviors such as drug use. How well are adolescents prepared to choose wisely from among the many options available to them?

Researchers have begun to understand adolescent risk taking and decision making by focusing on two different types of cognitive skills that emerge during child and adolescent development (Albert & Steinberg, 2011). On the one hand, many decisions that adolescents make involve rational, logical processes. Such "cold" decisions, as they are called, rely on the kind of analytical reasoning that underlies formal operational thought—the ability to consider possibilities, to solve logical problems, to anticipate consequences, and to remember previously learned solutions and apply them in new settings. These are the kinds of problems that are included on standardized tests of intelligence, which measure the degree to which individuals can reason their way through logical problems. Cold decision processes guide

imaginary audience
Adolescents' assumption that others are focusing a great deal of critical attention on them

Watch *Imaginary Audience* on **MyDevelopmentLab**

personal fable
Adolescents' belief that they are so special that they should be exempt from the laws of nature, that nothing bad can happen to them, and that they will live forever

a good share of our behavior. For example, if an adolescent is asked to stop at the grocery store on the way home from school and pick up the ingredients to make spaghetti, this is the type of activity that can easily be handled using a "cold" decision-making processes. However, in life, not all problems can be solved with logic and not all situations rest on logical reasoning. Suppose, for example, that, as the adolescent just mentioned leaves school, he is invited to stop over at his friend's house to "smoke a little weed." Will he stop by before he heads to the store? Logic, of course, would suggest not—he needs to get the groceries and take them to his family so that dinner can be prepared, and smoking marijuana is, of course, an illegal activity. However, other intuition-based decision processes are also in play: If he stops at his friend's house, will he get caught? Will he be able to hurry through the grocery store and still make it home without being late? Emotions are also involved: What will his friend think if he declines the offer? What does he *want* to do? For many adolescents, these "hot" decision processes—which rely on intuition and sometimes involve emotion regulation—guide important aspects of behavior.

One way of explaining the risky behavior that characterizes adolescence is to consider how decision-making skills develop. If "hot" processing is especially important during adolescence, then this might help explain why this period of the lifespan is especially characterized by high-risk behaviors. One set of studies that has explored the development of decision-making strategies using a lifespan approach has relied on a technique called the Iowa Gambling Task (IGT). The IGT was developed to measure cognitive deficits among brain-injured individuals who seemed to have good cognitive functioning, but who lacked the ability to make good decisions in social and emotional contexts (Anderson, Bechara, Damasio, Tranel, & Damasio, 1999). The IGT is a card game that involves gambling to win money. Participants can choose to play with any of four decks of cards, each of which offers the opportunity to both win and lose. Two of the decks are rigged so that rewards are high, but losses are even higher—these are the "risky" decks. The other two decks offer smaller winnings, but the probability of winning exceeds that of losing. Participants play games over and over, and can choose which deck to play with every game. Normal adults eventually learn which decks offer the best chances of winning, and over the course of the game eventually shift to choosing the winning strategy, which is to play with the decks that are less risky. Do adolescents use the same decision strategy?

Interestingly, they generally do not. In fact, when the ITG is played by people of varying ages, a clear pattern emerges: Although younger children and adults eventually figure out how to win at the game, adolescents generally persist in choosing the riskier, but less effective strategy (Cauffman, et al., 2010; Smith, Xiao, & Bechara, 2011). So, although logical decision processes continue to advance throughout childhood and adolescence, the "hot" decision processes that are measured by tasks like the IGT do not. Rather, adolescence seems to be a period in which individuals possess good logical thinking abilities, but have an especially hard time reasoning through problems that involve intuition and emotion. This deficit in decision-making skills is linked to the impulsive and reward-driven responses that are so often associated with adolescent risk-taking behaviors (Smith, Ratner, & Hobart, 2011). Only later in adolescence or early adulthood do individuals regain the ability to avoid high-risk, low-reward situations.

Most researchers believe the development of cognition and decision making corresponds to the development of the brain. When researchers study brain activity during risky decision-making tasks, they, too, find age-linked results. For example, in one study using fMRI brain-imaging technology, children, adolescents, and young adults were found to show different levels of brain activity in different regions of their brains. In particular, children and adults showed the highest level of activity in the parts of the cortex involved in reasoning and memory. In contrast, adolescents showed higher activation in the brain regions that are involved in reward systems and high-risk situations (Paulsen, Carter, Platt, Huettel, & Brannon, 2012). Thus, it appears that brain development also follows the same path as does decision making.

Moral Development in Adolescence The cognitive and brain changes that occur during adolescence lay the groundwork for the adolescent's moral development (Baird, 2008; Moshman, 2011). As they progress toward adulthood, adolescents must confront aspects of morality that they have not encountered previously. Now that they are capable of having sex, for example, they have to decide what sex means to them and whether to have sex before marriage. They have to evaluate the behaviors and attitudes of peers who might be involved with drugs or gangs. They have to decide whether doing well in school is important, how they feel about fitting into a society that measures success largely in terms of wealth and power, and what role, if any, religion will play in their lives. As a result, adolescents start to consider the broader issues that will define their adult years, and their ability to reason through choices—both good and bad—is instrumental to their behavior (Eisenberg, Morris, McDaniel, & Spinrad, 2009).

Some of the decisions that adolescents face—including those about sex and drugs—have complex, even life-threatening consequences. Yet, research suggests that wide differences in the pace of moral development exist among individuals during the period of adolescence (Krettenauer, 2011; Lehalle, 2006). Unfortunately, some adolescents may not develop the moral framework and cognitive skills to effectively deal with real-world pressures until well into adolescence or even into early adulthood—long after they have faced tough moral decisions. For example, when the moral reasoning of 18- and 22-year-olds was investigated on the subject of risky sexual behavior that could lead to STDs, including HIV/AIDS, only the 22-year-olds carefully considered the moral dilemmas associated with STDs (Jadack, Hyde, Moore, & Keller, 1995). Apparently, even the ability to make moral judgments about life-threatening behaviors takes time to develop.

As you may recall, Kohlberg's view of moral development (see Chapter 9) specifies that the ability to reason through moral dilemmas proceeds developmentally, from *preconventional,* through *conventional*, to *postconventional* thinking. By the time they reach their teens, most U.S. children have moved beyond Kohlberg's preconventional level of moral development and arrived at the conventional level, which is based in large part on conformity to social expectations and stereotypes.

In many day-to-day situations, conventional moral thinking works well because it encourages people to conform to society's expectations; however, conventional thinking can lead adolescents into difficulty. Their desire to conform to the standards of the peer group can get adolescents into trouble, which sometimes can be serious, especially if drugs, sex, or illegal activity is involved. Although much of adolescent and adult life involves conforming to society's rules and expectations, adults are expected to make sound moral choices, which sometimes require the ability and the wisdom to stand up against social conventions that are unfair or that do not apply (Nunner-Winkler, 2009).

In a society in which adolescents have both freedom and access to harmful choices, sometimes at quite young ages, how are they to make wise choices? Can more advanced moral thinking be learned? In the early days of his theorizing, Kohlberg and his colleagues tried setting up experimental moral education classes for children and adolescents from a variety of social backgrounds. The results, even with juvenile delinquents, suggested that higher levels of moral judgment *can* be taught. Kohlberg's classes centered on discussions of hypothetical moral dilemmas. Adolescents were presented with a problem and asked to give a solution. If the answer was argued at Stage 4 of Kohlberg's stages of moral development, the discussion leader suggested a Stage 5 rationale to see if the teenager thought it was a good alternative. The students almost always found that slightly more advanced reasoning was more appealing and, through repeated discussions, they sooner or later began to form judgments at higher stages (Kohlberg, 1966). Thus, it seems that presenting a child with increasingly complex moral issues creates *disequilibrium* in the child's mind, forcing the child to think and try to resolve the contradictions. Indeed, moral decisions are rarely simple, and adolescents must learn to weigh various perspectives as they determine their thoughts and actions (Killen & Smetana, 2007). Fortunately, their developing cognitive skills eventually provide adolescents and emerging adults with a solid foundation against which these moral decisions can be considered.

Can you suggest an instance in which a moral decision you made was defined by conventional thinking? Can you provide an example in which your moral judgment reflected postconventional themes?

As we conclude this chapter, we should offer some summary comments about the period of adolescence and emerging adulthood. Perhaps foremost among these is the idea that the period between childhood and adulthood is complex, involving dramatic growth and change. A critically important developmental event during this period is the attainment of sexual maturity because it is accompanied by new, important responsibilities and opportunities. Brain development continues during adolescence, giving rise to new cognitive abilities. Although adolescent thought still is more limited than adult cognition—especially with respect to adolescent egocentrism—their advancing cognitive abilities give adolescents new ways of thinking about the world and their place in it. Adolescence and emerging adulthood, at least in Western cultures, is a time of remarkable transition from child to adult—from near total dependency on parents to a lifestyle of considerable choice and freedom. In the next chapter, we continue to explore the personality and sociocultural development that adolescents and emerging adults experience—how new powers of thought are turned inward to a close examination of the self and, at the same time, outward to a world that has suddenly grown much more complex.

REVIEW THE FACTS 10-4

1. What two processes characterize brain development during adolescence?
2. According to a study reported in the text, whereas adults solving emotional problems showed more activity in the brain's frontal lobes, adolescents showed more activity in the ________.
3. List Piaget's stages of cognitive development that are appropriate to the following age groups:
   Birth to 2 years: ________ stage
   Age 2 to age 6 or 7: ________ stage
   Age 6 or 7 to age 12: ________ stage
   Age 12 and over: ________ stage
4. Adolescents' tendency to see themselves as the center of everyone's scrutiny is an aspect of adolescent egocentrism called the ________.
5. Joshua tells his father, "Don't worry about my driving! I'm not going to get into an accident!" Joshua's statement reflects the core of the concept referred to as
   a. second-order process.
   b. the imaginary audience.
   c. negotiation of shared goals.
   d. the personal fable.
6. "Cold" decision processes rely on ________; "hot" decision processes rely on ________.
7. According to Kohlberg, adolescence is a time when moral reasoning begins to shift from the ________ stage toward the ________ stage.

Practice on **MyDevelopmentLab**

CHAPTER SUMMARY

Adolescent Development in a Cultural and Historical Context

Do adolescents in cultures around the world, or who lived in different historical periods, experience the period of adolescence and emerging adulthood in much the same way?

- Adolescence is the period of development between childhood and adulthood that is present in all cultures. In less industrialized countries, the transition from childhood to adolescence typically begins when children enter their reproductive years, which usually is marked by a transitional ritual called a *rite of passage.* However, adolescence is more complex, it lasts longer, and its beginning and ending points are less well-defined in industrialized cultures, where the skills necessary for adult life are more difficult to master. Many scholars today refer to the period between the end of high school and the adoption of adult roles and responsibilities as *emerging adulthood.*

- Adolescents are very sensitive to their social worlds, and they adapt to the environments in which they live. Adolescence must therefore be considered in the broader social context.
- Adolescence is often divided into early adolescence (about ages 10 to 14), later adolescence (corresponding to the high school years), and emerging adulthood (about ages 18–25).

What features best characterize the developmental niche occupied by adolescents in the United States today?

- In the United States, the period of adolescence is heavily segregated by age: Teenagers generally spend more time with peers their age than with younger children or adults.
- Economic dependence is another characteristic of adolescence found in U.S. culture because teenagers usually are financially dependent on their parents during their years of schooling. This situation typically leads to some frustration and restlessness.
- Adolescents in the United States are often deeply affected by the events of the time in which they live. Many also are heavily influenced by the mass media.
- From a sociocultural perspective, adolescence in an industrialized culture like the United States often is a period characterized by instability, uncertainty, and challenge.

Physical Development and Adaptation

What physical changes occur as individuals move into adolescence, and what changes are specifically associated with puberty?

- Adolescence is a time of rapid biological changes. Adolescents often are preoccupied with these changes, and they compare themselves to others and to idealized images of how they wish to be.
- Secondary sex characteristics develop rapidly in early adolescence, as do the reproductive organs. Physical changes are largely controlled by the increased production of *hormones,* which are biochemical substances that are secreted into the bloodstream in very small amounts by internal organs called endocrine glands. This causes the *adolescent growth spurt,* which is a period of rapid growth in physical size and strength accompanied by changes in body proportions that is followed about a year later by *puberty* (sexual maturation).
- Both male and female hormones are present in members of both sexes. However, at adolescence, boys begin producing more of the male sex hormones called *androgens,* such as *testosterone,* and girls begin producing more of the female sex hormones, such as *estrogen* and *progesterone.* The balance of hormones is regulated by the brain's hypothalamus and the pituitary gland. The pituitary also produces several hormones, including growth hormone and the trophic hormones, which regulate the functioning of other glands.
- Hormones have a powerful effect on the brain, influencing its development. However, the emotionality often seen in teenagers results not only because of hormone action but also because of complex sociocultural and environmental factors.
- In girls, puberty is marked by *menarche*—the time of the first menstrual period, which usually occurs between the ages 9½ and 16½. The average age of menarche today in the United States is just under age 12½. In boys, puberty is marked by the first emission of semen that contains viable sperm, which usually occurs between the ages of 11 and 16.
- In many industrialized parts of the world, puberty occurs at younger ages now than in the historical past, which is a pattern referred to as the *secular trend.* Girls of average height usually reach menarche when they weigh about 100 pounds, but they usually do not ovulate until about a year later. The secular trend is related to nutrition and general health, although genetics probably also is involved, as are more subtle environmental factors.

Why do adolescents focus so intensely on issues of body image, and in what ways are their concerns about their appearance expressed?

- Adolescents comprise a *marginal group,* meaning that they are on the fringe of the dominant culture and therefore feel a strong pressure toward conformity. They especially are concerned with body image, and they engage in social comparison, comparing their body shape to that of other teenagers and to idealized images of the "perfect" body.
- In terms of body-image comparisons, boys generally are most concerned with physical size and strength. Girls more often worry about being too fat or too tall. Extreme focus on weight can lead to obesity or to eating disorders, the latter of which are much more common among adolescent girls than boys. *Anorexia nervosa* is an eating disorder in which a person is obsessed by thoughts of an unattainable image of thinness, which can result in death. Bingeing and purging characterize another eating disorder, which is called *bulimia nervosa.* Generally, girls also have a lower satisfaction with their body image.

Is it better to sexually mature before or after most of one's peers?

- Although there is a wide spread in age among both boys and girls with respect to when they reach physical maturity, girls mature on average about 2 years earlier than boys. Late maturation is often a disadvantage for boys. Early maturation can be a problem for both boys and girls because it abbreviates the period during which childhood experiences are accumulated. Later maturation can be an advantage for girls because this is when many of their male peers are maturing.

Gender Identity and Sexual Practices

How have sexual practices and expectations changed in the United States over the past six decades?

- Before the mid-1960s, attitudes in the United States about sexuality were more restrictive than they are today, and a *sexual double standard* existed, where sexual activity was viewed as more permissible for boys than for girls. In the 1970s, sexual attitudes and behaviors became more liberal, especially for girls. Also, during this decade attitudes about *same-sex orientation*, which involves attraction to members of one's own sex or engagement in same-sex activity, became somewhat more tolerant. By the 1980s, the sexual revolution was winding down, and social views about sexuality became more conservative, although never returning to pre-1960s levels. From the 1990s to the present, sexual values have largely stabilized, although there are very wide variations among individuals, families, religions, and cultures about what constitutes appropriate sexual behavior.
- Teenagers today continue to be highly sexually active. Almost two-thirds of White 12th graders have had sexual intercourse. Sexual activity typically begins earlier for Black boys and girls and for Hispanic boys. Early sexual activity is associated with adolescents who are raised in single-parent families and families who communicate poorly, with early maturation, and with low academic achievement. Later maturation and high academic achievement are associated with becoming sexually active at later ages.
- In the United States, about 20% of sexually active teenagers have an STD. Among adolescents, the most common STDs are genital herpes and chlamydia, although rates of HIV infection are rising.
- About 7% of teenage girls become pregnant, and about half of them give birth. Pregnancy rates vary dramatically by racial/ethnic background, and are higher for Black and Hispanic teenagers. Pregnancy rates for adolescents have fallen sharply over the past three decades, especially among Black and Hispanic teens.
- One factor that influences pregnancy rates among adolescence is the use of contraception. In the United States, 22% of adolescent girls and 15% of adolescent boys did not use contraception during their first sexual intercourse.
- Cultures and subcultures vary widely in the prevalence of births to teenage mothers. In the United States, becoming a teenage mother often is associated with difficult economic circumstances and personal challenges. Being a teenage father also may have negative consequences, especially due to the need to financially support the child. Marriage under such circumstances generally does not produce positive outcomes in part because early marriage often leads to dropping out of school.
- Although some children of teenage parents develop in very positive ways, others are at a disadvantage. Teenage parents often are stressed, frustrated, inexperienced in raising a child, and economically challenged; however, their success at nurturing their children depends on the individual parents, on the available resources, on the parents resilience, and on the skills that parents bring to parenting.

Cognitive Changes in Adolescence

What brain changes are associated with development through the period of adolescence and emerging adulthood?

- Although earlier research suggested that brain development was nearly complete by adolescence, new longitudinal studies using advanced fMRI techniques have shown that important changes still are taking place throughout this period.
- During adolescence, a second wave of neural pruning occurs and additional synapses develop in the brain. Gray matter (composed of neurons) increases until about age 9½ for girls and about age 10½ for boys, after which it declines until about age 25 due to pruning and then levels off. White matter (composed of heavily myelinated neurons and fibers) continues to increase in volume during adolescence until about age 40, thereby making neural communication more efficient.
- Brain development in adolescence begins first in the back of the brain in the regions that are largely responsible for sensory functioning and proceeds toward the front, to the prefrontal cortex, where decision making, problem solving, and thought occur. Cognitive skills involving judgment and self-concept are among the last to develop.
- Hormones produced during puberty affect brain development, especially in the amygdala, where emotions are regulated. Risky behavior and emotional outbursts may result from the pace at which different areas of the brain develop throughout adolescence.

What are "formal operations," and how does cognitive development change as the individual moves through adolescence?

- Cognitive development in adolescence centers on acquiring more knowledge and an increasing ability to use abstract thought and metacognition, which involves understanding how one thinks about things.
- Piaget noted that at about age 12, adolescents become able to think about abstract and hypothetical issues. He called

the stage of cognitive development associated with adolescence *formal operations.*

- In addition to their new abilities for abstract and hypothetical (scientific) reasoning, adolescents also become better at planning ahead. Thus, formal operations is a *second-order process,* where adolescents are now able to think about their thoughts, see the links between relationships, and consider the differences between reality and possibility.
- Theorists who emphasize an information-processing view see cognitive development as more gradual and flexible than Piaget did. Although Piaget suggested that all normal adolescents develop formal thought, research has shown that a certain level of intelligence is probably necessary and cultural factors are probably involved.
- As adolescents acquire improved cognitive skills, they often develop new interests. Parent–child relationships sometimes suffer as adolescents become more critical of their parents, and the negotiation of new relationships and rules becomes common. As teens become more independent, parents should change their expectations but continue to offer guidance and support.

What is adolescence egocentrism, and how is it linked to the changes in cognitive development that teenagers and emerging adults typically experience?

- Teenagers often develop an increased concern with social, political, and moral issues, especially in middle and later adolescence, as their knowledge of their own viewpoints develops. This absorption in their own thoughts leads to adolescent egocentrism.
- The *imaginary audience* concept refers to adolescents' tendency to see themselves as the center of everyone's scrutiny. Thus, adolescents are very sensitive to their own minor imperfections, to criticism, and to invasions of their privacy.
- Some adolescents develop a *personal fable,* which is the belief that they are special and they are invulnerable. Research suggests this egocentric thinking may extend well into emerging adulthood.
- Adolescent decision making is characterized by a higher level of risk taking than is either childhood or adulthood thought. Research suggests that although "cold" processes that rely on logic develop linearly from childhood to adulthood, the development of "hot" processes that involve the ability to accurately deal with intuition and emotions are delayed in adolescence.
- Most adolescents can move beyond Kohlberg's conventional stage (at least occasionally), where judgments conform to social expectations and stereotypes. When adolescents are able to make moral choices that do not conform to social standards but rather rely on internalized moral principles, they are exhibiting postconventional moral reasoning. Moral reasoning can be advanced by giving adolescents practice in solving increasingly complex moral dilemmas.

KEY TERMS

rites of passage (p. 275)
emerging adulthood (p. 276)
hormones (p. 278)
adolescent growth spurt (p. 278)
puberty (p. 278)
androgens (p. 279)
testosterone (p. 279)
estrogen (p. 279)
progesterone (p. 279)
menarche (p. 280)
secular trend (p. 280)
marginal group (p. 281)
anorexia nervosa (p. 281)
bulimia nervosa (p. 281)
sexual double standard (p. 285)
same-sex orientation (p. 285)
formal operations (p. 292)
imaginary audience (p. 296)
personal fable (p. 296)

MyVirtualLife

What decisions would you make while raising a child? What would be the consequences of those decisions?

Find out by accessing **MyVirtualLife** at
www.MyDevelopmentLab.com
to raise a virtual child and live your own virtual life.

11 ADOLESCENCE AND EMERGING ADULTHOOD
Personality and Sociocultural Development

LEARNING OBJECTIVES

- What sociocultural forces shape the transition from childhood to adulthood, and how do young people in developed economies typically move through this period of the lifespan?
- What factors are involved in developing a sense of autonomy as the young person moves through the period of adolescence and emerging adulthood?
- What is an identity crisis, and how is it linked to the formation of a secure self-identity?
- What factors exert the most influence on how one's identity is forged during adolescence and emerging adulthood?
- What are the most important roles that parents play during the teenage years?
- Why do adolescents place so much importance on how their peers regard them, and how is the explosion of electronic media impacting peer relationships?
- What roles do friends play during adolescence and emerging adulthood, and how do friendships change as teenagers mature?
- Why is adolescence and emerging adulthood a period of the lifespan characterized by risky behavior?
- Compared to previous generations, are adolescents in the United States today more, or less, likely to engage in various forms of risky behavior?
- How do adolescents typically cope with the pressures they feel during the teenage and emerging adult years?

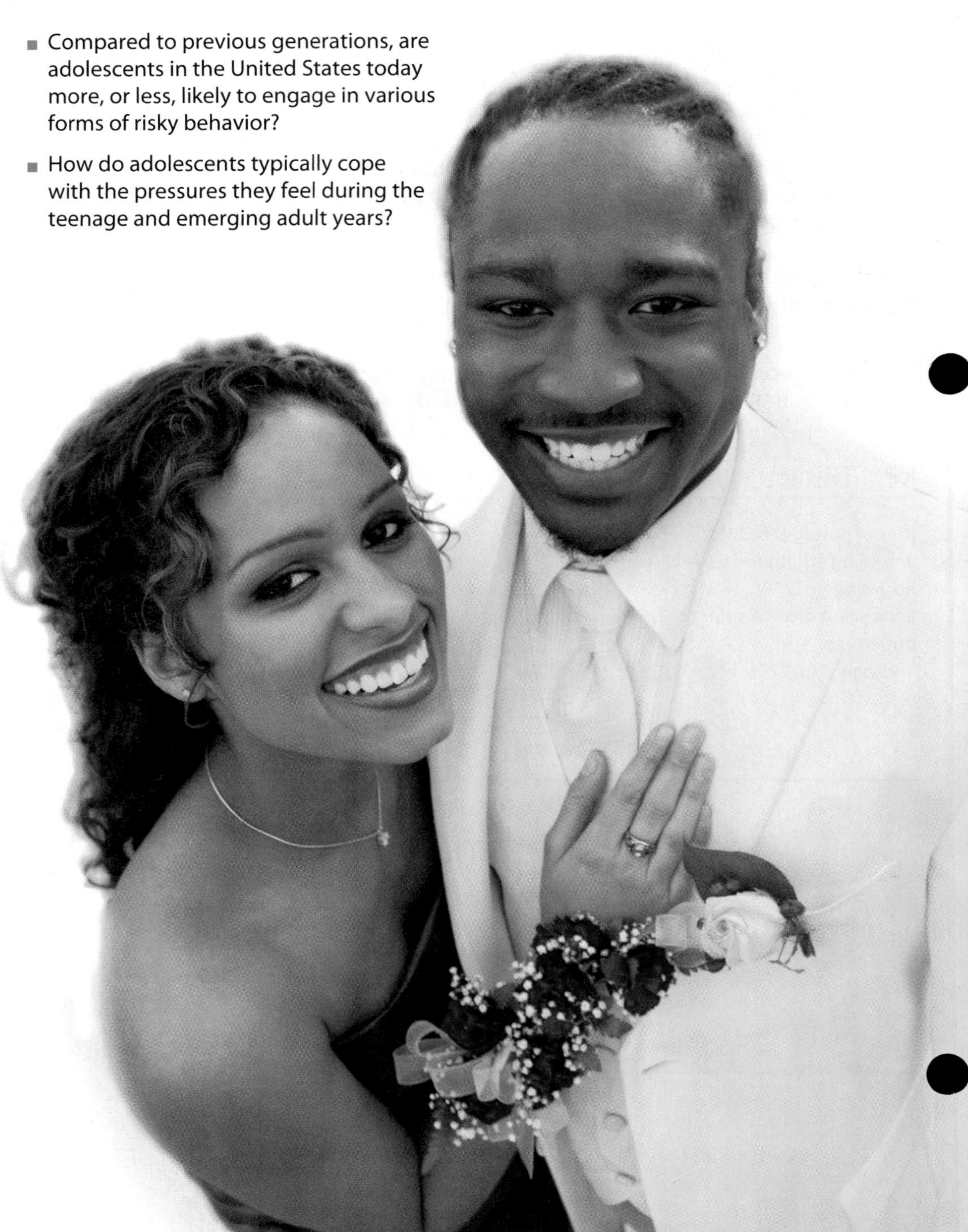

CHAPTER OUTLINE

Developmental Tasks of Adolescence
- Achieving Autonomy
- Forming an Identity
- Identity Formation, Culture, and Context
- "Generation Me"

Family Dynamics
- Intergenerational Communication

Peer Relationships During Adolescence
- Social Comparison
- Cliques and Crowds
- Dating
- Peers and Parents: A Clash of Cultures

Risk and Resilience in Adolescence
- Risk Taking
- The Use of Tobacco, Alcohol, Marijuana, and Other Drugs
- Delinquency
- Sexual Abuse of Adolescents

Stress, Depression, and Coping
- Depression
- Risk Factors for Psychological Problems
- Protective Factors and Coping Responses

In many important ways, adolescence serves as the bridge between childhood and adulthood—it is an important journey of transition in life. As we saw in the previous chapter, not only does the person reach sexual maturity during this stage, but developments in the brain and body also are reflected in changed thought processes, which shape how adolescents view themselves and their roles in the larger world.

Although the transition into adulthood is relatively brief and the roles of individuals are clearly and narrowly defined in some societies, in industrialized nations, the successful transition to adult status often requires lengthy education and occupational training. In these societies, adolescence often stretches from puberty to the late teenage years and often well beyond. As you learned in the previous chapter, researchers today often refer to the period between the end of high school and the full adoption of adult roles and responsibilities as "emerging adulthood," which for many U.S. adolescents spans the ages between 18 and about 25 (Arnett, 2000, 2010a). Today, emerging adults thus live in an extended period of limbo: Despite their physical and intellectual maturity, many have not yet assumed meaningful work and other adult responsibilities. This period of delay can be good or bad, depending on one's point of view. On the one hand, prolonged adolescence gives the young person repeated opportunities to experiment with different adult styles without making irrevocable commitments. On the other hand, a decade or more of adolescence generates certain pressures and conflicts, such as the need to appear independent and sophisticated while still being financially dependent on one's parents.

Adolescence differs from middle childhood in many important ways, not the least of which involves coping with a much wider range of interrelated contexts. Thus, generalizations about development in adolescence and emerging adulthood are difficult to make, since each person's experiences are unique. However, at least in Westernized cultures, most young people experience similar pressures and challenges. As children become teenagers, they must make more choices for themselves, and these choices are made in increasingly complex social environments. Parents protect their adolescents less than they did when they were younger children; therefore, adolescents encounter a broader array of peers, adults, and settings that call on them to exercise good judgment.

Today's adolescents live in an information age, and they are bombarded with messages on every conceivable topic, from how white their teeth should be to how to build a pipe bomb or buy a handgun. In many parts of the world, physical safety and security is a concern. Some adolescents experience a great deal of pressure from their parents, who may transfer to them their own aspirations or unfulfilled dreams to succeed and attain a higher social status. Adolescents must cope with these pressures, as well as with those that come from within themselves. They also must accomplish significant developmental tasks and weave the results into a coherent, functioning identity. Regardless of their particular situations, adolescents draw on the skills, competencies, attitudes, and relationships they have developed with others throughout their childhood in order to meet the challenges and developmental tasks of this period. As they navigate through the choices and experiences that they encounter, the self-concepts and identities that adolescents have developed serve to guide them through this period.

In this chapter, we look at how young people cope with the dilemmas of adolescence and the resulting triumphs and setbacks. We examine how they adopt values, form loyalties, and become more mature through their involvement with their parents and

◀ Contrary to popular belief, adolescence is not inevitably marked by rebellion against parents.

peers—including crowds, cliques, and intimate friends—as well as through the choices they make, which are as wide and varied as society itself. In addition, we explore the stresses and maladaptive coping patterns that also play a role in adolescent development, which sometimes lead to risk-taking behaviors, drug abuse, delinquency, and even depression and suicide. How adolescents cope with the stresses created by their changing bodies and their new roles, of course, depends in part on their personality development in earlier years. To meet new challenges, adolescents and emerging adults draw upon the skills, resources, and strengths they began to develop much earlier as they face the tasks associated with this period of development.

DEVELOPMENTAL TASKS OF ADOLESCENCE

In Western nations, adolescence traditionally has been viewed as a period of "storm and stress," a dramatic upheaval of emotions and behavior. Do most teenagers experience the period of adolescence as traumatic? Research suggests they do not. In fact, perhaps surprisingly, studies generally show that the large majority of adolescents are emotionally healthy and well adjusted and have few major conflicts with their parents, peers, or selves (Smetana, 2005, 2010). Nevertheless, adolescence and emerging adulthood is a period of the lifespan in which many individuals experience somewhat more conflict, greater extremes of mood, and riskier behavior than they did in childhood or will in adulthood. Even so, most scholars now agree that adolescence should not be thought of as a period characterized by dramatic or extreme emotional or psychological upheaval (Arnett, 2007, 2010b).

In thinking about your own adolescence, was achieving autonomy or forming an identity the more significant task?

This conclusion is supported cross-culturally. For example, in a study of about 27,000 adolescents in 24 different countries (including countries in Asia, Africa, the Caribbean, Europe, the Middle East, United States, and Australia), adolescents were asked to rate their own behavioral and emotional problems, along with their own positive qualities (Petot & Rescorla, 2011; Rescorla et al., 2007). Results showed striking similarities in the ways in which adolescents rated their lives. Although some adolescents did report emotional and behavioral problems—most typically mood swings, arguments, self-criticism, and distractibility—the percentage of individuals experiencing significant issues was small. Furthermore, the percentage of parents who reported observing these problems in their adolescent children was even smaller, suggesting that teenagers' judgments of their problems might be overestimated. Taken together with other cross-cultural studies (e.g., Offer, Ostrov, Howard, & Atkinson, 1988), these results suggest that around the world the vast majority of teenagers are well adjusted, get along reasonably well with their parents, and have positive attitudes toward their families.

Thus, media stories with a "generation gap" theme, although dramatic and interesting, have limited evidence to support them. Even though the emotional distance between teenagers and their parents tends to increase in early adolescence, this typically does not lead to rebellion or rejection of parents' values (Smetana, 2005). In fact, the modest amount of resistance to parental authority that is typical of adolescence may be developmentally appropriate, given the adolescent's need to achieve autonomy—a major developmental goal of this period of the lifespan.

As is true in other developmental periods, adolescence and emerging adulthood presents developmental challenges and difficulties that require new skills and responses. Most theorists agree that adolescents must confront two major tasks:

1. Achieving autonomy and independence from their parents (although the form this takes varies across cultures); and
2. Forming an identity, which means creating an integrated self that harmoniously combines different elements of the personality.

Achieving Autonomy

The developmental needs for autonomy and independence that have characterized development from around age 2 on, of course, do continue on through adolescence. However, autonomy and independence for the teenager do not imply that parental influence must be rejected. Most adolescents continue to depend on their family for support and guidance throughout adolescence and even into adulthood (Smetana, 2011; Smetana, Crean, & Campione-Barr, 2005). Perhaps a better way to consider these needs in adolescence is to focus on the concepts of self-regulation and interdependence.

Self-regulation, in the context of the need for independence, means making one's own judgments and regulating one's own behavior, as in the expression, "Think for yourself." Many adolescents learn to do precisely that. They reevaluate the rules, values, and boundaries that they experienced as children at home and at school. Sometimes they encounter considerable resistance from their parents, which may lead to conflict. More often, however, their parents work through the process with them, minimizing areas of conflict and helping them develop independent thought and self-regulated behavior.

When parents and teens can cooperate in problem solving and share with each other their needs, thoughts, and feelings, their relationship is characterized by **interdependence**. Interdependence can be defined as *reciprocal* dependence, where both parties depend on each other. Interdependence is a characteristic of most adult relationships, such as husband and wife or work supervisor and subordinate, and it involves long-term commitments and personal attachments. When parents are able to encourage their teenage children toward self-regulation and

self-regulation
In adolescence, making one's own judgments and regulating one's own behavior

interdependence
Reciprocal dependence, where both parties depend on each other

interdependent relationships, they are preparing them well for their future as adults.

Forming an Identity

Adolescence is a time when young people begin to consider the possibilities that are open to them in life (Moshman, 2011). They reflect on who they are, who they wish to be, and how these two states match up against one another. In the process of **identity formation**, adolescents gain a sense of who they are and how they fit into society, answering the question, "Who am I?"

In the process of identity formation, teenagers are exposed to a wide array of roles and values, particularly in Western cultures, where many lifestyle and career alternatives are available. Adolescents in these cultures are surrounded by a bewildering variety of roles offered by a multitude of **social reference groups** with which they may identify, and in so doing help to define themselves. These groups may include parents, friends, and various social groups to which adolescents belong. Roles that are accepted must be integrated into a personal identity, and this process is harder when role models represent conflicting values. For example, adolescents may face conflicting pressures when their parents want them to pursue college and a professional career but their friends plan to go directly into jobs or into the military following high school. Another example is an adolescent whose friends are "partiers" but whose parents expect strict adherence to conservative religious and social norms. The process of sorting through these competing roles and values is not easy, but it is of central importance in laying the foundation for adulthood. In recognition of its critical role for adolescents, Erik Erikson saw this process—the formation of an identity—as the critical developmental task of adolescence, one which focuses on forging an answer to the question, "Who am I?" Erikson referred to the central task of this period as one involving **identity versus identity confusion**.

Erikson's Concept of Identity Erikson spent much of his professional life as a clinical psychologist, working with adolescents and young adults (Erikson, 1959, 1968). His conception of adolescence as a period of searching for one's identity is widely regarded as the foundation for understanding the personal development that occurs during this period (Kroger, 2003; Kroger & Marcia, 2011). In Erikson's view, adolescence is a period in which young people *try out* various alternative identities as they attempt to sort through the available options and forge their unique sense of who they are. Adolescents who are able to integrate the various aspects of their choices into a coherent view of their *self* thereby attain a secure and stable sense of personal identity. Those who remain confused or conflicted about their various roles feel pulled in different directions by various forces and experience identity confusion. When identity formation is successful, adolescents move into adulthood with clear directions for what they hope to achieve in life. When adolescents are confused about their future roles, they often cope by withdrawing, becoming isolated from their friends and family, or by conforming to the expectations of whatever individuals or groups exert the greatest power over their lives.

Modes of Identity Formation Erikson believed that forming one's identity typically involved an **identity crisis**, during which individuals grapple with the options available and ultimately make a choice and commitment as to which paths their lives will take. Other researchers have taken Erikson's ideas and transformed them into testable research strategies (Archer, 2008). For example, James Marcia (1966) carefully defined the types of identity formation into four modes, or **identity statuses**: *foreclosure, diffusion, moratorium,* and *identity achievement.* The mode of an individual's identity formation at any one time is determined by the degree to which that person experienced an identity crisis and whether or not that person made a **commitment** to a specific set of choices, such as a system of values or a plan for a future occupation (see Table 11-1).

There is some professional debate about how significant the adolescent identity crisis is for healthy development. Did you experience such a crisis?

Adolescents who are in **foreclosure status** have made commitments without going through much decision making or an identity crisis. They have chosen an occupation, a religious outlook, an ideological viewpoint, and other aspects of their identity, but the choices were made early and determined more by their parents or teachers than by themselves. Their transition

Table 11-1 Modes of Identity Formation

Mode of Identity Formation	Identity Crisis?	Commitment?
Foreclosure	No	Yes
Diffusion	No	No
Moratorium	Yes	No
Identity achievement	Yes	Yes

identity formation
Gaining a sense of who you are and how you fit into society

identity crisis
A period during which individuals grapple with the options available and ultimately make a choice and commitment as to which path their lives will take

foreclosure status
The identity status of those who have made commitments without going through much decision making or through an identity crisis

social reference groups
Narrowly or broadly defined groups with which people identify, and in so doing, help to define themselves

identity status
According to Marcia, the type of identity formation experienced by a young person, which is determined by the degree to which that person has experienced an identity crisis and whether or not that person has made a commitment to a specific set of lifestyle choices

identity versus identity confusion
For Erikson, the critical developmental task for adolescents, which focuses on forging an answer to the question, "Who am I?"

commitment
For Marcia, the part of identity formation that involves making a personal investment in the paths one chooses

▲Identity formation is often supported by positive relationships with peers during the period of adolescence and emerging adulthood. By identifying with others, adolescents help define the roles they will adopt.

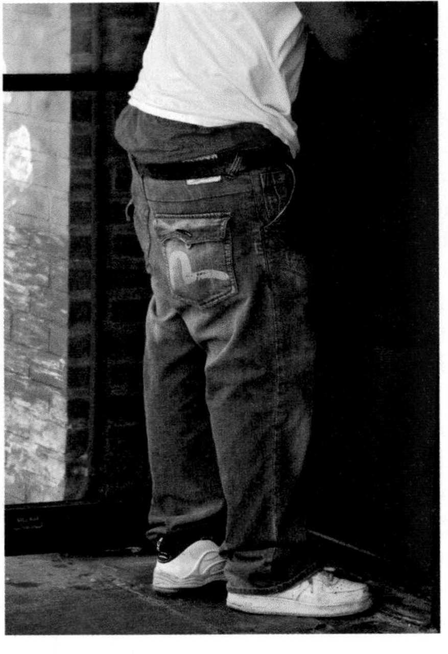

◄ Group identity can also be reflected in freely chosen hairstyles, athletic footwear, and joint activities. Individuality and group identity are developed simultaneously. Here, low-hanging jeans identify this young man as belonging to a certain group.

to adulthood occurs smoothly and with little conflict, but also with little experimentation and self-reflection.

Young people who lack a sense of direction and who seem to have little motivation to find one are in **diffusion status**. They have not experienced a crisis, nor have they selected an occupational role or a moral code. They are simply avoiding the issue. For some, life revolves around immediate gratification; others experiment, seemingly at random, with various kinds of attitudes and behaviors.

Adolescents or young adults in **moratorium status** are in the midst of an ongoing identity crisis or decision-making period. Their decisions may concern occupational choices, religious or ethical values, political philosophies, as well as other aspects of their future lives. Young people in this status are preoccupied with "finding themselves." College students, particularly those who have not identified a particular career path or even a major field of study, often are in this state, sometimes for a year or more, even if they were more decisive in high school. An extended period of decision making, although it may be uncomfortable, often can lead to more thoughtful resolutions.

Finally, **identity achievement** is the status attained by people who have passed through an identity crisis and have made commitments. As a result, they pursue work of their own choosing and attempt to live by their own individually formulated moral code. Identity achievement is usually viewed as the most desirable and the most mature status (Kroger & Marcia, 2011; Marcia, 1980). Identity achievement is difficult, however, and research suggests that perhaps only about half of those entering young adulthood have achieved this status, despite many years spent in emerging adulthood (Kroger, 2007). Generally, however, the period of adolescence and emerging adulthood is characterized by steady progress in achieving a well-integrated sense of personal identity (Klimstra, Hale, Branje, & Meeus, 2010; Meeus, Keijsers, & Branje, 2010). As individuals move into adulthood, they are increasingly likely to move out of moratorium and into identity achievement (Kroger, Martinussen, & Marcia, 2010). Clearly, the period of late adolescence and emerging adulthood is complex and filled with many choices and challenges for those growing up in modern societies (See Table 11-2).

Influences on Identity Formation Marcia's model describing identity formation in adolescence and emerging adulthood has provided researchers with a very useful conceptualization of the changes that take place during this developmental period (Schwartz, Adamson, Ferrer-Wreder, Dillon, & Berman, 2006). Most studies find that patterns of identity development are consistent across various cultures (Graf, Mullis, & Mullis, 2008; Schwartz,

Do any of Marcia's statuses accurately describe your own identity formation?

diffusion status
The identity status of those who have neither gone through an identity crisis nor committed to an occupational role or moral code

moratorium status
The identity status of those who are currently in the midst of an identity crisis or decision-making period

identity achievement
The identity status of those who have gone through an identity crisis and have made commitments

Table 11-2 Characteristics of the Four Modes of Identity Formation

Mode of Identity Formation	Description	Identity Crisis?	Commitment?
Diffusion	• Often associated with parental rejection or neglect • Associated with dropping out of school • Linked to alcohol and drug abuse	No	No
Moratorium	• High anxiety over unresolved choices • High confusion over conflicting options • Struggle for freedom from parents but unable or afraid to break away	Yes	No
Foreclosure	• Low anxiety because choices are made • Often linked to strong, dependent ties to others • Often results from holding authoritarian, rule-following values • May involve lower self-esteem or being easily influenced by others	No	Yes
Identity achievement	• Low anxiety • Low confusion • Self-confident approach to most issues and problems • Usually develops in later adolescence or early adulthood	Yes	Yes

et al., 2006) and ethnic groups (Crocetti, Rubini, Luyckx, & Meeus, 2008; Meeus, 2011; Seaton, Sellers, & Scottham, 2006). Thus, research supports the notion that identity development is a relatively universal developmental process, at least in cultures characterized by an extended period of adolescence and an individualist orientation (Stegarud, Solheim, Karlsen, & Kroger, 1999).

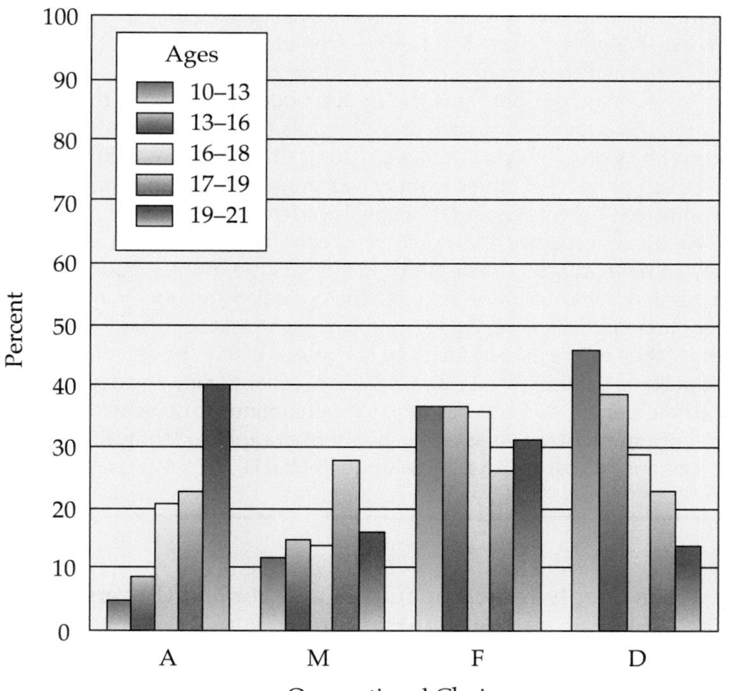

FIGURE 11-1 Changes in Identity Status with Age
The numbers indicate the percentage of people in each identity status category at each age. A = Achievement, M = Moratorium, F = Foreclosure, D = Diffusion.

SOURCE: From "Issues of identity formation revisited: United States and the Netherlands," by A. S. Waterman, *Development Review* (1999, December). Published by Elsevier and reprinted by permission.

However, individuals do take somewhat different paths as they develop their sense of identity (Meeus, Iedema, Helsen, & Vollebergh, 1999). Furthermore, identity development changes with age: For example, there are far more younger adolescents in diffusion and foreclosure status than in moratorium and identity achievement status, and the proportion of people in identity achievement status naturally increases with age (see Figure 11-1). Identity status may also vary according to what aspect of identity is under consideration: A high school student may be in foreclosure status regarding sex-role preference, in moratorium status regarding vocational choice or religious beliefs, and in diffusion status regarding political philosophy. Finally, not all adolescents experience identity formation in predictable patterns (Kroger, Martinssen, & Marica, 2010).

Gender, too, can influence how an adolescent experiences identity formation, typically reflecting the gender stereotypes and expectations of the culture (Berzonsky, 2011; Clemans, DeRose, Graber, & Brooks-Dunn, 2010). For example, although both boys and girls say that they plan to marry, have children, and pursue careers, girls traditionally have been more likely to express concern about possible conflicts between family and career (Archer, 1985, 2002). It has also been found that boys primarily develop *intrapersonal* identity, which focuses on aspects of the self, whereas girls more often develop a blend of intrapersonal and *interpersonal* identity, which includes defining oneself based on relationships with others (Lytel, Bakken, & Romig, 1997). However, gender differences in identity development appear to be shrinking, as opportunities for men and women are becoming more equalized (Alsaker & Kroger, 2006; Kroger, 2002).

Identity Formation, Culture, and Context

As noted in Chapter 1, Erikson's psychosocial theory largely reflects development in Western societies that stress individual accomplishments over group or collective accomplishments. Nowhere is this more evident than in his conceptualization of identity formation during adolescence and emerging adulthood. The emphasis on becoming a distinct, relatively autonomous individual as opposed to becoming a contributing

CURRENT ISSUES

Ethnic Identity—A Key Component of Self-Definition

When teenagers write descriptions about who they are, the portraits they construct usually are rich with comments about the varying facets of their personality and about their relationships with a wide range of people. As they move from early to late adolescence, these narratives become more detailed about personal beliefs, standards, and moral values; most adolescents also gain a more balanced perspective of both their positive and negative attributes (Harter, 1999; Schwartz & Pantin, 2006). By late adolescence or early adulthood the varying components of self-definition—gender, ethnicity, social class status and options, and personality—need to come together to form an integrated self-identity and self-concept.

The teenager's definition of his or her own identity relies considerably on processes that involve social comparison and knowledge of group norms. By comparing themselves to others in and out of their peer groups, individuals come to see how they are similar to and different from others, and they incorporate these perceptions into their definitions of who they are. One aspect of personal identity is the individual's ethnic identity, which represents the values of the cultural or ethnic group to which the person belongs. Adolescents' ethnic identity is influenced by whether they are part of the majority or minority ethnic culture. For most Americans who are White, a close exploration of ethnic identity is not terribly important to identity development, although some adolescents may be interested in their family origins. For these youth, their ethnicity fits nicely within their culture, and therefore crafting an identity that incorporates their ethnicity is not much of an issue. However, for those adolescents who belong to an ethnic minority that is immersed in a majority culture, concerns that focus on the issues of ethnic identity often are of vital importance (Kroger, 2003; Kroger & Marcia, 2011).

One important consideration to keep in mind is that adolescents generally do not have to search for the racial or ethnic group to which they belong—their racial or ethnic origin typically is a highly visible feature in their lives. Thus, by the time children move into the period of early adolescence, they already have a secure sense of their own ethnicity. The task, then, becomes more one of *integrating* their ethnic identity into their more general sense of personal identity (Meeus, 2011).

Because adolescence and early adolescence in particular is a time when peers and social comparison processes both contribute to self-definition and the construction of one's identity, teenagers who are members of ethnic minorities are particularly vulnerable to cultural conflicts. Healthy identity formation is particularly difficult if there is racial prejudice or ethnic targeting (Dubois, Burk-Braxton, Swenson, Tevendale, & Hardesty, 2002; Harris-Britt, Valrie, Kurtz-Costas, & Rowley, 2007). Even "daily hassles," such as teasing, taunting, or minor harassment, can have a cumulative effect on adolescent identity formation. In today's increasingly diverse world, forging a clear sense of cultural identity that integrates the various dimensions of one's life has, indeed, become a rather complex process (Arnett, 2011).

On an individual level, adolescents who identify with an ethnic culture different from that of the majority, such as Asian, Hispanic, or Black youths, often find themselves caught between the standards and values of the majority culture and those embraced by members of their ethnic minority group (Arnett, 2010a; Phinney, 2006). For example, many immigrant children want to honor their family values and traditions; however, they sometimes find these beliefs to be in direct contradiction to their peers' expectations (Phinney, Ong, & Madden, 2000).

On a societal scale, standards that are defined by the majority culture may be in conflict with those embraced by an ethnic minority culture: Consider, for example, how the majority culture in the United States defines perfection in body shape, facial characteristics, hair, speech, and dress. Adolescents who belong to ethnic minorities must take note of their ethnicity, but they must also acknowledge that the majority culture may not reflect or may actually be hostile to the characteristics valued within the ethnic group. Sometimes this means that individuals will experience an *ethnic identity crisis* much like the more general adolescent identity crisis that Erikson described (Phinney, 1989, 2008).

Most researchers believe that developing a strong ethnic identity in adolescence usually leads individuals to a more realistic self-understanding, to the formation of more effective goals, and to higher personal achievement. However, when adolescents reject the standards for achievement set by the majority culture, sometimes less positive adjustment results. One way of understanding why individuals within the same ethnic group adjust in different directions is to view ethnic identity as a complex trait. In one study of low-achieving Black teens, for example, ethnic identity was considered to be comprised of three factors: *race centrality* (the importance of race to the person's self-definition), *private regard* (group pride about belong to the racial group), and *public regard* (how one interprets the majority culture's beliefs about one's group) (Byrd & Chavous, 2011; Chavous, et al., 2003). Each of these components of ethnic identity was shown to have an impact on how minority adolescents viewed traditional academic achievement.

As we all recognize, individuals vary considerably with respect to how they come to interpret their ethnic identity. Some develop counterculture values and behaviors in response to the prejudice and discrimination they feel; others somehow manage to ignore negative attitudes directed at members of their ethnic group and go on to succeed within the definitions set by the majority culture (French, Kim, & Pillado, 2006). Clearly, the development of ethnic identity is an area of study that will continue to generate both interest and important results as researchers further explore identity formation in adolescence (Cross & Cross, 2008; Kroger & Marcia, 2011; Meeus, 2011).

---

member of a cooperative group directly bears this out. In collectivist societies, for the most part, the good of the individual is subordinated to the good of the group—where *group* can refer to family, peers, neighborhood, town, or society at large. That is, collectivist societies place much less emphasis on autonomy and much more on a child or adolescent becoming and remaining interdependent with others. Erikson's theory certainly has been found to have a high degree of universality with regard to development, but what a given culture views as a *favorable* resolution of each developmental period can vary considerably (Matsumoto, 2000). Identity and self-concept are thus deeply rooted in culture and context (Beyers & Çok, 2008; Solomontes-Kountouri & Hurry, 2008).

Cultural variations in identity development also are reflected in Marcia's conceptualization of identity statuses. Although there is evidence that Marcia's four modes of identity development can be found in most cultures, the timing at which different statuses emerge varies considerably from culture to culture, as do gender differences in the statuses (Waterman, 1999). In addition, as various researchers have found, the relative proportion of adolescents in each identity status differs according to culture, especially with respect to views on religion and social philosophy (e.g., Good & Willoughby, 2007; see the box Current Issues: Ethnic Identity—A Key Component of Self-Definition).

Identity formation is a general process experienced in various ways by all adolescents (Kroger & Marcia, 2011; Meeus, 2011). However, the process of forging a secure and positive sense of self generally is more difficult when one belongs to a group defined as being outside the majority culture (Cohler & Hammack, 2007). Identity formation is particularly hard when homosexuality is an issue, especially for boys. Many lesbians and gay male adolescents come to understand that they are different by age 6 or 7, but at this age they generally do not have names for their concerns or ways to discuss their feelings with others. These issues often crystallize in adolescence as they discover how different their thoughts and feelings are from their peers, as well as how others respond to their sexual orientation (Worthington, Navarro, Savoy, & Hampton, 2008). (We discuss homosexuality in greater detail in Chapter 12.) It is no accident that adolescent gay males have one of the highest suicide rates of any group; the guilt sometimes experienced by gay teens can be overwhelming, especially when their peer groups judge this central aspect of their identity to be unacceptable. However, recent research suggests that today's generation of youth are much more accepting of sexual diversity, and this is lessening the trauma associated with identity formation for gay men, lesbian women, and other youth who embrace nonmainstream forms of sexual identity (Dillon, Worthington, & Moradi, 2011; Savin-Williams, 2011). Families, and especially mothers, also play a large role in how adolescents—homosexual and otherwise—develop their concepts of who they are and who they will become (Koepke & Denissen, 2012; Missotten, Luyckx, Branje, Vanhalst, & Goossens, 2011).

What steps do you think families should take to support the identity development of a gay or lesbian family member?

"Generation Me"

Because environmental circumstances exert an impact on identity formation during adolescence, it seems reasonable that broad social and cultural forces might shape adolescent development in general, population-wide patterns. There is no doubt that American culture has changed significantly over the past few decades, leading those in the popular media to describe the resulting history-graded age cohorts with catchy-sounding names. For example, the "Baby Boomers," who were born between the years 1946 and 1961, grew up during the Vietnam War era, and their experiences were strongly shaped by the civil rights and women's movements. As noted in Chapter 10, Baby Boomers as a group typically subscribe to more liberal social and sexual practices than either their parents or their children, reflecting the social movements of importance during their own adolescence. People born in the United States between 1962 and 1981 are referred to as members of "Generation X," a group characterized as more conservative, better educated, and much more diverse than the generation that preceded it. People born in the two decades following the early 1980s belong to the cohort referred to as "Generation Y," "the Millennials," or "Generation Me."

How do the member of Generation Me compare to those who belong to earlier cohort generations? Researchers who study generational patterns often cite evidence to suggest that members of Generation Me are individuals interested in their own lives and their own happiness. For example, research conducted by Jean Twenge and her colleagues suggests that college-age students today are significantly more concerned with their own financial success than were members of previous generations (Twenge, Campbell, & Freeman, 2012). Based on data gathered in several large, ongoing, national surveys of youth and emerging adults, these researchers found that among today's Generation Me members, the most important life goal was "being well off financially." Generation Me members also were found to be less concerned with others, less engaged in community and civic affairs, and less interested in preserving the environment. They also placed more value on leisure time and on working at a job in which they could maintain a balance between their professional and personal life goals (Twenge & Campbell, 2010b). Members of the Baby Boomer cohort, on the other hand, usually gave top priority to personal fulfillment of goals of a different sort. When they were emerging adults, members of the Boomer generation placed most value on crafting a meaningful and purposeful philosophy of life, along with keeping up to date with political affairs and working to improve the environment. Results from this study, and similar studies, suggest that today's adolescents and emerging adults place more value on money and on "doing their own thing" and less value on being involved in governmental and civic affairs than did members of their parents' generation (Twenge & Campbell, 2010a; Twenge, Campbell, & Hoffman, 2010).

However, not all researchers agree that today's generation of youth is more self-centered, narcissistic, or materialistic than were members of previous generations (Trzesniewski & Donnellan, 2010). Although there do seem to be some meaningful cohort differences between the Generation Me cohort and those growing up in earlier generations, these differences may be due to the general way in which adults of *any* generation see those in the "next generation." For example, young people today seem to be less fearful of social problems than were those of their parents' generation. If this is the case, then lower ratings on questions asking about their concern for the environment make sense not as a case of diminished interest but rather of greater confidence in our ability to address these issues successfully. Thus, changes in the patterns of how young people answer questions about their values may reflect not so much on how their *values* differ from those of their parents, but rather on how their *lives* differ. Compared to adults of a generation ago, young people today spend more years in education, have greater debt and expenses to contend with, and delay marriage and childbearing until later in their lives. These sorts of changes in life patterns make it easier for older adults to see the Generation Me members as selfish, somewhat lazy, and self-centered (Arnett, 2012).

Regardless of the point of view one takes in this debate, it is clear that development in adolescence and emerging adulthood is heavily conditioned by relationships with others. Young people's experiences in their families and with their peers are powerful forces that shape their development. It is to these topics that we now turn.

REVIEW THE FACTS 11-1

1. What are the two fundamental developmental tasks of adolescence?
2. Do the majority of adolescents experience a period of "storm and stress"?
3. When teens and parents can cooperate and share their needs, thoughts, and feelings, the result is ________.
4. The developmental task of adolescence, according to Erikson, is one involving ________.
5. Match each of Marcia's types of identity status to its definition:

a. diffusion | b. identity achievement
c. moratorium | d. foreclosure

i. Being in the midst of exploring options
ii. A resolution that is reached too quickly, without enough self-exploration
iii. A successful resolution of an identity crisis
iv. A failure to explore options or make a commitment

6. Is identity formation typically more difficult or less difficult for members of ethnic minority groups?

FAMILY DYNAMICS

Throughout the process of identity formation, adolescents are forced to assess their own values and behaviors in relation to those of their family. In turn, the most important tasks of parenthood often seem paradoxical. On the one hand, successful parents provide their children with a sense of security and roots in an environment in which the children feel loved and accepted. On the other hand, successful parents encourage their children to become self-directing adults who can function independently in society. Furthermore, family systems are dynamic: Behavioral changes in one family member influence every other member of the family. Such changes sometimes produce conflict, which is reflected in intergenerational communication.

Intergenerational Communication

The adolescent's emerging need for autonomy and self-definition normally leads to at least some conflict within the family and an increased need to talk with parents about certain issues. Adolescents remain very much influenced by their families, although at times their ties to the family may become strained. However, studies have consistently shown that there is much less conflict between adolescents and their families than often is assumed (Smetana, 2005, 2011). Most conflicts revolve around ordinary issues, such as family chores, curfew hours, dating, grades, personal appearance, and eating habits. Conflicts between parents and adolescents about core economic, religious, social, and political values are much less common, probably because the relatively few adolescents who form truly independent opinions about ideological matters generally do so late in high school or in college.

However, research does show that conflict with parents peaks in early to middle adolescence (see Figure 11-2), especially if sons or daughters mature early (Collins & Laursen, 2006). Conflict then begins to subside in later adolescence (Granic, Dishion, & Hollenskin, 2003). When teenagers and their parents are older, both are better able to come to grips with potentially difficult autonomy and separation issues. It is important for parents and adolescents alike to realize that if they can maintain communication and share their respective views during adolescence, the difficult issues that arise almost always can be negotiated successfully.

Family Alliances Family alliances play a powerful role in communication. Like parenting styles, they begin to shape behavior long before adolescence. An older brother who dominated his younger brother during childhood will probably have the same influence in adolescence; a daughter who was "Daddy's girl" at age 6 will probably remain close to her father when she is 16.

Although alliances between various family members are natural and healthy, it is important that parents maintain a united front and a distinct boundary between themselves and their children. Parents also need to work together to nurture and discipline their children; a close bond between a child and one parent that excludes the other parent can be especially disruptive because the excluded parent loses stature as a socializing agent and an authority figure. Problems also arise from other kinds

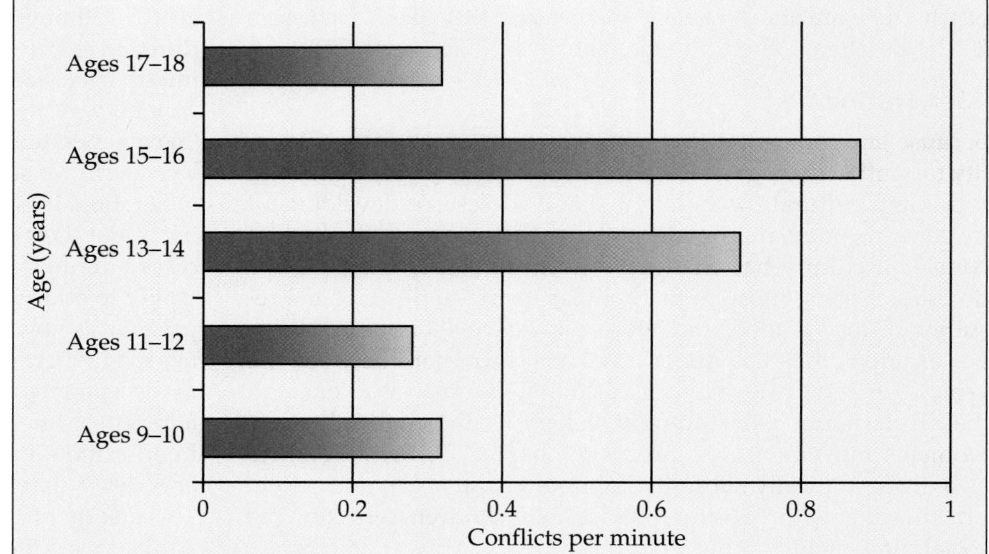

FIGURE 11-2 Mother–Son Conflict Patterns During Adolescence
Observed conflicts per minute between mother and son in 30-minute videotaped interactions over an 8-year period.

SOURCE: Graph in "The family ecology of adolescence," by I. Granic, T. J. Dishion, and T. Hollenstein, 2003, in G. R. Adams and M. D. Berzonsky (Eds.), *Blackwell handbook of adolescence*, pp. 66–91, UK: Blackwell Publishing. Copyright © 2003. Reprinted by permission of Blackwell Publishing, UK.

▲ In general, the greater involvement of mothers in their adolescent children's daily life activities, such as homework, tends to make these mother–adolescent relationships more complex than those that adolescents and their fathers experience.

of imbalance, such as the absence of one parent because of divorce or separation (Bachman, Coley, & Carrano, 2012). When an adolescent is testing new roles and struggling to achieve a new identity, parental authority may be severely tested, especially in a single-parent home.

Parenting Styles and Parental Monitoring In Chapter 7, we discussed the influences of different parenting styles on children's psychological makeup. As you would expect, these influences continue into adolescence. The link between parenting style and identity formation appears in a variety of different cultural and ethnic groups, indicating the general nature of these relationships (Lamborn, Dornbusch, & Steinberg, 1996).

As you may recall, *authoritarian* parents are low in warmth and high in their demand of control over their children's behavior; *permissive* parents are the opposite—high in warmth but low in control. Adolescents who have experienced authoritarian parenting, which centers on enforcement of inflexible rules for behavior, often become dependent and anxious in the presence of authority figures or may become defiant and resentful. Permissive parents provide little structure, and their adolescent children may have difficulty setting boundaries and defining appropriate behavior.

Normal and healthy adolescent behavior is most likely to result when parenting is *authoritative,* because this style encourages children toward taking responsible, independent actions and establishing good self-acceptance and self-control (Baumrind, 1991). You may recall that authoritative parents are high in warmth and they set reasonable, somewhat flexible limits for their children. Authoritative parenting also takes into account the adolescent's increased cognitive ability: For the first time, both parents and children can communicate using the same or similar levels of reasoning and logic. The warmth and the confident control provided by authoritative parents also is reassuring to most adolescents (Wang, Dishion, Stormshak, & Willett, 2011).

Mothers and fathers, however, influence their teenagers in somewhat different ways. To begin with, mothers generally know more about their adolescents' activities than fathers, and more maternal knowledge is associated with lower levels of adolescent deviance (Urry, Nelson, & Padilla-Walker, 2011; Waizenhofer, Buchanan, & Jackson-Newsom, 2004). Furthermore, mothers exert a stronger influence than fathers on both parent–child acceptance and conflict (Shearer, Crouter, & McHale, 2005). Especially when communication between mothers and adolescents breaks down, adolescent identity formation may be thwarted (Laursen, DeLay, & Adams, 2010; Reis & Youniss, 2004). What aspects of the mother–child relationship seem especially important? In one study of 1,893 sixth graders, results showed that when mothers adopted a harsh attitude, children were more likely to display problem behaviors. When mothers were overly intrusive into their young adolescents' lives or when they demonstrated little acceptance of their children's choices, the children in this study were more likely to develop emotional difficulties. Finally, when mothers were inconsistent in their relationships with their children, both behavioral and psychological difficulties emerged (Benson, Buehler, & Gerard, 2008).

Were the roles played by your mother and father during your adolescence typical of most parents? Why or why not?

Mothers' roles have undergone considerable change over the past few decades, as we will discuss more fully in Chapter 13. More mothers now work outside the home, often in full-time jobs. More children also are being raised in homes in which fathers are absent. Not surprisingly, as mothers' roles have changed, so have the roles of other members of the family, often in surprising ways (see the box Changing Perspectives: Family Obligation and Assistance During Adolescence).

Thus, it is difficult to make generalizations about family dynamics. However, it is clear that fathers and other family members play an important role in adolescent development and that family relationships are complex. Studies often show that children in the same family have quite different experiences with parents during adolescence. For example, as children enter adolescence, parental warmth generally declines, both from mothers and from fathers. However, this decline in outward affection is greater for first-born children in the family than for younger children (Shanahan, McHale, Crouter, & Osgood, 2007). Similarly, family conflict typically escalates when first-born children enter adolescence, but the level of conflict generally does not increase when younger children enter this developmental period (Shanahan, McHale, Crouter, & Osgood, 2007).

Not surprisingly, adolescents are influenced by their parents' conflict resolution style. In a study that looked at how parents solved problems and resolved conflicts with each other, adolescents were seen to have adopted a similar problem-solving style and approach to dealing with conflict 2 years later (Van Doom, Branje, & Meeus, 2007). Family stress is important in adolescent development. When problems exist within the family, the stress often spills over, leading to a variety of problems for the adolescent, including poorer performance in school (Flook & Fuligni, 2008; Fosco, Caruthers, & Dishion, 2012).

CHANGING PERSPECTIVES

Family Obligation and Assistance During Adolescence

Many cultural traditions embrace values of family solidarity, respect, and commitment. Historically in the United States, this often meant that adolescents, and even children, were expected to take on obligations and responsibilities for the greater good of the family (Fuligni, Alvarez, Bachman, & Ruble, 2005). Similar values continue to be expressed in many traditional U.S. families today, especially when children live in single-parent or dual-career households or in households headed by immigrant parents. Furthermore, in today's information age, families often recognize that the best way for children to support the family's welfare is to not only perform household tasks but also to attain high academic achievement. How do teens today handle these multiple responsibilities?

In one study of the coping patterns of dual-career families, researchers investigated when and under what conditions parents were likely to call on their children to take on more household obligations and responsibilities. This effort, the Penn State Family Relations project, involved interviews not only of children but of mothers and fathers as well (Crouter, Head, Bumpus, & McHale, 2001). Parents were interviewed about their jobs—the hours, the stress, the work pressures, and the work overload. The tasks that parents assigned to their children were assessed in two ways—by asking parents what their children were expected to do and by interviewing children on the phone about their duties and responsibilities to the family. Results showed that teens of working parents were asked to take on some family responsibilities, especially when the mother's job (but not necessarily the father's) was particularly stressful. When the mother's job was especially demanding, the oldest child typically rose to the occasion and took on greater responsibility, and younger siblings usually increased their duties a little bit. However, one of the more notable findings was that daughters, far more than sons, assumed the obligations when the parents needed help. This was true even when there was an older brother, and it reflects a general historical tradition for women to assume household responsibilities.

What about cultural differences in the expectations placed on teens? In one ongoing longitudinal study of the responsibilities assigned to teenagers in the United States, Andrew Fuligni (2001b, 2006) and his colleagues have been following about 1,000 adolescents from an ethnically diverse district in the San Francisco Bay area. Two-thirds of the adolescents in the study have at least one parent who was foreign-born. Participants who represent five ethnic backgrounds—Chinese, Filipino, Mexican, Central and South American, and European ancestry—were studied in 8th, 10th, and 12th grades. After participating in focus group discussions about family duties and obligations, students were surveyed about three types of family obligations. The first type of family obligation, called *current assistance,* included running errands, performing household chores, and babysitting. The second type was labeled was *family respect,* and it included showing respect to older family members, making sacrifices, and performing well for the sake of the family. Finally, the third type of family obligation, called *future support,* was assessed with questions about plans to send money from future earnings to the family or assume obligations for educating younger siblings. Included in the assessment were the adolescents' attitudes about doing well in school, both in general, and in math and English in particular.

Contrary to popular belief, many teens maintain regular family chores and responsibilities, and most pitch in during illness or family difficulties, as demonstrated by this adolescent girl who is helping out with home maintenance chores.

Did adolescents in families of different ethnic backgrounds approach their responsibilities in different ways? In many respects, yes. In comparison to adolescents whose parents represented European backgrounds, those from the other four ethnic traditions reported feeling greater obligation to their families in all three types of family obligation. Findings such as these are typical: Children of immigrant parents experience a greater sense of family obligation—and a sense of well-being when they perform these obligations (Fuligni & Masten, 2010; Telzer & Fuligni, 2009). This seems particularly true for children of non-European immigrants (Kiang & Fuligni, 2009).

Furthermore, adolescents from non-European groups also were more likely to recognize the value of school success, especially in the areas of math and English, although they did not *like* these subjects any more than the adolescents from the European background did. In terms of results, in every ethnic group studied, children of immigrant parents persisted longer and achieved higher education attainments than did children of American-born comparison groups (Fuligni & Witkow, 2004). In particular, persistence in difficult subjects such as math is more likely when students receive high levels of encouragement from their parents—a key dimension in many immigrant families (Witkow & Fuligni, 2011). Given that nearly one-fifth of children living in the United States today have immigrant parents, the remarkable success of these adolescents in school is notable.

As you think about the results of these studies, do you see how gender, culture, and work pressures on parents might be reflected in your own family or in the families of your friends? In your family, are adolescents expected to share household tasks with parents or siblings? Are there gender issues involved? Do you know students from immigrant families who work especially hard in school? Do you know of some who do not? What changes do you think currently are occurring in the expectations of adolescents to participate in family obligations? What family roles and responsibilities do you think are reasonable and appropriate for parents to expect of teenagers?

Watch *Adolescence: Identity and Role Development* on **MyDevelopmentLab**

Increasingly, as adolescents move closer to adulthood, parental control usually gives way to *parental monitoring*. Parents discuss, give advice, and supervise, but only to the extent with which the teen is comfortable. Parents who have built a strong relationship of mutual trust with their children are likely to have teenagers who provide more detail on their activities, relationships, and so forth (Smetana, Villalobos, Tasopoulos-Chan, Gettman, & Campione-Barr, 2009). Children whose parents engage in successful parental monitoring typically develop more positive behaviors, and fathers seem to play an especially important role in forging strong connections with their adolescent children (Fosco, Stormshak, Dishion, & Winter, 2012; Véronneau & Dishion, 2010). But at times, especially when there are clashes in values or breakdowns in the relationship, there is less disclosure by teens, and hence less parental monitoring. Because parents cannot follow a teenager around or force a conversation when the teen is unwilling, a better approach may be to try to improve the relationship or to discover the nature of the clash in values (Kakihara, Tilton-Weaver, Kerr, & Stattin, 2010; Kerr & Stattin, 2000).

Regardless of the specific nature of relationships within a family, as adolescents become more independent of their families, they depend increasingly on friendships to provide emotional support and serve as testing grounds for new values. Feeling accepted and liked by others is important to identity formation, and studying peer relationships during adolescence provides an important key in understanding the developmental events associated with this period of the lifespan, which we explore in the next section.

REVIEW THE FACTS 11-2

1. Is family conflict generally greater in early adolescence or in late adolescence?
2. Which of the following parenting styles appears to be most effective during adolescence?
   a. authoritative parenting
   b. permissive parenting
   c. authoritarian parenting
   d. retroactive parenting
3. Does family conflict increase most when the oldest, the middle, or the youngest child enters adolescence?
4. Parents' ability to know what their teens are thinking and doing is referred to as parental ________.

Practice on **MyDevelopmentLab**

PEER RELATIONSHIPS DURING ADOLESCENCE

During adolescence, the importance of peer groups increases enormously. Teenagers seek support from others in coping with the physical, emotional, and social changes of adolescence. Understandably, they are most likely to seek support from peers who are going through the same experiences, and close friends in particular help in identity formation. Not surprisingly, adolescents spend large amounts of time with their friends—often more than twice as much as they spend with their parents (Larson, 2004). The development of social media and the widespread availability of cellular telephones has made it virtually possible to "be with" friends at any hour of the day. Whether they rely on media or on face-to-face communication, peer networks are particularly important to the development of social skills. Teenagers learn from their friends and others their age the kinds of behavior that will be socially rewarded and the roles that suit them best, often by making *social comparisons,* which involves evaluating the characteristics of friends, as compared to various aspects of the self.

Can you think of cultures or subcultures in which adolescents spend less time with peers than is typical among middle-class U.S. teenagers? Are there some cultures in which more time is spent with peers?

Social Comparison

Social comparison is the process we all use to evaluate our abilities, behaviors, personality characteristics, appearance, reactions, and general sense of self in comparison to those of others, and it takes on tremendous importance during adolescence. Social comparison begins in early childhood and evolves during the adolescent years (Bagwell & Schmidt, 2011).

During early adolescence, teenagers spend their time and energy defining themselves in a diverse *peer arena* made up of many different kinds of young people; they use this arena to explore various roles and define who they are and who they want to become. Often, in their early teenage years, adolescents focus on their appearance and on those personality characteristics that make them popular, such as a sense of humor and friendliness.

Peers serve as audience, critic, and emotional support for their friends' ideas, innovations, and behavior.

Watch *Adolescence: Identity and Role Development and Sexual Orientation* on **MyDevelopmentLab**

Watch *Peer Groups in Adolescence* on **MyDevelopmentLab**

social comparison
The process of evaluating oneself and one's situation relative to others

Their activities typically involve a wide circle of acquaintances but few close friends; many of their relationships lack intimacy. Teenagers also need time by themselves during this stage to sort out the different messages they receive, to consolidate their identity, and to develop a secure sense of self. Social comparison changes during later adolescence. During these years, teenagers usually seek friends with whom they share similar characteristics, as they come to prefer the quality provided by a few close friendships to a larger quantity of relatively loose friendships that was more typical of earlier adolescence. Intimacy in same-sex friendships also increases (Engels, Kerr, & Stattin, 2007).

As friendships become more intimate, teenagers tend to turn to close friends instead of to their parents for advice (Nomaguchi, 2008). Friends serve as important consultants for many adolescents. As Table 11-3 shows, adolescents are likely to ask their peers for advice on many matters, particularly those relating to style and social concerns. However, they continue to seek advice from their parents on more important matters such as education, finances, and career plans (Brown & Klute, 2003).

Intimacy in adolescent friendship typically extends beyond asking for advice; it also involves sharing personal feelings and concerns (Bukowski, Simard, Dubois, & Lopez, 2011). For example, between ages 12 and 17, adolescents increasingly are likely to agree with statements such as "I feel free to talk with my friend about almost anything" and "I know how my friend feels about things without his or her telling me." Most adolescents report that they have one or two "best friends" as well as several "good friends." These friendships tend to be stable and usually last for at least a year. Not surprisingly, the stability and closeness of relationships increase as adolescence progresses, and friendships exist within the context of larger social groups that contribute to adolescents' personal development.

Table 11-3 Percentage of Teenagers Seeking Advice from Peers on Specific Issues

Issues	Percentage of Girls	Percentage of Boys
• What to spend money on	2%	19%
• Whom to date	47%	41%
• Which clubs to join	60%	54%
• Where to get advice on personal problems	53%	27%
• How to dress	53%	43%
• Which courses to take at school	16%	8%
• Which hobbies to take up	36%	46%
• How to choose a future occupation	2%	0%
• Which social events to attend	60%	66%
• Whether to go to college	0%	0%
• What books to read	40%	38%
• What magazines to buy	51%	46%
• How often to date	24%	35%
• Whether to participate in drinking parties	40%	46%
• How to choose a future spouse	9%	8%
• Whether to go steady	29%	30%
• How intimate to be on a date	24%	35%
• Where to get information about sex	44%	30%

SOURCE: Adapted from "Adolescents' peer orientation: Changes in the support system during the past three decades," by H. Sebald, *Adolescence*, Winter 1989, 940–941.

Friendships and Electronic Media Increasingly, children and adolescents are using media both to seek advice from and to stay in touch with their friends. Technology is advancing so rapidly that it is difficult to keep pace with how today's teenagers are responding (Subrahmanyam & Šmahel, 2011). In 1980, the typical U.S. home included one television set that received about 10 different channels (Warren & Sroufe, 2004). Media use, thus, was a negotiated and shared activity, as parents and children usually watched the same shows together. Today, of course, there is an entirely different landscape of media choices, ranging from TVs that receive hundreds of different channels to the widespread availability of the Internet, which is instantaneously available to anyone who has a smartphone. Phones, too, are a part of nearly every teenager's life: It is difficult to find a U.S. teenager who does not own some sort of cell phone, which is used not only for voice communication but also for instant messaging, texting, shopping, research, and even occasionally for completing assignments for school. Clearly, adolescents today have virtually unlimited access to virtually unlimited information, and they can communicate with virtually anyone on Earth.

Anyone who spends any time at all with teenagers today knows that they use this technology, and they use it a lot. For example, in a recent national survey of 8- to 18-year-olds in the United States, researchers found that adolescents were using some form of media more than 7.5 hours per day—more time than they spent in school or with their parents or peers (Rideout, Foehr, & Roberts, 2010; see Figure 11-3). Furthermore, more than a quarter of the time spent involved using two or more media sources simultaneously—talking on the phone while surfing the Internet, for example, or watching TV while typing a homework paper. Added together, the typical U.S. teen spends nearly 11 hours a day in the presence of media—more time than in any other activity, including sleep, school, or interacting with parents and peers. What effect on development has this technological revolution had?

Generally speaking, the rampant use of and reliance on media among adolescents raises two overarching questions: Is the exposure to largely unmonitored media programming leading teens to be more aggressive, more sexual, or to engage in less healthy behaviors? Is the reliance of teens on media displacing or changing the nature of adolescent friendships?

In response to the first question, the answer seems to be mixed (Roberts, Henriksen, & Foehr, 2009). Children have long been exposed to violent programming on television, and thousands of studies have investigated the impact that viewing violent programming has on aggression (see Chapter 7). Most research suggests that the impact is relatively modest, although it may be significant among a small number of vulnerable

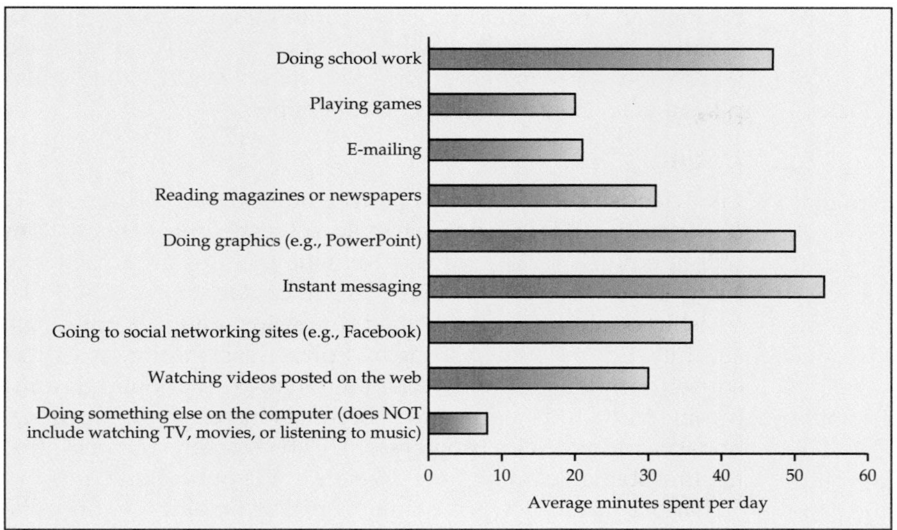

FIGURE 11-3 Minutes per Day Spent on Various Computer-Related Activities Among U.S. High School Students Who Use a Computer on a Regular Basis

SOURCE: *Generation M²: Media in the lives of 8- to 18-year olds, a Kaiser Family Foundation Study* (p. 74), by V. J. Rideout, U. G. Foehr, and D. F. Roberts, 2010, Menlo Park, CA: Henry J. Kaiser Family Foundation: Menlo Park, CA, retrieved from http://www.kff.org/entmedia/upload/8010.pdf.

individuals (Holtz & Appel, 2011). As the number of platforms by which violent programming is presented expands—to video games, Internet sites, virtual reality simulations, and beyond—it remains to be seen if these more "real" forms of violent interactions have a stronger impact on teens who use them. With respect to sexuality, a slightly clearer picture emerges. Research shows, for example, that teens who express a heavier interest in programming and games with explicit sexual content also are more likely to engage in their first sexual intercourse at younger ages (Bleakley, Hennessy, Fishbein, & Jordan, 2008; Brown, et al., 2006). Research also shows that teens who view sexually explicit programming, or who listen to music with sexually degrading language and themes, are more likely to become pregnant (Chandra et al., 2008; Martino et al., 2006). Of course, these results are correlational, and therefore circular: We don't know if teens more interested in sex seek out sexually explicit media, or if the media predisposes teens toward earlier sexual behavior. In any case, however, the link is there, and most researchers suspect that early exposure accelerates the emergence of sexual behavior among adolescents, at least some degree (Brown & Bobkowski, 2011). Early exposure to sexually explicit content also encourages a more gender-stereotyped view of sexuality and—for inexperienced teens—contributes to sexual knowledge. Some researchers speculate that having more knowledge about sex may encourage teens who otherwise would worry about their performance to have more confidence in knowing how to engage in sexual relationships. Whether this is good or bad depends on one's point of view.

With respect to general health, it is not hard to conclude that when teens are using media, they are not out exercising, and their physical fitness may suffer. Also, media programming is supported by advertisers, and many of the messages aimed at teens involve the promotion of unhealthy food choices, on the one hand, and an unrealistic image of body thinness, on the other (see Chapter 9). Indeed, about one-quarter of all ads pitched to U.S. adolescents are for food, beverages, or fast-food restaurants; the average U.S. teenager will see about 17 food-related ads a day—virtually all for high-calorie, low-nutritional-value food options (Gantz, Schwartz, Angelini, & Rideout, 2007). As the authors of one paper point out, the media world is populated with beautiful, thin women and muscular, fit men who apparently can eat all of the junk food advertised and still keep their "perfect" appearance (Brown & Bobkowski, 2011). It is difficult to imagine that the bombardment of teens with these images contributes to the development of positive views of the self.

With respect to friendships, yet a different concern about media emerges. On the one hand, given that the typical teenager is absorbed with media for more than 7 hours a day, this leaves relatively little time for face-to-face conversations with peers, or for just "hanging out." However, much of the time teens spend using media involves *social* media, such as Facebook or MySpace, through which they communicate with their peers, either alone or in groups of users. In a national survey of U.S. children ages 8 to 18 years, over 80% of high school students reported that they had visited a social networking site, and nearly three-fourths had created a profile (Rideout, Foehr, & Roberts, 2010). Because the explosion of social media technology is so new, very little research has been published that investigates the longer-term impact that its use has on the development of friendships and social relationships. Early reports suggest that adolescent friendship patterns have not changed all that much (Reich, Subrahmanyam, & Espinoza, 2012; Williams & Merten, 2011). Although some researchers suggest that online relationships cannot adequately substitute for face-to-face friendships (Donchi, Moore, Valkenburg, & Peter, 2010), others suggest that the wide availability of electronic access may actually have positive implications for adolescent development, as it allows teenagers to gather information on topics of interest to them, to stay connected to their peers, and to support the face-to-face friendships they already have as well as develop positive relationships with others whom they would not meet without the assistance of technology (Mesch & Talmud, 2010). Perhaps at this point the best conclusion to draw is that media use among teenagers appears to be here to stay, and it remains to be seen if it will influence significantly how adolescents interact with their peers—the topic to which we now turn.

Cliques and Crowds

In adolescence, there are two basic types of peer groups, which are distinguished by size. The larger type, with perhaps 15 to 30 members, is called a **crowd**; the smaller type, which might have as few

crowd
Adolescent peer group with perhaps 15 to 30 members

as 3 members or as many as 9, is called a **clique**, and is more cohesive. Peer crowds typically have two or more cliques within them.

Clique members typically share similar backgrounds, characteristics, interests, or reputations; examples include "jocks," "populars," "brains," and "druggies." During early adolescence, cliques tend to be all male or all female; later, teenagers become involved in opposite-sex cliques as well, which is a change that coincides with the beginning of dating. Interestingly, the process of forming groups that include members of both sexes typically involves combining same-sex cliques that were formed earlier (Atwater, 1996): For example, a clique of girls might join a clique of boys to form a new mixed-sex group.

Loners Although about 80% of adolescents belong to identifiable cliques and crowds, 20% don't and are therefore "loners." Most of us think of being alone as a sad state of affairs that no one would willingly choose, but this is not necessarily the case. Some people experience a sense of renewal or healing when alone. When aloneness is *voluntary*, it can provide a welcomed opportunity for creativity, relief from pressures, or psychological renewal.

More often, however, adolescents wind up as loners because they feel that they are different and strange and cannot really "belong." This can happen for many reasons, but a striking reason is having grown up in a markedly different family, ethnic group, or even region of the country. Adolescents who have been raised abroad and then return to their home country often have a particularly difficult time adjusting (Smith, 1994).

For adolescents who are *different* from others, identity formation may be particularly challenging because they are frequently treated as outsiders by their peers. These adolescents often find it difficult to gain acceptance in already established crowds or cliques, especially if their outlooks and values are very different from those of their peers. Because teenagers tend to choose friends based on shared interests and activities, those who enjoy unusual activities or interests often become loners, at least for a time. Of course, having a unique perspective on the world is not the only factor involved in spending time as a loner. Some children become loners because they are shy or become anxious in the presence of other children (Woodhouse, Dykas, & Cassidy, 2012). Given the mixing up of childhood friends that often takes place as children move into middle school, and then again into high school, it is not difficult to see how socially anxious children can feel left out or unsure of themselves (Rubin, Bowker, & Gazelle, 2010). This form of loneliness generally is lessened if the loner child has even a few good friends (Erath, Flanagan, Bierman, & Tu, 2010). Most children, in fact, do manage to forge friendships with peers during adolescence, as groups of friends shuffle around. However, some children and teens will never feel that they truly belong. *Involuntary* aloneness imposed by others through arguments and rejection can bring on severe feelings of isolation and depression (Asher & Paquette, 2004), as can awkwardness with members of the opposite sex because dating also plays a major role in adolescent development.

What specific factors might predispose an adolescent toward involuntarily becoming a loner?

Dating

Like friendship, dating evolves throughout adolescence (Connolly & McIsaac, 2011). During early adolescence, most interactions with members of the opposite sex take place in group settings. Many 14- or 15-year-olds prefer group contact to the closer relationship of dating. In the United States, just hanging out—such as sitting around and chatting in a pizzeria, standing on a street corner, or milling around a shopping mall—is a popular pastime throughout adolescence, and it becomes increasingly "coeducational" as adolescence progresses. This type of interaction is often the first step in learning how to relate to the opposite sex.

Early adolescence is a stage of testing, imagining, and discovering what it is like to function in mixed groups and pairs. It gives adolescents a trial period to collect ideas and experiences from which to form basic attitudes about gender roles and sexual behavior without feeling pressured to become too deeply involved. At some point, however, most teenagers begin to date, pairing up by twos for a variety of activities (Connolly, Furman, & Konarsky, 2000). Although girls usually begin dating at an earlier age—consistent with their earlier development of sexual maturity—dating serves similar functions for both boys and girls. Table 11-4 presents several of the most important functions of dating.

Dating also follows developmental trends, and these describe both opposite-sex and same-sex dating. At younger ages, adolescents tend to think in terms of immediate gratification; they consider recreation and status to be the most important reasons for dating. Young adolescents look for dates who are physically attractive, dress well, and are liked by others. Older adolescents are less superficial in their attitudes toward

Table 11-4 Functions of Dating

Function	Description
Recreation	An opportunity to have fun with a person of the opposite sex
Socialization	An opportunity for people of opposite sexes to get to know each other and to learn how to interact appropriately
Status	An opportunity to increase status by being seen with someone who is considered desirable
Companionship	An opportunity to have a friend of the opposite sex with whom to interact and to share experiences
Intimacy	An opportunity to establish a close, meaningful relationship with a person of the opposite sex
Sex	An opportunity to engage in sexual experimentation or to obtain sexual satisfaction
Mate selection	An opportunity to associate with members of the opposite sex for the purpose of selecting a husband or wife

clique
Adolescent peer group with as few as three members or as many as nine; more cohesive than a crowd

Watch *Adolescent Cliques* on **MyDevelopmentLab**

dating; they are more concerned about personality characteristics and the person's plans for the future. Older adolescents consider companionship and mate selection important reasons for dating, and dating may move into serious romantic relationships, where partners become each other's best friend (Furman, 2004). Not all teen romances are smooth, however. Many are stormy, at least at times, and some may involve sexual abuse. Thus, dating experiences vary widely from teen to teen, as well as from relationship to relationship (Furman, Ho, & Low, 2007).

Regardless of age, however, adolescents generally select friends and dating partners who are similar to themselves in terms of social class, interests, moral values, and academic ambitions. Although typically teenage girls are more interested in emotional intimacy and teenage boys in sexual intimacy, nearly all adolescents are concerned about how their dating partners affect their own status within their peer groups. From a psychological perspective, status is important. For example, teenagers who belong to high-status groups tend to have high self-esteem. In addition, teenagers who have a strong sense of ethnic identity and derive their status in part from ethnic group membership tend to have higher self-esteem than those who do not (French, Seidman, Allen, & Aber, 2006; Kiang, Yip, & Fuligni, 2008).

Peers and Parents: A Clash of Cultures

As we have seen, peer relationships are critically important to teenagers in virtually every respect. During adolescence, peers begin to replace parents as the primary socializing force in teenagers' lives. For teenagers who have enjoyed warm, supportive relationships with their parents, and whose parents have set clear yet flexible limits, the transition is usually fairly smooth (Parade, Supple, & Helms, 2012). When parents' values are mostly consistent with those embraced by the adolescent's peer group and dating partners, there generally is little serious conflict. However, when adolescents associate with peers whose values and world views are dramatically different from those of their parents, parents often become concerned, and the process of identity formation for the adolescent can be filled with turmoil, anger, and disappointment.

A *clash of cultures* can occur, of course, in any situation in which the adolescents' friends are different from those the parents would prefer. Some situations, however, are especially difficult. Consider, for example, the pressures faced by Hindu adolescents whose parents have immigrated to the United States from India (Miller, 1995). These adolescents often face a double set of standards, many of which are in direct conflict. They must decide how to dress and wear their hair—in the traditional way, perhaps demanded by their parents, or in a way that conforms to that of their new peers who were born in the United States. Furthermore, such conflicts usually are more serious for girls than for boys because disparities in hairstyles and dress are greater for women than men.

Watch Conflict with Parents in Adolescence on **MyDevelopmentLab**

Conflicts also occur when Hindu values about dating and premarital sex clash with the more liberal values of the U.S. adolescent culture. As Indian psychoanalyst Sudhir Kakar (1986) explains,

> In sexual terms, the West is perceived as a gigantic brothel, whereas the "good" Indian woman is idealized nostalgically in all her purity, modesty, and chastity. For Indians living in the West, this idealization and the splitting that underlies it are more emotionally charged and more intense than would be the case in India itself. The inevitable Westernization of wives and daughters is, therefore, the cause of deep emotional stress in men, and of explosive conflicts in the family. (p. 39)

It is not difficult to imagine that immigrant families from many cultures view life in the United States in similar fashion.

The difficult act of negotiating the borders between parental versus peer values and practices is of course common to all adolescents, not just to new immigrants. Tensions are highest when the gap in values is wide and their importance is central to both parents and the adolescent. For example, adolescents who are lesbians or gay males often experience considerable difficulty when their parents hold negative views about same-sex romantic relationships. (The topic of same-sex relationships receives more attention in Chapter 12.) Some adolescents also must negotiate between a peer culture that glorifies drugs and crime and parental values that stress working within the system and obeying the rules. As noted earlier, parental monitoring can only extend as far as the teen is willing to disclose feelings and behaviors to parents.

Do you believe you would express, or have you expressed, concern about your own adolescent children's choice of friends? What factors would you define as meriting a parent's concern?

Although most adolescents successfully negotiate whatever disparity exists between their peers and their parents, in terms of attitudes and values, some adolescents do have difficulty in reconciling contrary sets of expectations. For this reason and for others, adolescents sometimes turn to drugs or other illegal substances or act out in other ways that are not productive for their overall health or development, which are the topics of the next section.

REVIEW THE FACTS 11-3

1. The process in which adolescents compare themselves to their peers is called ________.
2. According to studies in the United States, the typical teenager today spends about ________ a day using various forms of media.
   a. 1 to 2 hours b. 3 to 4 hours
   c. 5 to 6 hours d. 7 to 8 hours
3. A crowd is usually made up of two or three ________.
4. In general, girls are more interested in ________ intimacy, whereas boys are more interested in ________ intimacy.
5. Do adolescents generally have an easier time with identity development if their parents and peers hold different values or similar values?

Practice on **MyDevelopmentLab**

RISK AND RESILIENCE IN ADOLESCENCE

Experimenting with different attitudes and behaviors, defining and redefining oneself, and gradually moving away from parental control are hallmarks of adolescence that serve an important and healthy purpose—they help transform a child into an adult. Fortunately, for most teenagers, the increase in energy and intellectual curiosity that accompanies adolescence is harnessed mostly in constructive ways, in school and perhaps in sports, in volunteer work, or in a job. These same tendencies, however, can yield extremely unhealthy behaviors during adolescence, such as risk taking in general and drug use in particular. Naturally, some teenagers are more prone to participate in high-risk activities than others and they often engage in more of these types of activities as they move through adolescence. Although only a minority of adolescents engage in seriously destructive high-risk behaviors, most adolescents take more risks than their parents would prefer. Why is this so?

▲ High-risk behaviors, such as fast driving while drinking, are often supported and maintained with peer encouragement, status, and support.

Risk Taking

Adolescence and emerging adulthood is a period of the lifespan that often is characterized by risk-taking behaviors. Many adolescents engage in sex, sometimes without protection or sometimes with multiple partners. Serious consequences of these behaviors range from unwanted pregnancy to life-threatening diseases, as noted in the preceding chapter. Teenagers are notorious for reckless driving (although only a minority do it) and a variety of other dangerous activities. Many also abuse drugs or alcohol. In some environments, violence, which often is gang related, continues at an alarming rate—or so the media would have us think.

Did you engage in high-risk behavior during your adolescence that you would not pursue at this point in your life? If so, why do you think your behavior has changed?

Adolescents and emerging adults engage in high-risk behaviors for a variety of reasons. In the preceding chapter, we saw that brain development continues throughout the teens and early 20s and that brain regions controlling decision-making functions are among the last to develop. Thus, adolescent judgment may be less than fully developed: Teenagers and emerging adults may get into trouble because they do not understand the risks they are taking (Galván, 2012; Jacobus, et al., 2012). Many researchers believe that adolescents who take risks also underestimate the likelihood of bad outcomes; in other words, they see themselves as invulnerable, which is consistent with the concept of the *personal fable* (see Chapter 10). Rather than considering the risks, they instead focus mainly on the anticipated benefits of their high-risk behaviors, such as higher status with some peers or the rush of adrenaline that comes from skirting danger (Steinberg, 2010).

The results of over two decades of research on adolescent risk-taking behaviors point to multiple causes (Jessor, 1992; Romer, et al., 2011). In general, adolescents who engage in high-risk behavior are more likely than others to have a history of aggressiveness, to enjoy the thrill involved in risky behavior, to have difficulty in controlling their impulsiveness, and to experience low school achievement (Arnett, 2007, 2010a). All of these forces interact to cause adolescents to engage in high-risk behaviors or lifestyles. Given the multiple forces at work propelling the adolescent toward risky behavior, what protective factors can help counteract these risks?

In general, when adolescents develop high self-esteem, a sense of competence, and a sense of belonging to a stable family and social order, they are less likely to engage in high-risk behaviors (Deptula, Henry, & Schoeny, 2010; Jessor, 1993; Perkins & Borden, 2003). Therefore, families are well advised to increase parent–child communication and parental monitoring, help build the teen's areas of competence, and increase communication between the school and home. Some families even move their child to a safer environment, and to a better school, to avoid the negative neighborhood or peer group influences (Jessor, 1993; Perkins & Borden, 2003). However, there is no truly safe environment, and no child is completely invulnerable to the destructive forces that are part of U.S. society. Perhaps the most common of high-risk behaviors among adolescents is their use of alcohol and other drugs.

The Use of Tobacco, Alcohol, Marijuana, and Other Drugs

A pervasive high-risk behavior during adolescence and young adulthood is the use of tobacco, alcohol, marijuana, and other illegal drugs. Use of these drugs is especially prevalent in the latter part of the teenage years and in emerging adulthood. The age period with the highest usage of illicit drugs is from 18 to 20 (see Figure 11-4). Nearly a quarter of U.S. teens and emerging adults in this group report having used illegal drugs—which in this age group includes alcohol—during the previous month (Substance Abuse and Mental Health Services Administration [SAMHSA], 2011).

Binge drinking is especially problematic for 18- to 25-year-olds (see Figure 11-5), and it is a major problem on most college campuses. As you can see in the figure, for example, among

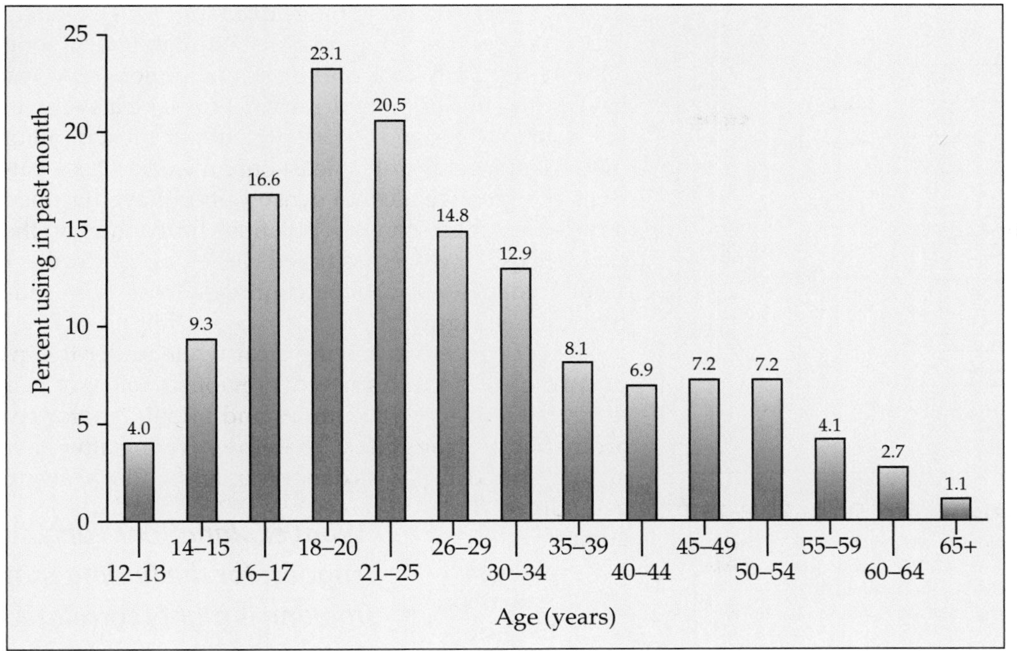

FIGURE 11-4 Individuals Reporting the Use of Any Illicit Drug in the Past Month, by Age, 2010
As shown, the highest incidence of drug use occurs between the ages of 16 and 25. Illicit drug use drops off dramatically in the adult population.

SOURCE: From *Results from the 2010 National Survey on Drug Use and Health: Summary of national findings*, NSDUH Series H-41, HHS Publication No. (SMA) 11-4658, Substance Abuse and Mental Health Services Administration (SAMHSA), 2011, Rockville, MD: Author.

21- to 25-year-olds, 70% used alcohol in the past month; of these, 15% were considered "heavy users," and an additional 30% were "binge users" (SAMHSA, 2011). Experimentation with other drugs also peaks during these teenage and emerging adult years. In the United States, the use of legal drugs of abuse, such as alcohol and tobacco, is illegal for teenagers because they are underage. Thus, these drugs are particularly problematic for adolescents because they are widely available as well as highly addictive. Furthermore, there are plenty of attractive role models who use these drugs and make them seem glamorous and appealing. Despite public service messages and education, many adolescents consider smoking and drinking to be *safe* habits that make them look more adult, and these drugs are the most frequently abused by adolescents. Fortunately, the use of alcohol and cigarettes by younger adolescents has been declining in recent years. However, the use of marijuana among teens in this age group has not. In 2010, nearly as many 12- to 17-year-olds smoked pot as smoked cigarettes (see Figure 11-6).

Tobacco Although fewer teens use tobacco products today than in previous years, cigarettes remain an alluring symbol of maturity to some teenagers, despite the overwhelming evidence that cigarette smoking is a serious health hazard. Smoking increases heart rate, constricts blood vessels, irritates the throat, and deposits foreign matter in sensitive lung tissues—thus limiting lung capacity. Years of smoking can lead to premature heart attacks, lung and throat cancer, emphysema, and other respiratory diseases. Studies suggest that even moderate smoking shortens a person's life by an average of 7 years (Eddy, 1991), and smoking-related illnesses are the single most preventable cause of illness and death in the United States today (National Center for Health Statistics [NCHS], 2011a).

Tobacco smoking by U.S. adolescents showed a sharp decline in the late 1970s; since that time smoking by teenagers has gradually declined (see Figure 11-6). Nevertheless, more than half of high school seniors have tried smoking. In 2010 about 15% of 16- to 17-year-olds and 32% of 18- to 20-year olds reported "current" smoking (defined as at least once within the past month). Among those age 21 to 25, the percent of smokers is 36% (SAMHSA, 2011). In the past, boys began smoking earlier than girls and they smoked more. Since the 1970s, however, the gender gap has narrowed: In some years, more adolescent girls than boys have reported daily smoking, often citing the desire to control weight as a reason for using

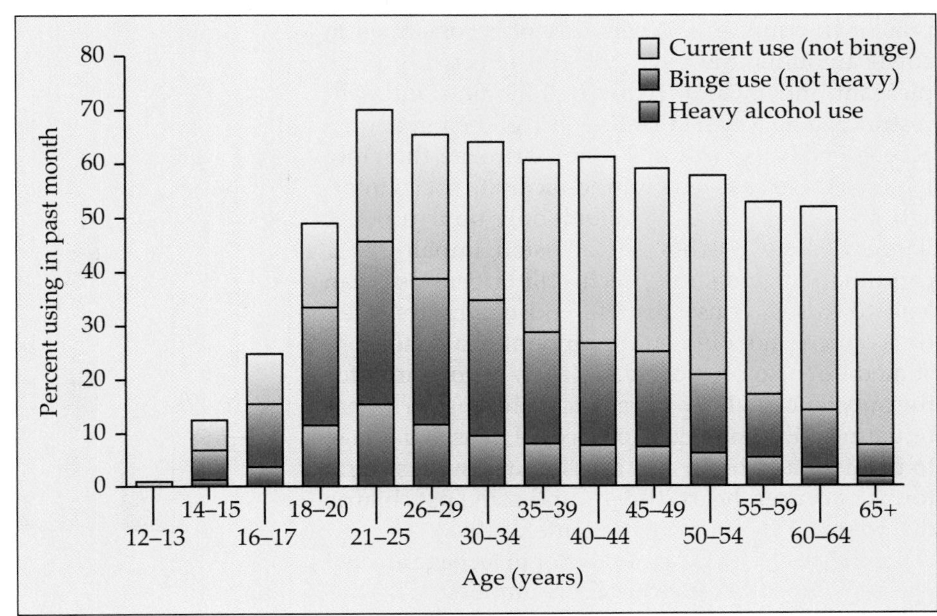

FIGURE 11-5 Current, Binge, and Heavy Alcohol Use Among Persons Aged 12 or Older, by Age: 2010

SOURCE: From *Results from the 2010 National Survey on Drug Use and Health: Summary of national findings*, NSDUH Series H-41, HHS Publication No. (SMA) 11-4658, Substance Abuse and Mental Health Services Administration (SAMHSA), 2011, Rockville, MD: Author.

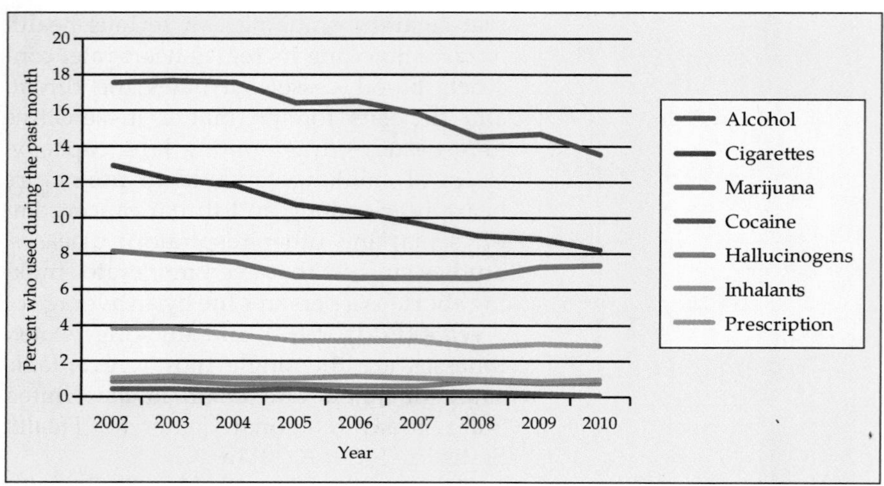

FIGURE 11-6 Percent of 12- to 18-Year-Olds Using Selected Illicit Drugs, 2002–2010

SOURCE: Substance Abuse and Mental Health Services Administration, *Results from the 2010 National Survey on Drug Use and Health: Summary of National Findings*, NSDUH Series H-41, HHS Publication No. (SMA) 11-4658. Rockville, MD: Substance Abuse and Mental Health Services Administration, 2011.

Note: Percent of drug use increases dramatically between the ages 12 and 18, as reflected in the relatively low rates of use when averaged across these ages.

cigarettes. More than half of the boys and girls who smoke begin by the ninth grade, often as a result of peer pressure. Because nicotine is a highly addictive drug, light or occasional smoking in high school often develops into a serious habit, accompanied by various health issues, as noted previously. Smoking, often of cigars, also is used by some teens as a way of covering up their use of other drugs, especially marijuana.

Alcohol Alcohol is a central nervous system (CNS) depressant with effects similar to those of sleeping pills or tranquilizers. When alcohol is consumed in small amounts, the psychological effects are often pleasant and include reduced inhibition and self-restraint, a heightened feeling of well-being, and an accelerated sense of time. Many drinkers therefore use alcohol to ease tension and facilitate social interaction—which it does, although only up to a point. Larger doses of alcohol distort vision, impair motor coordination, and slur speech; still larger doses can lead to loss of consciousness and death. These effects depend not only on the amount of alcohol consumed but also on individual levels of tolerance for the substance, which increases with long-term, habitual use. Excessive use of alcohol causes damage to the liver and brain and is associated with several forms of cancer, heart disease, and some psychiatric disorders (O'Connor & Schottenfeld, 1998).

Like cigarettes, a powerful factor in teenage alcohol use is the notion that alcohol consumption is a symbol of adulthood and social maturity. By early adolescence, more than half of U.S. teenagers have tried alcohol; the proportion grows to 70% by the end of high school (Johnston, O'Malley, Bachman & Schulenberg, 2012). Today, about 1 in 20 high school seniors reports drinking every day, and binge drinking, which usually occurs on weekends, has become quite common among adolescents: Fully 28% of high school seniors reported having had five or more drinks in a row at least once in the past 2 weeks, and 24% reported that most or all of their friends get drunk at least once a week. These patterns of excessive alcohol consumption have declined modestly in high school populations from a high in the early 1980s. However, as noted earlier, binge drinking among college-age groups continues to be a serious concern (see Figure 11-5).

Also of concern is driving a car while under the influence of alcohol. As noted previously, alcohol is a drug that slows reaction times and impairs motor coordination and judgment. Therefore, driving after having consumed alcohol is dangerous and is illegal at any age. Given that adolescence is a period in which risky behavior is at a peak—and that alcohol use is also at a high point during this period of the lifespan—it is not surprising that the percentage of U.S. teenagers and adults reporting that they have driven while under the influence of alcohol during the previous year is highest among those age 21 to 25—the period that corresponds to emerging adulthood (see Figure 11-7). Nearly a quarter of people in this age group have engaged in this high-risk behavior (SAMHSA, 2011).

What explanations can you suggest for the finding that smoking is highly correlated with the use of alcohol and other drugs?

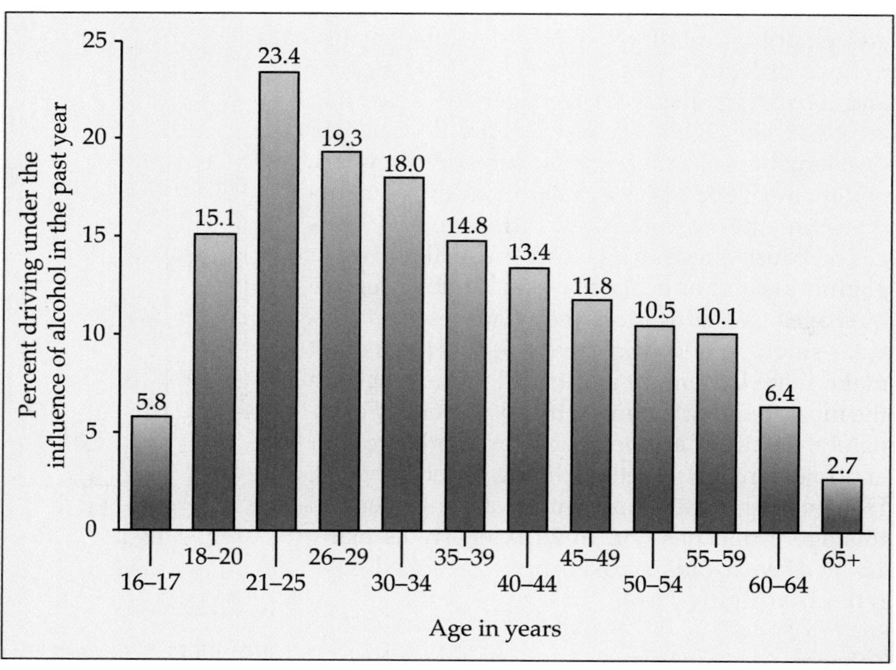

FIGURE 11-7 Percent Driving Under the Influence of Alcohol by Age Group, 2010

SOURCE: From *Results of the 2010 National Survey on Drug Use and Health: National Findings*, by Substance Abuse and Mental Health Services Administration (SAMHSA), 2011, Rockville, MD: Author.

Alcohol consumption by young people varies according to age, ethnic and religious background, locality, and gender (SAMHSA, 2011). Although alcohol abuse is found in every category of teenagers, the typical alcohol-abusing adolescent is a male with low grades and a family history of alcohol abuse. He is likely to have friends who also drink; he may also use other drugs. Many alcohol abusers also have serious psychological problems, such as depression, a poor sense of identity, a lack of goals, or a tendency to constantly seek new sensations and experiences. In addition, poor self-efficacy and low personal competence are predictors of adolescent alcohol use (Scheier & Botvin, 1998). Although in earlier generations boys were more likely to use alcohol than girls, today this gender difference has disappeared (SAMHSA, 2011).

Marijuana After alcohol and tobacco, marijuana is the most widely used drug in the United States, and the reported use of all three of these drugs increases between ages 18 to 25 (SAMHSA, 2011). Marijuana, which is illegal (except for medicinal purposes in some states), produces a mild euphoria and an altered sense of time, as well as physical and psychological symptoms in those who use it regularly.

The active ingredient in marijuana is delta-9-tetrahydrocannabinal, or THC. THC rapidly passes from the lungs into the bloodstream, which carries it to the brain and other major organs. In the brain, THC affects specific receptors that are involved in the experience of pleasure, as well as memory, concentration, perception, and coordination. Recent research using brain-imaging methods has shown that the regular use of marijuana may be more damaging than previously thought. Marijuana intoxication can cause distorted perceptions, impaired coordination, difficulty in thinking and problem solving, and problems with learning and memory. These problems are especially troublesome for those who also suffer from mental disorders such as depression and schizophrenia, and marijuana use often makes the symptoms of these disorders worse. Marijuana's adverse effects on thinking, problem solving, and memory can last for several days or weeks, so people who use the drug regularly may be functioning with impairment all of the time (National Institute on Drug Abuse [NIDA], 2008). Marijuana also is an addictive drug, and those who use it over a long period of time often have considerable difficulty in quitting. Marijuana use causes heart rate to increase and blood pressure to rise; because it is most typically smoked, users incur the same sorts of respiratory problems that chronic smokers confront.

▲ Experimenting with marijuana during adolescence is often done in the company of trusted companions.

The use of marijuana by adolescents and young adults rose sharply during the 1970s, and then declined but rose moderately again around the turn of the 21st century (see Figure 11-6). Since about 2006, marijuana use among high school students has been increasing gradually. In 2010, about 7% of 12- to 17-year-olds and 19% of 18- to 25-year olds reported current use (SAMHSA, 2011). Marijuana also became a much more "egalitarian" drug in the 1990s. Whereas White adolescents were significantly more likely to use marijuana in the 1980s, Hispanic and Black adolescents now use marijuana at virtually the same rate (SAMHSA, 2011).

What factors might account for the recent increase in the rate of marijuana use among adolescents who identify themselves as Black and Hispanic?

Other Drugs Although adolescents most often abuse alcohol, tobacco, and marijuana, there are a plethora of other available illegal drugs. Fortunately, the use of hard-core drugs—such as cocaine, heroin, LSD, and other hallucinogens—always has been relatively low, in part because these drugs are expensive and are harder to get. Usage of different types of drugs also varies somewhat by age: Predictably, the average age of first drug use is during later adolescence for inhalants and marijuana but during emerging adulthood for other illicit drugs (see Figure 11-8).

Drug use by adolescents has varied somewhat over the years, peaking in the 1970s, declining somewhat in the 1980s, increasing in the 1990s, and declining again or leveling in the early years of the 21st century. In particular, adolescents' use of so-called designer or club drugs, such as ecstasy ("X") and other amphetamine derivatives rose sharply in the late 1990s. These drugs became popular at nightclub-like events called *raves*. According to a survey of high school students, 9% of seniors and 6% of sophomores reported using ecstasy in 2000 (Johnston, O'Malley, & Bachman, 2001). However, ecstasy use had dropped by half by 2004, and in 2011, only 2.3% of high school seniors reported using this drug (Johnston, O'Malley, Bachman, & Schulenberg, 2012). Like ecstasy, other manufactured amphetamine drugs show periodic increases in popularity. Many such drugs, including methamphetamine (called *meth* or *ice*), can be produced from commonly available products; the use of this type of drug by adolescents peaked about 2001 and has fallen by about half since then (Johnson et al., 2012). Understandably, parents

Watch *Substance Abuse: Dr. Jean Obert* on **MyDevelopmentLab**

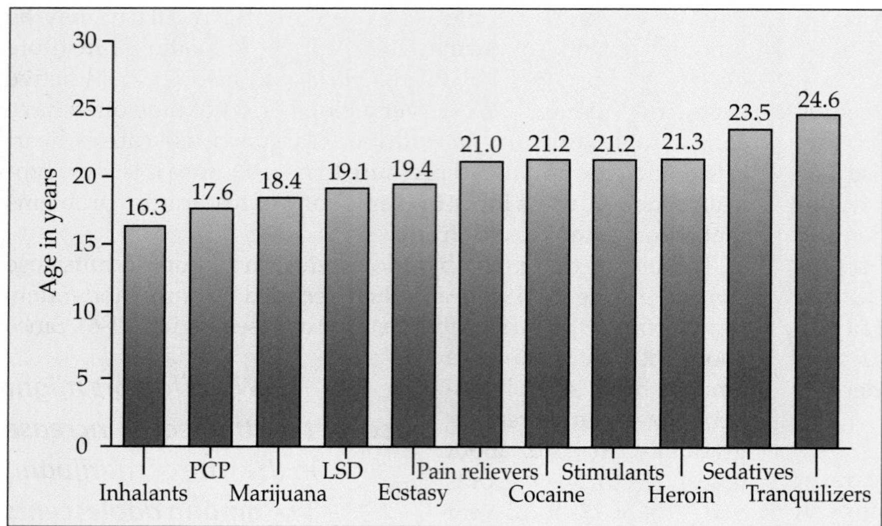

FIGURE 11-8 Average Age at First Use for Specific Illicit Drugs Among Past Year Initiates Aged 12 to 49, 2007

SOURCE: Substance Abuse and Mental Health Services Administration, *Results from the 2010 National Survey on Drug Use and Health: Summary of National Findings*, NSDUH Series H-41, HHS Publication No. (SMA) 11-4658. Rockville, MD: Substance Abuse and Mental Health Services Administration, 2011.

and others are concerned about the apparent attractiveness to adolescents of these highly addictive drugs, both because of their direct effects and because of their association with other risky behaviors: Teenagers, like adults, sometimes turn to stealing or prostitution to obtain the money needed to buy addictive drugs. Drug use among adolescents is not only dangerous and illegal; it can also lead to other behaviors that are violations of the law.

Delinquency

When adolescents break the law, their crimes are termed *delinquency*. Delinquent acts range in seriousness from shoplifting and vandalism to robbery, rape, and murder. Adolescents under age 16 or 18 who commit criminal acts are called **delinquents**; the age cutoff varies by state and by the nature of the crime. At some point in their lives, most adolescents engage in some form of delinquent behavior. Shoplifting is very common, as are minor acts of vandalism—damage to or desecration of property. Whether individuals are labeled as delinquent depends mainly on the frequency with which they commit crimes, the seriousness of their crimes and, of course, on whether they are caught.

What factors contribute to delinquency? Sociologists often note the association between crime and living in disadvantaged or stressful environments that arise from poverty, overcrowding, a racist culture, or the lack of a positive male role model. Yet these factors alone do not explain why some adolescents commit crimes—not all adolescents living in such situations become delinquents. Undoubtedly, many factors are involved. Often family characteristics are instrumental: When adolescents perceive their parents exhibit little warmth or when parents are neglectful or, conversely, are too intrusive or do not allow their adolescent children enough autonomy, acting-out behavior can be the likely result (Goldstein, Davis-Kean, & Eccles, 2005; Hoeve, Dubas, Gerris, van der Laan, & Smeenk, 2011; White & Renk, 2012). For some delinquents, the problems may be psychological, involving mental illness, or the inability to control anger and impulsive behavior. Some adolescents also become delinquent mainly because they seek to be members of delinquent peer groups (Vitaro, Tremblay, Kerr, Pagani, & Bukowski, 1997); in some circumstances, delinquency provides acceptance and status within deviant peer groups, such as gangs, thereby addressing the adolescent's needs for self-esteem and autonomy. Some delinquents engage in high-risk behaviors just for thrills.

The mass media also may play a role in the development of violent or delinquent behaviors among vulnerable teenagers. Movies, for example, may affect troubled adolescents through social learning. Identification with a violent movie and its characters may produce heightened arousal and lead to imitation of the characters' behaviors, such as assault and battery, stealing, using and selling drugs, or copycat acts of violence. Media also portrays sexuality in often explicit and sometimes violent detail, and the depiction of the thrill associated with forced sex may contribute to sexual abuse or even rape, which are problems some adolescents face, not only as perpetrators but more likely as victims.

Can you suggest the titles of specific films that portray forced sex in a positive or glamorized manner? Do you think such films should be censored?

Sexual Abuse of Adolescents

Sexual abuse, which also can be directed at younger children, is a problem for a significant number of adolescents. For example, national surveys of U.S. high school students typically report that about 11% of girls and 4% of boys have been forced to have sexual intercourse at some point in their lives (Black, et al., 2011; Centers for Disease Control [CDC], 2011k). Notably, these percentages are probably low due to underreporting errors that often are associated with estimates of sexual abuse. Furthermore, older adolescents sometimes are subjected to date (or acquaintance) rape, which is a significant problem on college campuses: As many as half of college men report that they have had forced sexual activity (Finkelson & Oswalt, 1995), and 20 to 25% of college women report that they have been the victim of an attempted or completed rape (CDC, 2011k). Increasingly, sexual abuse relationships may be initiated by "online predators"—adults who meet and develop relationships with adolescents on the Internet, which later lead to

delinquents
People under age 16 or 18 (depending on each state's definition) who commit criminal acts

Watch *Special Topics: Risk Taking and Brain Development* on **MyDevelopmentLab**

a forcible sexual assault and perhaps statutory rape (Wolak, Finkelhor, Mitchell, & Ybarra, 2008).

When rape occurs, it most often involves forced sexual relations by someone the victim knows—an intimate partner, friend, or acquaintance. For women, these three groups of perpetrators account for about half of all rapes; family members are involved in about one-quarter of the rapes of girls and women, and people in positions of authority and strangers make up the balance. For men, nearly two-thirds of rapes are committed by acquaintances, friends, and intimate partners; just under 20% are committed by family members; and people in positions of authority and strangers commit about 15% of rapes against men and boys. Although rape and other forms of sexual abuse can occur at any age, most victims are first raped when they are children or adolescents—this is particularly the case for males. According to national statistics, nearly three-quarters of male victims were raped before their 18th birthday; about three-quarters of female victims were raped before age 25 (Black, et al., 2011; CDC, 2011m).

Sexually abused and traumatized adolescents often feel depressed, guilty, and ashamed; yet they are often powerless to avoid the abuse. They may feel isolated and alienated from their peers and distrustful of adults in general. Because of the abuse, some of these adolescents have academic problems, others have physical complaints, and still others—especially girls—become sexually promiscuous or run away. Some victims turn their anger inward and become depressed or contemplate suicide (Dunn, Gilman, Willett, Slopen, & Moinar, 2012). A particularly troubling aspect of sexual abuse is that its effects are often long term (Fergusson, Boden, & Horwood, 2008). Sexual abuse affects adolescents' self-identity and their ability to form healthy relationships later in life. As adults, for example, men and women who were sexually abused in adolescence may have difficulty establishing normal sexual relationships; they may even have difficulty establishing normal relationships with their own children.

Women who were abused sexually seem to have particular problems. For example, they often develop distorted views of sexuality and they are actually more likely than nonabused women to marry abusive men or turn to substance abuse (Berlin & Dodge, 2004). If abuse occurs in their own family, such as if their husband abuses their daughter, they may deny the problem or feel powerless to do anything about it (Barnett, Miller-Perrin, & Perrin, 1997). Of course, boys also may be sexually abused. As is the case also for girls, abusers of boys are most likely to be a male who is not a family member. Typically, when boys are abused, the abuse takes place outside the home. Molestation by a man is often especially traumatic for boys; they typically report that they feel ashamed that they were forced to engage in same-sex acts and that they were powerless to defend themselves against their attacker (Bolton, McEacheron, & Morris, 1990). Particularly when the abuser is in a position of power or authority, the long-term effects on identity formation of sexually abused boys can be significant.

Watch *Coping with Grief* on **MyDevelopmentLab**

The impact of sexual abuse on children and adolescents depends on a variety of factors, including the nature of the abusive act, the age and vulnerability of the victim, whether the abuser was a stranger or a family member, whether there was a single incident or an ongoing pattern of abuse, and the reactions of the adults in whom the child confided (McCarthy & Breetz, 2010). The recognition of the problem and the provision of appropriate support and counseling typically reduce the impact on the child or adolescent.

Effective intervention and treatment are also highly important in successfully coping with other kinds of psychological disorders that arise in adolescence, such as depression and anxiety. In the final section of this chapter, we turn our attention to these issues.

REVIEW THE FACTS 11-4

1. The age period during which peak experimentation and use of alcohol and other drugs occurs is
   a. 12 to 16. b. 16 to 18.
   c. 18 to 25. d. 25 to 30.
2. About what percentage of high school seniors try smoking cigarettes?
   a. 30% b. 50%
   c. 70% d. 90%
3. Which of the following drugs does the largest proportion of adolescents use?
   a. alcohol b. tobacco
   c. marijuana d. methamphetamines
4. A person who commits a crime while a teenager is called a(n) ________.
5. Are boys or girls more likely to be sexually abused during adolescence?

Practice on **MyDevelopmentLab**

STRESS, DEPRESSION, AND COPING

Many articles and discussions about adolescents are filled with dramatic rhetoric. One article may suggest that adolescents typically are depressed or rebellious; another may state: "Wait until your child turns 12; then the parenting fun *really* begins!" Two problems arise from such overstatements of the psychological traumas of adolescence. First, all adolescents are labeled as experiencing psychological distress, which is not the case. Second, adolescents who need help may not be taken seriously because their behavior and feelings are considered part of a normal developmental phase (Connelly, Johnston, Brown, Mackay, & Blackstock, 1993). Clearly, it is important to distinguish between behavior that is considered normal for adolescents and that which indicates adolescents are experiencing real psychological distress.

Distress, of course, accrues from many sources. As we've learned, adolescents live in a complex world and many must cope with difficult relationships among their family members as well as their peers. Adolescence and emerging adulthood also is the developmental period when many forms of mental illness first emerge. For example, the average age at onset for many of the anxiety disorders, including phobias and impulse-control disorders, is late childhood or early adolescence. Other common anxiety disorders, such as obsessive-compulsive disorder and panic disorder, typically onset in emerging or early adulthood (Kessler, et al., 2007). Schizophrenia, a serious mental disorder that involves impaired cognition, emotion, and behavior, usually onsets in the late teen or early adulthood years as well. Although there is often a lag of between the onset of symptoms and the diagnosis of mental disorder, researchers estimate that about half of all cases of mental illness begin by age 14, and about three-quarters are apparent by age 24 (National Alliance on Mental Illness [NAMI], 2012c). One disorder that is especially common in adolescence and emerging adulthood is depression.

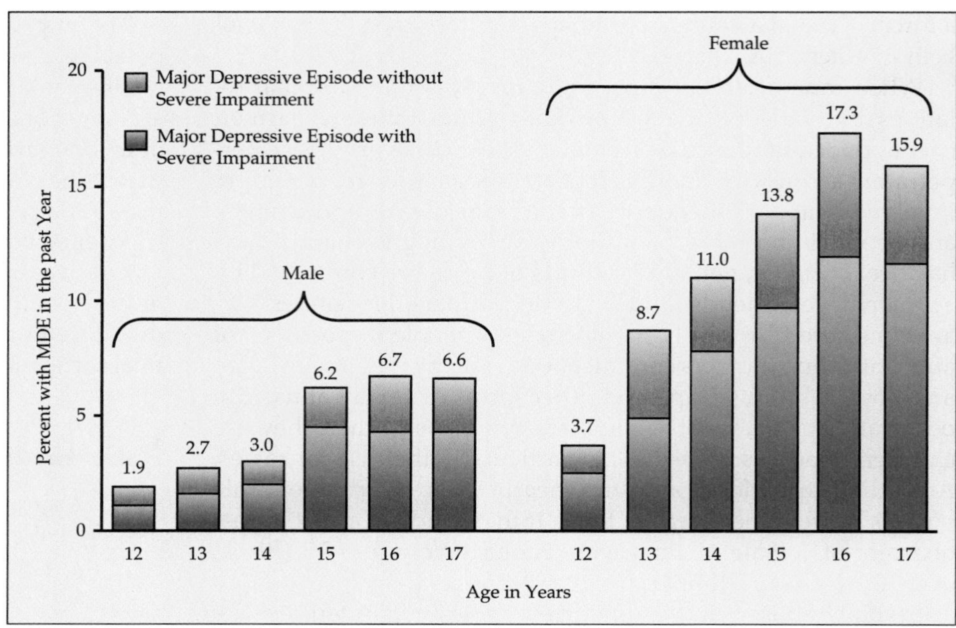

FIGURE 11-9 **Major Depressive Episode in the Past Year Among Youths Aged 12 to 17, by Severe Impairment, Age, and Gender**

SOURCE: From *Results of the 2010 National Survey on Drug Use and Health: National Findings*, Substance Abuse and Mental Health Services Administration (SAMHSA), 2011, Rockville, MD: Author.

Depression

Although it is difficult to cite accurate statistics about adolescent depression, a reasonable estimate is that at any given point in time about 8% of adolescents suffer from moderate to severe depression, with 15 to 20% of college students reporting having had a period of serious depression at some point in their teens (SAMHSA, 2011; Seroczynski, Jacquez, & Cole, 2003; see Figure 11-9). As is also true for adults, females are especially vulnerable: About twice as many female adolescents have the disorder as do males. The reasons for this gender difference are unclear, although part of the explanation most likely involves biology (Goodyer, 2009). For example, brain development may be involved: There are structural differences in the way male and female brains develop during adolescence (Durston, et al., 2001; Naninck, Lucassen, & Bakker, 2011). It is also possible that hormonal changes associated with puberty play a role (Ge, Conger, & Elder, 2001; Thapar, Collishaw, Pine, & Thapar, 2012). Some women complain of heightened depression just before they menstruate—a condition referred to as premenstrual syndrome (PMS). Gender differences also are observed in other mental disorders, such as attention deficit-hyperactivity disorder (ADHD; see Chapter 8), as well as in a wide variety of other behaviors, such as aggression and delinquency. In any case, it is clear that biological forces are involved in depression. For example, depression is a genetically linked disorder; that is, it runs in families (Weir, Zakama, & Rao, 2012). It also responds well to drug treatments that regulate the balance of important neurotransmitters in the brain.

What reasons might a depressed college student give for not seeking treatment? How might you address each of these concerns?

Depression also is associated with psychological variables, and these, too, may account for the gender differences observed. For example, adolescent depression is related to the substantial drop in self-esteem that sometimes occurs in particularly vulnerable girls when they enter junior high school (Costello, Swendsen, Rose, & Dierker, 2008). Indeed, low self-esteem has been shown to be the strongest predictor of depression in both male and female adolescents (Macphee & Andrews, 2006). Supporting this view that social stressors can be causal factors is the finding that lesbian and gay male adolescents show higher rates of depression (Bos, Sandfort, de Bruyn, & Hakvoort, 2008) and are two to three times more likely to commit suicide than heterosexual adolescents (Connelly et al., 1993; Marshal et al., 2011). This presumably is because of the extremely negative social pressures they often encounter. For similar reasons, adolescents who are bullied by others also are more likely to experience the symptoms of depression and to think more often about committing suicide (Pranjić & Bajraktarević, 2010). Indeed, many factors are linked to adolescent depression and suicide (see the box Try This! Taking a Look at Adolescent Depression).

What factors do you think best explain why White girls are at especially high risk for loss of self-esteem in adolescence?

An Interactive Approach Most likely, depression—like many other mental disorders—results from a combination of risk factors that interact, including biological, psychological, and social-systems variables. Supporting this view is evidence that depression in adolescence is often accompanied by other problems, ranging from anxiety disorders, to anorexia and bulimia

Watch *Sarah: Depression* on **MyDevelopmentLab**

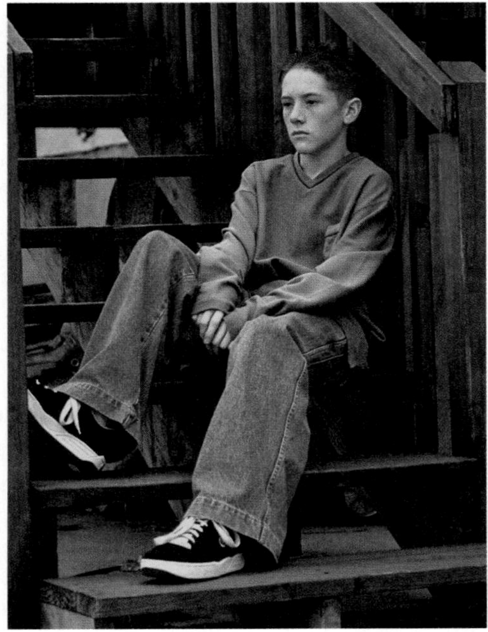

This boy's depression and loneliness may be temporary, but prolonged depression may signal a suicide risk.

(which are especially common in adolescent girls, see Chapter 10), to conduct disorders (which are especially common in adolescent boys), to substance abuse (Comer, 2013; Seroczynski, Jacquez, & Cole, 2003). Depression is also linked with chronic illness, and this situation highlights the interactive nature of causal forces: Chronic illness is depressing, and depression can increase the vulnerability to illness. In like manner, depression can both cause and result from problems of interpersonal functioning. When an individual is depressed, social relationships are much harder to maintain. For example, poor social functioning may worsen the parent–child relationship during adolescence and may negatively affect friendships and romantic relationships. Poor social functioning may also contribute to poor judgment and planning: For example, pregnancy is three times more likely among depressed teenage girls than among those who are not depressed (Horowitz, Klerman, Sungkuo, & Jekel, 1991). When personal relationships are difficult or unfulfilling, depression is not an uncommon result. Having high self-esteem and feeling connected to parents and peers are among the strongest protective factors related to adolescent depression (Costello, Swendsen, Rose, & Dierker, 2008).

Fortunately, most people, including adolescents, who have depression can be treated effectively. Several prescription drugs are available that are effective for about 80% of the people who suffer depression (Comer, 2013). Medications are even more effective when psychotherapy and counseling are available. If you suspect that someone you know is depressed, your best course of action is to urge them to seek treatment. Left untreated, depression is likely to take a serious toll on adolescent self-concept and may even result in a suicide attempt.

Watch *Interaction of Cognition and Emotion: Jutta Joormann* on **MyDevelopmentLab**

Adolescent Suicide In recent years, public concern over the increasing rate of adolescent suicide has led to increased suicide prevention efforts at the local, state, and federal levels. The concern is justified: Suicide is the third leading cause of death among adolescents after accidents and homicide, and the statistics probably underestimate the actual number of suicides (American Foundation for Suicide Prevention, 2012). Suicide rates have *nearly tripled* for those between ages 15 and 24 since 1950, owing in large part to rapidly rising suicide rates among young males. In 1950, the suicide rate for males age 15 to 19 was 3.5 deaths per 100,000 population; in 2008 this rate was 11.6. Suicide rates for teenage girls have also increased, but are much lower: 1.8 in 1950 compared to 3.1 in 2008 (NCHS, 2011a). Fortunately suicide rates among adolescents and emerging adults have declined somewhat in recent years, but thoughts of suicide are very common among young people in the United States. Surveys of high school students have found that as many as half have either engaged in suicidal behavior or have thought about suicide (Goldman & Beardslee, 1999).

What would cause a young person to commit suicide? Studies of adolescents who have attempted suicide, together with "psychological autopsies" of successful suicides, have revealed certain risk factors (Bridge, Goldstein, & Brent, 2006; Norton, 1994; Schusterbauer, 2009), which are outlined in Table 11-5. Although many adolescents who experience these risk factors do not contemplate or attempt suicide, such factors can provide early warnings that suicide is a possibility.

One significant risk factor is mental illness. Among those people who do commit suicide, an estimated 90% would have a diagnosable mental illness (NAMI, 2012b). Another set of risk factors has to do with personal issues. Some teens struggle more than others with such concerns, ranging from sexual orientation to rejection by peers, and these can put a vulnerable individual at higher risk for suicide. For example, suicide is estimated to be more common among gay, lesbian, bisexual and transgendered youth (Suicide Prevention Resource Center, 2008).

In general, adolescents who attempt suicide usually are not responding to one particular upsetting event. Instead, suicides typically occur within the context of long-standing personal or family problems. However, specific events may trigger a suicide attempt. For example, children growing up today may face excessive pressure and responsibility, and these forces may

Table 11-5 Risk Factors Associated with Adolescent Suicide

- A previous suicide attempt (the best single predictor)
- Depression, including strong feelings of helplessness and hopelessness (perhaps the next best predictor)
- Other psychiatric problems, such as conduct disorder or antisocial personality
- Abuse of alcohol and other drugs
- Stressful life events, such as serious family turmoil, divorce, or separation
- Access to and use of firearms

SOURCE: From "Adolescent suicide: Risk factors and consequences," by R. D. Norton, 1994, *Journal of Health Education*, *25*, 358–361. Copyright © 1994. Reprinted by permission of Copyright Clearance Center on behalf of American Alliance for Health, Physical Education, Recreation & Dance.

propel a vulnerable young person to attempt suicide (Elkind, 1998). Mass media also may play a role (Stack, 2001). There often is a significant increase in adolescent suicidal behavior following dramatic television or newspaper coverage of suicides, and reading fictional stories about suicide also has been found to be associated with an increase in suicidal behavior (Garland & Zigler, 1993). "Copycat suicides" are particularly likely in adolescence, when individuals are most vulnerable to the belief that the future is beyond their control or is unlikely to meet their dreams.

What can we do to prevent teenage suicide? In response to the dramatic rise in suicide attempts, crisis intervention services and telephone hotlines have been established throughout the nation to help prevent suicide. Currently, there are over 1,000 suicide hotlines available to adolescents. Educational programs delivered through the schools also can help (Joe & Bryant, 2007; Miller, 2011). Often these programs are designed to be consistent with the suicide prevention program developed by the American Psychological Association, the major points of which are reflected in Table 11-6 (Garland & Zigler, 1993; NAMI, 2012; National Institute of Mental Health [NIMH], 2012b). Given the severity of the problem, a comprehensive program such as this may offer the best means of preventing adolescent suicide.

Table 11-6 American Psychological Association Guidelines for Suicide Prevention

- Provide professional education for educators, health workers, and mental health workers
- Restrict access to firearms by passing strict gun control laws
- Provide suicide education for media personnel to ensure correct information and appropriate reporting
- Identify and treat at-risk youth

SOURCE: From "Adolescent suicide prevention: Current research and social policy implications," by A. F. Garland and E. Zigler, 1993, *American Psychologist, 48,* 169–182.

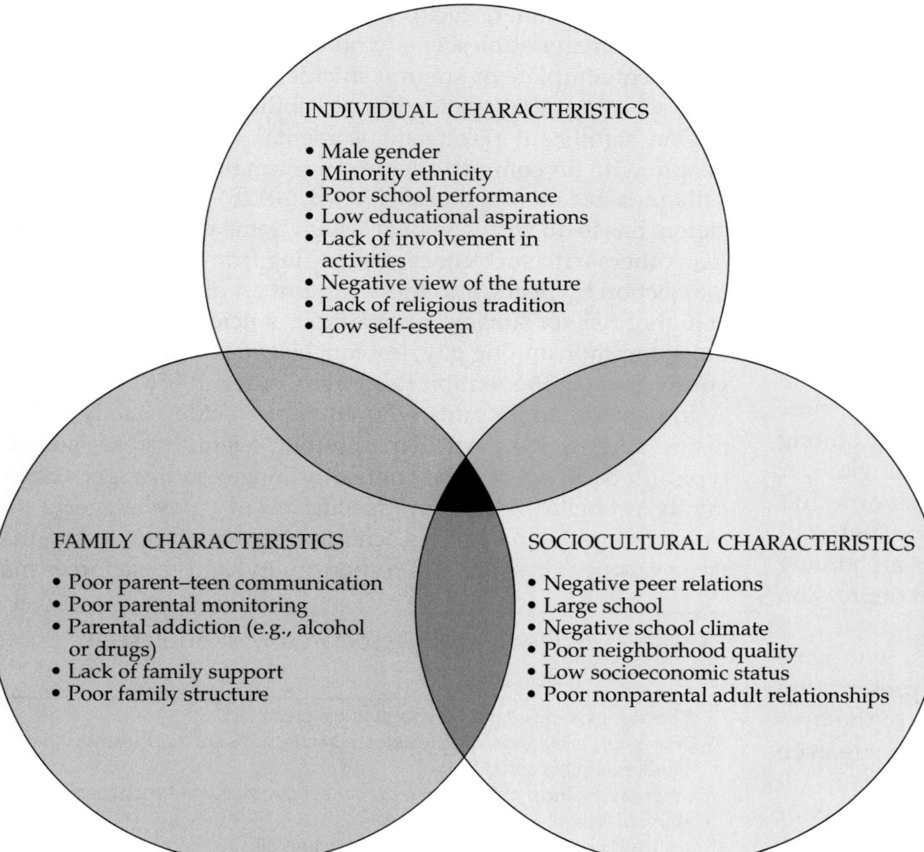

FIGURE 11-10 Selected Characteristics Associated with High-Risk Behavior
High-risk behaviors in adolescence are linked to many different factors.

SOURCE: Adapted from "Positive behaviors, problem behaviors, and resiliency in adolescence," by D. F. Perkins and L. M. Borden, 2003, in R. Lerner, M. A. Easterbrooks, and J. Mistry (Eds.), *Handbook of psychology: Vol. 6. Developmental psychology,* New York: Wiley.

Risk Factors for Psychological Problems

Although a discussion of psychological disorders and treatments is beyond the scope of this text, a few summary comments are in order. For teenagers of all groups, adolescence is a period in the lifespan generally characterized by change. Consequently, the period of adolescence and emerging adulthood involves adjustment, coping, and stress. A large majority of teenagers move through this period with few serious or long-term negative effects. However, adolescence follows a less positive course for some.

What factors determine how an individual adolescent will confront and resolve the challenges of these years? Perhaps the best way to conceptualize the risk factors most closely associated with adolescence is to note that they tend to fall into four categories: teenage sexual activity, abuse of alcohol and other drugs, antisocial and unproductive behavior, and—often as a consequence of these other factors—poor school performance. These broadly defined risk factors are complex and stem from a variety of sources; they also are typically associated with certain characteristics. Some appear to represent forces within the individual, others result from less than positive family situations, and others are present in the larger sociocultural environment in which the adolescent lives. Biological forces are also involved; genetic vulnerabilities put some individuals at especially high risk for certain types of problems that typically arise in adolescence and emerging adulthood. Figure 11-10 shows many of the more important characteristics associated with high-risk behaviors.

Protective Factors and Coping Responses

For those adolescents whose lives have been relatively easy and free of strain, most risk factors pose relatively minor problems and positive adjustment is a likely outcome. For those whose lives involve higher risks, adjustment may be more difficult. Although most

TRY THIS!

Taking a Look at Adolescent Depression

Depression is a term used in a variety of ways. Adolescents say they are depressed when they believe they have performed poorly on an important exam. Other adolescents say they are depressed following an argument or a breakup with a romantic partner. Used in these contexts, the term *depression* refers to a negative emotional state that generally is caused by an external event. However, depression also is a label for a psychological disorder that can be very serious. What are the symptoms of a psychological depression, and how does a person determine whether a low, blue mood is just a temporary, normal fluctuation of emotions or is indicative of a condition for which the person should seek treatment?

Generally speaking, the psychological disorder called *depression* can include symptoms that affect not only how we feel (the *emotional* aspects of this condition) but also can affect our motivation, our behavior, our cognition, and our physical functioning (Comer, 2009). When people are clinically depressed, they usually feel sad, they often lose their sense of humor, and they fail to get much pleasure from anything, even activities they used to enjoy. When depressed, people often have to force themselves to perform their daily activities. Merely arising from bed, getting dressed, and going to school can be formidable tasks for a depressed teenager. Depressed people usually are less active than they once were. They often stay in bed for long periods and they frequently complain that they do not have enough energy to undertake even simple tasks. Depressed individuals usually hold exceptionally negative views of themselves, and they typically believe that their circumstances will not improve. Sometimes they complain that they are unable to concentrate or to think clearly. Finally, people who are depressed sometimes experience physical symptoms, such as uncontrolled and frequent crying, headaches, dizzy spells, pain, or gastrointestinal problems. Disturbances of sleep (either sleeping too much or not being able to sleep) and appetite (either gaining or losing weight without trying) are especially common.

How does an adolescent who is experiencing some of the symptoms of depression—which almost all people experience occasionally—know if the psychological condition of depression is present? To explore how difficult it is to determine if normal highs and lows have crossed over the boundary to become psychological depression, try this. Rate yourself on the symptoms listed below that are associated with depression. Note whether you have experienced each symptom in the past 2 weeks, in the past year, or never.

Reflect on What You Observed

If you are like most people, you occasionally experience all or most of the symptoms noted in the table. However, most people are not psychologically depressed. How does someone know how serious these symptoms are? According to the *Diagnostic and Statistical Manual of Mental Disorders* (American Psychiatric Association, 2000), which is used by most U.S. clinicians as the standard guide for identifying mental disorders, depression may be diagnosed when at least five of the symptoms listed in the table are present during the same 2-week period. Furthermore, a diagnosis of depression is generally made only *if* the symptoms represent a change from previous functioning; *if* they cause significant distress or impairment in the individual's functioning in social, school, work, or other important areas; and *if* they are not caused by other factors, such as drug abuse, a medical condition, or grief over the death of a loved one. Finally, the symptoms of psychological depression must be *extreme*. Feeling sad over a lower grade on a test than you expected and feeling so sad that you have considered dropping out of school and moving back in with your parents are two different things.

For most people, occasionally experiencing some of the symptoms of depression does not pose continual or serious impediments to normal functioning. However, clinical depression is not as rare as many people might think. About 15 to 20% of college students report having experienced a depressive episode during their teenage years. Determining the difference between what is *normal* and what may represent psychological depression can be difficult, and only well-trained clinicians who usually are medical doctors, psychologists, or specially trained social workers or nurses are capable of making a diagnosis. Fortunately, the large majority of people with psychological depression can be treated effectively, and the best first step for those who may need to confront depression is to seek the appropriate diagnosis and treatment from a medical professional.

Our purpose in presenting the exercise discussed here is not to cause students undue concern about their level of psychological health. However, depression is a serious risk for adolescents, as it is for people at all stages of adulthood. If you have *any* concerns about your own responses to this exercise, please consult with someone you trust.

Consider the Issues

What experiences, if any, do you have in dealing with issues of depression? Have any of your friends or family members displayed symptoms like those noted? What factors might lead a person to feel depressed? How can life circumstances play a role in leading to feelings of despair? What special risks do adolescents face in coping with negative feelings? How might the other developmental issues of adolescence, such as forming an identity, dealing with peers, and determining the course of one's future, interact with or affect the kinds of feelings that often are linked to depression?

Symptom	I have experienced these symptoms within the past 2 weeks	I have experienced these symptoms within the past year	I have never experienced these symptoms
Depressed mood for most of the day; in teenagers, the mood may be irritable rather than depressed			
Markedly diminished interest or pleasure in all activities or in nearly all activities			
Significant weight loss or weight gain (more than 5% of body weight) without dieting or a noticeable decrease or increase in appetite			
Sleep disturbance; sleeping either noticeably more or less than usual			
Heightened or diminished levels of activity that are observable by others			
Fatigue or loss of energy			
Feelings of worthlessness or excessive or inappropriate guilt			
Diminished ability to think or concentrate; indecisiveness			
Recurrent thoughts of death			

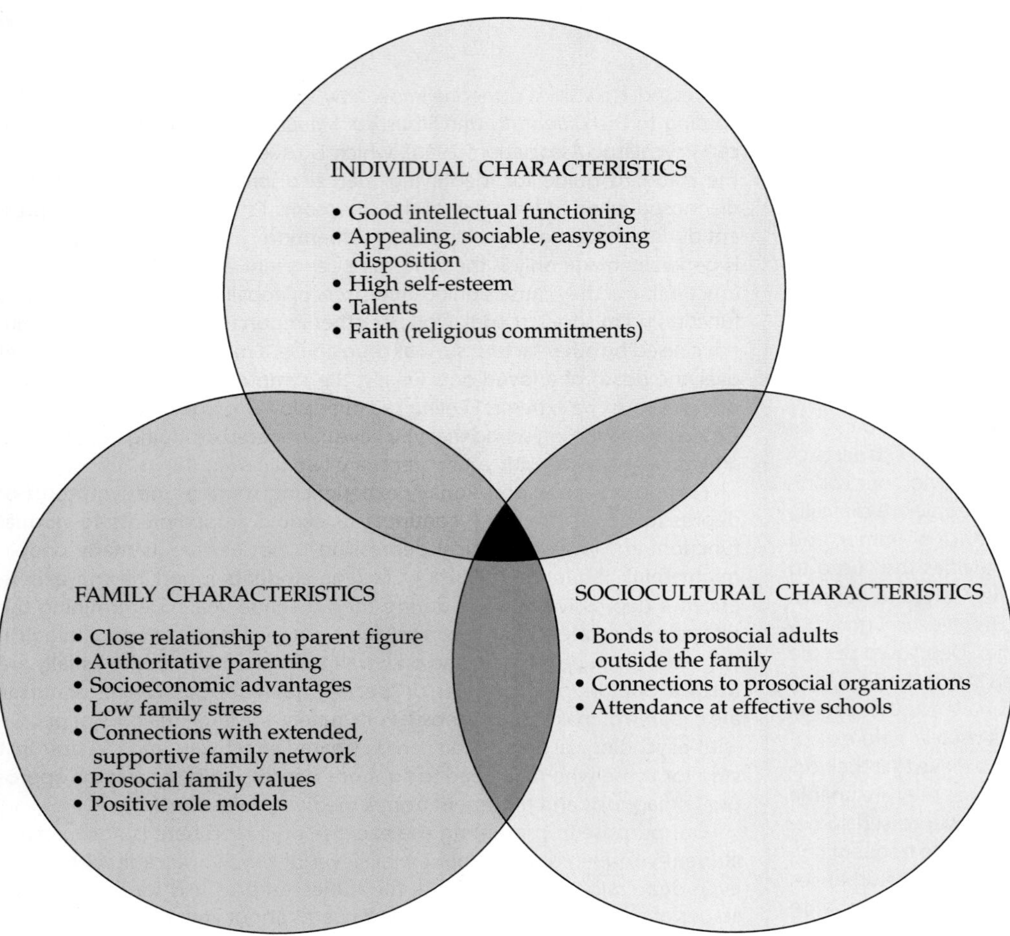

FIGURE 11-11 Selected Characteristics of Resilient Children and Adolescents
Multiple factors also are associated with positive functioning in adolescence.

SOURCE: Adapted from "Positive behaviors, problem behaviors, and resiliency in adolescence," by D. F. Perkins and L. M. Borden, 2003, in R. Lerner, M. A. Easterbrooks, and J. Mistry (Eds.), *Handbook of psychology: Vol. 6. Developmental psychology*, New York: Wiley.

adolescents, including those raised under the most difficult of circumstances and who are exposed to the highest levels of risk, develop positive coping mechanisms, some do not. Given equally challenging lives, why do some teenagers experience better outcomes than others?

Problematic adjustment is usually the result of experiencing several negative risk factors that typically interact with each other, piling up and aggravating the overall situation for the individual (Perkins & Borden, 2003). Seldom does a single event or difficulty derail a young person's positive adjustment. Furthermore, some individuals appear to be more *resilient* to negative pressure and risks (see Figure 11-11). Those with such positive attributes as good intellectual functioning and appealing personalities, who experience solid and positive family support, and who live in neighborhoods with good schools and other favorable organizations are more likely to confront the risks associated with adolescence and to deal effectively with them (Fergus & Zimmerman, 2005; Perkins & Borden, 2003). Those adolescents who lack such resources are at greater risk for negative outcomes.

What can be done to help young people move through adolescence with a minimum of trauma? First, we can support and strengthen families. Good relationships with parents and peers serve as buffers against stress. The importance of protective, supportive relationships cannot be overstated. Second, we can encourage adolescents to find activities they enjoy and pursue them. Competence in a particular area of expertise, such as sports, music, a craft, or an academic subject, can give the teenager a base from which to establish realistic self-confidence. Third, we can ask adolescents to contribute to others' welfare. Taking on a role that includes responsibility for others, perhaps team members or younger siblings, can help an adolescent set priorities and respond to challenges or crises with greater resilience.

Strategies such as these can help adolescents and emerging adults cope with the stresses, disappointments, and difficulties that, at times, characterize life for all of us. Learning to use positive coping techniques, such as careful planning and organization, setting priorities, and finding a close friend and confidant, also can help ease the tension all adolescents face from time to time. Acquiring successful coping skills also helps prepare adolescents for the tasks associated with becoming an adult, a topic we explore in the next two chapters of this book.

REVIEW THE FACTS 11-5

1. At any given point in time, about ________ of adolescents suffer from depression.
   a. 1%   b. 3%
   c. 8%   d. 15 to 20%
2. About what percentage of adolescents who experience depression can be treated successfully?
   a. 20%   b. 40%
   c. 60%   d. 80%
3. Are adolescent suicide attempts most likely to result from problems that arise quickly or from problems that are long-standing?
4. Adolescents who are better able to cope with negative risk factors in their lives are called
   a. resilient.   b. productive.
   c. ego enriched.   d. high risk–high reward.

Practice on **MyDevelopmentLab**

CHAPTER SUMMARY

Developmental Tasks of Adolescence

What sociocultural forces shape the transition from childhood to adulthood, and how do young people in developed economies typically move through this period of the lifespan?

- Adolescence is the bridge between childhood and adulthood. Experiences in childhood set the stage for adolescent development. In industrialized nations, adolescents in the period of emerging adulthood often are physically and intellectually mature before they assume independent lifestyles, which can cause conflict.
- Although Western cultures often portray adolescence as a stressful, emotional period, most adolescents adjust quite well, a finding common to many cultures around the world. Although conflict, stress, and risk-taking behaviors typically are high in adolescence, most adolescents do not experience this period as traumatic.

What factors are involved in developing a sense of autonomy as the young person moves through the period of adolescence and emerging adulthood?

- Adolescents must confront two developmental tasks: achieving autonomy and independence from their parents and forming an identity.
- Adolescents must learn to make their own judgments and to control their own behavior—a process called *self-regulation.* When teens and parents can cooperate and share their thoughts and feelings, *interdependence,* which also is called reciprocal dependence, is possible.

What is an identity crisis, and how is it linked to the formation of a secure self-identity?

- *Identity formation* in adolescence involves teenagers gaining a sense of who they are and how they fit into society through their exposure to many roles and values. *Social reference groups* are groups with which adolescents identify, and in so doing, they help in self-definition.
- Erikson viewed the critical developmental task of adolescence as *identity versus identity confusion,* which requires the teen to sort through various choices in order to establish an answer to the question, "Who am I?" Erikson believed that establishing one's identity involves an *identity crisis,* in which individuals grapple with the options available and ultimately make a choice and a commitment as to which path their lives will take.

What factors exert the most influence on how one's identity is forged during adolescence and emerging adulthood?

- For Marcia, identity formation involves both resolving an identity crisis and making a personal investment in the paths one chooses, a concept he referred to as making a *commitment.*
- Identity crisis may be defined according to four types of *identity statuses*: *foreclosure* (commitment without going through an identity crisis or much decision making), *diffusion* (no identity crisis nor is there a selection of an occupational role or moral code), *moratorium* (describing those who are currently in the midst of an identity crisis or decision-making period), and *identity achievement* (commitment that results from resolving the identity crisis).
- Although adolescents from different cultures appear to experience identity formation in much the same way, individuals often take quite different paths in how they resolve the identity crisis, and they can be in different statuses with respect to different aspects of their identity (e.g., career choice versus religious beliefs). Men more often develop an intrapersonal (self-oriented) identity, whereas women often blend this with an interpersonal identity that emphasizes relationships with others.
- Erikson's view of identity formation reflects Western values. Collectivist societies generally place less emphasis on autonomy and more on interdependence with others.
- Identity formation is more difficult when individuals belong to groups outside the majority culture. It is particularly difficult for adolescents who are lesbians or gay males, especially when their parents and peers judge their preferences or behavior to be unacceptable.
- Because identity formation involves adaptation to sociocultural forces, people growing up in different historical time periods fall into generational cohorts. Today's adolescents belong to the "Millennial" generation, also called "Generation Me." Although some research suggests that members of Generation Me are more self-centered and driven to achieve financial success than previous generational cohorts, other researchers view this generation as being more diverse, with greater financial needs and with a longer time spent in emerging adulthood.

Family Dynamics

What are the most important roles that parents play during the teenage years?

- Successful parents must provide support to teenage children but also allow them independence, and family conflict during adolescence is common. Maintaining communication helps reduce serious conflict.
- Parents are more successful when they work together yet maintain an appropriate boundary between themselves and their teenage children.
- Adolescents with authoritarian parents may become dependent and anxious or defiant and resentful. Those with permissive parents may have difficulty setting boundaries and defining appropriate behavior. Authoritative parenting usually is best because it involves warmth and control and also good communication.

- Mothers typically know more than fathers do about their adolescent's activities, and they exert a stronger influence on parent–child acceptance and conflict. Family dynamics are complex, and oftentimes first-born children forge the way in which families cope more so than later-born children do.
- Parental monitoring is based on open communication and adolescent willingness to disclose the details of the adolescent's life.

Peer Relationships During Adolescence

Why do adolescents place so much importance on how their peers regard them, and how is the explosion of electronic media impacting peer relationships?

- The importance of peers increases enormously during adolescence. Through *social comparisons,* teens compare themselves to their peers as a means of defining themselves.
- Teenagers turn both to parents and to peers for advice, although peers are more often consulted on issues of style and social concerns and parents on more far-reaching global matters. Teens also establish intimate relationships with some peers.
- The explosion of electronic media has dramatically changed how all people—including teenagers—communicate with each other. Although some research suggests that violent programming may encourage teens to be more aggressive, little evidence supports this view. Teens who are exposed to explicit sexuality do appear to engage in sexual activity at younger ages, but this finding is correlational, and many other factors undoubtedly are involved. Early research exploring how electronic media affects friendship seems to indicate that the impact is minimal.

What roles do friends play during adolescence and emerging adulthood, and how do friendships change as teenagers mature?

- Peer groups involve larger crowds and smaller cliques. *Crowds* consist of perhaps 15 to 30 members, whereas *cliques* have as few as 3 members or as many as 9, and cliques are more cohesive than crowds. About 20% of adolescents are loners who are not members of social groups. When being a loner is involuntary, it can contribute to difficulty in identity formation, as well as in dating.
- Early on, dating serves to give young adolescents experience without deep emotional involvement. Later, adolescents who date may develop emotional closeness and serious romantic relationships. Girls usually begin dating at younger ages.
- Adolescents usually select dates who are similar to themselves in social class, values, and academic ambitions. Both boys and girls are concerned with how their date affects their status, but during adolescence boys generally are more interested in sexual intimacy and girls are more interested in emotional intimacy.
- Adolescent development is harder and involves more conflict when peers' values are widely different from those of parents. This frequently is true in immigrant families where parents hold to traditional cultural values. Adolescents who are lesbians or gay males also may have turbulent relationships with their parents if parents hold negative views about same-sex romantic relationships.

Risk and Resilience in Adolescence

Why is adolescence and emerging adulthood a period of the lifespan characterized by risky behavior?

- Adolescence and emerging adulthood is often characterized by risk-taking behaviors. Because the brain regions related to judgment and emotional control are still developing, adolescents may take risks without fully appreciating the consequences.
- Risk-taking behaviors occur less frequently in adolescents who have high self-esteem, belong to a stable family with good parent–child communication, and have a sense of competence.

Compared to previous generations, are adolescents in the United States today more, or less, likely to engage in various forms of risky behavior?

- The use of alcohol and other drugs peaks during adolescence and early adulthood (ages 18 to 25). Tobacco and alcohol are the drugs most commonly used by adolescents.
- Tobacco use among teens is lower now than in the 1970s, but still more than half of high school seniors try smoking. Both boys and girls smoke, in roughly equal numbers, although smoking is associated with serious long-term health risks.
- Alcohol depresses activity in the central nervous system, causing slowed responses and a heightened sense of well-being. By the end of high school, 80% of seniors have tried alcohol and about 25% of high school students report binge drinking during the previous 2-week period. Binge drinking is common among college-age students. So, too, is driving while under the influence of alcohol, which also peaks in emerging adulthood.
- After alcohol and tobacco, marijuana is the most widely used drug in adolescence. The effects of marijuana's active ingredient, THC, last for several days, and regular users may be functioning with learning and memory impairments all of the time. Many other drugs also are available to teens.
- People under age 16 or 18 who commit crimes are called *delinquents.* Delinquent behavior is linked to living in disadvantaged or stressful conditions, impulsive or otherwise problematic behavior, and belonging to deviant peer groups. Media may encourage delinquent behavior and violence through modeling.

- Rates of sexual abuse before age 18 are high for both boys and girls. Sexual abuse often has long-term negative effects on identity formation and healthy adult development.

Stress, Depression, and Coping

How do adolescents typically cope with the pressures they feel during the teenage and emerging adult years?

- About 15 to 20% of college students report having been depressed. At any point, about 8% of adolescents experience depression. Girls are about twice as likely to be depressed as boys, perhaps a reflection of gender differences in adolescent brain development.
- Depression is associated with disruptions in brain chemistry and is genetically linked. It also is associated with psychological and sociocultural variables. About 80% of people who have depression can be treated effectively with medication, counseling, or with both.
- Suicide is the third-leading cause of death during adolescence, and the rate of suicide in this age group is rising. Over half of high school students have considered suicide.
- Suicide is linked to mental illness, to long-standing personal or family problems, to excessive pressure and responsibility, and to the belief that future goals are unattainable. Suicide attempts are sometimes patterned after suicides described or portrayed in mass media.
- Risk factors associated with adolescence cluster in the following groups: teenage sexual activity, abuse of alcohol and other drugs, antisocial behavior, and poor school performance. All are more likely to result when multiple negative forces interact in an adolescent's life. When negative forces are present, those adolescents who are *resilient* are more likely to develop positive coping mechanisms. Resilient teens are more likely to have positive personal qualities and supportive and functional families, as well as being more likely to live in good neighborhoods with good schools.
- To support positive adolescent development, we should support and strengthen families, provide teens with activities in which they can be successful, encourage them to help others, and teach them positive coping skills.

KEY TERMS

self-regulation (p. 304)
interdependence (p. 304)
identity formation (p. 305)
social reference groups (p. 305)
identity versus identity confusion (p. 305)
identity crisis (p. 305)
identity status (p. 305)
commitment (p. 305)
foreclosure status (p. 305)
diffusion status (p. 306)
moratorium status (p. 306)
identity achievement (p. 306)
social comparison (p. 313)
crowd (p. 315)
clique (p. 316)
delinquents (p. 322)

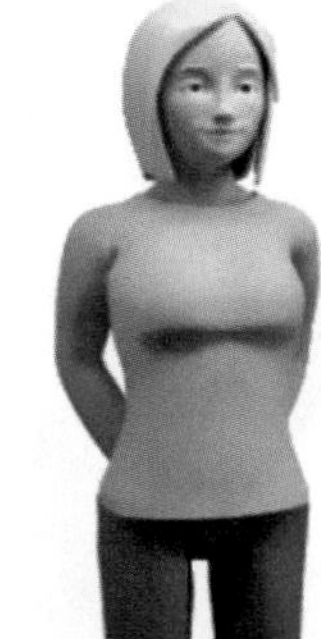

12 YOUNG ADULTHOOD
Physical and Cognitive Development

LEARNING OBJECTIVES

- How do normative and idiosyncratic events shape human developmental trajectories?
- Are adults who were born in the same year always of the same *age*?
- In recent decades, have young adults in the United States become more, or less, physically fit?
- What challenges do young adults typically face with respect to their sexual health?
- How have attitudes about sexuality and sexual behavior changed in the United States from the 1970s to the present?
- How does sexual orientation affect how a person experiences young adulthood?
- How do the thought processes used by young adults differ from those that guide adolescent cognition?
- How do stage models of development differ from context models?
- What are the primary developmental tasks most young adults growing up in the United States confront?
- How do an individual's cognitions and worldviews change during the period of young adulthood?

CHAPTER OUTLINE

Perspectives on Adult Development
- Age Clocks and Social Norms
- Contextual Paradigms

General Physical Development
- Strength and Stamina
- Fitness and Health

Sex and Sexuality
- Fertility
- Sexually Transmitted Diseases
- Sexual Attitudes and Behavior
- Sexual Identity and Sexual Orientation

Cognitive Development in Adulthood
- Beyond Formal Operations
- Postformal Thought
- Emotional Intelligence
- Schaie's Stages of Adult Thinking

Frameworks for Understanding Adult Development
- Stages and Contexts
- Havighurst's Developmental Tasks
- Erikson's Theory of Development
- Levinson's Seasons of a Man's Life
- The Limitations of Normative Models
- Gould's Transformations in Early Adulthood
- A Closing Comment

Although development throughout the lifespan is continuous, with earlier events establishing the foundation for later changes, once we reach the part of the lifespan called *adulthood,* these changes become both less predictable and more variable. One reason is that the events marking the major transitions from one stage to the next within adulthood are less closely tied to chronological age or specific biological events, such as the rapid brain maturation that occurs in infancy or the maturation of sexual functions in adolescence. Rather, the major markers within adulthood are more closely linked to personal, social, and cultural forces or events—such as getting married, starting a job or career, or having a child.

Because the major turning points in adulthood are more defined by culture, they also are more variable, both across cultures and within a given culture as well. Although the major life events that children typically experience are much the same, the pathways that individuals select throughout adulthood are quite divergent, even within a particular cultural context. For example, in the United States and other industrialized countries, all children are expected to enter school at about age 5 with certain skills in place, and they move through the educational system in much the same way. Not all adults, however, progress along a common path or structure their lives according to a common plan. Some adults marry in their teenage years, others do not marry at all. Some young adults begin jobs and become independent immediately after high school, others spend many years in a kind of "postadolescent–preadult limbo" while they attend college and perhaps several years of professional school beyond their undergraduate education. Some adults have several children at a young age, whereas others wait until their 30s or 40s or perhaps do not have children at all. Indeed, the transition from adolescence to adulthood for many young people in developed societies has come to occupy a unique period of the lifespan, often referred to as "emerging adulthood" (see Chapter 10). Because of the wide variety of paths these young people take, adults generally have less in common than children.

Can you suggest normative events in addition to those mentioned that are experienced by most adults in the United States? Which of these typically occur in young adulthood?

Despite the variety of lifestyle choices that adults make, there are, however, some commonalties in the developmental processes of adulthood. Although in adulthood there are few stage-defining physical events and no clear-cut cognitive transitions that unfold, we do have culturally defined social milestones against which to mark adult development. Adult development, thus, is defined largely by our choices of roles and relationships, the most important of which involve the cycles of family and of career.

Many social events, and the transitions that surround them, are considered to be **normative events**; that is, they occur at relatively specific times and are shared by most people in a particular age cohort. Normative events often define the transition points for early, middle, and later adulthood (such as getting married, starting a job, raising children, retiring from work, and so forth). Normative events usually are anticipated in advance, and because they are common within the culture, there typically are reasonably clear expectations about how they should be experienced and dealt with. Accordingly, they usually are associated with minimal stress. Sometimes, though, major life-changing events happen unexpectedly, such as when a spouse or a child dies, a person loses a job, or—on the bright side—someone wins the lottery. Events such as these are termed **idiosyncratic events**. Because these events usually are not anticipated and often are not emotionally shared with others, they can create considerable stress and a need for major reorganization of the person's life both personally and socially.

In this chapter, in addition to exploring physical and cognitive development in young adulthood, we lay the groundwork for the chapters that follow by examining fundamental concepts and theories that define the adult years. We note that adult development is especially complex because social and emotional development is blended in with the gradual physical changes that take place as we age. We also address young adulthood, first in terms of physical development and then in terms of cognitive development, considering especially how cognitive

normative events
Events, and the transitions that surround them, that occur at relatively specific times in the lifespan, which most people in an age cohort experience, such as marriage and retirement

idiosyncratic events
Events in the lifespan that are unanticipated, such as the death of a spouse, that typically cause considerable stress and readjustment in a person's life both personally and socially

▶ Age clocks let us know when important life events typically occur, although in today's U.S. society, age clocks are more flexible for many people than they have been for previous generations. For example, today many people, like this woman, are returning to school in their 30s or even later.

functioning interacts with social and personality development. Finally, we look at some of the developmental tasks that most young adults face. In the first section of this chapter, we explore various perspectives on adult development, the concepts of age clocks and social norms, and the basic ideas that underlie contextual approaches to the study of human development.

PERSPECTIVES ON ADULT DEVELOPMENT

As discussed in Chapter 1, we conventionally divide the adult years into young adulthood (the 20s and 30s), middle adulthood (the 40s and 50s), and later adulthood (age 60 or 65 and up). We also have noted that what age means to a given individual can vary considerably. In recognition of both cultural expectations and individual lifestyle choices, we often turn to the concepts of *age clocks* and *social norms* to explain adult development.

Age Clocks and Social Norms

It is difficult if not impossible to pinpoint stages of adult development solely on the basis of age. To address this problem, researchers often rely on the concept of the **age clock** (Neugarten & Neugarten, 1996). Age clocks are a form of internal timing; they let us know if we are progressing through life too slowly or too quickly. For example, 35-year-olds who are still in college might be considered to be lagging behind their peers; conversely 35-year-olds who are thinking about retirement might be considered to be far ahead of them. Age clocks let us know when certain events in our life *should* occur, relative to standards typical in our culture. If important life events happen earlier or later than expected, individuals may experience distress and less peer support than when such developments are accomplished according to a more typical schedule.

In other words, we have built-in expectations, constraints, and pressures for various periods of life that we apply to ourselves and others. Although these boundaries sometimes have a biological or psychological basis—a woman normally cannot conceive after menopause or a young adult might not be prepared to handle the stress of a complex, high-level job—the boundaries are more often socially based. For example, if we observe a couple proudly introducing their newborn child, we might have quite different reactions depending on whether the couple is in their late teens or their late 40s. We may well interpret the motivations of the couple differently, and we may also behave differently toward them. Thus, cultural norms and expectations define in important ways how we evaluate our lives—and the lives of others—based on whether or not significant life events correspond to what our age clocks specify.

Cultural norms, of course, vary from culture to culture and they change across time (Jones & Higgs, 2010). Perhaps the most significant historical change affecting the life course of people in the United States and other industrialized nations is the increasing length of the lifespan. For example, whereas in 1900 only about 14% of U.S. women reached age 80 or older, now more than half of the female population is expected to reach that age (U.S. Census Bureau, 2012d). This shift and others like it have changed how we define our age clocks and how our culture has adjusted the responsibilities most people are likely to encounter at various points in the adult lifespan.

Can you suggest two examples of the text's statement that the United States has become an "age-irrelevant" society?

Partly because more people are living longer and partly because our society is becoming more flexible with respect to the roles and opportunities available to both women and men, the lines that traditionally have separated the stages of adulthood are becoming more blurred (Butler, 2005). The result is that age clocks are more flexible now than they were in earlier decades. Nontraditional students return to school at ages 35, 45, or even older; many couples postpone having their first child until they are in their mid to late 30s; and marriage, divorce, and remarriage occur throughout the lifespan, not just during early adulthood. In many respects, the United States has become an "age-irrelevant" society in which members of a given adult age cohort may be involved in vastly different activities and life events.

Three Components of Age The very concept of age, too, is more complex than it at first might seem. When we refer to a person's age, we usually mean *chronological age*—how many years

age clock
A form of internal timing used as a measure of adult development; a way of knowing that we are progressing too slowly or too quickly in terms of key social events that occur during adulthood

Watch *Experiences of a Non-traditional College Student* on **MyDevelopmentLab**

and months have elapsed since birth. However, two adults of the same chronological age might be very different from each other with respect to health, physical capabilities, responsibilities, and adaptability. To more accurately describe the age of individuals, it is often useful to consider their *biological, social,* and *psychological* ages (Westerhof, Whitbourne, & Freeman, 2012; Whitbourne, 2008). **Biological age**, which is a person's position with regard to his or her expected lifespan, varies tremendously from one individual to another. A 40-year-old with emphysema and a severe heart condition who is likely to die in the near future differs greatly in biological age from a healthy 40-year-old who can expect to live another 35 years or more. In turn, **social age** refers to how an individual's current status compares to cultural norms. A 40-year-old married person with three children is developmentally different from a 40-year-old single person who engages in casual dating and does not plan to have children. Finally, **psychological age** refers to how well a person can adapt to social and other environmental demands. It includes such things as intelligence, learning ability, motor skills, and subjective dimensions like feelings, attitudes, and motives.

Contextual Paradigms

Considering how biological, social, and psychological ages interact throughout development provides an example of a *contextual paradigm* (approach). A *paradigm* is a hypothetical model or framework or, more simply, a systematic way of looking at things. **Contextual paradigms**—such as those that attempt to explain, for example, intelligence, health, or parenting—seek to describe and organize the effects of different kinds of forces on development. The term *context* is used here as it has been used at other points in the text: We speak of the physical environmental context, the social context, the psychological context, and the historical context—each of which influences development in complex ways that involve the interaction of all of the factors that are involved in an individual's life (Gruenewald, Mroczek, Ryff, & Singer, 2008; Hess, 2005). As you can see, contextual paradigms are complicated, but so is human development. Contextual paradigms focus on developmental forces as a whole, including those forces that are within as well as external to the individual. One especially dramatic change in many people's lives today—as compared to a generation ago—involves the rapid transition into the information age (see the box Changing Perspectives: History, Culture, and the Information Age). Clearly, the widespread use of computers and cellular phones and the development of the Internet are having an impact not only on the way individuals spend their time but also on the structure of the family, the workplace, and society in general.

Needless to say, contextual approaches are complex. They also apply throughout the lifespan, beginning in early childhood. At no point, however, do contextual considerations become more important than in adult development when, as noted earlier, pathways of life begin to diverge markedly. To establish a reference point for the subsequent exploration of adult development across various contexts, in the next section we look at the general physical development of young adulthood, including strength and stamina and fitness and health.

REVIEW THE FACTS 12-1

1. Events that typically occur at a particular time during the lifespan and are experienced by most people are termed ________ events.
2. Martin has a sense that he needs to make a career move before he is age 30 and "too old" to change directions. He is feeling pressure from his
   a. idiosyncratic life events. b. postformal paradigm.
   c. biological age. d. age clock.
3. Suppose Leila is concerned that she is the only 40-year-old among her friends who is not yet married. Her concern is most directly related to the concept of
   a. social age. b. chronological age.
   c. psychological age. d. personal age.
4. The number of days, weeks, and years a person has been alive is called ________.
5. An approach that emphasizes the impact on development of several factors interacting together is called a ________.

Practice on **MyDevelopmentLab**

GENERAL PHYSICAL DEVELOPMENT

Strength and Stamina

One thread in any contextual approach to understanding development is to consider issues involving physical health and the impact of health on other aspects of adult life. Our responses to life events are determined, in part, by our physical capacity—our health, fitness, strength, and stamina. In young adulthood—the 20s and 30s—most people enjoy peak vitality, strength, and endurance compared to people in other age ranges. Most cultures capitalize on these prime years by sending the young to do battle, idolizing young athletes and fashion models, expecting women to have children during these years, and prescribing the hardest and most consuming aspects of career development to this period of adulthood.

biological age
An individual's position with regard to his or her expected lifespan

contextual paradigms
Theories that emphasize the interaction of numerous environmental, social, psychological, and historical factors that influence development

social age
An individual's current status as compared with cultural norms

psychological age
An individual's current ability to cope with and adapt to social and environmental demands

CHANGING PERSPECTIVES

History, Culture, and the Information Age

Adult development is forcefully influenced by broad social, cultural, and historical factors. Such forces direct how adults define their personal expectations and also affect crucial transitions in adults' lives, often in dramatic ways (Arnett, 2011; Rogoff, 2003). It is important, therefore, to examine how social, cultural, and historical contexts affect adult development.

In the 20th century, one of the most important contextual shifts was a dramatic increase in life expectancy for those living in the United States and in other developed countries. Although there have been people who lived into their 80s, 90s, and beyond in every known historical period, many more people now are living into later adulthood, and this is reflected in life expectancies, which continue to rise. Increasing life expectancy has been due, for the most part, to decreased rates of infant and childhood mortality. For example, in Germany in 1600, nearly half of all children never reached adulthood (Imhof, 1986). By the time an average woman reached age 35 in 1800, she had lost one-third of her children. Now, in the United States and in other developed countries, less than 1% of 35-year-old women have lost a child. Thus, death during childhood was once a normal and expected event; it is now an abnormal part of the social script. As a result, the death of a child is now a shattering personal loss instead of an event that touches almost every parent's life at one time or another.

Like the periods that have preceded it, the 21st century brings a whole new set of historical circumstances. In this information age, we have become a global society with a global culture and instant communication throughout much of the world. In developed countries, knowledge often is no longer transmitted from adult to child or from older adults to younger trainees with the usual checks and balances of tradition. Instead, national and international television brings news, advertising, and information of every sort into almost every home; and then there is the Internet, which is changing language, work life, trade, and family communication in countless ways. By 2009 in the United States, nearly 80% of the adult population were regular users of e-mail and the Internet, and this percentage is even higher for young adults (Rainie, 2010). Only a decade earlier fewer than 40% of U.S. adults used the Internet.

The growth of Internet usage has slowed in some developed countries because of the saturation of computer technology throughout the culture. However, usage in many countries in Asia and the Middle East and in some countries in Latin America and Africa is still growing rapidly, and many people in these countries hope that access to global technology will provide the necessary bridge to cultural and economic development. Many younger adults in countries such as these hope to make the leap from developing countries to full partnership with other developed nations through the use of online education, business, and commerce. Internationally, adolescents and young adults are at the forefront of learning the tools and developing the customs associated with these new *cultural pathways* that are emerging through the information age (Greenfield, 2009).

What impact will this shift to a global information age imply for developmental processes and sequences? Researchers are just beginning to discover how the revolution in information technology is affecting our development and our lives. For example, Dinesh Sharma, a contemporary scholar of rapid social change in India, has been studying the impact of the new technologies on the cognitive development of children, on the functioning of families, and on cultural patterns in a more general sense. Sharma suggests that we are at the cusp of a new digitally connected world, which is giving rise to a radically different interactive culture. A flurry of current research is looking to find answers to important questions about how technology may be influencing human developmental processes (Sharma, 2004). Some of these investigations are revealing results like the following:

- The increased use of the computer can pull the family apart or bring members together. Computers can absorb time formerly spent in family interactions or can foster cooperative activity as parents help children find resources on the computer and have instant access to information to answer questions or make shopping or travel plans.
- Whereas formerly culture and wisdom were generally transmitted from older adults to those younger, now younger adults can reverse this process as they teach their parents how to become familiar with and to use the new technologies.
- The individual can create a *cyberself* in a cyberworld with anonymity and an air of mystery. With code words and shorthand and carefully controlled disclosure, individuals can try on a new identity or develop a point of view that may be inconsistent with their daily non-cyber self.

As you can see, information technology is having a powerful impact on the entire context in which development unfolds. Consider for a moment how your life would be different if you had lived at a time before computers and the Internet were available. How do you think computers are affecting the course of lifespan development? Are such changes positive, negative, or both?

Although our sense of vision begins a very slight decline in middle childhood (Rawson et al., 1998), for the most part, organ functioning, reaction time, strength, motor skills, and sensorimotor coordination are at their maximum in the early to mid-20s; after that they gradually decline (Gabbard, 2012). However, the decline that occurs during the 30s and 40s is less than most people imagine. As Figure 12-1 illustrates, the major functional drop-off of most of the body's biological systems occurs after about age 40. Thus, although the decline from peak performance that occurs after the mid-20s may be important to star athletes, it barely affects the rest of us.

Some employers encourage physical fitness by providing facilities and convenient times for employees to exercise.

Declines in physical skills and capabilities are most noticeable in emergency situations and at other times when physical demands are extreme. For example, when a woman is in her late 30s, a pregnancy draws more heavily on her reserve physical stamina than if she were in her 20s; in addition, it may take longer

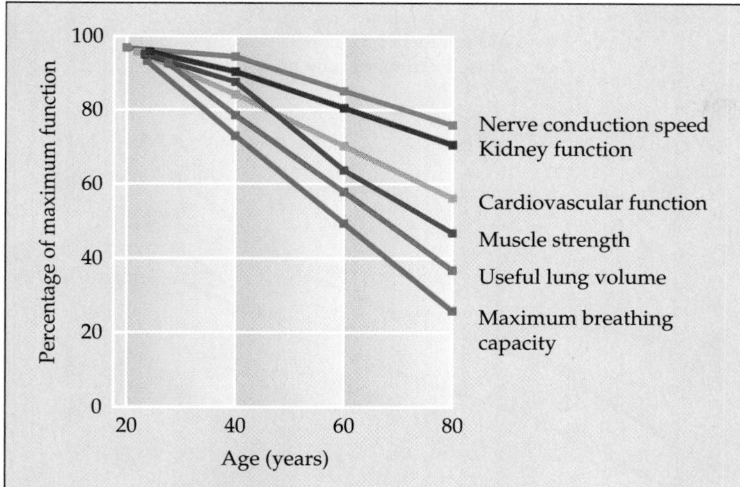

FIGURE 12-1 Average Declines in Biological Systems
These declines can be improved dramatically by health and fitness practices, including regular exercise.

SOURCE: Adapted from *Vitality and aging*, by J. F. Fries and L. M. Crapo, 1981, San Francisco: W. H. Freeman.

for the older woman to return to normal after the child is born. Similarly, it is typically easier for a 25-year-old to work at more than one job to get the family through a financial crisis than it is for a 40-year-old.

Fitness and Health

By and large, young adulthood is a healthy period. This is especially true for people who follow a sensible diet; get regular exercise; avoid tobacco and other drugs, and consume alcohol in moderation, if at all. Compared to older adults, young adults also are least likely to be overweight. However, not all individuals enter adulthood with good habits in place. As noted in the previous chapter, the rate of alcohol and drug use is highest in the 18- to 25-year-old category, and it remains high throughout the next decade of life (Substance Abuse and Mental Health Services Administration [SAMHSA], 2012). Fully 50% of 18- to 25-year-olds report binge drinking at least monthly, and this statistic applies equally to those in and out of college. Although some young adults eventually move away from such unhealthy behaviors, others do not, setting themselves up for significant health problems that typically emerge during middle adulthood.

Compounding the impact that unhealthy behavior has on later development, the health and exercise habits formed during young adulthood often persist throughout the adult years. Thus, although attitudes and behaviors related to health and fitness can change at any point, people often tend to resist such change, making it especially important to establish good health habits in young adulthood.

Physical Fitness Many athletes reach their peak skills and conditioning during young adulthood. Between the ages of 23 and 27, the striated (voluntary) muscles, including the biceps and triceps, achieve their maximum physical strength. Peak leg strength comes between the ages of 20 and 30, peak hand strength comes at about age 20. Of course, the age at which athletes reach their peak performance varies according to the sport. Swimmers and gymnasts generally peak during adolescence, short-distance runners and tennis players usually peak in their early 20s (Schulz & Salthouse, 1999). In contrast, and with some notable exceptions, golfers tend to perform best in their late 20s and on into their 30s (Gabbard, 2012). Major league baseball players generally peak around ages 27 to 30, although the players with the greatest ability may peak several years after that (Schulz, Musa, Staszewski, & Siegler 1994).

In recent decades, improvements in exercise training and diet have added so much to adult fitness that older adults are now capable of higher performance levels than adults in their prime a century ago. For example, when the winning times of younger runners in the 1896 Olympics were compared against the best performances of "master" athletes ages 40 to 69 a century later, the older athletes were sometimes faster than the younger gold-medal winners. As a case in point, in 1896 the winning time for a marathon was 2 hours 59 minutes; in 2012, the winning time for master athletes running the same distance ranged from 2 hours 23 minutes for those in the 40 to 49 age group to 3 hours 10 minutes for those in the 60 to 69 age group. Although women did not run in the Boston Marathon in the 1890s, the winning time for women in 1972 was 3 hours 10 minutes. In 2012, merely four decades later, the top woman finished in 2 hours 32 minutes, lopping 38 minutes off the 1972 winning time. In general, better nutrition and training throughout the adult years often more than compensates for advanced age.

Do you believe we will see comparable increases in maximum physical performance in the next 50 years as we have in the past 50? Why or why not?

In contrast to the peak fitness experienced by top athletes and other fit young adults, however, a large percentage of people in this age group report getting little or no exercise on a regular basis. In 2008 the federal government published guidelines for the amount of aerobic exercise and the amount of muscle-strengthening activity that Americans should include in their leisure-time activities. Today, about one-third of men age 18 to 44 meet both of these guidelines, as do about 20% of 18- to 44-year-old women (National Center for Health Statistics [NCHS], 2012f; see Figure 12-2). However, more than a third of young adult men, and nearly half of young adult women fail to meet either guideline, choosing instead to lead sedentary lifestyles. Furthermore, the proportion of those who lead lives with little physical activity increases with age (see Figure 12-2). Those who establish low activity levels in early adulthood tend to persist in that lifestyle, with clear risks of overweight and obesity and consequent health problems later in life. Obesity is now the second leading cause of preventable death, ranked just behind smoking and just ahead of alcohol consumption (Mokdad, Marks, Stroup, & Gerberding, 2004; see Figure 12-4).

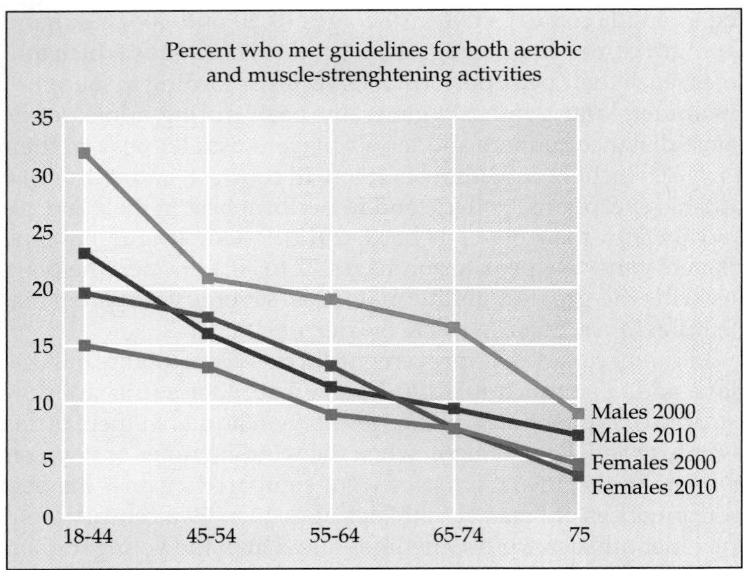

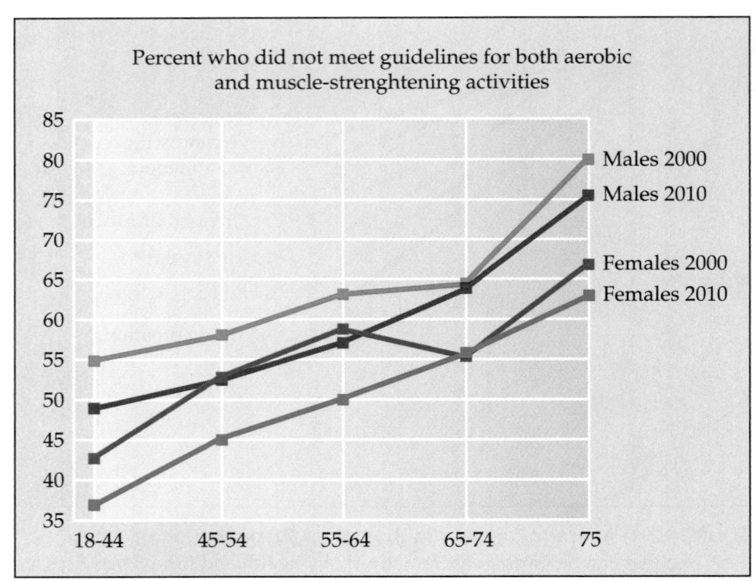

FIGURE 12-2 Percent of Adults Meeting the Federal Physical Activity Guidelines for Adults, 2000 and 2010

SOURCE: "Participation in leisure-time aerobic and muscle-strengthening activities that meet the 2008 federal physical activity guidelines for adults 18 years of age and over, by selected characteristics: United States, selected years 1998–2010," National Center for Health Statistics (NCHS), 2012, in *Health, United States*, 2012 (p. 252), Hyattsville, MD: Author.

Lifestyles established in the 20s and 30s often predict later practices and their associated outcomes. Not surprisingly, general healthiness is linked to physical activity. Adults with active lifestyles attain substantially higher levels of physiological functioning than do adults with more sedentary lifestyles, and this advantage is retained throughout adulthood (see Figure 12-3). Adults who remain active into their 80s retain physiological abilities characteristic of sedentary adults in their 40s (Gabbard, 2012).

Death Rates Among Young Adults Death rates are lower for U.S. young adults than for any other adult age group owing mostly to advances in medicine. Today, few younger women die in childbirth. Tuberculosis is no longer a leading killer of young adults, and diseases like diabetes and heart and kidney disease are often manageable over a normal lifespan. Death due to heart disease and cancers becomes somewhat more common in early adulthood than in childhood or adolescence, although these health problems

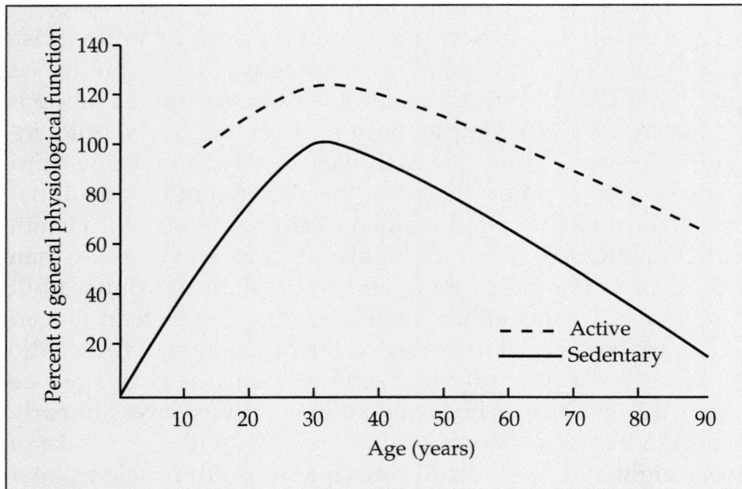

FIGURE 12-3 General Physiological Function Across the Lifespan for Active and Sedentary Persons

SOURCE: From Figure 11.5 in *Lifelong motor development* (p. 368), by C. P. Gabbard, 2004, Upper Saddle River, NJ: Pearson Education. Reprinted by permission.

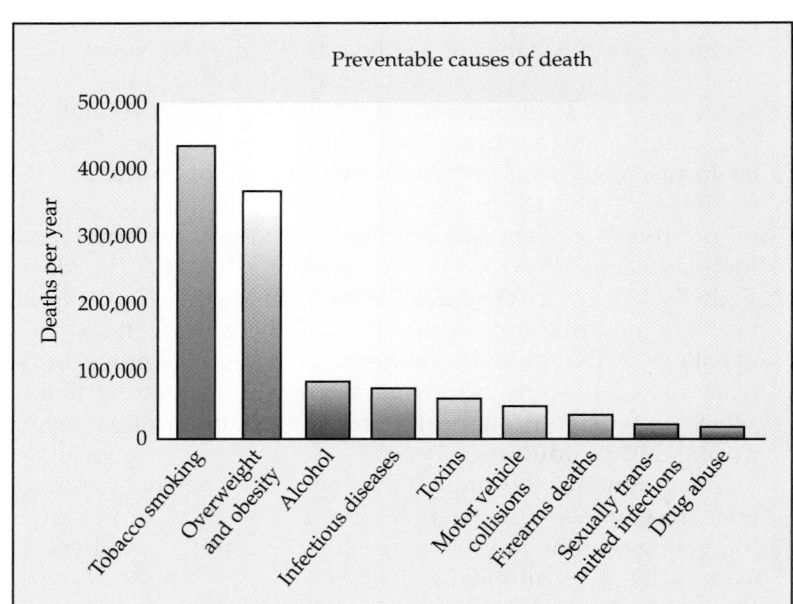

FIGURE 12-4 Leading Causes of Preventable Death

SOURCE: "Actual causes of death in the United States, 2000," by A. H. Mokdad, J. S. Marks, D. F. Stroup, and J. L. Gerberding, March 2004, *JAMA, 291*(10), 1238–1245. DOI:10.1001/jama.291.10.1238. PMID 15010446

Watch *Young Adulthood: Health, Mak* on **MyDevelopmentLab**

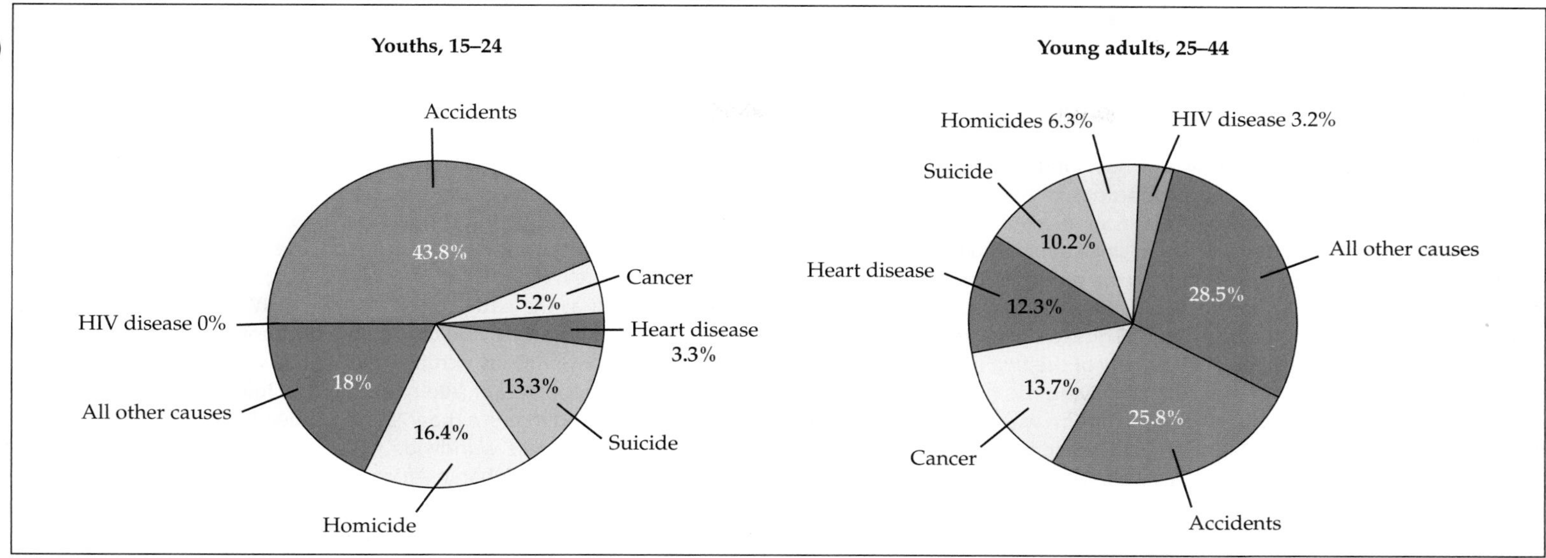

FIGURE 12-5 Major Causes of Death in the United States, 2008, for Youths and Young Adults, Ages 15 to 24 and 25 to 44, in Percent of Total Deaths

SOURCE: From *Health, United States, 2012: With special feature in socioeconomic status and health*, National Center for Health Statistics (NCHS), 2012, Hyattsville, MD: National Center for Health Statistics.

are more likely to arise later in adulthood. However, health habits that lead to these and other major causes of *preventable* deaths (e.g., smoking, obesity, and alcohol use) often are established during young adulthood (NCHS, 2012; see Figure 12-4). The leading cause of *actual* deaths during this period is accidents—which is also the case in infancy, childhood and adolescence (see Figure 12-5). Deaths due to accidents in young adulthood are about three times more common among males than females. Over the past two decades, death from AIDS has dropped from the second to the sixth leading cause of death in early adulthood in the United States due to the availability of new combinations of effective drugs. In other parts of the world, however, and especially in many countries in Africa, AIDS is ravaging the early adult population (see the box Current Issues: The Changing Face of HIV/AIDS).

Disease, Disability, and Physical Limitations Although death rates for young adults are much lower than those for other adult age groups, it has long been known that many of the diseases that will cause trouble later in life begin during young adulthood. Young adults may feel no symptoms; however, lung, heart, and kidney diseases, arthritis, joint and bone problems, atherosclerosis, and cirrhosis of the liver may be in their initial stages. Diseases and disorders that do yield symptoms during young adulthood include multiple sclerosis and rheumatoid arthritis; stress-linked diseases, such as hypertension and ulcers; some psychiatric disorders, such as schizophrenia and depression; and some genetically based diseases, such as diabetes or sickle-cell anemia. Drug abuse, including alcoholism, which often begins in adolescence, also poses significant problems for some young adults. As noted previously, people ages 18 to 25 have the highest rates of alcohol use, smoking, and illicit drug use of any age period. Young adults also have the highest reported rate of driving while drunk (see Figure 12-6), which is one factor that contributes to the fact that accidents are the leading cause of death for people in early adulthood. In addition, as noted earlier, alcohol-related conditions are the

What factors do you think might be responsible for the fact that adolescents and young adults are the age groups most likely to use tobacco, alcohol, and other illegal drugs?

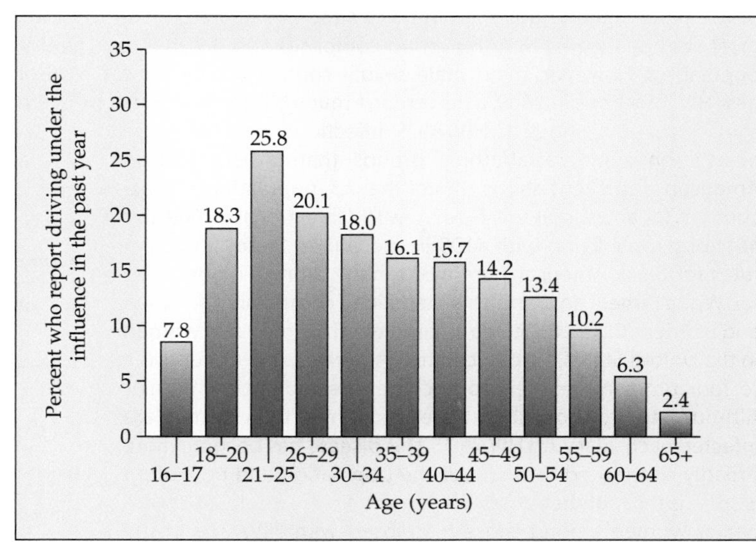

FIGURE 12-6 Driving Under the Influence of Alcohol in the Past Year by Age, 2007

Note that about one in four young adults in their early 20s reports driving under the influence within the last year, a behavior that drops off sharply with age.

SOURCE: From *The 2007 National Survey on Drug Abuse and Health*, Substance Abuse and Mental Health Services Administration (SAMHSA), 2007, SMA 03-3774, Rockville, MD: Author.

CURRENT ISSUES

The Changing Face of HIV/AIDS

Although issues related to HIV/AIDS seldom attract the national publicity they did in the 1980s, this disease has not gone away in the United States, and it has reached epidemic proportions in many other parts of the world. In the United States, the rate of diagnosis peaked in the mid-1990s to over 70,000 new cases per year. However, since about 2000, the number of new cases has been gradually declining to the present rate of about 33,000 in 2010 (Centers for Disease Control [CDC], 2012c).

Like other communicable diseases, AIDS hits some pockets of the population harder than others. In the 1980s, many of the first people diagnosed in the United States were gay men, initially giving rise to the concern that AIDS was a gay man's disease. This misperception was quickly checked by the finding that by the late 1980s HIV/AIDS infections were being transmitted through heterosexual activity as well, which has long been the way other common sexually transmitted diseases like chlamydia, gonorrhea, herpes, and syphilis usually are contracted (refer to Table 12-1). In the 1990s, there also was a dramatic increase in the number of young children who were dying from AIDS after contracting the disease from their infected mothers during the prenatal period (UNICEF, 2005).

By the mid-1990s, HIV infection was much better understood. In the United States, broad public health and educational efforts were launched to reduce its spread. In many cases, these efforts were successful, and—as previously noted—the rates of new infections declined. In addition, in the 1990s, antiretroviral therapies like AZT and various drug combinations called *drug cocktails* were shown to delay the onset of AIDS symptoms for most people infected with HIV. Although AIDS still is considered a terminal disease, these drug therapies—now referred to as HAARTs (highly active antiretroviral therapies)—have substantially reduced the death rate from AIDS, at least in developed countries where many individuals can afford these expensive drugs.

However, HIV/AIDS infections are still prevalent in the United States, with some subgroups being more heavily affected than others. Foremost among these are men who have sex with other men. Although estimates of the percentage of gay men in the United States are difficult to make, most studies suggest that this group comprises about 2 to 8% of the U.S. population. However, male–male sexual contact accounted for 61% of new HIV infections in 2009, a percentage much higher than the population statistics would suggest. HIV/AIDS infections also fall more heavily on some racial/ethnic groups than others. African Americans represent about 14% of the U.S. population, but accounted for an estimated 44% of new HIV infections in 2009 and 46% of people living with AIDS in the United States. Infection rates for Black Americans are more than 15 times higher than for White Americans, and this statistic is comparable for men and women (CDC, 2012c). Compared to White men and women in the United States, Hispanic/Latino Americans are about three to four times more likely to become infected with HIV/AIDS. Although today about three times more men than women are infected each year with HIV/AIDS, this disease has become more broadly distributed throughout the population and now often is spread through heterosexual contact. For example, the number of women among those diagnosed with HIV/AIDs in the United States increased from one in seven in 1995 to one in four in 2010 (CDC, 2012c).

No age group is spared from infection with HIV, despite the widely held impression that AIDS is a young person's disease. For example, older women have discovered that they also are vulnerable to HIV infection. In the "age of Viagra," south Florida has reported a large increase in HIV-positive tests among widows, widowers, and other seniors who have found a new social life by relocating to retirement communities. For example, in Broward County in Florida, one in six women over age 50 who were tested for AIDS were found to be HIV-positive (CNN, November 26, 2004; Inge Corless, personal communication, 2004). This population thought condoms were used to prevent childbirth and therefore thought they were not necessary after menopause.

As significant as the issues associated with HIV/AIDS are in the United States, they pale in comparison to the problems posed in many other parts of the world, where AIDS is virtually wiping out significant proportions of the young adult population (see the table that follows). Worldwide, AIDS has already resulted in more than 25 million deaths, and, in 2010, an estimated 34 million people worldwide were living with AIDS (AVERT, 2012). In some regions of sub-Saharan Africa, where the prevalence of AIDS currently is greatest, estimates indicate that as many as 70% of the population has been infected with the HIV virus. Families are decimated; children, who may be ill themselves, are left without parents to care for them; and the workforce has become seriously compromised due to the death and illness of large numbers of workers. Infection rates in some other parts of the world are still rising, especially among women (Associated Press, 2004; AVERT, 2012), to whom the disease is easily transmitted. Worldwide, more women than men are now diagnosed each year (UNAIDS, 2008). These facts have caused the World Health Organization (WHO) to call the global HIV/AIDS epidemic the "greatest threat to human health and development

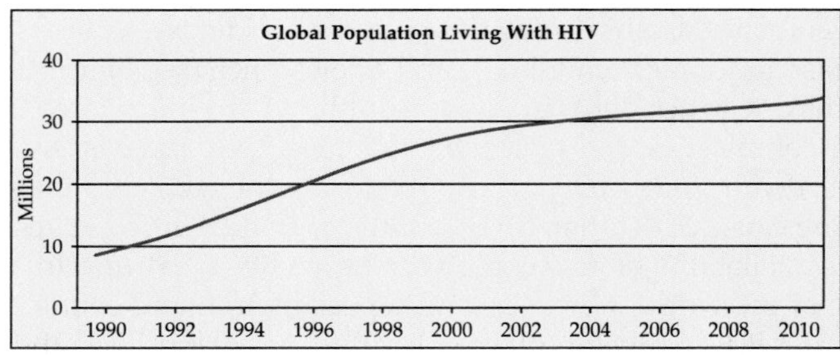

Regional Statistics for HIV/AIDS, 2010

Region	Adults and children living with HIV/AIDS in 2010	Percent of adult population living with AIDS	Deaths of adults and children in 2010
Sub-Saharan Africa	22.9 million	5.0%	1.2 million
North Africa and Middle East	470,000	0.2%	35,000
Asia	4.8 million	0.1%	306,000
Oceania	54,000	0.3%	1,600
Latin America	1.5 million	0.4%	67,000
Caribbean	200,000	0.9%	9,000
Eastern Europe and Central Asia	1.5 million	0.9%	90,000
North America, Western and Central Europe	2.1 million	0.6%	29,900
Global Total	34.0 million	0.8%	1.8 million

SOURCE: From "Worldwide HIV & AIDS statistics including deaths," AVERT, retrieved from http://www.avert.org/worldstats.htm.

since the bubonic plague and the advent of tobacco consumption" (WHO, 2004). AIDS is particularly a threat to developing nations where health care is poor or nonexistent and resources of all types are severely strained. What can be done?

The World Health Organization has called for a five-pronged assault on AIDS, focusing on both prevention and treatment. One major initiative is to provide drug therapies at costs that poor nations can afford. Some success has been achieved: In the late 1990s, a year's supply of antiretroviral drugs cost about $10,000 per patient; now similar therapies can be obtained for about $80 per year for the least expensive drugs to about $660 for the most expensive HAARTs (WHO, 2012b). Consequently, the number of people receiving antiretroviral therapy in low- and middle-income countries increased dramatically, rising 13-fold between 2003 and 2009 (WHO, 2012b). As of 2009, drug therapy was being provided to more than a third of HIV-infected people living in these countries (WHO, 2012b). In response, for the first time since the beginning of the epidemic, in 2006, the number of AIDS deaths worldwide began to decline (UNAIDS, 2012). However, at present, drugs provide a treatment, not a cure: Prevention is still the most pressing need in fighting the AIDS pandemic. People need to be tested for HIV, and they need to be persuaded to modify their sexual behavior. Progress on these fronts poses a challenge, but the alternatives at present are few.

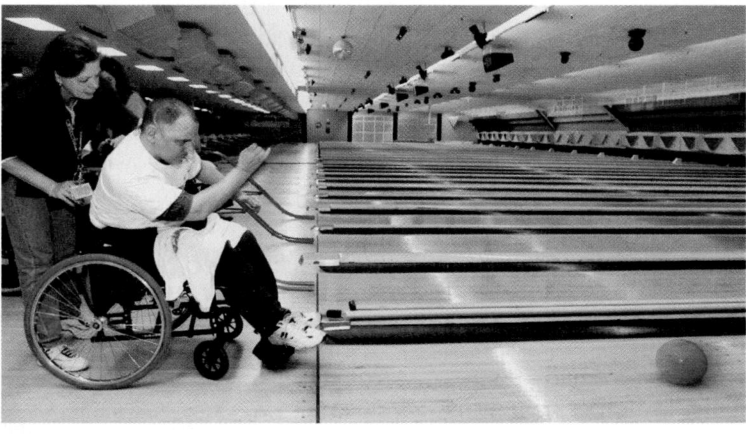

▲ Physical recreational activities such as bowling are particularly important for people with disabilities who have years of rehabilitation ahead of them. This veteran prepares for an upcoming tournament.

third-leading cause of preventable deaths in the United States, and most of these conditions trace their origins to heavy use of alcohol in adolescence and early adulthood.

Physical disabilities, which are difficult to adjust to at any age, are often especially trying during adolescence and early adulthood. At this stage in life, individuals normally are developing intimate relationships and making major decisions, such as choosing an occupation. People with physical disabilities may become overwhelmed by their limitations during this future-oriented period. This normally small population of young adults with physical disabilities becomes enlarged in times of war, reflecting the impact of combat-related injuries.

Understandably, young adults with physical disabilities have been in the forefront of efforts to change social attitudes and laws that affect all disabled people. As a result of their actions and of those of other interested individuals and groups, the Americans with Disabilities Act (ADA) was passed in the United States in 1990. This law makes it illegal to discriminate against individuals with disabilities in employment, public accommodations, transportation, and telecommunications. Among other things, it requires companies to make *reasonable accommodations* for the needs of employees with disabilities so that they can do the work for which they are trained; if that is not possible, they must be trained for comparably skilled work. Most important, people cannot be fired because of a disability alone. The ADA also requires that buildings, sidewalks, and other facilities and services used by the public be made *handicap accessible* to the degree possible. The ADA demands a policy of inclusion rather than exclusion and expects that organizations will be proactive in helping people with disabilities of all sorts live as full and productive lives as possible.

Despite the fact that young adulthood is a time of relatively few health problems for most people, it is not a time completely free of health concerns. Among these are issues related to sex and sexuality, which, along with topics including fertility, sexually transmitted diseases, sexual attitudes and behavior, and sexual identity and orientation, we discuss in the next section.

Watch *AIDS* on **MyDevelopmentLab**

REVIEW THE FACTS 12-2

1. Physical decline generally occurs earliest in which of the following?
   a. heart b. respiratory system
   c. vision d. digestion
2. In terms of voluntary muscle strength, such as the strength of the bicep muscles in the arm, you would expect a person to be strongest at ________ years of age.
   a. 16 b. 18
   c. 25 d. 32
3. The leading cause of *preventable* death in the United States is ________.
4. Which of the following is the leading cause of death for young adults in the United States?
   a. heart attack b. cancer
   c. accidents d. HIV/AIDS
5. The law that protects the rights of people with disabilities is referred to as the ________.

Practice on **MyDevelopmentLab**

SEX AND SEXUALITY

Although today sexual interest and often sexual activity begin in adolescence, early adulthood is usually the time of life where mature sexual behavior unfolds. As a rule, young adults are more sexually active and responsive than at any other point in the lifespan, and by this age, they are likely to have a clear sense of their sexual identity. Early adulthood is also the time of life when many adults plan to have children, so *fertility*—a couple's ability to have a child—becomes a central issue during this period of the lifespan.

Fertility

Although both males and females become fertile during early adolescence when they reach puberty, peak fertility occurs for both groups during late adolescence and early adulthood. Men and women do, however, exhibit different patterns of fertility across the lifespan. Men produce sperm continually from puberty on. Most men remain fertile throughout their later adult years, although as they age seminal emissions contain progressively fewer viable sperm. Women, on the other hand, are fertile only up until menopause, which typically occurs at around age 50, at which time ova are no longer released. As you may recall, females are born with their lifetime supply of about 400,000 ova that are released monthly, beginning soon after menarche. Ovulation is relatively stable between the ages of 25 and 38. After age 38, and up until menopause, however, there is a rapid decline in the number and regularity of ova released.

What reasons might a prospective parent give for wanting to have children at a young age? What reasons might he or she give for wanting to have children later in adulthood?

This does not mean that older women cannot or should not become pregnant. On the contrary: Increasing numbers of women are choosing to have children in their late 30s and into their 40s when they typically are more secure emotionally and financially and perhaps well established in a career. If becoming pregnant is difficult, several different techniques can be used to enhance a woman's fertility, including hormone injections that trigger the release of ova and *in vitro* fertilization, which involves extracting an ovum, fertilizing it in a laboratory, and reinserting it into the uterus where it develops. Because genetic defects are more likely to occur as a woman ages, genetic screening procedures, such as amniocentesis, allow older women to anticipate many issues associated with having a child with genetic abnormalities. (See Chapter 3 for more detailed coverage of assisted reproductive technologies and genetic and prenatal screening techniques.)

Sexually Transmitted Diseases

Difficulty in conceiving a child can result from many different kinds of problems, one of which is having had an untreated sexually transmitted disease (STD). Among the most common of STDs among young adults in the United States are chlamydia, gonorrhea, syphilis, herpes, and HIV/AIDS (CDC, 2012c). Chlamydia, which results from a bacterial infection, usually can be treated successfully with a course of antibiotics once it is identified. Chlamydia is the most commonly reported bacterial STD in the United States today. In some studies, the incidence of chlamydia has been reported to be as high as 10 to 15%, although it is difficult to establish the rates of occurrence for this as well as other STDs because young people often do not seek medical help, and they may not report their disease history accurately. Gonorrhea, another bacterial infection which also can be effectively treated with antibiotics, is also quite common. Both chlamydia and gonorrhea can result in serious consequences, including sterility, if left untreated. Although today syphilis, a third type of bacterial infection, usually is curable with antibiotic therapies, if left untreated it can result in neurological damage and can cause death. It also can produce difficulties with conception, although it is not as common in the United States today as are other STDs. Another common STD is genital herpes, which is caused by a virus that currently is incurable. The main symptom associated with herpes is the appearance of blisters, which erupt into sores, around the genitals or rectum. However, in many people genital herpes presents few or no symptoms, so individuals may be unaware that they are infected. Today, about one in four women and one in nine men in the United States has a genital herpes infection (CDC, 2012c). There are, of course, many additional types of diseases that are transmitted through sexual contact, although the five noted in Table 12-1 are the most common in the United States.

Can you suggest reasons in addition to the existence of HIV/AIDs that might be encouraging young adults toward more conservative sexual behavior?

Despite the fact that STDs affect millions of sexually active adolescents and adults each year, they have not attracted the public attention that accompanied the outbreak of HIV/AIDS, which in the United States was first identified in the early 1980s. AIDS is produced by a virus called the *human immunodeficiency virus (HIV)* that eventually causes the disease of acquired immune deficiency syndrome (AIDS); hence, it is often referred to by the combined name HIV/AIDS. The first incidences of AIDS reported in the United States were mostly among gay men, leading some to view this disease as somehow linked to homosexuality. HIV/AIDS, of course, is not a gay disease: It is spread through contact with infected blood or other body fluids, and thus it is seen in anyone who is exposed to these infected substances. Increasingly, AIDS is seen among members of the heterosexual population.

AIDS rates are especially high among particular groups of adults (refer to the box Current Issues: The Changing Face of HIV/AIDS), although the overall incidence of this disease in the United States is still very small in comparison to the prevalence of other STDs. Even for high-risk groups, the likelihood of contracting HIV is about 0.1%; the rates for contracting other STDs is in the range of 5 to 15%.

Table 12-1 Major Sexually Transmitted Diseases for All Ages in the United States

Disease	Description
CHLAMYDIA	Causes urinary tract infections in men; also responsible for testicular infection. In women, chlamydia can cause inflammation of the cervix and fallopian tubes. Although the infection is easily treated with antibiotics, failure to treat it may result in permanent damage, including infertility. Approximately 1.3 million new cases of chlamydia occur each year, and infection rates appear to be rising. Many cases go undetected and /or untreated, as symptoms are often mild or absent.
GONORRHEA	Can cause sterility and other chronic problems if left untreated or if treated at an advanced stage. Over 700,000 new people are infected with gonorrhea each year, and infection rates appear to be rising. Symptoms include a burning sensation while urinating and sometimes a discharge; these often are mild or absent, especially in women.
HERPES	A group of viruses that includes herpes simplex virus, types I and II, and affects about 1 out of 6 U.S. adolescents and adults (1 in 4 women; 1 in 9 men). Although there is no cure for herpes, there are treatments that can limit the severity of outbreaks. Infection usually occurs through contact with sores or outbreaks on the skin, so abstinence or use of condoms is recommended, especially during outbreaks.
HIV/AIDS	Human immunodeficiency virus (HIV) is a virus that destroys the body's immune system, leading to the development of acquired immune deficiency syndrome (AIDS), the disease that results from HIV infection. Although combinations of drugs, including AZT, can be effective in suppressing the virus, AIDS is currently considered an incurable disease. Its incidence in the United States has declined, but it exists in epidemic proportion throughout many parts of the world, especially in sub-Saharan Africa.
SYPHILIS	Can cause severe health problems, including sterility and even death if left untreated. Pregnant women with untreated syphilis can infect their developing fetus. Affects about 36,000 new people in the United States each year. Rates among men have increased to nearly 6%, with nearly two thirds of cases reported for men who have sex with men. Symptoms often are silent for years, even though complications are developing.
TRICHOMONIASIS ("trich")	Very common STD caused by infection with a protozoan parasite. Affects about 3.7 million people in the United States, making it a very common STD. Only 30% of people infected develop symptoms, which involve irritation and/or inflammation, especially during urination. Antibiotic treatment is effective.

SOURCE: Adapted from "Sexually transmitted diseases," by the Centers for Disease Control and Prevention, 2012, retrieved from http://www.cdc.gov/std/healthcomm/fact_sheets.htm.

Nevertheless, the public attention that was generated in the 1980s by the AIDS epidemic was dramatic. In fact, it can be argued that the publicity associated with AIDS, at least in part, appears to be behind a shifting in sexual behavior in the United States that began in the late 1980s and has affected the sexual activities of many young people. Today, most young adults report exercising greater caution in their sexual behavior than was the case 20 or 30 years ago. For example, in comparison to 1982, in 2008 fewer young people reported having had sexual intercourse, and the proportion of those who did but used condoms more than tripled (CDC, 2012c). In a detailed study conducted at the University of Chicago, for example, 76% of those who reported having five or more sex partners in the past year claimed either to be decreasing their sexual activity, going for HIV tests regularly, or always using condoms (Laumann, Gagnon, Michael, & Michaels, 1994, 2000). Prostitution without condoms also has sharply declined.

Sexual Attitudes and Behavior

Even in advance of the social changes generated by AIDS, trends in adult sexual attitudes and behavior had shifted considerably across the past several decades. In 1959, for example, only 22% of the U.S. population condoned premarital sex for both men and women (Hunt, 1974), a figure much lower than would be reported today. By the mid-1970s, sexual attitudes were beginning to shift (see Chapter 10). Not only were adults in the United States adopting more permissive attitudes, but their expectations about sex were also changing. Whereas in the first half of the 20th century sexual intercourse was narrowly scripted, properly involved only married man–woman couples, and was undertaken primarily for the purpose of procreation, by the 1970s, more couples were seeking to maximize the pleasure associated with sexuality. For example, the median duration of intercourse increased markedly, suggesting that partners were experiencing greater enjoyment, relaxation, and mutuality during intercourse (Hunt, 1974). Flexibility also increased; intercourse could now include previously "undesirable" acts, such as initiation of sex by the woman, masturbation, and oral sex (Hunt, 1974; King, Kante, & Feigenbaum, 2002).

Since the 1970s, sexual attitudes and behavior have continued to shift. A now-classic, comprehensive study conducted in the mid-1990s at the University of Chicago on the sexual habits of 3,500 U.S. participants ages 18 to 59 revealed the following findings (Laumann, Gagnon, Michael, & Michaels, 1994, 2000):

- The vast majority of adults in the United States are monogamous. More than 8 out of 10 have just one sexual partner a year or no partner at all. Over the course of a lifetime, a typical woman has just two partners; a typical man has six.
- There are three basic patterns of sexual relations: About one-third of individuals have sex at least twice a week, one-third

several times a month, and one-third a few times a year or not at all.

- Married couples have the most sex and are most likely to have orgasms during sex. Only about one out of four single people has sex twice a week; nearly two out of five married people do.
- Contrary to popular stereotypes, there are only very minor variations across ethnic groups with regard to frequency of sex.
- As expected, the highest frequencies of sexual activity regardless of marital status were reported by people in their 20s and 30s.
- A person's satisfaction with sex is not closely tied to having an orgasm.

Perhaps the overall conclusion is this: Compared to the 1970s, sexual satisfaction of most U.S. adults had improved markedly by the mid-1990s. As Figure 12-7 indicates, large percentages of married or cohabiting men and women reported being physically and emotionally satisfied by sex with their primary partner.

Since the mid-1990s, attitudes about sex and sexuality have continued to evolve, as social changes have taken place. Since that time, for example, sex education has become more available to youth, the incidence of STDs—including HIV/AIDs—has increased, same-sex marriage has become legal in some states, and the Internet has developed as an important information-disseminating tool. Sexual behavior also has changed; for example, it is estimated that today 95% of the married U.S. population has had sex before marriage (Finer, 2007). In the largest, most comprehensive survey since the Chicago study, researchers at the University of Indiana asked nearly 6,000 U.S. adults about their sexual attitudes and practices, and their results were published in a series of nine articles in a special issue of the *Journal of Sexual Medicine* (e.g., Herbenick et al., 2010; Reece et al., 2010). Among their most significant findings were the following:

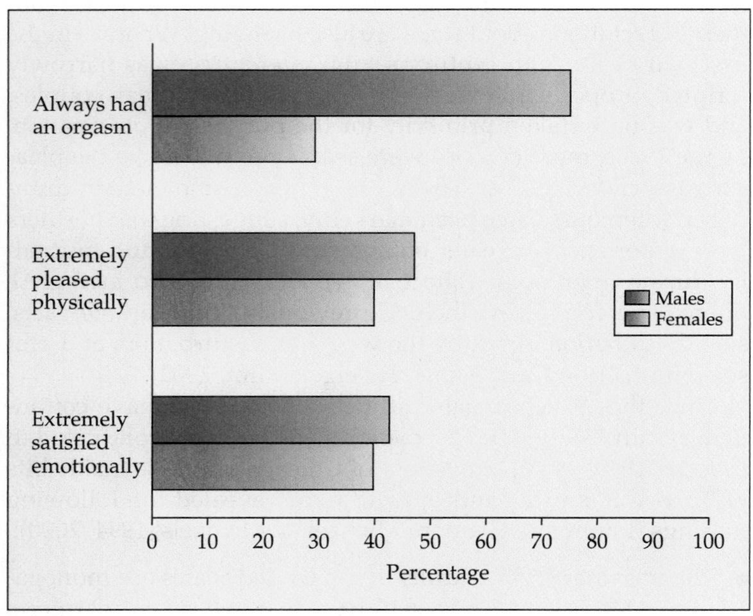

FIGURE 12-7 Three Measures of Sexual Satisfaction with Primary Partner

SOURCE: From Figure 9, "Three measures of sexual satisfaction with primary partner," in *Sex in America*, by R. T. Michael, E. O. Laumann, and G. Kolata, copyright © 1994 by CSG Enterprises, Inc. By permission of Little, Brown and Co., Inc., and Brockman, Inc.

- The use of condoms has increased significantly. In 2010, one in four acts of vaginal intercourse involved the use of a condom; the rate was one in three for single adults. Adults using condoms reported equally pleasurable sexual experiences.
- There is enormous diversity in the types of sex acts performed by adults. Although vaginal intercourse remains the most common form of sexual activity, many sexual events do not involve intercourse but only partnered masturbation or oral sex.
- Masturbation is common throughout the lifespan, and it is more common than partnered sexual activities during adolescence and in older adulthood.
- Oral sex is also common. About 20% of 16- to 17-year-olds performed oral sex during the previous year with an opposite-sex partner. More than half of women and men ages 18 to 49 engaged in oral sex.
- Anal sex is less common than oral sex, but more than 20% of men ages 25 to 49 and women ages 20 to 39 engaged in this behavior during the previous year.
- About 7% of adult women and 8% of adult men identified themselves as gay, lesbian, or bisexual. (Note: These percentages are higher than those found in many other studies.) However, male–male sexual contact is more common than even these percentages would suggest. For example, 15% of men aged 50 to 59 reported that they had received oral sex from a man at some point in the past.
- Most sexual encounters involve orgasm: 85% of men and 64% of women reported having had an orgasm at their most recent sexual event. Men are more likely to experience an orgasm when engaged in vaginal sex, whereas women's orgasms are more likely to be associated with oral sex or with a variety of sex acts.
- Many older adults reported having active, pleasurable sex lives.

As these results make clear, there is considerable diversity in the sexual attitudes and behaviors among adolescents and adults living in the United States today. Not surprisingly, teens and adults often hold strong views about sexuality, and in some cases these views are diverse as well. One especially important social issue of our time concerns how society addresses sexual orientation, the topic of the next section.

Sexual Identity and Sexual Orientation

Certainly no one living in contemporary culture in the United States could argue that sex and sexuality are not important dimensions of adult life. In fact, our *sexual identity*, which defines our sense of who we are sexually, is an important component of self-concept and one that develops throughout later childhood, adolescence, and into adulthood (see Chapter 10). Perhaps the most central aspect of our sexual identity is our sexual orientation.

Negotiating sexual identity formation and the relationships that accompany it can be difficult for anyone in a society as diverse as the United States, where our definitions of appropriate gender attributes and sexual behaviors vary considerably and continue to be in a state of transition. However, forming a secure, stable sexual identity can be especially challenging for those whose sexual orientation is toward others of their same gender. **Sexual orientation** refers to the direction of a person's sexual interest toward, and sexual activity with, members of the same, opposite, or both sexes. Sometimes sexual orientation is referred to as *sexual preference*. Partly because sexual orientation is closely linked to a person's romantic and emotional connections with others, it is usually an important part of most people's self-concept and sense of identity.

Discussions of sexual orientation often dichotomize individuals into two groups, *homosexuals* or *heterosexuals*, despite the fact that sexual preference is a much more complex and variable characteristic than any "either-or" approach can accommodate. Those considered to be heterosexual—who express a clear sexual orientation toward members of the opposite sex—generally receive considerable acceptance and support from family and peers. However, for young people who discover in themselves a nonheterosexual orientation, sexual identity formation can be difficult (Carrion & Lock, 1997; Meyer & Northridge, 2007). Realizing that one is sexually and romantically attracted to members of one's own sex—that is, that one is a **lesbian** female, a **gay** male, or to varying degree a **bisexual** person of either sex—generally is accompanied by feelings of being different in some important way, by an intense *self-questioning* process, and by an inner struggle to reconcile this aspect of oneself with one's overall identity as a person (D'Augelli, 2012). Moreover, as many authors have noted, gay male, lesbian, and bisexual adolescents and adults who "come out" and openly acknowledge their sexual orientation can face a gamut of negative reactions from the much larger heterosexual majority. When one's sexual identity is deemed "abnormal" or "undesirable" by others, this can have markedly detrimental effects on psychosocial development.

In your experience, what kinds of negative reactions have you observed when others "discover" that an individual is a lesbian, a gay male, or a bisexual person?

Origins of Same-Sex Orientation Perhaps the million-dollar question is, "What causes a person to develop a same-sex orientation?" The best answer is clearly, "We don't know," beyond the likelihood that sexual orientation, like other traits, results from a complex interaction of heredity and environment. Biological factors are almost certainly involved, and most researchers view male homosexuality and female homosexuality as quite different phenomena (Jenkins, 2010; Mustanski, 2002). Genetic research that has studied gene sequences in families with several gay brothers or lesbian sisters suggests that a particular gene sequence on the X chromosome may be implicated for male homosexuality, although no such link appears for female homosexuality; however, some researchers question the validity of these findings (Hu et al., 1995; Hyde, 2005). Genes do seem to be involved, however, and genetic mechanisms may operate by causing the brain to develop a slightly different structure, perhaps in response to atypical levels of androgenic (male) hormones that circulate during the fetal period of development (Blanchard, 2008; Byne, 2007; Hines, 2004).

Social factors, however, may also be involved; although the consensus view is that homosexuality is much more complex than simply making a *choice* about which sexual orientation one prefers (Jenkins, 2010; West, 2008). Reflecting the current understanding, an extensive review of the literature concluded that theorists remain sharply divided on the relative contributions of biology and social learning. Although there is evidence for each position, much of the evidence is inconclusive (Bily, 2009; Hines, 2004). Other researchers have reiterated this observation (e.g., Cohler & Galatzer-Levy, 2000), adding that it is much more important to understand what it means to be a member of the homosexual minority than it is to understand where homosexuality comes from.

Understanding Sexual Orientation In almost every important respect, individuals with a same-sex orientation are no different from members of the heterosexual community. They form friendships that deepen in young adulthood and that may or may not involve sex, they seek out and form intimate relationships that may or may not last, and they pursue goals in life and succeed or fail and move on (Basseri, Willoughby, Chalmers, & Bogaert, 2006; Roisman, Clausell, Holland, Fortuna, & Elieff, 2008).

Furthermore, the apparent dichotomy between being homosexual versus being heterosexual is not real. First of all, sexual orientation is not an "either–or" thing; it is best thought of as a continuum (Neill, 2009; see Figure 12-8). Second, gay males, lesbians, and bisexual people are as individual as anyone (Cohler, & Hammack, 2007). The popular conception that gay males are effeminate and lesbians are macho is also for the most part a myth (Bailey, Kim, Hills, & Linsenmeier, 1997; Lippa, 2008). Furthermore, the concept of androgyny (see Chapter 7) applies equally well to men and women regardless of their sexual orientation.

There are some important differences between homosexual and heterosexual individuals, however, that revolve around feeling and being different (D'Augelli & Patterson, 2001). The homosexual experience is distinct, as is the African-American experience, the Hispanic-American experience, and the experience of other groups who suffer or have suffered at the hands of a majority (Coyle & Kitzinger, 2002). Not surprisingly, there are some demographic differences when homosexual and heterosexual groups are compared. For example, a higher proportion

sexual orientation
The direction of a person's sexual interest toward, and sexual activity with, members of the same sex, opposite sex, or both sexes

bisexual
A person who is attracted both to males and to females

lesbian
A female with a sexual orientation toward other females

gay
A male with a sexual orientation toward other males

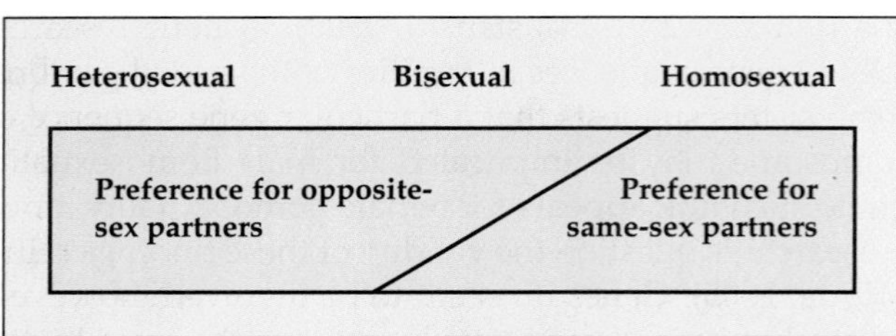

FIGURE 12-8 A Continuum Approach for Understanding Sexual Orientation
A continuum approach to understanding sexual preferences implies that many people can have both homosexual and heterosexual preferences, although some people are strongly heterosexual and others are strongly homosexual.

of self-reported homosexuals attend or complete college, and a higher proportion live in large cities than in other locales. It is difficult to interpret data such as these, however, because multiple explanations are possible. Although it is likely that urban areas include a broader base of compatible friends and partners, and that educated people are more open-minded about same-sex lifestyles, it is also quite possible that demographic trends such as these result from reporting bias. Lesbians and gay males living in uneducated or rural environments may be less willing to disclose their sexual orientation. Perhaps a more meaningful comparison is between lesbians and gay males, where demographic disparities are also seen (see Figure 12-9).

There also are some clear psychological differences between groups of homosexual versus heterosexual adults, which generally reflect cultural prejudices. For example, in comparison to heterosexual adolescents, lesbian, gay male, and bisexual adolescents are at higher risk for loneliness, distress, depression, substance abuse, and suicide. This is true even if they have not yet fully disclosed their same-sex orientation (Haas et al., 2011; Hong, Espelage, & Kral, 2011; Marshal et al., 2011). Researchers also have found that by young adulthood, some same-sex-oriented individuals *internalize* the larger society's prejudiced views of them, with the effect that they accept and live with a sense of shame and lowered self-esteem as a result of their sexual orientation (Allen & Oleson, 1999; Legate, Ryan, & Weinstein, 2012). Although views and values are changing in the United States, the prejudice that surrounds same-sex orientation is pervasive, and it often significantly influences identity formation. 👁

Homophobia Homophobia—a term that refers to the prejudice, aversion, fear, and other negative attitudes held by some individuals and directed toward lesbians, gay males, and/or bisexuals—remains pervasive in the United States. Although homophobia is not a true phobia and is perhaps better called *sexual prejudice* (Ahmad & Bhugra, 2010; Herek, 2000), the term continues to be used both in everyday language and in professional journals, as does the somewhat ill-defined term *homosexual*. Homophobia refers to a set of sharply negative attitudes that can include unreasoned fear, intense loathing, revulsion, and anger directed toward people entirely on the basis of their same-sex orientation. Openly same-sex-oriented people are sometimes blatantly scorned, shunned, condemned as immoral, and discriminated against (Herek, 2009). For example, one large-scale study of lesbians, gay men, and bisexuals in a California city (Herek, Gillis, & Cogan, 1999) found that about one-quarter of the men and one-fifth of the women had in the year prior to the study been victims of a hate crime, such as verbal harassment, being threatened with violence, being chased or followed, having an object thrown at them, or being spat on. Much worse treatment—including beatings and murders—surfaces regularly in the media. Homophobia seems especially intense when it involves men. For example, heterosexual men have been shown to express more negative attitudes toward same-sex-oriented people than heterosexual women, especially where the targets are gay men (Davies, Austen, & Rogers, 2011; Nagoshi et al., 2008).

Have you observed evidence of homophobia? If so, what particular aspects of homosexuality formed the basis of the prejudice?

Of course, not all heterosexual adults are homophobic. Homophobia does, however, raise particular concerns when these attitudes are held by people in positions of power, or by professionals responsible for treating or counseling individuals with same-sex orientations. Yet prejudice is sometimes present even among health practitioners. For example, one study found significant sexually prejudiced attitudes among second-year

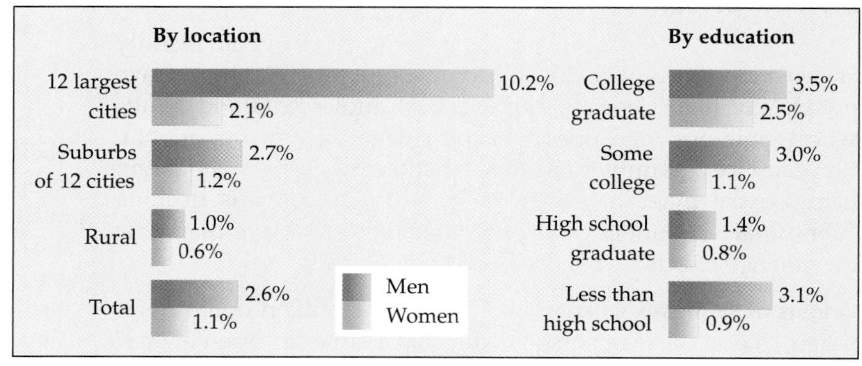

FIGURE 12-9 Demographic Differences Among People Who Reported Having Same-Sex Partners in the Preceding Year, Men and Women
Note that in all of these settings, a larger percentage of men than women report having a same-sex partner in the last year.

SOURCE: Table in *The social organization of sexuality*, by E. O. Laumann, J. H. Gagnon, R.T. Michael, and S. Michaels, copyright © 2004. Reprinted by permission of the University of Chicago Press.

👁 **Watch** *Straightening Out Homosexuals* on **MyDevelopmentLab**

homophobia
Prejudice, aversion, fear, and other negative attitudes held by individuals and directed toward lesbians, gay men, and/or bisexuals

medical students (Klamen, Grossman, & Kopacz, 1999), with 9% endorsing the outdated belief that homosexuality is a mental disorder: Homosexuality was removed as a classification within the *Diagnostic and Statistical Manual of Mental Disorders* nearly 50 years ago. Similarly, the American Psychological Association's (APA's) Division 44 Committee on Lesbian, Gay, and Bisexual Concerns Joint Task Force (APA, 2005) has established guidelines for psychotherapy with lesbian, gay male, and bisexual clients, citing numerous studies that indicate "heterosexist" bias among clinical psychologists and other therapists. Others have pointed out that although recent textbooks in psychology and sociology no longer explicitly characterize homosexuality as a disorder, many still implicitly do so in the way in which the topic is discussed (Weitz & Bryant, 1997).

What kind of backdrop does this provide for adolescent and young adult development? Often the situation is so harsh that many nonheterosexual adolescents conceal their sexual orientation except perhaps among their closest friends or partners, which can pose problems for identity development. Sometimes young people choose to come out later as young adults in college or after they have relocated to an urban setting. In these more open environments homosexual youth may still experience significant abuse and rejection by homophobics, but they also are more likely to find companionship and support. Also, later in development, a person's greater maturity generally provides more resilience for coping. Understandably, some homosexuals never publicly acknowledge their sexual preference, or they come out only to their closest confidants and not to the broader public. This is especially likely if they choose a vocation that places them among coworkers who are openly homophobic.

Of course, U.S. society is changing, as are laws concerning discrimination on the basis of sexual preference (Patterson, 2008; Savin-Williams, 2011). For example, researchers today are more likely to emphasize the commonalities of identity development experienced by all individuals, rather than focus on small, and largely insignificant, differences in experience between members of the sexual majority and those whose gender identities are gay, lesbian, or bisexual in orientation (Dillon, Worthington, & Moradi, 2011). This more inclusive approach is suggested by research findings showing that, as society is becoming more accepting of individuals with nonmajority sexual orientations, one's sexual orientation is becoming a less important factor in overall development. Supporting this view is a body of research suggesting that differences in adjustment between heterosexual and nonheterosexual adults, as well as between their children, are small, if they exist at all (e.g., Balsam, Beauchaine, Rothblum, & Solomon, 2008; Wainright & Patterson, 2008).

As society's tolerance for diverse forms of sexual expression and gender orientation has increased, the ways in which we think and talk about sexuality have become less rigid. For example, many people today use the *transgendered* as a generic description for all forms of sexuality that do not conform to a strict heterosexual orientation. Indeed, the acronym "LGBT" (lesbian, gay, bisexual, transgendered) is often used—especially by young people—to refer to this diverse group of individuals.

Despite the lingering prejudices that sometimes are applied to those who are "different," most young adults have developed cognitive processes during adolescence that allow them to respond maturely to issues involving sexuality, and these intellectual skills continue to expand long past the teenage years. In the next section, we explore various facets of cognitive development in young adulthood, including postformal thought and emotional intelligence.

▲ Young adulthood is a period of the lifespan in which forming deep and significant intimate relationships is an important goal for most people, regardless of their sexual orientation.

Watch *Prejudice* on **MyDevelopmentLab**

REVIEW THE FACTS 12-3

1. At about what age does a woman's fertility generally terminate?
2. The usual course of treatment for chlamydia, gonorrhea, and syphilis is ________.
3. Can genital herpes be cured?
4. According to the results of national surveys, does orgasm play a major role in determining whether or not a person is sexually satisfied with his or her primary partner?
5. To state that homosexuality exists on a "continuum" means that ________.

Practice on **MyDevelopmentLab**

COGNITIVE DEVELOPMENT IN ADULTHOOD

Most of human behavior is directly linked to *cognitive development*—our ability to learn, remember, solve problems, and make judgments about a wide variety of situations. Our ability to use thought to assess situations, form action plans, and guide behavior becomes more mature as we move out of adolescence and into adulthood. In addition to the development of better processes for thinking, we also accumulate a larger, broader knowledge base as we grow older. We come to know more about ourselves and the physical and social world around us. In particular, skills involving speed and rote memory are typically at their highest level in late adolescence and early adulthood, perhaps owing to biological factors or to the fact that young adults are more likely to be immersed in educational tasks that rely on such skills on a daily basis. Although overall intelligence quotient (IQ) scores generally remain high throughout most of adulthood, they often are observed to peak between the ages of 20 and 34, especially when the tests involve speed and memory in addition to more complex, context-based problem solving (Cohen, Swerdlik, & Sturman, 2013).

As we have seen in previous chapters, cognition is not simply a matter of processing speed or acquiring more and more information. At least through childhood and into adolescence, the patterns of thought themselves change. Thus, thinking becomes not just better and faster, but *different,* as we move through various transition phases that bridge our cognitive capacities from one stage to the next.

The most influential model of cognitive development was proposed by Jean Piaget, who identified four periods (stages) of cognitive development: the sensorimotor, preoperational, concrete operational, and formal operational. According to Piaget's view, the final shift in cognitive development begins at about age 12, when the child develops the ability to consider abstract concepts and ideas and to reason hypothetically. Although Piaget did not study adult cognition extensively, his perspective was that once formal thinking was acquired in early adolescence cognitive development was largely complete. According to Piaget, although adults continue to accumulate additional facts and experiences, the logic and problem-solving skills they apply are largely the same as they used when they developed formal operational skills in adolescence.

Beyond Formal Operations

Not all researchers have agreed with Piaget's notion that cognitive development is for the most part completed in adolescence. We know, for example, that development of those brain functions most closely associated with the development of formal thinking extends into early adulthood (see Chapter 10). Such research suggests that there may be subtle qualitative differences between the way an adult understands the world and the way an adolescent understands it.

One early, classic study that examined shifts in cognitive ability in young adulthood examined the change in thought processes that 140 Harvard and Radcliffe students experienced during their 4 years in college (Perry, 1970). At the end of each year, the students were asked questions about how they interpreted their college experiences. Of particular interest was how the students came to grips with the many conflicting points of view and frames of reference they encountered in their studies.

The results from this study showed that, early in their college years, students interpreted their world in a simpler, more dualistic manner. They focused on truth and knowledge and expressed frustration when their questions were met with ambiguous or conditional answers. By the end of college, however, they had become more comfortable in accepting contradictory points of view. They began to adopt the perspective that people have a right to hold different opinions, and they began to understand that things can be seen in different ways, depending on context. Ultimately, many of these students developed a personal orientation that represented their own set of values and points of view. Thus, students moved from a thinking style characterized by basic dualism (e.g., truth vs. falsehood), through one that emphasized tolerance for many competing points of view, to one that embraced self-chosen ideas and convictions. Studies such as this suggest that cognitive development—at least for well-educated young adults—extends past adolescence into early adulthood.

Do you think the college seniors you know approach problems differently than do first year students? If so, how?

Other theorists have elaborated on the types of thinking that are characteristic of young adulthood, often focusing on how people try to bring together and integrate opposing or conflicting views. For example, a young mother may value the role she can play if she stays at home to care for her children. Yet she may also value her role as a professional and may want to continue working and furthering her career. The conflict inherent in such a situation involves careful analysis of the pros and cons of a set of complex possibilities, which therefore involves **dialectical thought** (Riegel, 1973, 1975; Vukman, 2005; Wu & Chiou, 2008), which is the style of thinking that seeks to integrate opposing or conflicting ideas and observations. Such reasoning is seldom seen in adolescence and reflects a type of thought process beyond that described by Piaget's stage of formal operations.

Many contemporary theorists suggest that adult thought moves beyond the formal logic described by Piaget. Although

dialectical thought
Thought that seeks to integrate opposing or conflicting ideas and observations

formal operations may be fairly well mastered by midadolescence, as individuals gain exposure to complex social issues, different points of view, and the practicalities of real life they correspondingly develop broader styles of thinking (Labouvie-Vief, 2003; Sinnott, 2008, 2009). For example, it is through exposure to the world that we are able to construct the systems of beliefs and values that help us organize our thoughts, feelings, and shape our behavior. Adult cognitive maturity, thus, is marked by the development of independent decision-making skills.

The professional decisions of this nurse are contextualized and require knowledge, logic, experience, mature judgment, and the interpersonal skills to influence staff and patients. These skills develop more fully in adulthood.

Postformal Thought

The thinking of adults also is often highly *contextualized*, meaning that it draws on many aspects of intellect—including logic, intuition, and experience—as well as on emotion and interpersonal skills. When adults face complex problems, they often are able to weigh various alternatives, take creative approaches that address specific aspects of the situation, and deal with inconsistent and even contradictory information. These adult abilities are often referred to as **postformal thought** to denote that this type of thinking goes beyond the simpler, more logic-driven approach seen in formal operational thinking (Sinnott, 2003, 2009).

Postformal thinking typically involves both cognitive and emotional aspects in problem solving and often is seen when issues are framed within a social context (Labouvie-Vief, 2006). Consider the following dilemma, which was presented to people of various ages for analysis (Labouvie-Vief, Adams, Hakim-Larson, Hayden, & DeVoe, as cited in Papalia, Olds, & Feldman, 2004):

> John is a heavy drinker. His wife, Mary, warns him that if he gets drunk once more, she will take the children and leave him. John does come home drunk after an office party. Does Mary leave John?

As you can see, this dilemma includes not only cognitive aspects of intellect but also social and emotional issues. Interestingly, older children and younger adolescents typically responded by saying that, yes, Mary should leave John because she set up rules and he broke them. Older adolescents and adults, however, were able to focus on the human dimensions of the problem, and their answers were more complex, often concluding that Mary would probably not leave John. The most mature responses involved the ability to consider multiple factors in making the decision to act. This more mature approach to problem solving, which reflects postformal thinking, was not seen in participants' responses until late adolescence or adulthood, although it was no more likely to occur in the thinking of 40-year-olds than in 20-year-olds. Other research, however, suggests that postformal thinking does increase as adults grow older, especially when there is an emotional component involved in the dilemma (Commons & Richards, 2003) or when creativity is involved (Wu & Chiou, 2008).

Thus, one way in which thinking changes as young people move into adulthood is that it becomes more reflective and complex (Galupo, Cartwright, & Savage, 2010; Labouvie-Vief, 2006; Labouvie-Vief & Diehl, 1999). Adults come to understand that different solutions are appropriate in different situations; for example, that the way to approach a disagreeable coworker might need to be different than how a disagreeable friend could be addressed. Another dimension of adult thought is that it is more realistic, reflecting not just what is ideal but also what is possible (see the box Try This! Exploring Postformal Thought). Because postformal thought relies on the person's ability to integrate reason and emotion and to understand and weigh multiple concerns, some researchers believe that it is closely linked to the development of wisdom—a concept we explore in more depth in Chapter 16 (Benovenli, Fuller, Sinnott, & Waterman, 2011).

How well-supported is the existence of a fifth postformal stage of cognitive development? Although a number of studies support the notion that thinking changes as adolescents become adults (Sinnott, 2008, 2009), there is still considerable discussion about how universal these changes might be and how clearly different from Piaget's formal operations postformal thinking actually is. Regardless, the research on postformal thought has contributed to our understanding of adult thought as being broader and more complex than the logic-driven reasoning used by adolescents. In particular, it has focused our attention on the role that emotion plays in adult thinking.

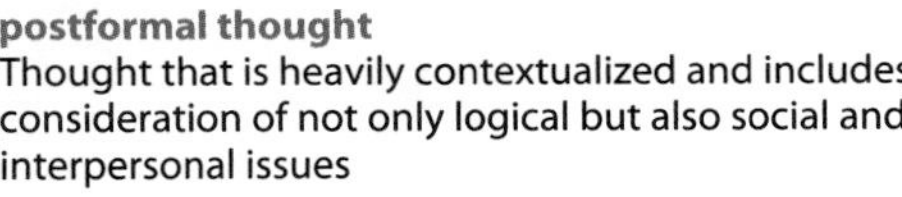

postformal thought
Thought that is heavily contextualized and includes consideration of not only logical but also social and interpersonal issues

Emotional Intelligence

Not all problems that adults face are primarily logical in nature; many involve understanding how individuals relate to each other and react to various kinds of situations. Furthermore, some people are more skilled than others in working in settings that require understanding perspectives of others or that involve the cooperation of other people.

Psychologists have long recognized such individual differences. For example, Gardner's theory of multiple intelligences (see Chapter 8) includes factors he calls interpersonal intelligence

TRY THIS!

Exploring Postformal Thought

As individuals move through childhood and adolescence and into young adulthood, their thought processes become more complex, especially with respect to being able to integrate both cognitive and emotional aspects of a situation into their problem-solving processes. To demonstrate the development of postformal thought, recruit two adolescents (maybe about 14 to 16 years of age) and two young adults (maybe in their mid to late 20s) to respond to a dilemma you pose.

The dilemma cited in the text by Labouvie-Vief and her colleagues works well for this exercise, although you could construct one with similar features to use in this investigation. Here's the dilemma used by Labouvie-Vief and her colleagues to explore the development of postformal thought: *John is a heavy drinker. His wife, Mary, warns him that if he gets drunk once more, she will take the children and leave him. John does come home drunk after an office party. Does Mary leave John?*

Read this dilemma to the four people you have identified and ask them the following questions:

- Does Mary leave John? Why or why not?
- What should Mary think about in deciding what she should do?
- Is leaving John the best solution for the children?
- What other choices does Mary have?

Reflect on What You Observed

What differences did you note in how adolescents and young adults responded to this dilemma? Were the adolescent respondents more likely to think that Mary should leave? Did they give more detailed or less detailed reasons for how Mary should think about the situation? What about the children: Were there age group differences in how the individuals you questioned thought Mary's actions would impact the children? Which group, the adolescents or the young adults, gave more thoughtful, complete responses when asked what other options Mary might have?

Consider the Issues

What predictions would you have made about how adolescents and young adults would respond to the dilemma presented? Did the people you questioned respond as you would have predicted? If not, what factors might have led to a different result? Do you think there might be differences other than age that could determine how an individual might react to the dilemma posed? Do you think, for example, that a person whose parents had divorced might respond differently than one who grew up in a peaceful home environment? Do you think there might be gender differences in the way adolescents or young adults might approach this situation? What other factors could account for the responses given by the people you talked with? How do you think thought processes change as adolescents become adults?

---

and intrapersonal intelligence, reflecting our knowledge of others and of ourselves, respectively. Sternberg's triarchic theory of intelligence (see Chapter 8) also addresses the abilities that revolve around relating to others within his concept of "practical intelligence."

The specific focus on social- and emotional-based aspects of problem solving, however, emerged more fully in the 1990s with the publication of Daniel Goleman's best-selling book, *Emotional Intelligence* (1995/2006), in which he argued that **emotional intelligence (EQ)**, in contrast to IQ, involved the way individuals understand and manage their own and others' emotions and emotional responses. Table 12-2 outlines Goleman's four areas of emotional intelligence. Goleman's view of EQ involves concepts—such as empathy, motivation, optimism, conscientiousness, and competence in social settings—which he believes are even more important to success on the job and in personal relationships than intelligence (Goleman, Boyatzis, & McKee, 2007).

Does EQ make a difference in personal effectiveness? At least some research studies suggest that it does (Bar-On, Maree, & Elias, 2007; Mayer, Salovey, Caruso, & Cherkasskiy, 2011). For example, people who possess higher levels of emotional intelligence enjoy better job success (O'Boyle, Humphrey, Pollack, Hawver, & Story, 2011) and may also be able to better weather periods of emotional distress (Cherniss, 2002; Martins, Ramalho, & Morin, 2010). Many psychologists, however, remain skeptical about the concept of EQ. They note that emotional intelligence overlaps significantly with traditional measures of intelligence and with some personality traits, especially with conscientiousness and emotional

emotional intelligence (EQ)
The term given to those aspects of the intellect that relate to understanding others' and one's own emotions and emotional responses

Table 12-2 Goleman's Four Areas of Emotional Intelligence

Area of Emotional Intelligence	Description
Developing emotional self-awareness	Separating feelings from actions *Example:* Although Shaynell does not like one of her coworkers, she is able to work effectively as part of a team.
Managing emotions	Controlling emotional responses, such as anger *Example:* Although Bob is angry with his boss's suggestion, he responds politely and appropriately.
Reading emotions	Understanding the emotional reactions of others *Example:* Maria understands why a subordinate is upset at being asked to do an unpleasant task.
Handling relationships	Solving relationship problems effectively *Example:* Jack is able to create a work situation where two employees who do not like each other are able to cooperate on work-related tasks.

SOURCE: From *Emotional intelligence*, by D. Goleman, 1995/2006. New York: Bantam Books.

In Schaie's acquisition period, young adults use their intellectual abilities to choose a lifestyle and pursue a career.

stability. Thus, it may provide little more than a popular and convenient label for psychological processes that already have been described and investigated. Other researchers, however, see emotional intelligence as contributing uniquely in predicting how people are able to interact with each other (Joseph & Newman, 2010; Zeidner, Matthews, & Roberts, 2009). Regardless of how useful this concept is as a personal characteristic, however, it does not provide a clear means of understanding cognitive abilities within a developmental context; that is, it does not explain how thinking changes as people move through the lifespan. One perspective that does weigh the role of social and emotional factors across the lifespan is the view advanced by Warner Schaie.

Schaie's Stages of Adult Thinking

Warner Schaie (2005; Schaie & Zanjani, 2006) proposed that the distinctive feature of adult thinking is the flexible way in which adults use the cognitive abilities they already possess. He suggested that during childhood and adolescence we acquire increasingly complex structures for understanding the world. The powerful tools of formal operational thinking are the key achievement of this period, which he called the *acquisition* period. In young adulthood, we use our intellectual abilities to pursue a career and to choose a lifestyle; Schaie called this the *achieving* period. We apply our intellectual, problem-solving, and decision-making abilities toward accomplishing goals and crafting a life plan—aspects of cognition that do not show up on traditional IQ tests.

Watch *What's In It For Me?: The Myth of Multitasking* on **MyDevelopmentLab**

Individuals who successfully complete the achieving period are able to move on to another phase in the application of cognitive skills, a period involving *social responsibility*. As we undertake the tasks of middle adulthood, according to Schaie, we use our cognitive abilities to solve problems for others in the family, in the community, and on the job. For some people, these social responsibilities may be quite complex. When individuals successfully combine their understanding of organizations, their different types of knowledge, and their social responsibilities, they become capable of *executive functions*, which allow them to address complex, multidimensional issues.

Which of Schaie's stages do you think you are in? If your parents and/or grandparents are alive, which are they in?

As people reach the age of retirement, they often focus on *reorganization*, where they learn to reallocate their time from work to other activities and to find meaning in nonwork-related aspects of their life. Finally, in the later years, the nature of problem solving shifts again. The central task at this stage is one of *reintegrating* the elements experienced earlier in life—making sense of life as a whole and exploring questions of purpose. Near the end of life, people may also focus on *legacy creation*, where they finish the business of their lives. In this period, individuals, for example, may make plans for their own death or make sure they have passed along to the next generation the stories, objects, or lessons they have learned or come to value.

Although Schaie's model is age-related, specifying that different stages correspond to different periods within adulthood, as shown in Figure 12-10, it does not argue that all adults experience all stages, nor that the stages occur only during the time frame Schaie describes. Rather, Schaie's view emphasizes that the focus of cognitive development in adulthood is not on expanded intellectual capacity or on a change in cognitive structures. Instead, it emphasizes the flexible use of intelligence in different ways at different stages of the lifespan. Many perspectives on adult development similarly point out the adaptive nature of human development throughout adulthood. In the final section of this chapter, we explore some of the more important theories for understanding this period of the lifespan.

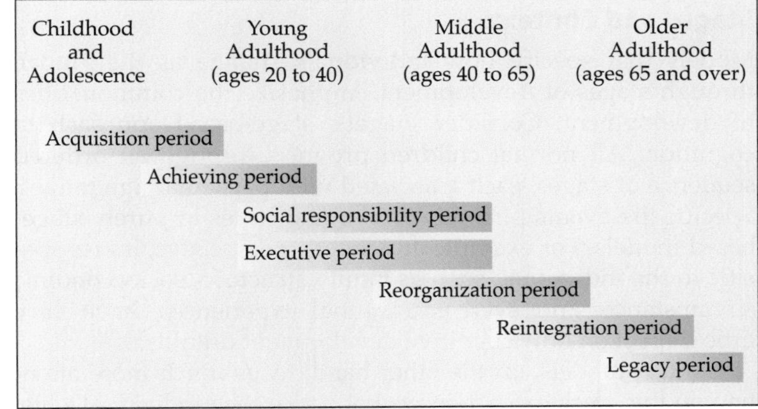

FIGURE 12-10 Schaie's Lifespan Model of Cognitive Development

REVIEW THE FACTS 12-4

1. IQ, especially when it is measured by tests of cognitive speed and memory, is normally highest during which period of life?
   a. the teenage years b. the 20s and 30s
   c. the 40s and 50s d. the 60s and 70s
2. According to Piaget, individuals achieve the highest level of cognitive development beginning at about age ________.
3. Adult thought is often referred to as ________ thought to reflect that it goes beyond Piaget's stage of formal operations.
4. Which of the following is *not* one of the ways that adult thought differs from adolescent thought?
   a. Adult thought is much faster.
   b. Adult thought is more complex.
   c. Adult thought is better able to consider the emotional aspects of a situation.
   d. Adult thought is based more on reality.
5. A person's EQ represents the ability to understand the person's own and others'
   a. extroversion tendencies. b. exceptional characteristics.
   c. excellence. d. emotion.
6. According to Warner Schaie, early adulthood is a period in which individuals typically focus on
   a. legacy creation. b. achieving.
   c. acquisition. d. reorganization.

Practice on MyDevelopmentLab

FRAMEWORKS FOR UNDERSTANDING ADULT DEVELOPMENT

Understanding the developmental changes that occur in adulthood is a difficult task. On the one hand, it does appear that there are reasonably predictable adjustments that nearly all adults experience as they grow older: Thinking becomes more complex and individuals become better able to understand social and emotional perspectives, for example. On the other hand, however, the specific paths we take in life can have major consequences for how our adult lives unfold. For psychologists, these two perspectives on the lifespan are often referred to as *stage-based* versus *context-based* perspectives.

Stages and Contexts

Models that specify how individuals change as they move through stages of development emphasize the commonalities of development. Consider Piaget's stage-based approach to cognition: All normal children progress through an ordered sequence of stages, each associated with particular age ranges. Specific life events play relatively minor roles in purely stage-based models. For example, in Piaget's perspective, issues specific to the individual, such as family structure, socioeconomic circumstance, and even educational experiences, have very little impact on how cognitive development unfolds.

Context models, on the other hand, focus much more attention on the specific experiences that shape each individual's life. Consider the literature on parenting styles: Here, how parents treat children plays an important role in the type of personality the children develop. Theories that emphasize context also imply that multiple factors are influential in development. Thus, context models view the individual's development at many levels: as an individual with specific genetic endowments and life experiences, as a member of a family, as belonging to various social reference groups, and within a broader social community and culture.

In adulthood, as throughout the lifespan, a blending of stage and contextual approaches is perhaps the most useful way to conceptualize development. Particularly when stage models describe narrowly defined cohorts of individuals (e.g., middle-class men who are fathers or women who are stay-at-home mothers), they often are describing development within a context that is quite limited and may not be typical of development in a broader population. Yet, especially within a given society, there usually are fairly standard contexts within which most people live their lives. In the United States, for example, nearly all people spend most of their childhood and adolescence in school, and most enter the workforce and establish a close intimate relationship with another person. Many also become parents. Later in life, children leave home and most people retire from work. When the context is so similar for large groups of people, this allows us to focus on the common threads in development, where we sometimes see similar patterns of development that occur for most people at particular points in the lifespan.

Would stage models and context models be equally useful in explaining developmental trends in societies that are in rapid social transition as opposed to those that are fairly stable?

Numerous influential models have guided our understanding of adulthood over the past 60 years. In each model, trends in development emerge. In the final section of this chapter, we outline the major ideas of four of these theories. As you will see, often for simplicity's sake alone, adulthood is discussed in terms of stages. However, especially during adulthood, please keep in mind that there can be wide individual variations in how particular people move through their adult years. In addition, it is always important to consider the context that applies to the group upon which conclusions are based.

Havighurst's Developmental Tasks

One of the earliest perspectives on adult development was proposed by Robert Havighurst (1953). In a classic and very pragmatic description of development over the lifespan, Havighurst proposed that adulthood could be viewed as a series of periods in which certain developmental tasks must be accomplished (see Table 12-3). In a sense, these tasks provide the broad context in which development takes place: They are demands that shape our use of intelligence. In young adulthood, the tasks mostly involve starting a family and establishing a career. In middle adulthood, they center on maintaining what was established earlier and on adjusting to physical changes, as well as to changes in the family. In the later years, still other adjustments must be made as aging occurs.

Table 12-3 Havighurst's Developmental Tasks

TASKS OF EARLY ADULTHOOD
• Selecting a mate • Learning to live with a marriage partner • Starting a family • Rearing children • Managing a home • Getting started in an occupation • Taking on civic responsibility • Finding a congenial social group
TASKS OF MIDDLE ADULTHOOD
• Achieving adult civic and social responsibility • Establishing and maintaining an economic standard of living • Developing adult leisure-time activities • Assisting teenage children to become responsible and happy adults • Relating to one's spouse as a person • Accepting and adjusting to the physiological changes of middle age • Adjusting to aging parents
TASKS OF OLDER ADULTHOOD
• Adjusting to decreasing physical strength and health • Adjusting to retirement and reduced income • Adjusting to death of spouse • Establishing an explicit affiliation with one's age group • Meeting social and civic obligations • Establishing satisfactory physical living arrangements

SOURCE: From *Development tasks and education* (3rd ed.), by R. J. Havighurst, copyright © 1972 by Pearson Education. Reprinted by permission of Allyn and Bacon, Boston, MA.

There are, of course, much broader definitions that apply to adults and their lifestyles now in the 21st century than were available to most people represented by Havighurst's study. However, most of these same tasks still must be addressed by many adults living in the United States, especially by those in the middle-class majority. Thus, Havighurst's three-stage model of adulthood serves as a useful starting point, and it typically is reflected in more contemporary approaches that describe the development of adults.

Erikson's Theory of Development

Erik Erikson argued that adult development, like that in earlier stages of the lifespan, is characterized by a series of conflicts, or crises, in which the individual confronts the major developmental task associated with that period of the lifespan, and resolves it, for better or worse (see Chapter 1). Erikson viewed adulthood as comprised of three such periods, each involving a crisis through which individuals redefine themselves, their priorities, and their place in the world (Hoare, 2002).

According to Erikson, the crisis of **intimacy versus isolation** is the developmental task that is most characteristic of young adulthood. Intimacy involves establishing a mutually satisfying, close relationship with another person. It represents the union of two identities without the loss of each individual's unique qualities. By contrast, isolation involves the inability or failure to achieve mutuality, sometimes because the individual's identity is too weak to risk a close union with another person (Erikson, 1968, 1983; Erikson & Erikson, 1997).

In Erikson's view, resolution in each stage of development rests on the stages that precede it. The stage of intimacy is especially dependent on how individuals grapple with the primary developmental task of adolescence—the construction of a clear sense of personal identity (see Chapters 10 and 11). Recent research on emerging adulthood suggests that establishing a clear sense of personal identity may extend well past adolescence, into the 20s and early 30s, and identity concerns may reemerge on multiple occasions throughout adulthood (Born, 2007; Sneed, Whitbourne, & Culang, 2006). Thus, many young adults are focused on both identity and intimacy concerns, although one or the other of these is often at the forefront of development at any given point in time. Although Erikson's view represents a stage approach, it is also heavily contextualized because it acknowledges the specific and unique experiences each individual faces in his or her own life.

In what ways does U.S. culture encourage the development of intimacy during young adulthood? Are there ways in which U.S. culture frustrates this developmental priority?

Levinson's Seasons of a Man's Life

Daniel Levinson (1978, 1986) conducted an intensive study of male adult development in the United States through which he identified three major *eras* in the adult male life cycle, each extending for roughly 15 to 20 years—early adulthood, middle adulthood, and late adulthood. Levinson believed that during each era, the person confronts a series of developmental tasks, such as finding a mate or selecting a career. By taking on and resolving the tasks of life, the person is able to develop a **life structure**, which is the overall pattern that underlies and unifies a person's life. According to Levinson, as the tasks in each era near completion, the person typically is moved to question his existing life structure. This questioning culminates in a transition, which bridges from one era to the next, and results in a reformulated life structure that is more consistent with the person's current needs and life circumstances. According to Levinson, major male life transitions occur at about ages 17 to 25, as the man enters early adulthood; at about ages 40 to 45, as he enters middle adulthood; and at about age 60 or so, as he enters older adulthood.

In early adulthood, which Levinson defined as corresponding to ages 17 to 45, young men must resolve adolescent conflicts, create a place for themselves in adult society, and commit themselves to stable and predictable patterns of behavior and life. For most men, relationships at work and within the family are

intimacy versus isolation
For Erikson, a crisis in young adulthood characterized by the conflict between establishing a mutually satisfying relationship with another person as opposed to failing to find such an intimate relationship

life structure
The overall pattern that underlies and unifies a person's life

Table 12-4 Levinson's Developmental Tasks for Entry into Adulthood

DEFINING A DREAM
Establishing an ideal goal for what one hopes to accomplish in adulthood
FINDING A MENTOR
Finding a trusted person who is approving of one's dream, supportive, and helpful in giving advice without being authoritative
DEVELOPING A CAREER
Using the dream and mentor to identify and enter a career that will be fulfilling
ESTABLISHING INTIMACY
Discovering one's own strengths and vulnerabilities and finding a special person with whom one can be emotionally intimate

SOURCE: From *The seasons of a man's life*, by D. J. Levinson, 1978, New York: Knopf; and *The seasons of a woman's life*, by D. J. Levinson, 1996, New York: Ballantine.

central. In order to make a successful transition into adulthood, according to Levinson, a young man must master four developmental tasks: (1) defining a "dream" of what adult accomplishment will consist of, (2) finding a mentor, (3) developing a career, and (4) establishing intimacy (see Table 12-4). Levinson specified comparable tasks for each stage throughout adulthood, and these are briefly described in Chapters 14 and 17.

Seasons of a Woman's Life As you might imagine, Levinson's research stimulated numerous criticisms, of which the most persistent was that he had not included women in his study. That criticism was addressed in subsequent research (Levinson, 1990, 1996), which demonstrated that women experience adult development in much the same way as men. For example, Levinson believed that women, like men, experience a critical transition at about age 40, a time of stress as career objectives and lifestyle choices are reexamined. Women also must address the same developmental tasks: Entry into adulthood involves defining a dream, finding a mentor, choosing an occupation, and establishing a relationship with a special person.

▲ Young adults who are successful tend to be practical, organized individuals with an integrated personality.

Table 12-5 Comparison of Men's and Women's Entry into Careers, According to Levinson

DEFINING A DREAM
Men: A unified vision of their future Women: "Split" dreams that involve a sense of having to trade off a career against having to raise a family
FINDING A MENTOR
Men: Learning from a more experienced yet supportive role model Women: Less likely to find a mentor due to fewer women mentors being available; male mentors can involve sexual attraction or confusion over appropriate roles
DEVELOPING A CAREER
Men: Most are fully immersed in their career by age 40 Women: Many delayed by conflicting family or personal goals; career immersion often does not occur until middle age

SOURCE: From *The seasons of a man's life*, by D. J. Levinson, 1978, New York: Knopf; and *The seasons of a woman's Life*, by D. J. Levinson, 1996, New York: Ballantine.

How women experience these tasks, however, appears to be quite different from how men move through this segment of the lifespan (see Table 12-5). For example, Levinson's research suggests that for women, the early phase of adulthood is much more likely to include role conflict because women value *both* establishing a career and assuming primary responsibility for child care and family life. Furthermore, at the time of Levinson's original work—the 1980s—fewer accomplished female mentors were available in the workforce, and expectations of how women should balance family versus career responsibilities were not well defined. Although Levinson claimed that both men's and women's transitions are closely linked to age, other researchers have found that, perhaps not surprisingly, the stage of the family life cycle seems to be a better indicator of when transitions for women occur (Harris, Ellicott, & Hommes, 1986). Women's transitions (and crises) may be linked less to their own age than to the pacing of major family events like the birth or the departure of children.

The Limitations of Normative Models

Levinson's models have been heavily criticized on a variety of grounds, perhaps most substantially because they were based on in-depth interviews with a small number of people (40 men and 45 women), all of whom lived very similar, middle-class lives. When groups of individuals who embrace different lifestyles are considered, normative models such as Levison's are less useful as descriptions of developmental transitions and stages (e.g., Wheeler-Scruggs, 2008). Nevertheless, Levinson's life-stage model is a good example of how *normative* models—those that link development to life events that most people experience—reflect the lifestyle trends of a particular group in a particular place or time (Bentley, 2007).

One of the strengths of normative models is that they recognize the important impact social roles play in adult development.

Watch *Workforce* on MyDevelopmentLab

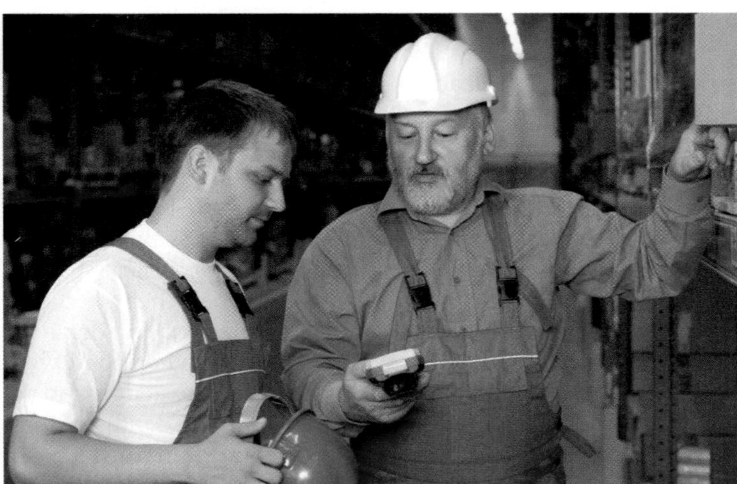

▲ The availability of a helpful mentor can make a major difference in the success of a novice. This senior engineer is assisting his trainee in learning to use a specialized instrument.

◄ Normative models provide good explanations for typical development during stable periods. However, the dramatic increase in dual-career families—where both mother and father work—has created a greater variety of acceptable roles for both men and women.

However, when societal changes occur, such models must adapt to the new roles that emerge. Particularly during times of social transition, in which role expectations are in flux, normative models have difficulty keeping pace (refer to the box Changing Perspectives: History, Culture, and the Information Age). At such times, not only are the general expectations for appropriate behavior less well defined, but also individuals often elect quite different paths—some conforming to traditional roles, others to newly emerging opportunities.

In the United States, the decades of the 1970s and 1980s were particularly transitional, as the women's movement, among others, propelled sweeping changes in social expectations, especially for women. It is therefore not surprising that Levinson's studies identified more role confusion for women than men. In the late 1950s and 1960s, for example, most women had little role confusion. The majority had a clear dream: to be a full-time homemaker (Helson & Picano, 1990). That dream became outdated as social changes brought women into the workforce at all levels. The roles open to young adult women today are wide, and most women elect those that combine both career and family. Roles for young adult men also are changing in response to their partners' career responsibilities and their increased involvement in family obligations. Perhaps the important point is that social expectations must be considered in any perspective on adult development, but individual responses to those broad societal trends must also be acknowledged.

Do you think that the tendency for women to link developmental transitions more to their family's life cycle than to their own age is becoming stronger, weaker, or remaining static in U.S. culture and subculture?

Watch *Gender Roles in the Family: Florence Denmark* on **MyDevelopmentLab**

Gould's Transformations in Early Adulthood

Part of the reason Levinson's model of adult development reflected so clearly the social changes of the late 20th century is that he emphasized the role of careers. Especially for women, changes in the workforce represented the most obvious point of social transition in that period of time, which Levinson's model was able to capture. However, Levinson's model did not focus on intellectual development.

A model of adult development that adopts a more cognitive focus is one proposed by Roger Gould (1978). Gould was interested in how an individual's assumptions, ideas, myths, and world views shifted during different periods of adulthood. Gould's examination of the life histories of a large group of U.S. women and men from ages 16 to 60 formed the basis of his view that people look at the world differently in different stages of adulthood. To describe how an individual's system of cognitive understanding shapes his or her behavior and life decisions, Gould argued that adults must challenge and resolve certain basic assumptions that characterize thinking earlier in life.

According to Gould's view of early adulthood, from the ages of 16 to 22, the major false assumption to be challenged is: "I'll always belong to my parents and believe in their world." To penetrate and discard this illusion, young adults must start building an adult identity that their parents cannot control or dominate. Young people's sense of self, however, is still fragile at this point, and self-doubt makes them highly sensitive to criticism. Yet, young adults also begin to see their parents as imperfect and fallible people rather than the all-powerful, controlling forces they once were. This helps them understand that their own perspectives have value, and this allows them to move forward in forging their own adult self-concept.

Between the ages of 22 and 28, young adults often make another false assumption that reflects their continuing doubts about self-sufficiency: "Doing things my parents' way, with willpower and perseverance, will bring results. But if I become too frustrated, confused, or tired, or am simply unable to cope, they will step in and show me the right way." To combat this notion, young adults must accept full responsibility for their own life, surrendering the expectation of continuous parental assistance. This involves far more than removing oneself from a mother's or a father's domination; it requires the active, positive construction of an adult life. Conquering the world on one's own also diverts energy from constant introspection and self-centeredness. Gould found that the predominant thinking mode during this period progresses from flashes of insight to perseverance, discipline, controlled experimentation, and goal orientation.

From the ages of 28 to 34, a significant shift toward adult attitudes occurs. The major false assumption during this period is: "Life is simple and controllable. There are no significant coexisting contradictory forces within me." This impression differs from those of previous stages in two important respects: It indicates a sense of competence and an acknowledgment of limitations. Enough adult understanding has been achieved to admit inner turmoil without calling strength or integrity into doubt. Talents, strengths, and desires that were suppressed during the 20s because they did not fit into the unfolding blueprint of adulthood may resurface. Gould cited the examples of an ambitious young partner in a prestigious law firm who begins to consider public service, or a suave and carefree single person who comes to realize that having many intimate relationships is not satisfying. Even those who have fulfilled youthful ambitions typically still experience some doubt, confusion, and depression during this period, and they may begin to question the very values that helped them gain independence from their parents. Growth involves breaking out of the rigid expectations of the 20s and embracing a more reasonable attitude: "What I get is directly related to how much effort I'm willing to make." Individuals cease to believe in luck and begin to put their faith in disciplined, well-directed work. At the same time, they begin to cultivate the interests, values, and qualities that will endure and develop throughout adult life.

Based both on your own experience and on your observations of individuals in the stage of young adulthood, what aspects of Gould's description of this period seem especially accurate?

In Gould's view, the years between ages 35 and 45 bring full involvement in the adult world. At this stage of adulthood, parents no longer control these adults, and their children have not yet effectively challenged them. At the same time, however, adults at this stage experience time pressure and they fear that they will not accomplish all of their goals. The physical changes of middle adulthood also frighten and dismay them; reduced career mobility often makes them feel penned in. The drive for stability and security, which was paramount when they were in their 30s, is replaced by a need for immediate action and results: There can be no more procrastination. The deaths of their parents and their awareness of their own mortality bring them face to face with the frequent unfairness and pain of life; they let go of their childish need for safety. This, Gould proposed, represents a full and autonomous adult consciousness, thereby setting the stage for the rest of adult life (see Table 12-6).

A Closing Comment

In closing, it is important to remember that theories that emphasize periods or stages are valuable in understanding adult development but should not be interpreted too rigidly for several reasons (Bentley, 2007; Whitbourne & Whitbourne, 2011). First, the notion of stages tends to obscure the stable, consistent aspects of personality during adulthood, instead focusing on points of transition or crisis. Most people experience adulthood with a well-integrated, consistent sense of self that does not change substantially from one part of adulthood to another. Second, these theories pay little attention to the unpredictability of life events. Because stage theories are largely normative, they do not fully acknowledge the variety and uniqueness of individuals' roles and responsibilities. For example, if a divorce or death in the family occurs, that may drastically affect how an individual experiences the remainder of the lifespan. Third, stage theories tend to undervalue the role of multiple contexts: Instead, they often focus too narrowly on particular aspects of development, such as starting a career, separating from parents, or establishing a close

Table 12-6 Gould's Transformations in Early Adulthood

Period	False Assumption	Response
Ages 16 to 22	"I'll always belong to my parents and believe in their world."	Young adults must construct their own identity that parents cannot control.
Ages 22 to 28	"Doing things my parents' way will bring results; if I fail on my own, they will rescue me."	Young adults become less self-centered and more disciplined and accept full responsibility for their lives.
Ages 28 to 34	"Life is simple and controllable, and there are no major contradictions I must face."	Young adults begin to recognize repressed and unfulfilled needs because they have developed a sense of their own limitations, yet remain confident of their abilities.
Ages 35 to 45	Young adults cast off false assumptions and become fully involved in adult life.	Adults in this stage begin to feel the need for action and results and to develop a full, independent sense of themselves as competent adults.

SOURCE: From *Transformations, growth and change in adult life*, by R. L. Gould, 1978, New York: Simon & Schuster.

Watch *Young Adulthood: Work, Jessica* on **MyDevelopmentLab**

Table 12-7 Selected Theorists' Views of the Major Tasks of Early Adulthood

Theorist	Major Task of Early Adulthood
Schaie	Flexibly applying intellectual, cognitive abilities to accomplish personal and career goals
Havighurst	Starting a family and establishing a career
Erikson	Establishing a meaningful and deep personal relationship that involves intimacy while continuing to develop a secure personal identity
Levinson	Developing an early life structure, which includes establishing a career and an intimate relationship with a special partner
Gould	Casting off erroneous assumptions about dependency, developing competence, acknowledging personal limitations, and accepting responsibility for one's own life

and meaningful intimate relationship. Individuals must integrate the various features of their lives into a meaningful whole, and important developmental events are in constant interaction, influencing each other in dynamic fashion. Finally, stage theories often reflect the experiences of a particular cohort group within a particular culture or subculture at a particular point in history. Thus, they may be of limited applicability as general theories that describe human development. A comparison summary of the theories discussed in this chapter is presented in Table 12-7. We address the issues these theories raise more fully in the next chapter when we discuss the personality and sociocultural issues that arise in early adulthood.

REVIEW THE FACTS 12-5

1. A developmental theory that emphasizes events and experiences that many people have is referred to as a __________ model; one that focuses more on the unique experiences of the individual is called a __________ model.
2. Havighurst proposed that the two central tasks of young adulthood are __________ and __________.
3. For Erikson, the crisis of early adulthood is __________.
4. According to Levinson, when young adults accomplish the tasks of a particular era of their lives, they typically
   a. experience relief.
   b. become depressed or anxious.
   c. regress back to an earlier set of concerns.
   d. question their existing life structure.
5. Are normative models more useful or less useful during times of rapid cultural change?
6. In comparison to other theories, Gould's view of adulthood focuses more on
   a. emotional development.
   b. family structure.
   c. cognitive issues.
   d. historical events.
7. Suggest three limitations of normative theories.

Practice on **MyDevelopmentLab**

CHAPTER SUMMARY

Perspectives on Adult Development

How do normative and idiosyncratic events shape human developmental trajectories?

- Compared to earlier developmental periods, changes in adulthood are less predictable and individuals vary more in the paths their lives take. Major markers in adulthood are more closely tied to personal, social, and cultural forces.
- Many key events in adulthood are *normative events;* that is, they occur at relatively predictable times for most people in an age cohort. *Idiosyncratic events* are events that are not anticipated and these typically cause considerable stress and readjustment.

Are adults who were born in the same year always of the same age?

- An *age clock* represents our internal sense of time for when major life events should occur. Age clocks are often influenced by cultural factors and are more flexible now than in the past because more people pursue many activities at nontraditional ages.
- Age is a complex concept that represents *biological age* (how old one is from a physiological perspective), *social age* (how one's status compares with current cultural norms), and *psychological age* (how well one can adapt to social and environmental demands).
- *Contextual paradigms* examine the effect of multiple factors interacting together that influence development and are especially important for understanding adult development.

General Physical Development

In recent decades, have young adults in the United States become more, or less, physically fit?

- Most people enjoy peak vitality, strength, and good health during young adulthood. Most biological systems begin to decline slightly during the 30s and 40s and more rapidly thereafter.
- Some individuals begin or continue habits that likely will produce health problems later in life, such as overeating; overuse of alcohol, tobacco, or other drugs; and lack of exercise.
- Peak performance in many physical abilities occurs in the decade of the 20s, although improved diets and exercise training are contributing to higher performance levels for athletes of all ages today than in previous generations.
- The leading cause of death in early adulthood is accidents, and men are three times more likely to die from accidents than are women. Other diseases also occur, and many conditions that will be problematic later in life (e.g., heart disease, respiratory disease) begin at this time, although their symptoms are often masked. Physical disabilities often are difficult for young adults to cope with.

Sex and Sexuality

What challenges do young adults typically face with respect to their sexual health?

- Early adulthood is often the time during which people are most sexually active, and many plan to have children during this period. Most men remain fertile from puberty on. Women, however, are only fertile until menopause, which occurs at about age 50. After age 38, women's fertility typically declines.
- If fertility is a problem, various alternatives now exist, including hormone therapy and *in vitro* fertilization.
- Sexually transmitted diseases (STDs) affect millions of young adults. The most common bacterial infections are chlamydia, gonorrhea, and syphilis. The herpes virus is also common.
- AIDS is caused by infection by the HIV virus. Although in the United States, HIV/AIDS was at first associated with the gay community, it is not a gay disease. Rather, HIV/AIDS is spread by contact with the body fluids of an infected person. In fact, today about half of those with AIDS are women. The overall incidence of HIV/AIDS in the United States has declined since the 1990s and now is relatively stable, affecting about 0.1% of the U.S. population. AIDS may be at least partly responsible for a shift to more cautious sexual behavior.

How have attitudes about sexuality and sexual behavior changed in the United States from the 1970s to the present?

- In the 1950s, sexual behavior was quite private and conservative. In the 1970s, both sexual attitudes and behaviors became more open and liberal, although more conservative practices emerged again in the 1990s, in part to response to the AIDS epidemic.
- Today, young adults are more likely to use condoms, and they report engaging in a wide variety of sexual practices in addition to vaginal intercourse, including oral and anal sex and masturbation.

How does sexual orientation affect how a person experiences young adulthood?

- *Sexual orientation* defines which sex a person is attracted to, as well as which sexual partners a person might wish to become involved with emotionally. Individuals with a homosexual orientation—that is, who are gay, lesbian, or bisexual—often have difficulty with identity formation because of social prejudice and discrimination. A *lesbian* is a female with a sexual orientation toward other women; a *gay* male has a sexual orientation toward other men. A *bisexual* is a person who is attracted both to males and females. Homosexuality results from complex causes that probably include both biological and social factors.
- Individuals with same-sex orientations experience development in much the same way as those with opposite-sex preferences. Sexual orientation is not "either–or" but rather exists on a continuum. Nevertheless, those who have any homosexual orientation often experience prejudice, which contributes to group differences in risk factors as well as life choices.
- *Homophobia* is prejudice, aversion, fear, or other negative attitudes directed against those who have a same-sex orientation. Homophobia is particularly problematic when it is exhibited by helping professionals, such as physicians and psychologists. Today, attitudes about transgendered individuals—those whose sexual orientation is not strictly heterosexual—have become somewhat more open and accepting.

Cognitive Development in Adulthood

How do the thought processes used by young adults differ from those that guide adolescent cognition?

- Cognitive skills, especially those involving response speed and memory for facts, are typically at their peak in young adulthood.
- Piaget argued that cognitive development reaches its highest level—that of formal operations—beginning at about age 12. However, other researchers suggest that as people enter adulthood, their thinking becomes more complex, reflecting further development of the brain during this period. Adult thinking often involves *dialectical thought*, which includes being able to consider ambiguous situations and problems that require judgment and decision making.
- *Postformal thought,* which is thought that is heavily contextualized and includes both social and interpersonal aspects, is believed to develop during early adulthood. Postformal thought involves both the cognitive and the emotional aspects of problem solving. In adulthood, thought becomes more complex and is more often based on reality.
- Many theories of intelligence recognize the importance of the social and emotional aspects of intelligence. *Emotional intelligence (EQ)* is the term given to those aspects of the intellect that relate to the way people manage their own and others' emotions and emotional responses. Although psychologists debate whether the concept of EQ contributes significantly to our overall understanding of cognition, individuals who possess high EQ are sometimes found to perform better and to better weather stress.
- Warner Schaie proposed that the distinctive feature of adult thinking is cognitive flexibility—the ability to use intelligence in different ways during different periods throughout the lifespan.

Frameworks for Understanding Adult Development

How do stage models of development differ from context models?

- Stage-based models of human development emphasize the common life events and adjustments that most individuals experience. In stage-based perspectives, specific, idiosyncratic events play a relatively minor role.
- Context-based models focus more attention on the specific experiences that shape each unique individual's life and

also emphasize the multiple points of view that contribute to an understanding of development.

- Both stage and context models are useful in explaining adult development.

What are the primary developmental tasks most young adults growing up in the United States confront?

- Havighurst proposed that adulthood could be divided into three periods in which specific developmental tasks must be accomplished. Young adulthood typically involves starting a family and establishing a career.
- Erikson also viewed adulthood as being comprised of three periods, each involving a crisis. Young adulthood centers on *intimacy versus isolation,* where the person seeks to establish a satisfying, close relationship with another person. However, young adults also may continue to work on establishing their identity—the developmental task associated with adolescence.
- Primarily through detailed interviews with men, Levinson identified three major eras in the male life cycle, each associated with different tasks. As the tasks in one stage are accomplished, men begin to question their existing *life structure,* the overall pattern that underlies and unifies a person's life. This questioning leads to a transition to the next era of life. The transition to adulthood involves defining a dream, finding a mentor, developing a career, and establishing intimacy. Women experience similar issues, but they are more likely than men to experience role conflict, and their transitions are linked more to life events than to age.
- Normative models—those organized around major life events—often reflect the experiences of culture and gender. Normative models are less useful in times of rapid cultural change or when individuals have many different roles available.

How do an individual's cognitions and worldviews change during the period of young adulthood?

- Gould's model focused more on cognitive views than social changes, finding that adults of different ages tend to look at the world somewhat differently. At first, young adults believe their parents define their roles; therefore, they focus on developing their own sense of personal identity. Then they come to accept responsibility for their choices. Finally they develop a sense of personal competence and acceptance of their limitations.
- Theories that describe adult development should not be interpreted too rigidly because they often place undue emphasis on life crises, they tend to ignore the uniqueness of individuals' lives, they undervalue the interactive nature of multiple contexts, and they often reflect the values and experiences of a particular cohort group.

KEY TERMS

normative events (p. 333)
idiosyncratic events (p. 333)
age clock (p. 334)
biological age (p. 335)
social age (p. 335)
psychological age (p. 335)
contextual paradigms (p. 335)
sexual orientation (p. 345)
lesbian (p. 345)
gay (p. 345)
bisexual (p. 345)
homophobia (p. 346)
dialectical thought (p. 348)
postformal thought (p. 349)
emotional intelligence (EQ) (p. 350)
intimacy versus isolation (p. 353)
life structure (p. 353)

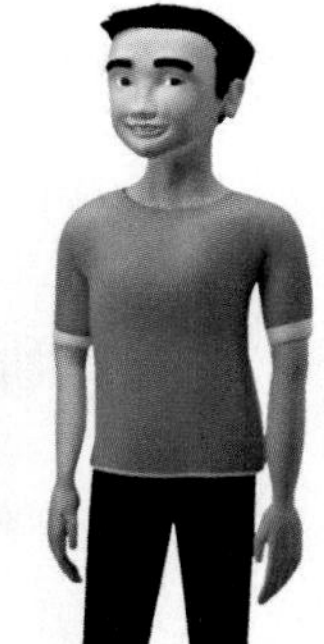

MyVirtualLife

What decisions would you make while living your life? What would be the consequences of those decisions?

Find out by accessing **MyVirtualLife** at www.MyDevelopmentLab.com to raise a virtual child and live your own virtual life.

13 YOUNG ADULTHOOD
Personality and Sociocultural Development

LEARNING OBJECTIVES

- How is the *self* generally defined by young adults?
- How does friendship in young adulthood differ from love?
- What is love, and why is it especially important to young adults?
- How does choosing a romantic partner differ for young adults living in United States versus other cultures around the world?
- How are marriage trends changing in the United States and in other parts of the world?
- What are the main features of the transitions that occur when a person becomes a parent?
- Why is single parenting becoming more common in the United States, and what special challenges are often associated with this form of parenting?
- How do people decide which career or job will be the best choice for them?
- How has work in the United States been changing for women over the past several decades?
- How have family members' roles changed as women have entered the workforce in increasing numbers?

CHAPTER OUTLINE

Self, Family, and Work
- The Personal Self
- Self as Family Member
- Self as Worker

Forming Close Relationships
- Adult Friendships
- Couple Formation and Development
- Marriage
- Cohabitation
- Gay and Lesbian Couples
- Staying Single

The Family Life Cycle and Adult Development
- The Family Life Cycle
- The Transition to Parenthood
- Coping with Children's Developmental Stages
- Single Parenthood

The Occupational Cycle
- Stages of Occupational Life
- Gaining a Place in the Workforce
- Careers and Career Choices
- Occupational Choice and Preparation

Work and Gender
- Changes in Women's Work Patterns
- The Many Meanings of Work
- The Role of Women in Careers
- The Dynamics of Dual-Earner Couples

In the preceding chapter, we discussed several views of adult development. A common theme among these various perspectives is that early adulthood is a time for establishing meaningful personal relationships that involve intimacy, for finding a direction for one's work and professional growth, and for becoming more aware of and comfortable with one's sense of personal identity. For many individuals in developed nations, these goals begin to be addressed during a period psychologists call *emerging adulthood*—a transition time between adolescence and the full assumption of adult roles and responsibilities. However, it is during *young adulthood*, which typically extends to about age 40 or 45, that these developmental tasks are addressed in full.

Clearly, a successful journey into and throughout adulthood is, for most people, closely tied to a person's involvement with a career and with a romantic partner and a family. Our ability to find meaningful work and to establish satisfying intimate relationships socializes us to new roles, usually involving increased personal and financial independence. Although the role changes of young adulthood typically are subtler and less systematic than those of childhood and adolescence, they nevertheless constitute transitions and turning points in our lives (Arnett, 2010a), and we are changed by them.

Increasingly, young adults in the United States are taking longer to make the commitments that typically define the challenges of this period. As noted in previous chapters, more and more young people are postponing marriage and taking longer to enter a career. Some experience a kind of panic as they worry about how to settle into an adult lifestyle. For most, early adulthood is a period of adaptation. Compared to adolescents, young adults see things differently; they behave differently; and they adjust their beliefs, attitudes, and values in accord with the roles and contexts they experience.

Work roles and family relationships define the parameters for much of adult development, especially in early adulthood when basic life patterns are established. Furthermore, both work and family relationships influence how we structure and restructure our sense of identity; as such, work and family relationships form the context in which personal identity—our sense of self—unfolds.

◄ In young adulthood, work and family roles tend to structure much of one's time and sense of identity. This father is attending his daughter's high school baseball game and enjoying time with his younger son.

SELF, FAMILY, AND WORK

Adult development can be described in the context of three separate but interacting systems that focus on various aspects of the *self*. These involve the development of the self as an individual, the self as a family member (adult child, member of a couple, or parent), and the self as a worker (see Figure 13-1). Interactions abound. For example, research has shown that the more positive a father's work experience, the higher is his self-esteem and the more likely he is to have an accepting, warm, and positive parenting style (Grimm-Thomas & Perry-Jenkins, 1994; Lamb, 2010b, 2012). Before we address the main topics of this chapter—family and work—and their impact on personality and sociocultural development, we first discuss some basic features of the self.

The Personal Self

There are many conceptualizations of self, as we have seen in previous chapters describing childhood and adolescence. Often, such views adopt a humanistic approach, emphasizing

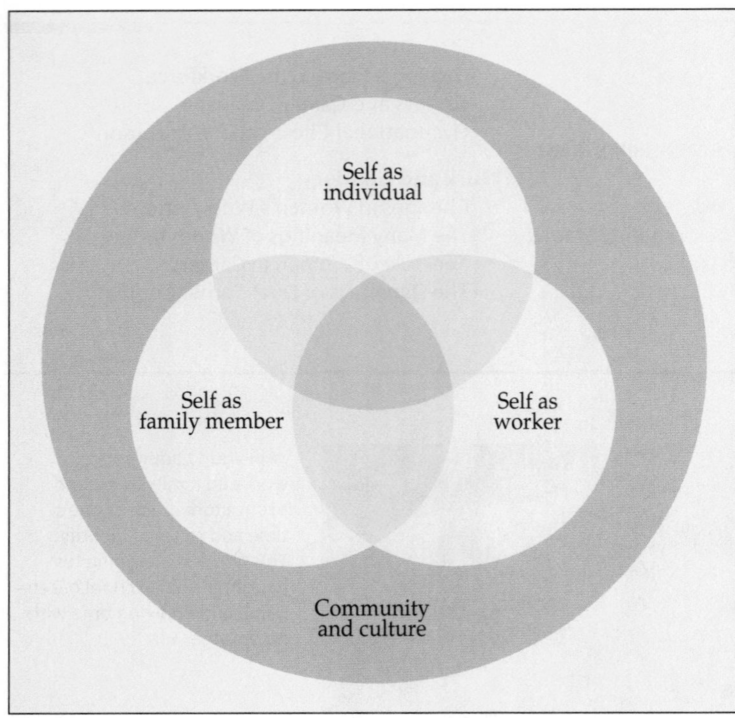

FIGURE 13-1 Domains of Self
The three domains of adult development involve dynamic interactions among the self as an individual, a family member, and a worker. These interactions take place in the broad context of community and culture.

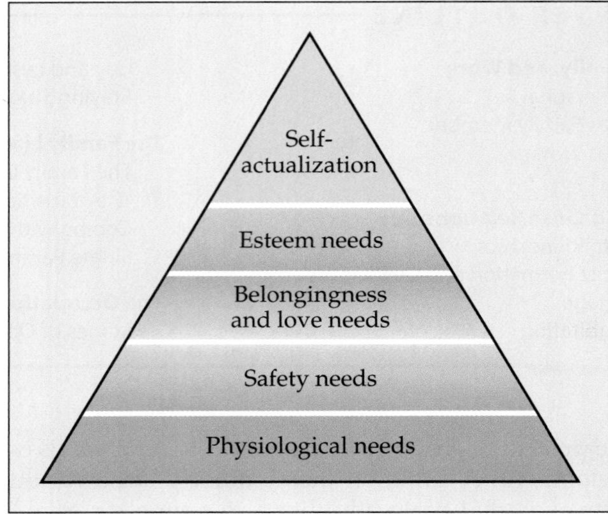

FIGURE 13-2 Maslow's Hierarchy of Needs
Although higher needs are no less important than lower needs, individuals must satisfy lower needs, such as those for survival and safety, before meeting higher needs, such as belongingness and esteem. Throughout life, adults must work out their needs for self-actualization in order to develop their fullest potential.

SOURCE: From *Motivation and personality* (3rd ed.), by A. H. Maslow, 1987, R. D. Frager and J. Fadiman (Eds.), copyright © 1987. Adapted by permission of Pearson Education, Inc., Upper Saddle River, NJ.

that individuals are innately motivated toward self-fulfillment and that they strive to make positive choices about their lives.

Abraham Maslow's Hierarchy of Needs A classic view of self-development was proposed by Abraham Maslow (1908–1970), who emphasized the *needs* that individuals must meet as they strive to reach their unique potential and sense of self. For Maslow, the ultimate goal of self-development was **self-actualization**, which involves realizing one's full development by optimally utilizing one's talents and abilities (Maslow, 1954, 1979).

For most people, however, life's responsibilities require a focus on more basic needs, such as those for food and safety, at least most of the time. To recognize the priority of the various needs we experience, Maslow proposed a *hierarchy of needs,* with self-actualization at the top (see Figure 13-2). According to Maslow, when our basic physiological and safety needs are satisfied, we can direct our energy toward attaining higher-level needs: to love, to feel loved, and to belong to our family and community; to earn the respect and esteem of others, as well as ourselves; and, ultimately, to become self-actualized. According to Maslow, our identity is upwardly focused. We seek self-fulfillment, even if it can only be achieved from time to time and in somewhat narrow contexts. Progress toward this goal often begins in young adulthood.

Carl Rogers's Unconditional Positive Regard Like Maslow, Carl Rogers (1902–1987) also believed that individuals are motivated toward self-actualization and self-fulfillment and that the core of human nature consists of healthy and constructive impulses (Rogers, 1980). However, as we develop, various significant others, beginning with our parents, often impose **conditions of worth** with their implicit messages: "Do this, don't do that, or you will be a worthless human being." An individual who internalizes these conditions develops low self-esteem, a sense of failure, and recurrent anxiety and despair because conditions of worth are often impossible to fulfill.

Why do you think Maslow's theory and Rogers's theory are usually identified as humanistic perspectives?

To develop a healthier self-concept and a more realistic sense of what we can attain in life, Rogers proposed that we should view ourselves and others with **unconditional positive regard,**

self-actualization
Realizing one's full potential through the development of one's talents and abilities

conditions of worth
Conditions others impose upon us if we are to be worthwhile as human beings; these often involve the withdrawal of affection and approval unless behavior conforms to another's expectations

unconditional positive regard
Rogers's proposition that we should warmly accept another person as a worthwhile human being without reservations or conditions of worth

Table 13-1 Aspects of Achieving Independence in Young Adulthood

HOW DO THESE DEFINITIONS OF INDEPENDENCE DESCRIBE THE TRANSITION INTO YOUNG ADULTHOOD IN YOUR OWN LIFE?

Type of Independence	Description
Emotional	The young adult becomes less dependent on parents for social and psychological support
Attitudinal	The young adult develops attitudes, values, and beliefs that are independent from, and may be different from, those held by parents
Functional	The young adult becomes financially independent and can take care of day-to-day problems
Conflictual	The young adult's separation from parents is accomplished without feelings of guilt or betrayal

SOURCE: Adapted from "The dynamics between dependency and autonomy: Illustrations across the life span," by M. M. Baltes and S. B. Silverberg, 1999, in D. L. Featherman, R. M. Lerner, and M. Perlmutter (Eds.), *Life-span development and behavior: Vol. 1* (pp. 41–90), Hillsdale, NJ: Erlbaum; and "Varieties of empathy-based guilt," by M. L. Hoffman, 2007, in J. Bybee (Ed.), *Guilt and children* (pp. 91–112), San Diego: Academic Press.

by which he meant being warmly accepting without imposing reservations or conditions. As a parent, love your child unconditionally, regardless of his or her behavior. When the child misbehaves, correct the behavior if necessary, but never attack the child's sense of being loved and having worth as a person. As a spouse, express your concerns in the context of a secure and supportive relationship.

Modern Perspectives on the Self The concept of self-actualization has been of interest to many theorists and researchers working within the field of psychology. For example, Mihály Csíkszentmihályi has proposed that a similar concept, which he calls "flow," serves to motivate us to accomplish our very best (Csíkszentmihályi, 2009; Nakamura & Csíkszentmihályi, 2009). According to Csíkszentmihályi (pronounced "chicks-send-me-high"), flow is a mental state during which the person is completely absorbed and involved with a particular activity. It is experienced as a state of deep enjoyment, concentration, and focus "in the moment." As such, flow provides a sort of optimal experience, much like the concept of self-actualization that was described by Maslow and Rogers. Like self-actualization, states of flow are rare; and flow usually involves the feeling of being challenged. For example, many people enjoy watching television, but this activity normally does not involve a state of flow. Rather, flow is experienced when we are fully concentrating on a task—perhaps writing a perfect paper, or perfecting a physical skill such as calligraphy. Given the reemergence of interest in positive psychology, with its focus on health and personal satisfaction, the concept of flow has re-enlivened research and interest in the concepts that Maslow and Rogers first described (Engeser & Schiepe-Tiska, 2012).

In addition to their focus on the positive aspects of human experience, modern perspectives also often emphasize *identity*, which includes both the individual's personal traits and abilities and the roles the person assumes—worker, parent, spouse, citizen. Furthermore, identity is considered fluid, meaning that it changes throughout life and in response to the dynamic interaction of one's role and one's developing personality (Bensen & Elder, 2011; Coté, 2009).

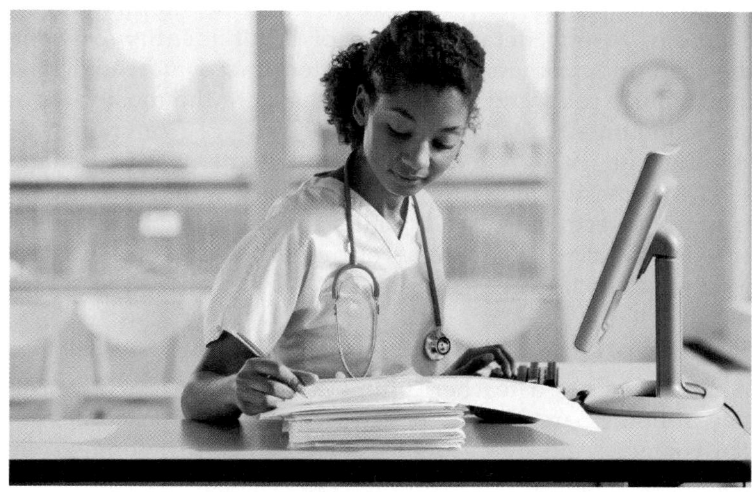

▲ A job that is interesting, challenging, and provides opportunity for professional growth tends to be more rewarding. This nurse works with patients, complex technologies, and other medical professionals, resulting in a complex career setting that allows her to express creativity and achieve a high level of performance.

Self as Family Member

Identity formation, of course, begins in childhood and is the major task of adolescence (see Chapter 11). It continues into adulthood, however, where it often centers on establishing independence from one's parents and taking on adult responsibilities that involve work and personal relationships.

A useful way to conceptualize this transition in identity formation from adolescence to adulthood is to consider how various aspects of independence emerge and how they are defined. Becoming independent, of course, is a complex process, involving separating from one's parents emotionally, attitudinally, functionally, and conflictually (see Table 13-1). Gaining independence from parents in early adulthood is linked to parental attachment: When adolescents and emerging adults have secure supportive relationships with parents, independence is typically easier to achieve (Koepke & Denissen, 2012; Lapsley & Edgerton, 2002). Furthermore, young people typically make progress in all areas of independence—emotional, attitudinal, functional, and conflictual—although not necessarily in any particular order. For example, studies of college students indicate substantial progress in each form of independence over the college years, although functional dependence often remains even in the senior year because many students still rely on their parents financially (Kroger, Martinussen, & Marcia, 2010). Achieving independence also involves cultural dimensions. For example, Asian Americans and adolescents in immigrant families place more importance on family interdependence, making independence more difficult to achieve (Tseng, 2004). Regardless of culture, however, achieving independence as one moves into adulthood is a gradual but important part of development in early adulthood.

The establishment of new family relationships also forms an extremely important context for adult development. For example, in one detailed study of adult identity, 90% of the men and women who were interviewed indicated that their family roles and responsibilities were the most important components in defining who they were (Vanmanen & Whitbourne, 1997). Very few men and women defined themselves primarily in terms of their career rather than their family. Nevertheless, career paths are important; our choice of work contributes greatly to our identity—who we are and who we are not.

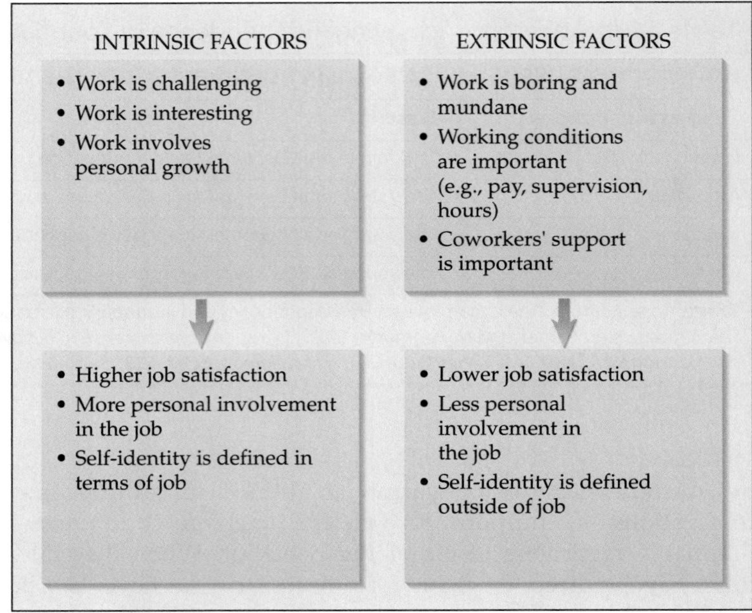

FIGURE 13-3 Intrinsic Versus Extrinsic Motivations Toward Work
People who work in jobs that are characterized by intrinsic factors are more likely to define their personal identity and satisfaction in terms of their job. People who work in jobs that involve primarily extrinsic factors are more likely to find life satisfaction outside of their work.

Self as Worker

Whether we are a teacher, plumber, corporate executive, or stay-at-home parent, our work defines our daily schedule, social contacts, and opportunities for personal development in important ways. In addition, our jobs often define our status, income, and prestige, as well as provide us with money to feed, clothe, and shelter ourselves and our families. Some jobs may also encourage personal growth and provide opportunities for creativity, self-development, and enhanced self-esteem. In short, our work provides an important context in which self and identity develop.

When jobs involve repetitive, mundane, and boring work, people usually focus on the **extrinsic factors** of their job. These include salary, status, the comfort or convenience of the work environment and hours of work, the adequacy of supervision and other employer practices, the attitudes and support of coworkers, and the opportunities for advancement. When jobs provide a chance to be creative or productive, or when they offer welcome challenges and provide an opportunity to gain self-esteem or respect, people more often focus on the **intrinsic factors** of their job. They describe their work in terms of its interest, and they focus on their own competence and achievements, obtaining satisfaction from doing the work in and of itself (see Figure 13-3).

Not surprisingly, how workers experience their jobs depends in large part on the job itself. Many jobs in our society offer little challenge and opportunity for personal growth, and the people who perform them focus on their extrinsic factors and financial survival. For people working in jobs such as these, their friendships with coworkers often form an important dimension of their work.

The fortunate workers whose jobs emphasize intrinsic factors typically report more job satisfaction and higher motivation and personal involvement in their jobs: When a worker is intrinsically motivated, there is more job involvement, better job performance, and stronger identity as a competent worker (Riggio, 2013). This in turn increases intrinsic work motivation, thereby perpetuating a work cycle characterized by high performance, as well as by positive self-concept as it relates to work. Understandably, workers in intrinsically motivated jobs are more likely to define their identity largely in terms of their work or career.

However, even for those people who enjoy their jobs, work is but one factor that contributes to identity formation in early adulthood. Also important is the person's need for family and friends. In the next section, we focus on the significance of close relationships in young adulthood.

extrinsic factors
In work, satisfaction in the form of salary, status, and other external rewards for work

intrinsic factors
In work, satisfaction workers obtain from doing the work in and of itself

REVIEW THE FACTS 13-1

1. What are the three primary developmental tasks of early adulthood?
2. If a person is constantly told that "If you do that, I won't love you anymore," the person making the threat is imposing what Rogers called ________.
3. According to Csíkszentmihályi, the concept of "flow" is most similar to that of
   a. love. b. respect.
   c. esteem. d. self-actualization.
4. Which of the following types of independence is often the last to develop among traditional college-aged students?
   a. functional b. emotional
   c. attitudinal d. conflictual
5. Approximately what percentage of adults note that their most important responsibilities involve family?
   a. 30% b. 60%
   c. 90% d. 100%
6. Focusing on how much a job pays emphasizes its ________ factors; focusing on how enjoyable it is emphasizes its ________ factors.

Practice on **MyDevelopmentLab**

FORMING CLOSE RELATIONSHIPS

As the self develops in early adulthood, most people focus their attention on two developmental tasks—work and family, with the latter of these being more important for most people. Finding a partner, building a close emotional bond, making a long-term commitment to another person—these are important tasks for most young adults. Whether involving friends or romantic partners, close relationships are critically important to healthy adult development, and many of these significant relationships are formed as people enter their adult years.

Adult Friendships

Friendships are a core aspect of adult life. Although friendship may be defined in various ways (Bukowski, Motzoi, & Meyer, 2009; Fehr, 1996), there are some things that friendships have in common. Close friends are trusted and relied on in times of difficulty, they are always ready to help, and they are enjoyable to spend time with. Friendships are usually characterized by positive emotional attachment, need fulfillment, and interdependence (Monsour, 2002). Close friends confide in each other, they help each other, and they try to support each other's well-being. Adult friendships that last over time have *reciprocity* and *mutuality*; that is, friendships are two-way, and friends care about each other (Regan, 2011; Samter, 2003). Although we discuss the topic of adult friendship more extensively in Chapters 15 and 17, friendships are important in young adulthood, as they are throughout life (Chow, Roesle, & Underwood, 2012). In many respects, they resemble romantic relationships, which also are of central importance, especially for young adults.

What characteristics of your best friends are most important to you?

Couple Formation and Development

The pairing of romantically attracted couples is an important aspect of the development of most young adults (Greif & Deal, 2012). Individuals often achieve part of their personal identity as a member of a relatively stable couple. For example, as you may recall, Erik Erikson proposed that establishing a meaningful intimate relationship was the primary developmental task in early adulthood (see Chapter 12). It is therefore important to understand how people choose their mates and why some decide to marry, some decide to cohabit, and others decide to remain single.

Studying such trends is challenging, especially during times in which cultural shifts are occurring. This is presently the case in the United States (Pew Social Trends, 2007, 2010; U.S. Conference of Catholic Bishops, 2006). Since the 1950s, there has been a dramatic and pervasive weakening of the norms requiring couples to marry, to remain married, to have children, to engage in intimate relations only within the marriage, and to maintain separate roles for males and females. Nevertheless, most people, including those with gay or lesbian sexual preferences, eventually choose a traditional family lifestyle—one that includes marriage, or a permanent marriage-like commitment, and parenthood. In addition, regardless of whether couples choose the formal acknowledgment that marriage implies, nearly all couples cite love as a central aspect of their relationships.

Sternberg's Triangular Theory of Love Love, owing at least in part to its elusive nature, has been one of the most difficult human constructs to define and study from a psychological perspective (Hsia & Schweinle, 2012). Robert Sternberg's (2006a) triangular theory of love is one approach that provides a developmental perspective on how love evolves. Sternberg suggested that love has three components—intimacy, passion, and decision/commitment—as illustrated in Figure 13-4. **Intimacy** is the feeling of closeness that occurs in love relationships. Intimacy is the sense of being connected or bonded to the people we love. We genuinely like them and are happiest when they are around. We count on them to be there when we need them, and we try to provide the same support in return. People who

Watch *Changes in Friendship with Age* on **MyDevelopmentLab**

intimacy
The feeling of closeness that occurs in love relationships

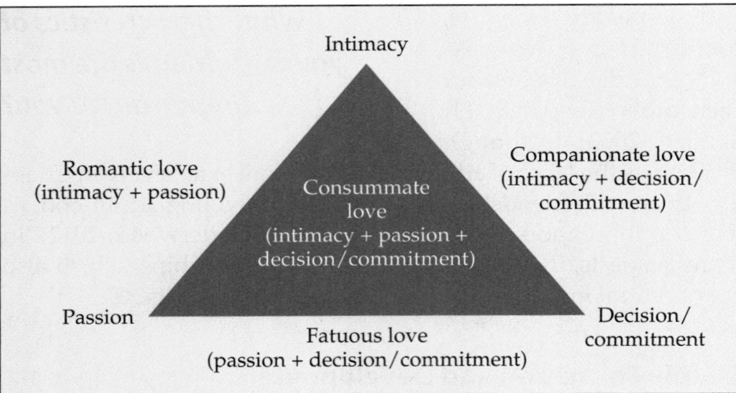

FIGURE 13-4 Sternberg's Triangular Theory of Love
Robert Sternberg has identified three components of love: intimacy, passion, and decision/commitment. These are incorporated in various ways to define different types of love-based relationships.

SOURCE: Adapted by Feldman, 1998, from "A triangular theory of love," by R. J. Sternberg, 1986, *Psychological Review, 93*, 119–135.

Table 13-2 Taxonomy of the Kinds of Love Based on Sternberg's Triangular Theory

	Component*		
Kind of Love	**Intimacy**	**Passion**	**Decision/Commitment**
Liking	yes	no	no
Infatuated love	no	yes	no
Empty love	no	no	no
Romantic love	yes	yes	no
Companionate love	yes	no	yes
Fatuous love	no	yes	yes
Consummate love	yes	yes	yes

**Yes* indicates the component is present; *no* indicates the component is absent. These kinds of love represent limiting cases based on the triangular theory. Most loving relationships fit between categories because the various components of love are expressed along continuums, not discretely.

SOURCE: Adapted from "A triangular theory of love," by R. J. Sternberg, 1986, *Psychological Review, 93*, 119–135; "Construct validation of a triangular love scale," by R. J. Sternberg, 1997, *European Journal of Social Psychology*, 27, 313–335; and "A duplex theory of love," by R. J. Sternberg, 2006, in R. J. Sternberg and K. Weiss (Eds.), *The new psychology of love* (pp. 184–199), New Haven, CT: Yale University Press.

are in love share activities, possessions, thoughts, and feelings. Indeed, sharing may be one of the most crucial factors in turning a dating relationship into a loving marriage or marriage-like relationship.

Passion is the second component of love. This refers to physical attraction, arousal, and sexual behavior in a relationship. Sometimes intimacy leads to passion; at other times passion precedes intimacy. In still other cases, there is passion without intimacy (as in a one-night affair) or intimacy without passion (as in a sibling relationship). The final component of Sternberg's love triangle is **decision/commitment**, which includes both the decision, or realization, of being in love and the commitment to maintain that love.

Love can be comprised of various combinations of intimacy, passion, and decision/commitment (see Table 13-2). Clearly, those of us who are interested in marriage hope for a relationship marked by consummate love, which includes intimacy, passion, and commitment. However, other forms of love are possible, as Sternberg's model makes clear, and not all close relationships are necessarily based on love. Some involve ritual dating—carrying on a relationship out of a sense of obligation or convenience. Others are centered on sexual needs, which can be manipulative or at least block the possibility that intimacy might develop. Others are lopsided, with one partner willing to become committed to an intimate relationship when the other partner is not.

Perhaps not surprisingly, the type of love that characterizes relationships changes across time (Furman & Winkles, 2012). For example, one group of researchers who conducted a large-sample Internet survey found that love dimensions shift in importance as people move through adulthood (Ahmetoglu, Swami, & Chamorro-Premuzic, 2010). Adolescents and younger adults were more likely to experience passion in their relationships, which gives way to intimacy and commitment later in adulthood. The length of the relationship also matters. Passionate love tended to diminish as relationships extended over longer periods of time. Intimacy and commitment, on the other hand, grew stronger over time, and also were more important to older, rather than younger, adults. Personality traits also seem to make a difference in how love is experienced. For example, in the

According to Sternberg, intimacy is a key characteristic of a love relationship.

passion
The component of love that refers to physical attraction, arousal, and sexual behavior in a relationship

decision/commitment
The realization of being in love and the establishment of a commitment to maintain it

Watch *Triangluar Theory of Love: Robert Sternberg* on **MyDevelopmentLab**

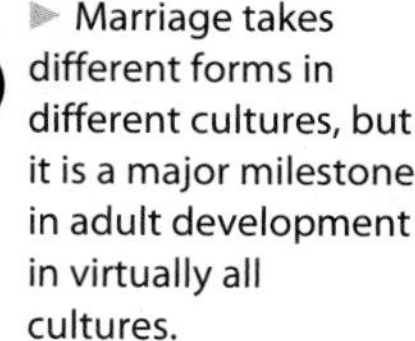

▶ Marriage takes different forms in different cultures, but it is a major milestone in adult development in virtually all cultures.

▲ Here, a bride and bridegroom prepare to be married in a South Asian Hindu wedding ceremony.

Internet survey just mentioned, people who were high in conscientiousness tended to forge relationships based on intimacy and commitment, but not necessarily on passion. People who were more agreeable and who generally got along well with others were more likely to experience all three of Sternberg's types of love. Clearly, love relationships in adulthood follow many different paths.

Choosing a Romantic Partner As important as love is, it is not the only factor that plays a role when choosing a romantic partner. Another perspective that some researchers believe comes into play focuses on more pragmatic considerations of how one's future life will be affected by the partner one chooses (Colyvan, 2010). For example, according to *stimulus-value-role theory* (Murstein, 1982, 1999), mate selection is motivated by each partner's attempt to get the best possible "deal." Each person in the relationship examines the assets and liabilities of the other partner to determine whether the relationship is worthwhile.

According to stimulus-value-role theory, couple formation takes place during three stages of courtship. During the *stimulus* stage, when a couple meets or sees each other for the first time, they make initial judgments about each other's appearance, personality, intelligence, and perhaps other rather superficial characteristics. If the mutual first impressions are favorable, the couple then progresses to the second stage of courtship, *value-comparison*. During this stage, their conversations reveal whether their interests, attitudes, beliefs, and needs are compatible. During the final *role* stage, the couple determines whether they can function in compatible roles in a marriage or similar long-term relationship.

Online dating services, such as eHarmony and Match.com, operate using decision-making models similar to this perspective. If a person subscribes to an online dating service, the first step typically is to fill out a detailed questionnaire about one's preferences and values and submit a picture and some biographical information, such as educational background, employment, family structure, and income. Then, profiles are matched by a computer program and a list of possible partners who share similar interests, values, and life objectives is generated. The next step is for the subscribers to evaluate the profiles of possible compatible partners and determine if a face-to-face meeting is desired. Through the conversations that follow, subscribers can further explore these values and determine if they and their match would be compatible partners in a longer-term relationship context.

Arranged Marriages Of course, as has been true in different historical periods, and is still true in many cultures today, finding a partner is much less a matter for the couple to consider in some cultures than others, because in some cultures marriages are arranged by families. Although allowing one's parents to choose one's life partner seems strange to many people living in the United States today, it is important to understand that arranged marriages are the norm in many parts of the world, and especially in Asia, India, and the Middle East. Today, as in years past, these marriages usually are crafted with religious, cultural, or financial goals in mind (Merali, 2012). It is important to understand that arranged marriages generally are not forced marriages. Rather, cultural expectations are such that young people expect that their parents, or other matchmakers, will find an appropriate life partner for them. For the most part, these young people are in agreement that such a system is desirable. For example, in India, traditional families negotiate the marriages of their children, often early in childhood. When the children reach the appropriate age, they are married in an elaborate marriage ceremony, steeped with tradition, joy, and fanfare.

People raised in contemporary Western society often find the concept of an arranged marriage an abridgement of free choice and a violation of their ideas about "true love" as the guiding force in marriage (Penn, 2011). For example, in an international survey of university students from around the world, 80% of students from the United States, England, and Australia reported that they would not marry a person without being in love, even if that person had all of the other spousal qualities that were desired (Levine, Sato, Hashimoto, & Verma, 1995). Yet, within the cultures where arranged marriages are practiced and honored, no such perception typically occurs (Ahluwalia, Suzuki, & Mir, 2009). In the university student survey mentioned, less than 40% of the students from India, Pakistan, and Thailand viewed love as a critically important feature when contemplating marriage. Thus, even among modern, professional young people, in cultures that embrace it the concept of arranged marriages remains a part of their expectations and traditions. For example, in one study of young Indian professionals, results suggest that when contemplating their ideal marriage partner, these young adults focused on achieving specific, desirable goals that were linked to both arranged and self-determined marriages. Thus, young Indian professionals are likely to consider such things as intimacy, equality, and personal choice alongside goals of "growing into love," the bride becoming a part of the groom's family, and the role of God in the forging of strong marital partnerships. In this way, the marriages that result are somewhat based on a compromise of older and newer views (Netting, 2010).

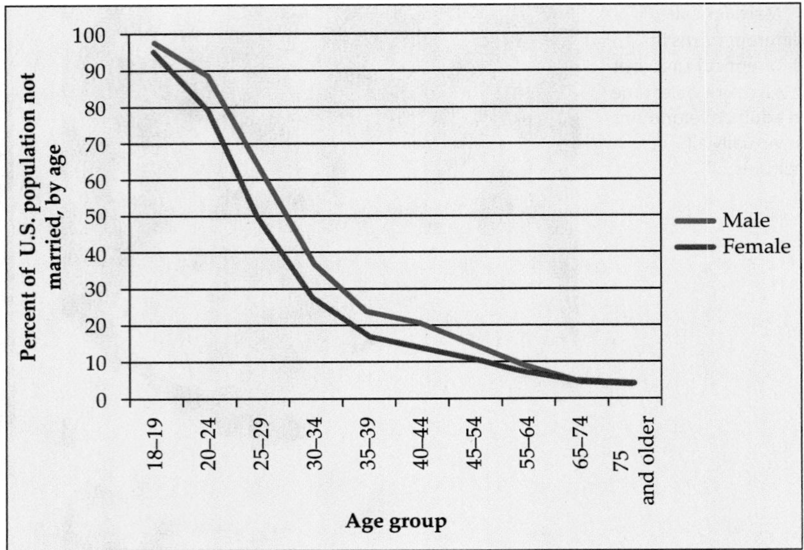

FIGURE 13-5 Percent of the U.S. Population That Is Not Married, by Sex and Age Group, 2010

SOURCE: Table 57, "Marital status of the population by sex and age: 2010," in "**America's families and living arrangements: 2010,**" U.S. Census Bureau, 2012, retrieved from http://www.census.gov/compendia/statab/cats/population.html.

Marriage

The United States is a nation of subcultures with many different patterns of adult lifestyles. Yet monogamous marriage is by far the most popular and most frequently chosen lifestyle. As you can see in Figure 13-5, people are more likely to marry as they grow older. For example, by age 40, only about 20% of men and 14% of women have never married. Among those age 75 and older, only 3.5% of men and 3.9% of women living in the United States in 2010 reported that they had never been married. Although it is difficult to estimate with precision, a reasonable conclusion is that about 90% of people living in the United States today will marry at some point during their lives.

The major reason that it is difficult to estimate marriage trends on a population-wide basis is that marriage patterns and rates are changing rather dramatically in the United States. Compared to just a few decades ago, the percent of the U.S. population that is currently married has fallen rather dramatically (see Figure 13-6). The reasons for this decline are many. For instance, people are choosing to marry at somewhat later ages today than in previous decades, and thus more young adults are still single, even though they ultimately will marry at some point in their lives. According to U.S. Census records, in 1970 57% of men and 88% of women were married for the first time between the ages of 20 and 24; in 2009, these percentages had fallen by more than half, to 24% and 38%, respectively (see Figure 13.7). Thus, young adulthood in particular is becoming a period of the lifespan in which many people are single. Also, people are living somewhat longer today than in past decades, and it is much more common to be widowed at the end of life than earlier in life. This, too, contributes to an overall decline in the percent of the population that is married. Divorce is also part of the picture. In 2010, for example, there were just over 2 million marriages performed in the United States; there

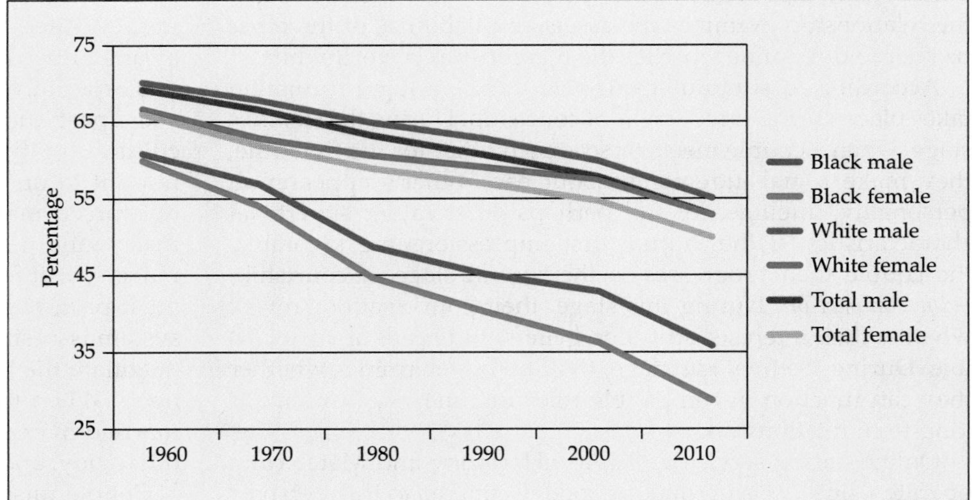

FIGURE 13-6 Percentage of All Persons Age 15 and Older Who Were Married, by Sex and Race, 1960–2010, United States

SOURCE: Table UC3 in "America's families and living arrangements: 2010," U.S. Census Bureau, 2012, retrieved from http://www.census.gov/population/www/socdemo/hh-fam/cps2010.html.

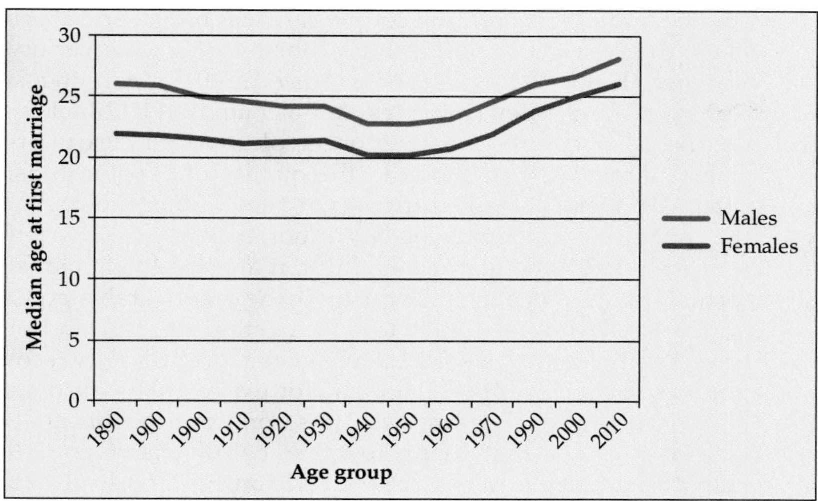

FIGURE 13-7 Average (Median) Age at First Marriage, 1890–2010, United States

SOURCE: Data from U.S. Census Bureau, accessed at Information Please Database, Pearson Education, Inc., http://www.infoplese.com/i9pa/A0005061.html.

were also just under 900,000 divorces (Centers for Disease Control [CDC], 2012a). Although the divorce rate in the United States has been relatively stable for the past two decades, in the last half of the 20th century it climbed dramatically. Also, cohabitation is much more common today than in the past; many more couples are choosing to live together without being married. For example, in 2010 there were 7.5 million unmarried couples living together—a 13% increase from the previous year (Kreider, 2010). Despite these trends, however, it still remains that marriage is a common event in the lives of most people living in the United States today.

In mainstream U.S. culture, preparation for marriage often involves rituals of dating, courtship, and engagement, and the selection of one's partner is typically a matter of one's own choice and is based on being in "love." The marriage bond is symbolized by a wedding rite, which may be simple or involve an elaborate and public wedding celebration. Regardless of the scope of the wedding, however, two extended families become linked. The marriage itself is expected to provide emotional sustenance, sexual gratification, and financial security for couples and their families. Like most social institutions, however, marriage is defined quite differently, depending on culture.

In traditional Arab cultures, for example, the transition to married life is carefully orchestrated by older relatives and the extended family. As soon as girls reach puberty, maintaining chastity through family vigilance may take on an urgent, even life-or-death quality in the interest of family honor. All contact with men—including the fiancé—is forbidden once the future husband has been selected. Marriages often are arranged: Older relatives of the young man screen eligible young girls and their families. Male elders conduct bride-price negotiations. To conserve family assets and protect family honor, "cousin marriages" with the daughter of the father's brother are traditionally favored. In this manner, a family can be sure that the young bride will be chaperoned and guarded in an acceptable manner. Customs in the diverse Arab cultures of the world are changing, but family honor and loyalty are highly valued, and marriage is still a central part of that system (Schvaneveldt, Kerpelman, & Schvaneveldt, 2005; Sharifzadeh, 1998).

Marriages are very important as cultural traditions in all parts of the world, and men and women play quite different roles in marriage, depending on their culture (Arnett, 2010a). In many regions in Africa, for example, young men desiring to marry must pay a dowry in order to gain permission to marry a family's daughter. Sometimes the dowry is quite high—a bride may cost the groom many cattle, for example—perhaps so many that he must work for some time to be able to afford to marry. In many regions of Africa, the practice of having multiple wives is quite common. Typically, the "first wife" occupies a special position of influence among the wives, but each is afforded time with the husband, and all children born are considered his legitimate heirs. In Northern Africa, where the Moslem region predominates, most families conform to a traditional, paternalistic family structure. Here, the father of the family is expected to be obeyed without questioning. Thus, marriages are determined and negotiated by the father and perhaps other male relatives, much as they are in Arab cultures. Women in these cultures have few rights, and are expected to conform their behavior to these very traditional values. Those who do not conform often are treated very harshly. As you can see, marriages vary considerably depending on culture, as do the roles occupied by husbands and wives. A discussion of these broad cultural traditions is well beyond the scope of this text. However, many resources highlight the traditions and rituals that define mate selection and marriage in various cultures, and you may find it interesting to consult these and other sources for more information (e.g., Hamon & Ingoldsby, 2003; Jankowiak, 2008).

How do your parents feel about the prospects of your entering a "mixed" marriage? What are your opinions on this issue?

Although most U.S. marriages are free of prenuptial investigation and negotiation, there remain strong constraints for relationships that violate social, economic, religious, or ethnic boundaries. For many groups within contemporary U.S. culture, sexual intimacy, for example, is expected to be reserved for marriage. Many people living in the United States today view marriage as an institution to be entered into only by one man and one woman, and view gay marriage as illegitimate. As of July 2012, marriages between two members of the same sex were prohibited by law in all but six states, although the national debate on gay marriage is far from concluded. Also, community groups and social institutions, as well as parents, often frown on "mixed" marriages of any kind.

There is, however, some indication that cultural prescriptions are relaxing, perhaps in response to the increasing diversity of the U.S. population. For example, statistics gathered in the 2010 U.S. Census show that interracial or interethnic opposite-sex married couple households grew by nearly a third over the previous decade—from 7% in 2000 to 10% in 2010 (U.S. Census Bureau, 2012n). This trend toward more interracial/interethnic relationships was even more pronounced among cohabiting partners (18%) and same-sex partners (21%). Clearly, the nature of relationships in the United States is reflecting the growing diversity of the country's population.

Cohabitation

More couples also are choosing to *cohabit*, or live together without the legal contract of marriage to bind them. Depending on the couple, cohabiting, or "living together," may or may not be similar to marriage. Just over one-half of cohabiting couples (57%) have no children, but that leaves over 2 million such households that do include children. Accurate statistics about cohabitation are hard to come by because of the reluctance of some couples to proclaim their relationship and because of the often transient nature of cohabitation. Nevertheless, for the U.S. population as a whole, cohabitation increased more than 15-fold from 1970 to 2010, from about half a million couples to 7.5 million couples during this 40-year period (Kreider, 2010). Most cohabitants are young adults: In 2011, 62.5% of cohabiting men and 66.4% of cohabiting women were under age 40 (U.S. Census Bureau, 2012k). However, this pattern of domestic partnership extends across adulthood, and cohabitation is present in all adult age groups.

Living together in an informal cohabiting arrangement entails many of the same relationship-building tasks that married couples face. Conflicts must be resolved, and constant and effective communication is essential. Like those who are married, couples that live together must deal with issues of commitment, fidelity, and permanence. There are some differences, however, between married and cohabiting couples. Both men and women in cohabiting relationships are more likely than married people to have affairs outside the relationship, which may contribute to the finding that cohabiting heterosexual couples experience more tension than either married heterosexual or gay male or lesbian couples (Wilson & Daly, 2001).

What factors might explain why couples who cohabit before marriage sometimes are not as happy in their marriages as couples who do not live together before marriage?

Although the great majority of cohabiting heterosexual couples plan to marry, only about one-third actually do. The reasons for why some of these relationships persist and others do not are as varied as the people involved in them (Lamanna & Reidmann, 2012). Correspondingly, some studies find that cohabiting couples are as well adjusted and equally committed to each other as are married couples; other studies find that cohabiting couples are less happy and more likely to experience relationship problems of a wide variety of types (Kulik & Havusha-Morgenstern, 2011; Manning & Cohen, 2012; Stanley, Rhoades, & Fincham, 2011). Much of the discussion about cohabitation involves a complex interaction of factors that play into the quality of relationships, such as poverty, family support for the couple, the age of the cohabiting partners, whether or not marriage is expected at some point, whether or not children are involved, and so forth. Perhaps one major conclusion to be drawn at this point is that some couples prefer to live together for a period of time, and those with a strong sense of personal identity, economic and social support, and realistic expectations for their relationship generally fare best. A second is probably that, despite the idea that living together before marriage will help "work out the kinks" in the relationship and lead to a happier and more stable marriage, cohabitation seldom leads to more positive outcomes than does marriage without prior cohabitation.

Gay and Lesbian Couples

The picture for cohabiting homosexuals, however, is somewhat different. Because gay men and lesbian women are, in most places, legally prevented from marrying their partners, their situations are necessarily described as cohabitation; however, the statistics that describe their relationships are more comparable to those describing married, rather than cohabiting, heterosexuals (Hyde & DeLamater, 2011). For instance, homosexual couples prefer long-term, committed relationships, as do heterosexual couples (Peplau & Beals, 2002), although gay men (but not lesbian women) are somewhat more accepting of nonromantic sexual encounters outside their romantic relationships.

Discussions about gay and lesbian cohabitation become particularly shrill when the topics of homosexual marriage and adoption are raised. Although at the time this book was written only six states and a few countries outside the United States legally sanctioned marriage between two members of the same sex, that may well have changed by the time you read this text. Adoptions are becoming less prohibitive for gay and lesbian couples, supported in part by research that shows that children raised in the homes of homosexual couples are just as popular and well adjusted as other children (Farr, Forssell, & Patterson, 2010; Hyde & DeLamater, 2011). As is the case for children raised in traditional families, the vast majority of children raised by homosexual parents develop a heterosexual orientation (Goldberg, 2010; Herek, 2006; Patterson, 2006). In recognition of these and other similar findings, the American Academy of Pediatrics (AAP) in 2002 adopted the position in support of allowing homosexuals to adopt their partner's children (AAP, 2002).

The shifts in gay male and lesbian cohabitation and family patterns highlight the social changes that are occurring in U.S. society. Another shift that is occurring is an increase in the proportion of young adults who are choosing not to marry or cohabit at all.

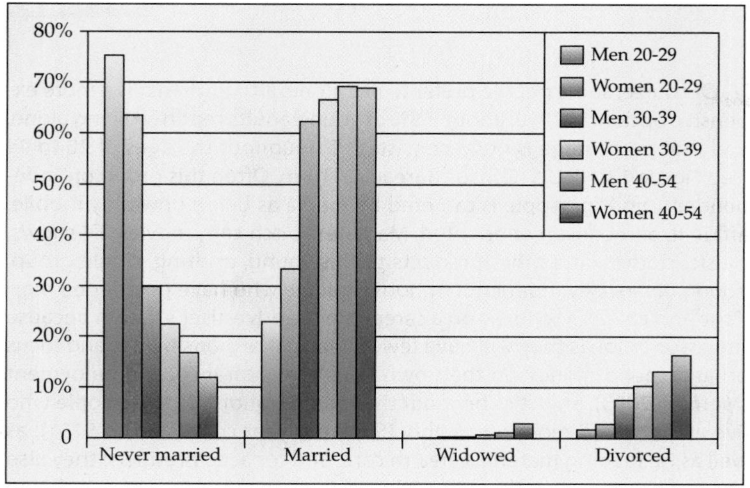

FIGURE 13-8 Marital Status, Young Adult Men and Women, 2010

SOURCE: U. S. Census Bureau. (2012). Table 57. Marital Status of the Population by Sex and Age: 2010. **Statistical Abstract of the United States, 2011.** Author.

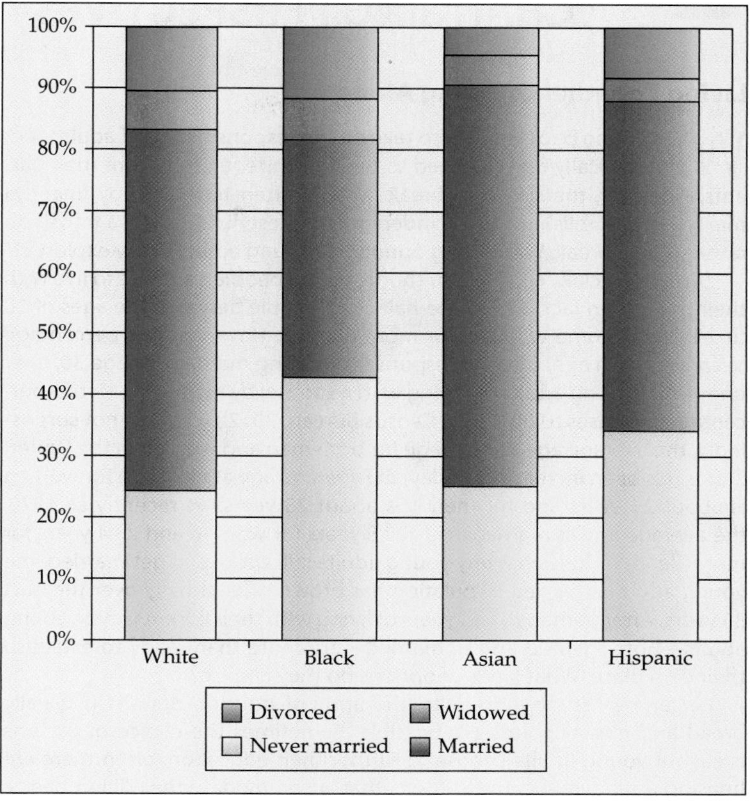

FIGURE 13-9 Marital Status of All U. S. Adults Age 15 and Over by Race/ Ethnicity, 2010

SOURCE: U. S. Census Bureau. (2012). Table 56. Marital Status of the Population by Sex, Race and Hispanic Origin, 1990 to 2010. **Statistical Abstract of the United States, 2011.** Author.

Staying Single

To understand the "single" lifestyle, it is useful to understand that the choice to remain unmarried or uncommitted to a relationship has fluctuated historically, often in response to social transition. During the late 1930s, for example, when the country was recovering from the Great Depression, fewer people married, and those who did marry did so at later ages. This trend continued during World War II when millions of temporarily single women joined the labor force while their boyfriends or husbands were overseas fighting and dying. After the war, the picture changed dramatically. By the mid-1950s, only 4% of marriage-age adults remained single, and the age at first marriage was the youngest on record. Remaining single became more popular once again in the 1970s and 1980s: The marriage rate among single people under 45 years of age fell to equal the post-Depression low and has remained low, taking a further recent dip in response to the economic downturn of 2008–2009. Perhaps not surprisingly, the proportion of adults who are unmarried varies somewhat by racial/ethnic group (see Figure 13-8). White Americans are least likely to remain single; Black Americans are most likely to never marry.

For contemporary young adults, remaining single may simply mean postponing marriage (see Figure 13-9). In 2010, 88.7% of U.S. men and 79.3% of U.S. women ages 20 to 24 were never married. The comparable percentages for never-married men and women in older young adult age groups were 36.5% and 27.1%, respectively, for those 30 to 34 years of age, and 20.4% and 13.8%, respectively, for those in the 40 to 44 age group (U.S. Census Bureau, 2012l). As these statistics clearly show, the older a person becomes, the greater is the chance of having been married. However, it is important to note that in each age group, the percentages of never-married young adults are higher now than at any time during the past 50 years. This increase in the number of young unmarried adults has many implications for society (see the box Changing Perspectives: Living Together or Living Alone).

Whether or not this trend will continue, intensify, or decline remains unclear. People offer different reasons for why they choose the single life. For some, economic hardship plays a role: Some people choose to delay marriage until they have a stable job and some money in the bank. For others, remaining single is not so much a choice as it is an unwanted consequence of being unable to find a suitable partner. Others choose the single life as a way of enjoying intimate relationships while avoiding the possible constraints and problems of marriage: They may not wish to feel trapped by a mate who stands in the way of their own personal development, and they may fear feelings of boredom, unhappiness, anger, sexual frustration, or loneliness with a person from whom they have grown apart. In addition, they may not feel sufficiently drawn to anyone to undertake one of the most consuming of adult responsibilities—parenthood—which we explore in the next section as we look at the family life cycle and adult development.

CHANGING PERSPECTIVES

Living Together or Living Alone

When young people begin to take on the responsibilities of adulthood, they typically feel the need to become independent from their parents. However, the desire to break away is often tempered by financial reality, and establishing a fully independent lifestyle is usually a transition rather than a break. What living options do young adults today explore?

Often, especially early in adulthood, young people continue to live with their parents. In fact, about one-half of all people between the ages of 18 to 24 live at home with one or more parents. However, this percentage decreases with age, often in response to getting married. By age 30, over one-half of young adults are living with a spouse; by ages 35 to 45, this percentage increases to 68% (U.S. Census Bureau, 2012l). Perhaps not surprisingly, the average age of marriage for both men and women in the United States has been increasing. Today, the average age at marriage for women is about 26 years and for men it is about 28 years. As recently as 1970, the average age at marriage was 20.8 years for women and 23.4 years for men. Clearly, although many young adults still choose to get married, the young adult unmarried population has grown substantially over the past 35 years. After perhaps a few years of living with their parents, most young adults—both married and unmarried—are more than ready to establish their own place. What kinds of options do they choose?

For unmarried young adults, the array of housing options is usually broad and many choices are possible. Sometimes the choice of options is easy. If young adults choose to further their education, often there are housing arrangements for students that accommodate their living needs. Many colleges and universities offer an array of housing options, ranging from single-sex dormitories to co-ed residence halls and even apartments for groups of students who want to assume more responsibilities for daily chores like cooking.

Sometimes young adults choose to live together because they are romantically involved. As noted previously, the U.S. Census Bureau (2012m) reports that in the most recent census about 7.5 million heterosexual couples declared themselves to be unmarried partners, and a little more than half of them (4.3 million) were young adults. The census also noted that more than 600,000 people identified themselves as same-sex cohabiting partners, and many of these people were young adults, too.

Sometimes housing choices are harder. Over three-quarters of emerging adults report living with someone other than their spouse. This could be their parents, one or more roommates, or a significant person in their life. Or, in this era of economic challenge, the young person might live with a stranger in order to make expenses. When a young person follows a job, especially if it involves relocating to a different community, finding a place to live can be a significant challenge. Often single people cannot find an affordable place unless they are willing to take one or more roommates. And, increasingly, young adults are moving back in with their parents, at least until they can save enough money to be able to launch themselves successfully. Although the percentage of young adults who live with others decreases with age, still nearly a quarter of adults between the ages of 35 and 44 live with someone who is not their spouse (see Figure 13-10).

Early adulthood is also a period during which many people marry—most for the first time. In fact, the percentage of young adults who marry increases dramatically across the ages of 20 to 44. Whereas about 15% of emerging adults ages 20 to 24 are married, the percentage increases to about 50% by ages 25 to 34 (see Figure 13-7). By ages 30 to 34, about two-thirds of U.S. adults are married.

Of course, some people prefer to live alone, although that is a more expensive option. In 2010, about 8.5% of young adults reported living alone, and that percentage is quite consistent throughout the ages of 20 to 44 (see Figure 13-10; U.S. Census Bureau, 2012m). Often this group of "independent" young people is targeted by media as being upwardly mobile, affluent, and consumer oriented. Marketers pitch cars, movies, TV shows, music, clothes, and other products to this young, aspiring, single group. Young, financially independent householders who have postponed marriage and children to focus on a career are the advertiser's dream because the assumption is they will have fewer financial responsibilities and focus on and spend money on their own health, appearance, and enjoyment (Morrow, 2003). Statistics bear out these assumptions: Single people who live alone spend more on alcohol ($314 per year compared to $181), as well as on reading materials, health care, and tobacco products; they also are more likely to buy themselves luxuries, even in the face of a declining economy, than are married people and those who live with roommates (Morrow, 2003).

However, living alone is not always glamorous. Young adults often do not command high salaries, and living expenses can eat up most of their income, leaving little money for such luxuries as eating out, buying expensive clothing and shoes, and belonging to the right club or gym. For most young adults, independent living allows flexibility with creating a lifestyle that the person wishes to pursue but usually with significant financial limitations.

What do you think about the living arrangements that are available to young adults today? If you are in your late teens or early 20s, what kind of living arrangement do you have? What is good and bad about it? What would you prefer? What are the impediments you experience? What are your plans for housing for the next 10 years? If you have already lived through your 20s, what living arrangements did you choose? Why did you decide to live the way you did? Were there options you rejected? What options would you choose if you were age 21 again?

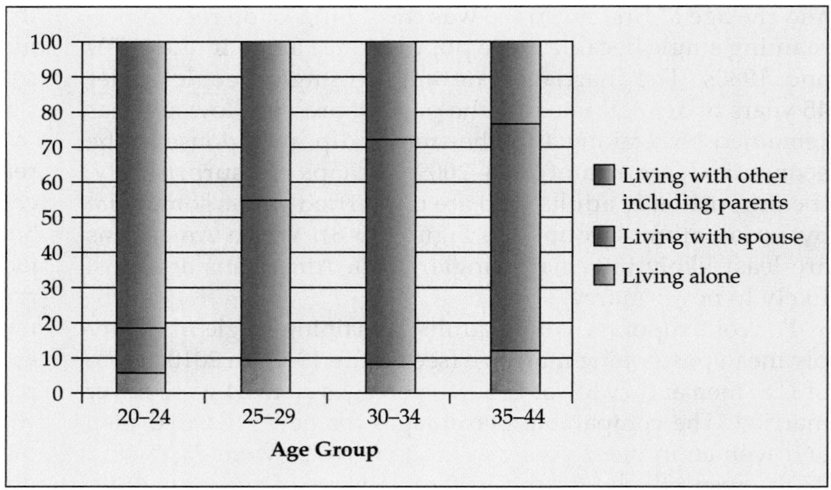

FIGURE 13-10 Living Arrangements of Young Adults in the United States, by Age, 2010
Note that living alone is a relatively uncommon arrangement throughout the young adult years.

SOURCE: From Table 58. Living arrangements of persons 15 years-old and over by race and age, 2010. *Statistical abstract of the United States: 2012*, U.S. Census Bureau, 2012, Washington, DC: Author.

REVIEW THE FACTS 13-2

1. What are Robert Sternberg's three components of love?
2. According to stimulus-value-role theory, we select romantic partners according to
   a. the assets and liabilities they bring to the relationship.
   b. the "fit" between their personality and our own personality.
   c. the passion we feel.
   d. whether or not our families approve.
3. If current trends hold, approximately what percentage of people in the United States will marry at some point in their lives?
4. Do the relationships of cohabiting homosexuals more resemble those of heterosexuals who are cohabiting or heterosexuals who are married?
5. What is the American Academy of Pediatrics' official stand on allowing homosexual couples to adopt children?
6. Currently, the average age at which individuals marry is ________ for men and ________ for women.
   a. increasing; decreasing
   b. increasing; increasing
   c. decreasing; increasing
   d. decreasing; decreasing

Practice on **MyDevelopmentLab**

THE FAMILY LIFE CYCLE AND ADULT DEVELOPMENT

The Family Life Cycle

Most adults experience a series of major life changes as the patterns of their lives unfold. Although not all adults experience all of the major events in the adult life cycle, and there can be considerable variability in the impact any event has on different people, viewing the adult lifespan as a cycle punctuated with significant milestones is a useful way to conceptualize the continuity of this phase of life (see Figure 13-11). Parenthood is one of a set of significant events in the typical family life cycle, and its challenges and demands comprise a major developmental phase for the parents as individuals and for the couple as a system (Carter, McGoldrick, & Petkov, 2011; Harwood, McLean, & Durkin, 2007).

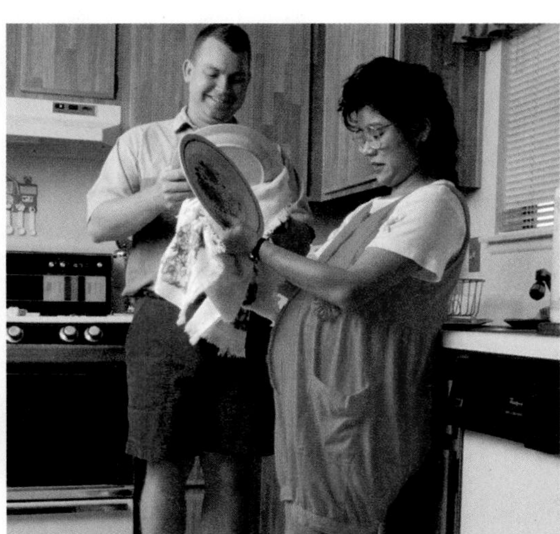

During the woman's pregnancy, both partners can offer emotional support to each other.

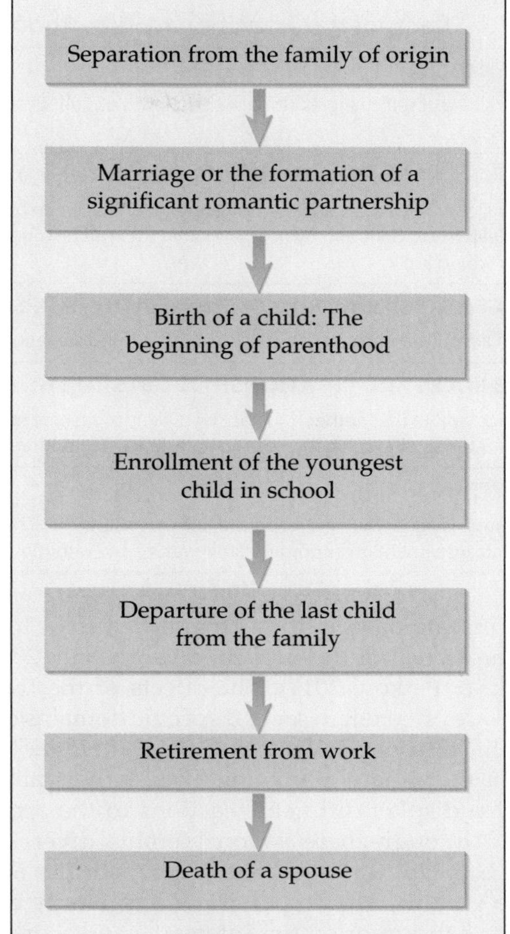

FIGURE 13-11 **Examples of Major Events in the Adult Life Cycle** Although the specific events that shape the adult life cycle are unique to each individual, most adults experience similar patterns in the way their lives unfold.

The Transition to Parenthood

The arrival of the first child changes the direction of family life irrevocably. Parenthood imposes new roles and responsibilities—involving challenges and wonderment—for both the mother and the father. For most new parents, the actual birth brings an onslaught of physical and emotional strains—disruption of sleep and other routines, financial drain, and increased tension and conflicts of various kinds. The mother is often tired, the father may feel neglected, and both partners sense that their freedom has been curtailed. The closeness and companionship of the husband and wife can be diluted by the introduction of a new family member, as the focus of either or both partners may shift to the baby.

The transition to parenthood is one of the major periods in the family life cycle, and it is usually irrevocable: Parents do not "divorce" their children. Parenthood calls for numerous adaptations and adjustments. For example, some newlywed couples enjoy a relatively high standard of living when both spouses are working and there is no child to provide for. They buy cars, furniture, and clothes. They eat out often and enjoy

Table 13-3 Effects of the Transition to Parenthood

CHANGES IN IDENTITY AND INNER LIFE Each parent's sense of self changes, along with assumptions about how family life works.
SHIFTS IN ROLES AND RELATIONSHIPS WITHIN THE MARRIAGE The division of labor between the parents changes at a time when both are stressed by sleep disruptions and by not being able to be alone together as much as they would like.
SHIFTS IN GENERATIONAL ROLES AND RELATIONSHIPS The transition affects grandparents as well as parents as roles are renegotiated.
CHANGING ROLES AND RELATIONSHIPS OUTSIDE THE FAMILY Outside changes affect the mother most, as she is likely to assume more responsibility for child care and to put her career on hold, at least temporarily.
NEW PARENTING ROLES AND RELATIONSHIPS The couple must navigate the new responsibilities associated with raising a child and reach agreement on important family values and priorities.

numerous recreational activities. This all may come to an abrupt end with the arrival of the first child (Bornstein, 2012; Carter, McGoldrick, & Petkov, 2011). The effects of the transition to parenthood are often felt in several specific domains of personal and family life (Strong, DeVault, & Cohen, 2011; see Table 13-3).

Although they share many concerns, fathers and mothers typically also display different reactions to the arrival of the first child. Although there is considerable diversity in contemporary U.S. culture, women characteristically adjust their lifestyles to give priority to parenting and family roles. Men, on the other hand, more often intensify their work efforts to become better or more stable providers (Feldman, Sussman, & Zigler, 2004). When the child arrives, there are new stresses and challenges, and role changes are rapid. Both parents usually experience new feelings of pride and excitement coupled with a greater sense of responsibility that can be sometimes overwhelming (Lawrence, Rothman, Cobb, & Bradbury, 2010). Although some couples experience greater marital satisfaction after the birth of a child, sexual problems, less communication and sharing of interests, and increased conflict occur in many marriages (Carter & McGoldrick, 2005; Lawrence et al., 2008). Couples with a new baby to care for also need to find time for each other and for other interests.

The arrival of the first child usually constitutes a transition rather than a crisis, however (Harwood, McLean, & Durkin, 2007; Mitnick, Heyman, & Smith, 2009). A variety of factors influence how well new parents adjust to their roles. Social support, especially from the husband, is crucial to a new mother (Cowan, Cowan, Pruett, & Pruett, 2006; Feinberg & Kan, 2008). Marital happiness during pregnancy is another important factor in the adjustment of both husband and wife; in fact, the father's adjustment is strongly affected by the mother's evaluation of her marriage and pregnancy (Wallace & Gotlib, 1990). The baby's characteristics are also important. For example, parents of "difficult" babies (see Chapter 5) more often report a decline in marital satisfaction than do those whose babies have easier temperaments (Belsky & Rosenberger, 1995; Crockenberg & Leerkes, 2003). Altogether, it is important to remember that the first few years of marriage—with or without children—require adjustment and can be stressful (Mitnick, Heyman, & Smith, 2009). Thus, global conclusions about how new parents react to the birth of their child are difficult to offer, as every couple, every baby, and every set of family circumstances is unique.

Coping with Children's Developmental Stages

The demands on parents vary at each period in the family life cycle. A young infant, for example, requires almost total and constant nurturance, which some parents provide more easily than others. Each critical period for the child produces or reactivates a critical period for the parents (Crockenberg & Leerkes, 2003; Strong, DeVault, & Cohen, 2011). As children grow, their needs change dramatically, and so do the tasks that parents must fulfill (see Table 13-4). Parents who are unable to deal effectively with children at one stage may be quite good at dealing with them at another stage. For example, parents who have a lot of difficulty with an infant may cope quite effectively with a preschool child or adolescent. The reverse may also be true; the parent who is quite at ease with a helpless baby may have problems with an increasingly independent teenager.

Table 13-4 Stages of Parenthood

Stage	Age of the Child	Tasks for Parents
Image making	Conception to birth	Couples create an image of the kind of parents they will be
Nurturing	Birth to age 2	Parents become attached to the child and learn to balance their commitments to family versus personal and professional life
Authority	Ages 2 to 5	Parents evaluate their parenting styles and determine rules and responsibilities
Interpretive	Ages 6 to 12	Parents continue to evaluate and test their theories of parenting
Interdependence	Age 13 to children's leaving home	Parents must redefine their lines of authority to accommodate their children's increasing needs for freedom
Departure	When grown children leave home	Parents must let go and also must face their successes and failures as parents

Watch *Adoption: Jane Marie and Dale* on **MyDevelopmentLab**

At each phase in the family life cycle, parents not only have to cope with the new challenges and demands of their changing and developing children, but they must also renegotiate their own relationship (Carter & McGoldrick, 2005). Couples must establish ways of making decisions and resolving conflicts that will maintain the integrity and respect of each partner. The new pressures created by adolescent rebellion and the quest for independence, for example, require that the couple adapt the family system to make room for the nearly autonomous child. A family system that is either too rigid or, on the other hand, too unstructured usually does not adapt well to a child's continually changing needs. Unresolved tensions may interfere with the marriage relationship or with the ability to function well as parents.

What period in your development do you think your parents found to be the most challenging? Why do you think this stage was the most difficult for your parents?

Single Parenthood

The pressures of parenthood are particularly acute for single parents, the overwhelming majority of whom are working mothers. Single-parent families became increasingly common in the United States up until about 2000, at which point the percent of single-family households stabilized at about 26% (see Figure 13-12). In 2010, 26.5% of all families with children were maintained by a single parent, 23.1% by a single mother, and 3.4% by a single father (U.S. Census, 2012).

Single parenting is associated with various types of stress. Not only does the single parent need to make all family decisions and handle all child-care complexities without the support of a partner, but there are financial implications as well. With only one income to support the family rather than two, single-parent families are much more likely to experience financial strain. For example, in 2010, the median family income in two-parent families in the United States was $71,627. For single-parent families headed by a male the median income was $41,501, compared to $29,770 for single-parent families headed by a female (U.S. Census, 2012).

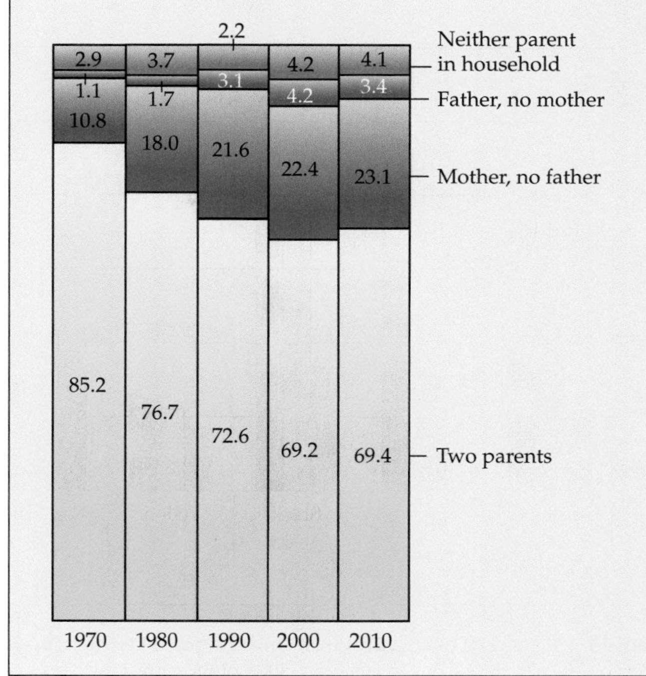

FIGURE 13-12 Living Arrangements of Children for Selected Years, 1970 to 2010

SOURCE: From Table 69, "Children under 18 years old by presence of parents: 2000 to 2010," in *Statistical Abstract of the United States, 2012*, U.S. Census Bureau, 2012. Washington, DC: Author.

Parents may be better at dealing with children at one stage of development than at another. Here, these parents seem to be enjoying their young children.

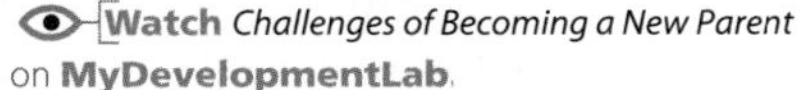

Single-Mother Families What is responsible for the exploding number of single-parent families headed by women? One factor is the rising divorce rate, accompanied by the tradition of awarding custody of the children to the mother. Although divorces can happen at any age, they are most common in the first 10 years of marriage and, therefore, particularly affect young adults during their parenting years. There also has been a substantial increase in the number of mothers who are separated from their spouses but not divorced. Another major factor is the increase in births to unmarried mothers. In 2009, 41.07% of all births were to unmarried women; for women who indicated that they were Black, the figure was 72.3% (Martin et al., 2011).

Reinforcing all of these trends, better job opportunities and improved status for women now allow at least some mothers and children to survive without support from fathers, at least in the short run. However, single parenthood can be an

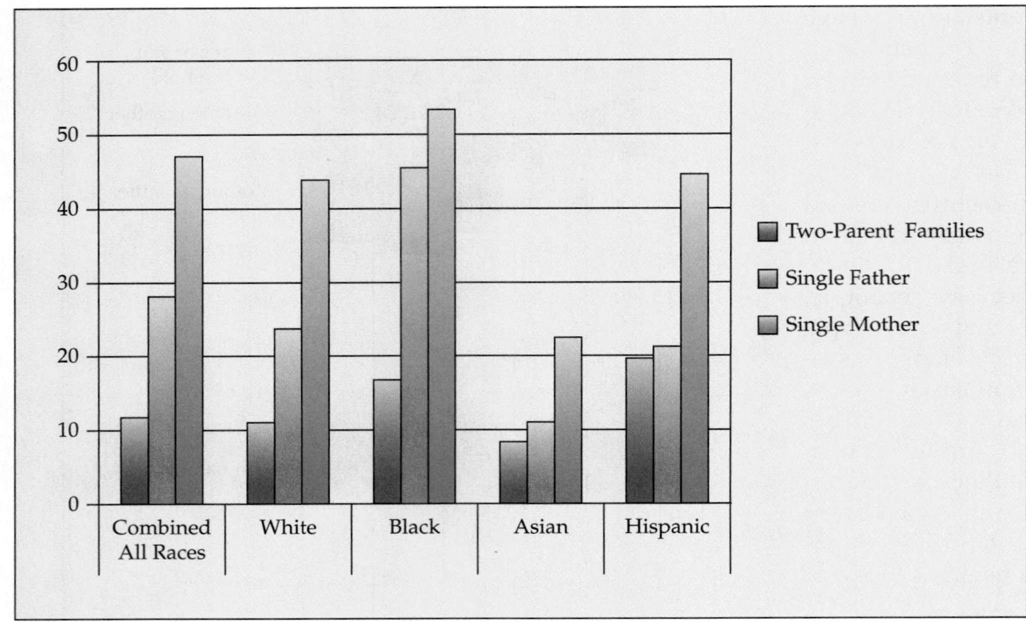

FIGURE 13-13 Percent of U.S. Children Under Age 18 Living in Poverty, by Race/Ethnicity, 2010

NOTE: Poverty is defined as living in families at 100% of the current government poverty level for families of their size. For a family of four, the 2012 poverty level = $23,050.

SOURCE: "People in families by family structure, age, and sex, iterated by Income-to-Poverty ratio and race: 2010," U.S. Census Bureau, 2012, in *Current population survey, 2011, annual social and economic supplement*, retrieved from http://www.census.gov/hhes/www/cpstables/032011/pov/new02_100_01.htm.

exhausting struggle for families of all economic levels. Single parents sometimes experience destructive levels of stress (McAdoo, 1995). Yet most single parents cope well with the challenges of parenting, especially if economic issues can be dealt with successfully.

Single Mothers and Poverty As data presented earlier make clear, economic challenges are likely to exist for most single parents, and especially for single mothers. Single mothers consistently earn less than single fathers. In 2010, the families maintained by single mothers were almost twice as likely to have incomes below the poverty line than were families maintained by single fathers—46.9% compared to 28.1%. The dramatic relationship between single parenthood and poverty is depicted in Figure 13-13. Especially for single mothers without adequate education, making ends meet often is extremely difficult. Although few families in poverty remain in poverty indefinitely, children in families headed by a single parent who has a limited educational background may spend at least half of their childhood in poverty.

This situation is particularly problematic among those belonging to disadvantaged racial and ethnic groups. For example, single-mother homes are more numerous and more often below the poverty level among African American families. Fully 65% of all Black families with children under 18 years are headed by a single parent (U.S. Census, 2012). On the other hand, Black and Hispanic people who live in poverty are also more likely to live in intergenerational households (Antonucci, Jackson, & Biggs, 2007; Fields, 2004). These extended families most often include one of the single mother's parents, in addition to other family or nonfamily members. In these situations, additional financial, psychological, and social resources often are available to the single mother, and consequently she may feel less isolated and overwhelmed.

Until 1996, families with children who qualified for public assistance fell under the guidelines of the Aid to Families with Dependent Children (AFDC) program. In 1996, Congress enacted the Personal Responsibility and Work Opportunity Reconciliation Act (PRWORA), which was the first major welfare reform effort in 60 years. The intent of the PRWORA, which was reauthorized in 2005 as the Deficit Reduction Act, was to transform public assistance into a system that helps mothers on welfare become independent, self-sufficient workers instead of being a program that encourages them to be dependent, passive aid recipients who tend to pass their dependency along to the next generation. Exactly how to accomplish this was to be determined by the states, within guidelines that (1) set a relatively tight schedule for implementation of state programs, (2) established immediate and lifetime limits on a mother's receipt of welfare payments, and, most important, (3) required the mother to work to receive payments and other assistance. The intent, in other words, was to reverse the welfare and poverty cycle.

What advantages and disadvantages would living in an intergenerational household typically imply?

In the initial period, the welfare reform act was quite successful, although women who were semiskilled and had some work history often made the transition back to employment more easily than those who were capable of only unskilled labor or had little or no work history. Job training and the expanding job market of the late 1990s allowed many women to move into full-time jobs. However, the PRWORA creates some problems for single parents, 90% of whom are women. Perhaps the most significant problem is child care. The available federal funds for child care are limited, and program requirements and restrictions have resulted in increasing numbers of women being ineligible for child-care assistance (Cherlin, 2004, 2008; Collins & Mayer, 2010; Thorne, 2004).

The day-care problem is compounded by the fact that most women who receive funding under the PRWORA work at jobs that pay minimum wage, which is still well below the poverty line for a family of three. The simple fact is that many single mothers cannot support their children adequately even when they work, and the disparity between what people earn and what they can buy with their earnings is increasing (Bernstein, 2004; Collins, Mayer, Morgan, Acker, & Weigt, 2010). Although the aim of the PRWORA is noble—to cut the cycle of generations of poverty—it remains to be seen whether this welfare "reform" can achieve the positive outcomes promised, and whether it will be modified significantly in an attempt to make it more responsive to its intended outcomes.

Single-Father Families Although single-parent families are less likely to be headed by a father than a mother, the number of single-father families is growing. At least 10% of fathers who divorce gain custody of their children, and another 16% participate in joint custody settlements. Although they are usually better off financially, single fathers experience many of the same problems and tensions as single mothers (Amato & Dorius, 2010).

Like single mothers, most single fathers maintain high-levels of emotional involvement with their children (Tamis-LeMonda & McFadden, 2010). They are heavily invested in and committed to their children's care, and they worry about failing them or not spending enough time with them. Most single fathers have already taken on extensive parenting roles before the divorce, which helps to prepare them for single parenthood. Despite this experience, the demands of maintaining a family and a job simultaneously are a challenge. Not surprisingly, many single fathers have the same feelings of loneliness and depression that many single mothers have. Single fathers also find, as do single mothers, that it is difficult to maintain an active circle of friends and other sources of emotional support. However, like single mothers, they often can find meaningful friendships at work, and work can satisfy not only economic needs but social and intellectual ones as well. We explore the occupational cycle in the next section.

Single parenting is challenging, for fathers as well as for mothers.

REVIEW THE FACTS 13-3

1. Which of the following groups in the United States is increasing in size at the fastest rate?
   a. families headed by two parents
   b. families headed by single mothers
   c. families headed by single fathers
2. About what percentage of Black families with children under age 18 are headed by a woman?
   a. 33% b. 44%
   c. 65% d. 74%
3. What was the aim of the PRWORA, which was passed by Congress in 1996?
4. What is the primary challenge faced by most single mothers who depend on the PRWORA?
5. Approximately what percentage of fathers who divorce are awarded custody of their children?
   a. 1% b. 10%
   c. 30% d. 50%

Practice on MyDevelopmentLab

THE OCCUPATIONAL CYCLE

To a great extent, people's work influences their attitudes and lifestyle. Their work may determine the life they will lead, either mobile or relatively settled; the kind of community they will live in; and the kind of home and standard of living they will have. Work may also influence friendships, opinions, prejudices, and political affiliations.

An adult's working life follows what is called the **occupational cycle**, which is a variable sequence of periods or stages in a worker's life. Usually, the occupational cycle begins in childhood, with thoughts and experiences that lead to a choice of occupation; it continues with pursuit of the chosen career or careers; and it ends with retirement from the workforce. Of course, every person's occupational cycle is unique and filled with numerous events, choices, and decisions. Work is such an important aspect of life, especially for young adults. How do individuals go about making career choices, and what do they experience in their jobs?

Stages of Occupational Life

Every working adult's job history can be broken down into a series of choices and experiences, which often begin in childhood and extend throughout the working years and into retirement. In a classic developmental model of the occupational cycle, Robert Havighurst (1964) described how people

occupational cycle
The sequence of periods or stages in a worker's life—from occupational exploration and choice, through education and training, to novice status, through promotions, ending in positions that build on earlier experiences

Table 13-5 Havighurst's Developmental Model of the Traditional One-Career Work Cycle

Stage	Developmental Period	Description or Task
Identifying with a worker	Ages 5 to 10	Children identify with working fathers and mothers and the idea of working enters their self-concept
Acquiring basic habits of industry	Ages 10 to 15	Students learn to organize their time and efforts and learn to give work priority over play when necessary
Acquiring an identity as a worker	Ages 15 to 25	People choose an occupation and begin to prepare for it
Becoming a productive person	Ages 25 to 40	Adults perfect skills required for their chosen occupation and move ahead in their career
Maintaining a productive society	Ages 40 to 70	Workers are at the high point of their career and begin to attend to civic and social responsibilities
Contemplating a productive and responsible life	Ages 70 and over	Workers, now retired, look back on their careers and contributions, hopefully with satisfaction

SOURCE: Adapted from "Stages of vocational development," by R. J. Havighurst, 1964, in H. Borow (Ed.), *Man in a world at work* (pp. 560–578), Boston: Houghton Mifflin.

traditionally develop their attitudes about work and how their careers might unfold (see Table 13-5). Despite the somewhat dated context of Havighurst's model, it does still contribute to our present understanding of how people approach the selection of careers (Patton & McMahon, 2006; Seiffge-Krenke & Gelhaar, 2008). For example, it appears that individuals begin to consider career choice very early in life, although children's views of jobs are often quite stereotypical (Palladino Schultheiss, 2008).

Havighurst's model, of course, was developed in the 1960s—a time characterized by a boom economy and a relatively stable occupational landscape. Today, the world of work is strikingly different. Most people, for example, no longer work in one job for their entire career; rather, a typical pattern is to change jobs and change companies several times throughout one's working years. In addition, many adults make one or more major midcareer shifts in which they not only change jobs, but they also change careers, which can involve retraining as well as relocating to a new city or town. Furthermore, these shifts may be the result of factors beyond the person's control, such as when a company downsizes and lays off the worker or when the worker's job simply becomes obsolete. Alternatively, such shifts may result from personal career reevaluation, as when people hit a "ceiling" and can progress no further in their present occupation, or perhaps they simply "burn out" and feel compelled to find something else to do.

Another way work has changed is that it has become increasingly technical. Jobs often require considerable technical training or education beyond that obtained in high school. For many people, college is considered a mandatory step in preparing for a career, although educational attainment (especially college) and other job-related training opportunities vary considerably across nations.

Gaining a Place in the Workforce

Having made at least tentative occupational choices and acquired appropriate training or education, young adults are ready to enter the workforce. Regardless of the type of job a person enters, most adults go through an adjustment process as they enter and move through their careers (Hutchison & Niles, 2009).

Formal and Informal Preparation Before entering the workforce, people acquire certain skills, values, and attitudes, both formally and informally. Formal occupational preparation includes structured learning in high school, vocational-training programs, college, as well as on-the-job training. Informal occupational preparation takes subtler forms. It involves adopting the attitudes, norms, and role expectations that are appropriate to a particular job. Long before we begin formal preparation, we are acquiring informal norms and values from our parents and teachers, from members of the trades and professions, and even from television and movie portrayals. We learn by observing others and from our day-to-day experiences. Informal socialization is so pervasive that it often determines our choice of the formal steps taken to prepare for a career.

Expectation Meets Reality When young adults start working, they may experience what could be termed *reality shock*. During adolescence and the preparation for a career, people often have high expectations about what their work will be like and what they will accomplish. When the training ends and the job begins, novices often quickly learn that some of their expectations were unrealistic. Their work may be dull and mechanical, their supervisors may be unfair, and their peers may be difficult to work with. The goals of the job may be lost in a maze of bureaucratic politics or subject to the whims of superiors, and the job may be harder or more complex than anticipated. The shock of reality may result

Do you think that most students experience a version of reality shock when they enter college? If so, what aspects of college life might be most surprising to new students?

in a period of frustration as the young worker adjusts to the new situation.

The Role of Mentors Gradually, the entry phase usually gives way to growing competence and autonomy. In the context of work, apprentices acquire skills and self-confidence, often with the assistance of mentors, who help them learn appropriate values and norms.

Several researchers have noted the positive role of good mentors in the development of young workers (e.g., Brewer, 2012; Ramaswami & Dreher, 2007; Tonidandel, Avery, & Phillips, 2007). Mentors perform teaching and training roles. They sponsor the young workers' advancement. They serve as models for social behavior, as well as work-related behavior. Generally, they ease the transition to independent work status. Mentors, however, are easier for some workers to find than they are for others. Women in high-level and technical careers still sometimes have difficulty finding a mentor because of the relatively few women who have ascended to positions at the top level in such fields. Also, the mentoring experience, although generally positive, is not always a benefit in one's career development (Tolar, 2012). For example, both men and women can learn from opposite-sex mentors, but issues of sexuality can get in the way. In an effort to help more women achieve executive, administrative, and managerial roles, it has been suggested that one of the most successful strategies would be to promote a formal, company-based system of mentor relationships (Young, Cady, & Foxon, 2006).

Achievement at Midcareer For most young adults, the midcareer period is a time of consolidation; work becomes routine and job-related expectations are clear. Typically, once people select a career and establish a path within it, they usually forget about attractive alternate careers and instead buckle down and strive for advancement and success. For those who do well, the mentor often is left behind, as the person becomes more autonomous in the job and may even serve as a mentor for others.

Climbing the ladder of success generally, however, is not as easy as anticipated. The higher one climbs, the less room there is for advancement. Hence, by their early 40s, some workers become disillusioned and somewhat cynical. For most people, however, the plateau that often comes in midcareer is not necessarily crucial to life satisfaction. Instead, other areas of life—such as family, volunteer work, and recreation—become more important and allow for personal fulfillment and satisfaction. In addition, some people reevaluate their work at this point, perhaps making a change to an entirely different occupation. A teacher, for example, may decide to retrain as a computer operator and undertake additional schooling in order to change career directions. Indeed, given the U.S. economic transition from a manufacturing to an information-based economy and the frequency with which people change companies and change jobs, such midcareer shifts are becoming more common. Thus, traditional models of work are being reexamined and updated to accommodate such changes.

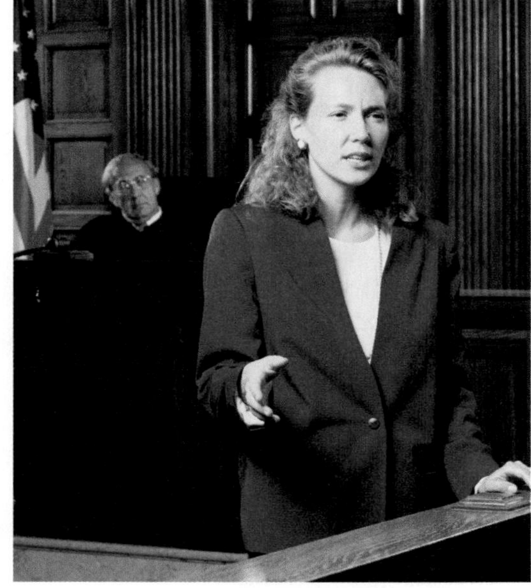

Career choice is often a defining feature in self-concept. By choosing to become a lawyer, this young woman also has elected a defined occupational course for her professional life.

Careers and Career Choices

In today's economy, individuals are faced with a staggering array of career options. How do people, at whatever stage in life, choose which job or career to pursue? Sometimes people enter careers after a thorough self-inquiry process, which involves the exploration of various types of work. The field of **career counseling** has emerged to help people select jobs that will be a good match to their talents and interests.

Holland's Theory of Careers Finding a job that is a good match to one's talents and interests is no small task. One method that is sometimes used by career counselors is to classify jobs into categories that represent different types of work and to attempt to match these jobs to an individual's personality style. Perhaps the most widely used method of job matching is derived from John Holland's theory of careers.

Holland (1996, 1997) proposed that individuals can be categorized into six career-related personality types: *realistic, investigative, artistic, social, enterprising,* and *conventional* (see Table 13-6). Furthermore, jobs also can be categorized according to the personal characteristics they require. The key for career placement is to find a person–job match. For example, a person who has high social and low investigative interests would be much better matched to a career as a social worker than to one as a medical technologist. Through the process of career

career counseling
A career field that attempts to match the talents and interests of individuals to the characteristics of a job

Watch *Discover Me: Match Personalities to Careers* on **MyDevelopmentLab**

Table 13-6 Holland's Theory of Careers

Type	Characteristics	Representative Career
Realistic	• Robust • Practical • Physically strong and active • Good motor skills	Carpenter
Investigative	• Introspective • Analytical • Curious • Task oriented	Medical technologist
Artistic	• Unconventional • Creative • Introspective • Independent	Reporter
Social	• Sociable • Responsible • Humanistic • Sometimes religious	Public health nurse
Enterprising	• High verbal abilities • Popular • Self-confident • High energy	Realtor
Conventional	• Conscientious • Efficient • Obedient • Orderly	Secretary

SOURCE: Adapted from "Relative importance of personality and general mental ability in mangers' judgments of applicant qualifications," by W. S. Dunn, M. R. Barnick, and D. S. Ones, 1995, *Journal of Applied Psychology, 80*(4), 500–509.

counseling, individuals can become more aware of their basic interests and preferences and can use this knowledge to make informed career choices. Although both people and jobs typically are more complex than Holland's model implies, the idea that people work best in jobs that match their interests and personalities is well supported in career development literature (Gottfredson & Johnstun, 2009; Herr, Cramer, & Niles, 2004; see the box Try This! Exploring the Type of Career Best Matched to You.

Occupational Choice and Preparation

People, of course, elect an occupation or a job for a variety of reasons, not just because it promises to be a good "fit" to their personality. Often an individual's background and opportunity also enter in, sometimes to a significant degree. For example, in times of recession and high unemployment people may not have much choice and may be forced to focus on simply finding some kind of job that will make ends meet. Under such conditions, it is not uncommon to hear about individuals who want to be architects or musicians but instead wind up as civil servants or hospital workers, depending on what jobs are available. Alternatively, people without definite plans or with varied interests and abilities may take any job that is available and frequently change jobs.

Watch *Career and Personality* on **MyDevelopmentLab**

Sometimes people let family pressures determine their choice of a career. Some children are groomed to take over family businesses or to follow in a parent's footsteps, although they might have preferred to pursue a different career. The need to support a spouse or children also may cause people to look for a job in a different field than they would choose if they did not have these constraints. In addition, one's gender or ethnicity sometimes can limit the available career options.

Gender and Ethnicity For a variety of reasons, women and members of some minority groups are overrepresented in lower-status jobs and in lower-paying jobs, and they are underrepresented in more highly paid professions, as shown in Table 13-7 (Leicht, 2008; U.S. Census, 2012). Researchers explain these discrepancies in two ways. One explanation is that individuals make early choices that ultimately determine what occupations they can or cannot pursue. For example, in the United States, Blacks and Hispanics are less likely to finish high school than are Whites, and those who drop out cannot compete for the jobs that require a high school or college education. Women may limit their choices if they question their competence in the sciences and avoid careers in technology-based fields, such as engineering. Some women choose careers that will give them the flexibility to raise a family. They may choose part-time work, move in and out of the job market during their child-rearing years, or look for jobs that involve limited stress and time pressure—which also have limited career and financial potential. Role modeling by parents may also influence career choice.

Do you think colleges and universities should actively encourage women and members of minority groups to enter occupations that historically have been saturated by White men? Should such institutions actively encourage men to enter female-dominated occupations such as teaching and nursing? Why or why not?

A second explanation for these occupational patterns is discrimination. Women and members of some minority groups may be subtly (or not so subtly) channeled into some jobs rather than others, in spite of federal equal opportunity requirements. Some research indicates, for example, that the better positions still tend to be given to men more frequently than to women—even when women have equal skills (Bendl, 2010; Bobbitt-Zeher, 2011). Promotions also may not be equally available. Although women and minorities continue to make gains in the workplace, education and skills that predict high salaries for White men frequently do not result in equally high salaries for Blacks, for Hispanics, or for women. In the next section, we take a closer look at work and gender.

Table 13-7 Representation in Various Occupations of Women of All Ethnicities and of People Who Identify Themselves as Black or Hispanic, United States, 2010

	Percentage of Total			
Occupation	**Women**	**Black**	**Hispanic**	**Asian**
Total employed	47.2	10.8	14.3	4.8
Dental assistants	97.5	5.7	20.0	5.6
Teachers, prekindergarten and kindergarten	97.0	13.4	9.6	2.7
Secretaries and administrative assistants	96.1	8.6	9.4	1.9
Teacher aides	92.4	12.7	15.1	2.9
Registered nurses	91.1	12.0	4.9	7.5
Maids and house cleaners	89.0	16.3	40.8	5.0
Nursing aides, orderlies, home health aides	88.2	34.6	14.7	4.0
Teachers, elementary school	81.8	9.3	7.3	2.4
Social workers	80.8	22.9	11.3	3.3
Bus drivers	47.0	25.1	12.3	2.2
Teachers, college and university	45.9	6.3	5.0	11.0
Postal service clerks	45.3	29.5	11.1	8.3
Janitor and office-building cleaners	33.2	17.1	30.9	3.2
Physicians and surgeons	32.3	5.8	8.8	15.7
Correctional officers	26.1	22.0	13.3	1.2
CEOs	25.5	2.8	4.8	3.2
Architects	24.4	2.1	7.8	1.9
Butchers and fish processing workers	21.2	14.0	36.2	10.4
Civil engineers	9.7	4.9	6.9	8.9
Aircraft pilots and flight engineers	5.2	1.0	6.3	1.0
Carpenters	1.4	4.0	25.7	1.4

SOURCE: From Table 616, "Employed civilians by occupation, sex, race, and Hispanic origin: 2010," in *Statistical abstract of the United States: 2012*, retrieved from http://www.census/gov/prod/2011pubs/12statab/labor.pdf.

REVIEW THE FACTS 13-4

1. The path that a person's working life follows is called the ________.
2. Cite the two major ways work has changed since the 1960s.
3. At what point in an individual's career is reality shock typically experienced?
   a. in high school, when planning a career
   b. soon after entering a career
   c. in midcareer
   d. when nearing retirement
4. According to Holland's theory of careers, people should seek jobs that
   a. pay well.
   b. have good working conditions.
   c. provide a good "fit" with their personalities.
   d. promise a long-term career path that is not likely to change.
5. Suggest two reasons why women may be paid less than men.

Practice on **MyDevelopmentLab**

WORK AND GENDER

In the United States today, the establishment of a job or career is a significant developmental event in the lives of most young adults. Work implies developmental consequences for U.S. women in particular, partly because—whether working or not—women are more likely than men to assume the primary family responsibilities. Thus, family cycle development is tied closely to how women approach their vocational goals. Although women have always been a part of the U.S. workforce, especially since the 1970s the entry of women into the world of work has been increasing steadily, with important consequences for the family. As more women have entered the U.S. labor force, roles for men and women have changed, both at home and at work. Thus, it is appropriate that we close this chapter with a brief discussion of work and gender.

Changes in Women's Work Patterns

Paid employment for women is not a new phenomenon, of course. Women have always worked outside the home, especially during periods of economic hardship. Before the rise of industrialism in the early 1800s, men and women often combined their efforts in family businesses and farms, as some still do. Not until the late 19th century did men come to be regarded as the "natural" providers for their families (Padavic & Reskin, 2002), while women cared for the children and the home. In modern times, women entered the workforce in record numbers during World War II when large numbers of male workers were overseas fighting. At the war's end, women's workforce participation fell back to make way for returning veterans. In the 1970s, however, the picture changed again as more and more women entered the workforce and established careers.

Do you believe typical work roles for men in the 21st century in the United States are becoming more flexible to allow them greater opportunity to assume family-care responsibilities? What evidence can you cite in support of your opinion?

One of the most notable developments in the employment world, in fact, is the significant increase in the percentage of women in the U.S. workforce in recent decades. In 1950—5 years following the end of WWII—about one in three U.S. women ages 16 and over were in the workforce. Today, that percentage has grown to nearly 60%. In addition, today most women do not enter the labor force until they are finished with high school, and many wait until they are finished with college or additional technical education before they begin their jobs. For example, compared to 1970, when only about one-fifth of women in the civilian labor force had gone to college or technical school, today about two-thirds of working women fall into this category (see Figure 13-14). Thus, although the 2010 labor force participation rate for all women ages 16 and over is 58.6%, that rate is 75.2% for women ages 25 to 54 (U.S. Bureau of Labor, 2011a). This compares to labor participation rates for men of 71.2% and 89.3%, respectively.

As these statistics demonstrate, today women in the United States are almost as likely to work at paid jobs as are men. In 2010, women made up about 47% of the labor force, and this percentage appears to be slowly increasing. For example, since 1970, the percent of women in the civilian labor force increased steadily until about 1990, at which time it began to level off. However, the percent of men in the civilian labor force has slowly but steadily declined since 1970 (U.S. Bureau of Labor, 2011b; see Figure 13-15). The economic downturn that began in 2008 seems to be fueling this effect, although it remains to be seen how this trend might change as the economy recovers. The most recent economic downturn also has hit members of racial and ethnic minority groups harder than it has White workers. For example, although historically White women have been the group least likely to work outside the home, today White women are actually more likely to have jobs than are Black or Hispanic women, owing in part to layoffs among those least advantaged in the workforce (U.S. Bureau of Labor, 2011c).

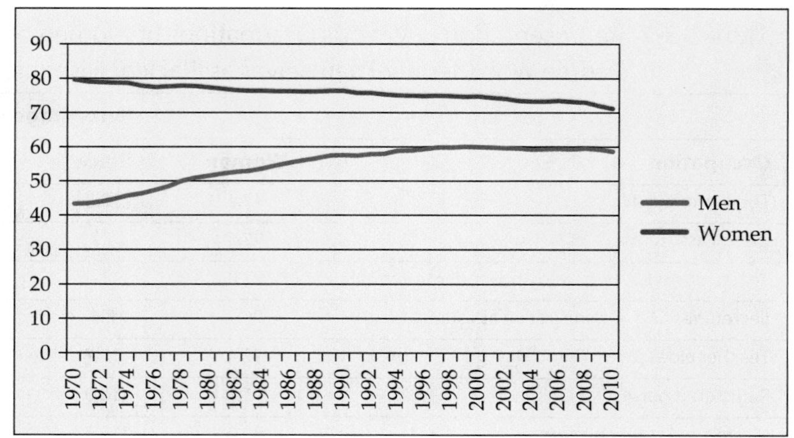

FIGURE 13-15 Percent of Men and Women in the U.S. Civilian Labor Force, 1970–2010.

SOURCE: Table 2, "Employment status of the civilian noninstitutional population 16 years and over by sex, 1970–2010 annual averages," in *Women in the labor force: A databook (2011 edition)*, U.S. Bureau of Labor Statistics, 2011, retrieved from http://www.bls.gov/cps/wlf-databook2011.htm.

Also important to consider are the gains women have been making among highly compensated occupations. Today, women hold positions of authority and influence in all economic sectors (see again Table 13-7). For example, in 2010, women made up more than half of all medical scientists; nearly a third of all lawyers, physicians, and surgeons; a quarter of all dentists and corporate CEOs; and two-thirds of all psychologists. Of those employed as managers in professional and related occupations, slightly more than half were women (U.S. Census Bureau, 2011a). Furthermore, these figures are generally about two to three times higher than they were only two decades ago, documenting the gains women have made as equal working partners with men. However, women still hold the majority of jobs in many low-paying occupations, such as teaching assistants, maids and housekeepers, and secretaries. In fact, in 2010, one out of every two women was employed in a low-paying, low-advancement job. Moreover, women still make less money on average than men—in 2010 about 81 cents for every dollar men earn (U.S. Department of Labor, 2011). Although this percentage has grown dramatically since 1979—the first year these statistics were tracked, and when women earned 62% of what men earned—the percentage has remained static at about 80 to 81% since 2004. Not surprisingly, there are racial/ethnic differences in this so-called "gender gap" in earnings. Whereas White women earned 81% as much as their White male counterparts in 2010, Asian women earned 83%, Hispanic women earned 91%, and Black women earned 94%. Unfortunately, for the most part this is not due to the high quality of jobs held by minority women, but rather to the abundance of low-paying jobs held by Black and Hispanic men (U.S. Department of Labor, 2011).

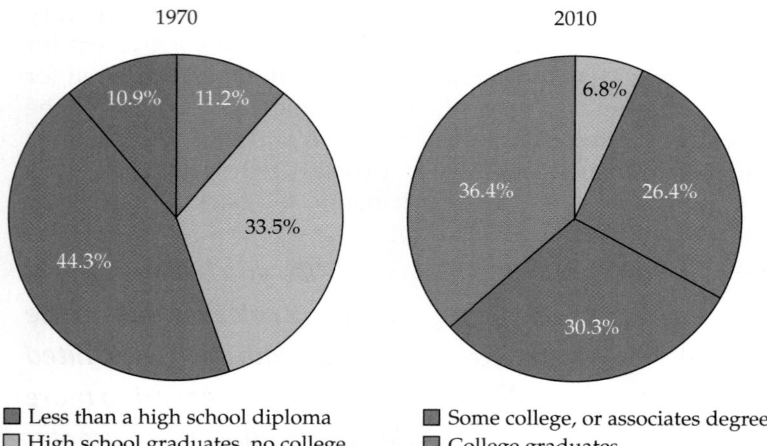

FIGURE 13-14 Distribution of Women in Workforce and Education, 1970 and 2010

SOURCE: "Women at work," Bureau of Labor Statistics, March 2011, retrieved from http://www.bls.gov/spotlight/2011/women.

The Many Meanings of Work

Like men, women participate in the world of work for many reasons; for both men and women, the primary reason is usually economic necessity. Single mothers are often the sole source of income for their families; even many married couples could not make ends meet without income from both spouses. Today, in two-parent families, wives' earnings make up nearly 40% of total family income, compared to only about 27% in 1980 (U.S. Bureau of Labor Statistics, 2011d). Like many men, many women find satisfaction and fulfillment in employment outside the home. They find their work interesting and challenging; they consider it an opportunity for self-direction or increased responsibility; they like the benefits of salary, greater future security, and the possibility of advancement (Whitbourne & Whitbourne, 2011).

Whatever the reasons, working women tend to be both physically and psychologically healthier than nonworking women (Barnett & Hyde, 2001), even into later adulthood (Vandewater & Stewart, 2006). Taking on multiple roles has been shown to contribute to, not detract from, mental health. Furthermore, women who enjoy their work benefit more from it. This may be one reason that professional women actually gain more physical and psychological benefits from their work than do clerical workers, despite the greater responsibilities and stresses of these professional women's jobs. Given the potential role strains, family problems, and stress, it is surprising that there is virtually no evidence indicating that employment, regardless of the types of work, is detrimental to women's physical or psychological health.

The Role of Women in Careers

Women who work outside the home do not necessarily follow the same type of career trajectories that are typical for men. Instead they follow a variety of career paths. Although an increasing number of women follow the traditional male pattern of pursuing a career without interruption, others stop work when they have children, perhaps returning to the workforce later. Another career pattern is elected by those women who wish to devote themselves exclusively to raising a family in early adulthood but establish careers outside the home after the last child has entered first grade or perhaps later, when the child enters college. In the 21st century, the average woman can devote 10 years to full-time child care while her children are young and still have 35 years left to enter the workforce, establish a career, or pursue other interests. Perhaps not surprisingly, many women still interrupt work at least temporarily to take care of children, whereas men rarely do so. These interruptions contribute to the wage gap between men and women.

Although there are real differences in the ways in which men and women approach work, there also are persistent myths and stereotypes. One such myth is that women in managerial, professional, or technical positions are less willing to take risks or make the sacrifices associated with career advancement. Another is that women do not want, need, or expect the same salaries as men, even when they accept a promotion. Myths such as these may contribute to gender disparities in pay and working conditions for women. Women do not have less motivation to achieve or less specific career plans than men. Women do, however, often choose occupations that allow for more flexibility. Consequently, women in traditionally *female* professions, such as education, social work, and nursing, may sometimes be perceived as less ambitious because they expect their jobs to accommodate their marriage and family responsibilities. Increasingly, men are choosing to work in these historically female occupations, presumably for many of the same reasons that women have elected them—good working conditions, flexibility, decent pay, and interesting, meaningful work. It remains to be seen how the influx of men into traditionally female positions may change the nature of work, and of pay, in these occupations. Women in traditionally *male* professions, such as business, law, and medicine, generally have career plans that are very similar to those of men pursuing the same careers.

Women who hold jobs outside the home usually are afforded quite wide latitude in how they define the centrality of their careers to their lives. Some women find homemaking meaningful and fulfilling and they view their jobs as contributing little to their positive view of themselves; others consider homemaking to be sheer drudgery and they center their view of themselves largely on their professional accomplishments. In one survey (Pietromonaco, Manis, & Markus, 1987), reports of self-esteem, life satisfaction, and self-perception differed dramatically between working women who were career oriented and working women who were not. Those who described themselves as career oriented were much happier and had higher self-esteem and more positive self-concepts when they were employed full-time than when they were temporarily unemployed or were working at part-time jobs or jobs that underutilized their skills. The results were quite different for women who described themselves as not being career oriented. Their self-esteem and life satisfaction were not related to whether they were employed full-time or part-time.

The Dynamics of Dual-Earner Couples

Regardless of why they work, the fact remains that most women in the United States today are employed. The dramatic increase in the number of women in the workforce has led to an increasingly common phenomenon known as the **dual-earner couple**, or *dual-earner marriage,* where a married or unmarried

dual-earner couple
A married or unmarried couple sharing a household in which both contribute to family income as members of the paid labor force

TRY THIS!

Exploring the Type of Career Best Matched to You

According to John Holland (1996, 1997), most people can be categorized in terms of six basic personality types, each representing a common outcome of growing up in our culture. Although all people, to a greater or lesser degree, are a blend of these types, most can be identified as fitting better into one type than others. Similarly, different types of jobs, which also involve many different skill sets, can be categorized according to their most important dimensions. The key to career success, according to person–job match models like Holland's, is to find a career that involves the same kinds of skills and tasks that you possess and prefer.

To explore how your personality type might be matched to the job or career you either have or intend to have, try ranking yourself on the six basic Holland types, which are represented in the following table. First, consider your own characteristics. What do you like to do? What kinds of skills do you think are your strongest? What kinds of tasks do you least like to do? Rank from 1 (highest) to 6 (lowest) your strongest attributes by circling the appropriate number next to each of the Holland types noted.

Now, look at the list of representative jobs in the table. Although there are many jobs that fit into each of the six job types in Holland's theory, the ones in this table should give you some idea about what kinds of work fit into each type. Which jobs appeal most to you? Which would you most like to have? Which are least attractive? Which would you most want to avoid? As you did before, now rank, from 1 (highest) to 6 (lowest) the job types you would prefer to have.

Holland Type		Characteristics of People of This Type		Representative Jobs of This Type	Match?
Realistic	1 2 3 4 5 6	Prefer systematic manipulation of tools; robust, practical, physically strong and active; have athletic interests; good motor skills; poorer verbal and interpersonal skills	1 2 3 4 5 6	Carpenter, corrections officer, electrician, farmer, radiology technician, tool and die maker	Yes? No?
Investigative	1 2 3 4 5 6	Have a scientific orientation; introspective, analytical, curious, independent, somewhat unconventional values; task-oriented; dislike repetitious work; see themselves as reserved and lacking in leadership abilities	1 2 3 4 5 6	Biologist, internist, pediatrician, scientific researcher, social scientist, electronics technician	Yes? No?
Artistic	1 2 3 4 5 6	Enjoy creative expression; introspective but value individual expression; unconventional; nonconforming; original; independent	1 2 3 4 5 6	Art teacher, author, broadcaster, librarian, reporter, poet, foreign language teacher	Yes? No?

couple share a household in which both contribute to family income as members of the paid labor force. Today, millions of women fully share the provider role with their husbands, and dual-earner households are now the norm (U.S. Department of Labor, 2011).

There are obvious advantages to dual-earner marriages. A higher total income makes possible a higher standard of living. There is more money for daily necessities, emergencies, a better place to live, and a better education for the children. Fathers benefit by playing a more active role in the family, especially with respect to interacting with children. For college-educated dual-earner couples in particular, perhaps the most important benefit is the wife's equal chance to gain self-fulfillment through a job or career.

There are, however, stresses and role conflicts. These stem in part from the need to juggle the roles of the wife as a worker, the husband as a worker, and both partners as family members. At times, one role may require more time and energy than the others. Especially during early adulthood, when parents must accommodate both the significant needs of their young children and their own struggles to establish a career, roles often collide, forcing the couple to set priorities and resolve conflicts. Because work demands are seldom negotiable, these discussions most often center around how household and child-care responsibilities will be shared by the working parents.

Domestic tasks—especially child care—are shared more equally in some dual-earner families than in others, and the national trend is for a more gender-balanced distribution of domestic tasks (Shirley & Wallace, 2004). Nevertheless, most U.S. women who work still tend to have the primary responsibility for housework and child care, and any perceived

Reflect on What You Observed

In the final column on the right side of the table, note whether you have a "match" between how you rated your characteristics and how you rated the various kinds of jobs in each type. If your rankings matched perfectly (say, a *5* and a *5*), or if they only differed by 1 or 2 points (a *6* and a *4*), consider that a match. If they differed by 3 or more (a *5* and a *1*), consider that as not a match. How well did your personality type match up to the career you have or to the types of jobs you might like to have?

Consider the Issues

Many theories about careers emphasize that an important dimension in choosing a career involves matching the skills and preferences of the person to the skills demanded and the working conditions of the job. Do you think that the characteristics, or personality types, described in Holland's theory represent an important classification scheme according to which people can be categorized? Would there be other ways to identify how people differ with respect to their basic values and preferences? Do you think that matching people to jobs according to a person–job match model like Holland's provides a useful way of counseling people about career selection? Do you believe that certain types of people fit best into certain types of jobs? What kind of job do you think represents a perfect match for you? Would your own person–job match be consistent with Holland's view? If not, why do you think you are attracted to this job?

Holland Type		Characteristics of People of This Type		Representative Jobs of This Type	Match?
Social	1 2 3 4 5 6	Like to work around others and in groups; sociable, responsible, humanistic, and sometimes religious; have effective verbal and interpersonal skills; solve problems through interpersonal relationships rather than through physical or intellectual means	1 2 3 4 5 6	Elementary education teacher, priest or minister, playground director, public health nurse, licensed practical nurse, special education teacher	Yes? No?
Enterprising	1 2 3 4 5 6	Like to be leaders and influence others; high energy, high in verbal abilities; popular, self-confident, and sociable; drawn to positions of power; avoid tasks that involve sustained intellectual effort or conformity	1 2 3 4 5 6	Athletic director, beautician, department store manager, funeral director, realtor, traveling salesperson, personnel director	Yes? No?
Conventional	1 2 3 4 5 6	Conscientious, efficient, obedient, orderly, conforming, and practical; value material possessions, like well-ordered environments and systematic tasks; prefer subordinate positions that involve clear directions and little physical exertion or interpersonal skills	1 2 3 4 5 6	Accountant, dental assistant, hospital records clerk, production manager, secretary, statistician	Yes? No?

unfairness in child-care responsibilities is especially likely to result in distress for mothers. Mothers, for example, are much more likely than fathers to "multitask," performing child care and housework at the same time (Offer & Schneider, 2011). Working night shifts or rotating shifts, which some parents do to reduce their reliance on child care, is particularly likely to cause problems, as parents who work different hours have little time together to work through decisions or share relaxing time with each other (Perry-Jenkins, Goldberg, Pierce, & Sayer, 2007). Parents who return to work part-time also are especially vulnerable because they may be reluctant to ask their partners for help at home, feeling that they should pick up the responsibility for household and child-care tasks, yet they may find that the combination of tasks is exhausting (Goldberg & Perry-Jenkins, 2004). Indeed, some people have suggested that working parents really have two full-time jobs—when they come home from work they begin a "second shift" of child care, housework, cooking, and other tasks that managing a household requires (Hochschild & Machung, 2012). Balancing work and family responsibilities requires long days; during the evenings and weekends, working parents often face a mountain of household chores—everything from child care to cooking to laundry to cleaning.

Do you believe that the partner who has the lower-paying job should assume more responsibility for family obligations and child care? Why or why not?

It would seem logical and fair to assume that dual-earner couples should share household chores equally, but that is rarely the case (Hochschild & Machung, 2012; van Hooff,

CURRENT ISSUES

Juggling Work and Family Roles—The Special Challenge for Low-Income Dual-Career Couples

The dual-earner family is now the norm in the United States, particularly for young adults in their 30s. Dual-earner couples must work out a partnership and negotiate roles of who does what and when. Work schedules, child-care arrangements, time for themselves, and who assumes responsibility for which household chores and roles must be regularly negotiated by the couple. Furthermore, the decisions reached must be seen as fair. How do individuals balance their roles as parent, spouse, and worker?

Generally, negotiations between partners in dual-earner families do not take place without a history. Each adult comes to family tasks with expectations not only about what men and women should and can do but also about the importance of each person's work. Each partner also has a particular set of skills and interests. For some couples, the most critical negotiations may focus on who will manage the family's financial obligations; for others these may center on who will prepare meals, help with homework, or shuttle children to school and events. Some families also must negotiate how much help they will need and are able to afford. Will the grandparents be actively involved? Is full-time day care an acceptable option? Each couple must work out an agreeable arrangement for how the family will be cared for given the confines of each person's work schedule and job responsibilities.

At all income levels, it is difficult for both men and women to juggle work and family responsibilities. However, especially for those whose incomes fall at the lower end of the socioeconomic scale, the pressures associated with handling the demands of the family, along with those imposed by work, may be especially difficult. Low wages, difficult work hours, nonflexible schedules, periods of layoff, and difficulty finding affordable child care arrangements, among many other factors, pose issues that low-income, dual-career couples must address (Crouter & Booth, 2004; Plotnick, 2011). For some families, the big problems of dovetailing work schedules, paying bills, finding affordable child care, finding affordable housing in an acceptable neighborhood, and having any free time for themselves may not have reasonable solutions.

One increasingly familiar challenge faced by low-income dual-career families involves the expansion of the traditional 40-hour workweek to meet the demands of a near 24/7 economy (Presser, 2004). Shopping and services available 24 hours a day and 7 days a week may be great for consumers, but the toll on workers—many of whom have jobs on the low end of the wage scale—can be damaging to family life and to the worker's health. Young people with low seniority and low income do much of the night shift and weekend shift work. These are often exactly the same individuals who are parents with small children. Researchers have long understood that "shift work" can have negative effects on the individuals who work irregular or off-peak hours, but what are the consequences for the family lives of these workers?

To investigate questions such as these, Marie Perry-Jenkins has been directing a longitudinal study of 150 working-class dual-earner families (Perry-Jenkins, 2004). In her study, Perry-Jenkins has found that about one-third of dual-earner families with children have at least one "off-shift" worker. Although, in general, most off-shift workers do not prefer this schedule, among low-income two-parent families, as many as one-third of those who work on off-shift hours actually choose such a schedule so that another family member can perform the child care. When one parent works from 9:00 a.m. to 5:00 p.m. and another works 11:00 p.m. to 7:00 a.m., child-care needs are reduced or eliminated. However, there may be other costs associated with the juggling and stresses such schedules require.

Perry-Jenkins's investigation of the impact of off-shift work on dual-career couples included interviewing parents about their daily lives and then following up with surveys and a second interview a year later. Results indicate that in the early stages of parenting when children are young, off-shift work was more detrimental to maternal health and well-being than to paternal health. Mothers working off-shifts got less sleep and had more difficulty juggling baby care with work demands, and they were more often depressed than those on regular work schedules. A year later, shift work for either the mother or father typically began to interfere with the couple's relationship with each other—wives reported less marital love. By the second year of shift work, fathers also were reporting less marital love. Clearly, over time, the quality of couple's relationships can deteriorate as difficult work–family arrangements take their toll (Perry-Jenkins, Goldberg, Pierce, & Sayer, 2007; Sheely, 2010).

High work demands affect the larger family system as well. Many low-income couples use other relatives for low-cost child care. However, these arrangements may have a social cost. New parents often feel indebted to their own parents, friends, and other relatives who help with child care; they feel obligated to pay back the gifts of time and care. Furthermore, when others care for children, the kind of care the children receive—and the lessons and rules the children are taught—are often out of parents' control. Sometimes this causes conflicts between the parents and the family members who are providing the free care; sometimes the conflicts are between the couple who may disagree about what constitutes acceptable arrangements for the children. Regardless, the stresses and strains of negotiating such complex and conflict-prone arrangements can take a toll on everyone concerned.

What can be done? The issues involved are not only complex, but they also are incredibly difficult to resolve. What possible solutions do you see? How would you advise a low-income dual-career couple to cope with the demands that work and family imply?

2011). In fact, when the gender gap in housework narrows, it most often is because women are doing less rather than because men are doing more (Shirley & Wallace, 2004). Studies have shown that even when both spouses are employed full-time, wives continue to do two to three times more of the daily housework than their husbands (Bianchi, Milkie, Sayer, & Robinson, 2000). Studies also have shown that the work men do around the house generally decreases as their income increases (Antial & Cottin, 1988), although how housework is defined provides some qualification of this result (Eichler & Albanese, 2007).

In addition to coping with the volume of work to be done, there are other strains in dual-earner marriages. For example, many dual-earner couples report experiencing severe role conflicts in their attempts to meet both work and family responsibilities. Sometimes it is very difficult to keep up

Parents in a dual-earner family often experience the understandable stresses of multiple roles and responsibilities. Time pressures of demanding and conflicting schedules can affect children as well as the adults in such families.

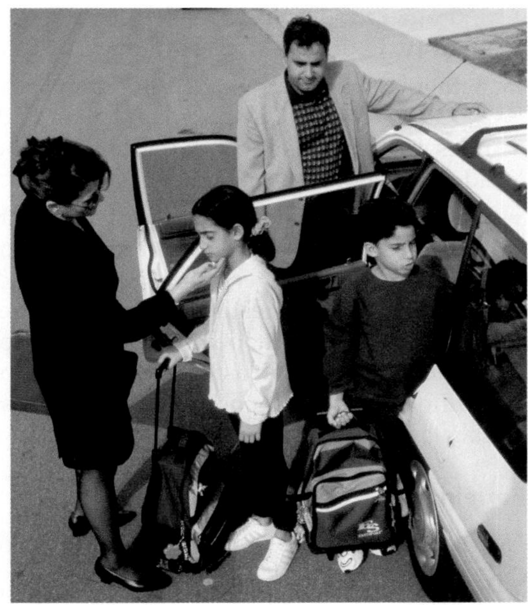

with the demands of the job while at the same time meeting the needs of the family. Not surprisingly, such conflicts stem from job demands, work hours, family and work-scheduling conflicts, and family crises. Although both men and women in dual-earner couples experience these conflicts, women typically report higher levels of conflict between work and family roles. The role conflict experienced by professional women is particularly acute when they work long hours and are under time pressures. Especially when family income is low, stress is often a part of daily life (see the box Current Issues: Juggling Work and Family Roles—the Special Challenge for Low-Income Dual-Career Couples)

What factors might explain why many people feel uncomfortable about wives earning as much or more income than their husbands? How do you feel about this issue?

Stress resulting from work–family role conflict is somewhat mediated by the fact that women who work are the norm today, rather than the exception. Thus, mothers who work outside the home are no longer perceived as "odd" or "selfish" in the way they might have been considered in decades past. However, there is still some disapproval of mothers of very young children working full-time, especially if their economic need is not acute. In addition, even in two-earner families, traditional values often persist. In one study, 78% of the men and 65% of the women recognized the necessity of the wives' income, but they were uncomfortable about it (Deutsch, 1999). Perceptions about role conflict and fairness are important—perhaps even more important than reality. Where overall marital satisfaction is concerned, how fair each spouse *perceives* the distribution of labor to be can be as important as the actual amount of housework each spouse does (Braun, Lewin-Epstein, Stier, & Baumgärtner, 2008; Goldberg & Perry-Jenkins, 2004).

Regardless of how working parents negotiate their household responsibilities, concerns typically are accentuated when dual-career parents have difficulty finding adequate, affordable day care for their children. Parents may feel particularly uneasy about leaving a new baby in someone else's care; yet, they may be subject to financial pressures that require them to do so as early in the infant's life as is possible. When a new baby is born, the mother typically is granted some medical leave, usually not extending past 6 weeks. However, this is seldom enough time to make all of the adjustments necessary to provide for the extra demands of caring for an infant, especially if the child is the first in the family and child-care decisions must be negotiated for the first time. Fathers seldom have the option of paternity leave, although the Family and Medical Leave Act of 1993 (FMLA) does apply to pregnancy, childbirth, and adoption, so families do have the option of taking some time away from work to establish new routines. However, **family leave** extends for only 12 weeks and—more important—is generally unpaid, so many families simply cannot afford to elect this option. For some families, the best option is for one of the parents—usually the mother—to quit working, at least for a period of time while the children are young.

Yet, as we have seen, this may not be the best option, especially for the parent who stays at home. Financially, most families have difficulty maintaining their lifestyle when one of the working parents no longer holds a paying job. When there is less money than before, tensions can arise and conflict may become more likely. Furthermore, despite all the strains, women, like men, generally gain substantial benefits from working. Why might this be? One possibility is social support. Women can turn to their colleagues at work for friendship, advice, and emotional bolstering. Work also can contribute to positive self-esteem; this is the case for both men and women who take pride in what they are able to accomplish in their jobs. Work, too, can provide a sense of control when things are going poorly at home (Rodin & Ickovics, 1990; Vandewater & Stewart, 2006). Thus, work may serve as a buffer against family related stresses, especially for women, but also for men. Work also can serve as a stabilizing force as young adults make the transition to middle age. We will discuss the period of middle adulthood and the physical, cognitive, personality, and sociocultural development that takes place in this period in the chapters that follow.

family leave
Leave required by law for the purpose of dealing with family affairs and problems

REVIEW THE FACTS 13-5

1. Men first came to be considered the "natural providers" for their families
   a. in the 1600s. b. in the late 1800s.
   c. after World War I. d. after World War II.
2. Since the 1970s, has the increase in the percentage of women in the workforce been greater for White or for Black women?
3. Today, women comprise _________ of the U.S. labor force.
   a. 37% b. 47%
   c. 57% d. 67%
4. For every dollar U.S. men earn, U.S. women earn about _________.
5. In comparison to women who do not work, working women typically have _________ physical health and _________ psychological health.
   a. worse; better b. better; worse
   c. worse; worse d. better; better
6. In the United States, the Family Leave Act guarantees all employees a minimum of _________ weeks of _________ leave per year.
   a. 2; paid b. 6; unpaid
   c. 8; paid d. 12; unpaid

✓ Practice on **MyDevelopmentLab**

CHAPTER SUMMARY

Self, Family, and Work

How is the self *generally defined by young adults?*

- As people become adults, they focus on establishing intimate relationships, finding a job or career, and becoming more comfortable with their personal identity. Finding a satisfying intimate relationship and a career involves role changes, although such adjustments are usually more subtle than in earlier stages of life.
- According to Abraham Maslow, the ultimate goal of self-development is *self-actualization,* which is realizing one's full development by utilizing one's talents and abilities. Life circumstances, however, often require people to focus on more immediate needs that are lower in the hierarchy of needs.
- Carl Rogers noted that personal development is thwarted when *conditions of worth,* which involve the withdrawal of affection and approval unless behavior conforms to another's expectations, are placed on an individual. Like Maslow, Rogers also believed that individuals are motivated toward self-fulfillment and self-actualization. Positive development is encouraged when people are treated with warmth and acceptance, which Rogers called *unconditional positive regard.*
- Mihály Csíkszentmihályi has proposed a concept called *flow,* which is similar to self-actualization. This perspective and other modern perspectives on the self often focus on identity, which includes both one's traits and one's roles.
- Achieving independence from parents is an important aspect of identity development in early adulthood. Family roles are often the most important component in young adults' identities.
- Work usually provides another important context in identity development. When jobs are dull, people typically focus on their *extrinsic factors,* such as salary and convenience. When jobs are interesting and provide the opportunity for personal growth, people more often focus on the job's *intrinsic factors,* such as the opportunity to achieve and make a difference. When jobs emphasize intrinsic factors, job satisfaction and performance are often higher.

Forming Close Relationships

How does friendship in young adulthood differ from love?

- Friendships are important in early adulthood, as they are throughout life.
- Erik Erikson emphasized the importance of establishing a meaningful intimate relationship in early adulthood. Nowadays, there is greater flexibility and acceptance of the various ways in which intimate relationships can exist, although most adults continue to embrace traditional family choices of marriage and parenthood.

What is love, and why is it especially important to young adults?

- Robert Sternberg defined love as having three components: *intimacy* (emotional closeness), *passion* (physical attraction and arousal), and *decision/commitment* (the decision to be and stay in a relationship). Many forms of love are possible, reflecting different balances of these three components. Close relationships also can be painful or destructive.
- According to the stimulus-value-role theory, we choose our romantic partners so that we get the best "deal." Relationships begin with an initial stimulus stage in which partners make initial judgments about attraction; they then move through a value-comparisons stage, during which partners determine their compatibility; and they finally end at a role stage, which involves making long-term commitments to each other. Computer dating services take a similar approach in identifying romantic partners who provide a good match for each other.

How does choosing a romantic partner differ for young adults living in United States versus other cultures around the world?

- Choosing a romantic partner is usually left to the individual in contemporary Western cultures. However, dating and marriage customs very widely around the world, and in many cultures marriages are arranged by parents. Consequently, the concept of "being in love" is less important in these settings.

How are marriage trends changing in the United States and in other parts of the world?

- Over 90% of U.S. men and women will marry at some point, although marriage rates in the United States have been declining in recent years. Courtship and marriage customs often are heavily defined by culture.
- More U.S. couples are deciding to cohabit, with rates increasing more than tenfold since 1970. Although most cohabiting couples plan to marry, only about one-third actually do. Cohabiting is not linked to better or happier marriages, and it may be linked to less positive relationship outcomes.
- Perhaps because gay and lesbian couples cannot legally marry in most places, their cohabitation patterns more closely resemble those of married, rather than cohabiting, heterosexuals. When gay male or lesbian couples adopt or have children, these children develop in patterns like those seen in families with heterosexual parents.
- The percentages of adults who do not marry have fluctuated throughout history, often in response to historical events. Remaining single has been increasing in popularity among young adults since the 1970s, although this trend also reflects the fact that U.S. adults are choosing to marry at somewhat later ages than in previous decades.

The Family Life Cycle and Adult Development

What are the main features of the transitions that occur when a person becomes a parent?

- Parenthood involves new roles and responsibilities and calls for numerous adaptations and adjustments. In the United States, women are more likely than men to adjust their lives to give priority to parenting, although both parents usually make some adjustments.
- The transition to parenthood generally is smoother when social support is available, marital happiness is high, parents have high self-esteem, and the baby is not too difficult.
- As children grow, their needs change, and so do the demands on parents. Parents must renegotiate their own relationship as families adjust and adapt.

Why is single-parenting becoming more common in the United States, and what special challenges are often associated with this form of parenting?

- Single-parent families are becoming increasingly common in the United States, with most being headed by mothers. In 2010, 26.5% of all families with children were headed by a single parent. This trend is the result of a rising divorce rate, an increase in the number of marital separations without divorce, and an increase in the number of unmarried mothers, especially among Black women.
- Single parents are especially prone to experience stress if economic pressures are involved, and single mothers are almost twice as likely to live below the poverty line as are single fathers. Economic challenges are even more likely among Black families headed by single mothers, especially when those mothers have limited education. However, Black and Hispanic families who live in poverty are more likely to have extended families who can provide some additional support.
- In 1996, Congress enacted the Personal Responsibility and Work Opportunity Reconciliation Act (PRWORA), the first major welfare reform in 60 years. The goal of this program is to help mothers on welfare become self-sufficient workers. Early indications show that the program is quite successful, especially for mothers with some work skills and experience. However, limited and affordable day care remains a challenge for many mothers.
- Single fathers face many of the same challenges as single mothers, although they usually are better off financially.

The Occupational Cycle

How do people decide which career or job will be the best choice for them?

- An *occupational cycle* is a variable sequence of periods or stages in a worker's life. Every person's occupational cycle is unique and filled with events and decisions. Havighurst's classic model of occupational choice suggests that individuals begin to think about work early in life, perhaps even in childhood.
- Today, most people have several different jobs and may change careers in midlife. Jobs today are becoming increasingly technical.
- Before entering the workforce, people acquire formal skills (such as education or training) and informal skills (such as attitudes and expectations about work).
- The entry phase of the occupational cycle, when young adults start working, may involve reality shock as people learn that their jobs may be different than expected. Mentors often can help younger workers acquire appropriate job skills and attitudes. Women sometimes have more difficulty in finding an appropriate mentor than do men.
- For most midcareer adults, work becomes routine, and mentors often are left behind. If one's career does not advance as fast or as far as expected, sometimes the person will change careers or look for satisfaction in noncareer areas of life.
- The field of *career counseling* has emerged to help people determine which careers are best suited to their talents and interests. Holland's theory of careers involves categorizing both personality types and job requirements and finding a "match."
- Sometimes people select careers or jobs because of family expectations or economic necessity. In the United States, women are overrepresented in low-status, low-paying jobs, and underrepresented in more highly paid positions and professions. Two explanations are possible: Women choose less demanding work due to family considerations, and women may be victims of discrimination.

Work and Gender

How has work in the United States been changing for women over the past several decades?

- Most women try to combine work and family roles, often taking a more flexible approach to their careers. Women always have worked outside the home, although changing societal expectations and historical events have had an impact on the number of women in the workforce in any given era.
- Especially since the 1970s, the proportion of women in the U.S. workforce has been increasing. Although White women made up the larger share of this trend, recently—owing to the economic downturn that began in 2008—minority women are more likely than White women to be unemployed. Women now comprise about 47% of the U.S. workforce. Women are making gains in many professions formerly dominated by men.
- About half of working women have low-paying, low-advancement jobs. Women, on average, make 81 cents today for every dollar men earn.
- Women, like men, work for many reasons, including financial necessity and personal fulfillment. Working women tend to be physically and psychologically healthier than nonworking women, especially if they enjoy their work.
- Career women elect a variety of work paths. Most women still interrupt work at least temporarily to care for children, whereas men seldom do.
- Career-oriented working women have been found to be happier and have higher self-esteem than those who were unemployed, working at part-time, or working in low-skilled jobs. However, noncareer-oriented women were equally happy whether they were employed full- or part-time.

How have family members' roles changed as women have entered the workforce in increasing numbers?

- The increase of women in the labor force has produced an increase in *dual-earner couples,* who benefit from higher combined family incomes. Although fathers usually benefit because they take a more active family role, there are many stresses associated with both partners juggling family and work responsibilities.
- Women who work still assume more responsibility than men for housework and child care, especially if they work part-time. Women also report higher levels of conflict between work and family roles than do men.
- In the United States, under the Family and Medical Leave Act of 1993 (FMLA), all employees are legally entitled to 12 weeks per year of unpaid *family leave.*
- Stress in dual-earner families is common, especially when parents have difficulty finding acceptable child care.
- There is still some social disapproval of women who "choose" to work when their children are young, and some people hold traditional values that reflect discomfort about mothers who work. Nevertheless, women can gain substantial benefits from working, perhaps due to the social support work colleagues provide and to the contribution working makes to a woman's self-esteem. Work may serve as a buffer against family-related stresses, especially for women, and it can be a stabilizing force in young adults' lives.

KEY TERMS

self-actualization (p. 362)
conditions of worth (p. 362)
unconditional positive regard (p. 362)
extrinsic factors (p. 364)
intrinsic factors (p. 364)
intimacy (p. 365)
passion (p. 366)
decision/commitment (p. 366)
occupational cycle (p. 377)
career counseling (p. 379)
dual-earner couple (p. 383)
family leave (p. 387)

MyVirtualLife

What decisions would you make while living your life? What would be the consequences of those decisions?

Find out by accessing **MyVirtualLife** at www.MyDevelopmentLab.com to raise a virtual child and live your own virtual life.

MIDDLE ADULTHOOD
Physical and Cognitive Development

14

LEARNING OBJECTIVES

- How do people in middle adulthood generally approach this period of development—as the best part of life or the beginning of decline?
- Is there such a thing as the midlife crisis?
- What changes in physical functions are associated with the middle adult years?
- What is the climacteric, and how is it typically experienced by men and women?
- How does sexuality change as men and women move through middle age?
- What health-related problems are most common during middle adulthood?
- How do habits established earlier in life begin to assert their effects in middle adulthood?
- What cognitive changes are most closely associated with the middle adult years?
- How do adults adapt to the mild cognitive declines associated with moving through middle age?

CHAPTER OUTLINE

Development in Middle Adulthood
- Prime Time or the Beginning of the End?
- Midlife Crisis: Is It Real?
- Perceptions and Realities at Midlife

Physical Continuity and Change
- Changes in Capabilities
- The Climacteric
- Sexuality in the Middle Years

Disease and Health
- The Cumulative Effects of Health Habits
- Stress and Health
- Ethnicity, Poverty, and Health

Cognitive Continuity and Change
- Fluid Versus Crystallized Intelligence
- Experience and Expertise
- Cognitive Skills in the Workplace

Up to this point in the text, we have looked at infancy, childhood, adolescence, emerging adulthood, and young adulthood. We have explored the developmental transitions that shape people's lives and that lead them to the development of a relatively stable outlook and personality. We have noted the social milestones that mark the entry into the world of adulthood—moving away from home, getting married, becoming a parent, and establishing a career. What's next? Is that all there is?

Middle adulthood, arbitrarily considered to span the years from ages 40 to 60 or 65, constitutes a substantial portion of a person's normal lifespan. Does it pose new challenges or is it merely a time in which to live out the decisions made earlier in life, possibly making a few corrections and adjustments here and there? In this chapter, we explore the significant physical and cognitive changes that typically occur in middle adulthood, paying close attention to important life events that direct the course of an individual's experiences in this period of life.

DEVELOPMENT IN MIDDLE ADULTHOOD

Developmental theorists tend to see middle adulthood as a cultural construction of the 20th century (Wahl & Kruse, 2005; Wethington, Kessler, & Pixley, 2004). As for when it begins and ends, much depends on the life experiences the person is going through. Does a 43-year-old woman with a newborn baby think of herself as middle-aged? Does a 41-year-old man in a training program for a new job consider himself in the middle years of his career—and life—or does he view himself as making a new start? In contemporary U.S. culture, we often define the beginning of middle age as age 40. On a person's 40th birthday, it is common practice to proclaim the milestone loudly, tell jokes about being "over the hill," send disparaging greeting cards, and maybe dress in black in mock sympathy for the 40-year-old's lost youth.

Do you think that in the future the period of middle age will be defined differently than at present? What social and cultural shifts could produce such a change?

The period defined as middle adulthood may begin earlier or later than age 40, however, and it may be longer or shorter for different people because there are so many different cues associated with aging (Brim, Ryff, & Kessler, 2004). Some of these cues have to do with *social* and *family status*. Middle adulthood is an in-between period, a bridge between two generations. People in midlife are aware of being separate not only from youngsters and young adults but also from older people, especially retirees. Some people feel that they are middle-aged when their children begin to leave home.

Other cues may be *physical* and *biological*. A woman may suddenly realize that her son is taller than she is; a man may find that he has lost a step on the basketball court or that his movement is hampered by the beginnings of arthritis. Health is a factor, too. How much do 40-year-olds who are physically fit and full of vim and vigor have in common with 40-year-olds who have let themselves go through alcohol or drug use, obesity, or lack of exercise?

There are also *psychological* cues, most of which involve issues of continuity and change. People realize that they have made certain basic decisions about their work and family that most likely will direct the future course of their lives. The future is never certain, but it no longer holds as many different possibilities as it once did. Cues also come from people's *jobs or careers*; by middle age, most people have established a clear work history and have a good picture of what their future responsibilities will be. This is especially true for workers in situations where job seniority is honored. Finally, the economic conditions, social class, and the times in which people live also affect how we view middle adulthood.

Prime Time or the Beginning of the End?

How do people feel about being middle-aged? Theorists and middle-aged people themselves do not agree on whether middle adulthood is a time of new fulfillment, stability, and potential leadership or a period of dissatisfaction, inner turmoil, and depression. The main reason for this disparity in perspectives is that individuals experience middle life in different ways. Many middle-aged adults realize that they are no longer young, yet they feel satisfied and believe that they are now in the "prime of life." Middle-aged people often feel "safe," settled, and secure (Helson & Soto, 2005; Ryff, 2008). For many middle-aged people, physical abilities may be slightly diminished, but experience and self-knowledge allow them to manage their own lives to a greater extent than at any other age. They can make decisions with ease, expertise, and self-confidence that were previously beyond their grasp. This is why the 40- to 60-year-old age group has been called the **command generation** and why most of the decision makers in government, corporations, and society

command generation
A term for the generation of middle-aged people; reflects the idea that this age group makes most of the policy decisions that affect our lives

at large are middle-aged. In the United States, today's generation of adults in midlife is better educated and healthier than ever before, and many of them report a strong sense of self-efficacy, at least in some important areas of their lives (Brim, Ryff, & Kessler, 2004; Clark-Plaskie & Lachman, 1999).

Of course, many middle-aged people do not make weighty decisions and run corporations or government agencies, and some do not feel that they even control their own lives, let alone those of others. Some also experience poor health. From this perspective, middle adulthood can be viewed as a period of declining activity, the onset of which can be marked by both psychological and biological crises (Levinson 1978, 1996).

Indeed, most people experience a sense of ambivalence during middle adulthood. It may be the prime of life with respect to family, career, or creative talents, but most people also are keenly aware of their own mortality and have recurrent thoughts about how their time is running out and that the years seem to pass more quickly. How people interpret this sense of urgency, together with the particular events they experience, determines whether middle adulthood is a period of gradual transition and reassessment or a period of crisis.

▲ What might it mean to this man in his 50s to be able to drive a red convertible from a vintage year? Perhaps he is having a midlife crisis, but more likely he is simply taking the opportunity to continue to enjoy the pleasures of good health, economic well-being, and adult independence.

Midlife Crisis: Is It Real?

A popular conception of midlife is that it involves a crisis of identity centered around the issue of growing old. Daniel Levinson's view of the "seasons of life" (see Chapter 12) reflects this **crisis model** perspective, which emphasizes that changes in midlife are abrupt and often stressful (Levinson, 1978, 1996). In Levinson's model, early adulthood is seen as a period of relative stability in which activity is directed at establishing a career and a fulfilling family life. At the end of this period, though, a midlife crisis occurs in which earlier decisions are questioned and life patterns must be reestablished.

According to Levinson, the midlife crisis for men typically occurs between the ages of 40 and 45 and revolves around a handful of core issues: being young versus old, being masculine versus feminine, being destructive versus constructive, and being attached to others versus being alienated. In his study of middle-aged men, Levinson found that about three-quarters of the participants experienced considerable turmoil centered around issues such as these; therefore, he concluded that most men do experience a midlife crisis of identity, after which they reenter a period of relative emotional and psychological stability. A typical midlife crisis might go something like this: At about the age of 40, a man may begin to question, or at least put into perspective, the driven life he has been leading. If he has been successful in reaching his goals, he may suddenly ask, "Was it worth the struggle?" If he has not achieved what he wanted in life, he may become keenly aware that he does not have many more chances to change things. Thus, he questions his entire life structure, including both work and family relationships (Levinson, 1986). Although Levinson's original sample included primarily highly successful middle-class White men, his subsequent work has led him to conclude that the midlife crisis is a common developmental event, and that it also is experienced in much the same way by women (Levinson, 1978, 1996).

More recent conceptualizations of middle adulthood often are critical of the concept of midlife crisis, at least as described by Levinson. Pointing out obvious methodological flaws, theorists advocating a **transition model** reject the idea that midlife crisis is the norm (Helson, 1997; Wethington, Kessler, & Pixley, 2004). Most longitudinal studies of adult development do not support the occurrence of a dramatic shift in personality or life adjustment related to the onset of middle age (Willis, Marti, & Rocke, 2010). Instead, researchers find more continuities than discontinuities in problem solving, personality, lifestyle, and general orientation to life (Whitbourne & Whitbourne, 2011). Furthermore, when crises do occur in life, they most often occur around specific events, such as the death of a friend or parent, a sudden illness, unemployment, a new job, a child going off to war, the birth or adoption of a child, divorce, and so forth. Also, life crises, when they do occur, often affect men and women differently (see Chapter 15). For example, a stay-at-home mother is likely to be much more impacted by the youngest child's leaving home than is the father, who may have been less directly involved in the day-to-day care of that child. Furthermore, transitional events can occur at any point in the lifespan, not just at ages 40 to 45.

What cultural stereotypes can you cite that suggest the existence of a midlife crisis? Are there different midlife crisis stereotypes for men versus women?

crisis model
The view that changes in midlife are abrupt and often stressful

Watch *Emotion Processes and Aging: Susan Charles* on **MyDevelopmentLab**

transition model
The view that changes in midlife are gradual and midlife crisis is not the norm

Although adulthood may be interrupted by crises like those noted, according to various transition models, development is more often marked by a series of expected major life events that can be anticipated and planned for. Although the transitions associated with these events can be difficult both psychologically and socially, most people adapt successfully because they know that these life changes are coming. For example, knowing that she will probably retire sometime in her 60s, a 40-year-old small-business owner makes regular deposits into a tax-deferred individual retirement account (IRA). By the time she is 50, she may have found the ideal home to retire in, and she regularly discusses her retirement plans with her spouse and children. Transition models recognize that people plan for major life changes and make a series of adjustments in anticipation. Thus, many age-related midlife crises are dealt with before they occur.

Regardless of how a person moves through middle adulthood, this period is a time when most people begin to take stock of their lives. Some may feel effective, competent, and at the peak of their powers; others may find it painful to examine their lives. Although the effects of aging (e.g., graying hair, an expanding midsection, or menopause) may combine with unexpected, nonnormative events (e.g., divorce or unemployment), if these situations are anticipated or regarded as normal, they are less likely to lead to a crisis (Mason, 2011; Neugarten & Brown-Rezanka, 1996; Sneed, Whitbourne, Schwartz, & Huang, 2012). A substantial and persuasive body of research supports the view that most adults experience the middle years simply as years of gradual transitions—both positive and negative—associated with growing older (Willis, Martin, & Rocke, 2010).

Perceptions and Realities at Midlife

It is difficult for many adolescents and young adults to think of middle age as anything but a giant black hole in which they will spend at least 20 years of their lives. Younger people often view middle age as a time when growth and development are over, as are youthful dreams and passions about careers and relationships: Whereas youth is about hope, middle age is about being stuck in a quagmire. Research, however, supports the opposite conclusion. According to Ronald Kessler, a sociologist and fellow at the MacArthur Foundation Research Network on Successful Midlife Development:

> The data show that middle age is the very best time in life. When looking at the total U.S. population, the best year is 50. You don't have to deal with the aches and pains of old age or the anxieties of youth: Is anyone going to love me? Will I ever get my career off the ground? Rates of general distress are low—the incidences of depression and anxiety fall at about 35 and don't climb again until the late 60s. You're healthy. You're productive. You have enough money to do some of the things you like to do. You've come to terms with your relationships, and the chance of divorce is very low. Midlife is the "it" you've been working toward. You can turn your attention toward being rather than becoming. (as cited in Gallagher, 1993, p. 53)

Research also suggests that midlife crisis is the exception rather than the rule (Freund & Ritter, 2009; Wethington, Kessler, & Pixley, 2004). The overwhelming majority of people shift gently into midlife as they trade their youthful goals of fame, wealth, accomplishment, and beauty for more realistic expectations. A 42-year-old wife and mother who at 18 wanted to be an actress, for example, may have accepted that she would never make it to Hollywood and now performs in the local community theater instead.

Those who are most likely to experience a midlife crisis tend to avoid introspection. They also use denial to avoid thinking about their changing bodies and lives. For example, a 45-year-old who thinks he is still a great athlete may be emotionally devastated when his 15-year-old son beats him at basketball. In addition, midlife crises are more common among the affluent than among the poor or working class. Perhaps it is easier to delude oneself about the realities of middle adulthood when money in the bank shields one from the burdens and struggles of life (Gallagher, 1993). Finally, when midlife crises do occur, they often are linked to the specific life events of an individual; therefore, they also reflect social forces that affect different cohorts of people in specific ways. Today's middle-aged adults may be more likely to hit their midlife crises—if they occur at all—in their mid-30s or mid-50s rather than their mid-40s (Rosenberg, Rosenberg, & Farrell, 1999; Whitbourne, & Willis, 2006), reflecting the issues most important to their particular generation (see the box Try This! Just What *Is* Middle Age?).

Regardless of when and how individuals confront the fact that they are growing older, physical changes occur in middle adulthood. Perhaps for the first time individuals in this stage of life begin to feel and look older. We consider what these changes are and how most people adjust to them in the following section.

REVIEW THE FACTS 14-1

1. In the United States, middle adulthood usually is considered to span which of the following age ranges?
   a. 35 to 55 or 60 b. 40 to 60 or 65
   c. 35 to 65 or 70 d. 50 to 70 or 75
2. Most decision makers in business and government are in their middle-adult years. Thus, they are sometimes called the ________ generation.
3. Perhaps the best word to describe the way most people experience middle age is
   a. high-energy. b. depressing.
   c. joyful. d. ambivalent.
4. Transition models generally argue that people's movement through middle adulthood is best characterized by
   a. continuity. b. crisis.
   c. discontinuity. d. nearly continuous turmoil.
5. If a man denies the fact that he is getting older and he tries to appear youthful, is he more likely or less likely to experience a midlife crisis?

Practice on MyDevelopmentLab

TRY THIS!

Just What *Is* Middle Age?

Life expectancy for people living in the United States, as well as in many other developed nations, has increased dramatically in the past 100 years. Consequently, the middle of life has shifted upward. Furthermore, people's perspectives on age usually change as they grow older—at age 18, 30 seems old; but to a 50-year-old, age 30 seems young. To explore the concept of middle age, try this!

Identify 10 adults (or more) who represent various age groups. Preferably, some should be in their late teens or in their 20s, some in their 30s or 40s, some in their 50s or 60s, and some in their 70s or older. Ask them the following three questions and record their answers, as well as their ages:

- At what age do you think middle age begins?
- At what age do you think middle age ends?
- What age do you think represents the *prime* of life?

To summarize the information you collect, it may be helpful to make a table like the one that follows. Your table should include a row for each of the 10 or more people you question. It is probably easiest to explore the data you collected if you organize it according to the ages of the people you questioned. Try listing each person's responses in order from youngest to oldest to see if any age-related trends appear in your data.

Reflect on What You Observed

What were the youngest and oldest ages that were noted as the beginning and the end of middle age? Was there a lot of variability in the answers your participants gave or did their answers cluster around a particular age? What about the age they identified as the prime of life? Compute the average age that your participants gave for each of the three questions asked. What was the average age given as the beginning of middle age? What was the average age given as the end of middle age? What was the average age given as the prime of life? Did these responses surprise you in any way?

Consider the Issues

Did the age of the people you questioned affect the ages they considered to correspond to middle age? Did their age affect the age they considered to be the prime of life? Did the younger people you questioned see middle age and the prime of life as occurring at younger ages than did the older people? Were you surprised at the results you obtained? How do you think people's perspective on getting older changes as *they* get older? Do your data support your view?

Do you think there might be gender or ethnic differences in the responses people would give to these questions? For example, it is known that women in the United States live longer on average than do men and that White Americans live longer than do members of various ethnic and racial minority groups. People in middle- and upper-class socioeconomic groups also live longer than do people in lower socioeconomic categories. Do you think people's answers to your questions reflect the demographics of their own particular group or do you think that their judgments about age reflect more generally the characteristics of our overall society? Do you see any trends in your data that would suggest an answer to this question? What do you think are the most important factors that enter into how a person defines middle age?

At what age do you think middle age begins?	At what age do you think middle age ends?	What age do you think represents the prime of life?	Age of each participant

PHYSICAL CONTINUITY AND CHANGE

The most obvious changes associated with the middle years are physical. Most physical abilities peak during adolescence or early adulthood and level off in early middle adulthood; then the first signs of physical decline begin to appear. For many middle-aged people, there is a moment of truth when the mirror reveals new wrinkles, midriff bulge, a receding hairline, or gray hair at the temples that no longer seems distinguished—just depressing.

These warning signals are more disturbing to some than to others, often depending on a person's attitudes toward aging and eventually dying. Are these physical changes signs of maturity or of decline? Some obvious biological events, such as menopause for women, increased difficulty in achieving erection for men, and decreasing visual acuity for both sexes, are events that require a change in self-image or activities and must be incorporated into a satisfactory lifestyle. Fortunately, even though most adults experience a gradual decline in their overall health during middle adulthood, their sense of well-being and satisfaction with life remain intact during these years (Cavanaugh & Blanchard-Fields, 2011; Röcke & Lachman, 2008). This is particularly the case for those who are high in the personality trait of conscientiousness (Goodwin & Friedman, 2006). Of course, many factors influence aging, and people age

Do you think that women in the United States are more concerned with the effects of aging than are men? What evidence can you cite to support your view?

Watch *Cosmetic Surgery* on **MyDevelopmentLab**

Table 14-1 Physical Changes of Middle Adulthood

SENSATION
• Decline in visual acuity, except for distant objects • Hearing loss, especially for high-frequency sounds • Decline in taste
REACTION TIME
• Slow decline in reaction time
INTERNAL CHANGES
• Slowing of the nervous system • Stiffening and shrinking of the skeleton • Loss of elasticity in the skin and the muscles; development of wrinkles • Accumulation of subcutaneous fat • Decrease in heart and lung capacity
SEX-RELATED CHANGES IN WOMEN
• Menopause (cessation of ovulation and menstruation) • Reduced production of estrogen • Shrinking of the uterus and reduction of breast size • Hot flashes; night sweats • Loss of bone mass (osteoporosis) • Vaginal atrophy
SEX-RELATED CHANGES IN MEN
• Gradual decline in the production of androgens • Increased difficulty in achieving erection

and develop at different rates. Typically, though, by age 50, there is enough physical change that aging becomes noticeable (Merrill & Verbrugge, 1999). Table 14-1 presents a summary of the physical changes of middle adulthood.

Changes in Capabilities

The decline in physical abilities experienced in middle age involves sensory and motor skills, as well as the body's internal functioning (Cleary, Zaborski, & Ayanian, 2004; Erber, 2010).

Sensation Visual capabilities are fairly stable from adolescence through the 40s or early 50s; then visual acuity declines (Fozard & Gordon-Salant, 2001; Whitbourne & Whitbourne, 2011). A partial exception is nearsightedness: People often see distant objects better in middle adulthood than they could as young adults. Hearing typically becomes less acute after age 20 and declines gradually, especially with regard to high-frequency sounds (Fozard & Gordon-Salant, 2001). This hearing loss is more common in men than in women, a fact that may be attributable to environmental factors in jobs such as construction work that include sustained exposure to loud or high-frequency noises. In any case, hearing loss is rarely severe enough to affect normal conversation in middle adulthood (Olsho, Harkins, & Lenhardt, 1985). Taste, smell, and sensitivity to pain decline at different points in middle adulthood, although these changes are more gradual and less noticeable than visual or auditory changes (Bartoshuk & Weiffenbach, 1990; Whitbourne & Whitbourne, 2011). Sensitivity to temperature changes remains high in middle adulthood (Newman, 1982). Although the sensory decline that occurs in middle age typically is modest, oftentimes individuals must focus more of their attention on seeing clearly, hearing, and so forth. Thus, even these small age-related changes can tax other cognitive resources such as memory and attention (Scheiber, 2006). Hence, sensory aging may involve a loss of adaptability, and the beginning of a more general age-related decline (Sosnoff, Vallantine, & Newell, 2007).

Motor Skills and Reaction Time As we age, and especially after age 50, our reaction speed slows (Gabbard, 2012; Newell, Vaillancourt, & Sosnoff, 2006). Oftentimes, however, actual performance remains constant, probably because practice and experience compensate for slower reaction times (Stones & Kozma, 1996). For example, someone who chops firewood, enters data at a keyboard, or plays tennis every day will usually experience little decline in performance during middle adulthood. Adults who adopt a positive orientation about their futures generally experience less physical decline with age (Kahana, Kahana, & Zhang, 2005). Learning new motor skills, however, gradually becomes increasingly difficult as middle adulthood progresses.

Internal Changes Reaching middle age is associated with changes to other parts of the body as well. For example, the skeleton stiffens and shrinks a bit over the course of adulthood; gravity gradually takes its toll, and the person becomes shorter in stature. Skin and muscles begin to lose elasticity and wrinkles develop. There is a greater tendency to accumulate more subcutaneous fat, especially in areas like the midriff, often causing people to become concerned about their appearance. One recent study showed that 87% of middle-aged women and 59% of middle-aged men had dieted to control their weight (Ziebland, Robertson, Jay, & Neil, 2002).

Cardiovascular efficiency also is affected. The heart pumps an average of 8% less blood to the body for each decade after the beginning of adulthood. By middle adulthood, the opening of the coronary arteries typically is nearly one-third less than it was in the 20s. Good cardiovascular health in middle adulthood is associated with better quality of life and lower risk of diseases in older age (Daviglus, et al., 2003). Lung capacity decreases as well. Because endurance depends on the amount of oxygen supplied to body tissues, people generally cannot perform as much sustained hard labor in middle adulthood as they can in young adulthood (Siegler, Kaplan, Von Dras, & Mark, 1999), although the extent of decline depends on lifestyle.

Watch *Cognitive Changes Secondary to Menopause in Middle Adulthood* on **MyDevelopmentLab**

Watch *Physical Changes in Middle Adulthood* on **MyDevelopmentLab**

▶ Many menopausal and postmenopausal women feel happy, now that their active mothering is drawing to an end, to have more time to themselves.

The Climacteric

Sometime in middle age, both men and women experience the **climacteric**, which refers to the overall complex of physical and emotional effects that accompany hormonal changes in middle adulthood. In women, the most dramatic aspect of the climacteric is **menopause**—the permanent cessation of ovulation and menstruation, which may be accompanied by physical symptoms and intense emotional reactions. As noted earlier, men continue to produce sperm and male hormones throughout the lifespan; thus, they do not experience a comparable male menopause, despite its occasional coverage in the popular media. Nevertheless, men undergo more gradual biological changes in middle adulthood that are accompanied by emotional readjustments and changes in sexual behavior, much like women experience during menopause.

The Physical Changes and Symptoms of Menopause On average, women experience their last menstrual period between ages 45 and 55, although for some women it may occur somewhat earlier or considerably later (Carlson, Eisenstat, & Ziporyn, 2004; Rossi, 2004). As menopause approaches, ovulation and the menstrual cycle become erratic at first and then stop altogether. These changes usually occur over a period of 7 or 8 years. Thus, menopause is a *process*, not an *event* (Rossi, 2004).

The early phase of the menopause process is often referred to as premenopause. During this period, levels of estrogen—one of the key female hormones—begin to fluctuate, and the menstrual cycle becomes less regular. Because of the estrogen fluctuations, in some months no ovum is released. For many women, premenopausal symptoms begin to occur as early as the late 30s or 40s, making it more difficult for women who wait until these years to become pregnant to conceive. Levels of progesterone—the other major female hormone—also begin to fluctuate during this period. Typically during their later 40s, most women enter perimenopause, which is associated with even more radical fluctuations of estrogen. During this phase, the menstrual cycle becomes less predictable, pregnancy becomes much more difficult, and most women experience an uncomfortable sensation referred to as "hot flashes." During a hot flash, the woman's skin temperature raises significantly, giving rise to the sensation of being suddenly very hot. Hot flashes are reported by 50 to 60% of women (Avis, 1999; Carlson, Eisenstat, & Ziporyn, 1996) and when they are bothersome and occur at night, they can lead to sleep deprivation (Xu, et al., 2012). In fact, many of the menopause-related problems women report, such as headaches, mental confusion, and emotional instability, are probably the result of sleep deprivation that results from hot flashes. In all, only about 20% of women who experience menopausal symptoms rate them as bothersome (Avis, 1999). However, a minority of women do have considerable difficulty adjusting to their changing hormone levels. Eventually, levels of estrogen and progesterone drop to consistently low levels, and menstruation ceases. During this postmenopausal stage, other physical changes occur in response to the lower levels of hormones. For example, the breasts become less firm, and the uterus and genitals shrink somewhat. Perhaps most significantly, the lining of the vaginal walls thins, becomes less elastic, and produces less lubricating fluids (Rossi, 2004). Consequently, after menopause many women prefer to use artificial forms of lubrication during sexual intercourse to improve comfort.

The Emotional Effects Associated with Menopause For a small proportion of women, the physical changes of menopause are accompanied by emotional changes, such as feelings of depression and a sense of being somehow less feminine because their reproductive function is gone (Wang-Cheng, Neuner, & Barnabei, 2007). In particular, research suggests that women who have more trouble with depression earlier in life may be at heightened risk both for greater difficultly with menopausal symptoms and for postmenopausal depression (Strauss, 2011). Thus the sometimes-reported link between menopause and depression appears to be more the result of factors other than menopause itself (Bromberger, et al., 2010). Nevertheless, women who have not had children and had not completely made up their minds about childbearing may experience some sense of regret, loss, or depression. Most women, however, do not encounter such difficulties during menopause (see Table 14-2). Indeed, some researchers report a *decrease* in emotional difficulties during and after menopause compared with the years immediately preceding it. A large national survey of menopausal women reported that fewer than 4% indicated feelings of regret over the cessation of their menstrual cycles; about half reported feeling only relief (Rossi, 2004).

In general, considerable research indicates that most women do not respond negatively to menopause in either the short term or the long term (Judd, Hickey, & Bryant, 2012). In one Pennsylvania study of over 500 healthy menopausal and postmenopausal women over a 5-year period, more than 50% reported that they were not more depressed or moody and that "the change" was easier than they had expected (Matthews, Wing, Kuller, Meilahn, & Owens, 2000). Many women feel freer and

climacteric
The broad complex of physical and emotional symptoms that accompanies reproductive changes in middle adulthood, affecting both men and women

menopause
The permanent end of menstruation; occurs in middle adulthood and may be accompanied by physical symptoms and emotional reactions, more so in some women and in some cultures than in others

Watch *Menopause* on **MyDevelopmentLab**

Table 14-2 Degree of Worry Women Express About Getting Older, on Three Issues

Issue	Percent Reporting "Not at All"	Percent Reporting "a Little"	Percent Reporting "Some or a Lot"
Being too old to have children	82.0	7.8	10.2
Being less attractive as a woman	36.3	34.6	29.1
Having more illness as you get older	21.6	38.0	40.4

NOTE: Participants were women included in the Midlife in the United States (MIDUS) survey, ages 25 to 74.
SOURCE: From "The menopausal transition and aging processes," by A. S. Rossi, 2004, in O. D. Brim, C. D. Ryff, and R. C. Kessler (Eds.), *How healthy are we? A national study of well-being at midlife* (pp. 153–204). Copyright © 2004. Reprinted by permissions of the University of Chicago Press.

more in control of their own lives, with a sense of elation because they no longer need to be concerned with menstrual periods or the possibility of pregnancy. At the same time, their active mothering role is usually ending; consequently, they often have more time for themselves. Even women who are not particularly pleased about menopause tend not to be worried or distressed—they simply take it in stride.

The cultural context of menopause can also affect the woman's feelings about herself, her behavior, and her actual physical symptoms (Lock, 1993). In some castes in India, for example, menopause traditionally brings with it a new positive status for women because they no longer are required to remain isolated from much of society, associating only with their husbands and immediate families. After menopause, they may enjoy the company of both men and women in a greater variety of social circumstances. In one study of a group of Indian women, none reported the range of negative symptoms—such as excessive moodiness, depression, or headaches—often associated with menopause in the United States (Flint, 1982). In fact, in cross-cultural studies of menopause, results typically reveal that reports of negative symptoms vary widely by culture, as well as among different women of the same culture. Results such as these suggest that menopausal symptoms are the result of not only physical factors but psychological and cultural factors as well (Robinson, 2002).

Long-Term Effects Menopausal symptoms, however, are not just a product of cultural interpretation. The estrogen loss that accompanies menopause produces long-term physiological changes in bone mass and the genitals, and probably increases the risk of coronary disease as well.

Although both men and women begin to experience a loss in bone mass as they approach the end of middle age, the loss is about twice as great in women and occurs more rapidly (Whitbourne & Whitbourne, 2011). As a result, bone fractures are much more common in older women than in older men. Women's loss of bone mass accelerates greatly after menopause, apparently because of estrogen deprivation. In the United States, **osteoporosis**, the medical term for loss of bone mass and increased bone fragility (regardless of the cause), is quite common. According to a report issued by the U.S. Surgeon General (2004), by 2020, half of Americans over age 50 are expected to have or be at risk of developing osteoporosis of the hip; most of those people will be postmenopausal women. Nearly half of all postmenopausal women over the age of 50 will experience a bone fracture related to osteoporosis (McBean, Forgac, & Finn, 1994).

The link between heart disease and menopause has been more difficult to establish. Our current understanding is that estrogen provides some protective mechanism that reduces a premenopausal woman's risk of heart disease. This conclusion is supported by data that show that women have a much lower rate of cardiovascular disease than men until menopause; then the rate for women rises nearly as high as the male rate. Young women who have had their ovaries removed (creating surgical menopause) also experience a dramatic increase in cardiovascular risk factors unless they take artificial hormones to replace the estrogen they no longer produce.

What particular aspects of culture do you think might be most important with respect to how women perceive the symptoms of menopause?

Hormone Replacement Therapy Because of the health risks and unpleasant symptoms associated with a decreased estrogen supply, some menopausal women have chosen to go on hormone replacement therapy (HRT). HRT—in the form of either estrogen or progesterone supplements or a combination of the two—helps alleviate symptoms, such as hot flashes and vaginal changes. In 1998, about one in three U.S. women between the ages of 45 and 64 were on HRT (Pinn & Bates, 2003).

The effectiveness of HRT in alleviating the unpleasant symptoms of menopause is generally well accepted. However, recent research presents a somewhat mixed picture about the potential side effects that may accompany its use over an extended period of time, some of which may be beneficial and some of which appear to be harmful (Canderelli, Leccesse, & Miller, 2007; Lobo, 2007; National Institutes of Health [NIH], 2012b). For example, research generally shows that HRT appears to be of

osteoporosis
The loss of bone mass and increased bone fragility; increases significantly in middle adulthood and beyond

some value in slowing or even stopping the progression of bone loss (NIH, 2012b; U.S. Food and Drug Administration, 2012; Yarbrough, Williams, & Allen, 2004). Early studies offered promise that HRT could also reduce a postmenopausal women's risk of heart disease (Grodstein, et al., 1997; Hu, et al., 1999). However, more recent research suggests that HRT may actually *increase* a woman's risk for cardiovascular problems as well as increase the risk for developing certain types of cancer, and especially breast cancer (American College of Obstetricians and Gynecologists, 2012). Early studies indicated that HRT might also be beneficial in preventing the onset of Alzheimer's disease and other forms of dementia, although the results of such studies presently appear mixed. Although some studies find no link between HRT and cognitive functions (e.g., Luetters et al., 2007), other studies do show some cognitive benefits to be associated with HRT (e.g., Ryan, et al., 2012). Although the mechanism by which hormones may protect cognitive functions are at present unknown, recent functional magnetic resonance imaging (fMRI) studies have shown that HRT users have higher levels of brain activity than nonusers in some parts of the brain linked to memory (e.g., Maki et al., 2011). Research such as this suggests that estrogen may have a positive effect on preventing the development of dementia if its use begins early enough when neurons are still in a healthy state.

Thus, the picture regarding the risks and benefits associated with HRT is mixed and difficult to decipher. To help consumers better understand the plethora of research, some of which is contradictory, the North American Menopause Society in 2012 issued a set of guidelines for women to consider. These guidelines make the following points:

- HRT remains the most effective treatment for menopausal symptoms and many women can take it safely.
- Women who have had blood clots, heart disease, stroke, or breast cancer should discuss these risk factors with their personal physician before taking HRT.
- Different forms of HRT appear to have different links to breast cancer. In particular, estrogen-only HRT can be taken for as many as 7 years with no increased risk, but HRT that contains both estrogen and progesterone should perhaps be discontinued sooner than this.
- Most healthy women under the age of 60 will not experience significantly increased risks of heart disease with HRT.

HRT delivered by patch, cream, gel, or spray may have lower risks of blood clots than oral medication, but this conclusion is still speculative and will require further study. Because HRT has been associated with significant health risks as well as benefits, the decision about whether to use HRT is now more questionable than it was previously. The best advice at present for women considering HRT is to consult with a trusted physician to tailor a program of treatment appropriate to each woman's particular symptoms and risk profile. (American College of Obstetricians and Gynecologists, 2012; Lobo, 2007).

Changes in Men For men, there is no single, relatively abrupt event comparable to menopause (Finch, 2001). Androgens (male hormones) decline very gradually beginning in middle age (Seidman, 2003), but they do not produce a precipitous drop in either sexual desire or performance. We do know, though, that many men undergo changes in sexual interest and activity, which generally occur in their late 40s. As with women, there are wide individual differences among people. Although most men remain fertile throughout middle age and often into their later adulthood, many men experience somewhat reduced sexual desire, although this is often related to job stress, family issues, or generally reduced energy. Of special concern to men are the issues associated with *erectile dysfunction* (impotence), which is more common than is often assumed. Studies report that about 50% of men over the age of 40 will experience some erectile dysfunction (Paduch, Bolyakov, Beardsworth, & Watts, 2012). Perhaps 10 to 20% of middle-aged men experience such problems on more than an infrequent basis (Korfage, et al., 2008).

Until quite recently, erectile dysfunction—in which erections are less frequent, less complete, or require more stimulation to achieve—was thought to be most often the result of psychological issues and was treated with counseling, if treated at all. Newer research, however, suggests that most cases have a physiological basis (McVary, 2007; Steggall, 2007). Sometimes performance problems result as a side effect of medicines taken for other health problems; in such cases medications can sometimes be adjusted to relieve the sexual side effects. Sometimes they are related to other health-related conditions: Cardiovascular disease, high cholesterol, diabetes, and smoking all increase a man's risk of erectile dysfunction (Goldstein, 2004; Slowinski, 2007a). Undoubtedly, the factors that enter into sexual dysfunction are complex and may reflect physiological issues, psychological issues, or a combination of both (Bodie, Beeman, & Monga, 2003; Ducharme, 2004).

To address erectile problems, many men elect to take prescription medicines that are now widely available—Viagra, Cialis, and Levitra are examples. Such drugs, which have been widely advertised since they came on the market in 1998, are effective in 60 to 80% of the men for whom they are prescribed (Padma-Nathan & Giuliano, 2001). These drugs work by affecting the dilation of blood vessels; they are widely used and appear to have few serious side effects, with headaches being the most common. When physiological problems do not seem to be at the root of sexual performance problems, often counseling can help (Slowinski, 2007b).

Watch *Estrogen and Memory* on **MyDevelopmentLab**

Watch *Middle Adulthood: Health, Jeff* on **MyDevelopmentLab**

Sexuality in the Middle Years

As we have seen, the physiological and psychological changes associated with middle adulthood markedly affect sexual functioning in both men and women (Hock, 2012; Tepper & Owens, 2007). How people respond to midlife changes can of course have an influence on their sexual satisfaction.

Frequency of sexual activity—as well as the number of different sexual partners a person is likely to have—generally slows down in middle adulthood (Burgess, 2004; Moore, Strauss, Herman, & Donatucci, 2003). Physiological changes account for some of the slowdown, but sexual activity also may drop off in the middle years because of ill health. Health problems that inhibit sexual activity include physical conditions, such as hypertension, diabetes, and coronary artery disease; and emotional problems, such as depression. In addition, medications used to treat these illnesses may have adverse effects on sexual activity. For example, the drugs used in the treatment of coronary artery disease may cause impotence as a side effect. Similarly, many tranquilizers and antidepressant drugs tend to reduce sexual desire. Lack of opportunity is also a factor; the time pressures associated with the middle-adult years may interfere with sexual interest. The pressures of career and family leave many couples with little time or energy for sex. For many people, interpersonal and family problems further interfere with sexual interactions (Hyde & LeLamater, 2011).

Do you think that the media portray the sexual activity of men at midlife as being high or low? What evidence can you cite in support of your view?

When men experience sexual anxiety and dissatisfaction in middle age, causes often include job stresses or boredom with a long-term sexual partner (Featherstone & Hepworth, 1985). Poor physical conditioning also may affect men's sexual activity. Men who are anxious about sex and have even a single episode of impotence or partial erection may start believing that age has diminished their sexual ability. To protect themselves from additional failures, some men may avoid sex or perhaps turn to alternative techniques, such as masturbation. However, as noted previously, since Viagra was introduced to the market, many men now choose to see their physicians and, if health factors are not an issue, to take this, or a similar, medication.

For women, the physiological changes associated with menopause often imply that more time may be needed to achieve orgasm. A similar slowdown occurs in men; they may take longer to achieve an erection and to reach orgasm, but they also can often maintain an erection for a longer time. Thus, because both men and women require more time during sex, the result is often a more sharing kind of lovemaking—in contrast to lovemaking in former years, which may have been directed more urgently toward orgasm (Hyde & DeLamater, 2011; Laumann, Gagnon, Michael, & Michaels, 1994).

▲ Although sexual capabilities decline during middle adulthood, sexual and romantic interests continue for both women and men.

Middle-aged adults who engage in sex infrequently often mistakenly believe that others around them are enjoying active, fulfilling sex lives (Laumann, Gagnon, Michael, & Michaels, 1994), and such misconceptions can compound their own dissatisfaction. Indeed, media give the impression that everyone is doing it all the time, both within their marriage and extramaritally as well; however, this is not the case. The results of a broad-scale survey (Michael, Gagnon, Laumann, & Kolata, 1994) support an extraordinarily conventional view of love, sex, and marriage, with monogamy predominating and with many people having sex infrequently.

Sex, of course, implies more than simply a physical act—sexuality is a complex of physical behaviors, emotions, values,

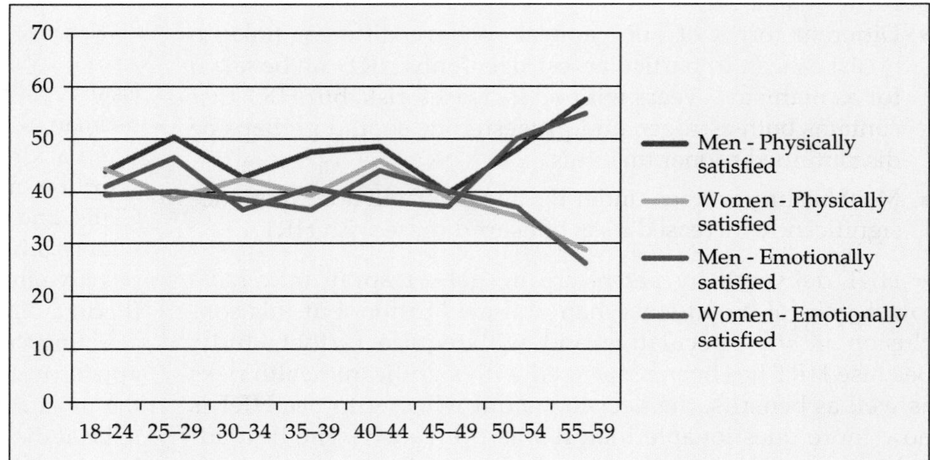

FIGURE 14-1 Percent of U.S. Men and Women Who Reported Being Extremely Physically and Emotional Satisfied with Their Primary Sexual Partners During the Past Year

SOURCE: Table 3.7, "Percentage of sexual satisfaction/substance use in self-reported 'primary' partnership last year. In E. O. Laumann, J. H. Gagnon, R. T. Michael, and S. Michaels, 1994, *The social organization of sexuality: Sexual practices in the United States*, Chicago: University of Chicago Press.

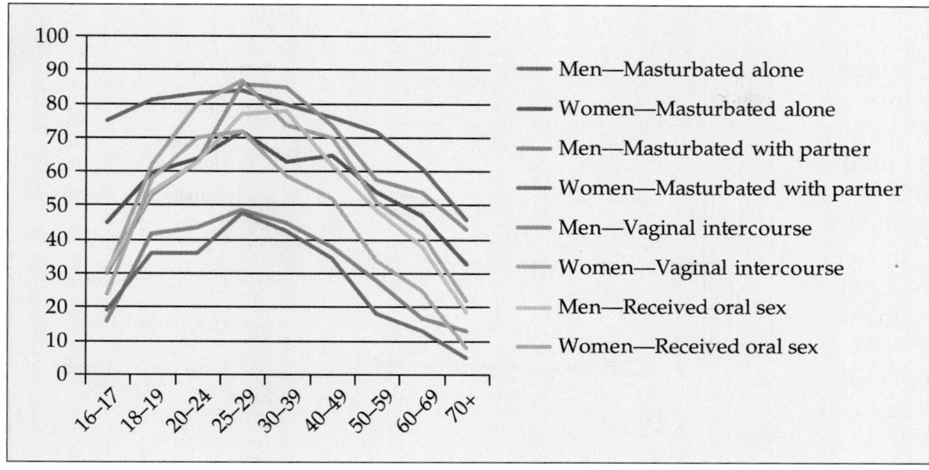

FIGURE 14-2 Percentage of Americans Performing Certain Sexual Behaviors in the Past Year by Age Group

SOURCE: "Percentage of Americans performing certain sexual behaviors in the past year," Center for Sexual Health Promotion, 2010, retrieved from http://www.nationalsexustudy. Indiana.edu/.

and cognitions, all of which take place in a sociocultural context. What do we know about sexuality in middle adulthood? Because sex is inherently a private act, it is difficult to know with any degree of accuracy what types of sexual activities adults prefer and in what types they engage. However, two large and fairly recent national surveys of sexuality provide us some opportunity to understand sexuality during this period of the lifespan.

The first of these was conducted in the early 1990s by researchers at the University of Chicago (Laumann, Gagnon, Michael, & Michaels, 1994), and the second in the mid-2000s by researchers at the University of Indiana (Center for Sexual Health Promotion, 2010). Although these surveys looked at somewhat different issues, both found that many adults in middle age were still engaging in sex, most were enjoying their sexuality about as much as they had earlier in adulthood, and many were interested in a variety of sexual behaviors. For example, most men and women reported being at least somewhat physically and emotionally satisfied with sex, and these percentages did not change much throughout emerging and young adulthood, nor in the early years of middle adulthood. However, beginning at about age 50, some shifts typically occur with regard to sexual satisfaction. Although men continue to find sex enjoyable, and in fact their satisfaction with sex becomes even greater as they age, women's overall satisfaction with sex begins to decline at about this point in the lifespan (Laumann, Gagnon, Michael, & Michaels, 1994; see Figure 14-1). A somewhat different picture emerges with respect to sexual behavior, which for both men and women reaches a peak in young adulthood, but declines as people move into middle adulthood and beyond (Center for Sexual Health Promotion, 2010; see Figure 14-2). Various factors have been identified to help explain why sexual behaviors decline in middle adulthood and beyond. For women, becoming widowed begins to increase in middle adulthood, and this is linked to the decline in sexual behaviors that involve a partner; for men, the decline is more closely tied to poorer physical health at older ages (Karraker & DeLamater, 2011). Women also begin to experience less satisfaction with sex during menopause, and this, too, contributes to less interest in and participation in sexual activities (Woods & Mitchell, 2010).

Thus, for many adults, sexuality is redefined during the middle years with more emphasis placed on **sensuality**, which includes a range of physical expressions that may or may not lead to a sexual act. Hugging, hand holding, touching, and stroking are as much expressions of mature sexuality as they are of caring and affection. Such expressions of caring and concern serve a variety of functions during the middle adult years and are especially important during times of illness, the topic we discuss in the next section.

sensuality
Hugging, touching, stroking, and other behaviors that may or may not lead to sex

REVIEW THE FACTS 14-2

1. In middle adulthood, reaction time usually ________ and performance usually ________.
   a. slows down; remains constant
   b. remains constant; decreases
   c. slows down; increases
   d. becomes faster; decreases
2. The overall complex of physical and emotional changes that middle-aged men and women experience due to hormonal changes is called the ________.
3. According to the text, about what percentage of U.S. women report that symptoms of menopause are bothersome?
   a. 20% b. 50%
   c. 70% d. 95%
4. All of the following are changes typically associated with menopause, *except*
   a. increased risk of osteoporosis.
   b. decreased production of estrogen.
   c. enlargement of the vagina.
   d. less production of lubricating fluids during sexual intercourse.
5. About what percentage of men over the age of 40 experience some erectile dysfunction?
   a. 5% b. 15%
   c. 50% d. 85%
6. Toward the end of middle adulthood, satisfaction with the physical and emotional dimensions of sex ________ for men and ________ for women.
   a. increases; increases b. decreases; decreases
   c. increases; decreases d. decreases; increases

Practice on **MyDevelopmentLab**

DISEASE AND HEALTH

As the body ages, many changes gradually occur. Among these is an increasing vulnerability to disease. Many people assume that deaths due to disease continue to increase uniformly throughout adulthood; however, this is not the case. In middle age, deaths are most likely to result from cancers and heart attacks (U.S. Census Bureau, 2012r), the prevalence of which increases throughout this period (see Figure 14-3). In later adulthood (here defined as over age 65), deaths are increasingly due to infectious diseases, respiratory disorders, mental disorders (especially dementias such as Alzheimer's), as well as cancers, heart failure, and degenerative cardiovascular disease (see Chapter 16). Thus, death in middle adulthood can be characterized as the result of chronic diseases that develop prematurely in high-risk individuals. In many cases, there are gender differences in the rates at which these chronic diseases occur (see Table 14-3); these often reflect lifestyle differences in the paths chosen by men and women, but may also reflect different patterns of vulnerability between the sexes. Death from disease in later adulthood is better described as resulting from age-related processes that are common to almost all people.

Although cancer and heart disease are the most common causes of death in middle age, other disease processes also can be involved. Some diseases of middle adulthood are not life threatening but nonetheless cause considerable discomfort and interfere with daily living. Arthritis, for example, troubles many middle-aged people of both sexes (see Figure 14-4).

In general, women maintain their earlier health advantages over men throughout middle age (see Figure 14-5). For example, throughout much of the lifespan, the death rate of

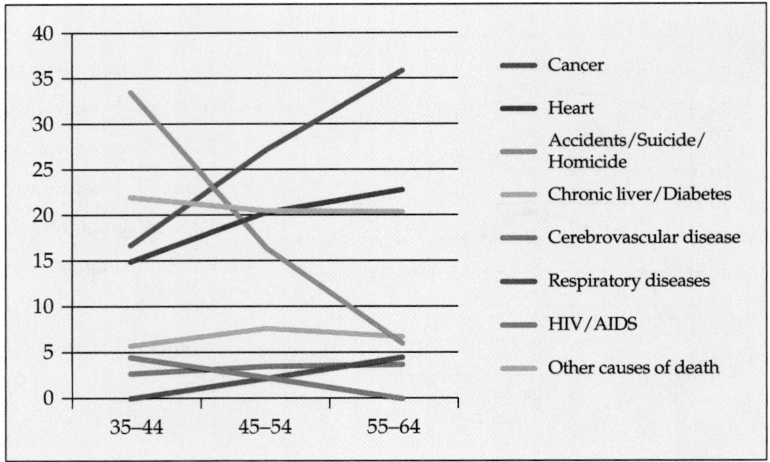

FIGURE 14-3 **Causes of Death in Early, Early-Middle, and Later-Middle Adulthood, Percent of All Deaths by Age Group**

SOURCE: Table 122, "Deaths and death rates by leading casus of death and age: 2007," in *Statistical abstract of the United States: 2012*, U.S. Census Bureau, 2012, Washington, DC: Author.

Table 14-3 Age-Adjusted Death Rates for Selected Causes of Death by Sex (per 100,000 population)

	Men	Women
Overall risk, all causes	900.6	643.4
Heart diseases	232.3	150.4
Stroke	40.9	39.9
Cancers	213.6	148.5
Respiratory diseases (including influenza and pneumonia)	71.3	54.1
Liver diseases	12.7	6.0
Diabetes	25.6	18.8
HIV	4.8	1.9
Accidents	53.6	25.1
Suicide	18.9	4.8
Homicide	9.3	2.4
Alzheimer's disease	20.6	26.7

*Age-adjusted rates are computed to compare risks of two or more groups at a given point in time. Thus, they are relative indices that do not convey information about actual risk. Here they provide a means of comparing death risk for men versus women across all age categories.

SOURCE: From Table 24, "Age-adjusted death rates for selected causes of death, by sex, race, and Hispanic origin: United States, selected years 1950–2008," in *Health, United States, 2011*, National Center for Health Statistics (NCHS), 2012, Hyattsville, MD: Author.

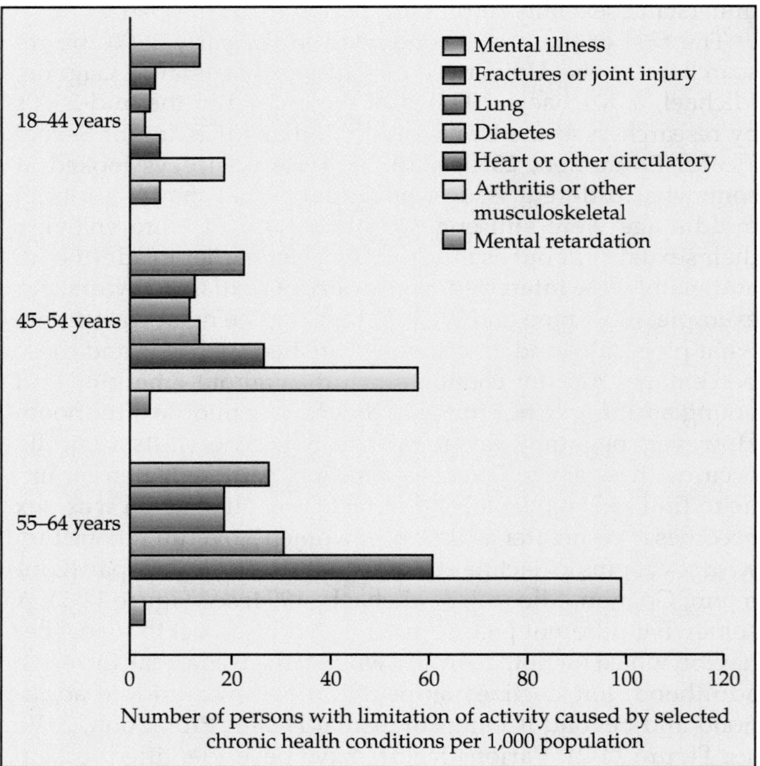

FIGURE 14-4 **Limitation of Activity Caused by Selected Chronic Health Conditions Among Working-Age Adults, by Age: United States**

SOURCE: From "Limitation of activity caused by chronic conditions: Working-age and older adults," National Center for Health Statistics (NCHS), 2010, *Health, United States, 2009: With special feature on medical technology*, Hyattsville, MD: Author.

men at any particular age is about twice that of women of the same age. This is partly because men are more likely to work in dangerous occupations. It is also likely that men have a higher genetic predisposition to certain diseases than women do. Psychological factors may also contribute: Men are likely to be less concerned about their health and are less likely to visit a doctor when ill or for a checkup. Men also are more likely to commit suicide. Educational level also has a major impact on death rates in middle adulthood (see Figure 14-6). People with more than a high school education are at less than half the risk of dying early than are those with 12 years of schooling or less (Xu, Kochanek, Murphy, & Tejada-Vera, 2010).

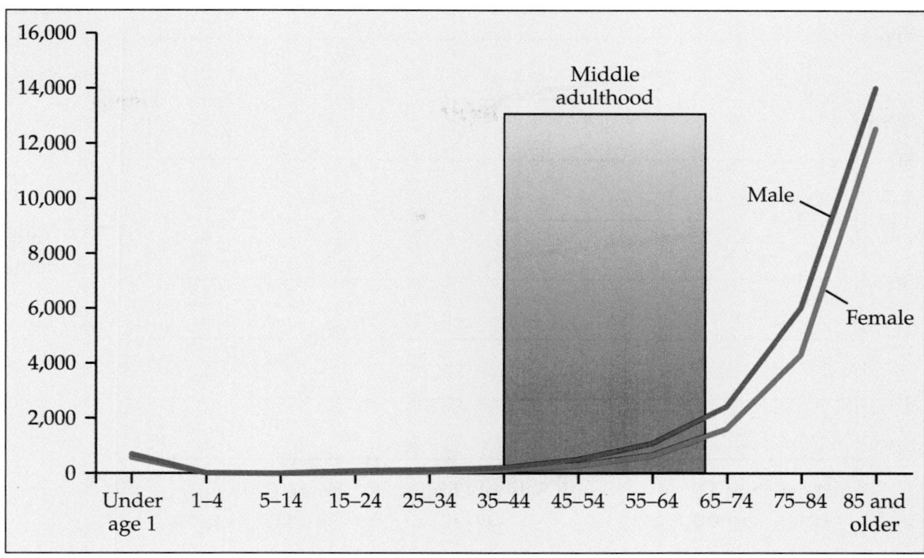

FIGURE 14-5 Age-Adjusted Death Rates by Sex Across the Lifespan

NOTE: Age-adjusted rates are computed to compare risks of two or more groups at a given point in time. Thus, they are relative indices that do not convey information about actual risk. Here, they provide a means of comparing death risk for men versus women.

SOURCE: Table 29, "Death rates for all causes, by sex, race, Hispanic origin, and age: United States, selected years 1950–2008," National Center for Health Statistics (NCHS), 2012, *Health, United States, 2011: With special feature on socioeconomic status and health*, Hyattsville, MD: Author.

The Cumulative Effects of Health Habits

Fortunately, most middle-aged people will not suffer serious, life-threatening forms of any disease. There also is some good news about aging and health, as outlined in Table 14-4. For example, the life expectancy for individuals who make it to age 45 in the United States is about 80 years, and over 80% of people who reach age 45 survive and remain in reasonably good health at least until age 65 (U.S. Census Bureau, 2012i). Although the average lifespan has not increased much beyond 85 years for any subset of the population, a sizable proportion of adults in the United States maintain relatively good health throughout middle adulthood.

Good Health Habits In part, longevity is attributable to good health habits. With a balanced and nutritious diet, a reasonable amount of exercise, and regular health care, many people will experience an active and extended adulthood. Indeed, many health experts believe that by following a program of regular exercise, reduced stress, and a good diet people can slow the aging process and continue to function with youthful vitality and a sense of well-being throughout middle adulthood and beyond (Katzel & Steinbrenner, 2012; Merrill & Verbrugge, 1999; Spiro, 2001).

The life expectancy at birth for people born 45 years ago was about 68 years. The life expectancy for this same group of people, who now are age 45, is about 80 years. What factors most likely account for the difference in these statistics?

Exercise is especially important: Numerous studies have shown that exercise before and during middle adulthood can increase physical capacities and endurance. Certain kinds of exercise—especially aerobic exercises—are designed to increase heart and lung capacity, thus supplying the body with more oxygen and, in turn, more energy. Even short-term, mild exercise-training programs for formerly sedentary middle-aged adults produce impressive gains in strength and heart and lung functioning. Regular exercise can slow the deterioration of muscle tissue, reduce body fat, help prevent deterioration of the joints, and combat some kinds of arthritis.

Poor Health Habits The cumulative effects of poor health habits during early adulthood often take their toll in middle adulthood—most chronic disorders begin to develop long before they are diagnosed. Chief among these chronic disorders are conditions related to cigarette smoking. Smoking contributes to cancer of the lung, mouth, pharynx, larynx, esophagus, colon,

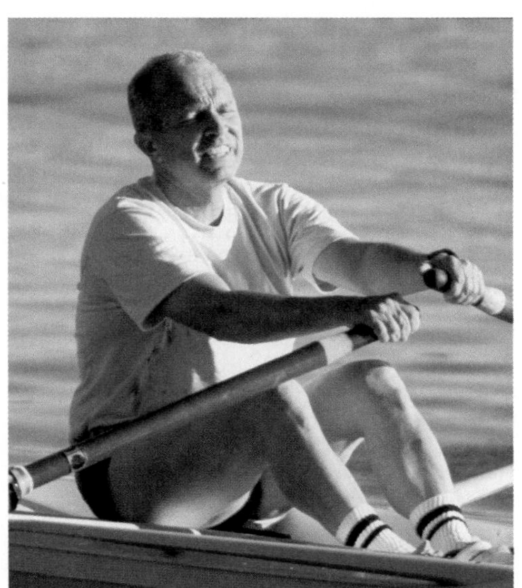

◀ Middle-aged people who exercise tend to maintain their youthful vitality and sense of well-being.

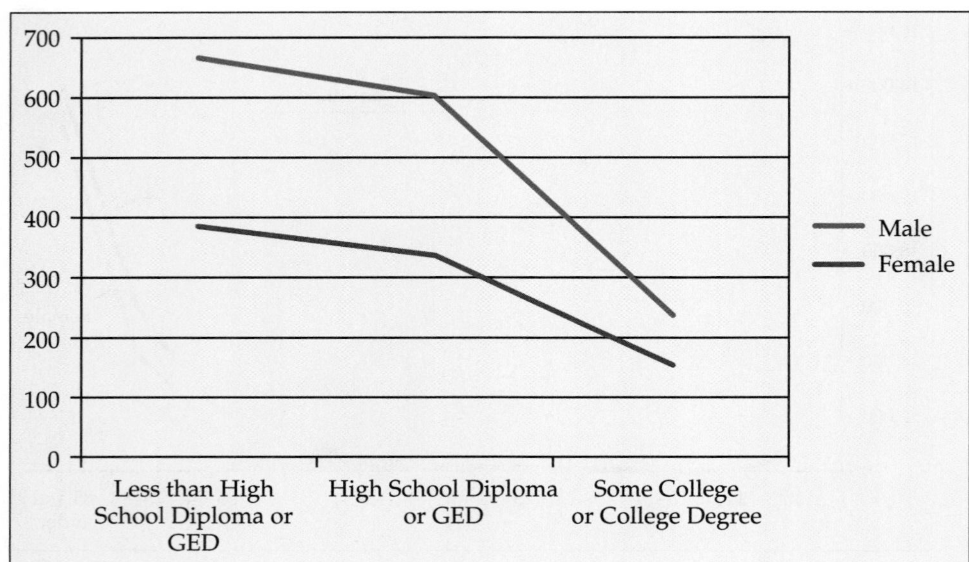

FIGURE 14-6 Death Rates from All Causes, Ages 25 to 64, According to Educational Level

NOTE: Age-adjusted rates are computed to compare risks of two or more groups at a given point in time. Thus, they are relative indices that do not convey information about actual risk. Here they provide a means of comparing death risk for men versus women.

SOURCE: "Deaths: Final data for 2007," by J. Q. Xu, K. D. Kochanek, S. L. Murphy, & B. Tejada-Vera, 2010, *National Vital Statistics Reports, 58*(19), National Center for Health Statistics (NCHS), Hyattsville, MD.

stomach, pancreas, uterus, cervix, kidney, ureter, and bladder; to various respiratory diseases including emphysema; to cardiovascular diseases; to arteriosclerosis; to hypertension; and to other diseases as well. Of the more than 2.4 million deaths in the United States today, it is estimated that 20% (about 480,000) are caused by smoking-related illnesses (American Cancer Society, 2011). Smoking accounts for about 30% of all deaths due to cancer, and for 80% of all lung cancer deaths. Lung cancer is the leading cause of cancer deaths among both men and women. The link between cancer and smoking is not surprising when one considers that cigarettes contain not only nicotine, but also more than 60 other chemicals known to cause cancer (American Cancer Society, 2011).

Despite 50 years of media campaigns about the dangers of smoking, about 20% of U.S. adults continues to smoke, although the percentage has dropped significantly since 1965, when nearly 42% of adults smoked (National Center for Health Statistics [NCHS], 2012a). The health risks associated with cigarette smoking are well known, but nicotine is a highly addictive drug. Although about 70% of those who smoke want to quit, and 35% attempt to quit each year, less than 5% succeed (American Cancer Society, 2011). Demographic groups that are disproportionately affected by the lure of cigarette smoking include people with the least education, those living below the poverty level, and those in the period of the lifespan referred to as emerging adulthood (American Cancer Society, 2011; NCHS, 2012a).

Regular smoking is just one habit that can lead to chronic disorders. Heavy use of any drug, including alcohol, has long-term consequences. As the liver and kidneys age, they become less efficient at clearing unusual amounts of drugs from the body. Cumulative damage to these two organs often begins to become apparent in middle adulthood (Horiuchi, Finch, Mesle, & Vallin, 2003). According to recent national surveys, more than half of the U.S. adult population drank alcohol in the past 30 days. Among those age 35 and over, 5% drank heavily, and nearly 20% engaged in binge drinking, and both trends are increasing (CDC, 2011c). Correspondingly, alcohol-related deaths are high. Nearly 80,000 people die each year as the result of excessive alcohol use, making alcohol consumption the third-leading cause of preventable death in the United States, following tobacco use and obesity (CDC, 2011c).

Although cigarette smoking and alcohol consumption are common practices for U.S. adults, other drugs also are linked to serious negative health consequences. Today, nearly

Table 14-4 The Good News About Aging and Health

- Many of the losses of function associated with aging can be stopped or slowed.
- Even past age 70, only 20 to 30% of people have symptoms of heart disease.
- Much of the cognitive decline that older people experience is attributable to treatable diseases.
- It actually is healthy to gain a pound or so a year from age 40 on—middle-aged people should avoid obesity, of course, but being concerned about losing 5 or 10 pounds is trivial.
- Finally, an aside: People do not get crankier as they age. Cranky older people were just as cranky when they were younger.

SOURCE: From "A study for the ages," by N. Shute, 1997, *U.S. News and World Report, 122*(22), 67–70, 72, 76–78, 80.

The long-term effects of alcohol abuse and smoking often become apparent in middle age.

▲ The cumulative hassles and stresses of daily life, including events like this simple traffic jam, can exert a toll on health and well-being.

40,000 deaths each year are tied directly to drug use, including deaths due to overdose, suicide, accidental injuries while using drugs, and deaths to newborns as a consequence of their mother's drug use (Kochanek, Xu, Murphy, Miniño, & Kung, 2011). Furthermore, drug use—like the use of cigarettes and alcohol—is indirectly linked to death from many different causes because these substances are associated with other habits that are unhealthy. Foremost among these are poor nutrition, obesity, and the lack of regular exercise.

Obesity, in particular, has become a more prevalent problem. Today, over 70% of U.S. adults between the ages of 20 and 74 are either overweight or obese. This percentage has increased dramatically in recent years—about 60% since 1980 (FIFARS, 2010d). Weight problems become more prevalent as adults move through the period of middle adulthood; about 40% of men and women between the ages of 45 and 65 are obese, meaning that their body mass index (BMI) is greater than 30.0 (Ogden, Carroll, Kit, & Flegal, 2012; see Chapter 8 for a discussion of BMI). Being overweight is now considered the second largest preventable cause of death and disease in adulthood, just behind smoking and just ahead of alcohol abuse. In addition, it is during middle adulthood that many of the health-related effects of obesity are seen, as diabetes, high blood pressure, and other forms of cardiovascular disease become more prevalent and problematic. Sustained overweight also affects muscles and joints—hip and knee replacements are not only becoming more common but also are being performed earlier in life—and low back pain also is a chronic problem for many overweight adults. As noted in previous chapters, obesity typically involves poor nutrition and the lack of regular exercise, and programs designed to help overweight adults lose weight usually focus on making healthier food choices and working appropriate exercise into one's daily life.

Stress and Health

Increasing evidence shows that the way people live has a marked effect on their health. Stress in particular plays a role in many of the diseases of middle adulthood. In the case of heart disease, for example, there is a complex interrelationship among lifestyle, personality, genetic factors, and stress.

Stress, however, is a normal part of life. This leads us to ask, are all stressful events equally dangerous? A classic approach to understanding how life events are linked to stress resulted from a study of hospital patients who were asked to rate the stressfulness of a variety of life events that occurred before they became ill (Holmes & Rahe, 1967). Not surprisingly, some life events were associated with more stress than were others, as shown in Table 14-5. The death of a spouse, for example, was judged in 1967 to be the highest stress producer and was assigned a value of 100. At the other extreme, a change in eating habits was rated as only mildly disruptive and was assigned a value of only 15. Stressful events, of course, occur in a social context. Accordingly, the amount of stress associated with life events can change over time, a premise that caused Richard Rahe to revise this rating scale in 1997, noting that life today is more stressful than in earlier decades (Miller & Rahe, 1997). Recently, data gathered through an online survey of 10 of the original life events have served to point out that, while some events generally cause less stress for adults today than they did 40 years ago, others cause more (Jayson, 2008; see Table 14-5).

Of course, each person experiences stressful events in somewhat unique ways. How an individual perceives and interprets an event can play an important role in how much stress that event causes. For example, a divorce may be devastating to a 50-year-old man whose wife leaves him to marry his best friend, but may seem much less traumatic to a couple who have agreed they both will be better off apart. Also, some people are simply better able to handle stress (Zautra & Reich, 2011). Researchers have repeatedly pointed out that the same event may cause considerable distress for one person but be viewed as a positive challenge by another person (Lazarus,

Table 14-5 Stress Scale for Selected Life Events, 1967 and 2007

	1967	2007
Death of a spouse	100	80
Death of a family member	63	70
Divorce/separation	73	65
Job layoff or firing	47	62
Pregnancy/birth of a child	40	60
Death of a friend	37	58
Marriage	50	50
Retirement	45	49
Marital reconciliation	45	48
Change of job field	36	47
Child leaves home	29	43

SOURCE: Adapted from "Point values add up to far more stress these days," by S. Jayson, USA Today (2008, May 5), Life section, p. 4D.

1981, 1999, 2000). Age, too, can make a difference: The events that college students find stressful are somewhat different from those that cause stress in later life (Aldwin, 2011; Renner & Mackin, 2002). In addition, if an event is anticipated or expected, it usually is less stressful than if it occurs suddenly and without warning. Finally, it is important to recognize that stressful events are additive: If several stressful events occur at the same time, the impact is much worse than if only one or two occur. Thus, the impact of any particular stressful event depends to some extent on what other conditions are present (Cooper & Dewe, 2007).

Stress, of course, results not only from major life events but also from the accumulation of the little *hassles* we face every day. Waiting in lines, driving in heavy traffic, arguing with children, being unhappy about one's appearance, not having enough money, or just feeling like there's too much to do all cause stress, and these stresses are associated with one's physical and mental health (Aldwin, 2007, 2011; Harrington, 2013; Lazarus, 1981). In addition, major life stresses often trigger an increased supply of little hassles. For example, a divorced person must cope with the emotional impact of this major life event and also with an array of smaller problems and adjustments, such as having less income, having more responsibility for housework and cooking, and having to arrange for children's visits. Experiencing a major stressful event can contribute in many ways to the stress of daily life.

Perhaps the important point is this: Regardless of the sources of stress, when too much stress if present, illness is more likely to result (Folkman, 2011). Because middle adulthood is a time when some people do lose spouses through death, divorce, and separation and also a time when they may experience other stress-producing changes such as early retirement and serious illness, it is easy to see that the middle years have the potential for extremely high stress levels.

Which major life events do you think cause the most stress? Are these events consistent with the rating scheme summarized in Table 14-5?

How does stress take its toll? We have long observed the connection between stressful lifestyles and the increased risk of certain illnesses, including heart disease, stroke, diabetes, stomach ulcers, and some forms of cancer. Evidence suggests that extreme or prolonged stress contributes to illness by weakening the immune system (Caserta, et al., 2008; Hamilton-West, 2011; Segerstrom, 2007). Stress also may affect our ability or willingness to take care of ourselves: When we are under stress, we may exercise less, eat poorly, experience problems sleeping, and engage more in unhealthy behaviors like smoking and drinking alcohol (Biondi et al., 2001). Fortunately, by middle age, most adults have settled into lifestyles that involve manageable levels of stress and have acquired good coping skills to deal with most hassles that come their way (Aldwin, 2011; Aldwin, Yancura, & Boeninger, 2004).

Ethnicity, Poverty, and Health

Some adults, of course, live in more stressful conditions than others do. Many members of disadvantaged minority groups and those who live in poverty often experience special challenges that contribute to stress, and these conditions are reflected in the greater incidence of poor health and earlier death associated with these groups. This burden is present throughout life, but it is especially evident during the middle and older adult years. For example, in the 45- to 64-year-old group, the death rate for Blacks is nearly twice the rate for Whites (NCHS, 2012c). Statistics show that Blacks are more likely to die during this period of life from heart disease, hypertension, cancer, diabetes, accidents, and AIDS than are Whites. Similarly, Hispanics have higher death rates from infectious and parasitic diseases, diabetes, hypertension, and AIDS than Whites do (NCHS, 2012c). Higher murder rates in some low-income or minority neighborhoods are also a factor.

Numerous social forces are at least partly responsible for these differences (see the box Current Issues: Health and Social Issues—Why Are Some Groups at Risk?). Many features of life for a low-income minority person involve a significant amount of stress, and stress contributes to unhealthy behaviors, increased health risks, and earlier death (Aldwin, 2011; Aldwin & Levenson, 2001). Cigarettes, alcohol, drugs, and overeating help people cope with daily stresses, which may be one reason why the incidence of these bad habits is higher in minority groups. Although these health habits are associated with negative long-term consequences, they provide immediate physiological and psychological compensations that enable people to cope with the stresses of their daily lives (Hamilton-West, 2011). The stress associated with racism can also take a toll (Peters, 2006; Williams & Mohammed, 2009).

Can you suggest why the relationships among ethnicity, stress, and health care are best considered as resulting from interactions among these variables?

Access to health care when needed is another issue that contributes to disparities in health outcomes between members of the majority and those who belong to disadvantaged minority groups or who have limited financial resources. Many low-wage jobs do not offer health-care insurance, yet the wages earned are sufficiently high that families do not qualify for government-supported health-care programs. Families of the working poor therefore tend to underutilize the health-care system until they are in a state of emergency (and therefore will not be turned away from hospital emergency rooms). In addition, low-wage jobs without health insurance virtually prevent many people

Watch *Gender Differences in Stress Vulnerability* on **MyDevelopmentLab**

Watch *Urban Sprawl and Obesity* on **MyDevelopmentLab**

CURRENT ISSUES

Health and Social Issues—Why Are Some Groups at Risk?

Middle adulthood for any individual is in part a "playing out" of what has gone before—the opportunities, the challenges, the hard work, the misfortunes, the stresses, and the coping styles one has learned in order to survive. National statistics make clear that people who live in poverty or who are victims of discrimination enjoy less healthy lifestyles, and the impact of these lifestyles becomes more apparent as people get older. For people in these groups, the pressures and strains of life are reflected in increased rates of disease, stress, obesity, early death, and financial tension.

What factors best explain why people in these groups are at risk? In order to probe such complex issues, as well as to better understand how all adults experience middle age, the MacArthur Foundation established the Research Network on Successful Midlife Development—MIDMAC, for short. As part of their effort to better understand midlife, an interdisciplinary team of social scientists constructed a large and detailed national multidisciplinary survey—the National Survey of Midlife in the United States (MIDUS)—that was administered to over 7,000 randomly selected U.S. adults (Brim, Ryff, & Kessler, 2004; MIDUS, 2011). The first interview—about 45 minutes by phone—was followed by a detailed questionnaire, which took about 2 hours to complete. Due to the nature of the survey procedure, researchers expected that the low-income portion of the middle-aged population would be underrepresented, making conclusions difficult to extend to members of this group. Consequently, an additional sample was recruited from low-income residents of New York and Chicago. In-depth interviews about peoples' lives, both in the present and in the past, were conducted by sensitive interviewers of similar ethnic and language backgrounds.

Because an extra effort was made to include people who often are left out of research reports, the MIDUS study has provided researchers with insight into what life for low-income and minority middle-aged adults is like. Results generally show that hard-working, proud, low-income minority adults in their 40s and 50s have usually done the best they could with the cards they were dealt. Sometimes that means that they care for their grandchildren out of necessity because their adult child is a single parent, is disabled or ill, or is in jail. Often they themselves, or perhaps a spouse or parent, must wrestle with a chronic disease like high blood pressure or diabetes. They work hard to make ends meet, perhaps at a restaurant or service job, but they often do not get much in the way of retirement benefits or health care beyond what Social Security and Medicare provide. Not surprisingly, making it the hard way takes its toll on lifestyle and on health.

According to Arline Geronimus, a researcher at the University of Michigan, economically poor minorities experience what she calls "weathering" (Newman, 2006). According to this weathering hypothesis, those who live in poverty or experience chronic discrimination because of their ethnic or racial status must deal with an accumulating burden of stress. This stress produces the onset of early disease and chronic health conditions and ultimately contributes to earlier death. To answer questions specifically related to health, a second phase of the MIDUS project was launched in 2002 (MIDUS, 2011). MIDUS II has involved the re-interviewing of 75% of the respondents in the original MIDUS survey. Its focus has been on health-related issues and on levels of cognitive functioning experienced by adults during middle age. Thus, this part of the project aims particularly to help us better understand how aging processes unfold. A third phase of the MIDUS project was recently funded, based on the success of the first two phases. MIDUS III, which is funded from 2011 to 2016, involves the recruitment of 2,600 new participants and is keyed to look especially at how the recent economic recession is impacting the lives of U.S. adults during midlife. This part of the project, known as the "MIDUS refresher" component, will focus not only on employment status, but also on the economic and emotional well-being of middle-aged adults, and on the quality of their family lives. MIDUS III also will re-interview the original respondents, gaining a longitudinal perspective on how the lives of middle-aged U.S. adults unfold.

These follow-up studies are especially important because research shows that *both* low-income status and minority group membership contribute to health risks. It has long been understood that financial struggles are linked to poor health habits, lack of appropriate health care, and consequently poorer health and earlier death. However, even when they have comparable economic positions with Whites, Blacks in the United States suffer higher rates of chronic disease and earlier death. Thus, both minority status and low income are linked to the development of ill health (Newman, 2003).

What factors account for the diminished health that low-income and minority adults experience? When people live in poverty or experience chronic discrimination, stress is a significant issue (Peters, 2006; Williams & Mohammed, 2009). Life in the inner city is hard, and daily challenges are significant. Access to health care is another issue. Control over one's environment is also a factor. If people believe that they cannot control the events of their lives, stress results, and it is often chronic and unrelenting. Education also is a key: People who report good mental and physical health are much more likely to have a college degree or at least a high school degree.

Of course, all of these challenges are woven together in each person's life, and they are cumulative. Most people can deal with manageable levels of stress, especially if one stressful event can be dealt with before another occurs. For the working poor, however, stressful events pile up with little opportunity for relief, especially if ethnic-based or racial discrimination is also involved. Yet, for most individuals, there is resilience, even when the challenges are significant. In comparison to White Americans, for example, members of minorities are less likely to suffer from depression. Nevertheless, life is more challenging for those in some segments of the population than in others, and most researchers believe it is the stress of facing these continuing issues that explains, at least in part, the health risks associated with poverty and minority status.

---

in low-income or minority groups from having regular or preventative health screenings, physical examinations, and access to other early detection methods. For those who do not speak English or who are intimidated by the complex bureaucracy that surrounds health care delivery in the United States today, access to quality care is even further threatened.

To address these, and many other, health-care-related issues, Congress enacted legislation that became law in 2010. Called the Affordable Care Act, and known colloquially as "Obamacare," this act seeks to extend health-care benefits to many people in the United States who formerly were uninsured or underinsured. The Affordable Care Act has been highly controversial, and it remains to be seen how its provisions will be implemented. Regardless, however, the act does recognize the disparity between rich and poor in the health-care options that presently exist.

REVIEW THE FACTS 14-3

1. The two most common causes of death in middle adulthood are ________ and ________.
2. The life expectancy of a 45-year-old person in the United States is now about age
   a. 72. b. 80.
   c. 88. d. 93.
3. The three leading preventable causes of death during middle adulthood are (in order from first to third):
   a. alcohol abuse, smoking, obesity.
   b. obesity, alcohol abuse, smoking.
   c. obesity, smoking, alcohol abuse.
   d. smoking, obesity, alcohol abuse.
4. About what percentage of U.S. adults today are overweight or obese?
   a. 35% b. 45%
   c. 60% d. 70%
5. Stress appears to contribute most directly to the increased susceptibility of disease leading to early death by weakening the
   a. immune system.
   b. vessels of the heart.
   c. brain.
   d. way in which the digestive system can process nutrients.
6. Suggest three reasons why members of low-income minority groups have on average higher rates of illness and early death.

Practice on **MyDevelopmentLab**

COGNITIVE CONTINUITY AND CHANGE

Although some cognitive functions decline as we age, we now know that many of these declines occur later and are much more gradual than researchers assumed as recently as 20 years ago (Berg, 2000). Furthermore, serious cognitive decline is not a universal aspect of aging. When it does occur, it often affects only certain areas of intellectual functioning (see Chapter 16).

Although some minor age-related cognitive declines may begin early in adulthood (Salthouse, 2009), most cognitive abilities remain strong through middle adulthood. In fact, some important aspects of intelligence actually increase during middle adulthood and beyond, especially for college-educated adults who remain active (Gour et al., 2011; Li, et al., 2004; Schaie, 2007; Tucker-Drob, 2009). Contrary to the stereotype that intellectual development peaks in adolescence or young adulthood, middle adulthood is the time of maximum performance of many higher-order cognitive abilities, especially in areas related to work and daily living (Schaie, 1996, 2007; Willis, 1989).

Fluid Versus Crystallized Intelligence

A useful way to examine how cognition changes with advancing age is to consider the various kinds of abilities a person uses in solving problems of different types. One common method of categorizing intellectual skills is to divide them into those that involve **crystallized intelligence** versus those that involve **fluid intelligence** (see Table 14-6). Crystallized intelligence refers to the accumulated knowledge and skills that come with education and life experiences. Crystallized intelligence is also referred to as *cognitive pragmatics*, reflecting the notion that it is learned and therefore influenced by culture (Baltes, 1993; Nisbett, et al., 2012). Fluid intelligence consists of the abilities involved in acquiring new knowledge and skills, including memorizing, reasoning inductively, and perceiving new relationships between objects and events. Also referred to as *cognitive mechanics*, these abilities reflect neurological functioning more closely and are more likely to be affected when brain damage occurs (Baltes, 1993; Nisbett et al., 2012; Sternberg, Grigorenko, & Oh, 2001). Thus, it is not surprising that fMRI brain scanning studies find that although general intelligence is associated with activity in a wide variety of brain regions, fluid and crystallized intelligence are each associated with distinctly different regions of the brain (Blair, 2010; Nisbett et al., 2012).

Early research examining how crystallized intelligence and fluid intelligence change throughout adulthood typically showed that crystallized intelligence remained high and perhaps even increased throughout middle age, whereas fluid intelligence began to decline in early adulthood and continued to get worse with age (Horn & Blankson, 2005; Horn & Noll, 1997; see Figure 14-7). These early studies, however, employed cross-sectional research methods, which compare groups of various ages to each other (see Chapter 1). Consequently, it was impossible to determine if the age-related decrements observed were the result of mental deterioration or of different learning and life experiences that existed between the different cohort groups who were born in different eras and led different types of lives. Because younger cohorts were better educated, had better health, and had better nutrition, it is reasonable to suspect that the age-related declines observed were in part the result of these factors rather than the effects of aging.

What happens when a longitudinal approach is used to examine crystallized and fluid intelligence? The results vary somewhat from one study to the next, but when measured among well-educated populations, many intellectual abilities actually are seen to increase throughout middle age. For example, according to results of the broad-based Seattle Longitudinal Study of Age and Intellectual Function (Schaie, 2007), it appears that several different kinds of intellectual abilities, both fluid and crystallized, either increase or are maintained throughout much of adulthood, declining only after age 60 if at all (see Figure 16-8). Indeed, some studies show that middle-aged adults are more knowledgeable than are younger adults in a variety of task domains (Ackerman, 2000; Tucker-Drob, 2009).

Implications for Intellectual Functioning It appears that the large majority of adults maintain a high level of functioning across

crystallized intelligence
Accumulated knowledge and skills based on education and life experiences; also referred to as *cognitive pragmatics*

fluid intelligence
Abilities involved in acquiring new knowledge and skills; also referred to as *cognitive mechanics*

Table 14-6 A Comparison of Crystallized Versus Fluid Intelligence

	Crystallized Intelligence	**Fluid Intelligence**
Definition	The body of knowledge and skills accumulated through education and life experiences; also called cognitive pragmatics	The ability to acquire new knowledge and skills; also called cognitive mechanics
Source	Influenced largely by culture	Influenced largely by neurological functioning
Representative tasks	Vocabulary General information Experiential evaluation	Figural relations Inductive reasoning
Age-related changes	Remains mostly unaffected by age	Begins to diminish somewhat in adulthood and continues to get worse with age, especially when tasks are associated with speed of mental processing

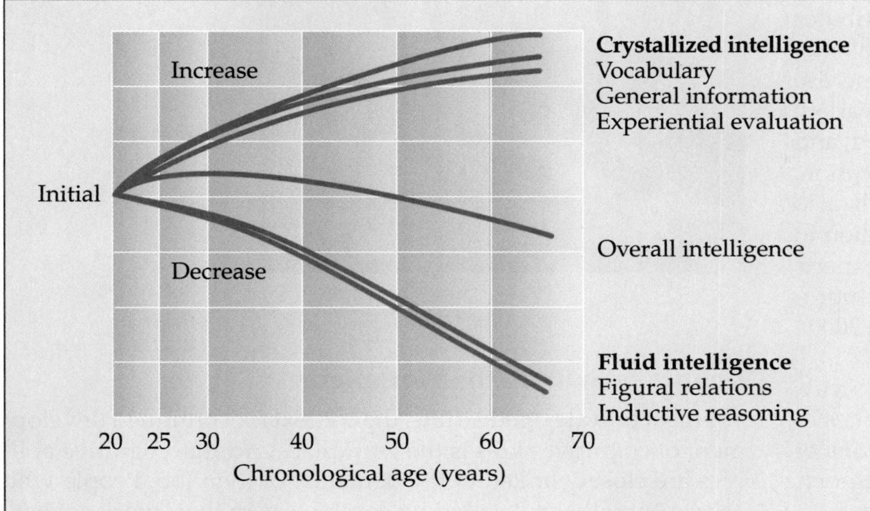

FIGURE 14-7 **A Cross-Sectional Comparison of Changes in Intellectual Abilities with Age, Based on Early Research**

a broad spectrum of intellectual abilities throughout middle adulthood (Gerstorf, Ram, Hoppmann, Willis, & Schaie, 2011; Willis & Schaie, 2006). There are, however, rather wide individual differences (Tucker-Drob & Salthouse, 2011). When we look at how individuals change as they grow older, results generally show that 45 to 60% of people maintain a stable level of overall intellectual performance—both fluid and crystallized—well into their 70s. About 10 to 15% of people even show increases in performance until their mid-70s. However, a slightly larger group of roughly 30% show declines by the time they reach their 60s; the cognitive decline of many of these individuals probably is the result of disease processes in the brain or of brain degeneration associated with the use of drugs or alcohol (Schaie, 2007; Willis & Schaie, 1999).

If there is a decline in intellectual functioning associated with age, it is most likely to be seen in tasks involving speed, since various psychomotor processes gradually begin to slow down in middle age because of physical and neurological decline (Nisbett et al., 2012; refer to Figure 14-7). For example, studies have linked the slower speed with which adults solve complex problems with shrinkage in the prefrontal regions of the brain as measured by fMRI scans (Head, Rodrigue, Kennedy, & Raz, 2008). Usually, however, this general slowing is not noticed in middle age because adults automatically compensate for declines in speed with increases in efficiency and general knowledge (Hess, 2005; Mata, Schooler, & Rieskamp, 2007). Indeed, some researchers speculate that as brain shrinkage occurs, the affected regions of the brain actually show higher levels of activation (Greenwood, 2007a). Thus, it may be that the aging brain is able to compensate for structural losses by reorganizing itself to be more efficient. Although not all researchers agree that this explanation is valid (e.g., Greenwood, 2007b), most researchers do agree that in healthy middle-aged adults, brain changes are not strongly linked to cognitive declines (Salthouse, 2011, 2012).

It is also true, of course, that middle-aged adults have had many more life experiences than younger adults, and they simply *know* more as a result. On many tasks, this larger warehouse of knowledge and experience can help compensate for any age-related declines in functioning. Furthermore, keeping mentally active appears to contribute to one's ability to avoid age-related cognitive decline. Individuals who undertake intellectual pursuits, especially if they are outside the person's primary profession, or who explore new activities and ways of thinking are especially likely to maintain their level of intellectual functioning in middle age (Pirttila-Backman & Kajanne, 2001; Valenzuela et al., 2012). Even into old age, carrying out complex mental tasks is believed to have a positive effect on intellectual processes (Carlson et al., 2009; Gow, Johnson, Pattie, & Brett, 2011; Hess, 2005).

What types of jobs do you think are particularly hard for middle-aged adults to do equally as well as younger adults? What kinds of skills and abilities do these jobs require?

It is clear that much of cognition in middle adulthood relies on the wealth of past life experience. Thus, if you think about it, it is a bit odd to conduct learning and memory studies comparing college students and older people on tests that use exclusively novel tasks and new, perhaps meaningless, information as most studies do. Older adults tend to place problems in context and make them concrete, thinking in terms of practical meaning and downplaying abstract reasoning—often to the detriment of their scores on such tests. College students, on the other hand, are in a period of life in which coping with new information is an important adaptive skill. Perhaps rather than measuring the cognitive capacities of middle-aged adults according to strategies more appropriate to young adults, we should measure adult cognition in terms of experience and expertise (Ackerman, 2011; Salthouse, 1987).

Experience and Expertise

Given that a person remains intellectually active, age brings *more* knowledge—both **declarative knowledge**, which is factual knowledge (knowing *what*), and **procedural knowledge**, which is action-oriented knowledge (knowing *how to*): Both are improved through deliberate practice and the refinement of skills. The accumulation of knowledge through experience contributes to one's *expertise*, which often can compensate for cognitive declines that may be experienced in middle adulthood. Expertise in a particular area is linked to higher performance in a variety of ways. For example, expert knowledge is better organized, and there are more interconnections between units of information, thus making problem solving more efficient. Expert skills also are more *automatic* (see Chapter 6), allowing mental attention to be directed at other aspects of complex tasks. In addition, experts quickly and easily recognize patterns and link these to appropriate procedures and responses (Staudinger & Pasupathi, 2000), reaching solutions much faster than nonexperts do.

Experience, of course, does not prevent or reverse the occurrence of age-related declines, which are the result of changes in the brain: As people age, shrinkage occurs in many regions of the brain, including those most closely associated with memory, spatial abilities, the ability to attend to several different tasks at once, and to think quickly (Raz & Kennedy, 2009). Spatial abilities also appear to decline with age (Pak, Czaja, Sharit, Rogers, & Fisk, 2008). These changes in the aging brain are reflected in performance: Older typists are slower under controlled conditions; older architects suffer losses in visual-spatial skills (Salthouse, Babcock, Skovronek, Mitchell, & Palmon, 1990). However, experience *compensates*. The more experienced architect knows almost automatically which building materials will work best. The older typist may read longer spans of words, thereby maintaining typing speed. These compensations allow adults in their middle and later years to remain productive at work (Krampe & Charness, 2006; Salthouse, 1990), often exceeding the performance of younger but less-experienced workers.

Thus, aging often involves a trade-off: As one skill declines, another improves. As they gain experience, individuals continually restructure their knowledge system to make it more cohesive, correct, and accessible, and these improvements contribute to performance. This may be true for common knowledge, such as how to use the Yellow Pages, or for occupational knowledge, such as how to perform a technical procedure more efficiently. Indeed, our ability to perform work at high levels of competence is often a key to maintaining a positive view of the aging process throughout middle adulthood.

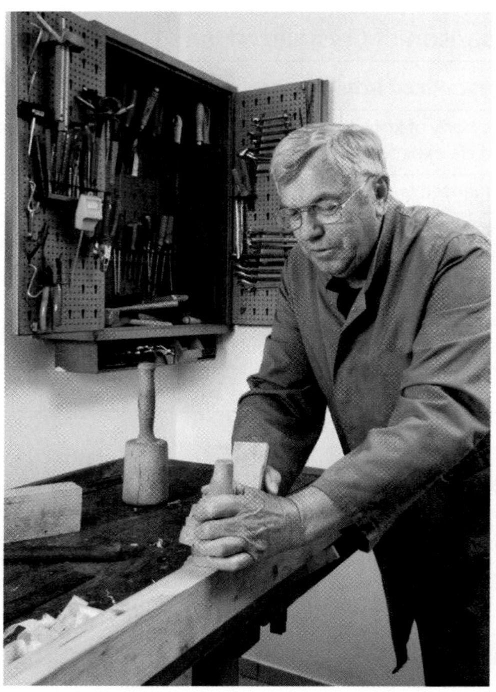

Experience is one factor that enables middle-aged adults to continue being productive. Here, this carpenter uses the woodworking experience he has acquired throughout his life, as well as specific skills, to build a piece of furniture.

Cognitive Skills in the Workplace

For most middle-aged adults, the context for continued development of cognitive skills is the workplace. Adults' cognitive abilities are closely linked to the demands of their job. People who are continually challenged by complexity in their work achieve higher scores on tests of intellectual flexibility than those who perform routine work (Kohn, 1980; Schooler, 2009; Schooler, Mulatu, & Oates, 2004). That is, adults with a high degree of *occupational self-direction*—regular use of thought, initiative, and independent judgment—also have a high degree of intellectual flexibility (Schooler, 2001, 2009).

Do you think that the complexity of your intellectual life will increase or decrease once you finish your college education? What might this imply for your cognitive development in later adulthood?

Increasingly, workers need intellectual flexibility in today's workplace. Technological change demands that most of us learn new skills, either to keep our jobs or to find new ones. Middle-aged adults who have the cognitive ability and skill to learn new tasks and the flexibility to take on more challenging assignments are better able to meet the demands of a changing workplace. This is especially true in fields such as medicine, engineering, and computer technology, where knowledge quickly becomes obsolete as new requirements and changes in the disciplines occur.

The concept of obsolescence is particularly important in middle adulthood because formal schooling typically ends years

declarative knowledge
Factual knowledge; knowing *what*

procedural knowledge
Action-oriented knowledge; knowing *how to*

CHANGING PERSPECTIVES

Retraining for Today's Technological Jobs

In today's information age, worker retraining is a fact of life. Many middle-aged workers find that job training is required to maintain their job, to advance to another position, to transfer to a new department, or to find a new job. Layoffs can necessitate finding a new career or specialty, which often also requires considerable retraining to learn new skills. Many jobs and careers, such as nursing, factory production work, secretarial positions, and the trades, have become dependent on technological innovation. Even jobs in the service industry often require far greater skill in managing technology than they did a decade ago. Much of the retraining required for jobs such as these occurs on the job. However, for a significant portion of the workforce, major reeducation is required. Such challenges can be stressful to middle-aged workers who may fear that they cannot compete with younger workers who often have grown up with technology and, therefore, have more advanced skills.

Thus, middle-aged workers may face both attitudinal and cognitive challenges as they discover that their current skills and abilities are becoming obsolete (Czaja et al., 2006; Czaja & Ownby, 2010). The rapid pace of technological change may cause anxiety and confusion even in otherwise healthy, effective workers. For those stressed by health or family strains, the prospect of major reeducation can be daunting.

As we have seen, cognitive and perceptual decline is not large for most people in middle adulthood. Most middle-aged workers retain good cognitive skills, but most also experience some decline in two areas in particular—speed of mental processing and responding and the ease of learning new information and procedures—and retraining often rests on just these skills (Charness, 2009; Van Gerven, Paas, & Tabbers, 2006). For example, many jobs involve rapid work processing or data entry, which are skills that tax motor dexterity and speed. Especially when middle-aged adults are unfamiliar with computer technology, the speed with which they can learn computer applications generally is slower than it is for younger workers (Charness, 2009; Priest, Nayak, & Stuart-Hamilton, 2007). Perceptual accuracy and memory for details may also pose issues for middle-aged workers, especially if the tasks are presented on a computer screen. Vision, particularly for close work, often deteriorates in middle adulthood, and reading glasses sometimes do not provide a perfect solution.

When substantive retraining is required, many adults turn to community colleges for job retraining and reeducation. In fact, in times of major layoffs, some community colleges can hardly keep up with the demand for workers trained in specifically needed skills. Each term, thousands of older students descend on community college campuses for short training courses, for year-long programs, or for 2-year degrees that will allow them access to jobs their previous level of skill and knowledge would not support.

Often the back-to-college adjustment involves major changes and challenges. Although some educational programs are carefully planned for midcareer adults, with courses offered at times that are convenient, others may require greater adjustment on the part of the students. The student role is generally very different from previous work responsibilities, especially when classes are populated largely with traditional 18- to 22-year-old students. The fact that younger students are fully acquainted and comfortable with a broad array of current technology is another factor that many middle-aged college students find intimidating. If English is a second language, the layers of challenges become even more difficult.

However, the field of human factors design offers the prospect for creating a better environment for older learners (Rogers & Fisk, 2000, 2010). Human factors engineers focus on understanding the cognitive and physical needs of older learners and work at designing machines and learning approaches that are suited to their abilities (Van Gerven, Paas, & Tabbers, 2006). For example, middle-aged adults often learn new technology more slowly, so lessons can be paced at a rate that makes learning success more likely. Many technologies are designed without consideration of older workers in mind. Human factors engineers study these situations and redesign machines to make them easier to use. For example, if visual displays are hard to read, they can be enlarged for the older learner; if machines are too heavy for older workers to manipulate, work may be able to be done in smaller steps that involve lighter loads. If a task requires the use of a computer, training programs can accommodate the needs of older adults by providing more time for learning skills, which often seem to an inexperienced user like learning a whole new language. Self-paced instruction, where individuals work at mastering units of material at their own pace, also provide the opportunity for additional practice that might be needed by middle-aged adults (Czaja et al., 2006; Czaja & Ownby, 2010). Training programs also can be written so that they engage the interests of older, more experienced workers, giving them security that their previous knowledge base and skills are not completely obsolete.

As you consider the issues involved in retraining an older workforce, consider the job or career that you intend to have. What pressure will there be in this field for retraining over the next 10 to 20 years? Do you think you will approach retraining more as an exciting opportunity or as a necessary evil? If you know midcareer adults who have entered retraining programs, how would you describe their experiences? Were they positive or negative? What further issues does retraining pose for the social and family demands that individuals face at midlife?

---

earlier, yet the length of time most adults are involved in active work has increased dramatically in the last century. In 1900, the average life expectancy at birth was 47.3 years; in 1950, it was 68.2 years; in 2000, it was 77.0 years; and by 2020, it is expected to be 79.5 years (U.S. Census Bureau, 2012d). Clearly, as people live longer, their working years have expanded accordingly. In addition, the speed of technological innovation is increasing, and the work years are often marked by multiple job changes that require the latest knowledge and skills. Consequently, the knowledge one needs in one's career cannot be fully obtained in the years of formal schooling. Rather, in nearly all jobs, individuals must continue to update their skills throughout their career (see the box Changing Perspectives: Retraining for Today's Technological Jobs).

Companies often assist their workers in updating their knowledge by offering training programs or by sending them to schools or workshops for further education. Many workers who are willing to learn are given promotions to jobs that require more complex skills. In some occupations, such as law, medicine, insurance, and accounting, there are requirements that practitioners must enroll in continuing education courses to maintain their certification or licensure. However, in other settings, additional training is the responsibility of the individual. For some, this might mean going back to college, perhaps to complete a degree or even to retrain for a different career. Indeed, the nontraditional student is a common fixture on most campuses across the United States.

Throughout middle adulthood, engaging in complex tasks seems to be a key in maintaining intellectual processes at their

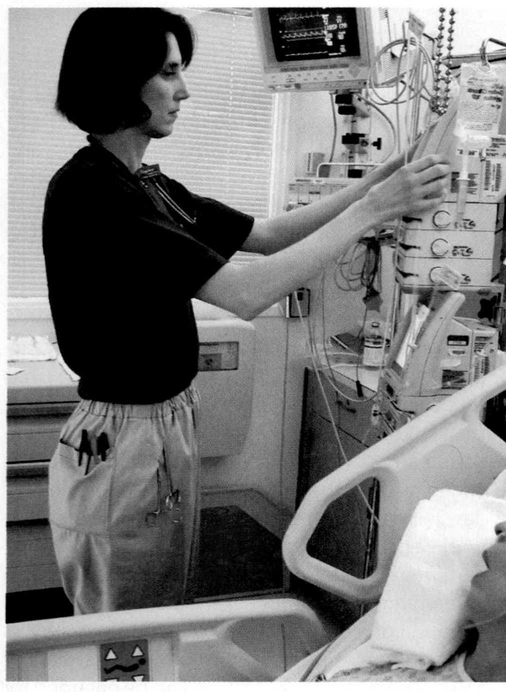

Cognitive skills in adulthood are closely linked to job complexity. Continued training, a complex work environment, and challenging yet meaningful work all contribute to mental growth and continued mental flexibility for this experienced nurse.

highest possible levels. Even participating in complex leisure-time activities can have a positive effect on maintaining intellectual vitality for workers and nonworkers alike (Schooler, 2009; Stern & Munn, 2010). Personality characteristics are also involved and help to explain why some adults continue to pursue intellectual tasks whereas others are content to adopt a more passive attitude (Charles & Horwitz, 2010; Lachman, Rosnick, & Röcke, 2009; Stine-Morrow, 2007). We explore such topics in more depth in the following chapter.

REVIEW THE FACTS 14-4

1. Is age-related intellectual decline in middle adulthood greater or less than previously thought?
2. The accumulated knowledge that we learn from education and life experiences is called __________ intelligence; abilities that involve acquiring new knowledge and skills and that more closely reflect neurological functioning are referred to as __________ intelligence.
3. In which of the following types of tasks would we expect to see the most age-related decline?
   a. knowledge of one's job
   b. memorized facts
   c. knowledge of how things work or how to do things
   d. tasks that involve quick responses
4. What is the best thing to do in order to maintain high intellectual functioning as one ages?
5. In 1900, the average life expectancy was __________; in 2000, it was __________.
   a. 37; 57　　b. 57; 67
   c. 47; 77　　d. 45; 91

Practice on **MyDevelopmentLab**

CHAPTER SUMMARY

Development in Middle Adulthood

How do people in middle adulthood generally approach this period of development—as the best part of life or the beginning of decline?

- Middle adulthood is usually defined as the ages of 40 to 60 or 65, although this period may begin and end earlier or later, depending on an individual's particular circumstances.
- Cues for entering and leaving middle adulthood can involve a person's social and family status, physical and biological status, psychological state, job or career path, and even the economic and historical events that affect a person's life.
- Many adults find that they are at their peak productivity during middle age—a situation that leads to referring to adults in this period as the *command generation*. For others, however, the middle-adult years can be a period of personal challenge and poor health. Most people express some ambivalence about being middle-aged, seeing it as a period of high productivity but also as linked to the end of life.

Is there such a thing as the midlife crisis?

- Daniel Levinson argued that men experience a midlife crisis between ages 40 to 45 when they recognize that they are aging. This *crisis model* views the changes in midlife as abrupt and stressful. Based on interviews primarily with highly successful middle-class White men, and later with women, Levinson viewed the midlife crisis as typical of life for U.S. adults, both men and women.
- Other theorists, however, reject the idea that a midlife crisis is the norm. Rather, they advocate a *transition model*, arguing that development in midlife is more continuous, and when crises do occur they are event related rather than age related. Many potential age-related crises can be averted by planning for them.
- Most adults do not experience a midlife crisis, but people have widely varying experiences in how they adapt to being middle-aged. People who do have a crisis in midlife often do so because they deny the fact that they are getting older or they experience a particular event (such as illness, death, or divorce) that triggers a reevaluation of their life.

Physical Continuity and Change

What changes in physical functions are associated with the middle adult years?

- The most obvious changes in middle adulthood are physical ones. Most physical abilities peak in early adulthood, remain stable in early middle adulthood, and then begin to decline, perhaps around age 50.
- Vision, hearing, and the other senses usually begin to decline in middle adulthood, but usually these declines are small. When declines do pose problems, they usually can be corrected, such as with glasses or hearing aids.

- Reaction time slows as people age, especially after age 50; however, during middle adulthood, actual performance usually stays constant due to practice and experience. Learning new motor skills, however, gradually becomes more difficult with age.
- In middle age, the skeleton begins to shrink, wrinkles develop, and many people accumulate more fat. Heart and lung capacity declines.

What is the climacteric, and how is it typically experienced by men and women?

- Both men and women experience the *climacteric* in middle age, which is the broad complex of physical and emotional symptoms that accompanies reproductive changes and that are associated with hormonal changes during this period. Women go through *menopause* when ovulation and menstruation stop.
- Menopause typically occurs between ages 45 to 55. During menopause, about 50 to 60% of U.S. women experience hot flashes, and some women have other symptoms as well. About 20% of women rate such symptoms as bothersome.
- Some women experience emotional changes during menopause, including depression. However, other women experience fewer emotional difficulties during this period. Emotional responses may be influenced by culturally based expectations.
- The estrogen loss that accompanies menopause triggers various physical responses, including loss of bone mass and increased bone fragility (called *osteoporosis*), shrinking of the genitals, and possibly developing an increased risk for heart disease.
- Because menopause is associated with both unpleasant symptoms and certain health risks, some women choose to go on hormone replacement therapy (HRT) that consists of supplements of estrogen, progesterone, or a combination of the two. However, HRT also is associated with an increased risk for cancer, especially breast cancer. Most doctors now suggest that HRT be used for short-term relief of symptoms, if at all.
- In men, androgens (male hormones) decline very gradually beginning in middle age, and some men experience decreased sexual desire. Often such decline in sexual desire is related to other life stresses and events rather than to hormonal decline.
- Erectile dysfunction (impotence) becomes more common with age. About 50% of men over age 40 will experience some erectile dysfunction. Many men take prescription medications to address this problem, and these drugs are effective for 60 to 80% of the men for whom they are prescribed. Counseling also can be useful for those whose performance problems do not appear to be physiological.

How does sexuality change as men and women move through middle age?

- Frequency of sexual activity typically declines during middle adulthood due to physiological changes, ill health, side effects of medication, time pressures, problems at work or at home, or boredom with one's partner. The time needed to achieve orgasm generally increases for both women and men in middle age.
- Surveys suggest that satisfaction with the physical and emotional aspects of sex remain fairly constant—and similar—for men and women until about age 50. However, later in life, men report increasingly greater satisfaction whereas women report increasing less.
- In terms of sexual behavior, surveys suggest that activity peaks in early adulthood, and steadily declines after that period of the lifespan.
- For many adults, sexuality in midlife is redefined and more emphasis is placed on *sensuality*, which includes hugging, touching, stroking, and other behaviors that may or may not lead to sex.

Disease and Health

What health-related problems are most common during middle adulthood?

- As people age they become more vulnerable to disease, but most deaths in middle age are from cancer and heart attacks. During this period, death is most often due to chronic disease that develops prematurely in high-risk individuals.
- Women generally are healthier than men are in middle age. People who have attained higher levels of education are also healthier than are those with 12 years of schooling or less.

How do habits established earlier in life begin to assert their effects in middle adulthood?

- Longevity is related to good health habits. A good diet, regular health care, and regular exercise also contribute to good health.
- Poor health habits often begin to take their toll in middle adulthood. Smoking, obesity, and excessive alcohol consumption are the three leading preventable causes of disease and early death.
- About 20% of adults smoke, and smoking is responsible for more than 20% of all deaths among people living in the United States today. Today, 70% of U.S. adults are overweight or obese, a percentage that has increased 60% since 1980. Weight problems are most acute during middle adulthood. Today about 40% of men and women age 45 to 65 in the United States are obese.
- Excessive stress plays a role in many diseases of middle adulthood. When stressful events pile up, illness is more likely. Stress can result from particular events, such as a death or job loss, and from dealing with the accumulation of daily hassles. Some people are better able to deal with stress than are others.
- Extreme or prolonged stress appears to contribute to illness by weakening the immune system. It may also make people less likely to take good care of themselves.

- Adults who live in poverty or are members of disadvantaged minority groups often must deal with special challenges that contribute to high levels of stress. They also experience poorer health and earlier death, and these trends are especially evident during middle adulthood.
- Low-income and minority adults are more likely to have poor health habits, less access to health care, and lower levels of educational attainment. All of these factors are linked to higher rates of chronic disease and early death.

Cognitive Continuity and Change

What cognitive changes are most closely associated with the middle adult years?

- Cognitive functioning declines as people age, although serious decline is not universal and, if it occurs, it usually affects only some areas of intellectual functioning. Middle adulthood is typically a time of maximum performance of many cognitive abilities, especially those related to work and daily living.
- *Crystallized intelligence* refers to the accumulated knowledge and skills that come with education and life experiences and are, therefore, learned and influenced by culture. *Fluid intelligence* involves abilities in acquiring new knowledge and skills and is more reflective of neurological functioning.
- Early cross-sectional research usually showed that crystallized intelligence remained high or even increased in middle adulthood, but fluid intelligence declined. Recent longitudinal research suggests that many intellectual abilities actually rise during this period, declining only after age 60. The exception involves tasks that require speed.

How do adults adapt the mild cognitive declines associated with moving through middle age?

- As people age, many regions of the brain shrink, especially those areas responsible for memory and decision making. Although most middle-aged adults do experience modest declines in memory functions and speed of responding, their actual mental performance typically remains high due to their greater general knowledge and experience. Wide individual differences do, however, occur. Remaining intellectually active in adulthood is linked to better functioning.
- Age brings more knowledge, often contributing to one's expertise. Expert knowledge is better organized and more automatic, and experts are faster at reaching solutions. Expertise can compensate for age-related intellectual losses, both with respect to *declarative knowledge*, which is factual knowledge (knowing "what"), and *procedural knowledge*, which is action-oriented knowledge (knowing "how to").
- People who are intellectually challenged in their work also have a higher degree of intellectual flexibility, which is becoming more important in our increasingly technical world.
- The average life expectancy in 1900 was 47.3 years; by 2020, it is expected to be 79.5 years. Thus, adults now have, on average, many more years to spend at work. Because most jobs change and workers also change jobs and careers, intellectual flexibility is very important to employment success. Many adults benefit from on-the-job training or additional education.
- Engaging in complex tasks throughout adulthood, in work, leisure, or both, seems to be a key to maintaining high levels of intellectual functioning.

KEY TERMS

command generation (p. 392)
crisis model (p. 393)
transition model (p. 393)
climacteric (p. 397)
menopause (p. 397)
osteoporosis (p. 398)
sensuality (p. 401)
crystallized intelligence (p. 408)
fluid intelligence (p. 408)
declarative knowledge (p. 410)
procedural knowledge (p. 410)

MyVirtualLife

What decisions would you make while living your life? What would be the consequences of those decisions?

Find out by accessing **MyVirtualLife** at
www.MyDevelopmentLab.com
to raise a virtual child and live your own virtual life

MIDDLE ADULTHOOD
Personality and Sociocultural Development

15

LEARNING OBJECTIVES

- How well does the theme "continuity and change" describe the adjustments that adults make in middle adulthood?
- What is implied when theorists note that generativity is the primary developmental task of middle adulthood?
- What differences exist in how men and women react to middle age?
- In what important ways can midlife adults be considered "the generation that runs things"?
- How do parents typically respond when their last child leaves home?
- What challenges are presented when the parents of midlife adults or children and grandchildren need assistance?
- How do friendships in middle adulthood differ from those developed during earlier periods of the lifespan?
- What challenges are associated with divorce and remarriage, and what factors help adults in midlife meet these challenges?
- How do career paths typically unfold in middle adulthood, and what occupational challenges do some midlife adults face?
- Is personality development in middle adulthood marked more by stability or by change?

CHAPTER OUTLINE

Personality Continuity and Change
- The Tasks of Middle Adulthood
- Personal Reactions to Middle Adulthood

Family and Friends: Interpersonal Contexts
- The Generation That Runs Things
- Relationships with Adult Children
- Relationships with Aging Parents
- Becoming a Grandparent
- Friendship: A Lifelong Perspective

The Changing Family
- Marriage, Divorce, and Remarriage
- Blended Families

Occupational Continuity and Change
- Job Change and Stress

Continuity and Change in the Structure of Personality
- The Five-Factor Model
- Stability or Change?

Middle adulthood—which encompasses the span of years from about age 40 to age 60 or 65—is a period when adults try to make sense of the continually changing demands of parenting, the shifting roles in intimate relationships, the changing world of work, and the issues in the larger world. Altogether, it is a period with a bewildering array of concerns. As life events race by and trigger a continual stream of social and cognitive changes, it seems as if there is little firm ground on which to stand during middle adulthood. Yet it can also be argued that the middle-adult years are a period of stability and continuity in personality and outlook. Even when we experience an onslaught of external changes and major life events, internal change can be gradual.

It is in this context of continuity and change during the middle years that reflection and reassessment occur. We review our life scripts as we experience major events and transitions, such as the death of a parent, a friend's serious illness, a new job, the birth of a midlife baby, or the launching of the youngest child into high school or college. We take stock; we contemplate our own mortality, especially when a relative or friend dies or becomes critically ill; and we sort out our values in a continuing attempt to decide what really matters in life. As we reflect, we think less about how long we've lived and more about how much time we have left.

These reflections and reassessments take place within the context of three interconnecting worlds: self, family, and work (see Chapter 13). Individuals express their development uniquely in each of these areas. For example, adults who choose to have a child at 40, to enter and leave the workforce many times during a career, or to divorce and remarry will have vastly different lifestyles and experiences than those who remain single or those who have children early, have a steady career, and maintain a lifelong commitment to one's spouse.

This chapter examines the complexity of personality and sociocultural development during middle adulthood, focusing on interpersonal relationships and work. Change—and the need to adjust to it—are central to contemporary living and require a reordering of our notion of the way things ought to be. Therefore, we begin this chapter by exploring the issues of personality continuity and change.

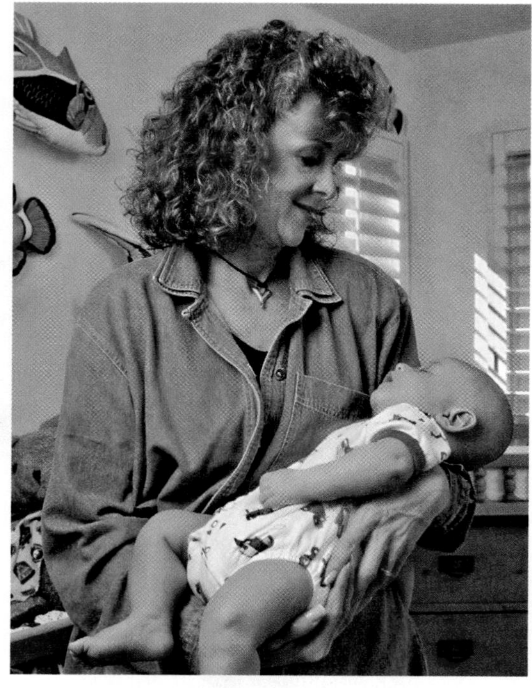

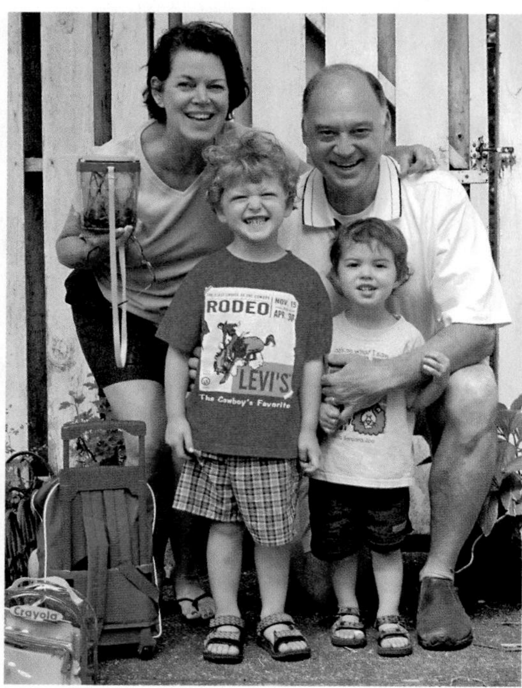

▲ In Erikson's theory, a sense of generativity is central to well-being in middle adulthood. This woman, new to motherhood in her early 40s, and this grandfather in his 50s are both expressing generativity in family life. Both may have jobs, social activities, or hobbies that include opportunities for contributing to the next generation as well.

PERSONALITY CONTINUITY AND CHANGE

When theorists consider the adult portion of the lifespan, they tend to focus on the significance of major life events, such as moving away from the parents' home, marrying, sending the oldest child into the world, retirement, and so forth. Thus, understanding adulthood is closely tied to considering how these life events affect the continuity of individuals' lives. Middle adulthood is defined largely by certain developmental tasks that form a common theme in theorists' views of this stage of life. Among the most important of these are marriage, work, parenting, and family relationships (Wethington, Kessler, & Pixley, 2004). Although these tasks differ somewhat for men and women and sometimes are mingled with those of early and late adulthood, they provide the context for understanding development in middle adulthood.

The Tasks of Middle Adulthood

The idea that common life events define and explain a person's experience in middle age, however, does not mean that understanding this period is easy. Numerous studies have provided evidence that the course of midlife is extremely diverse and varied and at times tumultuous. In other words, middle adulthood is a period of personal growth, often motivated by physical and social stressors (Chiriboga, 1996; Sutin, Costa, Wethington, & Eaton, 2010; Willis, Martin, & Röcke, 2010).

When you think about middle-aged adults you know well, whom do they identify as their best friends? Are these friends better described as age-peers or family life cycle–peers?

As you might guess, the stage of middle adulthood is defined as much by tasks as it is by age. For example, many middle-aged people are caring for their adolescent or young adult children as well as for their aging parents. However, the ages at which people in middle age undertake adult tasks varies widely—some people at age 45 are sending their last child off to college; others are starting their family at this same age. Either way, middle-aged adults tend to share activities and establish friendships with others who are at the same stage of the *family life cycle*, although they may not be the same age chronologically.

Erikson's Generativity Versus Self-Absorption Regardless of their different roles, according to Erik Erikson, the overarching task that adults face in middle age is one of **generativity versus self-absorption**, in which they develop either the feeling that they have contributed in worthwhile ways or that their lives have not been worthwhile. By generativity, Erikson meant that adults contribute positively to the good of others and their community. With regard to generativity, Erikson suggested that people act within three domains: a *procreative* domain, by giving and responding to the needs of the their children; a *productive* domain, by integrating work with family life or by caring for the next generation; and a *creative* domain, by contributing to society on a larger scale. Generativity may be expressed through prosocial community activities, through work, through immersion in parenting, or through caring for other loved ones. As such, the activities associated with generativity vary somewhat by culture, but in all societies adults take on the responsibilities for raising children and working for the well-being of future generations (McAdams, 2008; McAdams & Olson, 2010). These are the hallmarks of generativity. For many people, generativity is expressed across multiple roles, including both family and work settings (Peterson & Duncan, 2007; Westermeyer, 2004).

As summarized in Chapter 1, Erikson described the lifelong process of development as consisting of eight stages. One important point to emphasize is Erikson's belief that how one adjusts in earlier stages lays the foundation for later experiences. Another point is that during one's later years, all of the earlier developmental issues and their resolutions reappear from time to time—especially during times of stress or change. For example, a sudden physical impairment, such as a heart attack, may revive struggles with autonomy and dependence in a 45-year-old; the death of a spouse may renew strong intimacy needs in the survivor. In fact, each major life adjustment may necessitate reevaluations and revisions of earlier solutions. Erikson believed that when we are uprooted by major life circumstances—such as the death of a spouse or a serious illness—we must revisit the earlier developmental issues of basic trust, autonomy, initiative, industry, identity, and intimacy before we can pursue adult generativity.

Do you think different types of life traumas—for example, loss of a job, death of a spouse, divorce, or a major health problem—would prompt a person to refocus on different previous developmental solutions?

When adults fail to develop a sense of generativity, stagnation and boredom are often the result. Some people fail to find value in helping the next generation and have recurrent feelings of living an unsatisfying life. Others may be lacking in accomplishments or may devalue whatever accomplishments they have made. Rather than contributing to other people, they become self-absorbed and overly focused on their own experiences.

Extending Erikson's View Although Erikson's view provides an important perspective for understanding development across the lifespan, some theorists have argued that it may be too limited, especially in how it addresses adulthood (Magen, Austrian, & Hughes, 2002). In his now-classic work, Robert Peck (1968), for example, argued that Erikson's eight stages place too much emphasis on childhood, adolescence, and young adulthood. Although the developmental issues of those periods pose

generativity versus self-absorption
For Erikson, the overarching task of middle age in which adults develop either the feeling that they have contributed in worthwhile ways or that their lives have not been worthwhile

important crises that each individual must resolve, Peck suggested that far too many new issues and tasks arise in the middle and older years to be summed up in just two stages: *generativity versus self-absorption* and, later, *integrity versus despair* (when older adults look back and evaluate their lives; see Chapter 17).

In accounting for the special challenges of adult life, Peck proposed seven issues (conflicts) of adult development, which are summarized in Table 15-1. Although none of Peck's issues are strictly confined to middle or older adulthood, most people focus more attention on some conflicts earlier in life and on others later in life. Peck's view points out the significant role that middle adulthood plays in establishing the foundation for development throughout the remainder of the lifespan. In fact, the period from ages 50 to 60 is often a critical time for making adjustments that will determine the way people will live the rest of their lives (Newton & Stewart, 2012; Stanley & Isaacowitz, 2012).

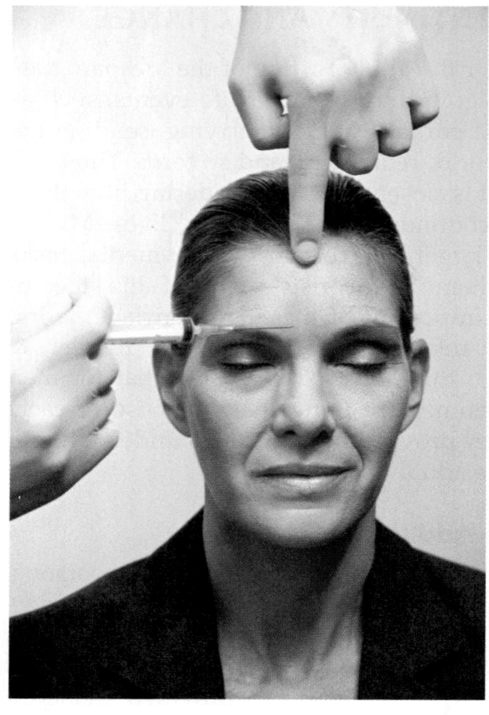

◀ At age 40, both men and women may pay particular attention to the signs of physical aging that begin to appear. Here, this woman is receiving Botox injections to soften the wrinkles in her forehead and make her look younger.

Personal Reactions to Middle Adulthood

One major aspect of midlife adjustment involves reassessing goals and life patterns that were established earlier in life. Traditionally, this process was somewhat different for men versus women because men were more likely to have focused on career goals and women on family goals during early adulthood. Of course, these stereotypical roles are still seen in many traditional families today; however, a blending of roles is becoming increasingly common: Both men and women work and both assume responsibility for raising the family (Marks, Bumpass, & Jun, 2004; Stewart & Newton, 2010). Of course, there is a wide array of individual reactions to the developmental issues encountered at midlife. Nevertheless, many men and women share similar experiences and assume comparable roles and responsibilities. Therefore, although men and women have

Table 15-1 Peck's Issues of Adult Development

MIDDLE ADULTHOOD

Valuing wisdom versus valuing physical powers
As physical stamina and health begin to wane, people must shift much of their energy from physical activities to mental ones.

Socializing versus sexualizing in human relationships
This also is an adjustment imposed by social constraints, as well as by biological changes. Physical changes may force people to redefine their relationships with members of both sexes—to stress companionship rather than sexual intimacy or competitiveness.

Cathectic (emotional) flexibility versus cathectic impoverishment
Emotional flexibility underlies the various adjustments that people must make in middle age as families split up, friends move away, and old interests cease being the central focus of life.

Mental flexibility versus mental rigidity
Individuals must fight the inclination to become too set in their ways or too distrustful of new ideas. Mental rigidity is the tendency to become dominated by past experiences and former judgments—to decide, for example, that "I've disapproved of Republicans (or Democrats or Independents) all my life, so I don't see why I should change my mind now."

OLDER ADULTHOOD

Ego differentiation versus work-role preoccupation
If people define themselves exclusively in terms of job or family, events such as retirement, a change in occupation, a divorce, or a child leaving home will create a gulf in which they are likely to flounder. Ego differentiation means defining yourself as a person in ways that go beyond what work you do or what family roles you fulfill.

Body transcendence versus body preoccupation
This centers on the individual's ability to avoid becoming preoccupied with the increasing aches, pains, and physical annoyances that accompany the aging process.

Ego transcendence versus ego preoccupation
This is particularly important in old age. It requires that people not become mired in thoughts of death (the "night of the ego," as Peck calls it). People who age successfully transcend the prospect of their own mortality by becoming involved in the younger generation—the generation that will outlive them.

SOURCE: Adapted from "Psychological developments in the second half of life," by R. C. Peck, 1968, in B. L. Neugarten (Ed.), *Middle age and aging* (pp. 88–92), Chicago: University of Chicago Press.

somewhat different experiences in middle adulthood, it is not surprising that some patterns of development are common to many men and women.

Men's Reaction to Middle Adulthood Research on midlife adjustment sometimes focuses on only one gender or the other. Consequently, we have somewhat different sources of information upon which to base conclusions for how men and women experience the middle adult years. For many men, midlife reflects earlier commitments to family and career. By this stage, most men have developed a routine way of life that helps them cope as problems arise. Indeed, survey results show that many men are engaged with similar developmental challenges (Rosenberg, Rosenberg, & Farrell, 1999)—such as caring for aging and dependent parents, dealing with adolescent children, coming to terms with personal limitations, and recognizing increasing physical vulnerability—issues that are relevant today for both men and women.

It should be noted that U.S. society traditionally has expected men to conform to a single and narrow standard of success and masculinity, and many men still try to conform to this standard. Men's psychological well-being traditionally has been linked primarily to their job roles. However, today it is increasingly common that family relations at midlife also are extremely important to most men. Indeed, midlife has been characterized as the *prime time* for fathers, as their influence over their young adult children tends to increase (Nydegger & Mitteness, 1996). Other research also supports the importance of family to men during midlife.

Indeed, men today usually experience middle adulthood in much the same way that women do. For example, even though men's satisfaction with sex is higher than women's in middle age, both men and women associate their sexual satisfaction with emotional aspects of their relationships as well as with the physical pleasure they experience (Carpenter, Nathanson, & Kim, 2009; Center for Sexual Health Promotion, 2012). Also, parenthood typically has similar psychological effects on mothers and fathers during midlife (Pudrovska, 2008). When differences do emerge, results often show that men benefit more in midlife from parenting than do women (Marks, Bumpass, & Jun, 2004).

Women's Reactions to Middle Adulthood Women, like men, often experience difficult transitions and reassessments in middle adulthood. Although there are wide individual differences, many women whose lives have reflected traditional female roles define themselves more in terms of the family cycle than by their place in the career cycle (McGoldrick & Carter, 2003). For example, one study of midwestern women (Reinke, 1985) found that they tended to report major life transitions at three points in the family cycle. The first major life transition occurs in young adulthood; fully 80% reported major role changes associated with the birth of their children and their early child-rearing years. In middle adulthood, about 40% reported a major life transition when their children left home, although very few described the transition as particularly traumatic. The final major life transition reported by 33% of the women was menopause.

Of course, women—like men—elect different paths through adulthood and many women focus on goals that vary considerably from those associated with the traditional role of women as wife and mother. Nevertheless, despite the variations in women's lifestyle choices, key events in their family life cycle and in their careers often define women's status, lifestyle, and options at middle adulthood. The timing of key life events also defines the specific nature of the stresses that women—and men—experience (see Chapter 13). One kind of stress that many midlife adults face is called **role conflict**, which occurs when an individual faces an overload of conflicting demands because of the various roles the person assumes. Common role conflicts for middle-aged women involve finding time for both family and career. For example, how does a busy executive cook an evening dinner, go to a child's soccer game, and still meet business deadlines that may require overtime work?

In comparison to middle-aged men, how concerned do you think middle-aged women are about their changing physical appearance?

Role strain results when there is an overload of demands within a given role, such as when a parent tries to give each of three teenage children the attention they need and feels incapable of fully satisfying any of them. Men and women who work may experience career-related role strain when multiple job demands exceed the time that can be allotted to work. For many middle-aged adults, role strain and role conflict also may occur when they are called on to care for aging parents. Yet combining work and family or addressing the needs of children or parents is not inherently stressful and, in fact, is often rewarding (Lee, Zarit, Rovine, & Birditt, 2012). In fact, research suggests that midlife adults—both men and women—experience greater well-being when they are engaged in multiple roles (Chrouser Ahrens, & Ryff, 2006). For many people, finding a balance among various work and family roles produces better mental health and adjustment than focusing too narrowly on a single aspect of life (Putney & Bengtson, 2001).

Goals and Choices Regardless of the paths they have chosen, men and women in middle adulthood usually reassess their priorities and reflect on whether their original goals have been met by taking a second look at their choices. By middle adulthood, most people realize that their families are established and that they have made career choices that they must live with. Some adults whose children are disappointments or who are dissatisfied with their work become bitter and discouraged. Others simply rearrange their priorities. For example, some people at midlife may decide to direct less attention toward occupational development and more toward family or other interpersonal relationships (Ryff, Singer, & Seltzev, 2002). Finding a way to contribute to other people defines generativity

role conflict
An overload of demands from competing roles, such as from work, household duties, and being a parent

role strain
An overload of demands within a given role, such as being a mother or father

and is a healthy adjustment to life in middle adulthood (Cox, Wilt, Olson, & McAdams, 2010; Jeong & Cooney, 2006). (See the box Current Issues: Studying Generativity in African American and White U.S. Families). Family, friends, and interpersonal relationships can all contribute to generativity in middle adulthood, and we focus on these important relationships during the period of middle adulthood in the next section.

REVIEW THE FACTS 15-1

1. Are women or men more likely to define their own tasks in terms of their family's life cycle?
2. Suppose that Andre is 50 years old and is directing much of his energy toward raising money for a child-care center for low-income families in his neighborhood. Erikson would most likely see this as contributing to the ________ domain.
   a. creative b. procreative
   c. productive d. organizational
3. Peck's major criticism of Erikson's view of adulthood is that Erikson saw this period as too
   a. long. b. simple.
   c. important. d. depressing.
4. According to research cited in the text, which of the following is *not* one of the three primary life transitions for women?
   a. children leaving home
   b. menopause
   c. declining sexual interest
   d. having children
5. When a person feels overloaded by too many responsibilities in one role of life, this is called ________.

FAMILY AND FRIENDS: INTERPERSONAL CONTEXTS

For men and women, interpersonal relationships are crucial during the middle-adult years. Although friendships again take greater priority in life, middle-aged people also act as a bridge between the younger generation (which usually means their children) and the older generation (their aging parents).

The Generation That Runs Things

As middle-aged adults adjust to their changing roles in a wide range of interpersonal and family relationships, they often gain a new perspective on their own lives. They are now the generation that must run things. This new responsibility often requires that middle-aged adults take stock of their lives and view their accomplishments with a realistic focus. At midlife, adults often become acutely aware of their successes, both personally and professionally. They also, however, may regret goals not achieved and may have to acknowledge that some goals will never be reached.

More than any other group, middle-aged adults must live in the present. Young people can look ahead, and older people often look back. People in their middle years often have shifting responsibilities to two generations, as well as to themselves. Consequently, middle-aged adults often assume the role of family **kinkeepers** (Richlin-Klonsky & Bengtson, 1996): They maintain family rituals, celebrate achievements, keep family histories alive, reach out to family members who are far away, and gather the family together for holiday celebrations—all of which helps keep the family close.

Who are the kinkeepers in your family? Do you think kinkeepers are more likely to be men or women?

Relationships with Adult Children

During middle adulthood, relationships with adult children typically include launching the children into their own independent lives and adjusting to life without them. At midlife, adults also must learn to relate to their adult children in a reciprocal way.

Launching Adolescents and Young Adults A redefinition of the parent–child relationship begins with the **launching of adolescents** into the adult world. There is no doubt that the launching of adolescents can be an important transition for parents, as well as for their nearly grown children. Despite the

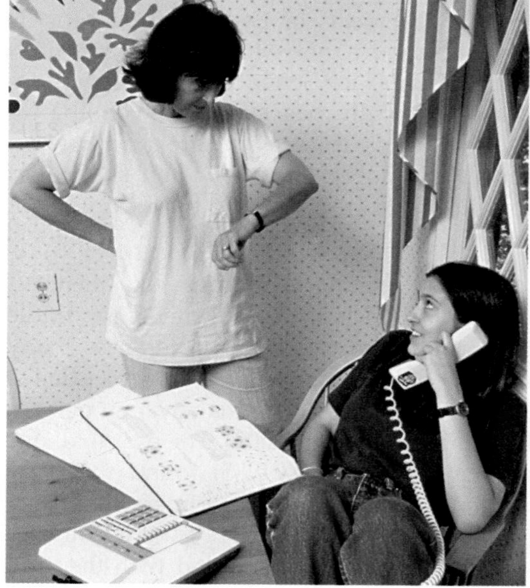

At this point in their lives, many middle-aged parents must begin to let go of their teenage children so that they may start the process of entering the adult world.

kinkeeper
The role assumed by middle-aged people that includes maintaining family rituals, celebrating achievements, keeping family histories alive, reaching out to family members who are far away, and gathering the family together for holiday celebrations—all of which helps keep the family close

Watch *Changing Parent-Child Relationships* on MyDevelopmentLab

launching of adolescents
Parents letting go of older adolescent children so that they can assume responsible adult roles

CURRENT ISSUES

Studying Generativity in African-American and White U.S. Families

Most theorists, including Erikson and Peck, view middle adulthood as a period of life in which much of adult activity is focused on *generativity*. Generativity involves an adult's concern for the next generation and includes various activities, such as raising and mentoring children, serving as a role model for younger people, supporting social causes that assist the next generation to develop in ways that are valued, and creating a legacy for others.

Although Erikson's concept of generativity provides a useful means of describing and interpreting the activities that middle-aged adults find rewarding, it is a difficult construct to measure. Furthermore, the conceptualization of middle adulthood as the period of *generativity versus self-absorption* was developed over half a century ago when adult life patterns were considerably different than they are today. Does the concept of generativity still make sense in today's world? How can it be measured? Does it apply equally well to people of different cultural backgrounds? What factors contribute to low or high levels of personal generativity in midlife?

Questions such as these recently have attracted more attention from researchers who are finding that middle adulthood is much more than a waiting period between becoming an adult and the decline of old age (Willis, Martin, & Röcke, 2010). In fact, it appears that there are wide individual differences in how adults experience generativity. Some adults express it in their work; others express generativity in their family or in their community; and still others are interested in mentoring, tutoring, or caring for the younger generation in other ways at this point in their lives. Because individuals experience generativity in such widely varying ways, researchers have had to be creative in developing methods to measure this trait, which involves behaviors that occur over wide spans of time in a broad array of contexts and relationships. Researchers often have asked adults to construct a "personal biography," in which they write about themselves, using questions such as "Who am I?" or "What do I find most meaningful in life?" Responses from individuals offer a rich picture about how they live and how they come to value their lives.

However, these qualitative measures are hard to summarize. To further explore the concept of generativity, researchers have developed measures like the Loyola Generativity Scale that consists of 20 statements about how adults might display generative concerns, such as "I try to pass along knowledge I have gained through my experiences" and "I do not feel that other people need me" (de St. Aubin, McAdams, & Kim, 2004; McAdams & de St. Aubin, 1992). Respondents quickly rate each of the 20 statements on a 4-point scale from "never applies to me" to "nearly always applies to me." Behaviors can also be assessed. When individuals are high in generativity, we expect that they will be involved in their families and communities. Respondents can be asked to check off how frequently they participate in such activities, and they also can be asked to make lists of things they value or things they are trying to do in their daily lives.

As better measures are being developed to assess the concept of generativity, researchers are beginning to explore how culture and different roles affect the patterns of generativity that adults adopt. For example, in one study—the first to investigate how both African-American and White adults experience generativity—researchers explored how generativity was related to social involvement (Hart, McAdams, Hirsch, & Bauer, 2001). Using several of the measures noted previously, researchers studied 253 U.S. adults between the ages of 34 and 65 years. Approximately half of the participants were African American and half were White. Interestingly, each of the ways of measuring generativity revealed the same findings, indicating that different measurement methods were tapping the same thing. For both African Americans and Whites, generativity was related to social support from family and friends—those higher in generativity were more involved with others. Generativity was also tied to participation in both religious and political activities, and parents who were high in generativity were more likely to see themselves as having an active role in their children's lives. In particular, adults high in generativity emphasized prosocial values and viewed themselves as role models. They often focused on the psychological theme of redemption—working through periods of adversity to gain a better position in life (McAdams, 2006).

Regarding the differences between African Americans and Whites, African Americans generally scored higher on measures of generative concern and on measures of social support, and religion played an especially important role in their lives. African American parents also were more likely to view themselves as role models and to serve as sources of wisdom for their children. In particular, they adopted a more vigilant approach to parenting, perhaps in response to their own experiences of racism and difficulty in their lives. Interestingly, many people in both cultural groups found their greatest inspiration from difficult or challenging life experiences that they had managed to overcome. Certainly results such as these help us better understand the central issues of middle adulthood, and research undoubtedly will continue to focus on how adults find meaning during this period of their lives.

---

worries that often accompany a child taking on the responsibilities of adult life, most parents enjoy the increase in freedom, privacy, and discretionary income once the children are gone (Berman & Napier, 2000; Gorchoff, John, & Helson, 2008).

Some families, of course, are better at letting go than are others (Nelson, Padilla-Walker, Christensen, Evans, & Carroll, 2011). Mothers often are better prepared than fathers to see their children leave home, in part because they are more likely to adopt an authoritative parenting style (Devries, Kerrick, & Oetinger, 2007; Koepke & Denissen, 2012). Adolescents on the verge of assuming responsible adult roles are best supported by parents who maintain a dialogue with them and increasingly trust and respect their judgments, decisions, and progress toward maturity (Kins, Beyers, Soenens, & Vansteenkiste, 2009). Parents must learn to let go and accept who their children are. Sometimes this means that children who leave home may return. Not all children who are launched into the world manage to stay independent the first time or two on their own. Because of failed marriages, job loss, and the difficulty of earning enough to live independently in today's world, an estimated 30 to 40% of adult children return home to recuperate before giving the outside world another try (Pew Research Center, 2012). A few adult children even return home with the intent to stay.

The "Boomerang Generation" Today, increasing numbers of emerging adults are "moving back in" with mom and dad. Whereas only about 11% of adults ages 25 to 34 lived at home with their parents in 1980, since that time this percentage has been climbing. A recent survey by the Pew Research Center (2012; see Figure 15-1) indicates that today nearly 22% of emerging adults in this age range currently are living with their parents—twice the percentage of only 30 years ago. Furthermore, many more have lived with their parents or will live with their parents at some point in time during their early adulthood. Most of these young adults—members of the so-called "boomerang generation"—are happy with living arrangements at home.

Although there are many factors that contribute to a young person's need or desire to move back home with parents, the primary force is the economy. Adult children living with their parents are more likely to be unemployed, to not have a college education, and to lack the financial resources needed to live on their own. About a third of these young adults reports that they have delayed marriage, parenthood, or both (Pew Research Center, 2012). Interestingly, gender and racial differences are small: Men and women are equally likely to move back in with parents, and the percent of White, Black, and Hispanic emerging adults who had lived with parents at some point during their early adult years in the Pew survey was 38%, 32%, and 45%, respectively. For the most part, these young adults get along well living at home: Only about one-fourth report that their living arrangement has been bad for their relationship with their parents.

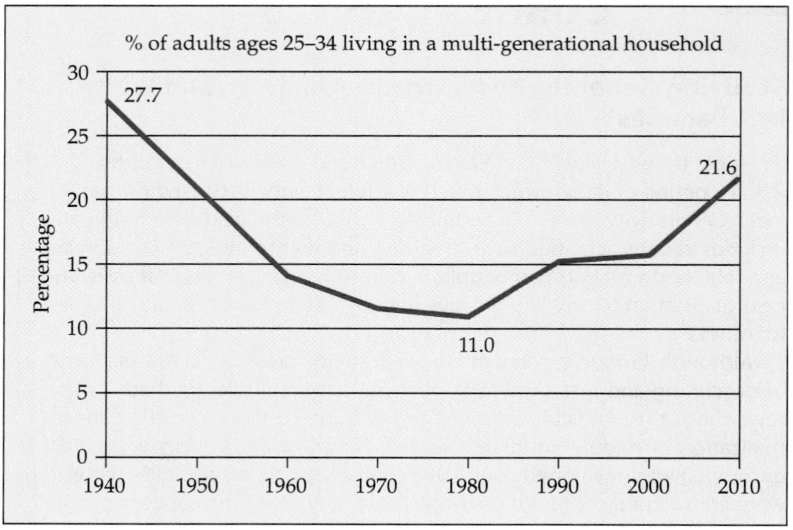

FIGURE 15-1 Percentage of Young Adults in the United States Who Live with Their Parents, 1940–2010
The percentage of young adults living at home with their parents reached a low point in 1980, but has been rising since that time, in part due to increasing economic pressures.

SOURCE: "The boomerang generation: Feeling OK about living with Mom and Dad," Pew Research Center, 2012, retrieved from http://www.pewsocialtrends.org/2012/03/15/the-boomerang-generation/?src=prc-headline.

How does a returning adult child affect the parents? In most cases, the impact is positive. From a financial point of view, having an adult child living at home can provide an additional source of income to help pay for living expenses. According to the Pew Research Center survey, about half of adult children living with parents pay rent, and nearly 90% contribute to some extent to help with household expenses. Only 8% of adult children living at home reported that they receive financial support from their parents. On a personal level, for most parents, having an adult child return home is not a source of challenge or frustration. In fact, parents whose children have moved back home report being just as satisfied with their family life as are parents whose adult children have not moved back home (Pew Research Center, 2012).

Of course, having any additional person in the family involves adjustments and in some cases these can involve challenges. In addition to issues as simple as sharing their space and resources with another adult, a young adult's return to economic dependency may violate the parents' expectations about their child's development and thereby can lower parental satisfaction. It can put a strain on the parent–child relationship (Aquilino, 1996). Moreover, the return of adult children often happens just as their parents are dealing with their own midlife issues, complicating matters further. When adult children return home, both parents and children need to renegotiate roles and expectations, and parents need to understand the new status of their children as adults.

Cultural factors come into play as well. For example, in Italy it is normal for children to reside in their parents' home until marriage (Rossi, 1997). Cultural differences also exist among various ethnic groups in the United States. For example, adult children in Asian and Latin American families were found to live with parents longer out of respect and the desire to assist the family than were children in families of other ethnicities (Fuligni & Pedersen, 2002; Kiang & Fuligni, 2009). Other studies show that young adults reside with parents longer in rural than in urban areas (Nave-Herz, 1997). Regardless of the cultural context, however, when families can adapt, coresidence often provides long-term educational and economic benefits for the entire family (Putney & Bengtson, 2001).

The Empty Nest As most parents who have dropped off their child for the first year at college would agree, the transition of having a "child in high school" to having a "child in college" is a notable family event, filled with pride and happiness, but usually also some sadness as well. This transition is especially felt when the *last* child in the family leaves home, and the parents—who for many years have lived in a family with children—now will live by themselves. Regardless of why children leave home—for college, for marriage, for military service, or for a job—when they do leave home, this implies changes to the family structure and to the relationships among all family members. Parents must renegotiate their roles and responsibilities and, in particular, their relationship with each other. In earlier generations, researchers often focused on the negative aspects of this transition, noting that having the last child leave home was a time of depression and emotional distress, especially for the mother, whose roles in a traditional family were thought to change dramatically and negatively. They used the term "**empty nest**" to describe this

Watch *Family Relationships in Middle Adulthood Across Cultures* on **MyDevelopmentLab**

empty nest
The period in the family life cycle that occurs after the last child has left home

transition when the last child leaves, usually focusing on the difficult adjustment that mothers in particular were expected to have, as they grieved for their lost children and their lost status as primary caretaker of the family.

Indeed, parental roles do change when children no longer live at home, and family dynamics may need to be renegotiated (Lewis & Gorman, 2011). However, today most researchers find that the empty-nest transition generally involves far more positive emotions and adjustments than negative ones. For example, studies of empty-nest parents generally find that only a minority of parents feel a sense of loss that is not more than compensated for by other, more positive emotions (Mitchell & Lovegreen, 2009). Marital satisfaction, for example, generally increases following the transition to an empty nest—an adjustment that results from an increase in the enjoyment of time that parents can now spend with each other (Gorchoff, John, & Helson, 2008).

Of course, there are wide differences among individuals at this, as well as most other, life transitions. For partners who have grown apart over the years, who have developed different interests, or who have become unaccustomed to spending much time together, the empty nest transition may be more dramatic, and may involve greater adjustment. Parents with widely different lifestyles can share a common focus on their children during the years the children live at home, but may find themselves at a loss when the last child becomes independent. Most middle-aged couples, however, have a history of shared traditions, values, and experiences and these form a positive base on which to reestablish a successful relationship. Even couples who do not have a high degree of companionship often rely on each other for emotional support, and they share resources successfully. Although marital satisfaction for some couples is not necessarily based on the same patterns of interactions that were present early in life before children were born, by far the majority of middle-aged parents not only survive, but thrive, after their children become adults (Lauer & Lauer, 2012).

In most ways, research shows that the impact of the empty-nest transition has been softening for most midlife parents in the United States today. In particular, the wider opportunities for women and the broader definition of roles in contemporary U.S. culture have expanded the options for parents, both before and after children leave home. However, the empty-nest transition is becoming more important in one particular way: People are living longer today than at any point in history, so the years partners can expect to spend together after their children become independent are longer. For example, in 1900, the average life expectancy of people in the United States was 47.3 years, in 1950 it was 68.2 years, and today it is 78.5 years (U.S. Census Bureau, 2012q; see Table 15-2). Thus, today most partners can expect to live 30 or 40 years after their children leave home, making the empty-nest transition an important dimension of their adult lives.

Mutually Reciprocal Relationships Of course, the way parents experience the empty nest depends somewhat on the nature of their relationships with their adult children. Ideally, as children reach adulthood, they interact with their parents on a more equal basis than they did earlier in life, thereby establishing a *reciprocal* give-and-take relationship. The shift to a reciprocal relationship rarely takes place suddenly or smoothly; it usually occurs in a series of jolts over a period of years. Adolescent and young adult children often feel the need to distance themselves, at least for a while, from their parents—and from perceived parental judgment—before they can see their parents in a realistic way. When this happens, middle-aged parents may feel cut off or unappreciated.

Table 15-2 Life Expectancy for U.S. Men and Women

Year	Men	Women	Overall
1900	46.3	48.3	47.3
1950	65.6	71.1	68.2
1975	68.8	76.6	72.6
2009	76.0	80.9	78.5
2025 (projected)	77.0	81.2	-
2050 (projected)	79.4	83.2	-
2100 (projected)	83.1	86.4	-

SOURCE: From *Statistical abstract of the United States, 2011*, U.S. Census Bureau, 2011, Washington, DC: U.S. Government Printing Office; and "Life tables for the United States Social Security area 1900–2100," by F. C. Bell & M. L. Miller, 2012, retrieved from http://www.ssa.gov/oact/NOTES/as/20/LifeTables_body.html.

Reciprocal relationships are easier to establish when parents and children relate positively to each other during childhood and adolescence. When family tensions are high during this period, such as when parents adopt a harsh, authoritarian style, the establishment of reciprocal relationships becomes more difficult. In extreme cases, it may take a family crisis—such as the death or illness of a family member, financial hardship, divorce, or unemployment—to prompt parents and adult children to find ways to renegotiate their relationship so that they can interact with each other in new, more reciprocal ways. However, most parents in midlife are happy in their parenting roles (Mitchell, 2010). Especially when family members are healthy and the family is intact, parenting in this stage in the lifespan is usually regarded as a positive experience (Keyes & Ryff, 1999).

Relationships with Aging Parents

One of the most dramatic population changes of the 20th century was the rise in life expectancy (see Table 15-2). In 1900, one in four children experienced the death of a parent before they were 15 years old; in 2000, fewer than 1 in 20 children did. In the United States today, most middle-aged adults can expect that one or both of their parents will be alive; therefore, many middle-aged adults must adjust to the changing needs and roles of their aging parents.

When parents are in good health and can live independently, their relationships with their middle-aged children are often characterized by reciprocity; parents and adult children help each other in concrete ways (Lowenstein, Katz, & Gur-Yaish, 2007; McIlvane, Ajrouch, & Antonucci, 2007). These relationships often change, however, when parents become ill or too frail to live on their own. Indeed, the primary reason for adult children and parents sharing a household is an elderly parent's disability (Brody, Litvin, Hoffman, & Kleban, 1995b). Yet, because independence is valued by each generation, fewer than 10% of aging parents in the United States share a home with their middle-aged children, and many do so only when economic hardship or physical disability gives them little choice.

The Reciprocal Exchange of Assistance Most middle-aged adults have ongoing relationships with their aging parents that include regular contact, shared memories, and a reciprocal exchange of assistance. Numerous surveys have revealed lasting social, emotional, and material exchanges between adult children and their parents (Bookman & Harrington, 2007; Troll & Fingerman, 1996). For example, many older parents provide financial assistance to their middle-aged children and to their grandchildren (Killian, 2004), at least in middle- and upper-middle-class families. When the older generation does not have the financial resources to contribute, they are likely to provide social support and perhaps babysitting services to their adult children—especially those who are coping with single parenthood (Ruiz & Silverstein, 2007).

How have members of your family dealt with older relatives who needed extra care? Do you think there are cultural differences in patterns of caring for frail older adults?

How adult children behave toward their parents largely depends on their life experiences and on their stage in the family life cycle. A 42-year-old woman with grown children who is at the peak of her professional life and living 1,000 miles away from her parents must take a different approach to her parents than a woman of similar age who is a full-time homemaker living nearby. Family history is also important: Each parent–child relationship is unique, and this leads to different patterns of interaction and coping. Moreover, the degree to which children are called on to help their parents varies from one individual to another and from one family to another. Gender differences often characterize these relationships. Traditionally, the primary parent–child relationship at this stage of life generally involves the daughter as caregiver to the parents. Ethnicity and social class, however, may also influence intergenerational relationships.

Role Reversals With age, role reversals gradually take place for middle-aged adults and their parents (Bengtson & Putney, 2006). Middle-aged adults become the generation in charge—working, raising children, and generally functioning as the "doers" in society. Their parents, if they are still living, may be in poor health, retired, or in need of financial aid. Over a period of years, power gradually and naturally shifts from older parents to their middle-aged children. Unless both generations realize that this role reversal is a common and often inevitable part of the life cycle, it can cause resentment on both sides and lead to conflict (Albert & Brody, 1996; Brody, 2006). Fortunately, it appears that most middle-aged people are concerned about and close to their parents and their children, despite the fact that many stereotypes and myths suggest that intergenerational relationships are full of misunderstanding and conflict.

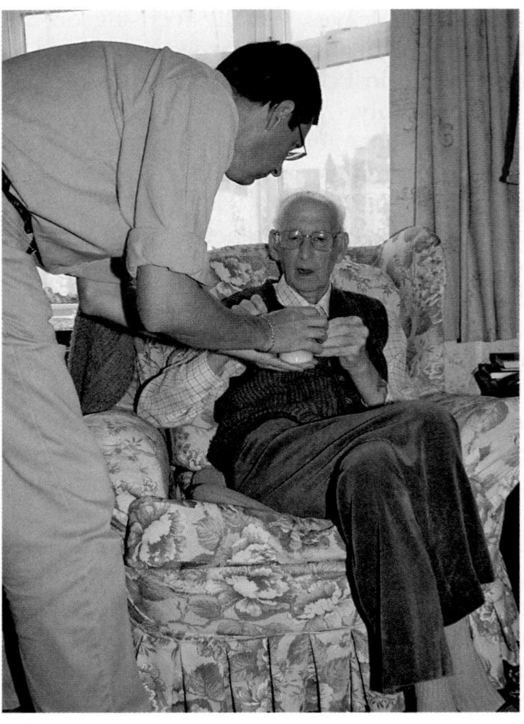

◀ Caring for an aged parent is often part of middle-age responsibilities, a role that is likely to be both rewarding and stressful. Sometimes there is a role reversal from earlier years, in which a son or daughter needs to take control or make decisions for the parent.

Caring for Elderly Parents Today, people are living longer after the onset of chronic diseases or disabilities, and few people reach the end of life without experiencing a period in which they are dependent on their children. The responsibility of long-term care for parents has become more the norm than the exception (Bookman & Harrington, 2007). One study (Marks, 1996) found that one in five adults from ages 35 to 64 had cared for a relative or a friend in the last year.

Although many people assume that care of the elderly is relegated to nursing homes and other formal facilities, this is actually the exception rather than the rule: Only a small percentage of caregivers use formal services. The majority of adults—80 to 90%—care for their aging parents at home, either by providing the necessary assistance that allows the parent to live independently or by having the parent move in with the family (Bookman & Harrington, 2007; Spector & Fleishman, 2001). For most middle-aged caregivers, the responsibility for parent care is both rewarding and stressful. In some instances, these arrangements create tension between dependence and independence and may reactivate old dependency conflicts or other relationship problems between parent and child or between siblings. Old loyalties, alliances, or rivalries sometimes reappear. The need to care for parents also foreshadows the future of the caregivers who come to understand that they also may be dependent on their children when they become old. Thus,

Why do you think daughters and daughters-in-law are more likely to provide living assistance for elderly relatives than are sons and sons-in-law?

caring for one's aged parents may be an unwelcome preview and model for relinquishing autonomy, control, and responsibility. These emotion-based conflicts—together with the very real demands on time and freedom, competing responsibilities, and interference with lifestyle and social and recreational activities—can create a stressful environment (Brody, 2006).

Regardless of whether or not they hold jobs, daughters and daughters-in-law are much more likely than male family members to provide care to aging parents (Bracke, Christiaens, & Wauterickx, 2008; Spector & Fleishman, 2001). How a daughter responds to the needs of her aging parents depends to a large extent on her life circumstances, including her age (is she in her 30s, 40s, or 50s?), her position in the family life cycle (does she have grown children or is she raising preschoolers?), and her involvement in the workforce (does she have a full-time job or is she a full-time homemaker?) (Brody, 2006). Regardless of the circumstances, daughters often experience strain because of their caregiving efforts. Stress is especially acute when the daughter does not have the help and support of a husband or children of her own (Brody, 2006). Despite their efforts, most middle-aged caregivers feel inadequate to the task. In one study, 60% of caregiving women reported that they felt guilty about not doing enough, and 75% agreed that middle-aged children do not take care of their older parents to the extent that they did in the past (Brody, 1985). Even so, many midlife caregivers find it rewarding to "give back" to their parents at this point in their lives (Putney & Bengtson, 2001).

Becoming a Grandparent

At the same time that middle-aged adults may be called on to help care for their parents, they may also find themselves assuming a new role in the family—that of being a grandparent. The majority of people in the United States become grandparents in middle age, although women and members of some minority groups tend to become grandparents at somewhat earlier ages (Szinovacz, 1998). Today in the United States, the average age of becoming a grandmother is 50; grandfathers' average age is about 52 (Legacy, 2012). Indeed, as life expectancy has increased, more children have living grandparents: Today over 90% of U.S. adolescents have two or more grandparents alive (Legacy, 2012).

Being a grandparent is highly satisfying for many people, although the roles played by grandparents vary widely. Grandparents can help raise a new generation without the daily responsibilities of being a parent and without the intense relationship and conflicts that may develop between parent and child. However, especially if their adult children divorce or encounter other problems, some grandparents become full-time surrogate parents to their grandchildren; others care for their grandchildren part-time, although they themselves may still be working full-time. Thus, in many ways, the concept of a grandparent that presently predominates in U.S. culture has evolved from that of an old person in a rocking chair to that of an active, involved family member.

Although the role of a grandparent is a highly individualized activity, there are some distinct roles that grandparents can play, depending on their relationships with their grandchildren (see Table 15-3). Some grandparents, for example, become "fun people" to their grandchildren, taking them on trips, shopping, or to interesting places. Sometimes grandparents live in the same household as their grandchildren, and their roles are therefore more like those of parents.

Table 15-3 Important Roles Played by Grandparents

BEING THERE

Sometimes grandparents describe their most important role as simply being there. They are a calming presence in the face of family disruption or external catastrophe. They provide an anchor of stability to both grandchildren and parents. Sometimes they even act as a deterrent to family disruption.

FAMILY NATIONAL GUARD

Some grandparents report that their most important function is to be available in times of emergency. During these times, they often need to go well beyond the role of simply being there and actively manage the grandchildren.

ARBITRATOR

Some grandparents see their role as one of imparting and negotiating family values, maintaining family continuity, and assisting in times of conflict. Although there are often differences in values between generations, some grandparents see themselves as better able to handle the conflicts between their adult children and their grandchildren because of their relative distance and greater experience.

MAINTAINING THE FAMILY'S BIOGRAPHY

Grandparents can provide a sense of continuity for the family, teaching grandchildren about the heritage and traditions of their family.

SOURCE: From "Diversity and symbolism in the grandparent role," by V. L. Bengtson, 1985, in V. L. Bengtson and J. F. Robertson (Eds.), *Grandparenthood* (pp. 11–25), Beverly Hills, CA: Sage.

Today many grandparents, about 10 to 11%, are raising their grandchildren, and even more provide significant support and serve in a near-parent role (Lumpkin, 2008; U.S. Census Bureau, 2012p). If a single mother or both parents work, grandparents sometimes take care of children during the day, playing roles more like parents than grandparents. In the United States today, nearly a third of children under the age of 5 whose mothers are employed are cared for on a regular basis by a grandparent during their mother's working hours (U.S. Census Bureau, 2012e). Not surprisingly, grandparents often help children form their values and set their priorities. For example, it is common for grandparents to influence the religious beliefs and behaviors of their grandchildren, playing a direct role in this aspect of socialization (Bengtson, Copen, Putney, & Silverstein, 2008; Ruiz & Silverstein, 2007). However, grandparents who assume the role of parents may find this role challenging. The financial demands of raising a child may make it difficult for grandparents—who often are living on low and fixed incomes—to take care of their own needs. Providing full-time childcare also limits grandparents' freedom and can reduce the time they spend in leisure activities or with friends. Thus, becoming a custodial grandparent usually involves challenges, as well as opportunities (Dolbin-MacNab, 2009). Nevertheless, grandparents can provide the support that safeguards the development of their grandchildren, and most are willing to make this investment (Coall & Hertwig, 2011).

Watch *Becoming a Grandparent* on **MyDevelopmentLab**

When it comes to grandparenting, cultural and ethnic differences are often observed. Asian, Black, Hispanic, Native-American, and Inuit families are far more likely to be three-generation households than are non-Hispanic White families. These multigenerational households come in all forms, and the grandchildren often live in the grandparent's home. In Black and Native-American families, more than 50% of grandparents are their grandchildren's primary caregivers. In these families, grandfathers often maintain their status and position as the formal head of the family. Regardless of the specific role they elect, becoming a grandparent is an important dimension of family life for many middle-aged adults (see the box Try This! What Makes a Great Grandparent?).

Friendship: A Lifelong Perspective

Although family responsibilities and interactions play a very large part in the lives of most middle-aged adults, maintaining relationships with friends who are peers is also a fulfilling and satisfying part of their lives (Hruschka, 2010; Mason, 2011). Friends serve an especially important function for adults who do not marry or have children because friendships often are a central part of their lives. For these adults, important life tasks, such as establishing intimacy, must be accomplished through friendships rather than through marriage and family. For older people who are widowed, friendship also fills many vital emotional needs.

Throughout adulthood, we tend to value a consistent set of characteristics in our friends. For example, in a study where groups of high school students, newlyweds, and people in early adulthood and late middle adulthood were asked to describe their friendships, similar descriptions were given. Reciprocity, in particular, was considered very important, with a strong emphasis on helping and sharing. People also saw their friends as similar to themselves in many ways and stressed the importance of shared experiences and being able to communicate well (Fiske & Chiriboga, 1990).

One age-related difference in friendships did emerge from the study; the most complex friendships generally occurred among the late middle-aged group. In early middle adulthood, most people were more involved with their families and jobs and therefore they had less time to devote to friends. On the other hand, by late middle adulthood, highly complex and multidimensional relationships among friends were the rule. For example, people at this stage were likely to appreciate the unique characteristics of their friends. It is possible that as people mature and become aware of the subtleties of their own natures, they also begin to appreciate complexity in others more than they did earlier in life (Fiske & Chiriboga, 1990).

How do you expect your friendships to change as you move through the various periods of adulthood?

Interestingly, sex differences in friendship are sometimes more significant than age differences (Adams, 2006; Greif, 2009; Rose, 2007). Oftentimes, women are more deeply involved in their friendships and consider reciprocity and intimacy to be their most important dimensions, whereas men tend to choose their friends on the basis of similarity (Felmlee & Muraco, 2009). Friendships between men and women also have a special quality (Hruschka, 2010), and middle-aged friendships today are more heterogeneous with respect to ethnicity and gender than was typical in previous generations. Despite the fact that most friendships are sex-segregated throughout the lifespan, some adults do develop strong friendship ties with members of opposite sex (Mehta & Strough, 2009). Indeed, friendships in midlife provide adults with an outlet for their interests and support, especially during periods of personal challenge. However, during middle adulthood many people have trouble finding time to devote to friendships, since they often are focused most intensely on their families.

▲ Friendships continue to be important in middle age. These women may enjoy bowling, but their conversations and social support through the major events of life may be the real reason for getting together regularly.

REVIEW THE FACTS 15-2

1. Middle-aged adults often are responsible for maintaining family ties; they serve as the family's ________.
2. Today about what percentage of adult children who leave home return to live with parents, at least for a period of time?
   a. 10 to 15% b. 20 to 25%
   c. 30 to 40% d. 50 to 60%
3. When the last child leaves the parent's home, this situation is referred to as the ________.
4. Are more aging relatives cared for today in formal facilities, such as nursing homes, or by family members?
5. Are sons or daughters more likely to provide care for elderly parents?
   a. sons b. daughters
   c. sons and daughters are equally likely to provide care
6. Men, more than women, are likely to base friendships in middle adulthood on
   a. honesty. b. age.
   c. intimacy. d. similarity.

Practice on MyDevelopmentLab

TRY THIS!

What Makes a Great Grandparent?

Although families exist in an almost infinite number of variations, most college students have one or more grandparents whom they have had the opportunity to know. Sometimes we get to know our grandparents very well. Perhaps we have lived in the same household with our grandparents or have spent many hours at their home or in their care. Sometimes we know them less well, especially if we grew up a long distance from where our grandparents live. Regardless of how well you know your grandparents, you probably have some experiences with them that will allow you to think about what kind of grandparents they have been to you. If you do not remember or have never known any of your grandparents, you can complete this exercise by asking your parents about their parents or by asking another student about his or her experiences with grandparents.

Based on your reflections of your own experiences, complete the following table for each of the grandparents you know or remember. Rate each of your grandparents on a scale of 1 to 5, where 1 indicates that you strongly agree with the statement and 5 indicates that you strongly disagree. You may wish to extend this survey with questions that you would like to add.

Reflect on What You Observed

As you were thinking about your grandparents, what general thoughts about each of them came to your mind? For each of the grandparents you evaluated, consider the following questions: Did you have a warm, close, personal relationship or were you more distant and formal when you interacted? Was your grandparent more of a disciplinarian or more of a fun playmate? Were your grandparent's rules stricter or more lax than the rules your parents enforced? Do you have a generally positive, negative, or neutral overall relationship with your grandparent? Why do you think you have the kind of relationships you do?

Consider the Issues

Grandparents can fill many different roles in their grandchildren's lives. Much depends on the specific circumstances that surround these relationships: The grandparent's age and health, their geographic closeness to you and your family, the kind of relationship the grandparent has with your parent, the grandparent's financial circumstances, and cultural expectations and norms all can make a difference. To what extent do factors such as these figure into how your relationships with your grandparents have developed? Do you feel emotionally close to your grandparents? What do you most admire and least admire about them? If you are a grandparent yourself, what do you think your grandchildren would say about you? Do you expect to be (or are you) a grandparent? If so, what kind of grandparent would you hope to be? What do you see as the greatest joys and the greatest challenges that grandparents face as they interact with their grandchildren? How do you think you might meet these challenges?

Life events	Grandparent 1	Grandparent 2	Grandparent 3	Grandparent 4
Celebrated most major holidays and birthdays with me				
Provided child care for me as I was growing up				
Interacted with my parent (grandparent's child) in positive ways				
Lived in my home or very close to my home				
Was involved in disciplining me				
Gave me thoughtful and appropriate presents				
Supported my family financially				
Was a great role model for me as I was growing up				
I like this grandparent as a person				
I admire the accomplishments of this grandparent				
I believe that this grandparent is proud of me				
Was more involved in my life when I was younger				
Approves of my current lifestyle and choices				

THE CHANGING FAMILY

Middle adulthood is a period when careers are often at their peak demand, when family dynamics are shifting as children are launched and perhaps other family members need care, and when people must adapt and adjust their own expectations in light of reality. Social changes also play a role. Although no one—not even the most radical social critic—would claim that the traditional *nuclear* family is dead or even dying, today only a minority of families—about 20%—still fit the traditional mold in which the father works and the mother stays home to care for the children (Brookings, 2011). According to the 2011 U.S. Census, about two-thirds of children live in families with both parents, and in most of these households both parents hold jobs. Changes in family structure in the United States are the result of many social forces, such as enhanced opportunities for women and minorities, economic pressures, and shifts in cultural values and norms. Just as individuals are tailoring their lifestyles to suit their own needs and priorities, the definition of *family* is broadening to accommodate changes in the social and personal needs and priorities of its members (Coleman, Ganong, & Warzinik, 2007; Wiseman, 2008).

Marriage, Divorce, and Remarriage

Statistics about marriage and divorce often are difficult to interpret. In the United States in 2009, about 2.08 million people were married and about 1.19 million people were divorced (U.S. Census Bureau, 2012l). Statistics such as these lead to the often cited conclusion that more than half of all marriages end in divorce. However, the people who are divorcing in a given year are not the same as those marrying, and therefore a simple comparison of marriage and divorce rates usually leads to an erroneous conclusion.

To arrive at an accurate estimate of the probability that a marriage today will end in divorce requires the consideration of many factors. For example, most divorces occur in early adulthood (see Figure 15-2). In 2009, the average age at which first marriages ended in divorce was 32.0 years for men and 30.1 years for women. For second marriage and divorce, the average age at divorce was 42.0 for men and 39.3 for women (U.S. Census Bureau, 2011c). However, the average age at which people first marry has been increasing in the United States, and this will likely affect the divorce rate projected forward in time. Marriage and divorce statistics look very different depending on which age group one is considering (see Figure 15-3). For example, by age 40, 77% of men and 83% of women have been married; 18% of men and 23% of women have also been divorced. By age 60, 89% of men and 91% of women have been married, and 36% of men and 37% of women have been divorced (U.S. Census Bureau, 2011c). Because second and third marriages are more likely to end in divorce than are first marriages, this is another complicating factor. Thus, it is difficult to calculate what the actual divorce rate is, as so many factors must be taken into consideration. Taking all of these trends into the calculation, a reasonable estimate of the chances of a given marriage ending in divorce today is close to 40%.

Why Couples Divorce In middle adulthood, couples divorce for many of the same reasons that younger couples do. Sometimes, for example, divorce is associated with misconceptions about marriage. Churches, lawyers, marriage counselors, media, family, and friends all pay homage to myths about what marriage is supposed to be. These myths often include unrealistic expectations that set the stage for failure (Fine & Harvey, 2006; see Table 15-4). When people at any stage of life want more from their marriage, divorce often appears preferable to continuing an unhappy relationship (Coleman, Ganong, & Warzinik, 2007; Lamanna & Reidmann, 2012).

Marriages rarely fall apart suddenly, especially during middle adulthood. More often, a break up is the culmination of a long process of emotional distancing. If the marriage is shaky, the empty-nest stage of the family life cycle may create a personal or marital crisis. Couples may observe that it is no longer necessary to stay together for the sake of their children; they may wonder whether they want to spend the rest of their lives together.

Regardless of the circumstances, the final months of a marriage are usually remembered as unhappy by both partners, although the eventual decision to divorce is usually made by one partner. Wives usually raise the issue of divorce first because they often are dissatisfied with their marriage earlier than are their husbands, and they are much more often the initiators of divorce (Hewitt, Western, & Baxter, 2006).

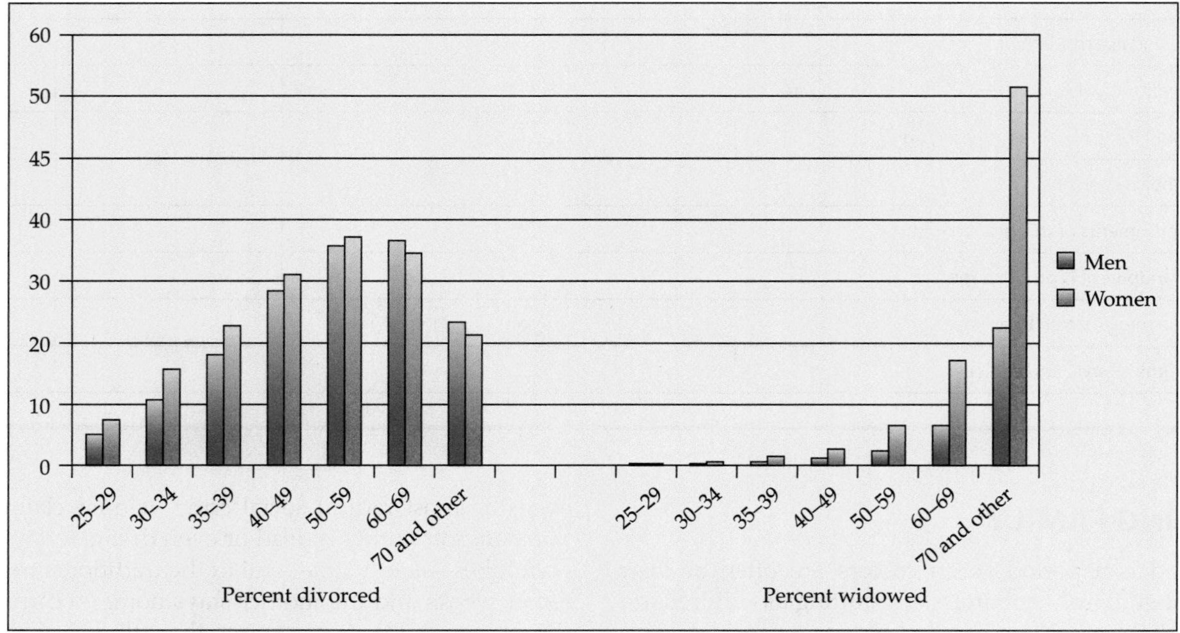

FIGURE 15-2 Divorce and Widowhood in the United States in Adulthood by Age Cohort and Gender

SOURCE: "Number, timing, and duration of marriages and divorces: 2009," U.S. Census Bureau, 2011, retrieved from http://www.census.gov/prod/2011/pubs/p70-125.pdf.

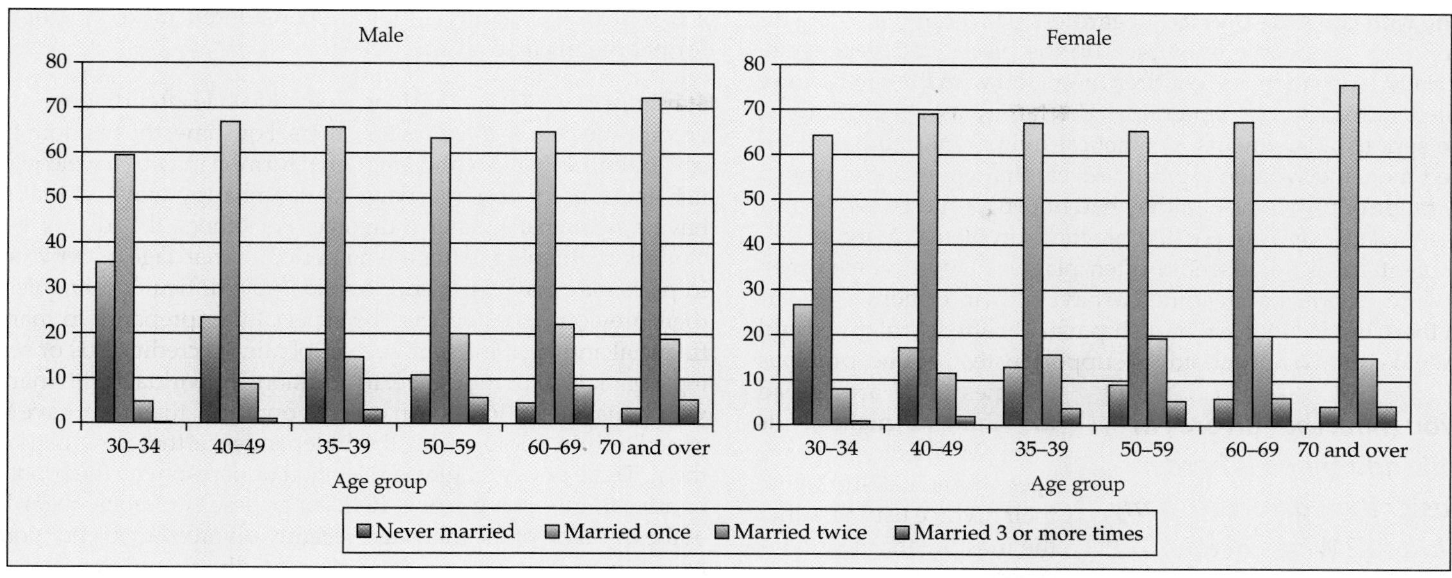

FIGURE 15-3 Marriage in the United States in Middle and Older Adulthood by Age Cohort and Gender
Here we see the result of several trends that affect men and women differently in each age bracket: Men stay single longer and marry younger women; men remarry more often after divorce or death of a spouse; and women are widowed earlier.

SOURCE: From "Number, timing, and duration of marriages and divorce: 2009," U.S. Census Bureau, 2011, in *Current populations reports*, retrieved from http://www.census.gov/prod/2011/pubs/p70-125.pdf.

Table 15-4 Myths and Facts About Marriage and Divorce

	Myth	Fact
1	Having children usually increases marital satisfaction for both partners.	Having the first child usually decreases marital satisfaction for both partners.
2	Men reap far greater benefits from marriage than women.	Men and women both benefit substantially from marriage, living longer, happier, healthier, and wealthier lives.
3	Single people have more sex and more satisfying sex lives than married couples.	Married people have sex more often than single people and report that sex is more physically and emotionally satisfying.
4	Divorce proceedings are usually initiated by men.	Women initiate about two-thirds of divorces.
5	Children do better in stepfamilies than in single-parent homes.	Children seem to do no better in stepfamily homes, and some do worse, than in single-parent homes.
6	Husbands' marital satisfaction is higher when wives are full-time homemakers than when they are employed.	Although early studies suggested this was true in the 1960s, studies today generally show that wives' employment is unrelated to husbands' satisfaction.
7	Husbands must make more adjustments to marriage than do wives.	Wives typically make more adjustments and find marriage more stressful than husbands.
8	Successfully married couples most often cite their romantic love and good luck as reasons for their long marriages.	Most couples do not view romantic love as the kind of love that helps maintain marital satisfaction over the lifespan; rather they cite the quality of their friendship as most important.
9	Children are better off with divorced parents than with parents who are unhappily married.	Divorce is usually traumatic for children; even unhappy marriages provide children with greater economic standing, stronger family bonds, stronger connections with the community, more time for parent–child interactions, and better overall emotional health.
10	Half of all marriages today will end in divorce.	If today's divorce rates continue unchanged into the future, the chance that a marriage will end in divorce is estimated to be about 40%.

SOURCE: Adapted from "Marriage and family therapists' endorsement of myths about marriage," by B. E. Caldwell and S. R. Woolley, 2008, *The American Journal of Family Therapy, 36*, 367–387; and "Top ten myths of divorce," by D. Popenoe and B. D. Whitehead, 2002, Rutgers, RI: The National Marriage Project, retrieved from http://marriage.rutgers.edu.

Coping with Life After Divorce Regardless of who initiates the divorce, divorced people must pick up the pieces and start again. Especially when there are children, going on with life can be complicated indeed (see Chapter 13). The family as a system must make serious adjustments in practical living, and studies of divorced men and women typically reveal that many suffer from a wide range of problems that they had not encountered while they were married. For example, the practical problems of organizing and maintaining a household often plague many divorced men who were generally accustomed to having their former wives perform these tasks. Financial hardship usually affects both men and women. With two households to support instead of one, previous incomes often are spread too thin to make ends meet. Women who have been homemakers before their divorce usually suffer the most financial strain—especially if their husbands fail to make court-ordered alimony or child support payments. Strapped by these new economic burdens, many women must enter the workforce—sometimes for the first time. If they were working before the divorce, they may need to work longer hours or take a second job; therefore, they have less time with their children and little or no time for themselves. Men also may need to work longer hours or take a second job; therefore, men may experience many of the same problems as their former wives do.

Do you think that divorce in middle adulthood is harder or easier than divorce in early adulthood? What factors should be considered in framing an answer to this question?

Disruption of the marital relationship, whether through divorce or death, is a stressful event (Coleman, Ganong, & Leon, 2006; Fine & Harvey, 2006; Howe, 2011). There is often grief and mourning over the loss of an intimate relationship. Even when the marriage was unhappy, people usually have second thoughts about whether they should have divorced. There is a disruption of normal routines and patterns, as well as sheer loneliness at times. Most people who are experiencing divorce perceive it as a kind of failure. For the partner who did not make the decision to divorce, there is often a feeling of rejection. Feelings of humiliation and powerlessness are common. Even if the marriage was unsatisfactory, the final decision often comes as a shock. For the partner who makes the decision, the stress is often higher during the agonizing months or years before the separation. The spouse who initiates the divorce may feel sadness, guilt, and anger. However, there is at least a compensating sense of control because the spouse has rehearsed and mentally prepared for the separation, which may come as a complete surprise to the other partner, making adjustment all the more difficult (Amato & Dorius, 2010).

When divorce occurs in middle adulthood, it is often especially difficult because both partners have grown accustomed to their previous way of life. The new financial and social circumstances that result from divorce often are wrenching to people in middle adulthood, especially if they are forced to concentrate on developmental tasks—such as going back to school, finding a new job, and dating—that are considered more appropriate for people in early adulthood.

Starting a New Life Establishing a new lifestyle after divorce is easier for some people than it is for others. For some, the freedom from constraint, obligation, and emotional turmoil may be a welcome relief, and those whose marriages were unhappy may feel that they have a new chance after a divorce. For others, the idea of living alone is frightening. After a long period of marriage, older women in particular may experience considerable difficulty relinquishing their previous role and may be especially unprepared to manage financial and legal matters, such as obtaining credit cards or securing a bank loan or mortgage. In addition, individuals who married young may never have been on their own and, therefore, have little experience in coping with the independence that now confronts them. These newly single people often underestimate the problems of adjusting to being alone. Reflecting these situations, regardless of the duration of the marriage, recently divorced men and women have higher rates of alcoholism, physical illness, and depression.

Most divorced individuals experience considerable improvement in well-being within 2 or 3 years of the final separation (Amato & Dorius, 2010; Greene, Anderson, Hetherington, Forgatch, & Degarmo, 2003), and many remarry. Divorced people who develop new intimate relationships are more likely to experience a positive adjustment after divorce, partly because their new relationships diminish their attachments to their ex-spouse (Coleman, Ganong, & Leon, 2006; Demo & Fine, 2010; Fine, Coffelt, & Olson, 2008). Of course, not all divorces end in positive adjustment. A sizable minority of divorced people remain bitter and isolated even 10 years after the divorce. Some men virtually lose contact with their children as the result of a bitter divorce and, despite adequate resources, refuse to help cover their expenses, such as college costs. Some divorced women use their children as weapons against their ex-husbands, in an effort to produce guilt and shame. When conflict and hatred endure, family relationships are very difficult to maintain. Adjustment following a divorce is better when both parties focus on growth rather than on resentment and past failures (Hetherington & Kelly, 2002; Sarrazin & Cyr, 2007; see Table 15-5).

What factors do you think contribute to the finding that divorced men are much more likely to remarry than are divorced women?

Marriages That Succeed Although we sometimes focus on divorce as a developmental issue, it is important to remember that more marriages succeed than fail. What makes for a successful marriage?

Although middle-aged men and women cite different reasons for remaining married, both list "My spouse is my best friend" as their primary reason (Lauer & Lauer, 2012; Lauer, Lauer, & Kerr, 1990). Interestingly, the top seven reasons listed by men

Watch *Leroy and Geneva: Divorce Is Not a Choice* on **MyDevelopmentLab**

Table 15-5 Recommended Strategies for Making a Positive Adjustment Following a Divorce

- Focus more on the future than the past.
- Focus on building new, more fulfilling relationships and developing opportunities for personal growth.
- Focus on your strengths, not your weaknesses, and look for ways in which you can use the resources available to you.
- Take a realistic approach to happiness and success. Remember that no one is happy all the time and success is not achieved without trials and failures along the way.
- Recognize that you have choices. There are always alternatives available no matter how hopeless things appear.
- Choose carefully and consider the long-term impact of decisions you make about children, romance, and work.

and women who have been married for 15 years or more are the same:

- My spouse is my best friend.
- I like my spouse as a person.
- Marriage is a long-term commitment.
- Marriage is sacred.
- We agree on aims and goals.
- My spouse has grown more interesting.
- I want the relationship to succeed.

Although most happily married couples are satisfied with their sex lives, it usually is not a primary factor in happiness or marital satisfaction. Men listed satisfaction with sex as the 12th most important reason for staying together; women listed it as the 14th.

Perhaps not surprisingly, studies generally report that middle-aged people who remain married experience higher levels of general happiness and satisfaction than do those who are single. One reason is that people in successful, happy marriages usually have learned to communicate effectively (Celello, 2012; Gottman, 2007), and this ability is a key to providing many of marriage's benefits. For example, marriage helps older people deal with stressful life events, such as retirement, loss of income, illness, or disability. These positive effects stem from the sense of intimacy, interdependence, and belonging that marriage brings. These same benefits also accrue to those who remarry if their new marriages are successful. Remarriage often requires considerable adjustment, however, just as the original marriage did. Adjustments typically are greater when children are involved and the marriage involves blending families together.

Blended Families

When divorced or widowed people with children remarry, they form *reconstituted* or **blended families**, also known as *stepfamilies*. Especially for the parent who has custody of the children, remarriages can reduce stress (Fine & Harvey, 2006; Pruett & Donsky, 2011). A partner who is willing to share financial responsibilities,

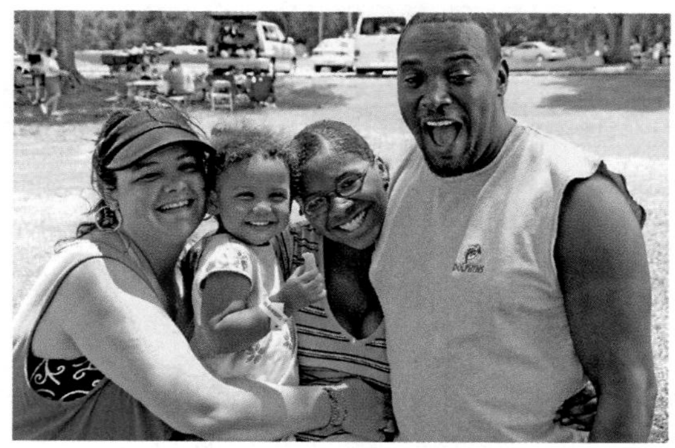

Among couples who have remained married for 15 or more years, the most common reason reported by both men and women is "my spouse is my best friend."

household tasks, child-rearing decisions, and so on can offer welcome relief to a divorced parent. The dynamics of reconstituted families, however, are complex (see Figure 15-4). Members of blended families often go through a period of adjustment as relationships and expectations are defined (Ganong, Coleman, & Hans, 2006; Pruett & Barker, 2009).

Blended Families in Perspective There is a tendency to think that because of the current high divorce and remarriage rate, blended families are an entirely new phenomenon; however, this is not the case. In fact, the current remarriage rate closely parallels remarriage rates in Europe and the United States in the 17th and 18th centuries. There is, however, a major difference: Today, most reconstituted families are created as a result of a marriage–*divorce*–remarriage sequence. In the past, most reconstituted families were a result of a marriage–*death*–remarriage sequence (Visher, Visher, & Pasley, 2003).

Can you think of reasons why stepmothers often have a more difficult adjustment than do stepfathers?

The difference between these two types of blended families is, of course, the presence of a living former spouse. Contact with the former spouse often continues and may include shared child custody, financial support, or visitation. In some families, it is difficult to maintain appropriate emotional distance, resolve conflicts, and avoid feelings of rejection. For the children, remarriage can create a situation characterized by ambivalence, conflict, uncertainty, and divided loyalties. It is therefore not surprising that previously widowed stepparents often report more positive relationships with each other and with their children following remarriage than do previously divorced stepparents (Visher, Visher, & Pasley, 2003).

In any event, second marriages are different from first marriages (Coleman & Ganong, 2009; Mason, 2007; Visher & Visher, 1998). They operate within a more complex family organization—stepchildren, ex-spouses, and former in-laws, for example—that can cause considerable conflict (Hennon & Schedle, 2008; Hetherington & Kelly, 2002). However, second marriages often are characterized by more open communication, by greater acceptance of conflict, and by more trust that any disagreements that arise can be resolved satisfactorily.

blended family
A family in which partners with children have remarried or formed a cohabiting relationship; also called a *reconstituted family* or *stepfamily*

Watch *Blended Families* on MyDevelopmentLab

CHANGING PERSPECTIVES

Blended Families—Themes and Variations

At the beginning of the 21st century, nearly half of all marriages are remarriages for one or both partners. As a consequence, nearly one-third of the children in the United States will spend some time in a stepparent household before they reach adulthood (Ganong & Coleman, 2004). Some couples—and some children—will experience more than one divorce and remarriage. Clearly, the nature of the *typical* family is changing.

Families are dynamic interrelated systems of relationships, customs, rules, and traditions (Gosselin & David, 2007). They each have a structure and a long-term history. If we consider grandparents and extended kin, families are often more complex than we imagine. When one family is disrupted and another forms in its place, there is a need for reevaluation and sometimes for reconstruction and repair.

Because of the complicated way that blended families come into being, the structures of various reconstituted families have wide variation. Some of these families, especially those formed later in life, involve primarily the couple as domestic partners because their children already have been raised and live on their own. However, family arrangements when children are still living at home are often much more complicated, particularly because of the increasingly common joint-custody arrangements where children are part of more than one family simultaneously. For example, consider Figure 15-4. These families have different members on weekdays as compared to Saturday and Sunday. Most of the children are part of two households. On weekdays, for example, Mary lives with her mother and stepfather; on Saturday she lives with her father, stepmother, and stepbrother; on Sunday she returns to her mother's household and is joined by her stepfather's three children. Beyond these immediate family relationships, there are often a tangle of grandparents, aunts, uncles, and cousins.

How do children untangle and adapt to the differing expectations in each household? How do they form new attachments to stepparents, stepbrothers, and stepsisters? How do parents and stepparents cope with part-time family members, set clear and reasonable expectations, and manage complex arrangements? Lawrence Ganong and Marilyn Coleman (e.g., Ganong & Coleman, 2004; Ganong, Coleman, & Hans, 2006; Ganong, Coleman, & Jamison, 2011) contend that several characteristics of reconstituted families should be understood if researchers are to consider and address the challenges that members of blended families face and to understand how these families function. Among these characteristics of reconstituted families are the following:

- Blended families are more structurally complex than other family forms.
- Children often are members of two households.
- A child's parent is often elsewhere, in actuality or in memory.
- Blended family members have different family histories.
- Parent–child bonds are older than adult partner bonds.
- Individual, marital, and family life cycles are likely to be on different clocks.
- Blended families begin after many losses and changes have occurred.
- Children and adults come to blended families with expectations from previous families.
- Blended families often have unrealistic expectations.
- Blended families are not supported well by society.
- Legal relationships between stepparent and stepchild are ambiguous or nonexistent.

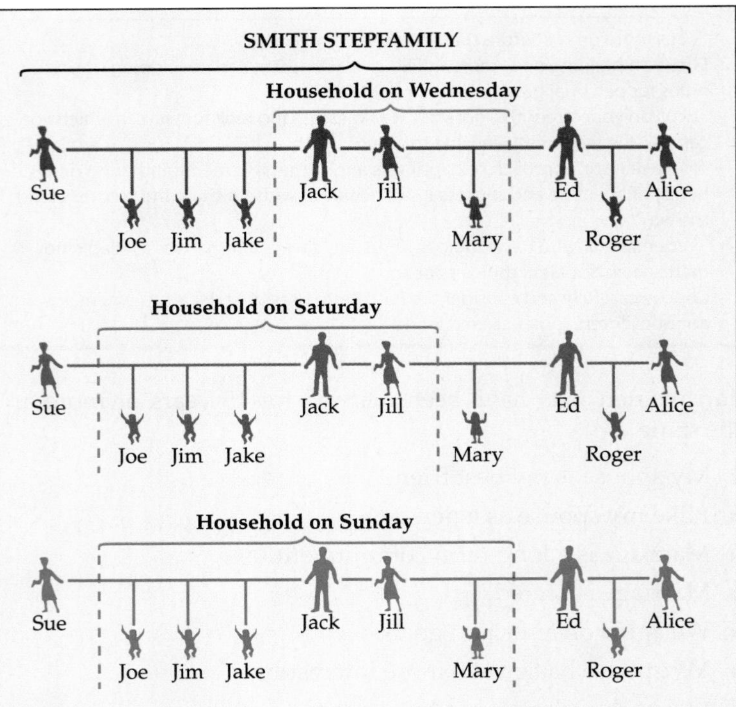

FIGURE 15-4 **Stepfamilies: A Complex Picture**
In this family, the children live with their custodial parent on weekdays and visit the other parent on weekends, resulting in different households on different days. Five parents as well as five children must continually adjust to changing roles, relationships, and responsibilities.

SOURCE: Figure, "Family tree/Smith family," in *Stepfamily relationships: Development, dynamics and interventions* (p. 197), by L. H. Ganong and M. Coleman, 2004, New York: Kluwer Academic/Plenum. Copyright © 2004. Reprinted by permission of Springer Science & Business Media.

Although some of these statements seem obvious, in fact they reflect a very complex system of personal relationships and histories.

In addition to the often overwhelming emotional and interpersonal aspects of managing reconstituted families, there also are formal arrangements to manage and obligations to fulfill. Custody, child support, guardianship, and even ensuring that children get to the places they are supposed to be are difficult arrangements to negotiate and honor. Holidays can be particularly difficult as family members are shuttled back and forth so that old and new family ties can be maintained. Building any family that supports each member is not an easy task, and blended families are more complicated than most. It takes time, understanding, and a willingness to listen to and address each family member's concerns and preferences to work out the details that living in a reconstituted family requires.

What experiences do you have with blended family situations? Are you part of a reconstituted family? Do you have close friends who are stepchildren or stepparents? How have family arrangements been negotiated in the cases with which you are most familiar? What coping strategies do you think work especially well in negotiating the arrangements required? Which characteristics noted in the previous list seem more significant to you, based on your experiences with reconstituted family situations?

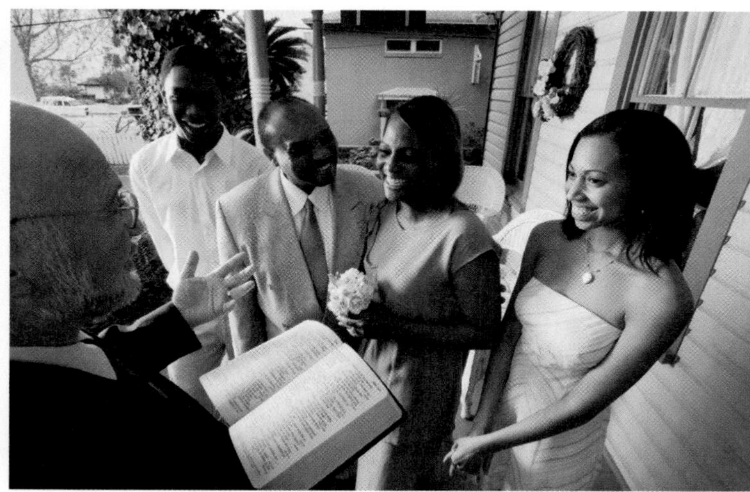

▲ Most stepparents and stepchildren ultimately make a positive adjustment to each other.

Learning to Live in a Blended Family The expectation that reconstituted families can simply pick up where the primary family left off is unrealistic and inevitably leads to frustration and disappointment. Both stepparents and stepchildren need time to adjust to one another—to learn about and test each other's personalities.

When asked what the greatest difficulties are in a stepparent–stepchild relationship, most stepparents mention discipline, adjusting to the habits and personalities of the children, and gaining the children's acceptance (Ganong & Coleman, 2004; Pruett & Barker, 2009). Stepmothers often have more problems than do stepfathers in adjusting to their new roles, partly because stepmothers spend more time with children than stepfathers do and usually are expected to do more and assume more of the child-care role.

There is also the popular stereotype of the stepchild, who is conceptualized as neglected, perhaps abused, and definitely not loved as much as the stepparent's biological child. Surveys of the public, and even of professionals who help blended families, find that such stereotypes are fairly widespread, but inaccurate (Coleman & Ganong, 2009; Ganong & Coleman, 2004). In those few cases where such a situation does exist, the stepparent is not always to blame. The stepchildren themselves may stand in the way. If they have not accepted their parents' divorce or the loss of their biological parent, if they have been used as pawns in a bitter and angry divorce, or if they hold an idealized view of the missing parent, children may reject the stepparent's love and make family harmony impossible.

Taking time to develop mutual trust, affection, a feeling of closeness, and respect for the child's point of view often helps in forming a workable relationship between stepchildren and stepparents. Defining the stepparent's role as different from the role held by the missing biological parent also is helpful. If stepparents try to compete with the stepchild's biological parent, they are more likely to fail. Although stepparents rarely duplicate the idealized biological parent's place in the child's life, they often can provide a loving, nurturing, and secure environment—one that often is more satisfactory than the one the child experienced before the divorce. Indeed, most stepparents and stepchildren eventually make positive adjustments (Cartwright & Auckland, 2008; Visher & Visher, 1998), although these often are harder to establish between girls and stepfathers and boys and stepmothers (Hetherington, 1992; Linder & Heatherington, 2004). In any case, a satisfactory resolution is more likely to occur if the reconstituted family creates a new social unit that blends familiar routines and expectations with new relationships, communication styles, methods of discipline, and problem-solving strategies (see the box Changing Perspectives: Blended Families—Themes and Variations).

Creating a happy, functional, stable family is a challenge for parents, whether they are biological parents or stepparents. So, too, is finding success and satisfaction at work, a topic we explore in the next section.

REVIEW THE FACTS 15-3

1. During which period of adulthood is divorce most likely?
   a. young adulthood
   b. middle adulthood
   c. older adulthood
2. The average age at which a first divorce occurs in the United States today is about ________ years for men and ________ years for women.
   a. 28; 26 b. 32; 34
   c. 34; 41 d. 32; 30
3. Are husbands or wives more likely to initiate a divorce?
4. When asked why they remain married, men are most likely to list ________ whereas women are most likely to list ________.
   a. sex; security
   b. sex; being best friends
   c. agreement on goals; religion
   d. being best friends; being best friends
5. The prevalence of reconstituted families today is ________ that found in Europe and the United States in the 17th and 18th centuries.
   a. much higher than b. about the same as
   c. a little lower than d. much lower than
6. Do stepmothers or stepfathers generally have a harder time adjusting to the presence of stepchildren?
7. When forming a blended, or reconstituted, family, is it generally better to try to create a new family as much like the old one as possible or to create a new social unit?

✓ Practice on **MyDevelopmentLab**

OCCUPATIONAL CONTINUITY AND CHANGE

As the preceding section makes clear, middle adulthood is a time of life characterized by both continuity and change in family relationships and structure. The workplace also serves as a vehicle for continuity and change, depending on how a person's career unfolds during middle adulthood.

Until quite recently, it was thought that a person's working life consisted of—or should consist of—entering a particular occupation or career as a young adult and remaining in that occupation until retirement. Obviously, this "preferred" career course required a thoughtful choice of occupation and careful preparation at the outset. Once individuals had begun a job, they were expected to lay the foundation for a lifetime career and to climb the ladder of success as quickly as possible.

This scenario has changed considerably, partly because in today's technologically advanced and economically unstable world, jobs change so quickly or are eliminated in such numbers that the one-career pattern no longer applies to most people. Occupational change is particularly appropriate to consider within the context of middle adulthood. Both corporate *downsizing* that eliminates jobs and *outsourcing* that farms out work to other companies—often outside the United States—involve the loss of jobs to workers, regardless of how competent and dedicated they have been. These practices are especially likely to be the cause of job loss during middle adulthood.

Job Change and Stress

When job loss occurs in midlife, it is often difficult for a displaced worker to find another job, especially one with comparable pay and benefits. With the other adjustments that occur in middle adulthood, changes to one's career—even if they are anticipated and desirable—can create temporary instability and stress, both for the individual and for the family (McKee-Ryan, Song, Wanberg, & Kinicki, 2005; Moen, Sweet, & Hill, 2010; Rudisill, Edwards, & Hershberger, 2010).

For many people, career changes are not welcome and may not go smoothly. When career progress and promotions do not occur as expected or when forced career shifts or sudden unemployment occur, high levels of stress, anxiety, and disequilibrium may be found. Situations that involve role conflict are problematic as well. For both mothers and fathers, family responsibilities may be in conflict with changing work requirements, for example, if relocation or a change in working hours is involved. The result is often increased stress, which is reflected in relationships at home and on the job. Many work-related situations can contribute to stress and challenge a worker's mental health (see Table 15-6).

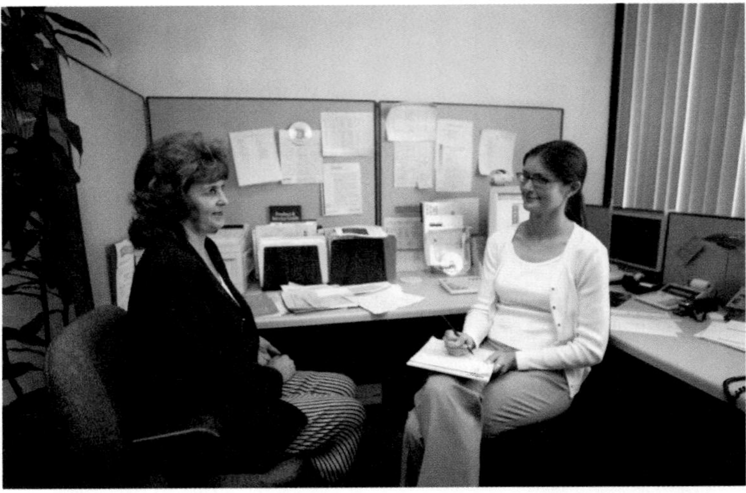

▲ For this middle-aged woman, the stress of hunting for a new job is increased when she finds she is being interviewed by a supervisor who is scarcely older than her own daughter.

Especially serious, in most cases, are situations in which middle-aged workers find themselves unexpectedly out of a job.

Job Loss People who are fired, laid off indefinitely, or who experience forced retirement often face emotional problems that may even outweigh the problem of loss of income. Responses to job loss can be serious. People's self-concept may be destroyed and their self-esteem shattered. Individuals often react to career loss in ways that are similar to the grief response triggered by the death of a loved one—initial shock and disbelief followed by anger and protest. Some people bargain and plead for a second chance, and some become depressed. Jobless workers may feel panic, guilt about the loss, or resentment; and they may develop physical ailments or become unable to participate in their normal activities, although these are unrelated to work (Niles, Jacob, & Nichols, 2010; Warr, 2007).

Table 15-6 Environmental Influences on Mental Health

Opportunity for control	Mental health is enhanced when individuals believe they have some control over the events in their lives. When demands are high and individuals' control over the situation is low, mental health often is challenged.
Opportunity for skill use	Individuals benefit from being able to use the skills they have and develop new skills of value.
Externally generated goals	Mental health is well served when individuals are stimulated to pursue goals, especially if they have some role in setting them.
Environmental variety	Environments that provide choices and options stimulate good mental health adjustments. Lack of variety often produces apathy.
Environmental clarity	People do best in environments where rules and standards of appropriate behavior are clear and in which they receive accurate feedback about their own performance.
Availability of money	Although money does not ensure good mental health, the lack of money (poverty) often diminishes it by decreasing peoples' control and reducing the number of choices when making life decisions.
Physical security	It is difficult to be healthy mentally if basic freedoms and needs (personal safety, sufficient food, adequate housing) are not met.
Opportunity for physical contact	When situations require isolation from other people, mental health can be challenged.
Valued social position	People are mentally healthier when they have a positive sense of their own self-esteem. When self-esteem is threatened, such as when a job is lost, mental health sometimes deteriorates.

SOURCE: Adapted from *Psychology applied to work*, by P. M. Muchinsky, 2009, Summerfield, NC: Hypergraphic Press; and *Work, happiness, and unhappiness*, by P. B. Warr, 2007, Mahwah, NJ: Lawrence Erlbaum Associates.

Table 15-7 Factors in Coping with Job Loss

PHYSICAL HEALTH

One of the first ways of coping with losing a job is to find another one, and it is easier for individuals to present themselves effectively during job interviews if they are in good health. Being in good physical condition also adds to the ability to handle the stress, unforeseen challenges, and fatigue associated with losing a job.

PHYSICAL AND FINANCIAL RESOURCES

Losing a job places greater stress on individuals who have no financial resources than it does on those who can pay their bills while they are looking for work. Individuals without financial resources may be forced to sell their house and scale down their lifestyle—all of which adds to the stress created by the job loss.

SPECIFIC SKILLS

Individuals with marketable job skills will probably have less difficulty finding a job than will those with inadequate or outmoded training.

SOCIAL SUPPORT

An individual who is surrounded by a loving, supportive family can often cope better with job loss than someone who is alone or has troubled family relationships.

COGNITIVE UNDERSTANDING OF EVENTS

The ability to understand the reasons behind a job loss (was it corporate downsizing, poor performance, or a personality clash?) helps the individual handle the dislocation and gather the energy to search for a new job. This ability comes partly from education and past experience.

ANTICIPATION AND PREPARATION

People who understood that new technology would make much of the work they do obsolete can anticipate the possibility of job loss and train for employment in related fields well in advance of being laid off. People who cannot or do not anticipate job loss are left with fewer options.

PERSONALITY FACTORS

Personality traits, such as flexibility, openness to experience, and resilience, prepare the individual to handle the pressures associated with finding a new job.

LIFE HISTORY

Individuals who have lost jobs before and have lived through periods of unemployment may react differently to a job loss than those who have never had these experiences.

Job loss is generally more difficult for middle-aged adults than for young adults. First, it is likely that middle-aged individuals have more of their identity invested in their job. Second, older people are likely to have a harder time finding a new job due to the mismatch between outdated skills and new technological requirements of many jobs. In some cases, older adults may experience age discrimination in hiring and in training programs—despite federal laws barring such discrimination. Older workers also are more likely to face significant financial obligations, since midlife typically is a time when family needs are high (Repetti & Wang, 2010). Finally, whatever job the worker can find is likely to have a lower salary and status than the previous job (Sterns & Huyck, 2001). This is particularly true during times of economic recession. People who have worked their way up the job hierarchy in a company to a position that is beyond their educational qualifications are particularly vulnerable to reduced salary and loss of status because their skills often are specific to that particular company or their particular job.

Why might the loss of a job in middle adulthood be perceived as a more serious threat to a person's self-concept than would be loss of a job in early adulthood?

In general, those who cope best with job loss try to take it in stride and not turn their anger inward by blaming themselves or considering themselves professional and personal failures. Additional factors that determine how well people cope with job loss are summarized in Table 15-7. Unfortunately, as disruptive as losing one's job is, this is not the only career setback experienced by middle-aged workers. Sometimes careers are unsatisfying or unfulfilling, either because the work is dull and repetitive or because supervision is inadequate (see Chapter 13). Another problem is job burnout.

Job Burnout **Job burnout** is characterized by emotional exhaustion that results from working in high-stress professions or trades. Of course, job burnout is not restricted to middle adulthood, although this is the time of life when it most often emerges. Job burnout is especially prevalent among individuals in the helping professions (Maslach & Leiter, 2008; Shirom, 2011). Social workers, police officers, nurses, therapists, teachers, day-care workers, and others who must work in close personal contact with those whom they serve—often in strained, tension-filled situations—are especially at risk.

People in the helping professions who suffer job burnout generally are idealistic, highly motivated, extremely competent workers who finally realize that they cannot make the difference they once thought they could. Those high in the personality trait of neuroticism are especially at risk (Kim, Shin, & Swanger, 2009; Langelaan, Bakker, van Doornen, & Schaufeli, 2006). Early warning signs include increasingly frequent anger,

job burnout
The emotional exhaustion that often affects people in high-stress professions and trades

▲ Social service workers who juggle multiple tasks and personalities and see little day-to-day progress or client improvement can be particularly prone to job burnout.

frustration, and despair. Burned-out workers may even turn on the people they are supposed to help or they may withdraw from emotional involvement into cold detachment. Physical exhaustion, psychosomatic illnesses, low morale, mediocre performance, and absenteeism commonly accompany job burnout (Akhtar & Lee, 2010; Rossi, Quick, & Perrewe, 2009).

The general cause of job burnout is the lack of rewards in a work situation in which great effort has been expended and high hopes originally predominated. Thus, job burnout is not the result of incompetence or personal failings; rather, burnout in the helping professions and in other settings is a function of the situation in which the individual works (Bakker, Schaufeli, Demerouti, & Euwema, 2007; Maslach & Leiter, 2008). Workers can avoid or minimize job burnout by learning to be realistic in their approach to their work and their goals, by promoting changes in their job requirements or work flow so job pressures do not mount excessively, by attempting to keep the rest of their life separate from their work (for example, by not taking their work troubles home with them), and by developing interests outside of their jobs. This is actually good advice for all workers, not just for potential job burnout victims.

Midcareer Reassessment Sometimes the best solution to a career-related problem, whether from the loss of a job, job burnout, or the need to increase income or job satisfaction, is to reevaluate one's career options with an eye toward making a change. Career reassessment in middle adulthood occurs for a number of reasons. Some workers may find that they are not being promoted as rapidly as they had expected; others may discover that a job may turn out to be less desirable than anticipated. When middle adulthood brings a more general shift in values and goals, this also can lead people to consider changing the course of their career as they realistically and systematically assess their own abilities and the pluses and minuses of their current occupational position (Barclay, Stoltz, & Chung, 2011; Sterns & Huyck, 2001). For example, people now live longer and can work longer; when their responsibilities to their children end, they are free to make changes that may reduce their income or transform their way of living. In comparison to earlier times, there also is greater tolerance for deviations from traditional social norms, including a wife financially supporting her husband. These more broadly defined expectations make it easier for people to act upon their newfound interests and ideals. Perhaps one spouse might work while the other makes a career change. In addition, women who have not held jobs while their children were at home may choose to enter the workforce. At middle age, they are ready to channel their energies into another form of generativity. In the workplace, these women may gain a new sense of accomplishment and form meaningful, sustaining relationships.

Indeed, with respect to occupations, families, and other relationships, the years that comprise middle adulthood are often characterized by change as well as by continuity. Middle-aged adults must adapt to changes in family structure and perhaps changes in jobs or in their health while generally maintaining a steady course through life. In the final section of this chapter, we look one more time at the issue of continuity and change, this time focusing on the structure of adult personality. Are we the same people at age 65 that we were at age 40 or have we changed in fundamental ways?

REVIEW THE FACTS 15-4

1. In comparison to previous generations, are adults today less likely or more likely to stay in the same job or career for much of their lives?
2. Is job loss generally more difficult for young adults or for middle-aged adults?
3. State two difficulties that workers typically face when they lose their jobs during middle adulthood.
4. When workers feel anger and frustration because their hard work does not make as much difference as they had hoped, they are said to experience ________.
5. As people live and work longer, is midcareer reassessment becoming less common or more common?

Practice on **MyDevelopmentLab**

CONTINUITY AND CHANGE IN THE STRUCTURE OF PERSONALITY

One of the major issues in studying how personality might change throughout the lifespan involves answering the fundamental question, "What is personality?" Over the years, many methods have been used to assess the various dimensions, or *traits*, that describe the normal personality.

The Five-Factor Model

In the past three decades or so, a consensus has emerged within the field of psychology that personality can be well described by assessing five traits, or factors, that appear to capture the most important dimensions on which individuals differ from each other (e.g., McCrae & Costa, 2008; McCrae, 2009, 2011). These traits, which are often referred to as the "Big Five" factors, are *emotional stability (also called neuroticism), extroversion, openness to experience, agreeableness,* and *conscientiousness.* The five-factor model argues that each of these traits exists on a continuum from high to low and that an individual is characterized by a certain amount of each trait. The five-factor model thus provides a useful vocabulary to describe how personality might change across the lifespan. Table 15-8 offers a summary of the five factors of personality.

Stability or Change?

Many people believe that their personalities are relatively stable, changing little as they move through their adult years (Herbst, McCrae, Costa, Feanganes, & Siegler, 2000). Why might this be? To the extent that personality is biologically determined, we would expect to see consistency in the traits that characterize the personality profile across the stages of the lifespan as well as across various cultures (Kandler, Rieman, Spinath, & Angelitner, 2010; Moore, Schermer, Paunonen, & Vernon, 2010). Most people move through their lives along relatively stable paths, which would also contribute to the consistency of personality throughout adulthood.

Data collected from cross-sectional and longitudinal studies of men and women of various ages have oftentimes shown considerable consistency in personality profiles across adulthood (e.g., Allemand, Gomez & Jackson, 2010; Terracciano, McCrae, & Costa, 2010), even when personality change was examined in other cultures (McCrae et al., 2004b; Saucier & Ostendorf, 1999). These study results suggest that the basic structure of personality is established relatively early in life—perhaps by age 30—and remains consistent throughout adulthood (Terracciano, Costa, & McCrae, 2006; Terracciano, McCrae, & Costa, 2010).

As we have seen repeatedly, however, individuals often take quite different paths through life. A consistent theme in adult development is that key life events can shape the course of an individual's life (Baltes, Lindenberger, & Staudinger, 2006). From this point of view, we might expect that personality traits would reflect these changes. For example, as we move through adulthood, we generally take on more responsibility and develop better interpersonal skills. Thus, greater conscientiousness and agreeableness would most likely develop in response.

Support for this view comes from a large-scale study of over 100,000 adults ages 21 to 60 that showed agreeableness increased significantly for both men and women as they moved through middle adulthood and that conscientiousness also increased after age 30 (Allemand, Zimprich, & Hendriks, 2008; see Figure 15-5). Indeed, some studies show that middle adulthood is the period of the lifespan in which conscientiousness is at its highest point (Donnellan & Lucas, 2008). A follow-up study using data gathered in the Midlife in the United States (MIDUS) project (see Chapter 14) showed similar results: Conscientiousness and agreeableness increased through early and middle adulthood. Neuroticism and openness to experience remained relatively stable through these periods, although all four of these factors declined as adults moved into old age (Zimprich, Allemand, & Lachman, 2012). Interestingly, in these studies and in other studies (Caprara, Caprara, & Steca, 2003), emotional stability was observed to change throughout adulthood as well, and the change depended on gender: Although women increased in emotional healthiness throughout middle adulthood, men did not. Thus, it may be that women are better able than men to adjust to the tasks of aging, although this result may also be due to a generally lower starting point in self-concept for women. As adolescents, girls generally have less self-confidence than boys do; however, as they move through adulthood, they develop higher self-esteem and a more confident sense of their own value and competence, and this may be reflected in lower levels of neuroticism (Caprara, Caprara, & Steca, 2003).

What is the best way to understand the findings of personality studies such as these? One conclusion seems to be that for most adults there is some general consistency in the structure of basic personality traits and this structure changes gradually, if at all, throughout adulthood. However, it also seems clear that personality is not set in plaster; that is, the major life events that occur throughout adulthood probably do, at least for some people, shape personality in predictable ways. Furthermore, personality also influences how we perceive and react to life events (see Figure 15-5; Allemand, Gomez, & Jackson, 2010; Allemand, Zimprich, & Hendriks, 2008). For example, when adults high in neuroticism encountered a stressful event in midlife, they were likely to see it as a negative turning point in their lives. Adults high in extraversion, on the other hand, saw the event more as an opportunity to learn, and focused more on the value they perceived to result from the challenge (Sutin, Costa, Wethington, & Eaton, 2010).

Thus, perhaps the best conclusion to draw is that in many ways middle adulthood is characterized by both stability and change. While stability is critical for preserving one's core identity and personal relationships throughout life, the ability to change and adjust to life's circumstances provides a means of adapting. Furthermore, there probably are individual differences in the degree that these adjustments occur. In a study that asked middle-aged adults how much they believed their personalities had changed

Table 15-8 Characteristics Associated with the Five Factors of Personality

Characteristic	Traits Associated with Low End	Traits Associated with High End
Emotional stability (Neuroticism)	Moody	Relaxed
	Jealous	Not jealous
	Touchy	Unexcitable
Extroversion	Introverted	Extroverted
	Shy	Talkative
	Quiet	Assertive
Openness to experiences	Unintellectual	Intellectual
	Unimaginative	Imaginative
	Uncreative	Creative
Agreeableness	Cold	Warm
	Unkind	Kind
	Unsympathetic	Sympathetic
Conscientiousness	Disorganized	Organized
	Careless	Dependable
	Inefficient	Persistent

SOURCE: Adapted from "Relative importance of personality and general mental ability in managers' judgments of applicant qualifications," by W. S. Dunn, M. K. Mount, M. R. Barrick, and D. S. Ones, 1995, *Journal of Applied Psychology, 80*(4), 500–509.

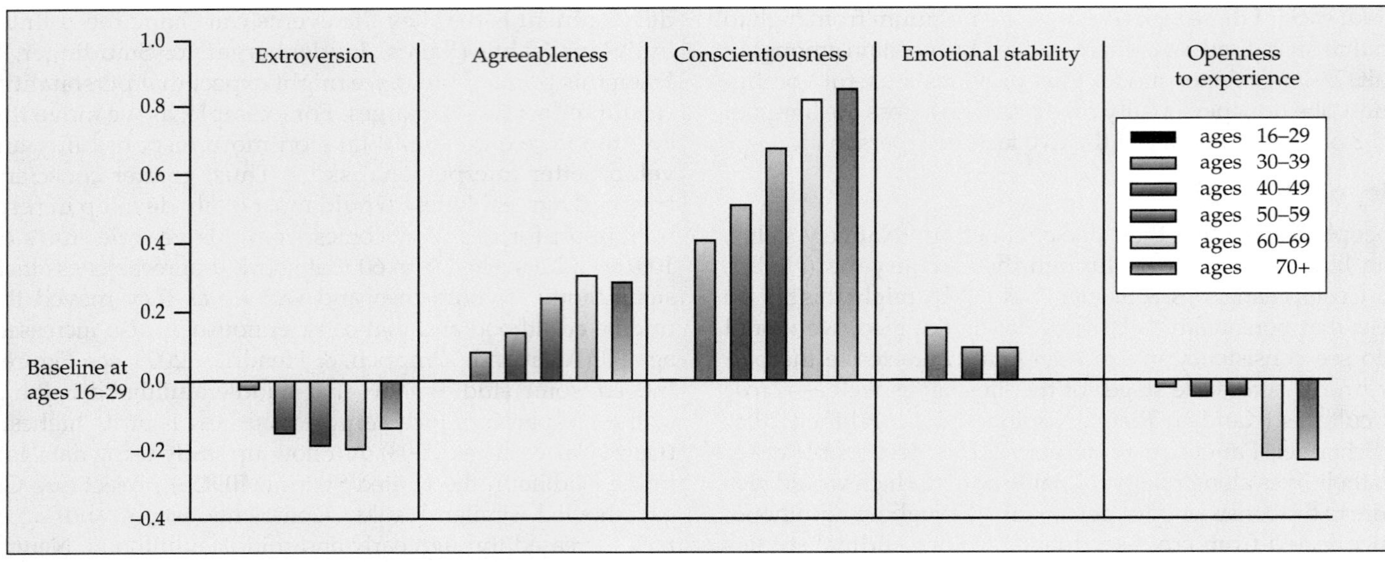

FIGURE 15-5 Changes in the Five Factors of Personality Across the Lifespan
As people move through adulthood, they typically become more conscientious and more agreeable, but somewhat less extroverted and less open to new experiences.

SOURCE: From "Age differences in five personality domains across the life span," by M. Allemand, D. Zimprich, and A. A. Hendriks, 2008, *Developmental Psychology, 44*(3), 758–770.

during the previous 6 years (Herbst, McCrae, Costa, Feaganes, & Siegler, 2000), 52.5% responded they had "stayed the same," and 38.5% reported they had "changed a little." Nevertheless, 9% of the adults responded that they had "changed a good deal." Thus, it seems likely that individuals are capable of change, and some adults change more than others. Regardless of whether a person's development is characterized more by stability or change, or a blending of the two, development in middle adulthood sets the stage in important ways for how people experience their later years in adulthood, the subject of the next two chapters.

REVIEW THE FACTS 15-5

1. Which of the following is *not* one of the "Big Five" traits of personality?
   a. conscientiousness b. emotional stability
   c. agreeableness d. generativity
2. To the extent that personality traits are determined by biology, would they be expected to be stable or to vary during adulthood?
3. Research suggests that the basic structure of one's personality is established by about age
   a. 2. b. 12.
   c. 30. d. 50.
4. Which of the following traits was shown to increase in adulthood in women but not in men?
   a. agreeableness b. emotional stability
   c. conscientiousness d. extroversion
5. Does personality change as a person moves through adulthood?

Practice on **MyDevelopmentLab**

CHAPTER SUMMARY

Personality Continuity and Change

How well does the theme "continuity and change" describe the adjustments that adults make in middle adulthood?

- Middle adulthood (ages 40 to 60 or 65) is a period of continuity and change, as reflection and reassessment occur within the context of self, family, and work.
- Middle-aged adults vary considerably in their places in the family life cycle: Some have young children, others are not married, and others have adult children and are again on their own. Middle adulthood is defined as much by task as it is by age.

What is implied when theorists note that generativity is the primary developmental task of middle adulthood?

- Erikson saw the overarching task of middle adulthood as one of *generativity versus self-absorption*, where adults develop either the feeling that they have contributed in worthwhile ways or that their lives have not been worthwhile. Generativity can be expressed by giving and responding to the needs of one's children (a procreative focus), by integrating work with family life or by caring for the next generation (a productive focus), and by contributing to society on a larger scale (a creative focus).
- In Erikson's view, adjustment in middle age depends on how the earlier stages are resolved. Especially during times of stress, adults may reexperience conflicts characteristic of earlier stages.

- Peck argued that Erikson's view of adulthood was too limited. Peck theorized that adults face seven major issues (or conflicts) and that middle adulthood, especially from ages 50 to 60, sets the stage for the rest of a person's life.

What differences exist in how men and women react to middle age?

- Although increasingly men and women adopt similar work and family roles, there are some gender differences in how they experience middle age. Men traditionally have focused on work-related roles, but family is also important to men at midlife.
- For women in traditional female roles, their place in the family life cycle is usually more significant than their work accomplishments. In one study, women reported three major life transitions: the birth of their children and their early child-rearing years, when their children left home, and menopause. Women, like men, often experience *role conflict* when balancing the needs of work and family. *Role strain* can result from an overload of demands within a given role. Both men and women may experience role conflict and role strain.
- Men and women may reassess their lives at midlife and may shift their attention to other goals and choices.

Family and Friends: Interpersonal Contexts

In what important ways can midlife adults be considered "the generation that runs things"?

- Interpersonal relationships are crucial for men and women throughout middle adulthood. Middle-aged adults must live in the present and assume the role of *kinkeeper* for their parents and their children by maintaining family rituals, celebrating achievements and holidays, and keeping family histories alive.

How do parents typically respond when their last child leaves home?

- When parents launch their adolescent and young adult children into the adult world so that they can assume responsible adult roles, parents must redefine their relationship with their children. At this age, parental success is tied to maintaining open communication with their children, respecting their judgment, and letting go.
- If children return home as adults, this may cause problems because their return may violate parents' expectations. However, if families can successfully renegotiate roles and expectations, long-term educational and economic outcomes for the adult children are often positive.
- When the last child leaves home, parents experience the *empty nest*, forcing them to focus more on their own relationship. Most parents today experience the empty nest as a positive life transition.

What challenges are presented when the parents of midlife adults or children and grandchildren need assistance?

- Life expectancy in the United States has risen dramatically over the last 100 years. Consequently, many middle-aged adults must adjust to caring for their aging parents. However, fewer than 10% of U.S. parents live with their adult children, usually doing so only if illness or economic necessity gives them little choice.
- Most middle-aged adults maintain reciprocal relationships with their parents; however, these usually depend somewhat on specific family circumstances.
- Traditionally, daughters and daughters-in-law assume the primary role as caregivers for aging parents. Although 20% of adults from ages 35 to 64 have cared for a friend or relative in the last year, this usually does not involve placing older relatives in nursing homes or other formal facilities. Only about 10 to 20% of the elderly are placed in these types of facilities. Most elderly adults live independently or move into a relative's home. Although caring for an aged relative can be stressful, it also can provide the caregivers with satisfaction for "giving back."
- Many middle-aged adults become grandparents, although how they assume this role varies widely by culture, proximity to grandchildren, and personal preferences. Three-generation households are more common arrangements among several ethnic minorities than they are for White families.

How do friendships in middle adulthood differ from those developed during earlier periods of the lifespan?

- Especially for people who do not marry or have children, friendships provide an opportunity for intimacy; for all adults, friendships fulfill many important emotional needs. Friends become more important and friendships become more complex as people move through middle adulthood. Women tend to be more deeply involved in their friendships; men's friendships more often are based on similarity.

The Changing Family

What challenges are associated with divorce and remarriage, and what factors help adults in midlife meet these challenges?

- Few U.S. families today fit the "traditional" mold of stay-at-home mom, dad who works, and children. Many social and economic forces are influencing various transitions in family structures.
- About 40% of first marriages in the United States today end in divorce, usually during young adulthood. Today, the average age of first-marriage divorce is about 32 for men and 30 for women. Wives are more often the initiators of divorce.
- Divorce usually involves adjustments and often is accompanied by economic pressures. When divorce occurs in middle adulthood, it is especially difficult because partners usually have grown accustomed to their previous married way of life.
- Recently divorced men and women experience higher rates of alcoholism, physical illness, and depression. However, most divorced people experience considerable improvement in well-being 2 or 3 years after the final separation and many

remarry. Some divorced people, however, remain bitter or have great difficulty coping.

- Men and women in successful marriages respond in very similar ways when asked why they stay married. Both men and women note that "My spouse is my best friend" is the top-ranked reason, and both rank satisfaction with sex well down on the list.
- Compared to those who are single, people who are married report higher levels of happiness during middle adulthood. Marriage helps middle-aged adults cope with stressful events and provides intimacy and interdependence.
- When remarriage involves children, *blended families* (also known as reconstituted families, or stepfamilies) result. Remarriage may help a single parent with children cope, both emotionally and financially, although redefining relationships and making adjustments can produce stress as well.
- The prevalence of blended families today is comparable to that in the 17th and 18th centuries, although reconstituted families in earlier periods usually resulted from parental death rather than from divorce. When parents remarry, family structures often become complex.
- Members of newly blended families need time to make adjustments. Stepparents note that discipline, gaining stepchildren's acceptance, and adjusting to their habits are especially difficult. Stepmothers often have more difficulty than do stepfathers in making adjustments.
- Members of reconstituted families generally make positive adjustments, although relationships between girls and stepfathers and between boys and stepmothers tend to be the most difficult. Resolution typically is best if the blended family creates a new social unit.

Occupational Continuity and Change

How do career paths typically unfold in middle adulthood, and what occupational challenges do some midlife adults face?

- Until recently, most adults expected to have the same job or career throughout life. However, most people today change jobs, perhaps several times, sometimes by choice and sometimes due to job loss or failure to progress in a career.
- When job loss occurs in middle adulthood, finding another job with comparable pay and benefits is often difficult. Job loss, thus, often produces considerable stress. Both economic and emotional problems are often involved, and the loss of income and the loss of self-esteem both can be problematic.
- Job loss at midlife is especially difficult because workers often have more of their identity invested in their jobs, because older workers face discrimination in hiring and in training, and because new jobs often pay less.
- *Job burnout*, which is characterized by emotional exhaustion due to working in high-stress professions or trades, is especially prevalent among those who work in the helping professions. Most people who experience job burnout are idealistic, competent, highly motivated workers who find that, despite their best efforts, they cannot make enough of a difference. Burned-out workers typically experience anger, frustration, and despair. Workers can help avoid job burnout by being realistic about investing too much of themselves in their jobs.
- People now live and work longer, and social expectations about work are more flexible. Consequently, career reassessment during middle adulthood is becoming more common.

Continuity and Change in the Structure of Personality

Is personality development in middle adulthood marked more by stability or by change?

- Middle adulthood is characterized by both change and continuity.
- Many researchers today believe that one's personality can be described by noting how high or low one falls on each of the "Big Five" personality traits: emotional stability (also called neuroticism), extroversion, openness to experience, agreeableness, and conscientiousness.
- For many people, basic personality seems to be established quite early in life—perhaps by age 30—and is relatively stable throughout adulthood. However, some people experience key life events that can affect personality traits, and personality also affects how life events are interpreted.
- Research suggests that agreeableness and conscientiousness increase through adulthood. Emotional stability increases more for women during adulthood than it does for men.
- Although there is some consistency in personality throughout adulthood, for some adults personality can be shaped by life events. There probably are individual differences in the degree to which personality changes throughout life.

KEY TERMS

generativity versus self-absorption (p. 417)
role conflict (p. 419)
role strain (p. 419)
kinkeeper (p. 420)
launching of adolescents (p. 420)
empty nest (p. 422)
blended family (p. 431)
job burnout (p. 435)

OLDER ADULTHOOD
Physical and Cognitive Development

16

LEARNING OBJECTIVES

- What positive and negative stereotypes are typically invoked to describe how "old people" should think and act?
- In what ways does each of the four decades of older adulthood typically differ from the other decades?
- How does a person's body change during the four decades that define older adulthood?
- What are the common health problems people typically face as they move through older adulthood?
- What problems are associated with drug use by the elderly today?
- What theories are used to explain why people grow old and die?
- How do thinking and memory change as a healthy person moves through older adulthood?
- How do older adults compensate for brain-related declines in their cognitive processes?
- What are the differences between normal aging and senility?
- How does having a stroke or ministroke, or developing Alzheimer's disease, change one's ability to move through older adulthood?

CHAPTER OUTLINE

Aging Today
- Ageism and Stereotypes
- Four Decades of Later Life

The Physical Aspects of Aging
- The Changing Body
- Health, Disease, and Nutrition

The Causes of Aging
- Theories of Aging

Cognitive Changes in Advanced Age
- Understanding Various Aspects of Cognition
- Cognitive Decline
- Compensating for an Aging Mind

What is it like to grow old? As is true of other periods in the lifespan, older adulthood is associated with physical, intellectual, and social changes that typically accompany this part of life. However, the ways that people experience becoming old also are heavily dependent on their cultural context. In some societies, for example, people in their older adult years are recognized as elders and awarded high status. In contrast, Western societies often have marginalized the elderly. Only recently, as this older segment of our population has grown and become more visible, have we focused on achieving a better understanding of the changes associated with becoming old.

In this chapter, we explore the physical and cognitive changes that people typically experience as they enter and move through the period of older adulthood. We also recognize that the view of the elderly as empty, decrepit, unhappy people is based on stereotypes, and most older adults experience a life much more full and rich than younger people often imagine.

AGING TODAY

For many people currently living in the United States, the prospects of becoming old appear so grim that they avoid thinking about how they will experience their own old age. In fact, many younger people seem to view older adulthood as a state of marginal existence. They fear the losses of energy, control, flexibility, sexuality, physical mobility, memory, and even intelligence that they think go hand in hand with aging.

Ageism and Stereotypes

Older people are often stereotyped in Western nations. Stereotypes usually reflect **ageism**, which refers to the set of widely prevalent negative attitudes that many people hold of older adults (Nelson, 2009, 2011). Ageist stereotypes typically overvalue youth and degrade older people.

Stereotypes of any sort—regardless of whether they are negative or positive—make it difficult to see other people accurately and to understand them as the varied individuals they are. Ageist stereotypes, in particular, may lead to attitudes and policies that discourage older adults from active participation in work and leisure activities, and these stereotypes are often harshest when they concern older women (Hummert, 2011). For example, a survey of popular movies over the last several decades (Bazzini, McIntosh, Smith, Cook, & Harris, 1997) found that older women are more often portrayed as unattractive, unfriendly, and unintelligent than are older men. In particular, older women's sexuality most often is depicted in humorous contexts, and then is generally shown only for slim, White, middle-class women with male partners of the same age (Weitz, 2010). Apparently, older women's bodies are generally perceived to become less attractive as they age. For example, the fashion industry seldom includes images of women over age 40 in its magazines and publications, and rather promotes its products using young, thin, and exotic-looking models (Lewis, Medvedev, & Seponski, 2011).

If you could choose between being the age you are now or being 80 years old, which would you choose? Why? Does your choice reflect ageism?

A Sociocultural Perspective Looking across cultures and historical periods, we see that people have not always dreaded getting old. In many of the world's religions, for example, elders are considered to possess great wisdom. Among Native Americans throughout the western hemisphere, older people traditionally have been venerated as wise elders and transmitters of culture and have been respected as a storehouse of historical lore. In China, Japan, and other Asian nations, older people are honored in a tradition known as **filial piety**. In Japan, for example, more than three out of four older adults live with their children, and respect is demonstrated through a variety of everyday activities: At home, meals are prepared with everyone's tastes in mind and, in public, people bow with respect when they pass an older person. Filial piety may be changing, however. Although respect for older people remains strong in countries throughout Asia, it is more pronounced among middle-aged and rural people than among young adults and urban residents, who reflect to a greater degree the influence of Western traditions (Hsiu-Hsin, Mei-Hui, & Yun-Fang, 2008; Jenike & Traphagan, 2009; Lam, 2006).

From a historical context, the biblical tradition of veneration for elders was a powerful cultural influence, even in Western cultures such as the United States. For example, in colonial times, long life was viewed as an outward manifestation of divine grace and favor, the reward for an extraordinarily upright life. Benjamin Franklin played a major role in drafting the Constitution

ageism
In Western societies, the widely prevalent negative attitudes, which many people hold of older adults, that overvalue youth and degrade older people

filial piety
The veneration given to the elderly in Asian and other cultures, which is manifested in cultural traditions as well as in everyday encounters

Watch *Aging and Culture* on **MyDevelopmentLab**

not only because he was a shrewd parliamentarian but also because he was over 80 years old at the time and was viewed as "crowned" with the glory of his years.

Part of the reason that reverence for age was powerful in earlier times was that so few people managed to achieve old age. The demographic contrast between then and now is startling. In the colonial period, the median age of the population was 16 and only 2% of the population reached the age of 65; today, the median age of the U.S. population is 37.2 and climbing (U.S. Census Bureau, 2011a), and approximately one in eight people is age 65 or older.

Are there ways today in which older adults are revered, honored, or treated with respect due to their age? If so, what might these be?

As a result of the aging of Baby Boomers, the trend toward lower birth rates, better health care, and declining death rates, the percentage of the population over age 65 is projected to rise even more dramatically in the next three decades. According to U.S. Census Bureau (2010) projections, by the year 2030, nearly one out of every five people living in the United States will be 65 years of age or older (see Table 16-1). Clearly, we are witnessing the unprecedented emergence of a sizable group of older people, at least in the United States and other developed nations.

Table 16-1 Aging: Percentage of the Population 65 Years of Age and Over

Actual Year	Percentage of Population	Projected Year	Percentage of Population
1950	8.1	2010	13.0
1960	9.2	2020	16.1
1970	9.8	2030	19.3
1980	11.3	2040	20.0
1990	12.5	2050	20.0
2000	12.4		

SOURCE: From *Statistical abstract of the United States, 2012*, U.S. Census Bureau, 2012, Washington, DC: U.S. Government Printing Office; and *The next four decades: The older population in the United States, 2010 to 2050*, U.S. Census Bureau, 2010, Washington, DC: U.S. Government Printing Office.

Is Ageism Alive and Well? Do ageist stereotypes still exist now that people over age 65 have become a significant and growing minority, and public awareness of them has greatly increased? In general, and especially in the United States, the answer seems to be a qualified *yes*. People of all ages tend to assign more negative stereotypes to older people and more positive ones to younger people (Kite, Stockdale, Whitley, & Johnson, 2005; Nelson, 2009), although, to some extent, these negative images may reflect the particular cohort that today constitutes the elderly population. For example, today's average older adults have a lower educational level than the younger population, and most have lived through the Great Depression and World War II. Thus, their experiences—and not just their age—have contributed to their values and attitudes, which may seem out of step to some younger people.

Furthermore, when we hear about the elderly, the context is often negative. Newspapers are filled with dramatic stories about such issues as nursing home abuses and desperate older people shoplifting hamburger meat or living on canned dog food. Such stories create powerful images, which often reinforce ageist stereotypes. Negative stereotypes not only instill fear of aging in young people, but they also have a powerful grip on older people. Polls have shown that, although most older adults have a high opinion of their own economic and social condition, they often believe that they are among the lucky few who have escaped the misery of aging in the United States.

Despite the cultural context that ageist stereotypes imply, most people recognize that there are wide individual differences in how adults experience old age; failing health and loneliness do not have to be part of aging any more than acne and awkwardness have to be part of adolescence. The population over age 65 has its marathoners and executives, as well as its shut-ins and bench sitters. Furthermore, several studies demonstrate that attitudes toward older people are not simply negative but also often are ambivalent, if not contradictory. Older people are often seen as both wise and senile, both kind and grouchy, and both concerned for others and inactive and unsociable (Angus & Reeve, 2006; Palmore, 2001).

Indeed, perceptions about older adults usually include both positive and negative stereotypes (see Table 16-2). Furthermore, these perceptions seem to generalize widely among cultures around the world. For example, in a survey about perceptions of aging conducted among individuals living in 26 different cultures, remarkably similar results were found (Löckenhoff et al., 2009). In general, people perceived older adults as having more knowledge and wisdom than younger adults, and as deserving of more respect and having more authority within the family. However, older adults were also perceived as being less physically attractive and as being less able to learn new things and perform everyday tasks (see Figure 16-1). Thus, it appears that basic patterns of aging perceptions are shared among individuals from widely different cultures, including those of the United States, Argentina, France, India, Japan, Poland, Slovakia, and Uganda, among several others. In part, these perceptions match reality: Older adults do experience some decline in their later years and therefore perceptions about learning and the ability to perform daily tasks probably are somewhat consistent with developmental trajectories into older adulthood (Löckenhoff et al., 2009).

Responses to Changes in Appearance It seems clear that older people are thought of differently than they were when they were younger, despite the degree to which age has actually influenced their ability to carry on the same tasks that they routinely accomplished earlier in life. The fact that older adults *look* old changes how people respond to them and think about them. In today's youth-oriented culture, older adults often find that their changing physical appearance is especially bothersome as

Watch *Aging Stereotypes* on **MyDevelopmentLab**

Table 16-2 Common Misperceptions About the Elderly Based on Stereotypes

EXAMPLES OF MISPERCEPTIONS BASED ON NEGATIVE STEREOTYPES

- Most older people are poor.
- Most older people do not have incomes that allow them to keep up with inflation.
- Most older people are ill-housed.
- Most older people are frail and in poor health.
- The aged are impotent as a political force and require advocacy.
- Most older people are inadequate employees; they are less productive, efficient, motivated, innovative, and creative than younger workers.
- Most older workers are accident-prone.
- Older people are mentally slower and more forgetful; they are less able to learn new things.
- A majority of older people are socially isolated and lonely. Most are disengaging or disengaged from society.
- Most older people are confined to long-term-care institutions.

EXAMPLES OF MISPERCEPTIONS BASED ON POSITIVE STEREOTYPES

- The aged are relatively well off; they are not poor but in good economic shape. Their benefits are generously provided by working members of society.
- The aged are a potential political force that votes and participates in unity and in great numbers.
- Older people make friends very easily. They are kind and amiable.
- Most older people are mature, experienced, wise, and interesting.
- Most older people are good listeners and are especially patient with children.
- A majority of older people are very kind and generous to their children and grandchildren.

SOURCE: From "Congressional perceptions of the elderly: The use of stereotypes in the legislative process," by S. Lubomudrov, 1987, *The Gerontologist, 27*(1), pp. 77–81. Copyright © 1987 by The Gerontological Society of America. Reproduced by permission of Oxford University Press.

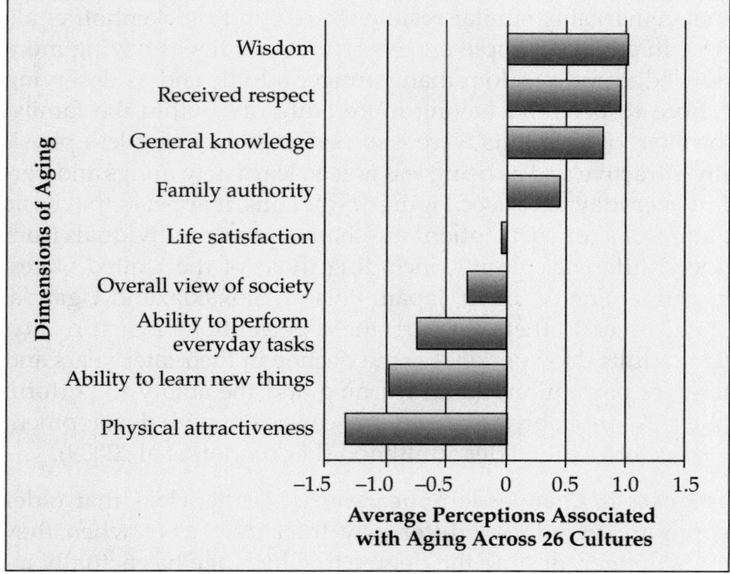

FIGURE 16-1 Perceptions of Aging Across Cultures

NOTE: Positive numbers mean that older adults are rated more favorably than younger adults; negative numbers mean that older adults are rated less favorably on these dimensions.

SOURCE: "Perceptions of aging across 26 cultures and their culture-level associates," by Corinna E. Löckenhoff et al., 2009, *Psychology and Aging, 24*(4), 941–954.

In many non-Western societies, including China, Japan, and other Asian nations, older people tend to be venerated and respected.

they age. In response to age-related negative assessments about body image, older adults—and women in particular—are turning to the use of beauty aids to make themselves look younger, and hence more attractive.

When older adults use these techniques, they generally are trying to address one or more concerns. For older women, these typically include the desire to attract or retain a romantic partner, the desire to appear younger so they are perceived to be more competent in their jobs, their interest to continue to "look good" and thereby maintain their lifelong investment in their physical appearance, and their view that looking younger makes them seem more vital and visible to others (Clarke & Griffin, 2008). Most often, women use simple cosmetic procedures such as hair dye, makeup, and perhaps the removal of facial hair to produce a more youthful appearance. Increasingly, men, too, are using similar products to darken graying hair, or perhaps re-grow it. But cosmetic approaches do not stop at the beauty counter in the drug store. Especially in recent years, more and more older women—and some older men—are turning to cosmetic surgery techniques to restore a more youthful appearance. For example, the American Society for Aesthetic Plastic Surgery (ASAPS) recently announced that in 2011 nearly 9.2 million cosmetic procedures were performed in the United States, 92% of which were done for women (ASAPS, 2011). This number compares to 2 million procedures performed in 1997—an increase of nearly 500% over just 15 years.

Not surprisingly, minimally invasive procedures were the most common techniques performed, accounting for about 82% of all cosmetic surgical techniques. Among these, injections with botulinum toxin ("Botox") were the most common;

in 2011, over 4 million Botox injections were given, the large majority to middle-aged and older women. Botox is a poison that temporarily paralyzes muscles. When it is injected into the forehead, it relaxes the facial muscles that cause wrinkles, thereby giving the face a more youthful appearance. Other common minimally invasive cosmetic procedures include facial peels, where mild acid is applied to the facial skin so that older skin cells are peeled away, leaving younger-looking skin with fewer lines, and microdermabrasion, which buffs off surface skin cells, again with the result of leaving behind younger-looking skin. Not all cosmetic procedures, of course, are so minor, and major surgical interventions, too, are becoming much more commonly performed. In 2011, cosmetic surgeons performed 325,000 liposuction surgeries to remove unwanted body fat deposits, 316,000 breast augmentations, 149,000 abdonimoplasties ("tummy tucks"), 147,000 eyelid surgeries to make eyelid wrinkles disappear, 128,000 face lifts, and 127,000 breast lift surgeries (ASAPS, 2011). Not surprisingly, as cosmetic surgery is becoming more common, it is also being seen as a more acceptable response to aging. In 2011, about half of U.S. men and women agreed that they approve of cosmetic surgery, and about a third indicated they would consider cosmetic surgery for themselves. Interestingly, it is older Americans—age 77 and older—who are most likely to say they would not be embarrassed to have cosmetic surgery themselves (ASAPS, 2011).

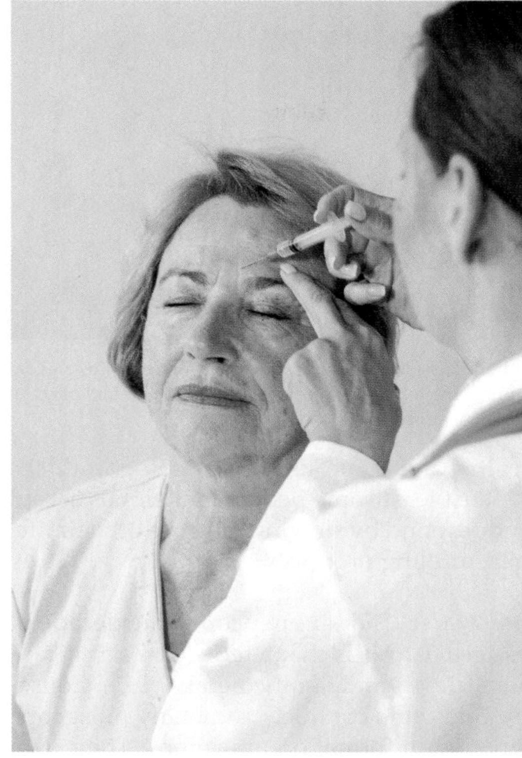

◀ This woman is preparing for a Botox injection that will reduce the wrinkles in her forehead. Do you approve or disapprove of this technique as a way of addressing ageist prejudices?

Four Decades of Later Life

In the United States today, an average 65-year-old can expect to live about another 18.7 years; those who are now 75 years old can look forward to about 12.0 more years (U.S. Census Bureau, 2009b). It is not uncommon for people to live into their 90s and beyond. An obvious but important point is that individuals in later adulthood—which can span 40 or more years—are not a homogeneous group. Indeed, the period of the lifespan defined as "older adulthood" is long, and the individuals within this group are very diverse. For example, a newly retired and relatively hardy 65-year-old and his frail 85- or 90-year-old parent are both older adults; however, they also are members of two separate generations. They represent not only clearly different cohorts with respect to historical events, but they may also have disparate interests, capabilities, and perhaps overall health and functioning. Thus, to recognize the differences among cohorts in the *over-60* portion of the population, it is often useful to subdivide the period of older adulthood by decades.

Young-Old: Ages 60 to 69 For most adults in the United States, the decade of life that encompasses the ages of 60 to 69 is accompanied by a major transition in roles, because this is often the period during which people retire from work (Whitbourne & Whitbourne, 2011). Along with other adjustments associated with retirement or cutting back in working hours, many older adults find that their income is also reduced, and this sometimes forces additional changes in lifestyle and choices. However, there is tremendous variation concerning retirement in this age group. Whereas most people retire at about age 65, others retire at age 55, and still others retire at age 75. Retirement decisions at any age depend heavily on various issues, such as health, energy level, and the type of work that people perform. Those who work in jobs that required hard physical labor will likely be forced to retire earlier than those who perform white-collar jobs. The decision to retire also depends on interpersonal factors, such as the health of a spouse and the relocation of friends. Economic issues, such as family finances are often especially important. Whereas one 68-year-old with little savings may be forced to continue working to pay the bills, another may be able to retire in comfort on a pension and invested savings supplemented by Social Security or other benefits.

Retirement is important in a developmental context because it implies a transition in roles. This transition centers on two developmental challenges: adjustment to the loss of activities and relationships associated with work, and the development of a satisfactory postretirement lifestyle (van Solinge & Henkens, 2008). Individuals meet these challenges in widely varying ways (Pinquart & Schindler, 2007). Many recently retired people are healthy, hardy, and well educated, and many people in their 60s have plenty of energy and seek out new and different activities. They may use their new leisure time for self-enhancement or for community or political activities. Some retirees enjoy regular athletic and sexual activity, and some are determined to remain givers, producers, and mentors. They may become volunteer executives in small businesses, visitors to hospitals, or foster grandparents.

However, society frequently reduces its expectations of people in their 60s, demanding less energy, independence, and creativity, which thereby can demoralize older adults, especially

(a)

(b)

(c)

▲ The period of older adulthood may span four decades and a range of lifestyles. (a) These men in their 60s are participating in senior Olympics. (b) This retired doctor of 88, lives in a retirement community; she regularly enjoys playing the piano and plays her church organ on Sundays. (c) An infirm man of 91 is comforted by his wife of 64 years on returning home from the hospital after a stroke.

those who remain healthy and vigorous (Hoyer & Roodin, 2009; Schaie & Abeles, 2008). At least some people in their 60s accept these expectations and respond by slowing the pace of their life, thereby creating a self-fulfilling prophecy.

Middle-Aged-Old: Ages 70 to 79 For many people, the decade of life that encompasses ages 70 to 79 is characterized by significant illness and loss as more friends and family members die. Consequently, their social world often contracts and many must cope with reduced participation in formal organizations. Their own health problems also tend to become more troublesome during this decade. Men and women in their 70s, called **septuagenarians**, often experience a decline in sexual activity, in many cases because of the loss of a sexual partner. Not surprisingly, many septuagenarians sometimes exhibit restlessness and irritability.

However, increasingly larger proportions of adults in their 70s are able to maintain relatively good health. People who have suffered heart attacks, strokes, or cancer often survive—most without serious disability—because of improved medical care and healthier lifestyles. Despite their losses, many people cope successfully with the challenges of this decade of life and maintain the central aspects of their personality despite changing circumstances.

Old-Old: Ages 80 to 89 Although age is certainly one of the markers of the transition from young-old to old-old, it is not the only one. Being *old* has been poignantly described as a "gradual process that begins the very first day one begins to live in his (or her) memories" (Burnside, Ebersole, & Monea, 1979). We often consider people to be old when they no longer look forward to their future.

Of course, people in their 80s, called **octogenarians**, have a range of perspectives, as well as various levels of health or disability. Most 85-year-olds are frail; however, frailty does not necessarily imply disability or total dependence. Although 25% of U.S. people in this age group were hospitalized for some time in the previous year, only 10% are seriously disabled. Most people over age 85 live in their own homes; only 14% reside in nursing homes (Federal Interagency Forum on Age-Related Statistics [FIFARS], 2008), and this percentage is declining as more intermediate-care options are becoming available (see also Figure 17-9). However, most people in their 80s experience increased difficulty in adapting to and interacting with their surroundings, and many need help in maintaining social and cultural contacts.

Providing care for frail, older adults is increasingly a matter of social and economic concern because people over age 85 make up the fastest growing group in the U.S. population. In the United States in 1980, there were 2.24 million people over age 85; in 2010, there were 5.75 million—nearly 60% of whom were women (U.S. Census Bureau, 2012i). By 2050, the number of people over age 85 is projected to swell to over 19 million (U.S. Census Bureau, 2012j; see Figure 16-2), which will put a strain on U.S. health-care systems and Social Security, with important political considerations.

Very Old-Old: Ages 90 and Over There are fewer data on people in their 90s, called **nonagenarians**, than on 60-, 70-, or 80-year-olds;

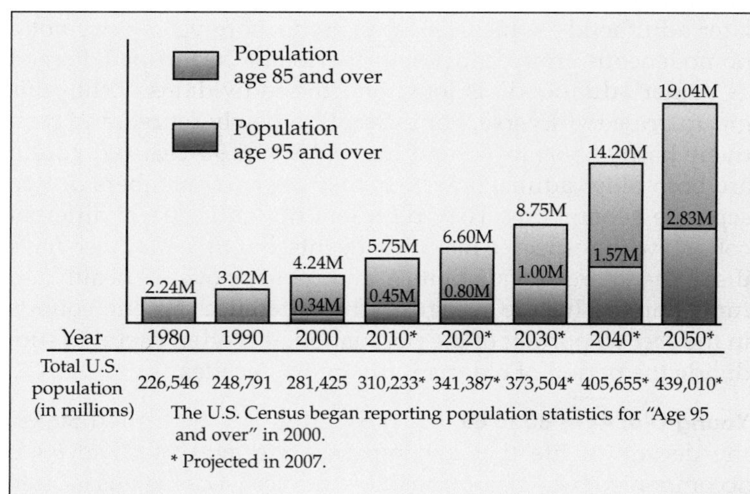

FIGURE 16-2 **U.S. Population Age 85 and Over and Age 95 and Over (in Millions)**

SOURCE: From *Statistical abstract of the United States, 2012,* by the U.S. Census Bureau, 2012, Washington, DC: U.S. Government Printing Office.

septuagenarians
People in their 70s

octogenarians
People in their 80s

nonagenarians
People in their 90s

Table 16-3 The "DARE" Strategy for Healthy Aging

Guideline	Description
Diet	Eat a well-balanced diet on a regular schedule.
Attitude	Keep an optimistic, positive attitude about your health and future.
Renewal	Pick yourself up after losses associated with aging.
Exercise	Maintain a regular program of vigorous exercise appropriate to your physical capabilities.

SOURCE: From "The centenarians are coming," by C. G. Wagner, 1999, *The Futurist, 33*(5), 16–23. Copyright © 1999. Reprinted by permission of World Future Society.

however, the generally emerging picture suggests that the changes that shape life for people in their 90s occur gradually and over a long period. People who survive into their 90s are generally hearty, having survived the diseases and other afflictions that cause other people to die in their 70s and 80s. Thus, people who survive to their 90s typically experience only minimal cognitive decline and often are healthier, more agile, and more active than people 20 years younger (Christensen, McGue, Petersen, Jeune, & Vaupel, 2008). However, health problems generally become more severe with advancing age (Berlau, Corrada, Peltz, & Kawas, 2012; Sarkeala et al., 2011). Nevertheless, many nonagenarians can successfully alter their activities so that they make the most of what they have. Remaining physically active is closely associated with good health among the oldest-old (Formiga, Ferrer, Perez-Castejon, Olmedo, & Pujol, 2007; Frisard et al., 2007). A healthy diet, a positive attitude about the future, taking life's setbacks in stride, and various strategies to prevent strokes and falls also help the very old-old adjust to their advanced age (see Table 16-3). Despite some limitations, if previous crises have been resolved in satisfactory ways, this decade can be joyful, serene, and fulfilling.

Aging: In Perspective To reiterate, older adults are not a single cohesive group but, rather, are best thought of as a collection of subgroups, ranging from the active 65-year-old to the frail nonagenarian (see Table 16-4). There also are wide individual differences. All people experience older adulthood in their own unique way, and the issues associated with a given decade of life may come earlier, later, or not at all to a particular person. Yet, for most older adults, each decade of life brings with it common problems and issues, and most older adults must adjust to the age-related difficulties of reduced income, failing health, and the loss of loved ones. As the popular adage goes, "Getting old is not for sissies." However, *having* a problem is not the same as *being* a problem. The all-too-popular view of people over age 65 as needy, unproductive, and unhappy is an inaccurate one indeed, as is the perception that older adulthood is always accompanied by ill health. There are, however, physical aspects of aging that typically occur during this period. We explore these, and the topics of health, disease, and nutrition, in the next section.

If you were to live to be 100 years old, which decade of older adulthood would you most look forward to? Which do you think would be the most difficult? What factors did you consider as you prepared your responses?

Table 16-4 Major Issues Commonly Faced by Older Adults at Different Ages

Decade	Major Issues Typical of This Decade
60 to 69 (young-old)	Coping with role changes, often centering on retirement
70 to 79 (middle-aged-old)	Coping with illness, the loss of loved ones, and the social isolation this produces
80 to 89 (old-old)	Coping with increasing frailty and maintaining meaningful social and cultural contacts
90 and over (very old-old)	Retaining one's abilities and keeping a positive attitude; people surviving into their 90s often are especially hearty

REVIEW THE FACTS 16-1

1. In Asian nations, the tradition of honoring older people is called ________.
2. Are negative ageist stereotypes more commonly associated with older men or with older women?
3. In the United States today, about 1 person in ________ is age 65 or older.
   a. 3 b. 5
   c. 8 d. 13
4. Which of the following cosmetic procedures is the most commonly performed?
   a. face lift
   b. tummy tuck
   c. breast augmentation
   d. Botox injection
5. About what percentage of people over the age of 85 reside in nursing homes?
   a. 5% b. 14%
   c. 27% d. 33%
6. Why are people in their 90s often heartier than are people in their 70s?

Practice on **MyDevelopmentLab**

THE PHYSICAL ASPECTS OF AGING

The physical aspects of aging determine many of the changes and limitations that occur in later adulthood. However, these physical effects of age often are more the result of

Watch *Successful Aging, Independent Lifestyle: Thelma, 81 Years Old* on **MyDevelopmentLab**

pathological aging factors that result from earlier events and lifestyle choices—accidents, previous illnesses, or bad health habits—than they are of aging processes per se (Gabbard, 2012; Leventhal, Rabin, Leventhal, & Burns, 2001). For example, many people who become partially or completely deaf in older adulthood do so because of experiences earlier in life, such as a firecracker that went off close to their ear or frequent attendance at loud music concerts. Lifelong smokers may develop breathing problems in later years. An older woman who develops diabetes may have been seriously overweight throughout adulthood. Thus, not all of the physical changes that come with age are part of a normal aging process.

Nevertheless, there are biological aging processes at work. Although physical aging comes sooner for some people and later for others, it is inevitable. The processes of aging for most bodily systems actually begin in early and middle adulthood; however, many of the effects of aging are not noticed until later adulthood because aging is gradual, and most physical systems have considerable reserve capacity. Thus, most individuals do not experience interruptions in daily living or major health problems until well into their 70s. However, as people age, their bodies change in a number of predictable ways, affecting their appearance, senses, habits, and general health.

The Changing Body

Appearance A look in the mirror provides clear evidence of the aging process; the gray or thinning hair, a shift in posture, and deepening wrinkles are telltale signs (Whitbourne & Whitbourne, 2011). Changes in the skin are especially noticeable. Wrinkles caused partly by loss of fat tissue under the skin and partly by the skin's thinning and decrease in elasticity give it the crisscrossed look of soft, crumpled paper or fine parchment. Laid on top of wrinkles formed earlier by the use of particular muscles, the face gains the appearance of age. Aging also may produce an increase in warts on the trunk, face, and scalp; small blood vessels often break, producing tiny black-and-blue marks. Age spots may appear; these brown areas of pigmentation are popularly called *liver spots,* although they have nothing to do with the liver's functioning.

Genetic factors also are involved in age-related changes in appearance. Identical twins, for example, show very similar patterns of aging. For many people, however, skin changes are closely related to exposure to wind, climate, abrasions, and especially ultraviolet rays from the sun, which diminishes the skin's ability to renew itself. A "healthy tan" thus leads to thin, wrinkled skin for some people and to skin cancer for others. Some of these signs of aging skin can be controlled by eating well, staying healthy, and protecting the skin against lengthy exposure to the sun—either by avoiding exposure or by using high-level sunblocking lotions.

pathological aging factors
The cumulative effects that result from earlier events and lifestyle choices—accidents, previous illnesses, or bad health habits—that may accelerate aging

Muscles, Bones, and Mobility As we age, we generally become weaker, shorter, and less able to maintain our balance (Newell, Vaillancourt, & Sosnoff, 2006). Muscle weight—and therefore strength and endurance—generally decreases with age, and it takes older muscles longer to restore themselves after physical activity. Muscle function also depends on the cardiovascular system to provide oxygen and nutrients and to remove waste. As blood vessels become less elastic, or if some become clogged, there is less blood flow to the muscles. Decreased lung functioning also may reduce the supply of oxygen to the muscles, further limiting strength and endurance, and fine motor coordination and speed of reaction time typically decrease as we age (Bonder & Bello-Haas, 2009; Wahl, 2010).

This age-related decline in strength and mobility, however, often can be delayed or partially offset by high-intensity exercise training. Done within age-appropriate limits, exercise helps counteract muscle weakness and related physical frailty even in very old people. For example, in a study of 63 women and 37 men with an average age of 87 years, regular exercise increased muscle strength by more than 113% (Fiatarone et al., 1994). Similarly, a 3-year study conducted by the National Institute on Aging and the National Center for Nursing Research showed how strength and balance exercises can benefit frail people in their 80s and 90s: Those who engaged in muscle-building exercises were able to double and even triple their strength and, for the first time in years, perform many strength-related tasks without assistance (Krucoff, 1994). In general, physical activity is linked to better health in older adulthood (Seeman & Chen, 2002; Singh, 2002).

Age often is accompanied by changes not only to the muscles but also to the structure and composition of the skeleton. For example, older adults are usually an inch or more shorter than they were in early adulthood as a result of the compression of cartilage in the spine, which is a long-term effect attributable to the effects of gravity (Whitbourne & Whitbourne, 2011). *Osteoporosis*—an age-related condition where bones become weaker, more hollow, and more brittle—makes bones more likely to fracture and take longer to mend (see Chapter 14). Osteoporosis, which can strike at any age, is a major health threat, especially for older adults, and accounts for 1.5 million bone fractures a year, including 300,000 hip fractures, 700,000 vertebral fractures, and 250,000 wrist fractures (National Institutes of Health [NIH], 2005, 2012a). Older women—and especially White and Asian women—are particularly susceptible to this condition (Whitbourne & Whitbourne, 2011). Osteoporosis is often the cause of the bent or stooped posture that some people develop as they age.

Muscle weakness and osteoporosis often contribute to problems with mobility. As people age, they sometimes develop problems in getting around. Particularly dangerous are problems associated with changes in the *vestibular system* that regulates balance because these often increase a person's risk of falling (Gabbard, 2012; Ketcham & Stelmach, 2001; Ochs, Newberry, Lenhardt, & Harkins, 1985). The sensitivity of vestibular sensory receptors, which are located in the inner ear and detect bodily movement and changes in position, declines markedly in older adulthood, often leading to balance-related accidents. An estimated 33% of

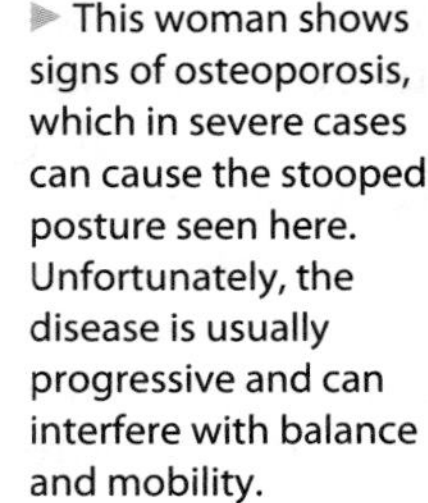

▶ This woman shows signs of osteoporosis, which in severe cases can cause the stooped posture seen here. Unfortunately, the disease is usually progressive and can interfere with balance and mobility.

individuals over age 65 and 40% of those over age 80 fall at least once a year (NIH, 2012a; Simoneau & Leibowitz, 1996). Falls can be prevented to some degree by strengthening muscles through exercise (Baker, Atlantis, & Singh, 2007), which generally improves balance (Orr et al., 2006; Orr, Raymond, & Singh, 2008).

The Internal Organs Aging typically is accompanied by the reduced functioning of most internal organs. For example, as we age, the function of the immune system declines, leaving us less protected from infection and disease (Miller, 1996; Whitbourne & Whitbourne, 2011). This is why annual flu shots are routinely recommended for older people, as well as for those with compromised immune functions. Influenza can be lethal to older people because it makes them vulnerable to secondary bacterial infections, such as pneumonia. Respiratory infections are particularly worrisome because aging is accompanied by a lower capacity for oxygen intake.

Although age-related problems can arise in any of the organ systems, particularly problematic are changes in the heart. Like other muscles, the strength and efficiency of the heart typically declines with age, and it is vulnerable to any alterations in the respiratory or cardiovascular systems that diminish the supply of oxygen in the blood. Furthermore, when the heart muscle weakens with age, the result is decreased circulation. Such congestive heart failure causes problems in all of the body's systems. When there is decreased or disrupted blood flow to the brain, cognitive impairment typically results (Rozzini et al., 2005; Sabatini et al., 2000).

The first signs of age-related problems with the heart or other internal organs often are detected when our bodies experience stress because the *reserve capacity* of the heart, lungs, and other organs also decreases with age. During early adulthood, these organs can function at between 4 and 10 times their normal level when under stress. Reserve capacity, however, drops slowly but steadily in middle adulthood and beyond. Older people may not notice their diminished capacity in day-to-day living; however, they may realize it when, for example, they attempt to shovel snow after the first storm of the season.

Diminished reserve capacity may be especially severe in extreme heat or cold. For example, many older people adapt more slowly to cold environments than they did when they were younger, and they may chill more easily, with a resulting low body temperature that can be a serious health risk. Thus, older people often complain of being cold, even at temperatures that younger people find normal or on the warm side. Older people often have similar difficulty coping with heat, particularly if they exert themselves, such as when mowing the lawn on a hot summer day. Nevertheless, most older adults can perform many of the tasks they did when they were younger as long as they perform them more slowly; take frequent breaks; and consume extra liquids, such as water, or nutrient-replenishing products, such as sports drinks.

Sleep problems About half of the people over age 65 who live at home and about two-thirds of those in nursing homes and other long-term care facilities suffer from sleep problems (Neikrug & Ancoli-Israel, 2010). To understand these problems, it is useful to consider the sleep patterns that typify older adults, which are summarized in Table 16-5. Generally, as people get older, they sleep less; they also spend less time in deep sleep, both of which contribute to feelings of tiredness and fatigue (Morgan, 2008).

Beyond this general trend toward less sleep and less time in deep sleep, some adults experience sleep disorders, including *insomnia* (the inability to sleep) and *sleep apnea* (repeated waking due to interruptions or pauses in breathing). Many sleep disorders can be treated quite effectively, either with medication or through a change of habits, such as not drinking caffeinated beverages before bedtime. When sleep problems result from trauma or loss, such as when a loved one is ill or dies, counseling and support often can help. When loss of sleep is due to mental or

Table 16-5 Sleep Patterns Typical of Older Adulthood

- Older adults average between 6 to $6^1/_2$ hours of sleep a night, although many remain in bed for up to 8 hours.
- Although many older adults sleep more than younger adults, the amount of nightly sleep that older adults get varies from fewer than 5 hours to more than 9 hours.
- Many older adults have trouble going to sleep, and they may toss and turn for up to 30 minutes before falling asleep.
- After older adults fall asleep, they experience significantly more early awakenings than younger people. It is considered normal for older adults to spend up to 20% of their time in bed awake and to compensate by spending more time in bed.
- A change in the distribution of sleep stages results in an increase in stage 1 sleep (light sleep) and a decrease in stages 3 and 4 sleep (deep sleep). Thus, even when sleep occurs, generally it is not deep, satisfying sleep.

SOURCE: From "Common sleep disorders in the elderly: Diagnosis and treatment," by P. M. Becker and A. O. Jamieson, 1992, *Geriatrics, 47,* 41–52.

physical illness, such as depression or painful arthritis, medications that address the underlying problems can be prescribed.

The Senses Although there are wide individual variations in the extent of age-related declines, our senses—hearing, vision, taste, and smell—generally become less efficient as we age, and our ability to perceive sensory information slows down (Ross et al., 1997). Of all the senses, the sense of taste is probably the least affected by age, although many older people do begin to add more salt to their food in order to add flavor—a practice that sometimes contributes to **hypertension**, which is abnormally high blood pressure. Taste also is affected by the sense of smell, which does appear to undergo some age-related decline (Fukunaga, Uematsu, & Sugimoto, 2005; Whitbourne & Whitbourne, 2011). Smokers typically experience the greatest decrease in sensitivity for both taste and smell, although people who quit smoking often recover at least some of their losses (Schiffman, 2009). Viral infections also can damage smell receptors. Declines in taste and smell, however, are not generally associated with problems as severe as those experienced by people who have difficulty with hearing or vision.

Age-related hearing deficits are quite common; in fact, over 40% of men and 30% of women age 65 and older report at least some trouble with their hearing; about 60% of adults over age 85 experience this problem (FIFARS, 2010i). These age-related hearing impairments are usually mild to moderate and often involve difficulty with detecting voices in the midst of background noise (Fozard & Gordon-Salant, 2001) or with hearing high-frequency tones, such as those that occur in speech sounds like *s, sh, ch,* and *f*, or low-frequency tones (Hull, 2012). Sometimes hearing aids are helpful in dealing with these problems; however, these devices also often are frustrating. Most hearing aids amplify all sound frequencies, including background noise, and therefore do not provide much help in picking out the details of what someone is saying. With or without hearing aids, older individuals with hearing loss may appear inattentive or embarrassed when, in fact, they simply cannot understand what is being said, leading some to withdraw or become suspicious of what they cannot hear.

Do you know older adults who have experienced a noticeable decline in one or more of their senses? Which sensory declines seem to be most troublesome?

Difficulties with hearing are often worse when they are accompanied by difficulties with vision (Schneider et al., 2011). Several kinds of visual impairments are common in aging individuals (Schieber, 2006). For example, the ability to focus on objects declines as the lenses of the eyes become less flexible and able to accommodate (Schneider & Pichora-Fuller, 2000). Depth perception also may be affected by loss of flexibility in the lens. Another problem associated with aging is that the lens may become cloudy and may eventually develop a **cataract**, which is a clouding of the lens of the eye that obstructs light and visual sensation. Another problem is **glaucoma**, an increase of pressure within the eyeball that can result in damage and the gradual loss of vision (see Figure 16-3). However, most cataracts can be removed through outpatient laser surgery, and glaucoma often can be treated with medication. Fortunately, most visual problems experienced by older adults can be remedied: Fewer than 20% of adults age 65 and older report significant trouble with their ability to see (FIFARS, 2010i).

However, older individuals typically lose some **visual acuity**, which is the ability to distinguish fine detail. It is not uncommon for older people to have difficulty perceiving visual details—whether they are threading a sewing needle, distinguishing the edge of a stair step that is covered by a carpet with a confusing pattern, or simply reading a newspaper (Whitbourne & Whitbourne, 2011). This may be due partly to the inflexibility of the lens and partly to the loss of visual receptor cells in the rear of the eye. Visual acuity usually can be increased with corrective lenses, including bifocals and trifocals, and surgical procedures to improve visual acuity also are an option for many people.

For many older adults, concerns about declining eyesight lead to anxiety about their ability to drive a car, which for many people in the United States is critically important to remaining

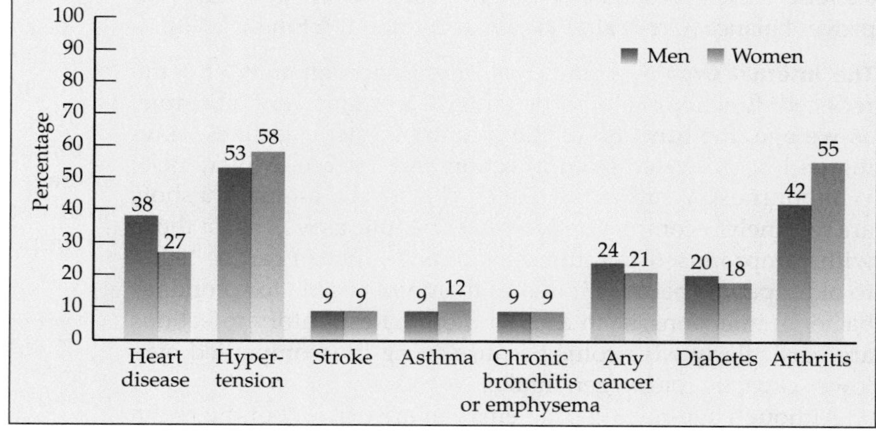

FIGURE 16-3 People Age 65 and Over Who Reported Having Selected Chronic Conditions, by Gender

SOURCE: From "Chronic health conditions," Older Americans: Key indicators of well-being, 2010. Federal Interagency Forum on Aging-Related Statistics, 2010. Washington, DC: U.S. Government Printing Office. Available online at http://www.agingstats.gov/agingstatsdotnet/Main_Site/Data/2010_Documents/Docs/OA_2010.pdf.

hypertension
Abnormally high blood pressure, sometimes accompanied by headaches and dizziness

visual acuity
The ability to distinguish fine detail

cataract
The clouding of the lens of the eye that obstructs light and thereby limits vision

glaucoma
An increase of pressure within the eyeball that can result in damage and the gradual loss of vision

FIGURE 16-4 Changes in Vision Due to Cataracts and to Glaucoma
These images represent what adults with the visual impairments of cataracts and glaucoma typically would see.

SOURCE: http://www.foxcenter.pitt.edu/15/what-is-vision-impairment.

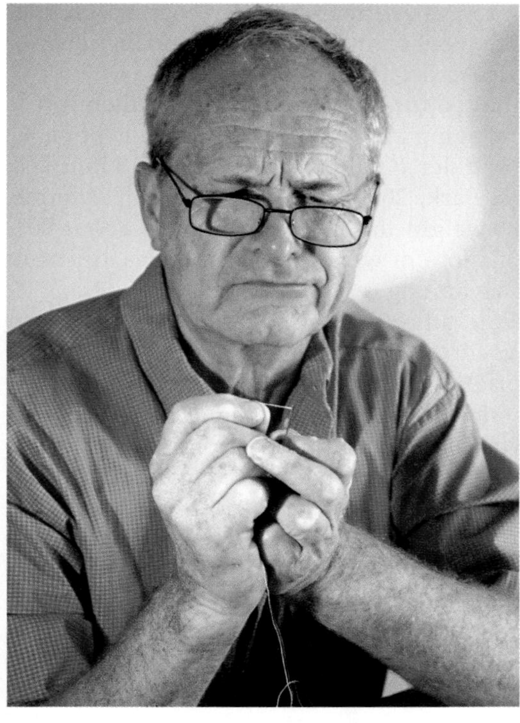

Visual and hearing problems are common among older adults, as well as minor tremors. Routine tasks, like threading a needle may require minor adaptations, like bracing one's arms to hold one's hands still.

independent—especially so for those who live in rural areas or at some distance from relatives. Yet visual acuity problems generally are not the source of problems with driving (Fiorentino, 2008; Schultheis & Manning, 2011). Rather, it is the more general slowing down of certain cognitive abilities that can lead older adults into difficulties with driving. In particular, as people age, they increasingly have trouble ignoring irrelevant stimuli. Their ability to perform visual search tasks, locating the correct "place to look" in a complex display of visual information, tends to become slower and less accurate with age (Madden, 2007). When multiple images must be attended to quickly, such as when a driver in traffic approaches a traffic light that is changing, it is difficult for the older driver to make decisions about stopping or going on quickly enough to avoid being a hazard. Not surprisingly, older drivers are overrepresented in car accidents, especially those involving left turns at intersections, which require quick and complex responses to rapidly changing traffic conditions. These attention-related problems, especially when coupled with even small age-related declines in elbow control and speed of movement, can make driving dangerous—especially in heavy traffic, in low-light conditions, on strange roads, or at high speeds (Aksan et al., 2012; Ketcham, Dounskaia, & Stelmach, 2004). The good news, however, is that older drivers generally are aware of their limitations and most restrict their driving so as to be more safe—perhaps by not driving in bad weather, at night, on long trips, at high speeds, or in heavy traffic. In one study, 95% of older drivers practiced one or more of these strategies to improve the safety of their driving (Betz & Lowenstein, 2010). Also encouraging is the finding that older drivers can learn better strategies for safer driving (e.g., Hunt & Arbesman, 2008; Klavora & Heslegrave, 2002; Kua, Korner-Bitensky, Desrosiers, Man-Son-Hing, & Marshall, 2007). Even simple physical exercises can improve reactions and contribute to safer driving practices (Marmeleira, de Melo, Tlemcani, & Godinho, 2011).

The Brain and the Nervous System When we think of the elderly adult, we are often struck with the image of a general slowdown in intellectual functioning. Reaction times are slower; words, and especially names, are harder to remember. We also may associate older age with **dementia**, which is a disorder that includes a broad array of cognitive deficiencies, such as impaired learning and memory ability, a deterioration of language and

dementia
A disorder associated with older age that includes a broad array of cognitive deficiencies, such as impaired learning and memory ability, a deterioration of language and motor functions, a progressive inability to recognize familiar people and objects, frequent confusion, and personality changes

motor functions, a progressive inability to recognize familiar people and objects, frequent confusion, and personality change (American Psychiatric Association, 2000).

Although dementia is a function of disease, and therefore is not part of the normal aging process, the brain does experience changes as we grow older (Galluzzi, Beltramello, Filippi, & Frisoni, 2008; Goh & Park, 2009). After age 30, for example, the brain declines in weight until, by age 90, it is about 90% of its earlier size. This loss of weight appears to be the result of fewer connections among neurons (Hogan et al., 2011; Raz, 2005; West, 1996), rather than a reduction in the number of total neurons present. The shrinkage appears to be greatest in the frontal cortex, which is heavily involved in higher cognitive functions such as problem solving and memory. Interestingly, those who experience the least brain atrophy are more likely to engage regularly in complex cognitive tasks. Apparently, keeping our brains active and engaged in old age may help ward off some of the neurological decline that typically accompanies aging (Mast, Zimmerman, & Rowe, 2009). In addition, the lateralization (sorting) of functions into the left or right hemispheres that is characteristic of the brain during adolescence and young adulthood becomes at least somewhat diminished in old age (Angel, Fay, Bouazzaoui, & Isingrini, 2011; Cabeza, 2001; Smeets et al., 2010). Whether this is a consequence of general brain deterioration or is, rather, a beneficial response that directs more of the brain's function to tasks that are important is a matter of current speculation.

Recent advances in technology are providing new insights into how the brain ages (Dennis & Cabeza, 2008; Rodrigue & Kennedy, 2011). For example, it is now known that neurons are able to repair themselves to a much greater degree than was previously thought (Doetsch & Scharff, 2001). In addition, new neurons can continue to be added, even late in life (Nottebohm, 2002; Riddle & Lichtenwalner, 2007), a finding that again contradicts our earlier understanding of the extent to which the adult brain is capable of change. Nevertheless, aging is accompanied by a general slowing of the central nervous system that can affect coordination and the speed of reactions and reflexes, and this general slowing probably underlies the poorer performance of older adults on timed tests of cognitive abilities.

What are the most noticeable ways that older adults display the general slowing down of the nervous system? Do you think that sociocultural factors may also be involved in these types of slowing? If so, how?

Despite the fact that some brain deterioration probably is age-related, most adults do not exhibit meaningful neurological deficiencies unless disease processes, such as Alzheimer's and Parkinson's diseases, are involved. Age-related changes, thus, vary considerably from one person to the next (Rogers & Fisk, 2010). It does appear, however, that most people experience some age-related declines in brain functioning, probably beginning in middle age, although the rate of decline is not great for most people. As we will see later in this chapter, the primary cognitive effect for most people is a general slowing of responses, both in physical movement and in cognitive processing speed (Buckner, Head, & Lustig, 2006). Although there can be significant cognitive impairment when brain functions are disrupted by disease, this is the exception rather than the rule. For most older adults, brain-related cognitive declines are manageable, especially when people learn to use effective strategies to compensate (Green & Bavelier, 2008) and when they maintain an active intellectual curiosity about life.

Health, Disease, and Nutrition

Fortunately, most older people report that they have good to excellent health most of the time. Although they may be forced to adapt, such as to the slow development of arthritis or to the side effects of medication to control high blood pressure and other disorders, they usually can do this easily and with little inconvenience or disruption to their lives. When older adults experience major health-related problems, these are most likely the result of a chronic condition, poor nutrition, or the misuse of prescription drugs.

Chronic Health Problems One major difference between childhood and late adulthood is in the incidence of acute versus *chronic* (lasting or recurrent) diseases. In childhood, acute diseases—which last a brief time and often climax with a fever and a rash—are very common. Older adults, however, more often suffer from chronic conditions—illnesses that never go away. In the United States, the most common chronic conditions associated with age are hypertension (high blood pressure), arthritis, and heart disease (FIFARS, 2010a; see Figure 16-4). Visual and hearing impairments and the aftereffects of accidental falls also affect a large percentage of older adults. Type 2 diabetes is another chronic, age-related health condition. Not only does this disease become more prevalent as adults grow older, but also the damage it causes to the body accumulates over time. Type 2 diabetes is linked to obesity, which is becoming more prevalent among older adults (FIFARS, 2010a; see Figure 16-5, and the box Changing Perspectives: Diabetes—Will Type 2 Diabetes Be the New Lifestyle Disease Epidemic?). Obesity contributes in several ways to deteriorating health and quality of life as extra weight strains the cardiovascular system, as well as muscles and joints. In all, chronic diseases and impairments touch the lives of a substantial number of older adults, perhaps affecting nearly three-quarters of the U.S. population over age 75 (National Center for Health Statistics [NCHS], 2012).

The age-related increase in chronic health problems largely reflects the body's decreased ability to cope with stress, including the stress of disease. A disease that a young person can handle easily, such as a respiratory infection, may linger in an older person and cause permanent damage. Ironically, as

Watch *Coping with Diabetes* on **MyDevelopmentLab**

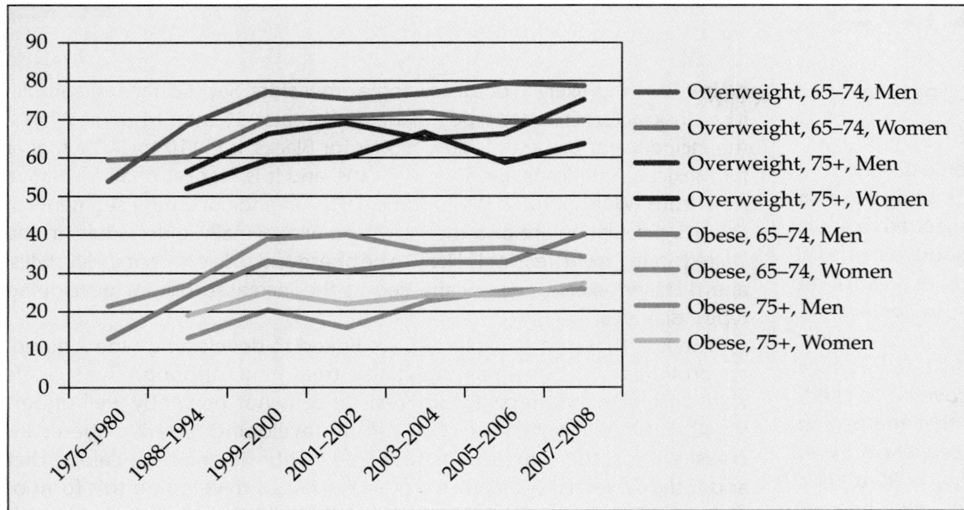

FIGURE 16-5 People Age 65 and Over Who Are Overweight and Obese, by Gender and Age Group, Selected Years 1976–2008

Note the dramatic rise in overweight and obesity for both men and women in the past 3 decades, and particularly among men aged 65–74, where the percentage has more than doubled.

SOURCE: From "Obesity," Federal Interagency Forum on Aging-Related Statistics, 2010, in *Older Americans: Key indicators of well-being, 2010*, Washington, DC: U.S. Government Printing Office, retrieved from http://www.agingstats.gov/agingstatsdotnet/Main_Site/Data/2010_Documents/Docs/OA_2010.pdf.

the ability to cope with stress declines with age, the number of stressful events in the person's life tends to increase. Aside from health problems, stress also comes from life-cycle crises, such as retirement and widowhood.

Sociocultural factors often play a part in the prevalence of illness among older adults. Rates of disease incidence are reflected in life expectancies, which are longer for women than for men and longer for Whites than for Blacks (NCHS, 2012h; see Figure 16-6), with the latter difference attributable to the disparities in socioeconomic conditions among the groups (Hayward, Crimmins, Miles, & Yang, 2000). As this finding makes apparent, healthier lifestyles and better medical care have a positive impact on lifespan, and increasing numbers of adults in the United States therefore are living longer. Indeed, the dramatic increase in life expectancy in the United States over the last century is astonishing. Yet, it also is fueling substantial changes throughout our culture and economy. For example, today a much larger number of older adults must cope with chronic medical conditions and must sometimes deal with disabilities, which also become more common at advanced age. Medical care for older adults is often expensive, and there is considerable debate about how much—and what kind—of care is the responsibility of the government. Yet, even among adults age 85 and over, more than half report having good to excellent health (see also Figure 17-1).

atherosclerosis
Hardening of the arteries, which is a common condition of aging caused by the body's increasing inability to use excess fats in the diet; these fats are stored along the walls of arteries, where they restrict flow of blood when they harden; responsible for many of the heart conditions prevalent among older people

Nutrition Because of their reduced physical activity and their slowdown in body metabolism, older adults do not require as much food as do younger adults. In fact, by the time they reach age 65, older adults require at least 20% fewer calories than younger adults do; however, they still need nearly as many basic nutrients. Consequently, it is not unusual for older U.S. adults to be both overweight and undernourished (Salerno-Kennedy, 2008).

A particular problem, especially in Western diets, is the overconsumption of fats. As the body ages, it becomes less able to use the various kinds of fat that are present in many foods. Fat that is not used is stored in special lipid cells, as well as within the walls of the arteries where it may harden and form plaques that reduce the flow of blood. This condition, called **atherosclerosis**, or hardening of the arteries, is responsible for many of the heart conditions that are prevalent among older people. Atherosclerosis is very common in older people in the United States and in Western Europe; however, in non-Western countries, it is much less common, and this is reflected in better cardiovascular health. This trend also is seen in ethnic populations within the United States: In 2000, the rate of cardiovascular disease for Asian Americans was substantially lower than that of White people living in the United States (NCHS, 2012c). The prevalence of cardiovascular disease appears to be changing as diets around the world increasingly reflect Western tastes. Fat consumption, of course, is also linked to obesity, which is a major risk factor for early death. Due to increasing prevalence of obesity among the U.S. population, the steady rise in life expectancy experienced during the past century may soon come to an end, and even begin to decline (Olshansky et al., 2005; see Figure 16-6).

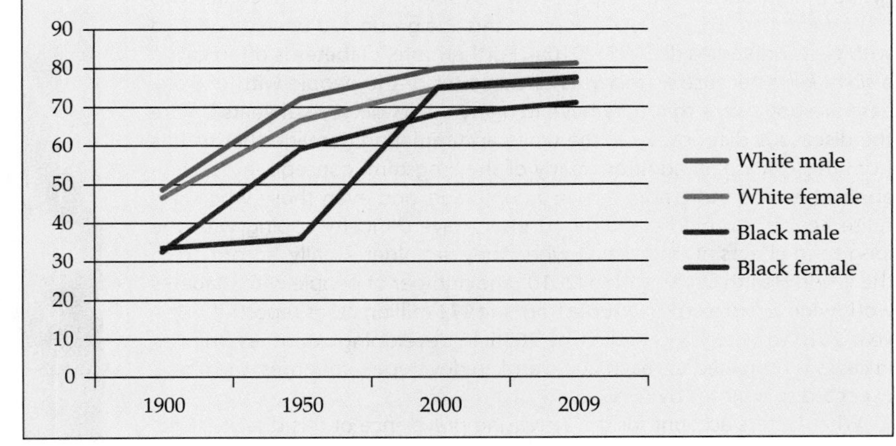

FIGURE 16-6 Life Expectancies at Birth, by Gender and Race 1900–2009

SOURCE: Table 22, "Life expectancy at birth, at 65 years of age, and at 75 years of age, by sex, race, and Hispanic origin: United States, selected years 1900–2009," in *Health, United States, 2011*, National Center for Health Statistics (NCHS), 2012, Hyattsville, MD: Author.

CHANGING PERSPECTIVES

Diabetes—Will Type 2 Diabetes Be the New Lifestyle Disease Epidemic?

Diabetes (technically termed *diabetes mellitus*) is a chronic disease that involves a problem with the production of, or with the body's use of, *insulin*. Insulin is a protein produced in the pancreas that is needed to break down and process *glucose*, a type of sugar that is a major source of energy for the body's cells. Although the causes of diabetes are complex and not yet perfectly understood, it is known that diabetes occurs in two major forms—type 1 and type 2. In type 1 diabetes (formerly called *insulin-dependent diabetes* or *juvenile diabetes*), the individual's pancreas fails to produce a sufficient amount of insulin. This disease is usually discovered in childhood and is treated vigorously with insulin injections so that the person can survive. Type 2 diabetes (formerly called *noninsulin-dependent diabetes* or *adult-onset diabetes*) is much more common, accounting for 90 to 95% of all cases (Burant, 2012; CDC, 2011h). In type 2 diabetes, the pancreas does produce insulin, but the body's cells are *insulin resistant;* therefore, the insulin that is produced cannot trigger the cells to absorb the available sugar molecules and break them down for energy.

In both types of diabetes, the unused glucose eventually is filtered through the kidneys to be excreted in urine; however, the chronically high level of glucose in the blood often damages many body systems in the process, especially the blood vessels and nerves. Common symptoms of diabetes include excessive thirst and urination (to dilute the unused sugar and excrete it), fatigue (because energy levels are low), and several long-term problems that result from this system-wide breakdown in body chemistry. For example, diabetes sometimes causes blood vessel problems in the retina of the eye, and this disease is the leading cause of blindness in adults. Nearly one-half of the cases of end-stage kidney disease are the result of diabetes (American Diabetes Association, 2012). People with diabetes also are at higher risk for various chronic ailments, ranging from heart disease and stroke to circulation problems, especially in the feet and legs. Diabetes is listed as the sixth leading cause of death in people ages 65 and over (FIFARS, 2010a). Furthermore, as many as 65% of the deaths of people with diabetes are attributed to heart disease or stoke, conditions that may well have been brought on or made worse by diabetes.

Why is diabetes of such concern, and why is it especially a concern for older adults? To begin with, the prevalence of type 2 diabetes in this age group is high, affecting perhaps as many as one-fifth or more of adults ages 65 and older; in 2010, 19% of people in this age group had been diagnosed with type 2 diabetes (FIFARS, 2010a). Furthermore, diabetes is often called a *silent killer* because as many as one-quarter of the people with this disease are not aware that they have it; many adults go several years before the disease is diagnosed, all the while accumulating damage that results from this disease. In addition, many of the long-term consequences of diabetes become more apparent as people age, and even those who were quite healthy in middle adulthood often have difficulty coping with the long-term effects of the disease when they get older. Finally, according to the World Health Organization (2010), the number of people with diabetes worldwide is expected to double from the 171 million cases reported in the year 2010 to nearly 350 million by 2030; in developing countries, the rise in cases is projected to reach 200% and, in developed countries, the rate is expected to increase by 45%.

What factors account for the increasing prevalence of this disease? First, as is the case in the rest of the world, the U.S. population is aging, and type 2 diabetes is more likely to occur as people grow older. Second, race and ethnicity are risk factors linked to type 2 diabetes. Compared to non-Hispanic Whites, the incidence of diabetes is 60% higher for Blacks, it is 110 to 120% higher for Mexican Americans and Puerto Ricans, and it is highest of all for Native Americans (Whitbourne & Whitbourne, 2011). In addition, these segments of the U.S. population are also the fastest growing. Finally, older adults in the United States are increasingly likely to be obese and to live sedentary lifestyles, and diet and exercise are clearly tied to the increased risk for developing type 2 diabetes.

The fact that diet and exercise are linked to developing type 2 diabetes provides both an explanation and a treatment. Although the specific ways that obesity affects insulin resistance is not presently well understood, as people get fatter, their risk of developing type 2 diabetes increases. Thus, the same things that lead to obesity—a high-calorie diet and lack of exercise—increase a person's risk of developing this form of diabetes. The correlation between obesity and type 2 diabetes is very high: 13.5% of obese people in a survey conducted by the CDC had this disease, whereas only 3.5% of those of normal weight were affected (FIFARS, 2008).

Type 2 diabetes often can be controlled without insulin treatment by maintaining a diet that is low in sugar and high in fruits and vegetables, with limited or moderate use of alcohol. Exercise also can help. The good news about type 2 diabetes is that many people who develop this disease later in life can minimize its harmful effects through a program of moderate exercise—such as walking 30 minutes a day—and moderate diet. Even though such lifestyle changes are not easy, they are effective, and they make a difference in death rates and the onset of complications. Although some adults must resort to taking insulin or other newer medications, many people can successfully treat their diabetes by carefully monitoring their blood glucose levels and by adjusting their lifestyle toward healthier habits. Such an approach has secondary benefits as well because, over the long term, healthy habits contribute in a variety of ways to better health and a longer, more active life.

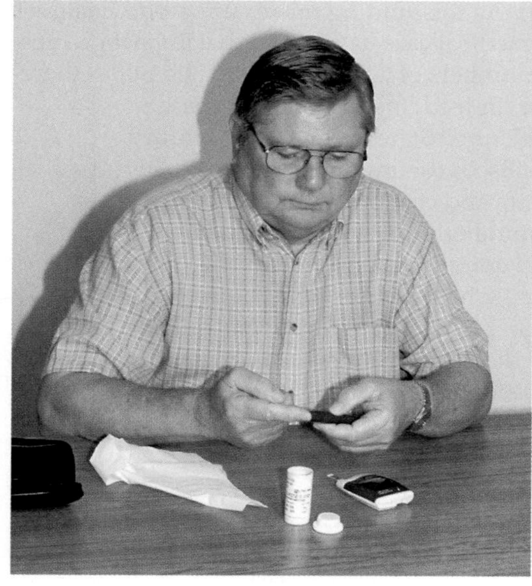

◀ Many seniors are now learning to monitor their blood glucose levels and adjust their diets in ways that contrast with a lifetime of habits.

The most common dietary deficiencies in old age are iron, calcium, and vitamins A and C. Vitamin supplements often are recommended for older adults, especially if they are unlikely to include sufficient quantities of these nutrients in their regular diets. Because constipation is also associated with old age, the elderly generally are encouraged to eat diets high in fiber and to drink plenty of water, which usually are better alternatives than laxatives.

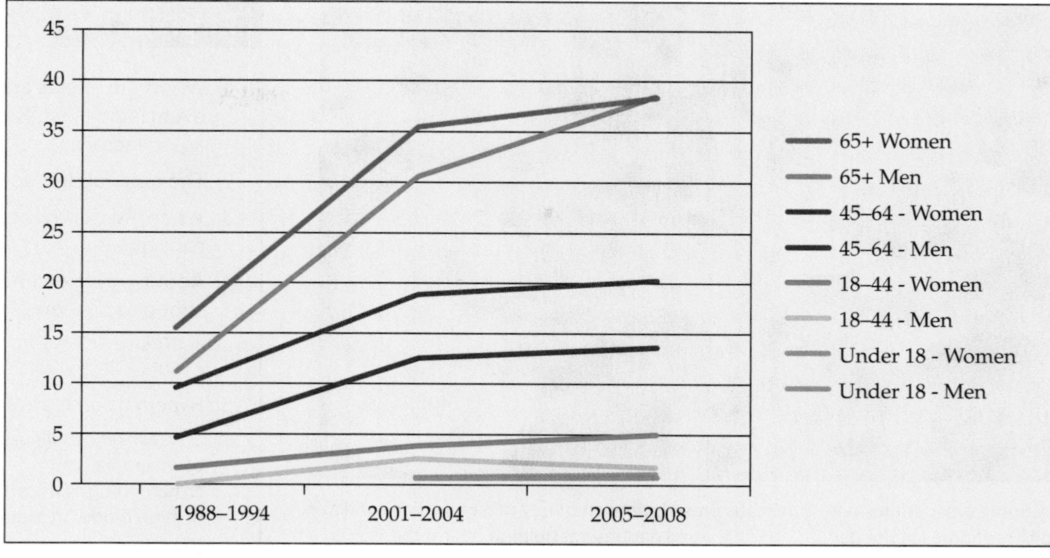

FIGURE 16-7 Percentage of Men and Women in the United States with 5 or More Drug Prescriptions in the Previous Month, by Age Group

SOURCE: Table 99, "Prescription drug use in the past 30 days, by sex, age, race, and Hispanic origin: United States selected years 1988–1994 through 2005–2008," in *Health, United States, 2011*, National Center for Health Statistics (NCHS), 2012, retrieved from http://www.cdc.gov/nchs/data/hus/hus11.pdf.

The Misuse of Prescribed Medication Serious intentional drug abuse is not a major problem among older adults. In fact, the most popular recreational drug used by this age group is alcohol, and older U.S. adults generally are more moderate drinkers than members of younger age groups (Substance Abuse and Mental Health Services Administration [SAMHSA], 2010). Nevertheless, as many as one-third of older adults are treated or hospitalized because of overuse, misuse, or abuse of drugs (Offerhaus, 1997). Why?

The answer to this question relates to the abundance of medications that are prescribed to the elderly. Over the past two decades, the use of prescription medications by adults in the United States has skyrocketed, nearly tripling among adults age 65 and older in just 20 years (NCHS, 2012g; see Figure 16-7). Not surprisingly given the volume of drugs that are prescribed, errors occur. For example, surveys show that inappropriate medicines were prescribed during nearly 8% of doctor visits made by people ages 65 and older, especially when more than one drug was prescribed or when the person was a woman (Lisby, Nielsen & Mainz, 2005). In addition, older people often take combinations of medications for different conditions, and interactions between medications can produce toxic effects. Compounding this problem is the fact that older adults may become confused or simply forget when and how much of each medication to take. Errors occur frequently, especially when several medications are involved. Medication mistakes occur with caregivers, too. For example, in a study of 12 different assisted living facilities spread across three states, errors were observed in 28.2% of the medication deliveries (Young et al., 2008). About 70% of these errors were for the right medicine delivered at the wrong time. However, more than a quarter of the medication errors involved either the wrong dose of a prescribed medication or the wrong medication. Older adults also may fail to mention all of their medications to their nurses or their physicians. In a study of older people in residential facilities, 20 to 25% of these people had at least one inappropriate prescription (Spore, Mor, Parrat, Hawes, & Hiris, 1997). Finally, as people age, their body chemistry may shift, thereby changing the action of drugs in their system or making previously acceptable dosages too strong. Older people also have greater difficulty clearing drugs through declining organ systems, such as the liver and kidneys, with the effect that larger amounts of the drugs remain in their systems longer.

What things can older adults do to reduce the possibility that they will take incorrect doses of prescription medications?

In the United States, although it is not uncommon for older people to be overweight and undernourished, it is important to note that many others are well nourished.

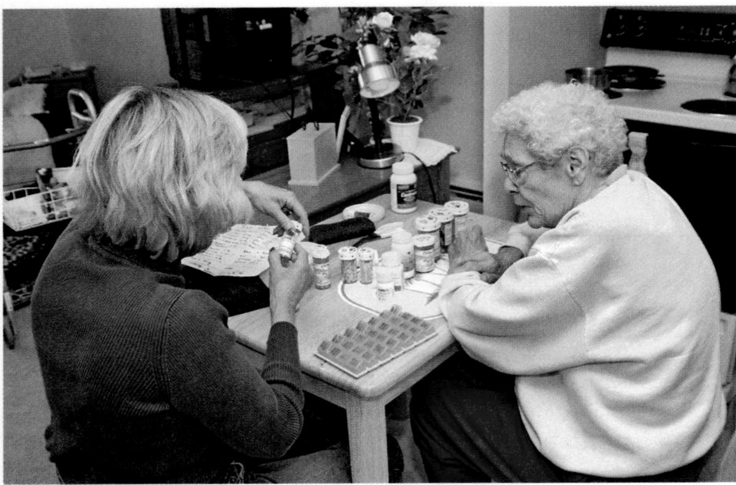

▲ Some older adults have numerous prescriptions that they must take daily and at different times of the day. This middle-aged daughter is helping her mother sort a week's supply of pills into a pill box.

REVIEW THE FACTS 16-2

1. When the effects associated with aging are the result of earlier events and lifestyle choices, these are referred to as ________ aging factors.
2. The general deterioration of bone is called ________.
3. When we experience stress, we rely on our body's ________ capacity.
4. About what percentage of adults over age 65 who live at home experience sleep problems?
   a. 10% b. 30%
   c. 50% d. 70%
5. *Hypertension* is another term for
   a. stress-related illness.
   b. insomnia.
   c. hardening of the arteries.
   d. high blood pressure.
6. What are the three most common chronic diseases associated with aging?
7. What food substance poses the most problems in typical Western diets?
   a. fat b. sugar
   c. protein d. water

Practice on MyDevelopmentLab

Increasing reliance on medicines among the elderly is, of course, accompanied by increasing costs for the drugs. In 2005, more than half of U.S. adults over age 65 spent more than $1,000 on their medicines; nearly a quarter spent more than $2,500 (FIFARS, 2010a). During the 1990s and up until about 2004, drug costs rose dramatically, both because so many more prescriptions were written and because many new drugs are expensive (see Figure 16-8). However, since that time, the costs of medicines have leveled off, increasing perhaps 1 to 3% per year (Kaiser Family Foundation, 2010). In part, this leveling is the result of the increased availability and use of low-cost generic drugs—a trend being encouraged by the health insurance industry. Nevertheless, paying for prescription drugs is a serious challenge for many older adults in the United States. As the U.S. population includes an increasingly larger proportion of older adults, the costs associated with advancing age will need to be addressed. In the next section, we explore the causes of aging and several theories of aging.

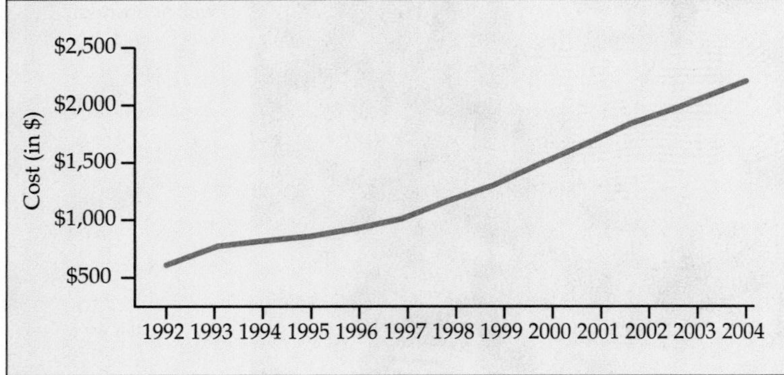

FIGURE 16-8 Average Annual Prescription Drug Costs (in Dollars) Among Noninstitutionalized Medicare Enrollees Age 65 and Over

SOURCE: From *Older Americans: Key indicators of well-being, 2010*, Federal Interagency Forum on Aging-Related Statistics, March 2010, Washington, DC: U.S. Government Printing Office.

THE CAUSES OF AGING

Many factors affect how long an individual will live. Some people are predisposed to developing chronic illnesses, such as cancer and heart disease; others seem immune. Socioeconomic factors are also involved: Those who are economically disadvantaged live in more dangerous environments, have poorer nutrition, have more limited access to health care, and are more likely to engage in destructive habits such as smoking and drinking.

Regardless of risk factors, however, everyone ages and ultimately dies. The lifespan is finite, and no one lives much past 110 years of age. Aging is a natural, universal process. Although, at present, aging processes are not well understood, several theories have been advanced to describe why and how humans age.

Theories of Aging

How does aging actually happen? Does the "genetic clock" simply run down or is the process more one of wear and tear? **Senescence**, which is the normal aging not connected with the occurrence of disease in an individual, refers to the universal biological processes of aging. The majority of theories of senescence can be grouped into two categories—the stochastic

senescence
The normal aging process, not connected with the occurrence of disease in an individual; refers to the universal biological process of aging

theories and the preprogrammed biological clock theories (Bengtson, 2009; Masoro & Austad, 2011; Moody, 2009).

Stochastic Theories According to **stochastic theories of aging**, the body ages as a result of random assaults from internal and external environments (Murphy & Partridge, 2008). These theories, which are sometimes called *wear-and-tear* theories, compare the human body to a machine that simply wears out because of constant use and accumulated cellular insults and injuries.

A popular stochastic theory involves the action of *free radicals* (Gilca, Stoian, Atanasiu, & Virgolici, 2007; Lustgarten, Muller, & Van Remmen, 2011; Rattan, 2006). Free radicals, which are unstable oxygen molecules left over from cellular processes, are believed to react with other chemical compounds in the cells, thereby interrupting normal cell functioning and causing damage. Normally, cells have repair mechanisms that reduce the damage done by free radicals. However, after a major injury—such as a heart attack—or sustained exposure to toxins, substantial free radical damage often occurs. Some dietary substances, such as vitamins C and E, seem to reduce the negative effects of free radicals (Galli, Shukitt-Hale, Youdim, & Joseph, 2002). Research on changes in diet and the use of dietary supplements has been promising in reducing the risk of cancer and arthritis (Aldwin, Spiro, & Park, 2006).

Free radical theory is but one example of the stochastic theories of aging. Other agents, such as certain toxins or radiation from the sun, also are suspected of causing cellular damage that, over time and with more abuse, becomes increasingly difficult to repair. Wear and tear from whatever source may affect some tissues or systems more than it does others. Sunlight, for example, is especially damaging to skin cells, greatly increasing a person's risk of developing skin cancers. Recent research often focuses on stochastic effects within the immune system, which is likely implicated in many age-related diseases, including arthritis, lupus, diabetes, and multiple sclerosis.

In summary, although stochastic theories are appealing, they do not fully explain aging. They do not, for example, explain why the functions of the body's internal repair shop decline. In addition, they do not explain why exercise—a potential form of wear and tear—can have beneficial rather than negative effects.

Biological Clock Theories The second general type of theory of aging focuses on genetic programming that determines the pace and the process of aging (Ossa & Crews, 2006). According to one version of **biological clock theories of aging**, there is a limit to the number of times each cell can divide before it dies. One limiting mechanism that appears to be involved centers on DNA sequences, called *telomeres*, that lie at the tips of chromosomes. Research shows that with each cell division, the length of the telomere becomes shorter; after about 60 to 80 cell divisions, there is no longer enough telomere left for cells to reproduce, and they ultimately die (Geddes, 2008). Referred to as the "Hayflick limit," after the researcher who advocated the telomere theory of aging, this view suggests that regardless of how healthy our lifestyles become, there is a maximum age for the lifespan, which seems to be about 110 years (Hayflick, 1996, 2004). Support for this view comes from studies that suggest that many of the factors associated with stress and vulnerability to disease—such as smoking, obesity, lack of exercise, and depression—are also linked to telomere shortening (Adler, 2011; Aviv, 2011).

Which of the two models of aging—stochastic theories or biological clock theories—seems more appealing to you? How might your answer reflect your underlying ideas about what aging is?

Another biological clock theory suggests that there is some sort of cellular pacemaker, or timer, probably controlled by the hypothalamus or the pituitary gland. In one such model, the pituitary gland is believed to release a hormone shortly after puberty that begins the process of cellular decline at a programmed rate throughout the rest of the lifespan. The theory that a biological clock might control aging is bolstered by the fact that such clocks control other age-related processes. For example, biological clocks in humans appear to control the female menstrual cycle, which begins at around age 12 and ends somewhere around age 50. A biological clock also appears to control the human immune system, which gains strength until age 20 and then gradually weakens. It appears that this decline in immune function may underlie many age-related conditions, including the susceptibility to cancer and infections such as influenza and pneumonia, as well as to the alteration in the walls of the blood vessels and arteriosclerosis (Jones, 2011; Mastropieri & Hoffman, 2011; Schneider, 1992).

At present, we do not understand the process of aging very well (Bengtson, Gans, Putney, & Silverstein, 2009). Although ongoing research efforts continue to make progress in advancing our views of aging, much of the work that offers current promise focuses on how to prevent conditions that are known to be related to longevity, such as understanding the actions of viruses, the way in which immunological mechanisms work, and how cancer causes cellular changes.

Particularly important in this work is the research directed at understanding cellular changes in the brain. Neurological mechanisms are almost certainly involved in the normal process of aging, and they underlie many age-related disease processes as well, such as Alzheimer's disease and other forms of dementia. They also are instrumental in the more subtle cognitive changes

stochastic theories of aging
Theories suggesting that the body ages as a result of assaults from both internal and external environments; also referred to as "wear-and-tear" theories

Watch *Effects of Sun Tanning on Skin* on **MyDevelopmentLab**

biological clock theories of aging
Theories suggesting that genetic programming determines the pace and process of aging

of advanced age, those affecting thought, emotion, and intellect, that we examine in the next section of this chapter.

REVIEW THE FACTS 16-3

1. The normal process of aging is called ________.
2. The theory that aging results from wear and tear on the body is referred to as the ________ theory of aging.
3. Which of the following has been shown to reduce the presence of free radicals in the body?
   a. a diet high in protein
   b. surgery to remove the spleen
   c. exposure to sunlight
   d. vitamins C and E
4. The tips of chromosomes are called
   a. telomeres.
   b. free radicals.
   c. stochastic elements.
   d. biological clocks.
5. The idea that cells can divide only about 60 to 80 times before they die is referred to as the
   a. allostatic load.
   b. free radical freeze.
   c. Hayflick limit.
   d. stress-disease model of aging.

Practice on **MyDevelopmentLab**

COGNITIVE CHANGES IN ADVANCED AGE

Many people assume that the intellects of older people automatically decay with advancing age. For example, if a young or middle-aged man prepares to leave a party and does not remember where he left his coat, people think nothing of it. If the same forgetfulness is observed in an older person, however, people more often attribute the error to the loss of memory associated with age. The idea that cognitive functions decline with age is common; however, a careful consideration of how older adults think and solve problems indicates that—in the absence of disease processes—mental skills remain largely intact, and declines associated with normal aging processes, although sometimes significant, are not as great as most people assume (Salthouse, 2004, 2010; Zacks & Hasher, 2006).

Understanding Various Aspects of Cognition

Cognition is a general term used to describe overall intellectual functioning. Many different skills are involved in cognition, and some of these are affected by aging more than are others.

Speed of Cognition Many studies have shown that the intellectual functions that depend heavily on speed of performance decline in older people. Older people have slower reaction times, slower perceptual processing, and slower cognitive processes in general (Craik & Salthouse, 2008; Park & Bischof, 2011). Studies of performance on standard memory tasks, for example, typically reveal a difference in speed between the performances of 30- and 70-year-olds. In relatively simple cognitive tasks, such as those that ask participants to compare the size of different objects, older people typically take approximately 50% longer to complete the task than do younger people. As cognitive problems become more complex, requiring, for example, simultaneous comparisons of size and location, older adults generally require about twice as much time as do younger adults to complete the task (Baltes, 1993; Madden, 2001). Why?

What types of tasks might be most appropriate to use in memory studies that compare the performance of college-age adults to that of older adults?

Although some of this comparative slowness is clearly attributable to the neurological changes associated with aging, some of it also may be due to the different strategies that older people use (Schaie, 2005). For example, older adults often value accuracy more than younger people do; when tested, they make fewer guesses and try to answer each item correctly. In addition, older people may be less familiar with some of the tasks used in testing situations. For example, older people are often compared with college students in tests of recall of nonsense syllables. Students regularly practice learning new vocabularies for examinations, but older people usually have not engaged in comparable practice for a long time. On many such tasks, older people may be slower because they have not practiced the relevant cognitive skills recently. Thus, although the decline in cognitive processing associated with aging is real, in many studies it may well be exaggerated.

Older people often learn new strategies to compensate for their loss of speed. In one study, older typists typed as fast as younger typists despite their slower visual processing, slower

Older adults working in highly technical fields may find they have a wealth of experience but less perceptual speed or dexterity. These older data processing workers may be somewhat slower in entering information, but they also likely use more effective strategies so their overall work quality does not suffer.

Watch *Living Better Living Longer* on **MyDevelopmentLab**

reaction time, and reduced dexterity. However, when the number of words that the typists could read ahead was controlled and limited, the older typists' speed slowed considerably more than did the younger typists. Thus, it appears that older typists had learned to look farther ahead, using this strategy to compensate for their slower reactions (Lawton & Salthouse, 1998; Salthouse, 1994). By using more effective strategies, older people are often able to compensate for their loss of speed on many tasks and, in many cases, to recover much of their former performance level (Salthouse, 1996, 2000; Schaie, 2005).

Memory Perhaps no single aspect of aging has been studied more thoroughly than memory. Recall the information-processing model of memory discussed in Chapter 6: Information is first fleetingly retained in sensory memory in the form of visual or auditory images, then transferred to short-term memory for organization and encoding, and finally transferred to long-term memory for retention. Aging has been shown to affect various memory processes, and some more than others, as shown in Table 16-6 (Hoyer & Verhaeghen, 2006).

Sensory memory is very brief visual or auditory memory that holds sensory input for fractions of a second while the information is being processed. With respect to memory capacity, it appears that older individuals are able to pick up and hold slightly less sensory information than are young adults. However, an important part of sensory memory is attention, which involves being able to screen out irrelevant stimuli while focusing on a particular message. As we age, our ability to attend without being distracted declines somewhat, although older adults can often learn to compensate (Lindenberger, Lövdén, Schellenbach, Li, & Krüger, 2008; Passow et al., 2012; Rogers & Fisk, 2001). Thus, it is unlikely that the modest sensory memory losses observed in later adulthood have much effect on most tasks of daily living (Moulin & Gathercole, 2008; Salthouse, 2012).

However, these memory declines do make some things harder for older adults. For example, attention limitations can make it difficult for older adults to shift their attention among several speakers in a conversation (Passow et al., 2012). When coupled with mild-to-moderate hearing loss, the aging process of sensory memory can pose some difficulties, especially when older adults are trying to listen to several channels of information. Of particular concern, of course, is driving. Highway signs that whiz by can create difficulty for older drivers who require relatively more sensory input for skilled performance (Baldock, Berndt, & Mathias, 2008). Again, age-related declines usually are slight, and generally can be accommodated by driving more cautiously.

Short-term memory, which is limited-capacity storage that holds things that are "in mind" at the moment, also changes little with age in terms of capacity. Most studies find no significant difference between older and younger adults in short-term memory capacity. However, short-term memory is also the home of our *working memory*, where we process information that we retrieve from long-term memory, using various strategies to apply the stored information to make decisions and solve problems. Considerable research suggests that there are age-related declines associated with working memory (Braver & West, 2008; Nettelbeck & Burns, 2010). For example, it appears that older individuals are less efficient in organizing, rehearsing, and encoding material to be learned—all of which are short-term memory functions. Yet, with careful instruction and a little practice, older people can improve markedly. Even people near age 80 show some benefits from training in how to organize and rehearse information for permanent retention (McDaniel, Einstein, & Jacoby, 2008; Richmond, Morrison, Chein & Olson, 2011; Stine-Morrow & Basak, 2011; Zinke, Zeintl, Eschen, Herzog, & Kliegel, 2012).

Older adults, by virtue of their greater age and experience, have much more information stored in their brains. How might this relatively larger storehouse of knowledge affect the speed with which they can make decisions and solve problems?

The ability to remember, of course, depends on more than the strategies we use. We also must be able to remember past events and tap into our vast stores of information. *Long-term memory* is the warehouse for these facts and images, and it

Table 16-6 Memory Functions and Their Sensitivity to Aging Processes

Memory Type or Function	Description	Example	Declines with Age?
Sensory memory	Retention of a sensory image for a very brief time, perhaps 1 or 2 seconds	Remembering the illuminated pixels on a computer screen long enough to carry the image until the next pixels refresh	Slight or none
Short-term memory	Memory for things we are presently and actively thinking about	Remembering a phone number just looked up long enough to dial it	Slight or none
Working memory	Active processing of information while it is held in short-term memory; active thinking	Using our memory of the multiplication tables as we work through a set of math problems	Yes, although more effective strategies can limit decline
Episodic long-term memory	Recollection of past events and personally relevant information	Remembering the events of your last birthday party	Yes, but decline may be due to slower processing speed
Semantic long-term memory	Retrieval of facts, vocabulary, and general knowledge	Remembering how to add, how to speak a language, what you learned in school	Minimal

SOURCE: Adapted from "Aging and cognition," by R. W. Keefover, 1998, *Neurologic Clinics of North America, 16*(3), 635–648.

appears to undergo some deterioration with advancing age (Park & Reuter-Lorenz, 2009; Salthouse, 2010).

In particular, older adults experience more decline in their ability to recall *episodic memories* than *semantic memories* (Charlton, Barrick, Markus, & Morris, 2010). Episodic memories are those recollections of past events, or episodes: Remembering your first kiss is an example. Semantic memory includes the factual knowledge that we learn, such as the colors of the rainbow, the words to the "Star-Spangled Banner," how to convert a fraction to a decimal number, and so forth. Semantic memory appears to be largely unaffected by age; however, episodic memory does appear to decline despite the fact that older adults often *believe* they remember past events with excellent clarity. In healthy older adults, however, this apparent memory decline, may be mostly a product of slower processing speed (Kennedy & Raz, 2009; Park & Bischof, 2011).

The decline of memory associated with aging is, for most people, gradual and nonconsequential. It is most likely associated with changes in the brain, including the general slowing of the central nervous system and the age-related shrinkage of the brain's frontal lobes (Raz et al., 2010; Salthouse, 2010, 2011). Yet the brain appears to compensate for its declining size. Recent studies that employ brain-imaging technology demonstrate that, somewhat surprisingly, older individuals show increased levels of neural activity when compared to younger adults, especially in regions of the prefrontal cortex—that part of the brain most intimately connected with thinking and executive functions (Park & Bischof, 2011; Park & Reuter-Lorenz, 2009). Apparently, the regions of the brain responsible for decision-making functions become increasingly active at older ages in order to compensate for age-related declines. This increase in brain activity helps older adults maintain higher levels of cognitive functioning (Reuter-Lorenz & Cappell, 2008). In this way, the brain's plasticity is enhanced and at least some of the age-related deterioration that occurs as a normal part of advanced aging can be offset.

Research also shows that not all kinds of cognitive abilities undergo age-related decline to the same degree or at the same rate and that noticeable age-related decline generally does not begin until later adulthood. K. Warner Schaie has been studying the age-related changes in various types of cognitive abilities for over 50 years. His study, referred to as the Seattle Longitudinal Study, has tracked adults ages 20 to 70 since 1956; the oldest participants in his study are now about 100 years old (Schaie & Willis, 2011). Although Schaie's study has examined a multiplicity of factors related to aging, perhaps the most important results pertain to the tracking of six cognitive factors: verbal ability, spatial orientation, inductive reasoning, numeric facility, perceptual speed, and verbal memory (see Table 16-7).

Part of the reason that Schaie's work is important is that he uses both cross-sectional and longitudinal methods to study age-related changes. As noted in Chapter 1, cross-sectional studies compare individuals in various age groups at the same point in time; longitudinal studies, in contrast, follow a single group of individuals across time, looking at how they change as they age. Longitudinal studies have the advantage of being able to factor out age-graded cohort effects, which can be significant when the groups under study represent different generations, each with unique social and historical experiences (Raz & Lindenberger, 2011).

By following individuals both cross-sectionally and longitudinally across an extended period of time, Schaie's work presents an important picture of how cognitive abilities change with age. Looking at cross-sectional data (see Figure 16-9), Schaie's results suggest that inductive reasoning, perceptual speed, spatial orientation, and verbal memory decline rather

Table 16-7 Six Cognitive Abilities Included in the Seattle Longitudinal Study

Ability	Description	Example
Verbal ability	The ability to understand ideas expressed in words; closely linked to vocabulary	How are a cat and a dog alike?
Spatial orientation	The ability to visualize and mentally manipulate objects in two or three dimensions; to perceive relationships among objects in space; to understand a map; to imagine what objects would look like when assembled from pieces	If you were to rotate the following figure 180 degrees, what would it look like? oooo x
Inductive reasoning	The ability to recognize and understand new concepts and ideas; to solve logical problems, foresee consequences, analyze situations based on past experience, and make and carry out plans based on facts	If you found a small child alone and crying in a store, what should you do?
Numeric facility	The ability to understand numerical relationships; to work with figures and to solve simple quantitative problems rapidly and accurately	If you have $1.50 and you bought two notebooks that each cost $.59, how much change should you receive?
Perceptual speed	The ability to find figures, make comparisons, and carry out other simple tasks involving visual perceptions with speed and accuracy	Are these two names the same or different (timed)? Arthur P. Dusselhorst Arthur P. Dusellherst
Verbal memory	The ability to memorize and recall verbal information accurately	What are the six cognitive abilities followed in the Seattle Longitudinal Study?

SOURCE: Adapted from "What can we learn from longitudinal studies of adult development?" by K. W. Schaie, 2005, *Research in human development, 2*(3), 133–158; and *Developmental influences on adult intelligence: The Seattle Longitudinal Study*, by K. W. Schaie, 2007, New York: Oxford University Press.

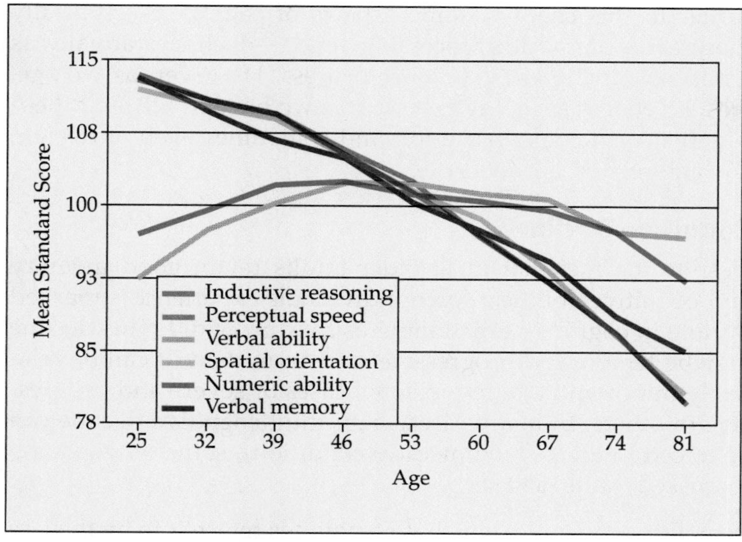

FIGURE 16-9 Age-Related Changes in Six Cognitive Abilities: Cross-Sectional Data

SOURCE: From *Developmental influences on adult cognitive development: The Seattle Longitudinal Study* (Figure 3, p. 103), by K. W. Schaie, 2005. Copyright © 2005 by Oxford University Press, New York. Reprinted by permission of Oxford University Press, Inc.

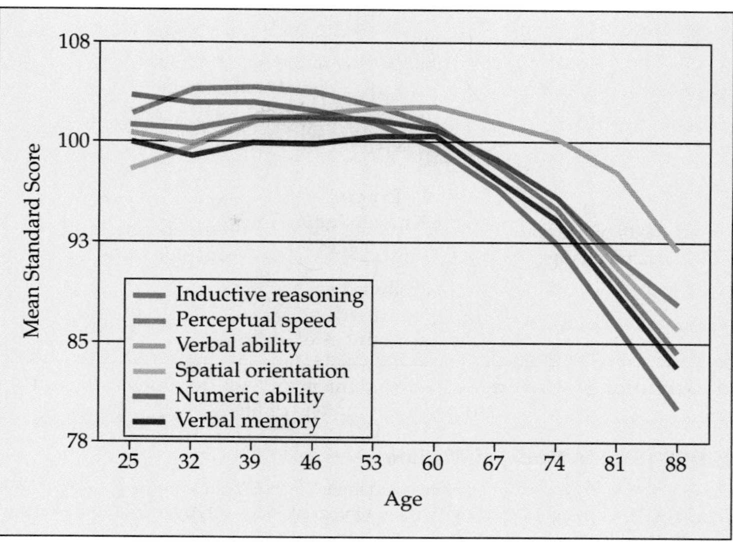

FIGURE 16-10 Age-Related Changes in Six Cognitive Abilities: Longitudinal Data

SOURCE: From *Developmental influences on adult cognitive development: The Seattle Longitudinal Study* (Figure 4, p. 127), by K. W. Schaie, 2005. Copyright © 2005 by Oxford University Press, New York. Reprinted by permission of Oxford University Press.

steadily with age, beginning in early adulthood; verbal ability and numerical ability show quite a different age trajectory, improving through most of adulthood, with only modest declines in later years. However, because these results are based on comparisons of different groups of individuals, the results cannot factor out the effect of generational experience. Adults age 70 today are quite different, on average, from adults age 30 in many dimensions important to cognitive functioning, including education, health care, and practice with technology. Thus, it is important to understand age-related differences *within* individuals, and a longitudinal approach provides a means of doing this. When individuals are tracked across time as they age, a quite different picture of age-related cognitive decline appears (see Figure 16-10). Here we see that adults maintain their early levels of cognitive functions throughout early and middle adulthood, with very little decline occurring until about age 65. By age 75, some gentle decline in most functions has begun, and by age 85 this decline is more significant.

It is important to note, however, that the age-related decline in cognitive functioning, although present, is for the most part modest. As noted previously, much of the decline older adults experience can be compensated for, either through additional effort or better use of problem-solving strategies. Furthermore, the gentle decline in cognitive functioning observed as a normal part of aging is often compensated for by the experience that older adults have gained. One form that such experience takes is often referred to as *wisdom.*

Wisdom Although the mechanics of memory are somewhat stronger in young adults than in older adults, the reverse is often true about **wisdom**, which refers to an expert knowledge system that involves excellent judgment and advice on critical and practical life issues (Karelitz, Jarvin, & Sternberg, 2010; Kunzmann, 2007; Scheibe, Kunzmann, & Baltes, 2007). Wisdom is more than the accumulation of information; rather, it has several characteristics that set it apart from fact-based problem solving (Ardelt, 2011; Kunzmann & Baltes, 2003). First, wisdom appears to focus on important and difficult matters that are often associated with the meaning of life and the human condition. Second, the level of knowledge, judgment, and advice reflected in wisdom is superior. Third, the knowledge associated with wisdom has extraordinary scope, depth, and balance, and it can be applied to address specific situations or problems. Fourth, wisdom combines mind and virtue (character) and is employed for personal well-being, as well as for the benefit of humankind. Fifth, although difficult to achieve, wisdom is easily recognized by most people, and it represents the capstone of human intelligence.

A person's degree of wisdom typically is assessed by posing a series of dilemmas and evaluating the degree to which a person's responses approach the five criteria of wisdom-related knowledge: factual knowledge, procedural knowledge, life-span contextualism, value relativism, and recognition and management of uncertainty (see Figure 16-11). Answers can be rated to evaluate how much and what kind of wisdom-related knowledge an individual possesses (see the box Current Issues: Wisdom—Cross-Cultural or Culture Specific? and Table 16-8).

wisdom
An expert knowledge system that focuses on the practicalities of life and that involves excellent judgment and advice on critical life issues, including the meaning of life and the human condition; wisdom represents the capstone of human intelligence

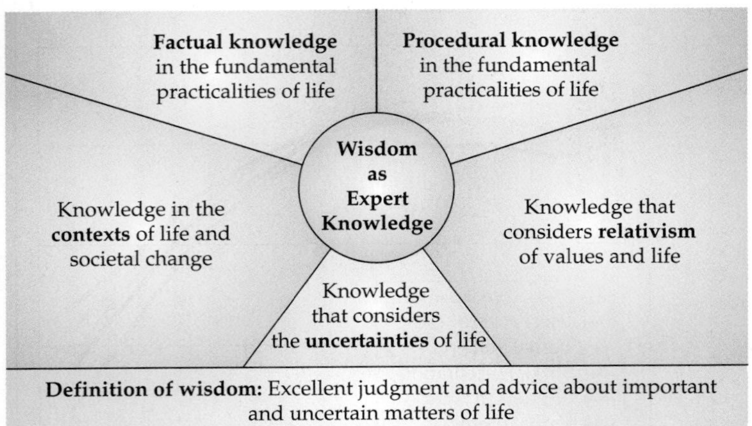

FIGURE 16-11 A Model of Wisdom

SOURCE: From "The aging mind: Potential and limits" by P. B. Baltes, *The Gerontologist*, 1993, 33(5), 580–594. Copyright © 1993 by The Gerontological Society of America. Reproduced by permission of Oxford University Press, New York.

As you might guess, wisdom is related to age, although the relationship between age and wisdom is complex (Sternberg, 2005a). Although the thought processes associated with wisdom are mostly present by the end of the college years, the development of wisdom also requires a certain level of social intelligence, openness to experience, and exposure to positive role models. Thus, one reason that wisdom is often associated with older adulthood is that it depends on life experiences. It is rare that a young person could accumulate the breadth and depth of learning that wisdom requires. In addition, as adults age, they develop personal attributes that are conducive to the development of wisdom. Both the development of personality and cognitive growth contribute to wisdom (Birney & Sternberg, 2011; Kunzmann, 2007; Staudinger & Gluck, 2011).

The emergence of wisdom in older adulthood makes clear the point that cognitive abilities change as we grow older. As noted earlier in this chapter, some aspects of cognition—especially those associated with processing speed—decline gradually as a normal function of the aging process. However, as we age, we also benefit from the experiences we have in life, and these benefits often compensate for, and sometimes even outweigh, any age-related declines.

Table 16-8 Use of the Wisdom-Related Criteria to Evaluate Discourse About Life Matters

Suppose a 15-year-old girl wants to get married right away. What should she consider and do?	
An abbreviated illustration of two extreme responses	
Low score	A 15-year-old girl wants to get married? No, no way; marrying at age 15 would be utterly wrong. Someone has to tell the girl that marriage is not possible. (After further probing) It would be irresponsible to support such an idea. No, this is just a crazy idea.
High score	Well, on the surface, this seems like an easy problem. On average, marriage for 15-year-old girls is not a good thing. I guess many girls might think about it when they fall in love for the first time. Then there are situations where the average case does not fit. Perhaps, in this instance, special life circumstances are involved, such as the girl has a terminal illness or this girl may not be from this country. Perhaps she lives in another culture and historical period. Before I offer a final evaluation, I would need more information.

SOURCE: Adapted from "The aging mind: Potential and limits," by P. B. Baltes, 1993, *The Gerontologist, 33*, 580–594.

Cognitive Decline

Despite the fact that most older adults retain good memory and cognitive abilities, some individuals experience a marked decline in cognitive functioning as they grow old. This decline may be temporary, progressive, or intermittent. It can be relatively minor and fleeting in some cases or severe and progressive in others. In many cases, significant cognitive decline can be traced to underlying medical conditions, some of which are discussed in the next section.

Dementia Dementia, which is sometimes referred to by the less technical term *senility,* refers to the chronic confusion, forgetfulness, and accompanying personality changes that are sometimes associated with advanced age. People who suffer from dementia have a limited ability to grasp abstractions. They may lack ideas, repeat the same statements over and over again, lose their train of thought in the middle of a sentence, think more slowly than healthier people, or lack the ability to pay attention to those around them. Memory for recent events also is often impaired: A person suffering from dementia may clearly recall a childhood event but be unable to remember something that happened an hour ago.

Dementia is usually a serious, often life-altering problem. For example, because of their mental deterioration, people with dementia may be unable to cope with routine tasks, such as keeping clean and groomed, and may be unable to think, behave, or relate to people normally (American Psychiatric Association, 2000; Lerner & Lerner, 2009; Shigeta & Homma, 2007). Many people fear dementia in the mistaken belief that it is an inevitable curse of growing old. To them, growing old means losing emotional and intellectual control and becoming a helpless, useless person who becomes a burden to their family. However, dementia results from specific causes, and it is not simply an aspect of growing old.

Environmental Factors What causes some people to develop dementia, whereas others live long lives with no significant cognitive decline? Several factors are most likely involved. Sometimes dementia is the result of environmental factors that affect a person's overall welfare, such as poor general health or living in a nonstimulating environment. Both of these situations, as well as others, can produce symptoms associated with dementia (see Table 16-9). When environmental factors are the cause of dementia, they can sometimes be addressed, and the associated mental confusion and cognitive decline may improve. For example, when older adults can reduce the number

Watch *Alzheimers and Dementia* on **MyDevelopmentLab**

CURRENT ISSUES

Wisdom—Cross-Cultural or Culture Specific?

What is wisdom? Philosophers, religion scholars, psychologists, and many others have pondered this question across the centuries (Ardelt, 2011; Sternberg, 2005b). From the perspective of science, the best approach to the study of such complex and multifaceted areas of human behavior is to establish a program of research—one that extends across several years and includes many interrelated studies. By establishing a program of research, basic questions can be addressed from various perspectives and knowledge becomes cumulative, allowing for the development of theories and a broader understanding. One of the first research groups to tackle the different problems inherent in the study of a trait so diffuse as wisdom was headed by Paul Baltes (e.g., Baltes & Kunzmann, 2003, 2004; Kunzmann, 2007; Staudinger, 2008). Although Baltes died in 2006, researchers using his methods and guided by his views have continued to advance work on this important topic.

One question that the study of wisdom raises is the degree to which wisdom is linked to a particular culture's definition. Is Asian wisdom the same as that of Western European philosophers? Is the European idea that wisdom is a body of knowledge or a set of theoretical principles at odds with the Eastern tradition of viewing wisdom as what is possessed by wise people? Baltes and colleagues believe that wisdom involves a kind of complex decision making that is common across cultures, although the products of wise thinking—the specific decisions or choices—may vary by culture (Baltes & Kunzmann, 2003, 2004). Thus, although the decisions reached by wise people may differ, the processes these people take in making their decisions may actually be quite similar.

To study how people make wise choices, Baltes and colleagues posed dilemmas and asked people to answer questions about the dilemmas that require the consideration of various kinds of judgments involved in wisdom (Baltes, 1993; Baltes & Kunzmann, 2004; Stange & Kunzman, 2008). For example, if you were a volunteer in one of these studies, you might be asked, "A 15-year-old girl wants to get married right away. What should she consider and do?" Your answer would be evaluated according to several criteria that characterize wise judgments: how you understand the facts of the situation, how you analyze the situation, how you consider the special circumstances that apply, how you understand your own values as being different from others' values, and how you reflect the uncertain nature of the various outcomes that might be attained (see Table 16-8). Baltes and his colleague, Ute Kunzmann, argued that people who score higher on wisdom on tasks such as this also have higher levels of openness to experience, psychological mindedness, and creativity, as well as higher emotional involvement, value orientation, and a stronger preference for cooperative rather than competitive conflict management. People who score higher on wisdom also focus more on personal growth rather than on attaining a pleasant life (Kunzmann & Baltes, 2003).

Thus, these researchers, and others who have adopted a similar approach, view wisdom not just as a set of specific decisions or as the beliefs and values reflected by a wise person (Birney & Sternberg, 2011; Staudinger & Gluck, 2011). Rather, they see wisdom as reflecting a general theory of expert knowledge and judgment that speaks to the combination of excellence in mind together with virtue. Wisdom is not just a cold cognition; it is a rich combination of thinking and judgment related to life experience. People who score high on wisdom have not hidden away from life to think great thoughts but rather have lived full and thoughtful lives, aware of others and of their own emotions. Wise people, according to this view, are those who are able to see the ramifications and consequences of different choices in the important decisions of life.

Wisdom, thus, develops within a social context (Karelitz, Jarvin, & Sternberg, 2010; Staudinger, Kessler, & Dörner, 2006). In real life, wisdom is most likely to be earned by helping others, by contributing to society, by deciding and developing one's own path through life, by resolving difficult problems, and by maintaining a lifestyle that is satisfying. Also wisdom is linked to an insistence on doing what one believes is "right," especially in the face of adversity (Yang, 2008).

Is wisdom cross-cultural or culture specific? If, as Baltes's research suggests, wise people arrive at decisions using similar processes and experiences, it would seem that wisdom would reflect a set of universal principles that is not much affected by one's culture. Indeed, researchers today view wisdom as a broadly defined trait, linked not only to cognitive variables such as intelligence, but also to personality factors and even to cultural and spiritual traditions (Scheibe, Kunzmann, & Baltes, 2009; Walsh, 2011). Their research, which attempts to address one of the most difficult concepts of which humans are capable, expands our knowledge about what it means to be human and it allows us to better understand how individuals change as they develop across the lifespan.

Table 16-9 Environmental Factors That Are Linked to Cognitive Decline in Older Adults

General Factors	Characteristics
Negative expectations about aging	• When older adults expect that their capabilities will decline, they often do as the result of a self-fulfilling prophecy.
Physical illness	• Some disease processes—such as heart, kidney, or liver problems—are associated with general cognitive decline.
Loneliness, depression, and other mental illnesses	• When people grow old, they sometimes limit their cognitive, social, and physical activities and their experiences become mundane. • Depression is a common reaction to the losses associated with aging, and it lowers a person's level of cognitive functioning. • Other psychiatric conditions can also reduce mental functioning.
Drugs	• Some drugs have side effects that affect alertness and cognitive functions. • Alcohol, especially when used over an extended period, impairs cognitive abilities. • Prescription drugs often interact, causing confusion or other cognitive impairments.
Exercise	• There is a clear link between regular physical exercise and good cognitive functioning.
Nutrition	• Some nutritional deficiencies (e.g., anemia, some vitamins) are linked to poor performance on intellectual tasks.
Mental activity	• "Use it or lose it" refers to the finding that engaging in complex thinking keeps a person's mind sharp.

or the dosage of prescription drugs they take, they sometimes find that their thinking improves.

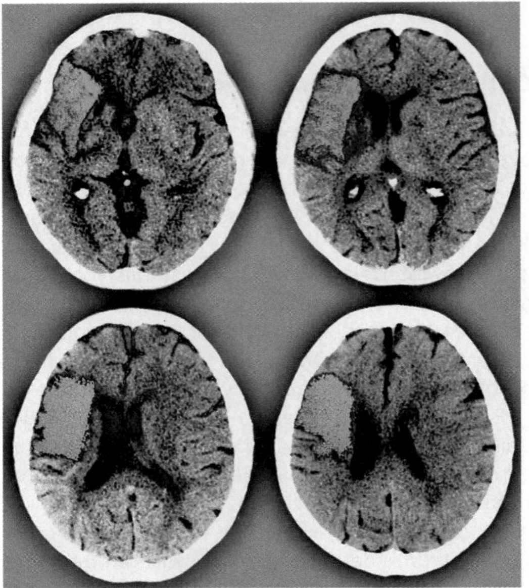

This is a colored computed tomography (CT) scan of the brain of a 68-year-old stroke patient. The red coloring indicates the interruption of the blood flow and damage to a significant area of the left side of the brain. The images show horizontal sections through the brain at different levels.

Cardiovascular and Circulatory Problems Sometimes dementia results from problems with blood flow to, or throughout, the brain. **Strokes**, including ministrokes, produce a form of cognitive decline that is sometimes called *multi-infarct dementia (MID)*. An *infarct* is an obstruction of a blood vessel that prevents a sufficient supply of blood from reaching a particular area of the brain. This causes the destruction of brain tissue and is commonly referred to as a *stroke* or a *ministroke*. Major strokes, of course, can produce substantial impairment in those functions that were formerly controlled by the stroke-affected part of the brain. If, however, the area of damage is small and if the effects of the stroke are relatively temporary, these episodes are usually referred to as *transient ischemic attacks (TIAs)*. Normally, if a person experiences only a few minor TIAs, there is little noticeable effect. However, if a series of events that damage brain tissue occurs over a period of time, the damage accumulates. When enough damage has occurred that the person experiences cognitive impairment, the diagnosis is MID.

Can you suggest steps that can be taken to reduce the general factors that might be contributing to an older person's cognitive decline?

Often the underlying cause of ministrokes and the resulting destruction of brain tissue is *atherosclerosis*—the buildup of fatty plaques on the lining of the arteries. People who have atherosclerosis or existing heart problems, hypertension, or diabetes are at particular risk for strokes. Those at risk are advised to pay attention to measures that improve their circulation, such as moderate exercise, and to control their hypertension and diabetes through diet and medication. In fact, maintaining a regular program of physical exercise is one of the best ways to protect against events that can produce decline—both mental and physical—in older adulthood (Chang et al., 2010; Middleton, Lui, & Yaffe, 2010).

Alzheimer's Disease Although the effects of TIAs and ministrokes can be cumulative and ultimately cause significant impairment in thinking, they are relatively rare in comparison to the incidence of the leading cause of dementia, **Alzheimer's disease**, which is the fifth leading cause of death among people age 65 and older and—perhaps even more surprising—the sixth leading cause of all deaths in the United States today (Alzheimer's Association, 2012; FIFARS, 2010j).

Because Alzheimer's is a disease closely linked to aging, and because the older segment of the U.S. population is growing dramatically (see Figure 16-12), the prevalence of Alzheimer's is increasing correspondingly. Today, 5.4 million people in the United States are living with Alzheimer's disease; by 2050, that number is expected to be 16 million—nearly three times larger (Alzheimer's Association, 2012). Clearly, Alzheimer's disease is a major health-care challenge for those living in the United States or in other developed countries of the world (see Figure 16-13).

Alzheimer's disease involves the progressive deterioration of brain cells, especially those in the cerebral cortex, where

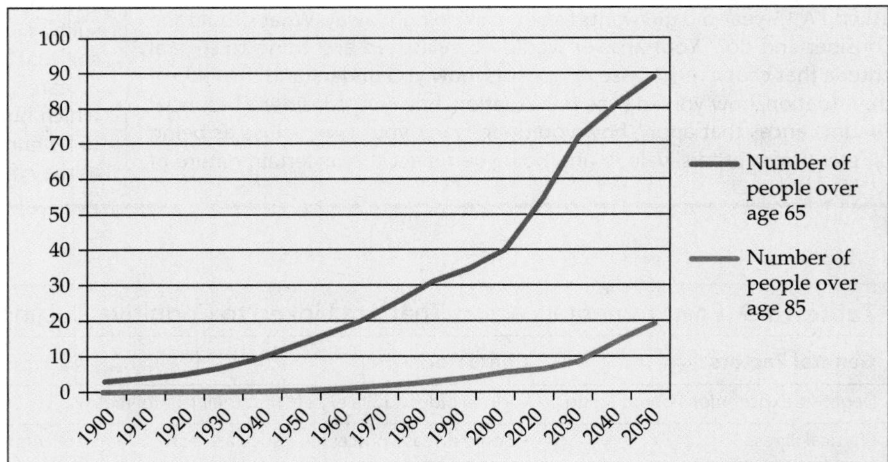

FIGURE 16-12 Number of People Age 65 and over and 85 and over, Selected Years 1900–2050, United States (in millions)

SOURCE: Table 1a, "Number of people age 65 and over and 85 and over, selected years 1900–2008 and projected 2010–2050," Federal Interagency Forum on Aging-Related Statistics, 2010, in *Older Americans 2010*, retrieved from http://www.agingstats.gov/agingstatsdotnet/Main_Site/Data/2010_Documents/docs/OA_2010.pdf.

stroke
Blockage of blood to a region in the brain, which can cause brain damage

Alzheimer's disease
A disease that causes dementia due to a progressive deterioration of brain cells, especially those in the cerebral cortex

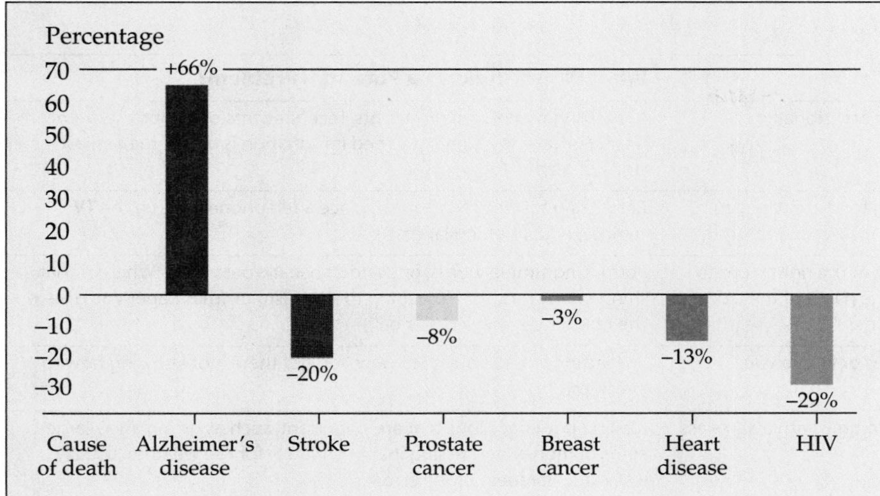

FIGURE 16-13 Percentage Changes in Selected Causes of Death (All Ages), 2000 to 2008

SOURCE: "Factsheet," Alzheimer's Association, 2012, retrieved from http://www.alz.org/alzheimers_disease_facts_and_figures.asp.

much of thinking and memory is located. At the present time, the definitive diagnosis of Alzheimer's disease is possible only at autopsy, when the brain degeneration associated with the disease can be examined. Consequently, Alzheimer's disease is diagnosed according to the symptoms that generally occur as the disease process advances (see Table 16-10). Although many of these symptoms in mild form are commonly associated with aging, in the case of Alzheimer's the symptoms are more severe and keep progressing until substantial disability, and ultimately death, result. Generally, the first problems noticed are forgetfulness and minor disruptions in speech. In the beginning, only little things are forgotten; however, as the disease progresses, places, names, and routines may not be recalled; and finally, even events that may have just occurred are forgotten. Forgetfulness is often accompanied by a sense of confusion, and people with Alzheimer's disease often experience difficulty in performing even simple routines; for example, it is hard to get something to eat because the person cannot find the refrigerator. This loss of contact with the routine and familiar aspects of life, of course, causes serious disorientation, confusion, and anxiety. At this point, it usually becomes clear that the person cannot be left alone because of the potential for injury. Finally, full dementia sets in. The person is unable to complete the simplest tasks, such as dressing or even eating. Familiar people are not recognized; even a devoted spouse who has cared for the person through years of decline may be perceived as a complete stranger.

Not surprisingly, Alzheimer's disease typically has a substantial impact on the family of the person with the disease. In the early stages, adaptations are relatively easy. The environment can be simplified and objects—even furniture—can be labeled. The person can still be alone, at least for short periods, and things like a sandwich prepared earlier by a family member may prevent an accident in the kitchen at mealtime. Later, however, when 24-hour care becomes necessary, major adaptations must be made. Caring for a loved one with Alzheimer's disease is both physically and emotionally difficult. According to the Alzheimer's Association (2012), more than 60% of caregivers rate their level of emotional stress as high or very high. Aside from practical matters, family members often must also deal with grief and despair and perhaps with anger and frustration; at this stage, the support of others and the availability of counseling services are particularly helpful (Gaugler, Roth, Haley, & Mittelman, 2008). In some cases, the difficult decision to place the person in a memory care facility or nursing home must be made. Sometimes this decision is easier if the person seems not to know where he or she is. Also, the simpler, more predictable environment of the institution may make life easier for a person with Alzheimer's disease (see Chapter 18), and this often provides some comfort to grieving families (see the box Try This! Exploring Alzheimer's Disease).

Despite the fact that major research efforts are currently under way to find effective treatments or a cure for Alzheimer's disease, not much is known about its cause. Researchers now identify two forms of the disease, which appear to have somewhat different causes. One form, which is called *early-onset Alzheimer's disease*, is characterized by the onset of symptoms in the 40s through the mid-50s. Fortunately, early-onset Alzheimer's is quite rare, and accounts for only about 1% of all cases. This form of the disease seems to be closely tied to one of three genetic mutations, labeled *APP*, *PS-1*, and *PS-2*, which fall on chromosomes 1, 14, and 21. If a person inherits one of these gene mutations, it is believed that at some point the disease process will begin (Alzheimer's Association, 2012). Other genes that control how cells use calcium have also been implicated in early-onset Alzheimer's (Bertram & Tanzi, 2008; Juncosa, 2008), and the picture about what causes this disease is probably a complex one.

The other, much more common form of Alzheimer's disease is associated with later-developing symptoms, which typically do not onset before age 65. Although this form of the disease is most likely associated with a variety of genetic markers (Serretti, Olgiati, & De Ronchi, 2007), one gene that has been linked to its development is a gene on chromosome 19 referred to as *APOE-e4*. This gene is a variant of the gene that instructs the protein synthesis for apolipoprotein E, which is thought to play a role in repairing damaged connections between brain cells (Alzheimer's Association, 2012). Although it appears that *APOE* and perhaps other genes play an important role in the development of

Watch *What Happens with Alzheimers* on MyDevelopmentLab

Watch *Speaking Out: Alvin: Living with Dementia* on MyDevelopmentLab

Table 16-10 Ten Warning Signs of Alzheimer's Disease

Symptom	What's Normal?	What Would Indicate a Potential Problem?
Memory loss	Forgetting names or appointments occasionally, which everyone does	Forgetting names, appointments, recent events on a more frequent basis. Forgetting recently learned information is one of the earliest signs of Alzheimer's disease
Difficulty performing familiar tasks	Forgetting what you were planning to say or why you came into a room	Forgetting how to cook a meal, place a telephone call, run the TV remote, or play a familiar game
Problems with language	Sometimes having trouble thinking of the right word to use in conversation (e.g., "what is the name of that zoo animal like a lion but with black stripes?")	Forgetting simple words, or using unusual words (e.g., "Where is that thing for my mouth?" [meaning toothbrush] or "that paper you give the man" [meaning a dollar bill])
Disorientation to time and place	Forgetting what day of the week it is or where you parked your car in the lot	Forgetting where you are or how you got there; not knowing how to get home
Poor or decreased judgment	Making a poor decision from time to time with awareness afterward that it was a mistake	Making poor decisions that are important, such as giving away large sums of money or dressing inappropriately for the weather, usually without awareness of the error
Problems with abstract thinking	Having some difficulty with complex decisions, such as balancing a checkbook or understanding tax issues	Forgetting what numbers are or how they can be used
Misplacing things	Misplacing things such as keys or a wallet from time to time	Misplacing things frequently, sometimes in odd places, such as putting the iron away in the refrigerator or a wristwatch in the sugar bowl
Changes in mood or behavior	Occasionally experiencing sadness or moodiness, but to a normal degree	Exhibiting much more extreme and rapid mood swings, such as going from calmness to tears and anger for no apparent reason
Changes in personality	Personality changes are gradual with age, if they occur at all	Personality changes that can be dramatic, characterized by confusion, fearfulness, suspiciousness, or dependence
Loss of initiative	Feeling fatigued and tired of work or social events from time to time	Exhibiting extremely passive behavior, such as staring at TV for hours, sleeping more than usual, and not wanting to engage in usual activities

SOURCE: Adapted from "10 Signs of Alzheimer's," Alzheimer's Association, 2009, retrieved from http://www.alz.org/alzheimers_disease_10_signs_of_ alzheimers.asp.

Alzheimer's disease, researchers have much to learn before a definitive cause of the disease can be identified. For example, some individuals that have the *APOE-e4* genetic variant never develop the symptoms of the disease; others who have the symptoms do not have the *APOE* gene variant. Environmental factors also seem to influence the development of the disorder. Thus, epigenetic processes are almost certainly involved (see Chapter 2).

How does Alzheimer's disease affect the brain? Autopsies of deceased people in the advanced stages of Alzheimer's disease have revealed a characteristic pattern of damaged brain areas where neurons are no longer neatly ordered but instead are disorganized, looking like little bits of braided yarn. Cortical shrinkage is also revealed in the brain scans of people living with Alzheimer's disease, although it is difficult to sort out how much shrinkage is associated with normal aging versus the disease processes associated with Alzheimer's disease.

Although at present there is no cure for Alzheimer's, nor are there drugs available that can slow or stop the progress of this disease, there are two types of drugs that sometimes are prescribed to address symptoms of memory loss. One of these types—the *cholinesterase inhibitor* drugs—works by preventing the breakdown of the neurotransmitter *acetylcholine*. The drugs Aricept and Cognex are examples of this type of drug, and for some people they appear to slow the progression of symptoms associated with the disease. The other type of drug, which is newer to the market, also works on a brain neurotransmitter—in this case *glutamate*. Namenda is currently the only glutamate-regulating medication recommended to treat the memory symptoms of Alzheimer's. Physicians sometimes prescribe both of these types of medicines together, and they also may prescribe high doses of vitamin E—an

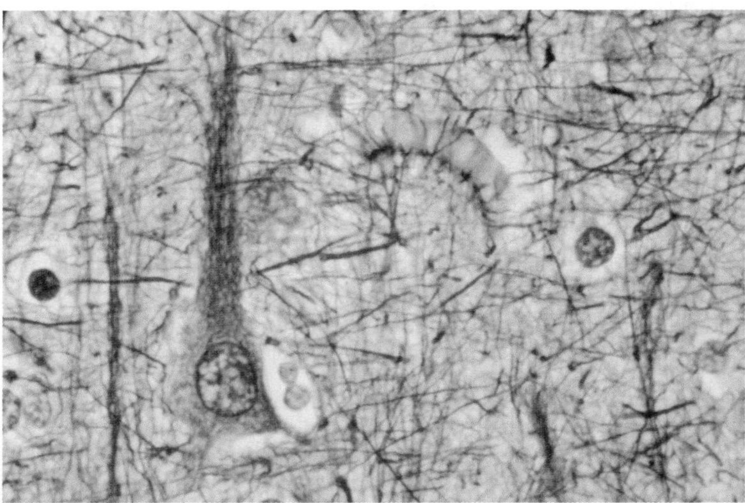

▲ This is a light micrograph (with yellow stain) of a section of the brain of a person affected by Alzheimer's disease. It shows the neural tangles and plaques that are characteristic features of this disease. The long elongated "dart" on the left side is a tangle of twisted neural filaments.

TRY THIS!

Exploring Alzheimer's Disease

Alzheimer's disease is a progressive, degenerative disease of the cells of the brain. Over time, it involves the development of multiple cognitive deficits, including language disturbances, motor impairments, the inability to recognize familiar people and objects, and the impairment in all forms of thinking and problem solving (refer to Table 16-10). Nearly everyone is familiar with the symptoms of this disease, and most people know someone—a grandparent, another relative, or a family friend—who has been affected by Alzheimer's.

However, reading about Alzheimer's disease and its symptoms fails to adequately capture this illness, which ultimately and progressively robs older individuals of their cognitive functions. To better understand the often devastating impact that Alzheimer's disease can have on those it affects, conduct an in-depth interview with a person who has observed first hand the effects that Alzheimer's disease has had on a friend, a family member, or a person in their care. You may know such a person or you may need to ask around to identify a person who is willing to discuss their story of a loved one with Alzheimer's. If you have difficulty finding a person to interview, you might call a care facility in your town or city and ask to speak with one of the caregivers who has taken care of institutionalized people with Alzheimer's disease. Perhaps you know of a person who has this disease. If so, you might wish to reflect on your own experiences as you think about the following questions.

As part of your interview, you might consider asking questions such as the following:

- How did the person affected first notice the early signs of Alzheimer's disease? What were the first clues that this disease might be present?
- What were the early symptoms like? What functions were first affected? How did the disease progress? How quickly did various cognitive impairments develop?
- How did the person with Alzheimer's disease react to the progressive symptoms? How did the person cope with the cognitive difficulties he or she experienced?
- How did the loved ones react to the person with Alzheimer's? Was there a point at which a decision needed to be made about providing more care than was available at home for the person? How difficult were these circumstances?
- What was (or is) the hardest aspect of Alzheimer's disease to deal with, both for the person with the disease and for those who love and care for that person?

Reflect on What You Observed

Did the symptoms of the person whose life you discussed reflect those typically associated with Alzheimer's disease? Were there any symptoms that stand out as being particularly problematic or difficult to deal with? How well do you think the person with Alzheimer's disease learned to cope with the disease? How well did the loved ones cope? What kind of care was (or is) required for the person affected by the disease? What kinds of support services are available for people with Alzheimer's disease? Did the person you spoke with discuss the use of any services? If so, were they helpful? How difficult was it for the person you interviewed to deal with the diagnosis and the eventual cognitive decline of the person you discussed?

Consider the Issues

Alzheimer's is a particularly difficult disease because it affects a person's cognitive functions—the very aspects that define one's personality, intellect, and character. Many caregivers report that one of the most devastating aspects of this disease is that it robs the affected person of who they are and, therefore, changes long-standing relationships. Caregivers often report great sadness and grief over the loss of their loved one's mental abilities, especially when memories are so severely disrupted that the person with Alzheimer's no longer remembers who the loved ones are or what their relationships have meant. As you reflect on the story you heard, what do you think is the hardest part of dealing with Alzheimer's disease? How do you think you would cope if a person you loved developed this illness (or how have you coped)? What things do you think can (or should) be done to help a family adjust to a loved one's diagnosis of Alzheimer's disease? What advice do you think might be helpful to family members who must deal with a loved one in the advanced stages of this disease?

---

antioxidant—to address the memory problems that develop as Alzheimer's disease advances. They also can prescribe other types of drugs to address other symptoms, such as depression, anxiety, hallucinations, or difficulty with sleep. Of course, drug researchers are aggressively working to develop drugs that can more effectively manage symptoms, as well as those that might offer some promise of slowing or halting the disease processes themselves.

Compensating for an Aging Mind

Regardless of whether advanced age brings minimal cognitive disruptions or the dramatic deterioration of advanced Alzheimer's disease, as adults grow older, they learn to make adjustments for the declines they experience. As older adults recognize the changes in their cognitive abilities, they reorganize and adjust their sense of self in response (Baltes, Lindenberger, & Staudinger, 2006; Resnick, Gwyther, & Roberto, 2011; Scheibe, Kunzmann, & Baltes, 2009). This readjustment may explain why most older adults do not experience a major reduction in their sense of either subjective well-being or personal control.

Furthermore, factors such as higher education (Sando et al., 2008) and sustained overall activity level have been linked with a person's ability to compensate for and minimize some aspects of cognitive decline in very old adulthood (Andel et al., 2008; Chang et al., 2010; Middleton, Lui, & Yaffe, 2010; Sando et al., 2008; Stine-Morrow & Basak, 2011). For example, when the concert pianist Arthur Rubinstein was asked how he managed to remain a successful pianist in his old age, he mentioned three strategies: In old age (a) he performed fewer pieces, (b) he practiced each piece more frequently, and (c) he introduced more ritarandos (slowing down of passages) in his playing before fast segments so that the playing speed sounded faster than it was in reality (Baltes, 1993, p. 590).

Rubinstein's strategy reflects processes that older adults use to cope with the cognitive declines that accompany advanced age: They select fewer tasks on which to focus; they devote more attention to the tasks they select; and they optimize their outcomes, compensating for poorer skills by relying on those they still possess.

Older adulthood, like the periods of the lifespan that come before it, is thus a time of change and challenge. As such, it involves not only adjustments to physical and cognitive processes but to personality and sociocultural dimensions as well. We explore these dimensions of older adulthood in the next chapter.

REVIEW THE FACTS 16-4

1. The major cognitive decline associated with normal aging concerns tasks that involve
   a. expert knowledge. b. judgment.
   c. complex decision making. d. speed.
2. The short-term memory function that usually is most affected by normal aging is called ________ memory.
3. *Senility* is another word for
   a. dementia. b. senescence.
   c. episodic memory. d. semantic memory.
4. Multi-infarct dementia is caused by
   a. overuse of prescription medications.
   b. long-term use of alcohol.
   c. strokes or ministrokes.
   d. a brain disease similar to Alzheimer's.
5. The most common cause of age-related dementia is
   a. ministrokes. b. transient ischemic attacks (TIAs).
   c. major strokes. d. Alzheimer's disease.

CHAPTER SUMMARY

Aging Today

What positive and negative stereotypes are typically invoked to describe how "old people" should think and act?

- How people experience growing old is heavily dependent on their cultural context, which varies widely. In the United States, ageist stereotypes reflect common assumptions—often negative—about older adults. *Ageism* refers to the widely prevalent negative attitudes in Western societies that overvalue youth and degrade older people. Most people, however, recognize that wide individual differences in the effects of aging exist.
- In some cultures and historical periods, older people are honored: In many Asian nations, this tradition is known as *filial piety*, where respect for the elderly is manifested in cultural traditions, as well as in everyday activities. However, in contemporary Asian society, filial piety may be declining.
- In developed countries, old age is typically associated with negative assessments. Some people choose to change their physical appearance—using hair dye, make-up, or cosmetic surgery—to make themselves appear younger.
- The percentage of the population over age 65 has been increasing as a result of the aging of baby boomers, the trend toward lower birth rates, better health care, and declining death rates. It is expected to rise even more dramatically over the next 3 decades. By 2030, nearly one out of every five U.S. people is projected to be age 65 or older.

In what ways does each of the four decades of older adulthood typically differ from the other decades?

- People in older adulthood—age 60 or 65 and beyond—are a very heterogeneous group, partly because this part of the lifespan includes people in such a wide age range. Thus, a 65- and an 85-year-old are both included but belong to different cohort groups and may have quite different interests, abilities, and health status. For this reason, older adulthood often is broken down into different decades.
- The young-old period (ages 60 to 69) often involves role transition, especially retirement and the reduced income that often accompanies it. Society generally expects less of people in their 60s, which can demoralize members of this age cohort.
- People in the middle-aged-old cohort (ages 70 to 79) are called *septuagenarians.* During this decade, people frequently experience loss, as friends and family members become ill or die. Many people also must cope with their own illnesses, although improved health care and healthier lifestyles allow many in this group to remain active and to cope successfully.
- Members of the old-old age group (ages 80 to 89), called *octogenarians,* often are frail and sometimes need assistance in maintaining social contacts. However, only 10% in this group are seriously disabled and only about 14% reside in nursing homes. The over-85 age group is the fastest growing U.S. cohort, thereby putting a strain on health-care systems and Social Security.
- The very old-old cohort (ages 90 to 99), called *nonagenarians,* are often very hearty people to have survived so long. They often are healthier and more active than people 20 years younger.
- Although there is wide diversity in the people belonging to each age group of older adults, many people experience common challenges in each decade. The negative stereotype of older adults as needy, unproductive, and unhappy generally is inaccurate.

The Physical Aspects of Aging

How does a person's body change during the four decades that define older adulthood?

- The cumulative effects of aging often result from earlier events and lifestyle choices—called *pathological aging factors*—rather than from advancing age itself. Aging, however, is inevitable, although it usually is gradual.
- Age-related changes in appearance are especially noticeable in the skin, with the appearance of wrinkles, warts, broken blood vessels, and age spots. Genes are involved in such changes, as are environmental factors, especially damage from the ultraviolet light from the sun.
- Muscles gradually become lighter and weaker with age. Endurance and reaction times decline. Regular physical exercise can delay or offset some of these age-related declines, and physical exercise is linked to better overall health.

- Osteoporosis, an age-related condition in which bone mass declines, is responsible for 1.5 million bone fractures per year. Older White and Asian women are especially at risk for developing osteoporosis. The vestibular system, which maintains our sense of balance, declines with age, often leading to falls.
- Most organ systems decline in function with age, including the immune system, the heart, and the respiratory system. The first signs of aging in these systems often are experienced when the body is stressed and must use reserve capacity, which declines with age.
- About one-half of 65-year-olds living at home and two-thirds of those in nursing homes or other long-term care facilities experience sleep problems. Generally, older people sleep less and have less time in deep sleep, both of which contribute to fatigue. Sleep disorders, such as insomnia and sleep apnea, may also develop.
- The senses generally become less sensitive as we age. Taste usually is least affected. Hearing and visual impairments become increasingly common with age. A *cataract* is a clouding of the lens of the eye that obstructs light and visual sensation. *Glaucoma* is an increase of pressure within the eyeball that can result in damage and the gradual loss of vision. Both of these conditions contribute to reduced vision; however, cataracts can usually be treated with surgery and glaucoma can usually be treated with medication. It also is relatively common for older adults to lose some *visual acuity*, which is the ability to distinguish fine detail, and some people have trouble ignoring irrelevant stimuli. Visual problems sometimes result in the loss of a driver's license, which generally is a difficult adjustment.
- The brain also changes with age, declining in weight because fewer connections exist among neurons, especially in the frontal cortex. Engaging in complex cognitive tasks appears to ward off some of the neurological decline associated with aging. In addition, the lateralization of functions into left and right hemispheres declines, perhaps due to deterioration or perhaps to redirecting functions to improve mental processing efficiency.
- New brain-imaging techniques show that the brain is somewhat able to repair itself and add new neurons even later in life. However, with age, the central nervous system slows. Nevertheless, most older adults do not experience significant cognitive impairments unless dementia is involved. *Dementia* is a disorder associated with older age that includes a broad array of cognitive deficiencies, such as impaired learning and memory ability, a deterioration of language and motor functions, a progressive inability to recognize familiar people and objects, frequent confusion, and personality changes.

What are the common health problems people typically face as they move through older adulthood?

- As people age, chronic, long-term conditions become more apparent. In the United States, the most common of these are hypertension (high blood pressure), arthritis, and heart disease, although sensory impairments and type 2 diabetes are also quite common. Stress and sociocultural factors also play a role in chronic, age-related diseases.
- Older adults have slower metabolisms, and obesity becomes more common with age. Diets heavy in fat are especially problematic because they contribute to atherosclerosis. *Atherosclerosis*, or hardening of the arteries, is a common condition of aging caused by the body's increasing inability to use excess fats in the diet and it is responsible for many of the heart conditions prevalent among older people. These fats are stored along the walls of the arteries and restrict the flow of blood when they harden.

What problems are associated with drug use by the elderly today?

- The misuse of medication is common among the elderly due to inappropriate prescriptions, drug interactions, confusion over whether or not the drugs have been taken, and changes in body metabolism. The use and cost of prescription drugs has increased dramatically over the past several years.

The Causes of Aging

What theories are used to explain why people grow old and die?

- *Senescence* refers to the normal, biological processes associated with aging and excludes the effects of disease.
- *Stochastic theories of aging* (wear-and-tear theories) argue that aging results from random assaults from both internal and external environments. Free radicals, which are unstable oxygen molecules, may be involved as may other agents, such as toxins, or radiation, such as sunlight.
- *Biological clock theories of aging* argue that the pace and the process of aging are genetically programmed. One such theory suggests that chromosome tips (telomeres) become shorter with each cell division and, after dividing about 80 times, become too short for cells to reproduce, at which point they die. Another biological clock model suggests that changes in the pituitary gland or the hypothalamus may initiate a slow physiological decline. Biological clocks control other age-related processes, such as the menstrual cycle and the immune system's action.
- At present, aging processes are not well understood, although we are making progress in understanding diseases associated with aging—such as cancer, viruses, and various forms of neurological degeneration.

Cognitive Changes in Advanced Age

How do thinking and memory change as a healthy person moves through older adulthood?

- In the absence of illness, mental skills remain largely intact as we age and declines are not as great as most people assume. The major exception is the speed of cognition, which slows as we age.

- Older people do have slower reaction times, slower perceptual processing, and slower cognitive processes in general. Slower processing may be due to a variety of factors, including a general neurological decline and the use of more time-consuming mental strategies. Older people often learn to compensate for their slower cognition by learning to use more effective strategies.
- Aging affects memory processes, and it affects some memory processes more than it does others. With respect to *sensory memory*, older adults hold slightly less information and have a bit more trouble attending to important stimuli. These small declines generally cause little trouble, although they can make driving more challenging.
- The storage capacity of short-term memory changes little with age, but the speed of working memory does decrease. Thus, older adults may take longer to organize, rehearse, and encode information to be learned, although compensatory strategies can improve performance.
- Long-term memory also experiences some age-related decline, and episodic memories (for past events) are more affected by aging than are semantic memories (for factual, learned knowledge).

How do older adults compensate for brain-related declines in their cognitive processes?

- Age-related shrinkage in the brain is partially offset by an increase in brain activity, especially in the prefrontal cortex, the brain region most closely linked to executive functions. In general, age-related declines in memory are gradual and nonconsequential, unless disease processes are involved. Often such gentle declines are compensated for by experience.
- The Seattle Longitudinal Study has followed adults for over 50 years. Although cross-sectional studies show that several cognitive abilities decline throughout adulthood, longitudinal studies show little decline before age 65.
- *Wisdom*—an expert knowledge system that involves excellent judgment and advice on critical and practical life issues—generally increases with age because of accumulating life experience. Not all older adults are wise, but wisdom is rare in younger people.
- Although most older adults retain good memory and cognitive abilities, some do experience a marked decline in mental abilities. Such declines can be temporary, progressive, or intermittent, and they can range in severity.

What are the differences between normal aging and senility?

- Dementia (also called senility) refers to chronic confusion, forgetfulness, and personality changes that sometimes develop with advanced age. Dementia is not an inevitable consequence of growing old; however, for those affected, it can involve substantial impairments.
- Sometimes dementia results from environmental factors, such as poor general health, living in an unstimulating environment, or the side effects of medication. Sometimes it results from biological factors that involve damage to the brain. Ministrokes and Alzheimer's disease are two biological factors that often are associated with dementia.

How does having a stroke or ministroke, or developing Alzheimer's disease, change one's ability to move through older adulthood?

- Strokes and ministrokes are caused by obstructions in blood vessels that supply the brain, and can cause brain damage. When brain damage is minimal and temporary, such ministrokes are called transient ischemic attacks (TIAs). If enough damage occurs, the result is called multi-infarct dementia. Strokes are linked to atherosclerosis, heart problems, hypertension, and diabetes.
- Strokes are rare in comparison to the leading cause of dementia, *Alzheimer's disease,* which is the fifth leading cause of death in people age 65 and older and the sixth leading cause of death in the United States. Alzheimer's disease involves a progressive deterioration of brain cells, especially those in the cerebral cortex. As the symptoms of Alzheimer's disease progress, the deterioration of memory and other cognitive abilities occurs.
- The causes of Alzheimer's disease are presently unknown, although genetic links have been identified. Two forms of the disease have been identified—early onset and later onset. Alzheimer's disease becomes more prevalent with advancing age. Drugs have been developed that can delay the progress of symptoms, but no effective treatments or cure have been developed to date.
- Most adults effectively compensate for age-related cognitive declines. Both higher education and overall activity level are linked with less cognitive decline.

KEY TERMS

ageism (p. 442)
filial piety (p. 442)
septuagenarians (p. 446)
octogenarians (p. 446)
nonagenarians (p. 446)
pathological aging factors (p. 448)
hypertension (p. 450)
cataract (p. 450)
glaucoma (p. 450)
visual acuity (p. 450)
dementia (p. 451)
atherosclerosis (p. 453)
senescence (p. 456)
stochastic theories of aging (p. 457)
biological clock theories of aging (p. 457)
wisdom (p. 461)
stroke (p. 464)
Alzheimer's disease (p. 464)

17

OLDER ADULTHOOD
Personality and Sociocultural Development

LEARNING OBJECTIVES

- How does the status passage from middle adulthood to older adulthood differ from earlier developmental transitions?
- What did Erik Erikson mean when he identified the critical conflict of older adulthood as one of integrity versus despair?
- How do older adults adapt to and cope with the changes that come with advancing age?
- What transitions are typically experienced when an older adult retires, and what changes—good and bad—does retirement usually bring?
- How do older adults adapt to the typical changes in family structure that usually accompany this stage of the lifespan?
- How do older adults typically cope with loss?
- How is the age structure of the U.S. population changing, and what impact will this change have on society and social programs?
- What are the pros and cons associated with the two major government-supported social programs for older adults, Social Security and Medicare?
- What options are available when older adults need assistance in living, and how should families choose among them?

CHAPTER OUTLINE

Personality and Aging
- Developmental Tasks in Older Adulthood
- Emotional Development in Older Adulthood
- Continuity and Change in Older Adulthood
- Successful Aging

Retirement: A Major Change in Status
- Adjusting to Retirement
- Retirement Options

Family and Friends: Interpersonal Contexts
- When Parenting Is Over
- Caring for an Ill Spouse or Partner
- Widows and Widowers

U.S. Social Policy and Older Adulthood
- The Demographics of Aging
- Lifestyle Options for Older Adults
- Goals for the Care of Older Adults

Changes in a person's *status*—how one views oneself and others—occur throughout the lifespan. The adolescent becomes a young adult; the young adult enters middle adulthood. In each case, the person takes on enlarged roles and responsibilities, typically with gains in status and power. Such changes in role and social position are called **status passages**, and they mark each of the transitions we make from one period of the lifespan to the next.

The status passages associated with entering older adulthood, however, are quite different than those that have come before. Although becoming old can yield new freedoms and fewer burdensome responsibilities, it also is typically associated with losses—of power, of responsibility, and of autonomy.

It is important to keep in mind, however, that the events that define status passages in people's lives are often less important than the way in which each person *interprets* them. Events that seem like losses to other people may not be interpreted as losses by the older adults who experience them. For example, some people may view retirement as signaling the end of their usefulness or productiveness in the workforce, perhaps the end of a major part of their identity. Others, however, may view retirement quite differently if they have spent the last 30 to 40 years hating their job and everything about it; in this case, retirement may mean a release from tedium, drudgery, and subservience to authority. Indeed, one factor that is closely linked to adjustment to retirement is how much people have enjoyed their jobs. Retirement also can be interpreted positively if it provides an impetus to explore new activities, such as reading or gardening, that were overlooked or put off during earlier periods of life. Thus, retirement can signal the beginning of what may be the best time of a person's life—the years spent in the period of older adulthood. In this chapter, we explore the personality and sociocultural development that takes place in older adulthood, covering the topics of personality and aging, retirement, family and personal relationships, and U.S. social policies and their impact on older adults.

PERSONALITY AND AGING

Much of each person's experience with growing older depends on that individual's interpretation of events. Thus, it is easy to overgeneralize about personality, life satisfaction, and developmental tasks in later adulthood. Also, each individual, regardless of age, has a unique pattern of attitudes, values, beliefs, and specific life experiences. These unique events accumulate across the lifespan, making older adulthood a developmental period that is especially dependent on each person's earlier life experiences (Freund, Nikitin, & Ritter, 2009). These differences among individuals make generalizing about the period of older adulthood even more difficult. Furthermore, as noted previously in Chapter 16, there are significant differences between the vigorous, healthy, and recently retired young-old adult and the old-old adult who is often frail: The experience of older adulthood depends heavily on health, fitness, and which limitations, if any, are imposed by aging.

Despite the wide individual differences that typify older adulthood, there are, however, some events and concerns that are common to most people in later life. Older adulthood, like the stages of life that came before, involves adjusting and coping; it is accompanied by developmental tasks that many individuals confront and resolve. How these challenges are dealt with, plays a major role in successful aging.

Developmental Tasks in Older Adulthood

Erikson's Stage of Integrity Versus Despair According to Erik Erikson, the final developmental task that people face in older adulthood is one that focuses on **integrity versus despair** (Erikson, Erikson, & Kivnick, 1986/1994). Indeed, research suggests that this last developmental stage unfolds much as Erikson described it, with some individual variability but also with much of its structure determined by how the individual has negotiated earlier developmental stages (Sneed, Whitbourne, & Culang, 2006). According to Erikson, this final period in the lifespan is a time when people ponder about how their lives have fulfilled their earlier expectations. Those

status passages
The changes in role and social position that occur when a person enters adolescence, becomes a parent, retires, or becomes a widow or widower

integrity versus despair
According to Erikson, the final developmental task in the lifespan when people think about how their lives have fulfilled their earlier expectations

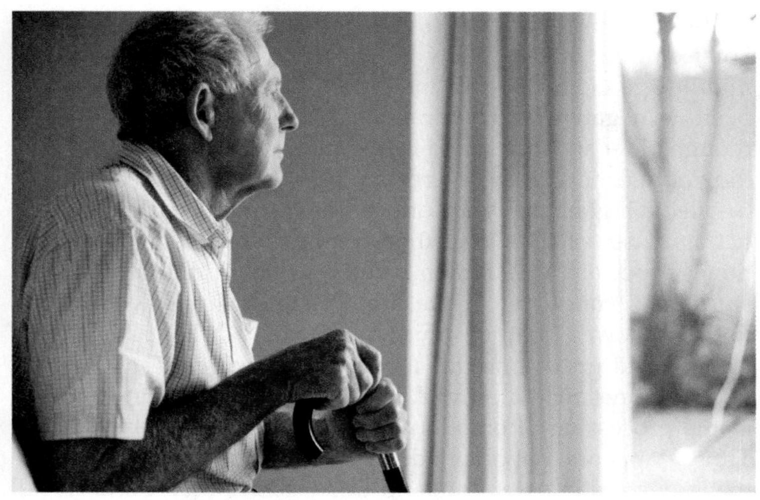

▲ Most older people must cope with a sense of their own vulnerability.

who can look back and feel satisfied that their lives have had meaning and that they have done the best they could to develop a strong sense of personal *integrity*. Those who look back and see nothing but a long succession of wrong turns, missed opportunities, and failures develop a sense of *despair*.

Do you think men and women in U.S. culture approach the tasks associated with establishing integrity in substantially similar or dissimilar ways? What factors would be important to consider in framing an answer to this question?

Part of the adjustment to older adulthood includes the psychological need to reminisce and reflect on past events. Older people often spend time searching for themes and images that give their lives meaning and coherence. Some people ruminate over what type of legacy they will leave, what contributions they have made, and how the world will remember them—whether through works of art, social service, accomplishments at work, the children they bore and raised, or the material wealth they will pass along to their children or to society. Many older adults look to their children and grandchildren as a legacy in whom traces of their own personality and values will live on.

Although younger people often think of older adulthood as depressing and empty, most older adults actually adjust quite well to this stage of life. The wisdom that people acquire with age often enables older adults to maintain dignity and an integrated self in the face of physical deterioration and even impending death. In their 60s, many older adults experience a wonderful combination of good health and freedom from work and worry. In their 70s and beyond, these same adults fine-tune their priorities and focus on what they *can* do rather than on what they cannot do any longer.

This does not mean, however, that well-adjusted older adults have no regrets; rather, their regrets are balanced against a sense that their lives have been well lived. An 85-year-old woman eloquently expressed some of the musings and expressions of minor regrets that are typical of this process:

> If I had my life to live over, I'd dare to make more mistakes next time. I'd relax. I'd limber up. I'd be sillier than I've been this trip. I'd take fewer things seriously. I'd take more chances. I'd take more trips. I'd climb more mountains and swim more rivers. I'd eat more ice cream and less beans. I'd perhaps have more actual troubles, but I'd have fewer imaginary ones. You see, I'm one of those people who lived sensibly and sanely hour after hour, day after day. Oh, I've had my moments and if I had it to do over again, I'd have more of them. In fact, I'd try to have nothing else. Just moments, one after another, instead of living so many years ahead of each day. (Burnside, 1979, p. 425)

Thus, in Erikson's view, a satisfactory resolution of the developmental tasks of older adulthood involves accepting that not everything in life has worked out as ideal, yet realizing that one's life has been of value; that is, that integrity has predominated over despair (Erikson, Erikson, & Kivnick, 1986/1994).

Maintaining Identity Establishing a sense of ego integrity while facing the challenges of older adulthood requires that individuals have a firmly established *identity*; that is, that they have a clear and consistent view of their physical, psychological, and social attributes. One way to view the process of maintaining a consistent identity emphasizes the process of adaptation, much as Jean Piaget described it (see Chapters 1 and 4). It involves *assimilating* new events and changing circumstances into one's existing self-concept and *accommodating* (changing) one's self when major life events cannot be readily assimilated.

Ideally, according to Piaget's view, people maintain a balance between assimilation and accommodation. Refusal to accommodate may mean that the person is denying reality. Such a person may be defensive, rigid, and may unjustifiably blame other people. On the other hand, accommodating too readily can make a person hysterical, impulsive, or hypersensitive. Maintaining a balance between protecting the consistency of one's identity, yet remaining open to new experiences, is an important developmental task of older adulthood, just as it is in earlier periods of the lifespan (Whitbourne & Connolly, 1999; Whitbourne & Whitbourne, 2011).

Why might a shift in focus from present functioning to past accomplishments be a healthy adjustment for adults nearing the end of life?

For the very old, maintaining a sense of consistency in personal identity may be particularly important. In one study of over 600 people, mostly in their 70s and 80s, who had experienced major changes in their health and living arrangements, researchers found that accommodating was an enormously difficult task, especially for those who were frail and highly dependent on others (Lieberman & Tobin, 1983). Those who were most successful in adapting managed to do so by maintaining and validating their identities. Despite adversity, they were able to say, "I am who I have always been." How were they able to do this when faced with very real shifts in their lives and in their physical abilities? Generally, they shifted from thinking about the present to thinking about the past. For example, one woman first described herself by saying, "I am important to my family and friends; you should see how many birthday cards I got." Two years later, after some major changes in her life, she instead defined herself by saying, "I think I am important to my family; I have always done the best I could for my family, and they appreciate it." Thus, she maintained a concept of her present personal identity that was consistent with the person she used to be (Ruth & Coleman, 1996).

Emotional Development in Older Adulthood

Stereotypical views of old age often depict the older adult's emotional and social world as one of narrowness and emptiness. Research, however, suggests the opposite (Sneed & Whitbourne, 2005; Weir, Meisner, & Baker, 2010). This life stage is usually experienced as one of continued emotional growth. If well-being declines at all, it generally does so only in the period immediately preceding a person's death, or when cognitive and physical problems seriously impact a person's critical areas of functioning (Baltes, 1998; Grühn, Gilet, Studer, & Labouvie-Vief, 2011).

During the majority of older adulthood most older people experience more satisfaction with their interpersonal relationships than they have throughout their earlier lives (Orth, Robins, & Widaman, 2012). Their awareness of the fragility of human life often leads older adults to make greater investments in emotionally close relationships. Although they may reduce the number of acquaintance relationships they maintain, older adults often focus on deepening those connections that they find meaningful; they may not maintain as many relationships, but the ones they keep do not diminish in intensity (Charles & Carstensen, 2007, 2010). Furthermore, this preference for narrowing social networks to focus on particularly meaningful relationships is seen across cultures. For example, researchers in one study found that older people in Hong Kong showed a greater preference for familiar social partners than did younger people (Fung, Carstensen, & Lutz, 1999).

Emotional adjustment in older adulthood is generally positive. Indeed, the ability to regulate emotions generally is spared from age-related decline and is perhaps enhanced with advancing old age (Carstensen & Mikels, 2005; Holahan & Velasquez, 2011). For example, older adults show no reduction in their capacity to feel positive emotions, such as happiness and joy (Lawton, Parmelee, Katz, & Nesselroade, 1996); in addition, negative emotions surface less frequently than they previously did. In studies across cultures, older adults consistently reported fewer mood swings, less agitation, and a greater ability to control their emotions than did young adults, which contributes to a greater sense of well-being (Gross et al., 1997).

Interestingly, emotional information seems resistant to age-related decline (Carstensen & Mikels, 2005). Although working memory functions decline somewhat with advancing age (see Chapter 16), when the content to be remembered involves emotional information, no such age-related decrement occurs (Charles & Carstensen, 2007). Furthermore, older adults seem to attend more to positive information than negative information, and they remember positive information better as well. This well-documented finding is referred to as the *positivity effect*. For example, in one study, groups of younger (ages 18–29), middle-aged (ages 41–53), and older (ages 65–85) adults viewed positive, negative, and neutral images on a computer screen. Although older adults recalled fewer images of all three types than did younger adults, the interesting finding was that older adults recalled a higher *proportion* of positive images (Charles, Mather, & Carstensen, 2003). To further examine why positive information is especially well remembered by older adults, a follow-up study was conducted while brain-imaging scans were taken. Results showed that, relative to younger adults, older adults experienced greater neural activation for positive images than negative ones in the amygdala, an area in the brain involved in the processing of emotional responses (Mather et al., 2004). Thus, it appears that older adults pay more attention to positive than negative information, and this leads to their better recall (Goeleven, De Raedt, & Dierckx, 2010). They also are able to distance themselves from feelings of regret over missed opportunities (Brassen, Garner, Peters, Gluth, & Büchel, 2012), and this, too, contributes to a more positive adjustment in older adulthood. Thus, the positivity effect seems to be the result of goal-directed memory processes that allow the older individual to allocate attention and shape memory in ways that preserve, and even enhance, well-being.

As people grow older, their sense that time is fleeting usually deepens and makes for more complex emotionality, in which sadness may be a significant component. For example, each visit with an intimate friend may be pervaded by a sense that this may be one of the last occasions to be together. The rich mix of sadness and joy that results from this kind of awareness often causes older people to report that life has never been better (Carstensen & Charles, 1998; Charles & Cartensen, 2010). As they approach older adulthood, individuals become better able to negotiate the conflicts between what they believe they should do and what they want to do. This, too, contributes to a greater sense of well-being (Riediger & Freund, 2008). Thus, the view that the majority of older adults spend their later years in sadness and despair is not the typical pattern. Instead, despite the fact that older adults must confront loss, they most often remain emotionally well adjusted and are often happier and more satisfied than they were in previous periods of their lives.

Continuity and Change in Older Adulthood

As we have seen in earlier chapters, most contemporary theorists tend to see development as a lifelong phenomenon; thus, adjustment to older adulthood rests on personality styles that developed earlier in life. Theorists differ, however, on the balance they assign to continuity versus change, with some placing a greater emphasis on change and others placing a greater emphasis on continuity.

For example, *stage* theorists believe that new life structures or organizations emerge in older adulthood, although they are built on earlier stages. For example, Daniel Levinson (1978, 1986, 1996) believed there is a period of transition during ages 60 to 65 that links a person's previous life structure to that of late adulthood; thus, Levinson argued that older adulthood is *different* from earlier stages and is not just an extension of what has come before. Likewise, Erik Erikson and his colleagues saw the emergence of ego integrity (or its counterpart, despair) as comprising a discreet stage that was separate from earlier developmental periods (Erikson, Erikson, & Kivnick, 1986).

Other theorists emphasize the role of smaller, continuous adjustments as people respond to aging. For example, Robert Atchley (1999; Atchley & Barusch, 2004) suggested that *continuity* provides people with an identity, a sense of who they are. Continuity enables people to say things like "I would never do that" or "That's just like me" with confidence. People strive to be consistent in their behavior because it makes them feel more secure. In addition, other people expect us to be consistent, and they often become uncomfortable if we seem unpredictable. Atchley was quick to emphasize, however, that continuity does not mean that there are no changes at all. People's roles, abilities, and relationships all change; and people do make corresponding alterations in their behaviors, their expectations, and even their values. However, according to Atchley's view, these changes generally are not abrupt; rather, they are consistent with the *inner core* that we use to define ourselves.

Continuity and Change in Personality Although the core of personality does appear to be largely established by early adulthood, as noted in Chapter 15, some adults nevertheless do undergo changes in their basic personality traits as they respond to their changing circumstances. When considering how personality adjusts as adults move through older adulthood, there is evidence of both continuity and change (Ryff, 2008). For example, many studies support the view that personality dimensions remain largely consistent throughout older adulthood (Allemand & Gomez, 2010; Terracciano, McCrae, & Costa, 2010). Even the oldest old have organized, coherent, integrated patterns or beliefs about themselves (Troll & Skaff, 1997), and they tend to act in ways that are consistent with their self-image. Furthermore, when they are able to judge themselves as having acted in accordance with their self-concept despite major life changes, the majority of the oldest old express more life satisfaction and self-esteem (Charles & Carstensen, 2010). Consistent with this positive view of life is the finding that emotional stability generally increases as adults enter the period of older adulthood, especially among older women (Caprara, Caprara, & Steca, 2003; Zimprich, Allemand, & Lachman, 2012).

Thus, the negative stereotype of older adulthood as a time of despair and futility does not correspond to the actuality of life for most older people. In fact, well-being in adulthood is linked to several facets of life. Carol Ryff and her colleagues have suggested a six-component model that lays out the qualities that are most closely associated with positive development throughout adulthood (see Table 17-1; Ryff, 1995; Ryff & Singer, 2006). Some of these components appear to increase and others to decrease as adults grow older (see the box Current Issues: Psychological Well-Being in Later Adulthood).

Table 17-1 Six Components of Well-Being in Adulthood

Dimension	Characteristics of a High Scorer	Characteristics of a Low Scorer
Self-acceptance	• Possesses positive attitude toward self • Acknowledges and accepts multiple aspects of self, including good and bad qualities • Feels positive about past life	• Feels dissatisfied with self • Is disappointed with what has occurred in past life • Is troubled about certain personal qualities • Wishes to be different than what he or she is
Positive relations with other people	• Has warm, satisfying, trusting relationships with others • Is concerned about the welfare of others • Is capable of strong empathy, affection, and intimacy • Understands the give-and-take of human relationships	• Has few close, trusting relationships with others • Finds it difficult to be warm, open, and concerned about others • Is isolated and frustrated in interpersonal relationships • Is not willing to make compromises to sustain important ties with others
Autonomy	• Is self-determining and independent • Is able to resist social pressures to think and act in certain ways • Regulates behavior from within • Evaluates self by personal standards	• Is concerned about the expectations and evaluations of others • Relies on judgments of others to make important decisions • Conforms to social pressures to think and act in certain ways
Environmental mastery	• Has a sense of mastery and competence in managing the environment • Controls a complex array of external activities • Makes effective use of surrounding opportunities • Is able to choose or create contexts suitable to personal needs and values	• Has difficulty managing everyday affairs • Feels unable to change or to improve surrounding context • Is unaware of surrounding opportunities • Lacks a sense of control over the external world
Purpose in life	• Has goals in life and a sense of direction • Feels there is meaning to present and past life • Holds beliefs that give life purpose • Has aims and objectives for living	• Lacks a sense of meaning in life • Has few goals or aims and lacks a sense of direction • Does not see a purpose in past life • Has no outlooks or beliefs that give life meaning
Personal growth	• Has a feeling of continued development • Sees self as growing and expanding • Is open to new experiences • Has a sense of realizing own potential • Sees improvement in self and behavior over time • Is changing in ways that reflect more self-knowledge and effectiveness	• Has a sense of personal stagnation • Lacks a sense of improvement or expansion over time • Feels bored and uninterested with life • Feels unable to develop new attitudes or behaviors

SOURCE: Adapted from "Psychological well-being in adult life," by C. D. Ryff, 1995, *Current Directions in Psychological Science, 4*, 99–104.

CURRENT ISSUES

Psychological Well-Being in Later Adulthood

When we consider psychological well-being, it is often easier to define and study the negative aspects of people's functioning, such as depression, anxiety, or other psychological problems (Ryff, 1995). Most personality theories, however, focus on *positive* adjustment, such as self-actualization, coping mechanisms, and happiness. Drawing from a number of developmental theorists, such as Erikson, Jung, Rogers, Neugarten, Birren, and many others, Carol Ryff has constructed a model of psychological well-being that focuses on these positive factors of personality.

According to Ryff, well-being is not just the absence of illness or stress; rather, it is the presence of several positive qualities, attitudes, and coping methods. Ryff's model goes beyond ideas such as *happiness* and *life satisfaction,* which have been studied extensively but often seem superficial as a means of capturing the challenges and adjustments of older adults. Ryff argues that well-being can be conceptualized by considering six components: self-acceptance, positive relations with other people, autonomy, environmental mastery, purpose in life, and personal growth (Ryff, 1995; Ryff & Singer, 2006; refer to Table 17-1).

Theories that address global concepts like *well-being,* such as Ryff's, often make intuitive sense, but the question remains if they accurately capture the core concepts that adults actually experience. To study the validity of her theory, Ryff and colleagues have developed measures of each of these six components and have studied the responses of adults in over 22 countries and among several racial and ethnic groups (e.g., Brim, Ryff, & Kessler, 2004). One such large-scale study is the Midlife in the United States (MIDUS) project (described in Chapter 14). In the MIDUS project, the focus of study was on adults in middle age; however, younger and older cohorts were included to provide a context for understanding midlife issues. Because the study was constructed to include multiple representative subgroups in the U.S. population, data allow for comparisons among various racial and ethnic minorities, as well as among adults in different age categories.

Perhaps the most interesting of the MIDUS project's cross-cultural findings is that members of U.S. racial minorities generally scored *higher* in well-being than did Whites. Furthermore, this positive advantage remained even when such factors as education, socioeconomic background, and perceived discrimination were taken in account (Brim, Ryff, & Kessler, 2004; Ryff & Singer, 2008). These results suggest that certain aspects of well-being, such as self-acceptance, environmental mastery, and personal growth, may be developed by coping through adversity. Furthermore, these results support the view that "the presence of the negative in the lives of oppressed groups does not automatically imply an absence of the positive" (Brim et al., 2004, p. 418).

With respect to the development of well-being in older adulthood, it appears that some factors of well-being increase with age, whereas other factors may diminish for most people (Brim et al., 2004; Friedman & Ryff, 2012). For example, young adults generally scored higher in personal growth and purpose—components that seem to decline with age. On the other hand, older adults generally scored higher on environmental mastery measures than did young and middle-aged adults. Older and middle-aged adults also scored higher than young adults on autonomy measures in many of the subsamples included in this study. Among Mexican Americans living in Chicago and Blacks living in New York, older adults scored higher on positive relations with others as well, although this result was not found among White adults in the study. In most groups, measures of self-acceptance did not vary significantly by age.

Data from extensive large-scale studies, such as the MIDUS project, help us understand more accurately the typical development of large numbers of individuals. However, it is important to remember that not all people conform to the findings that these data suggest. Certainly, the life experiences of individuals play a large role in how they experience such complex psychological constructs as well-being (Friedman & Ryff, 2012). For example, it may be difficult to experience environmental mastery if a person is a poor, immigrant woman who must struggle to simply survive; an older man who is immobilized by a stoke may find it difficult to retain a strong sense of autonomy. Yet, over time, most individuals do adapt, and such adjustments may be important to psychological well-being in adulthood (Ryff, 2008; von Faber et al., 2001). Although culture undoubtedly plays a role in how we experience life, basic psychological processes extend across culture and often shape the unfolding aspects of personality development in important ways.

Yet, all adults do not develop in the same ways. Well-being, self-concept, and other psychological variables reflect how adults experience and manage major life changes throughout the lifespan, and they are influenced by critical events that occur in earlier developmental periods (Friedman & Ryff, 2012; Ryff, Kwan, & Singer, 2001). Especially important are the person's health, finances, and adjustment to retirement, all of which can have an important impact on how individuals change as they move into older adulthood (Allemand, Zimprich, & Hertzog, 2007). Furthermore, life events such as these sometimes affect a particular aspect of personality, while other personal characteristics remain unaffected. For example, many people, especially men, become more introverted as they age (Costa & McCrae, 1989); however other personality characteristics, such as agreeableness and openness to experience, generally increase or remain consistent throughout adulthood and old age (McCrae & Costa, 2006; Zimprich, Allemand, & Lachman, 2012). Perhaps it is not surprising that as older adults adjust to major events in their lives, both continuity and change are reflected in their overall view of themselves.

Coping Styles As adults experience the formidable changes that often come with advanced age, they develop coping strategies that allow them to deal effectively with these changes. Not surprisingly, coping styles appear to become increasingly mature as we grow older and gain experience in how best to confront and resolve problems.

Can you suggest a specific example from your own experience that demonstrates an older adult's use of a passive, emotion-focused style of coping?

For example, some researchers have found that older adults tend to be more passive and focused on emotions, whereas younger adults are more likely to use active coping styles that focus on specific problems (Aldwin, 2011; Martin,

Brooks-Gunn, Klebanov, Buka, & McCormick, 2008). For instance, an older woman might downplay the importance of the traffic accident she just had or might view it in a more positive light by saying "I really needed to get rid of that car anyway" or "At least no one was injured." A younger woman might instead handle the situation by confronting the other driver, getting the other driver's name and address, contacting the insurance company, and getting estimates to repair the damage. Older adults also are more likely to use humor and be accepting when they are faced with setbacks in their life (Vaillant, 2002).

Gender differences also emerge when coping styles are examined across adulthood, although coping styles vary somewhat depending on what the individual is coping with (Brennan, Holland, Schutte, & Moos, 2012). In general, women tend to express more emotion when coping and may also cope less effectively (Kato & Pedersen, 2005). Coping strategies may become more androgynous in older adulthood, however; that is, older men tend to become more passive whereas older women become more aggressive and domineering (Gutmann, 1994). Gender differences, of course, reflect the cultural context in which development occurs, and some cultural differences in the ways older adults cope have been identified (Conway, Magai, & Milano, 2010). However, differences in coping mostly reflect the particular circumstances of each individual's life, and in general most older adults cope with stresses in fairly generic ways.

In summary, adjustments in later life are often very similar to the adjustments that occur in earlier life. People develop an identity; in so doing, they create consistent themes that they carry with them through life. When people reach old age, their reactions to aging and to new situations will be highly individual; however, personal adjustments to aging most often will reflect the core identity that has guided each individual's personality development throughout earlier periods of the lifespan.

Successful Aging

Eventually, older adults must confront the many problems of aging. For example, the longer individuals live, the more likely they are to experience the death of their friends and family members, including their partner or spouse. For a few older adults, the problems that result from aging are overwhelming; in response, these people become preoccupied with their health, loneliness, restricted circumstances, hardships, and increasing lack of autonomy. Despite the challenging nature of their circumstances, however, the majority of older adults perceive themselves in quite positive ways. In a national survey of older Americans in 2010, nearly three-quarters of adults age 65 and older rated their health and well-being as good to excellent (Federal Interagency Forum on Aging-Related Statistics [FIFARS], 2010g), although significant differences emerged among White, Black, and Hispanic Americans (see Figure 17-1).

When researchers tried to determine why many older people maintain a positive outlook despite their failing health and declining abilities, they found that *social comparison* played a crucial role (Yin et al., 2011; see Chapter 11). When people use social comparison, they evaluate themselves and their own situation against the experiences of others they perceive to be similar. One way older adults do this is to compare themselves to middle-aged, rather than older, adults. For example, in a study in which older adults were first confronted with negative age-related information, and then asked to look at pictures of adults of various ages, they tended to look away from pictures of older adults and look longer at pictures of middle-aged adults (Weiss & Freund, 2012). Another social comparison strategy is to compare oneself to others of the same age but with poorer life quality. For example, a woman with failing eyesight who

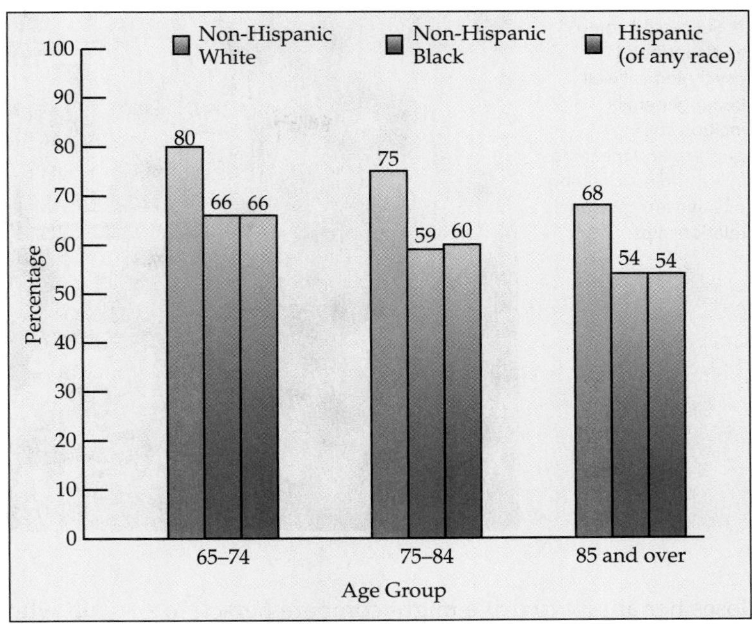

FIGURE 17-1 Percentage of People Age 65 and over Who Reported Having Good to Excellent Health, by Age Group and Racial/Ethnic Group

NOTE: Data are for 2008.

SOURCE: From *Older Americans 2010: Key indicators of well-being*, Federal Interagency Forum on Aging-Related Statistics, July 2010, Washington, DC: U.S. Government Printing Office.

There is great diversity among older people, with many adopting active lifestyles.

Watch *Getting Old* on **MyDevelopmentLab**

Successful aging and continued psychological well-being generally include finding purpose and meaning in life and maintaining positive interpersonal relationships.

loses her ability to drive might compare herself to a friend who is in a wheelchair and must lead an even more restricted life. When older adults are able to make social comparisons with those who are worse off than themselves, their mental health is generally better, even when they are faced with severe physical problems. In one study, the women who were in poorest health showed the strongest effects of social comparison and achieved a degree of psychological adaptation comparable to that of healthy women—they came to perceive themselves as better off than they actually were (Bauer, Wrosch, & Jobin, 2008). When social comparison is combined with the ability to maintain personal relationships and a meaningful life, people generally are able to minimize their psychological distress, to maintain their sense of well-being, and to successfully confront the negative effects of poor physical health.

Health, of course, is not the only factor that determines satisfaction in older adulthood, although it is the most important. Money, social class, marital status, adequacy of housing, amount of social interaction, and even transportation are also important factors that influence whether older adults feel satisfied with their lives. Interestingly, age itself bears little relationship to happiness in old age.

As people grow older, however, their satisfaction with life may change. Younger adults, for example, gain the most satisfaction from their achievements and advances in work, self-development, and other aspects of their lives. Older adults tend to define psychological well-being in terms of an "other" orientation—being a caring, compassionate person and having good relationships with others that lead to satisfaction with one's own life. Older adults also point to the acceptance of change as an important quality of positive functioning; they tend to focus less on striving for gains and more on maintaining current functions and preventing losses (Ebner, Freund, & Baltes, 2006). In addition, many older adults look to religion and an extended social network of friends for support and validation. Especially for adults who lack economic resources, friends and family, and a reliance on their church, can provide substantial support during the later years (Blazer & Meador, 2010; Klemmack et al., 2007).

Successful aging also involves maintaining physical and cognitive functioning, and staying engaged in social and productive activities is especially important (Freund & Baltes, 2007; Whitbourne & Whitbourne, 2011). Maintaining a regular schedule of physical activities, such as walking, has many positive benefits, including better cognitive functioning and a stronger sense of self-efficacy (Deary, Whalley, Batty, & Starr, 2006; Rejeski et al., 2008). Also, participating in activities that the person is good at and actively compensating for any physical or mental decline are important coping responses (see Chapter 16). Keeping a positive attitude and emphasizing the advantages over the difficulties that a person experiences also are keys to good adjustment. However, regardless of how positive a person is about becoming old, older adulthood does require major life adjustments. For most people, one task is to successfully make the transition from work to retirement, which we explore in the next section.

REVIEW THE FACTS 17-1

1. How is the transition to older adulthood different from the transitions between earlier stages in life?
2. Erik Erikson saw the final developmental task of older adulthood as one that involves ________ versus ________.
3. In older adulthood, do people tend to have fewer friends or more friends than they did in early adulthood?
4. Theories that emphasize the differences that exist between different periods of the lifespan are often referred to as ________.
   a. stage theories
   b. consistency theories
   c. theories of accommodation
   d. lifespan models
5. If James copes by convincing himself that his ailments are not as bad as Andre's ailments, he is using a strategy called ________.
6. The most important factor in determining satisfaction in older adulthood is a person's ________.
   a. financial situation
   b. gender
   c. age
   d. health

Practice on **MyDevelopmentLab**

RETIREMENT: A MAJOR CHANGE IN STATUS

Retirement requires different adjustments for different people, depending on the circumstances that surround what retirement means to the individual. In traditional families, where the father holds a paying job and the mother assumes child-rearing responsibilities and household duties, retirement often affects men and women differently. Men suddenly have much more leisure time; women experience a substantial reduction in their autonomy, at least in those activities that fall into the 9-to-5 workday schedule. Today, changing roles for many women and men are blurring these gender-based distinctions; however, regardless of a person's work status, retirement implies substantial change.

Regardless of how an older person experiences retirement—whether as the retiring worker or the spouse, or as a choice that is eagerly anticipated or one that is dreaded or unexpected—retirement typically is the most significant status change of later adulthood. However, fewer adults today are retiring from work at the traditional ages of 62 or 65; complete retirement at this traditional point in the lifespan seems to have peaked in the 1980s or early 1990s. For example, in 1985, only 24% of men over the age of 65 remained in the U.S. labor force; by 2008 this percentage had increased to 36% (FIFARS, 2010e). One significant factor that is contributing to delayed retirement for many older adults today is the economy. Whereas adults who retired in previous decades could count on earnings of perhaps 5 to 8% on their invested retirement savings, in 2012 interest rates were much lower—perhaps on the order of 1 to 2%, depending on investments. Even a substantial retirement savings account today does not generate enough annual income to support the lifestyle that would have been attainable a decade ago. Thus, difficult economic circumstances may require additional years at work. Also, longer lifespans and better health and fitness for many older adults allow many older people to select from a wider range of retirement choices, although about a third of older adults still choose to retire in the traditional sense—that is, to quit working entirely at around age 65.

However retirement occurs, it involves much more adaptation than just dealing with greatly increased free time. Because work establishes a context for many important social relationships and is usually an important component of an individual's personal identity, retirement often requires considerable adjustments.

Although retirement is a significant event that marks the beginning of a new stage of life for most people, it actually is a process, requiring a series of adaptations. One view of how these events typically occur has been proposed by Robert Atchley (2003; Atchley & Barusch, 2004), who has outlined six distinct stages that most people go through as they leave the workforce and enter full retirement (see Table 17-2). Throughout these stages, retirees must work out choices, negotiations, and coping patterns consistent with their personal identity. How easily the individual adapts to the new role of retirement depends on a number of factors. If the shift to retirement is sudden and dramatic, if the person's standard of living is compromised, or if an individual's identity has been closely tied to an occupational role, the transition may be very difficult.

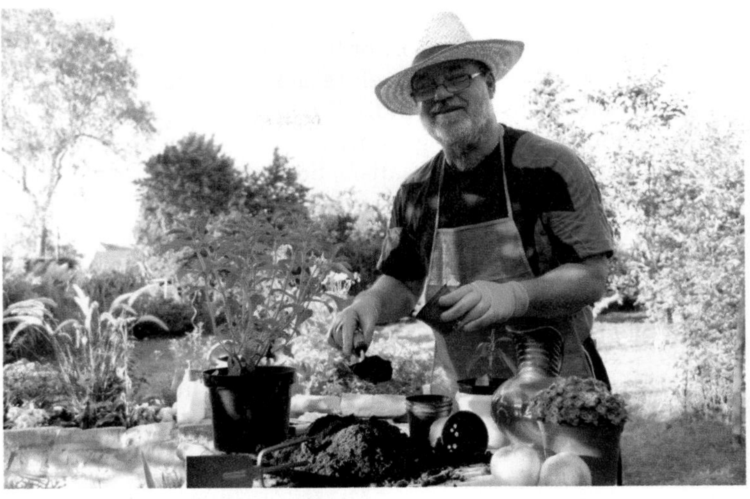

▲ Of those who retire, healthy people generally fare better psychologically than those who must retire because of poor health.

Adjusting to Retirement

Several factors exert an important influence on how a person experiences the transition to retirement. One factor is the person's lifelong *attitude toward work*. In some segments of the United States, there is an almost religious devotion to work. Many people have invested so much time and energy in their

Table 17-2 Six Stages of Retirement as Outlined by Robert Atchley

Stage	Characteristics
Phase 1: Pre-retirement	• Occurs before retirement actually begins • Involves considerable planning, especially about financial matters

Phase 2: Retirement	• Usually involves one of three paths:
	  • feeling like one is on indefinite vacation, with lots of fun activities planned
	  • taking life easy, with little activity, lots of rest, and a feeling of relief from work stress
	  • easily falling into a comfortable retirement routine and schedule

Phase 3: Disenchantment	• Some, but not all, people experience feelings of loss, or miss their work colleagues and structure • Disenchantment is more likely if unexpected events change retirement plans (e.g., death of a spouse, serious illness, loss of income)
Phase 4: Reorientation	• After a period of adjustment, people usually reestablish a routine that better fits their preferences, activity level, and values
Phase 5: Retirement Routine	• This stage involves settling into a comfortable, rewarding routine of activities, which may be maintained for many years • Establishing a satisfying retirement routine can occur shortly after retirement, or may take much longer to develop
Phase 6: Termination of Retirement	• The comfortable and rewarding retirement routine may end if the person becomes unable to carry out satisfying and enjoyable activities due to ill health or other limiting circumstances • If retirement routine is terminated, then a "disabled elder" status typically takes its place

SOURCE: *Continuity and adaptation in aging: Creating positive experiences*, by R. C. Atchley, 1999, Baltimore, MD: Johns Hopkins University Press; and *Social forces and aging: An introduction to social gerontology*, by R. C. Atchley & A. S. Barusch, 2004, Baltimore, MD: Wadsworth.

jobs that their overall sense of self-worth and self-esteem depends on the work they do. For these people, leisure activities often seem superficial and therefore lack meaning. In a very real sense, retirement for these individuals means stepping out of their previous lives. Disengagement is especially hard for people who have never found satisfaction outside of their jobs in the form of hobbies, reading, continued education, or involvement in civic organizations. The problem tends to be worse for people who are less educated, who are financially strained, and who are involved with few social or political outlets; however, professionals or business executives may also have difficulty finding something to do with their greatly increased leisure time. This is one reason why today a substantial number of people—perhaps as many as half—continue to work part-time or return to work after retiring (FIFARS, 2010e).

Economic status is another major factor that affects a retiree's adjustment to a new way of life. Although very few people experience an increase in their economic standard of living when they retire, most older adults in the United States have sufficient financial assets with which to live. In terms of net worth, older adults tend to be wealthier than younger adults. Still, about 10% of adults ages 65 or older live below the poverty line (FIFARS, 2010a), and about two-thirds of retired U.S. adults ages 65 and over rely on Social Security benefits as a significant source of income. For nearly 40% of retirees, Social Security benefits are virtually their only source of income (FIFARS, 2010a).

The fact that most retired adults can survive economically, however, masks the circumstances of certain subgroups of older adults. For example, older women are more likely than are older men to be poor: In 2008, 12% of older women lived in poverty, compared to 7% of older men. Those suffering the discrimination that typically comes with being both female and a member of a minority group are the most likely to be poor: 27% of older African-American women are impoverished, as are 20% of older Hispanic women (FIFARS, 2010a).

Part of the reason that women experience more poverty in retirement is that they often have worked for lower wages; therefore, they receive lower Social Security benefits than people who had higher levels of income during their working years. Women also generally have accumulated less savings to fall back on in times of need. Furthermore, on average, women live longer than men do; therefore, the money they have must last for a longer period.

What factors might support a conclusion that retirement is harder for men than women? What factors would support the conclusion that retirement is harder for women than men?

Not surprisingly, a third factor that influences how a person experiences retirement is *health*. For example, one study of a large group of men who were about to retire found that healthy men who wanted to retire fared best (Richardson, 1999). Those in ill health fared poorly, whether they wanted to retire or not. This may be because retirement frequently occurs more suddenly for people in ill health (Brockman, Müller, & Helmert, 2009); therefore, they may be less prepared financially and psychologically than those who have time to anticipate and plan for their retirement. In addition, good health allows the retiree broader participation in postretirement activities and perhaps a more hopeful and positive outlook about the years ahead.

Watch *Transitioning to Retirement: Mary and George* on **MyDevelopmentLab**

Retirement Options

Complete withdrawal from the workforce, of course, is not the only option for people in later adulthood. Although formerly there was little or no financial incentive for older workers to remain in the labor force, changes in Social Security and other pension regulations have made it advantageous for older people to continue to work either full- or part-time. Consequently, some older adults continue to work at their same jobs, but for fewer hours per week, or perhaps with more vacation time. Others prefer to work part-time; still others change jobs so that they are working in situations that are more enjoyable or more flexible (Sterns & Chang, 2010). For example, retired businesspeople have been hired to train young and inexperienced workers, and older people have been trained to work with children with disabilities. When such flexible options have been tried as pilot programs, they generally have been remarkably successful. If health or mobility are issues, in some cases older adults can work from home.

Retirement options, of course, are heavily influenced by historical and social contexts. Consequently, retirement patterns have shifted—sometimes quite substantially—over the past few decades. For example, in 1950, about 50% of all men over age 65 were still working; however, in the 1980s and early 1990s, only about 12% of this age group still held a job or were looking for work (Kaye, Lord, & Sherrid, 1995; Sterns & Gray, 1999). In the last decade or so, the percentage of older workers has increased over rates in the 1980s and 1990s: In 2008, 36% of men and 26% of women ages 65 through 69 were still in the labor force (FIFARS, 2010e). These rates drop off dramatically, however, after age 70 (see Figure 17-2).

Are you concerned that Social Security may be underfunded to the extent that retirement benefits may not be available when today's young adults reach retirement age? What solutions do you see for this potential problem?

Regardless of when they retire, careful financial planning before retirement is important to guarantee older adults an adequate source of income in retirement. If current economic trends continue (in which interest rates and investment returns remain low), fewer people may have the option of working only part-time or of taking early retirement in the years to come. Many experts predict that a large proportion of the 76 million baby boomers (those people born between 1946 and 1964) will be forced to continue working to age 70 and beyond because they

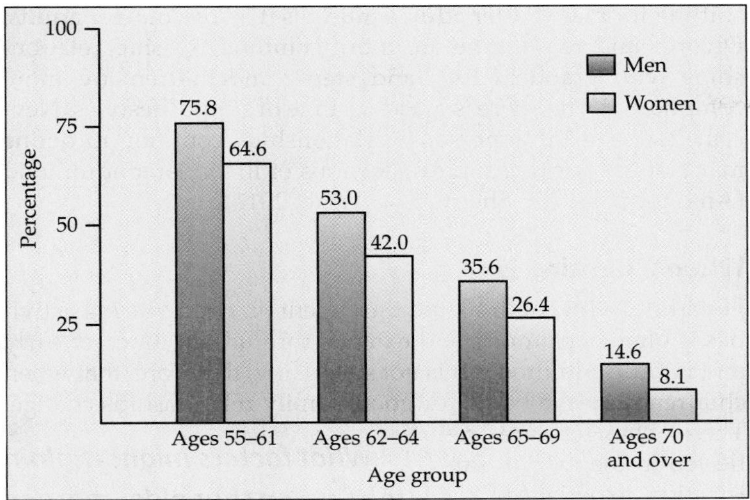

FIGURE 17-2 Percentage of Older Men and Women in the U.S. Labor Force by Age Group and Gender, 2006

NOTE: Data are for 2008.

SOURCE: From *Older Americans 2010: Key indicators of well-being*, Federal Interagency Forum on Aging-Related Statistics, July 2010, Washington, DC: U.S. Government Printing Office.

▲ Many recently retired people become involved in community or political activities during their new leisure time.

will not have sufficient funds to retire. Limited access to health insurance coverage, higher levels of educational attainment, and lower rates of personal savings in pension funds are all accelerating this trend toward delayed retirement (Mermin, Johnson, & Murphy, 2007). The government's decision to raise the minimum age for Social Security retirement benefits (see Table 17-3), the uncertain future of the Social Security system, increasing life expectancy, dramatically accelerating costs of health and nursing home care, and the notoriously poor rate of savings by baby boomers are also contributing factors (Kaye, Lord, & Sherrid, 1995).

However, financial pressures are not the only reason that retirement statistics are shifting. Another factor for the shift in retirement patterns is that more options are now available for older adults, and trends are occurring in a couple of directions at once. On the one hand, many people are retiring earlier, making a clear choice to take a break or perhaps to change careers. Others, however, are working longer (perhaps due to financial necessity) or are remaining active as volunteers in work-related ways for causes that they deem worthwhile, such as volunteering

Table 17-3 Social Security Retirement Benefits Schedule

The Social Security Administration is raising the age at which Americans can receive their retirement benefits. Here is a look at how the changes will affect recipients.

If You Were Born in:	You Will Turn Age 62 in:	The Percentage of Benefits You Receive if You Retire Then Is:	To Collect 100% of Your Benefits, You Need to Retire When You Turn:
1937 or before	1999 or before	80%	65 years
1938	2000	79 1/6%	65 years, 2 months
1939	2001	78 1/3%	65 years, 4 months
1940	2002	77 1/2%	65 years, 6 months
1941	2003	76 2/3%	65 years, 8 months
1942	2004	75 5/6%	65 years, 10 months
1943 to 1954	2005 to 2016	75%	66 years
1955	2017	74 1/6%	66 years, 2 months
1956	2018	73 1/3%	66 years, 4 months
1957	2019	71 1/2%	66 years, 6 months
1958	2020	71 2/3%	66 years, 8 months
1959	2021	70 5/6%	66 years, 10 months
1960 or later	2022 or later	70%	67 years

SOURCES: From "Waiting longer for Social Security," by A. A. Love, *Terre-Haute Tribune Star*, 1999, November 30; and "Retirement planner: Full retirement age," retrieved from http://www.ssa.gov/pubs/10035.html#retirement.

for Habitat for Humanity, volunteer counseling, or tutoring and mentoring young people. Thus, the options for many older adults are expanding (Sheaks, 2007; Vickerstaff & Cox, 2005).

Despite the dramatic changes retirement usually implies, most people adjust positively. In fact, about a third of retirees report an improvement in their mental and physical health in the period immediately after retirement; another 50% report no change. Overall, many recent retirees experience an increase in life satisfaction (Sterns & Chang, 2010; Sterns & Gray, 1999). As noted previously, the adjustment to retirement also is easier when people are prepared (Choi, 2001). Some companies provide retirement counselors who can guide people through the process and help them determine the best time to retire. Several specific factors are considered, such as how long the potential retiree has worked and if the retiree has adequate savings, income, a place to live, and plans for further work or activities after retirement. Some retirement counselors refer to the answers to these considerations as an index of **retirement maturity**—how prepared a person is to retire. In general, people with a higher degree of retirement maturity have better attitudes toward retirement and an easier time adjusting to it. Adjustment to retirement is also conditioned by the quality of family and personal relationships, which are topics we address in the next section.

REVIEW THE FACTS 17-2

1. About what percentage of U.S. adults today choose to *retire* in the traditional sense?
   a. 10% b. 33%
   c. 50% d. 67%
2. Do older adults tend to be less wealthy or wealthier than younger adults are?
3. Who is more likely to be poor, older men or older women?
4. In comparison to retirement rates in the 1980s and 1990s, the current percentage of adults ages 65 through 69 who are continuing to work has ________.
   a. decreased
   b. remained steady
   c. increased
5. The degree to which a person is ready to retire is reflected in an index called ________.

Practice on **MyDevelopmentLab**

FAMILY AND FRIENDS: INTERPERSONAL CONTEXTS

Just as retirement requires an adjustment for older adults who must find new ways of defining themselves and spending their time, when family structures change—whether through death, divorce, remarriage, or changed relationships with other close family members—older adults must adjust accordingly.

As in any period of the lifespan, the social context of family and personal relationships helps define our roles, responsibilities, and life satisfactions. In today's world, this social context is shifting for many older adults, much as it is for younger adults. Divorce and remarriage are more common, kinship relationships with grandchildren and step-grandchildren are more complicated, and there is a wider range of single lifestyles. Nevertheless, close interpersonal relationships continue to define many of the stresses and satisfactions of life in later adulthood (Antonucci, Birditt, Sherman, & Trinh, 2011).

When Parenting Is Over

For adults with children, the time spent on child-rearing activities is often consuming and extends throughout much of early and middle adulthood. It is not surprising, therefore, that when children do leave home for good, family relationships change. These changes are reflected in the marital satisfaction experienced by older adults. Although there may be some initial difficulty in adjusting to each other as a couple, most empty nest couples report decreased stress and increased feelings of satisfaction and harmony; on average, older married couples report being more satisfied with their marriage after their children leave home (Whitbourne & Whitbourne, 2011).

What factors might explain the finding that older married couples are generally more satisfied with their marriage after their children leave home?

Couples whose marriage has been at the emotional center of their lives are generally among the most satisfied. Marriage now brings them more comfort, emotional support, and intimacy. Happy marriages that survive into later adulthood also are often more egalitarian and cooperative (Schmitt, Kliegel, & Shapiro, 2007). In these relationships, there is a reasonable equality of love, status, and money; traditional gender roles become less important; and the partners are more likely to experience greater happiness. In older adulthood, marital satisfaction is especially influenced by each partner's willingness and ability to resolve interpersonal conflicts, which at this stage of life often center on illness, or aging, and ultimately on death (Field, 1996; Story et al., 2007).

Relationships with Children and Grandchildren Although older adults are generally happier once their children are launched into independent lives, they usually enjoy remaining connected with their adult children. Most older adults report having relatively frequent contact with their children and grandchildren—if not in person, at least by phone. Typically, they also still feel responsible for helping their children as needed, although most older adults are also anxious not to interfere. They often provide their adult children with advice, as well as with various forms of assistance—such as money and babysitting.

Furthermore, grandparenthood (see Chapter 15) is often seen as one of the most satisfying roles of older adulthood. Studies have shown that many grandparents develop strong,

retirement maturity
A measure of how well prepared a person is to retire

▲ This grandson and grandfather can maintain their mutually supportive relationship while reading the sports page together. Each adjusts and compensates a little for the reduced mobility of the grandfather.

companionable relationships with their grandchildren. These bonds are based on regular contact and are the basis for close, loving relationships (Harper, 2005; Thiele & Whelan, 2006). In addition, with longer lifespans, the role of a great-grandparent has taken on increasing significance for many older adults (Bengtson, 2001). In general, great-grandparents are pleased with their role, and they attach emotional significance to it. Being a great-grandparent can provide a sense of personal and family renewal, a new diversion in life patterns, and a proud marker of longevity (Bengtson, 2001; Doka & Mertz, 1988). Thus, great-grandparents may be given a special status in the family.

Kinship patterns, however, have undergone stress and change in the past few decades. The high rates of divorce and remarriage, in particular, have made many family patterns more complex (Birditt & Wardjiman, 2012). Grandparents often play a particularly important role in helping to maintain stability and a sense of values during periods of family disruption. For example, the role of being a grandparent increasingly includes accepting the primary responsibility for the care of grandchildren. Although 2.3 million grandchildren lived in grandparent-maintained households in 1980, by 1997, that number had doubled to 7.5 million, which included 6.5% of all U.S. children under the age of 18 (Tavernise, 2010; see the box Try This! Exploring the Dimensions of Grandparenting). The number of children living in households that include one or more grandparents continues to increase, partly due to increasing lifespans and partly to difficult economic circumstances. In 2009, for example, about 6.7 million grandparents were living in households with their under-age-18 grandchildren. In over 40% of these situations, the grandparents were responsible for their grandchildren (U.S. Census, 2012).

Watch *Caring for an Ill Spouse* on **MyDevelopmentLab**

Caring for an Ill Spouse or Partner

At the same time that older adults are being called on more than ever to care for the younger members of their families, they also must often respond to the needs of an ill spouse or life partner. Although most older adults do not need much help with daily living, those who do tend to rely heavily on their families (Putney & Bengtson, 2001). If there is a surviving spouse or partner, she or he is the most likely caregiver.

Caring for a person who is both elderly and ill can be a taxing experience for anyone. This is particularly true when the caregiver is older or also is in poor health. When an illness or a disability is temporary, it is relatively easy to make short-term adjustments in daily routines that accommodate the need to provide care for a spouse. When an illness is terminal or the disability is permanent or progressive, however, caregiving takes a larger toll. For example, caring for someone with Alzheimer's disease entails unique strains (Gwyther & Meglin, 2012; Pearlin, Pioli, & McLaughlin, 2001). Not only does Alzheimer's disease cause physical disability; often, the most difficult aspects of the illness are the changes in personality and memory that typically accompany its advanced stages. Caring for a spouse with Alzheimer's is particularly stressful when the afflicted person's behavior becomes disruptive or socially embarrassing. Even organized respite programs do not seem to be particularly helpful (Lawton, Brody, & Saperstein, 1989; Zarit & Femia, 2008). Yet, despite the stresses and strains, caregivers often report considerable gratification from providing care for a person who has meant so much to them (Sanders, 2005).

Widows and Widowers

As with Alzheimer's disease, many conditions associated with the long-term care of older adults ultimately result in death. Consequently, the surviving partner must adjust to a new life pattern that is no longer governed by the daily routine and needs of the dependent person. The surviving partner also must adjust to a sense of loss, a lack of activity, and a new structure for the events of the day. In other cases, death may be sudden, leaving the surviving partner unprepared. Of course, some individuals are better prepared to cope with the loss of a spouse than others, and those who have had a long and positive relationship with their partner typically find the adjustment to widowhood to be especially difficult (Ong, Fuller-Rowell, & Bonanno, 2010). Regardless of the circumstances, however, the death of one's spouse brings with it a change in status—to that of widower or widow. Comparable status changes also occur for life partners who are not married. Such status passages often are extended and difficult because survivors must not only grieve, but they also must establish new routines and relationships, as well as cope with new responsibilities.

Based on your experience, what do you think the most difficult adjustments are for recent widows? Which adjustments are hardest for widowers?

TRY THIS!

Exploring the Dimensions of Grandparenting

Grandparenting can mean many different things to different people. For some people, becoming a grandparent is an exciting, long-awaited joy in life. For others, becoming a grandparent prompts mixed or even negative feelings and adjustments. What aspects of grandparenting do adults find positive? What aspects of grandparenting are more likely to prompt negative responses? To explore questions such as these, try this!

First, construct a list of the various roles and responsibilities that grandparents often assume. Consider the list in the following table, which you may adapt or expand, as you think about the various dimensions that best capture the array of activities that grandparents perform. When you have completed your list, ask two or three people who are grandparents whether they think each item on the list is a positive benefit, a negative challenge, or a neutral aspect associated with being a grandparent. Record each person's responses as you conduct each interview. You may find it helpful to use a format, such as the format suggested in the following table, to record the responses you collect. You also may wish to briefly interview each of the grandparents about their specific situation. Feel free to explore questions that interest you. It may be useful to ask the grandparents to describe, in general, their feelings about being a grandparent. As you interview each grandparent, note any specific circumstances that you think might be important as you think about each grandparent–grandchild situation (e.g., the grandparent's approximate age, gender, socioeconomic status, or cultural characteristics).

Reflect on What You Observed

In general, what types of activities did the grandparents you talked with view as positive? Which did they view as negative? Did the items you asked about seem to capture the most important activities these grandparents shared with their grandchildren? Did the grandparents mention any other things they especially liked or disliked about being a grandparent? How old were the grandparents you interviewed? Were the people you interviewed grandmothers, grandfathers, or did you include members of both groups? How many grandchildren did each grandparent have? What were the specific circumstances of their situations? For example, did their grandchildren live nearby? How would you describe the family situations of the grandchildren? What socioeconomic groups did the grandparents and grandchildren represent?

Consider the Issues

How a person views grandparenting depends on a multitude of factors. Important factors include the age, health, and gender of the grandparent; the degree that the grandchildren and their parents need the grandparent's support and assistance; the economic situations of the families involved; the specific role the grandparent is required or expects to play; the cultural traditions of the families; and how geographically close the grandparents live to their grandchildren. To what extent did you observe the influence of each of these factors in the responses given by the grandparent you spoke to? In general, how do you think each of these factors influences how grandparents approach the task of grandparenting? What do you see as the most important aspects that determine an individual's grandparenting style? What factors do you think contribute most positively to how a grandparent thinks about this role? What factors might be most likely to contribute negatively to a person's view about becoming a grandparent?

Activities Commonly Performed by Grandparents	Do You Find That This Activity is Generally Positive (+), Negative (–), Neutral (0), or Not Applicable (NA)?		
	Grandparent 1	Grandparent 2	Grandparent 3
Playing with grandchildren			
Buying toys or clothing for grandchildren			
Babysitting or providing care for grandchildren			
Paying for educational expenses for grandchildren			
Disciplining grandchildren			
Offering advice to parents about how to raise grandchildren			
Helping grandchildren with schoolwork or special projects			
Asking grandchildren for assistance with household tasks			
Vacationing with grandchildren			
Other			

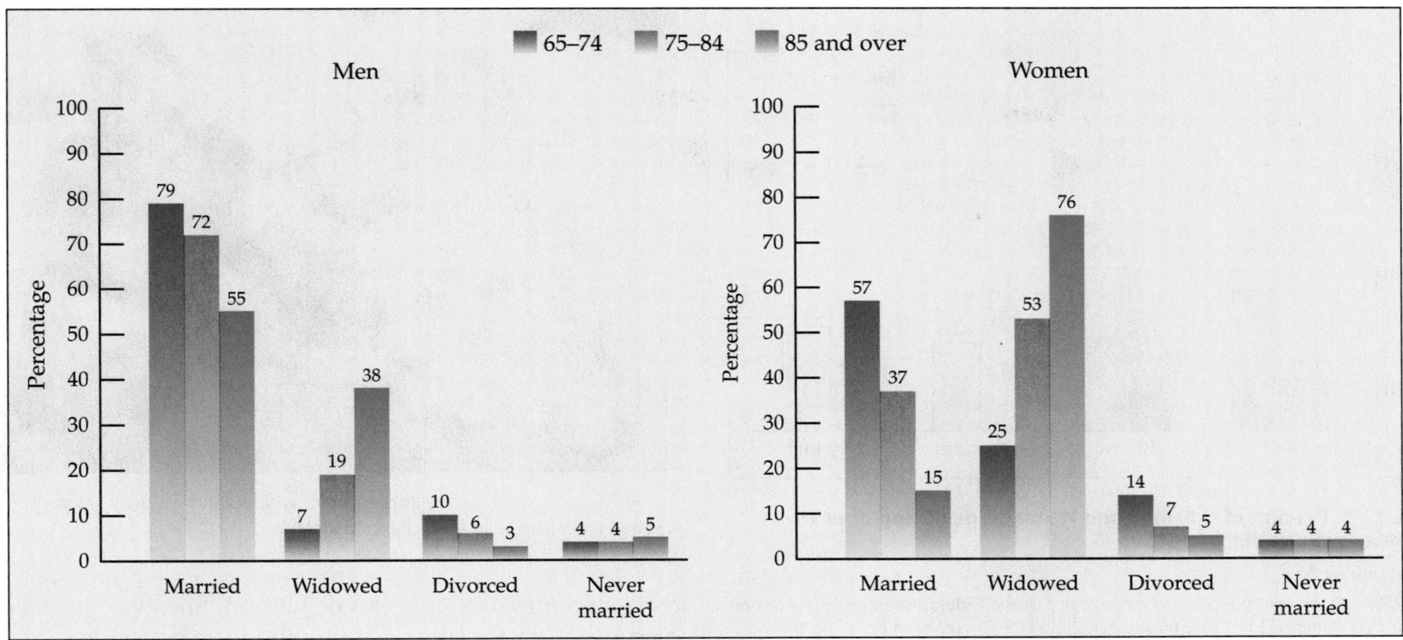

FIGURE 17-3 Marital Status of the U.S. Population Age 65 and over, by Age and Gender

Note that a far greater proportion of men than women is still married after age 65, and that a far greater proportion of women over 65 is widowed.

NOTE: Data are for 2008.

SOURCE: *Older Americans 2010: Key indicators of well-being*, Federal Interagency Forum on Aging-Related Statistics, July 2010, Washington, DC: U.S. Government Printing Office.

Living Arrangements Perhaps not surprisingly, a widow's experience of the loss of her spouse is often quite different from that of a widower's experience. Today in the United States the total number of older adult women who are widows is about three times the number of older adult men who are widowers (see Figure 17-3). By age 85, over 75% of women are widows (FIFARS, 2010c). These statistics reflect women's greater longevity and also their younger average age at marriage. Women also are less likely than men to remarry. This is partly because U.S. cultural attitudes traditionally favored the pairing of older men and younger women, which is a practice that contributes to the disproportionate number of widows in the first place.

Therefore, both because women tend to survive their spouses or partners and because of cultural attitudes, it is much more likely for older women to live alone than it is for older men (see Figure 17-4). This is particularly true for older women who identify themselves as White or Black (see Figure 17-5). For both widows and widowers, living alone involves many practical and psychological challenges. Single widows and widowers must run errands, maintain social contacts, and make financial decisions on their own. Some of these people may welcome the opportunity; others may have difficulty because their spouses had always taken care of certain matters, such as cooking or handling the finances.

Regardless of their specific circumstances, widows and widowers usually face the prospect of being *alone*, perhaps for the first time in their lives, along with all that being alone entails. Often widows and widowers experience loneliness (Ben-Zur, 2012). Therefore many older adults whose spouse has just died seek out companionship and assistance from friends, family members, and perhaps organizations that can help them cope with the tasks and the emotional aspects of living alone.

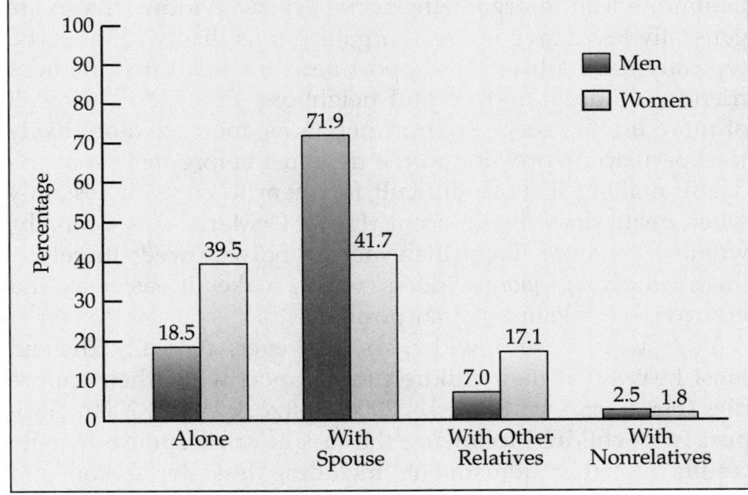

FIGURE 17-4 Living Arrangements of the U.S. Population Age 65 and over, by Gender

In older adulthood, men are more likely to live with a spouse, whereas women are more likely to live alone or with another person who is not a spouse.

NOTE: Data are for 2008.

SOURCE: *Older Americans 2010: Key indicators of well-being*, Federal Interagency Forum on Aging-Related Statistics, July 2010, Washington, DC: U.S. Government Printing Office.

Social Support Widows often have an easier time than widowers do in maintaining a social life (Whitbourne & Meeks, 2011). One reason for this is that women traditionally maintain

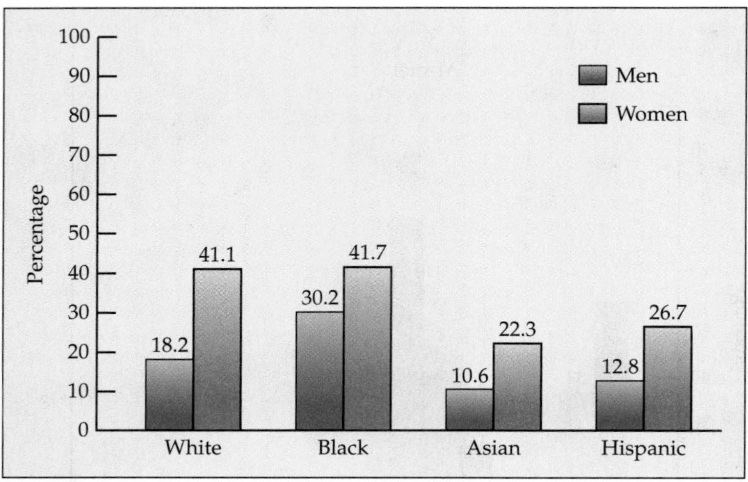

FIGURE 17-5 Percent of U.S. Men and Women Age 65 and over Who Live Alone, by Racial/Ethnic Group

NOTE: Data are for 2008.

SOURCE: *Older Americans 2010: Key indicators of well-being*, Federal Interagency Forum on Aging-Related Statistics, July 2010, Washington, DC: U.S. Government Printing Office.

▲ Friends can be particularly important for widows and widowers as they cope with loss and learn new skills for a changed lifestyle.

communication with family members and initiate social activities with friends. Thus, widowers are not as experienced in making social arrangements, and they often have more difficulty in taking the lead in organizing social events. Widowers also are generally less active in social organizations than widows, who typically have a broader support network that often includes friends, children, and helpful neighbors. Perhaps as a result of more limited social support networks, men are more likely to experience depression in the time just before their spouse's death, making it more difficult for them to cope successfully when death does finally occur (Lee & DeMaris, 2007). Finally, women are more likely than men to be widowed; therefore, there simply are *more* widows, which makes it easier to find groups of people in a similar position.

Both widows and widowers, however, typically depend most heavily on their children for support when their spouse dies (Ha, Carr, Utz, & Nesse, 2006; Spitze & Ward, 2000). Support from children following the loss of one's spouse usually results in better adjustment, including less depression and anxiety (Ha, 2010). In the United States, the majority of older adults have at least one child living within 10 miles of them, and adult children who have moved away often return when their parents need help (Lin & Rogerson, 1995). In the immediate aftermath of the spouse's death, there typically is increased contact, help, and perception of kinship obligations. Both widows and widowers are likely to receive assistance from their children, especially if they have daughters (Ha & Carr, 2005; Suitor & Pillemer, 2006). Of course, having a child step into one's life can be helpful; however, it also can be disruptive, despite the good intentions on both sides of the relationship. Nevertheless, adult children often play an important role in helping their mothers or fathers adjust to living alone.

What factors might account for the finding that fathers generally find it more difficult than mothers to accept help from children following the death of a spouse?

Siblings, too, can contribute to helping an older adult adjust to the loss of their spouse; in general, older adults often have close relationships with their siblings. In later adulthood, many people report increased contact with and concern for their siblings, as relationships that were quite distant in the busy, middle part of adult life are sometimes renewed and revitalized. Siblings sometimes share living quarters, they typically provide comfort and support in times of crisis, and they often nurture each other in times of ill health. Siblings are especially valuable companions for the kind of reminiscing that leads to ego integrity. Sibling relationships are not always smooth and congenial, of course. Nevertheless, at least a modicum of kinship responsibility among siblings is a common part of the social network of the majority of older adults, especially among those who are single or who need care and assistance but do not have grown children who can help.

Friendships also provide considerable stability and life satisfaction for both married and unmarried older individuals (Blieszner & Roberto, 2012; Ha, 2008). However, most studies that compare friendships and family relationships find clear distinctions. Most older adults think of kinship relationships as permanent; they believe they can call upon kin for long-term commitments. They cannot, however, make quite the same demands on a friendship. The prevailing view is that friends will help in an immediate emergency, such as a sudden illness, but kin should handle long-term responsibilities (Aizenberg & Treas, 1985; Stephens & Franks, 1999). Friends can, however, assume special importance for adults who lack close family members. Friendships are also an important source of social support for older adults who live in retirement communities (Potts, 1997), and they can form the basis for rich and positive interactions that support the older adult's emotional and social needs. Having friends also can serve a valuable function when the bereaved person can provide help as well as receive it.

Indeed, when grieving older adults were called on to help others, their loss-related grief and depression subsided more rapidly (Brown, Brown, & Smith, 2008).

Both family members and friends can serve as important sources of support for older adults. Older adults who live in the United States can also benefit from government policies and programs that aim to provide an adequate standard of care. In the final section of this chapter, we explore the impact of U.S. social policy decisions on older U.S. adults.

REVIEW THE FACTS 17-3

1. Do older married couples generally report an increase or a decrease in marital satisfaction when their children leave home?
2. Happy marriages that survive into older adulthood typically are __________ egalitarian and __________ cooperative.
   a. more; less b. less; more
   c. more; more d. less; less
3. By age 85, about what percentage of women are widows?
   a. 33% b. 50%
   c. 75% d. 95%
4. Suggest two major reasons why there are more widows than widowers.
5. Generally, do widows or widowers have a harder time adjusting to the death of a spouse?

Practice on MyDevelopmentLab

U.S. SOCIAL POLICY AND OLDER ADULTHOOD

Each age cohort brings to older adulthood different expectations, skills, and ways of adapting. The speed at which social change has occurred in the past 20 years—as we have moved into the information age—has required today's older adults to make numerous adaptations. For example, consider what a typical 80-year-old—who likely first saw television at about age 30 and may never have used a computer at work or at home—must learn in order to negotiate satellite TV, computerized health insurance forms, and even voicemail options. Each generation must adjust to changing circumstances in their historical and cultural environment as the lifespan unfolds. Undoubtedly, today's baby boomers will not experience older adulthood in the same way as previous generations.

Understanding the needs of today's older adults requires not only considering the circumstances of individuals but considering social policies that affect them as well. Furthermore, once social policy is adopted, it defines the options available to individuals in ways that often are critically important.

The Demographics of Aging

Perhaps the most important point to understand when considering the context for social policy discussions is to recognize that older adults are becoming a much larger proportion of the population. Whereas there were only 3.1 million older adults in the United States in 1900—about 1 in 25 people in the general population—there were 40 million in 2010, which is about 1 in every 8 people. By 2050, this segment of the population is expected to grow to nearly 90 million people and to represent 1 in every 5 people (FIFARS, 2010j). This is a dramatic and meaningful shift.

Other population changes are also important. As Figure 17-6 shows, the demographics of the older adult population in the United States have changed dramatically since 1950, and they will continue to change as we move toward 2050 (U.S. Census, 2008). For example, although the majority of older people today are White, this group will become more ethnically diverse in the

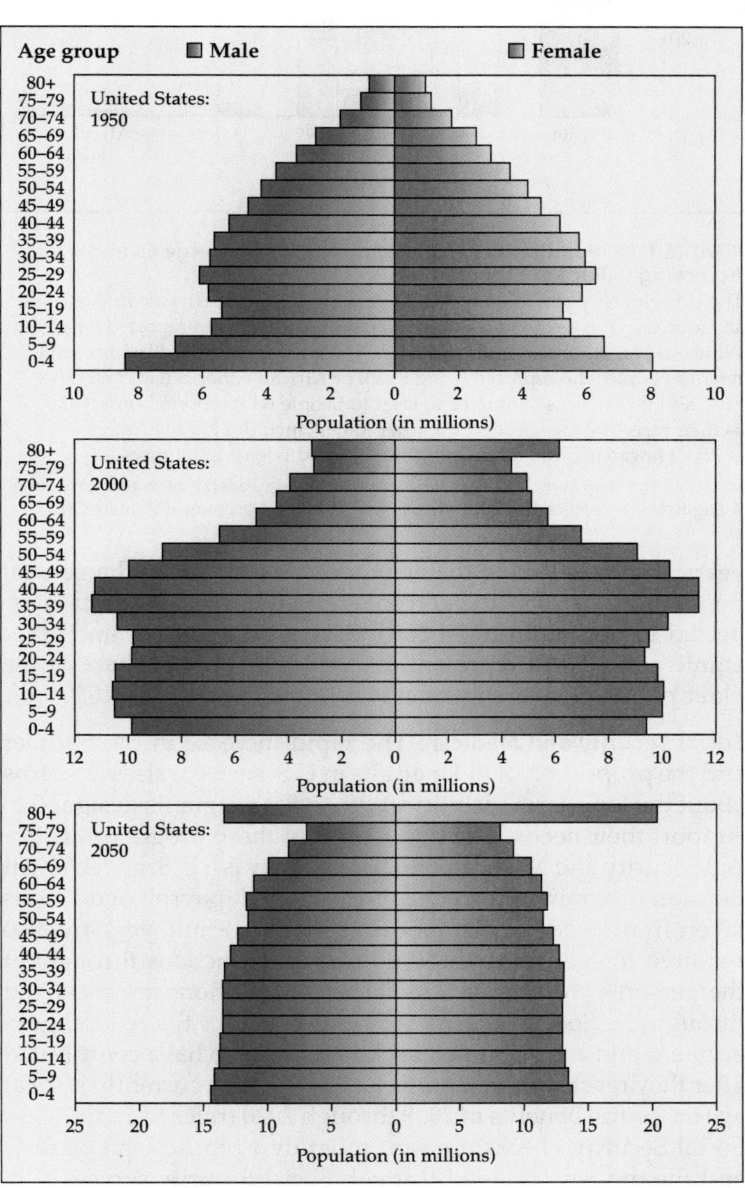

FIGURE 17-6 U.S. Population Pyramids: Percent of Males and Females in Various Age Groupings, 1950, 2000, and 2050
In 1950, most U.S. citizens were clustered in the younger age groups. By 2050, this triangle-shaped population distribution will have become rectangular, as members of the baby-boom generation enter middle and older adulthood.

SOURCE: From "Population pyramids," in *International data base (IDB)*, U.S. Census Bureau, 2008, Washington, DC: International Programs Center, retrieved from http://www.census.gov/ipc/www/idbpyr.html.

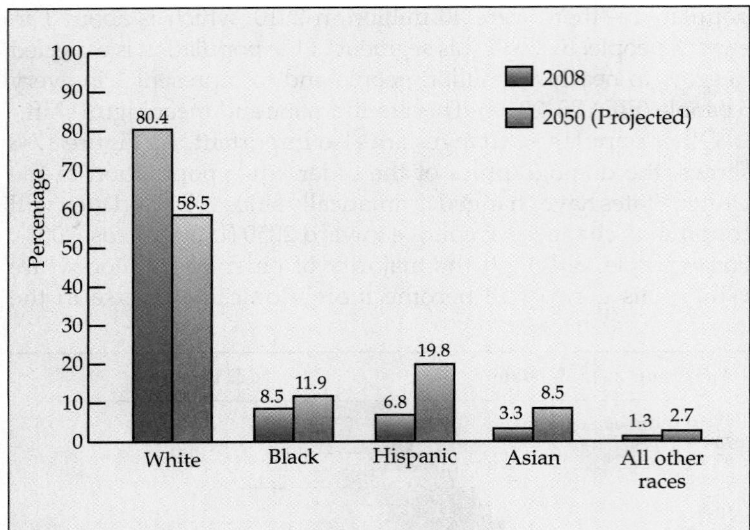

FIGURE 17-7 Population Percentages of U.S. Adults Age 65 and over, According to Race or Ethnic Origin

The U.S. elderly population will become more ethnically diverse in the years ahead. Note: The term *White* is used to refer to people who reported being White and no other race and who are not Hispanic. The term *Black* is used to refer to people who reported being Black or African American and no other race, and the term *Asian* is used to refer to people who reported only Asian as their race. The race group "All other Races" includes Native Americans, Native Hawaiians, and all people who reported two or more races.

SOURCE: *Older Americans 2010: Key indicators of well-being*, Federal Interagency Forum on Aging-Related Statistics, July 2010, Washington, DC: U.S. Government Printing Office.

years ahead, reflecting the demographic changes in the general population. By 2050, the percentage of White older adults is expected to decline from its 2008 level of 80% to 59%, and other ethnic groups will represent a significantly larger share of the older population, as shown in Figure 17-7 (FIFARS, 2010f).

Social Security and Medicare The rapid increase in the number and the proportion of older adults in U.S. society raises concerns about the long-term viability of the social programs designed to support their needs. The two largest of these programs are Social Security and Medicare. **Social Security** is a U.S. government pension program of forced savings through payroll deductions taken from every working adult's income; employers are also required to contribute through payroll deductions throughout the person's working years. These contributions are managed through the Social Security Administration of the federal government and are disbursed back to those who have contributed after they reach a certain minimum age, which currently is set at age 66 for full benefits in 2009 through 2020 (refer to Table 17-3). Social Security checks are sent monthly to those who qualify, and the money provided through Social Security serves as an important source of income for a very large majority of retired adults in the United States (see Chapter 16).

Medicare is a U.S. government program subsidized by taxes that provides payments for many basic health-care services for older adults, although most adults with the financial means also buy supplemental health insurance coverage to pay for expenses that are not covered by Medicare. Medicare is available for most hospital and physician charges, and, since 2005, it also covers some of the costs of prescription drugs, which for many older adults totals several hundred dollars each month. Individuals who are financially able also can purchase additional drug insurance coverage that further assists them in paying for their prescription drugs under a program titled *Medicare–Part D*. The Affordable Care Act, which was passed in 2010, will further expand the benefits of Medicare when it is fully implemented.

Social Security and Medicare programs are of great interest to most people living in the United States. Social Security, for example, provides the largest proportion of retirement income for older adults, eclipsing the savings and assets that retired people have accumulated throughout their lives. With a population that is growing increasingly older, many people worry that Social Security will become bankrupt, thus leaving older adults with incomes that are drastically insufficient to meet their needs (International Monetary Fund, 2012).

The long-term funding of Medicare also is a topic of concern, especially considering that the number of older adults will increase markedly in the decades to come (Whitbourne & Whitbourne, 2011). As noted in Chapter 16, the fastest-growing group in the U.S. population is those age 85 and older. The strain on Medicare is not likely to occur, however, because of extravagant expenses incurred by the oldest segment of the population. In fact, current data indicate that the oldest old may actually be about as healthy as people in the young-old age group (Parker & Thorslund, 2007). Moreover, the oldest old often die quickly as a result of an illness, such as pneumonia, and they are less likely to suffer prolonged—and expensive—hospitalizations than are people in their 60s and 70s.

Do you think an appropriate proportion of federal dollars is currently being directed to fund Medicare? If not, what changes would you support?

Thus, the expected strain on Medicare will not be from the increased costs per person as much as it will be from the increased number of people who will become eligible for this benefit. When researchers at the Centers for Medicare and Medicaid Services (CMMS) calculated the impact of increased longevity on Medicare spending, they found that improved life expectancy had only a small financial impact on the system (Calfo, Smith, & Zezza, 2008; CMMS, 2004). Instead, it is the sheer size of the baby-boomer generation—the vast number of people who will reach age 65 over the next decades—and the increasing concentration of health-care costs that occur in the final part of the lifespan at whatever age death occurs

Social Security
A U.S. government pension program of forced savings through payroll deductions from working adults' income and corporate contributions, with money disbursed to the adults after they reach a certain minimum age, usually at retirement

Medicare
A U.S. government program subsidized by taxes that provides payment for many basic health-care services and some of the cost of the drugs needed by older adults

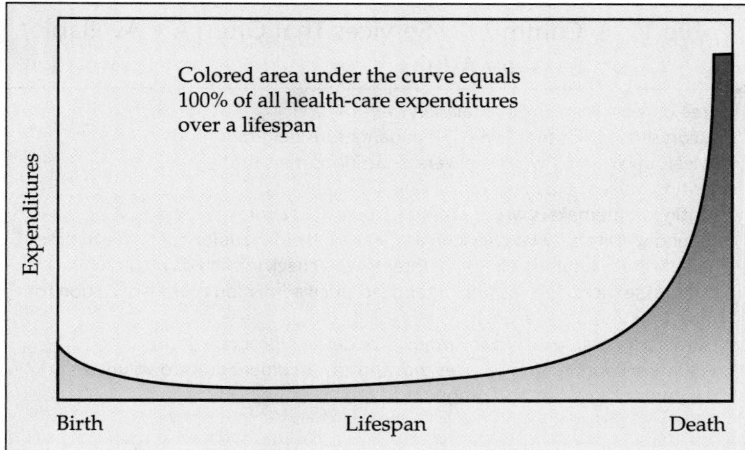

FIGURE 17-8 Americans' Current Health-Care Expenditures Are Concentrated in the Final Part of the Lifespan
A very large majority of all money spent on health care currently is spent during the final months of life. This raises important social policy questions.

SOURCE: From *Living well at the end of life*, by J. Lynn, copyright © 2003. Reprinted by permission of Copyright Clearance Center on behalf of RAND Corporation, Santa Monica, CA.

(see Figure 17-8) that are expected to drastically increase annual Medicare costs (Rice, 2004).

Social Security and Medicare, of course, are only two programs that serve the needs of older adults. Certainly, providing an economic safety net and attending to the medical needs of older adults have improved the later years for many people living in the United States. However, other needs exist; and many of these are concentrated among the economically poor. For example, public housing does not always accommodate the requirements of older adults. Some facilities fail to provide necessary services; in other cases, it might not be safe to walk in the corridors of community projects. Indeed, finding an appropriate living arrangement is often the most challenging need that older adults face, especially when they become frail and have difficulty caring for themselves.

Lifestyle Options for Older Adults

Nursing Homes When we think about caring for frail, older adults who can no longer care for themselves, we often consider the possibility of placing these older adults in a nursing home. Sometimes such a placement is temporary. For example, after an older person is hospitalized, it may be advisable for that person to spend a short period in a nursing home or rehabilitation center to regain strength before returning home. In a small percentage of cases, long-term placement, which typically is permanent, becomes necessary.

Although nursing homes provide an important and needed alternative for caring for those with substantial needs, the institutional care received by older adults can vary widely in quality. Today, most long-term care facilities are well-planned and caring institutions that meet national and local standards. However, some facilities still exist that seem to be boring, meaningless places where people often have little to do but wait for the end of their lives—at least that is the popular image. Thus, people who are about to enter a nursing home often feel great anxiety and dread, and their children often feel guilty. Even when high-quality care is assured, many people are reluctant to enter a nursing home. They understandably dread the break in the continuity of their lives, the loss of their independence, and the separation from many of their possessions and familiar routines. Once they do enter a nursing home, they may find that their identity is further eroded. For example, they may now be called "Honey" or "Dearie" instead of "Mr." or "Mrs." or "Ms. Somebody." They also may have to conform to unfamiliar and unpleasant daily routines and eat food that—even if high in quality—does not taste like their own cooking. Perhaps not surprisingly, people entering nursing homes sometimes exhibit the characteristics of people who are already institutionalized, such as apathy, passivity, bitterness, or depression. Fortunately, the majority of older adults do not require the intensive services that nursing homes provide. Today, only about 4% of people over age 65 reside in nursing homes. However, as people age, this percentage increases significantly (see Figure 17-9). Of those who reside in nursing homes, most are over the age of 85, and most are single and have some form of mental impairment, such as Alzheimer's disease (see Chapter 16).

Watch *Caring for Alzheimer's Patients* on **MyDevelopmentLab**

Although most older adults do not require the level of care that nursing homes provide, they may need some assistance in living. For example, they may require education, counseling, legal aid, social networking, or just more interesting things to do. These needs are especially acute for older adults who lack the social support of family or friends, who display unusual

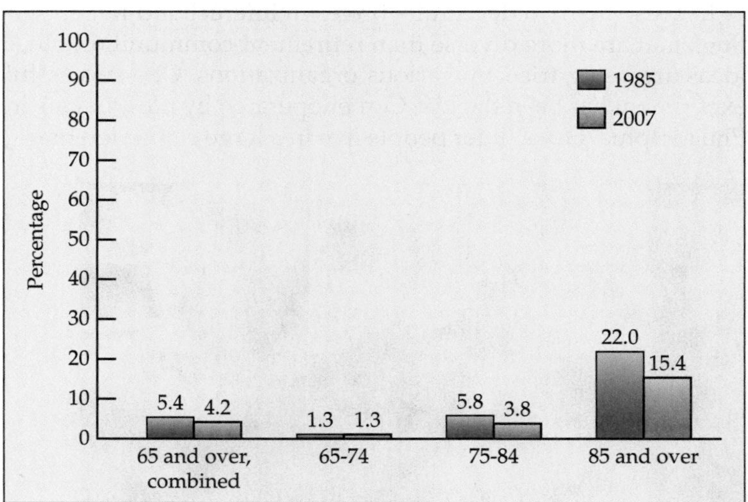

FIGURE 17-9 Percentage of People in the United States Age 65 and over Living in Nursing Homes, by Age Group, 1985 and 2007
Although the size of the age-65-and-over population in the United States is growing, the proportion of that population, as well as the actual number of individuals, who live in nursing homes is decreasing.

SOURCE: *Older Americans 2010: Key indicators of well-being*, Federal Interagency Forum on Aging-Related Statistics, July 2010, Washington, DC: U.S. Government Printing Office.

behavior patterns, or who have trouble with self-care. Consequently, other options continue to be developed for those frail, older adults who need assistance with their lives but do not require the extent of services that only an institutional setting can provide. Increasingly popular are *assisted-living facilities (ALFs)*, where older adults live in their own apartments but also receive some support in meeting their daily needs (see the box Changing Perspectives: Assisted Living—The In-Between Choice for Frail, Older Adults).

Day-Care Centers for Older Adults Day-care centers provide another option for older adults who require some assistance in living. Consider the case of a 77-year-old stroke victim. She lived with her daughter and son-in-law, but she spent her days in a day-care center where she received therapy, kept busy, and made new friends. Her morale and temperament improved dramatically after only a few weeks of attendance, which made her family's burden of care much lighter. For families who care for their older relatives in the evenings and throughout the night, day-care centers offer periods of relief and the opportunity to maintain a normal work schedule. They also can provide a stimulating and agreeable environment for the older adult. However, the cost of day-care centers usually is not covered by health insurance policies, although these centers are a more cost-effective option than nursing homes. Thus, they may be prohibitively expensive for some families.

Other Options For older adults in good health, various other lifestyle options exist. For example, retirement communities allow older adults to maintain their own apartment, condominium, or home in complexes comprised of other older residents who live together and share interests and activities in safe surroundings. However, they often also tend to isolate older adults by limiting their contact to other older people living in the retirement setting.

Because many older adults prefer to interact and live in settings that are more diverse than retirement communities, other ideas are being tried by various organizations. One successful experiment has been the Life Center operated by the Quakers in Philadelphia. Here, older people live in a large converted house with students and people in other age groups. Costs, housework, and meals are shared, and the resulting sense of community keeps older adults in the mainstream of life rather than segregated into age-defined groups. This type of home sharing has worked for older adults in a variety of locations. A similar approach is to establish an intergenerational program within a retirement community. When group meetings include younger and older people working together on a common project, all parties can benefit (Lawrence-Jacobson, 2006).

▲ Day-care centers for older adults provide a good option for many frail older people, who enjoy the company of their age peers during the day, but who return to the home of a family member for care overnight and on weekends.

Table 17-4 Community Services That Often Are Available to Older Adults

- Free or reduced-fee bus or taxi services
- Escort services for those who live in dangerous neighborhoods
- "Meals on Wheels," which delivers a nutritious meal each day
- Visiting nurses who make house calls
- Visiting homemakers who assist with household chores
- "Friendly Visitors," who check on and visit with older adults from time to time
- Telephone reassurance from volunteers who check in each day
- Cultural services, such as free or reduced-price admission or transportation to museums and other events
- Library services, such as book mobiles or delivery programs
- Volunteer coordination services that arrange for older adults to volunteer in community agencies and programs
- Free legal assistance

For older adults who need only limited support, community services can sometimes provide enough assistance so that they can stay in their own homes, which is a preference that is widely shared by most older adults in the United States. In many communities, an array of services has increasingly become available to older adults, as shown in Table 17-4. These programs improve the lives of those they serve. In addition, they often are a very cost-effective means of providing the needed support so that older adults can remain in their homes, which is a goal of policymakers not only in the United States but also in Great Britain, Sweden, Denmark, the Netherlands, Australia, and in many other countries of the world (Davies, 1993; World Health Organization, 2003). Other community-based programs include senior centers where older adults can participate in varied activities, attend classes and parties, and receive needed services. Still other communities have experimented with community care programs where people who would otherwise be institutionalized receive around-the-clock care in a private home.

Goals for the Care of Older Adults

As we have seen throughout this chapter, older adults constitute a remarkably varied group; they are not a single, uniform mass of humanity. Catchall phrases, such as "the elderly" and "senior citizens," are inadequate to describe the multitude of individual qualities found among aging individuals. Moreover, the period of older adulthood covers a long span of time. Consequently, there are sharp differences between the young-old, who are recently retired and often healthy and vigorous, and the old-old, who are more likely to experience ill health, restricted mobility, and social isolation. Social policies designed to assist older adults must consider this diversity if they are to be effective.

CHANGING PERSPECTIVES

Assisted Living—The In-Between Choice for Frail, Older Adults

Assisted-living facilities (ALFs) are the fastest growing noninstitutional long-term care alternatives for frail, older adults in the United States. These facilities serve the population of individuals who need some help with daily living activities but do not need extensive nursing care. ALFs typically provide small individual apartments or condominiums that allow for privacy and independence. They also usually provide meals in a common dining room, some management of medications as needed, housekeeping and laundry services, and transportation to doctors' visits or for shopping. On-site recreational facilities—such as a card room, a library, and an exercise center—and perhaps programs that teach crafts such as painting, sculpting, or woodworking also may be part of the facility's services. Most ALFs can provide additional personal-care services to residents if needed, although these services usually are offered at additional expense. Some ALFs are affiliated with long-term care facilities, which may be in close physical proximity, so the residents of the ALF may easily visit a spouse, a friend, or a neighbor who requires more care than ALFs can provide. In general, ALFs provide an intermediate array of support services—more than are available to older adults who live in their own homes but less than the services provided in nursing homes.

Given the array of options and services that are now available to frail, older adults, how does a person make an appropriate choice of living arrangements? Despite the fact that most states regulate ALFs and have established standards for various aspects of care, choosing which type of group residence will best meet an individual's needs is sometimes confusing because not all facilities of a given type provide the same set of services.

It is also sometimes difficult to know exactly what services a person requires. To help determine the level of support required, health-care professionals typically assess how well a person can manage two types of daily activities (Reuben et al., 2011). The first type includes six basic self-maintenance capabilities, which are called *activities of daily living*. The six activities measured are bathing, dressing, toileting, feeding, grooming, and physical mobility (e.g., walking or getting in and out of bed). The second type is called *instrumental activities of daily living*. It includes areas of functioning, such as telephoning, shopping, housekeeping, laundering, food preparation, transportation, and managing one's own medications and finances. Both sets of activities are important for living alone outside of a care facility. If a person lacks a few of these skills, community services may be sufficient to meet the person's needs, and the person may be able to live independently. However, when more help is needed, ALFs may be a good option. Today, among adults ages 85 and older, 15% are in nursing homes, 78% are living on their own, and 7% are in some form of ALF, which is an option that is becoming increasingly popular (FIFARS, 2010b).

Research on the outcomes associated with ALFs usually reveals favorable results (Robison et al., 2011; Zimmerman et al., 2005). For example, residents of ALFs generally have fewer chronic diseases than do residents in nursing homes. Of the people with more capabilities at the beginning of their residence, those who reside in ALFs generally maintain better functioning longer than do those who reside in nursing homes (Franks, 2004; Golant, 2011). Positive outcomes have been observed both in expensive ALFs and in those provided for low-income older adults. In one study, low-income residents of an affordable ALF maintained their function or coped well with their functional decline, in ways similar to and in some ways better than a comparison group of community-dwelling older adults—especially in maintaining stable, high levels of functioning (Fonda, Clipp, & Maddox, 2002; Robison et al., 2011). Of course, these results need to be interpreted very carefully, given the wide array of older adults' needs and the specific characteristics of various facilities. Assisted-living options currently are being studied in the United States, in Europe, and in Asia.

The rapidly expanding popularity of assisted-living arrangements seems to reflect, in part, a better understanding of the components necessary for well-being at older ages. The availability of some health care support and daily living assistance, together with regular social contacts and the availability of interesting recreational options that ALFs provide, supports a more positive perception of well-being for many frail, older adults. New friendships after losses, new activities to replace those that can no longer be performed, and increased mobility with assistance can make a major difference in reducing the stress associated with diminished capabilities. In particular, ALFs provide needed personal care, allowing family members to focus on providing social support that contributes to better quality of life (Gaugler & Kane, 2007). ALFs thereby can increase the well-being of older adults who no longer can live independently without some support. Perhaps not surprisingly, residents of ALFs tend to retain a strong value for independence. Such attitudes encourage these older adults to perceive themselves as independent and to find satisfaction in their remaining abilities (Ball et al., 2004). ALFs therefore provide individuals who need some help, but who also desire to remain as independent as possible, another option in living arrangements. What services for seniors are widely available in your community? Which do you think are the most valuable?

Addressing the needs of older adults implies a complicated series of considerations—one that recognizes their widely varying needs and preferences, as well as their differing financial and social circumstances (Golant, 2011). For example, older adults whose children live nearby and who are capable of and willing to provide care present a quite different set of social challenges than do single older adults with no family to support them or to help them make decisions. Regardless of their specific circumstances, however, the needs of older adults must be addressed not only by their families and friends but also by society.

To advance the issues that are especially important to older adults, several activist groups have been formed. Notable among them are the Gray Panthers, which is a coalition of older and younger people, and the American Association of Retired Persons (AARP), which brings older people together as a political and social force. Members of these and other groups are working to obtain more rights for older adults in the workplace and in society as a whole. Their work has led to greater autonomy and better living conditions for older adults, as well as for other members of society. For example, one badly disabled older woman made a great impact in Philadelphia by publicly demonstrating that the urban transportation system could not accommodate the weak or the old. The most serious shortcoming found was that the steps for getting onto buses were too high. Efforts like this have led to the use of "kneeling buses" and special vans for the handicapped. Finally, organizations like the Gray Panthers and the AARP are giving older adults a better self-image, which is something that has long been neglected in a world that equates youth with beauty, middle-age with power, and old age with obsolescence.

It is important for everyone to recognize that a larger population of older adults does not necessarily imply a larger or unfair burden on the rest of society. In fact, social programs in most industrialized nations increasingly are recognizing the needs of older adults and are working to address those needs (see Table 17-5). Globally, the World Health Organization (WHO), for example, publishes scores of guidelines pertaining to the needs of older adults and makes policy recommendations about how those needs can best be met. As the proportion of older adults in the population continues to grow, their needs are likely to receive a greater amount of focus, and societal assumptions, behaviors, and practices will continue to evolve as we respond to the challenges posed.

Table 17-5 Goals for Social Programs That Address the Needs of Older Adults

1. To do as much as possible to keep older adults integrated in society while at the same time trying to improve the quality of their lives and the care they receive
2. To recognize the burdens and stresses experienced by caregivers and devise programs to help avoid caregiver burnout
3. To improve the effectiveness and efficiency of elder-care programs, thereby limiting costs

SOURCE: From "Caring for the frail elderly: An international perspective," by B. Davies, *Generations*, Winter 1993, *17*(4), 51–54. Copyright © 1993 by American Society on Aging, San Francisco, CA.

REVIEW THE FACTS 17-4

1. In 1900, about 1 in ______ people were older adults; in 2010, this proportion rose to 1 in ______; by 2050, it will be 1 in ______.
   a. 100; 30; 8 b. 50; 15; 3
   c. 100; 50; 10 d. 25; 8; 5
2. The proportion of White older adults in the U.S. population is ______.
   a. becoming larger b. remaining constant
   c. becoming smaller
3. Over the next 30 years, the age at which a person can elect to begin withdrawing Social Security benefits will ______.
   a. increase b. remain the same
   c. decrease
4. What are the two major reasons that Medicare will become increasingly strained in the next decade?
5. What is the approximate percentage of people age 65 and older who reside in nursing homes?
   a. 4% b. 9%
   c. 18% d. 25%
6. If a family chooses to care for an older relative in the evenings and overnight but wishes to place the person in a managed care facility during the workday, their best option would most likely be a(n) ______.

Practice on **MyDevelopmentLab**

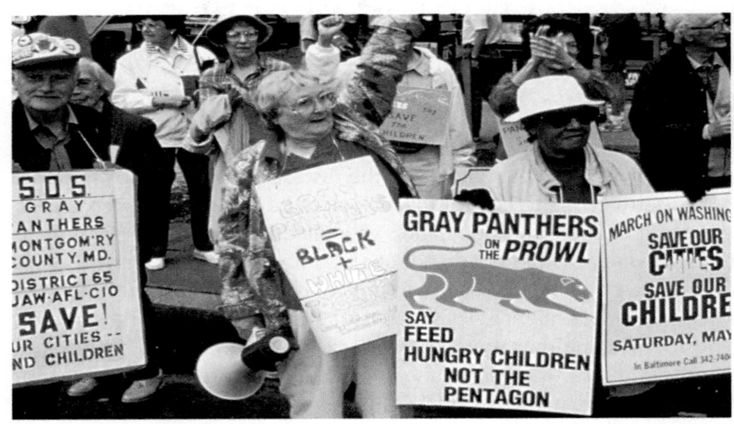

▲ These older citizens have joined together as the Gray Panthers to inform the public and do their own political activism. The Gray Panthers began organizing to combat the stereotypes of rocking-chair seniors and for better recognition of the real needs of older citizens—for better public transportation, for example. Now they often speak out on behalf of other social groups.

CHAPTER SUMMARY

Personality and Aging

How does the status passage from middle adulthood to older adulthood differ from earlier developmental transitions?

- Changes in role and social position are called *status passages*, and these passages mark transitions in life, such as entering adolescence, becoming a parent, retiring, or becoming a widow or widower. The status passage to older adulthood is unique, however, because it typically involves losses as well as gains. How a person interprets life events has a major impact on how status passages are experienced, so individual differences can vary greatly.

What did Erik Erikson mean when he identified the critical conflict of older adulthood as one of integrity versus despair?

- Erik Erikson viewed the final developmental task in the lifespan as one of *integrity versus despair*, when older adults think about how their lives have fulfilled their earlier expectations. Most older adults adjust quite well to advancing age. Regrets tend to be balanced against a sense that their lives have been well-lived and that integrity has predominated over despair.

How do older adults adapt to and cope with the changes that come with advancing age?

- Maintaining a secure sense of identity is accomplished by assimilating new circumstances into one's existing self-concept and by accommodating (adjusting) one's self-concept when major life events cannot be assimilated. Maintaining a balance between assimilation and accommodation is an important developmental task in older adulthood, as it is in earlier stages of life.
- Accommodation may be especially difficult in older adulthood, particularly if a person must face major restrictions or limitations. Accommodation is easier when older adults

shift their orientation from thinking about the present to thinking about the past.

- Although older adulthood is often stereotyped as narrow and empty, research suggests it usually is experienced as a stage of continued emotional growth, at least until shortly before death. Older adults often focus on close, personal relationships rather than on maintaining large numbers of friends.
- Older adults typically experience no reduction in positive emotions, and they typically experience fewer negative emotions and greater control of their emotions. They also experience more complex emotionality, which often includes sadness about losses. Older adults generally are well adjusted and often are happier and more satisfied than they were earlier in life.
- Stage theorists such as Daniel Levinson and Erik Erikson tend to focus on important changes that occur in development, rather than on continuity, seeing each new developmental stage as distinctly different from earlier stages. Other theorists, such as Robert Atchley, argue that continuity is what establishes a person's sense of identity; although changes occur, they are general and consistent, rather than abrupt. Themes of both continuity and change are reflected in adult development.
- Carol Ryff and colleagues have characterized well-being as a set of six components, which tend to change as adults grow older. Yet all individuals do not change in the same ways because major life events also can affect development—sometimes in important ways.
- Coping styles become more mature with age and experience, and older adults generally become more passive and focused on emotions, whereas younger adults are more likely to use active coping strategies that focus on the problem. As both men and women enter older adulthood, gender-specific roles may be relaxed.
- As people age, their reactions are highly specific to their unique experiences; however, they also reflect a consistent core identity that has guided their personality development throughout earlier life.
- As people grow older, they must confront the problems associated with aging. However, nearly three-quarters of adults who are age 65 and older report their health and well-being as good to excellent. Social comparison seems to play a role in maintaining a positive outlook. Health, more than age, appears to be more closely related to satisfaction in older adulthood; however, other factors also are important.

Retirement: A Major Change in Status

What transitions are typically experienced when an older adult retires, and what changes—good and bad—does retirement usually bring?

- Making the transition from work to retirement is an important developmental task for most older adults, for the retiring workers as well as for their spouses or partners. According to Robert Atchley, retirement consists of a series of adjustments, rather than a single transition.
- Changes in retirement patterns are occurring in response to changing gender roles and more diverse career paths. With longer lifespans and better health and fitness, many adults are opting for a wider range of retirement options, although about a third of older workers still choose to retire in the traditional sense.
- Factors that influence people's adjustment to retirement include their attitude toward work, their economic status, and their health. Adjustment is generally easier when people have interests outside their job, have adequate retirement income, and are in good health.
- Changes in Social Security and pension regulations have reduced incentives to retire at age 62 or 65, and more adults are choosing to continue working, often part-time or as volunteers. Economic pressures are also contributing to the trend for people to work longer, which will likely continue.
- Most people adjust positively to retirement, especially if they are well prepared emotionally and financially to retire—a dimension referred to as *retirement maturity.* Those with higher retirement maturity have a better attitude about retirement and adjust to it more successfully.

Family and Friends: Interpersonal Contexts

How do older adults adapt to the typical changes in family structure that usually accompany this stage of the lifespan?

- Family social contexts are shifting in response to longer lifespans, higher divorce and remarriage rates, and a wider range of single lifestyles.
- On average, older married couples experience greater satisfaction after their children leave home. Happy marriages tend to be more egalitarian and cooperative.
- Parents usually stay connected with their children and most enjoy being a grandparent and a great-grandparent. More grandparents today accept the primary responsibility for the care of their grandchildren.
- Caring for an ill spouse can be taxing, especially if the illness is chronic or terminal or if the caregiver is also older or in poor health. Despite the stress involved, most spouses report considerable gratification in providing care for their spouse.

How do older adults typically cope with loss?

- When a spouse or life partner dies, the survivor must undertake a status passage that usually is extended and difficult. In the United States, the number of older adult women who are widows is about three times the number of older adult men who are widowers. By age 85, over 75% of women are widows. Widows are more common because women live longer than men and they are less likely than men to remarry, and partly because men are more likely to marry younger women.
- Older women are more likely to live alone than are older men. Widows often adjust better than widowers do after the loss of a spouse because they have more experience in communicating with family members and in initiating

social activities, they have broader support networks, and there are more of them, so companions are easier to find. Children usually help their surviving parent cope.

- Siblings also help with adjustment following the loss of their sibling's spouse. Siblings often report increased contact in older adulthood, and they often provide valuable support and companionship. Friends also can contribute to stability and life satisfaction in older adulthood; however, they are less likely than family to be viewed as providing a permanent support system.

U.S. Social Policy and Older Adulthood

How is the age structure of the U.S. population changing, and what impact will this change have on society and social programs?

- The rapid speed of social change in the United States over the past 20 years has hit today's adults with numerous changes, especially with respect to technology. Each cohort of adults adapts in unique ways to such changes.
- Older adults are becoming a much larger percentage of the U.S. population, and this trend will continue as baby boomers age. In addition, this older group is becoming and will continue to become more racially and ethnically diverse, reflecting general population trends.

What are the pros and cons associated with the two major government-supported social programs for older adults, Social Security and Medicare?

- The increase in the number and proportion of older adults raises concerns about the viability of *Social Security,* which is a U.S. government pension program of forced savings through payroll deductions from working adults' income and corporate contributions. The viability of the Medicare program also is a concern. *Medicare* is a U.S. government program subsidized by taxes that pays for many basic health-care services for older adults. Beginning in 2005, Medicare benefits were extended to cover some of the cost of prescription drugs, and the Affordable Care Act passed in 2010 will further extend Medicare benefits when fully implemented. Individuals with financial means often purchase additional health insurance to pay for drugs and services not covered by Medicare.
- The strain on Medicare comes not so much from longer life expectancy, but rather from the increase in the number of people who will reach age 65 over the next decades, as well as the large medical costs associated with the end of the lifespan at whatever age death occurs.

What options are available when older adults need assistance in living, and how should families choose among them?

- About 4% of adults over the age of 65 reside in nursing homes, which provide intensive services. Most residents of nursing homes are single and have some form of mental impairment, such as Alzheimer's disease, and the large majority are over age 85.
- Most older adults feel great anxiety and dread about moving to a nursing home. Consequently, other options for those who need less extensive assistance than nursing homes provide, such as assisted-living facilities (ALFs), are becoming increasingly popular.
- Day-care centers provide another option for those who need limited assistance and whose families can care for them in the evenings and throughout the night. Retirement communities provide yet another choice for older adults who can care for themselves but desire the companionship of other older adults. For older adults who require only limited support, communities often provide services, such as transportation and assistance with tasks, which allow them to stay in their own homes. Senior centers provide opportunities for socializing and recreation.
- Older adults are a remarkably varied group, and this period of life covers a long span of time. To address the needs of this group, several activist groups have been formed, such as the Gray Panthers and the American Association of Retired Persons (AARP). These groups can be effective by pushing for social policy changes, as well as by providing a better self-image for older adults.

KEY TERMS

status passages (p. 472)
integrity versus despair (p. 472)
retirement maturity (p. 482)
Social Security (p. 488)
Medicare (p. 488)

DEATH AND DYING

18

LEARNING OBJECTIVES

- How has the consideration and study of death changed during the past 50 to 100 years?
- How do most people in Western cultures think about death today, and how do they react to it?
- How can knowledge of one's own death serve to enhance one's self-esteem and as a basis for inspiration?
- How do most terminally ill people and their caregivers cope with the knowledge that death will soon come?
- What trajectories of dying are most desirable, and how does suicide fit into a discussion about the trajectories associated with dying?
- What characterizes a humane death, and how can we make death more humane?
- What methods can individuals employ in order to gain some control over the circumstances that will surround them as they die?
- What factors generally influence how people deal with grief and bereavement?
- What special circumstances are associated with the death of a child?
- How can death be considered as part of the lifespan?

CHAPTER OUTLINE

Thoughts and Fears of Death
- Denial of Death
- Reactions to Death
- Managing the Anxiety Associated with One's Own Death

Confronting One's Own Death
- Death as the Final Developmental Task
- Stages of Adjustment
- Coping with Terminal Illness
- Alternative Trajectories

The Search for a Humane Death
- Hospice
- The Right to Die

Grief and Bereavement
- Grieving
- Bereavement in Cross-Cultural Perspective
- Rituals and Customs
- The Death of a Child
- Grieving When a Child Dies

Completing the Life Cycle

Death is an integral part of every person's life cycle. When it comes at the end of a long life, it is the ultimate developmental milestone—the end of life as we know it. When it occurs earlier—in infancy, in childhood, in adolescence, or early in adulthood—it often seems unfair and out of place. Whenever death occurs and however it occurs—whether it is sudden or the end stage of a long illness—it is the final chapter in a person's life.

Physiologically, death is an irrevocable cessation of life functions. Psychologically, of course, death has intense personal significance to the dying person, as well as to the person's family and friends. To die means to cease experiencing, to leave loved ones, to leave unfinished business, and to enter the unknown. For all of us, death is a natural event—whether it occurs prematurely because of disease or accident or at the end of a full and rich life. All creatures die; death is as much a part of development as it is a part of living (DeSpelder & Strickland, 2011).

A person's death is deeply embedded in a cultural context. There often are collective meanings, many of which are expressed in the culture's literature, art, music, religion, and philosophy. In most cultures, death is associated with particular rituals and rites. Depending on a person's culture—and on a person's personal beliefs and interpretations—death may be an event that is feared, dreaded, abhorred, and postponed as long as possible. Alternatively, a person may view death more as a transition than as an end—as a passage into another life and, it is hoped, into a better world or a higher plane of existence. For some people, death may be a welcome relief from the extreme suffering that can accompany disease or aging. For others—such as those who commit suicide—it may be a final, desperate escape from a life replete with pain and misery. Indeed, death has many meanings.

Historically, developmental psychologists largely ignored the subject of death. Granted, death is not easy to study, and perhaps they thought it was inappropriate to scrutinize the attitudes and reactions of people who were dying. In recent decades, however, death has been studied thoroughly. We now have a better understanding of how people typically confront the prospect of death—their own as well as others'—and how we cope with the psychological loss that death implies. Although each person experiences death in her or his own unique way, there are common issues and patterns that many people share as they anticipate death or react to it. Therefore, from a developmental perspective, death can be considered as the final stage of life. In this final chapter of the text, we consider what it means to complete the life cycle, beginning with an exploration of people's thoughts and fears of death.

▲ Funerals can help survivors by providing, among other things, a sense of continuity and closure.

THOUGHTS AND FEARS OF DEATH

Birth and death are natural events; they constitute the beginning and the end of a life. However, their emotional impact and personal meanings are vastly different. Birth is usually anticipated with excitement and optimism; however, discussions of death are usually avoided, even by those who believe in an afterlife. In contemporary Western culture, death is most often something that is feared; therefore, our reactions to death are often complex and sometimes contradictory.

Denial of Death

In earlier historical periods, death was a familiar event. It usually occurred at home, with family members caring for the dying person until the end. Even after death, the details of preparing the body for burial and for performing the final rituals were family and community events. Burial rituals prescribed the roles that grieving family members played, and family members and friends usually opened and closed the grave.

In the latter half of the 20th century, however, death became something of a technological marvel. In Western nations today, most people die in hospitals, with medical staff attending to their needs and with family members standing by. Contact with the dying person before and after death is often greatly restricted. Thus, some theorists have suggested that we currently live in an era of "invisible death," where we cope with death through psychological *denial*. Although we know that everyone dies, we distance ourselves emotionally from the realization that death will eventually come to *us*. By denying the reality of our own death, we are able to cope with the stress associated with the ending of life.

However, denial is an imperfect method of coping with death. It often leads a person to the brink of facing death, whether one's own or that of a loved one, ill prepared and with few successful means of coping. Furthermore, in youth-oriented and technologically sophisticated cultures, such as that found in the United States today, many people exhibit the curious habit of denying and avoiding death while being strangely preoccupied with it. Especially in the media, people are fascinated by gruesome murders and fatal accidents. However, by engaging in denial, we tend to believe that these events only happen to other people.

As we are moving through the 21st century, however, the cultural taboo about discussing death in the United States has been weakening. For example when researchers began to study the dying process in the mid-1960s, they often noted considerable resistance and denial on the part of hospital staff members when dealing with patients who were dying (Kübler-Ross, 1969). Once a diagnosis of a terminal illness was made, nurses and doctors paid less attention to the patient, and they seemingly avoided all but the most necessary contact. They talked to the patient less, they provided less routine care, and they usually did not tell the patient that he or she was in a terminal state—even when the patient asked. Patients who were dying also were discouraged from discussing their feelings about dying.

What evidence can you present that reinforces the position that today in the United States most people deny the reality of death?

Today this has changed (Kastenbaum, 2012). All nursing programs, and many programs for doctors, include seminars on death education that stress maintaining contact with the patient who is dying and respecting the patient's right to know. It is now widely recognized that medical professionals who understand the dying process are better able to set realistic goals for good outcomes, where patients have a chance to express their final sentiments to their family and friends, to express their feelings about death in a manner that is consistent with their lifestyle, and to die with dignity. The assistance of caregivers who are specially trained to assist the patient and their loved ones can be especially important when the dying person is young. In these circumstances well-trained caregivers can provide helpful assistance through the illness, as well as with the grief associated with loss (Field & Behrman, 2003). Furthermore, books, articles, and death education classes are beginning to change people's attitudes by providing a more realistic perspective on what happens as we die.

Watch *Children's Perception of Death* on **MyDevelopmentLab**

Although denial often is still an initial reaction to the prospect of death or the fact that the death of a loved one has occurred, it no longer is considered the end stage of coping. We are learning to think about death in ways that are centered more on reality, recognizing that death is a natural consequence of having lived.

Reactions to Death

Most psychological perspectives view a certain amount of anxiety or fear about death as an appropriate and expected response (Doka, 2007). Yet there are wide individual variations in how people view and anticipate death. For some people, death is clearly incorporated in their understanding of the purpose of their lives. Dying gives meaning to life, and the way a person accepts death is emblematic of that life. For others, death is terrifying and no belief system can be found that gives meaning to the finality of death.

Can you suggest another example where cultural expectations seem to shape how individuals think about their own mortality?

For the wide range of people who fall somewhere between these extremes, researchers find that personal and cultural meanings of death often play an important role in determining how people cope with death; age also is a factor. For example, studies have found that older adults generally are somewhat less anxious about death than younger people are. Although some older adults think about death often, most feel surprisingly calm at the prospect of death (Kastenbaum, 2012). Religious beliefs are also important in coping with death (Hays & Hendrix, 2008). Research has repeatedly shown that people with strong religious convictions and a deep belief in an afterlife experience less depression and anxiety about death (Greeff & Human, 2004; Harding, Flannelly, Weaver, & Costa, 2005). However, it is the personal conviction itself that is important: People who attempt to lower their anxiety about dying by increasing their religious participation and by trying to force themselves to believe do little to address the anxiety associated with death. Also, people with a strong sense of purpose in life fear death less.

Although many older people report low levels of anxiety about death, not all older people feel this way. There are substantial individual differences in how people react to death. Is there a pattern that identifies those who will be the most or the least anxious? The research findings are difficult to interpret. In some studies, people who are psychologically well adjusted and who seem to have achieved Erikson's stage of personality integrity are the least anxious. In other studies, older people who are both physically and mentally healthy and feel in control of their own lives are the most anxious. Furthermore, anxiety levels often change as people move closer to death. For example, people often experience high anxiety about death when they are diagnosed with a potentially fatal disease; however, they gradually become less anxious over a period of several weeks or months thereafter (Kastenbaum, 1999, 2012).

Managing the Anxiety Associated with One's Own Death

Although people have widely varying reactions to their impending death, nearly all people experience some anxiety and

▲ This couple survived the devastating tornado in Joplin, Missouri in May of 2011, but their immediate reaction to such widespread destruction and death is likely to be shock and disbelief.

dread about the ending of their life. One view of how we deal with this anxiety suggests that we manage the terror associated with death by enhancing our *self-esteem*, which refers to evaluating and strengthening our attitude about ourselves (Greenberg, 2012; Greenberg & Arndt, 2012; Gurari, Strube, & Hetts, 2009). According to this view—referred to as *terror management theory*—our biologically motivated desire for life is in direct contradiction with our knowledge that we will die at some point. This conflict gives rise to terror. If this terror is not addressed, it can be psychologically paralyzing and lead to despair and depression over the hopelessness of our situation. According to terror management theory, we cope with this terror by developing our self-esteem. We work on becoming competent, attached, and important to other people, and on attending to the needs of others, as well as ourselves. Thus, according to terror management theory, the universal need for self-esteem is ultimately motivated by our reaction against the anxiety triggered by our awareness of death. Stated another way, people develop their self-esteem to buffer their anxiety about their own death.

According to the terror management view, death can thus be a force that encourages us to move forward in our lives and attempt to accomplish the goals we have set for ourselves. In this context, death is not a source of fear; instead, it is the basis for inspiration. The view that increased self-esteem is a reaction to our awareness of our own death is supported by research that demonstrates that people with high levels of self-esteem generally experience less death-related anxiety. Research shows that when people are reminded of their own mortality, they often work harder at securing a positive view of themselves (Kesebir & Pyszczynski, 2012; Pyszczynski, Solomon, & Greenberg, 2003b). They also may attempt to protect their positive self-concept against criticism. Further support for the terror management view is found in cross-cultural comparisons. Anxiety over death is particularly acute in individualist cultures where the focus is on personal accomplishments. When the cultural context is more collectivist and group welfare is emphasized over that of an individual, there is less anxiety about death and the need to achieve self-esteem is not as important (Ma-Kellams & Blascovich, 2011; Ryan & Deci, 2004). For example, individualism is generally found to be stronger in Australia than it is in Japan. As predicted by terror management theory, when Australian and Japanese adults were forced to consider their own mortality, the Australians experienced an enhanced individualism, whereas the Japanese participants focused less on their own self-esteem (Kashima, Halloran, & Yuki, 2004).

However, research suggests that older adults do not respond to reminders of their own mortality in the same way that younger persons do (Maxfield et al., 2007). Perhaps because they are closer to their own death, older adults may be more aware of its reality; with advancing age, death becomes a more expected, normative event. Thus, terror management theories may better explain the relationship between self-esteem and anxiety for younger, compared to older, adults. Furthermore, not all researchers see the development of self-esteem as the outcome of our fear of our own mortality. They argue that the terror management view is too pessimistic. Rather, they view self-esteem as arising out of our positive desire for competence, autonomy, and relatedness to others and not as a reaction to our fears about death (Ryan & Deci, 2004). Death, thus, is not necessarily a source of energy, resolve, and enthusiasm; rather, it is an inevitable event that people must adapt to. How they adapt is often related to the particular circumstances they face at the end of their lives (see the box Current Issues: Searching for Meaning in Natural Disasters, Accidents, Terrorism, and Personal Tragedies). In the next section, we explore how people confront their own death.

REVIEW THE FACTS 18-1

1. In the early 21st century, is the cultural taboo against discussing death weakening or strengthening?
2. In the 1960s, the typical reaction of physicians and other health-care workers when a person was diagnosed as being terminally ill was to
   a. discuss the upcoming death with the terminally ill patient at every opportunity.
   b. encourage relatives to spend a lot of time with the dying patient.
   c. offer sympathy but little medical attention to the dying patient.
   d. avoid the terminally ill patient.
3. Does research show that people who believe in religion and an afterlife are less or more afraid of death when compared to those who do not hold such beliefs?
4. Terror management theory argues that we cope with the awareness of our own death by
   a. denying we will die.
   b. rejecting religious beliefs.
   c. developing positive self-esteem.
   d. becoming depressed and unproductive.
5. In which of the following cultures would you expect that the anxiety about death is least pervasive?
   a. Australia b. the United States
   c. Germany d. China

✓ Practice on MyDevelopmentLab

CURRENT ISSUES

Searching for Meaning in Natural Disasters, Accidents, Terrorism, and Personal Tragedies

Periodically, we are exposed to seemingly senseless death. Terrible disasters—natural and otherwise—are brought into our homes, often with graphic and relentlessly repeated detail, by television coverage of the events. Few people will have difficulty recalling vivid images of recent catastrophes—tsunamis and earthquakes, terrorist attacks, plane crashes, school shootings, suicide bombings, and so forth—that cause death and destruction to innocent people. Sometimes we experience tragedy in a more personal way. Perhaps a close friend dies of a drug overdose, a car accident, cancer, or a suicide. These tragedies often seem to make little sense. Why do events such as these happen to innocent people, young and old? Why is there such needless pain and suffering? When death comes at the end of a long and productive life, we usually can accept the death, although we may grieve over the loss of a loved one. However, when people are victims of unexpected tragedies—especially when they are infants, children, or teenagers—these events seem particularly cruel.

Although disasters and tragedies are more commonplace in many parts of the world than they are in the United States, a particularly transforming event occurred in the United States on September 11, 2001. On this date, terrorists crashed two jetliners into the twin towers of the World Trade Center in New York City, another into the Pentagon, and another into a field in Pennsylvania. In the aftermath of 9/11, numerous psychologists began to study the impact of catastrophic events on the victims, the observers, and the terrorists themselves. How do people think about such sweeping acts of violence against innocent victims? What conscious, or perhaps unconscious, processes shape our understanding, impressions, and judgments about the circumstances surrounding a tragedy?

Although it is early in the research effort to untangle the complex psychological features that characterize the cognitive and emotional aspects of how we cope with disaster, some interesting results have emerged. Many of these results support the idea that we manage the terror associated with death by establishing a positive self-concept—one that provides a day-to-day buffer against the uncertainty and tragedy in our daily lives (Greenberg, 2012; Pyszczynski et al., 2003a). Thus, according to this *terror management theory*, we deal with the anxiety surrounding death by developing our sense of positive self-esteem. Belief in a life after death, especially one that rewards us for our good acts, is another way that some people cope with the anxiety caused by our acknowledgment of death (Pyszczynski & Kesebir, 2012).

Tragedies often accentuate our awareness that life is finite and that death will occur sometimes without warning and without regard to fairness. When we are forced to confront the issues of mortality, such as when a national or personal tragedy occurs, we try to cope. One consequence of our coping seems to be that we try to reestablish more control over the events of our own lives. For example, research suggests that we tend to become more materialistic following disasters: Conspicuous consumption—buying wanted things that enhance our status—may help us cope with the uncertainty about when our lives might end (Arndt, Solomon, Kasser, & Sheldon, 2004). Another response to tragedy involves developing prejudices against groups that we perceive to be different from our own, and therefore potentially threatening (Greenberg, Landau, Kosloff, & Solomon, 2009; Lieberman, 2010). When we experience a threat that triggers our sense of mortality we also respond by viewing strong leaders as more attractive. In a study that examined how thoughts about the 9/11 terrorist attack affected Americans' attitudes about President George W. Bush, researchers found that reminding people about their own mortality or refreshing their memories about the 9/11 disaster increased their support for the President and his antiterrorist policies (Landau et al., 2004). Apparently, in times of crisis, many people—and especially those who feel insecure—seek to support charismatic leaders who present a strong face of resistance to threats (Greenberg & Arndt, 2012; Weise et al., 2008).

Can understanding terror management theory help improve world peace and global health and safety? Can we channel the threat imposed by disasters of various types into positive, productive efforts to improve the lives of others, as well as our own personal sense of well-being? Some theorists are optimistic about the resolution of questions such as these (Pyszczynski, Rothschild, & Abdollahi, 2008). They argue that people need to feel their lives are worthwhile. One way that we demonstrate the value of our existence is to contribute to a cause that is greater than our own self-interest. When our mortality is threatened, as it is when we experience tragedy, we can cope by helping others. People need to have a sense that they exercise some control over their own lives, and they need to feel that their efforts make a positive impact on the lives of others. Thus, coping with the terror caused by tragedy can have a positive effect on our lives, as well as on the lives of those to whom we contribute.

CONFRONTING ONE'S OWN DEATH

The age at which a person dies is an important factor in determining reactions to death, as are the specific circumstances that lead up to it. As adults grow older or become ill, they begin to realize that death is no longer a distant event. Young and healthy people usually have the luxury of pushing these thoughts into the background; however, in illness or in older adulthood, thoughts of death become unavoidable. How do people react to the growing realization of their own mortality?

When young people were asked how they would spend the remaining 6 months of their life if they knew that was all they had, they typically described activities, such as traveling and trying to do things that they wanted to do but not yet had a chance to do. Older people had different priorities. Sometimes they talked about contemplation, meditation, and other inner-focused pursuits. They often talked about spending time with their families and those closest to them (Kalish, 1987). Indeed, studies show that most older people accept the approach of death, although many note that they fear a prolonged and painful death (M. J. Field & Behrman, 2003).

What occurrences in everyday life might serve to remind older adults of their impending death? Do you think these occurrences are generally helpful or harmful to the personal adjustment of older adults?

These findings raise the obvious point that people come to death in different ways—some die suddenly and unexpectedly, whereas others move through protracted and perhaps painful phases of a progressive terminal illness, such as cancer. Some people die at young ages; others experience death as the natural ending of a long life. When people have time to contemplate their own death, they often are able to adjust successfully to its impact.

Death as the Final Developmental Task

People who are not faced with the prospect of immediate death can spend more time adjusting to the idea. Death in these circumstances often prompts a kind of life review; therefore, it comprises a final developmental task. When adults reach old age, they often spend their last years looking back and reliving old pleasures and pains. This review of one's life is a very important step in the lifelong growth of the individual. At no other time is there as strong a force toward self-awareness as in older adulthood. The process of life review often leads to real personality growth; individuals resolve old conflicts, reestablish meaning in life, and even discover new things about themselves. In coping with the reality of approaching death, we can make crucial decisions about what is important and who we really are—we can establish a secure sense of self-esteem (Arndt, 2012; Maxfield et al., 2007). Death, thus, can lend the necessary perspective to evaluating our lives.

Stages of Adjustment

Not all people have the luxury of advanced years in which to gradually adjust to the idea of dying. When a person is told that death is imminent, such as when a diagnosis of a serious terminal illness is made, the person must address the issues of mortality in an abbreviated way. One of the first people to investigate how individuals react to knowledge that their own death was imminent was Elisabeth Kübler-Ross (1969/2009). Today her work is regarded with some skepticism, but Kübler-Ross's interviews with terminally ill adults led her to identify a sequence of five stages of coping as individuals adjust to the idea of death: denial, anger, bargaining, depression, and acceptance (see Table 18-1)—a view that still has some merit.

Kübler-Ross's stage theory of coping with death has received widespread attention in the popular press and health care profession. However, many researchers today are critical of this view, noting that Kübler-Ross's methods lacked the rigor associated with scientific investigation (Konigsberg, 2011). In particular, critics note that the five stages of coping are not universal—people deal with their impending deaths in unique ways that do not follow a closely prescribed sequence of predictable stages. Nevertheless, the idea that there are different ways that people cope with their own death, and that these often proceed in some sort of sequence, is useful in helping caregivers understand how dying people feel. Today, most professional caregivers recognize that not all people experience all of the five stages, and only a few people experience the stages in the specified order. For example, some people remain angry or depressed until the end; others come to welcome death as a release from their pain. In helping a loved one adjust to the reality of death, it is important to remember that people cope with death in individual ways; therefore, they should not be forced or expected to adjust according to a set pattern of stages. Instead, they should be allowed to follow their own paths to dying (DeSpelder & Strickland, 2011; Kastenbaum, 2012). If they want, they should talk about their feelings, concerns, and experiences; have their questions answered; set their lives in order; see relatives and friends; and forgive or ask for forgiveness for quarrels or petty misdeeds. These actions are more important to the person than experiencing broad emotional states in a particular order.

Caregivers' Adjustments Caregivers also must grieve and cope with the anxiety associated with the death of a loved one, and they often feel inadequate in their task. Support from other family members often can make caregiving easier. A sense of personal optimism is also important in coping (Greeff & Human, 2004; Greeff, Vansteenweger, & Herbiest, 2011). Those who hold religious beliefs, especially if they are practiced, are often better able to cope with the demands of caring for a dying loved one (Herbert, Dang, & Schulz, 2007; Kelley & Chan, 2012; Wortmann, 2008). In addition, professional counseling sometimes can serve a useful function for caregivers who are supporting a person who is dying.

Coping with Terminal Illness

Especially when the ill person's needs are excessive, as is often the case when terminal illnesses like cancer or Alzheimer's disease are involved, the caregiver may be physically and emotionally

Table 18-1 Kübler-Ross's Five Stages of Death and Dying

Stage	Term	Description
First	Denial	People reject the possibility of their death and search for more promising opinions and diagnoses
Second	Anger	People realize their death is imminent and experience anger, resentment, and envy; they feel frustrated because plans and dreams will not be fulfilled
Third	Bargaining	People look for ways to buy time, making promises and negotiating with their God, doctors, nurses, or others for more time and for relief from pain and suffering
Fourth	Depression	Helplessness and hopelessness take hold when bargaining fails or time runs out; people mourn both for the losses that have already occurred and for the death and separation from family and friends that will soon occur
Fifth	Acceptance	People accept the fact of imminent death and await death calmly

SOURCE: From *On death and dying*, by E. Kübler-Ross, 1969, New York: Macmillan. Republished in 2009, New York: Routledge.

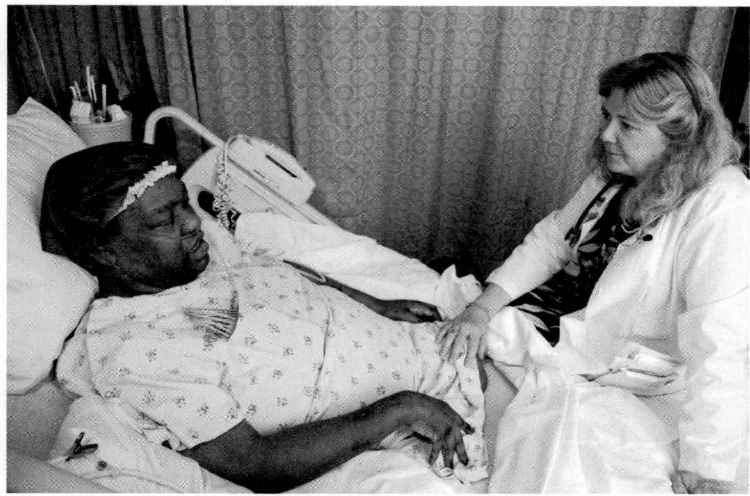

▲ This doctor is discussing the diagnosis with a terminally ill patient. These are never easy discussions, but there needs to be honest, two-way communication so that both can make reasonable decisions.

▲ This grandmother and her small grandchild have come to visit the child's dying great-grandmother. All three can benefit, in their own way, from the recognition of meaningful links across generations.

drained from the multitude of responsibilities that are required in daily care. For example, in one study of end-of-life care of those with dementia, half of the caregivers surveyed reported being "on duty" 24 hours a day, and half spent at least 46 hours per week providing care (Schultz et al., 2003). In dealing with a loved one's terminal illness, depression and despair among caregivers are common during the illness, although many caregivers show remarkable resilience after their loved one's death. In one study, 72% of caregivers reported that the death of their loved one was a relief to them, and over 90% reported that they felt it provided a welcome relief to the person who was dying (Schultz et al., 2003). Thus, for caregivers and those who are dying, the specific circumstances surrounding the end of life are of paramount importance in determining how this event will be experienced.

What circumstances might caregivers find especially difficult to cope with as they care for a terminally ill loved one?

As noted previously, the course of an illness often affects people's reactions to the dying process. If death is sudden, there is little time for life review and integration. An illness that causes considerable pain, limited mobility, or requires frequent and complex medical intervention may leave a person with little time or energy to adjust to death. Therefore, medical personnel and family members should not assume that a dying person is adjusting in any particular way when, in fact, the illness has progressed so rapidly that the dying person has little time for adjustment of any sort to his or her own death.

Alternative Trajectories

Just as there are numerous and unique life *trajectories*—or patterns—in adult development, there also is a wide range of dying trajectories. In the United States today, the commonly accepted *ideal* trajectory is to be healthy to age 85 or more, put your affairs in order, and die suddenly and without pain, perhaps while asleep (Lang, Baltes, & Wagner, 2007; Whitbourne & Whitbourne, 2011). Indeed, surveys show that far more people would prefer a sudden death—particularly the young (M. J. Field & Cassel, 1997). In other cultures, different trajectories are idealized (Rosenblatt, 2008), as they were in other historical periods—perhaps an early but valiant death in glorious battle or a death caused by defending one's principles, values, family, or culture.

Yet many people must cope with a death that does not conform to an ideal trajectory. Sometimes the trajectory of death is a long, slow steady decline, with progressive loss of function. Deaths from Alzheimer's disease and ALS, for example, typically follow this trajectory. In other cases, the trajectory of death is erratic: The person experiences significant bouts of ill health, only to recover temporarily, and then again slip into

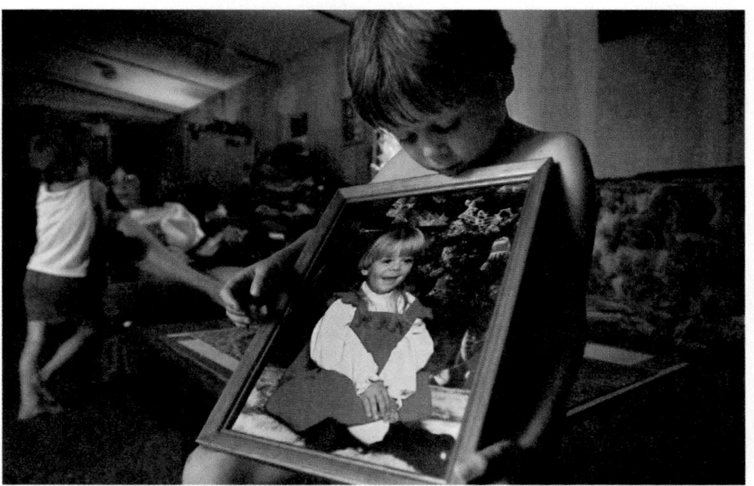

▲ For many people, the ideal death trajectory is to die peacefully and without pain in old age. Death is harder to accept when the trajectory is not ideal, as in this case where a young boy grieves over the death of his little sister.

another health crisis in which death may again be imminent. Some deaths from cancer follow trajectories similar to this.

For those who are confronting a terminal illness, the trajectory of the illness often seems beyond their control. Some people attempt to influence the course of their disease by accepting or rejecting treatment, by exerting their will to live, or by resigning themselves to the inevitable. For many people with a terminal illness, the need to maintain some control and dignity in this final trajectory is paramount. It is not uncommon for people with a terminal illness to contemplate suicide as a means to gain control over the process of dying, to relieve their loved ones of the difficult caretaking process, or to avoid the suffering and pain they may associate with their final days.

Suicide Although the most highly publicized suicides typically are those of young adults, adolescents, and even schoolchildren, by far the greatest proportion of suicides occurs among older men (see Figure 18-1). Indeed, men over age 85 are about twice as likely to die as the result of suicide than are young men of age 30. This trend is especially apparent among White older men (see Figure 18-2). Indeed, about 1 in 20 White men age 85 and over dies as the result of suicide (National Center for Health Statistics [NCHS], 2012). Furthermore, this rate is probably an underestimate of the actual number of suicides. In some cases, deaths that actually are suicides are committed so that they look like accidents—for example, a single-vehicle car wreck or an "accidental" fall. Furthermore, official statistics do not record the more passive forms of suicide. One such passive form is called **submissive death**, where people simply let themselves die by not caring for themselves. Another, called **suicidal erosion**, occurs when people intentionally engage in high-risk activities, such as excessive drinking, smoking, or other drug abuse. Both of these forms of passive suicide are especially common among older men.

What factors do you think might explain why suicide in older adulthood is much more common among men than among women? Do you foresee these statistics changing over the next 20 years? If so, why? If not, why not?

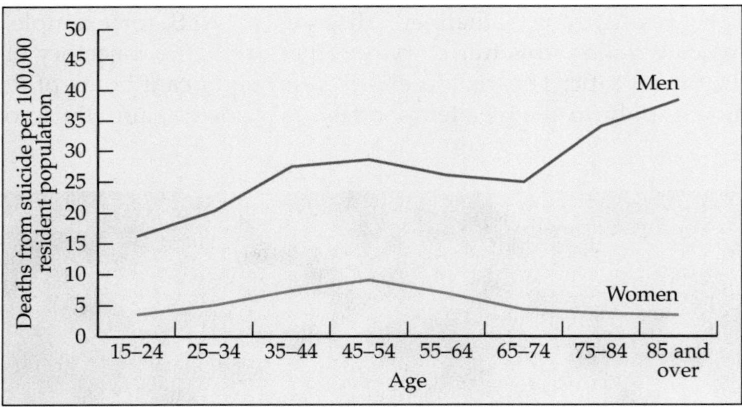

FIGURE 18-1 Suicide Rates (Per 100,000 Population) for Adult Men and Women in the United States, by Age Group

NOTE: Data are for 2008.

SOURCE: "Death rates for suicide, by sex, race, Hispanic origin, and age: United States, selected years 1950–2008," in *Health, United States, 2011: With special feature on socioeconomic status and health*, National Center for Health Statistics (NCHS), 2012, Hyattsville, MD: Author.

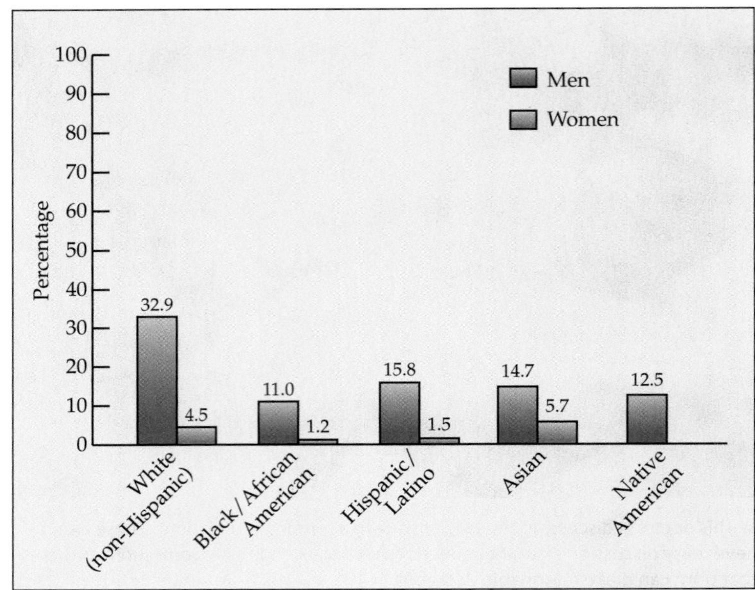

FIGURE 18-2 Suicide Rates (Per 100,000 Population) for Adult Men and Women in the United States over Age 65, by Racial/Ethnic Group

NOTE: Data are for 2008.

SOURCE: "Death rates for suicide, by sex, race, Hispanic origin, and age: United States, selected years 1950–2008," in *Health, United States, 2011: With special feature on socioeconomic status and health*, National Center for Health Statistics (NCHS), 2012, Hyattsville, MD: Author.

Interestingly, men at all ages are more likely to actually commit suicide than are women, even though women are more likely to make oftentimes dramatic, but unsuccessful, suicide attempts. Not surprisingly, this is especially the case among older White men, where the suicide rate for White men age 85 and over is about 10 times higher than the rate for White women in this same age group (NCHS, 2012b). Why are older men—and older White men in particular—so much more likely to die as the result of suicide?

Especially among older men, suicide is sometimes used as a means of coping with a terminal illness. It can also be the result of "vital losses," such as retirement shock or diminished capabilities. Widowers particularly are at a higher risk for suicide than the general population, especially during the first year of

submissive death
Suicide where people simply let themselves die by not caring for themselves

suicidal erosion
An indirect form of suicide pursued by engaging in high-risk activities, such as excessive drinking, smoking, or other drug abuse

bereavement (G. Li, 1995). Although the suicide rates for married and widowed women are nearly identical, the suicide rate for widowers is about five times greater than the rate for married men (Hansson & Stroebe, 2007).

Although the increased risk of suicide for surviving spouses undoubtedly reflects a complex interplay of several factors, one issue is often the grief survivors feel about the events surrounding the death of their loved one. Did they provide enough support? Did they make the correct decisions about care? Caregivers generally receive little guidance about the best way to address the issues surrounding their loved one's death; however, suggestions about how to care for a dying loved one are becoming more widely available (Jordan & McIntosh, 2011). Hopefully, as health-care professionals become more aware that prolonging a life needs to be considered in the context of providing for a humane death, suicide rates among older and terminally ill people will decline. In the next section, we explore topics associated with a humane death.

REVIEW THE FACTS 18-2

1. When young people are asked how they would spend time if they only had 6 months to live, they typically mention ________; when older adults are asked the same question, they usually mention ________.
   a. doing activities such as traveling; spending time with family and friends
   b. killing themselves to ease the pain; waiting patiently for death to come
   c. reading and thinking; completing undone life tasks, such as traveling
   d. being sad; being happy
2. According to the stage theory proposed by Kübler-Ross, when people are told that they have a terminal illness, they typically first respond with
   a. bargaining. b. acceptance.
   c. anger. d. denial.
3. In the United States today, what is the *ideal* trajectory for death?
4. Statistically, who is the most likely to commit suicide?
   a. a teenage boy b. a young adult woman
   c. an older man d. an older woman
5. When people simply stop caring for themselves and consequently die, this is called ________.

Practice on **MyDevelopmentLab**

THE SEARCH FOR A HUMANE DEATH

As we have seen, a great deal of study has been conducted on the experience of dying; former ignorance and neglect of the subject are giving way to a more realistic view. It may be a long time, however, before society's general attitude toward death catches up to the needs of dying patients and their loved ones. Although doctors and other health-care professionals are remarkably good at providing health care in the form of medication and life-support systems to patients who are dying, they too often are poor at dealing head-on with patients' and caregivers' worries and thoughts.

Fortunately, in recent years, doctors and other health-care professionals have become more honest with patients who are dying. Care of the terminally ill has generally become more humane. Along these lines, those who are terminally ill often are given some measure of autonomy. Having a say in how much pain medication or sedatives they receive, for example, can give patients who are dying a sense that they still control some aspects of their lives. This is very important for people who may otherwise feel that they are being swept along by forces beyond their control. In recognition of the benefits associated with allowing terminally ill patients greater control over their lives and more influence in the decisions that will affect their care, patients' rights groups have developed methods for communicating the intentions of the person who is dying. One of the best known of these methods is called the "Five Wishes" (see Table 18-2), which is further discussed later in this chapter.

When people feel that they can no longer control their own lives in any meaningful way, they often respond by giving up the struggle. Supporting this view are the results of a study of adults with congestive heart failure; those who became more disengaged were more likely to die from their illness (Murberg, Furze, & Bru, 2004). In contrast, people who attempt to control their environment tend to cope better and live longer (Connor-Smith & Flachsbart, 2007; M. J. Field & Cassel, 1997; Shaver & Mikulincer, 2012). Thus, providing people who are seriously or terminally ill with active coping skills and the ability to determine at least some aspects of managing their illness appears to be important not only to their quality of life, but to their longevity as well.

Often—especially if there is adequate time to prepare—people who are dying express more fear about *how* they will die than about their death itself. Typically, most people want to avoid a long and painful terminal period, they do not want to be dependent on others, and they want to maintain their mental functions and their dignity. The quest for a *good death* has led to several proposed changes in how services are provided to people who are dying. These changes include hospice care and the right to die.

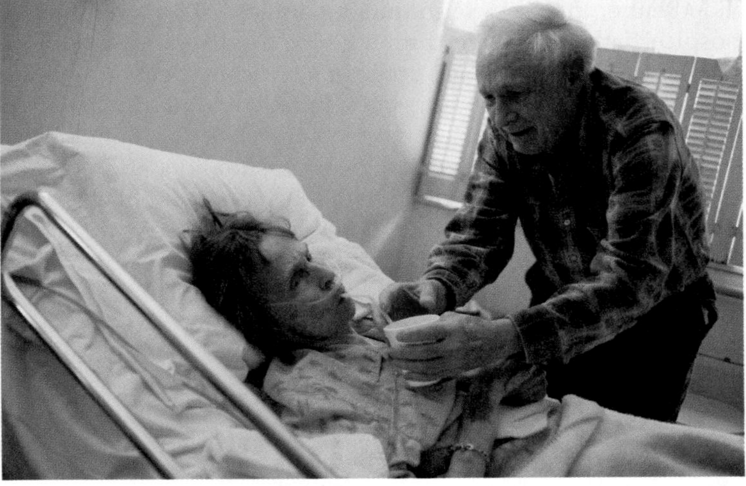

In hospices, death is seen as a normal stage of life to be faced with dignity.

Table 18-2 Five Wishes for Terminally Ill Patients

Wish	
Wish 1: The person I want to make care decisions for me when I can't	• Wish 1 is considered a legal document, similar to the power of attorney. • Once the dying person identifies a "health-care agent," this person is able to make decisions about the delivery or nondelivery of care when the ill person no longer can make these decisions.
Wish 2: The kind of medical treatment I want or don't want	• Wish 2 functions as a living will, and is also a legal document. • This wish identifies which life-support treatments the ill person wants, and which should not be used. • An example would be whether the person wanted a feeding tube used once he or she can longer eat or swallow.
Wish 3: How comfortable I want to be in my final days and hours	• Several medications (e.g., morphine) can be given to ease or eliminate pain, but these usually cause drowsiness and sleep. • The dying person decides where the line should be between remaining alert and being without pain.
Wish 4: How I want people to treat me	• Here, the person can identify where he or she wishes to be cared for in his or her final days (e.g., at home, in a hospice, in a hospital). • The dying person can also express personal preferences, such as whether or not prayers will be given, whether young children will be present at the death, and so forth.
Wish 5: What I want my loved ones to know	• Here, the dying person can make requests about funeral and memorial plans. • The person may also make final statements about forgiveness or advice that would be given to loved ones.

SOURCE: Information pertaining to the Five Wishes is available at http://www.agingwithdignity.org/five-wishes.php/. The Five Wishes documents are available at this site for a charge of $5.00.

Hospice

Hospice is designed to help people with a terminal illness live out their days as fully and independently as possible by giving needed care, counseling, support, and other assistance both to patients and to their families and loved ones. It is based on the philosophy that death is a natural process and that individuals should be allowed to maintain some control over how they die. The first hospice for the dying was started in England in 1967, and the hospice concept has spread rapidly (see Figure 18-3). In 2009, there were more than 3,400 Medicare-certified hospice programs throughout the United States, and over 5,000 total hospice programs (National Hospice and Palliative Care Organization [NHPCO], 2012; Hospice Association of America, 2010; see the box Try This! Exploring the Dimensions of Hospice Care).

It is important to note that hospice is not a *place;* it is a philosophy. According to the National Hospice and Palliative Care Organization (2012), about two-thirds of hospice care is provided either in homes or in nursing homes. About one-third of hospice patients receive care either in a hospital or a hospice inpatient facility. Hospice programs typically deliver comprehensive services, including both inpatient units in hospitals and home-care programs comprised of a variety of home-based services, medical and psychological consultation, and ongoing medical and nursing services that relieve pain and help control symptoms. Like hospital care, home-based hospice care is usually covered by insurance, and in many cases it is much more cost-effective than hospitalization.

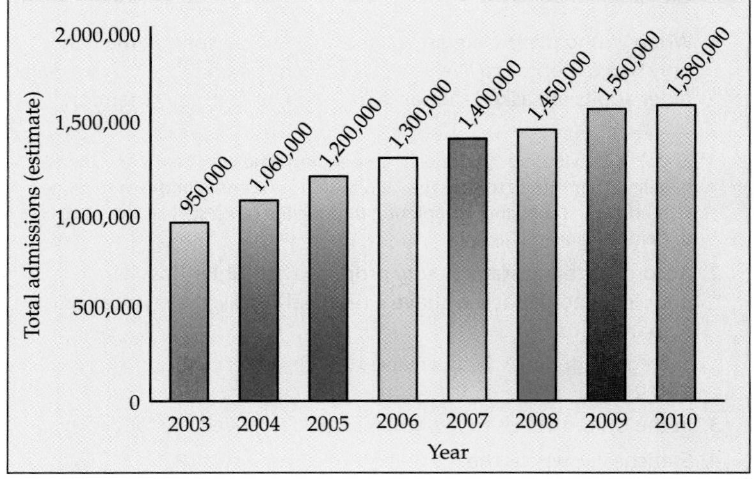

FIGURE 18-3 Total Annual Hospice Patients Served in the United States, 2003–2010

Hospice care has grown significantly in the United States in recent years. In 2010, nearly 42% of all deaths in the United States were under the care of a hospice program.

SOURCE: *Hospice care in America, 2011 edition*, National Hospice and Palliative Care Organization (NHPCO), 2012, Alexandria, VA: Author. Retrieved from http://www.nhpco.org/files/public/Statistics_Research/2011_Facts_Figures.pdf.

Both hospital care and hospice have an appropriate role in the care of the dying, and it is useful to consider the philosophies that guide these institutions. Hospitals are devoted to life and life support; hospital personnel tend to see death as the enemy, and they often work to prolong life, sometimes in ways that are not sensitive to the wishes of the patient. The hospice concept emphasizes that death is a normal and natural stage of life to be approached with dignity. According to the hospice philosophy,

hospice
A philosophy of care designed to help people with a terminal illness live out their days as fully and independently as possible by giving the needed care, counseling, support, pain management, and other assistance for people with a terminal illness and their families

Watch *Hospice Care* on MyDevelopmentLab

TRY THIS!

Exploring the Dimensions of Hospice Care

The hospice movement has grown dramatically in the United States in recent years. One reason for this dramatic growth is that hospice provides the kind of end-of-life support and care that many people with terminal illnesses and their families find responsive and supportive. To better understand how people experience the kind of care that hospice organizations provide at the end of life, try this!

Identify and interview a person who has had firsthand experience with hospice care—what it provided and what it meant in the context of the loss of a loved one. Perhaps you know a person who lost a family member or a close friend to a terminal illness who received hospice care during the final days or weeks leading up to the death. If so, you might ask if he or she would be willing to talk with you about the hospice care experience. If you do not know anyone who has firsthand experience with hospice, you might call your local hospital or hospice chapter and ask to speak to a hospice nurse or caregiver. Any person who has been involved with hospice is likely to be willing to talk about how this program works.

The focus of your interview should be based on the following three general themes:

- What services did (or does) hospice provide, and what is the philosophy of care that hospice care embraces?
- What specific difficulties did hospice address, and how successful was hospice in helping to ease the challenges in the final stages of terminal illness? In particular, you may wish to explore how pain medication typically was administered and how the hospice personnel worked with the patient and the family to balance the effectiveness of pain management with the need for the patient to remain alert and aware.
- How did the services that hospice provided affect the final weeks, days, and hours of life, both for the person who was dying and for the person's family and friends?

Reflect on What You Observed

Many people, and younger people in particular, have trouble discussing the subject of death, especially when it becomes *real*, that is, when it is associated with the real death of a specific individual. Interviewing a person about his or her experiences with hospice care may involve emotional issues that you will need to be aware of, both for the person who talks with you and for yourself as well. Try to be sensitive and flexible as you discuss how care was provided to the person who was dying that you are talking about. Was it difficult for the person you interviewed to discuss the circumstances surrounding the loved one's death? Was it difficult for you to conduct your interview without becoming too involved or without remaining too distant and detached? What did you learn about hospice care? What seemed to be the goal or goals of the hospice program involved in the specific situation you discussed? Did the person you interviewed generally have positive or negative feelings about hospice care? What factors contributed to the person's overall impression of hospice care?

Consider the Issues

Based on what you learned, what do you think about hospice care programs? If a person close to you were in the final stages of a terminal illness, would you want to rely on hospice care? If you were terminally ill, what would you think about using hospice services? In the specific case you investigated, were the hospice services appreciated? What specific aspects of hospice care seemed to make the most difference? Do you think the circumstances of a person's illness would affect the usefulness of hospice care? Under what circumstances do you think hospice care would be most advantageous?

death is viewed as natural, as is birth. Like birth, death sometimes requires assistance; hospice care is designed to provide that assistance and comfort. The primary goal of hospice care is to manage pain of all types, including physical, mental, social, and spiritual pain. Beyond that, hospice workers try to respect the dying person's rights concerning their choices about death whenever possible (DeSpelder & Strickland, 2011; Knee, 2010). In addition, they help the family understand the dying person's experience and needs, and they keep the lines of communication open so that the person who is dying feels less isolated. Hospice contact with the family continues up to and beyond their loved one's death, extending throughout the period of bereavement.

The Right to Die

If, as many people believe, death is a natural and essentially positive experience, should we use artificial means to prolong a person's life? Do we rob people of a dignified death if we use technology to maintain their bodily systems beyond the point at which they can ever recover? Is there a time when a person of whatever age is *meant* to die, when it would be better to let nature take its course? Do we prolong life because we fear death, although the patients themselves may be ready to die? These questions have received a great deal of attention in recent years, and many people now demand a **right to die**, which advocates that death is a right to be exercised at the individual's discretion. People who embrace the right to die concept believe that individuals should be able to control when and how their life should end.

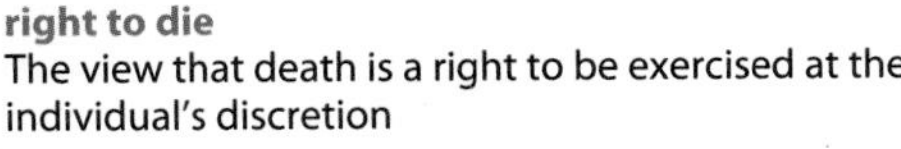

right to die
The view that death is a right to be exercised at the individual's discretion

Active Euthanasia The idea that individuals should decide when to die, of course, is not entirely new. *Euthanasia*, or *mercy killing*, was practiced in ancient Greece and probably earlier. One of the more notable advocates of euthanasia in the 20th century was Sigmund Freud. In 1939, the 83-year-old Freud, who had been suffering from painful cancer of the jaw for 16 years, decided that he had had enough: "Now it is nothing but torture, and makes no sense any more" (cited in Shapiro, 1978). Freud had previously made a pact with his physician to administer a lethal dose of morphine should he decide that he could no longer bear his intense pain and frustration. Freud asked that the agreement be put into effect, and the doctor honored his wish.

In Freud's case, nature was not simply allowed to take its course; positive steps were taken to bring about death. This is generally called **active euthanasia**, although many would consider the term euphemistic. In U.S. society, active euthanasia is legally considered to be murder, although it is sometimes treated with leniency. This is especially true in cases where the final act of euthanasia is carried out by the person who is dying so that it legally can be considered a suicide. Termed **assisted suicide**, this is what happens in the widely publicized cases of people with terminal illnesses who are provided with "death machines" that allow them to self-administer a lethal drug (Corr, Corr, & Bordere, 2013; Lewy, 2011).

The question of how far a physician should go in easing a person's death is a hotly debated question. Most polls indicate that the majority of U.S. people now support the right of individuals with a terminal illness to receive a lethal drug from their physician if they wish (Harris Poll, 2005, 2007). Some health-related professional organizations also endorse this view. On the other hand, the majority of these organizations, including the American Medical Association (AMA), strongly oppose suicide with the assistance of a physician. What are some of the issues?

Why do you think the AMA is opposed to physician-assisted suicide when most of the adults in the United States support this practice? What are the central issues involved in this debate?

Proponents of assisted suicide argue that a significant number of people die in pain and agony after lengthy battles with diseases such as cancer and AIDS. Despite major advances in the management of pain, modern narcotics often do not eliminate it. Moreover, current laws often prohibit doctors from prescribing excessive dosages of painkillers. Bear in mind that a person's tolerance for narcotics increases with sustained use, requiring continuously increasing dosages that render the patient immobile and unconscious much of the time. Thus, for many people with a terminal illness, the quality of life declines rapidly as death approaches.

Opponents of assisted suicide argue that it constitutes a form of active euthanasia, which they see as murder. They are extremely wary of the precedent that would be set by legalizing assisted suicide. Particularly troubling are the issues of informed consent. Are people in the later stages of disease, who often are heavily medicated, fully competent to make these decisions about assisted suicide? Would family members or medical professionals be granted the right to make these decisions for others? Opponents worry that endorsing assisted suicide provides a foothold for legalizing euthanasia, which they see as an unacceptable practice.

The debate about active euthanasia will continue to unfold as people with terminal illnesses, their families, their physicians, and the courts search for a means of providing a "good death" for those who choose to take an active role in the decision about when and how their life should end (Smith, 2012). Alternatives to active euthanasia continue to be developed as we gain more knowledge about managing pain and providing appropriate care for those in the terminal stage of an illness. Less controversial—but posing equally difficult philosophical issues—is the practice of passive euthanasia.

Passive Euthanasia **Passive euthanasia** involves withholding or disconnecting life-sustaining equipment so that death can occur naturally. Passive, voluntary euthanasia has become a conspicuous issue because of relatively recent medical advances in the ability to sustain life—in some cases almost indefinitely. Indeed, a major issue is how to determine when to disconnect life-support machines. Part of the issue surrounding passive euthanasia concerns defining when death technically occurs. Although there are criteria in place for determining death, as outlined in Table 18-3, these definitions do not fully resolve all of the issues (Kastenbaum, 2012). For example, do functioning and blood flow have to be absent in all areas of the brain for the person to be considered dead, or is cessation of activity in the cerebral cortex sufficient? Such questions are most likely to be raised—and the criteria are most likely to be invoked—when there are differing opinions among family members or medical staff and a judge is asked to make the decision about terminating life support.

For adults who wish to make their preference clearly understood that extravagant efforts or artificial means should not be used to sustain their lives, a **living will** can be prepared (see Figure 18-4). A living will informs a person's family, or others who may be concerned, of the person's wish to avoid the use of heroic or extraordinary measures to maintain life in the event of irreversible illness. Although it is not legally binding, a living will does clarify a person's wishes and provides both comfort and some legal protection to a loved one who makes the decision to discontinue the use of artificial means to sustain life. Another important document is a **medical power of attorney**, which is a legal document prepared and notarized while a person is still of sound mind. This document authorizes a loved one or other

active euthanasia
Taking steps to bring about another person's death, specifically in cases of terminal illness; in the United States, active euthanasia is considered to be murder

living will
A legal directive signed by a person indicating that the person does not wish that extraordinary measures be employed to sustain life in case of terminal illness

assisted suicide
Providing people with a terminal illness the means to end their own lives, such as by allowing them to self-administer a lethal drug

medical power of attorney
A legal document by which a person authorizes another to make life-or-death medical decisions on his or her behalf

passive euthanasia
Withholding or disconnecting life-sustaining equipment so that death can occur naturally

Table 18-3 The Harvard Criteria for the Determination of a Permanently Nonfunctioning (Dead) Brain

Criteria	Description
Unreceptive and unresponsive	• No awareness is shown for external stimuli or inner need • The unresponsiveness is complete, even under the application of stimuli that ordinarily would be extremely painful
No movements or breathing	• There is a complete absence of spontaneous respiration and all other spontaneous muscular movement
No reflexes	• The usual reflexes that can be elicited in a neurophysiological examination are absent (e.g., when a light is shined in the eye, the pupil does not constrict)
Flat electroencephalogram (EEG)	• Electrodes attached to the scalp elicit a printout of electrical activity from the living brain, popularly known as *brain waves,* but the brain does not provide the usual pattern of peaks and valleys • Moving automatic stylus essentially records a flat line, which is taken to demonstrate the lack of electrophysiological activity
No circulation to or within the brain	• Lack of oxygen and nutrition provided to the brain by the blood supply will soon terminate its functioning; length of time the brain can retain its viability without circulation currently under investigation and varies somewhat with condition

SOURCE: From *Death, society, and human experience* (6th ed.), by R. J. Kastenbaum, 1998, Boston: Allyn & Bacon.

trusted person to make life-or-death medical decisions on the person's behalf if the person becomes mentally incapacitated due to an injury or during a protracted illness—particularly an illness such as Alzheimer's disease, in which dementia can precede the loss of crucial bodily functions by years.

The concepts upon which a living will and a medical power of attorney are centered are extended somewhat when individuals prepare and sign another type of legal document called the "Five Wishes" (Aging with Dignity, 2012; see Table 18-2). The concept behind the Five Wishes document is to combine the legal protections afforded by a living will and a medical power of attorney with specific personal directions from the terminally ill patient. In completing the Five Wishes document, the ill person reads a series of statements about various types of end-of-life care that are available, and chooses which statements best correspond to his or her own desires about the treatment preferred at the end of life. For example, the person may either agree or disagree with a statement requesting that prayers or meaningful poems be read during the final hours of life. The Five Wishes also gives the dying person the option of communicating any final messages to loved ones and to express wishes about final arrangements, such as funeral or memorial services. In completing the Five Wishes document, which is now legally binding in 42 states, the person has a chance to anticipate the decisions that will be made at the end of life and to participate in how these decisions will be made.

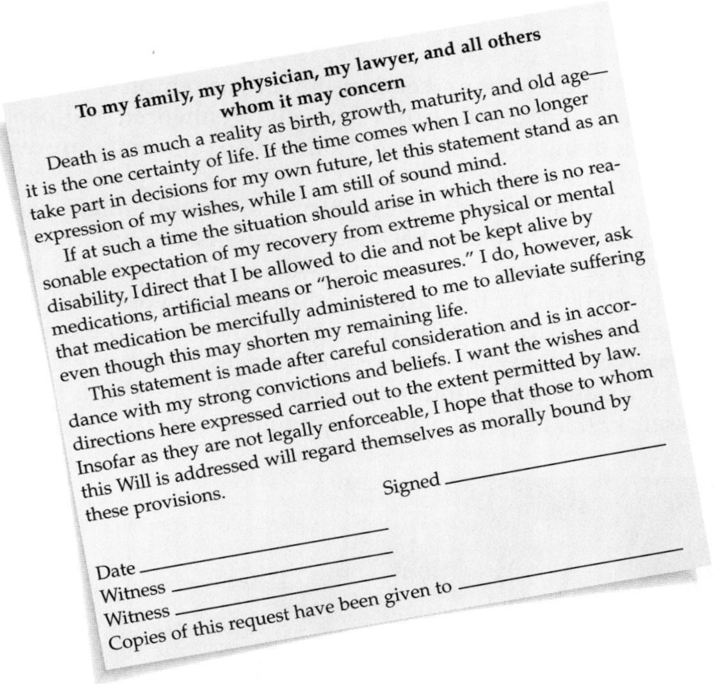

To my family, my physician, my lawyer, and all others whom it may concern

Death is as much a reality as birth, growth, maturity, and old age—it is the one certainty of life. If the time comes when I can no longer take part in decisions for my own future, let this statement stand as an expression of my wishes, while I am still of sound mind.

If at such a time the situation should arise in which there is no reasonable expectation of my recovery from extreme physical or mental disability, I direct that I be allowed to die and not be kept alive by medications, artificial means or "heroic measures." I do, however, ask that medication be mercifully administered to me to alleviate suffering even though this may shorten my remaining life.

This statement is made after careful consideration and is in accordance with my strong convictions and beliefs. I want the wishes and directions here expressed carried out to the extent permitted by law. Insofar as they are not legally enforceable, I hope that those to whom this Will is addressed will regard themselves as morally bound by these provisions.

Signed ______

Date ______
Witness ______
Witness ______
Copies of this request have been given to ______

FIGURE 18-4 A Living Will
This is a formal request prepared by Concern for Dying and the Educational Council. It informs the signer's family, or others who may be concerned, of the signer's wish to avoid the use of "heroic measures" to maintain life in the event of irreversible illness.

Decisions about living wills and powers of attorney and end-of-life care, of course, apply when people who are terminally ill are adults and therefore can make decisions about their own lives. When a life-threatening illness affects a child, a different set of legal options is available. Parents, or guardians, and medical professionals must determine the course of treatment. In some instances, especially when there is disagreement, legal challenges ensue and courts become involved.

Palliative and End-of-Life Care Controversies about choices available to people who are dying focus attention on what is the best strategy for managing life-threatening illnesses. A useful distinction concerns the differences between palliative care and end-of-life care. **Palliative care** can be defined as care that attempts to prevent or relieve the emotional distress and physical difficulties associated with a life-threatening illness. The aim of palliative care is to allow people with terminal illnesses

palliative care
Care that attempts to prevent or relieve the emotional distress and physical difficulties associated with a life-threatening illness

and their families to live as normal a life as possible (Matzo & Sherman, 2010; Werth & Blevins, 2009). Palliative care can be provided along with medical treatments. For example, if a child who has cancer must be hospitalized for an extended period, palliative care seeks to provide that child and the child's family with as normal a lifestyle as possible, perhaps by arranging for nearby living facilities for the family, by providing access to favorite foods and TV shows, and by ensuring the child and the family private time to be alone.

End-of-life care, on the other hand, specifically addresses the concerns and the circumstances associated with impending death. Providing opportunities for the person who is dying to express his or her concerns and wishes; to settle affairs; and to manage how, and how much, medical intervention will be used are examples of considerations in end-of-life care (Gillick, 2009). When palliative care and end-of-life care are emphasized, communication among all parties typically is enhanced and people who are dying and their family members generally are well-served (Connor, 2009).

Are you aware of any palliative care services provided in your community? What services do you think would be most useful?

Because the final stages of a terminal illness sometimes are difficult to manage and because so many issues are involved, in 1997 the American Medical Association approved a set of new guidelines for providing quality care to people at the end of their life (AMA, 1997). These guidelines were the result of an extensive study, a series of conferences, and a report written by a national committee on end-of-life care (M. J. Field & Cassel, 1997). In particular, the guidelines specify that people with a terminal illness or their decision makers should be provided with the opportunity for full information about their condition, as well as to the decisions and plans for end-of-life care. They also should be assured that their wishes will be followed and that they will be treated with dignity and respect throughout all stages of their illness. Finally, active provisions should be arranged so that pain is reduced, to the degree possible, and comfort is increased. These guidelines, of course, reflect the principles that already govern the delivery of high-quality end-of-life care, and they support the continuing expansion of improved end-of-life care in hospitals and nursing homes and the increased use of hospice services.

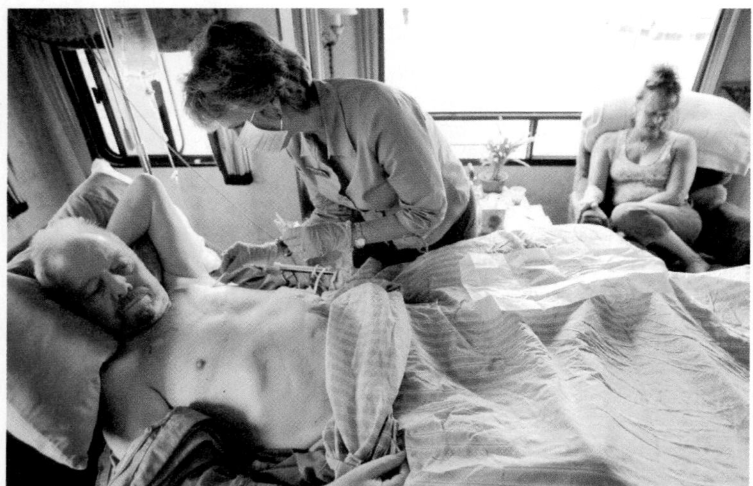

▲ Palliative, end-of-life care includes the provision of effective pain medication that the patient can control to the extent possible.

Despite the increasing availability of more humane care at the end of life, death is still usually a sad event that is characterized by grieving. In the next section of this chapter, we explore grief and bereavement, including patterns of grief, cross-cultural perspectives on grieving, rituals and customs associated with grieving, and grieving when a child dies.

REVIEW THE FACTS 18-3

1. When people with a terminal illness are able to retain a sense of control in their lives, do they often die sooner or live longer?
2. The philosophy and support organization that assists people who are terminally ill to live out their final days as fully and independently as possible is called ________ care.
3. The word currently used for what used to be called *mercy killing* is ________.
4. When people sign over the legal responsibility to make medical decisions should they become mentally or physically incapable, such a document is called a(n) ________.
5. Care that is intended to prevent or relieve the emotional distress and physical difficulties associated with a life-threatening illness is called ________ care.

Practice on **MyDevelopmentLab**

GRIEF AND BEREAVEMENT

Although preliminary steps, such as signing a medical power of attorney, preparing a living will, and arranging for end-of-life care, can help caregivers make decisions about how a person should be cared for at the end of life, no amount of preparation can eliminate the sense of loss that occurs when a loved one actually dies. Surviving family members and close friends often must make major adjustments to a loved one's death; for them, life must go on. **Bereavement** is the process during which people cope and eventually come to terms with a loved one's death.

A useful way of conceptualizing the bereavement process is according to the **dual-process model of stress and coping**

end-of-life care
Care that specifically addresses the concerns and the circumstances associated with impending death

Bereavement
The process during which people cope with a loved one's death

Dual-process model of stress and coping
Model that suggests that bereavement consists of two dimensions of stress, the emotional grief felt as the result of loss and the life changes and adaptations that must be made to move forward with life

(Stroebe & Schut, 2010). According to this view, the bereavement process must accommodate two sources of stress, which are quite different from each other. The first involves coping with grief—the emotional sense of loss and longing that comes with losing contact with a person to whom one is closely attached. To work through the grieving process, people often cling to their connections with the person who has died. For example, a widow may be reluctant to part with her husband's favorite shirt, and may take comfort in wearing it to bed at night. Many people like to keep pictures of lost loved ones on display, and they take comfort in remembering the fine qualities of the person who died (Whitbourne & Whitbourne, 2011). The second process involves learning to live in a world without the person who died. When it is one's spouse or partner who dies, this usually involves not only absorbing many more chores and tasks, such as cooking or servicing the car, but also learning to think of oneself as a single person, rather than as one-half of a couple (Stroebe, Schut, & Boerner, 2010). If the death involves a parent or child, similar adjustments are usually required. Healthy adjustment to a loved one's death involves attending to both of these tasks.

Another way of thinking about bereavement is to consider the time dimension associated with various sorts of coping tasks. Some of the adjustments to be made following the death of a loved one are best described as short-term adjustments. These include coping with initial emotional reactions—often called **grief work**—in addition to coping with practical matters, such as arranging for a funeral and taking care of legal and financial issues. Long-term adjustments—particularly for a widow, widower, or life partner—include changes in life patterns, routines, roles, and activities that may be necessary as these people cope with the social void left by their loved one's death (see Chapter 17). The degree to which survivors must adjust depends on a myriad of factors, including the degree of independence the survivor maintained prior to the loved one's death, the financial resources available, the amount and kind of social support available, and so forth. For many older adults, the loss of a spouse or life partner comes at a time in the lifespan when their own resources are taxed, and coping can be especially difficult (Hansson & Stroebe, 2007). The extent of grief is also related to the circumstances surrounding the death. When an older person is suffering from a painful or debilitating terminal condition, the grieving process is quite different than when a younger person—and especially a child—dies. Nevertheless, whenever a loved one dies, grief is a consistent response.

Grieving

Does grieving serve a purpose? The prevailing view is that certain psychological tasks need to be accomplished after the loss of a loved one (Stroebe, 2011; Weiss, 2008). The survivor needs to accept the reality of the loss and the pain associated with it. In addition, the survivor must rechannel the emotional energy that previously was invested in the relationship with the deceased person. Grieving addresses these issues and helps the person cope.

Many experts hesitate to define specific phases of grieving on the grounds that it might encourage people to *force* what are widely varying patterns of grieving into some prescribed sequence (Lieberman, 2010; Stroebe, 2008). Also, research suggests that individuals vary quite widely in how much grief they experience following the death of a loved one (Bonanno, Boerner, & Wortman, 2008; Wortman & Silver, 2001). Yet, for many people, grieving does tend to follow a predictable course. Immediately after a loved one's death, for example, most people experience a shock phase that often lasts for several days and sometimes much longer. Especially after a sudden, unanticipated death, the people closest to the deceased may participate in the funeral ceremonies and burial in a robotlike fashion, not yet fully believing that the loss has occurred. As the shock of the loss eases, survivors typically experience active grief in the form of weeping or other expressions of sorrow. They may yearn for the deceased person. Some people have symptoms, such as feelings of weakness or emptiness, as well as appetite loss and sleep disturbances. They often lose interest in normal pursuits and become preoccupied with thoughts of the deceased, and they may exhibit the full range of symptoms associated with depression.

Eventually, however, most survivors begin to recover; they adjust to their new life circumstances. They let go of their loved one, invest time and energy in new relationships, and reconstruct an identity apart from their relationship with the deceased. Grieving can involve personal growth, as the person increases in self-understanding, maturity, coping skills, and the ability to adapt to change (Field, 2008; Schaefer & Moos, 2001). This does not, however, mean that grieving individuals forget their loved ones and cease to think about them. Instead, what seems to happen is that the emotional pain associated with thoughts of the loved one gradually diminishes.

There are, of course, many patterns of grieving; these depend on personality, age, sex, cultural traditions, and on the quality of the relationship with the deceased. Regardless of how a person experiences grief, certain grieving tasks must be accomplished (Corr, Corr, & Bordere, 2013; Kaslow, 2004; see Table 18-4). The first task typically involves *healing,* where the person adjusts to the sense of loss and the new roles and responsibilities forced by the death of their loved one. Eventually, the person enters the *renewal* phase of grieving, in which new life patterns are established and the person reestablishes a future-oriented focus.

Healing and renewal are, of course, experienced differently by different individuals. For example, when death is preceded by a long illness, some of the grief tasks can be addressed early on. In these cases, survivors may experience **anticipatory grief** by emotionally preparing themselves for the death of a loved

grief work
Methods of dealing with the emotional reactions to the loss of a loved one

Watch *Death of a Spouse* on **MyDevelopmentLab**

anticipatory grief
Grief experienced as people emotionally prepare themselves for the death of a loved one, as in cases of prolonged terminal illness

Table 18-4 Tasks Associated with Coping in the Healing and Renewal Phases of Loss

TASKS IN THE HEALING PHASE OF GRIEVING

- Relinquishing roles, particularly the roles of a spouse
- Forming a new identity that is separate from the person who has died
- Caring for self
- Assuming control and responsibility for one's own decisions
- Centering or soothing and calming oneself
- Forgiving the loved one for dying
- Searching for meaning in the loved one's death
- Attaining closure, often through conducting a ritual or ceremony to mark the loved one's passing
- Renewing hope and realistically remembering both sad and happy times

TASKS IN THE RENEWAL PHASE

- Keeping loneliness in perspective while learning to live without the loved one
- Enduring anniversaries without undue longing and grief
- Accepting new roles and learning to enjoy life again
- Focusing attention on setting and achieving new goals
- Reaching out and establishing new relationships with others
- Understanding the long process of grieving

SOURCE: Adapted from "Death of one's partner: The anticipation and the reality," by F. W. Kaslow, 2004, Professional Psychology: Research and Practice, 35(3), 227–233.

▲ When this Russian community experienced the sudden death of several community members including several schoolchildren, many of the adults were left with that empty, prolonged grief reaction and depression characteristic of bereavement overload.

one. Although anticipatory grief does not eliminate postdeath grieving, it may make it easier to cope with the death when it occurs. If an illness lasts too long, however, the emotional drain of caring for the person tends to outweigh the benefits of anticipatory grief. Moreover, when an illness is prolonged, the survivor may become convinced that the person who is terminally ill will not really die, and that the person has beaten the odds. In such cases, the person's eventual death can be even more shocking than a sudden death would have been.

In what ways might social support assist a person during the grieving process? Are there ways in which social support can prolong the grieving process as well?

Social support can play a positive role in grieving, especially when it comes from others who have experienced a similar loss (Steiner, 2006). Self-help support groups for widowed people can be of significant value (Walter, 2005), as can groups organized to support those left behind following a death by suicide (Jordan, 2011). Parents who have lost a child often find it comforting to interact with others whose children have died, and children and adolescents who have lost loved ones also benefit from support groups (Balk, 2011; Cacciatore, 2007; Schuurman & DeCristofaro, 2010). People who participate in these self-help groups often find comfort in sharing their fears and feelings with others who may understand, better than even well-meaning family members, what their grieving is like. Self-help support groups also provide a protective setting in which to form new relationships and to try out new roles so that people become less isolated and become better able to help themselves.

However, even with the support of others, grieving still implies a significant adjustment, and research suggests that emotional disclosure to others does not necessarily compensate for the grieving person's loss or contribute significantly to that person's adjustment in normal bereavement situations (Stroebe, Schut, & Stroeke, 2005). Also, there is wide variation in patterns of coping with grief. Men and women often adopt different coping styles, as do members of different ethnic groups and those with various personality styles (Martin & Doka, 2011; Rosenblatt, 2008). No one approach to grieving fits all.

There are circumstances where grief may be particularly overwhelming. For example, people who experience the loss of several friends or family members in a relatively short span of time may experience **bereavement overload**, which is a stress reaction that often is characterized by depression. Bereavement overload also affects communities that may lose many members in a short span of time—such as those who lose several close friends to AIDS, whose family or friends perish in a natural disaster or accident, or who simply have the misfortune to experience multiple losses from a variety of factors. Depression then becomes a serious risk during bereavement, especially for men (Corr, 2003; M. S. Stroebe, Hansson, Stroebe, & Schut, 2001), as do drug and alcohol abuse. Not surprisingly, physical health also may be affected as people cope with their losses and deal with the stress these losses cause. Sometimes grieving becomes an ingrained, pathological mourning process

bereavement overload
A stress reaction experienced by people who lose several friends or loved ones during a short period of time; often characterized by depression

in which the person never overcomes the grief. Some researchers are suggesting that a new diagnostic category—prolonged grief disorder—be added to the next edition of the *Diagnostic and Statistical Manual* (American Psychiatric Association, 2000), the guide that is used throughout the United States to diagnose mental disorders (Prigerson, Vanderwerker, & Maciejewski, 2008). This **chronic grief** is especially difficult to address because it pervades the overall context of the grieving person's life.

Bereavement in Cross-Cultural Perspective

Although the grief process is different for every person, cultural expectations often shape, at least in a general way, how grief is experienced. Cultural norms also generally prescribe how individuals are expected to cope (Hayslip & Peveto, 2005; Klass & Chow, 2011; Walter, 2012). The modern Western view of grief typically requires that people engage in "proper grieving" by recovering from their grief and returning to normal functioning as quickly as possible. This perspective, however, is not generally shared by other cultures around the world (DeSpelder & Strickland, 2011). For example, many non-Western cultures stress maintaining a continuing bond with the deceased. In the Japanese tradition, for instance, mourners have an altar in their home dedicated to the family's ancestors. They offer food at the altar and talk to the ancestors, whom they believe are accessible to them. In Egypt, mourners are encouraged to express their grief through emotional outpourings. In Mexico, there is a traditional celebration of ancestors called *Dia de los Muertos* (translated as the *Day of the Dead*), which involves offerings and a joyful community celebration where the deceased family members are reintegrated into the family as ancestors.

Even in Western cultures, grief is recognized differently today than it was in the historical past. Although current Western thought about grief emphasizes a rational response as the means of returning to normal functioning, grief was viewed differently during the 19th century. For example, it was common for widows 150 years ago to dress in black, to mourn for at least a year, and to expect grief to occupy a significant and extended role in their life. In contrast, as noted earlier, adults today often are expected to quickly resume normal activities, perhaps returning to work a day or two after the funeral (Doka, 2008). Interestingly, this rapid return to normal life does not appear to reduce the grief that people feel. Research shows that despite their return to routine, most people whose loved ones die do not adjust quickly to their loss (Carmelley, Wortman, Bolger, & Burke, 2006; Stroebe et al., 2001). Rather, many widows and widowers tend to maintain their ties to the deceased, just as the bereaved did during earlier historical periods. Widows and widowers may sense their spouse's presence for years after their spouse has died, and the deceased continues to have a strong psychological influence on the survivor's life.

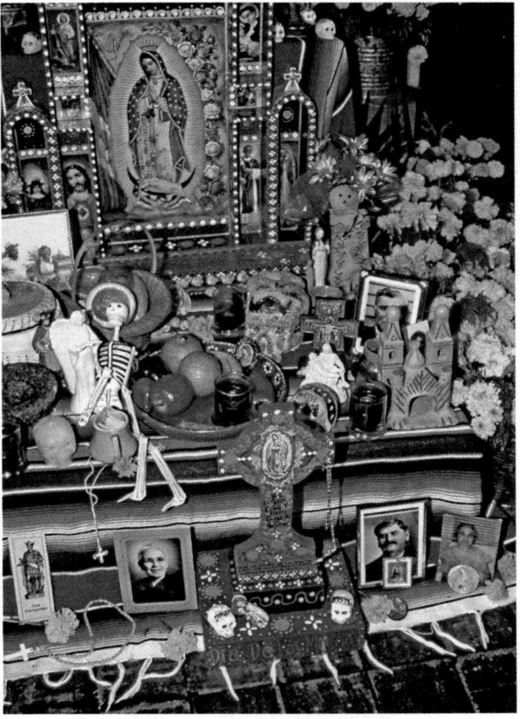

In the Mexican celebration of *Dia de los Muertos*, there is both sadness over the recent loss of a loved one but also joyous celebration that recognizes that those who have recently died have joined their family ancestors. Here, an altar commemorates those who have died, as part of the celebration of the *Day of the Dead*.

Rituals and Customs

Culture-based views of death and grieving are often reflected in the specific kinds of rituals and customs that are used to mark the end of a person's life, to celebrate the impact the person had while living, and to bring closure to the family and loved ones. In Western cultures, funerals and memorial services are common, and they can impart a sense of order, decorum, and continuity. They can reaffirm the values and beliefs of the individuals and the community, as well as demonstrate the support of family and friends. The deceased person's life can be reviewed and celebrated in a public, shared forum. Many other cultures have similar rituals.

What are the typical features of the rituals and ceremonies that are used in your family when a loved one dies? How are your customs similar to and different from those common to other groups of which you are aware?

Survivors often take considerable comfort from the rituals and customs common to their culture's acknowledgement of death. Sometimes, however, such ceremonies clash with the values and experiences of some of the survivors, leaving them feeling further isolated. Yet it is hard for most people to conceive of following a loved one's death with no ritual whatsoever; rituals make the end "official," and they often are helpful in allowing the survivors to deal with their grief.

chronic grief
An ingrained, pathological mourning process in which the person never overcomes the grief

Watch *Death, Grief, and Mournig* on **MyDevelopmentLab**

In summary, grief reactions and the rituals and customs that surround the process and the fact of dying differ markedly from person to person and from culture to culture. Perhaps the important point is that there is not a universal, right way to grieve, although societal expectations are powerful influences that can make it appear that there is.

The Death of a Child

The death of a child often involves special sorrow and grief. If a child's death follows an extended illness, loved ones—parents, siblings, grandparents, and friends—must prepare for and cope with the child's difficult period of declining health leading up to death. When death is sudden, perhaps the result of an accident or a rapidly progressing illness, there is little time to adjust, and the grieving process often is extremely painful.

Regardless of the age of the person who is dying, caregivers and loved ones usually play a major role in managing the circumstances surrounding the person's death. When the person who is dying is young, this poses special challenges. This partly is due to the out-of-sequence nature of children's deaths. In developed countries like the United States, the death rates for infants and children have fallen dramatically. In 1900, only a little more than a century ago, the death rate of U.S. children under the age of 5 was 30%; by 2009, it had dropped to about 1.5%. Similarly, infant mortality has declined from about 10% in 1915 to less than 1% today (NCHS, 2012d). Reflecting these dramatic changes in demographic trends, we simply do not expect infants and children to die. When they do die, the tragedy seems especially acute.

Nevertheless, young people do die. According to U.S. Census data, in 2010 about 63,700 U.S. children and adolescents between the ages of 0 and 24 died (Murphey, Xu, & Kochanek, 2012). Most of these deaths occurred in infancy, as shown in Figure 18-5. Nearly everyone can recall the death of a child whom they knew.

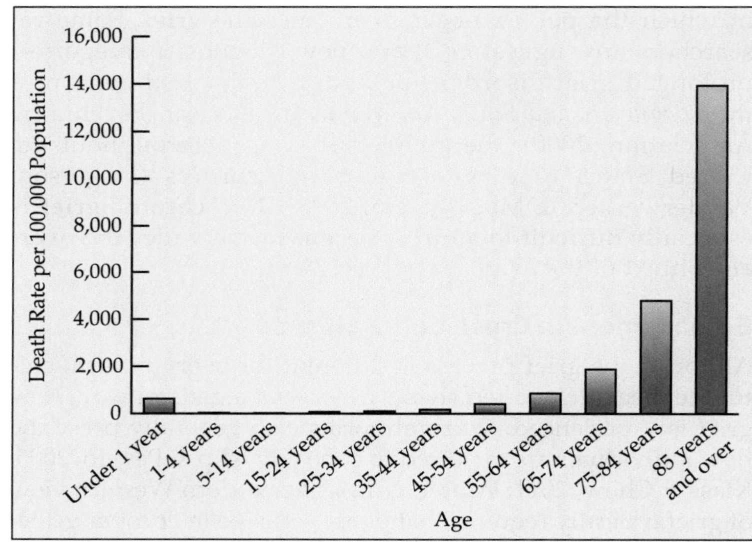

FIGURE 18-5 Percentage of Deaths in the United States, by Age Group

NOTE: Data are for 2010.

SOURCE: "Deaths: Preliminary data for 2010, by S. L. Murphy, J. Xu, & K. D. Kochanek, January 2012, *National Vital Statistics Reports, 60*(4). Retrieved from http://www.cdc.gov/nchs/data/nvsr/nvsr60/nvsr60_04.pdf

Individuals with Disabilities A special set of circumstances applies when a family includes one or more members who have significant intellectual or developmental disabilities. This is true both when it is the disabled person who is dying, and also when the death involves a family member. If a death occurs within such a family, it is of course the case that the disabled person will experience loss and will need to adjust to changes within daily routines, just as do other members of the family (Doka, 2010). In previous decades, many individuals with disabilities were placed in institutional care as babies or young children, where the death of a family member did not disrupt so significantly their daily routines or attachments to family members. Today, most people with disabilities live at home, at least until they reach adulthood. Thus, when a family member dies, they—like all members of the family—experience grief and go through a bereavement process. Furthermore, whereas in previous decades it was more typical for individuals with significant disabilities to die early in life, today—owing to life-extending medical advances—most people with intellectual disabilities live normal or near-normal lifespans. For example, 50 years ago, most individuals with Down's syndrome died in childhood, adolescence, or in their early adult years. Today, these people typically live into middle adulthood, and sometimes beyond. Therefore, it is much more likely today that an intellectually or developmentally disabled person will experience the death of parents, and perhaps other family members. Families, therefore, must plan for and cope with these realities.

If the disabled person is the one who is terminally ill, a different set of issues emerges. For example, if the disability is severe, caregivers need to establish what constitutes a good quality of life (Hauer, 2010; Runswick-Cole, 2010). Also, family members are emotionally attached to disabled members of the family, just as they are to members who do not have a disability. It is therefore expected that the family left behind when a disabled child dies will grieve over this loss, even if—and perhaps especially if—the disabled child needed significant levels of care (Doka, 2010). Counseling can be especially helpful for family members who must struggle with reestablishing routines and who may question whether or not they had "done enough" to provide the best level of care for the disabled child.

During which developmental period—infancy and toddlerhood, early childhood, middle childhood, or adolescence—do you think death provokes the most difficult coping responses? Why?

Watch *Jewish and Islamic Funeral Rituals* on **MyDevelopmentLab**

CHANGING PERSPECTIVES

Humane End-of-Life Care for Children Who Are Dying and for Their Families

Everyone wants humane care for anyone who is dying—perhaps most of all for children and for their families—because an early death seems especially unfair and tragic. No one, least of all family members and those who care for children who are dying, seeks to provide anything but the best, most responsive, and most appropriate care for these children. Yet it is not always easy to understand what constitutes the best care. Sometimes well-meaning people who are caught up in saving lives or preserving the life of a loved one at all costs fail to make the most humane decisions, although this is precisely their intention.

Doctors and medical-care professionals are very good at finding and delivering life-saving treatments; however, these treatments sometimes may be painful and invasive, and they may not necessarily extend the life of the patient. Administering these procedures to children is often especially challenging because children are difficult to medicate for pain, especially if they are too young to speak or too ill or weak to respond accurately. Families also may cling to any hope that their child will survive, asking for extravagant treatments that may briefly extend their child's life; however, they may subject their child to prolonged suffering in the process. No one wants to cause pain or to extend suffering; therefore, when a child experiences a life-threatening illness, what can—and should—be done?

To better understand how to sensitively and humanely care for children who are dying and for their families, the Institute of Medicine launched a major effort to study this problem and to make national policy recommendations (M. J. Field & Behrman, 2003). In the course of their investigation, the researchers identified several pertinent problems in caring for children with life-threatening illnesses. Sometimes family members who must make decisions about the kind of care that will be delivered receive confusing or misleading explanations of the treatment options that are available. Much information about medicine is still unknown, and treatments do not provide clear outcomes for all people. For example, a painful chemotherapy treatment may extend life, statistically, by 2 to 3 years on average. However, this does not mean that a particular child will experience a prolonged life, and it also does not mean that the quality of whatever extra days or years the treatment provides will be positive for the child or for the child's family. The most serious illnesses of childhood often are rare, and little information is available about what the best treatment options are. In addition, when a disease is unusually rare or complex, children are often treated in hospitals far from their homes. When this occurs, family members must face the additional burden of finding appropriate and affordable lodging, and they must maintain a normal life for their other children while continuing to concentrate on their jobs and on their other responsibilities that cannot be put on hold.

Adding to the strain, negotiating insurance provisions and social service systems is very complex; family members who already are stressed by trying to deal with the shock and sadness that caring for a seriously ill child imposes may be ill equipped to deal with these additional details. The financial strain imposed by medical expenses during a serious illness, especially for families without insurance, is very difficult. Another problem of caring for a child with a serious illness involves the speed with which treatment decisions must sometimes be made. When a child is dying, there may be little opportunity to consider the various options and what they mean in terms of quality-of-life issues for the child. Furthermore, because caregivers and family members often are reluctant to discuss negative outcomes, such as death, decisions about care sometimes must be made without time for adequate emotional adjustment. As noted previously, the management of a child's pain is also a challenge.

What can be done to improve the outcomes for people who must cope with the impending death of a child? First, all parties involved must recognize that children are not just small adults; they have their own developmental needs for attachment and autonomy, and their understanding of what is happening necessarily will be limited by their general level of cognitive development. Their concerns and fears will not be the same as those of an adult, and caregivers must recognize their children's needs and ability to understand the realities of their situation (Corr, 2010). This is particularly true when the dying child has an intellectual disability that further limits the degree to which the child can understand what is happening and that may make changes in routine especially traumatic (Hauer, 2010). Furthermore, parents are not just decision makers—they *love* their child, and their intense emotional attachment may make it difficult to objectively decide the best course of treatment or the best way of dealing with their child's situation.

To assist people in recognizing the special concerns that accompany caring for children with life-threatening illnesses, a report was issued by the Institute of Medicine that suggested a set of working principles (M. J. Field & Behrman, 2003). Of special note are the following items:

- The need to attend to the pain and suffering of the ill child
- The need to expand funding options for more home-based services, such as hospice care, that provide more humane options and that are generally more cost-effective than hospital-based care, although these expenses sometimes are not covered by insurance
- The need to provide effective, ongoing education to health-care professionals that teaches them about the special circumstances that often surround a child's death

When children die, the lives of loved ones will likely be altered forever by this experience and loss. The goal of recommendations like those offered by the Institute of Medicine is to better understand and address more effectively the special circumstances that surround the death of a child. This is a noble goal and one worth pursuing.

Grieving When a Child Dies

Regardless of the specific circumstances, when death comes to a child, many aspects of grief and bereavement may be intensified. There is, however, considerable variability in how parents and others cope with a child's death (Arnold, 2008; Grinyer, 2012; Meij et al., 2008; Stroebe, Folkman, Hansson, & Schut, 2006). Some grieving parents, for example, appear to be hardier than others. They are better able to maintain a greater sense of personal control, a more active orientation toward meeting life's challenges, and a stronger belief in the ability to make sense of their own existence following a tragedy (A. Lang, Goulet, & Amsel, 2003). Gender differences also are often observed, reflecting the gender-role socialization that predominates within a culture (Alam, Barrera, D'Agostino, Nicolas, & Schneiderman, 2012). For example, in a study of parents who lost children in the Arab–Israeli conflict, mothers were more likely than fathers to see the forces surrounding their children's death as externally controlled, and they also expressed greater feelings of hopelessness about their loss (Rubinstein, 2004).

Regardless of the circumstances surrounding a child's death, confusion, guilt, and attempts to assign blame for the loss often result (M. J. Field & Behrman, 2003). Especially if the child's death is violent, parents generally have difficulty in dealing with their grief (Keesee, Currier, & Niemeyer, 2008). The death of a child, of course, affects everyone in the family. The brothers and sisters of a dying child may be particularly confused and disoriented (Koehler, 2010). Parents who are coping with their own grief often may be unable to help the other children in the family or even to answer a child's questions on an appropriate developmental level. Many grieving children do not disclose their secret fears, feelings of guilt, or misunderstandings; and yet many of the thoughts and feelings that arise during such a family crisis may last a lifetime (Davies, 2000).

When a child dies slowly of a terminal illness, there also are other issues to deal with (see the box Changing Perspectives: Humane End-of-Life Care for Children Who Are Dying and for Their Families). What should the dying child be told? How can the child be helped to confront death? How do the parents deal with their own feelings of failure, guilt, and helplessness? Medical caregivers often become personally involved in the child's hopes for recovery. They also experience feelings of failure and anticipatory grief. There is a tendency for all involved to deny these painful feelings.

A crisis of values is common among survivors after the death of a child. Certainly, the child did not deserve to die. The survivors often struggle, questioning and reevaluating their most closely held beliefs and values—especially religious ones—at the same time that they are suffering from numerous symptoms of sorrow and depression. Sometimes parents have trouble addressing their guilt, wondering what they have done to warrant such punishment; at the same time, they also recognize that the death was neither their fault nor under their control. Parents who find some way to resolve these issues often report sensing a deeper meaning in their own lives; those who do not resolve them may live out a lifetime in despair (Rogers, Floyd, Seltzer, Greenburg, & Hong, 2008; Rubin & Malkinson, 2001). Sometimes survivors derive comfort from channeling their energies into programs or initiatives that may benefit others. Parents may raise money for research leading to cures for the disease that claimed their child's life. In the case of fatal accidents, they may also find meaning and resolution in joining advocacy groups, such as Mothers Against Drunk Driving (MADD), that seek to prevent needless childhood deaths in the future. Support from the community in which the family lives is another factor affecting how well members of the family will be able to cope (Greeff, Vansteenwegen, & Herbiest, 2011). In any case, parents and other survivors cope in their own ways as best they can.

Regardless of the specific means through which individuals cope with the death of a loved one, there is a sense that death is final. In this sense, death completes the life cycle, which is the topic we address in the concluding section of this book.

REVIEW THE FACTS 18-4

1. What is the typical order of the following three phases of grief: active grief, shock, and letting go?
2. When a person experiences several major losses over a short time span, this may lead to
   a. chronic grief. b. suicidal erosion.
   c. bereavement overload. d. anticipatory grief.
3. In comparison to earlier historical periods, in the United States today, survivors are more likely to
   a. return quickly to a normal routine.
   b. grieve less.
   c. develop chronic grief.
   d. follow elaborate grieving rituals.
4. In 1900, about ________% of U.S. children under the age of 5 died; today that percentage is about ________%.
   a. 50; 10 b. 30; 1.5
   c. 10; 1.8 d. 10; 0.1
5. In comparison to grief experienced over an older person's death, when a child dies, are the grief responses of survivors frequently less or more intense?

Practice on **MyDevelopmentLab**

COMPLETING THE LIFE CYCLE

Ultimately, whether death involves a child; a frail, older adult; or a person at any stage of life; it marks the completion of that person's life cycle. We close the chapter—and this book—with some thoughts about what this completion means.

First, from the perspective of human lifespan development, it is useful to consider an individual's life as a cycle that begins at conception, ends at death, and encompasses the unfolding development that occurs between these points. Some cultural practices make the links between death, birth, and the life cycle explicit. For example, in Jewish culture, it is customary to name a newborn child after a deceased member of the immediate family; renewal and continuity are thus celebrated in the new birth. In traditional Chinese culture, a grandparent's death may prompt a grandchild of the appropriate age to marry or to have a child at the urging of family members. Hence, what seem like polar opposites—birth and death—are linked as part of a continuous family thread.

Can you suggest a specific example of how an individual's death has inspired others in positive ways?

Second, the death of an individual can inspire and transform the lives of the people who are left to grieve. Whatever the cultural backdrop, death and its prospects often give life new meaning for the surviving family members and perhaps for the entire community. As we try to make sense of a particular person's life and death, we often reassess our own priorities and values. The death of a world or community leader may sharpen cultural values and inspire a sense of common purpose and community. Yet, quite ordinary deaths often help just as much in defining the meaning of courage, loyalty, kindness, or virtue for a person, often in lasting and personal ways.

Finally, death—regardless of the circumstances—is a part of nature. It is undeniable and clear-cut. It happens to all of us, as well as to all members of every other species. Death is the end of life. It provides the final closure against which our lives are lived and a context within which we mark the transitions across earlier stages in the lifespan. Death is the ending point for the study of development across the lifespan. In this respect, it provides a context for understanding much of the development that has come before. Therefore, it can be considered another point of demarcation that we use in studying how individuals change as they develop—the subject matter of human lifespan development.

Thus, we conclude this text by reviewing the central themes that guide human development throughout the lifespan. Development is best thought of as an intricate interaction of hereditary and environmental forces. Each person inherits specific biological instructions that set the stage for that person's development, and environmental forces acting on the individual shape how these biological predispositions will unfold and how the person will adjust and adapt throughout the lifespan. Importantly, each person's life cycle also is embedded in a cultural and historical context; clearly, a person's family and culture play especially significant roles. Birth, first steps, first words, schooling, coming of age, finding a mate, working, building a family, finding wisdom, and facing one's own mortality are developmental tasks faced by most people, and these milestones provide a framework for understanding the commonalities of human lifespan development. But developmental events are played out against a rich tapestry of individual biological and cultural patterns. Thus, all people experience development in their own special and unique way, as biological, social, and cultural threads are woven together throughout the lifespan. The challenge for those who study human lifespan development is to understand how these multiple factors interact to forge the lives of individuals, and to do so both in terms of the common themes that run through most people's experience and in terms of appreciating the uniqueness of every person. We hope you have found this book useful as you have wrestled with these issues and that you have come to appreciate the elegant complexity of the study of human development across the lifespan.

◀ Older people, when confronted with the question of what they would do if they had only 6 months to live, often focus on spending time with their families.

CHAPTER SUMMARY

Thoughts and Fears of Death

How has the consideration and study of death changed during the past 50 to 100 years?

- Death is an integral part of every person's life. A person's death has intense personal significance, but it is embedded in cultural traditions as well.
- Historically, developmental psychologists often largely ignored the subject of death; however, it has generated more interest and research recently. It is now a topic of considerable interest to scholars and laypersons alike.
- The emotional impact of death is very different from the emotional impact of birth.

How do most people in Western cultures think about death today, and how do they react to it?

- Today, many people in Western nations cope with death through denial. Although we know that everyone dies, we do not like to confront the reality of death. When we deny death, we sometimes fail to develop adequate coping mechanisms for dealing with it.
- The Western cultural taboo about discussing death is weakening. Today, people confront the reality of death more directly and with less secrecy.
- People vary widely in how they view death. Advanced age and religious beliefs in an afterlife typically are associated with less fearful conceptualizations of death. Research findings suggest that people who are psychologically well adjusted and who have achieved a sense of personality integrity are the least anxious about death. Other research findings suggest that people who are physically and mentally healthy and who feel in control of their own lives are often the most anxious about death. Anxiety levels, however, sometimes change with changing circumstances.

How can knowledge of one's own death serve to enhance one's self-esteem and serve as the basis for inspiration?

- Terror management theory argues that the anxiety we feel about our own deaths leads us to cope by developing positive self-esteem. Death, thus, is the basis for inspiration. Other theories, however, view self-esteem more as the result of our positive desire for competence, autonomy, and relatedness to others, and not as a reaction to our fears about death.
- Some research suggests that the anxiety about death is greater in individualistic cultures than it is in collectivist cultures.

Research also shows that people work harder at developing a positive self-concept when they are reminded of death.

Confronting One's Own Death

How do most terminally ill people and their caregivers cope with the knowledge that death will soon come?

- Younger and older people often have different reactions about death, with older people generally being more accepting of it. When people have time to contemplate their own deaths, they often are able to successfully adjust.
- When adults reach old age, they often look back and review their lives, and this can lead to personality growth and to a more secure sense of self-esteem.
- Although today her work is somewhat controversial, Elisabeth Kübler-Ross proposed five stages in the process of adjusting to a terminal illness: denial, anger, bargaining, depression, and acceptance. These stages are not universal; however, they can help us to understand how people who are dying may feel.
- Taking care of a person with a terminal illness often is taxing. A sense of optimism, as well as professional counseling, can help a caregiver cope. Depression and despair are common among those who care for loved ones with long-term illnesses that require extensive care. Yet many caregivers report remarkable resilience following the loved one's death.

What trajectories of dying are most desirable and how does suicide fit into a discussion about the trajectories associated with dying?

- There is a wide range of dying trajectories, or patterns. In the United States today, the majority of people would prefer a sudden death at advanced age rather than a lingering, terminal illness. Coping with deaths that do not conform to this "ideal" trajectory is especially difficult.
- Suicide is one response to terminal illness, and it is especially common among older White men. Suicide rates almost certainly would be higher if statistics included *submissive deaths,* which are a passive form of suicide where people simply let themselves die by not caring for themselves, and *suicidal erosion,* which is an indirect form of suicide accomplished by engaging in high-risk activities. These behaviors also are more common among older men. Men age 85 and older are about 10 times more likely to commit suicide than are women in this age group.

The Search for a Humane Death

What characterizes a humane death, and how can we make death more humane?

- Although doctors and health-care professionals today are quite good at providing competent medical care to people who are dying, they are relatively poor at helping people who are terminally ill to cope emotionally and psychologically. However, in recent years, the care of people with terminal illnesses has generally become more humane.
- People with terminal illnesses who have more control over their environment are more likely to live longer and to experience a better quality of life. Most people desire a "good death."
- *Hospice* is a philosophy that is designed to help people with terminal illnesses live out their days as independently as possible by giving needed care, support, and other assistance. Hospice care also emphasizes the management of pain and includes assistance to family members who must cope with the loss of a loved one. Hospice began in 1967 in England, and the hospice concept has grown rapidly in the United States. Hospice is a philosophy, not a place, and hospice care can be provided in a range of settings and throughout illness, death, and bereavement.

What methods can individuals employ in order to gain some control over the circumstances that will surround them as they die?

- Many people now demand a *right to die,* which is the view that death is a right to be exercised at a terminally ill individual's discretion. Discussions about the right to die often raise questions about *active euthanasia,* which involves taking steps to bring about another person's death. Currently, active euthanasia is illegal in the United States. However, in cases of assisted suicide, where death is carried out by the person who is terminally ill and who is provided with the means to end their own life, more leniency is sometimes awarded. In any form, these acts are controversial. Although most U.S. adults support the right to die, the American Medical Association (AMA) opposes physician-assisted suicide. The continued development of better pain management techniques is providing some people with better alternatives to active euthanasia.
- *Passive euthanasia* involves withholding or disconnecting life-sustaining equipment so that people with a terminal illness can die naturally. Often, the major issue is that it is difficult to determine when the person should be considered dead.
- In preparing for death, adults often formally express their wishes about the use of extraordinary measures to artificially sustain life. Although not legally binding, a *living will* is an advance directive signed by a person indicating that the person does not wish extraordinary measures to be employed to sustain life in case of terminal illness. A *medical power of attorney* is a legal document that authorizes a loved one to assume the power to make life-or-death medical decisions. The "Five Wishes" document can be used to convey instructions about how one wishes to be treated at the time of, and after, death.
- When the person with a terminal illness is a child, parents or legal guardians must make decisions about the child's care.
- *Palliative care* is designed to prevent or relieve the emotional distress and physical difficulties associated with a life-threatening illness, both for the person with the terminal illness and for his or her loved ones. *End-of-life care* specifically addresses the concerns and the circumstances associated with impending death. Both palliative and end-of-life care can improve communication and care for a person who is terminally ill, as well as for his or her loved ones.

- The AMA has issued guidelines for the care of people in the final stages of a terminal illness. These guidelines specify that these people and their families should receive full information, be treated with dignity, have their wishes followed, and receive effective pain management.

Grief and Bereavement

What factors generally influence how people deal with grief and bereavement?

- The *dual-process model of stress and coping* suggests that dealing with the loss of a loved one includes both coping with grief and learning how to live in a world without the person who died.
- Coping with the initial emotional reactions that occur after the loss of a loved one is called *grief work*. Grieving helps survivors cope with their loss, and it usually follows a predictable course. Shock usually is the first reaction, followed by active grieving, and eventually recovery. Thus, grieving includes healing, which is then followed by renewal.
- When death is preceded by a long illness, loved ones sometimes experience *anticipatory grief*, where they emotionally prepare themselves for the death of their loved one. Anticipatory grief may make the adjustment following death somewhat easier. People grieve in different ways, although many find that the support of others is helpful.
- *Bereavement overload* is a stress reaction that may occur when a person experiences multiple losses over a short span of time, and it often is characterized by depression. Sometimes *chronic grief* may develop, which is an ingrained, pathological mourning process in which the grieving person never overcomes the grief, leading some researchers to suggest that chronic grief responses be identified as a type of mental disorder.
- Cultural expectations play a role in how proper grieving is defined. In modern Western cultures, survivors are expected to quickly return to normal life, although this does not make their adjustment to the loss any quicker than if their grieving period were extended. In most cultures, rituals and customs mark the end of a person's life, and these often are helpful in allowing survivors to deal with their grief.

What special circumstances are associated with the death of a child?

- The death of a child often is especially difficult to deal with. This partly is because death in childhood has become much less common in developed nations, and partly because early death is considered to be out of sequence in our conceptualization of the normal lifespan.
- When families include one or more members who have intellectual or developmental disabilities, death and grieving may involve special considerations.
- When a child dies, grieving is often especially intense, although individual and cultural variations in grief responses exist. Grieving children may not have a clear understanding of death, and this makes their grief especially difficult to address. Sometimes parents can gain some relief by channeling their energy toward causes that support the social good.

Completing the Life Cycle

How can death be considered as part of the lifespan?

- Death—whenever it occurs—marks the end of a person's life cycle. As such, it can be viewed as the final step in human lifespan development.
- Death provides a closure to life against which we mark the transitions in earlier periods of the lifespan.
- Development is an intricate interaction among hereditary and environmental forces. Family and culture are especially important influences. Although many people experience similar developmental events that provide common themes across lifespan development, each person's life and developmental patterns are unique.

KEY TERMS

submissive death (p. 502)
suicidal erosion (p. 502)
hospice (p. 504)
right to die (p. 505)
active euthanasia (p. 506)
assisted suicide (p. 506)
passive euthanasia (p. 506)
living will (p. 506)
medical power of attorney (p. 506)
palliative care (p. 507)
end-of-life care (p. 508)
bereavement (p. 508)
dual-process model of stress and coping (p. 508)
grief work (p. 509)
anticipatory grief (p. 509)
bereavement overload (p. 510)
chronic grief (p. 511)

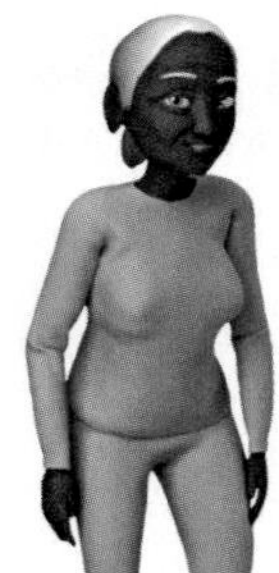

MyVirtualLife

What decisions would you make while living your life? What would be the consequences of those decisions?

Find out by accessing **MyVirtualLife** at
www.MyDevelopmentLab.com
to raise a virtual child and live your own virtual life.

ANSWERS TO REVIEW THE FACTS

CHAPTER 1 INTRODUCTION TO HUMAN DEVELOPMENT

REVIEW THE FACTS 1-1

1. age based
2. influence each other, usually in complex ways
3. biological factors and environmental factors
4. social context for development

REVIEW THE FACTS 1-2

1. A
2. with more rights and as more innocent
3. collectivist
4. individualist
5. cognitive domain
6. enculturation; socialization

REVIEW THE FACTS 1-3

1. B
2. Erik Erikson
3. classical conditioning principles
4. social learning theory
5. D
6. guided participation
7. systems theory; or the bioecological model
8. it is flexible and can take many paths

REVIEW THE FACTS 1-4

1. case study
2. laboratory observation; attachment
3. A
4. confounding
5. negative
6. how well the children read at the end of the program
7. the two different reading approaches, phonics versus whole word
8. Institutional Review Board

CHAPTER 2 HEREDITY AND ENVIRONMENT

REVIEW THE FACTS 2-1

1. D
2. A
3. they synthesize proteins
4. the DNA instructions that are transmitted from parent to child

REVIEW THE FACTS 2-2

1. karyotype (or karyogram)
2. mitosis
3. prenatal (before birth); puberty (or adolescent)
4. alleles
5. independent assortment
6. epigenetics

REVIEW THE FACTS 2-3

1. C
2. D
3. extra chromosome material on the 21st pair
4. B
5. retrovirus

REVIEW THE FACTS 2-4

1. Because it recognizes the role environmental factors can play in how or whether a gene will be expressed.
2. heritability
3. higher
4. D

REVIEW THE FACTS 2-5

1. habituation
2. classical conditioning
3. repeated in the future
4. shaping or successive approximations
5. self-concept

REVIEW THE FACTS 2-6

1. B
2. harder
3. ethnocentrism
4. socialization
5. B
6. C

CHAPTER 3 PRENATAL DEVELOPMENT AND CHILDBIRTH

REVIEW THE FACTS 3-1

1. The fertilized egg is implanted in the uterine wall.
2. 30 to 50%
3. C
4. spontaneous abortion
5. the age at which an infant has a 50% chance of surviving after birth
6. proximodistal trend

REVIEW THE FACTS 3-2

1. B
2. C
3. Any three of the following:
   (a) through the placenta,
   (b) through the amniotic fluid,
   (c) during the birth process, or
   (d) from breast milk
4. D
5. C

REVIEW THE FACTS 3-3

1. B
2. to prevent tearing of the mother's tissue around the vaginal opening
3. labor and delivery
4. B
5. A
6. A
7. small-for-date

REVIEW THE FACTS 3-4

1. B
2. neonate
3. C
4. Because the skull bones (fontanels) are not yet fused, and these are squeezed together during the birth process.
5. a cheesy-looking protective coating sometimes found on the newborn
6. colostrum

CHAPTER 4 INFANCY AND TODDLERHOOD: Physical, Cognitive, and Language Development

REVIEW THE FACTS 4-1

1. D
2. the 2-year-old
3. A
4. B

REVIEW THE FACTS 4-2

1. more predictable
2. 4 months
3. D
4. D

REVIEW THE FACTS 4-3

1. C
2. C
3. fine motor skill; or pincer grasp
4. B
5. impulsiveness, inattentiveness or attention deficit; depression, helplessness, or low energy
6. A

REVIEW THE FACTS 4-4

1. sensation; perception
2. mirror
3. monocular
4. human speech, especially the mother's voice
5. A

REVIEW THE FACTS 4-5

1. D
2. assimilation; accommodation
3. object permanence
4. deferred imitation
5. B

REVIEW THE FACTS 4-6

1. phonemes
2. C
3. holophrastic speech
4. D
5. C

CHAPTER 5 INFANCY AND TODDLERHOOD: Personality and Sociocultural Development

REVIEW THE FACTS 5-1

1. A
2. D
3. B
4. Any answer that demonstrates two highly different styles; for example, an easily excited baby raised in a noisy, unpredictable family or a difficult baby raised in a family that values schedules and calmness.

REVIEW THE FACTS 5-2

1. trust
2. feeding
3. oral
4. both should develop in balance, with trust predominating in most instances
5. no

REVIEW THE FACTS 5-3

1. resistant attachment
2. C
3. imprinting
4. synchrony
5. B
6. A

REVIEW THE FACTS 5-4

1. B
2. autonomy versus shame and doubt
3. prosocial
4. D
5. 21 months
6. attachment and separation *or* establishing trust and autonomy

REVIEW THE FACTS 5-5

1. more mothers are working outside the home
2. C
3. more likely
4. C
5. B

REVIEW THE FACTS 5-6

1. establishing synchronous communication and not feeling that their infant is unresponsive
2. talk or sing almost constantly to the child
3. a visual impairment
4. B
5. A

CHAPTER 6 EARLY CHILDHOOD: Physical, Cognitive, and Language Development

REVIEW THE FACTS 6-1

1. lower
2. more efficient (or faster)
3. is controlled by a particular region of the brain; or, is controlled by the left or right hemisphere
4. left hemisphere
5. D

REVIEW THE FACTS 6-2

1. gross; fine
2. B
3. functional subordination
4. the brain and the nervous system
5. B

REVIEW THE FACTS 6-3

1. assimilation; accommodation
2. egocentrism
3. symbolic representation
4. that the flatter ball had more clay; because the child has not yet mastered the conservation of mass
5. the zone of proximal development
6. D

REVIEW THE FACTS 6-4

1. overregularization
2. pragmatics
3. D
4. because they have more opportunities to practice language skills in the types of play they prefer
5. bilingual

REVIEW THE FACTS 6-5

1. D
2. parallel play
3. less egocentric
4. A
5. C

CHAPTER 7 EARLY CHILDHOOD: Personality and Sociocultural Development

REVIEW THE FACTS 7-1

1. phobia
2. defense mechanisms
3. D
4. B
5. A

REVIEW THE FACTS 7-2

1. frustration
2. (1) Children become less likely to misinterpret others' behavior as aggressive, and (2) they become better able to empathize.
3. It increases aggressive urges, even if the child avoids the behaviors that lead to punishment.
4. They are positively correlated: Children who view more violence also tend to be more aggressive.
5. prosocial
6. empathy
7. both

REVIEW THE FACTS 7-3

1. autonomy (or independence)
2. C
3. D

REVIEW THE FACTS 7-4

1. C
2. D
3. A
4. emotions
5. They are negatively correlated: More popular children generally are less aggressive.

REVIEW THE FACTS 7-5

1. self-concept
2. C
3. When heredity is especially significant we use the term sex; when influences are more environmental, we usually refer to *gender.*
4. D
5. inconsistent
6. A

REVIEW THE FACTS 7-6

1. authoritative; high but flexible control and high warmth
2. Any of the following: establish fair rules, enforce these rules, create a consistent set of expectations, be warm and caring, keep two-way communication open, make an emotional connection with children.
3. shared
4. are not the same
5. A
6. B

CHAPTER 8 MIDDLE CHILDHOOD: Physical and Cognitive Development

REVIEW THE FACTS 8-1

1. slower
2. D
3. A
4. nearly 19%
5. accidents
6. about 20%

REVIEW THE FACTS 8-2

1. no
2. a script
3. vocabulary increases and language structure (e.g., grammar, syntax) becomes more complex
4. 8 years
5. they have comparable average test scores

REVIEW THE FACTS 8-3

1. B
2. girls
3. achievement motivation
4. quantitative and spatial skills; verbal skills
5. C

REVIEW THE FACTS 8-4

1. a free and appropriate education in the least restrictive environment possible.
2. increased; decreased
3. D
4. dyslexia
5. understimulation
6. autism; or autism spectrum disorder; or ASD

CHAPTER 9 MIDDLE CHILDHOOD: Personality and Sociocultural Development

REVIEW THE FACTS 9-1

1. A
2. industry; inferiority
3. C
4. high (or low) achievement and positive (or negative) self-esteem influence and reinforce each other
5. D

REVIEW THE FACTS 9-2

1. social cognition
2. B
3. moral realism; moral relativism
4. C
5. justice; social relations or caring

REVIEW THE FACTS 9-3

1. first stage: friends are playmates; second stage: friends become aware of friends' feelings; third stage: friends help each other and trust develops; fourth stage: friends can understand a friend's perspective on the relationship
2. any two of the following answers: (a) groups become more formal, (b) groups have more rigid membership requirements, (c) groups become more gender-segregated
3. D
4. D
5. Prejudice is an attitude; discrimination is a behavior.

REVIEW THE FACTS 9-4

1. D
2. self-regulation
3. C
4. women (or mothers)
5. it is a good idea
6. a parent remarries

CHAPTER 10 ADOLESCENCE AND EMERGING ADULTHOOD: Physical and Cognitive Development

REVIEW THE FACTS 10-1

1. right of passage
2. longer
3. B
4. emerging adulthood

REVIEW THE FACTS 10-2

1. C
2. puberty
3. testosterone; estrogen and progesterone
4. menarche
5. secular trend
6. B
7. boys

REVIEW THE FACTS 10-3

1. B
2. sexual double standard
3. B
4. about 50%
5. B
6. A

REVIEW THE FACTS 10-4

1. two of the following answers: (a) some neurons are pruned away, (b) neural branching occurs, resulting in increased numbers of connections among neurons, (c) myelination continues and white matter increases
2. the amygdala
3. sensorimotor; preoperational; concrete operations; formal operations
4. imaginary audience
5. D
6. reasoning or logic; intuition or emotion
7. conventional; postconventional

CHAPTER 11 ADOLESCENCE AND EMERGING ADULTHOOD: Personality and Sociocultural Development

REVIEW THE FACTS 11-1

1. achieving independence (autonomy) from parents and forming an identity
2. no
3. interdependence, or reciprocal dependence
4. identity versus identity confusion

5. a. iv
   b. iii
   c. i
   d. ii
6. more difficult

REVIEW THE FACTS 11-2
1. early adolescence
2. A
3. the oldest child
4. monitoring

REVIEW THE FACTS 11-3
1. social comparison
2. D
3. cliques
4. emotional; sexual
5. similar values

REVIEW THE FACTS 11-4
1. C
2. B
3. A
4. delinquent
5. girls

REVIEW THE FACTS 11-5
1. C
2. D
3. long-standing problems
4. A

CHAPTER 12 YOUNG ADULTHOOD: Physical and Cognitive Development

REVIEW THE FACTS 12-1
1. normative
2. D
3. A
4. chronological age
5. contextual paradigm (or contextual approach)

REVIEW THE FACTS 12-2
1. C
2. C
3. Tobacco/smoking
4. C
5. Americans with Disabilities Act (ADA)

REVIEW THE FACTS 12-3
1. age 50
2. antibiotics
3. no
4. no
5. individuals may be strongly heterosexual, strongly homosexual, or may fall somewhere in between

REVIEW THE FACTS 12-4
1. B
2. 12
3. postformal
4. A
5. D
6. B

REVIEW THE FACTS 12-5
1. stage-based (or normative); context-based
2. starting a family and establishing a career
3. intimacy versus isolation
4. D
5. less useful
6. C
7. any three of the following: (a) they overemphasize life crises, (b) they ignore the significance of individual uniqueness and idiosyncratic events, (c) they undervalue the impact of multiple contexts, or (d) they overemphasize the experiences and values of a particular cohort group

CHAPTER 13 YOUNG ADULTHOOD: Personality and Sociocultural Development

REVIEW THE FACTS 13-1
1. establishing meaningful intimate relationships, identifying a career or job path, becoming more comfortable with one's self-identity
2. conditions of worth
3. D
4. A
5. C
6. extrinsic; intrinsic

REVIEW THE FACTS 13-2
1. intimacy, passion, and decision/commitment
2. A
3. 90%
4. heterosexuals who are married
5. they endorse adoption by homosexual couples
6. B

REVIEW THE FACTS 13-3
1. B
2. C
3. help welfare mothers get off welfare and become economically independent workers
4. funding adequate day care
5. B

REVIEW THE FACTS 13-4
1. occupational cycle
2. (a) people more frequently change jobs and careers (b) work has become more technical
3. B
4. C
5. (a) they may choose jobs that involve less stress or time (b) they may experience job-related discrimination

REVIEW THE FACTS 13-5
1. B
2. White women
3. B
4. 80 to 81 cents
5. D
6. D

CHAPTER 14 MIDDLE ADULTHOOD: Physical and Cognitive Development

REVIEW THE FACTS 14-1
1. B
2. command
3. D
4. A
5. more likely

REVIEW THE FACTS 14-2
1. A
2. climacteric
3. A
4. C
5. C
6. C

REVIEW THE FACTS 14-3
1. cancers; heart attacks (or heart disease)
2. B
3. D
4. D
5. A
6. any of the following: poor health habits, more life stress, poor access to health care, less education, living in dangerous neighborhoods

REVIEW THE FACTS 14-4
1. less
2. crystallized; fluid
3. D
4. stay intellectually active or engage in regular physical exercise
5. C

CHAPTER 15 MIDDLE ADULTHOOD: Personality and Sociocultural Development

REVIEW THE FACTS 15-1
1. women
2. A
3. B
4. C
5. role strain

REVIEW THE FACTS 15-2
1. kinkeepers
2. C
3. empty nest
4. by family members
5. B
6. D

REVIEW THE FACTS 15-3
1. A
2. B
3. wives
4. D
5. B
6. stepmothers
7. create a new social unit

REVIEW THE FACTS 15-4
1. less likely
2. middle-aged adults
3. any of the following: (a) have more identity invested in their previous jobs, (b) may face age discrimination, (c) have lower pay, less benefits, or lower status in new jobs
4. job burnout
5. more common

REVIEW THE FACTS 15-5
1. D
2. be stable
3. C
4. B
5. depends on the individual and his or her life experiences; some experience more change and others more continuity

CHAPTER 16 OLDER ADULTHOOD: Physical and Cognitive Development

REVIEW THE FACTS 16-1
1. filial piety
2. older women
3. C
4. D
5. B
6. People in their 90s have lived past the age when chronic health problems have caused the death of those who had them and therefore they are healthier.

REVIEW THE FACTS 16-2
1. pathological
2. osteoporosis
3. reserve
4. C
5. insomnia; sleep apnea
6. hypertension, arthritis symptoms, and heart problems
7. A

REVIEW THE FACTS 16-3
1. senescence
2. stochastic
3. D
4. A
5. C

REVIEW THE FACTS 16-4
1. D
2. working
3. A
4. C
5. D

CHAPTER 17 OLDER ADULTHOOD: Personality and Sociocultural Development

REVIEW THE FACTS 17-1

1. typically involves losses, as well as gains
2. integrity; despair
3. fewer friends
4. A
5. social comparison
6. D

REVIEW THE FACTS 17-2

1. B
2. wealthier
3. older women
4. C
5. retirement maturity

REVIEW THE FACTS 17-3

1. an increase
2. C
3. C
4. (a) women live longer; (b) men tend to marry younger women
5. widowers

REVIEW THE FACTS 17-4

1. D
2. C
3. A
4. (a) more people will reach age 65; (b) health-care costs are largest at the end of life
5. A
6. day-care center

CHAPTER 18 DEATH AND DYING

REVIEW THE FACTS 18-1

1. weakening
2. D
3. less afraid
4. C
5. D

REVIEW THE FACTS 18-2

1. A
2. D
3. to die suddenly in old age with no suffering
4. C
5. submissive death

REVIEW THE FACTS 18-3

1. live longer
2. hospice
3. euthanasia (or active euthanasia)
4. medical power of attorney
5. palliative

REVIEW THE FACTS 18-4

1. shock, followed by active grief, followed by letting go
2. C
3. A
4. B
5. more intense

REFERENCES

Abecassis, M. (2004). I hate you just the way you are: Exploring the formation, maintenance, and need for enemies. In E. Hodges & N. Card, *New Directions for Child and Adolescent Development, 102*, 5–22.

Abler, R. M., & Sedlacek, W. E. (1989). Freshman sexual attitudes and behaviors over a 15-year period. *Journal of College Student Development, 30*, 201–209.

Ackerman, P. L. (2000). Domain-specific knowledge as the "dark matter" of adult intelligence: Gf/Gc, personality, and interest correlates. *Journal of Gerontology, 55B*(2), 69–84.

Ackerman, P. L. (2011). Intelligence and expertise. In R. J. Sternberg & S. B. Kaufman (Eds.), *The Cambridge handbook of intelligence* (pp. 847–860). New York: Cambridge University Press.

Adams, R. G. (2006). Middle-aged and older adult men's friendships. In V. Bedford & B. Turner (Eds.), *Men in relationships: A new look from a life course perspective* (pp. 103–124). New York: Springer Publishing.

Adams, R. J., & Courage, M. L. (1995). Development of chromatic discrimination in early infancy. *Behavioural Brain Research, 67*, 99–101.

Adler, N. E. (2011). Cell aging and social disadvantage: Perspectives on mechanisms underlying health disparities from "across the pond." *Brain, Behavior, and Immunity, 25*(7), 1290–1291.

Adolph, K. (2008). Learning to move. *Current Directions in Psychological Science, 17*(3), 213–218.

Adolph, K. D., & Berger, S. E. (2006). Motor development. In D. Kuhn, R. S. Sigler, W. Damon, & R. M. Lerner (Eds.) *Handbook of child psychology: Vol 2, Cognition, perception, and language (6th ed.).* (161–213). Hoboken, NJ: John Wiley & Sons, Inc.

Aging with Dignity. (2012). Five Wishes. Retrieved online on October 15, 2012 at http://www.agingwithdignity.org/forms/5wishes.pdf.

Ahluwalia M. K., Suzuki, L. A., & Mir, M. (2009). Dating, partnerships, and arranged marriages. In N. Tewari & A. N. Alvarez (Eds.), *Asian American psychology: Current perspectives* (pp. 273–294). New York: Routledge/Taylor & Francis Group.

Ahmad, S., & Bhugra, D. (2010). Homophobia: An updated review of the literature. *Sexual and Relationship Therapy, 25*(4), 447–455.

Ahmetoglu, G., Swami, V., & Chamorro-Premuzic, T. (2010). The relationship between dimensions of love, personality, and relationship length. *Archives of Sexual Behavior, 39*(5), 1181–1190.

Aikins, J., & Litwack, S. D. (2011). Prosocial skills, social competence, and popularity. In A. Cillessen, D. Schwartz, & L. Mayeux (Eds.), *Popularity in the peer system* (pp. 140–162). New York: Guilford Press.

Ainsworth, M. D. (1985). Patterns of attachment. *Clinical Psychologist, 38*(2), 27–29.

Ainsworth, M. D. S. (1995). On the shaping of attachment theory and research: An interview with Mary D. S. Ainsworth (Fall 1994). *Monographs of the Society for Research in Child Development, 60*(2–3), 3–21.

Ainsworth, M. D. S. (2010). Security and attachment. In R. Volpe (Ed.), *The secure child: Timeless lessons in parenting and childhood education* (pp. 43–53). Greenwich, CT: IAP Information Age Publishing.

Ainsworth, M. D., & Bell, S. M. (1970). Attachment, exploration, and separation: Illustrated by the behavior of one-year-olds in a strange situation. *Child Development, 41*, 49–67.

Ainsworth, M. S. (1983). Patterns of infant–mother attachment as related to maternal care. In D. Magnusson & V. Allen (Eds.), *Human development: An interactional perspective* (pp. 35–53). New York: Academic Press.

Ainsworth, M. S. (1979). Infant-mother attachment. *American Psychologist, 34*(10), 932–937.

Ainsworth, M. S., & Bowlby, J. (1991). An ethological approach to personality development. *American Psychologist, 46*(4), 333–341.

Ainsworth, M. S., Blehar, M., Waters, E., & Wall, S. (1978). *Patterns of attachment.* Hillsdale, NJ: Erlbaum.

Akhtar, S., & Lee, J. S. Y. (2010). Job burnout: Toward an integration of two dominant resource-based models. *Psychological Reports, 107*(1), 193–208.

Akiba, D., Szalacha, L., & Garcia Coll, C. (2004). Multiplicity of ethnic identification during middle childhood: Conceptual and methodological considerations. In M. E. Mascolo & J. Li (Eds.), *Culture and developing selves: Beyond dichotomization* (pp. 45–60). San Francisco, CA: Jossey-Bass.

Aksan, N., Anderson, S. W., Dawson, J. D., Johnson, A. M., Uc, E. Y., & Rizzo, M. (2012). Cognitive functioning predicts driver safety on road tests 1 and 2 years later. *Journal of the American Geriatrics Society, 60*(1), 99–105.

Alam, R., Barrera, M., D'Agostino, N., Nicolas, D. B., & Schneiderman, G. (2012). Bereavement experiences of mothers and fathers over time after the death of a child due to cancer. *Death Studies, 36*(1), 1–22.

Alanis, I., & Rodriguez, M. A. (2008). Sustaining a dual language immersion program: Features of success. *Journal of Latinos and Education, 7*(4), 305–319.

Albert, D., & Steinberg, L. (2011). Judgment and decision making in adolescence. *Journal of Research on Adolescence, 21*(1), 211–224.

Albert, S. M., & Brody, E. M. (1996). When elder care is viewed as child care: Significance of elder's cognitive impairment and caregiver burden. *American Journal of Geriatric Psychiatry, 4*, 121–130.

Aldwin, C. (2011). Stress and coping across the lifespan. In S. Folkman (Ed.), *The Oxford handbook of stress, health, and coping* (pp. 15–34). New York: Oxford University Press.

Aldwin, C. M. (2007). *Stress, coping, and development: An integrative perspective* (2nd ed.). New York: Guilford Press.

Aldwin, C. M., & Levenson, M. R. (2001). Stress, coping, and health at midlife: A developmental perspective. In M. E. Lachman (Ed.), *Handbook of midlife development* (pp. 188–214). New York: John Wiley & Sons, Inc.

Aldwin, C. M., Spiro, A., & Park, C. L. (2006). Health, behavior, and optimal aging: A life-span developmental perspective. In J. E. Birren & K. Schaire (Eds.), *Handbook of the psychology of aging* (6th ed., pp. 85–104). Amsterdam, Netherlands: Elsevier.

Aldwin, C. M., Yancura, L. A., & Boeninger, D. K., (2010). Coping across the life span. In C. M. Aldwin, L. A. Yancura, & D. K. Boeninger (Eds.) *The handbook of life-span development, Vol 2: Social and emotional development* (pp. 298–340). Hoboken, NJ: John Wiley and Sons Inc.

Alexandroni, S. (2007). Swedish model. *New Statesman, 136*(4854), 18.

Alink, L. R. A., Cicchetti, D., Kim, J., & Rogosch, F. A. (2012). Longitudinal associations among child maltreatment, social functioning, and cortisol regulation. *Developmental Psychology, 48*(1), 224–236.

Allemand, M., Gomez, V., Jackson, J. J. (2010). Personality trait development in midlife: Exploring the impact of psychological turning points. *European Journal of Aging, 7*(3), 147–155.

Allemand, M., Zimprich, D., & Hendriks, A. A. (2008). Age differences in five personality domains across the life span. *Developmental Psychology, 44*(3), 758–770.

Allemand, M., Zimprich, D., & Hertzog, C. (2007). Cross-sectional differences and longitudinal age changes of personality in middle adulthood and old age. *Journal of Personality, 75* (2), 323–358.

Allen, D. J., & Oleson, T. (1999). Shame and internalized homophobia in gay men. *Journal of Homosexuality, 37*, 33–43.

Alsaker, F. D., & Kroger, J. (2006). Self-concept, self-esteem and identity. In S. Jackson & L. Goossens (Eds.), *Handbook of adolescent development* (pp. 90–113). New York: Psychology Press.

Alzheimer's Association. (2009). *Standard treatments.* Retrieved February 10, 2009 from http://www.alz.org/alzheimers_disease_standard_prescriptions.Asp

Alzheimer's Association. (2012). 2012 Alzheimer's disease fact and figures. Retrieved from http://www.alz.org/documents_custom/2012_facts_figures_fact_sheet.pdf

Amato, P. R. (2001). Children of divorce in the 1990s: An update of the Amato and Keith (1991) meta-analysis. *Journal of Family Psychology, 15*(3), 355–370.

Amato, P. R. (2006). Marital discord, divorce, and children's well-being: Results from a 20-year longitudinal study of two generations. In A. Clarke- Stewart & J. Dunn (Eds.), *Families count: Effects on child and adolescent development* (pp. 179–202). New York: Cambridge University Press.

Amato, P. R. (2007). Life span of children to their parents' divorce. In S. Ferguson (Ed.), *Shifting the center: Understanding contemporary families* (3rd ed., pp. 567–588). New York: McGraw-Hill.

Amato, P. R., & Dorius, C. (2010). Fathers, children, and divorce. In M. E. Lamb (Ed.), *The role of the father in child development* (5th ed., pp. 177–200). Hoboken, NJ: John Wiley & Sons, Inc.

American Academy of Child & Adolescent Psychiatry. (2009). Child and adolescent mental illness and drug abuse statistics. Retrieved from http://www.aacap.org/cs/root/resources_for_families/child_and_adolescent

American Academy of Pediatrics (AAP). (1999). The lure of technology. *Pediatrics, 103,* 1037.

American Academy of Pediatrics (AAP). (2002). Coparent or second-parent adoption by same-sex parents. *Pediatrics, 109*(2), 339–340. Retrieved on January 27, 2009, from http://www.aappolicy.aappublications.org/cgi/content/abstract/pediatrics;109/2/339

American Academy of Pediatrics (AAP). (2008). *TV and your family.* Retrieved on December 8, 2008 from http://www.aap.org/publiced/BR_TV.htm

American Academy of Pediatrics. (2011a). Abusive head trauma: A new name for shaken baby syndrome. Retrieved from http://www.aap.org/en-us/about-the-app/app-press-room/pages/Abusive

American Academy of Pediatrics. (2011b). Children, adolescents, obesity, and the media. *American Academy of Pediatrics, 128*(1), 201–208.

American Academy of Pediatrics. (2012a). Intellectual disability. Retrieved from http://www.healthychildren.org/English/health-issues/conditions

American Academy of Pediatrics. (2012b). Nutrition: What every parent needs to know. Retrived from http://healthchildren.org/English/health-issures/conditions/obesity

American Association on Intellectual and Developmental Disabilities (AAIDD). (2010). *Intellectual disability: Definition, classification, and systems of supports* (11th ed.). Washington, DC: Author.

American Cancer Society. (2011). Cigarette smoking. Retrieved from http://www.cancer.org/Cancer/CancerCauses/TobaccoCancer

American College of Obstetricians and Gynecologists. (2010). Your pregnancy and childbirth: Month to month. Washington, DC: Author.

American College of Obstetricians and Gynecologists. (2012). Hormone therapy. Retrieved from http://www.acog.org

American Diabetes Association. (2012). Diabetes statistics. Retrieved from http://www.diabetes.org/diabetes-basics/diabetes-statistics/

American Foundation for Suicide Prevention. (2012). Facts and figures, national statistics. Retrieved from http://www.afsp.org/index.cfm?fuseaction=home.viewpage&page_id=

American Lung Association. (2011). Asthma & child fact sheet. Retrieved from http://www.lung.org/lung-disease/asthma/resources/facts-and-figures/asthma-children-fact-sheet.html

American Medical Association (AMA). (1997). AMA guidelines for caring for patients in the last phase of life. *CQ Researcher, 7*(33), 774.

American Medical Association (AMA). (2011). Human cloning. Retrieved from http://www.ama-assn.org/ama/pub/physician-resources

American Pregnancy Association. (2006). *Amniocentesis.* Retrieved from http://www.americanpregnancy.org/prenataltesting/amniocentesis.html

American Pregnancy Association. (2012a). *Amniocentesis.* Retrieved from http://www.americanpregnancy.org/prenataltesting/amniocentesis.html

American Pregnancy Association. (2012b). Ovulation frequently asked questions. Retrieved from http://www.americanpregnancy.org/gettingpregnant/ovulationfaq.htm

American Pregnancy Association. (2012c). VBAC: Vaginal birth after cesarean. Retrieved from http://americanpregnancy.org/labornbirth/vbac.html

American Psychiatric Association. (1994). *Diagnostic and statistical manual of mental disorders* (DSM-IV, 4th ed.). Washington, DC: Author.

American Psychiatric Association. (2000). *Diagnostic and statistical manual of mental disorders: DSM-IV-TR.* Washington, DC: Author.

American Psychological Association. (2010). Ethical principles of psychologists and code of conduct. Retrieved from http://www.apa.org/ethics/code/index.aspx

American Psychological Association. (2005). Guidelines for psychotherapy with lesbian, gay, and bisexual clients. Washington, DC: Author.

American Psychological Association (APA). (2006). *Report of the working group on psychoactive medications for children and adolescents. Psychopharmacological, psychosocial, and combined interventions for childhood disorders. Evidence base, contextual factors, and future directions.* Washington, DC: Author.

American Psychological Association. (2012). More research needed on the effects medications have on children. *APA Monitor, 43*(16), 41.

American Society for Aesthetic Plastic Surgery (ASAPS). (2011). Statistics, surveys & trends. Retrieved from http://www.surgery.org/media/news-releases/statistics-survey-and-trends

Amsel, E. (2011). Hypothetical thinking in adolescence: Its nature, development, and applications. In E. Amsel & J. Smetana (Eds.), *Adolescent vulnerabilities and opportunities* (pp. 86–116). New York: Cambridge University Press.

Andel, R., Crowe, M., Pedersen, N. L., Fratiglioni, L., Johansson, B., & Gatz, M. (2008). Physical exercise at midlife and risk of dementia three decades later: A population-based study of Swedish twins. *Journals of Gerontology Series A: Biological Sciences and Medical Sciences, 63A*(1), 62–66.

Andersen, A. N., Wohlfahrt, P. C., Christens, J. O., Olsen, J., & Melbye, M. (2000). Maternal age and fetal loss: Population based register linkage study. *British Medical Journal, 320,* 1708–1712.

Anderson, C. A., & Bushman, B. J. (2001). Effects of violent video games on aggressive behavior, aggressive cognition, aggressive affect, physiological arousal, and prosocial behavior: A meta-analytic review of the scientific literature. *Psychological Science, 12,* 353–359.

Anderson, S. W., Bechara, A., Damasio, H., & Damasio, A. R. (1999). Impairment of social and moral behavior related to early damage in human prefrontal cortex. *Nature Neuroscience, 2*(11), 1032–1037.

Andersson, B.-E. (1989). Effects of public day-care: A longitudinal study. *Child Development, 60*(4), 857–866.

Aneja, A., Iqbal, M. M., & Ahmed, K. (2006). The effects of amphetamine use during pregnancy and lactation. *Directions in Psychology, 26*(3), 237–251.

Angel, L., Fay, S., Bouazzaoui, B., & Isingrini, M. (2011). Two hemispheres for better memory in old age: Role of executive functioning. *Journal of Cognitive Neuroscience, 23*(12), 3767–3777.

Angus, J., & Reeve, P. (2006). Ageism: A threat to "aging well" in the 21st century. *Journal of Applied Gerontology, 25*(2), 137–152.

Annunziata, J. & Nemiroff, M. (2009). *Sometimes I'm scared.* Washington, DC: Magination Press/American Psychological Association.

Anthonysamy, A., & Zimmer-Gembeck, M. J. (2007). Peer status and behaviors of maltreated children and their classmates in the early years of school. *Child Abuse and Neglect, 31*(9), 971–991.

Antial, J. K., & Cottin, S. (1988). Factors affecting the division of labor in households. *Sex Roles, 18,* 531–553.

Antonucci, T. C., Birditt, K. S., Sherman, C. W., & Trinh, S. (2011). Stability and change in the intergenerational family: A convoy approach. *Ageing & Society, 31*(7), 1084–1106.

Antonucci, T. C., Jackson, J. S., & Biggs, S. (2007). Intergenerational relations: Theory, research, and policy. *Journal of Social Issues, 63*(4), 679–693.

Anzures, G., Pascalis, O., Quinn, P. C., Slater, A. M., & Lee, K. (2011). Minimizing skincolor differences does not eliminate the own-race recognition advantage in infants. *Infancy, 16*(6), 640–654.

Apfelbaum, E. P., Pauker, K., Ambady, M., Sommers, S. R., & Norton, M. I. (2008). Learning (not) to talk about race: When older children underperform in social categorization. *Developmental Psychology, 44*(5), 1513–1518.

Apperly, I. (2010). *Mindreaders: The cognitive basis of theory of mind.* Hove, UK: Psychology Press.

Aquilino, W. S. (1996). The returning child and parental experience at midlife. In C. D. Ryff & M. M. Seltzer (Eds.), *The parental experience in midlife* (pp. 423–458). Chicago: University of Chicago Press.

Archambault, I., Eccles, J. S., & Vida, M. N. (2010). Ability self-concepts and subjective value in literacy: Joint trajectories from grades 1 through 12. *Journal of Educational Psychology, 102*(4), 804–816.

Archer, S. L. (1985). Identity and the choice of social roles. In A. S. Waterman (Ed.), *New Directions for Child Development, 30,* 79–100. San Francisco: Jossey-Bass.

Archer, S. L. (2002). Commentary on "feminist perspectives on Erikson's theory: Their relevance for contemporary identity development research." *An International Journal of Theory and Research,* 2(3), 267–270.

Archer, S. L. (2008). *Identity and interventions: An introduction.* United Kingdom: Taylor & Francis; United States: Lawrence Erlbaum.

Archibald, A. B., Graber, J. A., & Brooks-Gunn, J. (2008). Pubertal processes and physiological growth in adolescence. In G. R. Adams & M. D. Berzonsky (Eds.), *Blackwell handbook of adolescence.* Oxford, UK: Blackwell Publishing Ltd. doi: 10.1002/9780470756607.ch2

Ardelt, M. (2011). Wisdom, age, and well-being. In K. Warner Schaie & S. L. Willis (Eds.), *Handbook of the psychology of aging* (7th ed., pp. 279–291). San Diego, CA: Elsevier Academic Press.

Ariès, P. (1962). *Centuries of childhood: A social history of family life.* New York:Vintage Books.

Armstrong, T. (1996). A holistic approach to attention deficit disorder. *Educational Leadership, 53,* 34–36.

Arndt, J. (2012). A significant contributor to a meaningful cultural drama: Terror management research on the functions and implications of self-esteem. In P. R Shaver & M. Mikulincer (Eds.), *Meaning, mortality, and choice: The social psychology of existential concerns* (pp. 55–73). Washington, DC: American Psychological Association.

Arnett, J. (2000). Emerging adulthood: A theory of development from the late teens through the twenties. *American Psychologist, 55*(5), 469–480.

Arnett, J. J. (2007). Suffering, selfish, slackers? Myths and reality about emerging adults. *Journal of Youth and Adolescence, 36*(1), 23–29.

Arnett, J. J. (2009). *Adolescence and emerging adulthood: A cultural approach* (4th ed.). Upper Saddle River, NJ: Prentice Hall.

Arnett, J. J. (2010a). *Adolescence and emerging adulthood: A cultural approach.* Upper Saddle River, NJ: Pearson.

Arnett, J. J. (2010b). Oh, grow up! Generational grumbling and the new life stage on emerging adulthood—commentary on Trzeniewski & Donnellan (2010). *Perspectives on Psychological Science, 5*(1), 89–92.

Arnett, J. J. (2012). *Adolescent psychology around the world.* New York: Psychology Press.

Arnett, J. J., et al. (2011). *Debating emerging adulthood: stage or process?* New York: Oxford University Press.

Arnett, L. A. (2011). *Bridging cultural and developmental approaches to psychology: New syntheses in theory, research, and policy.* New York: Oxford University Press.

Aronson, J. (2002). *Improving academic achievement: Impact of psychological factors on education.* Boston: Academic Press.

Arthur, A. E., Bigler, R. S., Liben, L. S., Gelman, S. A., & Ruble, D. N. (2008). Gender stereotyping and prejudice in young children: A developmental intergroup perspective. In S. R. Levy & M. Killen (Eds.), *Intergroup attitudes and relations in childhood through adulthood* (pp. 66–86). New York: Oxford University Press.

Asato, M. R., Terwilliger, R., Woo, J., & Luna, B. (2010). White matter development in adolescence: A DTI study. *Cerebral Cortex, 20*(9), 2122–2131.

Asch, A., & Marmor, R. (2008). Assisted reproduction. In M. Crowley (Ed.), *From birth to death and bench to clinic: the Hastings Center bioethics briefing book for journalists, policymakers, and campaigns* (pp. 5–10). Garrison: The Hastings Center.

Asendorph, J. B., Denissen, J., & Van Aken, M. (2008). Inhibited and aggressive preschool children at 23 years of age: Personality and social transitions into adulthood. *Developmental Psychology, 44*(4), 997–1011.

Asher, S. R., & Paquette, J. A. (2004). Loneliness and peer rejection in childhood. In J. Lerner & A. Alberts (Eds.), *Current directions in developmental psychology* (pp. 101–107). Upper Saddle River, NJ: Prentice Hall.

Asher, S. R., Rose, A. J., & Gabriel, S. W. (2001). Peer rejection in everyday life. In M. R. Leary (Ed.), *Interpersonal rejection* (pp. 105–142). London: London University Press.

Aslin, R. N. (1987). Visual and auditory development in infancy. In J. D. Osofsky (Ed.), *Handbook of infant development* (2nd ed., pp. 5–97). New York: Wiley.

Aslin, R. N., & Smith, L. B. (1988). Perceptual development. *Annual Review of Psychology, 39,* 435–473.

Aslin, R. N., Clayards, M. A., & Bradhan, N. P. (2008). Mechanisms of auditory reorganization during development: From sounds to words. In C. A. Nelson & M. Luciana (Eds.), *Handbook of developmental cognitive neuroscience* (2nd ed., pp. 97–116). Cambridge, MA: MIT Press.

Aspy, C. B., Vesely, S. K., Oman, R. F., Rodine, S., Marshall, L., & McLeroy, K. (2007). Parental communication and youth sexual behaviour. *Journal of Adoelscence,* 30(3), 449–466.

Associated Press. (2004, November 23). U.N. links HIV fight to women's rights: United Nations says global battle against HIV will fail unless progress is made on women's rights.

Ata, R., Ludden, A., & Lally, M. (2007). The effects of gender and family, friend, and media influences on eating behaviors and body image during adolescence. *Journal of Youth and Adolescence, 36*(8), 1024–1037.

Atala, A., & Yoo, J. J. (2008). Tissue engineering in urology. *World Journal of Urology, 26*(4), 293–294.

Atance, C. M., & Hanson, L. K. (2011). Making predictions: A developmental perspective. In M. Bar (Ed.), *Predictions in the brain: Using our past to generate a future* (pp. 311–324). New York: Oxford University Press.

Atchley, R. C. (1999). *Continuity and adaptation in aging: Creating positive experiences.* Baltimore, MD: Johns Hopkins University Press.

Atchley, R. C. (2003). Why most people cope well with retirement. In J. L. Ronch & J. A. Goldfied (Eds.), *Mental wellness in aging: Strengths-based approaches* (pp. 123–138). Baltimore, MD: Health Professions Press.

Atchley, R. C., & Barasch, A. S. (2004). *Social forces and aging: An introduction to social gerontology.* Baltimore, MD: Wadsworth.

Atkinson, R. C., & Shiffrin, R. M. (1971). The control of short-term memory. *Scientific American, 225,* 82–90.

Atwater, E. (1996). *Adolescence* (4th ed.). Englewood Cliffs, NJ: Prentice Hall.

AVERT. (2012). *Worldwide HIV & AIDS statistics.* Retrieved from http://www.avert.org/workstats.htm

Avis, N. E. (1999). Women's health at midlife. In S. L. Willis & J. D. Reid (Eds.), *Life in the middle: Psychological and social development in middle age* (pp. 105–146). San Diego, CA: Academic Press.

Aviv, A. (2011). Leukocyte telomere dynamics, human aging, and life span. In E. J. Masoro & S. N. Austad (Eds.), *Handbook of the biology of aging* (7th ed., pp. 163–176). San Diego, CA: Elsevier Academic Press.

Azar, B. (1997). Defining the trait that makes us human. *APA Monitor, 28*(11), 1, 15.

Bachman, H. J., Coley, R., & Carrano, J. (2012). Low-income mothers' patterns of partnership instability and adolescents' socioemotional well-being. *Journal of Family Psychology, 26*(2), 263–273.

Baer, J. C., & Martinez, C. D. (2006). Child maltreatment and insecure attachment: A meta-analysis. *Journal of Reproductive and Infant Psychology, 24*(3), 187–197.

Bagwell, C. L., & Schmidt, M. E. (2011). *Friendships in childhood and adolescence.* New York: Guilford Press.

Bailey, J. M., Kim, P. Y., Hills, A., & Linsenmeier, J. A. W. (1997). Butch, femme, or straight acting? Partner preferences of gay men and lesbians. *Journal of Personality and Social Psychology, 73,* 960–973.

Baillargeon, R. (2004). Infants' physical world. *Current Directions in Psychological Science, 13*(3), 89–94.

Baillargeon, R., Jie, L., Gertner, Y., & Wu, D. (2011). How do infants reason about physical events? In U. Goswami (Ed.), *The Wiley-Blackwell handbook of childhood cognitive development* (2nd ed., pp. 11–48).

Baird, A. A. (2008). Adolescent moral reasoning: the integration of emotion and cognition. In W. Sinott-Armstrong (Ed.), *Moral psychology, Vol. 3: The neuroscience of morality: Emotion, brain disorders, and development* (pp. 323–342). Cambridge, MA: MIT Press.

Bakeman, R., Adamson, L. B., Konner, M., & Barr, R. G. (1990). !Kung infancy: The social context of object exploration. *Child Development, 61*(3), 796.

Bakeman, R., Adamson, L., Konner, M., & Barr, R. G. (1997). Sequential analyses of !Kung infant communication: Inducing and recruiting. In E. Amsel & K. Renninger (Eds.), *Change and development: Issues of theory, method, and application* (pp. 173–192). Mahwah, NJ: Lawrence Erlbaum Associates Publishers.

Baker, M. K., Atlantis, E., & Singh, M. A. (2007). Multi-modal exercise programs for older adults. *Age and Aging, 36*(4), 375–381.

Bakker, A. B., Schaufeli, W. B., Demerouti, E., & Euwema, M. C. (2007). An organizational and social psychological perspective on burnout and work engagement. In M. Hewstone, H. Schut, J. De Wit, K. Van Den Bos, & M. S. Stroebe (Eds.), *The scope of social psychology: Theory and applications* (pp. 227–250). New York: Psychology Press.

Balas, B., Westerlund, A., Hung, K., & Nelson, C. A. (2011). Shape, color and the other-race effect in the infant brain. *Developmental Science, 14*(4), 892–900.

Baldock, M. R. J., Berndt, A., & Mathias, J. L. (2008). The functional correlates of older drivers' on-road driving test errors. *Topics in Geriatric Rehabilitation, 24* (3), 204–223.

Balk, D. E. (2011). Adolescence, sibling death, and bereavement. In J. Caspi (Ed.), *Sibling development: Implications for mental health practitioners* (pp. 359–376). New York: Springer Publishing.

Ball, M. M., Perkins, M. M., Whittington, F. J., Hollingsworth, C., King, S. V., & Combs, B. L. (2004). Independence in assisted living. *Journal of Aging Studies, 18,* 445–465.

Balsam, K. F., Beauchaine, T. P., Rothblum, E. D., & Solomon, S. E. (2008). Three-year follow-up of same-sex couples who had civil unions in Vermont, same-sex couples not in civil unions, and heterosexual married couples. *Developmental Psychology, 44*(1), 102–116.

Baltes, M. M. (1998). The psychology of the oldest-old: The fourth age. *Current Opinion in Psychiatry, 11,* 411–418.

Baltes, P. B. (1987). Theoretical propositions of life-span developmental psychology: On the dynamics of growth and decline. *Developmental Psychology, 23,* 611–626.

Baltes, P. B. (1993). The aging mind: Potential and limits. *The Gerontologist, 33*(5), 580–594.

Baltes, P. B., & Kunzmann, U. (2003). Wisdom. *Psychologist, 16*(3), 131–133.

Baltes, P. B., & Kunzmann, U. (2004). The two faces of wisdom: Wisdom as a general theory of knowledge and judgment about excellence in mind and virtue versus wisdom as everyday realization in people and products. *Human Development, 47*(5), 290–299.

Baltes, P. B., Reuter-Lorenz, P. A., & Rosler, F. (2006). *Lifespan development and the brain: The perspective of biocultural co-constructivism.* New York: Cambridge University Press.

Baltes, P. B., Lindenberger, U., & Staudinger, U. M. (2006). Lifespan theory in developmental psychology. In R. M. Lerner & W. Damon (Eds.) *Handbook of child psychology (6th ed.): Vol 1. Theoretical models of human development* (pp. 569–664). Hoboken, NJ: John Wiley & Sons, Inc.

Baltes, M. M., & Silverberg, S. B. (1999). The dynamics between dependency and autonomy: Illustrations across the life span. In D. L. Featherman, R. M. Lerner, & M. Perlmutter (Eds.), *Life-span Development and Behavior: Vol. 1* (pp. 41–90), Hillsdale, NJ: Erlbaum.

Baltes, P. B., & Smith, J. (2004). Lifespan psychology: From developmental contextualism to developmental biocultural co-constructivism. *Research in Human Development, 1*(3), 123–144.

Bandura, A. (1965). Influence of models' reinforcement contingencies on the acquisition of imitative responses. *Journal of Personality and Social Psychology, 1,* 589–595.

Bandura, A. (1969). *Principles of behavior modification.* New York: Holt, Rinehart and Winston.

Bandura, A. (1997). *Self-efficacy: The exercise of control.* New York: Freeman.

Barac, R., & Bialystok, E. (2012). Bilingual effects on cognitive and linguistic development: Role of language, cultural background, and education. *Child Development, 83*(2), 413–422.

Barclay, S. R., Stoltz, K. B., & Chung, Y. (2011). Voluntary midlife career change: Integrating the transtheoretical model and the life-span, life-span approach. *The Career Development Quarterly, 59(5),* 386–399.

Barkley, R. A. (2006). *Attention-deficit hyperactivity disorder: A handbook for diagnosis and treatment* (3rd ed.). New York: Guilford Press.

Barnes, G. M., Hoffman, J. H., Welte, J. W., Farrell, M. P., & Dintcheff, B. A. (2007). Adolescents' time use: Effects on substance use, delinquency and sexual activity. *Journal of Youth and Adolescence, 36*(5), 697–710.

Barnett, D. (1997). The effects of early intervention on maltreating parents and their children. In M. J. Guralnick (Ed.), *The effectiveness of early intervention* (pp. 146–170). Baltimore: Brookes.

Barnett, D. (2007). Who should be considered at risk for maltreating their children? *Child Maltreatment, 12*(4), 383–384.

Barnett, M. (2008). Economic disadvantage in complex family systems: Expansion of family stress models. *Clinical Child and Family Psychology Review, 11*(3), 145–161.

Barnett, M. A., Min, D., Mills-Koonce, W. R., Willoughby, M., & Cox, M. (2008). Interdependence of parenting of mothers and fathers of infants. *Journal of Family Psychology, 22*(4), 561–573.

Barnett, O. W., Miller-Perrin, C. L., & Perrin, R. D. (1997). *Family violence across the life span: An introduction.* Thousand Oaks, CA: Sage.

Barnett, R. C., & Hyde, J. S. (2001). Women, men, work, and family. *American Psychologist, 56,* 781–796.

Baroody, A. J. (2000). Does mathematics instruction for three- to five-year-olds really make sense? *Young Children, 55*(4), 61–67.

Baroody, A. J., Lai, M., & Mix, K. S. (2006). The development of young children's early number and operation sense and its implications for early childhood education. In B. Spodex & O. N. Saracho (Eds.), *Handbook of research on the education of young children* (2nd ed., pp. 187–221). Mahwah, NJ: Erlbaum.

Barr, R. G. (2011). Mother and child: Preparing for a life. In D. P. Keating (Eds.), *Nature and nurture in early child development* (pp. 70–96). New York: Cambridge University Press.

Barr, R., Dowden, A., & Hayne, H. (1996). Developmental changes in deferred imitation by 6- to 24-month-old infants. *Infant Behavior and Development, 19,* 159–170.

Barry, C. T., & Pickard, J. D. (2008). Developmental issues. In M. Hersen & D. Reitman (Eds.), *Handbook of psychological assessment, case conceptualization, and treatment* (pp. 76–101). Hoboken, NJ: Wiley.

Bartlett, D. (1997). Primitive reflexes and early motor development. *Journal of Developmental and Behavioral Pediatrics, 18,* 151–157.

Bartoshuk, L. M., & Weiffenbach, J. M. (1990). Chemical senses and aging. In E. L. Schneider & J. W. Rowe (Eds.), *Handbook of the biology of aging* (3rd ed., pp. 429–444). San Diego, CA: Academic Press.

Bau, A. M. (2009). Is there a further acceleration in the age at onset of menarche? A cross-sectional study in 1840 school children focusing on age and bodyweight at the onset of menarche. *European Journal of Endocrinology, 160*(1), 107–13.

Bauer, I., Wrosch, C., & Jobin, J. (2008). I'm better off than most other people: The role of social comparisons for coping with regret in young adulthood and old age. *Psychology and Aging, 23*(4), 800–811.

Bauer, P. J. (2004). Getting explicit memory off the ground: Steps toward contruction of a neuro-developmental account of changes in the first two years of life. *Developmental Review, 24*(4), 347–373.

Bauer, P. J. (2007). Recall in infancy: A neuro-developmental account. *Current Directions in Psychological Science, 16*(3), 142–144.

Bauer, P. J. (2009). The cognitive neuroscience of the development of memory. In M. L. Courage & N. Cowan (Eds.), *The development of memory in infancy and childhood* (2nd ed., pp. 115–144). New York: Psychology Press.

Baumrind, D. (1975). *Early socialization and the discipline controversy.* Morristown, NJ: General Learning Press.

Baumrind, D. (1980). New directions in socialization research. *American Psychologist, 35,* 639–650.

Baumrind, D. (1989). Rearing competent children. In W. Damon (Ed.), *Child development today and tomorrow* (pp. 349–378). San Francisco: Jossey-Bass.

Baumrind, D. (1991). The influence of parenting style on adolescent competence and substance use. *Journal of Early Adolescence, 11,* 56–95.

Bauserman, R. (2002). Child adjustment in joint-custody versus sole-custody arrangements: A meta-analytic review. *Journal of Family Psychology, 16*(1), 91–102.

Bayley, N. (2005). *Bayley Scales of Infant and Toddler Development* (3rd ed.). Pearson Clinical Assessment.

Bazzini, D. G., Mcintosh, W. D., Smith, S. M., Cook, S., & Harris, C. (1997). The aging woman in popular film: Underrepresented, unattractive, unfriendly, and unintelligent. *Sex Roles, 36,* 531–543.

Beaton, E. A., Schmidt, L. A., Schulkin, J., Antony, M. M., Swinson, R. P., & Hall, G. B. (2009). Different fusiform activity to stranger and personally familiar faces in shy and social adults. *Social Neuroscience, 4*(4), 308–316.

Becker, J. (1993). Young children's numerical use of number words: Counting in many-to-one situations. *Developmental Pscyhology, 29,* 458–465.

Beckett, C., Castle, J., Rutter, M., & Sonuga-Barke, E. J. (2010). Institutional deprivation, specific cognitive functions, and scholastic achievement: English and Romanian adoptees (ERA) study findings. *Monographs of the Society for Research in Child Development, 75*(1), 125–142.

Beckman, S., Aksu-Koc, A., & Kagitcibase, C. (2009). *Perspectives on human development, family and culture.* Cambridge, UK: Cambridge University Press.

Beeghly, M., & Cicchetti, D. (1994). Child maltreatment, attachment, and self system: Emergence of an internal state lexicon in toddlers of high social risk. *Development and Psychopathology, 6,* 5–30.

Beelman, A., & Brambring, M. (1998). Implementation and effectiveness of a home-based early intervention program for blind infants and preschoolers. *Research in Developmental Disabilities, 19,* 225–244.

Beins, B. C. (2012). Jean Piaget: Theorist of the child's mind. In W. E. Pickren, D. A. Dewsbury, & M. Wertheimer (Eds.), *Portraits of pioneers in developmental psychology* (pp. 89–107).

Bell, D. (2010). *The dynamics of connection: How evolution and biology create caregiving and attachment.* Lanham, MD: Lexington Books/Rowman & Littlefield.

Bell, F. C., & Miller, M. L. (2012). Life tables for the United States Social Security area 1900–2100. Retrieved from http://www.ssa.gov/oact/NOTES/as120/LifeTables_Body.html

Bell, J. H., & Bromnick, R. D. (2003). The social reality of the imaginary audience: A grounded theory approach. *Adolescence, 38*(150), 205–219.

Bell, S. M., & Ainsworth, M. D. (1972). Infant crying and maternal responsiveness. *Child Development, 43,* 1171–1190.

Belsky, J. (2008). War, trauma and children's development: Observations from a modern evolutionary perspective. *International Journal of Behavioral Development, 32*(4). Special issue: *Chronic exposure to catastrophic war experiences and political violence: Links to the well-being of children and their families,* 260–271.

Belsky, J., & Rosenberger, K. (1995). Maternal personality, marital quality, social support and infant temperament: Their significance for infant–mother attachment in human families. In C. Pryce, R. Martin & D. Skuse (Eds.), *Motherhood in human and nonhuman primates: Biosocial determinants* (pp. 115–124). Basel, Switzerland: Karger.

Belsky, J., Vandell, D., Burchinal, M., Clarke-Stewart, K. A., McCartney, K., & Owen, M. (2007). Are there long-term effects of early child care? *Child Development, 78*(2), 681–701.

Bendl, R. (2010). From "glass ceilings" to "firewalls"—different metaphors for describing discrimination. *Gender, Work, and Organization, 17*(5), 612–634.

Bengtson, V. L. (1985). Diversity and symbolism in grandparents' role. In V. L. Bengtson & J. F. Robertson (Eds.), *Grandparenthood* (pp. 11–25). Beverly Hills, CA: Sage.

Bengtson, V. L. (2009). *Handbook of theories of aging* (2nd ed.). New York: Springer.

Bengtson, V. L., & Putney, N. M. (2006). Future "conflicts" across generations and cohorts? In J. A. Vincent, C. R. Phillipson & M. Downs (Eds.), *The futures of old age* (pp. 20–29). Thousand Oaks, CA: Sage Publications.

Bengtson, V. L., Copen, C. E., Putney, N. M., & Silverstein, M. (2008). Religion and intergenerational transmission over time. In K. Schaie & R. P. Abeles (Eds.), *Social structures and aging individuals: Continuing challenges* (pp. 305–333). New York: Springer Publishing.

Bengtson, V. L., Gans, D., Putney, N. M., & Silverstein, M. (2009). Theories about age and aging. In V. L. Bengston, D. Gans, N. M. Pulney, & M. Silverstein (Eds.), *Handbook of theories of aging* (2nd ed., pp. 3–23). New York: Springer Publishing Co.

Bengtsson, H., & Arvidsson, A. (2011). The impact of developing social perspective-taking skills on emotionality in middle and late childhood. *Social Development, 20*(2), 353–375.

Bennett, D. S., Bendersky, M., & Lewis, M. (2008). Children's cognitive ability from 4 to 9 years old as a function of prenatal cocaine exposure, environmental risk, and maternal verbal intelligence. *Developmental Psychology, 44*(4), 919–928.

Benovenli, L., Fuller, E., Sinnott, J., & Waterman, S. (2011). Three applications of the theory of postformal thought: Wisdom, concepts of God, and success in college. *Research in the Social Scientific Study of Religion, 22,* 141–154.

Benson, M. J., Buehler, C., & Gerard, J. M. (2008). Interparental hostility and early adolescent problem behavior: Spillover via maternal acceptance, harshness, inconsistency, and intrusiveness. *Journal of Early Adolescence, 28*(3), 428–454.

Bentley, E. (2007). *Adulthood: Developmental psychology.* New York: Routledge/Taylor & Francis Group.

Ben-Zur, H. (2012). Loneliness, optimism, and well-being among married, divorced, and widowed individuals. *Journal of Psychology: Interdisciplinary and Applied, 146*(1–2), 23–36.

Beresin, E. V. (2010). The impact of media violence on children and adolescents: Opportunities for Clinical Interventions. American Academy of Child and Adolescent Psychiatry. Retrieved from http://www.aacap.org/cs/root/develomentor/the_impact_of_media_violence_on_chidren_and_adolescents_opportunites_for_clinical_interventions

Berg, C. A. (2000). Intellectual development in adulthood. In R. J. Sternberg (Ed.), *Handbook of intelligence* (pp. 117–137). New York: Cambridge University Press.

Berger, A. (2011a). Developmental neuroprocesses supporting the emergence of self-regulation. In A. Berger (Ed.), *Self-regulation: Brain, cognition, and development* (pp. 45–60). Washington, DC: American Psychological Association.

Berger, A. (2011b). Individual differences in self-regulation. In A. Berger (Ed.), *Self-regulation: Brain, cognition, and development* (pp. 61–90). Washington, DC: American Psychological Association.

Berger, A. (2011c). *Self-regulation: Brain, cognition, and development.* Washington, DC: American Psychological Association.

Berger, L. M., & Waldfogel, J. (2000). Prenatal cocaine exposure: Long-run effects and policy implications. *Social Science Review, 74,* 28–43.

Berger, S., Theuring, C., & Adolph, K. (2007). How and when infants learn to climb stairs. *Infant Behavior and Development, 30*(1), 36–49.

Berk, L. E. (1994b). Why children talk to themselves. *Scientific American, 271*(1), 78–83.

Berk, L. E., Mann, T. D., & Ogan, A. T. (2006). Make-believe play: Wellspring for development of self-regulation. In L. Berk, T. Mann, & A. Ogan (Eds.), *Play = learning: How play motivates and enhances children's cognitive and socialemotional growth* (pp. 74–100). New York: Oxford University Press.

Berlau, D. J., Corrado, M. M., Peltz, C. B., & Kawas, C. H. (2012). Disability in the oldest-old: Incidence and risk factors in The 90+ study. *The American Journal of Geriatric Psychiatry, 20*(2), 159–168.

Berlin, L. J., & Cassidy, J. (1999). Relations among relationships: Contributions from attachment theory and research. In J. Cassidy & P. R. Shaver (Eds.), *Handbook of attachment: Theory, research, and clinical applications* (pp. 688–712). New York: Guilford Press.

Berlin, L.J., Cassidy, J., & Appleyard, K. (2010). The influence of early attachments on other relationships. In J. Cassidy & P. Shaver (Eds.), *Handbook of attachment: Theory, research, and clinical applications* (2nd ed., pp. 48-77). New York, NY: Guilford Press.

Berlin, L. J., & Dodge, K. A. (2004). Relations among relationships. *Child Abuse and Neglect, 28*(11), 1127–1132.

Berman, E., & Napier, A. Y. (2000). The midlife family: Dealing with adolescents, young adults, and the marriage in transition. In W. C. Nichols, M. E. Pace-Nichols, et al. (Eds.), *Handbook of family development and intervention* (pp. 208–234). New York: John Wiley & Sons, Inc.

Bernier, A., Carlson, S. M., & Whipple, N. (2010). From external regulation to self-regulation. Early parenting precursors of young children's executive functioning. *Child Development, 81*(1), 326–339.

Bernstein, J. (2004). The low-wage labor market: Trends and policy issues. In A. C. Crouter & A. Booth (Eds.), *Work–family challenges for low-income parents and their children* (pp. 3–34). Mahwah, NJ: Erlbaum.

Bersamin, M. M., Walker, S., Fisher, D. A., & Grube, J. W. (2006). Correlates of oral sex and vaginal intercourse in early and middle adolescence. *Journal of Research on Adolescence, 16*(1), 59–68.

Bertenthal, B. I., & Clifton, R. K. (1998). Perception and action. In D. Kuhn & R. Siegler (Eds.), *Handbook of child psychology: Vol. 2. Cognition, perception, and language* (5th ed., pp. 51–102). New York: Wiley.

Bertram, L., & Tanzi, R. E. (2008). Thirty years of Alzheimer's disease genetics: The implications of systematic meta-analyses. *Nature Reviews Neuroscience, 9*(10), 768–778.

Berzonsky, M. D. (2011). A social-cognitive perspective on identity construction. In S. J. Schwartz, K. Luyckx, & V. L. Vignoles (Eds.), *Handbook of identity theory and research* (Vols. 1 and 2, pp. 55–76). New York: Springer Science +Business Media.

Betancourt, T., & Khan, K. (2008). The mental health of children affected by armed conflict: Protective processes and pathways to resilience. *International Review of Psychiatry, 20*(3), 317–328.

Betz, M. E., & Lowerstein, S. R. (2010). Driving patterns of older adults: Results from the second injury control and risk survey. *Journal of the American Geriatrics Society, 58*(10), 1931–1935.

Beyers, W., & Çok, F. (2008). Adolescent self and identity development in context. *Journal of Adolescence, 31*(2), 147–150.

Bhatt, R. S., & Quinn, P. C. (2011). How does learning impact development in infancy? The case of perceptual organization. *Infancy, 16*(1), 2–38.

Bialystok, E. (2007). Acquisition of literacy in bilingual children: A framework for research. *Learning Language, 57*(Suppl 1), 45–77.

Bialystok, E. (2011). Reshaping the mind: The benefits of bilingualism. *Canadian Journal of Experimental Psychology/Revue canadienne de psychologie experimentale, 65*(4), 229–235.

Bialystok, E., Luk, G., Peets, K. F., & Yang, S. (2010). Receptive vocabulary differences in monolingual and bilingual children. *Bilingualism: Language and Cognition, 13*(4), 525–531.

Bianchi, S. M., Milkie, M. A., Sayer, L. C., & Robinson, J. P. (2000). Is anyone doing the housework? Trends in the gender division of household labor. *Social Forces, 79*, 191–228.

Bibok, M. B., Muller, U., & J. I. M. Carpendale (2009). Childhood. In U. Muller, J. I. M. Carpendale, & L. Smith (Eds.), *The Cambridge companion to Piaget* (pp. 229–254). New York: Cambridge University Press.

Biehl, M., Natsuaki, M., & Ge, X. (2007). The influence of pubertal timing on alcohol use and heavy drinking trajectories. *Journal of Youth and Adolescence, 36*(2), 153–167.

Bigelow, A. (2005). Blindness. In B. Hopkins (Ed.), *The Cambridge encyclopedia of child development* (pp. 409–413). New York: Cambridge University Press.

Bigner, J. J. (2010). *Parent–child relations: An introduction to parenting* (8th ed.). Upper Saddle River, NJ: Prentice Hall.

Bily, C. A. (2009). *Homosexuality.* Detroit: Greenhaven Press.

Binet, A., & Simon, T. (1905). Methodes nouvelles pour le diagnostic du niveau intelectual des anormaux. *L'Annee Psychologique, 11*, 191–244.

Binet, A., & Simon, T. (1916). *The development of intelligence in children.* Baltimore: Williams & Wilkins.

Biondi, M., Moynihan, J. A., Stevens, S. Y., Lysle, D. T., Drusnecov, A. W., Sved, A., et al. (2001). Part V: Stress and immunity. In R. Ader & D. L. Felten (Eds.), *Psychoneuroimmunology:* Vols. 1–2 (3rd ed., pp. 189–345). San Diego, CA: Academic Press.

Birditt, K. S., & Wardjiman, E. (2012). Intergenerational relationships and aging. In S. K. Whitbourne & M. J. Sliwinski (Eds.) *Handbook of adulthood and aging* (pp. 399–415). Malden, MA: Wiley-Blackwell.

Birkeland, M., Melkevik, O., Holsen, I., & Wold, B. (2012). Trajectories of global self-esteem development during adolescence. *Journal of Adolescence, 35*(1), 43–54.

Birney, D. P., & Sternberg, R. J. (2011). The development of cognitive abilities. In M. H. Bornstein & M. E. Lamb (Eds.), *Developmental science: An advanced textbook* (6th ed., pp. 353–388). New York: Psychology Press.

Bjorklund, D. F. (2004). Special issue: Memory development in the new millennium. *Developmental Review, 24*(4), 343–346.

Bjorklund, D. F. (2007). *Why youth is not wasted on the young: Immaturity in human development.* Malden, MA: Blackwell Publishing.

Bjorklund, D. F., Dukes, C., & Brown, R. D. (2009). The development of memory strategies. In M. L. Courage & N. Cowan (Eds.), *The development of memory in infancy and childhood* (2nd ed., pp. 145–175). New York: Psychology Press.

Black, M. C., Basile, K. C., Breiding, M. J., Smith, S. G., Walters, M. L., Merrick, M. T., Chen, J., & Stevens, M. R. (2011). *The National Intimate Partner and Sexual Violence Survey (NISVS): 2010 Summary Report.* Atlanta, GA: National Center for Injury Prevention and Control, Centers for Disease Control and Prevention.

Black, M. M., Dubowitz, H., Krishnakumar, A., & Starr, R. H. (2007). Early intervention and recovery among children with failure to thrive: Follow-up at age 8. *Pediatrics, 120*(1), 59–69.

Black, M. M., & Hurley, K. M. (2010). Infant nutrition. In J. G. Bremner & T. D. Wachs (Eds.), *The Wiley Blackwell Handbook of infant development* (pp. 33–61). Malden, MA: Wiley-Blackwell.

Blair, C. (2010). Fluid cognitive abilities and general intelligence: A life-span neuroscience perspective. In W. F. Overton & R. M. Lerner (Eds.), *The handbook of life-span development, Vol. 1: Cognition, biology, and methods* (pp. 226–258). Hoboken, NJ: Wiley & Sons.

Blakemore, S. (2008). The social brain in adolescence. *Nature Reviews Neuroscience, 9*(4), 267–277. doi: http://dx.doi.org/10.1038/nrn2353

Blakemore, J. E., Berenaum, S. A., & Liben, L. S. (2009). *Gender development*. New York: Psychology Press.

Blanchard, R. (2008). Review and theory of handedness, birth order, and homosexuality in men. *Laterality, 13*(1), 51–70.

Blasco, P. A., Johnson, C., & Palomo-Gonzalez, S. A. (2008). Supports for families of children with disabilities. In P. J. Accardo (Ed.), *Capute and Accardo's neurodevelopmental disabilities in infancy and childhood, Vol. 1: Neurodevelopmental diagnosis and treatment* (3rd ed., pp. 445–468). Baltimore, MD: Paul H. Brookes Publishing.

Blazer, D. G., & Meador, K. G. (2010). The role of spirituality in healthy aging. In C. A. Depp & D. V. Jeste (Eds.), *Successful cognitive and emotional aging* (pp. 73–85). Arlington VA: American Psychiatric Publishing.

Bleakley, A., Hennessy, M., Fishbein, M., & Jordan, A. (2008). It works both ways: The relationship between exposure to sexual content in the media and adolescent sexual behavior. *Media Psychology, 11*, 443–461.

Blieszner, R., & Roberto, K. A. (2012). Partners and friends in adulthood. In S. K. Whitbourne & M. J. Sliwinski (Eds.), *Handbook of adulthood and aging* (pp. 381–398). Malden, MA: Wiley-Blackwell.

Bloom, B., Cohen, R. A., & Freeman, G. (2011). Summary health statistics for U.S. children: National health interview survey, 2010. *National Center for Health Statistics. Vital Health Stat 10(250).*

Bloom, L. (1998). Language acquisition in its developmental context. In D. Kuhn & R. Sigler (Eds.), *Handbook of child psychology: Vol. 2. Cognition, perception, and language* (5th ed., pp. 309–370). New York: Wiley.

Blumenthal, H., Leen-Feldner, E. W., Babson, K. A., Gahr, J. L., Trainor, C. D., & Frala, J. L. (2011). Elevated social anxiety among early maturing girls. *Developmental Psychology, 47*(4), 1133–1140.

Blythe, S. G. (2000). Early learning in the balance: Priming the first ABC. *Support for Learning, 15*(4), 154–158.

Bobbitt-Zeher, D. (2011). Gender discrimination at work: Connecting gender stereotypes, institutional policies, and gender composition of workplace. *Gender & Society, 25*(6), 764–786.

Bodie, J. A., Beeman, W. W., & Monga, M. (2003). Psychogenic erectile dysfunction. *International Journal of Psychiatry in Medicine, 33*, 273–293.

Bolton, F. G., MacEachron, A. E., & Morris, L. A. (1990). *Males at risk: The other side of child abuse* (3rd ed.). Newbury Park, CA: Sage.

Bonder, B., & del Bello-Haas, V. (2009). *Functional performance in older adults.* Philadelphia, PA: F. A. Davis.

Bonham, V. L., Warshauer-Baker, E., & Collins, F. S. (2005). Race and ethnicity in the genome era: The complexity of the constructs. *American Psychologist, 60*(1), 9–15.

Bookman, A., & Harrington, M. (2007). Family caregivers: A shadow workforce in the geriatric health care system? *Journal of Health Politics, Policy and Law, 32*(6), 1005–1041.

Boom, J. (2010). Measuring moral development: Stages as markers along a latent developmental dimension. In W. Koops, D. Brugman, T. J. Ferguson, & A. F. Sanders (Eds.), *The development and structure of conscience* (pp. 151–167). New York: Psychology Press.

Born, A. (2007). Well-diffused? Identity diffusion and well-being in emerging adulthood. In M. Watzlawik & A. Born (Eds.), *Capturing identity: Quantitative and qualitative methods* (pp. 149–161). Lanham, MD: University Press of America.

Bornstein, M. H. (2012). *Handbook of parenting being and becoming a parent.* Psychology Press.

Bornstein, M. H., Putnick, D. L., Suwalsky, J. T. D., Venuti, P., & Gini, M. (2012). Emotional relationships in mothers and infants: Culture-common and community-specific characteristics of dyads from rural and metropolitan settings in Argentina, Italy, and the United States. *Journal of Cross-Cultural Psychology, 43*(2), 171–197.

Bornstein, M. H., & Tamis-LeMonda, C. S. (2010). Parent-infant interaction. In J. G. Bremner & T. D. Wachs (Eds.), *The Wiley Blackwell handbook of infant development* (pp. 458–482). Malden, MA: Wiley-Blackwell.

Bornstein, M. H., Cote, L. R., Maital, S., Painter, K., Park, S., Pascual, L., et al. (2004). Cross-linguistic analysis of vocabulary in young children: Spanish, Dutch, French, Hebrew, Italian, Korean, and American English. *Child Development, 75*(4), 1115–1139.

Bornstein, M. H., Tamis-Lemonda, C. S., Chun-Shin, H., & Haynes, O. M. (2008). Maternal responsiveness to young children at three ages: Longitudinal analysis of a multidimensional, modular, and specific parenting construct. *Developmental Psychology, 44*(3), 867–874.

Bos, H., Sandfort, T., de Bruyn, E. H., & Hakvoort, E. M. (2008). Same-sex attraction, social relationships, psychosocial functioning, and school performance in early adolescence. *Developmental Psychology, 44*(1), 59–68.

Boutwell, B. B., Beaver, K. M., Gibson, C. L., & Ward, J. T. (2011). Prenatal exposure to cigarette smoke and childhood externalizing behavioral problems: A propensity score matching approach. *International Journal of Environmental Health Research, 21*(4), 248–259.

Boutwell, B. B., Franklin, C. A., Barnes, J. C., & Beaver, K. M. (2011). Physical punishment and childhood aggression: The role of gender and gene-environment interplay. *Aggressive Behavior, 37*, 559–568.

Boutwell, J., & Klare, M. T. (2000). A scourge of small arms. *Scientific American, 282*(6), 48–53.

Bowlby, J. (1980). *Attachment and loss: Vol. 1. Attachment.* New York: Basic Books. (Original work published 1969)

Bowlby, J. (1988). *A secure base: Parent-child attachment and healthy human development*. New York: Basic Books.

Bowlby, J. (1989). The role of attachment in personality development and psychopathology. In S. I. Greenspan & G. H. Pollock (Eds.), *The course of life, Vol. 1: Infancy* (pp. 229–270). Madison, CT: International Universities Press, Inc.

Bowlby, J. (1999a). *Attachment* (2nd ed.). New York: Basic Books.

Bowlby, J. (1999b). *Attachment and loss*, (2nd ed.). New York: Basic Books.

Bowlby, J. (2007). *A secure base: Clinical applications of attachment theory*. London: Routledge.

Boyce, P., Condon, J., Barton, J., & Corkindale, C. (2007). First-time fathers' study: Psychological distress in expectant fathers during pregnancy. *Australian and New Zealand Journal of Psychiatry, 41*(9), 718–725.

Braaten, E. B. (2011). Learning disabilities. In E. B. Braaten (Ed.), *How to find mental health care for your child* (pp. 121–137). Washington, DC: American Psychological Association.

Brackbill, Y., & Nevill, D. (1981). Parental expectations of achievement as affected by children's height. *Merrill-Palmer Quarterly, 27*, 429–441.

Bracke, P., Christiaens, W., & Wauterickx, N. (2008). The pivotal role of women in informal care. *Journal of Family Issues, 29*(10), 1348–1378.

Bracken, S., & Fischel, J. E. (2008). Family reading behavior and early literacy skills in preschool children from low-income backgrounds. *Early Education and Development, 19*(1), 45–67.

Braddick, O., & Atkinson, J. (2011). Development of human visual function. *Vision Research, 51*(13), 1588–1609.

Bradley, R. A., Hathaway, M., Hathaway, J., & Hathaway, J. (2008). *Husband-coached childbirth: The Bradley method® of natural childbirth* (5th ed.). New York: Bantam Books.

Brady, S. A., Braze, D., & Fowler, C. A. (2011). *Explaining individual differences in reading: Theory and evidence.* New York: Psychology Press.

Brambring, M. (2006). Divergent development of gross motor skills in children who are blind or sighted. *Journal of Visual Impairment and Blindness, 100*(10), 620–634.

Brambring, M. (2007). Divergent development of verbal skills in children who are blind or sighted. *Journal of Visual Impairment and Blindness, 101*(12), 749–762.

Brandone, A. C., Salkind, S. J., Golinkoff, R. M., & Hirsh-Pasek, K. (2006). Language development. In G. Bear & K. M. Minke (Eds.), *Children's needs III: Development, prevention, and internvention* (pp. 499–514). Washington, DC: National Association of School Psychologists.

Bransford, J. D., Brown, A. L., & Cocking, R. R. (2008). Mind and brain. In M. Immordino-Yang (Ed.), *The Jossey-Bass reader on the brain and learning* (pp. 89–105). San Francisco, CA: Jossey-Bass.

Bransford, J. D., Brown, A. L., Donovan, M. S., & Pellegrino, J. W. (2003). *How people learn: Brain, mind, experience, and school* (8th ed.). Washington, DC: National Academy Press.

Brassen, S., Garner, M., Peters, J., Gluth, S., & Büchel, C. (2012). Don't look back in anger! Responsiveness to missed chances in successful and nonsuccessful aging. *Science, 336*(6081), 612–614.

Bratko, D., Butkovic, A., & Chamorro-Premuzic, T. (2010). The genetics of general knowledge: A twin study from Croatia. *Personality and Individual Differences, 48*(4), 403–407.

Braun, M., Lewin-Epstein, N., Stier, H., & Baumgärtner, M. K. (2008). Perceived equity in the gendered division of household labor. *Journal of Marriage and Family, 70*(5), 1145–1156.

Brazelton Institute (2012). *The Newborn Behavioral Observations system: What is it?* Accessed online on April 25, 2012 from http://www.brazelton-institute.com/clnbas.html.

Brazelton, T. B., & Nugent, K. J. (2011). *Neonatal behavioral assessment scale* (4th ed.), Hoboken, NJ: John Wiley & Sons.

Brennan, P. L., Holland, J. M., Schutte, K. K., & Moos, R. H. (2012). Coping trajectories in later life: A 20-year predictive study. *Aging & Mental Health, 16*(3), 305–316.

Bretherton, I. (2010). Fathers in attachment theory and research: A review. *Early child development and care, 180*(1–2), 9–23.

Brewer, A. M. (2012). Positive mentoring relationships: Nurturing potential. In S. Roffey (Ed.), *Positive relationships: Evidence based practice across the world* (pp. 197–214). New York: Springer Science + Business Media.

Brick, J. (2008). *Handbook of the medical consequences of alcohol and drug abuse.* New York: Routledge.

Bridge, J. A., Goldstein, T. R., & Brent, D. A. (2006). Adolescent suicide and suicidal behavior. *Journal of Child Psychology and Psychiatry, 47*(3/4), 372–394.

Brim, O. G., Ryff, C. D., & Kessler, R. C. (2004). The MIDUS national survey: An overview. In O. G. Brim, C. D. Ryff, & R. C. Kessler (Eds.), *How healthy are we? A national study of well-being at midlife* (pp. 1–34). Chicago: University of Chicago Press.

Brockmann, H., Müller, R., & Helmert, U. (2009). Time to retire—time to die? A prospective cohort study of the effects of early retirement on long-term survival. *Social Science and Medicine, 69*(2), 162–164.

Brody, E. M. (1985). *Parent care as a normative family stress.* Donald P. Kent Memorial Lecture presented at the 37th annual scientific meeting of the Gerontological Society of America, San Antonio, TX.

Brody, E. M. (2006). *Women in the middle: Their parent care years* (2nd ed.). New York: Springer Publishing.

Brody, E. M., Litvin, S. J., Hoffman, C., & Kleban, M. H. (1995b). On having a "significant other" during the parent care years. *Journal of Applied Gerontology, 14,* 131–149.

Brody, G. H. (2004). Siblings' direct and indirect contributions to child development. *Current Directions in Psychological Science, 13*(3), 124–126.

Broeren, S., & Muris, P. (2009). The relation between cognitive development and anxiety phenomena in children. *Journal of Child and Family Studies, 18,* 702–709.

Broesch, T., Callaghan, T., Henrich, J., Murphy, C., & Rochat, P. (2011). Cultural variations in children's mirror self-recognition. *Journal of Cross-Cultural Psychology, 42*(6), 1018–1029.

Bromberger, J. T., Schott, L. L., Kravitz, H. M., Sowers, M., Avis, N. E., Gold, E. B., Randolph, J., & Matthews, K. (2010). Longitudinal change in reproductive hormones and depressive symptoms across the menopausal transition: Results from the Study of Women's Health across the Nation (SWAN). *Archives of General Psychiatry, 67*(6), 598–607.

Bronfenbrenner, U. (1970). *Two worlds of childhood: U.S. and U.S.S.R.* New York: Russell Sage Foundation.

Bronfenbrenner, U. (1979). *The ecology of human development.* Cambridge, MA: Harvard University Press.

Bronfenbrenner, U. (2005). The bioecological theory of human development. In U. Bronfenbrenner, (Ed.), *Making human beings human: Bioecological perspectives on human development* (pp. 3–15). Thousand Oaks, CA: Sage Publications.

Bronfenbrenner, U., & Morris, P. A. (2006). The bioecological model of human development. In R. M. Lerner & W. Damon (Eds.), *Handbook of child psychology, Vol. 1, Theoretical models of human development* (6th ed., pp. 793–828). Hoboken, NJ: John Wiley & Sons Inc.

Bronstein, P. (2006). The family environment: Where gender role socialization begins. In J. Worell & C. D. Goodheart (Eds.), *Handbook of girls' and women's psychological health: Gender and well-being across the lifespan* (pp. 262–271). New York: Oxford University Press.

Brookings. (2011). Five things the census revealed about America in 2011. Retrieved from http://www.brookings.edu/research/opinions/2011/12/20-census-demographics

Brooks-Gunn, J., & Furstenberg, F. F., Jr. (1986). The children of adolescent mothers: Physical, academic, and psychological outcomes. *Developmental Review, 6,* 224–251.

Brooks-Gunn, J., Berlin, L. J., Leventhal, T., & Fuligni, A. S. (2000). Depending on the kindness of strangers: Current national data initiatives and developmental research. *Child Development, 71,* 257–268.

Brown, B. B., & Bakken, J. P. (2011). Parenting and peer relationships: Reinvigorating research on family-peer linkages in adolescence. *Journal of Research on Adolescence, 21*(1), 153–165.

Brown, B., & Dietz, E. L. (2009). Informal peer groups in middle childhood and adolescence. In K. H. Rubin, W. M. Bukowski, & B. Laursen (Eds.), *Handbook of peer interactions, relationships, and groups* (pp. 361–376). New York: Guilford Press.

Brown, J. D., & Bobkowski, P. S. (2011). Older and newer media: Patterns of use and effects on adolescents' health and well-being. *Journal of Research on Adolescence, 21*(1), 95–113.

Brown, J. D., L'Engle, K. L., Pardun, C. J., Guo, G., Kenneavy, K., & Jackson, C. (2006). Sexy media matter: Exposure to sexual content in music, movies, television, and magazines predict Black and White adolescents' sexual behavior. *Pediatrics, 117,* 1018–1027.

Brown, J. E., Nicholson, J. M., Broom, D. H., & Bittman, M. (2011). Television viewing by school-age children: Associations with physical activity, snack food consumption and unhealthy weight. *Social Indicators Research, 101*(2), 221–225.

Brown, L., Lamb, S., & Tappan, M. (2009). *Packaging boyhood: Saving our sons from superheroes, slackers, and other media stereotypes.* New York: St. Martin's Press.

Brown, R. (1973). *A first language: The early stages.* Cambridge, MA: Harvard University Press.

Brown, S. L., Brown, R. M., & Smith, D. M. (2008). Coping with spousal loss: Potential buffering effects of self-reported helping behavior. *Personality and Social Psychology Bulletin, 34*(6), 849–861.

Brown, T. A. (2010). *Gene cloning and DNA analysis* (6th ed.). Hoboken, NJ: Wiley-Blackwell.

Brownell, C. A., & Kopp, C. B. (2007). *Socioemotional development in the toddler years: Transitions and transformations.* New York: Guilford Press.

Brownell, C. A., Romani, G. B., & Zerwas, S. (2007). Becoming a social partner with peers: Cooperation and social understanding in one- and two-yearolds. *Child Development, 77*(4), 803–821.

Bruner, J. S. (2006). *In search of pedagogy: The selected works of Jerome S. Bruner.* London: New York: Routledge.

Bublitz, M. H., & Stroud, L. R. (2012). Maternal smoking during pregnancy and offspring brain structure and function: Review and agenda for future research. *Nicotine & Tobacco Research, 14*(4), 388–397.

Buchbinder, M. & Timmermans, S. (2011). HYPERLINK "http://www.experts.scival.com/reachnc/pubDetail.asp?t=pm&id=78651289152&n=Mara+Buchbinder&u_id=720162700" Medical technologies and the dream of the perfect newborn. *Medical Anthropology: Cross Cultural Studies in Health and Illness, 30*(1), 56-80.

Buchmann, C., Diprete, T. A., & McDaniel, A. (2008). Gender inequalities in education. *Annual Review of Sociology, 34*(1), 319–337.

Buckley, S., & Johnson-Glenberg, M. C. (2008). Increasing literacy learning for individuals with Down syndrome and fragile X syndrome. In J. E. Roberts, R. S. Chapman, & S. F. Warren (Eds.), *Speech and language development and intervention in Down syndrome and fragile X syndrome* (pp. 233–254). Baltimore Paul H. Brookes Publishing.

Buckley, S. J. (2009). *Gentle birth, gentle mothering: The wisdom and science of gentle choices in pregnancy*, birth, and parenting. Berkeley, CA: Celestial Arts.

Buckner, R. L., Head, D., & Lustig, C. (2006). Brain changes in aging: A lifespan perspective. In E. Bialystok & F. Craik (Eds.), *Lifespan cognition: Mechanisms of change* (pp. 27–42). New York: Oxford University Press.

Bukowski, W. M., Motzoi, C., & Meyer, F. (2009). Friendship as process, function, and outcome. In K. H. Rubin, W. M. Bukowski, & B. Laursen (Eds.), *Handbook of peer interactions, relationships, and groups* (pp. 217–231). New York: Guilford Press.

Bukowski, W. M., Simard, M., Dubois, M., & Lopez, L. S. (2011). Representations, process, and development: a new look at friendship in early adolescence. In E. Amsel & J. Smetana (Eds.), *Adolescent vulnerabilities and opportunities* (pp. 159–181). New York: Cambridge University Press.

Bullock, J. (2002, Spring). Bullying among children. *Childhood Education,* 130–133.

Bunge, S. A. (2008). Changing minds, changing brains. *Human Development, 51*(3). 162–164.

Burant, C. F. (2012). *Medical management of type 2 diabetes* (7th ed.). Alexandria, VA: American Diabetes Association.

Bureau of Labor Statistics. (2010). Employment status of women by presence and age of youngest child, March 1975–2009. *Women in the labor force: A databook*, retrieved on May 3, 2012 from http://www.bls.gov/cps/wlf-databook-2010.htm/

Bureau of Labor Statistics. (2011). Women at work. Retrieved from http://www.bls.gov/spotlight/2011/women

Burgess, E. O. (2004). Sexuality in midlife and later life couples. In J. Harvey, A. Wenzel, & S. Sprecher (Eds.), *The handbook of sexuality in close relationships* (pp. 437–454). Mahwah, NJ: Lawrence Erlbaum Associates Publishers.

Burnham, D., & Mattock, K. (2011). Auditory development. In J. G. Bremner & T. D. Wachs (Eds.), *The Wiley-Blackwell handbook of infant development, Vol. 1: Basic research* (2nd ed.). Malden, MA: Wiley Blackwell.

Burnside, I. M. (1979). The later decades of life: Research and reflections. In I. M. Burnside, P. Ebersole, & H. E. Monea (Eds.), *Psychosocial caring throughout the life span* (pp. 405–436). New York: McGraw-Hill.

Burnside, I. M., Ebersole, P., & Monea, H. E. (Eds.). (1979). *Psychosocial caring throughout the life span.* New York: McGraw-Hill.

Bushnell, I. W. R. (2001). Mother's face recognition in newborn infants: Learning and memory. *Infant & Child Development, 10*(1/2), 67–74.

Bushnell, I. W. R. (2003). Newborn face recognition. In O. Pascalis & A. Slater (Eds.) *The development of face processing in infancy and early childhood: Current perspectives,* (41–53). Hauppauge: Nova Science Publishers.

Buss, A. H. (2012a). Temperament I: Activity and emotionality. In A. H. Buss (Ed.), *Pathways to individuality: Evolution and development of personality traits* (pp. 43–67). Washington, DC: American Psychological Association.

Buss, A. H. (2012b). Temperament II: Sociability and impulsiveness. In A. H. Buss (Ed.), *Pathways to individuality: Evolution and development of personality traits* (pp. 69–88). Washington, DC: American Psychological Association.

Buss, K. A. (2011). Which fearful toddlers should we worry about? Context, fear, regulation, and anxiety risk. *Developmental Psychology, 47*(3), 804–819.

Butler, C. B. (2005). Age-related paradigms. *New Directions for Adult & Continuing Education, Winter 2005* (108), 61–68.

Butler, J., Floccia, C., Goslin, J., & Panneton, R. (2011). Infants' discrimination of familiar and unfamiliar accents in speech. *Infancy, 16*(4), 392–417.

Buysse, V., Goldman, B. D., West, T. & Hollingsworth, H. (2008). Friendships in early childhood: Implications for early education and intervention. In W. H. Brown, S. L. Odom, & S. R. McConnell (Eds.), *Social competence of young children: Risk, disability, and intervention* (pp. 77–97). Baltimore, MD: Paul H Brookes Publishing.

Byne, W. (2007). Biology and sexual minority status. In I. H. Meyer & M. E. Northridge (Eds.), *The health of sexual minorities: Public health perspectives on lesbian, gay, bisexual, and transgender populations* (pp. 65–90). New York: Springer Science + Business Media.

Byrd, C. M., & Chavous, T. (2011). Racial identity, school racial climate, and school intrinsic motivation among African American youth: The importance of person-context congruence. *Journal of Research on Adolescence, 21*(4), 849–860.

Cabeza, R. (2001). Cognitive neuroscience of aging: Contributions of functional neuroimaging. *Scandinavian Journal of Psychology, 42,* 277–286.

Cabrera, N. J., Shannon, J. D., & Tamis-LeMonda, C. (2007). Fathers' influence on their children's cognitive and emotional development: From toddlers to pre-K. *Applied Developmental Science, 11*(4), 208–213.

Cabrera, N. J., Tamis-Lemonda, C. S., Bradley, R. H., Hofferth, S., & Lamb, M. E. (2000). Fatherhood in the twenty-first century. *Child Development, 71*(1), 127–136.

Calfo, S., Smith, J., & Zezza, M. (2008, August 4). Last year of life study. Centers for Medicare & Medicaid Services, Office of the Actuary. Retrieved February 23, 2009 from http://www.cms.hhs.gov/ActuarialStudies/downloads/Last_Year_of_Life. Pdf

Calkins, S. D., & Mackler, J. S. (2011). Temperament, emotion regulation, and social development. In M. K. Underwood & L. H. Rosen (Eds.), *Social development: Relationships in infancy, childhood, and adolescence* (pp. 44–70). New York: Guilford Press.

Callaghan, T., Rochat, P., Lillard, A., Claux, M., Odden, H., Itakura, S., et al. (2005). Synchrony in the onset of mental-state reasoning. *Psychological Science, 16*(5), 378–384.

Camann, W., & Alexander, K. (2006). *Easy labor: Every woman's guide to choosing less pain and more joy during childbirth.* New York: Ballantine Books.

Cameron, C. E., Connor, C., Morrison, F. J., & Jewkes, A. M. (2008). Effects of classroom organization on letter-word reading in first grade. *Journal of School Psychology, 46*(2), 173–192.

Campbell, B. C. (2011). An introduction to the special issue on middle childhood. *Human Nature, 22*(3), 247–248.

Cantor, J., Bushman, B. J., Huesmann, L. R., Groebel, J., Malamuth, N. M., Impett, E. A., et al. (2001). In D. G. Singer & J. L. Singer (Eds.), *Handbook of children and the media* (pp. 207–307). Thousand Oaks, CA: Sage.

Capone, G. T., & Kaufmann, W. E. (2008). Human brain development. In P. J. Accardo (Ed.), *Capute and Accardo's neurodevelopmental disabilities in infancy and childhood, Vol. 1: Neurodevelopmental diagnosis and treatment* (3rd ed., pp. 27–59). Baltimore, MD: Paul H Brooks Publishing.

Caprara, G. V., Caprara, M., & Steca, P. (2003). Personality's correlates of adult development and aging. *European Psychologist, 8*(3), 131–147.

Cardena, E., & Gleaves D. H. (2007). Dissociative disorders. In M. Hersen, S. M. Turner, & D. C. Beidel, (Eds.), *Adult psychopathology and diagnosis* (pp. 473–503). Hoboken, NJ: John Wiley & Sons.

Carlson, K. J., Eisenstat, S. A., & Ziporyn, T. D. (1996). *The Harvard guide to women's health.* Cambridge, MA: Harvard University Press.

Carlson, K. J., Eisenstat, S. A., & Ziporyn, T. D. (2004). *The new Harvard guide to women's health.* Cambridge, MA: Harvard University Press.

Carlson, M. C., et al. (2009). Evidence for neurocognitive plasticity in at-risk older adults: The Experience Corps program. *The Journals of Gerontology: Series A: Biological Sciences and Medical Sciences, 64A*(12), 1275–1282.

Carlson, M. J., & Hognas, R. S. (2011). Coparenting in fragile families: Understanding how parents work together after a nonmarital birth. In J. P. McHale & K. M. Lindahl (Eds.), *Coparenting: A conceptual and clinical examination of family systems* (pp. 81–103).

Carlson, M. J., & McLanahan, S. S. (2010). Fathers in fragile families. In M. E. Lamb (Ed.), *The role of the father in child development* (5th ed., pp. 241–269). Hoboken, NJ: John Wiley & Sons, Inc.

Carlson, V., & Harwood, R. L. (2003). Attachment, culture, and the caregiving system: The cultural patterning of everyday experiences among Anglo and Puerto Rican mother–infant pairs. *Infant Mental Health Journal, 24*(1), 53–73.

Carmody, D. P., Bennett, D. S., & Lewis, M. (2011). The effects of prenatal cocaine exposure and gender on inhibitory control and attention. *Neurotoxicology and Teratology, 33*(1), 61–68.

Carpendale, J. (2009). Piaget's theory of moral development. In U. Müller, J. Carpendale, & L. Smith (Eds.), *The Cambridge companion to Piaget* (pp. 270–286). New York: Guilford Press.

Carpendale, J., Sokol, B. W., & Müller, U. (2010). Is a neuroscience of morality possible? In P. D. Zelazo, M. Chandler, & E. Crone (Eds.), *Developmental social cognitive neuroscience* (pp. 289–311). New York: Psychology Press.

Carpenter, L. M., Nathanson, C. A., & Kim, Y. J. (2009). Physical women, emotional men: Gender and sexual satisfaction in midlife. *Archives of Sexual Behavior, 38*(1), 87–107.

Carr, P. B., & Dweck, C. S. (2011). Intelligence and motivation. In R. J. Sternberg & S. B. Kaufman (Eds.), *The Cambridge handbook of intelligence* (pp. 748–770). New York: Cambridge University Press.

Carrion, V. G., & Lock, J. (1997). The coming out process: Developmental stages for sexual minority youth. *Clinical Child Psychology and Psychiatry, 2,* 369–377.

Carter, B., McGoldrick, M., & Petkov, B. (2011). Becoming parents: The family with young children. In M. McGoldrick, E. A. Carter, & N. Garcia-Preto (Eds.), *The expanded family life cycle: individual, family, and social perspectives* (pp. 211–231). Boston, MA: Pearson Allyn & Bacon.

Carter, E. A., & McGoldrick, M. (2005). *The expanded family life cycle: Individual, family, and social perspectives* (3rd ed.). New York: Pearson Allyn & Bacon.

Carter, R. C., et al. (2010). Iron deficiency anemia and cognitive function in infancy. *Pediatrics, 126*(2), e427–e434.

Cartwright, C., & Auckland, T. (2008). Resident, parent-child relationships in stepfamilies. In J. Pryor (Ed.), *The international handbook of stepfamilies: Policy and practice in legal, research, and clinical environments* (pp. 208–230). Hoboken, NJ: John Wiley & Sons Inc.

Caserta, M. T., O'Connor, T. G., Wyman, P. A., Wang, H., Moynihan, J., Cross, W., et al. (2008). The associations between psychosocial stress and the frequency of illness, and innate and adaptive immune function in children. *Brain, Behavior, and Immunity, 22*(6), 933–940.

Casey, B. J., Getz, S., & Galvan, A. (2008). The adolescent brain. *Developmental Review, 28*(1), 62–77.

Casey, B. J., Giedd, J. N., & Thomas, K. M. (2000). Structural and functional brain development and its relation to cognitive development. *Biological Psychology, 54,* 241–257.

Cashon, C. H. (2011). Development of specialized face perception infants: An information-processing perspective. In L. M. Oakes, C. H. Cashon, M. Casasola, & D. H. Rakison (Eds.), *Infant perception and cognition: Recent advances emerging theories, and future directions* (pp. 69–83). New York: Oxford University Press.

Casile, A., Caggiano, V., & Ferrari, P. (2011). The mirror neuron system: A fresh view. *The Neuroscientist, 17*(5), 524–538.

Caspi, A. (1998). Personality development across the life course. In N. Eisenberg (Ed.), *Handbook of child psychology: Vol. 3. Social, emotional, and personality development* (5th ed., pp. 779–862). New York: Wiley.

Cassidy, J., & Berlin, L. J. (1994). The insecure/ambivalent pattern of attachment: Theory and research. *Child Development, 65*(4), 971–991.

Cassidy, J., & Shaver, P. R. (2008). *Handbook of attachment: Theory, research, and clinical applications* (2nd ed.). New York: Guilford Press.

Cassidy, S. B., & Allanson, J. E. (2010). *Management of genetic syndromes* (3rd ed.). Hoboken, NJ: Wiley-Blackwell.

Cassidy, T. (2006). *Birth: The surprising history of how we are born.* New York: Atlantic Monthly Press.

Catts, H. W., & Adlof, S. (2011). Phonological and other language deficits associated with dyslexia. In S. A. Brady, D. Braze, & C. A. Fowler (Eds.), *Explaining individual differences in reading: Theory and evidence* (pp. 137–151).

Cauffman, E., Shulman, E. P., Steinberg, L., Claus, E., Banich, M. T., Graham, S., & Woolard, J. (2010). Age differences in affective decision making as indexed by performance on the Iowa Gambling Task. *Developmental Psychology, 46*(1), 193–207.

Ceballo, R., & McLoyd, V. (2002). Social support and parenting in poor, dangerous neighborhoods. *Child Development, 73,* 1310–1321.

Ceballo, R., McLoyd, V. C., & Toyokawa, T. (2004). The influence of neighborhood quality on adolescents' educational values and school effort. *Journal of Adolescent Research, 19*(6), 716–739.

Celello, K. (2012). *Making marriage work: A history of marriage and divorce in the twentieth-century United States.* Chapel Hill, NC: University of North Carolina.

Celera Genomics Corporation. (2000, June 26). *The heart, the moon, and the genome.* Retrieved on June 26, 2000 from http://www.celera.com/celera/press_releases/2000

Center for Research on Child Wellbeing. (2011). The fragile families and child well-being study. Retrieved from http://www.fragilefamilies.princeton.edu

Center for Sexual Health Promotion. (2010). National survey on sexual health and behavior. Retrieved from http://www.nationalsexstudy.indiana.edu/

Center for Sexual Health Promotion. (2012). National survey of sexual health and behavior. Retrieved from http://www.nationalsexstudy.indiana.edu

Centers for Disease Control and Prevention (CDC). (1997). *Guidelines for school and community health programs to promote lifelong physical activity among young people.* Hyattsville, MD: Author.

Centers for Disease Control and Prevention (CDC). (2004). *Surgeon General's Report 2004: Health Consequences of Smoking: Chapter 5.* Retrieved on July 26, 2005 from http://www.cdc.gov/tobacco/sgr_2004

Centers for Disease Control and Prevention. (CDC). (2006). *Achievements in public health: Reduction in perinatal transmission of HIV infection—United States, 1985–2005.* Retrieved on November 13, 2008 from http://www.cdc.gov/mmwr/preview/mmwrhtml/mm5521a3.htm

Centers for Disease Control and Prevention (CDC). (2000). *Stature-for-age and weight-for-age percentiles.* Retrieved on December 11, 2008 from http://www.cdc/gov/growthcharts

Centers for Disease Control and Prevention. (2010). *Sexual risk behavior: HIV, STD, & teen pregnancy prevention.* Retrieved from http://www.cdc.gov/HealthyYouth/sexualbehaviors/

Centers for Disease Control and Prevention. (2011). 2010 Sexually transmitted diseases surveillance. *STD Surveillance, 2010 – STDs in adolescents and young adults.* Retrieved June 19, 2012 from http://www.cdc.gov/std/stats10/adol.htm

Centers for Disease Control and Prevention. (2011a). Asthma in the US growing every year. *Vitalsigns, May 2011.* Retrieved from http://www.cdc.gov/vitalsigns/Asthma/

Centers for Disease Control and Prevention. (2011b). Breastfeeding among U.S. children born 2000–2008, CDC National Immunization survey. Retrieved on from http://www.cdc.gov/breastfeeding/data/NIS_data/

Centers for Disease Control and Prevention. (2011c). CDC fact sheets—alcohol use and health. Retrieved from http://www.cdc.gov/alcohol/fact-sheets/alcohol-use.htm/

Centers for Disease Control and Prevention. (2011d). Drinking while pregnant still a problem. Retrieved from http://www.cdc.gov/Features/dsAlcoholChildbearingAgeWomen

Centers for Disease Control and Prevention. (2011e). Infertility FAQs. Retrieved from http://www.cdc.gov/reproductivehealth/Infertility/index.htm

Centers for Disease Control and Prevention. (2011f). Mitochondrial disease. Retrieved from http://www.cdc.gov/ncbddd/autism/mitochondrial-faq.html.

Centers for Disease Control and Prevention. (2011g). Multiple births. Retrieved from http://www.cdc.gov/nchs/fastats/multiple.htm

Centers for Disease Control and Prevention. (CDC). (2011h). National diabetes fact sheet. Retrieved from http://www.cdc.gov/diabetes/pubs/pdf/ndfs_2011.pdf

Centers for Disease Control and Prevention. (CDC). (2011i). *National Vital Statistics Reports: Births: Final Data for 2009, 59*(4). Retrieved from http://www.cdc.gov/nchs/data/nvsr/nvsr59/nvsr59_04.pdf

Centers for Disease Control and Prevention. (2011j). Radiation and pregnancy: A fact sheet for clinicians. Retrieved from http://www.bt.cdc.gov/radiation/prenatalphysician.asp

Centers for Disease Control and Prevention. (2011k). Sexually transmitted diseases surveillance. STD Surveillance, 2010—STDs in adolescents and young adults. from http://www.cdc.gov/std/stats10/adol.htm

Centers for Disease Control and Prevention. (2011l). Table 45. Acquired immunodeficiency syndrome (AIDS) diagnoses, by year of diagnosis and selected characteristics: United States, 2006–2009. *Health, United States, 2011.*

Centers for Disease Control and Prevention. (2011m). Teen pregnancy. Retrieved from http://www.cdc.gov/chronicdisease/resources/publications/aag/teen-preg.htm

Centers for Disease Control and Prevention (CDC). (2012a). National marriage and divorce rate trends. Retrieved from http://www.cdc.gov/nchs/nvss/marriage_divorce_tables.htm

Centers for Disease Control and Prevention (CDC). (2012b). Prevalence of autism spectrum disorders—autism and developmental disabilities monitoring network, United States, 2008. *Mortal Weekly Report (MMWR), 61*(3).

Centers for Disease Control and Prevention (CDC). (2012c). Sexually transmitted diseases (STDs). Retrieved from http://www.cdc.gov/std

Centers for Disease Control and Prevention. (2012d). Teen pregnancy. Retrieved from http://www.cdc.gov/chronicdisease/resources/publications/aag/teen-preg.htm

Centers for Disease Control and Prevention (CDC). (2012e). The NHANES National Youth Fitness Survey. Retrieved from http://www.cdc/gov/nchs/nyfs.htm

Centers for Disease Control and Prevention. (2012g). What is assisted reproductive technology? Retrieved from http://www.cdc.gov/art/

Centers for Medicare and Medicaid Services. (2004). Last year of life study. Retrieved on October 28, 2005 at http://www.cms.hhs.gov/statistics/lyol/intro.asp

Central Intelligence Agency. (2012). The world factbook. Retrieved from http://www.cia.gov/library/publications/the-world-factbook/rankorder/2187rank.html

Cervone, D., Mor, N., Orom, H., Shadel, W. G., & Scott, W. D. (2011). Self-efficacy beliefs and the architecture of personality: On knowledge, appraisal, and self-regulation. In K. D. Vohs & R. F. Baumeister (Eds.), *Handbook of self-regulation: Research, theory, and applications* (2nd ed., pp. 461–484). New York: Guilford Press.

Chaffin, M., Hanson, R., Saunders, B. E., Nichols, T., Barnett, D., Zeanah, C., et al. (2006). Report of the APSAC task force on attachment therapy, reactive attachment disorder, and attachment problems. *Child Maltreatment, 11*(1), 76–89.

Chan, C. C., Tardif, T., Chen, J., Pulverman, R. B., Zhu, L., & Meng, X. (2011). English- and Chinese-learning infants map novel labels to objects and actions differently. *Developmental Psychology, 47*(5), 1459–1471.

Chandra, A., et al. (2008). Does watching sex on television predict teen pregnancy? Findings from a national longitudinal survey of youth. *Pediatrics, 122* (5), 1047–1054.

Chang, M., et al. (2010). The effect of midlife physical activity on cognitive function among older adult: AGES—Reykjavik Study. *Journals of Gerontology: Series A: Biological Sciences and Medical Science, 65A*(12), 1369–1374.

Chao, R. K. (2001). Extending research on the consequences of parenting styles for Chinese Americans and European Americans. *Child Development, 72*(6), 1832–1843.

Charles, S. T., & Carstensen, L. L. (2007). Emotion regulation and aging. In J. J. Gross (Ed.), *Handbook of emotion regulation* (pp. 307–327). New York: Guilford Press.

Charles, S. T., & Carstensen, L. L. (2010). Social and emotional aging. *Annual Review of Psychology, 61,* 383–409.

Charles, S. T., & Horwitz, B. N. (2010). Positive emotions and health: What we know about aging. In C. A. Depp & D. V. Jeste (Eds.), *Successful cognitive and emotional aging* (pp. 55–72). Arlington, VA: American Psychiatric Publishing.

Charles, S. T., Mather, M., & Carstensen, L. L. (2003). Aging and emotional memory: The forgettable nature of negative images for older adults. *Journal of Experimental Psychology: General, 132*(2), 310–324.

Charlton, R. A., Barrick, T. R., Markus, H. S., & Morris, R. G. (2010). The relationship between episodic long-term memory and white matter integrity in normal aging. *Neuropsychologia, 48*(1), 114–122.

Charness, N. (2009). Skill acquisition in older adults: Psychological mechanisms. In S. J. Czaja & J. Sharit (Eds.), *Aging and work: Issues and implications in a changing landscape* (pp. 232–258). Baltimore, MD: Johns Hopkins University Press.

Charpak, N. (2006). *Kangaroo babies: A different way of mothering.* London: Souvenir.

Chase-Lansdale, P. L., Brooks-Gunn, J., & Zamsky, E. S. (1994). Young African-American multigenerational families in poverty: Quality of mothering and grandmothering. *Child Development, 65*(2), 373–393.

Chasnoff, I. J., Anson A., Hatcher R., Stenson H., Kai, I. K., & Randolph, L. A. (1998). Prenatal exposure to cocaine and other drugs: Outcome at four to six years. *Annals of the New York Academy of Science, 846,* 314–328.

Chatoor, I., Surles, J., Ganiban, J., Beker, L., Paez, L., & Kerzner, B. (2004). Failure to thrive and cognitive development in toddlers with infantile anorexia. *Pediatrics, 113*(5), 440–447.

Chavous, T. M., Bernat, D. H., Schmeelk-Cone, K., Caldwell, C. H., Kohn-Wood, L., & Zimmerman, M. A. (2003). Racial identity and academicattainment among African American adolescents. *Child Development, 74,* 1076–1090.

Chavez, A., Martinez, C., & Soberanes, B. (1995). Effects of early malnutrition on late mental and behavioral performance. *Developmental Brain Dysfunction, 8,* 90–102.

Chavez, M., & Insel, T. R. (2007). Eating disorders. National Institute of Mental Health's perspective. *American Psychologist, 62*(3), 159–166.

Chedraui, P. (2008). Pregnancy among young adolescents: Trends, risk factors and maternal-perinatal outcome. *Journal of Perinatal Medicine, 36*(3), 256–259.

Chen, X., DeSouza, A. T., Chen, H., & Wang, L. (2006). Reticent behavior and experiences in peer interactions in Chinese and Canadian children. *Developmental Psychology, 42*(4), 656–665.

Chen, X. T., & Tse, H. (2008). Social functioning and adjustment in Canadianborn children with Chinese and European backgrounds. *Developmental Psychology, 44*(4), 1184–1189.

Chen, X., & K. H. Rubin (2011). *Socioemotional development in cultural context.* New York: Guilford Press.

Cheour-Luhtanen, M., Alho, K., Sainio, K., Rinne, T., & Reinikainen, K. (1996). The ontogenetically earliest discriminative response of the brain. *Psychophysiology, 33,* 478–481.

Cherlin, A. (2004). The growing compliance burden for recipients of public assistance. In A. C. Crouter & A. Booth (Eds.), *Work–family challenges for lowincome parents and their children* (pp. 265–272). Mahwah, NJ: Erlbaum.

Cherlin, A. J. (2008). Can the left learn the lessons of welfare reform? *Contemporary Sociology, 37*(2), 101–104.

Chess, S., & Thomas, A. (1996). *Temperament: Theory and practice.* Philadelphia: Brunner-Mazel.

Chin, R., & Hall, P. (2011). Father's experiences of their transition to fatherhood: A metasynthesis. *Journal of Reproductive and Infant Psychology, 29*(1), 4–18.

Chinnery, P. F. (2010). Mitochondrial disorders overview. Retrieved from http://www.ncbi.nlm.nih.gov/books/NBK1224/?report=printable

Chiriboga, D. A. (1996). In search of continuities and discontinuities across time and culture. In V. L. Bengtson (Ed.), *Adulthood and aging: Research on continuities and discontinuities* (pp. 173–199). New York: Springer-Verlag.

Chiu, M. M., & McBride-Chang, C. (2010). Family and reading in 41 countries: Differences across cultures and students. *Scientific Studies of Reading, 14*(6), 514–543.

Choi, C. Q. (2007). Speaking in tones. *Scientific American, 297*(3), 25–26.

Choi, N. G. (2001). Relationship between life satisfaction and postretirement employment among older women. *International Journal of Aging and Human Development, 52*(1), 45–70.

Chomsky, N. (1959). Review of *Verbal behavior* by B. F. Skinner. *Language, 35,* 26–58.

Chomsky, N. (1995). *The minimalist program.* Cambridge, MA: MIT Press.

Chow, C. M., Roesle, H., Buhrmester, D., & Undewood, M. (2012). Transformations in friend relationships across the transition to adulthood. In B. Laursen & W. A. Collins (Eds.), *Relationship pathways: from adolescence to young adulthood* (pp. 91–112). Thousand Oaks, CA: Sage.

Christensen, K., McGue, M., Petersen, I., Jeune, B., & Vaupel, J. W. (2008). Exceptional longevity does not result in excessive levels of disability. *Proceedings of the National Academy of Sciences of the United States of America, 105*(36), 13274–13279.

Christiansen, M. H., & Chater, N. (2008). Brains, genes, and language evolution: A new synthesis. *Behavioral & Brain Sciences, 31*(5), 537–558.

Chrouser Ahrens, C. J., & Ryff, C. D. (2006). Multiple roles and well-being: Sociodemographic and psychological moderators. *Sex Roles, 55*(11–12), 801–815.

Chumlea, W. C., Schubert, C. M., Roche, A. F., Kulin, H. E., Lee, P. A., Himes, J. H., et al. (2003). Age at menarche and racial comparisons in U.S. girls. *Pediatrics, 111,* 110–113.

Cicchetti, D. (2002). How a child builds a brain: Insights from normality and psychopathology. In W. Hartup & R. A. Weinberg (Eds.), *Child psychology in retrospect and prospect* (pp. 23–71). Mahwah, NJ: Erlbaum.

Cicchetti, D., & Cohen, D. J. (2006). *Developmental psychopathology: Volume 2, developmental neuroscience* (2nd ed.). Hoboken, NJ: John Wiley & Sons, Inc.

Cicchetti, D., & Curtis, W. J. (2006). The developing brain and neural plasticity: Implications for normality, psychopathology, and resilience. In D. Cicchetti & D. Cohen (Eds.), *Developmental psychopathology (2nd ed.): Developmental neuroscience* (Vol. 2). New York: Wiley.

Cicchetti, D., & Toth, S. L. (2000). Developmental processes in maltreated children. In D. J. Hanson (Ed.), *Nebraska Symposium on Motivation, Vol. 46, 1998: Motivation and Child Maltreatment* (pp. 85–160). Lincoln, NE: University of Nebraska Press.

Cicchetti, D., & Toth, S. L. (2005). Child maltreatment. *Annual Review of Clinical Psychology, 1*(1), 409–438.

Cicchetti, D., & Toth, S. L. (2010). Child maltreatment: The research imperative and the exportation of results to clinical contexts. In T. B. Brazleton, B. M. Lester, & J. D. Sparrow (Eds.), *Nurturing children and families: Building on the legacy of T. Berry Brazelton* (pp. 264–274). Malden, MA: Wiley-Blackwell.

Cicchetti, D., Rogosch, F. A., Toth, S. L. (2006). Fostering secure attachment in infants in maltreating families through preventive interventions. *Development and Psychopathology, 18*(3), 623–649.

Cillessen, A. H. (2011). Toward a theory of popularity. In A. Cillessen, D. Schwartz, & L. Mayeux (Eds.), *Popularity in the peer system* (pp. 273–299). New York: Guilford Press.

Claas, M. J., de Vries, L. S., Bruinse, H. W., van Haastert, I. C., Uniken Venema, M. M. A., Peelen, L. M., & Koopman, C. (2011). Neurodevelopmental outcome over time of preterm born children ≤ 750 g at birth. *Early Human Development, 87*(3), 183–191.

Clarke, L. H., & Griffin, M. (2008). Visible and invisible aging: Beauty work as a response to ageism. *Ageing & Society, 28*(5), 653–674.

Clark-Plaskie, M., & Lachman, M. E. (1999). The sense of control in midlife. In S. L. Willis & J. D. Reid (Eds.), *Life in the middle: Psychological and social development in middle age* (pp. 181–208). San Diego, CA: Academic Press.

Cleary, P. D., Zaborski, L. B., & Ayanian, J. Z. (2004). Sex differences in health over the course of midlife. In O. G. Brim, C. D. Ryff, & R. C. Kessler (Eds.), *How healthy are we? A national study of well-being at midlife* (pp. 37–63). Chicago: The University of Chicago Press.

Clemans, K. H., DeRose, L. M., Graber, J. A., & Brooks-Gunn, J. (2010). Gender in adolescence: Applying a person-in-context approach to gender identity and roles. In J. C. Chrisler & D. R. McCreary (Eds.), *Handbook of gender research in psychology, Vol. 1: Gender research in general and experimental psychology* (pp. 527–557). New York: Springer Science + Business Media.

Clifton, R. K., Rochat, P., Robin, D. J., & Berthier, N. E. (1994). Multimodal perception in the control of infant reaching. *Journal of Experimental Psychology: Human Perception and Performance, 20,* 876–886.

CNN. (2004, November 26). AIDS incidence in Broward County, Florida [Television broadcast].

Coalition to Stop the Use of Child Soldiers. (2011). Child soldiers: Global report 2008. Retrieved from http://www.childsoldiersglobalreport.org/files/country_pdfs/FINAL_2008_Global_Report.pdf

Coall, D. A., & Hertwig, R. (2011). Grandparental investment: A relic of the past or a resource for the future? *Current Directions in Psychological Science, 20*(2), 93–98.

Coch, D., Fischer, W., & Dawson, G. (2010). *Human behavior, learning, and the developing brain: Typical development.* New York: The Guilford Press.

Cohen, D. (2006). Pretending. In D. Cohen (Ed.), *The development of play* (pp. 84–105). New York: Routledge.

Cohen, L. B., & Cashon, C. H. (2003). Infant perception and cognition. In R. M. Lerner, M. A. Easterbrooks, & J. Mistry (Eds.), *Handbook of psychology: Vol. 6. Developmental psychology* (pp. 65–89). New York: Wiley.

Cohen, L. B., & Cashon, C. H. (2006). Infant cognition. In D. Kuhn, R. Siegler, D. William, & R. M. Lerner (Eds.), *Handbook of child psychology, Vol. 2: Cognition, perception, and language* (6th ed., pp. 214–251). Hoboken, NJ: John Wiley & Sons Inc.

Cohen, R. J., & Swerdlik, M. E. (2010). *Psychological testing and assessment: An introduction to tests and measurement* (7th ed.). Boston, MA: McGraw-Hill Higher Education.

Cohen, R. J., Swerdlik, M. E., & Sturman, E. (2013). *Psychological testing and assessment: An introduction to tests and measurement* (8th ed.). New York: McGraw-Hill.

Cohler, B. J., & Galatzer-Levy, R. M. (2000). *The course of gay and lesbian lives: Social and psychoanalytic perspectives.* Chicago: University of Chicago Press.

Cohler, B. J., & Hammack, P. L. (2007). The psychological world of the gay teenager: Social change, narrative, and "normality." *Journal of Youth and Adolescence, 36*(1), 47–59.

Colby, A., Lawrence, K., Gibbs, J., & Lieberman, M. (1994). A longitudinal study of moral judgment. In B. Puka (Ed.), *New research in moral development* (pp. 1–124) New York: Garland Publishing.

Cole, M. (2011). Culture in development. In M. H. Bornstein & M. E. Lamb (Eds.), *Cognitive development: An advanced textbook* (pp. 67–123). New York: Psychology Press.

Coleman, J. C. (2011). *The nature of adolescence* (4th ed.). New York: Routledge.

Coleman, M., & Ganong, L. H. (2009). *Handbook of contemporary families: Considering the past, contemplating the future.* Thousand Oaks, CA: Sage Publications.

Coleman, M., Ganong, L., & Leon, K. (2006). Divorce and postdivorce relationships. In A. L. Vangelisti & D. Perlman (Eds.), *The Cambridge handbook of personal relationships* (pp. 157–173). New York: Cambridge University Press.

Coleman, M., Ganong, L. H., & Warzinik, K. (2007). *Family life in the 20th-century America.* Westport, CT: Greenwood Press.

Collie, R., & Hayne, H. (1999). Deferred imitation by 6- and 9-month-old infants: More evidence for declarative memory. *Developmental Psychobiology, 35,* 83–90.

Collins, J. L., & Mayer, V. (2010). *Both hands tied: Welfare reform and the race to the bottom of the low-wage labor market.* Chicago, IL: The University of Chicago Press.

Collins, J. L., Mayer, V., Morgan, S., Acker, J., & Weigt, J. (2010). *Stretched thin: Poor families, welfare work, and welfare reform.* Ithaca: Cornell University Press.

Collins, W., & Laursen, B. (2006). Parent–adolescent relationships. In P. Noller and J. Feeney (Eds.), *Close relationships: Functions, forms and processes* (pp. 111–125). Hove, England: Psychology Press.

Colyvan, M. (2010). Mating, dating, and mathematics: It's all in the game. In K. Miller & M. Clark (Eds.), *Dating: Flirting with big ideas* (pp. 211–220). Malden, MA: Wiley-Blackwell.

Combs-Orme, T., & Renkert, L. E. (2009). Fathers and their infants: Caregiving and affection in the modern family. *Journal of Human Behavior in the Social Environment, 19*(4), 394–418.

Comer, R. J. (2009). *Abnormal psychology.* New York: Worth Publishers.

Comer, R. J. (2013). *Abnormal psychology.* New York: Worth Publishers.

Commons, M. L., & Richards, F. A. (2003). Four postformal stages. In J. Demick & C. Andreoletti (Eds.), *Handbook of adult development* (pp. 199–219). New York: Kluwer Academic/Plenum Publishers.

Conger, R. D., & Donnellan, M. B. (2007). An interactionist perspective on the socioeconomic context of human development. *Annual Review of Psychology, 58*(1), 175–199.

Connell-Carrick, K. (2010). Child abuse and neglect. In J. G. Bremner & T. D. Wachs (Eds.), *The Wiley Blackwell handbook of infant development* (2nd ed., pp. 165–191). Malden, MA: Wiley-Blackwell.

Connolly, J., & McIsaac, C. (2011). Romantic relationships in adolescence. In M. K. Underwood & L. H. Rosen (Eds.), *Social development: Relationships in infancy, childhood, and adolescence* (pp. 180–203). New York: Guilford Press.

Connolly, J., Furman, W., & Konarski, R. (2000). The role of peers in the emergence of heterosexual romantic relationships in adolescence. *Child Development, 71*(5), 1395–1408.

Connolly, M., Hoorens, T., & Chambers, G. M. (2010). The costs of consequences of assisted reproductive technology: An economic perspective. *Human Reproduction Update, 16*(6), 603–613.

Conradt, E., & Ablow, J. (2010). Infant physiological response to the still-face paradigm: Contributions of maternal sensitivity and infants' early regulatory behavior. *Infant Behavior & Development, 33*(3), 251–265.

Conway, F., Magai, C., & Milano, K. (2010). Synergy between molecular and contextual views of coping among four ethnic groups of older adults. *The International Journal of Aging & Human Development, 70*(4), 319–343.

Cook, C. R., Williams, K. R., Guerra, N. G., Kim, T. E., & Sadek, S. (2010). Predictors of bullying and victimization in childhood and adolescence: A meta-analysis investigation. *School Psychology Quarterly, 25*(2), 65–83.

Cooper, C. L, & Dewe, P. (2007). Stress: A brief history from the 1950s to Richard Lazarus. In A. Monat, R. Lazarus, & G. Reevy (Eds.), *The Praeger handbook on stress and coping* (pp. 7–31). Westport, CT: Praeger Publishers/Greenwood Publishing Group.

Corballis, M. C. (2010). Mirror neurons and the evolution of language. *Brain and Language, 112*(1). Special issue: *Mirror neurons: Prospects and problems for the neurobiology of language,* 25–35.

Corr, C. A. (2003). Loss, grief, and trauma in public tragedy. In M. Lattanzi-Licht & K. J. Doka (Eds.), *Living with grief: Coping with public tragedy* (pp. 63–76). New York: Brunner-Routledge.

Corr, C. A. (2010). Children, development, and encounters with death, bereavement, and coping. In C. A. Corr & D. E. Balk (Eds.), *Children's encounters with death, bereavement, and coping* (pp. 3–19). New York: Springer Publishing Co.

Corr, C. A., Corr, D. M., & Bordere, T. C. (2013). *Death & dying, life & living* (7th ed.). Belmont, CA: Wadsworth Cengage Learning.

Costa, A. L. (2004). *Developing minds: A resource book for teaching thinking.* Moorabbin, Vic.: Hawker Brownlow Education.

Costa, A. L. (2008). *The school as a home for the mind: Creating mindful curriculum, instruction, and dialogue* (2nd ed.). Thousand Oaks, CA: Corwin Press.

Costa, P. T., Jr., & McCrae, R. R. (1989). Personality continuity and the changes of adult life. In M. Storandt & G. R. VandenBos (Eds.), *The adult years: Continuity and change* (pp. 41–77). Washington, DC: American Psychological Association.

Costello, D. M., Swendsen, J., Rose, J. S., & Dierker, L. C. (2008). Risk and protective factors associated with trajectories of depressed mood from adolescence to early adulthood. *Journal of Consulting and Clinical Psychology, 76*(2), 173–183.

Costin, S. E., & Jones, D. C. (1992). Friendship as a facilitator of emotional responsiveness and prosocial interventions among young children. *Developmental Psychology, 28,* 941–947.

Côté, J. E. (2006). Emerging adulthood as an institutionalized moratorium: Risks and benefits to identity formation. In J. J. Arnett & J. L. Tanner (Eds.), *Emerging adults in America: Coming of age in the 21st century* (pp. 85–116). Washington, DC: American Psychological Association.

Côté, J. E. (2009). Identity formation and self-development in adolescence. In R. M. Lerner & L. Steinberg (Eds.), *Handbook of adolescent psychology, Vol. 1: Individual bases of adolescent development* (pp. 266–304). Hoboken, NJ: John Wiley & Sons Inc.

Côté, S. M. (2009). A developmental perspective on sex differences in aggressive behaviours. In R. E. Tremblay, M. A. van Aken, & W. Koops (Eds.), *Developmental perspective on sex differences in aggressive behaviours* (pp. 143–163). New York: Psychology Press.

Côté, S. M., Geoffreoy, M., Borge, A. I., Rutter, M., & Tremblay, R. E. (2008). Nonmaternal care in infancy and emotional/behavioral difficulties in 4 years old: Moderation of family risk characteristics. *Developmental Psychology, 44*(1), 155–168.

Côté, S. M., Vailancourt, T., Barker, E. D., Nagin, D., & Tremblay, D. (2007). The joint development of physical and indirect aggression: Predictors of continuity and change during childhood. *Development and Psychopathology, 19*(1), 37–55.

Cotrim, A. P., & Baum, B. J. (2008). Gene therapy: Some history, applications, problems, and prospects. *Toxicologic Pathology, 36*(1), 97–103.

Council for Excellence in Government. (2008). *Social programs that work: Nursefamily partnership.* Retrieved December 4, 2008 from http://www.evidencebasedprograms.org/Default.aspx?tabid=35

Cowan, C., Cowan, P. A., Pruett, M., & Pruett, K. (2006). An approach to preventing coparenting and divorce in low-income families: Strengthening couple relationships and fostering fathers' involvement. *Family Processes, 46*(1), 109–121.

Cowden, P. A. (2010). Social anxiety in children with disabilities. *Journal of Instructional Psychology, 37*(4), 301–305.

Cox, K. S., Wilt, J., Olson, B., & McAdams, D. P. (2010). Generativity, the Big Five, and psychosocial adaptation in midlife adults. *Journal of Personality, 78*(4), 1185–1208.

Coyle, A., & Kitzinger, C. (2002). *Lesbian and gay psychology.* Malden, MA: Blackwell Press.

Craik, F., & Salthouse, T. A. (2008). *The handbook of aging and cognition* (3rd ed.). New York: Psychology Press.

Crain, W. C. (2011). *Theories of development: Concepts and applications.* Boston, MA: Prentice Hall.

Crick, N., & Ladd, G. W. (1993). Children's perceptions of their peer experiences: Attributions, loneliness, social anxiety, and social avoidance. *Developmental Psychology, 29,* 244–254.

Crocetti, E., Rubini, M., Luyckx, K., & Meeus, W. (2008). Identity formation in early and middle adolescents from various ethnic groups: From three dimensions to five statuses. *Journal of Youth and Adolescence, 37*(8), 983–986.

Crockenberg, S., & Leerkes, E. (2003). Infant negative emotionality, caregiving, and family relationships. In A. C. Crouter & A. Booth (Eds.), *Children's influence on family dynamics: The neglected side of family relationships* (pp. 57–58). Mahwah, NJ: Erlbaum.

Crockett, L. J., Raffaelli, M., & Moilanen, K. L. (2003). Adolescent sexuality: Behavior and meaning. In G. R. Adams & M. D. Berzonsky (Eds.), *Blackwell handbook of adolescence* (pp. 371–392). Oxford, England: Basil Blackwell.

Crockett, L. J., & Silbereisen, R. K. (2011). *Negotiating adolescence in times of social change.* Cambridge: Cambridge University Press.

Crone, E. A., & Westenberg, P. (2009). A brain-based account of developmental changes in social decision making. In M. de Haan & M. R. Gunnar (Eds.), *Handbook of developmental social neuroscience* (pp. 378–396). New York: Guilford Press.

Crouter, A. C., & Booth, A. (Eds.). (2004). *Work–family challenges for low-income parents and their children.* Mahwah, NJ: Erlbaum.

Crouter, A. C., Head, M. R., Bumpus, M. F., & McHale, S. M. (2001). Household chores: Under what conditions do mothers lean on daughters? In A. J. Fuligni (Ed.), *New Directions for Child and Adolescent Development, 94,* 23–42. San Francisco: Jossey-Bass.

Crouter, A. C., MacDermid, S. M., McHale, S. M., & Perry-Jenkins, M. (1990). Parental monitoring and perceptions of children's school performance and conduct in single- and dual-earner families. *Developmental Psychology, 26,* 649–657.

Csikszentmihalyi, M. (2009). *Flow: The psychology of optimal experience.* New York: Harper & Row.

Cuevas, K., Rovee-Collier, & Learmonth, A. E. (2006). Infants form associations between memory representations of stimuli that are absent. *Psychological Science, 17*(6), 543–549.

Cummings, M. R. (2006). *Human heredity: Principles and issues* (7th ed.). Belmont, CA: Thompson Brooks/Cole.

Cummings, M. R. (2011). *Human heredity: Principles & issues.* Belmont, CA: Brooks/Cole, Cengage Learning.

Curtis, W. J., & Cicchetti, D. (2007). Emotion and resilience: A multilevel investigation of hemispheric electroencephalogram asymmetry and emotion regulation in maltreated and normal treated children. *Developmental Psychopathology, 19*(3), 811–840.

Czaja, S. J., & Ownby, R. L. (2010). Aging, cognition, and technology. In C. A. Depp & D. V. Jeste (Eds.), *Successful cognitive and emotional aging* (pp. 349–361). Arlington, VA: American Psychiatric Publishing.

Czaja, S. J., Charness, N., Fisk, A. D., Hertzog, C., Nair, S. N., Rogers, W. A., et al. (2006). Factors predicting the use of technology: Findings from the Center for Research and Education and Education on Aging and Technology Enhancement (CREATE). *Psychology and Aging, 21*(2), 333–352.

D'Angiulli, A., & Schibli, K. (2011). Mirror neurons and visuo-motor images in children: A meta-analysis of Piaget and Inhelder's data. *Imagination, Cognition and Personality, 31*(1–2), 129–142.

D'Augelli, A. R. (2012). Restoring lives: Developmental research on sexual orientation. *Human Development, 55*(1), 1–3.

D'Augelli, A. R., & Patterson, C. (2001). *Lesbian, gay, and bisexual identities and youth: Psychological perspectives.* New York: Oxford University Press.

D'Onofrio, B. M., Turkheimer, E., Emery, R. E., Slutske, W. S., Heath, A. C., Madden, P. A., et al. (2006). A genetically informed study of the processes underlying the association between parental marital instability and offspring adjustment. *Developmental Psychology, 42*(3), 486–499.

Dahinten, V., Shapka, J., & Willms. J. (2007). Adolescent children of adolescent mothers: The impact of family functioning on trajectories of development. *Journal of Youth and Adolescence, 36*(2), 195–212.

Daiute, C., Campbell, C. H., Griffin, T. M., Reddy, M., & Tivnan, T. (1993). Young authors' interactions with peers and a teacher: Toward a developmentally sensitive sociocultural literacy theory. In C. Daiute (Ed.), *New Directions for Child Development, 61,* 41–63. San Francisco: Jossey-Bass.

Daman, W. (1999). The moral development of children. *Scientific American, 281*(2), 72–78.

Damon-Wasserman, M., Brennan, B., Radcliffe, F., Prigot, J., & Fagen, J. (2006). Auditory-visual context and memory retrieval in 3-month-old infants. *Infancy, 10*(3), 201–220.

Daniels, H. (2011). Vygotsky and psychology. In U. Goswami (Ed.), *The Wiley-Blackwell handbook of childhood cognitive development* (2nd ed., pp. 673–696). Malden, MA: Wiley-Blackwell.

Daro, D. (1993). Child maltreatment research: Implications for program design. In D. Cicchetti & S. Toth (Eds.), *Child abuse, child development, and social policy* (pp. 331–367). Norwood, NJ: Ablex.

Daro, D. A., & McCurdy, K. P. (2007). Interventions to prevent child maltreatment. In L. S. Doll, S. E. Bonzo, J. A. Mercy, & D. A. Sleet (Eds.), *Handbook of injury and violence prevention* (pp. 137–155). New York: Springer Science + Business Media.

Daugherty, M., & White, C. S. (2008). Relationships among private speech and creativity in Head Start and low-socioeconomic status preschool children. *Gifted Child Quarterly, 52*(1), 30–39.

Davies, B. (1993). Caring for the frail elderly: An international perspective. *Generations, 17*(4), 51–54.

Davies, B. (2000). Sibling bereavement: We are grieving too. In K. J. Doka (Ed.), *Living with grief: Children, adolescents, and loss.* Washington, DC: Hospice Foundation of America.

Davies, M., Austen, K., & Rogers, P. (2011). Sexual preference, gender, and blame attributions in adolescent sexual assault. *The Journal of Social Psychology, 151*(5), 592–607.

Daviglus, M. L., Kiang, L., Pirzada, A., Yan, L. L., Garside, D. B., Feinglass, J., et al. (2003). Favorable cardiovascular risk profile in middle age and health-related quality of life in older age. *Archives of Internal Medicine, 163*(20), 2460–2469.

Davis, D. S. (2010). *Genetic dilemmas: Reproductive technology, parental choices, and children's futures* (2nd ed.). New York: Oxford University Press.

Davis, K., Seider, S., & Gardner, H. (2011). The theory of multiple intelligences. In R. Sternberg & S. Kaufman (Eds.), *The Cambridge handbook of intelligence* (pp. 485–503). New York: Cambridge University Press.

Davis, O., Arden, R., & Plomin, R. (2008). G in middle childhood: Moderate genetic and shared environmental influence using diverse measures of general cognitive ability at 7, 9 and 10 years in a large population sample of twins. *Intelligence, 36*(1), 68–80.

Davis, P. E., Meins, E., & Fernyhough, C. (2011). Self-knowledge in childhood: Relations with children's imaginary companions and understanding of mind. *British Journal of Developmental Psychology, 29*(3), 680–686.

Day, N. L., Leech, S. L., Richardson, G. A., Cornelius, M. D., Robles, N., & Larkby, C. (2002). Prenatal alcohol exposure predicts continued deficits in offspring size at 14 years of age. *Alcoholism: Clinical and Experimental Research, 26*(10), 1584–1591.

De Groot, A. M. B. (2011). *Language and cognition in bilinguals and multilinguals: An introduction.* New York: Psychology Press.

de Haan, M. (2008). Event-related potential (ERP) measures in visual development research. In L. A. Schmidt & S. J. Segalowitz (Eds.), *Developmental psychophysiology: Theory, systems, and methods* (pp. 103–126). New York: Cambridge University Press.

de Haan, M., & Nelson, C. A. (1999). Brain activity differentiates face and object processing in 6-month-old infants. *Developmental Psychology, 35,* 1113–1121.

de Souza, A. S., Fernandes, F. S., & do Carmo, M. G. (2011). Effects of maternal malnutrition and postnatal nutritional rehabilitation on brain fatty acids, learning, and memory. *Nutrition Reviews, 69*(3), 132–144.

de St. Aubin, E., McAdams, D. P., & Kim, T. (2004). The generative society: An introduction. In E. de St. Aubin, P. Dan, & T. Kim (Eds.), *The generative society: Caring for future generations* (pp. 3–13). Washington, DC: American Psychological Association.

Deangelis, T. (2004). Size-based discrimination may be hardest on children. *Monitor on Psychology, 35*(1), 62.

Deary, I. J., Whalley, L. J., Batty, G. D., & Starr, J. M. (2006). Physical fitness and lifetime cognitive change. *Neurology, 67*(7), 1195–1200.

DeCasper, A. J., Lecanuet, J. P., Busnel, M. C., & Granier-Deferre, C. (1994). Fetal reactions to recurrent maternal speech. *Infant Behavior and Development, 17,* 159–164.

Degnan, K. A., Hane, A., Henderson, H. A., Moas, O., Reeb-Sutherland, B. C., & Fox, N. A. (2011). Longitudinal stability of temperamental exuberance and social-emotional outcomes in early childhood. *Developmental Psychology, 47*(3), 765–780.

DeHart, T., Pelham, B. W., & Tennen, H. (2006). What lies beneath: Parenting style and implicit self-esteem. *Journal of Experimental Social Psychology, 42*(1), 1–17.

Delandtsheer, J. (2011). *Making all kids smarter: Strategies that help all students reach their highest potential.* Thousand Oaks, CA: Corwin Press.

DeLoache, J. S. (2011). Early development of the understanding and use of symbolic artifacts. In U. Goswami (Ed.), *The Wiley-Blackwell handbook of childhood cognitive development* (2nd ed., pp. 312–336). Malden, MA: Wiley-Blackwell.

Deloache, J. S., Cassidy, D. J., & Brown, A. L. (1985). Precursors of mnemonic strategies in very young children's memory. *Child Development, 56,* 125–137.

de Mause, L. (1995). *The history of childhood.* Northvale, NJ: J. Aronson.

Demo, D. H. & Fine, M.A. (2010). *Beyond the average divorce.* Thousand Oaks, CA: Sage Publications.

Denham, S. A., Bassett, H., Mincic, M., Kalb, S., Way, E., Wyatt, T., & Segal, Y. (2012). Social-emotional learning profiles of preschoolers' early school success: A person-centered approach. *Learning and Individual Differences, 22*(2), 178–189.

Denham, S. A., Bassett, H. H., & Wyatt, T. (2007). The socialization of emotional competence. In J. E. Grusec & P. D. Hastings (Eds.), *Handbook of socialization: Theory and research* (pp. 614–637) New York: Guilford Press

Denham, S. A., Blair, K. A., Demulder, E., Levitas, J., Sawyer, K., Auerbach- Major, S., et al. (2003). Preschool emotional competence: Pathway to social competence. *Child Development, 74,* 238–256.

Dennis, N. A., & Cabeza, R. (2008). Neuroimaging of healthy cognitive aging. In F. Craik & T. A. Salthouse (Eds.), *The handbook of aging and cognition* (3rd ed., pp. 1–54). New York: Psychology Press.

DePalma, R. (2010). *Language use in the two-way classroom: Lessons from a Spanish-English bilingual kindergarten.* Clevedeon, UK: Multilingual Matters.

DePaul, G. J. (2007). School-based interventions for students with attention deficit hyperactivity disorder: Current status and future directions. *School Psychology Review, 36*(2), 183–194.

Deptula, D. P., Henry, D. B., & Schoeny, M. E. (2010). How can parents make a difference? Longitudinal associations with adolescent sexual behavior. *Journal of Family Psychology, 24*(6), 731–739.

DeRose, L. M., Shiyko, M. P., Foster, H., & Brooks-Gunn, J. (2011). Associations between menarcheal timing and behavioral developmental trajectories for girls from age 6 to 15. *Journal of Youth and Adolescence, 40*(10), 1329–1342.

Dershewitz, R. A. (2006). Average age at menarche continues to decline. *Journal Watch General Medicine,* January 6.

DeSpelder, L. A., & Stickland, A. L. (2011). *The last dance: Encountering death and dying.* New York: McGraw-Hill.

Detweiler, M. F., Comer, J. S., & Albano, A M. (2010). Social anxiety in children and adolescents: Biological, developmental and social considerations. In S. G. Hofmann & P. M. DiBartolo (Eds.), *Social anxiety: Clinical developmental, and social perspectives* (2nd ed., pp. 223–270). San Diego, CA: Elsevier Academic Press.

Deutsch, F. M. (1999). *Having it all: How equally shared parenting works.* Cambridge, MA: Harvard University Press.

DeVries, H., Kerrick, S., & Oetinger, M. (2007). Satisfactions and regrets of midlife parents: A qualitative analysis. *Journal of Adult Development, 14,* 6–15.

Diamond, A. (2007). Interrelated and interdependent. *Developmental Science, 10*(1), 152–158.

Diamond, A. (2009). The interplay of biology and the environment broadly defined. *Developmental Psychology, 45*(1), 1–8.

Diamond, A., & Amso, D. (2008). Contributions of neuroscience to our understanding of cognitive development. *Current Directions in Psychological Science, 17*(2), 136–141.

Diamond, A., & Lee, K. (2011). Interventions shown to aid executive function development in children 4 to 12 years old. *Science, 333*(6045), 959–964.

Dias, M. S., Smith, K., deGuehery, K., Mazur, P., Li, V., & Shaffer, M. L. (2005). Preventing abusive head trauma among infants and young children: A hospital-based, parent education program. *Pediatrics, 115*(4), 470–477.

Diav-Citrin, O., & Koren, G. (2012). Human teratogens: A critical evaluation. Retrieved from http://www.nvp-volumes.org/p2_4.htm

Dick, D. M., et al. (2011). CHRM2 parental monitoring, and adolescent externalizing behavior: Evidence for gene-environment interaction. *Psychological Science, 22*(4), 481–489.

Dickens, W. T., & Flynn, J. R. (2001). Heritability estimates versus large environmental effects: The IQ paradox resolved. *Psychological Review, 108*(2), 346–369.

DiClemente, R. J., & Crosby, R. A. (2003). Sexually transmitted diseases among adolescents: Risk factors, antecedents, and preventive strategies. In G. R. Adams & M. D. Berzonsky (Eds.), *Blackwell handbook of adolescence* (pp. 573–605). Oxford, England: Basil Blackwell.

Dillon, F. R., Worthington, R. L., & Moradi, B. (2011). Sexual identity as a universal process. In S. J. Schwartz, K. Luyckx, & V. L. Vignoles (Eds.), *Handbook of identity theory and research* (Vols. 1 and 2, pp. 649–670). New York: Springer Science + Business Media.

Dimitry, L. (2012). A systematic review on the mental health of children and adolescents in areas of armed conflict in the Middle East. *Child: Care, Health and Development, 38*(2), 153–161.

Dishion, T. J., Ha, T., Nijmegen, N., & Veronneau, M. (2012). An ecological analysis of the effects of deviant peer clustering on sexual promiscuity, problem behavior, and childbearing from early adolescence to adulthood: An enhancement of the life history framework. *Developmental Psychology, 48*(3). *Special Section: Beyond Mental Health: An Evolutionary Analysis of Development Under Risky and Supportive Environmental Conditions,* 703–717.

Dixon, R., & Smith, P. K. (2011). *Rethinking school bullying: Towards an integrated model.* New York: Cambridge University Press.

Dodge, K. A., Coie, J. D., & Lynam, D. (2006). Aggression and antisocial behavior in youth. In N. Eisenberg, W. Damon, & R. M. Lerner (Eds.), *Handbook of child psychology. Vol. 3, social, emotional and personality development* (6th ed., pp. 719–788). Hoboken, NJ: Wiley.

Dodge, K. A., Pettit, G. S., & Bates, J. E. (1994). Effects of physical maltreatment on the development of peer relations. *Development and Psychopathology, 6,* 43–55.

Dodwell, P., Humphrey, G. K., & Muir, D. (1987). Shape and pattern perception. In P. Salapatek & L. Cohen (Eds.), *Handbook of infant perception: Vol. 2. From sensation to perception* (pp. 1–77). New York: Academic Press.

Doetsch, F., & Scharff, C. (2001). Challenges for brain repair: Insights from adult neurogenesis in birds and mammals. *Brain, Behavior, and Evolution, 58,* 306–322.

Doherty, M. J. (2009). *Theory of mind: How children understand others' thoughts and feelings.* New York: Psychology Press.

Doka, K. J. (2007). Historical and contemporary perspectives on dying. In D. Balk, C. Wogrin, G. Thornton, & D. Meagher (Eds.), *Handbook of thanatology: The essential body of knowledge for the study of death, dying, and bereavement* (pp. 19–25). Northbrook, IL: Association for Death Education and Counseling.

Doka, K. J. (2008). Disenfranchised grief in historical and cultural perspective. In M. Stoebe, R. Hansson, H. Schut, W. Stroebe, & E. Van den Blink (Eds.), *Handbook of bereavement research and practice: Advances in theory and intervention* (pp. 223–240). Washington, DC: American Psychological Association.

Doka, K. J. (2010). Struggling with grief and loss. In S. L. Friedman & D. T. Helm (Eds.), *End-of-life care for children and adults with intellectual and developmental disabilities* (pp. 261–271). Washington, DC: American Association on Intellectual and Developmental Disabilities.

Doka, K., & Mertz, M. (1988). The meaning and significance of great–grandparenthood. *The Gerontologist, 28,* 192–197.

Dolbin-MacNab, M. L. (2009). Becoming a parent again: An exploration of transformation among grandparents raising grandchildren. In J. A. Mancini & K. A. Roberto (Eds.), *Pathways of human development: Explorations of change* (pp. 207–226). Lanham, MD: Lexington Books/ Rowman & Littlefield.

Donchi, L., Moore, S., Valkenburg, P. M., & Peter, J. (2010). Do online friendships hurt adolescent development? In B. Slife (Ed.), *Clashing views on psychological issues* (16th ed., pp. 155–174). New York: McGraw-Hill.

Donnellan, M. B., & Lucas, R. E. (2008). Age differences in the big five across the life span: Evidence from two national samples. *Psychology and Aging, 23*(3), 558–566.

Donnelly, E. H., Smith, J. M., Farfan, E. B., & Ozcan, I. (2011). Prenatal radiation exposure: Background material for counseling pregnant patients following exposure to radiation. *Disaster Medicine and Public Health Preparedness, 5*(1), 62–68.

Donovan, M. S., & Cross, C. T. (Eds.). (2002). *Minority students in special and gifted education.* Washington, DC: National Academy Press.

Dosoky, M. El., & Amoudi, F. Al. (1997). Menarcheal age of school girls in the city of Jeddah, Saudi Arabia. *Journal of Obstetrics and Gynaecology, 17,* 195.

Dougherty, L. R. (2006). Children's emotionality and social status: A metaanalytic review. *Social Development, 15*(3), 394–417.

Dowshen, S. (2007). *Growing pains.* Retrieved on December 11, 2008 from http://kidshealth.org/parent/growth/growth/growing_pains.html

Doyle, A. B., Beaudet, J., & Aboud, F. (1988). Developmental patterns in the flexibility of children's ethnic attitudes. *Journal of Cross–Cultural Research, 19,* 3–18.

Doyle, R. (2000). Asthma worldwide. *Scientific American, 28*(6), 30.

Draper, T. W., & James, R. S. (1985). Preschool fears: Longitudinal sequence and cohort changes. *Child Study Journal, 15,* 147–155.

Drew, C. J., & Hardman, M. L. (2006). *Intellectual disabilities across the lifespan* (9th ed.). Columbus, OH: Pearson Merrill Prentice Hall.

Dreyer, P. H. (1982). Sexuality during adolescence. In B. Wolman (Ed.), *Handbook of developmental psychology* (pp. 559–596). Englewood Cliffs, NJ: Prentice Hall.

Dubois, D. L., Burk–Braxton, C., Swenson, L. P., Tevendale, H. D., & Hardesty, J. L. (2002). Race and gender influences on adjustment in early adolescence: Investigation of an integrative model. *Child Development, 73,* 1573–1592.

Dudek, R. W. (2010). *Genetics.* Baltimore, MD: Lippincott Williams & Wilkins.

Duncan, G. J., et al. (2007). School readiness and later achievement. *Developmental Psychology, 43*(6), 1428–1446.

Duncan, R. M., & Tarulli, D. (2003). Play as the leading activity of the preschool period: Insights from Vygotsky, Leont'ev, and Bakhtin. *Early Education and Development, 14*(3), 271–292.

Dunn, E. C., Gilman, S. E., Willett, J. B., Slopen, N. B., & Moinar, B. E. (2012). The impact of exposure to interpersonal violence on gender differences in adolescent-onset major depression: Results from the National Comorbidity Survey Replication (NCS-R). *Depression and Anxiety, 29*(5), 391–399.

Dunn, J. (1986). Growing up in a family world: Issues in the study of social development of young children. In M. Richards & P. Light (Eds.), *Children of social worlds: Development in a social context* (pp. 98–115). Cambridge, MA: Harvard University Press.

Dunn, J. (1993). *Young children's close relationships: Beyond attachment.* Newberry Park, CA: Sage.

Dunn, J. (2007). Siblings and socialization. In J. Grusec & P. Hastings (Eds.), *Handbook of socialization: Theory and research* (pp. 309–327). New York: Guilford Press.

Dunn, J. (2008). Relationships and children's discovery of the mind. In U. Müller, J. I. M. Carpendale, N. Budwig, & B. W. Sokol (Eds.), *Social life and social knowledge: Toward a process account of development* (6th ed., pp. 171–182). New York: Taylor & Francis Group/ Erlbaum.

DuPaul, G. J., & Kern, L. (2011a). Findings and future directions. In G. J. DuPaul & L. Kern (Eds.), *Young children with ADHD: Early identification and intervention* (pp. 185–201). Washington, DC: American Psychological Association.

DuPaul, G. J., & Kern, L. (2011b). Psychotropic medication treatment. In G. J. DuPaul & L. Kern (Eds.), *Young children with ADHD: Early identification and intervention* (pp. 149–165). Washington, DC: American Psychological Association.

Dupre, J. (2008). What genes are and why there are no genes for race. In B. A. Koenig, S. Lee, & S. S. Richardson (Eds.), *Revisiting race in a genomic age* (pp. 39–55). Piscataway, NJ: Rutgers University Press.

Durston, S., Hulshoff Pol, H. E., Casey, B. J., Giedd, J. N., Buitelaar, J. K., & Van Engeland, H. (2001). Anatomical MRI of the developing brain: What have we learned? *Journal of the American Academy of Child and Adolescent Psychiatry, 40,* 1012–1020.

Duwe, K. N., Reefhuis, J., Honein, M. A., Schieve, L. A., & Rasmussen, S. A. (2010). Epidemiology of fertility treatment use among U.S. women with liveborn infants, 1997–2004. *Journal of Women's Health, 19*(3), 407–416.

Dweck, C. S. (1986). Motivational processes affecting learning. *American Psychologist, 41*(10), 1040–1048.

Dweck, C. S. (2007). The perils and promises of praise. *Educational Leadership, 65*(2), 34–39.

Dweck, C. S. (2008). The secret to raising smart kids. *Scientific American Mind, 18*(6), 36–43.

Dweck, C. S., & Master, A. (2009). Self-theories and motivation: Student's beliefs about intelligence. In K. R. Wenzel & A. Wigfield (Eds.), *Handbook of motivation at school* (pp. 123–140). New York: Routledge/Taylor & Francis Group.

Dykens, E. M., & Roof, E. (2008). Behavior in Prader-Will syndrome: Relationship to genetic subtypes and age. *Journal of Child Psychology & Psychiatry, 49*(9), 1001–1008.

Dyson, L. L. (2003). Children with learning disabilities within the family context: A comparison with siblings in global self-concept, academic selfperception, and social competence. *Learning Disabilities Research and Practice, 18*(1), 1–9.

Eagly, A. H., & Wood, W. (2012). Social role theory. In P. Van Lange, A. W. Kruglanski, & E. T. Higgins (Eds.), *Handbook of theories of social psychology* (Vol. 2, pp. 458–476). Thousand Oaks, CA: Sage Publications Ltd.

Ebner, N. C., Freund, A. M., & Baltes, P. B. (2006). Developmental changes in personal goal orientation from young to late adulthood: From striving for gains to maintenance and prevention of losses. *Psychology and Aging, 21*(4), 664–678.

Eddy, D. M. (1991). The individual vs. society: Is there a conflict? *Journal of the American Medical Association, 265,* 1446–1450.

Eddy, K. T., Herzog, D. B., & Zucker, N. L. (2011). Diagnosis and classification of eating disorders in adolescence. In D. Le Grange & J. Lock (Eds.), *Eating disorders in children and adolescents: A clinical handbook* (pp. 126–134). New York: Guilford Press.

Edwards, C. P. (2005). Children's play in cross-cultural perspective: A new look at the 'Six Cultures' Study in F. F. McMahon, D. E. Lytle, & B. Sutton-Smith (Eds.), *Play: An interdisciplinary synthesis* (pp. 81–96). Lanham, MD: University Press.

Edwards, M. (2006). Preconception care. *Practice Nurse, 32*(2), 43–46.

Egelund, B., Pianta, R., & O'Brien, M. A. (1993). Maternal intrusiveness in infancy and child maladaptation in early school years. *Development and Psychopathology, 5,* 359–370.

Eggum, N. D., et al. (2011). Emotion understanding, theory of mind, and prosocial orientation: Relations over time in early childhood. *The Journal of Positive Psychology, 6*(1), 4–16.

Eichler, J., & Albanese, P. (2007). What is household work? A critique of assumptions underlying empirical studies of housework and an alternative approach. *Canadian Journal of Sociology, 32*(2), 227–258.

Eimas, P. D. (1999). Segmental and syllabic representations in the perception of speech by young infants. *Journal of the Acoustical Society of America, 105,* 1901–1911.

Eimas, P. D., & Quinn, P. C. (1994). Studies on the formation of perceptually based categories in young infants. *Child Development, 65,* 903–917.

Eisenberg, N. (1989a). *The development of prosocial moral reasoning in childhood and mid-adolescence.* Paper presented at the biennual meeting of the Society for Research in Child Development, Kansas City.

Eisenberg, N. (1989b). The development of prosocial values. In N. Eisenberg, J. Reykowski, & E. Staub (Eds.), *Social and moral values: Individual and social perspectives* (pp. 87–103). Hillsdale, NJ: Erlbaum.

Eisenberg, N. (2010). Empathy-related responding: Links with self-regulation, moral judgment, and moral behavior. In M. Mikulincer & P. Shaver (Eds.), *Prosocial motives, emotions, and behavior: The better angels of our nature* (pp. 129–148). Washington, DC: American Psychological Association.

Eisenberg, N., & Eggum, N. D. (2008). Empathy-related and prosocial responding: Conceptions and correlates during development. In B. Sullivan, M. Snyder, & J. Sullivan (Eds.), *Cooperation: The political psychology of effective human interaction* (pp. 53–74). Malden, MA: Blackwell Publishing.

Eisenberg, N., Eggum, N. D., & Edwards, A. (2010). Empathy-related responding and moral development. In W. F. Arsenio & E. A. Lemerise (Eds.), *Emotions, aggression, and morality in children: Bridging development and psychopathology* (pp. 115–135). Washington, DC: American Psychological Association.

Eisenberg, N., & Fabes, R. A. (1998). Prosocial development. In D. William & N. Eisenberg (Eds.), *Handbook of child psychology, Vol. 3: Social, emotional, and personality development* (5th ed., pp. 701–778). Hoboken, NJ: John Wiley & Sons Inc.

Eisenberg, N., Fabes, R. A., & Spinrad, T. L. (2006). Prosocial development. In N. Eisenberg, D. William, & R. M. Lerner (Eds.), *Handbook of child psychology: Vol. 3, social, emotional, and personality development* (6th ed., pp. 646–718). Hoboken, NJ: Wiley.

Eisenberg, N., Morris, A., McDaniel, B., & Spinrad, T. L. (2009). Moral cognitions and prosocial responding in adolesence. In R. M. Lerner & L. Steinberg (Eds.), *Handbook of adolescent psychology, Vol. 1: Individual bases of adolescent development* (3rd ed., pp. 229–265). Hoboken, NJ: John Wiley & Sons.

Eisenberg, N., Smith, C. J., & Spinrad, T. L. (2011). Effortful control: Relations with emotion regulation. In K. D. Vohs & R. F. Baumeister (Eds.), *Handbook of self-regulation: Research, theory, and applications* (2nd ed., pp. 263–283). New York: Guilford Press.

Eisenberg, N., Spinard, T. L., & Eggum, N. D. (2010). Emotion-related self-regulation and its relation to children's maladjustment. *Annual Review of Clinical Psychology, 6,* 495–525.

Eisenberg, N., & Sulik, M. J. (2012). Emotion-based self-regulation in children. *Teaching of Psychology, 39*(1), 77–83.

Ejei, J., Lavassani, M. G., Malahmadi, E., & Kherzi, H. (2011). The relationship between parenting styles and academic achievement through the mediating influences of achievement goals and academic self-efficacy. *Journal of Psychology, 15*(3), 284–301.

Ekehammer, B., Akrami, N., Hedlund, L., Yoshimura, K., Ono, K., Ando, J., & Yamagata, S. (2010). The generality of personality heritability: Big-five trait heritability predicts response time to trait items. *Journal of Individual Differences, 31*(4), 209–214.

Ekman, P. (1992). An argument for basic emotions. *Cognition and Emotion, 6*(3/4), 169–200.

Ekman, P., & Cordaro, D. (2011). What is meant by calling emotions basic. *Emotion Review, 3(4),* 364–370.

Elden, R. D., Edwards, E. P., & Leonard, K. E. (2007). A conceptual model for the development of externalizing behavior problems among kindergarten children of alcoholic families: Role of parenting and children's self regulation. *Developmental Psychology, 43*(5), 1187–1201.

Elder, G. H. (1998). The life course as developmental theory. *Child Development, 69,* 1–12.

Elder, G. H. , & Johnson, M. K. (2002). Perspectives on human development in context. In C. von Hofsten & L. Bäckman (Eds.), *Psychology at the turn of the millennium, Vol. 2: Social, developmental, and clinical perspectives* (pp. 153–172). Florence, KY: Taylor & Frances/Routledge.

Elder, G. H., Caspi, A., & Burton, L. M. (1988). Adolescent transition in developmental perspective: Sociological and historical insights. In M. R. Gunnar & W. A. Collins (Eds.), *Development during the transition to adolescence* (pp. 151–179). Hillsdale, NJ: Erlbaum.

Elfers, T., Martin, J., & Sokol, B. (2008). Perspective taking: A review of research and theory extending Selman's developmental model of perspective taking. In A. M. Columbus (Ed.), *Advances in psychology research* (Vol. 54, pp. 229–262). Hauppauge: Nova Science Publishers.

Elkind, D. (1967). Egocentrism in adolescence. *Child Development, 38*(4), 1025–1034.

Elkind, D. (1998). *All grown up and no place to go: Teenagers in crisis* (Rev. ed.). Reading, MA: Perseus.

Elliot, A. J., & Dweck, C. S. (2005). Competence and motivation: Competence as the core of achievement motivation. In A. J. Elliot & C. S. Dweck (Eds.), *Handbook of competence and motivation* (pp. 3–12). New York: Guilford Publications.

Elliot, A. J., & Dweck, C. S. (2007). *Handbook of competence and motivation.* New York: Guilford Press.

Elliott, D., Hayes, S. J., & Bennett, S. J. (2012). 125 year of perceptual-motor skill research. *The American Journal of Psychology, 125*(1), 9–23.

Engels, R., Kerr, M., & Stattin, H. (2007). *Friends, lovers, and groups: Key relationships in adolescence.* Hoboken, NJ: John Wiley & Sons. Brown, B. B., & Klute, C. (2003). Friendships, cliques, and crowds. In G. R. Adams & M. D. Berzonsky (Eds.), *Blackwell handbook of adolescence* (pp. 330–348). Oxford, England: Basil Blackwell.

Engeser, S., & Schiepe-Tiska, A. (2012). Historical lines and an overview of current research on flow. In S. Engeser (Ed.), *Advances in flow research* (pp. 1–22). New York: Springer Science + Business Media.

Ensor, R., & Hughes, C. (2008). Content or connectedness? Mother–child talk and early social understanding. *Child Development, 79*(1), 201–216.

Epstein, I., & Lutjens, S. L. (2008). *The Greenwood encyclopedia of children's issues worldwide: North America and the Caribbean.* Westport, CT: Greenwood Press.

Erath, S. A., Flanagan, K. S., Bierman, K. L., & Tu, K. M. (2010). Friendships moderate psychosocial maladjustment in socially anxious early adolescents. *Journal of Applied Developmental Psychology, 31*(1), 15–26.

Erber, J. T. (2010). *Aging and older adulthood* (2nd ed.). Malden, MA: Wiley-Blackwell.

Erickson, M., & Egeland, B. (2002). Child neglect. In J. Myers, L. Berliner, J. Briere, C. T. Hendrix, C. Jenny, and T. Reid (Eds.), *The APSAC Handbook on child maltreatment* (2nd ed., pp. 3–20). Thousand Oaks, CA: Sage Publications.

Erikson, E. H. (1984). Reflections on the last stage—and the first. *Psychoanalytic Study of the Child, 39*, 155–165.

Erikson, E. H. (1959). The problem of ego identity. In E. H. Erikson (Ed.), *Identity and the life cycle: Selected papers. Psychological Issues Monographs, 1*(1).

Erikson, E. H. (1964). *Childhood and society*. Oxford, England: W. W. Norton.

Erikson, E. H. (1968). *Identity, youth, and crisis*. New York: Norton.

Erikson, E. H. (1983). Reflections. *Adolescent Psychiatry, 11*, 9–13.

Erikson, E. H. (1989). Elements of a psychoanalytic theory of psychosocial development. In S. I. Greenspan & G. H. Pollock (Eds.), *The course of life, Vol. 1: Infancy* (pp. 15–83). Madison, CT: International Universities Press, Inc.

Erikson, E. H. (1993). *Childhood and society*. New York: Norton.

Erikson, E. H., & Erikson, J. M. (1997). *The life cycle completed*. New York: W. W. Norton.

Erikson, E. H., Erikson, J. & Kivnick, H. (1986). *Vital involvement in old age*. New York: Norton.

Erikson, E. H., Erikson, J. M., & Kivnick, H. Q. (1989/1994). *Vital involvement in old age*. New York: W. W. Norton.

Ernst, M., & Fudge, J. L. (2010). Adolescence: On the neural path to adulthood. In J. E. Grant & M. N. Potenza (Eds.), *Young adult mental health* (pp. 19–39). New York: Oxford University Press.

Espelage, D. L., & Holt, M. K. (2012). Understanding and preventing bullying and sexual harassment in school. In K. R. Harris, S. Graham, T. Urdan, S. Graham, J. M. Royer, & M. Zeidner (Eds.), *APA educational psychology handbook, Vol. 2: Individual differences and cultural and contextual factors* (pp. 391–416). Washington, DC: American Psychological Association.

Espy, K. A., Hua, F., Johnson, C., Stopp, C., Wiebe, S. A., & Respass, J. (2011). Prenatal tobacco exposure: Developmental outcomes in the neonatal period. *Developmental Psychology, 47*(1), 153–169.

Evans, G. W., & Kim, P. (2012). Childhood poverty and young adults' allostatic load: The mediating role of childhood cumulative risk exposure. *Psychological Science, 20*(10), 1–5. doi: 10.1177/0956797612441218.

Fabiano, G. A., Pelhan, W. E., Jr., Gnagy, E. M., Burrows-Maclean, L., Coles, E. K., Chacko, A., et al. (2007). The single and combined effects of multiple intensities of behavior modification and methylphenidate for children with attention deficit hyperactivity disorder in a classroom setting. *School Psychology Review, 36*(2), 195–216.

Fagen, J., Prigot, J., Carroll, M., Pioli, L., Stein, A., & Franco, A. (1997). Auditory context and memory retrieval in young infants. *Child Development, 68*, 1057–1066.

Farooqi, S. (2010). Genes and obesity. In P. G. Kopelman, I. D. Caterson, & W. H. Dietz (Eds.), *Clinical obesity in adults and children* (3rd ed., pp. 82–91). Malden, MA: Wiley-Blackwell.

Farr, R. H., Forssell, S. L., & Patterson, C. J. (2010). Parenting and child development in adoptive families: Does parental sexual orientation matter? *Applied Developmental Science, 14*(3), 164–178.

Farrant, B. M., Devine, T. A. J., Mayberry, M. T., & Fletcher, J. (2012). Empathy, perspective taking and prosocial behaviour. The importance of parenting practices. *Infant and Child Development, 21*(2), 175–188.

Farroni, T., Menon, E., Rigato, S., & Johnson, M. H. (2007). The perception of facial expressions in newborns. *European Journal of Developmental Psychology, 4*(1), 2–13.

Fass, P. S. (2004). *Encyclopedia of children and childhood: In history and society*. New York: Macmillan References USA.

Fearon, R. P., Bakersmans-Kranenburg, M. J., van IJzendoorn, M. H., Lapsley, A., & Roisman, G. I. (2010). The significance of insecure attachment and disorganization in the development of children's externalizing behavior: A meta-analytic study. *Child Development, 81*(2), 435–456.

Featherstone, M., & Hepworth, M. (1985). The male menopause: Lifestyle and sexuality. *Maturitas, 7*(3), 235–246.

Federal Interagency Forum on Aging-Related Statistics. (2008). *Older Americans 2008: Key indicators of well-being*. Washington, DC: U.S. Government Printing Office.

Federal Interagency Forum on Aging-Related Statistics. (2010a). *Chronic health conditions. Older Americans 2010: Key indicators of well-being. Federal Interagency Forum on Aging-Related Statistics.* Washington, DC: U.S. Government Printing Office.

Federal Interagency Forum on Aging-Related Statistics. (2010b). *Living arrangements. Older Americans 2010: Key indicators of well-being. Federal Interagency Forum on Aging-Related Statistics.* Washington, DC: U.S. Government Printing Office.

Federal Interagency Forum on Aging-Related Statistics. (2010c). *Marital status. Older Americans 2010: Key indicators of well-being. Federal Interagency Forum on Aging-Related Statistics.* Washington, DC: U.S. Government Printing Office.

Federal Interagency Forum on Aging-Related Statistics. (2010d). *Obesity. Federal Interagency Forum on Aging-Related Statistics.* Washington, DC: U.S. Government Printing Office.

Federal Interagency Forum on Aging-Related Statistics. (2010e). *Participation in the labor force. Older Americans 2010: Key indicators of well-being. Federal Interagency Forum on Aging-Related Statistics.* Washington, DC: U.S. Government Printing Office.

Federal Interagency Forum on Aging-Related Statistics. (2010f). *Racial and ethnic composition. Older Americans 2010: Key indicators of well-being. Federal Interagency Forum on Aging-Related Statistics.* Washington, DC: U.S. Government Printing Office.

Federal Interagency Forum on Aging-Related Statistics. (2010g). *Residential services. Older Americans 2010: Key indicators of well-being. Federal Interagency Forum on Aging-Related Statistics.* Washington, DC: U.S. Government Printing Office.

Federal Interagency Forum on Aging-Related Statistics. (2010i). *Sensory impairments and oral health. Older Americans 2010: Key indicators of well-being. Federal Interagency Forum on Aging-Related Statistics.* Washington, DC: U.S. Government Printing Office.

Federal Interagency Forum on Aging Related Statistics. (2010j). Table 1a. Number of people age 65 and over and 85 and over, selected years 1980–2008 and projected 2010–2050. *Older Americans 2010: Key indicators of well-being. Federal Interagency Forum on Aging-Related Statistics.* Washington, DC: U.S. Government Printing Office.

Federal Interagency Forum on Child and Family Statistics. (2011). America's children: Key national indicators of well-being, 2011. Retrieved from http://www.childstats.gov/americaschildren *Federal Interagency Forum on Aging-Related Statistics.* Washington, DC: U.S. Government Printing Office.

Feeney, J. A., Passmore, N. L., & Peterson, C. C. (2007). Adoption, attachment, and relationship concerns: A study of adult adoptees. *Personal Relationships, 14*(1), 129–147.

Feeney, S., Moravcik, E., & Nolte, S. (2013). *Who am I in the lives of children?: An introduction to early childhood education.* Boston, MA: Pearson.

Fehr, B. (1996). *Friendship processes.* Thousand Oaks, CA: Sage.

Feigenbaum, P. (2009). Development of communicative competence through private and inner speech. In A. Winsler, C. Fernyhough, & I. Montero (Eds.), *Private speech, executive functioning, and the development of verbal self-regulation* (pp. 105–120). New York: Cambridge University Press.

Feinberg, M. E., & Kan, M. L. (2008). Establishing family foundations: Intervention effects on co-parenting, parent/infant well-being, and parent–child relations. *Journal of Family Psychology, 22*(2), 253–263.

Feldman, R. (2011). Maternal touch and the developing infant. In M. J. Hertenstein & S. J. Weiss (Eds.), *The handbook of touch: Neuroscience, behavioral, and health perspectives* (pp. 373–407). New York: Springer Publishing.

Feldman, R., Sussman, A. L., & Zigler, E. (2004). Parental leave and work adaptation at the transition to parenthood: Individual, marital, and social correlates. *Journal of Applied Developmental Psychology, 25*(4), 459–479.

Felmlee, D., & Muraco, A. (2009). Gender and friendship norms among older adults. *Research on Aging, 31*(3), 318–344.

Femyhough, C. (2009). Dialogic thinking. In A. Winsler, C. Fernyhough, & I. Montero (Eds.), *Private speech, executive functioning, and the development of verbal self-regulation* (pp. 42–52). New York: Cambridge University Press.

Fergus, S., & Zimmerman, M. A. (2005). Adolescent resilience: A framework for understanding healthy development in the face of risk. *Annual Review of Public Health, 26*(1), 399–419.

Ferguson, C. J., & Kilburn, J. (2010). Much ado about nothing: The misestimation and overinterpretation of violent video game effects in eastern and western nations: Comment on Anderson et al. *Psychological Bulletin, 136*(2), 174–178.

Ferguson, T. J. (2010). Like snowflakes and memories: Affective, cognitive, and conative facets of conscience in middle and later childhood. In W. Koops, D. Brugman, T. J. Ferguson, & A. F. Sanders (Eds.), *The development and structure of conscience* (pp. 69–116). New York: Psychology Press.

Fergusson, D. M., Boden, J. M., & Horwood, J. L. (2008). Exposure to childhood sexual and physical abuse and adjustment in early adulthood. *Child Abuse and Neglect, 32*(6), 607–619.

Fernyhough, C. (2008). Getting Vygotskian about theory of mind: Mediation, dialogue, and the development of social understanding. *Developmental Review, 28*(2), 225–262.

Ferretti, P. (2006). *Embryos, genes, and birth defects* (2nd ed.). Hoboken, NJ: Wiley.

Fiatarone, M. A., O'Neill, E. F., Ryan, N. D., Clements, K. M., Solares, G. R., Nelson, M. E., et al. (1994). Exercise training and nutritional supplementation for physical frailty in very elderly people. *New England Journal of Medicine, 330*, 1769–1775.

Fidler, D. J., & Nadel, L. (2007). Education and children with Down syndrome: Neuroscience, development, and intervention. *Mental Retardation & Developmental Disabilities Research Reviews, 13*(3), 262–271.

Field, D. (1996). Awareness and modern dying. *Mortality, 1*, 255–265.

Field, M. J., & Behrman, R. E. (2003). *When children die: Improving palliative and end-of-life care for children and their families.* Washington, DC: National Academies Press.

Field, T., Diego, M., Hernandez-Reif, M., & Fernandez, M. (2007). Depressed mothers' newborns show less discrimination of other newborns' cry sounds. *Infant Behavior and Development, 30*(3), 431–435.

Fields, J. (2004). American's families and living arrangements: 2003. Current Population Reports (P20-553). Washington, DC: U.S. Census Bureau. Retrieved on January 4, 2005 from http://www.census.gov/prod2004pubs/p20-553.pdf.

Fields, M., Groth, L. A., & Spangler, K. (2008). *Let's begin reading right: A developmental approach to emergent literacy* (6th ed.). Upper Saddle River, NJ: Pearson/Merrill Prentice Hall.

Fields, R. D., & Stevens-Graham, B. (2002). New insights into neuron-glia communication. *Science, 298*(5593), 556.

Finch, C. (2001). Toward a biology of middle age. In M. E. Lachman (Ed.), *Handbook of midlife development* (pp. 77–108). New York: Wiley.

Fine, M. A., & Harvey, J. H. (2006). *Handbook of divorce and relationship dissolution.* Mahwah, NJ: Lawrence Erlbaum.

Fine, M. A., Coffelt, T. A., & Olson, L. N. (2008). Romantic relationship initiation following relationship dissolution. In S. Sprecher, A. Wenzel, & J. Harvey (Eds.), *Handbook of relationship initiation* (pp. 391–407). New York: Psychology Press.

Finer, L. B. (2007). Trends in premarital sex in the United States, 1954–2003. *Public Health Reports*, 122, 73–78.

Finer, L. B., & Kost, K. (2011). Unintended pregnancy rates at the state level. *Perspectives on Sexual Health and Reproductive Health, 43*(2).

Fingerman, K. L. (1998). The good, the bad, and the worrisome: Emotional complexities in grandparent's experiences with individual grandchildren. *Family Relations, 47*, 403–412.

Finkelhor, D., & Jones, L. (2006). Why have child maltreatment and child victimization declined? *Journal of Social Issues, 62*(4), 685–716.

Finkelhor, D., Ormrod, R., Turner, H., & Hamby, S. L. (2005). The victimization of children and youth: A comprehensive national survey. *Child Maltreatment, 10*, 5–25.

Finkelson, L., & Oswalt, R. (1995). College date rape: Incidence and reporting. *Psychological Reports, 77*, 526.

Fiorentino, D. D. (2008). Cognition, but not sensation, mediates age-related changes in the ability to monitor the environment. *Psychology and Aging, 23*(3), 665–670.

Fisanick, C. (2009). *Childbirth.* Detroit: Greenhaven Press.

Fischman, M. W. (2000). Informed consent. In B. D. Sales & S. Folkman (Eds.), *Ethics in research with human participants* (pp. 35–48). Washington, DC: American Psychological Association.

Fiske, M., & Chiriboga, D. A. (1990). *Change and continuity in adult life.* San Francisco: Jossey-Bass.

Flavell, J. H. (1985). *Cognitive development* (2nd ed.). Upper Saddle River, NJ: Prentice Hall.

Flavell, J. H. (2003). *Development of children's knowledge about the mind.* Worcester, MA: Clark University Press.

Flavell, J. H. (2007). Theory-of-mind development: Retrospect and prospect. In G. Ladd (Ed.), *Appraising the human developmental sciences: Essays in honor of Merrill-Palmer Quarterly* (pp. 38–55). Detroit: Wayne State University Press.

Flavell, J. H., Flavell, E. R., & Green, F. L. (2001). Development of children's understanding of connections between thinking and feeling. *Psychological Science, 12*(5), 430.

Flavell, J. H., Miller, P. H., & Miller, S. A. (2002). *Cognitive development* (4th ed.). Upper Saddle River, NJ: Prentice Hall.

Fleer, M. (2010). *Early learning and development: Cultural-historical concepts in play: Cultural-historical concepts in play*. Cambridge, MA: Cambridge University Press.

Fleer, M. (2011). Kindergartens in cognitive times: Imagination as a dialectical relation between play and learning. *International Journal of Early Childhood, 43*(3), 245–259.

Fletcher, A. C., Walls, J. K., Cook, E. C., Madison, K. J., & Bridges, T. H. (2008). Parenting style as a moderator of associations between maternal disciplinary strategies and child well-being. *Journal of Family Issues, 29*(12), 1724–1744.

Flint, M. (1982). Male and female menopause: A cultural put-on. In A. Voda, M. Dennerstein, & S. O'Donnel (Eds.), *Changing perspectives in menopause* (pp. 363–375). Austin: University of Texas Press.

Floccia, C., Christophe, A., & Bertoncini, J. (1997). High-amplitude sucking and newborns: The quest for underlying mechanisms. *Journal of Experimental Child Psychology, 64*, 175–198.

Flook, L., & Fuligni, A. J. (2008). Family and school spillover in adolescents' daily lives. *Child Development, 79*(3), 776–787.

Flouri, E. (2004). Subjective well-being in midlife: The role of involvement of and closeness to parents in childhood. *Journal of Happiness Studies, 5*(4), 335–358.

Fogel, A., King, B. J., & Shanker, S. G. (2008). *Human development in the twenty-first century: Visionary ideas from systems scientists*. New York: Cambridge University Press.

Folkman, S., (2011). Stress, health, and coping: an overview. In S. Folkman (Ed.), *The Oxford handbook of stress, health, and coping* (pp. 3–14). New York: Oxford University Press.

Folkman, S., & Sales, B. D. (2005). *Ethics in research with human participants*. Washington, DC: American Psychological Association.

Fonagy, P., & Target, M. (2005). Bridging the transmission gap: An end to an important mystery of attachment research? *Attachment and Human Development, 7*(3), 333–343.

Fonda, S. J., Clipp, E. D., & Maddox, G. L. (2002). Patterns in functioning among residents of an affordable assisted living housing facility. *The Gerontologist, 42*, 178–187.

Fontes, L. A., & O'Neill-Arana, M. R. (2008). Assessing for child maltreatment in culturally diverse families. In L. Suzuki & J. G. Ponterotto (Eds.), *Handbook of multicultural assessment: Clinical, psychological, and educational applications* (pp. 627–650). San Francisco: Jossey-Bass.

Formiga, F., Ferrer, A., Perez-Castejon, J., Olmedo, C., & Pujol, R. (2007). Risk factor for functional decline in nonagenarians: A one-year follow-up. *Gerontology, 53*, 211–217.

Foroud, A., & Whishaw, I. Q. (2012). The consummatory origins of visually guided reaching in human infants: A dynamic integration of whole-body and upper-limb movements. *Behavioural Brain Research.* doi: 10.1016/j.bbr.2012.01.045

Forrester, M. B., & Merz, R. D. (2007). Risk of selected birth defects with prenatal illicit drug use, Hawaii, 1986–2002. *Journal of Toxicology and Environmental Health: Part A, 70*(1), 7–18.

Fosco, G. M., Caruthers, A. S., & Dishion, T. J. (2012, June, 18). A six-year predictive test of adolescent family relationship quality and effortful control pathways to emerging adult social and emotional health. *Journal of Family Psychology.*

Fosco, G. M., Stormshak, E. A., Dishion, T. J., & Winter, C. E. (2012). Family relationships and parental monitoring during middle school as predictors of early adolescent problem behavior. *Journal of Clinical Child and Adolescent Psychology, 41*(2), 202–213.

Fozard, J. L., & Gordon-Salant, S. (2001). Changes in vision and hearing with aging. In J. E. Birren & K. W. Schaie (Eds.). *Handbook of the psychology of aging* (5th ed., pp. 241–266). San Diego, CA: Academic Press.

Frankenberger, K. D. (2000). Adolescent egocentrism: A comparison among adolescents and adults. *Journal of Adolescence, 23*(3), 343–354.

Franklin, A., Bevis, L., Ling, Y., & Hurlbert, A. (2010). Biological components of colour preference in infancy. *Developmental Science, 13*(2), 346–354.

Frankman, E. A., Wang, L., Bunker, C. H., & Lowder, J. L. (2009). Episiotomy in the United States: Has anything changed? *American Journal of Obstetrics and Gynecology, 200*(5), 573.

Franks, J. S. (2004). Comparing perceived quality of life in nursing homes and assisted-living facilities. *Journal of Gerontological Social Work, 43*, 119–130.

Fraser, J., Goswami, U., & Conti-Ramsden, G. (2010). Dyslexia and specific language impairment: The role of phonology and auditory processing. *Scientific Studies of Reading, 14*(1). Special issues: *The overlap between dyslexia and SLI: The role of phonology*, 8–29.

Freeman, H., Newland, L. A., & Coyl, D. D. (2010). New directions in father attachment. *Early Child Development and Care, 180*(1–2), 1–8. French, S., Seidman, E., Allen, L., & Aber, J. L. (2006). The development of ethnic identity during adolescence. *Developmental Psychology, 42*(1), 1–10.

Freund, A. M., & Baltes, P. B. (2007). Toward a theory of successful aging: Selection, optimization, and compensation. In R. Fernández-Ballesteros (Ed.), *Geropsychology: European perspectives for an aging world* (pp. 239–254). Ashland, OH: Hogrefe & Huber Publishers.

Freund, A. M., & Ritter, J. O. (2009). Midlife crisis: A debate. *Gerontology, 55*(5), 582–591.

Freund, A. M., Nikitin, J., & Ritter, J. O. (2009). Psychological consequences of longevity. *Human Development, 52*(1), 1–37.

Fried, P. A. (2008). Report of the thirty-first annual meeting of the Neurobehavioral Teratology Society, 2007. *Neurotoxicology and Tetratology, 30*(2), 131–132.

Friedler, G. (1996). Paternal exposures—Impact on reproductive and developmental outcome: An overview. *Pharmacology, Biochemistry, and Behavior, 55*, 691–700.

Friedman, E. M., & Ryff, C. D. (2012). Theoretical perspectives: A biopsychosocial approach to positive aging. In S. K. Whitbourne & M. J. Sliwinski (Eds.), *The Wiley-Blackwell handbook of adulthood and aging.* Oxford, England: Blackwell Publishing.

Friedman, H. S., Kern, M. L., & Reynolds, C. A. (2010). Personality and health, subjective well-being, and longevity. *Journal of Personality, 78*(1), 179–216.

Friedmann, T. (2007). A decade of accomplishments: Gene therapy and the SSGT. *Molecular Therapy, 15*(9), 1576–1578.

Frisard, M. I., Fabre, J. M., Russell, R. D., King, C. M., DeLany, J. P., Wood, R. H., et al. (2007). Physical activity level and physical functionality in nonagenarians compared to individuals aged 60–74 years. *Journals of Gerontology: Series A: Biological Sciences and Medical Sciences 62A*(7), 783–788.

Frisch, R. E. (1988). Fatness and fertility. *Scientific American, 258*(3) 88–95.

Frith, C. D., & Frith, U. (2012). Mechanisms of social cognition. *Annual Review of Psychology, 63*, 287–313.

Frontline. (2012). Ellen Galinsky. Retrieved from http://www.pbs.org/wgbh/pages/frontline/shows/teenbrain/interviews

Fujimura, J. H., & Rajagopalan, R. (2011). Different differences: The use of "genetic ancestry" versus race in biomedical human genetic research. *Social Studies of Science, 41*(1), 5–30.

Fujimura, J. H., Rajagopalan, R., Ossorio, P. N., & Doksum, K. A. (2010). Race and ancestry: Operationalizing populations in human genetic variation studies. In I. Whitmarsh & D. S. Jones (Eds.), *What's the use of race? Modern governance and the biology of difference* (pp. 169–183). Cambridge, MA: MIT Press.

Fukunaga, A., Uematsu, H., & Sugimoto, K. (2005). Influences of aging on taste perception and oral somatic sensation. *Journal of Gerontology: Series A: Biological Sciences and Medical Sciences, 60A*(1), 109–113.

Fuligni, A. J. (2001b). Family obligation and the academic motivation of adolescents from Asian, Latin American, and European backgrounds. In A. J. Fuligni (Ed.), *New Directions for Child and Adolescent Development, 94*, 61–76. San Francisco: Jossey-Bass.

Fuligni, A. J. (2006). Family obligation among children in immigrant families. Migration Information Source. Retrieved from http://www.migrationinformation.org/Feature/display.cfm?ID=410

Fuligni, A. J., & Pedersen, S. (2002). Family obligation and the transition to young adulthood. *Developmental Psychology, 38*(5), 856–868.

Fuligni, A. J., & Witkow, M. (2004). The postsecondary educational progress of youth from immigrant families. *Journal of Research on Adolescence, 14*(2),159–183.

Fuligni, A. J., Alvarez, J., Bachman, M., & Ruble, D. N. (2005). Family obligation and the academic motivation of young children from immigrant families. In C. R. Cooper, C. T. Coll, W. T. Bartko, H. Davis, & C. Chatman (Eds.), *Developmental pathways through middle childhood: Rethinking contexts and diversity as resources* (pp. 261–282). Mahwah, NJ: Lawrence Erlbaum Associates.

Fuligni, A. S., McCabe, L., McLanahan, S., & Roth, J. (2003). Four new national longitudinal surveys on children. In J. Brooks-Gunn, A. S. Fuligni, & L. J. Berlin (Eds.), *Early child development in the 21st century: Profiles in current research initiatives* (pp. 326–359). New York: Teachers College Press, Columbia University.

Fuligni, A., & Masten, C. L. (2010). Daily family interactions among young adults in the United States from Latin American, Filipino, East Asian, and European backgrounds. *International Journal of Behavioral Development, 34*(6), 491–499.

Fung, H., Carstensen, L. L., & Lutz, A. (1999). The influence of time on social preferences: Implications for life-span development. *Psychology and Aging, 14*, 595–604.

Furman, W. (2004). The emerging field of adolescent romantic relationships. In J. Lerner & A. Alberts (Eds.), *Current directions in developmental psychology* (pp. 128–133). Upper Saddle River, NJ: Prentice Hall.

Furman, W., & Winkles, J. K. (2012). Transformations in heterosexual relationships across the transition into adulthood: "Meet me at the bleachers…I mean the bar." In B. Laursen & W. A. Collins (Eds.), *Relationship pathways: From adolescence to young adulthood* (pp. 191–214). Thousand Oaks, CA: Sage.

Furman, W., Ho, M. J., & Low, S. M. (2007). The rocky road of adolescent romantic experience: Dating and adjustment. In R. Engels, M. Kerr, & H. Stattin (Eds.), *Friends, lovers and groups: Key relationships in adolescence* (pp. 61–80). New York: John Wiley & Sons.

Furukawa, E., & Tangney, J. (2012). Cross-cultural continuities and discontinuities in shame, guilt, and pride: A study of children residing in Japan, Korea and the USA. *Self and Identity, 11*(1), 90–113.

Gabbard, C. P. (2004). *Lifelong motor development* (4th ed.). San Francisco: Benjamin Cummings.

Gabbard, C. (2012). *Lifelong motor development* (6th ed.). San Francisco, CA: Pearson Benjamin Cummings.

Gaertner, B. M., Spinrad, T. L., & Eisenberg, N. (2008). Focused attention in toddlers: Measurement, stability, and relations to negative emotion and parenting. *Infant and Child Development, 17*(4), 339–363.

Gaertner, B. M., Spinrad, T. L., Eisenberg, N., & Greving, K.A. (2007). Parental child-rearing attitudes as correlates of father involvement during infancy. *Journal of Marriage and Family, 69*(4), 962–976.

Galinsky, E. (1999). *Ask the children: The breakthrough study that reveals how to succeed at work and parenting.* New York: HarperCollins.

Galinsky, E. (2005). Children's perspectives of employed mothers and fathers: Closing the gap between public debates and research findings. In D. F. Halpern & S. E. Murphy (Eds.), *From work-family balance to work-family interaction: Changing the metaphor* (pp. 219–236). Mahwah, NJ: Lawrence Erlbaum Associates Publishers.

Gallagher, W. (1993, May). Midlife myths. *Atlantic, 271* (5), 51–55, 58–62, 65, 68–69.

Galler, J. R. (Ed.) (1984). *Human nutrition: A comprehensive treatise: Vol. 5. Nutrition and behavior.* New York: Plenum.

Galler, J. R. et al. (2010). Early childhood malnutrition predicts depressive symptoms at ages 11–17. *Journal of Child Psychology and Psychiatry, 51*(7), 789–798.

Galler, J., Harrison, R., Ramsey, F., Chawla, S., & Taylor, J. (2006). Postpartum feeding attitudes, maternal depression, and breastfeeding in Barbados. *Infant Behavior and Development, 29*(2), 189–203.

Gallese, V., Fadiga, L., Fogassi, L., & Rizzolatti, G. (1996). Action recognition in the premotor cortex. *Brain, 119(2)*, 593–609.

Gallese, V., Gernsbacher, M. A., Heyes, C., Hickok, G., & Iacoboni, M. (2011). Mirror Neuron Forum. *Perspectives on Psychological Science, 6*(4), 369–407.

Galli, R. L., Shukitt-Hale, B., Youdim, K. A., & Joseph, J. A. (2002). Fruit polyphenolics and brain aging: Nutritional interventions targeting agerelated neuronal and behavioral deficits. In D. Harman (Ed.), *Increasing healthy life span: Conventional measures and slowing the innate aging process* (pp. 128–132). New York: New York Academy of Sciences.

Galluzzi, S., Beltramello, A., Filippi, M., & Frisoni, G. B. (2008). Aging. *Neurological Sciences, 29*(Suppl 3), S296–S300.

Galotti, K. M. (2011). *Cognitive development: Infancy through adolescence.* Thousand Oaks, CA: Sage Publications.

Galupo, M. P., Cartwright, K. B., & Savage, L. S. (2010). Cross-category friendships and post-formal thought among college students. *Journal of Adult Development, 17*(4), 208–214.

Galván, A. (2012). Risky behavior in adolescents: The role of the developing brain. In V. F. Reyna, S. B. Chapman, M. R. Dougherty, & J. Confrey (Eds.), *The adolescent brain: Learning, reasoning, and decision making* (pp. 267–289). Washington, DC: American Psychological Association.

Ganong, L., Coleman M., & Hans, J. D. (2006). Divorce as prelude to stepfamily living and the consequences of redivorce. In M. A. Fine & J. H. Harvey (Eds.), *Handbook of divorce and relationship dissolution* (pp. 409–434). Mahwah, NJ: Lawrence Erlbaum Associates Publishers.

Ganong, L. H., & Coleman, M. (2004). *Stepfamily relationships: Development, dynamics, and interventions.* New York: Kluwer Academic/Plenum Publishers.

Ganong, L. H., Coleman, M., & Jamison, T. (2011). Patterns of stepchild-stepparent relationship development. *Journal of Marriage and Family, 73*(2), 396–413.

Ganong, L., Coleman, M., & Hans, J. (2006). Divorce as prelude to stepfamily living and the consequences of redivorce. In M. Fine & J. Harvey (Eds.), *Handbook of divorce and relationship dissolution* (pp. 409–434). Mahwah, NJ: Lawrence Erlbaum Associates.

Gantz, W., Schwartz, N., Angelini, J., & Rideout, V. (2007). *Food for thought: Television food advertising to children in the United States.* Menlo Park, CA: The Henry J. Kaiser Family Foundation.

Garcia, E. E., & Nanez, J. E., Sr. (2011a). Bilingualism and cognition. In E. E. Garcia & J. E. Nanez, Sr. (Eds.), *Bilingualism and cognition: Informing research, pedagogy, and policy* (pp. 57–77).

Garcia, E. E., & Nanez, J. E. Sr. (2011b). *Bilingualism and cognition: Informing research, pedagogy, and policy.* Washington, DC: American Psychological Association.

Garcia, E. E., & Nanez, J. E. Sr. (2011c). Best practices and successful strategies. In E. E. Garcia & J. E. Nanez, Sr. (Eds.), *Bilingualism and cognition: Informing research, pedagogy, and policy* (pp. 131–156). Washington, DC: American Psychological Association.

Garcia, F., & Garcia, E. (2009). Is always authoritative the optimum parenting style? *Adolescence, 44*(173), 101–131.

Garcia, O. (2009). *Bilingual education in the 21st century: A global perspective.* Malden, MA; Oxford: Wiley-Blackwell.

Garcia, O. (2011). Educating New York's bilingual children: Constructing a future from the past. *International Journal of Bilingual Education and Bilingualism, 14*(2), 133–153.

Garcia-Sierra, A., Rivera-Gaxiola, M., Percaccio, C. R., Conboy, B. T., Romo, H., Klarman, L., Ortiz, S., & Kuhl, P. K. (2011). Bilingual language learning: An ERP study relating early brain responses to speech, language input, and later word production. *Journal of Phonetics, 39*(4), 546–557.

Gardner, H. (2004). *Frames of mind: The theory of multiple intelligences.* New York: Basic Books.

Gardner, H. (2011). The theory of multiple intelligences. In M. Gernsbacher, R. Pew, L. Hough, & J. Pomerantz (Eds.), *Psychology and the real world: Essays illustrating fundamental contributions to society* (pp. 122–130). New York: Worth Publishers.

Gardner, M., Roth, J., & Brooks-Dunn, J. (2008). Adolescents' participation in organized activities and developmental success 2 and 8 years after high school: Do sponsorship, duration, and intensity matter? *Developmental Psychology, 44*(3), 814–830.

Garland, A. F., & Zigler, E. (1993). Adolescent suicide prevention: Current research and social policy implications. *American Psychologist, 48,* 169–182.

Gathercole, S. E. (1998). The development of memory. *Journal of Child Psychology and Psychiatry and Allied Disciplines, 39,* 3–27.

Gathercole, S. E. (2007). Working memory: A system for learning. In R. K. Wagner, A. E. Muse, & K. R. Tannenbaum (Eds.), *Vocabulary acquisition: Implications for reading comprehension* (pp. 233–248). New York: Guilford.

Gaugler, J. E., & Kane, R. L. (2007). Families and assisted living. *Gerontologist, 47*(6), 83–99.

Gaugler, J. E., Roth, D. L., Haley, W. E., & Mittelman, M. S. (2008). Can counseling and support reduce burden and depressive symptoms in caregivers of people with Alzheimer's disease during the transition to institutionalization? Results from the New York University Caregiver Intervention Study. *Journal of American Geriatrics Society, 56*(3), 421–428.

Gavidia-Payne, S., & Stoneman, Z. (2004). Family predictors of maternal and paternal involvement in programs for very young children with disabilities. In M. A. Feldman (Ed.), *Early intervention: The essential readings* (pp. 311–338). Malden, MA: Blackwell Publishing.

Gazzaniga, M. S. (2009). *The cognitive neurosciences* (4th ed.). Cambridge, MA: MIT Press.

Gazzaniga, M. S., Ivry, R. B., & Mangun, G. R. (2009). *Cognitive neuroscience: The biology of the mind* (3rd ed.). New York: Norton.

Ge, X., Conger, R. D., & Elder, G. H., Jr. (1996). Coming of age too early: Pubertal influences on girls' vulnerability to psychological distress. *Child Development, 67*(6), 3386–3400.

Ge, X., Conger, R. D., & Elder, G. H., Jr. (2001). Pubertal transition, stressful life events, and the emergence of gender difference in adolescent depressive symptoms. *Developmental Psychology, 37*(3), 404–417.

Geddes, J. F., & Plunkett, J. (2004). "The evidence base for shaken baby syndrome": Authors' reply. *British Medical Journal, 328,* 1317.

Geddes, L. (2008). A small step closer to eternal youth. *New Scientist, 199*(2683), 8–9.

Gelman, S. A. (1998). Categories in young children's thinking. *Young Children, 1,* 20–26.

Gelman, S. A. (2003). *The essential child: Origins of essentialism in everyday thought.* London: Oxford University Press.

Gelman, S. A. (2007). *The essential child: Origins of essentialism in everyday thought.* New York: Oxford University Press.

Gelman, S. A., Taylor, M. G., & Nguyen, S. P. (2004). Mother–child conversations about gender: Understanding the acquisition of essentialist beliefs. *Monographs of the Society for Research in Child Development, 69*(1, Serial No. 275), 1–127.

Genbacev, O., McMaster, M. T., Zdravkovic, T., & Fisher, S. J. (2003). Disruption of oxygen-regulated responses underlies pathological changes in the placentas of women who smoke or who are passively exposed to smoke during pregnancy. *Reproductive Toxicology, 17*(5), 509.

Genesoni, L., & Tallandini, M. A. (2009). Men's psychological transition to fatherhood: An analysis of the literature. *Birth: Issues in Perinatal Care, 36*(4), 305–318.

Genro, J. P., Kieling, C., Rohde, L. A., & Hutz, M. H. (2010). Attention-deficit/hyperactivity disorder and the dopaminergic hypotheses. *Expert Review of Neurotherapeutics, 10*(4), 587–601.

Gentner, D., & Goldin-Meadow, S. (2003). *Language in mind: Advances in the study of language and thought.* Cambridge, MA: MIT Press.

Georgas, J., Berry, J. W., van de Vijver, F. J. R., Kagitcibasi, C., & Poorting, Y. H. (2009). Cultures and families: A 30-nation psychological study. *Psychology: The Journal of the Hellenic Psychological Society, 16*(1), 1–27.

Gershoff, E. T., & Bitensky, S. H. (2007). The case against corporal punishment of children. *Psychology, Public Policy, and Law, 13*(4) 231–272.

Gerstorf, D., Ram, N., Hoppmann, C., Willis, S. L., & Schaie, K. (2011). Cohort differences in cognitive aging and terminal decline in the Seattle Longitudinal Study. *Developmental Psychology, 47*(4), 1026–1041.

Gervain, J., & Mehler, J. (2010). Speech perception and language acquisition in the first year of life. *Annual Review of Psychology, 61*, 191–218.

Gesell, A. (1940). *The first five years of life: The preschool years.* New York: Harper & Brothers.

Gest, S. D., & Davidson, A. J. A. (2011). A developmental perspective on risk, resilience, and prevention. In M. K. Underwood & L. H. Rosen (Eds.), *Social development: Relationships in infancy, childhood, and adolescence* (pp. 427–454). New York: Guilford Press.

Gibson, E. J. (2000). Commentary on perceptual and conceptual processes in infancy. *Journal of Cognition and Development, 1*(1), 43–48.

Gibson, E. J., & Walk, R. D. (1960). The "visual cliff." *Scientific American, 202*(4), 64–71.

Giedd, J. N. (2008). The teen brain: Insights from neuroimaging. *Journal of Adolescent Health, 42*(4), 335–343.

Giedd, J. N., et al. (2010). Anatomic magnetic resonance imaging of the developing child and adolescent brain and effects of genetic variation. *Neuropsychology Review, 20*(4), 349–361.

Giedd, J. N., et al. (2011). Structural brain magnetic resonance imaging of typically developing children and adolescents. In E. Amsel & J. G. Smetana (Eds.), *Adolescent vulnerabilities and opportunities: Developmental and constructivist perspectives* (pp. 23–40). New York: Cambridge University Press.

Gil, E. (2010). Working with children to heal interpersonal trauma: The power of play. In E. Gil (Ed.), *Working with children to heal interpersonal trauma: The power of play* (pp. 3–11). New York: Guilford Press.

Gilca, M., Stoian, I., Atanasiu, V., & Virgolici, B. (2007). The oxidative hypothesis of senescence. *Journal of Postgraduate Medicine, 53*(3), 207–213.

Gillam, R. B., Bedore, L. M., & Davis, B. L. (2011). Communication across the life span. In R. B. Gillam, T. P. Marquardt, & F. N. Martin (Eds.), *Communication sciences and disorders: From science to clinical practice* (2nd ed., pp. 27–50). Boston, MA: Jones and Bartlett Publishers.

Gilligan, C. (1993). *In a different voice: Psychological theory and women's development.* Cambridge, MA: Harvard University Press.

Gilligan, C. (1994). In a different voice: Women's conceptions of self and mortality. In B. Puka (Ed.), *Caring voices and women's moral frames: Gilligan's view* (pp. 1–37). New York: Garland Publishing, Inc.

Gillis, J. J. (1992). Attention deficit disorder in reading-disabled twins: Evidence for a genetic etiology. *Journal of Abnormal Child Psychology, 20*, 303.

Giorgio, A., et al. (2010). Longitudinal changes in grey and white matter during adolescence. *NeuroImage, 49*(1), 94–103.

Gleason, R. R., Sebanc, A. M., & Hartup, W. W. (2000). Imaginary companions of preschool children. *Developmental Psychology, 36*, 419–428.

Glenberg, A. M. (2011a). Introduction to the mirror neuron forum. *Perspectives on Psychological Science, 6*(4), 363–368.

Glenberg, A. M. (2011b). Positions in the mirror are closer than they appear. *Perspectives on Psychological Science, 6*(4), 408–410.

Glick, B. R., Pasternak, J. J., & Patten, C. L. (2010). *Molecular biotechnology: Principles and applications of recombinant DNA* (4th ed.). Washington, DC: ASM Press.

Gliga, T., Mareschal, D., & Johnson, M. H. (2008). Ten-month-olds' selective use of visual dimensions in category learning. *Infant Behavior and Development, 31*(2), 287–293.

Goble, M. (2008). Medical and psychological complications of obesity. In D. Davies & H. Fitzgerald (Eds.), *Obesity in childhood and adolescence, Vol. 1: Medical, biological, and social issues* (pp. 229–269). Westport, CT: Praeger Publishers/Greenwood Publishing.

Goddard, S. (2009). *Attention, balance and coordination.* Oxford: Wiley-Blackwell.

Goeleven, E., De Raedt, R., & Dierckx, E. (2010). The positivity effect in older adults: The role of affective interference and inhibition. *Aging & Mental Health, 14*(2), 129–137.

Goh, J. O., & Park, D. C. (2009). Neuroplasticity and cognitive aging: The scaffolding theory of aging and cognition. *Restorative Neurology and Neuroscience, 27*(5), 391–403.

Golant, S. M. (2011). The changing residential environments of older people. In R. H. Binstock & L. K. George (Eds.), *Handbook of aging and the social sciences* (7th ed., pp. 207–220). San Diego, CA: Elsevier Academic Press.

Goldberg, A. E. (2010). Partners but not parents: Intimate relationships of lesbians and gay men. In A. E. Goldberg (Ed.), *Lesbian and gay parents and their children: Research on the family life cycle* (pp. 15–48). Washington, DC: American Psychological Association.

Goldberg, A. E., & Perry-Jenkins, M. (2004). Division of labor and workingclass women's well-being across the transition to parenthood. *Journal of Family Psychology, 18*, 225–236.

Goldberg, W. A., Prause, J., Lucas-Thompson, R., & Himsel, A. (2008). Maternal employment and children's achievement in context: A meta-analysis of four decades of research. *Psychological Bulletin, 134*(1), 77–108.

Goldin-Meadow, S. (2009). Using the hands to study how children learn language. In J. Colombo, P. McCardle, & L. Freund (Eds.), *Infant pathways to language: Methods, models, and research disorders* (pp. 195–210). New York: Psychology Press.

Goldin-Meadow, S. (2011). Creating and learning language by hand. In M. Gernsbacher, R. W. Pew, L. M. Hough, & J. R. Pomerantz (Eds.), *Psychology and the real world: Essays illustrating fundamental contributions to society* (pp. 90–97). New York: Worth Publishers.

Goldin-Meadow, S., & Mylander, C. (1998). Spontaneous sign systems created by deaf children in two cultures. *Nature, 391*, 279–281.

Goldman, L. (2007). Make over my period! *Health, 21*(7), 75–80.

Goldman, S., & Beardslee, W. R. (1999). Suicide in children and adolescents. In D. Jacobs (Ed.), *The Harvard Medical School guide to suicide assessment and intervention* (pp. 417–442). San Francisco: Jossey-Bass.

Goldrick-Rab, S., & Sorensen, K. (2010). Unmarried parents in college. *The Future of Children, 20*(2), 179–203.

Goldschmidt, A. B., Wall, M., Loth, K. A., Le Grange, D., & Neumark-Sztainer, D. (2012). Which dieters are at risk for the onset of binge eating? A prospective study of adolescents and young adults. *Journal of Adolescent Health.*

Goldschmidt, L., Richardson, G. A., Willford, J., & Day, N. L. (2008). Prenatal marijuana exposure and intelligence test performance at age 6. Journal of the American Academy of Child and Adolescent Psychiatry, 47(3), 254–263.

Goldschmidt, L., Richardson, G. A., Willford, J. A., Severtson, S. G., & Day, N. L. (2012). School achievement in 14-year-old youths prenatally exposed to marijuana. *Neurotoxicology and Teratology, 34*(1), 161–167.

Goldstein, I. (2004). Epidemiology of erectile dysfunction. *Proceedings of the Boston University School of Medicine Conference on Erectile Dysfunction, 22*(2), 113–120.

Goldstein, M. H., & Schwade, J. A. (2008). Social feedback to infants' babbling facilitates rapid phonological learning. *Psychological Science, 19* (5), 515–523.

Goldstein, S. E., Davis-Kean, P. E., & Eccles, J. S. (2005). Parents, peers, and problem behavior: A longitudinal investigation of the impact of relationship perceptions and characteristics on the development of adolescent problem behavior. *Developmental Psychology, 41*(2), 401–413.

Goldstein, S., & Devries, M. (2011). Attention-deficit/hyperactivity disorder in childhood. In S. Goldstein, J. A. Naglieri, & M. DeVries (Eds.), *Learning and attention disorders in adolescence and adulthood: Assessment and treatment* (2nd ed., pp. 59–86). Hoboken, NJ: John Wiley & Sons Inc.

Goleman, D., Boyatzis, R. E., & McKee, A. (2007). *The new leaders: Transforming the art of leadership into the science of results.* London: Sphere.

Goleman, D. (1995). *Emotional intelligence.* New York: Bantam Books.

Goleman, D. (2006). *Emotional intelligence.* New York: Bantam Books.

Golinkoff, R. M., & Hirst-Pasek, K. (2000). *How babies talk: The magic and mystery of language in the first three years of life.* New York: Plume.

Gomes, L., & Livesey, D. (2008). Exploring the link between impulsivity and peer relations in 5- and 6-year-old children. *Child: Care, Health and Development, 34*(6), 763–770.

Good, M., & Willoughby, T. (2007). The identity formation experiences of church attending rural adolescents. *Journal of Adolescent Research, 22*(4), 387–412

Goodwin, R. D., & Friedman, H. S. (2006). Health status and the five-factor personality traits in a nationally representative sample. *Journal of Health Psychology, 11*(5), 643–654.

Goodyer, I. M. (2009). Early onset depression: meanings, mechanisms, and processes. In S. Nolen-Hoeksema & L. M. Hilt (Eds.), *Handbook of depression in adolescents* (pp. 239–258). New York: Routledge/Taylor & Francis Group.

Gooren, E. M. J., van Lier, P. A. C., Stegge, H., Terwogt, M. M., & Koot, H. M. (2011). The development of conduct problems and depressive symptoms in early elementary school children: The role of peer rejection. *Journal of Clinical Child and Adolescent Psychology, 40*(2), 245–253.

Gopnik, A., Meltzoff, A. N., & Kuhl, P. K. (1999). *The scientist in the crib: Minds, brains, and how children learn.* New York: Morrow.

Gopnik, A., Meltzoff, A. N., & Kuhl, P. K. (2008). *The scientist in the crib: What early learning tells us about the mind.* Pymble, NSW; New York: HarperCollins e-books.

Gopnik. A. (2010). How babies think. *Scientific American, 303*(1), 76–81.

Gorchoff, S. M., John, O. P., & Helson, R. (2008). Contextualizing change in marital satisfaction during middle age: an 18-year longitudinal study. *Psychological Science, 19*(11), 1194–1200.

Gordon, R. A., Chase-Lansdale, P. L., & Brooks-Gunn, J. (2004). Extended households and the life course of young mothers: Understanding the associations using a sample of mothers with premature, low birth weight babies. *Child Development, 75*(4), 1013–1038.

Gosselin, J., & David, H. (2007). Risk and resilience factors linked with the psychology adjustment of adolescents, stepparents and biological parents. *Journal of Divorce and Remarriage, 48*(1/2), 29–53.

Goswami, U. (2008a). Reading, dyslexia and the brain. *Educational Research, 50*(2), 135–148.

Goswami, U. C. (2008b). *Cognitive development: The learning brain.* New York: Psychology Press.

Goswami, U. (2011). A temporal sampling framework for developmental dyslexia. *Trends in Cognitive Sciences, 15*(1), 3–10.

Gottfredson, G. D., & Johnstun, M. L. (2009). John Holland's contributions: A theory-ridden approach to career assistance. *The Career Development Quarterly, 58*(2), 99–107.

Gottlieb, G. (1998). Normally occurring environmental and behavioral influences on gene activity: From central dogma to probabilistic epigenesist. *Psychological Review, 105*(4), 792–802.

Gottlieb, G. (2007). Probabilistic epigenesist. *Developmental Science, 10*(1), 1–11.

Gottlieb, G., Wahlsten, D., & Lickliter, R. (2006). The significance of biology for human development: A developmental psychobiological systems view. In R. M., Lerner & W. Damon (Eds.) *Handbook of child psychology (6th ed.): Vol 1, Theoretical models of human development* (pp. 210–257). Hoboken, JH: John Wiley & Sons Inc.

Gottman, J. M. (2007). *Why marriages succeed or fail.* New York: Simon & Schuster.

Gottman, J. M., Katz, L. F., & Hooven, C. (1996). Parental meta-emotion philosophy and the emotional life of families: Theoretical models and preliminary data. *Journal of Family Psychology, 10,* 243–268.

Gottman, J., & Katz, L. (2002). Children's emotional reactions to stressful parent–child interactions: The link between emotion regulation and vagal tone. *Marriage and Family Review, 34*(3/4), 265.

Goubet, N., Rattaz, C., Pierrat, V., Allémann, E., Bullinger, A., & Lequien, P. (2002). Olfactory familiarization and discrimination in preterm and full-term newborns. *Infancy, 3*(1), 53–75.

Gow, A. J., Johnson, W., Pattie, A., & Brett, C.E. (2011). Stability and change in intelligence from age 11 to ages 70, 79, 87: The Lothian birth cohorts of 1921 and 1936. *Psychology and Aging, 26*(1), 232–240.

Graber, J. A., Seeley, J. R., Brooks-Gunn, J., & Lewinsohn, P. M. (2004). Is pubertal timing associated with psychopathology in young adulthood? *Journal of the American Academy of Child and Adolescent Psychiatry, 43*(6), 718–726.

Graf, S. C., Mullis, R. L., & Mullis, A. K. (2008). Identity formation of United States American and Asian Indian adolescents. *Adolescence, 43*(169), 57–69.

Graham, J., Tisher, R., Ainley, M., & Kennedy, G. (2008). Staying with the text: The contribution of gender, achievement orientations, and interest to students' performance on a literacy task. *Educational Psychology, 28*(7), 757–776.

Granic, I., Dishion, T. J., & Hollenstein, T. (2003). The family ecology of adolescence: A dynamic systems perspective on normative development. In G. R. Adams & M. D. Berzonsky (Eds.) *Blackwell handbook of adolescence* (pp. 60–91). Malden, MA: Blackwell Publishing.

Grant, K. E., McMahon, S. D., Duffy, S. N., Taylor, J. J., & Compas, B. E. (2011). Stressors and mental health problems in childhood and adolescence. In R. J. Contrada & A. Baum (Eds.), *The handbook of stress science: Biology, psychology, and health* (pp. 359–372). New York: Springer Publishing Co.

Grantham-McGregor, S., & Powell, C. (1994). The long-term follow-up of severely malnourished children who participated in an intervention program. *Child Development, 65*(2), 428–439.

Grantham-McGregor, S., Yin Bun, C., Cueto, S., Glewwe, P., Richter, L., & Strupp, B. (2007). Child development in developing countries 1: Developmental potential in the first 5 years for children in developing countries. *Lancet, 369*(9555), 60–70.

Graziano, W. G., Leone, C., Musser, L. M., & Lautenschlager, G. J. (1987). Self-monitoring in children: A differential approach to social development. *Developmental Psychology, 23,* 571–576.

Greeff, A. P., Vansteenwegen, A., & Herbiest, T. (2011). Indicators of family resilience after the death of a child. *Omega: Journal of Death and Dying, 63*(4), 343–358.

Greeff, A., & Human, B. (2004). Resilience in families in which a parent has died. *American Journal of Family Therapy, 32*(1), 27–42.

Green, B. L., Furrer, C. J., & McAllister, C. L. (2011). Does attachment style influence social support or the other way around? A longitudinal study of Early Head Start mothers. *Attachment & Human Development, 13*(1), 27–47.

Green, C. S., & Bavelier, D. (2008). Exercising your brain: A review of human brain plasticity and training-induced learning. *Psychology and Aging, 23*(4), 692–701.

Greenberg, J. (2012). Terror management theory: From genesis to revelations. In P. R. Shaver & M. Mikulincer (Eds.), *Meaning, mortality, and choice: The social psychology of existential concerns* (pp. 17–35). Washington, DC: American Psychological Association.

Greenberg, J., & Arndt, J. (2012). Terror management theory. In P. A. M. Lange, A. W. Kruglanski, & T. E. Higgins (Eds.), *Handbook of theories of social psychology* (Vol. 1, pp. 398–415). Thousand Oaks, CA: Sage Publications.

Greenberg, J., Landau, M., Kosloff, S., & Solomon, S. (2009). How our dreams of death transcendence breed prejudice, stereotyping, and conflict: Terror management theory. In T. D. Nelson (Ed.), *Handbook of prejudice, stereotyping, and discrimination* (pp. 309–332). New York: Psychology Press.

Greene, A. L. (1990). Great expectations: Construction of the life course during adolescence. *Journal of Youth and Adolescence, 19,* 289–303.

Greene, S. M., Anderson, E. R., Hetherington, E. M., Forgatch, M. S., & Degarmo, D. S. (2003). Risk and resilience after divorce. In F. Walsh (Ed.), *Normal family processes: Growing diversity and complexity* (3rd ed., pp. 96–120). New York: Guilford Press.

Greenfield, P. M. (2009). Linking social change and developmental change: Shifting pathways of human development. *Developmental Psychology, 45*(2), 401–418.

Greenman, P. S., Schneider, B. H., & Tomada, G. (2009). Stability and change in patterns of peer rejection: Implications for children's academic performance over time. *School Psychology International, 30*(2), 163–183.

Greenman, P. S., & Tardif, G. (2010). From the cradle to the grave: The clinical applications of attachment theory throughout the lifespan. In A. Columbus (Ed.), *Advances in psychology research* (Vol. 62, pp. 51–81). New York: Nova Science Publishers, Inc.

Greenspan, S. (2007a). *Great kids: Helping your baby and child develop the ten essential qualities for a happy, healthy life.* Cambridge, MA: Da Capo Press.

Greenspan, S. (2007b). Levels of infant–caregiver interactions and the DIR model: Implications for the development of signal affects, the regulation of mood and behavior, the formation of a sense of self, the creation of internal representation, and the construction of defenses and character structure. *Journal of Infant, Child and Adolescent Psychotherapy, 6*(3), 147–210.

Greenwood, P. M. (2007a). Functional plasticity in cognitive aging: Review and hypothesis. *Neuropsychology, 21*(6), 657–673.

Greenwood, P. M. (2007b). Reply to Grady (2007), Raz (2007), and Salthouse (2007): Can age and treachery triumph over youth and skill? *Neuropsychology, 21*(6), 680–683.

Greif, G. L. (2009). *Buddy system: Understanding male friendships.* New York: Oxford University Press.

Greif, G. L., & Deal, K. (2012). *Two plus two: Couples and their couple friendship.* London: Routledge.

Greitemeyer, T. (2011). Effects of prosocial media on social behavior: When and why does media exposure affect helping and aggression? *Current Directions in Psychological Science, 20*(4), 251–255.

Greven, C. U., Rijsdijk, F. V., & Plomin, R. (2011). A twin study of ADHD symptoms in early adolescence: Hyperactivity-impulsivity and inattentiveness show substantial genetic overlap but also genetic specificity. *Journal of Abnormal Child Psychology, 39*(2), 265–275.

Grigorenko, E. L. (2008). *Educating individuals with disabilities: IDEIA 2004 and beyond.* New York: Springer Publishing.

Grimm-Thomas, K., & Perry-Jenkins, M. (1994). All in a day's work: Job experiences, self-esteem, and fathering in working-class families. *Family Relations, 43,* 174–181.

Grinyer, A. (2012). *Palliative and end of life care for children and young people: Home, hospice and hospital.* Chichester, West Sussex, UK: John Wiley & Sons.

Grissmer, D., Grimm, K. J., Aiyer, S. M., Murrah, W. M., & Steele, J. S. (2010). Fine motor skills and early comprehension of the world: Two new school readiness indicators. *Developmental Psychology, 46*(5), 1008–1017.

Grodstein, F., Stampfer, M. J., Colditz, G. A., Willett, W. C., Manson, J. E., Joffe, M., et al. (1997). Postmenopausal hormone therapy and mortality. *New England Journal of Medicine, 336,* 1769–1775.

Groen-Blokhuis, M. M., van Beijsterveldt, C. E. M., & Boomsma, D. I. (2011). Evidence for a causal association of low birth weight and attention problems. *Journal of the American Academy of Child & Adolescent Psychiatry, 50*(12), 1247–1254.

Groeschel, S., Vollmer, B., King, M. D., & Connelly, A. (2010). Developmental changes in cerebral grey and white matter volume from infancy to adulthood. *International Journal of Developmental Neuroscience, 28*(6), 481–489.

Gross, J. J., Carstensen, L. L., Pasupathi, M., Tsai, J., Goetestam-Skorpen, C., & Hsu, A. Y. C. (1997). Emotion and aging: Experience, expression, and control. *Psychology and Aging, 12,* 590–599.

Gruenewald, T. L., Mroczek, D. K., Ryff, C. D., & Singer, B. H. (2008). Diverse pathways to positive and negative affect in adulthood and later life: An integrative approach using recursive partitioning. *Developmental Psychology, 44*(2), 330–343.

Gruhn, D., Gilet, A., Studer, J., & Labouvie-Vief, G. (2011). Age-relevance of person characteristics: Persons' beliefs about developmental change across the lifespan. *Developmental Psychology, 47*(2), 376–387.

Guay, F., Larose, S., & Boivin, M. (2004). Academic self-concept and educational attainment level: A ten-year longitudinal study. *Self & Identity, 3*(1), 53–68.

Guerra, N. G., Williams, K. R., & Sadek, S. (2011). Understanding bullying and victimization during childhood and adolescence: A mixed methods study. *Child Development, 82*(1), 295–310.

Gupta, R., & Karr, B. R. (2010). Specific cognitive deficits in ADHD: A diagnostic concern in differential diagnosis. *Journal of Child and Family Studies, 19*(6), 778–786.

Gupta, R., Karr, B. R., & Srinivasan, N. (2011). Cognitive-emotional deficits in ADHD: Development of a classification system. *Child Neuropsychology, 17*(1), 67–81.

Gurian, M. (2011). *Boys and girls learn differently!: A guide for teachers and parents.* San Francisco, CA: Jossey-Bass.

Gutmann, D. L. (1994). *Reclaimed powers: Men and women in later life.* Evanston, IL: Northwestern University Press.

Guttman, L., & Eccles, J. S. (2007). Stage-environment fit during adolescence: Trajectories of family relations and adolescent outcomes. *Developmental Psychology, 43*(2), 522–537.

Gwiazda, J., & Birch, E. E. (2001). Perceptual development: Vision. In E. B. Goldstein (Ed.), *Blackwell handbook of perception* (pp. 636–668). Malden, MA: Blackwell.

Gwyther, L. P., & Meglin, D. E. (2012). Working with families of older adults. In D. G. Blazer & D. C. Steffens (Eds.), *Essentials of geriatric psychiatry* (2nd ed., pp. 337–349). Arlington, VA: American Psychiatric Publishing.

Ha, J. (2008). Changes in support from confidants, children, and friends following widowhood. *Journal of Marriage and Family, 70*(2), 306–318.

Ha, J. (2010). The effects of positive and negative support from children on widowed older adults' psychological adjustment: A longitudinal analysis. *The Gerontologist, 50*(4), 471–481.

Ha, J., & Carr, D. (2005). The effect of parent–child geographic proximity on widowed parents' psychological adjustment and social integration. *Research on Aging, 27*(5), 578–610.

Ha, J., Can, D., Utz, R. L., & Nesse, R. (2006). Older adults' perceptions of intergenerational support after widowhood: How do men and women differ? *Journal of Family Issues, 27*(1), 3–30.

Haas, A. P., et al. (2011). Suicide and suicide risk in lesbian, gay, bisexual, and transgender populations: Review and recommendations. *Journal of Homosexuality, 58*(1), 10–51.

Hagerman, R. J. (2011). Fragile X syndrome and fragile X-associated disorders. In S. Goldstein & C. R. Reynolds (Eds.), *Handbook of neurodevelopmental and genetic disorders in children* (2nd ed., pp. 276–292). New York: Guilford Press.

Halberstadt, A. G., & Lozada, F. T. (2011). Emotion development in infancy through the lens of culture. *Emotion Review, 3*(2), 158–168.

Halford, G. S., & Andrews, G. (2011). Information-processing models of cognitive development. In U. Goswami (Ed.), *The Wiley-Blackwell handbook of childhood cognitive development* (2nd ed., pp. 697–721). Malden, MA: Wiley-Blackwell.

Halim, M. L., & Ruble, D. (2010). Gender identity and stereotyping in early and middle childhood. In J. C. Chrisler & D. R. McCreary (Eds.), *Handbook of gender research in psychology, Vol. 1: Gender research in general and experimental psychology* (pp. 495–525). New York: Springer Science + Business Media.

Halpern, D. F., et al. (2011). The pseudoscience of single-sex schooling. *Science, 333* (6050), 1706–1707.

Halpern, D. F. (2012). *Sex differences in cognitive abilities* (4th ed.). New York: Psychology Press.

Hamilton, B. E., Martin, J. A., & Ventura, S. J. (2011). Births: Preliminary data for 2010. *National Vital Statistics Reports, 60*(2). National Center for Health Statistics.

Hamilton-West, K. (2011). *Psychobiological processes in health and illness.* Los Angeles, CA: SAGE.

Hamon, R. R., & Ingoldsby, B. B. (2003). *Mate selection across cultures.* Thousand Oaks, CA: Sage Publications.

Hampton, M., McWatters, B., Jeffery, B., & Smith, P. (2005). Influence of teens' perceptions of parental disapproval and peer behavior on their initiation of sexual intercourse. *Canadian Journal of Human Sexuality, 14*(3/4), 105–121.

Handler, S. M., & Fierson, W. M. (2011). Learning disabilities, dyslexia, and vision. *Pediatrics, 127*(3), e818–e856.

Hannah, M. E., Hannah, W. J., Hodnett, E. D., Chalmers, B., Kung, R., et al. (2002). Outcomes at 3 months after planned cesarean versus planned vaginal delivery for breech presentation at term: The International Randomized Term Breech Trial. *Journal of the American Medical Association, 287*(14), 1822.

Harley, T. A. (2008). *The psychology of language: From data to theory* (3rd ed.). New York: Psychology Press.

Harlow, H. F. (1959). Love in infant monkeys. *Scientific American, 201*(6), 68–74.

Harlow, H. F., & Harlow, M. K. (1962). Social deprivation in monkeys. *Scientific American, 208*(5), 137–146.

Harms, R. W. (2010). Getting pregnant. Retrieved from http://www.mayoclinic.com/health/pregnancy/AN00281

Harms, R. W., & Wick, M. (2011). *Mayo Clinic guide to a healthy pregnancy.* Intercourse, PA: Good Books.

Harrington, R. (2013). *Stress, health & well-being: Thriving in the 21st century.* Belmont, CA: Wadsworth Cengage Learning.

Harris Poll. (2005). *Majorities of U.S. adult favor euthanasia and physician-assisted suicide by more than two-to-one.* Retrieved February 27, 2009 from http://www.harrisinteractive.com

Harris Poll. (2007). *Views on social issues and their potential impact on the presidential election.* Retrieved February 27, 2009 from http://www.harrisinteractive.com/harris_poll/index.asp?PID=907

Harris, R., Ellicott, A., & Hommes, D. (1986). The timing of psychosocial transitions and changes in women's lives: An examination of women aged 45 to 60. *Journal of Personality and Social Psychology, 51,* 409–416.

Harris-Britt, A., Valrie, C. R., Kurtz-Costas, B., & Rowley, S. J. (2007). Perceived racial discrimination and self-esteem in African American youth: Racial socialization as a protective factor. *Journal of Research on Adolescence 17*(4), 669–682.

Hart, B., & Risley, T. R. (1995). *Meaningful differences.* Baltimore: Brookes.

Hart, D. (2005). The development of moral identity. *Nebraska Symposium on Motivation, 51,* 165–196.

Hart, H. M., McAdams, D. P., Hirsch, B. J., & Bauer, J. J. (2001). Generativity and social involvement among African American and White adults. *Journal of Research in Personality, 35,* 208–230.

Hart, S. N., Brassard, M. R., Binggeli, N. J., & Davidson, H. A. (2002). Psychological maltreatment. In J. Myers, L. Berliner, J. Briere, C. T. Hendrix, C. Jenny, & T. Reid (Eds.), *The APSAC Handbook on Child Maltreatment* (2nd ed., pp. 79–104). Thousand Oaks, CA: Sage Publications.

Harter, S. (1999). *The construction of the self: A developmental perspective.* New York: Guilford Press.

Harter, S. (2006). The self. In N. Eisenberg, W. Damon, & R. M. Lerner (Eds.), *Handbook of child psychology: Vol. 3, social, emotional, and personality development* (6th ed., pp. 505–570). Hoboken, NJ: Wiley.

Harter, S. (2012). *The construction of the self* (2nd ed.). New York: Guilford Press.

Hartl, D. L. (2011). *Essential genetics: A genomics perspective* (5th ed.). Sudbury, MA: Jones and Bartlett Publishers.

Hartup, W. W. (1995). Personality development in social context. *Annual Review of Psychology, 46,* 655–687.

Hartup, W. W. (2006). Relationships in early and middle childhood. In A. J. Vangelisti & D. Perlman (Eds.), *The Cambridge handbook of personal relationships* (pp. 177–190). New York: Cambridge University Press.

Harwood, K., McLean, N., & Durkin, K. (2007). First-time mothers' expectations of parenthood: What happens when optimistic expectations are not matched by later experiences? *Developmental Psychology, 43*(1), 1–12.

Harwood, R. L., Schoelmerich, A., Schulze, P. A., & Gonzalez, Z. (1999). Cultural differences in maternal beliefs and behaviors: A study of middle-class Anglo and Puerto Rican mother–infant pairs in four everyday situations. *Child Development, 70,* 1005–1016.

Hasting, P. D., Nuselovici, J. N., Rubin, K. H., & Cheah, C. S. (2010). Shyness, parenting, and parent-child relationships. In K. H. Rubin & R. J. Coplan (Eds.), *The development of shyness and social withdrawal* (pp. 107–130). New York: Guilford Press.

Hauer, J. (2010). Medical treatment and management at the end of life. In S. L. Friedman & D. T. Helm (Eds.), *End-of-life care for children and adults with intellectual and developmental disabilities* (pp. 93–120). Washington, DC: American Association on Intellectual and Developmental Disabilities.

Häyry, M. (2010). *Rationality and the genetic challenge: Making people better?* New York: Cambridge University Press.

Havighurst, R. J. (1953). *Human development and education.* New York: Longman, Inc.

Havighurst, R. J. (1964). Stages of vocational development. In H. Borow (Ed.), *Man in a world at work* (pp. 560–578). Boston: Houghton Mifflin.

Hawley, P. H., Little, T. D., & Rodkin, P. C. (2007). *Aggression and adaptation: The bright side to bad behavior.* Mahwah, NJ: L. Erlbaum Associates.

Hay, D. F., et al. (2011). Known risk factors for violence predict 12-month-old infants' aggressiveness with peers. *Psychological Science, 20*(10), 1–7.

Haydon, J. (2007). *Genetics in practice: A clinical approach for healthcare practitioners.* Hoboken, NJ: Wiley.

Hayflick, L. (1996). *How and way we age.* New York: Ballantine Books.

Hayflick, L. (2004). The not-so-close relationships between biological aging and age-associated pathologies in humans. *The Journals of Gerontology: Series A: Biological Sciences and Medical Sciences, 59A*(6). Special issue: *Anti-aging medicine: The hype and the reality—part 1,* 547–550.

Hayne, H., & Rovee-Collier, C. (1995). The organization of reactivated memory in infancy. *Child Development, 66,* 893–906.

Hayslip, B., Jr., & Peveto, C. A. (2005). *Cultural changes in attitudes toward death, dying, and bereavement.* New York: Springer Publishing.

Hayward, M. D., Crimmins, E. M., Miles, T. P., & Yang, Y. (2000). The significance of socioeconomic status in explaining the racial gap in chronic health conditions. *American Sociological Review, 65,* 910–930.

Haywood, K., & Getchell, N. (2009). *Life span motor development* (5th ed.). Champaign, IL: Human Kinetics.

Head, D., Rodrique, K. M., Kennedy, K. M., & Raz, N. (2008). Neuroanatomical and cognitive mediators of age-related differences in episodic memory. *Neuropsychology, 22*(4), 491–507.

Hebebrand, J., & Hinney, A. (2009). Environmental and genetic risk factors in obesity. *Child and Adolescent Psychiatric Clinics of North America, 18*(1), 83–94.

Heckhausen, J., & Dweck, C. S. (2009). *Motivation and self-regulation across the life span.* New York: Cambridge University Press.

Heilbron, N., & Prinstein, M. (2008). A review and reconceptualization of social aggression: Adaptive and maladaptive correlates. *Clinical Child and Family Psychology Review, 11*(4), 176–217.

Heimann, M., & Meltzoff, A. N. (1996). Deferred imitation in 9- and 14-month-old infants: A longitudinal study of a Swedish sample. *British Journal of Developmental Psychology, 14,* 55–64.

Helson, R. (1997). The self in middle age. In M. E. Lachman & J. B. James (Eds.), *Multiple paths of midlife development* (pp. 21–43). Chicago: University of Chicago Press.

Helson, R., & Picano, J. (1990). Is the traditional role bad for women? *Journal of Personality and Social Psychology, 59,* 311–320.

Helson, R., & Soto, C. J. (2005). Up and down in middle age: Monotonic and nonmonotonic changes in roles, status, and personality. *Journal of Personality and Social Psychology, 89*(2), 194–204.

Helwig, C. C. (1995). Adolescents' and young adults' conceptions of civil liberties: Freedom of speech and religion. *Child Development, 66*(1), 152–166.

Helwig, C. C. (2006). Rights, civil liberties, and democracy across cultures. In M. Killen & J. Smetana (Eds.), *Handbook of moral development* (pp. 185–210). Mahwah, NJ: Lawrence Erlbaum Assocates.

Helwig, C. C. and Turiel, E. (2010) Children's Social and Moral Reasoning, In P. K. Smith & C. H. Hart (Eds.) The Wiley-Blackwell Handbook of Childhood Social Development, Second Edition, (pp. 562-583) Wiley-Blackwell, Oxford, UK. doi: 10.1002/9781444390933.ch30

Hendry, J. (2009). Many pregnant women take drugs harmful to babies. Reuters Health. Retrieved from http://www.reuters.com/article/2009/11/27/us-pregnant-drugs

Hennon, C. B., & Schedle, A. (2008). Stepfamilies and children. In T. P. Gullotta & G. M. Blau (Eds.), *Family influences on childhood behavior and development: Evidence-based prevention and treatment approaches* (pp. 161–185). New York: Routledge/Taylor & Francis Group.

Hepper, P. G., Wells, D. L., & Lynch, C. (2005). Prenatal thumb sucking is related to postnatal handedness. *Neuropsychologia, 43*(3), 313–315.

Herbenick, D., Reece, M., Schick, V., Sanders, S. A., Dodge, B., & Fortenberry, J. D. (2010). Sexual behavior in the United States: Results from a national probability sample of men and women ages 14–94. *Journal of Sexual Medicine, 7*(5), 255–265.

Herbst, J. H., McCrae, R. R., Costa, P. T., Feaganes, J. R., & Siegler, I. C. (2000). Self-perceptions of stability and change in personality at midlife: The UNC Alumni Heart Study. *Assessment, 7*(4), 379–388.

Herek, G. M. (2000). The psychology of sexual prejudice. *Current Directions in Psychological Science, 9,* 19–22.

Herek, G. M. (2006). Legal recognition of same-sex relationships in the United States. *American Psychologist, 61*(6), 607–621.

Herek, G. M. (2009). Sexual stigma and sexual prejudice in the United States: A conceptual framework. In D. A. Hope (Ed.) *Contemporary perspectives on lesbian, gay, and bisexual identities* (Vol. 54, pp. 65–111). New York: Springer Science + Business Media.

Herek, G. M., Gillis, J. R., & Cogan, J. C. (1999). Psychological sequelae of hate-crime victimization among lesbian, gay, and bisexual adults. *Journal of Consulting and Clinical Psychology, 67*, 945–951.

Herr, E. L., Cramer, S. H., & Niles, S. G. (2004). *Career guidance and counseling through the life span: Systematic approaches* (6th ed.). Needham Heights, MA: Allyn & Bacon.

Hersen, M., & Reitman, D. (2008). *Handbook of psychological assessment, case conceptualization, and treatment, children and adolescents.* New York: Wiley.

Hespos, S. J., & Spelke, E. S. (2007). Precursors to spatial language: The case of containment. In M. Aurnague, M. Hickmann, & L. Vieu (Eds.), *The categorization of spatial entities in language and cognition* (pp. 233–245). Amerstam, Netherlands: John Benjamins Publishing.

Hess, E. H. (1973). *Imprinting: Early experience and the developmental psychobiology of attachment.* New York: Van Nostrand Reinhold Co.

Hess, T. M. (2005). Memory and aging in context. *Psychological Bulletin, 131*(3), 383–406.

Hetherington, E. M. (1992). Coping with marital transitions: A family systems perspective. *Monographs of the Society for Research in Child Development, 57*(2-3, Serial No. 227), 1–14.

Hetherington, E. M. (2003). Social support and the adjustment of children in divorced and remarried families. *Childhood: A Global Journal of Child Research, 10*(2), 217–236.

Hetherington, E. M. (2006). The influence of conflict, marital problem solving and parenting on children's adjustment in nondivorced, divorced and remarried families. In A. Clarke-Stewart & J. Dunn (Eds.), *Families count: Effects on child and adolescent development* (pp. 203 –237). New York: Cambridge University Press.

Hetherington, E. M., & Blechman, E. A. (1996). *Stress, coping, and resiliency in children and families.* Hillsdale, NJ: Erlbaum.

Hetherington, E. M., & Kelly, J. (2002). *For better or for worse: Divorce reconsidered.* New York: Norton.

Hetzner, N. M., Razza, R. A., Malone, L. M., & Brooks-Gunn, J. (2009). Associations among feeding behaviors during infancy and child illness at two years. *Maternal and Child Health Journal, 13*(6), 795–805.

Hewitt, B., Western, M., & Baxter, J. (2006). Who decides? The social characteristics of who initiates marital separation. *Journal of Marriage and Family, 68*(5), 1165–1177.

Heywood, C. (2001). *A history of childhood.* Cambridge, UK; Malden, MA: Polity Press.

Hill, N. E., & Witherspoon, D. P. (2011). Race, ethnicity, and social class. In M. K. Underwood & L. H. Rosen (Eds.), *Social development: Relationships in infancy, childhood, and adolescence* (pp. 316–346). New York: Guilford Press.

Hines, M. (2004). *Brain gender.* New York: Oxford University Press.

Hirsh-Pasek, K., & Golinkoff, R. M. (1996). *The origins of grammar.* Cambridge, MA: MIT Press.

Hoare, C. (2002). *Erikson on development in adulthood: New insights from the unpublished papers.* New York: Oxford University Press.

Hochschild, A. R., & Machung, A. (2012). *The second shift: Working families and the revolution at home.* New York: Penguin Books.

Hock, E., & Lutz, W. (1998). Psychological meaning of separation anxiety in mothers and fathers. *Journal of Family Psychology, 2*, 41–55.

Hock, R. R. (2012). *Human sexuality* (3rd ed.). Upper Saddle River, NJ: Pearson.

Hoddinott, J., Maluccio, J. A., Behrman, J. R., Flores, R., & Martorell, R. (2008). Effect of a nutrition intervention during early childhood on economic productivity in Guatemalan adults. *Lancet, 371*(9610), 411–416.

Hodge, R. (2009). *Genetic engineering: Manipulating the mechanisms of life.* New York: Facts on File.

Hoefnagels, M., Lewis, R., Gaffin, D., & Parker, B. (2010). *Biology, concepts and investigations.* McGraw-Hill Science Engineering.

Hoeve, M., Dubas, J. S., Gerris, J. R. M., van der Laan, P. H., & Smeenk, W. (2011). Maternal and paternal parenting styles: Unique and combined links to adolescent and early adult delinquency. *Journal of Adolescence, 34*(5), 813–827.

Hofer, M. A. (2009). Developmental neuroscience. In G. G. Berntson, & J. T. Cacioppo (Eds.), *Handbook of neuroscience for the behavioral sciences* (Vol. 1, pp. 12–31). Hoboken, NJ: John Wiley & Sons Inc.

Hoff, E. (2009). *Language development* (4th ed.). Belmont, CA: Wadsworth/Cengage Learning.

Hoff, E. (2011). *Research methods in child language: A practical guide.* Malden, MA: Wiley-Blackwell.

Hoff, E. V. (2005). Imaginary companions, creativity, and self-image in middle childhood. *Creativity Research Journal, 17*(2/3), 167–180.

Hoff, E., Core, C., Place, S., Rumiche, R., Senor, M., & Parra, M. (2012). Dual language exposure and early bilingual development. *Journal of Child Language, 39*(1), 1–27.

Hogan, M. J., Staff, R. T., Bunting, B. P., Murray, A. D., Ahearn, T. S., Deary, I. J., & Whalley, L. J. (2011). Cerebellar brain volume accounts for variance in cognitive performance in older adults. *Cortex: A Journal Devoted to the Study of the Nervous System and Behavior, 47*(4), 441–450.

Hogart, A., Patzel, K., & LaSalle, J. (2008). Gender influences monoallelic expression of ATP10A in human brain. *Human Genetics, 124*(3), 235–242.

Holahan, C. K., & Velasquez, K. (2011). Perceived strategies and activities for successful later aging. *The International Journal of Aging & Human Development, 72*(4), 343–359.

Holahan, C. K., Sears, R. R., & Cronbach, L. J. (1995). *The gifted group in later maturity.* Palo Alto, CA: Stanford University Press.

Holbrook, M. (2006).*Children with visual impairments: A parent's guide.* Bethesda, MD: Woodbine House.

Holden, G. W. (2010). Childrearing and developmental trajectories: Positive pathways, off-ramps, and dynamic processes. *Child Development Perspectives, 4*(3). Special issue: *Special section on temperament and personality prospects for developmental psychopathology research*, 197–204.

Holland, J. L. (1996). Exploring careers with a typology: What we have learned and some new directions. *American Psychologist, 51*, 397–406.

Holland, J. L. (1997). *Making vocational choices: A theory of vocational personality and work environments* (3rd ed.). Odessa, FL: Psychological Assessment Resources.

Hollich, G. (2010). Early language. In J. G. Bremner & T. D. Wachs (Eds.), *Wiley-Blackwell handbook of infant development* (Vol. 1, 2nd ed.). Oxford, UK: Wiley-Blackwell. doi: 10.1002/9781444327564.ch14

Hollich, G., & Prince, C. G. (2009). Comparing infants' preference for correlated audiovisual speech with signal-level computational models. *Developmental Science, 12*(3), 379–387.

Holmes, T. H., & Rahe, R. H. (1967). The social readjustment rating scale. *Journal of Psychosomatic Research, 11*, 213–218.

Holtz, P., & Appel, M. (2011). Internet use and video gaming predict problem behavior in early adolescence. *Journal of Adolescence, 34*(1), 49–58.

Hong, J. S., Espelage, D. L., & Kral, M. J. (2011). Understanding suicide among sexual minority youth in America: An ecological systems analysis. *Journal of Adolescence, 34*(5), 885–894.

Hood, K. E. (2010). *Handbook of developmental science, behavior, and genetics.* Malden, MA: Wiley-Blackwell.

Hood, M., Conlon, E., & Andrews, G. (2008). Preschool home literacy practices and children's literacy development: A longitudinal analysis. *Journal of Educational Psychology, 100*(2), 252–271.

Hooper, C. J., Luciana, M., Conklin, H. M., & Yarger, R. S. (2004). Adolescents' performance on the Iowa Gambling Task: Implications for the development of decision making and ventromedial prefontal cortex. *Development Psychology, 40*(6), 1148–1158.

Hoover, J. R., Sterling, A. M., & Storkel, H. L. (2011). Speech and language development. In A. S. Davis (Ed.), *Handbook of pediatric neuropsychology* (pp. 71–78). New York: Springer Publishing, Co.

Hopkins, B. (1991). Facilitating early motor development: An intercultural study of West Indian mothers and their infants living in Britain. In J. K. Nugent, B. M. Lester, & T. B. Brazelton (Eds.), *The cultural context of infancy* (pp. 93–143). Norwood, NJ: Ablex.

Horiuchi, S., Finch, C. E., Mesle, F., & Vallin, J. (2003). Differential patterns of age-related mortality increase in middle age and old age. *Journal of Gerontology, 58A*(6), 495–507.

Horn, J. L., & Blankson, N. (2005). Foundations for better understanding of cognitive abilities. In

D. Flanagan & P. Harrison (Eds.), *Contemporary intellectual assessment: Theories, tests, and issues* (pp. 41–68). New York: Guilford Press.

Horn, J. L., & Noll, J. (1997). Human cognitive capabilities: Gf – Gc theory. In D. P. Flanagan, J. L. Genshaft, et al. (Eds.), *Contemporary intellectual assessment: Theories, tests, and issues* (pp. 53–91). New York: Guilford Press.

Horowitz, J., Galst, J., & Elster, N. (2010). *Ethical dilemmas in fertility counseling*. Washington, DC: American Psychological Association.

Horowitz, S. M., Klerman, L. V., Sungkuo, H., & Jekel, J. F. (1991). Intergenerational transmission of school-age parenthood. *Family Planning Perspectives, 23,* 168–177.

Horton-Ikard, R., & Weismer, S. E. (2007). A preliminary examination of vocabulary and word learning in African American toddlers from middle and low socioeconomic status homes. *American Journal of Speech-Language Pathology, 16,* 381–392.

Hospice Association of America. (2010). Hospice facts & statistics. Retrieved from http://www.nahc.org

Howe, T. R. (2011). *Marriages and families in the 21st century: A biological approach.* Malden, MA: Wiley-Blackwell.

Howell, K. K., Lynch, M. E., Platzman, K. A., Smith, G. H., & Coles, C. D., (2006). Prenatal alcohol exposure and ability, academic achievement, and school functioning in adolescence: A longitudinal follow-up. *Journal of Pediatric Psychology, 31*(1), *Special Issue: Prenatal substance exposure: Impact on children's health, development, school performance, and risk behavior*, 116–126.

Howes, C. (2009). Friendship in early childhood. In K. H. Rubin, W. M. Bukowski, & B. Laursen (Eds.), *Handbook of peer interactions, relationships, and groups* (pp. 180–194). New York: Guilford Press.

Howes, C. & Spieker, S. (2010).Attachmnet relationships in the context of multiple caregivers. In J. Cassidy & P. Shaver (Eds.), *Handbook of attachment: Theory, research, and clinical applications* (2nd ed., pp. 48-77). New York, NY: Guilford Press.

Hoyer, W. J., & Roodin, P. (2009). *Adult development and aging* (6th ed.). Boston: McGraw-Hill.

Hoyer, W. J., & Verhaeghen, P. (2006). Memory aging. In J. E. Birren & W. K. Schaire (Eds.), *Handbook of the psychology of aging* (6th ed., pp. 209–232). Amsterdam, Netherlands: Elsevier.

Hruschka, D. J. (2010). *Friendship: development, ecology, and evolution of a relationship*. Berkeley, CA: University of California Press.

Hsia, J. F., & Schweinle, W. E. (2012). Psychological definitions of love. In M. A. Paludi (Ed.), *The psychology of love* (Vols. 1–4, pp. 15–17). Santa Barbara, CA: Praeger/ABC-CLIO.

Hsiu-Hsin, T., Mei-Hui, C., & Yun-Fang, T. (2008). Perceptions of filial piety among Taiwanese university students. *Journal of Advanced Nursing, 63*(3), 284–290.

Hsu, H., & Lavelli, M. (2005). Perceived and observed parenting behavior in American and Italian first-time mothers across the first 3 months. *Infant Behavior & Development, 28*(4), 503–518.

Hu, F. B., Grodstein, F., Hennekens, C. H., Colditz, G. A., Johnson, M., Manson, J. E., et al. (1999). Age at natural menopause and risk of cardiovascular disease. *Archives of Internal Medicine, 159,* 1061–1068.

Hu, S., Pattatucci, A. M. L., Patterson, C., Li, L., Fulker, D. W., Cherny, S. S., et al. (1995). Linkage between sexual orientation and chromosome X 28 in males, but not in females. *Nature Genetics, 11,* 248–256.

Hunt, M. (1974). *Sexual behavior in the 1970s.* New York: Dell.

Hudley, C., & Irving, M. (2012). Ethnic and racial identity in childhood and adolescence. In K. R. Harris, S. Graham, T. Urdan, S. Graham, J. M. Royer, & M. Zeidner (Eds.), *APA educational psychology handbook, Vol. 2: Individual differences and cultural and contextual factors* (pp. 267–292). Washington, DC: American Psychological Association.

Hudson, J. A., & Mayhew, E. M. Y. (2009). The development of memory for recurring events. In M. L. Courage & N. Cowan (Eds.), *The development of memory in infancy and childhood* (2nd ed., pp. 69–91). New York: Psychology Press.

Huesmann L. R., & Miller, L. S. (1994). Long-term effects of repeated exposure to media violence in childhood. In L. R. Huesmann (Ed.), *Aggressive behavior: Current perspectives* (pp. 153–186). New York: Plenum Press.

Huesmann, L. R., Moise-Titus, J., Podolski, C. L., & Eron, L. D. (2003). Longitudinal relations between children's exposure to TV violence and their aggressive and violent behavior in young adulthood: 1977–1992. *Developmental Psychology, 39,* 201–221.

Huesmann, R. L., Dubow, E. F., & Boxer, P. (2011). The transmission of aggressiveness across generations: Biological, contextual, and social learning processes. In P. R. Shaver & M. Mikulincer (Eds.), *Human aggression and violence: Causes, manifestations, and consequences* (pp. 123–142). Washington, DC: American Psychological Association.

Hughes, C., & Dunn, J. (2007). Children's relationships with other children. In C. A. Brownell & C. B. Kopp (Eds.), *Socioemotional development in the toddler years: Transitions and transformations* (pp. 177–200). New York: Guilford Press.

Hughes, M., & Donaldson, M. (1979). The use of hiding games for studying the coordination of viewpoints. *Educational Review, 31,* 133–140.

Huizink, A. C., & Mulder, E. (2006). Maternal smoking, drinking or cannabis use during pregnancy and neurobehavioral and cognitive functioning in human offspring. *Neuroscience and Biobehavioral Reviews, 30*(1), 24–41.

Hull, R. H. (2012). *Hearing and aging.* San Diego, CA: Plural Publishing.

Hulme, C., & Snowling, M. J. (2011). Children's reading comprehension difficulties: Nature, causes, and treatments. *Current Directions in Psychological Science, 20*(3), 139–142.

Hummert, M. L. (2011). Age stereotypes and aging. In K. Warner Schaie & S. L. Willis (Eds.), *Handbook of the psychology of aging* (7th ed., pp. 249–262). San Diego, CA: Elsevier Academic Press.

Hund, A. M., & Naroleski, A. R. (2008). Developmental changes in young children's spatial memory and language in relation to landmarks. *Journal of Cognition and Development, 9*(3), 310–339.

Hunt, L. A., & Arbesman, M. (2008). Evidence-based and occupational perspective of effective interventions for older clients that remediate or support improved driving performance. *American Journal of Occupational Therapy, 62*(2), 136–148.

Huston, A. C., & Bentley, A. C. (2010). Human development in societal context. *Annual Review of Psychology, 61*(1), 411–437.

Hutchinson, J. (1991). What crack does to babies. *American Educator, 15,* 31–32.

Hutchison, B., & Niles, S. G. (2009). Career development theories. In I. Marini & M. A. Stebnicki (Eds.), *The professional counselor's desk reference* (pp. 467–476). New York: Springer Publishing Co.

Hutman, T., & Dapretto, M. (2009). The emergence of empathy during infancy. *Cognition, Brain, Behavior: An Interdisciplinary Journal, 13*(4). Special issue: *Empathy development—insights from early years,* 367–390.

Huttenlocher, J., Haight, W., Bryk, A., Seltzer, M., & Lyons, T. (1991). Early vocabulary growth: Relation to language input and gender. *Developmental Psychology, 27*(2), 236–248.

Hyde, J. (2005). The genetics of sexual orientation. In J. S. Hyde (Ed.), *Biological substrates of human sexuality* (pp. 9–20). Washington, DC: American Psychological Association.

Hyde, J. D., & DeLamater, J. D. (2011). *Understanding human sexuality* (11th ed.). New York: McGraw-Hill.

Hyde, J. S., Lindberg, S. M., Linn, M. C., Ellis, A. B., & Williams, C. C. (2008). Gender similarities characterize math performance. *Science, 321*(5888), 494–495.

Hyde, J., & DeLamater, J. D. (2008). *Understanding human sexuality* (10th ed.). Boston: McGraw-Hill Higher Education.

Iacoboni, M. (2012). The human mirror neuron system and its role in imitation and empathy. In F. B. M. de Waal & P. F. Ferrari (Eds.), *The primate mind: Built to connect with other minds* (pp. 32–47). Cambridge, MA: Harvard University Press.

Ihsen, E., Troester, H., & Brambring, M. (2010). The role of sound in encouraging infants with congenital blindness to reach for objects. *Journal of Visual Impairment & Blindness, 104*(8), 478–488.

Imai, M., Li, L., Haryu, E., Okada, H., Hirsh-Pasek, K., Golinkoff, R. M., & Shigematsu, J. (2008). Novel noun and verb learning in Chinese-, English-, and Japanese-speaking children. *Child Development, 79*(4), 979–1000.

Imhof, A. E. (1986). Life course patterns of women and their husbands. In A. B. Sorensen, F. E. Weinert, & L. R. Sherrod (Eds.), *Human devel-*

opment and the life course: Multidisciplinary perspectives (pp. 247–270). Hillsdale, NJ: Erlbaum.

Inhelder, B., & Piaget, J. (1958). *The growth of logical thinking: From childhood to adolescence.* New York: Basic Books.

Institute for Behavioral Genetics. (2011). *Colorado adoption project.* Retrieved from http://ibgwww.colorado.edu/cap

International Human Genome Sequencing Consortium. (2004). Finishing the euchromatic sequence of the human genome. *Nature, 431,* 931–945.

International Monetary Fund. (April, 2012). The financial impact of longevity risk. Retrieved from http://www.imf.org/external/pubs/ft/gfsr/2012/01/pdf/c4.pdf

Isaacs, S., & Swartz, A. (2010). On the front lines of childhood obesity. *American Journal of Public Health,* 11, 2018.

Israel, S. E., & Duffy, G. G. (2008). *Handbook of research on reading comprehension.* New York: Routledge.

Iverson, J. M. (2010). Developing language in a developing body: The relationship between motor development and language development. *Journal of Child Language, 37*(2), 229–261.

Iverson, P., Kuhl, P. K., Akahane-Yamado, R., Diesch, E., Tohkura, Y., Ketterman, A., & Siebert, C. (2003). A perceptual inference account of acquisition difficulties for non-native phonemes. *Cognition, 87*(1), B47–B57.

Iwayama, M., et al. (2011). Parental age and child growth and development: Child health check-up data. *Pediatrics International 53*(5), 709–714.

Jacobus, J., Thayer, R. E., Trim, R. S., Bava, S., Frank, L. R., & Tapert, S. F. (2012, May 7). White matter integrity, substance use, and risk taking in adolescence. *Psychology of Addictive Behaviors.*

Jadack, R. A., Hyde, J. S., Moore, C. F., & Keller, M. L. (1995). Moral reasoning about sexually transmitted diseases. *Child Development, 66*(1), 167–177.

Jaffee, S. R., Hanscombe, K. B., Haworth, C., David, O., & Plomin, R. (2012). Chaotic homes and children's disruptive behavior: A longitudinal cross-lagged twin study. *Psychological Science,* 1–8. doi: 10.1177/0956797611431693

James, W. (1950). *The principles of psychology.* New York: Dover. (Original work published 1890)

James, J., Thomas, P., Cavan, D., & Kerr, D. (2004). Primary care—Preventing childhood obesity by reducing consumption of carbonated drinks: Cluster randomised controlled trial. *British Medical Journal, 328,* 1237–1239.

Jankowiak, W. R. (2008). *Intimacies: Love and sex across cultures.* New York: Columbia University Press.

Jaswal, V. K., McKercher, D. A., & Vanderborght, M. (2008). Limitations on reliability: Regularity rules in the English plural and past tense. *Child Development, 79*(3), 750–760.

Jayson, S. (2008, May 4). Point values add up to far more stress these days. *USA Today.* Retrieved December 4, 2008 from http://www.usatoday.com/news/health/2008-05-04-life-changes-N.htm

Jedrychowski, W., et al. (2009). Gender specific differences in neurodevelopmental effects of prenatal cohort study in three-year olds. *Early Human Development, 85*(8), 503–510.

Jedrychowski, W., et al. (2011). Intrauterine exposure to lead may enhance sensitization to common inhalant allergens in early childhood: A prospective prebirth cohort study. *Environmental Research, 111*(1), 119–124.

Jenike, B. R., & Traphagan, J. W. (2009). Transforming the cultural scripts for aging and elder care in Japan. In J. Sokolovsky (Ed.), *The cultural context of aging: Worldwide perspectives* (3rd ed., pp. 240–258). Westport, CT: Praeger Publishers/Greenwood Publishing Group.

Jenkins, W. J. (2010). Can anyone tell me why I'm gay? What research suggests regarding the origins of sexual orientation. *North American Journal of Psychology, 12*(2), 279–296.

Jensen, L. A. (2011). *Bridging cultural and developmental approaches to psychology: New syntheses in theory, research, and policy.* Oxford; New York: Oxford University Press.

Jenvey, V. B. (2007). The relationship between television viewing and obesity in young children: A review of existing explanations. *Early Child Development and Care, 177*(8), 809–820.

Jeong, S., & Cooney, T. M. (2006). Psychological well-being in mid to late life: The role of generativity development and parent–child relationships across the lifespan. *International Journal of Behavioral Development, 30*(5), 410–421.

Jersild, A. T., & Holmes, F. B. (1935). Children's fears. *Child Development Monograph, 20.* New York: Teachers College Press, Columbia University.

Jessor, R. (1992). Risk behavior in adolescence: A psychosocial framework for understanding and action. *Developmental Review, 12,* 374–390.

Jessor, R. (1993). Successful adolescent development among youth in high-risk settings. *American Psychologist, 48,* 117–126.

Jin, K. M., Jacobvitz, D., Hazen, N., & Jung, S. H. (2012). Maternal sensitivity and infant attachment security in Korea: Cross-cultural validation of the Strange Situation. *Attachment & Human Development, 14(1),* 33–44.

Joe, S., & Bryant, H. (2007). Evidence-based suicide prevention screening in schools. *Children and Schools, 29*(4), 219–227.

Johnson, D. W., & Johnson, R. T. (2002). Teaching students how to cope with adversity: The three Cs. In E. Frydenberg (Ed.), *Beyond coping: Meeting goals, visions, and challenges* (pp. 195–216). New York: Oxford University Press.

Johnson, D. W., & Johnson, R. T. (2004). *Assessing students in groups: Promoting group responsibility and individual accountability.* Thousand Oaks, CA: Corwin Press.

Johnson, M. H. (2011). Developmental neuroscience, psychophysiology, and genetics. In M. H. Bornstein & M. E. Lamb (Eds.), *Cognitive development: an advanced textbook* (pp. 217–255). New York: Psychology Press.

Johnson, M. H., & de Haan, M. (2011). *Developmental cognitive neuroscience: An introduction.* Chichester, UK: Wiley-Blackwell.

Johnson, M. H., Munakata, Y., & Gilmore, R. O. (2008). *Brain development and cognition.* Malden, MA: Blackwell Publishing.

Johnson, W., Turkheimer, E., Gottesman, I. I., & Bouchard, T. J. (2009). Beyond heritability: Twin studies in behavioral research. *Current Directions in Psychological Science, 18*(4), 217–220.

Johnston, L. D., O'Malley, P. M., & Bachman, J. G. (2001). *Monitoring the Future: National survey results on drug use, 1975–1999. Volume I: Secondary school students* (NIH Publication No. 00-4802). Bethesda, MD: National Institute on Drug Abuse.

Johnston, L. D., O'Malley, P. M., Bachman, J. G., & Schulenberg, J. E. (2012). *Monitoring the future national survey results on drug use, 1975–2011. Volume 1: Secondary school students.* Ann Arbor, MI: Institute for Social Research, The University of Michigan.

Johnston, T. D. (2010). Developmental systems theory. In M. S. Blumberg, J. H. Freeman, & S. R. Robinson (Eds.), *Oxford handbook of developmental behavioral neuroscience* (pp. 12–29). New York: Oxford University Press.

Joint United Nations Programme on HIV/AIDS (UNAIDS). (2008). *Report on the global AIDS epidemic 2008: Executive summary.* Geneva, Switzerland.

Joint United Nations Programme on HIV/AIDS. (2010). Global report: UNAIDS report on the global AIDS epidemic 2010. Retrieved from http://www.unaids.org/globalreport/documents/20101123_GlobalReport_full_en.pdf

Jolley, R. P. (2010). *Children and pictures: Drawing and understanding.* Malden, MA: Wiley Blackwell.

Jones, C. M. (2011). Failing to adapt—the ageing immune system's role in cancer pathogenesis. *Reviews in Clinical Gerontology, 21*(3), 209–218.

Jones, E., & Herbert, J. S. (2006). Exploring memory in infancy: Deferred imitation and the development of declarative memory. *Infant and Child Development, 15*(2), 195–205.

Jones, I. R., & Higgs, P. F. (2010). The natural, the normal and the normative: Contested terrains in ageing and old age. *Social Science & Medicine, 71*(8), 1513–1519.

Jones, K. L., & Streissguth, A. P. (2010). Fetal alcohol syndrome and fetal alcohol spectrum disorders: A brief history. *Journal of Psychiatry & Law, 38*(4), 373–382.

Jones, L. M., Finkelhor, D., & Halter, S. (2006). Child maltreatment trends in the 1990s: Why does neglect differ from sexual and physical abuse? *Child Maltreatment, 11*(2), 107–120.

Jones, S. S. (1996). Imitation or exploration? Young infants' matching of adults oral gestures. *Child Development, 67,* 1952–1969.

Jordan, J. R. (2011). Group work with suicide survivors. In J. R. Jordan & J. L. McIntosh (Eds.), *Grief after suicide: Understanding the consequences and caring for the survivors* (pp. 283–300). New York: Routledge/Taylor & Francis Group.

Jordan, J. R., & McIntosh, J. L. (2011). *Grief after suicide: Understanding the consequences and caring for the survivors.* New York: Routledge.

Joseph, D. L., & Newman, D. A. (2010). Emotional intelligence: An integrative meta-analysis and cascading model. *Journal of Applied Psychology, 95*(1), 54–78.

Judd, F. K., Hickey, M., & Bryant, C. (2012). Depression and midlife: Are we overpathologising the menopause? *Journal of Affective Disorders, 136*(3), 199–201.

Juncosa, B. (2008). Another gene for Alzheimer's. *Scientific American, 399*(3), 36.

Junn, E., & Boyatzis, C. J. (2011). *Child growth and development* (18th ed.). New York: McGraw-Hill.

Just, M. A., Keller, T. A., Malave, V. L., Kana, R. K., & Varma, S. (2012). Autism as a neural systems disorder: A theory of frontal-posterior underconnectivity. *Neuroscience and Behavioral Reviews, 36*(4), 1292–1313.

Kagan, J. (1978). The baby's elastic mind. *Human Nature, 1,* 66–73.

Kagan, J. (2000). Inhibited and uninhibited temperaments: Recent developments. In W. R. Crozier (Ed.), *Shyness: Development, consolidation and change* (pp. 22–29). New York: Routledge.

Kagen, J., Reznick, J. S., & Gibbons, J. (1989). Inhibited and uninhibited types of children. *Child Development, 60*(4), 838–845.

Kagitçibasi, Ç. (1996). *Family and human development across cultures: A view from the other side.* Mahwah, NJ: Erlbaum.

Kagitçibasi, C. (2007). *Family, self, and human development across cultures: Theories and applications* (2nd ed.). Mahwah, NJ: Lawrence Erlbaum Associates Publishers.

Kahana, E., Kahana, B., & Zhang, J. (2005). Motivational antecedents of preventive proactivity in late life: Linking future orientation and exercise. *Motivation and Emotion, 29*(4), 438–464.

Kaiser Family Foundation. (2010). Prescription drug trends. Menlo Park, CA: The Henry J. Kaiser Family Foundation.

Kakar, S. (1986). Male and female in India: Identity formation and its effects on cultural adapatation in tradition and transformation. In R. H. Brown & G. V. Coelho (Eds.), *Asian Indians in America* (pp. 27–41). Williamsburg, VA: College of William and Mary Press.

Kakihara, F., Tilton-Weaver, L., Kerr, M., & Stattin, H. (2010). The relationship of parental control to youth adjustment: Do youths' feelings about their parents play a role? *Journal of Youth and Adolescence, 39*(12), 1442–1456.

Kandler, C., Riemann, R., Spinath, F. M., Angleitner A. (2010). Sources of variance in personality facets: A multiple-rater twin study of self-peer, peer-peer, and self-self (dis)agreement. *Journal of Personality, 78*(5), 1565–1594.

Kaneshiro, N. K. (2011). Failure to thrive. MedlinePlus. Retrieved from http://www.nlm.nih.gov/medlineplus/ency/article/000991.htm

Kaplan, N., Choy, M. H., & Whitmore, J. K. (1992). Indochinese refugee families and academic achievement. *Scientific American, 266*(2), 36–42.

Karasik, L. B., Adolph, K. E., Tamis-LeMonda, C. S., Bornstein, M. H., & Karasik, L. B. (2010). WEIRD walking: Cross-cultural research on motor development. *Behavioral and Brain Sciences, 33*(2–3), 95–96.

Karasik, L. B., Tamis-LeMonda, C. S., & Adolph, K. E. (2011). Transition from crawling to walking and infants' actions with objects and people. *Child Development, 82*(4), 1199–1209.

Karelitz, T. M., Jarvin, L., & Sternberg, R. J. (2010). The meaning of wisdom and its development throughout life. In W. Overton & R. M. Lerner (Eds.). *The handbook of life-span development, Vol. 1: Cognition, biology and methods.* (pp. 837-881). Hoboken, NJ: John Wiley and Sons, Inc.

Karen, R. (2008). Investing in children and society: What we have learned from seven decades of attachment research. In K. Kline (Ed.), *Authoritative communities: The scientific case for nurturing the whole child* (pp. 103–120). New York: Springer Science + Business Media.

Karraker, A., & DeLamater, J. (2011). Sexual frequency decline from midlife to later life. *The Journals of Gerontology: Series B: Psychological Sciences and Social Sciences, Vol. 66B*(4), 502–512.

Kärtner, J., Keller, H., & Chaudhary, N. (2010). Cognitive and social influences on early prosocial behavior in two sociocultural contexts. *Developmental Psychology, 46*(4), 905–914.

Kastenbaum, R. J. (1999). Dying and bereavement. In J. C. Cavanaugh & S. K. Whitbourne (Eds.), *Gerontology: An interdisciplinary perspective* (pp. 15–185). New York: Oxford University Press.

Kastenbaum, R. J. (2012). *Death, society, and human experience.* Boston, MA: Pearson. Kato, K., & Pedersen, N. L. (2005). Personality and coping: A study of twins reared apart and twins reared together. *Behavior Genetics, 35*(2), 147–157.

Katz, D. L., O'Connell, M., Njike, V. Y., Yeh, M. C., & Nawaz, H. (2008). Strategies for the prevention and control of obesity in the school setting: Systematic review and meta-analysis. *International Journal of Obesity, 32*(12), 1780–1789.

Katz, L. G., & McClellan, D. E. (1997). *Fostering children's social competence: The teacher's role.*Washington, DC: National Association for the Education of Young Children.

Katzel, L. I., & Steinbrenner, G. M. (2012). Physical exercise and health. In S. K. Whitbourne & M. J. Sliwinski (Eds.), *The Wiley-Blackwell handbook of adulthood and aging* (pp. 97–117). Malden, MA: Wiley-Blackwell.

Kavanaugh, R. D. (2006). Pretend play. In B. Spodek & S. Olivia (Eds.), *Handbook of research on the education of young children* (2nd ed., pp. 269–278). Mahwah, NJ: Lawrence Erlbaum Associates Publishers.

Kavšek, M., & Yonas, A. (2012). Infants' sensitivity to pictorial depth cues: A review and meta-analysis of looking studies. *Infant Behavior & Development, 35*(1), 109–128.

Kay, M. A. (2011). State-of-the-art gene-bases therapies: The road ahead. *Nature Reviews Genetics, 12*(5), 316–328.

Kaye, S. D., Lord, M., & Sherrid, P. (1995). Stop working? Not boomers. *U.S. News and World Report, 118*(23), 70–72, 75–76.

Keating, D. P. (2004). Cognitive and brain development. In R. Lerner & L. Steinberg (Eds.), *Handbook of adolescent psychology* (pp. 45–84). Hoboken, NJ: John Wiley & Sons Inc.

Keating, D. P. (2011). *Nature and nurture in early child development.* New York: Cambridge University Press.

Keesee, N. J., Currier, J. M., & Neimeyer, R. A. (2008). Predictors of grief following the death of one's child: The contribution of finding meaning. *Journal of Clinical Psychology, 64*(10), 1145–1163.

Kehrer-Sawatzki, H., & Cooper, D. (2007). Structural divergence between the human and chimpanzee genomes. *Human Genetics, 120*(6), 759–778.

Kelley, M. M., & Chan, K. T. (2012). Assessing the role of attachment to god, meaning, and religious coping as mediators in the grief experience. *Death Studies, 36*(3), 199–227.

Kelly, S.E., & Farrimond , H.R. (2011). Non-invasive genetic testing: A study of public attitudes. *Public health genomics, 15,* 73-81.

Kelly, S. J., Day, N., & Streissguth, A. P. (2000). Effects of prenatal alcohol exposure on social behavior in humans and other species. *Neurotoxicology and Teratology, 22,* 143–149.

Kennedy, K. M., & Raz, N. (2009). Aging white matter and cognition: Differential effects of regional variations in diffusion properties on memory, executive functions, and speed. *Neuropsychologia, 47*(3), 915–927.

Kermoian, R., & Campos, J. J. (1988). Locomotor experience: A facilitation of spatial cognitive development. *Child Development, 59,* 908–917.

Kern, M. L. (2009). Early educational milestones as predictors of lifelong academic achievement, midlife adjustment, and longevity. *Journal of Applied Developmental Psychology, 30*(4), 419–430.

Kerns, K. A., Aspelmeier, J. E., Gentzler, A. L., & Grabill, C. M. (2001). Parent–child attachment and monitoring in middle childhood. *Journal of Family Psychology, 15*(1), 69–81.

Kerr, M. E. (2008). Why do siblings often turn out very differently? In A. Fogel, B. J. King, & S. G. Shanker (Eds.), *Human development in the twenty-first century: Visionary ideas from system scientists* (pp. 206–215). New York: Cambridge University Press.

Kerr, M., & Stattin, H. (2000). What parents know, how they know it, and several forms of adolescent adjustment: Further support for a reinterpretation of monitoring. *Developmental Psychology, 36*(3), 366–380.

Kesebir, P., & Pyszczynski, T. (2012). The role of death in life: Existential aspects of human motivation. In R. M. Ryan (Ed.), *The Oxford handbook of human motivation* (pp. 43–64). New York: Oxford University Press.

Kesselring, T. (2011). The concept of egocentrism in the context of Piaget's theory. *New ideas in psychology, 29*(3), 327–345.

Kessler, R. C., Amminger, G. P., Aguilar-Gaziola, S., Alonso, J., Lee, S., & Ustun, T. B. (2007). Age of onset of mental disorders: A review of recent literature. *Current Opinion in Psychiatry, 20*(4), 359–364.

Ketcham, C. J., & Stelmach, G. E. (2001). Age-related declines in motor control. In J. E. Birren & K. W. Schaie (Eds.), *Handbook of the psychology of aging* (5th ed., pp. 313–348). New York: Academic Press.

Ketcham, C. J., Dounskaia, N. V., & Stelmach, G. W. (2004). Age-related differences in the control of multijoint movements. *Motor Control, 8*(4), 422–236.

Keyes, C. L. M., & Ryff, C. D. (1999). Psychological well-being in midlife. In S. L. Willis & J. D. Reid (Eds.), *Life in the middle: Psychological and social development in middle ages* (pp. 161–180). San Diego, CA: Academic Press.

Khan, F. A. (2012). *Biotechnology fundamentals.* Boca Raton: CRC Press.

Kiang, L., & Fuligni, A. (2009). Ethnic identity and family processes among adolescents from Latin American, Asian, and European backgrounds. *Journal of Youth and Adolescence, 38*(2), 228–241.

Kiang, L., Yip, T., & Fuligni, A. J. (2008). Multiple social identities and adjustment in young adults from ethnically diverse backgrounds. *Journal of Research on Adolescence, 18*(4), 643–670.

Kibbe, M. M., & Leslie, A. M. (2011). What do infants remember when they forget? Location and identity in 6-month-olds' memory for objects. *Psychological Science*, 1–6.

Killen, M., & Smetana, J. (2007). The biology of morality: Human development and moral neuroscience. *Human Development, 50*(5), 241–243.

Killgore, W. D., & Yurgelun-Todd, D. A. (2007). Unconscious processing of facial affect in children and adolescents. *Social Neuroscience, 2*(1), 28–47.

Killgore, W., Oki M., & Yurgelun-Todd, D. A. (2001). Sex-specific developmental changes in amygdala responses to affective faces. *Neuroreport: For Rapid Communication of Neuroscience Research, 12*, 427–433.

Killian, T. S. (2004). Intergenerational monetary transfers to adult children and stepchildren: A household level analysis. *Journal of Divorce and Remarriage, 42*(1–2), 105–130.

Kim, H. J., Shin, K. H., & Swanger, N. (2009). Burnout and engagement: A comparative analysis using the big five personality dimensions. *International Journal of Hospitality Management, 28*(1), 96–104.

Kim, P., & Evans, G. W. (2011). Family resources, genes, and human development. In A. Booth, S. M. McHale, & N. S. Landale (Eds.), *Biosocial foundations of family processes* (pp. 221–230). New York: Springer Science + Business Media.

Kim-Cohen, J., & Gold, A. L. (2009). Measured gene-environment interactions and mechanisms promoting resilient development. *Current Directions in Psychological Sciences, 18*(3), 138–142.

Kindermann, T. A. (1993). Natural peer groups as contexts for individual development: The case of children's motivation in school. *Developmental Psychology, 29*, 970–977.

Kindermann, T. A. (2007). Effects of naturally existing peer groups on changes in academic engagement in a cohort of sixth graders. *Child Development, 78* (4), 1186–1203.

King, B. M., Kante, S., & Feigenbaum, R. (2002). *Human sexuality.* Boston, MA: Pearson.

Kinnon, J. B. (1998). Special deliveries: New childbirth options for modern mothers (and fathers) range from high-tech to home again. *Ebony, 53*(7), 40–42.

Kinnunen, M., Pietilainen, K., & Rissanen, A. (2006). Body size and overweight from birth to adulthood. In L. Pulkkinen, J. Kaprio, & R. J. Rose (Eds.), *Socioemotional development and health from adolescence to adulthood* (pp. 95–107). New York: Cambridge University Press.

Kins, E., Beyers, W., Soenens, B., & Vansteenkiste, M. (2009). Patterns of home leaving and subjective well-being in emerging adulthood: The role of motivational processes and parental autonomy support. *Developmental Psychology, 45*(5), 1416–1429.

Kinsbourne, M. (2009). Development of cerebral lateralization in children. In C. R. Reynolds & E. Fletcher-Janzen (Eds.), *Handbook of clinical neuropsychology* (3rd ed., pp. 47–66). New York: Springer Science + Business Media.

Kirsh, S. J. (2012). *Children, adolescents, and media violence: A critical look at the research* (2nd ed.). Thousand Oaks, CA: Sage Publications.

Kite, M. E., Stockdale, G. D., Whitley, B. E., & Johnson, B. T. (2005). Attitudes toward younger and older adults: An updated meta-analytic review. *Journal of Social Issues, 61*(2), 241–266.

Klamen, D. L., Grossman, L. S., & Kopacz, D. R. (1999). Medical student homophobia. *Journal of Homosexuality, 37*, 53–63.

Klass, D., & Chow, A. (2011). Culture and ethnicity in experiencing, policing, and handling grief. In R. A. Neimeyer, D. L. Harris, H. R. Winokuer, & G. F. Thornton (Eds.), *Grief and bereavement in contemporary society: Bridging research and practice* (pp. 341–353). New York: Routledge/Taylor & Francis Group.

Klausen, E., & Passman, R. H. (2006). Pretend companions (imaginary playmates): The emergence of a field. *Journal of Genetic Psychology, 167*(4), 349–364.

Klavora, P., & Heslegrave, R. J. (2002). Senior drivers: An overview of problems and interventions strategies. *Journal of Aging and Physical Activity, 10*(3), 322–335.

Klein, R. G. (2011). Thinning of the cerebral cortex during development: A dimension of ADHD. *The American Journal of Psychiatry, 168*(2), 111–113.

Kleinhaus, K., Perrin, M., Friedlander, Y., Paltiel, O., Malaspina, D., & Harlap, S. (2006). Paternal age and spontaneous abortion. *Obstetrics and Gynecology, 108*(2), 369–377.

Klemmack, D. L., Roff, L. L. Parker, M. W., Koenig, H. G., Sawyer, P., & Allman, R. M. (2007). A cluster analysis typology of religiousness/spirituality among older adults. *Research on Aging, 29*(2), 163–183.

Klevens, J., & Whitaker, D. J. (2007). Primary prevention of child physical abuse and neglect: Gaps and promising directions. *Child Maltreatment, 12* (4), 364–377.

Klimstra, T. A., Hale, W. W. III, Branje, S. J., & Meeus, W. H. J. (2010). Identity formation in adolescence: Change or stability? *Journal of Youth and Adolescence, 39*(2), 150–162.

Knee, D. O. (2010). Hospice care for the aging population in the United States. In J. C. Cavanaugh & C. K. Cavanaugh (Eds.), *Aging in America, Vol. 3: Societal issues* (pp. 203–221). Santa Barbara, CA: Praeger/ABC-CLIO.

Knight, J. A. (2010). *Genetics & inherited conditions.* Pasadena, CA: Salem Press.

Kochanek, K. D., Xu, J. Q., Murphy, S. L., Miniño, A. M., & Kung, H. (2011, December 29). Deaths: Final data for 2009. *National Vital Statistics Reports, 60*(3). Kochanska, G., & Aksan, N. (2006). Children's conscience and self-regulation. *Journal of Personality, 74*(6), 1587–1618.

Koehler, K. (2010). Sibling bereavement in childhood. In C. A. Corr & D. E. Balk (Eds.), *Children's encounters with death, bereavement, and coping* (pp. 195–218). New York: Springer Publishing.

Koepke, S., & Denissen, J. J. A. (2012). Dynamics of identity development and separation—individuation in parent-child relationships during adolescence and emerging adulthood – A conceptual integration. *Developmental Review, 32*(1), 67–88.

Koh, C. J., & Atala, A. (2004). Therapeutic cloning applications for organ transplantation. *Transplant Immunology, 12*(3), 193–202.

Kohlberg, L. (1966). A cognitive developmental analysis of children's sex-role concepts and attitudes. In E. Maccoby (Ed.), *The development of sex differences* (pp. 82–173). Stanford, CA: Stanford University Press.

Kohlberg, L. (1978). Revisions in the theory and practice of moral development. In W. Damon (Ed.), *New Directions for Child Development, 2*, 83–87. San Francisco: Jossey-Bass.

Kohlberg, L. (1981). *Essays on moral development: Vol. 1. The philosophy of moral development.* New York: Harper & Row.

Kohlberg, L. (1984). *Essays on moral development: Vol. 2. The psychology of moral development.* New York: Harper & Row.

Kohlberg, L., & Puka, B. (1994). *Kohlberg's original study of moral development.* New York: Garland.

Kohn, A. (2006). *Unconditional parenting: Moving from rewards and punishments to love and reason.* New York: Atria Books.

Kohn, M. L. (1980). Job complexity and adult personality. In N. J. Smelser & E. H. Erikson (Eds.), *Theories of work and love in adulthood* (pp. 347–358). Cambridge, MA: Harvard University Press.

Konigsberg, R. D. (2011). *The truth about grief: The myth of its five stages and the new science of loss.* New York: Simon & Schuster.

Konner, M. (2010). *The evolution of childhood: Relationships, emotion, mind.* Cambridge, MA: Belknap Press of Harvard University Press.

Korb, R. (2012). *Motivating defiant and disruptive students to learn: Positive classroom management strategies.* Thousand Oaks, CA: Corwin Press.

Korfage, I. J., Roobol, M., de Koning, H. J., Kirkels, W. J., Schröder, F. H., & Essink-Bot, M. (2008). Does "normal" aging imply urinary, bowel, and erectile dysfunction? A general population survey. *Urology, 72*(1), 3–9.

Kostelny, K., & Garbarino, J. (2001). The war close to home: Children and violence in the United States. In D. Christie, R. Wagner, & D. Winter (Eds.), *Peace, conflict, and violence: Peace psychology for the 21st century* (pp. 110–199). Upper Saddle River, NJ: Prentice Hall/Pearson Education.

Kovelman, I., Baker, S. A., & Petitto, L. (2008). Age of first bilingual language exposure as a new window into bilingual reading development. *Bilingualism: Language and Cognition, 11*(2), 203–223.

Krampe, R., & Charness, N. (2006). Aging and expertise. In K. A. Ericsson, N. Charness, P. J. Feltovich, & R. R. Hoffman (Eds.), *The Cambridge handbook of expertise and expert performance* (pp. 723–742). New York: Cambridge University Press.

Kreider, R. M. (2010). Increase in opposite-sex cohabiting couples from 2009 to 2010 in the Annual Social and Economic Supplement (ASEC) to the Current Population Survey (CPS): Working paper. U.S. Bureau of the Census.

Krettenauer, T. (2011). The issue of highest stages in structural-developmental theories. In A. Pfaffenberger, P. W. Marko, & A. Combs (Eds.), *The postconventional personality: Assessing, researching, and theorizing higher development* (pp. 75–86). Albany: State University of New York Press.

Kroger, J. (2002). Feminist perspectives on Erikson's theory: Their relevance for contemporary identity development research. *Identity, 2*(3), 257–266.

Kroger, J. (2003). Identity development during adolescence. In G. R. Adams & M. D. Berzonsky (Eds.), *Blackwell handbook of adolescence* (pp. 205–226). Oxford, England: Basil Blackwell.

Kroger, J. (2007). Why is identity achievement so elusive? *An International Journal of Theory and Research, 7*(4), 331–348.

Kroger, J., & Marcia, J. E. (2011). The identity statuses: Origins, meanings, and interpretations. In S. J. Schwartz, K. Luyckx, & V. L. Vignoles (Eds.), *Handbook of identity theory and research* (Vols. 1 and 2, pp. 31–53). New York: Springer Science +Business Media.

Kroger, J., Martinussen, M., & Marcia, J. E. (2010). Identity status change during adolescence and young adulthood: A meta-analysis. *Journal of Adolescence, 33*(5), 683–698.

Krombholz, H. (2006). Physical performance in relation to age, sex, birth order, social class, and sports activities of preschool children. *Perceptual and Motor Skills, 102*(2), 477–484.

Kron-Sperl, V., Schneider, W., & Hasselhorn, M. (2008). The development and effectiveness of memory strategies in kindergarten and elementary school: Findings from the Würzburg and Göttingen longitudinal memory studies. *Cognitive Development, 23*(1), 79–104.

Krucoff, C. (1994). Use 'em or lose 'em. *Saturday Evening Post, 226*(2), 34–35.

Kruger, A. C., & Konner, M. (2010). Who responds to crying? Maternal care and allocare among the !Kung. *Human Nature, 21*(3), 309–329.

Kua, A., Korner-Bitensky, N., Desrosiers, J., Man-Son-Hing, M., & Marshall, S. (2007). Older driver retaining: A systematic review of evidence of effectiveness. *Journal of Safety Research, 38*(7), 81–90.

Kuhl, E. S., Clifford, L. M., & Stark, L. J. (2012). Obesity in preschoolers: Behavioral correlates and directions for treatment. *Obesity, 20*(1), 3–29.

Kuhl, P. K. (2011). Early language learning and literacy: Neuroscience implications for education. *Mind, Brain, and Education, 5*(3), 128–142.

Kuhl, P. K., & Iverson, P. (1995). Linguistic experience and the "perceptual magnet effect." In W. Strange (Ed.), *Speech perception and linguistic experience: Issues in cross-language research* (pp. 121–154). Timonium, MD: York Press.

Kuhl, P. K., & Meltzoff, A. N. (1988). Speech as an intermodal object of perception. In A. Yonas (Ed.), *Minnesota Symposia on Child Psychology: Vol. 20. Perceptual development in infancy* (pp. 235–266). Hillsdale, NJ: Erlbaum.

Kuhl, P., & Rivera-Gaxiola, M. (2008). Neural substrates of language acquisition. *Annual Review of Neuroscience, 31*(1), 511–534.

Kuhn, D. (2009). Adolescent thinking. In R. M. Lerner & L. Steinberg (Eds.), *Handbook of adolescent psychology, Vol. 1: Individual bases of adolescent development* (3rd ed., pp. 152–186). Hoboken, NJ: John Wiley & Sons.

Kuhn, D. (2011). What is scientific thinking and how does it develop? In U. Goswami (Ed.), *The Wiley-Blackwell handbook of childhood cognitive development* (2nd ed., pp. 497–523). Malden, MA: Wiley-Blackwell.

Kuhn, D., & Pease, M. (2006). Do children and adults learn differently? *Journal of Cognition and Development, 7*(3), 279–293.

Kuhn, D., & Pease, M. (2010). The dual components of developing strategy use: Production and inhibition. In H. Waters & W. Schneider (Eds.), *Metacognition, strategy use, and instruction* (pp. 135–159). New York: Guilford Press.

Kulik, L., & Havusha-Morgenstern, H. (2011). Does cohabitation matter? Differences in initial marital adjustment among women who cohabited and those who did not. *Families in Society, 92*(1), 120–127.

Kunzmann, U. (2007). Wisdom: Adult development and emotional motivational dynamics. In R. Fernandez-Ballesteros (Ed.), *Geropsychology: European perspectives for an aging world* (pp. 224–238). Ashland, OH: Hogrefe & Huber Publishers.

Kunzmann, U., & Baltes, P. B. (2003). Wisdom-related knowledge: Affective, motivational, and interpersonal correlates. *Personality and Social Psychology Bulletin, 29*(9), 1104–1119.

Kutner, L., Olson, C., Grimes, T., Anderson, J., & Bergen, L. (2008). *Media violence and aggression: Science and ideology.* Thousand Oaks, CA: Sage.

Labouvie-Vief, Adams, Hakim-Larson, Hayden, & DeVoe, as described in D. E. Papalia, S. W. Olds, & R. D. Feldman. (2004). Human development (9th ed.). (pp. 473–474). Boston: McGraw-Hill.

Labouvie-Vief, G. (2003). Dynamic integration: Affect, cognition, and the self in adulthood. *Current Directions in Psychological Science, 12,* 201–206.

Labouvie-Vief, G. (2006). Emerging structures of adult thought. In J. Arnett & J. Tanner (Eds.), *Emerging adults in America: Coming of age in the 21st century* (pp. 59–84). Washington, DC: American Psychological Association.

Labouvie-Vief, G., & Diehl, M. (1999). Self and personality development. In J. C. Cavanaugh & S. K. Whitbourne (Eds.), *Gerontology: An interdisciplinary perspective* (pp. 238–268). New York: Oxford University Press.

Lachman, M. E., Rosnick, C. B., & Rocke, C. U. (2009). The rise and fall of control beliefs and life satisfaction in adulthood: Trajectories of stability and change over ten years. In H. B. Bosworth & C. Hertzog (Eds.), *Aging and cognition: Research methodologies and empirical advances* (pp. 143–160). Washington, DC: American Psychological Association.

Ladd, G. W., Buhs, E. S., & Troop, W. (2002). Children's interpersonal skills and relationships in school settings: Adaptive significance and implications for school-based prevention and intervention programs. In P. K. Smith & C. H. Hart (Eds.), *Blackwell handbook of childhood social development* (pp. 394–415). Oxford, England: Basil Blackwell.

LaFontana, K. M., & Cillessen, A. H. N. (2010). Developmental changes in the priority of perceived status in childhood and adolescence. *Social Development, 19*(1), 130–147.

LaFreniére, P. (2010). *Adaptive origins: Evolution and human development.* New York: Psychology Press.

Lagasse, L. L., Van Vorst, R. F., Brunner, S. M., & Zucker, M. S. (1999). Infants' understanding of auditory events. *Infant and Child Development, 8,* 85–100.

Lagattuta, K., & Thompson, R. A. (2007). The development of self-conscious emotions: Cognitive processes and social influences. In J. L. Tracy, R. W. Robins, & J. Tangney (Eds.), *The self-conscious emotions: Theory and research* (pp. 91–113). New York: Guilford Press.

Lai, C. S. L., Fisher, S. E., Hurst, J. A., Vargha-Khadem, F., & Monaco, A. P. (2001). A forkhead-domain gene is mutated in a severe speech and language disorder. *Nature, 413*, 519–523.

Laird, R. D., Criss, M. M., Pettie, G. S., Dodge, K. A., & Bates, J. E. (2008). Parent's monitoring knowledge attenuates the link between antisocial friends and adolescent delinquent behavior. *Journal of Abnormal Child Psychology, 36*(3), 299–310.

Lam, R. C. (2006). Contradictions between traditional Chinese values and the actual performance: A study of the caregiving roles of the modern sandwich generation in Hong Kong. *Journal of Comparative Family Studies, 37*(2), 299–313.

Lamanna, M. A., & Reidmann, A. C. (2012). *Marriages and families: Making choices in a diverse society.* Belmont, CA: Wadsworth, Cengage Learning.

Lamaze, F. (1958). *Painless childbirth: Psychoprophylactic method.* London: Burke.

Lamaze, F. (1970). *Painless childbirth: The Lamaze method.* Chicago: Regnery.

Lamb, M. E. (1988). Social and emotional development in infancy. In M. H. Bornstein & M. E. Lamb (Eds.), *Developmental psychology: An advanced textbook* (2nd ed., pp. 359–410). Hillsdale, NJ: Lawrence Erlbaum Associates, Inc.

Lamb, M. E. (2010a). How do fathers influence children's development? Let me count the ways. In M. E. Lamb (Ed.), *The role of the father in child development* (5th ed., pp. 1–26). Hoboken, NJ: John Wiley and Sons, Inc.

Lamb, M. E. (2010b). *The role of the father in child development* (5th ed.). Hoboken, NJ: John Wiley & Sons Inc.

Lamb, M. E. (2012). Mothers, fathers, families, and circumstances: Factors affecting children's adjustment. *Applied Developmental Science, 16*(2), 98–111.

Lamb, M. E. (Ed.). (2004). *The role of the father in child development* (4th ed.). New York: Wiley.

Lamb, M. E., & Lewis. C. (2010). The development and significance of father-child relationships in two-parent families. In M. E. Lamb (Ed.), *The role of the father in child development* (5th ed., pp. 94–153). Hoboken, NJ: John Wiley and Sons, Inc.

Lamb, M. E., & Lewis, C. (2011). The role of parent-child relationships in child development. In M. H. Bornstein & M. E. Lamb (Eds.), *Developmental science: An advanced textbook* (6th ed., pp. 469–517). New York: Psychology Press.

Lamb, M. E., Hwang, P. C., Ketterlinus, R. D., & Fracasso, M. P. (1999). Parent–child relationships: Development in the context of a family. In M. H. Bornstein & M. E. Lamb (Eds.), *Developmental psychology: An advanced textbook* (4th ed., pp. 411–450). Hillsdale, NJ: Erlbaum.

Lamb, M. E., Ketterlinus, R. D., & Fracasso, M. P. (1992). Parent–child relationships. In M. H. Bornstein & M. E. Lamb (Eds.), *Developmental psychology: An advanced textbook* (3rd ed., pp. 465–518). Hillsdale, NJ: Erlbaum.

Lamborn, S. D., Dornbusch, S. M., & Steinberg, L. (1996). Ethnicity and community context as moderators of the relations between family decision making and adolescent adjustment. *Child Development, 67*(2), 283–301.

Land, K. C. (2008). 2008 special focus report: Trends in infancy/early childhood and middle childhood well-being, 1994–2006: The Foundation for Child Development child and youth well-being index (CWI) project: A composite index of trends in the well-being of America's children and youth. New York: Foundation for Child Development. (Available online at http://www.fcd-us.org/usr%5Fdoc/EarlyChildhoodWell-BeingReport.pdf)

Langelaan, S., Bakker, A. B., van Doornen, L., & Schaufeli, W. B. (2006). Burnout and work engagement: Do individual differences make a difference? *Personality and Individual Differences, 40*(3), 521–532.

Lansford, J. E. (2009). Parental divorce and children's adjustment. *Perspectives on Psychological Science, 4*(2), 140–152.

Lansford, J. E., Criss, M. M., Laird, R. D., Shaw, D. S., Pettit, G. S., Bates, J. E., & Dodge, K. A. (2011). Reciprocal relations between parents' physical discipline and children's externalizing behavior during middle childhood and adolescence. *Developmental and Psychopathology, 23*(1), 225–238.

Lansford, J. E., Malone, P. S., Dodge, K. A., Pettit, G. S., & Bates, J. E. (2010). Developmental cascades of peer rejection, social information processing biases, and aggression during middle childhood. *Developmental and Psychopathology, 22*(3). Special issue: *Developmental cascades: Part 1*, 593–602.

Lansford, J. E., Miller-Johnson, S., Berlin, L. J., Dodge, K. A., Bates, J. E., & Pettit, G. S. (2007). Early physical abuse and later violent delinquency: A prospective longitudinal study. *Child Maltreatment, 12*(3), 233–245.

Lapsley, D. K., & Edgerton, J. (2002). Separation–individuation, adult attachment style, and college adjustment. *Journal of Counseling and Development, 80*, 484–492.

Larouche, M., Galand, B., & Bouffard, T. (2008). The illusion of scholastic incompetence and peer acceptance in primary school. *European Journal of Psychology of Education—EJPE, 23*(1), 25–39.

Larson, R. W. (2004). How U.S. children and adolescents spend their time: What it does (and doesn't) tell us about their development. In J. Lerner and A. Alberts (Eds.), *Current directions in developmental psychology* (pp. 134–141). Upper Saddle River, NJ: Prentice Hall.

Larson, R. W., & Rickman, A. (2009). Globalization, societal change, and adolescence across the world. In R. M. Lerner & L. Steinberg (Eds.), *Handbook of adolescent psychology, Vol. 2: Contextual influences on adolescent development* (3rd ed., pp. 290–622).

Last, C. G. (2006). *Help for worried kids: How your child can conquer anxiety and fear.* New York: Guilford Publications.

Lauer, R. H., & Lauer, J. C. (2012). *Marriage & family: the quest for intimacy.* New York: McGraw-Hill.

Lauer, R. H., Lauer, J. C., & Kerr, S. T. (1990). The long-term marriage: Perceptions of stability and satisfaction. *International Journal of Aging and Human Development, 31*, 189–195.

Laumann, E. O., Gagnon, J. H., Michael, R. T., & Michaels, S. (1994). *The social organization of sexuality: Sexual practices in the United States.* Chicago: University of Chicago Press.

Laumann, E. O., Gagnon, J. H., Michael, R. T., & Michaels, S. (2000). *The social organization of sexuality: Sexual practices in the United States.* Chicago, IL: University of Chicago Press.

Laursen, B., Bukowski, W. M., Aunola, K., & Nurmi, J. E. (2007). Friendship moderates prospective associations between social isolation and adjustment problems in young children. Child Development, 78 (4), 1395–1404.

Laursen, B., DeLay, D. & Adams, R. E. (2010). Trajectories of perceived support in mother-adolescent relationships: The poor (quality) get poorer. *Developmental Psychology, 46*(6), 1792–1798.

Lawrence, E., Cobb, R. J., Rothman, A. D., Rothman, M. T., & Bradbury, T. N. (2008). Marital satisfaction across the transition to parenthood. *Journal of Family Psychology, 22*(1), 41–50.

Lawrence, E., Rothman, A. D., Cobb, R. J., & Bradbury, T. N. (2010). Marital satisfaction across the transition to parenthood: Three eras of research. In M. S. Schulz, M. K. Pruett, P. K. Kerig, & R. D. Parke (Eds.), *Strengthening couple relationships for optimal child development: Lessons from research and intervention* (pp. 97–114). Washington, DC: American Psychological Association.

Lawrence-Jacobson, A. R. (2006). Intergenerational community action and youth empowerment. *Journal of Intergenerational Relationships, 4*(1), 137–147.

Lawson, D. W., & Mace, R. (2010). Siblings and childhood mental health: Evidence for a later-born advantage. *Social Science & Medicine, 70*(12), 2061–2069.

Lawton, M. P., & Salthouse, T. A. (Eds.). (1998). *Essential papers on the psychology of aging.* New York: New York University Press.

Lawton, M. P., Brody, E., & Saperstein, A. (1989). A controlled study of respite service for care-givers of Alzheimer's patients. *The Gerontologist, 29*, 8–16.

Lawton, M. P., Parmelee, P. A., Katz, I., & Nesselroade, J. (1996). Affective states in normal and depressed older people. *Journals of Gerontology, 51*, 309–316.

Lazarus, R. S. (1981). Little hassles can be hazardous to health. *Psychology Today, 15*(7), 58–62.

Lazarus, R. S. (1999). *Stress and emotion: A new synthesis.* New York: Springer-Verlag.

Lazarus, R. S. (2000). Toward better research on stress and coping. *American Psychologist, 55*, 665–673.

Leaper, C., & Bigler, R. S. (2011). Gender. In M. K. Underwood & L. H. Rosen (Eds.), *Social development: Relationships in infancy, childhood, and adolescence* (pp. 289–315). New York: Guilford Press.

Learner, S. (2005). Home comforts in labour room deliver more relaxed birthing. *Nursing Standard, 19*(41), 9–9.

Lecanuet, J., Granier-Deferre, C., & DeCasper, A. (2005). Are we expecting too much from prenatal sensory experiences? In B. Hopkins & S. Johnson (Eds.), *Prenatal development of postnatal functions* (pp. 31–49) Westport, CT. Praeger Publishers/ Greenwood Publishing Group.

Lee, G. R., & DeMaris, A. (2007). Widowhood, gender, and depression. *Research on Aging, 29*(1), 56–72.

Lee, J., Zarit, S. H., Rovine, M. J., & Birditt, K. S. (2012). Middle-aged couples' exchanges of support with aging parents: Patterns and association with marital satisfaction. *Gerontology, 58*(1), 88–96.

Leerkes, E. M., & Burney, R. V. (2007). The development of parenting efficacy among new mothers and fathers. *Infancy, 12*(1), 45–67.

Legacy. (2012). Fast facts on grandparenting & intergenerational mentoring. Retrieved from http://www.legacyproject.org/specialreports/fastfacts.html

Legate, N., Ryan, R. M., & Weinstein, N. (2012). Is coming out always a "good thing"? exploring the relations of autonomy support, outness, and wellness for lesbian, gay, and bisexual individuals. *Social Psychological and Personality Science, 3*(2), 145–152.

Lehalle, H. (2006). Moral development in adolescence: How to integrate personal and social values? In S. Jackson & L. Goossens (Eds.), *Handbook of adolescent development* (pp. 118–134). New York: Psychology Press.

Lehman, C., Salaway, J. L., Bagnato, S. J., Grom, R. M., & Willard, B. (2011). Prevention as early intervention for young children at risk: Recognition and response in early childhood. In M. A. Bray & T. J. Kehle (Eds.), *The Oxford handbook of school psychology* (pp. 369–378). New York: Oxford University Press.

Leicht, K. (2008). Broken down by race and gender? Sociological explanations of new sources of earnings inequality. *Annual Review of Sociology, 34*(1), 237–255.

Lenroot, R. K., et al., (2009). Differences in genetic and environmental influences on the human cerebral cortex associated with development during childhood and adolescence. *Human Brain Mapping, 30*(1), 163–174.

Leo, J. (1984, April 9). The revolution is over. *Time, 123*, 74–83.

Lerner, A. W., & Lerner, A C. (2009). *Alzheimer's disease*. Detroit: Greenhaven Press.

Lerner, R. M. (2006). Developmental science, developmental systems, and contemporary theories of human development. In R. M. Lerner & D. William (Eds.), *Handbook of child psychology* (6th ed., pp. 1–17). Hoboken, NJ: John Wiley & Sons.

Lerner, R. M. (2011). Structure and process in relational, developmental systems theories: A commentary on contemporary changes in the understanding of developmental change across the life span. *Human Development, 54*(1), 34–43.

Lerner, R. M., Lewin-Bizan, S., & Warren, A. E. (2011). Concepts and theories of human development. In M. H. Bornstein & M. E. Lamb (Eds.), *Developmental science: An advanced textbook* (6th ed., pp. 3–49). New York: Psychology Press.

Lerner, R. M., & Steinberg, L. (2009). The scientific study of adolescent development: Historical and contemporary perspectives. In R. M. Lerner & L. Steinberg (Eds.), *Handbook of adolescent psychology, Vol. 1: Individual bases of adolescent development* (3rd ed., pp. 4–14). Hoboken, NJ: John Wiley & Sons.

Lester, B. M., & Sparrow, J. D. (2010). *Nuturing children and families: Building on the legacy of T. Berry Brazelton*. Malden, MA: Wiley-Blackwell.

Lester, B., Lagrasse, L., & Bigsby, R. (1998). Prenatal cocaine exposure and child development: What do we know and what do we do? *Seminars in Speech and Language, 19*, 123–146.

Let's Move. (2012). Learn the facts. Retrieved from http://www.letsmove.gov/learn-facts/epidemis-childhood-obesity

Leung, J. L. Y., & Pang, S. M. C. (2009). Ethical analysis of non-medical fetal ultrasound. *Nursing Ethics, 16*(5), 637–646.

Levay, S., & Baldwin, J. (2009). *Human sexuality*. Sunderland, MA: Sinauer Associates.

Leventhal, H., Rabin, C., Leventhal, E. A., & Burns, E. (2001). Health risk behaviors and aging. In J. E. Birren & K. W. Schaie (Eds.), *Handbook of the psychology of aging* (5th ed., pp. 186–214). San Diego, CA: Academic Press.

Leventhal, T., & Brooks-Gunn, J. (2004). A randomized study of neighborhood effects on low-income children's educational outcomes. *Developmental Psychology, 40*, 488–507.

Levin, D. E. (1998). *Remote control childhood: Combating the hazards of media culture*. Washington, DC: National Association for the Education of Young People.

Levine, J. A., Emery, C. R., & Pollack, H. (2007). The well-being of children born to teen mothers. *Journal of Marriage and Family, 69*(1), 105–122.

LeVine, R. A. (1989). Cultural environments in child development. In W. Damon (Ed.), *Child development today and tomorrow* (pp. 52–68). San Francisco: Jossey-Bass.

LeVine, R. A. (1990). Enculturation: A biosocial perspective on the development of self. In D. Cicchetti & M. Beeghly (Eds.), *The self in transition: Infancy to childhood* (pp. 99–117). Chicago: University of Chicago Press.

Levine, R., Sato, S., Hashimoto, T., & Verma, J. (1995). Love and marriage in eleven cultures. In H. T. Reis & C. E. Rusbult (Eds.), *Close relationships: Key readings* (pp. 229–238). Philadelphia, PA: Taylor & Francis.

Levinson, D. (1978). *The seasons of a man's life*. New York: Knopf.

Levinson, D. (1986). A conception of adult development. *American Psychologist, 41*, 3–13.

Levinson, D. (1996). *The seasons of a woman's life*. New York: Ballantine.

Levinson, D.J. (1990). A theory of life structure development in adulthood. In D. J. Levinson (Ed.) *Higher stages of human development: Perspectives on adult growth*. (pp. 35-53). New York: Oxford University Press.

Levrini, A., & Prevatt, F. (2012). Getting the most out of medication. In A. Lenrini & F. Prevatt (Eds.), *Succeeding with adult ADHD: Daily strategies to help you achieve your goals and manage your life* (pp. 231–252). Washington, DC: American Psychological Association.

Levy, T. M. (2007). *Handbook of attachment interventions* (2nd ed.). Amsterdam: Elsevier.

Lewis, D. C., Medvedev, K., & Seponski, D. M. (2011). Awakening to the desires of older women: Deconstructing ageism within fashion magazines. *Journal of Aging Studies, 25*(2), 101–109.

Lewis, L., & Gorman, E. (2011). Loss related to developmental milestones: An analysis of the postparental transition. In D. L. Harris (Ed.), *Counting our losses: Reflecting on change, loss, and transition in everyday life* (pp. 93–102). New York: Routledge/Taylor & Francis Group.

Lewis, L. J. (2010). Honoring diversity: Cultural competence in genetic counseling. In P. M. Veach & D. M. Bartels (Eds.), *Genetic counseling practice: Advanced concepts and skills* (pp. 201–233). Malden, MA: Wiley-Blackwell.

Lewis, M., & Kestler, L. (2012). *Gender differences in prenatal substance exposure*. Washington, DC: American Psychological Association.

Lewis, M. (2005). The child and its family: The social network model. *Human Development, 48*(1/2), 8–27.

Lewis, M., & Carmody, D. P. (2008). Self-representation and brain development. *Developmental Psychology, 44*(5), 1329–1334.

Lewis, M., Haviland-Jones, J. M., & Barrett, L. F. (2008). *Handbook of emotions* (3rd ed.). New York: Guilford Press.

Lewis, R. (2010). *Human genetics: The basics*. New York: Routledge.

Lewkowicz, D. J., & Hansen-Tift, A. M. (2012). Infants deploy selective attention to the mouth of a talking face when learning speech. *Proceedings of the National Academy of Sciences*. Retrieved from http://www.pnas.org/cgi/doi/10.1073/pnas.1114783109

Lewy, G. (2011). *Assisted death in Europe and America: Four regimes and their lessons*. Oxford; New York: Oxford University Press.

Li, S.-C., Lindenberger, U., Hommel, B., Aschersleben, G., Prinz, W., & Baltes, P. B. (2004). Transformations in the couplings among intellectual abilities and constituent cognitive processes across the life span. *Psychological Science, 15*, 155–163.

Lickliter, R., & Bahrick, L. E. (2000). The development of infant intersensory perception: Advantages of a comparative convergent-operations approach. *Psychological Bulletin, 126*, 260–280.

Lieberman, J. D. (2010). Inner terror and outward hate: The effects of mortality salience on bias motivated attacks. In B. H. Bornstein & R. L.

Wiener (Eds.), *Emotion and the law: Psychological perspectives* (pp. 133–155). New York: Springer Science +Business Media.

Lieberman, M. A., & Tobin, S. S. (1983). *The experience of old age: Stress, coping, and survival.* New York: Basic Books.

Lillard, A. (2007). Pretend play in toddlers. In C. A. Brownell & C. B. Kopp (Eds.), *Socioemotional development in the toddler years: Transitions and transformations* (pp. 149–176). New York, Guilford Press.

Lillard, A., & Curenton, S. (1999). Do young children understand what others feel, want, and know? *Young Children, 54*(5), 52–57.

Lillard, A., Pinkham, A. M., & Smith, E. (2011). Pretend play and cognitive development. *The Wiley-Blackwell handbook of childhood cognitive development* (2nd ed., pp. 285–311). Malden, MA: Wiley-Blackwell.

Lillycrop, K. A., & Burdge, G. C. (2011). Epigenetic changes in early life and future risk of obesity. *International Journal of Obesity, 35*(1), 72–83.

Lin, G., & Rogerson, P. A. (1995). Elderly parents and the geographic availability of their adult children. *Research on Aging, 17*, 303–331.

Lindenberger, U., Lövdén, M., Schellenbach, M., Li, S., & Krüger, A. (2008). Psychological perspectives of successful aging technologies: A mini-review. *Gerontology, 54*(1), 59–68.

Linder, M., & Hetherington, G. (2004). Stepchildren's perceptions of noncustodial mothers and noncustodial fathers: Differences in socioemotional involvement and associations with adolescent adjustment problems. *Journal of Family Psychology, 18*(4), 555–563.

Linke, D. B., & Kersebaum, S. (2005). Left out. *Scientific American Mind, 16*(4), 78–83.

Liotti, G. (2012). Disorganized attachment and the therapeutic relationship with people in shattered states. In J. Yellin & K. White (Eds.), *Shattered states: Disorganised attachment and its repair* (pp. 127–156). London, England: Karnac Books.

Lippa, R. (2008). Sex differences and sexual orientation differences in personality: Findings from the BBC Internet Survey. *Archives of Sexual Behavior, 37*(1), 173–187.

Lisby, M., Nielsen, L. P., & Mainz, J. (2005). Errors in the medication process: Frequency, type, and potential clinical consequences. *International Journal for Quality in Health Care, 17* (1), 15-22.

Liu, D., Wellman, H. M., Tardif, T., & Sabbagh, M. A. (2008). Theory of mind development in Chinese children: A meta-analysis of false-belief understanding across cultures and languages. *Developmental Psychology, 44*(2), 523–531.

Liu, J., & Graves, N. (2011). Childhood bullying: A review of constructs, concepts, and nursing implications. *Public Health Nursing, 28*(6), 556–568.

Liu, Y. (2011). When is the best age to have a child? *Issues in Perinatal Care, 38*(3), 276.

Llop, S., et al. (2012). Prenatal exposure to mercury and infant neurodevelopment in a multicenter cohort in Spain: Study of potential modifiers. *American Journal of Epidemiology, 175*(5), 451–465.

Lobo, R. A. (2007). *Treatment of the postmenopausal woman: Basic and clinical aspects* (3rd ed.). Burlington, MA: Academic Press.

Lo-Castro, A., D'Agati, E., & Curatolo, P. (2011). ADHD and genetic syndromes. *Brain & Development, 33*(6), 456–461.

Lock, M. (1993). *Encounters with aging.* Berkeley: University of California Press.

Löckenhoff, C. E., et al. (2009). Perceptions of aging across 26 cultures and their culture-level associates. *Psychology and Aging, 24*(4), 941–954.

Lohaus, A., et al. G. (2011). Infant development in two cultural contexts: Cameroonian NSO farmer and German middle-class infants. *Journal of Reproductive and Infant Psychology, 29*(2), 148–161.

Lohman, B. J., & Billings, A. (2008). Protective and risk factors associated with adolescent boys' early sexual debut and risky sexual behaviors. *Journal of Youth and Adolescence, 37*(6), 723–735.

Lonigan, C. J. (2006). Development, assessment, and promotion of preliteracy skills. *Early Education and Development, 17*(1), 91–114.

Loth, K. A., Mond, J., Wall, M., & Neumark-Sztainer, D. (2011). Weight status and emotional well-being: Longitudinal findings from project EAT. *Journal of Pediatric Psychology, 36*(2), 216–225.

Lowenstein, A., Katz, R., & Gur-Yaish, N. (2007). Reciprocity in parent–child exchange and life satisfaction among the elderly: A cross-national perspective. *Journal of Social Issues, 63*(4), 865–883.

Lowenthal, B. (1998). Early childhood traumatic brain injuries: Effects on development and interventions. *Early Child Development and Care, 146*, 21–32.

Lozoff, B., Corapci, F., Burden, M., Kaciroti, N., Angulo-Barroso, R., Sazawal, S., et al. (2007). Preschool-aged children with iron deficiency anemia show altered affect and behavior. *Journal of Nutrition, 137*(3), 683–689.

Lucock, M., Xiaowei, M., Veysey, M., & Zoe, Y. (2005). Folic acid: An essential nutrient with added health benefits. *Biologist, 52*(1), 21–27.

Luetters, C., et al. (2007). Menopause transition stage and endogenous estradiol and follicle-stimulating hormone levels are not related to cognitive performance: Cross-sectional results from the Women's Health Across the Nation (SWAN). *Journal of Women's Health, 16*(3), 331–344.

Lumpkin, J. R. (2008). Grandparents in a parental or near-parental role. *Journal of Family Issues, 29*(3), 357–372.

Lustgarten, M., Muller, F. L., & Van Remmen, H. (2011). An objective appraisal of the free radical theory of aging. In E. J. Masoro & S. N. Austad (Eds.), *Handbook of the biology of aging* (7th ed., pp. 177–202). San Diego, CA: Elsevier Academic Press.

Lykken, D. T. (2007). A more accurate estimate of heritability. *Twin Research and Human Genetics, 10*(1), 168–173.

Lynn, R., & Hattori, K. (1990). The heritability of intelligence in Japan. *Behavior Genetics, 20*, 545–546.

Lytel, L., Bakken, L., & Romig, C. (1997). Adolescent female identity development. *Sex Roles, 37*, 175–185.

Lyytinen, H., Erskine, J., Aro, M., & Richardson, U. (2007). Reading and reading disorders. In E. Hoff & M. Shatz (Eds.), *Blackwell handbook of language development* (pp. 454–474). Malden, MA: Blackwell Publishing.

Macchi, C., Valenza, E., Simion, F., & Leo, I. (2008). Congruency as a nonspecific perceptual property contributing to newborns' face preference. *Child Development, 79*(4), 807–820.

Maccoby, E. E. (1992). The role of parents in the socialization of children: An historical overview. *Developmental Psychology, 28*, 1006–1017.

Maccoby, E. E. (1998). *The two sexes: Growing up apart, coming together.* Cambridge, MA: Harvard University Press.

Maccoby, E. E., & Jacklin, C. N. (1974). *The psychology of sex differences.* Stanford, CA: Stanford University Press.

Maccoby, E. E., & Martin, J. A. (1983). Socialization in the context of the family: Parent–child interaction. In P. H. Mussen (Ed.), *Handbook of child psychology: Vol. 4. Socialization, personality, and social development* (pp. 1–102). New York: Wiley.

MacDorman, M. F., Menacker, F., & Declercq, E. (2010). Trends and characteristics of home and other out-of-hospital births in the United States, 1990–2006. *National Vital Statistics Report, 58*(11).

MacFarlane, A. (1978). What a baby knows. *Human Nature, 1*(2), 81–86.

MacPhee, A. R., & Andrews, J. W. (2006). Risk factors for depression in early adolescence. *Adolescence, 14*(163), 436–437.

Madden, D. J. (2001). Speed and timing of behavioral processes. In J. E. Birren & K. W. Schaie (Eds.), *Handbook of the psychology of aging* (5th ed., pp. 288–312). New York: Academic Press.

Madden, D. J. (2007). Aging and visual attention. *Current Directions in Psychological Science, 16* (2), 70–74.

Madsen, M. C. (1971). Developmental and cross-cultural differences in the cooperative and competitive behavior of young children. *Journal of Cross-Cultural Psychology, 2*, 365–371.

Magai, C. (2010). Attachment in middle and later life. In J. Cassidy & P. Shaver (Eds.), *Handbook of attachment: Theory, research, and clinical applications* (2nd ed., pp. 48-77). New York, NY: Guilford Press.

Magen, R. H., Austrian, S. G., & Hughes, C. S. (2002). Adulthood. In S. G. Austrian (Ed.), *Developmental theories through the life cycle* (pp. 181–263). New York: Columbia University Press.

Mahoney, D. H., Motil, K. J., Drutz, J. E., & Hoppin, A. G. (2012). Iron deficiency in infants and young children: Screening, prevention, clinical manifestations, and diagnosis. Retrieved from http://www.uptodate/com/contents/iron-defiency-in-infants-and-young-children-treatment

Main, M. (2000). Attachment theory. In A. Kazdin (Ed.), *Encyclopedia of psychology* (Vol. 1, pp. 289–293). Washington, DC: American Psychological Association.

Main, M., & Solomon, J. (1986). Discovery of an insecure-disorganized/disoriented attachment pattern. In T. B. Brazelton & M. W. Yogman (Eds.), *Affective development in infancy* (pp. 95–124). Westport, CT: Ablex Publishing.

Mainstream Science on Intelligence. (1994, December 13). *Wall Street Journal*, p. A18.

Majors, K. (2012). Friendships: The power of positive alliance. In E. Roffey (Ed.), *Positive relationships: Evidence based practice across the world* (pp. 127–143). New York: Springer Science + Business Media.

Ma-Kellams, C., & Blascovich, J. (2011). Culturally divergent responses to mortality salience. *Psychological Science, 22*(8), 1019–1024.

Maki, P. M., et al. (2011, March 16). Perimenopausal use of hormone therapy is associated with enhanced memory and hippocampal function later in life. *Brain Research, 1379*.

Makin, J. W., & Porter, R. H. (1989). Attractiveness of lactating females' breast odors to neonates. *Child Development, 60*, 803–810.

Malouff, J. M., Rooke, S. E., & Schutte, N. S. (2008). The heritability of human behavior: Results of aggregating meta-analyses. *Current Psychology, 27*(3), 153–161.

Mancilla-Martinez, J., & Lesaux, N. K. (2011). Early home language use and later vocabulary development. *Journal of Educational Psychology, 103*(3), 535–546.

Mandler, J. (2004a). *The foundations of mind: Origins of conceptual thought.* New York: Oxford University Press.

Mandler, J. (2004b). Thought before language. *Trends in Cognitive Sciences, 8*(11), 508–513.

Mandler, J. M. (1988). How to build a baby: On the development of an accurate representational system. *Cognitive Development, 3*, 113–136.

Mandler, J. M. (1992). Commentary. *Human Development, 35*, 246–253.

Mandler, J. M. (2007). On the origins of conceptual system. *American Psychologist, 62*(8), 741–451.

Mannarino, A. P. (December 13, 2011*). Written statement presented on behalf of the American Psychological Association before the Senate Subcommittee on Children and Families on protecting children from child abuse and neglect.* Retrieved from http://www.apa.org. Washington, DC: American Psychological Association.

Manning, W. D., & Cohen, J. A. (2012). Premarital cohabitation and marital dissolution: An examination of recent marriages. *Journal of Marriage and Family, 74*(2), 377–387.

March of Dimes. (2011). In the NICU. Retrieved from http://www.marchofdimes.com/baby/inthenicu_kangaroocare.html

March of Dimes. (2012). Feeding your baby. Retrieved from http://www.marchofdimes.com/baby/feeding _indepth.html

Marchman, V. A., & Thal, D. J. (2005). Words and grammar. In M. Tomasello & D. E. Slobin (Eds.) *Beyond nature-nurture: Essays in honor of Elizabeth Bates* (141–164). Mahway, NJ: Lawrence Erlbaum Associates Publishers.

Marcia, J. (1966). Development and validation of ego-identity status. *Journal of Personality and Social Psychology, 3*, 551–558.

Marcia, J. (1980). Identity in adolescence. In J. Adelson (Ed.), *Handbook of adolescent psychology* (pp. 159–187). New York: Wiley.

Marcus, G. F. (1996). Why do children say "breaked"? *Current Directions in Psychological Science, 5*(3), 81–85.

Mares, M., Palmer, E., & Sullivan, T. (2008). Prosocial effects of media exposure. In S. L. Calvert & B. J. Wilson (Eds.), *The handbook of children, media, and development* (pp. 268–289). Malden, MA: Malden Blackwell Publishing.

Marieb, E., & Hoehn, K. (2012). *Human anatomy & physiology* (9th ed.). Boston: Pearson.

Marks, N. F. (1996). Caregiving across the lifespan: National prevalence and predictors. *Family Relations, 45*, 27–36. *Users.* Retrieved February 3, 2009 from http://www.ahrq.gov/RESEARCH/ltcusers/index.html

Marks, N. F., Bumpass, L. L., & Jun, H. (2004). Family roles and well-being during the middle life course. In O. G. Brim, C. D. Ryff, & R. C. Kessler (Eds.), *How healthy are we? A national study of well-being at midlife* (pp. 514–549). Chicago: The University of Chicago Press.

Marmeleira, J. F., de Melo, F., Tiemcani, M., & Godinho, M. (2011). Exercise can improve speed of behavior in older drivers. *Journal of Aging and Physical Activity, 19*(1), 48–61.

Marschik, P. B., Einspieler, C., Strohmeier, A., Garzarolli, B., & Prechtl, H. (2008). From the reaching behavior at 5 months of age to hand preference at preschool age. *Developmental Psychobiology, 50*(5), 512–518.

Marshal, M. P., et al. (2011). Suicidality and depression disparities between sexual minority and heterosexual youth: A meta-analytic review. *Journal of Adolescent Health, 49*(2), 115–123.

Martin, A. C. (2008). Television media as a potential negative factor in the racial identity development of African American youth. *Academic Psychiatry, 32*(4), 338–342.

Martin, A., Brooks-Gunn, J., Klebanov, P., Buka, S. L., & McCormick, M. C. (2008). Long-term maternal effects of early childhood intervention: Findings from the Infant Health and Development Program (IHDP). *Journal of Applied Developmental Psychology, 29*(2), 101–117.

Martin, J. A., Hamilton, B. E., & Osterman, M. J. K. (2012*). Three decades of twin births in the United States, 1980–2009. NCHS Data Brief, No. 80.* Hyattsville, MD: National Center for Health Statistics.

Martin, J. A., Hamilton, B. E., Sutton, P. D., Ventura, S. J., Menacker, P. H., et al. (2007). Births: Final data for 2005. *National Vital Statistics Reports, 56* (6).

Martin, J. A., Hamilton, B. E., Ventura, S. J., Osterman, M. J. K., et al. (2011). Births: Final data for 2009. *National Vital Statistics Reports, 60*(1). Retrieved from http://www.cdc.gov/nchs/data/nvsr/nvsr60/.

Martin, T. L., & Doka, K. J. (2011). The influence of gender and socialization on grieving styles. In R. A. Neimeyer, D. L. Harris, H. R. Winokuer, & G. F. Thornton (Eds.), *Grief and bereavement in contemporary society: Bridging research and practice* (pp. 69–77). New York: Routledge/Taylor & Francis Group.

Martinez, G., Copen, C. E., & Abma, J. C. (2011). Teenagers in the United States: Sexual activity, contraceptive use, and childbearing, 2006–2010 National Survey of Family Growth. *Vital Health Stat 23*(31). National Center for Health Statistics.

Martínez, I., Garcia, J. F., & Yubero, S. (2007). Parenting styles and adolescents' self-esteem in Brazil. *Psychological Reports, 100*(3), 731–745.

Martins, A., Ramalho, N., & Morin, E. (2010). A comprehensive meta-analysis of the relationship between emotional intelligence and health. *Personality and Individual Differences, 49*(6), 554–564.

Marzano, R. J., & Marzano, J. S. (2003). The key to classroom management. *Educational Leadership, 61*(1), 6–13.

Marzolf, D. P., & De Loache, J. S. (1994). Transfer in young children's understanding of spatial representations. *Child Development, 65*(1), 1–15.

Maslach, C., & Leiter, M. P. (2008). Early predictors of job burnout and engagement. *Journal of Applied Psychology, 93*(3), 498–512.

Maslow, A. H. (1954). *Motivation and personality.* New York: Harper & Brothers.

Maslow, A. H. (1979). *The journals of A. H. Maslow* (R. J. Lowry & B. G. Maslow, Eds.). Monterey, CA: Brooks/Cole.

Mason, M. A. (2007). The modern American stepfamily: Problems and possibilities. In S. J. Ferguson (Ed.), *Shifting the center: Understanding contemporary families* (3rd ed., pp. 588–605). New York: McGraw-Hill.

Mason, M. G. (2011). *Adulthood and aging.* Boston, MA: Allyn & Bacon.

Masoro, E. J., & Austad, S. N. (2011). *Handbook of the biology of aging* (7th ed.). San Diego, CA: Elsevier Academic Press.

Massad, S., Nieto, F. J., Palta, M., Smith, M., Clark, R., & Thabet, A. (2009). Mental health of children in Palestinian kindergartens: Resilience and vulnerability. *Child and Adolescent Mental Health, 14*(2), 89–96.

Mast, B. T., Zimmerman, J., & Rowe, S. V. (2009). What do we know about the aging brain? Implications for learning in late life. In C. M. Smith & N. DeFrates-Densch (Eds.), *Handbook of research on adult learning and development* (pp. 695–731). New York: Routledge/Taylor & Francis Group.

Mastropieri, D., & Hoffman, C. L. (2011). Chronic stress, allostatic load, and aging in nonhuman primates. *Development and Psychopathology, 23*(4). Special issue: *Allostatic load: Part 2*, 1187–1195.

Mata, R., Schooler, L. J., & Rieskamp, J. (2007). The aging decision maker: Cognitive aging and the adaptive selection of decision strategies. *Psychology and Aging, 22*(4), 796–810.

Mather, M., Canli, T., English, T., Whitefield, S., Wais, P., Ochsner, K., et al. (2004). Amygdala responses to emotionally valenced stimuli in older and younger adults. *Psychological Science, 15*(4), 259–263.

Mathieson, K., & Banerjee, R. (2010). Pre-school peer play: The beginnings of social competence. *Educational and Child Psychology, 27*(1), 9–20.

Maton, K. (2003). Community violence and children: Preventing exposure and reducing harm. *Investing in children, youth, families, and communities: Strength-based research and policy* (pp. 303–320). Washington, DC: American Psychological Association.

Matsumoto, D. (2000). *Culture and psychology* (2nd ed.). Belmont, CA: Wadsworth.

Matthews, K. A., Wing, R. R., Kuller, L. H., Meilahn, E. N., & Owens, J. F. (2000). Menopause as a turning point in midlife. In S. B. Manuck, R. Jennings, B. S. Rabin, & A. Baum (Eds.), *Behavior, health, and aging* (pp. 43–57). Mahwah, NJ: Erlbaum.

Mattock, K., Amitay, S., & Moore, D. R. (2010). Auditory development and learning. In C. Plack (Ed.), *Oxford handbook of auditory science: Auditory perception*. Oxford, UK: Oxford University Press.

Matzo, M., & Sherman, D. (2010). *Palliative care nursing: Quality care to the end of life.* New York: Springer Publishing.

Maughan, A., Cicchetti, D., Toth, S., & Rogosch, F. (2007). Early-occuring maternal depression and maternal negativity in predicting young children's emotion regulation and socioemotional difficulties. *Journal of Abnormal Child Psychology, 35*(5), 685–703.

Mayer, J. D., Salovey, P., Caruso, D. R., & Cherkasskiy, L. (2011). Emotional intelligence. In R. J. Sternberg & S. B. Kaufman (Eds.), *The Cambridge handbook of intelligence.* New York: Cambridge University Press.

Mayer, R. E. (2012). Information processing. In K. R. Harris, S. Graham, T. Urdan, C. B. McCormick, G. M. Sinatra, & J. Sweller (Eds.), *APA educational psychology handbook, vol. 1: Theories, constructs, and critical issues* (pp. 85–99). Washington, DC: American Psychological Association.

Mayeux, L., Houser, J. J., & Dyches, K. D. (2011). Social acceptance and popularity: Two distinct forms of peer status. In A. Cillessen, D. Schwartz, & L. Mayeux (Eds.), *Popularity in the peer system* (pp. 79–102). New York: Guilford Press.

Mayo Clinic. (2010a). Chorionic villus sampling. Retrieved from http://www.mayoclinic.com/health/chorionic-villus-sampling/MY00154

Mayo Clinic. (2010b). Thalidomide: Research advances in career and other conditions. Retrieved from http://www.mayoclinic.com/health/thalidomide/HQ01507

Mayo Clinic. (2011). VBAC (vaginal birth after C-section). Retrieved from http://www.mayoclinic.com/health/vbac/MY01143

Mayo Clinic. (2012). Miscarriage: Risk factors. Retrieved from http://www.mayoclinic.com/health/miscarriage/DS01105

McAdams, D. P. (2006). The redemptive self: Generativity and the stories Americans live by. *Research in Human Development, 3*(2–3), 81–100.

McAdams, D. P. (2008). Generativity, the redemptive self, and the problem of a noisy ego in American life. In H. A. Wayment & J. J. Bauer (Eds.), *Transcending self-interest: Psychological explorations of the quiet ego* (pp. 235–242). Washington, DC: American Psychological Association.

McAdams, D. P., & de St. Aubin, E. (1992). A theory of generativity and its assessment through self-report, behavioral acts, and narrative themes in autobiography. *Journal of Personality and Social Psychology, 62,* 1003–1015.

McAdams, D. P., & Olson, B. D. (2010). Personality development: Continuity and change over the life course. *Annual Review of Psychology, 61,* 517–542.

McAdoo, H. P. (1995). Stress levels, family help patterns, and religiosity in middle- and working-class African American single mothers. *Journal of Black Psychology, 21,* 424–449.

McBean, L. D., Forgac, T., & Finn, S. C. (1994). Osteoporosis: Visions for care and prevention—A conference report. *Journal of the American Dietetic Association, 94,* 668–671.

McCarthy, B. W., & Breetz, A. (2010). Confronting sexual trauma and enhancing adult sexuality. In C. B. Risen, S. E. Althof, S. B. Levine (Eds.), *Handbook of clinical sexuality for mental health* (2nd ed., pp. 295–310). New York: Routledge/Taylor & Francis Group.

McCartney, K., Burchinal, M., Clarke-Stewart., A., Bub, K. L., Owen, M. T., & Belsky, J. (2010). Testing a series of causal propositions relating time in child care to children's externalizing behavior. *Developmental Psychology, 46*(1), 1–17.

McClelland, D. C. (1955). Some social consequences of achievement motivation. In M. R. Jones (Ed.), *Nebraska Symposium on Motivation*: Vol. 3. Lincoln: University of Nebraska Press.

McCrae, R. R. (2009). The five-factor model of personality traits: Consensus and controversy. In P. J. Corr & G. Matthews (Eds.), *The Cambridge handbook of personality psychology* (pp. 148–161). New York: Cambridge University Press.

McCrae, R. R. (2011). Personality theories for the 21st century. *Teaching of Psychology, 38*(3), 209–214.

McCrae, R. R., & Costa, P. T. (2006). *Personality in adulthood: A five factor theory perspective* (2nd ed.). New York: Guilford Press.

McCrae, R. R., & Costa, P. T. (2008). The five factor theory of personality. In O. P. John, R. W. Robins, & L. A. Pervin (Eds.), *Handbook of personality: Theory and research* (3rd ed., pp. 159–181). New York: Guilford Press.

McCrae, R. R., Costa, P. T., Jr., Martin, T. A., Oryol, V. E., Rukavishnikov, A. A., Senin, I. G., et al. (2004b). Consensual validation of personality traits across cultures. *Journal of Research in Personality, 38,* 179–201.

McCredie, J. (2007). *Beyond thalidominde: Birth defects explained.* Ashland, OH: Royal Society of Medicine Press.

McDaniel, M. A., Einstein, G. O., & Jacoby, L. L. (2008). New considerations in aging and memory: The glass may be half full. In F. Craik & T. A. Salthouse (Eds.), *The handbook of aging and cognition* (3rd ed., pp. 251–310). New York: Psychology Press.

McDonald, L., & Stuart-Hamilton, I. (2003). Egocentrism in older adults: Piaget's three mountains task revisited. *Educational Gerontology, 29*(5), 417.

McDowell, M. A., Brody, D. J., & Hughes, J. P. (2007). Has age at menarche changed? Results from the National Health and Nutrition Examination Survey (NHANES) 1999–2004. *Journal of Adolescent Health, 40,* 227–231.

McGoldrick, M., & Carter, B. (2003). The family life cycle. In F. Walsh (Ed.), *Normal family processes: Growing diversity and complexity* (3rd ed., pp. 375–398). New York: Guilford Press.

McHale, S. M., Dariotis, J. K., & Kauh, T. J. (2003). Social development and social relationships in middle childhood. In R. Learner, M. A. Easterbrooks, & J. Mistry (Eds.), *Handbook of psychology: Vol. 6. Developmental psychology* (pp. 267–291). New York: Wiley.

McIlvane, J. M., Ajrouch, K. J., & Antonucci, T. C. (2007). Generational structure and social resources in mid-life: Influences on health and well-being. *Journal of Social Issues, 63*(4), 759–773.

McIntosh, T. (2012). *A social history of maternity and childbirth: Key terms in maternity care.* New York: Routledge.

McKee-Ryan, F., Song, Z., Wanberg, C. R., & Kinicki, A. J. (2005). Psychological and physical well-being during unemployment: A meta-analytic study. *Journal of Applied Psychology, 90*(1), 53–76.

McLanahan, S., & Beck, A. N. (2010). Parental relationships in fragile families. *The Future of Children, 20*(2), 17–37.

McLoyd, V. C. (1998). Economic disadvantage and child development. *American Psychologist, 53,* 185–204.

McLoyd, V. C. (2011). How money matters for children's socioemotional adjustment: Family processes and parental investment. In G. Carlo, L. J. Crockett, & M. A. Carranza (Eds.), *Health disparities in youth and families: Research and applications* (pp. 33–72). New York: Springer Science + Business Media.

McVary, K. T. (2007). Erectile dysfunction. *New England Journal of Medicine, 357*(24), 2472–2481.

Meadows, D., Elias, G., & Bain, J. (2000). Mothers' ability to identify infant's communicative acts consistently. *Journal of Child Language, 27,* 393–406.

Meaney, M. (2010). Epigenetics and the biological definition of gene x environment interactions. *Child Development, 81*(1), 41—79.

MedlinePlus. (2010). In vitro fertilization (IVF). Retrieved from http://www.nlm.nih.gov/medlineplus/ency/article/007279.htm

MedlinePlus. (2012a). Chorionic villus sampling. Retrieved from http://www.nlm.nih.gov/medlineplus/ency/article/003406.htm

MedlinePlus. (2012b). Pregnancy ultrasound. Retrieved from http://www.nlm.nih.gov/medlineplus/ency/article/003778.htm

Meeus, W. (2011). The study of adolescence identity formation 2000–2010: A review of longitudinal research. *Journal of Research on Adolescence, 21*(1), 75–94.

Meeus, W., Iedema, J., Helsen, M., & Vollebergh, W. (1999). Patterns of adolescent identity development: Review of literature and longitudinal analysis. *Developmental Review, 19,* 419–461.

Meeus, W., Keijsers, L., & Branje, S. (2010). On the progression and stability of adolescent identity formation: A five-wave longitudinal study in early-to-middle and middle-to-late adolescence. *Child Development, 81*(5), 1565–1581.

Mehta, C. M., & Strough, J. (2009). Sex segregation in friendships and normative contexts across the life span. *Developmental Review, 29*(3), 201–220.

Mejía-Arauz, R., Rogoff, B., Dexter, A., & Najafi, B. (2007). Cultural variation in children's social organization. *Child Development, 78*(3), 1001–1014.

Meij, L., Stroebe, M., Stroebe, W., Schut, H., Van Den Bout, J., & Van Der Heijden, P.G.M., et al. (2008). The impact of circumstances surrounding the death of a child on parents' grief. *Death Studies, 32*(3), 237–252.

Melinder, A., Forbes, D., Tronick, E., Fikke, L., & Gredeback, G. (2010). The development of the still-face effect: Mothers do matter. *Infant Behavior & Development, 33*(4), 472–481.

Meltzoff, A. N. (1988a). Infant imitation and memory: Nine-month-olds in immediate and deferred tests. *Child Development, 59,* 217–225.

Meltzoff, A. N. (1988b). Infant imitation after a 1-week delay: Long-term memory for novel acts and multiple stimuli. *Developmental Psychology, 24,* 470–476.

Meltzoff, A. N. (2000). Infancy: Learning and cognitive development. In A. E. Kazdin (Ed.), *Encyclopedia of psychology* (Vol. 4, pp. 275–278). Washington, DC: American Psychological Association.

Meltzoff, A. N. (2007). Infants' causal learning: Intervention, observation, imitation. In A. Gopnik & L. Schulz (Eds.), *Causal learning: Psychology, philosophy, and computation* (pp. 37–47). New York: Oxford University Press.

Meltzoff, A. N., & Borton, R. W. (1979). Intermodal matching by human neonates. *Nature, 282,* 403–404.

Meltzoff, A. N., & Moore, M. K. (1977). Imitation of facial and manual gestures by human neonates. *Science, 198,* 75–78.

Meltzoff, A. N., & Moore, M. K. (2002). Imitation, memory, and the representation of persons. *Infant Behavior and Development, 25*(1), 39.

Meltzoff, A. N., Waismeyer, A., & Gopnik, A. (2012). Learning about causes from people: Observational causal learning in 24-month-old infants. *Developmental Psychology,* doi: 10.1037/a0027440

Meltzoff, A. N., & Williamson, R. A. (2010). The importance of imitation for theories of social-cognitive development. In J. G. Bremner & T. D. Wachs (Eds.), *The Wiley Blackwell handbook of infant development* (2nd ed., pp. 345–364). Malden, MA: Wiley-Blackwell.

Merali, N. (2012). Arranged and forced marriages. In M. A. Paludi (Ed.), *The psychology of love* (Vols. 1–4, pp. 143–168). Santa Barbara, CA: Praeger/ABC-CLIO.

Mermin, G. B., Johnson, R. W., & Murphy, D. P. (2007). Why do boomers plan to work longer? *Journals of Gerontology Series B: Psychological Sciences and Social Sciences, 62B*(5), S286–S294.

Merrill, S. S., & Verbrugge, L. M. (1999). Health and disease in midlife. In S. L. Willis & J. D. Reid (Eds.), *Life in the middle: Psychological and social development in middle age* (pp. 77–103). San Diego, CA: Academic Press.

Merrill, S. S., & Verbrugge, L. M. (1999). Health and disease in midlife. In S. L. Willis & J. D. Reid (Eds.), *Life in the middle: Psychological and social development in middle age* (pp. 77–103). San Diego, CA: Academic Press.

Mesch, G. S., & Talmud, I. (2010). *Wired youth: The social work of adolescence in the information age.* New York: Routledge/Taylor & Francis Group.

Metzger, S., Erdman, P., & Ng, K-M. (2010). Attachment in cultural contexts. In P. Erdman & K-M. Ng (Eds.) (pp. 3-12). *Attachment: Expanding the cultural connections.* Routledge/Taylor & Francis Group: New York.

Meyer, I. H., & Northridge, M. E. (2007). *The health of sexual minorities: Public health perspectives on lesbian, gay, bisexual, and transgender populations.* New York: Springer.

Michael, R. T., Gagnon, J. H., Laumann, E. O., & Kolata, G. (1994). *Sex in America: A definitive survey.* Boston: Little, Brown.

Middleton, L. E., Lui, L., & Yaffe, K. (2010). Physical activity over the life course and its association with cognitive performance and impairment in old age. *Journal of the American Geriatrics Society, 58*(7), 1322–1326.

MIDUS. (2011). Midlife in the United States: A national longitudinal study of health & well-being. Retrieved from http://www.midus.wisc.edu/puboverview.php

Mijovic, A., & Turk, J. (2008). Behavioral phenotypes and child and adolescent mental health. *Pediatrics, 21*(1), 1–9.

Milevsky, A. (2011). *Sibling relationship in childhood and adolescence: Predictors and outcomes.* New York: Columbia University Press.

Miller, B. C., Bayley, B. K., Christensen, M., Leavitt, S. C., & Coyl, D. D. (2003). Adolescent pregnancy and childbearing. In G. R. Adams & M. D. Berzonsky (Eds.), *Blackwell handbook of adolescence* (pp. 415–449). Oxford, England: Basil Blackwell.

Miller, B. C., Norton, M. C., Fan, X., & Christopherson, C. R. (1998). Pubertal development, parental communication, and sexual values in relation to adolescent sexual behavior. *Journal of Early Adolescence, 18,* 27–52.

Miller, B. D. (1995). Precepts and practices: Researching identity formation among Indian Hindu adolescents in the United States. In J. J. Goodnow, P. J. Miller, & F. Kessel (Eds.), *New Directions for Child Development, 67,* 71–85. San Francisco: Jossey-Bass.

Miller, D. N. (2011). *Child and adolescent suicidal behavior: School-based prevention, assessment, and intervention.* New York: Guilford Press.

Miller, M. A., & Rahe, R. H. (1997). Life changes scaling for the 1990s. *Journal of Psychosomatic Research, 43,* 279–292.

Miller, M., & Hinshaw, S. R. (2012). Attention-deficit/hyperactivity disorder. In P. C. Kendall (Ed.), *Child and adolescent therapy: Cognitive-behavioral procedures* (4th ed., pp. 61–91). New York: Guilford Press.

Miller, P. H. (2010). *Theories of developmental psychology* (5th ed.). New York: Worth.

Miller, P. H. (2011a). Piaget's theory: Past, present, and future. In U. Goswami (Ed.), *The Wiley-Blackwell handbook of childhood cognitive development* (2nd ed., pp. 649–672). Malden, MA: Wiley Blackwell.

Miller, P. H. (2011b). *Theories of developmental psychology* (5th ed.). New York: Worth Publishers.

Miller, R. A. (1996). The aging immune system: Primer and prospectus. *Science, 273,* 70–74.

Miller-Perrin, C. L., & Perrin, R. D. (2007). *Child maltreatment: An introduction* (2nd ed.). Thousand Oaks, CA: Sage Publications.

Mills, J. L. (1999). Cocaine, smoking, and spontaneous abortion. *New England Journal of Medicine, 340,* 380–381.

Minnesota Center for Twin & Family Research. (2011). Retrieved from http://mctfr.psych.umn.edu

Misago, C., Umenai, T., Noguchi, M., Mori, T., & Mori, T. (2000). Satisfying birthing experiences in Japan. *The Lancet, 3555,* 2256.

Missotten, L. C., Luyckx, K., Branje, S., Vanhalst, J., & Goossens, L. (2011). Identity styles and conflict resolution styles: Associations in mother-adolescent dyads. *Journal of Youth and Adolescence, 40*(8), 972–982.

Mistry, J., & Saraswathi, T. S. (2003). The cultural contest of child development. In R. Learner, M. A. Easterbrooks, & J. Mistry (Eds.), *Handbook of psychology: Vol. 6. Developmental psychology* (pp. 267–291). New York: Wiley

Mistry, R. S., Lowe, E. D., Benner, A. D., & Chien, N. (2008). Expanding the family economic stress model: Insights from a mixed-methods approach. *Journal of Marriage and Family, 70*(1), 196–209.

Mistry, R., Vandewater, E., Huston, A., & McLoyd, V. (2002). Economic well-being and children's social adjustment: The role of family process in an ethnically diverse low-income sample. *Child Development, 73,* 935–951.

Mitchell, B. A. (2010). Happiness in midlife parental roles: a contextual mixed methods analysis. *Family Relations: An Interdisciplinary Journal of Applied Family Studies, 59*(3), 326–339.

Mitchell, B. A., & Lovegreen, L. D. (2009). The empty nest syndrome in midlife families: A multimethod exploration of parental gender differences and cultural dynamics. *Journal of Family Issues, 30*(12), 1651–1670.

Mitnick, D. M., Heyman, R. E., & Smith Slep, A. M. (2009). Changes in relationship satisfaction across the transition to parenthood: A meta-analysis. *Journal of Family Psychology, 23*(6), 848–852.

Moen, P., Sweet, S., & Hill, R. (2010). Risk, resilience, and life-course fit: Older couples' encores following job loss. In P. S. Fry & C. L. M. Keyes (Eds.), *New frontiers in resilient aging: Life-strengths and well-being in later life* (pp. 283–309). New York: Cambridge University Press.

Moerk, E. L. (2000). *The guided acquisition of first language skills*. Stamford, CT: Ablex Publishers.

Moilanen, K. L., Crockett, L. J., Raffaelli, M., & Jones, B. L. (2010). Trajectories of sexual risk from middle adolescence to early adulthood. *Journal of Research on Adolescence, 20*(1), 114–139.

Mokdad, A. H., Marks, J. S., Stroup, D. F., & Gerberding, J. L. (2004). Actual causes of death in the United States, 2000. *JAMA, 292*(10), 1238–1245.

Molenberghs, P., Cunnington, R., & Mattingley, J. B. (2009). Is the mirror neuron system involved in imitation? A short review and meta-analysis. *Neuroscience and Biobehavioral Reviews, 33*(7), 975–980.

Monsour, M. (2002). *Women and men as friends: Relationships across the life span in the 21st century*. Mahwah, NJ: Erlbaum.

Moody, H. R. (2009). *Aging: Concepts and controversies* (6th ed.) Thousand Oaks, CA: Pine Forge Press.

Moore III, W. E., Pfeifer, J. H., Mazziotta, J. C., & Iacoboni, M. (2012). Facing puberty: Associations between pubertal development and neural responses to affective facial displays. *Social cognitive and affective neuroscience, 7*(1), 35–43.

Moore, M. K., & Meltzoff, A. N. (2008). Factors affecting infants' manual search for occluded objects and the genesis of object permanence. *Infant Behavior and Development, 31*(2), 168–180.

Moore, M., Schemer, J., Paunonen, S. V., & Vernon, P. A. (2010). Genetic and environmental influences on verbal and nonverbal measures of the Big Five. *Personality and Individual Differences, 48*(8), 884–888.

Moore, T. M., Strauss, J. L., Herman, S., & Donatucci, C. F. (2003). Erectile dysfunction in early, middle, and late adulthood: Symptom patterns and psychosocial correlates. *Journal of Sex and Marital Therapy, 29*, 381–399.

Morgan, K. (2008). Sleep and insomnia in later life. In R. Woods & L. Clare (Eds.), *Handbook of the clinical psychology of ageing* (2nd ed., pp. 219–233). New York: John Wiley & Sons.

Morgan, M. (2007). What do young people learn about the world from watching television? In S. R. Mazzarella (Ed.), *20 questions about youth and the media* (pp. 153–166). New York: Peter Lang Publishing.

Morrongiello, B. A., Fenwick, K. D., & Chance, G. (1998). Cross-modal learning in newborn infants: Inferences about properties of auditory–visual events. *Infant Behavior and Development, 21*, 543–553.

Morrow, J. (2003). A place for one. *American Demographics, 25*(9), 19.

Moses, A. M. (2008). Impacts of television on young children's literacy development in the USA: A review of the literature. *Journal of Early Childhood Literacy, 8*(1), 67–102.

Moshman, D. (2009). Adolescence. In U. Muller, J. Carpendale, & L. Smith (Eds.), *The Cambridge companion to Piaget* (pp. 255–269). New York: Cambridge University Press.

Moshman, D. (2011). *Adolescent rationality and development: Cognition, morality, and identity* (3rd ed.) New York: Psychology Press.

Moss, E., Bureau, J., Cyr, C., Mongeau, C., & St-Laurent, D. (2004). Correlates of attachment of age 3: Construct validity of the preschool attachment classification system. *Developmental Psychology, 40*(3), 323–334.

Moulin, C. J. (2011). *Human memory*. Los Angeles, CA: SAGE Publications.

Moulin, C. J., & Gathercole, S. E. (2008). Memory changes across the lifespan. In G. Cohen & M. A. Conway (Eds.), *Memory in the real world* (3rd ed., pp. 305–326). New York: Psychology Press.

Mullineaux, P. Y., Deater, Deckard, K., Petrill, S. A., & Thompson, L. A. (2009). Parenting and child behavior problems: A longitudinal analysis of non-shared environment. *Infanct and Child Development, 18*, 133–148.

Mulvaney, M. K., & Mebert, C. J. (2007). Parental corporal punishment predicts behavior problems in early childhood. *Journal of Family Psychology, 21*(3), 389–397.

Muris, P. (2007). *Normal and abnormal fear and anxiety in children and adolescents*. Amsterdam; Boston: Elsevier.

Muris, P. (2010). Anxiety-related reasoning biases in children and adolescents. In J. A. Hadwin & A. P. Field (Eds.), *Information processing biases and anxiety: A developmental perspective* (pp. 21–45). Malden, MA: Wiley-Blackwell.

Murphy, M. P., & Partridge, L. (2008). Toward a control theory analysis of aging. *Annual Review of Biochemistry, 77*(1), 777–798.

Murphy, S. L., Xu, J., & Kochanek, K. D. (2012). Deaths and death rates by age, sex, race, and Hispanic origin, and age-adjusted death rates, by sex, race, and Hispanic origin: United States final 2009 and preliminary 2010. *Deaths: Preliminary data for 2010. National Vital Statistics Reports, 60*(4).

Murray, J. P. (2008). Media violence: The effects are both real and strong. *American Behavioral Scientist, 51*(8), 1212–1230.

Murray, V., Brody, G. H., Simons, R. L., Cutrona, C. E., & Gibbons, F. X. (2008). Disentangling ethnicity and context as predictors of parenting within rural African American families. *Applied Developmental Science, 12*(4), 202–210.

Murray-Close, D., & Crick, N. R. (2006). Mutual antipathy involvement: Gender and associations with aggression and victimization. *School Psychology Review, 35*(3), 472–492.

Murray-Close, D., Han, G., Cicchetti, D., Crick, N. R., & Rogosch, F. A. (2008). Neuroendocrine regulation and physical and relational aggression: The moderating roles of child maltreatment and gender. *Developmental Psychology, 44*(4), 1160–1176.

Murstein, B. I. (1982). Marital choice. In B. Wolman (Ed.), *Handbook of developmental psychology* (pp. 652–666). Englewood Cliffs, NJ: Prentice Hall.

Murstein, B. I. (1999). The relationship of exchange and commitment. In J. M. Adams & M. H. Jones (Eds.), *Handbook of interpersonal commitment and relationship stability* (pp. 205–219). New York: Kluwer Academic/Plenum.

Murstein, B. I., Chalpin, M. J., Heard, K. V., & Vyse, S. A. (1989). Sexual behavior, drugs, and relationship patterns on a college campus over thirteen years. *Adolescence, 24*, 125–139.

Mustanski, B. S. (2002). A critical review of recent biological research on human sexual orientation. *Annual Review of Sex Research, 13*, 89.

Myers, J., Gramzow, E., Ornstein, P. A., Wagner, L., Gordon, B. N., & Baker-Ward, L. (2003). Children's memory of a physical examination: A comparison of recall and recognition assessment protocols. *International Journal of Behavioral Development, 27*(1), 66–73.

Nagoshi, J. L., Adams, K. A., Terrell, H. K., Hill, E. D., Brzuzy, S., & Nagoshi, C. T. (2008). Gender differences in correlates of homophobia and transphobia. *Sex Roles, 59*(7–8), 521–531.

Nagy, E. (2008). Innate intersubjectivity: Newborns' sensitivity to communication disturbance. *Developmental Psychology, 44*(6), 1779–1784.

Nagy, T. F. (2011). Informed consent. In T. F. Nagy (Ed.), *Essential ethics for psychologists: A primer for understanding and mastering core issues* (pp. 89–104). Washington, DC: American Psychological Association.

Nakamura, J., & Csikszentmihalyi, M. (2009). Flow theory and research. In S. J. Lopez & C. R. Snyder (Eds.), *Oxford handbook of positive psychology* (2nd ed., pp. 195–206). New York: Oxford University Press.

Naninck, E. F. G., Lucassen, P. J., & Bakker, J. (2011). Sex differences in adolescent depression: Do sex hormones determine vulnerability? *Journal of Neuroendocrinology, 23*(5), 383–392.

Narvaez, D., Holter, A., & Vaydich, J. L. (2011). Moral devlepment. In A. S. Davis (Ed.), *Handbook of pediatric neuropsychology* (pp. 79–87). New York: Springer Publishing.

Nathani, S., Oller, D. K., & Neal, A. R. (2007). On the robustness of vocal development: An examination of infants with moderate-to-severe hearing loss and additional risk factors. *Journal of Speech, Language, and Hearing Research, 50*(6), 1425–1444.

National Alliance on Mental Illness (NAMI). (2012a). Facts on children's mental health in America. Retrieved from http://www.nami.org/Template.cfm?Section=federal_and_state_policy

National Alliance on Mental Health (NAMI) (2012b). Mental illness. Retrieved from http://www.nami.org/Template.cfm?Section=By_Illness&Template

National Alliance on Mental Illness (NAMI). (2012c). Mental illness: Facts and numbers. Retrieved from http://www.nami.org/

Template.cfm?Section=About_Mental_Illness&Templates=/ContentManagement/ContentDisplay.cfm&ContentID=53155

National Association of Anorexia Nervosa. (2012). Eating disorders statistics. Retrieved from http://www.anad.org/get-information/about-eating-disorders/

National Cancer Institute. (2012). BRCA1 and BRCA2: Cancer risk and genetic testing. Retrieved October 15, 2012 from http://www.cancer.gov/cancertopics/factsheet/Risk/BRCA.

National Center for Biotechnology Information (NCBI). (2011a). Genomes and maps. Retrieved from http://www.ncbi.nlm.nih.gov

National Center for Health Statistics (NCHS). (2007a). *Health, United States, 2007 with Chartbook on trends in the health of Americans.* Hyattsville, MD: author. Available online at http://www.cdc.gov/nchs/hus/htm

National Center for Health Statistics (NCHS). (2007b). *New CDC study finds no increase in obesity among adults; but levels still high.* Retrieved on January 30, 2009 from http://www.cdc.gov/nchs/pressroom/07newsreleases/obesity.htm

National Center for Health Statistics (NCHS). (2007c). *Teen birth rate rises for first time in 15 years.* Retrieved on December 31, 2008 from http://www.cdc. gov/nchs/pressroom/07newsreleases/teenbirth.htm

National Center for Health Statistics. (2008, April 14). Estimated pregnancy rates by outcome for the United States, 1990–2004. *National Vital Statistics Reports, 56*(15).

National Center for Health Statistics. (2010). Limitation of activity caused by chronic conditions: Working-age and older adults. *Health, United States, 2009: with special feature on medical technology,* Hyattsville, MD: Author.

National Center for Health Statistics. (2011a). *Health, United States, 2010: With special feature on death and dying.* Hyattsville, MD: Author.

National Center for Health Statistics. (2011b). Table 24. Age-adjusted death rates for selected causes of death, by sex, race, and Hispanic origin: United States, selected years 1950–2008. *Health, United States, 2011.* Hyattsville, MD: Author.

National Center for Health Statistics. (2011c). Table 29. Death rates for all causes, by sex, race, Hispanic origin, and age: United States, selected years 1950–2008. *Health, United States, 2011: With special feature on socioeconomic status and health.* Hyattsville, MD: Author.

National Center for Health Statistics. (2011d). Table 64: Percentage of high school students who ever had sexual intercourse and who had sexual intercourse for the first time before age 13 years, by sex—selected U.S. sites, Youth Risk Behavior Survey, 2011. *Health, United States, 2011: With special feature on socioeconomic status and health.* Hyattsville, MD: Author.

National Center for Health Statistics. (2011e). Table 67: Health risk behaviors among students in grades 9–12, by sex, grade level, race, and Hispanic origin: United States, selected years, 1991–2009. *Health, United States, 2011: With special feature on socioeconomic status and health.* Hyattsville, MD: Author.

National Center for Health Statistics (2011f). Table 74. Healthy weight, overweight, and obesity among persons 20 years of age and over, by selected characteristics: United States, selected years 1960–1962 through 2007–2010. *Health, United States, 2011: With special feature on socioeconomic status and health.* Hyattsville, MD: Author.

National Center for Health Statistics. (2012a). Contraceptive use in the past month, among women 15–44 years of age, by age, race, and Hispanic origin, and method of contraception: United States, selected years 1982–2008. *Health, United States, 2011: With special feature on socioeconomic status and health.* Hyattsville, MD: Author.

National Center for Health Statistics. (2012b). Death rates for suicide, by sex, race, Hispanic origin, and age: United States, selected years 1950–2008. *Health, United States, 2011: With special feature on socioeconomic status and health.* Hyattsville, MD: Author.

National Center for Health Statistics. (2012c). *Health, United States, 2011: With special feature on socioeconomic status and health.* Hyattsville, MD: Author.

National Center for Health Statistics. (2012d). Infant, neonatal, and postneonatal mortality rates: United States, 1998–2008. *Health, United States, 2011: With special feature on socioeconomic status and health.* Hyattsville, MD: Author.

National Center for Health Statistics. (2012e). Leading causes of death and numbers of deaths, by age: United States, 1980–2008. *Health, United States, 2011: With special feature on socioeconomic status and health.* Hyattsville, MD: Author.

National Center for Health Statistics. (2012f). Participation in leisure-time aerobic and muscle-strengthening activities that meet the 2008 federal Physical Activity Guidelines for adults 19 years of age and over, by selected characteristics: United States, selected years 1998–2010. *Health, United States, 2011* (p. 252). Hyattsville, MD: Author.

National Center for Health Statistics. (2012g). Prescription drugs. *Health, United States, 2011: With special feature on socioeconomic status and health.* Hyattsville, MD: Author.

National Center for Health Statistics. (2012h). Table 22. Life expectancy at birth, at 65 years of age, and at 75 years of age, by sex, race, and Hispanic origin: United States, selected years 1900–2009. *Health, United States, 2011: With special feature on socioeconomic status and health.* Hyattsville, MD: Author.

National Center for Health Statistics. (2012i). Table 75. Obesity among children and adolescents 2–19 years of age, by selected characteristics: United States, selected years 1963–1965 through 2007–2010. *Health, United States, 2011: With special feature on socioeconomic status and health.* Hyattsville, MD: Author.

National Center for Health Statistics. (2012j). Table 99. Prescription drug use in the past 30 days, by sex, age, race and Hispanic origin: United States, selected years 1988–1994 through 2005–2008. *Health, United States, 2011: With special feature on socioeconomic status and health.* Hyattsville, MD: Author.

National Heart and Lung Institute. (2012). What is asthma? Retrieved from http://www.nhlbi.nih.gov/health/prof/lung/asthma/naci/asthma-info

National Hospice and Palliative Care Organization (NHPCO). (2012). *Hospice care in America, 2011 Edition.* Alexandra, VA: Author. Retrieved from http://www.nhpco.org/files/public/Statistics_Research/2011_Facts_Figures.pdf

National Institute of Child Health & Human Development. (2012). NICHD study of early child care and youth development. Retrieved from http://www.nichd.nih.gov/research/supported/seccyd/overview.cfm

National Institute of Child Health and Human Development (NICHD). (2006, September). *NICHD Study of Early Child Care and Youth Development (SECCYD).* Retrieved on November 24, 2008 from http://www.nichd.nih .gov/research/supported/seccyd.cfm

National Institute of Child Health and Human Development (NICHD). (2006, September). *Sudden Infant Death Syndrome (SIDS).* Retrieved on November 18, 2008 from http://www.nichd.nih.gov/health/topics/ Sudden_Infant_Death_Syndrome.cfm

National Institute of Child Health and Human Development. (2009). *The NICHD study of early child care and youth development: Findings for children up to age 4/12 years.* Accessed online on June 12, 2009 at http://nichd.nih.gov.

National Institute of Mental Health. (2012). Attention deficit hyperactivity disorder (ADHD). Retrieved from http://www.nimh.nih.gov/health/publications/attention-deficit-hyperactivity

National Institute of Neurological Disorders and Stroke. (2010). NINDS shaken baby syndrome information page. Retrieved from http://www.ninds.nih.gov/disorders/shakenbaby/shakenbaby.htm

National Institute of Neurological Disorders and Stroke. (2012). Autism fact sheet. Retrieved from http://www.ninds.nih.gov/disorders/autism/detail_autism.htm

National Institute on Drug Abuse (NIDA). (2008). *NIDA InfoFacts: Marijuana.* Retrieved on January 7, 2009 from http://www.nida.nih.gov/infofacts/marijuana.html

National Institute on Mental Health (NIMH). (2012). Suicide in the U.S.: Statistics and prevention. Retrieved from http://www.nimh.nih.gov/health/publications/suicide-in-the-us-statistics

National Institutes of Health (NIH). (2005, January). *International HumanGenome Sequencing Consortium describes finished human genome sequence.* Retrieved on January 15, 2005, from http://www.genome.gov/pfv.cfm?pageid=12513430

National Institutes of Health (NIH). (2005, October). *Osteoporosis and Related Bone Diseases National Research Center (2005). Osteoporosis Overview.*

Retrieved on October, 2005 from http://www.osteo.org/newfile.asp?doc=r106i&doctitle=Osteoporosis[]Overview[]%2D[]HTML[]Version&doctype=HTML[]Fact[]Sheet

National Institutes of Health. (2011a). Fragile X syndrome. Retrieved from http://www.nlm.nih.gov/medlineplus/fragilexsyndrome.html

National Institutes of Health. (2011b). Genetic disorders, genomics, and healthcare. Retrieved from http://www.genome.gov

National Institutes of Health. (2012a). Falls and older adults. Retrieved from http://www.nihseniorhealth.gov/falls/aboutfalls/01.html

National Institutes of Health. (2012b). Hormone replacement therapy. Retrieved from http://www.nichd.nih.gov/health/topics/Hormone_Replacement_Therapy.cfm

Nave-Herz, R. (1997). Still in the nest. *Journal of Family Issues, 18*(6), 671–689.

Neikrug, A. B., & Ancoli-Israel, S. (2010). Sleep disorders in the older adult—a mini-review. *Gerontology, 56*(2), 181–189.

Neil, P. A., Chee-Ruiter, C., Scheier, C., Lewkowicz, D. J., & Shimojo, S. (2006). Development of multisensory spatial integration and perception in humans. *Developmental Science, 9* (5), 454–464.

Neill. J. (2009). *The origins and role of same-sex relations in human societies*. Jefferson, NC: McFarland & Co.

Nelson, C. A. (1999). Neural plasticity and human development. *New Directions in Psychological Science, 8*(2), 42–45.

Nelson, C. A., & de Haan, M. (1996). Neural correlates of infants' visual responsiveness to facial expression of emotion. *Developmental Psychobiology, 29*, 577–595.

Nelson, C. A., de Haan, M., & Thomas, K. M. (2006). *Neuroscience of cognitive development: The role of experience and The developing brain*. Hoboken, NJ: Wiley.

Nelson, J. K., & Bennett, C. (2008). Introduction: Special issue on attachment. *Clinical Social Work Journal, 36*(1), 3–7.

Nelson, L. J., Padilla-Walker, L. M., Christensen, K. J., Evans, C. A., & Carroll, J. S. (2011). Parenting in emerging adulthood: An examination of parenting clusters and correlates. *Journal of Youth and Adolescence, 40*(6), 730–743.

Nelson, T. D. (2009). Ageism. In T. D. Nelson (Ed.), *Handbook of prejudice, stereotyping, and discrimination* (pp. 431–440). New York: Psychology Press.

Nelson, T. D. (2011). Ageism: The strange case of prejudice against the older you. In R. L. Wiener & S. L. Willborn (Eds.), *Disability and aging discrimination: Perspectives in law and psychology* (pp. 37–47). New York: Springer Science + Business Media.

Ness, R. B., Grisson, J. A., Hirshinger, N., Markovic, N., Shaw, L. M., Day, N. L., et al. (1999). Cocaine and tobacco use and the risk of spontaneous abortion. *New England Journal of Medicine, 340*, 333–339.

Nettelbeck, T., & Burns, N. R. (2010). Processing speed, working memory and reasoning ability from childhood to old age. *Personality and Individual Differences, 48*(4), 379–384.

Netting, N. S. (2010). Marital ideoscapes in 21st-century India: Creative combinations of love and responsibility. *Journal of Family Issues, 31*(6), 707–726.

Neugarten, B. L., & Brown-Rezanka, L. (1996). Midlife women in the 1980s. In B. L. Neugarten & D. A. Neugarten, *The meaning of age: Selected papers of Bernice L. Neugarten* (pp. 160–175). Chicago: University of Chicago Press.

Neugarten, B. L., & Neugarten, D. L. (1996). *The meanings of age: The selected papers of Bernice L. Neugarten.* Chicago: University of Chicago Press.

Neumark-Sztainer, D., Wall, M., Larson, N. I., Eisenberg, M. E., & Loth, K. (2011). Dieting and disordered eating behaviors from adolescence to young adulthood: Findings from a 10-year longitudinal study. *Journal of American Dietetic Association, 111*(7), 1004–1011.

New, R. S. (1989). The family context of Italian infant care. *Early Child Development and Care, 50*, 99–108.

New, R. S. (2008). Child's play in Italian perspective. In R. A. LeVine & R. S New (Eds.), *Anthropology and child development: A cross-cultural reader* (pp. 213–226). Malden, MA: Blackwell Publishing.

Newell, K. M., Vaillancourt, D. E., & Sosnoff, J. J. (2006). Aging, complexity, and motor performance. In J. E. Birren & K. Schaire (Eds.), *Handbook of the psychology of aging* (6th ed., pp. 163–182). Amsterdam, Netherlands: Elsevier.

Newland, L. A., Coyl, D. D., & Freeman, H. (2008). Predicting preschoolers' attachment security from fathers' involvement internal working models, and use of social support. *Early Child Development and Care, 178*(7/8), 785–801.

Newman, B. M. (1982). Midlife development. In B. Wolman (Ed.), *Handbook of developmental psychology* (pp. 617–625). Englewood Cliffs, NJ: PrenticeHall.

Newman, K. (2003). *A different shade of gray: Midlife and beyond in the inner city.* New York: New Press.

Newman, K. S. (2006). *A different shade of gray: Midlife and beyond in the inner city.* New York: New Press.

Newman, L. S. (1990). Intentional and unintentional memory in young children: Remembering vs. playing. *Journal of Experimental Child Psychology, 50*, 243–258.

Newton, E., & Jenvey, V. (2011). Play and theory of mind: Associations with social competence in young children. *Early Child Development and Care, 181*(6), 761–773.

Newton, N. J., & Stewart, A. J. (2012). In S. K. Whitbourne & M. J. Sliwinski (Eds.), *The Wiley-Blackwell handbook of adulthood and aging* (pp. 211–235). Malden, MA: Wiley-Blackwell.

Nichols, B. (1994). *Moving and learning: The elementary school physical education experience.* St. Louis, MO: Times Mirror/Mosby.

Nicoladis, E. (1999). "Where is my brush-teeth?" Acquisition of compound nouns in a French–English bilingual child. *Bilingualism, 2*, 245–256.

Nicoladis, E. (2008). Bilingualism and language cognitive development. In J. Altarraba & Heredia, R. R. (Eds.), *An introduction to bilingualism: Principles and processes* (pp. 167–181). Mahwah, NJ: Lawrence Erlbaum Associates.

Nicolopoulou, A. (2006). The interplay of play and narrative in children's development: Theoretical reflections and concrete examples. In A. Göncü & S. Gaskins (Eds.), *Play and development: Evolutionary, sociocultural, and functional perspectives* (pp. 247–273). Mahwah, NJ: Erlbaum.

Nihiser, A. J., Lee, S. M., Wechsler, H., McKenna, M., Odom, E., Reinold, C., et al. (2007). Body mass index measurement in schools. *Journal of School Health, 77*(10), 651–671.

Niles, S. G., Jacob, C. J., Nichols, L. M. (2010). Career development and self-esteem. In M. H. Guindon (Ed.), *Self-esteem across the lifespan: Issues and interventions* (pp. 249–262). New York: Routledge/Taylor & Francis Group.

Nilsson, L., & Hamberger, L. (2009). *A child is born* (5th ed.). London: Jonathan Cape.

Nisbett, R. E., Aronson, J., Blair, C., Dickens, W., Flynn, J., Halpern, D. F., & Turkheimer, E. (2012). Intelligence: New findings and theoretical developments. *American Psychologist, 67*(2), 130–159.

Norbis, S. S. (2004) *Different and alike (Diferentes y semejantes): An ethnographic study of language use in a dramatic play center.* Unpublished doctoral dissertation completed at the University of Massachusetts, Amherst.

North American Menopause Society (NAMS). (2012). Hormone therapy for women in 2012. Retrieved from http://www.menopause.org/psht12patient.pdf

Norton, R. D. (1994). Adolescent suicide: Risk factors and countermeasures. *Journal of Health Education, 25*, 358–361.

Nottebohm, F. (2002). Neuronal replacement in the adult brain. *Brain Research Bulletin, 57*, 737–749.

Nucci, L. P., & Gingo, M. (2011). The development of moral reasoning. In U. Goswami (Ed.), *The Wiley-Blackwell handbook of childhood cognitive development* (2nd ed., pp. 420–444). Malden, MA: Wiley-Blackwell.

Nugent, J. K. (1994, November 6). Cross-cultural studies of child development:Implications for clinicians. *Zero to Three.*

Nugent, J. K., & Brazelton, T. B. (2000). Preventive infant mental health: Uses of the Brazelton scale. In J. D. Osofsky & H. E. Fitzgerald (Eds.), *Handbook of infant mental health: Vol. 2. Early intervention, evaluation, and assessment* (pp. 157–202). New York: Wiley.

Nugent, J. K., Greene, S., & Mazor, K. (1990, October). *The effects of maternal alcohol and nicotine use during pregnancy on birth outcome.* Paper presented at Bebe XXI Simposio Internacional, Lisbon, Portugal.

Nugent, J. K., Keefer, C. H., Minear, S., Johnson, L. C., & Blanchard, Y. (2007). *Understanding newborn behavior and early relationships: The Newborn Behavioral Observations (NBO) systems handbook.* Baltimore: Paul H. Brookes Publishing Co.

Nugent, J. K., Petrauskas, B. J., & Brazelton, T. B. (2009). *The newborn as a person: Enabling health infant development worldwide.* Hoboken, NJ: Wiley.

Nunner-Winkler, G. (2009). Moral motivation from childhood to early adulthood. In W. Schneider & M. Bullock (Eds.), *Human development from early childhood to early adulthood: Findings from a 20 year longitudinal study* (pp. 91–118). New York: Psychology Press.

Nurse, A. D. (2009). *Physical development in the early years.* New York: Routledge.

Nurse-Family Partnership. (2012). Nurse family partnership: Helping first-time parents succeed. Retrieved from http://www.nursefamilypartnership.org/

Nydegger, C. N., & Mitteness, L. S. (1996). Midlife: The prime of fathers. In C. D. Ryff & M. M. Seltzer (Eds.), *The parental experiment in midlife* (pp. 533–559). Chicago: University of Chicago Press.

O'Boyle, E. H., Humphrey, R. H., Pollack, J. M., Hawver, T. H., & Story, P. A. (2011). The relation between emotional intelligence and job performance. *Journal of Organizational Behavior, 32*(5), 788–818.

O'Brien, M., & Nagle, K. J. (1987). Parents' speech to toddlers: The effect of play context. *Journal of Language Development, 14,* 269–279.

O'Brien, M., Nader, P. R., Houts, R. M., Bradley, R., Friedman, S. L., Belsky, J., et al. (2007). The ecology of childhood overweight: A 12-year longitudinal analysis. *International Journal of Obesity, 31*(9), 1469–1478.

O'Callaghan, F. V., O'Callaghan, M., Najman, J. M., Williams, G. M., & Bor, W. (2007). Prenatal alcohol exposure and attention, learning and intellectual ability at 14 years: A prospective longitudinal study. *Early Human Development, 83*(2), 115–123.

O'Connor, P. G., & Schottenfeld, R. S. (1998). Medical progress: Patients with alcohol problems. *New England Journal of Medicine, 338,* 592–602.

O'Dougherty Wright, M. (2007). *Childhood emotional abuse: Mediating and moderating processes affecting long-term impact.* Binghamton, NY: Haworth Maltreatment and Trauma Press.

Oak Ridge National Laboratory. (2008). *The science behind the Human Genome Project.* Retrieved November 10, 2008 from http://www.ornl.gov/sci/techresources/Human_Genome/project/info.shtml

Oak Ridge National Laboratory. (2012). Gene testing. Retrieved on October 15, 2012 from http://www.ornl.gov/sci/techresources/Human_Genome/medicine/genetest.shtml.

de Jong et al., 2011; Reference should be: de Jong, A, et al. (2011). Advances in prenatal screening: The ethical dimension. *Nature reviews genetics, 12* (9), 657-663.

Oakes, L. M. (2010). Using habituation of looking to time to assess mental processes in infancy. *Journal of Cognition and Development, 11*(3), 255–268.

Oakes, L. M., & Madole, K. L. (2000). The future of infant categorization research: A process-oriented approach. *Child Development, 71,* 119–126.

Oakes, L. M., Cashon, C. H., Cassasola, M., & Rakison, D. H. (2011). *Infant perception and cognition: Recent advances, emerging theories, and future directions.* New York: Oxford University Press.

Obeidallah, D., Brennan, R. T., Brooks-Gunn, J., & Earls, F. (2004). Links between pubertal timing and neighborhood contexts: Implications for girls' violent behavior. *Journal of the American Academy of Child and Adolescent Psychiatry, 43*(12), 1460–1468.

Ocampo, K. A., Knight, G. P., & Bernal, M. E. (1997). The development of cognitive abilities and social identities in children: The case of ethnic identity. *International Journal of Behavioral Development, 21,* 479–500.

Ochs, A., Newberry, J., Lenhardt, M., & Harkins, S. (1985). Neural and vestibular aging associated with falls. In J. E. Birren & K. W. Schaie (Eds.), *Handbook of the psychology of aging* (2nd ed., pp. 378–399). New York: Van Nostrand Reinhold.

Offer, D., Ostrov, E., Howard, K., & Atkinson, R. (1988). *The teenage world:Adolescents' self-image in ten countries.* New York: Plenum.

Offer, S., & Schneider, B. (2011). Revisiting the gender gap in time-use patterns: Multitasking and well-being among mothers and fathers in dual-earner families. *American Sociological Review, 76*(6), 809–833.

Offerhaus, L. (1997). *Drugs for the elderly: Second edition.* Copenhagen: WHO Regional Publications: European Series, No. 71.

Ogden, C. L., Carroll, M. D., Kit, B. K., & Flegal, K. M. (2012). *Prevalence of obesity in the United States, 2009–2010. NCHS Data Brief No. 82.*

Okamura, H., So, K., & Yamaguchi, M. K. (2007). Development of chromatic induction in infancy. *Infant and Child Development, 16*(6), 629–648.

Okanda, M., Moriguchi, Y., & Itakura, S. (2010). Language and cognitive shifting: Evidence from young monolingual and bilingual children. *Psychological Reports, 107*(1), 68–78.

Olds, D. L. (2010a). The nurse-family partnership. In B. M. Lester & J. D. Sparrow (Eds.), *Nurturing children and families: Building on the legacy of T. Berry Brazleton* (pp. 192–203). Malden, MA: Wiley-Blackwell.

Olds, D. L. (2010b). The nurse-family partnership: From trials to practice. In A. J. Reynolds, A. J. Rolnick, M. M. Englund, & J. A. Temple (Eds.), *Childhood programs and practices in the first decade of life: A human capital integration* (pp. 49–75). New York: Cambridge University Press.

Olshansky, S. J., Passaro, D. J., Hershow, R. C., Layden, J., Carnes, B. A., & Brody, J., et al. (2005). A potential decline in life expectancy in the United States in the 21st century. *New England Journal of Medicine, 352*(11), 1138–1145.

Olsho, L. W., Harkins, S. W., & Lenhardt, M. L. (1985). Aging and the auditory system. In J. E. Birren & K. W. Schaie (Eds.), Handbook of the psychology of aging (2nd ed., pp. 332–377). New York: Van Nostrand Reinhold.

Omoto, C. K., & Lurquin, P. F. (2004). *Genes and DNA: A beginner's guide to genetics and its applications.* New York: Columbia University Press.

Ong, A. D., Fuller-Rowell, T. E., & Bonanno, G. A. (2010). Prospective predictors of positive emotions following spousal loss. *Psychology and Aging, 25*(3), 653–660.

Orr, R., De Vos, N. J., Singh, N. A., Ross, D. A., Stavrinos, T. M., & Fiatarone-Singh, M.A. (2006). Power training improves balance in healthy older adults. *Journals of Gerontology Series A: Biological Sciences and Medical Sciences, 61A*(1), 78–85.

Orr, R., Raymond, J., & Singh, M. (2008). Efficacy of progressive resistance training on balance performance in older adults. *Sports Medicine, 38*(4), 317–343.

Ortega, S., Beauchemin, A., & Kaniskan, R. (2008). Building resiliency in families with young children exposed to violence: The safe start initiative pilot study. *Best Practices in Mental Health: An International Journal, 4*(1), 48–64.

Orth, U., Robins, R. W., & Widaman, K. F. (2012). Life-span development of self-esteem and its effects on important life outcomes. *Journal of Personality and Social Psychology, 102*(6), 1271–1288.

Osofsky, J. D. (2011). Young children and disasters: Lessons learned from Hurricane Katrina about the impact of disasters and postdisaster recovery. In J. Osofsky (Ed.), *Clinical work with traumatized young children* (pp. 295–312). New York: Guilford Press.

Ossa, K. L., & Crews, D. E. (2006). Biological and genetic theories of the process of senescence throughout life. In C. Sauvin-Dugerdil, H. Leridon, & N. Mascie-Taylor (Eds.), *Human clocks: The bio-cultural meanings of age* (pp. 61–84). New York: Peter Lang Publishing.

Ossorio, P. N. (2011). Myth and mystification: The science of race and IQ. In S. Krimsky & K. Sloan (Eds.), *Race and the genetic revolution: Science, myth, and culture* (pp. 173–194). New York: Columbia University Press.

Ostrov, J. M., Gentile, D. A., & Crick, N. R. (2006). Media exposure, aggression and prosocial behavior during early childhood: A longitudinal study. *Social Development, 15*(4), 620–626.

Overton, Willis, F. (2010). Life-span development: Concepts and issues. In W. F. Overton & R. M. Lerner (Eds.), *The handbook of life-span development, Vol. 1: Cognition, biology, and methods* (pp. 1–29). Hoboken, NJ: John Wiley & Sons Inc.

Owens, R. E. (2008). *Language development: An introduction* (7th ed.). Boston: Pearson/Allyn and Bacon.

Özyürek, A., Kita, S., Allen, S., Brown, A., Furman, R., & Ishizuka, T. (2008). Development of cross-linguistic variation in speech and gesture: Motion events in English and Turkish. *Developmental Psychology, 44*(4), 1040–1054.

Pace, C. S., Zavattini, G. C., D'Alessio, M., & Zavattini, G. C. (2012). Continuity and discontinuity of attachment patterns: A short-term longitudinal pilot study using a sample of late-adapted children and their adoptive mothers. *Attachment & Human Development, 14*(1), 45–61.

Padavic, I., & Reskin, B. F. (2002). Women and men at work (2nd ed.). Thousand Oaks, CA: Pine Forge Press.

Padma-Nathan, H., & Giuliano, F. (2001). Oral drug therapy for erectile dysfunction. *The Urologic Clinics of North America,* 28, 321–334.

Paduch, D. A., Bolyakov, A., Beardsworth, A., & Watts, S. D. (2012). Factors associated with ejaculatory and orgasmic dysfunction in men with erectile dysfunction: Analysis of clinical trials involving the phosphodiesterase type 5 inhibitor tadlafil. *BJU International, 109,* 1060–1067. doi: 10.1111/j.1464–410X.2011.1054.x

Pak, R., Czaja, S. J., Sharit, J., Rogers, W. A., & Fisk, A. D. (2008). The role of spatial abilities and age in performance in an auditory computer navigation task. *Computers in Human Behavior, 24*(6), 3045–3051.

Pal, S., Shyam, R., & Singh, R. (1997). Genetic analysis of general intelligence "g": A twin study. *Personality and Individual Differences,* 22, 779–780.

Palencia, R., Gafni, A., Hannah, M. E., Ross, S., Willan, A., Hewson, S. et al. (2006). The costs of planned cesarean versus planned vaginal birth in the Term Breech Trial. *Canadian Medical Association Journal, 174*(8), 1–11.

Palladino Schultheiss, D. E. (2008). Current status and future agenda for the theory, research, and practice of childhood career development. *Career Development Quarterly, 57*(1), 7–24.

Palmore, E. (2001). The Ageism Survey: First findings. *The Gerontologist, 42,* 572–575.

Paoloni-Giacobino, A. & Chaillet, J. R. (2004). Genomic imprinting and assisted reproduction. *Reproductive Health, 1*(6), 1–7.

Papadatou-Pastou, M., Martin, M., Munafò, M. R., & Jones, G. V. (2008). Sex differences in left-handedness: A meta-analysis of 144 studies. *Psychological Bulletin, 134*(5), 677–699.

Papousek, H. (1961). Conditioned head rotation reflexes in infants in the first three months of life. *Acta Paediatrica Scandanavica, 50,* 565–576.

Parade, S. H., Supple, A. J., & Helms, H. M. (2012). Parenting during childhood predicts relationship satisfaction in young adulthood: A prospective longitudinal perspective. *Marriage & Family Review, 48*(2), 150–169.

Paris, S. G., Yeung, A. S., Wong, H. M., & Luo, S. W. (2012). Global perspectives on education during middle childhood. In K. R. Harris, S. Graham, T. Urdan, A. G. Bus, S. Major, & H. L. Swanson (Eds.), *APA educational psychology handbook, Vol. 3: Application to teaching and learning* (pp. 23–41). Washington, DC: American Psychological Association.

Park, A. (2011). *The stem cell hope: How stem cell medicine can change our lives.* New York: Hudson Street Press.

Park, C. C. (2011). Young children making sense of racial and ethnic differences: A sociocultural approach. *American Educational Research Journal, 48*(2), 387–420.

Park, D. C., & Bischof, G. N. (2011). Neuroplasticity, aging, and cognitive function. In K. Warner Schaie & S. L. Willis (Eds.), *Handbook of the psychology of aging* (7th ed., pp. 109–119). San Diego, CA: Elsevier Academic Press.

Park, D. C., & Reuter-Lorenz, P. (2009). The adaptive brain: Aging and neurocognitive scaffolding. *Annual Review of Psychology, 60*(1), 173–196.

Park, H. (2008). Public policy and the effect of sibship on educational achievement: A comparative study of 20 countries. *Social Science Research, 37*(3), 874–887.

Parke, R. D. (1996). *Fatherhood.* Cambridge, MA: Harvard University Press.

Parkhurst, J. T., & Asher, S. R. (1992). Peer rejection in middle school: Subgroup differences in behavior, loneliness, and interpersonal concerns. *Developmental Psychology, 28,* 244–254.

Pascalis, O., & Kelly, D. J. (2009). The origins of face processing in humans: Phylogeny and ontogeny. *Perspectives on Psychological Science, 4*(2), 200–209.

Pascalis, O., de Haan, M., Nelson, C. A., & de Schonen, S. (1998). Long-term recognition memory for faces assessed by visual impaired comparison in 3- and 6-month-old infants. *Journal of Experimental Psychology: Learning, Memory, and Cognition, 24,* 249–260.

Pascalis, O., Kelly, D. J., & Schwarzer, G. (2009). Neural bases of the development of face processing. In M. de Haan & M. R. Gunnar (Eds.), *Handbook of developmental social neuroscience* (pp. 63–86). New York: Guilford Press.

Passow, S., Westerhausen, R., Wartenburger, I., Hugdahl, K., Keekeren, H. R., Lindenberger, U., & Li, S. (2012). Human aging compromised attentional control of auditory perception. *Psychology and Aging, 27*(1), 99–105.

Pasternak, C. (2003). *Quest: The essence of humanity.* Hoboken, NJ. Wiley.

Patrinos, A. (2004). "Race" and the human genome. *Nature Genetics, 36,* S1–S2.

Patterson, C. J. (2006). Children of lesbian and gay parents. *Current Directions in Psychological Science, 15*(5), 241–244.

Patterson, C. J. (2008). Sexual orientation across the life span: Introduction to the special section. *Developmental Psychology, 44*(1), 1–4.

Patton, W., & McMahon, M. (2006). The systems theory framework of career development and counseling: Connecting theory and practice. *International Journal for the Advancement of Counselling, 28*(2), 153–166.

Paulsen, D. J., Carter, R., Platt, M. L., Huettel, S. A., & Brannon, E. M. (2012). Neurocognitive development of risk aversion from early childhood to adulthood. *Frontiers in Human Neuroscience, 5.*

Paulussen-Hoogeboom, M., Stams, G., Hermanns, J., Peetsma, T., & Van Den Wittenboer, G. (2008). Parenting style as a mediator between children's negative emotionality and problematic behavior in early childhood. *Journal of Genetic Psychology, 169*(3), 209–226.

Paus, T. (2010). Mapping brain maturation and development of social cognition during adolescence. In C. L. Cooper, J. Field, U. Goswami, R. Jenkins, & B.J. Sahakian (Eds.) *Mental capital and wellbeing.* (pp. 87-99). London: Wiley-Blackwell.

Payne, V. G., & Isaacs, L. D. (2012). *Human motor development* (8th ed.). New York: McGraw-Hill.

Pearlin, L. I., Pioli, M. F., & McLaughlin, A. E. (2001). Care giving by adult children: Involvement, role disruption, and health. In R. H. Binstock & L. K. George (Eds.), *Handbook of aging and the social sciences* (5th ed., pp. 238–254). San Diego, CA: Academic Press.

Peay, H., & Austin, J. (2011). *How to talk with families about genetics and psychiatric illness.* New York: W. W. Norton.

Peck, R. C. (1968). Psychological developments in the second half of life. In B. L. Neugarten (Ed.), *Middle age and aging* (pp. 88–92). Chicago: University of Chicago Press.

Pedersen, S., Vitaro, F., Barker, E. D., & Borge, A. (2007). The timing of middlechildhood peer rejection and friendship: Linking early behavior to earlyadolescent adjustment. *Child Development, 78*(4), 1037–1051.

Pellegrino, J. E., & Pellegrino, L. (2008). Fetal alcohol syndrome and related disorders. In P. J. Accardo (Ed.), *Capute and Accardo's neurodevelopmental disabilities in infancy and childhood: Vol. 1: Neurodevelomental diagnosis and treatment* (3rd ed., 269–284). Baltimore, MD: Paul H. Brookes Publishing.

Pellegrini, A. D., Roseth, C. J., Ryzin, M. J., & Solberg, D. W. (2011). Popularity as a form of social dominance: An evolutionary perspective. In A. Cillessen, D. Schwartz, & L. Mayeux (Eds.), *Popularity in the peer system* (pp. 123–139). New York: Guilford Press.

Pelletz, L. (1995). *The effects of an interactive, interpersonal curriculum upon the development of self in seventh-grade girls.* Unpublished doctoral dissertation, University of Massachusetts, Amherst.

Peltonen, K., Qouta, S., El Sarraj, E., & Punamaki, R. (2010). Military trauma and social development: The moderating and mediating roles of peer and sibling relations in mental health. *International Journal of Behavioral Development, 34*(6), 554–563.

Penn, R. (2011). Arranged marriages in Western Europe: Media representatives and social reality. *Journal of Comparative Family Studies, 42*(5), 637–650.

Peplau, L. A., & Beals, K. P. (2002). Lesbians, gays, and bisexuals in relationships. In J. Worell (Ed.) *Encyclopedia of women and gender.* San Diego, CA: Academic Press.

Pergament, E., Toydemir, P. B., & Fiddler, M. (2007). Sex ratio: A biological perspective of "Sex and the City." *Reproductive Biomedicine Online, 14*(1). Retrieved from http://www.ncbi.nlm.nih.gov/pubmed/12470545

Perkins, D. F., & Borden, L. M. (2003). Positive behaviors, problem behaviors, and resiliency in adolescence. In R. Learner, M. A. Easterbrooks, & J. Mistry (Eds.), *Handbook of psychology: Vol. 6. Developmental psychology* (pp. 373–394). New York: Wiley.

Perkins, D. F., & Borden, L. M. (2003). Positive behaviors, problem behaviors, and resiliency in adolescence. In R. Learner, M. A. Easterbrooks, & J. Mistry (Eds.), *Handbook of psychology: Vol. 6.*

Developmental psychology (pp. 373–394). New York: Wiley.

Perner, J., Mauer, M., & Hildenbrand, M. (2011). Identity: Key to children's understanding of belief. *Science, 333*(6041), 474–477.

Perry, W. G., Jr. (1970). *Forms of intellectual and ethical development in the college years.* New York: Holt, Rinehart & Winston.

Perry-Jenkins, M. (2004). The time and timing of work: Unique challenges facing low-income families. In A. C. Crouter & A. Booth (Eds.), *Work–family challenges for low-income parents and their children* (pp. 107–115). Mahwah, NJ: Erlbaum.

Perry-Jenkins, M., Goldberg, A. E., Pierce, C. P., & Sayer, A. G. (2007). Shift work, role overload, and the transition to parenthood. *Journal of Marriage and Family, 69*(1), 123–138.

Pertea, M., & Salzberg, S. (2010, May 5). Between a chicken and a grape: Estimating the number of human genes. *Genome Biology, 11.*

Peters, R. M. (2006). The relationship of racism, chronic stress emotions, and blood pressure. *Journal of Nursing Scholarship, 38*(3), 234–240.

Peterson, B. E., & Duncan, L. E. (2007). Midlife women's generativity and authoritarianism: Marriage, motherhood, and 10 years of aging. *Psychology and Aging, 22*(3), 411–419.

Peterson, C. C., & Wellman, H. M. (2009). From fancy to reason: Scaling deaf children's theory of mind and pretence. *British Journal of Development Psychology, 27,* 297–310.

Petot, D., & Rescorla, L. (2011). Agreement between parent- and self-reports of Algerian adolescents' behavioral and emotional problems. *Journal of Adolescence, 34*(5), 977–986.

Pew Research Center. (2012). The boomerang generation. Feeling ok about living with mom and dad. Retrieved from http://www.pewresearch.org/pubs/2219/boomerang-kids

Pew Social Trends. (2007). *As marriage and parenthood drift apart, public is concerned about social impact.* Retrieved on January 27, 2009 from http://www.pewsocialtrends.org/pubs/526/marriage-parenthood

Pharo, H., Sim, C., Graham, M., Gross, J., & Hayne, H. (2011). Risky business: Executive function, personality, and reckless behavior during adolescence and emerging adulthood. *Behavioral Neuroscience, 125*(6), 970–978.

Philipsen, N., & Brooks-Gunn, J. (2008). Overweight and obesity in childhood. In T. P. Gullotta & G. M. Blau (Eds.), *Handbook of childhood behavioral issues: Evidence-based approaches to prevention and treatment* (pp. 125–146). New York: Routledge/Taylor & Francis Group.

Phillips, A. T., & Wellman, H. M. (2005). Infants' understanding of object-directed action. *Cognition, 98*(2), 137–155.

Phinney, J. S. (1989). Stages of ethnic identity development in minority group adolescents. *Journal of Early Adolescence, 9*(1–2), 34–49.

Phinney, J. S. (2006). Ethnic identity exploration in emerging adulthood. In J. Arnett & J. Tanner (Eds.), *Emerging adults in America: Coming of age in the 21st century* (pp. 117–134). Washington, DC: American Psychological Association.

Phinney, J. S. (2008). Ethnic identity exploration in emerging adulthood. In D. Browning (Ed.), *Adolescent identities: A collection of readings* (pp. 47–66). New York: The Analytic Press/Taylor & Francis Group.

Phinney, J. S., Ong, A., & Madden, T. (2000). Cultural values and intergenerational value discrepancies in immigrant and non-immigrant families. *Child Development, 71*(2), 528–539.

Piaget, J. (1950). *The psychology of intelligence.* New York: Harcourt Brace.

Piaget, J. (1970). Piaget's theory. In P. H. Mussen (Ed.), *Carmichael's manual of child psychology: Vol. 1.* (3rd ed., pp. 703–732). New York: Wiley.

Pietromonaco, P. R., Manis, J., & Markus, H. (1987). The relationship of employment to self-perception and well-being in women: A cognitive analysis. *Sex Roles, 17,* 467–476.

Pinn, V. W., & Bates, A. (2003). *NIH research and other efforts related to the menopausal transition.*Washington, DC: National Institutes of Health.

Pinquart, M., & Schindler, I. (2007). Changes of life satisfaction in the transition to retirement: A latent-class approach. *Psychology and Aging, 22*(3), 442–455.

Pirttila-Backman, A. M., & Kajanne, A. (2001). The development of implicit epistemologies during early and middle adulthood. *Journal of Adult Development, 8*(2), 81–97.

Plantin, L., Olukoya, A. A., & Ny, P. (2011). Positive health outcomes of fathers' involvement in pregnancy and childbirth paternal support: A scope study literature review. *Fathering, 9*(1), 87–102.

Pleck, J. H. (1997). Paternal involvement: Levels, sources, and consequences. In M. E. Lamb (Ed.), *The role of the father in child development* (3rd ed., pp. 66–103). New York: Wiley.

Plomin, R. (1990). *Nature and nurture: An introduction to human behavioral genetics.* Pacific Grove, CA: Brooks/Cole.

Plomin, R., & Daniels, D. (1987). Why are children in the same family so different from one another? *Behavioral and Brain Sciences, 10,* 1–60.

Plomin, R., Asbury, K., & Dunn, J. (2001). Why are children in the same family so different? Nonshared environment a decade later. *The Canadian Journal of Psychiatry, 46*(3), 225–233.

Plotnick, R. D., et al. (2011). *Old assumptions, new realities: Economic security for working families in the 21st century.* New York: Russell Sage Foundation.

Polivy, J., Herman, C., & Boivin, M. (2008). Eating disorders. In J. E. Maddux & B. A. Winstead (Eds.), *Psychopathology: Foundations for a contemporary understanding* (2nd ed., pp. 251–279). New York: Routledge/Taylor & Francis Group.

Polivy, J., Herman, C. P., Mills, J. S., & Wheeler, H. B. (2008). Eating disorders in adolescence. In G. R. Adams & M. D. Berzonsky (Eds.), *Blackwell handbook of adolescence.* Oxford, UK: Blackwell Publishing.

Polka, L., Rvachew, S., & Mattock, K. (2007). Experiential influences on speech perception and speech production in infancy. In E. Hoff & M. Shatz (Eds.), *Blackwell handbook of language development* (pp. 153–172). Malden, MA: Blackwell Publishing.

Polka, L., Rvachew, S., & Molnar, M. (2008). Speech perception by 6- to 8-month olds in the presence of distracting sounds. *Infancy, 13*(5), 421–439.

Pollitt, E. (1994). Poverty and child development: Relevance of research in developing countries to the United States. *Child Development, 65,* 283–295.

Pollitt, E., Gorman, K. S., Engle, P. L., Martorell, R., & Rivera, J. (1993). Early supplementary feeding and cognition: Effects over two decades. *Monographs of the Society for Research in Child Development, 58*(7, Serial No. 235).

Popenoe, D., & Whitehead, B. D. (2002). The top ten myths of marriage. Rutgers, RI: *National Marriage Project.* Retrieved February 4, 2009 from http://marriage.rutgers.edu

Porter, R. H., & Winberg, J. (1999). Unique salience of maternal breast odors for newborn infants. *Neuroscience and Biobehavioral Reviews, 23,* 439–449.

Posada, G., & Kaloustian, G. (2010). Attachment in infancy. In J. G. Bremner & T. D. Wachs (Eds.), *The Wiley Blackwell handbook of infant development* (2nd ed., pp. 483–509). Malden, MA: Wiley-Blackwell.

Posada, G., Gao, Y., WU, F., Posada, R., Tascon, M., Shoelmerich, A., et al. (1995). The secure-base phenomenon across cultures: Children's behavior, mothers' preferences, and experts' concepts. *Monographs of the Society for Research in Child Development, 60*(2–3, Serial No. 244), 27–48.

Posner, M. I., Rothbart, M. K., & Sheese, B. E. (2007). Attention genes. *Developmental Science, 10*(1), 24–29.

Posthuma, D., de Geus, J. C., & Deary, I. J. (2009). The genetics of intelligence. In T. Goldberg & D. R. Weinberger (Eds.), *The genetics of cognitive neuroscience* (pp. 97–121). Cambridge, MA: MIT Press.

Potts, M. K. (1997). Social support and depression among older adults living alone: The importance of friends with and outside of a retirement community. *Social Work, 42,* 348–361.

Poulsen, C., Picton, T. W., & Paus, T. (2007). Age-related changes in transient and oscillatory brain responses to auditory stimulation in healthy adults, 19–45 years old. *Cerebral Cortex, 17,* 1454–1467.

Powell, M. D., & Ladd, L. D. (2010). Bullying: A review of the literature and implications for family therapists. *The American Journal of Family Therapy, 38,* 189–206.

Powers, S. I., Hauser, S. T., & Kilner, L. A. (1989). Adolescent mental health. *American Psychologist, 44,* 200–208.

Pranjic, N., & Bajraktarevic, A. (2010). Depression and suicide ideation among secondary school adolescents involved in school bullying. *Primary Health Care Research and Development, 11*(4), 349–362.

Presser, H. B. (2004). Employment in a 24/7 economy: Challenges for the family. In A. C. Crouter & A. Booth (Eds.), *Work–family challenges for low-income parents and their children* (pp. 83–105). Mahwah, NJ: Erlbaum

Pressley, M., Gaskins, I. W., Solic, K., & Collins, S. (2006). A portrait of benchmark school: How a school produces high achievement in students who previously failed. *Journal of Educational Psychology, 98*(2), 282–306.

Preston, S. D., & de Waal, F. B. M. (2002). Empathy: Its ultimate and proximate bases. *Behavioral and Brain Sciences, 25,* 1–72.

Price, T. S., & Jaffee, S. R. (2008). Effects of the family environment: Gene–environment interaction and passive gene–environment correlation. *Developmental Psychology, 44*(2), 305–315.

Priddis, L., & Howieson, N. (2012). Insecure attachment patterns at five years. What do they tell us? *Early Child Development and Care, 182*(1), 45–58.

Priest, L., Nayak, L., & Stuart-Hamilton, I. (2007). Website task performance by older adults. *Behaviour and Information Technology, 26*(3), 189–195.

Principe, G. F., Guilliano, S., & Root, C. (2008). Rumor mongering and remembering: How rumors originating in children's inferences can affect memory. *Journal of Experimental Child Psychology, 99*(2), 135–155.

Prinstein, M. J., Meade, C. S., & Cohen, G. L. (2003). Adolescent oral sex, peer popularity, and perceptions of best friend's sexual behavior. *Journal of Pediatric Psychology, 28*(4), 243–249.

Pruett, K. D. (1987). *The nurturing father: Journey toward the complete man.* New York: Warner Books.

Pruett, M. K., & Barker, R. (2009). Children of divorce: New trends and ongoing dilemmas. In J. H. Bray & M. Stanton (Ed.), *The Wiley-Blackwell handbook of family psychology* (pp. 463–474). Malden, MA: Wiley-Blackwell.

Pruett, M. K., & Donsky, T. (2011). Coparenting after divorce: Paving pathways for parental cooperation, conflict resolution, and redefined family roles. In J. P. McHale & K. M. Lindahl (Eds.), *Coparenting: A conceptual and clinical examination of family systems* (pp. 231–250). Washington, DC: American Psychological Association.

Pudrovska, T. (2008). Psychological implications of motherhood and fatherhood in midlife: Evidence from sibling models. *Journal of Marriage and Family, 70,* 168–181.

Putney, N. M. & Bengtson, V. L. (2001). Families, intergenerational relationships, and kinkeeping in midlife. In M. E. Lachman (Ed.), *Handbook of midlifedevelopment* (pp. 528–570). Hoboken, NJ: John Wiley & Sons Inc.

Pyszczynski, T., & Kesebir, P. (2012). Culture, ideology, morality, and religion: Death changes everything. In P. R. Shaver & M. Mikulincer (Eds.), *Meaning, mortality, and choice: The social psychology of existential concerns* (pp. 75–91). Washington, DC: American Psychological Association.

Pyszcynski, T., Rothschild, Z., & Abdollahi, A. (2008). Terrorism, violence, and hope for peace: A terror management perspective. *Current Directions in Psychological Science, 17*(5), 318–322.

Pyszczynski, T., Solomon, S., & Greenberg, J., (2003b). *In the wake of 9/11: The psychology of terror.* Washington, DC: American Psychological Association.

Pyszczynski, T., Solomon, S., & Greenberg, J. (2003a). Give peace a chance. In T. Pyszczynski, S. Solomon, & J. Greenberg (Eds.), *In the wake of 9/11: The psychology of terror* (pp. 171–187). Washington, DC: American Psychological Association.

Qouta, S., Punamäki, R., & El Sarraj, E. (2008). Child development and family mental health in war and military violence: The Palestinian experience. *International Journal of Behavioral Development, 43*(4), 310–321.

Quackenbush, J. (2011). *The human genome: The book of essential knowledge.* New York: Imagine.

Quasem, I., Sloan, N. L., Chawdhury, A., Ahmed, S., & Winikoff, B. (2003). Adaptation of kangaroo mother care for community-based application. *Journal of Perinatology, 23*(8), 646–651.

Qui, M., Ye, Z., Li, Q., Liu, G., Xie, B., & Wang, J. (2011). Changes of brain structure and function in ADHD children. *Brain Topography, 24*(3–4), 243–252.

Quinn, P. C. (2002). Category representation in young infants. *Current Directions in Young Infants, 11*(2), 66.

Quinn, P. C., & Oates, J. (2004). Early category representation and concepts. In J. Oates & A. Grayson (Eds.), *Cognitive and language development in children.* Maidenhead, BRK, England: Open University Press.

Quinn, P. C., Eimas, P. D., & Tarr, M. J. (2001). Perceptual categorization of cat and dog silhouettes by 3- to 4-month-old infants. *Journal of Experimental Child Psychology, 79*(1), 78.

Quintana, S. M. (2008). Racial perspective taking ability: Developmental, theoretical, and empirical trends. In S. M. Quintana & C. McKown (Eds.), *Handbook of race, racism, and the developing child* (pp. 16–36). Hoboken, NJ: John Wiley & Sons.

Racine, S. E., Root, T. L., Klump, K. L., & Bulik, C. M. (2011). Environmental and genetic risk factors for eating disorders: A developmental perspective. In D. Le Grange & J. Lock (Eds.), *Eating disorders in children and adolescents: A clinical handbook* (pp. 25–33). New York: Guilford Press.

Racz, S. J., & McMahon, R. J. (2011). The relationship between parental knowledge and monitoring and child and adolescent conduct problems: A 10-year update. *Clinical Child and Family Psychology Review, 14*(4), 377–398.

Radke-Yarrow, M., Zahn-Waxler, C., & Chapman, M. (1983). Children's prosocial dispositions and behavior. In E. M. Hetherington (Ed.), *Handbook of child psychology: Vol. 4. Socialization, personality, and social development* (pp. 469–546). New York: Wiley.

Radvansky, G. A. (2011). *Human memory.* Upper Saddle River, NJ: Pearson Education.

Rainie, L. (2010). Internet, broadband, and cell phone statistics. PewResearchCenter. http://www.pewinternet.org/~/media/Files/Reports/2010/PIP_December08_stats.pdf

Rakison, D. H., (2010). Perceptual categorization and concepts. In J. G. Bremner & T. D. Wachs (Eds.) *Wiley-Blackwell handbook of infant development, Vol. 1, 2nd Ed.* Oxford, UK: Wiley-Blackwell.

Rakison, D., & Woodward, A. (2008). New perspectives on the effects of action on perceptual and cognitive development. *Developmental Psychology, 44*(5), 1209–1213.

Ramaswami, A., & Dreher, G. F. (2007). The benefits associated with workplace mentoring relationships. In T. Allen & L. Eby (Eds.), *The Blackwell handbook of mentoring: A multiple perspectives approach* (pp. 211–231). Malden, MA: Blackwell Publishing.

Ramus, F., & Szenkovits, G. (2008). What phonological deficit? *Quarterly Journal of Experimental Psychology, 61*(1), 129–141.

Raphael-Leff, J. (2010). Mothers' and fathers' orientations: Patterns of pregnancy parenting and the bonding process. In S. Tyano, M. Keren, H. Herman, & J. Cox (Eds.), *Parenthood and mental health: A bridge between infant and adult psychiatry* (pp. 9–22). Malden, MA: Wiley-Blackwell.

Rattan, A., Good, C., & Dweck, C. S. (2011, December 29). "It's ok—not everyone can be good at math": Instructors with an entity theory comfort (and demotivate) students. *Journal of Experimental Social Psychology.*

Rattan, S. (2006). Theories of biological aging: Genes, proteins, and free radicals. *Free Radical Research, 40*(12), 1230–1238.

Rauste-Von Wright, M. (1989). Body image satisfaction in adolescent girls and boys: A longitudinal study. *Journal of Youth and Adolescence, 18,* 71–83.

Rawson, N. E., Gomez, G., Coward, B., Restrepo, D., Meisami, E., Mikhai, L., et al. (1998). Part XVII: Aging and the chemical senses. In C. Murphy (Ed.), *Olfaction and taste: Vol 12. An international symposium* (pp. 701–737). New York: New York Academy of Sciences.

Ray, K., & Smith, M. C. (2010). The kindergarten child: What teachers and administrators need to know to promote academic success in all children. *Early Childhood Education Journal, 38*(1), 5–18.

Rayner, K., Pollatsek, A., Ashby, J., & Clifton, C. (2012). *Psychology of reading* (2nd ed.). New York: Psychology Press.

Raz, N. (2005). The aging brain observed in vivo: Differential changes and their modifiers. In R. Cabezo, L. Nyberg, & D. Parks (Eds.), *Cognitive neuroscience of aging: Linking cognitive and cerebral aging* (pp. 19–57). London: London University Press.

Raz, N., et al. (2010). Trajectories of brain aging in middle-aged and older adults: Regional and individual differences. *NeuroImage, 51* (2) 501–511.

Raz, N., & Kennedy, K. M. (2009). A systems approach to age-related change: Neuroacatomic changes, their modifiers, and cognitive correlates. In W. Jagust & M. D'Esposito (Eds.), *Imaging the aging brain* (pp. 43–71). New York: Oxford University Press.

Raz, N., & Lindenberger, U. (2011). Only time will tell: Cross-sectional studies offer no solution to the age-brain-cognition triangle: Comment on Salthouse. *Psychological Bulletin, 137*(5), 790–795.

Raznahan, A., et al. (2011). How does your cortex grow? *The Journal of Neuroscience, 31*(19), 7174–7177.

Reardon, L. E., Leen-Feldner, E. W., & Hayward, C. (2009). A critical review of the empirical literature on the relation between anxiety and puberty. *Clinical Psychology Review, 29,* 1–23. doi:10.1016/j.cpr.2008.09.005

Reddy, L. A. (2012). Group play skill sequences. In L. A. Reddy (Ed.), *Group play interventions for children: Strategies for teaching prosocial skills* (pp. 55–100). Washington, DC: American Psychological Association.

Reece, J. B., et al. (2011). *Campbell biology* (9th ed.). Boston: Pearson.

Reece, M., Herbenick, D. C., Schick, V., Sanders, S. A., Dodge, B., & Fortenberry, J. (2010). Background and considerations on the National Survey of Sexual Health and Behavior (NSSHB) from the investigators. *Journal of Sexual Medicine, 7*(5), 243–245.

Regan, P. (2011). *Close relationships.* New York: Routledge/Taylor & Francis Group.

Reich, S. M., Subrahmanyam, K., & Espinoza, G. (2012). Friending, IMing, and hanging out face-to-face: Overlap in adolescent's online and offline social networks. *Developmental Psychology, 48*(2), 356–368.

Reinke, B. J. (1985). Psychosocial changes as a function of chronological age. *Human Development, 28*(5), 266–269.

Reis, O., & Youniss, J. (2004). Patterns in identity change and development in relationships with mothers and fathers. *Journal of Adolescent Research, 19*(1), 31–44.

Rejeski, W. J., King, A. C., Katula, J. A., Kritchevsky, S., Miller, M. E., Walkup, M. P. et al. (2008). Physical activity in prefrail older adults: Confidence and satisfaction related to physical function. *Journals of Gerontology Series B: Psychological Sciences and Social Sciences, 63B*(1), 19–26.

Renner, M. J., & Mackin, R. S. (2002). A life stress instrument for classroom use. In R. A. Griggs (Ed.) *Handbook for teaching introductory psychology: Vol. 3: With an emphasis on assessment.* (pp. 236–238) Mahwah, NJ: Lawrence Erlbaum Associates Publishers.

Repetti, R., & Wang, S. (2010). Parent employment and chaos in the family. In G. W. Evans & T. D. Wachs (Eds.), *Chaos and its influence on children's development: An ecological perspective* (pp. 191–208). Washington, DC: American Psychological Association.

Rescorla, L., et al. (2007). Epidemiological comparisons of problems and positive qualities reported by adolescents in 24 countries. *Journal of Consulting and Clinical Psychology, 75*(2), 351–358.

Resnick, B., Gwyther, L. P., & Roberto, K. A. (2011). *Resilience in aging: Concepts, research, and outcomes.* New York: Springer.

Reuben, D. B., et al. (2011). *Geriatrics at your fingertips.* New York: American Geriatrics Society.

Reuter-Lorenz, P. A., & Cappell, K. A. (2008). Neurocognitive aging and the compensation hypothesis. *Current Directions in Psychological Science, 17*(3), 177–182.

Reynolds, B. M., & Juvonen, J. (2011). The role of early maturation, perceived popularity, and rumors in the emergence of internalizing symptoms among adolescent girls. *Journal of Youth and Adolescence, 40*(11), 1407–1422.

Reynolds, J. F., Dorner, L. M., & Orellana, M. F. (2011). Siblings as cultural educators and socializing agents. In J. Caspi (Ed.), *Sibling development: Implications for mental health practitioners* (pp. 107–121). New York: Springer Publishing.

Rhyner, P. M. (2009). *Emergent literacy and language development: Promoting learning in early childhood.* New York: Guilford Press.

Rice, D. P. (2004). Economic implications of increased longevity in the United States. *Annual Review of Public Health, 25,* 457–473.

Richards, C., & Leafstedt, J. M. (2010). *Early reading intervention: Strategies and methods for teaching struggling readers.* Boston: Pearson/Allyn & Bacon.

Richardson, R. A. (2005). Developmental contextual considerations of parent–child attachment in the later middle childhood years. In K. Kerns & R. Richardson (Eds.), *Attachment in middle childhood* (pp. 24–45). New York: Gilford Press.

Richardson, S. O., & Gilger, J. W. (2005). *Research-based education and intervention: What we need to know.* Baltimore: International Dyslexia Association.

Richardson, V. E. (1999). How circumstances of widowhood and retirement affect adjustment among older men. *Journal of Mental Health and Aging, 5,* 165–174.

Richmond, L. L., Morrison, A. B., Chein, J. M., & Olson, I. R. (2011). Working memory training and transfer in older adults. *Psychology and Aging, 26*(4), 813–822.

Riddle, D. R., & Lichtenwalner, R. J. (2007). Neurogenesis in the adult and aging brain. In D. R. Riddle (Ed.), *Brain aging: Models, methods, and mechanisms* (pp. 127–157). Boca Raton, FL: CRC Press.

Rideout, V. J., Vandewater, E. A., & Wartella, E. A. (2003). *Zero to six: Electronic media in the lives of infants, toddlers, and preschoolers.* Menlo Park, CA: The Henry J. Kaiser Family Foundation.

Rideout, V., Hamel, E., & Kaiser Family Foundation (2006). *The media family: Electronic media in the lives of infants, toddlers, preschoolers and their parents.* Menlo Park, CA: Henry J. Kaiser Family Foundation.

Rideout, V. J., Foehr, U. G., & Roberts, D. F. (2010). Generation M2 : Media in the lives of 8- to 18-year olds. Accessed online on October 25, 2012 from http://www.kff.org/entmedia/upload/8010.pdf

Riediger, M., & Freund, A. M. (2008). Me against myself: Motivational conflicts and emotional development in adulthood. *Psychology and Aging, 23*(3), 479–494.

Riegel, K. F. (1973). Dialectic operations: The final period of cognitive development. *Human Development, 16,* 346–370.

Riegel, K. F. (1975). Toward a dialectical theory of development. *Human Development, 18*(1–2), 50–64.

Rigby, K. (2002). Bullying in childhood. In P. K. Smith & C. H. Hart (Eds.), *Blackwell handbook of childhood social development* (pp. 549–568). Oxford, England: Basil Blackwell.

Rigby, K. (2012). Bullying in schools: Addressing desires, not only behaviours. *Educational Psychology Review, 24*(2), 339–348.

Rigby, K., & Bauman, S. (2010). How school personnel tackle cases of bullying: A critical examination. In S. R. Jimerson, S. M. Swearer, & D. L. Espelage (Eds.), *Handbook of bullying in schools: An international perspective* (pp. 455–467). New York: Routledge/Taylor & Francis Group.

Rigby, K., & Smith, P. K. (2011). Is school bullying really on the rise? *Social Psychology of Education, 14*(4), 441–455.

Riggio, R. E. (2013). *Introduction to industrial/organizational psychology.* Upper Saddle River, NJ: Pearson.

Rinaldi, C. M., & Howe, N. (2012). Mothers' and fathers' parenting styles and associations with toddlers' externalizing, internalizing, and adaptive behaviors. *Early Childhood Research Quarterly, 27*(2), 266–273.

Ritter, M. (2008). *Is technology rewiring our brains?* Retrieved on December 5, 2008 from http://dsc.discovery.com/news/2008/12/03/kids-internet-techprint.Html

Rittle-Johnson, B., Saylor, M., & Swygert, K. E. (2008). Learning from explaining: Does it matter if mom is listening? *Journal of Experimental Child Psychology, 100*(3), 215–224.

Rizzolatti, G., & Craighero, L. (2004). The mirror-neuron system. *Annual Review of Neuroscience, 27,* 169–192.

Rizzolatti, G., Fogassi, L., & Gallese, V. (2006). Mirrors in the mind. *Scientific American, 295*(5), 295–300.

Rizzolatti, G., & Sinigaglia, C. (2010). The functional role of the parieto-frontal mirror circuit: Interpretations and misinterpretations. *Nature Reviews Neuroscience, 11,* 264–274.

Rizzolatti, G., Sinigaglia, C., & Anderson, F. (2008). *Mirror in the brain: How our minds share actions and emotions.* New York: Oxford University Press.

Roberson, K. C. (2006). Attachment and caregiving behavioral systems in intercountry adoption: A literature review. *Children and Youth Services Review, 28*(7), 727–740.

Roberts, D. F., Henrikson, L., & Foehr, U. G. (2009). Adolescence, adolescents, and media. In R. M. Lerner & L. Steinberg (Eds.), *Handbook of adolescent psychology, Vol. 2: Contextual influences on adolescent development* (3rd ed., pp. 314–344). Hoboken, NJ: John Wiley & Sons.

Roberts, J. E., Rosenfeld, R. M. & Zeisel, S. A. (2004). Otitis media and speech and language: A meta-analysis of prospective studies. *Pediatrics, 113*(3), 238.

Robins, G. (2012). *Praise, motivation, and the child.* New York: Routledge.

Robinson, C. W., & Sloutsky, V. M. (2007). Visual processing speed: Effects of auditory input on visual processing. *Developmental Science, 10*(6), 734–740.

Robinson, G. (2002). Cross-cultural perspectives on menopause. In A. E. Hunter & C. Forden (Eds.), *Readings in the psychology of gender: Exploring our differences and commonalities* (pp. 140–149). Needham Heights, MA: Allyn & Bacon.

Robinson, I. E., & Jedlicka, D. (1982). Change in sexual behavior of college students from 1965–1980: A research note. *Journal of Marriage and the Family, 44,* 237–240.

Robison, J., et al. (2011). Community-based versus institutional supportive housing: Perceived quality of care, quality of life, emotional well-being, and social interaction. *Journal of Applied Gerontology, 30*(3), 275–303.

Robles, M., & McCoshen, J. A. (2008). *Kangaroo care: The human incubator for the premature infant.* Retrieved on November 13, 2008 from http://www.childbirthsolutions.com/articles/birth/roocare/index.php

Rochat, P. (2010). Emerging self-concept. In J. G. Bremner & T. D. Wachs (Eds.), *The Wiley Blackwell handbook of infant development* (2nd ed., pp. 320–344). Malden, MA: Wiley-Blackwell.

Rochat, P., Goubet, N., & Senders, S. J. (1999). To reach or not to reach? Perception of body effectiveness by young infants. *Infant and Child Development, 8,* 129–148.

Röcke, C., & Lachman, M. E. (2008). Perceived trajectories of life satisfaction across past, present, and future: Profiles and correlates of subjective change in young, middle-aged, and older adults. *Psychology and Aging, 23*(4), 833–847.

Rodin, J., & Ickovics, J. (1990). Women's health: Review and research agenda as we approach the 21st century. *American Psychologist, 45,* 1018–1034.

Rodkin, P. C., & Roisman, G. I. (2010). Antecedents and correlates of the popular-aggressive phenomenon in elementary school. *Child Development, 81*(3), 837–850.

Rodkin, P. C., Farmer, T. W., Pearl, R., & Van Acker, R. (2006). They're cool: Social status and peer group supports for aggressive boys and girls. *Social Development, 15*(2), 175–204.

Rodkin, P. C., Wilson, T., & Ahn, H. (2007). Social integration between African American and European American children in majority black, majority white, and multicultural elementary classrooms. *New Directions for Child and Adolescent Development, 2007* (118), 25–42.

Rodrigue, K. M., & Kennedy, K. M. (2011). The cognitive consequences of structural changes to the aging brain. In K. Warner Schaie & S. L. Willis (Eds.), *Handbook of the psychology of aging* (7th ed., pp. 73–91). San Diego, CA: Elsevier Academic Press.

Rogers, C. (1980). *A way of being.* Boston: Houghton Mifflin.

Rogers, C. H., Floyd, F. J., Seltzer, M., Greenburg, J., & Hong, J. (2008). Longterm effects of the death of a child on parents' adjustment in midlife. *Journal of Family Psychology, 22*(2), 203–211.

Rogers, L., Zosuls, K. M., Halim, M. L., Ruble, D., Hughes, D., & Fuligni, A. (2012). Meaning making in middle childhood: An exploration of the meaning of ethnic identity. *Cultural Diversity and Ethnic Minority Psychology, 18*(2), 99–108.

Rogers, W. A., & Fisk, A. D. (2000). Human factors, applied cognition, and aging. In F. I. M. Craik & T. A. Salthouse (Eds.), *The handbook of aging and cognition* (2nd ed., pp. 559–592). Mahwah, NJ: Erlbaum.

Rogers, W. A., & Fisk, A. D. (2001). Understanding the role of attention in cognitive aging research. In J. E. Birren & K. W. Schaie (Ed.), *Handbook of the psychology of aging* (5th ed., pp. 267–287). San Diego, CA: Academic Press.

Rogers, W. A., Fisk, A. D. (2010). Toward a psychological science of advanced technology design for older adults. *The Journal of Gerontology: Series B: Psychological Sciences and Social Sciences, 65B*(6), 645–653.

Rogoff, B. (1990). *Apprenticeship in thinking: Cognitive development in social context.* New York: Oxford University Press.

Rogoff, B. (2003). *The cultural nature of human development.* New York: Oxford University Press.

Rogoff, B., Correa-Chavez, M., & Silva, K. G. (2011). Cultural variation in children's attention and learning. In M. Gernsbacher, R. W. Pew, L. M. Hough, & J. Pomerantz (Eds.), *Psychology and the real world: Essays illustrating fundamental contributions to society* (pp. 154–163). New York: Worth Publishers.

Rogoff, B., Mistry, J., Goncu, A., & Mosier, C. (1993). Guided participation in cultural activity by toddlers and caregivers. *Monographs of the Society for Research in Child Development, 58*(8, Serial No. 236).

Roisman, G. I., & Grohl, A. M. (2011). Attachment theory and research in developmental psychology: An overview and appreciative critique. In M. K. Underwood & L. H. Rosen (Eds.), *Social development: Relationships in infancy, childhood, and adolescence* (pp. 101–156). New York: Guilford Press.

Roisman, G. I., Clausell, E., Holland, A., Fortuna, K., & Elieff, C. (2008). Adult romantic relationships as contexts of human development: A multimethod comparison of same-sex couples with opposite-sex dating, engaged, and married dyads. *Developmental Psychology, 44*(1), 91–101.

Romer, D., Betancourt, L. M., Brodsky, N. L., Giannetta, J. M., Yang, W., & Hurt, H. (2011). Does adolescent risk taking imply weak executive function? A prospective study of relations between working memory performance, impulsivity, and risk taking in early adolescence. *Developmental Science, 14*(5), 1119–1133.

Ronco, A. M., Garrido, F., & Llanos, M. N. (2006). Smoking specifically induces metallothionein-2 isoform in human placenta at term. *Toxicology, 223*(1/2), 46–53.

Rose, A. J., Glick, G. C., & Smith, R. L. (2011). Popularity and gender: The two cultures of boys and girls. In A. Cillessen, D. Schwartz, & L. Mayeux (Eds.), *Popularity in the peer system* (pp. 103–122). New York: Guilford Press.

Rose, S. M. (2007). Enjoying the returns: Women's friendships after 50. In V. Muhlbauer & J. C. Chrisler (Eds.), *Women over 50: Psychological perspectives* (pp. 112–130). New York: Springer Science + Business Media.

Rose-Krasnor, L., & Denham, S. (2009). Social-emotional competence in early childhood. In K. Rubin, W. Bukowski, & B. Laursen (Eds.), *Handbook of peer interactions, relationships, and groups* (pp. 162–179). New York: Guilford Press.

Rosen, D. S. (2004). Physiologic growth and development during adolescence. *Pediatrics in Review, 25*(6), 194–200.

Rosen, L. H., & Patterson, M. M. (2011). The self and identity. In M. K. Underwood & L. H. Rosen (Eds.), *Social development: Relationships in infancy, childhood, and adolescence* (pp. 73–100). New York: Guilford Press.

Rosenberg, S. D., Rosenberg, H. J., & Farrell, M. P. (1999). The midlife crisis revisited. In S. L. Willis & J. D. Reid (Eds.), *Life in the middle: Psychological and social development in middle age* (pp. 47–73). San Diego, CA: Academic Press.

Rosenstein, D., & Oster, H. (1988). Differential facial response to four basic tastes in newborns. *Child Development, 59,* 1555–1568.

Rosenthal, E. (1990, January 4). New insights on why some children are fat offers clues on weight loss. *New York Times,* pp. B7–B8.

Rosenzweig, M. R. (1969). Effects of heredity and environment on brain chemistry, brain anatomy, and learning ability in the rat. In M. Monosevitz, G. Lindzey, & D. D. Thiessen (Eds.), *Behavioral genetics.* New York: Appleton-Century-Crofts.

Roskos, K. A., & Christie, J. F. (2007a). *Play and literacy in early childhood: Research from multiple perspectives* (2nd ed.). Mahwah, NJ: Lawrence Erlbaum Associates Publishers.

Roskos, K. A., & Christie, J. F. (2007b). Play in the context of the new preschool basics. In K. A. Roskos & J. F. Christie (Eds.), *Play and literacy in early childhood: Research from multiple perspectives* (2nd ed., pp. 83–100). Mahwah, NJ: Lawrence Erlbaum Associates Publishers.

Roskos, K. A., Christie, J. F., Widman, S., & Holding, A. (2010). Three decades in: Priming for meta-analysis in play-literacy research. *Journal of Early Childhood Literacy, 10*(1), 55–96.

Ross, C. A. (2010). Symptom patterns in dissociative identity disorder patients and the general population. *Journal of Trauma & Dissociation, 11*(4), 458–468.

Ross, M. H., Yurgelun-Todd, D. A., Renshaw, P. F., Maas, L. C., Mendelson, J. H., Mello, N. K., et al. (1997). Age-related reduction in functional MRI response to photic stimulation. *Neurology, 48,* 173–176.

Rossi, A. S. (2004). The menopausal transition and aging processes. In O. G. Brim & C. D. Ryff (Eds.), *How healthy are we? A national study of wellbeing at midlife* (pp. 153–204). Chicago: The University of Chicago Press.

Rossi, A., Quick, J. C., & Perrewe, P. L. (2009). *Stress and quality of working life: The positive and the negative.* Charlotte, NC: Information Age Publishing.

Rossi, G. (1997). The nestlings. *Journal of Family Issues, 18*(6), 627–644.

Rothbart, M. K., & Bates, J. E. (2006). Temperament. In N. Eisenberg, W. Damon & R. M. Lerner (Eds.), *Handbook of child psychology: Vol. 3, Social, emotional, and personality development* (6th ed., pp. 99–166). Hoboken, NJ: John Wiley & Sons.

Rothbart, M. K., & Sheese, B. E. (2007). Temperament and emotion regulation. In J. Gross (Ed.), *Handbook of emotion regulation* (pp. 331–350). New York: Guilford Press.

Rothbart, M. K. (2007). Temperament, development, and personality. *Current Directions in Psychological Science, 16*(4), 207–212.

Rothbart, M. K., Sheese, B. E., Rueda, M. R., & Posner, M. I. (2011). Developing mechanisms of self-regulation in early life. *Emotion Review, 3*(2), 207–213.

Rothbaum, F., Morelli, G., & Rusk, N. (2011). Attachmnet, learning, and coping: The interplay of cultural similarities and differences. In M. J. Gelfand, C. Chiu, & Hong, Y. (Eds.) (pp. 153–215). *Advances in culture and psychology, Vol. 1.* New York: Oxford University Press.

Roth-Hanania, R., Davidov, M., & Zahn-Waxler, C. (2011). Empathy development from 8 to 16 months: Early signs of concern for others. *Infant Behavior & Development, 34*(3), 447–458.

Roze, E., Groningen, G., Meijer, L., Van Braeckel, K. N., Ruiter, S. A. J., Bruggink, J. L. M., & Bos, A. F. (2010). Developmental trajectories from birth to school age in healthy term-born children. *Pediatrics, 126*(5), e1134–e1142.

Rozzini, R., Sabatini, T., Cassinadri, A., Boffelli, S., Ferri, M., Barbisoni, P., et al. (2005). Relationships between functional loss before hospital admission and mortality in elderly persons with medical illness. *Journals of Gerontology Series A: Biological Sciences and Medical Sciences, 60A*(9), 1180–1183.

Rubin, K. H., Bowker, J., & Gazelle, H. (2010). Social withdrawal in childhood and adolescence: Peer relationships and social competence. In K. H. Rubin & R. J. Coplan (Eds.), *The development of shyness and social withdrawal* (pp. 131–156). New York: Guilford Press.

Rubin, K. H., Bukowski, W. M., & Parker, J. G. (2006). Peer interactions, relationships, and groups. In N. Eisenberg, W. Damon, & R. M. Lerner (Eds.), *Handbook of child psychology: Vol. 3, social, emotional, and personality development* (6th ed., pp. 571–645). Hoboken, NJ: Wiley.

Rubin, K. H., Coplan, R. J., & Bowker, J. C. (2009). Social withdrawal in childhood. *Annual Review of Psychology, 60,* 141–171.

Rubin, K. H., Coplan, R., Chen, X., Bowker, J., & McDonald, K. L. (2011). Peer relationships in childhood. In M. H. Bornstein & M. E. Lamb (Eds.), *Developmental science: An advanced textbook* (6th ed., pp. 519–570). New York: Psychology Press.

Rubin, K., Fredstrom, B., & Bowker, J. (2008). Future directions in: Friendship in childhood and early adolescence. *Social Development, 17*(4), 1085–1096.

Rubin, S. S., & Malkinson, R. (2001). Parental response to child loss across the life cycle: Clinical and research perspectives. In M. S. Stroebe, R. O. Hansson, W. Stroebe, & H. Schut (Eds.), *Handbook of bereavement research: Consequences, coping, and care* (pp. 219–240). Washington, DC: American Psychological Association.

Ruble, D. N., & Martin, C. L. (1998) Gender development. In N. Eisenberg (Ed.), *Handbook of child psychology: Vol. 3. Social, emotional, and personality development* (5th ed., pp. 553–618). New York: Wiley.

Ruble, D. N., Martin, C., & Berenbaum, S. A. (2006). Gender development. In N. Eisenberg, W. Damon, & R. Lerner (Eds.), *Handbook of child psychology: Vol. 3, Social, emotional, and personality development* (6th ed., pp. 858–932). Hoboken, NJ: Wiley.

Rudisill, J. R., Edwards, J. M., & Hershberger, P. J. (2010). Coping with job transitions over the work life. In T. W. Miller (Ed.), *Handbook of stressful transitions across the lifespan* (pp. 111–131). New York: Springer Science + Business Media.

Rudy, D., & Grusec, J. E. (2006). Authoritarian parenting in individualist and collectivist groups: Associations with maternal emotion and cognition and children's self-esteem. *Journal of Family Psychology, 20*(1), 68–78.

Ruiz, S. A., & Silverstein, M. (2007). Relationships with grandparents and the emotional well-being of late adolescent and young adult grandchildren. *Journal of Social Issues, 63*(4), 793–808.

Runswick-Cole, K. (2010). Living with dying and disabilism: Death and disabled children. *Disability & Society, 25*(7), 813–826.

Rushton, J. P., Bons, T. A., & Hur, Y. (2008). The genetics and evolution of the general factor of personality. *Journal of Research in Personality, 42*(5), 1173–1185.

Rutter, M. (2008). Biological implications of gene–environment interaction. *Journal of Abnormal Child Psychology, 36*(7), 969–975.

Rutter, M., & Sonuga-Barke, E. J. (2010). Conclusions: Overview of findings from the ERA study, inferences, and research implications. *Monographs of the Society for Research in Child Development, 75*(1), 212–229.

Rutter, M., Beckett, C., Castle, J., Colvert, E., Kreppner, J., Mehta, M., et al. (2007). Effects of profound early institutional deprivation: An overview of findings from a UK longitudinal study of Romanian adoptees. *European Journal of Developmental Psychology, 4*(3), 332–350.

Rutter, M., O'Conner, T. G., & the English and Romanian Adoptees (ERA) Study Team. (2004). Are there biological programming effects for psychological development? Findings from a study of Romanian adoptees. *Developmental Psychology, 40,* 81–94.

Rvachew, S., Nowak, M., & Cloutier, G. (2004). Effect of phonemic perception training on the speech production and phonological awareness skills of children with expressive phonological delay. *American Journal of Speech–Language Pathology, 13*(3), 250–263.

Rvachew, S., Slawinski, E. B., Williams, M., & Green, C. L. (1999). The impact of early onset otitis media on babbling and early language development. *Journal of the Acoustical Society of America, 105,* 467–475.

Ryan, R. M., & Deci, E. L. (2004). Avoiding death or engaging life as accounts of meaning and culture: Comment on Pyszczynski et al. *Psychological Bulletin, 130,* 473–477.

Ryan, C. L., & Siebens, J. (2012). *Educational attainment in the United States: 2009.* Washington, DC: U.S. Census Bureau.

Ryan, J., Stanczyk, F. Z., Dennerstein, L., Mack, W. J., Clark, M. S., Szoeke, C., Kildea, D., & Henderson, V. W. (2012). Hormone levels and cognitive function in postmenopausal midlife women. *Neurobiology of Aging, 33*(3), e11–e22.

Ryff, C. D. (1995). Psychological well-being in adult life. *Current Directions in Psychological Science, 4,* 99–104.

Ryff, C. D. (2008). Challenges and opportunities at the interface of aging, personality, and well-being. In O. P. John, R. W. Robins, & L. A. Pervin (Eds.), *Handbook of personality: Theory and research* (3rd ed., pp. 199–418). New York: Guilford Press.

Ryff, C. D., & Singer, B. (2008). Thriving in the face of challenge: The integrative science of human resilience; Postscript. In F. Kessel, P. L. Rosenfield, & N. B. Anderson (Eds.), *Interdisciplinary research: Case studies from health and social science* (pp. 198–227). New York: Oxford University Press.

Ryff, C. D., & Singer, B. H. (2006). Best news yet on the six-factor model of well-being. *Social Science Research, 35*(4), 1103–1119.

Ryff, C. D., Kwan, M. L., & Singer, B. H. (2001). Personality and aging: Flourishing agendas and future challenges. In J. E. Birren & K. W. Schaie (Eds.), *Handbook of the psychology of aging* (5th ed., pp. 477–499). New York: Academic Press.

Ryff, C. D., Singer, B. H., & Seltzer, M. M. (2002). Pathways through challenge: Implications for well-being and health. In L. Pulkkinen & A. Caspi (Eds.), *Paths to successful development: Personality in the life course* (pp. 302–328). New York: Cambridge University Press.

Sabatini, T., Frisoni, G. B., Barbisoni, P., Bellelli, G., Rozzini, R., & Trabucchi, M. (2000). Atrial fibrillation and cognitive disorders in older people. *Journal of the American Geriatrics Society, 48,* 387–390.

Sachdeva, S., Singh, P., & Medin, D. (2011). Culture and the quest for universal principles in moral reasoning. *International Journal of Psychology, 46*(3), 161–176.

Safron, M., & Cislak, A. (2011). Effects of school-based interventions targeting obesity-related behaviors and body weight change: A systematic umbrella review. *Behavioral Medicine, 37*(1), 15–25.

Sagiv, S. K., Thurston, S. W., Bellinger, D. C., Tolbert, P. E., Altshul, L. M., & Korrick, S. A. (2010). Prenatal organochlorine exposure and behaviors associated with attention deficit hyperactivity disorder in school-aged children. *American Journal of Epidemiology, 171*(5), 593–601.

Sahin, N. H. & Gungor, I. (2010). *Birth defects: Issues on prevention and promotion.* New York: Nova Science Publishers.

Salerno-Kennedy. R., (2008). Nutrition in older adults: An overview. In N. E. Bernhardt & A. M. Kasko (Eds.), *Nutrition for middle aged and elderly* (pp. 285–298). New York: Nova Biomedical Books.

Salihu, H. M., Wilson, R. E., Alio, A. P., & Kirby, R. S. (2008). Advanced maternal age and risk of antepartum and intrapartum stillbirth. *Journal of Obstetrics and Gynaecology Research, 34*(5), 843–850.

Salmivalli, C., & Peets, K. (2009). Bullies, victims, and bully-victim relationships in middle childhood and early adolescence. In K. H. Rubin, W. M. Bukowski, & B. Laursen (Eds.), *Handbook of peer interactions, relationships, and groups* (pp. 322–340). New York: Guilford Press.

Salthouse, T. (1987). The role of experience in cognitive aging. In K. W. Schaie & K. Eisdorfer (Eds.), *Annual review of gerontology and geriatrics: Vol. 7.* (pp. 135–158). New York: Springer-Verlag.

Salthouse, T. (1990). Cognitive competence and expertise in aging. In J. E. Birren & K. W. Schaie (Eds.), *Handbook of the psychology of aging* (3rd ed., pp. 310–319). San Diego, CA: Academic Press.

Salthouse, T. (1994). The nature of the influence of speed on adult age differences in cognition. *Developmental Psychology, 30,* 240–259.

Salthouse, T. (1996). General and specific speed mediation of adult age differences in memory. *Journal of Gerontology, 51A,* P30–P42.

Salthouse, T. (2000). Adulthood and aging: Cognitive processes and development. In A. Kazdin (Ed.), *Encyclopedia of psychology* (pp. 69–74). Washington, DC: American Psychological Association.

Salthouse, T. A. (2004). What and when of cognitive aging. *Current Directions in Psychological Science, 13*(4), 140–144.

Salthouse, T. A. (2009). When does age-related cognitive decline begin? *Neurobiology of Aging, 30*(4), 507–514.

Salthouse, T. A. (2010). *Major issues in cognitive aging.* New York: Oxford University Press.

Salthouse, T. A. (2011). Neuroanatomical substrates of age-related cognitive decline. *Psychological Bulletin, 137*(5), 753–784.

Salthouse, T. (2012). Consequences of age-related cognitive declines. *Annual Review of Psychology, 63,* 201–226.

Salthouse, T., Babcock, R., Skovronek, E., Mitchell, D., & Palmon, R. (1990). Age and experience effects in spatial visualization. *Developmental Psychology, 26,* 128–136.

Samter, W. (2003). Friendship interaction skills across the life-span. In J. Greene & B. Burleson (Eds.), *Handbook of communication and social interaction skills* (pp. 637–684). Mahwah, NJ: Lawrence Erlbaum Associates Publishers.

Samuels, B. (2011). Breaking the silence on child abuse: Protection, intervention, and deterrence. National Child Abuse and Neglect Data System (NCANDS). Retrieved from http://www.hhs.gov/asl/testify/2011/12/t20111213a.thml

Sanders, S. (2005). Is the glass half empty or half full: Reflections on strain and gain in caregivers of individuals with Alzheimer's disease. *Social Work in Health Care, 40*(3), 57–73.

Sanderson, S. C., & Faith, M. S. (2010). Obesity risk. In K. P. Tercyak (Ed.), *Handbook of genomics and the family: Psychosocial context for children and adolescents* (pp. 329–343). New York: Springer Science + Business Media.

Sando, S., Melquist, S., Cannon, A., Hutton, M., Sletvold, O., Saltvedt, I., et al. (2008). Risk-reducing effect of education in Alzheimer's disease. *International Journal of Geriatric Psychiatry, 23*(11), 1156–1162.

Sandstrom, M. (2011). The power of popularity: Influence processes in childhood and adolescence. In A. Cillessen, D. Schwartz, & L. Mayeux (Eds.), *Popularity in the peer system* (pp. 219–244). New York: Guilford Press.

Saracho, O. N., & Spodek, B. (2008). Fathers: The "invisible" parents. *Early Child Development and Care, 178*(7/8), 821–836.

Sarkadi, A., Kristiansson, R., Oberklaid, F., & Bremberg, S. (2008). Fathers' involvement and children's developmental outcomes: A systematic review of longitudinal studies. *Acta Paediatrica, 97*(2), 153–158.

Sarkeala, T., et al. (2011). Disability trends among nonagenarians in 2001–2007: Vitality 90+ study. *European Journal of Ageing, 8*(2), 87–94.

Sarrazin, J., & Cyr, F. (2007). Parental conflicts and their damaging effects on children. *Journal of Divorce and Remarriage, 47*(1/2), 77–93.

Saucier, G., & Ostendorf, F. (1999). Hierarchical subcomponents of the Big Five personality factors: A cross-language replication. *Journal of Personality and Social Psychology, 76,* 613–627.

Savin-Williams, R. C. (2011). Identity development among sexual-minority youth. In S. J. Schwartz, K. Luyckx, & V. L. Vignoles (Eds.), *Handbook of identity theory and research* (Vols. 1 and 2, pp. 671–689). New York: Springer Science +Business Media.

Sayfan, L. (2008). Grown-ups are not afraid of scary stuff, but kids are: Young children's and adults' reasoning about children's, infants', and adults' fears. *Child Development, 79*(4), 821–835.

Scararnella, L. V., Neppl, T. K., Ontai, L. L, & Conger, R. D. (2008). Consequences of socioeconomic disadvantage across three generations: Parenting behavior and child externalizing problems. *Journal of Family Psychology, 22*(5), 725–733.

Schaie, K. W., & Zanjani, F. A. K. (2006). Intellectual development across adulthood. In C. Hoare (Ed.) *Handbook of adult development and learning* (pp. 99–122). New York: Oxford University Press.

Schaie, K. W. (1996). Intellectual development in adulthood. In J. E. Birren & K. W. Schaie (Eds.), *Handbook of the psychology of aging* (4th ed., pp. 266–286). San Diego, CA: Academic Press.

Schaie, K. W. (2005). *Developmental influences on adult intelligence: The Seattle Longitudinal Study.* London: Oxford University Press.

Schaie, K. W. (2005). What can we learn from longitudinal studies of adult development? *Research in Human Development, 2*(3), 133–158.

Schaie, K. W. (2007). *Developmental influences on adult intelligence: The Seattle Longitudinal Study.* New York: Oxford University Press.

Schaie, K. W., & Abeles, R. P. (2008). *Social structures and aging individuals: Continuing challenges.* New York: Springer Publishing.

Schaie, K. W., & Willis, S. L. (2011). The Seattle Longitudinal Study. Retrieved from http://www.uwpsychiatry.org/sls/about/index.htm

Scheibe, S., Kunzmann, U., & Baltes, P. B. (2007). Wisdom, life longings, and optimal development. In J. A. Blackburn & C. N. Dulmus (Eds.), *Handbook of gerontology: Evidence-based approaches to theory, practice, and policy* (pp. 117–142). Hoboken, NJ: John Wiley & Sons.

Scheibe, S., Kunzmann, U., & Baltes, P. B. (2009). New territories of positive life-span development: Wisdom and life longings. In S. J. Lopez & C. R. Snyder (Eds.), *Oxford handbook of positive psychology* (2nd ed., pp. 171–183). New York: Oxford University Press.

Scher, M. S., Ludington-Hoe, S., Kaffashi, F., Johnson, M. W., Holditch-Davis, D., & Loparo, K. A. (2009). Neurophysiologic assessment of brain maturation after an 8-week trial of skin-to-skin contact on preterm infants. *Clinical Neurophysiology, 120*(10), 1812–1818.

Schieber, F. (2006). Vision and aging. In J. E. Birren & K. Schaire (Eds.), *Handbook of the psychology of aging* (6th ed., pp. 129–161). Amsterdam, Netherlands: Elsevier.

Schiffman, S. S. (2009). Effects of aging on the human taste system. *Annals of the New York Academy of Science, 1170,* 725–729.

Schipul, S. E., Williams, D. L., Keller, T. A., Minshew, N. J., Just, M. A. (2011). Distinctive neural processes during learning in autism. *Cerebral Cortex,* doi: 10.1093/cercor/bhr162

Schmidt, L. A., & Buss, A. H. (2010). Understanding shyness: Four questions and four decades of research. In K. H. Rubin & R. J. Coplan (Eds.), *The development of shyness and social withdrawal* (pp. 23–41). New York: Guilford Press.

Schmitt, M., Kliegel, M., & Shapiro, A. (2007). Marital interaction in middle and old age: A predictor of marital satisfaction. *International Journal of Aging and Human Development, 65*(4), 283–300.

Schneider, B. A., & Pichora-Fuller, M. K. (2000). Implications of perceptual deterioration for cognitive aging research. In F. I. M. Craik & T. A.

Salthouse (Eds.), *Handbook of aging and cognition* (2nd ed., pp. 155–219). Mahwah, NJ: Erlbaum.

Schneider, B. H., Atkinson, L., & Tardiff, C. (2001). Child-parent attachment and children's peer relations: A quantitative review. *Developmental Psychology, 37*(1), 86–100.

Schneider, J. M., Gopinath, B., McMahon, C. M., Leeder, S. R., Mitchell, P., & Wang, J. J. (2011). Dual sensory impairment in older age. *Journal of Aging and Health, 23*(8), 1309–1324.

Schneider, M. (2011). *Introduction to public health.* Sudbury, MA: Jones and Bartlett Publishers.

Schneider, W. (2011). Memory development in childhood. In U. Goswami (Ed.), *The Wiley-Blackwell handbook of childhood cognitive development* (2nd ed., pp. 347–376). Malden, MA:

Schneider, W., & Bjorklund, D. F. (1998). Memory. In D. Kuhn & R. Siegler (Eds.), *Handbook of Child Psychology: Vol. 2. Cognition, perception, and language* (5th ed., pp. 467–522). New York: Wiley.

Schooler, C. (2001). The intellectual effects of the demands of the work environment. In R. J. Sternberg & E. L. Grigorenko (Eds.), *Environmental effects of intellectual functioning* (pp. 363–380). Hillsdale, NJ: Erlbaum.

Schooler, C. (2009). The effects of the cognitive complexity of occupational conditions and leisure-time activities on the intellectual functioning of older adults. In W. Chodzko-Zajko, A. F. Kramer, & L. W. Poon (Eds.), *Enhancing cognitive functioning and brain plasticity* (Vol. 3, pp. 15–34). Champaign, IL: Human Kinetics.

Schooler, C., Mulatu, M. S., & Oates, G. (2004). Occupational self-direction, intellectual functioning, and self-directed orientation in older workers: Findings and implications for individuals and societies. *American Journal of Sociology, 110*(1), 161–197.

Schroeder, J. H., Desrocher, M., Bebko, J. M., & Cappadocia, M. C. (2010). The neurobiology of autism: Theoretical applications. Research in Autism Spectrum Disorders, 4(4), 555–564.

Schultheis, M. T., & Manning, K. J. (2011). Neuroscience and older drivers. In B. E. Porter (Ed.), *Handbook of traffic psychology* (pp. 127–136). San Diego, CA: Elsevier Academic Press.

Schulz, R., & Salthouse, T. (1999). *Adult development and aging: Myths and emerging realities* (3rd ed.). Upper Saddle River, NJ: Prentice Hall.

Schulz, R., Musa, D., Staszewski, J., & Siegler, R. S. (1994). The relationship between age and major league baseball performance: Implications for development. *Psychology and Aging, 9*, 274–286.

Schusterbauer, E. (2009). *Teen suicide.* Detroit, MI: Greenhaven Press.

Schuurman, D. L., & DeCristofaro, J. (2010). Principles and practices of peer support groups and camp-based interventions for grieving children. In C. A. Corr & D. E. Balk (Eds.), *Children's encounters with death, bereavement, and coping* (pp. 359–372). New York: Springer Publishing.

Schvaneveldt, P. L., Kerpelman, J. L., & Schvaneveldt, J. D. (2005). Generational and cultural changes in family life in the United Arab Emirates: A comparison of mothers and daughters. *Journal of Comparative Family Studies, 36*(1), 77–91.

Schwartz, P. D., Maynard, A. M., & Uzelac, S. M. (2008). Adolescent egocentrism: A contemporary view. *Adolescence, 43*(171), 441–448.

Schwartz, S. J., Adamson, L., Ferrer-Wreder, L., Dillon, F. R., & Berman, S. L. (2006). Identity status measurement across contexts: Variations in measurement structure and mean levels among White American, Hispanic American, and Swedish emerging adults. *Journal of Personality Assessment, 86*(1), 61–76.

Schwenkreis, P., El Tom, S., Ragert, P., Pleger, B., Tegenthoff, M., & Dinse, H. R. (2007). Assessment of sensorimotor cortical representation asymmetries and motor skills in violin players. *European Journal of Neuroscience, 26*(11), 3291–3302.

Scott, L. S., Pascalis, O., & Nelson, C. A. (2007). A domain-general theory of the development of perceptual discrimination. *Current Directions in Psychological Science, 16*(4), 197–201.

Seaton, E. K., Sellers, R. M., & Scottham, K. M. (2006). The status model of racial identity development in African American adolescents: Evidence of structure, trajectories, and well-being. *Child Development, 77*(5), 1416–1426.

Sebanc, A. M., Kearns, K. T., Hernandez, M. D., & Galvin, K. B. (2007). Predicting having a best friend in young children: Individual characteristics and friendship features. *Journal of Genetic Psychology, 168*(1), 81–96.

Sebastian, C., Burnett, S., & Blakemore, S. (2008). Development of the self-concept during adolescence. *Trends in Cognitive Sciences, 12*(11), 441–446.

Sedikides, C., & Spencer, S. J. (2007). *The self.* New York: Psychology Press.

Seeman, R., & Chen, X. (2002). Risk and protective factors for physical functioning in older adults with and without chronic conditions: MacArthur studies of successful aging. *Journal of Gerontology 57B*(3), S135–S144.

Segal, N. J., & Stohs, J. (2007). Resemblance for age at menarche in female twins reared apart and together. *Human Biology, 79*(6), 623–635.

Segal, N. L. (2000). *Entwined lives: Twins and what they tell us about human behavior.* New York: Dutton.

Segal, N. L. (2010). Twins: The finest natural experiment. *Personality and Individual Differences, 49*(4), 317–323.

Segerstrom, S. C. (2007). Stress, energy, and immunity: An ecological view. *Current Directions in Psychological Science, 16*(6), 326–330.

Seidman, S. M. (2003). The aging male: Androgens, erectile dysfunction, and depression. *Journal of Clinical Psychiatry, 64*(10), 31–37.

Seiffge-Krenke, I. (1998). *Adolescents' health: A developmental perspective.* Mahwah, NJ: Erlbaum.

Seiffge-Krenke, I., & Gellhaar, T. (2008). Does successful attainment of developmental tasks lead to happiness and success in later developmental tasks? A test of Havighurst's (1948) theses. *Journal of Adolescence, 31*(1), 33–52.

Selin, H., & Stone, P. (2009). *Childbirth across cultures: ideas and practices of pregnancy, childbirth and the postpartum.* Dordrecht; New York: Springer.

Seroczynski, A. D., Jacquez, F. M., & Cole, D. (2003). Depres sion and suicide during adolescence. In G. R. Adams & M. D. Berzonsky (Eds.), *Blackwell handbook of adolescence* (pp. 550–572). Oxford, England: Basil Blackwell.

Serretti, A., Olgiati, P., & De Ronchi, D. (2007). Genetics of Alzheimer's disease. A rapidly evolving field. *Journal of Alzheimer's Disease, 12*, 73–92.

Sesardic, N. (2010). *Making sense of heritability.* Cambridge, MA: Cambridge University Press.

Shahaeian, A., Peterson, C. C., Slaughter, V., & Wellman, H. M. (2011). Culture and the sequence of steps in theory of mind development. *Developmental Psychology, 47*(5), 1239–1247.

Shakib, S., Veliz, P., Dunbar, M. D., & Sabo, D. (2011). Athletics as a source for social status among youth: Examining variation by gender, race/ethnicity, and socioeconomic status. *Sociology of Sport Journal, 28*(3), 303–328.

Shamoo, A. E., & Resnik, D. B. (2009). *Responsible conduct of research.* (2nd ed.) New York: Oxford University Press.

Shanahan, L., McHale, S. M., Crouter, A. C., & Osgood, D. (2007). Warmth with mothers and fathers from middle childhood to late adolescence: Within- and between-families comparisons. *Developmental Psychology, 43*(3), 551–563.

Sharifzadeh, V. (1998). Families with Middle Eastern roots. In E. W. Lynch & M. J. Hanson. *Developing cross-cultural competence* (2nd ed., pp. 441–482). Baltimore: Brookes.

Sharma, D. (2004). Cultural pathways through the information age. In D. Sharma (Ed.), *New Directions for Child and Adolescent Development, 105*, 1, 3–23. San Francisco: Jossey-Bass.

Shatz, M. (1991). Using cross-cultural research to inform us about the role of language in development: Comparisons of Japanese, Korean, and English, and of German, American English, and British English. In M. H. Bornstein (Ed.), *Cultural approaches to parenting* (pp. 139–153). Hillsdale, NJ: Erlbaum.

Shatz, M., & Gelman, R. (1973). The development of communication skills: Modifications in the speech of young children as a function of the listener.

Shaver, P. R., & Fraley, R. C. (2010). Attachment, loss, and grief: Bowlby's views and current controversies. In J. Cassidy & P. Shaver (Eds.), *Handbook of attachment: Theory, research, and clinical applications* (2nd ed., pp. 48–77). New York: Guilford Press.

Shaver, P. R., & Mikulincer, M. (2012). *Meaning, mortality, and choice: The social psychology of existential concerns.* Washington, DC: American Psychological Association.

Shaywitz, S. E., Morris, R., & Shaywitz, B. A. (2008). The education of dyslexic children from childhood to young adulthood. *Annual Review of Psychology, 59*(1), 451–475.

Sheaks, C. (2007). The state of phased retirement: Facts, figures, and policies. *Generations, 31*(1), 57–62.

Shearer, C. L., Crouter, A. C., & McHale, S. M. (2005). Parents' perceptions ofchanges in mother–child and father–child relationships during adolescence. *Journal of Adolescent Research, 20*(6), 662–684.

Shears, J., & Robinson, J. (2005). Fathering attitudes and practices: Influences on children's development. *Child Care in Practice, 11*(1), 63–79.

Sheely, A. (2010). Work characteristics and family routines in low-wage families. *Journal of Sociology and Social Welfare, 37*(3), 59–77.

Sherar, L. B., Baxter-Jones, A. D. G., & Mirwald, R. L. (2007). The relationship between body composition and onset of menarche. *Annals of Human Biology, 34*(6), 673–677.

Shigeta, M., & Homma, A. (2007). Alzheimer's disease. In J. A. Blackburn & C. N. Dulmus (Eds.), *Handbook of gerontology: Evidence-based approaches to theory, practice, and policy* (pp. 336–366). Hoboken, NJ: John Wiley & Sons.

Shing, Y. L., Werkle-Bergner, M., Li, S., & Lindenberger, U. (2008). Associative and strategic components of episodic memory: A life-span dissociation. *Journal of Experimental Psychology, 137*(3), 495–513.

Shinskey, J. L. (2008). The sound of darkness: Why do auditory cues aid infants' search for objects hidden by darkness but not by visible occluders? *Developmental Psychology, 44*(4), 1715–1725.

Shipley, T. F., & Zacks, J. M. (2008). *Understanding events: From perception to action.* New York: Oxford University Press.

Shirley, C., & Wallace, M. (2004). Domestic work, family characteristics, and earnings: Reexamining gender and class differences. *Sociological Quarterly, 45*(4), 663–690.

Shirom, A. (2011). Job-related burnout: A review of major research foci and challenges. In J. C. Quick & L. E. Tetrick (Eds.), *Handbook of occupational health psychology* (2nd ed., pp. 223–241). Washington, DC: American Psychological Association.

Shum, D., Neulinger, K., O'Callaghan, M., & Mohay, H. (2008). Attentional problems in children born very preterm with extremely low birth weight at 7–9 years. *Archives of Clinical Neuropsychology, 23*(1), 103–112.

Shwalb, D. W., Nakazawa, J., & Shwalb, B. J. (2005). *Applied developmental psychology: Theory, practice, and research from Japan.* Greenwich, CT: Information Age Publishers.

Shwalb, D. W., Shwalb, B. J., & Lamb, M. E. (2013). *Fathers in cultural context.* New York: Psychology Press.

Shweder, R. A., & Bidell, T. R. (2009). *The child: An encyclopedic companion.* Chicago, IL: University of Chicago Press.

Siddique, J., Lauderdale, D. S., VanderWeele, T. J., & Lantos, J. D. (2009). Trends in prenatal ultrasound use in the United States 1995 to 2006. *Medical Care, 47*(11), 1129–1135.

Sieber, R. T., & Gordon, A. J. (1981). Socialization implications of school discipline or how first graders are taught to listen. In R. T. Sieber and A. J. Gordon (Eds.), *Children and their organizations: Investigations in American culture* (pp. 1–17). Boston: G. K. Hall.

Siegler, I. C., Kaplan, B. H., Von Dras, D. D., & Mark, D. B. (1999). Cardiovascular health: A challenge for midlife. In S. L. Willis & J. D. Reid (Eds.), *Life in the middle: Psychological and social development in middle age* (pp. 147–157). San Diego, CA: Academic Press.

Siegler, R. S., & Ellis, S. (1996). Piaget on childhood. *Psychological Science, 7,* 211–215.

Simkin, P. (2008). *The birth partner: A complete guide to childbirth for dads, doulas, and other labor companions* (3rd ed.). Boston: Harvard Common Press.

Simkin, P., et al. (2010). *Pregnancy, childbirth, and the newborn: The complete guide* (4th ed.). New York: Simon & Schuster.

Simoneau, G. G., & Leibowitz, H. W. (1996). Posture, gait, and falls. In J. E. Birren, K. W. Schaie, R. P. Abeles, M. Gatz, & T. A. Salthouse (Eds.), *Handbook of the psychology of aging* (4th ed., pp. 204–217). San Diego, CA: Academic Press.

Simpson, J. A., & Belsky, J. (2010) Attachment theory within a modern evolutionary framework. In J. Cassidy & P. Shaver (Eds.), *Handbook of attachment: Theory, research, and clinical applications* (2nd ed., pp. 131–157). New York: Guilford Press.

Singer, D. G., & Singer, J. L. (Eds.). (2000). *Handbook of children and the media.* Thousand Oaks, CA: Sage.

Singh, J. (2008). Bacterial infection as a cause of sudden infant death. *American Journal of Nursing, 108*(9), 22.

Singh, M. A. (2002). Exercise comes of age: Rationale and recommendations for a geriatric exercise prescription. *Journals of Gerontology Series A: Biological Sciences and Medical Sciences, 57A*(5), M262.

Sinnott, J. D. (2003). Postformal thought and adult development: Living in balance. In J. Demick & C. Andreoletti (Eds.), *Handbook of adult development* (pp. 221–238). New York: Kluwer Academic/Plenum Publishers.

Sinnott, J. D. (2008). Cognitive and representational development in adults. In K. Cartwright (Ed.), *Literacy processes: Cognitive flexibility in learning and teaching* (pp. 42–68). New York: Guilford Press.

Sinnott, J. D. (2009). Cognitive development as the dance of adaptive transformation: Neo-Piagetian perspectives on adult cognitive development. In C. M. Smith & N. DeFrates-Densch (Eds.), *Handbook of research on adult learning and development* (pp. 103–134). New York: Routledge/Taylor & Francis Group.

Slater, A., & Johnson, S. P. (1998). Visual sensory and perceptual ablities of the newborn: Beyond the blooming, buzzing confusion. In F. Simion & G. Butterworth (Eds.), *The development of sensory, motor, and cogntive capacities in early infancy: From perception to cognition* (pp. 121–141). Hove, England: Erlbaum.

Slater, A. M. et al. (2011). Visual perception. In J. G. Bremner & T. D. Wachs (Eds.), *The Wiley-Blackwell handbook of infant development, Vol. 1: Basic research* (2nd ed.). Malden, MA: Wiley-Blackwell.

Slaughter, V., Dennis, M. J., & Pritchard, M. (2002). Theory of mind and peer acceptance in preschool children. *British Journal of Developmental Psychology, 20*(4), 545–564.

Slavin, R. E. (2000). *Cooperative learning: Theory, research, and practice* (2nd ed.). Boston: Allyn and Bacon.

Slobin, D. I. (1972). Children and language: They learn the same way all around the world. *Psychology Today, 6*(2), 71–74, 82.

Slowinski, J. (2007a). Sexual problems and dysfunctions in men. In A. Owens & M. Tepper, *Sexual health Vol 4: State-of-the-art treatments and research* (pp. 1–14). Westport, CT: Praeger Publishers/Greenwood Publishing Group.

Slowinski, J. (2007b). Psychological and relationship aspects of male sexuality. In A. Owens & M. Tepper (Eds.), *Sexual health Vol 4: State-of-the-art treatments and research* (pp. 14–46). Westport, CT: Praeger Publishers/Greenwood Publishing Group.

Sluss, D., & Jarrett, O. (2007) *Investigating play in the 21st century.* Lanham, MD: University Press of America.

Small, G. W. (2008). *iBrain: Surviving the technological alteration of the modern mind.* New York: Collins Living.

Smeets, F., et al. (2010). Aging does not affect gray matter asymmetry. *Psychology and Aging, 25*(3), 587–594.

Smetana, J. G. (2010). The role of trust in adolescent-parent relationships: To trust you is to tell you. In K. J. Rotenberg (Ed.), *Interpersonal trust during childhood and adolescence* (pp. 223–246).

Smetana, J. G. (2005). Adolescent–parent conflict: Resistance and subversion as developmental process. In L. Nucci (Ed.), *Conflict, contradiction, and contrarian elements in moral development and education* (pp. 69–91). Mahwah, NJ: Lawrence Erlbaum Associates.

Smetana, J. G. (2011). Adolescents' social reasoning and relationships with parents: Conflicts and coordination's within and across domains. In E. Amsel & J. Smetana (Eds.), *Adolescent vulnerabilities and opportunities* (pp. 139–158). New York: Cambridge University Press.

Smetana, J. G., & Villalobos, M. (2009). Social cognitive development in adolescence. In R. M. Lerner & L. Steinberg (Eds.), *Handbook of adolescent psychology, Vol. 1: Individual bases of adolescent development* (3rd ed., pp. 187–228). Hoboken, NJ: John Wiley & Sons.

Smetana, J. G., Villalobos, M., Tasopoulos-Chan, M., Gettman, D. C., & Campione-Barr, N. (2009). Early and middle adolescents' disclosure to parents about activities in different domains. *Journal of Adolescence, 32*(3), 693–713.

Smetana, J., Crean, H. F., & Campione-Barr, N. (2005). Adolescents' and parents' changing conceptions of parental authority. *New Directions for Child and Adolescent Development, 108,* 31–46.

Smith, B. S., Ratner, H. H., & Hobart, C. J. (1987). The role of cueing and organization in children's memory for events. *Journal of Experimental Child Psychology, 44,* 1–24.

Smith, C. D. (1994). *The absentee American: Repatriates' perspectives on America.* Bayside, NY: Aletheia.

Smith, C., & Lloyd, B. (1978). Maternal behavior and perceived sex of infant: Revisited. *Child Development, 49*(4), 1263–1265.

Smith, D. G., Xiao, L., & Becharra, A. (2011 November 14). Decision making in children and adolescents: Impaired iowa gambling task performance in early adolescence. *Developmental Psychology*. Advance online publication. doi: 10.1037/a0026342Smith, L. B., Thelen, E., Titzer, R., & McLin, D. (1999). Knowing in the context of acting: The task dynamics of the A-Not-B Error. *Psychological Review, 106,* 235–260.

Smith, L. M., LaGasse, L. L., Derauf, C., & Newman, E., et al. (2011). Motor and cognitive outcomes through three years of age in children exposed to prenatal methamphetamine. *Neurotoxicology and Teratology, 33*(1), 176–184.

Smith, P. K. (2010). *Children and play.* Malden, MA: Wiley-Blackwell.

Smith, P.K., & Gosso, Y. (2010). *Children and play.* London: Wiley-Blackwell.

Smith, S. D. (2011). Approach to epigenetic analysis in language disorders. *Journal of Neurodevelopmental Disorders, 3*(4), 356–364.

Smith, S. W. (2012). *End-of-life decisions in medical care: Principles and policies for regulating the dying process.* New York: Cambridge University Press.

Smolak, L., & Stein, J. A. (2010). A longitudinal investigation of gender role and muscle building in adolescent boys. *Sex Roles, 63*(9–10), 738–746.

Sneed, J. R., & Whitbourne, S. K. (2005). Models of the aging self. *Journal of Social Issues, 61*(2), 375–388.

Sneed, J. R., Whitbourne, S. K., & Culang, M. E. (2006). Trust, identity, and ego integrity: Modeling Erickson's core stages over 34 years. *Journal of Adult Development, 13,* 148–157.

Sneed, J. R., Whitbourne, S. K., Schwartz, S. J. & Huang, J. R. (2012). The relationship between identity, intimacy, and midlife well-being: Findings from the Rochester Adult Longitudinal Study. *Psychology and Aging, 27*(2), 318–323.

Snow, C. E. (2006). What counts as literacy in early childhood? In K. McCartney & D. Phillips (Eds.), *Blackwell handbook of early childhood development* (pp. 274–294). Malden, MA: Blackwell Publishing.

Snow, C. E., Griffin, P., & Burns, M. S. (2005). Students change: What are teachers to learn about reading development? In C. Snow, P. Griffin, & M. Burns (Eds.), *Knowledge to support the teaching of reading: Preparing teachers for a changing world* (pp. 15–122). San Francisco: Jossey-Bass.

Snowling, M. J., & Hulme, C. (2011). Evidence-based interventions for reading and language difficulties: Creating a virtuous circle. *British Journal of Educational Psychology, 81*(1), 1–23.

Society for Research in Child Development. (2011). SRCD ethical standards for research with children. Retrieved from http://www.srcd.org/index.php?option=com_content&task+view&id=68

Soken, N. H., & Pick, A. D. (1999). Infants' perception of dynamic affective expressions. Do infants distinguish specific expressions? *Child Development, 70,* 1275–1282.

Solantaus, T., Leinonen, J., & Punamäki, R. (2004). Children's mental health in times of economic recession: Replication and extension of the Family Economic Stress Model in Finland. *Developmental Psychology, 40*(3), 410–429.

Solomon, J., & George, C. (2011). *Disorganized attachment and caregiving.* New York: Guilford Press.

Solomontes-Kountuori, O., & Hurry, J. (2008). Political, religious and occupational identities in context: Placing identity status paradigm in context. *Journal of Adolescence, 31*(2), 241–258.

Solway, A. (2009). *Using genetic technology*. Chicago: Heinemann Library

Sommer, I. E. C. (2010). Sex differences in handedness, brain asymmetry, and language lateralization. In K. Hugdahl & R. Westerhausen (Eds.), *The two halves of the brain: Information processing in the cerebral hemispheres* (pp. 287–312). Cambridge, MA: MIT Press.

Sommerville, J. A., & Hammond, A. J. (2007). Treating another's actions as one's own: Children's memory of and learning from joint activity. *Developmental Psychology, 43*(4), 1003–1018.

Song, H., & Baillargeon, R. (2008). Infants' reasoning about others' false perceptions. *Developmental Psychology, 44*(6), 1789–1795.

Sonuga-Barke, E., Schlotz, W., & Rutter, M. (2010). Physical growth and maturation following early severe institutional deprivation: Do they mediate specific psychopathological effects? *Monographs of the Society for Research in Child Development, 75*(1), 143–166.

Sorenson, R. C. (1973). *Adolescent sexuality in contemporary America: Personal values and sexual behavior, ages 13–19.* New York: World.

Sosnoff, J. J., Vallantine, A. D., & Newell, K. M. (2007). Aging: Loss of complexity or loss of adaptability. *Journal of Sport and Exercise Psychology, 29,* S131–S131.

Southgate, V., Csibra, G., Kaufman, J., & Johnson, M. H. (2008). Distinct processing of objects and faces in the infant brain. *Journal of Cognitive Neuroscience, 20*(4), 741–749.

Southgate, V., Gergely, G., & Csibra, G. (2009). Does the mirror neuron system and its impairment explain human imitation and autism? In J. A. Pineda (Ed.), *Mirror neuron systems: The role of mirroring processes in social cognition* (pp. 331–354). Totowa, NJ: Humana Press.

Spear, L. (2002). The adolescent brain and the college drinker: Biological basis of propensity to use and misuse alcohol. *Journal of Studies on Alcohol, Vol. Suppl 14, Mar 2002. Special issue: College drinking, what it is, and what to do about it: Review of the state of the science,* 71–81.

Spear, L. (2008). The psychobiology of adolescence. In K. Kline (Ed.), *Authoritative communities: The scientific case for nurturing the whole child* (pp. 263–280). New York: Springer Science + Business Media.

Spear, L. P. (2010). *The behavioral neuroscience of adolescence.* New York: W. W. Norton & Co.

Spector, W. D., & Fleishman, J. A. (2001). *The characteristics of long-term care users.* Retrieved February 3, 2009 from http://www.ahrq.gov/RESEARCH/ltcusers/index.html

Spelke, E. S. (2005). Sex differences in intrinsic aptitude for mathematics and science? *American Psychologist, 60*(9), 950–958.

Spencer, P. E., & Marschark, M. (2006). Advances in the spoken language development of deaf and hard-of-hearing children. In P. E. Spencer & M. Marschark (Eds.), *Perspectives on deafness.* New York: Oxford University Press.

Spencer-Rodgers, J., & Collins, N. L. (2006). Risk and resilience: Dual effects of perceptions of group disadvantage among Latinos. *Journal of Experimental Social Psychology, 42*(6), 729–737.

Spinrad, T. L., & Eisenberg, N. (2009). Empathy, prosocial behavior, and positive development in schools. In R. Gilman, S. E. Huebner, & M. J. Furlong (Eds.), *Handbook of positive psychology in schools* (pp. 119–129). New York: Routledge/Taylor & Francis Group.

Spinrad, T. L., & Stifter, C. A. (2006). Toddlers' empathy-related responding to distress: Predictions from negative emotionality and maternal behavior in infancy. *Infancy, 10*(2), 97–121.

Spinrad, T. L., Eisenberg, N., & Bernt, F. (2007). Introduction to the special issues on moral development: Part 1. *Journal of Genetic Psychology,* 168(2), 101–104.

Spiro, A. (2001). Health in midlife: Toward a lifespan view. In M. E. Lachman (Ed.), *Handbook of midlife development* (pp. 156–187). New York: Wiley.

Spiteri, E., Konopka, G., Coppola, G., Bomar, J., Oldham, M., Jing, O., et al. (2007). Identification of the transcriptional targets of FOXP2, a gene linked to speech and language, in developing human brain. *American Journal of Human Genetics, 81*(6), 1144–1157.

Spitze, G., & Ward, R. (2000). Gender, marriage, and expectations for personal care. *Research on Aging, 22*(5), 451–469.

Spivak, A. L., & Howes, C. (2011). Social and relational factors in early education and prosocial actions of children of diverse ethnocultural communities. *Merrill-Palmer Quarterly: Journal of Developmental Psychology, 57*(1), 1–24.

Spore, D. L., Mor, V., Parrat, P., Hawes, C., & Hiris, J. (1997). Inappropriate drug prescriptions for elderly residents of board and care facilities. *American Journal of Public Health, 87,* 404–409.

Springer, S. P., & Deutsch, G. (2003). *Left brain, right brain: Perspectives from cognitive neuroscience* (5th ed.). New York: Freeman.

Stack, D. M. (2010). Touch and physical contact during infancy: Discovering the richness of the forgotten sense. In J. G. Bremner & T. D. Wachs (Eds.), *The Wiley Blackwell handbook of infant development* (2nd ed., pp. 352–567). Malden, MA: Wiley-Blackwell.

Stack, D. M., Serbin, L. A., Enns, L. N., Ruttle, P. L., & Barrieau, L. (2010). Parental effects on children's emotional development over time and across generations. *Infants & Young Children, 23*(1), 52–69.

Stack, S. (2001). Sociological research into suicide. In D. Lester (Ed.), *Suicide prevention: Resources for the millennium* (pp. 17–29). New York: Brunner-Routledge.

Stange, A., & Kunzmann, U. (2008). Fostering wisdom: A psychological perspective. In M. Ferrari & G. Potworowski (Eds.), *Teaching for wisdom: Cross-cultural perspectives on fostering wisdom* (pp. 23–36). New York: Springer Science + Business Media.

Stanley, J. T., & Isaacowitz, D. M. (2012). In S. K. Whitbourne & M. J. Sliwinski (Eds.), *The Wiley-Blackwell handbook of adulthood and aging* (pp. 236–253). Malden, MA: Wiley-Blackwell.

Stanley, S. M., Rhoades, G. K., & Fincham, F. D. (2011). Understanding romantic relationships among emerging adults: the significant roles of cohabitation and ambiguity. In F. D. Fincham & M. Cui (Eds.), *Romantic relationships in emerging adulthood* (pp. 234–251). New York: Cambridge University Press.

Staudinger, U. M. (2008). A psychology of wisdom: History and recent developments. *Research in Human Development, 5*(2). Special issue: *Lifespan psychology: The Legacy of Paul Baltes,* 107–120.

Staudinger, U. M., & Gluck, J. (2011). Intelligence and wisdom. In R. J. Sternberg & S. B. Kaufman (Eds.), *The Cambridge handbook of intelligence* (pp. 827–846). New York: Cambridge University Press.

Staudinger, U. M., Kessler, & E., Dörner, J. (2006). Wisdom in social context. In K. Schaie & L. L. Carstensen (Eds.), *Social structures, aging, and self-regulation in the elderly* (pp. 33–67). New York: Springer Publishing.

Staudinger, U. M., & Pasupathi, M. (2000). Life-span perspectives on self, personality, and social cognition. In F. I. M. Craik & T. A. Salthouse (Eds.), *Handbook of aging and cognition* (2nd ed., pp. 633–688). Mahwah, NJ: Erlbaum.

Stegarud, L., Solheim, B., Karlsen, M., & Kroger, J. (1999). Ego identity in crosscultural context: A replication study. *Psychological Reports, 85,* 457–461.

Steggall, M. J. (2007). Erectile dysfunction: Physiology, causes and patient management. *Nursing Standard, 21*(43), 49–56.

Steinbock, B. (2007). *The Oxford handbook of bioethics.* New York: Oxford University Press.

Steinburg, L. (2010). A dual systems model of adolescent risk-taking. *Developmental Psychobiology, 52*(3). Special issue: *Psychobiological models of adolescent risk,* 216–224.

Steinburg, L. (2011). Adolescent risk taking: A social neuroscience perspective. In E. Amsel & J. Smetana (Eds.), *Adolescent vulnerabilities and opportunities* (pp. 41–64). New York: Cambridge University Press.

Stemmer, B., & Whitaker, H. A. (2008). *Handbook of the neuroscience of language.* Amsterdam; Boston: Elsevier/Academic Press.

Stenberg, G. (2009). Selectivity in infant social referencing. *Infancy, 14*(4), 457–473.

Stephens, M. A. P., & Franks, M. M. (1999). Intergenerational relationships in later-life families: Adult daughters and sons as caregivers to aging parents.

Stern, C., & Munn, Z. (2010). Cognitive leisure activities and their role in preventing dementia: A systematic review. *International Journal of Evidence-Based Healthcare, 8*(1), 2–17.

Sternberg, R. J. (2005a). Older but not wiser? The relationship between age and wisdom. *Ageing International 30*(1), 5–26.

Sternberg, R. J. (2005b). The triarchic theory of successful intelligence. In D. Flanagan & P. Harrison (Eds.), *Contemporary intellectual assessment: Theories, tests, and issues* (pp. 103–119). New York: Guilford Press.

Sternberg, R. J. (2006b). Creating a vision of creativity: The first 25 years. *Psychology of Aesthetics, Creativity, and the Arts, S*(1), 2–12.

Sternberg, R. J. (2006a). A duplex theory of love. In R. J. Sternberg & K. Weiss (Eds.), *The new psychology of love* (pp. 184–199). New Haven, CT: Yale University Press.

Sternberg, R. J. (2006b). *Thinking and problem solving.* San Diego: Academic Press.

Sternberg, R. J. (2011). The theory of successful intelligence. In R. Sternberg & S. Kaufman (Eds.), *The Cambridge handbook of intelligence* (pp. 504–527). New York: Cambridge University Press.

Sternberg, R. J., Bonney, C. R., Gabora, L., & Merrifield, M. (2012). WICS: A model for college and university admissions. *Educational Psychologist, 47*(1), 30–41.

Sternberg, R. J., Grigorenko, E. L., & Kidd, K. K. (2005). Intelligence, race, and genetics. *American Psychologist, 60*(1), 46–59.

Sternberg, R. J., Grigorenko, E. L., Kidd, K. K., & Stemler, S. E. (2011). Intelligence, race, and genetics. In S. Krimsky & K. Sloan (Eds.), *Race and the genetic revolution: Science, myth, and culture* (pp. 195–237). New York: Columbia University Press.

Sternberg, R. J., Kaufman, J. C., & Grigorenko, E. L. (2009). *The essential Sternberg: Essays on intelligence, psychology, and education.* New York: Springer.

Sternberg, R. L., Jarvin, L., & Grigorenko, E. L. (2011). *Explorations in giftedness.* New York: Cambridge University Press.

Sterns, H. L., & Chang, B. (2010). Workforce issues and retirement. In J. C. Cavanaugh & C. K. Cavanaugh (Eds.), *Aging in America, Vol. 3: Societal Issues* (pp. 81–105). Santa Barbara, CA: Praeger/ABC-CLIO.

Sterns, H. L., & Gray, J. H. (1999). Work, leisure, and retirement. In J. C. Cavanaugh & S. K. Whitbourne (Eds.), *Gerontology: An interdisciplinary perspective* (pp. 355–390). New York: Oxford University Press.

Sterns, H. L., & Huyck, M. H. (2001). The role of work at midlife. In M. E. Lachman (Ed.), *Handbook of midlife development* (pp. 447–486). New York: Wiley.

Stewart, A. J., & Newton, N. J. (2010). Gender, adult development, and aging. In J. C. Chrisler & D. R. McCreary (Eds.), *Handbook of gender research in psychology, Vol. 1: Gender research in general and experimental psychology* (pp. 559–580). New York: Springer Science + Business Media.

Stine-Morrow, E. (2007). The Dumbledore hypothesis of cognitive aging. *Current Directions in Psychological Science, 16*(6), 295–299.

Stine-Morrow, E. A. L., & Basak, C. (2011). Cognitive interventions. In K. Warner Schaie & S. L. Willis (Eds.), *Handbook of the psychology of aging* (7th ed., pp. 153–171). San Diego, CA: Elsevier Academic Press.

Stones, J. J., & Kozma, A. (1996). Activity, exercise, and behavior. In J. E. Birren & K. W. Schaie (Eds.), *Handbook of the psychology of aging* (4th ed., pp. 338–352). San Diego, CA: Academic Press.

Stoodley, C. J., & Stein, J. F. (2011). The cerebellum and dyslexia. *Cortex: A Journal Devoted to the Study of Nervous System and Behavior, 47*(1), 101–116.

Stoppard, M. (2012). *Preparing for childbirth: A practical guide to childbirth choices.* London: Dorling Kendersley.

Story, T. N., Berg, C. A., Smith, T. W., Beveridge, R., Henry, N. J., & Pearce, G. (2007). Age, marital satisfaction, and optimism as predictors of positive sentiment override in middle-aged and older married couples. *Psychology and Aging, 22*(4), 719–727.

Strauch, B. (2008). *The primal teen: What the new discoveries about the teenage brain will us about our kids.* Paw Prints.

Strauss, J. R. (2011). The reciprocal relationship between menopausal symptoms and depressive symptoms: A 9-year longitudinal study of American women in midlife. *Maturitas, 70*(3), 302–306.

Strid, K., Tjus, T., Smith, L., Melzoff, A. N., & Heimann, M. (2006). Infant recall memory and communication predicts later cognitive development. *Infant Behavior and Development, 29*(4), 545–553.

Stroebe, M., & Schut, H. (2010). The dual process model of coping with bereavement: A decade on. *Omega: Journal of Death and Dying, 61*(4), 273–289.

Stroebe, M., Folkman, S., Hansson, R. O., & Schut, H. (2006). The prediction of bereavement outcome: Development of an integrative risk factor framework. *Social Science and Medicine, 63*(9), 2440–2451.

Stroebe, M., Schut, H., & Boerner, K. (2010). Continuing bonds in adaptation to bereavement: Toward theoretical integration. *Clinical Psychology Review, 30*(2), 259–268.

Stroebe, M. S. (2008). *Handbook of bereavement research and practice: Advances in theory and intervention.* Washington, DC: American Psychological Association.

Stroebe, M. S., Hansson, R. O., Stroebe, W., & Schut, H. (Eds.). (2001). *Handbook of bereavement research: Consequences, coping, and care.* Washington, DC: American Psychological Association.

Stroebe, W., Schut, H., & Stroebe, M. S. (2005). Grief work, disclosure, and counseling: Do they help the bereaved? *Clinical Psychology Review*, 25(4), 395 -414.

Stroebe, M. S. (2011). Coping with bereavement. In S. Folkman (Ed.), *The Oxford handbook of stress, health, and coping.* New York: Oxford University Press.

Strong, B., DeVault, C., & Cohen, T. F. (2011). *The marriage and family experience: Intimate relationships in a changing society.* Belmont, CA: Wadsworth/ Cengage Learning.

Sturaro, C., van Lier, P. A. C., Cuijpers, P., & Koot, H. M. (2011). The role of peer relationships in the development of early school-age externalizing problems. *Child Development, 82*(3), 758–765.

Subbotsky, E. (1994). Early rationality and magical thinking in preschoolers: Space and time. *British Journal of Developmental Psychology, 12,* 97–108.

Subrahmanyam, K., & Smahel, D. (2011). *Digital youth: The role of media in development.* New York: Springer Science + Business Media.

Substance Abuse and Mental Health Services Administration (SAMHSA). (2007). Driving under the influence of alcohol in the past year by age, 2007. *The 2007 National Survey on Drug Use and Health, SMA 03-3774.* Rockville, MD: Substance Abuse and Mental Health Services Administration.

Substance Abuse and Mental Health Services Administration. (2011). *Results for the 2010 National Survey on Drug Use and Health: Summary of National Findings, NSDUH Series H-41, HHS Publication No. (SMA) 11–1–4658.* Rockville, MD: Author.

Substance Abuse and Mental Health Services Administration. (2012). *Results from the 2010 National Survey on Drug Use and Health: Mental Health Findings, NSDUH Series H-42, HHS Publication No. (SMA) 11–1–4667.* Rockville, MD: Author. Retrieved from http://www.store.samhas.gov/home

Suicide Prevention Resource Center. (2008). *Suicide risk and prevention for lesbian, gay, bisexual, and transgender youth.* Newton, MA: Education Development Center, Inc.

Suitor, J. J., & Pillemer, K. (2006). Choosing daughters: Exploring why mothers favor adult daughters over sons. *Sociological Perspectives, 49*(2), 139–161.

Suomi, S. J. (2010). Attachment in rhesus monkeys. In J. Cassidy & P. Shaver (Eds.), *Handbook of attachment: Theory, research, and clinical applications* (2nd ed., pp. 173–191). New York: Guilford Press.

Super, C. M., & Harkness, S. (2002). Culture structures the environment for development. *Human Development, 45*(4), 270–274.

Super, C. M., & Harkness, S. (2010). Culture and infancy. In J. G. Bremner & T. D. Wachs (Eds.), *The Wiley-Blackwell handbook of infant development* (2nd ed., pp. 623–649). Malden, MA: Wiley-Blackwell.

Super, C. M., Herrera, M. G., & Mora, J. O. (1990). Long-term effects of food supplementation and psychosocial intervention on the physical growth of Colombian infants at risk of malnutrition. *Child Development, 61,* 29–49.

Sussman, E. J., Dorn, L. D., & Schiefelbein, V. L. (2003). Puberty, sexuality, and health. In R. Learner, M. A. Easterbrooks, & J. Mistry (Eds.), *Handbook of psychology: Vol. 6. Developmental psychology* (pp. 295–324). New York: Wiley.

Sutin, A. R., Costa, P. T., Jr., Wethington, E., & Eaton, W. (2010). Turning points and lessons learned: Stressful life events and personality trait development across middle adulthood. *Psychology and Aging, 25*(3), 524–533.

Suy, A., Hernandez, S., Thorne, C., Lonca, M., Lopez, M., & Coll, O. (2008). Current guidelines on management of HIV-infected prenant women: Impact on mode of delivery. *European Journal of Obstetrics and Gynecology and Reproductive Biology, 139*(2), 127–132.

Suzuki, L. A., Short, E. L., & Lee, C. S. (2011). Racial and ethnic group differences in intelligence in the United States: Multicultural perspectives. In R. Sternberg & S. Kaufman (Eds.), *The Cambridge handbook of intelligence* (pp. 273–292). New York: Cambridge University Press.

Swanson, M. W., Streissguth, A. P., Sampson, P. D., & Olson, H. (1999). Prenatal cocaine and neuromotor outcome at four months: Effect of duration of exposure. *Journal of Developmental and Behavioral Pediatrics, 20,* 325–334.

SWEDNES.SE: The Official Gateway to Sweden. (2012). Swedish child care. Retrieved from http://www.sweden.se/eng/Home/society Childcare/

Swingley, D. (2008). The roots of the early vocabulary in infants' learning from speech. *Current Directions in Psychological Science, 17*(5), 308–312.

Szaflarski, J. P., et al. (2012). Left-handedness and language lateralization in children. *Brain Research, 1433,* 85–97.

Szinovacz, M. E. (1998). Grandparents today: A demographic profile. *The Gerontologist, 38,* 37–52.

Taimalu, M., & Lahikainen, A. R. (2007). Self-reported fears as indicators of young children's well-being in societal change: A cross-cultural perspective. *Social Indicators Research, 80*(1), 51–78.

Taki, Y., Kinomura, S., Sata, K., Goto, R., Kawashima, R., & Fukuda, H. (2011). A longitudinal study of gray matter volume decline with age and modifying factors. *Neurobiology of Aging, 32*(5), 907–915.

Tamis-LeMonda, C. S., & Cabrera, N. J. (2002). *Handbook of father involvement: Multidisciplinary perspectives.* Mahwah, NJ: Lawrence Erlbaum Associates.

Tamis-LeMonda, C. S., & McFadden, K. E. (2010). Fathers from low-income backgrounds: Myths and evidence. In M. E. Lamb (Ed.), *The role of the father in child development* (5th ed., pp. 296–318). Hoboken, NJ: John Wiley & Sons, Inc.

Tangney, J., Stuewig, J., & Mashek, D. J. (2007). Moral emotions and moral behavior. *Annual Review of Psychology, 58,* 345–372.

Tanner, J. M. (1962). *Growth at adolescence, with a general consideration of the effects of hereditary and environmental factors upon growth and maturation from birth to maturity* (2nd ed.). Oxford: Blackwell Scientific Publications.

Tanner, J. M. (1998). Sequence, tempo, and individual variation in growth and development of boys and girls ages twelve to sixteen. In R. E. Muuss & H. D. Porton (Eds.), *Adolescent behavior and society: A book of readings* (5th ed., pp. 34–46). Boston: McGraw–Hill.

Tardif, T., Gelman, S. A., & Xu, F. (1999). Putting the "noun bias" in context: A comparison of English and Mandarin. *Child Development, 70,* 620–635.

Tardif, W., Fletcher, P., Liang, W., Zang, Z., Kacirot, N., & Marchman, V. A. (2008). Baby's first 10 words. *Developmental Psychology, 44*(4), 929–938.

Tavernise, S. (2010). Grandparents' role grows as the economy struggles. *The New York Times.* Retrieved from http://www.nytimes.com/2010/11/11/us/11marriage.html

Taylor, C. A., Manganello, J. A., Lee, S. J., & Rice, J. C. (2010). Mother's spanking of 3-year-old children and subsequent risk of children's aggressive behavior. *Pediatrics, 125,* 1057–1065.

Taylor, H. G., & Espy, K. A. (2009). Mathematics deficiencies in children with very low birth weight or very preterm birth. *Developmental Disabilities Research Reviews, 15*(1). Special issue: *Pathways to mathematical learning difficulties and disabilities.*

Taylor, M. G., Rhodes, M., & Gelman, S. A. (2009). Boys will be boys; cows will be cows: Children's essentialist reasoning about gender categories and animal species. *Child Development, 80*(2), 461–481.

Taylor, M., Carlson, S. M., Maring, B. L., Gerow, L., & Charley, C. M. (2004). The characteristics and correlates of fantasy in school-age children: Imaginary companions, impersonation, and social understanding. *Developmental Psychology, 40*(6), 1173–1187.

Taylor, R. D., Seaton, E., & Dominguez, A. (2008). Kinship support, family relations, and psychological adjustment among low-income African American mothers and adolescents. *Journal of Research on Adolescence, 18*(1), 1–22.

Teller, D. Y. (1998). Spatial and temporal aspects of infant color vision. Proceedings of the International Colour Vision Society. *Vision Research, 38*(21), 3275–3282.

Telzer, E. H., & Fuligni, A. J. (2009). Daily family assistance and the psychological well-being of adolescents from Latin American, Asian, and European backgrounds. *Developmental Psychology, 45*(4), 1177–1189.

Temcheff, C. E., Serbin, L. A., Martin-Storey, A., Stack, D. M., Ledingham, J., & Schwartzman, A. E. (2011). Predicting adult physical health outcomes from childhood aggression, social withdrawal and likeability: A 30-year prospective, longitudinal study. *International Journal of Behavioral Medicine, 18*(1), 5–12.

Tepper, M., & Owens, A. (2007). *Sexual health.* Westport, CT: Praeger.

Terracciano, A., Costa, P. T., & McCrae, R. R. (2006). Personality plasticity after age 30. *Personality and Social Psychology Bulletin, 32*(8), 999–1009.

Terracciano, A., McCrae, R. R., & Costa, P. T. (2010). Intra-individual change in personality stability and age. *Journal of Research in Personality, 44*(1), 33–37.

Tessier, R., Charpak, N., Giron, M., Criston, M., de Calume, Z. F., & Ruiz-Peláez, J. G. (2009). Kangaroo mother care, home environment and father involvement in the first year of life: a randomized controlled study. *Acta Paediatrica, 98*(9), 1444–1450.

Tessier, R., Cristo, M. B., Velez, S., Giron, M., Line, N., Figueroa De Calume, Z., & Ruiz-Palaez, J. G. (2003). Kangaroo mother care: A method for protecting high-risk low-birth-weight and premature infants against developmental delay. *Infant Behavior and Development, 26*, 384–397.

Thabet, A. A., & Vostanis, P. (2000). Post-traumatic stress disorder reactions in children of war: A longitudinal study. *Child Abuse and Neglect, 24*, 291–298.

Thabet, A. A., Abed, Y., & Vostanis, P. (2004). Comorbidity of PTSD and depression among refugee children during war conflict. *Journal of Child Psychology and Psychiatry, 45*, 533–542.

Thabet, A. A., Ibraheem, A. N., Shivram, R., Winter, E. A., & Vostanis, P. (2009). Parenting support and PTSD in children of a war zone. *International Journal of Social Psychiatry, 55*(3), 226–237.

Thapar, A., Collishaw, S., Pine, D. S., & Thapar, A. K. (2012). Depression in adolescence. *The Lancet, 379*(9820), 1056–1067.

Thatcher, R. W., Walker, R. A., & Guidice, S. (1987). Human cerebral hemispheres develop at different rates and ages. *Science, 236*, 110–113.

The Arc. (2012). *What are the causes of intellectual disability?* Retrieved June 13, 2012 from http://www.thearc.org/page.aspx?pid=2453

The Brazelton Institute. (2012). The newborn behavioral observations system: What is it? Retrieved from http://www.brazelton-institute.com/clnbas.html

The Center for Effective Discipline. (2011). Legal reforms corporal punishment of children in the family. Retrieved from http://www.stophitting.com/index.php?page=laws-main

The College Board. (2011). Total group profile report. Retrieved from http://professionals.collegeboard.com/data-reports-research/sat/

The Elizabeth Glaser Pediatric AIDS Foundation. (2012). HIV and AIDS in the U.S. Retrieved from http://www.pedaids.org

The Partnership for Maternal, Newborn & Child Health. (2011). *A global review of the key interventions related to reproductive, maternal, newborn and child health (RMNCH).* Geneva, Switzerland: Author.

Thelen, E. (2008). Grounded in the world: Developmental origins of the embodied mind. In W. F. Overton, U. Muller, & J. L. Newman (Eds.), *Developmental perspectives on embodiment and consciousness* (pp. 99–129). New York: Taylor & Francis Group/Lawrence Erlbaum Associates.

Thelen, E., & Smith, L. B. (2006). Dynamic systems theories. In R. M. Lerner & W. Damon (Eds.), *Handbook of child psychology, Vol. 1: Theoretical models of human development* (6th ed., pp. 258–312). Hoboken, NJ: John Wiley & Sons.

Thomas, A., & Chess, S. (1977). *Temperament and development.* New York: Brunner-Mazel.

Thomas, M., & Johnson, M. H. (2008). New advances in understanding sensitive periods in brain development. *Current Directions in Psychological Science, 17*(1), 1–5.

Thompson, R. A., Easterbrooks, M. A., & Padilla-Walker, L. M. (2003). Social and emotional development in infancy. In R. Learner, M. A. Easterbrooks, & J. Mistry (Eds.), *Handbook of psychology: Vol. 6. Developmental psychology* (pp. 91–112). New York: Wiley.

Thompson, R. A., Winer, A. C., & Goodvin, R. (2011). The individual child: Temperament, emotion, self, and personality. In M. H. Bornstein & M. E. Lamb (Eds.), *Developmental science: An advanced textbook* (6th ed., pp. 427–468). New York: Psychology Press.

Thomson, N. R., Kennedy, E. A., & Kuebli, J. E. (2011). Attachment formation between deaf infants and their primary caregivers: Is being deaf a risk factor for insecure attachment? In D. H. Zand & K. J. Pierce (Eds.), *Resilience in deaf children: Adaptation through emerging adulthood* (pp. 27–64). New York: Springer Science + Business Media.

Thorne, B. (2004). The crisis of care. In A. C. Crouter & A. Booth (Eds.), *Work–family challenges for low-income parents and their children* (pp. 165–178). Mahwah, NJ: Erlbaum.

Tiemeier, H., Lenroot, R. K., Greenstein, D. K., Tran, L., Pierson, R., & Giedd, J. N. (2010). Cerebellum development during childhood and adolescence: A longitudinal morphometric MRI study. *NeuroImage, 49*(1), 63–70.

Tikalsky, F. D., & Wallace, S. D. (1988). Culture and the structure of children's fears. *Journal of Cross-Cultural Psychology, 19*, 481–492.

Tither, J. M., & Ellis, B. J. (2008). Impact of fathers on daughters' age at menarche: A genetically and environmentally controlled sibling study. *Developmental Psychology, 44*(5), 1409–1420.

Tolar, M. H. (2012). Mentoring experiences of high-achieving women. *Advances in Developing Human Resources, 14*(2), 172–187.

Tomasello, M. (2011). Language development. In U. Goswami (Ed.), *The Wiley-Blackwell handbook of childhood cognitive development* (2nd ed., pp. 239–357). Totowa, NJ: Human Press.

Tonidandel, S., Avery, D. R., & Phillips, M. G. (2007). Maximizing returns on mentoring: Factors affecting subsequent protégé performance. *Journal of Organizational Behavior, 28*(1), 89–110.

Torpy, J. M., Lynm, C., & Glass, R. M. (2005). Smoking and pregnancy. *Journal of the American Medical Association, 293*(10), 1286–1286.

Toth, S. L., & Cicchetti, D. (2006). Promises and possibilities: The application of research in the area of child maltreatment to policies and practices. *Journal of Social Issues, 62*(4), 863–880.

Toth, S., Manly, J., & Hathaway, A. (2011). Relational interventions for young children who have been maltreated. In J. Osofsky (Ed.), *Clinical work with traumatized young children* (pp. 96–113). New York: Guilford Press.

Toth, S. L., Harris, L. S., Goodman, G. S., & Cicchetti, D. (2011). Influence of violence and aggression on children's psychological development: Trauma, attachment, and memory. In P. R. Shaver & M. Mikulincer (Eds.), *Human aggression and violence: Causes, manifestations, and consequences* (pp. 351–365). Washington, DC: American Psychological Association.

Toth, S. L., Rogosch, F. A., Caplan, R., & Cicchetti, D. (2011). Illogical thinking and thought disorder in maltreated children. *Journal of the American Academy of Child & Adolescent Psychiatry, 50*(7), 659–668.

Trapolini, T., Ungerer, J. A., & McMahon, C. A. (2007). Maternal depression and children's attachment representations during the preschool years. *British Journal of Developmental Psychology, 25*(2), 247–261.

Tremblay, R. E. (2011). Origins, development, and prevention of aggressive behavior. In D. P. Keating (Ed.), *Nature and nurture in early child development* (pp. 169–187). New York: Cambridge University Press.

Tremblay, R. E. (2012). Environmental, genetic, and epigenetic influences on the developmental origins of aggression and other disruptive behaviors. In T. Bliesener, A. Beelmann, & M. Stemmier (Eds.), *Antisocial behavior and crime: Contributions of developmental and evaluation research to prevention and intervention* (pp. 3–16). Cambridge, MA: Hogrefe Publishing.

Trickett, P. K., & Nagriff, S. (2011). Child maltreatment and social relationships. In M. K. Underwood & L. H. Rosen (Eds.), *Social development: Relationships in infancy, childhood, and adolescence* (pp. 403–426). New York: Guilford Press.

Trionfi, G., & Reese, E. (2009). A good story: Children with imaginary companions create richer narratives. *Child Development, 80*(4), 1301–1313.

Troester, H., & Brambring, M. (1992). Early social/emotional development in blind infants. *Child: Care, Health, Development, 18*, 207–227.

Troll, L. E., & Fingerman, K. L. (1996). Connections between parents and their adult children. In C. Magai & S. H. McFadden (Eds.), *Handbook of emotion, adult development, and aging* (pp. 185–205). San Diego, CA: Academic Press.

Troll, L. E., & Skaff, M. M. (1997). Perceived continuity of self in very old age. *Psychology and Aging, 12*, 162–169.

Tronick, E. (2005). Why is connection with others so critical? The formation of dyadic states of consciousness and the expansion of individuals' states of consciousness: Coherence governed selection and the co-creation of meaning out of messy meaning making. In J. Nadel & D. Muir (Eds.), *Emotional development: Recent research advances* (pp. 293–315). New York: Oxford University Press.

Tronick, E. (2007). *The Norton series on interpersonal neurobiology: The neurobehavioral and social-emotion development of infants and children.* New York: W. W. Norton & Co.

Tronick, E. Z. (1989). Emotions and emotional communication. *American Psychologist Special Issue: Children and their development: Knowledge base, research agenda, and social policy application, 44*(2), 112–119.

Troseth, G. L., Bloom, M. E., & DeLoache, J. S. (2007). Young children 's use of scale models: Testing an alternative to representational insight. *Developmental Science, 10*(6), 763–769.

Trzesniewski, K. H., & Donnellan, M. B. (2010). Rethinking "Generation Me:" A study of cohort effects from 1976–2006. *Perspectives on Psychological Science, 5*(1), 58–75.

Tseng, V. (2004). Family interdependence and academic adjustment in college: Youth from immigrant and U.S.-born families. *Child Development, 75*(3), 966–983.

Tucker-Drob, E. M. (2009). Differentiation of cognitive abilities across the life span. *Developmental Psychology, 45*(4), 1097–1118.

Tucker-Drob, E. M., & Salthouse, T. A. (2011). Individual differences in cognitive aging. In T. Chamorro-Premuzic, T., S. von Stumm, & A. Furnham (Eds.), *The Wiley-Blackwell handbook of individual differences* (pp. 242–267). Malden, MA: Wiley-Blackwell.

Tudge, J. (2008). The everyday lives of young children: Culture, class, and child rearing in diverse societies. New York: Cambridge University Press.

Turati, C., Cassia, V., Simion, F., & Leo, I. (2006). Newborns' face recognition: Role of inner and outer facial features. *Child Development, 77*(2), 297–311.

Turiel, E. (2006). The development of morality. In N. Eisenberg, W. Damon, & R. Lerner (Eds.), *Handbook of child psychology: Vol. 3, social, emotional, and personality development* (6th ed., pp. 789–857). Hoboken, NJ: John Wiley & Sons Inc.

Turiel, E. (2008). The development of children's orientations toward moral, social, and personal orders: More than a sequence in development. *Human Development, 51*(1), 21–39.

Turiel, E. (2010). The development of morality: Reasoning, emotions, and resistance. In W. F. Overton & R. M. Lerner (Eds.), *The handbook of life-span development, Vol. 1: Cognition, biology, and methods* (pp. 554–583). Hoboken, NJ: John Wiley & Sons.

Turiel, E., & Killen, M. (2010). Taking emotions seriously: The role of emotions in moral development. In W. F. Arsenio, & E. A. Lemerise (Eds.), *Emotions, aggression, and morality in children: Bridging development and psychopathology* (pp. 33–52). Washington, DC: American Psychological Association.

Turkheimer, E., & Waldron, M. (2000). Nonshared environment: Atheoretical, methodological, and quantitative review. *Psychological Bulletin, 126*(1), 78–108.

Turnbull, A., & Turnbull, R. (2001). Self-determination for individuals with significant cognitive disabilities and their families. *Journal of the Association for Persons with Severe Handicaps, 6*(1), 56–62.

Twenge, J. M., & Campbell, W. K. (2010a). Birth cohort differences in the monitoring the future dataset and elsewhere: Further evidence for generation me—commentary on Trzesniewski & Donnellan. *Perspetives on Psychological Science, 5*(1), 81–88.

Twenge, J. M., & Campbell, S. M. (2010b). Generation me and the changing world of work. In A. P. Linley, S. Harrington, & Garcea, N. (Eds.), *Oxford handbook of positive psychology and work* (pp. 25–35). New York: Oxford University Press.

Twenge, J. M., Campbell, W. K., & Freeman, E. C. (2012). Generational differences in young adults' life goals, concern for others, and civic orientation, 1966–2009. *Journal of Personality and Social Psychology, 102*(5), 1045–1062.

Twenge, J. M., Campbell, S. M., & Hoffman, B. J. (2010). Generational differences in work values: Leisure and extrinsic values increasing, social and intrinsic values decreasing. *Journal of Management, 36*(5), 1117–1142.

U.S. Bureau of Labor Statistics. (2010). Employment status of women by presence and age of youngest child, March 1975–2009. Retrieved from http://www.bls.gov/cps/wlf-databook2010.htm

U.S. Bureau of Labor Statistics. (2011a). Employment status of the civilian noninstitutional population by age and sex, 2010 annual averages. Women in the labor force: A databook. Retrieved from http://www.bls.gov/cps/wlf-databook2011.htm

U.S. Bureau of Labor Statistics. (2011b). Employment status of the civilian noninstitutional population 16 years and over by sex, 1970–2010 annual averages. Women in the labor force: A databook. Retrieved from http://www.bls.gov/cps/wlf-databook2011.htm

U.S. Bureau of Labor Statistics. (2011c). Employment status by race, age, sex, and Hispanic or Latino ethnicity, 2010 annual averages. *Women in the labor force: A databook.* Retrieved from http://www.bls.gov/cps/wlf databook2011.htm

U.S. Bureau of Labor Statistics. (2011d). Contribution of wives' earnings to family income, 1970–2009. *Women in the labor force: A databook.* Retrieved July 5, 2012 from http://www.bls.gov/cps/wlf-databook2011.htm

U.S. Bureau of Labor Statistics. (2012a). Employment characteristics of families—2011. Retrieved from http://www.bls.gov/news.release/famee.nr0.htm

U.S. Bureau of Labor Statistics. (2012b). Table 4. Families with own children: Employment status of parents by age of youngest child and family type, 2010–2011, annual averages. Retrieved from http://www.bls.gov/news.release/famee.t04.htm

U.S. Census Bureau. (2008a). *America's families and living arrangements: 2008.* Retrieved on June, 26, 2009 from http://www.census.gov/population/www/socdemo/hh-fam/cps2008.html

U.S. Census Bureau. (2008b). Children under 18 years old by presence of parents: 1990–2006. *The 2008 Statistical Abstract.* Retrieved on November 20, 2008 from http://www.census.gov/compendia/statab/cats/population.html

U.S. Census Bureau. (2008c). *Weekly child care costs paid by families with employed mothers: 1985–2005: Table C2. from the Survey of Income and Program and Participation (SIPP).* Available online at www.census.gov.

U.S. Census Bureau (2009). *Statistical Abstract of the United States: 2009.* Retrieved February 25, 2009 from http://www.census.gov/prod/2008pubs/09statab

U.S. Census Bureau. (2010). The next four decades: The older population in the United States: 2010–2050. U.S. Department of Commerce.

U. S Census Bureau. (2010). Who's minding the kids? Child care arrangements: Spring 2010. Retrieved on April 3, 2012 from http://www.census.gov/hhes/childcare/data/sipp/2010/tables.html.

U.S. Census Bureau. (2011a). *Age and sex composition: 2010.* Washington, DC: Author.

U.S. Census Bureau. (2011b). America's families and living arrangements: 2011. Retrieved from http://www.census.gov/hhes/families/data/cps2011.html

U.S. Census Bureau. (2011c). Number, timing, and duration of marriages and divorces: 2009. Retrieved from http://www.census.gov/prod/2011pubs/p70_125.pdf

U.S. Census Bureau. (2012a). Age of own children under 18 years in families and subfamilies by living arrangements by employment status of parents. Retrieved from http://factfinder2.census.gov/faces/tableservices/jsf/pages/productview

U.S. Census Bureau. (2012b). Average weekly child care expenditures of families with employed mothers that make payments, by age groups and selected characteristics: Spring 2010. Survey of income and program participation (SIPP), 2008 Panel, Wave 5.Retrieved from http://www.census.gov/sipp/sourceac/S&A08_W1toW6%28S&A-13%29.pdf

U.S. Census Bureau. (2012c). Employed civilians by occupation, sex, race, and Hispanic origin: 2010. Labor force, employment, and earnings. *Statistical Abstract of the United States, 2012.* Washington, DC: Author.

U.S. Census Bureau. (2012d). Expectations of life at birth, 1970 to 2008, and projections, 2010 to 2020. *Statistical Abstract of the United States, 2012* (p. 77). Washington, DC: Author.

U.S. Census Bureau. (2012e). Facts for features: Grandchildren. Retrieved from http://www.census.gov/newsroom/releases/archives/facts_for_features_special_editions/cb11–ff17.html

U.S. Census Bureau. (2012f). Median age at first marriage, 1890–2010. Retrieved from http://www.infoplease.com/ipa/A0005061.html

U.S. Census Bureau. (2012g). People in families by family structure, age, and sex, iterated by income-to-poverty ratio and race: 2010. Retrieved from http://www.census.gov/hhes/www/cpstables/032011/pov/new02_100_01.htm

U.S. Census Bureau. (2012h). *Statistical Abstract of the United States, 2012* (131st ed.). Washington, DC: Author. Retrieved from http://www.census.gov/compendia/statab/

U.S. Census Bureau. (2012i). Table 7. Resident population by sex and age: 1980–2010. *Statistical Abstract of the United States, 2012*. Washington, DC: Author.

U.S. Census Bureau. (2012j). Table 9. Resident population projections by sex and age: 2010–2050. *Statistical Abstract of the United States, 2012.* Washington, DC: Author.

U.S. Census Bureau. (2012k). Table 56. Marital status of the population by sex race, and Hispanic origin: 1990–2010. *Statistical Abstract of the United States, 2012.* Washington, DC: Author.

U.S. Census Bureau. (2012l). Table 57. Marital status of the population by sex and age: 2010. *Statistical Abstract of the United States, 2012*. Washington, DC: Author.

U.S. Census Bureau. (2012m). Table 58. Living arrangements of persons 15 years old Andover by race and age: 2010. *Statistical Abstract of the United States, 2012.* Washington, DC: Author.

U.S. Census Bureau. (2012n). Table 60. Interracially married couples by race and Hispanic origin of spouses: 1980 to 2010. *Statistical Abstract of the United States, 2012.* Washington, DC: Author.

U.S. Census Bureau. (2012o). Table 69. Children under 18 years old by presence of parents: 2000 to 2010. *Statistical Abstract of the United States, 2012.* Washington, DC: Author.

U.S. Census Bureau. (2012p). Table 70. Grandparents living with grandchildren by race and sex: 2009. *Statistical Abstract of the United States, 2012*. Washington, DC: Author.

U.S. Census Bureau. (2012q). Table 104. Expectation of life at birth, 1970 to 2008, and projections, 2010–2020.

U.S. Census Bureau. (2012r). Table 105. Life expectancy by sex, age, and race: 2008. *Statistical Abstract of the United States, 2012*. Washington, DC: Author.

U.S. Census Bureau. (2012s). Table 122. Deaths and death rates by leading causes of death and age: 2007. Statistical Abstract of the United States, 2012. Washington, DC: Author.

U.S. Census Bureau. (2012t). Table 698. Money income of families—distribution by family characteristics and income level: 2009. *Statistical Abstract of the United States, 2012*. Washington, DC: Author.

U.S. Census Bureau. (2012u). Table UC3. Opposite sex unmarried couples by presence of biological children/1 under 18, and age, earnings, education, race and Hispanic origin/2 of both partners: 2011. *Current Population Survey, 2011 Annual Social and Economic Supplement, November 2011*. Washington, DC: Author.

U.S. Department of Education. (2012). Building the legacy of IDEA 2004. Retrieved June 13, 2012 from http://idea.ed.gov/explore/home

U.S. Department of Health and Human Services (USD-HHS). (2005). *U.S. surgeon general releases advisory on alcohol use in pregnancy.* Retrieved on November 13, 2008 from http://www.surgeongeneral.gov/pressreleases/sg02222005.html

U.S. Department of Health and Human Services, Administration for Children and Families, Administration on Children, Youth, and Families, Children's Bureau. (2011). Child Maltreatment 2010. Retrieved from http://www.hhs.gov/asl/testify/2011/12/t20111213a.html

U.S. Department of Labor. (2007). Women in the labor force: Adatabook (Report 1002). Available online at http://stats.bls.gov/cps/wlf-databook-2007.pdf.

U.S. Department of Labor. (2011). Women in the labor force: A databook. In *The Changing Nature of the Family* (pp. 246–247). Retrieved from http://www.bls.gov/cps/wlf-databook-2011.pdf

U.S. Food and Drug Administration. (2011). Animal & veterinary consumer FAQs. Retrieved from http://www.fda.gov/AnimalVeterinary/SafetyHealth/AnimalCloning

U.S. Food & Drug Administration. (2012). Menopause and hormones. Retrieved from http://www.fda.gov/ForConsumers/ByAudience/ForWomen/ucm118624.htm

U.S. Surgeon General. (2004). *Bone health and osteoporosis: A report of the surgeon general.* Retreived on January 29, 2009 from http://www.surgeongeneral.gov/library/bonehealth/chapter_4.html

Uleman, J. S., Saribay, S., & Gonzalez, C. (2008). Spontaneous inferences, implicit impressions, and implicit theories. *Annual Review of Psychology, 59,* 329–360.

UNAIDS. (2012). UNAIDS strategy 2011–2015. Retrieved from http://www.unaids.org/en/aboutunaids/unaidsstrategygoalsby2015

Underwood, M. K. (2011). Aggression. In M. K. Underwood & L. H. Rosen (Eds.), *Social development: Relationships in infancy, childhood, and adolescence* (pp. 207–234). New York: Guilford Press.

United Nations Children's Fund (UNICEF). (2005). *The state of the world's children: 2005.* New York: Author.

United Nations Children's Fund (UNICEF). (2008a). *Nutrition.* Retrieved on November 18, 2008 from http://www.unicef.org/media/media_45490.html

United Nations Children's Fund (UNICEF). (2011). Fact sheet: Child soldiers. Retrieved from http://www.unicef.org/emerg/files/childsoldiers.pdf

United Nations Children's Fund (UNICEF). (2012a). Breastfeeding. Retrieved from http://www.unicef.org/nutrition/index_24824.html

United Nations Children's Fund (UNICEF). (2012b). Children in urban world. In *The state of the world's children, 2012.* New York: Author.

United Nations Children's Fund (UNICEF). (2012c). Table 5, Education. *The state of the world's children, 2012.* New York: Author.

United Nations High Commissioner for Refugees. (2011). Global trends 2010. Retrieved from http://www.unhcr.org

Urry, S. A., Nelson, L. J., Padila-Walker, L. M. (2011). Mother knows best: Psychological control, child disclosure, and maternal knowledge in emerging adulthood. *Journal of Family Studies, 17*(2), 153–173.

Usmiani, S., & Daniluk, J. (1997). Mothers and their adolescent daughters: Relationship between self-esteem, gender role identity, and body image. *Journal of Youth and Adolescence, 26*(1), 45–62.

Uszynska-Jarmoc, J. (2007). Self-esteem and different forms of thinking in seven and nine year olds. *Early Child Development and Care, 177*(4), 337–348.

Vaillant, G. E. (2002). *Aging well: Surprising guideposts to a happier life from the landmark Harvard Study of Adult Development.* New York: Little, Brown.

Vaillant-Molina, M., & Bahrick, L. E. (2012). The role of intersensory redundancy in the emergence of social referencing in 5½ month-old infants. *Developmental Psychology, 48*(1), 1–9.

Valenzuela, M. (1997). Maternal sensitivity in a developing society: The context of urban poverty and infant chronic undernutrition. *Developmental Psychology, 33,* 845–855.

Valenzuela, M. J., Matthews, F. E., Brayne, C., Ince, P., Halliday, G., & Kril, J. J. (2012). Multiple biological pathways link cognitive lifestyle to protection from dementia. *Biological Psychiatry, 71*(9), 783–791.

Valla, J. M., & Williams, W. M. (2006). Cognitive-developmental psychology as the liaison between evolutionary theory and interdisciplinary studies of human development. *Applied Cognitive Psychology 20*(4), 557–560.

van den Dries, L., Juffer, F., van IJzendoom, & Bakermans-Kranenburg, M. J. (2009). Fostering security? A meta-analysis of attachment in adapted children. *Children and Youth Services Review, 31*(3), 410–421.

Van Doom, M. D., Branje, S., & Meeus, W. (2007). Longitudinal transmission of conflict resolution styles from marital relationships to adolescent–parent relationships. *Journal of Family Psychology, 21*(3), 426–434.

Van Gerven, P., Paas, F., & Tabbers, H. K. (2006). Cognitive aging and computer-based instructional design: Where do we go from here? *Educational Psychology Review, 18,* 141–157.

van Hooff, J. H. (2011). Rationalizing inequality: heterosexual couples' explanations and justifications for the division of housework along traditionally gendered lines. *Journal of Gender Studies, 20*(1), 19–30.

van Ijzendoorn, M. H., Bakermans-Kranenburg, M., & Juffer, F. (2007). Plasticity of growth in height, weight, and head circumference: Meta-analytic evidence of massive catch-up after international adoption. *Journal of Developmental and Behavioral Pediatrics, 28(4)*, 334–343. doi: http://dx.doi.org/10.1097/DBP.0b013e31811320aa

van IJzendoorn, M. H., & Sagi-Schwartz, A. (2010). Corss-cultural patterns of attachment: Universal and contextual dimensions. In J. Cassidy & P. Shaver (Eds.), *Handbook of attachment: Theory, research, and clinical applications* (2nd ed., pp. 48–77). New York, NY: Guilford Press.

Van Leijenhorst, L., Zanolie, K., VanMeel, C. S., Westenberg, P., Rombouts, S. A., & Crone, E. A. (2010). What motivates the adolescent? Brain regions mediating reward sensitivity across adolescence. *Cerebral Cortex, 20*(1), 61–69.

van Solinge, H., & Henkens, K. (2008). Adjustment to and satisfaction with retirement: Two of a kind? *Psychology and Aging, 23*(2), 422–434.

Vandell, D. L., Belsky, J., Burchinal, M., Steinberg, L., & Vandergrift, N. (2010). Do effects of early child care extend to age 15 years? Results from the NICHD study of early child care and youth development. *Child Development 81*(3), 737–756.

Vandenberg, K. A. (2007). Individualized developmental care for high risk newborns in the NICU: A practice guideline. *Early Human Development, 83*(7), 433–442.

Vandewater, E. A., & Stewart, A. J. (2006). Paths to late midlife well-being for women and men: The importance of identity development and social role quality. *Journal of Adult Development, 13*(2), 76–83.

Vandewater, E. A., Bickham, D. S., Lee, J. H., Cummings, H. E., Wartella, E. A., & Rideout, V. J. (2005). When the television is always on: Heavy television exposure and young children's development. *American Behavioral Scientist, 48*(5), 562–577.

VanFleet, R., & Topham, G. (2011). Filial therapy for maltreated and neglected children: Integration of family therapy and play therapy. In A. A. Drewes, S. C. Bratton, & C. E. Schaefer (Eds.), *Integrative play therapy* (pp. 153–175). Hoboken, NJ: John Wiley.

Van Gerven, P., Paas, F., & Tabbers, H. K. (2006). Cognitive aging and computer-based instructional design: Where do we go from here? *Educational Psychology Review, 18,* 141–157.

Vanmanen, K.-J., & Whitbourne, S. K. (1997). Psychosocial development and life events in adulthood. *Psychology and Aging, 12,* 239–246.

Varki, A., & Nelson, D. L. (2007). Genomic comparisons of human and chimpanzees. *Annual Review of Anthropology, 36*(1), 191–209.

Ventura, S. J., Curtin, S. C., & Abma, J. C. (2012). Estimated pregnancy rates and rates of pregnancy outcomes for the United States, 1990–2008. *National Vital Statistics Reports, 60*(7). U.S. Department of Health and Human Services.

Verissimo, M., Santos, A. J., Vaughn, B. E., Torres, N., Monteiro, L., & Santos, O. (2011). Quality of attachment to father and mother and nmber of reciprocal friends. *Early Child Development and Care, 181*(1), 27–38.

Verkuyten, M., & De Wolf, A. (2007). The development of in-group favoritism: Between social reality and group identity. *Developmental Psychology, 43*(4), 901–911.

Verma, S., & Larson, R. (2003b). *Examining adolescent leisure time across cultures: Development opportunities and risks.* San Francisco: Jossey-Bass.

Véronneau, M., & Dishion, T. J. (2010). Predicting change in early adolescent problem behavior in the middle school years: A mesosystemic perspective on parenting and peer experiences. *Journal of Abnormal Child Psychology, 38*(8), 1125–1137.

Véronneau, M., Vitaro, F., Brendgen, M., Dishion, T. J., & Tremblay, R. E. (2010). Transactional analysis of the reciprocal links between peer experiences and academic achievement from middle childhood to early adolescence. *Developmental Psychology, 46*(4), 773–790.

Vickerstaff, S., & Cox, J. (2005). Retirement and risk: The individualization of retirement experiences? *Sociological Review, 53*(1), 77–95.

Vigil, J. M., Geary, D. C., & Byrd-Craven, J. (2005). A life history assessment of early childhood sexual abuse in women. *Developmental Psychology, 41*(3), 553–561.

Vihman, M. (2013). *Language development: An introduction.* Hoboken, NJ: Blackwell Publishers.

Visher, E. B., & Visher, J. S. (1998). Stepparents: The forgotten family members. *Family and Conciliation Courts Review, 36,* 444–451.

Visher, E. B., Visher, J. S., & Pasley, K. (2003). Remarriage families and stepparenting. In F. Walsh (Ed.), *Normal family processes: Growing diversity and complexity* (3rd ed., pp. 153–175). New York: Guilford Press.

Visscher, P. M., Hill, W. G., & Wray, N. R. (2008). Heritability in the genomics era—concepts and misconceptions. *Nature Reviews Genetics, 9*(4), 255–266.

Vitaro, F., Tremblay, R. E., Kerr, M., Pagani, L., & Bukowski, W. M. (1997). Disruptiveness, friends' characteristics, and delinquency in early adolescence: A test of two competing models of development. *Child Development, 68*(4), 676–689.

Vitiello, B. (2008). Effectively obtaining informed consent for child and adolescent participation in mental health research. *Ethics & Behavior, 18*(2–3). 182–198.

Vogt, Y. (2010). Body perceptions, weight control behavior, and changes in adolescents' psychological well-being over time: A longitudinal examination of gender. *Journal of Youth and Adolescence, 39*(8), 927–939.

von Faber, M., Bootsma-Van Den Wiel, A., Van Exel, E., Gussekloo, J., Lagaay, A. M., et al. (2001). Successful aging in the oldest old: Who can be characterized as successfully aged? *Journal of the American Medical Association: Archives of Internal Medicine, 161,* 2694–2701.

Vorvick, L. J., & Storck, S. (2010). Miscarriage. MedlinePlus. Retrieved from http://www.nlm.nih.gov/medlineplus/ency/artical/001488.htm

Votruba-Drzal, E. (2006). Economic disparities in middle childhood development: Does income matter? *Developmental Psychology, 42*(6), 1154–1167.

Vukman, K. B. (2005). Developmental differences in metacognition and their connections with cognitive development in adulthood. *Journal of Adult Development, 12*(4), 211–221.

Vygotsky, L. S. (1978). *Mind in society: The development of higher psychological processes.* M. Cole, V. John-Steiner, S. Scribner, & E. Souberman (Eds.), Cambridge, MA: Harvard University Press. (Original work published 1935)

Vygotsky, L. S. (1987). Thinking and speech. In R. W. Rieber & A. S. Carton (Eds.), *The collected works of L. S. Vygotsky: Vol. 1. Problems of general psychology,* pp. 39–285. New York: Plenum. (Original work published 1934)

Wachs, T. D., & Bates, J. E. (2010). Temperament. In J. G. Bremner & T. D. Wachs (Eds.), *The Wiley Blackwell Handbook of infant development* (pp. 592–622). Malden, MA: Wiley-Blackwell.

Wadsworth, M. E., & Santiago, C. (2008). Risk and resiliency processes in ethnically diverse families in poverty. *Journal of Family Psychology, 22*(3), 399–410.

Wahl, H-W., Schmitt, M., Danner, D. & Coppin, A. (2010). Is the emergence of functional ability decline in early old age related to change in speed of cognitive processing and also to change in personality? *Journal of Aging and Health, 22*(6), 691–712.

Wahlstrom, D., White, T., & Luciana, M. (2010). Neurobehavioral evidence for changes in dopamine system activity during adolescence. *Neuroscience and Biobehavioral Reviews, 34*(5), 631–648.

Wainright, J. L., & Patterson, C. J. (2008). Peer relations among adolescents with same-sex parents. *Developmental Psychology, 44,* 117–126.

Waizenhofer, R. N., Buchanan, C. M., & Jackson-Newsom, J. (2004). Mothers'and fathers' knowledge of adolescents' daily activities: Its sources and its links with adolescent adjustment. *Journal of Family Psychology, 18*(2), 348–360.

Waldenstroem, U. (1999). Experience of labor and birth in 1,111 women. *Journal of Psychosomatic Research, 47,* 471–482.

Waldfogel, J., Craigie, T., & Brooks-Gunn, J. (2010). Fragile families and child wellbeing. *The Future of Children, 20*(2), 87–112.

Wahl, H-W & Kruse, A. (2005). Historical perspectives of middle age within the life span. In S. L. Willis & M. Martin (Eds.) *Middle adulthood: A lifespan perspective.* (pp. 3–34). Thousand Oaks, CA: Sage.

Walker, D. (2011). Evidence-based practice in early childhood intervention. In C. Groark, S. Eidelman, L. Kaczmarek, & S. P. Maude (Eds.), *Early childhood intervention: Shaping the future for children with special needs and their families* (pp. 147–167). Santa Barbara, CA: Praeger/ABC-CLIO.

Walker, R. F., & Murachver, T. (2012). Representation and theory of mind development. *Developmental Psychology, 48*(2), 509–520.

Walker, S. P., Change, S. M., Powell, C. A., Simonoff, E., & Grantham-McGregor, S. M. (2007). Early childhood stunting is associated with poor psychological functioning in late adolescence and effects are reduced by psychosocial stimulation. *Journal of Nutrition, 137*(11). 2664–2469.

Walker-Andrews, A. S., Bahrick, L. E., Raglioni, S. S., & Diaz, I. (1991). Infants' bimodal perception of gender. *Ecological Psychology, 3*, 55–75.

Wallace, P., & Gotlib, I. (1990). Marital adjustment during the transition to parenthood: Stability and predictors of change. *Journal of Marriage and the Family, 52*, 21–29.

Walsh, R. (2011). The varieties of wisdom: Contemplative, cross-cultural, and integral contribution. *Research in Human Development, 8*(2), 109–127.

Walter, C. (2005). Support groups for widows and widowers. In G. L. Greif & P. H. Ephross (Eds.), *Group work with populations at risk* (2nd ed., pp. 109–125). New York: Oxford University Press.

Walter, T. (2012). Why different countries manage death differently: A comparative analysis of modern urban societies. *British Journal of Sociology, 63*(1), 123–145.

Wang, M., Dishion, T. J., Stormshak, E. A., & Willett, J. B. (2011). Trajectories of family management practices and early adolescent behavioral outcomes. *Developmental Psychology, 47*(5), 1324–1341.

Wang-Cheng, R., Neuner, J. M., & Barnabei, V. M. (2007). *Menopause.* Philadelphia: American College of Physicians.

Warr, P. B. (2007). *Work, happiness, and unhappiness.* Mahwah, NJ: Lawrence Erlbaum Associates.

Warren, K. R., Hewitt, B. G., & Thomas, J. D. (2011). Fetal alcohol spectrum disorders: Research challenges and opportunities. *Alcohol Research & Health, 34*(1), 4–14.

Warren, S. L., & Sroufe, L. A. (2004). Developmental issues. In T. H. Ollendick & J. S. March (Eds.), *Phobic and anxiety disorders in children and adolescents: A clinician's guide to effective psychosocial and pharmacological interventions* (pp. 92–115). New York: Oxford University Press.

Waterhouse, L. (2008). Child abuse. In M. Davies (Ed.), *The Blackwell companion to social work* (3rd ed., pp. 18–26). Malden, MA: Blackwell Publishing.

Waterman, A. S. (1999). Issues of identity formation revisited: United States and the Netherlands. *Developmental Review, 19*(4), 462–479.

Waterman, A. S. (2012). Issues of identity formation revisited; United States and the Netherlands. *Developmental Review, 19*(4), 462–479.

Watson, A. J., & Valtin, R. (1997). Secrecy in middle childhood. *International Journal of Behavioral Development, 21*, 431–452.

Watson, J. B., & Raynor, R. (1920). Conditioned emotional reactions. *Journal of Experimental Psychology, 3*, 1–14.

Watson, J. D., & Crick, F. H. C. (1953). Molecular structure of nucleic acids: A structure for deoxyribose nucleic acid. *Nature, 171*, 737–738.

Wechsler, D. (1974). *Selected papers of David Wechsler.* Oxford, England: Academic Press.

Weinberg, R. A., Scarr, S., & Waldman, I. D. (1992). The Minnesota Transracial Adoption Study: A follow-up of IQ test performance at adolescence. *Intelligence, 16*(1), 117.

Weir, J. M., Zakama, A., & Rao, U. (2012). Developmental risk I: Depression and the developing brain. *Child and Adolescent Psychiatric Clinic of North America, 21*(2), 237–259.

Weir, P. L., Meisner, B. A., & Baker, J. (2010). Successful aging across the years: Does one model fit everyone? *Journal of Health Psychology, 15*(5), 680–687.

Weisner, T. S. (2011). Culture. In M. K. Underwood & L. H. Rosen (Eds.), *Social development: Relationships in infancy, childhood, and adolescence* (pp. 372–399). New York: Guilford Press.

Weiss D., & Freund, A. M. (2012). Still young at heart: Negative age-related information motivates distancing from same-aged people. *Psychology and Aging, 27*(1), 173–180.

Weitz, R. (2010). Changing the scripts: Midlife women's sexuality in contemporary U.S. films. *Sexuality & Culture: An Interdisciplinary Quarterly, 14*(1), 17–32.

Weitz, R., & Bryant, K. (1997). The portrayals of homosexuality in abnormal psychology and sociology of deviance textbooks. *Deviant Behavior, 18*, 27–46.

Wellman, H. M. (2011). Developing a theory of mind. In U. Goswami (Ed.), *The Wiley-Blackwell handbook of childhood cognitive development* (2nd ed., pp. 258–284). Malden, MA: Wiley-Blackwell.

Wellman, H. M., Fang, F., Liu, D., Zhu, L., & Liu, L. (2006). Scaling theory-of-mind understanding in Chinese children. *Psychological Science, 17*, 1075–1081.

Wenar, C. (1990). Childhood fears and phobias. In M. Lewis & S. M. Miller (Eds.), *Handbook of developmental psychopathology* (pp. 281–290). New York: Plenum.

Werner, E. E. (1995). Resilience in development. *Current Directions in Psychological Science, 4*(3), 81–85.

Werner, J. S., Frost, M. H., Macnee, C. L., McCabe, S. F., & Rice, V. H. (2012). Major and minor life stressors, measures, and health outcomes. In V. Rice (Ed.), *Handbook of stress, coping, and health: Implications for nursing research, theory, and practice* (2nd ed., pp. 125–154). Thousand Oaks, CA: Sage Publications.

Wertheim, E. H., & Paxton, S. J. (2011). Body image development in adolescent girls. In T. F. Cash & L. Smolak (Eds.), *Body image: A handbook of science, practice, and prevention* (2nd ed., pp. 76–84). New York: Guilford Press.

Wertsch, J. V. (2008). From social interaction to higher psychological processes. *Human Development, 51*(1), 66–79.

West, D. J. (2008). *Homosexuality: Its nature and causes.* New Brunswick, NJ: Aldine Transaction.

West, R. L. (1996). An application of prefrontal cortex function theory to cognitive aging. *Psychological Bulletin, 120*(2), 272–292.

Westerhof, G. J., Whitbourne, S. K., & Freeman, G. P. (2012). The aging self in a cultural context: The relation of conceptions of aging to identity processes and self-esteem in the United States and the Netherlands. *Journals of Gerontology Series B: Psychological Sciences & Social Sciences, 67B*(1), 52–60.

Westermeyer, J. F. (2004). Predictors and characteristics of Erikson's life cycle model among men: A 32-year longitudinal study. *International Journal of Aging and Human Development, 58*(1), 29–48.

Wethington, E., Kessler, R. C., & Pixley, J. E. (2004). Turning points in adulthood. In O. G. Brim, C. D. Ryff, & R. C. Kessler (Eds.), *How healthy are we? A national study of well-being at midlife* (pp. 586–613). Chicago: The University of Chicago Press.

Wheeler, P. L. (2001). Shaken baby syndrome: An introduction to the literature. *Child Abuse Review, 12*, 401–415.

Wheeler, P. L. (2003). Shaken-baby syndrome—An introduction to the literature. *Child Abuse Review, 12*(6), 401–415.

Wheeler-Scruggs, K. S. (2008). Do lesbians differ from heterosexual men and women in Levinsonian phases of adult development? *Journal of Counseling and Development, 86*, 39–46.

Whipple, N., Bernier, A., & Mageau, G. A. (2011). Broadening of study of infant security of attachment: Maternal autonomy-support in the context of infant exploration. *Social Development, 20*(1), 17–32.

Whitbourne, S. (2008). *Adult development & aging: Biopsychosocial perspectives* (3rd ed.). Hoboken, NJ: John Wiley.

Whitbourne, S. K., Connolly, L. A. (1999). Physical changes. In J. C. Cavanaugh & S. K. Whitbourne (Eds.), *Gerontology: An interdisciplinary perspective* (pp. 91–122). New York: Oxford University Press.

Whitbourne, S. K., & Meeks, S. (2011). Psychopathology, bereavement, and aging. In K. Warner Schaie & S. L. Willis (Eds.), *Handbook of the psychology of aging* (7th ed., pp. 311–323). San Diego, CA: Elsevier Academic Press.

Whitbourne, S. K., & Whitbourne, S. B. (2011). *Adult development and aging: Biopsychosocial perspectives* (4th ed.). Hoboken, NJ: Wiley.

Whitbourne, S. K., & Willis, S. L. (2006). *The baby boomers grow up: Contemporary perspectives on midlife.* Mahwah, NJ: Lawrence Erlbaum Associates.

White, D., & Rabago-Smith, M. (2011). Genotype-phenotype associations and human eye color. *Journal of Human Genetics, 56(1)*, 5–7.

White, K. J., & Kistner, J. (1992). The influence of teacher feedback on young children's peer preferences and perceptions. *Developmental Psychology, 28*, 933–940.

White, K. R. (2006). Early intervention for children with permanent hearing loss: Finishing the EHDI revolution. *Volta Review, 106*(3), 237–258.

White, R., & Renk, K. (2012). Externalizing behavior problems during adolescence: An ecological perspective. *Journal of Child & Family Studies, 21*(1), 158–171.

Whitebread, D., Coltman, P., Jameson, H., & Lander, R. (2009). Play, cognition and self-regulation: What exactly are children learning when they learn through play? *Educational and Child Psychology, 26*(2), 40–52.

Whiteley, L. B., & Brown, L. K. (2010). Adolescent pregnancy and parenting. *Current Psychiatry Reviews, 6*(4), 269–279.

Whiteman, S. D., Bernard, J. M., & Jensen, A. C. (2011). Sibling influence in human development.

In J. Caspi (Ed.), *Sibling development: Implications for mental health practitioners* (pp. 1–15). New York: Springer Publishing.

Whitman, B. Y. (2008). Family functioning. In P. J. Accardo (Ed.), *Capute and Accardo's neurodevelopmental disabilities in infancy and childhood, Vol. 1: Neurodevelopmental diagnosis and treatment* (pp. 445–468). Baltimore, MD: Paul H Brookes Publishing.

Wiebe, S. A., et al. (2009). Gene-environment interactions across development: exploring DRD2 genotype and prenatal smoking effects on self-regulation. *Developmental Psychology, 45*(1), 31–44.

Willford, J. A., Richardson, G. A., & Day, N. L. (2012). Sex-specific effects of prenatal marijuana exposure on neurodevelopment and behavior. In M. Lewis & L. Kestler (Eds.), *Gender differences in prenatal substance exposure* (pp. 121–136). Washington, DC: American Psychological Association.

Williams, A. L., & Merten, M. J. (2011). iFamily: Internet and social media technology in the family context. *Family and Consumer Sciences Research Journal, 40*(2), 150–170.

Williams, D. R., & Mohammed, S. A. (2009). Discrimination and racial disparities in health: Evidence and needed research. *Journal of Behavioral Medicine, 32*(1), 20–47.

Williams, J. D., & Jacoby, A. P. (1989). The effects of premarital heterosexual and homosexual experience on dating and marriage desirability. *Journal of Marriage and the Family, 51*, 489–497.

Williams, M. N. (2011). The changing roles of grandparents raising grandchildren. *Journal of Human Behavior in the Social Environment, 21*(8), 948–962.

Willis, S. L. (1989). Adult intelligence. In S. Hunter & M. Sundel (Eds.), *Midlife myths: Issues, findings, and practice implications* (pp. 97–111). Thousand Oaks, CA: Sage.

Willis, S. L., & Schaie, K. (2006). Cognitive functioning in the baby boomers: Longitudinal and cohort effects. In S. Whitbourne & S. Willis (Eds.), *The baby boomers grow up: Contemporary perspectives on midlife* (pp. 205–234). Mahwah, NJ: Lawrence Erlbaum Associates Publishers.

Willis, S. L., & Schaie, K. W. (1999). Intellectual functioning in midlife. In S. L. Willis & J. D. Reid (Eds.), *Life in the middle: Psychological and social development in middle age* (pp. 233–247). San Diego, CA: Academic Press.

Willis, S. L., Martin, M., & Rocke, C. (2010). Longitudinal perspectives on midlife development: Stability and change. *European Journal of Ageing, 7*(3), 131–134.

Wilson, B. J. (2008). Media violence and aggression in youth. In S. L. Calvert & B. J. Wilson (Eds.), *The handbook of children, media, and development* (pp. 237–267). Malden, MA: Blackwell Publishing.

Wilson, M., & Daly, M. (2001). The evolutionary psychology of couple conflict in registered versus de facto marital unions. In A. Booth, A. C. Crouter, & M. Clements (Eds.), *Couples in conflict* (pp. 3–26). Mahwah, NJ: Erlbaum.

Winer, G. A., Craig, R. K., & Weinbaum, E. (1992). Adult's failure on misleading weight-conservation tests: A developmental analysis. *Developmental Psychology, 28*, 109–120.

Winsler, A., De León, J. R., Wallace, B. A., Carlton, M. P., & Wilson-Quayle, A. (2003). Private speech in preschool children: Developmental stability and change, across-task consistency, and relations with classroom behaviour. *Journal of Child Language, 30*(3), 583–608.

Winsler, A., Díaz, R. M., Espinosa, L., & Rodriguez, J. L. (1999). When learning a second language does not mean losing the first: Bilingual language development in low-income, Spanish-speaking children attending bilingual preschool. *Child Development, 70*(2), 349–362.

Wiseman, D. G. (2008). The 21st century American family. In D. G. Wiseman (Ed.), *The American family: Understanding its changing dynamics and place in society* (pp. 5–19). Springfield, IL: Charles C Thomas Publisher.

Witherington, D. C., Campos, J. J., Harringer, J. A., Bryan, C., & Margett, T. E. (2010). Emotion and its development in infancy. In J. G. Bremner & T. D. Wachs (Eds.), *The Wiley Blackwell Handbook of infant development* (pp. 568–591). Malden, MA: Wiley-Blackwell.

Witkow, M. R., & Fuligni, A. J. (2011). Ethnic and generational differences in the relations between social support and academic achievement across the high school years. *Journal of Social Issues, 67*(3), 531–552.

Wolak, J., Finkelhor, D., Mitchell, K., & Ybarra, M. L. (2008). Online "predators" and their victims: Myths, realities, and implications for prevention treatment. *American Psychologist, 63*(2), 111–128.

Wolf, J. H. (2009). *Deliver me from pain: Anesthesia and birth in America.* Baltimore: John Hopkins University Press.

Wolfe, D. A., Wolfe, V. V., & Best, C. L. (1988). Child victims of sexual abuse. In V. B. VanHasselt, R. L. Morrison, A. S. Bellack, & M. Herson (Eds.), *Handbook of family violence* (pp. 157–185). New York: Plenum.

Wolff, P. H. (1987). T*he development of behavioral states and the expression of emotions in early infancy: New proposals for investigation.* Chicago, IL, US: University of Chicago Press, Chicago, IL.

Wolff, P. H. (1966). The causes, controls, and organization of behavior in the neonate. *Psychological Issues Monographs, 5*(1, Serial No. 17).

Wolraich, M. L. (2006). Attention-deficit/hyperactivity disorder. *Infants and Young Children: An Interdisciplinary Journal of Special Care Practices, 19*(2), 86–93.

Wong, F. Y., et al. (2011). Cerebral oxygenation is depressed during sleep in healthy term infants when they sleep prone. *Pediatrics, 127*(3), e558–e565.

Wood, W., & Eagly, A. H. (2010). Gender. In S. T. Fiske, D. T. Gilbert, & L. Gardner (Eds.), *Handbook of social psychology* (Vol. 1, 5th ed., pp. 629–667). Hoboken, NJ: John Wiley & Sons.

Woods, N. & Mitchell, E. (2010). Sexual desire during the menopausal transition and early postmenopause: Observations from the Seattle Midlife Women's Health Study. *Journal of Women's Health, 19*(2), 209–218.

World Health Organization (WHO). (2003). Key policy issues in long-term care. Retrieved from http://www.who.int/ncd/long_term_care/index.htm

World Health Organization (WHO). (2004). *Kangaroo mother care: A practical guide*. Geneva, Switzerland: Author.

World Health Organization (WHO). (2010). Child maltreatment. Retrieved from http://www.who.int/mediacentre/factsheets/fs150/en/

World Health Organization (WHO). (2011). Guidelines on optimal feeding of low birth-weight infants in low-and-middle-income countries. Geneva: Author.

World Health Organization (WHO). (2012a). Global database on child growth and malnutrition. Retrieved from http://www.who/int/nutgrowthdb/estimates/en/

World Health Organization (WHO). (2012b). Progress report 2010. Retrieved from http://www.who.int/hiv/pub/2010progressreport/ch4_en.pdf

World Health Organization (WHO). (2012c). Ten facts on breastfeeding. Retrieved from http://www.who.int/features/factfiles/breastfeeding.en/

World Health Organization (WHO). (2012d). World Health Statistics 2011. Retrieved from http://www.who.int/whosis/whostat/EN_WHS2011_Full.pdf

Worthington, R. L., Navarro, R. L., Savoy, H., & Hampton, D. (2008). Development, reliability, and validity of the Measure of Sexual Identity Exploration and Commitment (MOSIEC). *Developmental Psychology, 44*(1), 22–33.

Wortman, C. B., & Silver, R. C. (2001). The myths of coping with loss revisited. In M. S. Stroebe, R. O. Hansson, W. Stroebe, & H. Schut (Eds.), *Handbook of bereavement research: Consequences, coping, and care* (pp. 405–429). Washington, DC: American Psychological Association.

Wortmann, J. H. (2008). Religion and spirituality in adjustment following bereavement: An integrative review. *Death Studies, 32*(8), 703–736.

Wright, K. (1997). Babies, bonds, and brains. *Discover, 18*(10), 74–75.

Wu, P., & Chiou, W. (2008). Postformal thinking and creativity among late adolescents: A post-Piagetian approach. *Adolescence, 43*(170), 237–251.

Wu, R., Gopnik. A., Richardson, D. C., & Kirkham, N. Z. (2011). Infants learn about objects from statistics and people. *Developmental Psychology, 47*(5), 1220–1229.

Xinyin, C., & French, D. C. (2008). Children's social competence in cultural context. *Annual Review of Psychology, 59*(1), 591–616.

Xu, H., Matthews, K. A., Bryce, C. L., Hays, R. D., Kapoor, W. N., Ness, R. B., & Hess, R. (2012). Are hot flashes associated with sleep disturbance during midlife? Results from the STRIDE cohort study. *Maturitas, 71*(1), 34–38.

Xu, J. Q., Kochanek, K. D., Murphy, S. L., & Tejada-Vera, B. (2010). Deaths: Final data for 2007. National Vital Statistics Reports, *58*(19). Hyattsville, MD: National Center for Health Statistics.

Xu, Y. (2010). Children's social play sequence: Parten's classic theory revisited. *Early Child Development and Care, 180*(4), 489–498.

Yamamoto, S. L. (2011). Recognizing cesarean delivery on maternal request as a social problem: Utilizing the public arenas model. *Policy, Politics, & Nursing Practice, 12*(3), 168–174.

Yang, S. (2008). Real-life contextual manifestations of wisdom. *International Journal of Aging and Human Development, 67*(4), 273–303.

Yeung, W. J., Duncan, G. J., & Hill, M. S. (2000). Putting fathers back in the picture: Parental activities and children's adult outcomes. *Marriage and Family Review, 29*(2–3), 97–113.

Yeung, W. J., Sandberg, J. F., Davis-Kean, P. E., & Hofferth, S. L. (2001). Children's time with fathers in intact families. *Journal of Marriage and the Family, 63*(1), 136–154.

Yin, H., Lin, S., Kong, S., Benzeroual, K., Crawford, S. Y., Hedeker, D., Lambert, B. L., & Muramatsu, N. (2011). The associations between physical functioning and self-rated general health in later life: The implications of social comparison. *Applied Research in Quality of Life, 6*(1), 1–19.

Yip, T., & Douglass, S. (2011). Ethnic/racial identity and peer relationships across elementary, middle, and high schools. In X. Chen & K. H. Rubin (Eds.), *Socioemotional development in cultural context* (pp. 186–207). New York: Guilford Press.

Yolton, K. (2011). The role of environmental contaminants in ADHD. *Neurotoxicology and Teratology, 33*(4), 499–500.

Yonas, A., & Granrud, C. E. (2006). Infants' perception of depth from cast shadows. *Perception and Psychophysics, 68*(1), 154–160.

Young, A. (2010). The impact of early identification of deafness on hearing parents. In M. Marshark & P. E. Spencer (Eds.), *The Oxford handbook of deaf studies, language, and education* (Vol. 2, pp. 241–250). New York: Oxford University Press.

Young, A. M., Cady, S., & Foxon, M. J. (2006). Demystifying gender differences in mentoring: Theoretical perspectives and challenges for future research on gender and mentoring. *Human Resource Development Review, 5*(2), 148–175.

Young, H. M., Gray, S. L., McCormick, W. C., Sikma, S. K., Reinhard, S., Johnson, L., et al. (2008). Types, prevalence, and potential clinical significance of medication administration errors in assisted living. *Journal of the American Geriatrics Society, 56*(7), 1199–1205.

Young, K. M., Northern, J. J., Lister, K. M., Drummond, J. A., & O'Brien, W. H. (2007). A meta-analysis of family-behavioral weight-loss treatments for children. *Clinical Psychology Review, 27*(2), 240–249.

Young, S. E., Rhee, S. H., Stallings, M. C., Corley, R. P., & Hewitt, J. K. (2006). Genetic and environmental vulnerabilities underlying adolescent substance use and problem use: General or specific? *Behavioral Genetics, 36*(4), 603–15.

Young-Wolff, K. C., Enoch, M., & Prescott, C. A. (2011). The influence of gene-environment interactions on alcohol consumption and alcohol use disorders: A comprehensive review. *Clinical Psychology, 31*(5), 800–816.

Yu, J. W., Buka, S. L., McCormick, M. C., Fitzmaurice, G. M., & Indurkhya, A. (2006). Behavioral problems and the effects of early intervention on eightyear-old children with learning disabilities. *Maternal and Child Health Journal, 10*(4), 329–338.

Zacks, R. T., & Hasher, L. (2006). Aging and long-term memory: Deficits are not inevitable. In E. Bialystok & F. Craik (Eds.), *Lifespan cognition: Mechanisms of change* (pp. 162–177). New York: Oxford University Press.

Zahn-Waxler, C., & Radke-Yarrow, M. (1992). Development of concern for others. *Developmental Psychology, 28*(1), 126.

Zander, L., & Chamberlain, G. (1999). Place of birth. *British Medical Journal, 318*, 721–723.

Zarit, S. H., & Femia, E. E. (2008). A future for family care and dementia intervention research? Challenges and strategies. *Aging and Mental Health, 12*(1), 5–13.

Zeidner, M., Matthews, G., & Roberts, R. D. (2009). *What we know about emotional intelligence: How it affects learning, work, relationships, and our mental health.* Cambridge, MA: MIT Press.

Zembar, M. J., & Blume, L. B. (2009). *Middle childhood development: A contextual approach.* Upper Saddle River, NJ: Merrill/Pearson.

Zhao, J., & Wang, M. (2009). Developmental characteristics of preschoolers' anxiety. *Chinese Journal of Clinical Psychology, 17*(6), 723–725.

Ziebland, S., Robertson, J., Jay, J., & Neil, A. (2002). Body image and weight change in middle age: A qualitative study. *International Journal of Obesity and Related Metabolic Disorders, 26*, 1083–1091.

Zigler, E., & Gilman, E. (1998). The legacy of Jean Piaget. In G. A. Kimble & M. Wertheimer (Eds.), *Portraits of pioneers in psychology, Vol. 3* (pp. 145–160). Washington, DC: American Psychological Association.

Zimmer-Gembeck, M.J., & Helfand, M. (2008). Ten years of longitudinal research on U.S. adolescent sexual behavior: Developmental correlates of sexual intercourse, and the importance of age, gender and ethnic background. *Developmental Review, 28*(2), 153–224.

Zimmerman, S., Sloane, P. D., Eckert, J. K., Gruber-Baldini, A. L., Morgan, L. A., Hebel, J. R., et al. (2005). How good is assisted living? Findings and implications from an outcomes study. *Journals of gerontology: Series B: Psychological Sciences and Social Sciences, 60B*(4), S195–S204.

Zimprich, K., Allemand, M., & Lachman, M. E. (2012). Factorial structure and age-related psychometrics of the MIDUS personality adjective items across the lifespan. *Psychological Assessment, 24*(1), 173–186.

Zinke, K., Zeintl, M., Eschen, A., Herzog, C., & Kliegel, M. (2012). Potentials and limits of plasticity induced by working memory training in old-old age. *Gerontology, 58*(1), 79–87.

Zukow-Goldring, P. (2012). Assisted imitation: First steps in the seed model of language. *Language sciences, 34*(5), 569–582.

Zvolensky, M. J., McNeil, D. W., Porter, C. A., & Stewart, S. H. (2001). Assessment of anxiety sensitivity in young American Indians and Alaska Natives. *Behaviour Research and Therapy, 39*(4), 477–493.

PHOTO CREDITS

Chapter 1 **1** Dorling Kindersley, Ltd. **2** Mary Ann Kucera **3** Mary Ann Kucera **5** Giangi555/Fotolia **6** Reunion Des Musees Nationaux/Art Resource, NY **11** Phanie/SuperStock **12** Fatykhov/Fotolia **13** Petrenko Andriy/Shutterstock **15** (left) Pictorial Press Ltd/Alamy (right) Nina Leen/Time Life Pictures/Getty Images **16** (top) Benjamin Harris, Professor of Psychology (bottom) Tetra Images/Alamy **18** Kidstock/Blend Images/AGE Fotostock **22** Bruno Boissonnet/BSIP/AGE Fotostock **23** Pearson Education **25** Visions of America/UIG/Getty Images **26** Caro/Alamy **27** Michael Newman/PhotoEdit, Inc.

Chapter 2 **34** Ruth Jenkinson/Dorling Kindersley, Ltd **37** Kenneth Eward/Photo Researchers, Inc.. **38** Image Source/Getty Images **39** (left) Photo Researchers, Inc. (right) CNRI/SPL/Photo Researchers, Inc. **40** Pearson Education **47** (left) Pete Jenkins/Detail Photography (right) George Doyle/Stockbyte/Getty Images **52** David J. Phillip/AP Images **53** (left) Vanessa Davies/Dorling Kindersley, Ltd. (right) IS2 from Image Source/Alamy **54** Monkey Business Images/Shutterstock **55** Bonita R. Cheshier/Shutterstock **57** Peter Horree/Alamy **59** I love images/Alamy **60** Pearson Education

Chapter 3 **65** Robert Daly/Stone/Getty Images **67** (left) Pearson Education (right) Photo Researchers, Inc. **69** Pearson Education **72** (a) Raj Creationzs/Shutterstock (b) Findlay Kember/Bourn Hall Fertility Clinic/AP Images (c) Omikron/Photo Researchers, Inc. (d) Anatomical Travelogue/Photo Researchers, Inc. (e) Kage-Mikrofotografie/Alamy (f, g) Claude Edelmann/Photo Researchers, Inc. **73** Norbert Schiller/The Image Works **75** Pearson Education **77** Penny Tweedie/Alamy **79** Ting-Li Wang/The New York Times/Redux Pictures **82** Heinz Kluetmeier/Dot Pictures **85** Bananastock/JupiterImages **87** (bottom) Pearson Education (top) Mikael Damkier/Shutterstock/ Dorling Kindersley, Ltd **90** Phanie/SuperStock **93** Nicolas Bets/Getty Images **94** (left) Jules Selmes/Dorling Kindersley Ltd. (middle) Cantor Pannatto/Fotolia (right) Phanie/SuperStock

Chapter 4 **98** Dorling Kindersley, Ltd. **102** T. Berry Brazelton, MD, Brazelton Touchpoints Foundation **104** (top) Pearson Education (bottom) Pearson Education **105** (left) Galina Barskaya/Fotolia LLC (right) Hallgerd/Shutterstock **107** (left) Alena Ozerova/Fotolia (middle) Roddy Paine/Pearson Education Ltd/Pearson (right) Nataliiap/Shutterstock **110** Russel Sadur/Dorling Kindersley, Ltd. **114** From Discrimination and imitation of facial expression by neonates, Field, T. et al., American Association for the Advancement of Science, Oct. 1982. Reprinted with permission from AAAS **115** PhotoEdit **116** Michael Newman/PhotoEdit **118** Monkey Business/Fotolia **119** Elizabeth Crews/The Image Works **125** Exactostock/SuperStock **126** Dave King/Dorling Kindersley, Ltd.

Chapter 5 **130** Marlon Lopez/Shutterstock **135** (left) Andy Lim/Shutterstock (right) Jeff Greenberg/PhotoEdit **137** Johns Hopkins University **138** Nina Leen/Time & Life Pictures/Getty Images **139** Photo inc./Photo Researchers/Getty Images **140** Ellizabeth Crews/The Image Works **142** Brian Phillips/Syracuse Newspapers/The Image Works **144** Alison Williams/Shutterstock **147** Cindy Charles/PhotoEdit **148** Shutterstock **149** (bottom) Pearson Education (top) Tom Grill/Glow Images **152** Huntstock, Inc./Alamy

Chapter 6 **152** Huntstock, Inc./Alamy **157** Andy Crawford/Dorling Kindersley, Ltd. **158** Robert Brenner/PhotoEdit **159** Photo Researchers, Inc. **162** Barbara Peacock/Taxi/Getty Images **165** Cathy Datwani **166** Juice Images/Glow Images **168** Pearson Education **170** Morgan Lane Photography/Shutterstock **172** Mat Hayward/Fotolia **174** Robert Brenner/PhotoEdit **176** Bubbles Photolibrary/Alamy **177** Monkey Business/Fotolia

Chapter 7 **184** Stockbyte/Getty Images **186** Daniel Dempster Photography/Alamy **187** Michael Newman/PhotoEdit **190** Igor Yaruta/Shutterstock **194** Bob Daemmrich/The Image Works **195** Tom Prettyman/PhotoEdit **197** David Grossman/Alamy **199** Jim Pickerell/The Image Works **200** Rocio Alba Gonzalez/Workbook Stock /Getty Images **204** Catalin Petolea/Shutterstock **205** Altanaka/Shutterstock **206** Tom Prettyman/PhotoEdit **207** Christina Kennedy/PhotoEdit **210** Pixel Memoirs/Shutterstock

Chapter 8 **218** SW Productions/Photodisc/Getty Images **221** Photo Researchers, Inc. **223** Bill Aron/PhotoEdit **229** Michael Newman/PhotoEdit **231** Lisa F. Young/Fotolia **232** Ullstein Bild/Glow Images **233** Bob Daemmrich/PhotoEdit **237** Syracuse Newspapers/The Image Works **238** Michael Newman/PhotoEdit **240** Richard Hutchings/Photo Researchers/Getty Images **241** Wonderlandstock/Alamy

Chapter 9 **250** Mark Bowden/The Agency Collection/Getty Images **252** Image Source/SuperStock **256** Richard Hutchings/PhotoEdit **258** (left) Laima Druskis/Pearson Education (right) Myrleen Ferguson Cate/PhotoEdit **260** Ken Lax/Photo Researchers, Inc. **262** Tony Freeman/PhotoEdit **263** Mary Kate Denny/PhotoEdit **265** Myrleen Pearson/PhotoEdit **267** Thomas M Perkins/Shutterstock **271** Kayte Deioma/PhotoEdit

Chapter 10 **274** Tetra Images/SuperStock **277** Martha Cooper/National Geographic/Getty Images **279** David Grossman/Alamy **282** Jeff Greenberg/PhotoEdit **283** Wavebreakmedia Ltd./Shutterstock **284** Michael Newman/PhotoEdit **288** Bob Daemmrich/The Image Works **291** Konstantin Sutyagin/Shutterstock **292** Peter Muller/Glow Images **296** Myrleen Ferguson Cate/PhotoEdit

Chapter 11 **302** Digital Vision/Photodisc/Getty Images **303** Rhoda Sidney/PhotoEdit **306** (left) Imagesource/Glow Images (right) Martin Thomas Photography/Alamy **311** Jose Luis Pelaez Inc/Blend Images/Alamy **312** Lisa F. Young/Shutterstock **313** David Grossman/Alamy **318** Will & Deni McIntyre/Photo Researchers, Inc. **321** Ace Stock Limited/Alamy **325** Nancy Richmond/The Image Works

Chapter 12 **332** Dave & Les Jacobs/Blend Images/Alamy **334** Tom McCarthy/PhotoEdit **336** Peter Bernik/Shutterstock **341** Kathy McLaughlin/The Image Works **347** H&S Produktion/Corbis/Glow Images **349** Michal Heron/Pearson **351** Avava/Shutterstock **354** Daniel Korzeniewski/Shutterstock **355** (left) Endostock/Fotolia LLC (right) Blend Images/SuperStock

Chapter 13 **360** Ryan McVay/Digital Vision/Getty Images **361** Tom & Dee Ann McCarthy/Corbis/Glow Images **363** Blend Images/Alamy **366** Iuliia Sokolovska/Fotolia **367** (left) Don Tremain/Photodisc/Getty Images (right) Dinodia Photos/Alamy **373** PhotoEdit **375** Otnaydur/Shutterstock **377** PhotoAlto Sas/Alamy **379** PhotoLink/Photodisc/Getty Images **387** Spencer Grant/PhotoEdit

Chapter 14 **391** Graham Atkins-Hughes/Dorling Kindersley, Ltd **393** Ryan McVay/Digital Vision/Getty Images **397** Christopher Fitzgerald/The Image Works **400** Blend Images/Shutterstock **403** Bob Daemmrich/The Image Works **404** Eckphoto/Alamy **405** Robert Brenner/PhotoEdit **410** Lisa S./Shutterstock **412** David Bacon/The Image Works

Chapter 15 **415** Wong Yu Liang/Fotolia **416** (left) The Image Works (right) Erin Moroney LaBelle/The Image Works **418** Robert Kneschke/Fotolia **420** Michael Newman/PhotoEdit **424** Chris Smith/PhotoEdit **426** ColorBlind Images/Blend Images/Corbis **431** Jeff Greenberg/PhotoEdit **433** Golden Pixels LLC/Corbis **434** Spencer Grant/Photoedit **436** Mark Richards/PhotoEdit

Chapter 16 **441** DNF-Style Photography/Shutterstock **444** Inmagineasia/Alamy **445** Image Broker/Age Fotostock **446** (left) Bob Daemmrich/The Image Works (middle) Michael J. Doolittle/The Image Works (right) Christopher Fitzgerald/The Image Works **449** David Halbakken/Alamy **451** (left) National Eye Institute (right) John Neubauer/PhotoEdit **454** Nancy P. Alexander/PhotoEdit **455** Myrleen Ferguson Cate/PhotoEdit **456** Illene MacDonald/PhotoEdit **458** Yuri Arcurs/Shutterstock **464** Zephyr/Photo Researchers, Inc. **466** SPL/Photo Researchers, Inc.

Chapter 17 **471** Will & Deni McIntyre/Photo Researchers, Inc **473** Yuri Arcurs/Fotolia **477** Juice Images/Alamy **478** Tom McCarthy/PhotoEdit **479** K. U. Häbler/Fotolia **481** Myrleen Pearson/PhotoEdit **483** Alan Oddie/PhotoEdit **486** Amy Etra/PhotoEdit **490** Monkey Business Images/Shutterstock **492** Paul Conklin/PhotoEdit

Chapter 18 **495** Cohen/Ostrow/Digital Vision/Getty Images **496** Tony Freeman/PhotoEdit **498** Tom Uhlenbrock/UPI/Newscom **501** (left) Jim West/Alamy (top, right) Jeff Greenberg/PhotoEdit (bottom, right) Robert F. Bukaty/AP Photos **503** Steve Dunwell/Age Fotostock **508** Jerome A. Pollos/Coeur d'Alene Press/AP Photo **510** Ivan Sekretarev/AP Images **511** James Shaffer/PhotoEdit **515** Imagemore Co., Ltd./Alamy

NAME INDEX

A

Abecassis, M., 261
Abed, Y., 7
Abeles, R. P., 446
Abler, R. M., 285
Ablow, J., 132
Abma, J. C., 287, 288
Aboud, F., 264
Acker, J., 377
Ackerman, P. L., 408, 410
Adams, 349
Adams, K. A., 346
Adams, R. E., 311
Adams, R. G., 426
Adams, R. J., 112, 113
Adamson, L., 142, 306, 307
Adamson, L. B., 142
Adler, N. E., 457
Adlof, S., 242
Adolph, K., 105, 107
Adolph, K. D., 104
Adolph, K. E., 103, 105
Aguilar-Gaziola, S., 324
Ahearn, T. S., 452
Ahluwalia, M. K., 368
Ahmad, S., 346
Ahmed, K., 80
Ahmetoglu, G., 366
Ahn, H., 264
Aikins, J., 261
Ainley, M., 238
Ainsworth, M. D., 22, 136, 139
Ainsworth, M. D. S., 136
Ainsworth, M. S., 11, 136, 139
Aiyer, S. M., 163
Ajrouch, K. J., 423
Akahane-Yamado, R., 122
Akhtar, S., 436
Akiba, D., 263
Akrami, N., 52
Aksan, N., 451
Aksu-Koç, A., 180
Akter, N., 208
Alam, R., 513
Alanis, I., 179
Albanese, P., 386
Albano, A M., 187
Albert, D., 296
Aldwin, C., 406, 476
Aldwin, C. M., 406, 457
Alexander, K., 84
Alho, K., 122
Alink, L. R. A., 212
Alio, A. P., 73
Allanson, J. E., 48
Allemand, M., 437, 475, 476
Allémann, E., 115
Allen, D. J., 346
Allen, S., 175
Allman, R. M., 478
Alonso, J., 324
Alsaker, F. D., 307
Altshul, L. M., 81
Alvarez, J., 312
Alzheimer's Association, 464, 465
Amato, P. R., 146, 269, 271, 377, 430
Ambady, M., 264
American Academy of Pediatrics (AAP), 87, 106, 194, 227, 240, 370
American Association on Intellectual and Developmental Disabilities (AAIDD), 241
American Cancer Society, 404
American College of Obstetricians and Gynecologists, 81, 399
American Diabetes Association, 454
American Foundation for Suicide Prevention, 325
American Medical Association (AMA), 52
American Pregnancy Association, 67, 84, 85, 87
American Psychiatric Association, 242, 245, 246, 327, 452, 462, 511
American Psychological Association (APA), 29, 227, 347
American Society Aesthetic Plastic Surgery (ASAPS), 444, 445
Amitay, S., 115
Amminger, G. P., 324
Amoudi, F. Al, 280, 281
Amsel, E., 294
Amso, D., 10
Ancoli-Israel, S., 449
Andel, R., 467
Andersen, A. N., 73
Anderson, C. A., 193
Anderson, E. R., 430
Anderson, F., 114
Anderson, J., 193
Anderson, S. W., 297, 451
Andersson, B. E., 151
Ando, J., 52
Andrews, G., 171, 175, 231
Andrews, J. W., 324
Aneja, A., 80
Angel, L., 452
Angelini, J., 315
Angleitner, A., 437
Angulo-Barroso, R., 109
Angus, J., 443
Annunziata, J., 188
Anson, A., 80
Anthonysamy, A., 201
Antial, J. K., 386
Antonucci, T. C., 376, 423, 482
Antony, M. M., 11
Anzures, G., 113
Apfelbaum, E. P., 264
Appel, M., 315
Apperly, I., 166
Aquilino, W. S., 422
Arbesman, M., 451
Arc, The, 241
Archambault, I., 252
Archer, S. L., 305, 307
Archibald, A. B., 208
Ardelt, M., 461
Arden, R., 51
Ariès, P., 463
Armstrong, T., 245
Arndt, J., 498, 500
Arnett, J. J., 3, 275, 276, 277, 284, 295, 304, 308, 309, 318, 336, 361, 369
Aro, M., 242
Aronson, J., 235, 253, 408
Arthur, A. E., 204
Arvidsson, A., 254
Asato, M. R., 292
Asbury, K., 209
Asch, A., 91
Aschersleben, G., 408
Asendorph, J. B., 190
Ashby, J., 244
Asher, S. R., 200, 261, 316
Aslin, R. N., 112, 114, 115
Aspelmeier, J. E., 265
Associated Press, 341
Ata, R., 281
Atala, A., 52
Atanasiu, V., 457
Atance, C. M., 172
Atchley, R. C., 475, 479
Atkinson, J., 114
Atkinson, L., 138
Atkinson, R., 304
Atkinson, R. C., 171
Atlantis, E., 449
Atta, M., 208
Atwater, E., 316
Auckland, T., 433
Auerbach-Major, S., 190, 197, 200
Aunola, K., 257
Austad, S. N., 457
Austen, K., 346
Austin, J., 48
Austrian, S. G., 417
AVERT, 75, 340, 341
Avery, D. R., 379
Avis, N. E., 397
Aviv, A., 457
Ayanian, J. Z., 396
Azar, B., 143

B

Babcock, R., 410
Babson, K. A., 284
Bachman, J. G., 320, 321
Bachman, M., 312
Bagnato, S. J., 244
Bagwell, C. L., 252, 257, 313
Bahrick, L. E., 116, 141
Bailey, J. M., 345
Baillargeon, R., 119
Bain, J., 122
Baird, A. A., 297
Bajraktarevic, A., 324
Bakeman, R., 142
Baker, J., 474
Baker, M. K., 449
Baker, S. A., 176
Baker-Ward, L., 172
Bakermans-Kranenburg, M. J., 94, 137
Bakken, J. P., 294
Bakken, L., 307
Bakker, A. B., 435, 436
Bakker, J., 324
Balas, B., 113, 117
Baldock, M. R. J., 459
Baldwin, J., 89
Balk, D. E., 510
Ball, M. M., 491
Balsam, K. F., 347
Baltes, M. M., 474
Baltes, P. B., 2, 19, 59, 161, 408, 437, 458, 461, 462, 463, 467, 478
Bandura, A., 27, 28, 56
Banerjee, R., 178
Banich, M. T., 297
Barac, R., 177
Barasch, A. S., 475, 479
Barbisoni, P., 449
Barclay, S. R., 436
Barker, E. D., 261
Barker, R., 431
Barkley, R. A., 244, 245
Barnabei, V. M., 397
Barnes, G. M., 295
Barnes, J. C., 192
Barnett, D., 138, 154, 323
Barnett, M., 268
Barnett, M. A., 146
Barnett, R. C., 383
Baroody, A. J., 170
Barr, R., 120
Barr, R. G., 82, 142
Barrera, M., 513
Barrett, L. F., 144
Barrick, T. R., 460
Barrieau, L., 116
Barry, C. T., 225
Bartlett, D., 93
Barton, J., 89, 91
Bartoshuk, L. M., 396
Basak, C., 459, 467
Basile, K. C., 322, 323
Bassett, H., 197, 200
Bates, A., 398
Bates, J. E., 133, 192, 201, 213, 261, 265
Batty, G. D., 478
Bau, A. M., 281
Bauer, I., 478
Bauer, J. J., 421
Bauer, P. J., 10, 120
Baum, B. J., 50
Bauman, S., 261
Baumgärtner, M. K., 387
Baumrind, D., 206, 207
Bauserman, R., 269
Bava, S., 318
Bavelier, D., 452

Baxter, J., 428
Baxter-Jones, A. D. G., 281
Bayley, N., 108
Bazzini, D. G., 442
Beals, K. P., 370
Beardslee, W. R., 325
Beardsworth, A., 399
Beaton, E. A., 11
Beauchaine, T. P., 347
Beauchemin, A., 267
Beaudet, J., 264
Beaver, K. M., 79, 192
Becharra, A., 80, 297
Beck, A. N., 25
Becker, J., 170
Beckett, C., 243
Beckman, S., 180
Bedore, L. M., 122
Beeghly, M., 153
Beelman, W. W., 399
Behrman, J. R., 109
Beins, B. C., 169
Beker, L., 138
Bell, D., 11
Bell, F. C., 423
Bell, J. H., 296
Bell, S. M., 22, 139
Bellelli, G., 449
Bellinger, D. C., 81
Belsky, J., 138, 150, 188, 226, 374
Beltramello, A., 452
Bempohl, F., 160
Ben-Zur, H., 485
Bendersky, M., 80
Bendl, R., 380
Bengtson, V. L., 419, 422, 424, 425, 457, 483
Bengtsson, H., 254
Benner, A. D., 268
Bennett, C., 141
Bennett, D. S., 80
Bennett, S. J., 161
Benovenli, L., 349
Benson, M. J., 311
Bentley, A. C., 158
Bentley, E., 354, 356
Benzeroual, K., 477
Berenaum, S. A., 252
Berenbaum, S. A., 204, 205
Beresin, E. V., 192, 194
Berg, C. A., 408, 482
Bergen, L., 193
Berger, A., 11, 133, 188
Berger, L. M., 80
Berger, S., 107
Berger, S. E., 104
Berk, L. E., 120, 174
Berlau, D. J., 447
Berlin, L. J., 24, 148, 153, 213, 323
Berman, E., 421
Berman, S. L., 306, 307
Bernal, M. E., 264
Bernard, J. M., 147, 209
Berndt, A., 459
Bernier, A., 142
Bernstein, J., 377
Berry, J. W., 5
Bersamin, M. M., 286
Bertenthal, B. I., 163
Berthier, N. E., 115
Bertoncini, J., 102
Bertram, L., 465
Berzonsky, M. D., 307
Best, C. L., 212
Betancourt, L. M., 318
Betancourt, T., 267
Betz, M. E., 451
Beveridge, R., 482
Bevis, L., 113
Beyers, W., 308, 421
Bhatt, R. S., 113
Bhavaneswar, C., 80
Bhugra, D., 346
Bialystok, E., 177
Bianchi, S. M., 386
Bibok, M. B., 169
Bickham, D. S., 194
Bidell, T. R., 7
Biehl, M., 284
Bierman, K. L., 316
Bigelow, A., 151
Biggs, S., 376
Bigler, R. S., 203, 204, 238, 252
Bigner, J. J., 265
Bigsby, R., 80
Billings, A., 286
Bily, C. A., 345
Binet, A., 232
Binggeli, N. J., 212
Biondi, M., 406
Birch, E. E., 112
Birditt, K. S., 419, 482, 483
Birkeland, M., 281
Birney, D. P., 462
Bischof, G. N., 458, 460
Bitensky, S. H., 6
Bittman, M., 226
Bjorklund, D. F., 56, 171, 172
Black, M. C., 322, 323
Black, M. M., 108, 153
Blair, C., 235, 408
Blair, K. A., 190, 197, 200
Blakemore, J. E., 252
Blakemore, S., 291
Blanchard, R., 345
Blanchard, Y., 102
Blankson, N., 408
Blasco, P. A., 152
Blascovich, J., 498
Blazer, D. G., 478
Bleakley, A., 315
Blechman, E. A., 267
Blehar, M., 136
Blieszner, R., 486
Bloom, B., 224
Bloom, L., 174
Bloom, M. E., 167
Blume, L. B., 219, 257
Blumenthal, H., 284
Blythe, S. G., 163
Bobbitt-Zeher, D., 380
Bobkowski, P. S., 315
Boden, J. M., 323
Bodie, J. A., 399
Boerner, K., 509
Boffelli, S., 449
Boivin, M., 237, 283
Bolton, F. G., 323
Bolykov, A., 399
Bomar, J., 125
Bonanno, G. A., 483
Bonder, B., 448
Bonham, V. L., 38
Bonney, C. R., 234
Bons, T. A., 52
Bookman, A., 424
Boom, J., 256
Boomsma, D. I., 88
Booth, A., 386
Bootsma-Van Den Wiel, A., 476
Bor, W., 79
Borden, L. M., 318, 326, 328
Bordere, T. C., 506, 509
Borge, A., 261
Borge, A. I., 262
Born, A., 353
Bornstein, M. H., 103, 123, 135, 139
Borton, R. W., 116
Bos, A. F., 103
Bos, H., 324
Bouazzaoui, B., 452
Bouchard, T. J., 51
Bouffard, T., 237
Boutwell, B. B., 79, 192
Boutwell, J., 7
Bowker, J., 187, 200, 202, 257, 259
Bowlby, J., 11, 136, 139, 140
Boxer, P., 192
Boyatzis, C. J., 209
Boyatzis, R. E., 350
Boyce, P., 89, 91
Braaten, E. B., 244
Brackbill, Y., 283
Bracke, P., 425
Bracken, S., 175
Bradbury, T. N., 374
Braddick, O., 114
Bradhan, N. P., 115
Bradley, R., 226
Bradley, R. A., 84
Bradley, R. H., 146
Brady, S. A., 242
Brambring, M., 151
Brandone, A. C., 122
Branje, S., 306, 309, 311
Branje, S. J., 306
Brannon, E. M., 297
Bransford, J. D., 159, 229, 237
Brassard, M. R., 212
Brassen, S., 474
Bratko, D., 51
Braun, M., 387
Brayne, C., 409
Braze, D., 242
Brazelton Institute, The, 102, 103
Brazelton, T. B., 56, 92, 103, 116
Breetz, A., 323
Breiding, M. J., 322, 323
Bremberg, S., 147
Brendgen, M., 261
Brennan, B., 120
Brennan, P. L., 477
Brennan, R. T., 284
Brent, D. A., 325
Bretherton, I., 145
Brewer, A. M., 379
Brick, J., 80
Bridge, J. A., 325
Bridges, T. H., 207
Brim, O. G., 392, 393, 407, 476
Brockmann, H., 480
Brodsky, N. L., 318
Brody, D. J., 280, 281
Brody, E., 483
Brody, E. M., 424, 425
Brody, G. H., 147, 209
Brody, J., 453
Broeren, S., 186, 187, 188
Broesch, T., 144
Bromberger, J. T., 397
Bromnick, R. D., 296
Bronfenbrenner, U., 19
Bronstein, P., 203, 205
Brookings, 427
Brooks-Dunn, J., 24
Brooks-Gunn, J., 24, 25, 58, 194, 208, 226, 234, 268, 283, 284, 289, 307
Broom, D. H., 226
Brown, A., 175
Brown, A. L., 159, 172, 229, 237
Brown, B., 259
Brown, B. B., 294
Brown, J. D., 315
Brown, J. E., 226
Brown, L., 193
Brown, L. K., 289
Brown, R., 124
Brown, R. D., 172
Brown, R. M., 487
Brown-Rezanka, L., 394
Brown, S. L., 487
Brown, T. A., 35
Brownell, C. A., 143, 188
Bruggink, J. L. M., 103
Bruinse, H. W., 88
Bruner, J. S., 229
Brunner, S. M., 115
Bryan, C., 131
Bryant, C., 397
Bryant, H., 326
Bryant, K., 347
Bryce, C. L., 397
Bryce, C. P., 109
Bryk, A., 126
Brzuzy, S., 346
Bub, K. L., 150
Bublitz, M. H., 79
Buchanan, C. M., 311
Büchel, C., 474
Buchmann, C., 162
Buckley, S., 47
Buckner, R. L., 452
Buehler, C., 311
Buhrmester, D., 365
Buhs, E. S., 262
Buitelaar, J. K., 290, 324
Buka, S. L., 58, 244
Bukowski, W. M., 200, 257, 314, 322, 365

Bulik, C. M., 283
Bullinger, A., 115
Bullock, J., 260
Bumpass, L. L., 418
Bumpus, M. F., 312
Bunge, S. A., 10
Bunker, C. H., 82
Bunting, B. P., 452
Burant, C. F., 454
Burchinal, M., 150
Burden, M., 109
Burdge, G. C., 226
Bureau, J., 195
Bureau of Labor Statistics, 382
Burgess, E. O., 400
Burk–Braxton, C., 308
Burnett, S., 291
Burney, R. V., 58, 146, 147
Burnham, D., 115
Burns, E., 448
Burns, M. S., 231
Burns, N. R., 459
Burnside, I. M., 446, 473
Burrows-Maclean, L., 245
Burton, L. M., 60
Bushman, B. J., 193
Bushnell, I. W. R., 113
Busnel, M. C., 115
Buss, A. H., 133, 187
Buss, K. A., 187
Butkovic, A., 51
Butler, C. B., 334, 335
Butler, J., 122
Buysse, V., 202, 262
Byne, W., 345
Byrd, C. M., 308
Byrd-Craven, J., 280

C

Cabeza, R., 452
Cabrera, N. J., 145, 146, 147
Cady, S., 379
Caggiano, V., 114
Calfo, S., 488
Calkins, S. D., 200
Callaghan, T., 144, 166
Camann, W., 84
Cameron, C. E., 237
Campbell, B. C., 219
Campbell, C. H., 231
Campbell, S. M., 309
Campbell, W. K., 309
Campione-Barr, N., 304, 313
Campos, J. J., 115, 131
Canli, T., 474
Cannon, A., 467
Cantor, J., 193
Caplan, R., 213
Capone, G. T., 159
Cappell, K. A., 460
Caprara, G. V., 437, 475
Caprara, M., 437, 475
Cardeña, E., 22
Carlson, K. J., 397
Carlson, M. C., 409
Carlson, M. J., 25
Carlson, S. M., 142, 199
Carlson, V., 140
Carlton, M. P., 174
Carmody, D. P., 11, 80
Carnes, B. A., 453
Carpendale, J., 11, 169, 255
Carpendale, J. I. M., 169
Carpenter, L. M., 419
Carr, D., 486
Carr, P. B., 239
Carrion, V. G., 345
Carroll, J. S., 421
Carroll, M., 120
Carroll, M. D., 405
Carstensen, L. L., 474, 475
Carter, B., 374, 419
Carter, E. A., 374
Carter, R., 297
Carter, R. C., 109
Cartwright, C., 433
Cartwright, K. B., 349
Caruso, D. R., 350
Caruthers, A. S., 311
Caserta, M. T., 406
Casey, B. J., 11, 220, 290, 324
Cashon, C. H., 107, 113, 115, 117, 119, 120
Casile, A., 114
Caspi, A., 60, 190
Cassasola, M., 120
Cassia, V., 113
Cassidy, D. J., 172
Cassidy, J., 137, 138, 148, 153, 316
Cassidy, S. B., 48
Cassidy, T., 82
Cassinadri, A., 449
Castle, J., 243
Catts, H. W., 242
Cauffman, E., 297
Cavan, D., 226
Ceballo, R., 265, 269
Celello, K., 431
Celera Genomics Corporation, 10, 35
Center for Effective Discipline, The, 6
Center for Research on Child Well-being, 25
Center for Sexual Health Promotion, 401, 419
Centers for Disease Control and Prevention (CDC), 44, 48, 66, 68, 76, 77, 79, 81, 91, 109, 219, 222, 223, 246, 285, 286, 287, 322, 323, 340, 342, 343, 404, 405, 454
Centers for Medicare and Medicaid Services, 488
Central Intelligence Agency, 287
Cervone, D., 56
Chacko, A., 245
Chaffin, M., 138
Chahry, N., 144
Chaillet, J. R., 47
Chalmers, B., 87
Chalpin, M. J., 285
Chamberlain, G., 83
Chambers, G. M., 91
Chamorro-Premuzic, T., 51, 366
Chan, C. C., 126
Chan, K. T., 500
Chance, G., 116
Chang, B., 480, 482
Chang, G., 80
Chang, M., 464, 467
Change, S. M., 73
Chao, R. K., 208
Chapman, M., 143
Charles, S. T., 412, 474, 475
Charley, C. M., 199
Charlton, R. A., 460
Charness, N., 410, 411
Charpak, N., 90
Chase-Lansdale, P. L., 58, 268
Chasnoff, I. J., 80
Chater, N., 125
Chatoor, I., 138
Chavez, A., 73
Chavez, M., 283
Chavous, T., 308
Chawla, S., 109
Cheah, C. S., 187
Chedraui, P., 73
Chee-Ruiter, C., 116
Chein, J. M., 459
Chen, H., 201
Chen, J., 126, 322, 323
Chen, X., 201, 202, 208, 257, 259, 448
Cheour-Luhtanen, M., 122
Cherkasskiy, L., 350
Cherlin, A. J., 376
Cherny, S. S., 345
Chess, S., 133
Chien, N., 268
Chin, R., 91
Chinnery, P. F., 48
Chiou, W., 348, 349
Chiriboga, D. A., 417, 426
Chiu, M. M., 231
Choi, C. Q., 125
Choi, N. G., 482
Chomsky, N., 125
Chow, A., 511
Chow, C. M., 365
Choy, M. H., 235
Christens, J. O., 73
Christensen, K., 447
Christensen, K. J., 421
Christiaens, W., 425
Christiansen, M. H., 125
Christie, J. F., 180, 198
Christophe, A., 102
Christopherson, C. R., 286
Chrouser Ahrens, C. J., 419
Chumlea, W. C., 281
Chun-Shin, H., 139
Chung, Y., 436
Cicchetti, D., 99, 100, 138, 153, 154, 212, 213
Cillessen, A. H., 200
Cillessen, A. H. N., 261, 262
Cislak, A., 226
Claas, M. J., 88
Clark, L. H., 444
Clark, M. S., 399
Clark-Plaskie, M., 393
Clark, R., 7
Clarke-Stewart. A., 150
Clarke-Stewart, K. A., 150
Claus, E., 297
Clausell, E., 345
Claux, M., 166
Clayards, M. A., 115
Cleary, P. D., 396
Clemans, K. H., 307
Clements, K. M., 448
Clifford, L. M., 226
Clifton, C., 244
Clifton, R. K., 115, 163
Clipp, E. D., 491
Cloutier, G., 123
CNN, 340
Coalition to Stop the Use of Child Soldiers, 7
Coall, D. A., 425
Cobb, R. J., 374
Coch, D., 159
Cocking, R. R., 159, 229
Coffelt, T. A., 430
Cogan, J. C., 346
Cohen, D., 171
Cohen, D. J., 99
Cohen, G. L., 286
Cohen, J. A., 370
Cohen, L. B., 107, 113, 115, 117, 119, 120
Cohen, R. A., 224
Cohen, R. J., 234, 348
Cohen, T. F., 374
Cohler, B. J., 309, 345
Coie, J. D., 191
Çok, F., 308
Colby, A., 256
Colditz, G. A., 399
Cole, D., 324, 325
Cole, M., 7
Coleman, J. C., 276
Coleman, M., 428, 430, 431, 432, 433
Coles, C. D., 79
Coles, E. K., 245
Coll, O., 77
College Board, The, 203
Collie, R., 120
Collins, F. S., 38
Collins, J. L., 376, 377
Collins, N. L., 253
Collins, S., 237
Collins, W., 310
Collishaw, S., 324
Coltman, P., 198
Colvert, E., 243
Colyvan, M., 367
Combs, B. L., 491
Combs-Orme, T., 147
Comer, J. S., 187
Comer, R. J., 325, 327
Commons, M. L., 349
Compas, B. E., 267
Conboy, B. T., 176
Condon, J., 89, 91
Conger, R. D., 268, 284, 289, 324
Conklin, H. M., 290
Conlon, E., 175, 231
Connell-Carrick, K., 153
Connelly, A., 11, 159, 220
Connolly, J., 316

Connolly, M., 91
Connor, C., 237
Conradt, E., 132
Conti-Ramsden, G., 244
Conway, F., 477
Cook, C. R., 260
Cook, E. C., 207
Cook, S., 442
Cooney, T. M., 420
Cooper, C. L., 406
Cooper, D., 37
Copen, C. E., 287, 288, 425
Copian, R., 200, 202, 257, 259
Coplan, R. J., 187
Coppola, G., 125
Corapci, F., 109
Corballis, M. C., 114
Cordaro, D., 131
Core, C., 177
Corkindale, C., 89, 91
Corley, R. P., 51
Cornelius, M. D., 79
Corr, C. A., 506, 509, 510, 513
Corr, D. M., 506, 509
Corrado, M. M., 447
Correa-Chavez, M., 180
Costa, A. L., 237
Costa, P. T., 436, 437, 438, 475, 476
Costa, P. T. Jr., 417, 437, 476
Costello, D. M., 324, 325
Costin, S. E., 202
Côté, J. E., 3
Cote, L. R., 123
Côté, S. M., 192, 262
Cotrim, A. P., 50
Cottin, S., 386
Council for Excellence in Government, 83
Courage, M. L., 112, 113
Cowan, C., 374
Cowan, P. A., 374
Coward, B., 336
Cowden, P. A., 244
Cox, J., 482
Cox, K. S., 420
Cox, M., 146
Coyl, D. D., 145
Coyle, A., 345
Craig, R. K., 170
Craigie, T., 25, 58
Craik, F., 458
Crain, W. C., 18
Cramer, S. H., 380
Crawford, S. Y., 477
Crean, H. F., 304
Crews, D. E., 457
Crick, F. H. C., 35
Crick, N., 262
Crick, N. R., 193, 212, 260
Crimmins, E. M., 453
Criss, M. M., 192, 265
Cristo, M. B., 90
Criston, M., 90
Crocetti, E., 307
Crockenberg, S., 374
Crockett, L. J., 275, 286
Cronbach, L. J., 24
Crone, E. A., 290, 291
Crosby, R. A., 286
Cross, C. T., 240
Cross, W., 406
Crouter, A. C., 265, 311, 312, 386
Crowe, M., 467
Csibra, G., 113
Csikszentmihalyi, M., 363
Cueto, S., 108
Cuevas, K., 120
Cuijpers, P., 200
Culang, M. E., 353, 472
Cummings, H. E., 194
Cummings, M. R., 47, 69
Cunnington, R., 114
Curatolo, P., 45
Curenton, S., 170, 202
Currier, J. M., 214
Curtin, S. C., 287
Curtis, W. J., 100, 213
Cutrona, C. E., 209
Cyr, C., 195
Cyr, F., 430
Czaja, S. J., 410, 411

D

D'Agati, E., 45
D'Agostino, N., 513
Dahinten, V., 289
Daiute, C., 231
D'Alessio, M., 94
Daly, M., 370
Damasio, A. R., 297
Damasio, H., 297
Damon, W., 253, 256
Damon-Wasserman, M., 120
D'Angiulli, A., 120
Daniels, D., 209
Daniels, H., 18, 170
Daniluk, J., 283
Dapretto, M., 143
Dariotis, J. K., 261
Daro, D., 154
Daro, D. A., 154
D'Augelli, A. R., 345
Daugherty, M., 174
David, H., 432
David, O., 265
Davidov, M., 143
Davidson, A. J. A., 267
Davidson, H. A., 212
Davies, B., 490, 492
Davies, M., 346
Daviglus, M. L., 396
Davis, B. L., 122
Davis, D. S., 52
Davis, K., 233
Davis-Kean, P. E., 146, 322
Davis, O., 51
Davis, P. E., 199
Dawson, G., 159
Dawson, J. D., 451
Day, N., 79
Day, N. L., 79, 80
de Bruyn, E. H., 324
de Calume, Z. F., 90
de Geus, J. C., 51
de Groot, A. M. B., 177
de Haan, M., 112, 113, 120, 159, 160, 161
de Koning, H. J., 399
De León, J. R., 174
de Mause, L., 6
de Melo, F., 451
De Raedt, R., 474
De Ronchi, D., 465
De Schonen, S., 120
de Souza, A. S., 73
de St. Aubin, E., 421
De Vos, N. J., 449
de Vries, L. S., 88
de Waal, F. B. M., 114
De Wolf, A., 264
Deal, K., 365
DeAngelis, T., 222
Deary, I. J., 51, 452, 478
Deater, Deckard, K., 57
DeCasper, A., 115
DeCasper, A. J., 115
Declercq, E., 83
DeCristofaro, J., 510
Degarmo, D. S., 430
Degnan, K. A., 133
deGuehery, K., 106
DeHart, T., 207
del Bello-Haas, V., 448
DeLamater, J., 401
DeLamater, J. D., 238, 370, 400
Delandtsheer, J., 237
DeLany, J. P., 447
DeLay, D., 311
Deloache, J. S., 167, 172
DeMaris, A., 486
Demerouti, E., 436
Demulder, E., 190, 197, 200
Denham, S., 200
Denham, S. A., 190, 197, 200
Denissen, J., 190
Denissen, J. J. A., 309, 363, 421
Dennerstein, L., 399
Dennis, M. J., 200
Dennis, N. A., 452
DePalma, R., 179
DePaul, G. J., 245
Deptula, D. P., 318
Derauf, C., 80, 297
DeRose, L. M., 284, 307
Dershewitz, R. A., 280
Desouza, A. T., 201
DeSpelder, L. A., 496, 500, 505, 511
Desrosiers, J., 451
Detweiler, M. F., 187
Deutsch, F. M., 387
Deutsch, G., 160
DeVault, C., 509
Devine, T. A. J., 143
DeVoe, M., 349
DeVries, H., 421
Devries, M., 244
Dewe, P., 406
Dexter, A., 195
Diamond, A., 5, 10, 44, 158, 208
Dias, M. S., 106
Diav-Citrin, O., 76
Diaz, I., 116
Díaz, R. M., 176
Dick, D. M., 43
Dickens, W., 235, 408
Dickens, W. T., 53
DiClemente, R. J., 286
Diego, M., 102
Diehl, M., 349
Dierckx, E., 474
Dierker, L. C., 324, 325
Diesch, E., 122
Dietz, E. L., 259
Dillon, F. R., 306, 307, 309, 347
Dimitry, L., 267
Dinse, H. R., 194
Dintcheff, B. A., 295
Diprete, T. A., 162
Dishion, T. J., 261, 286, 294, 310, 311, 313
Dixon, R., 261
do Carmo, M. G., 73
Dodge, B., 344
Dodge, K. A., 191, 192, 201, 213, 261, 265, 323
Dodwell, P., 114
Doetsch, F., 452
Doherty, M. J., 166, 167
Doka, K. J., 510, 512
Doksum, K. A., 38
Dolbin-MacNab, M. L., 425
Dominguez, A., 268
Donaldson, M., 170
Donatucci, C. F., 400
Donchi, L., 315
Donnellan, M. B., 268, 309, 437
Donnelly, E. H., 81
D'Onofrio, B. M., 269
Donovan, M. S., 237, 240
Donsky, T., 431
Dorius, C., 146, 271, 377, 430
Dorn, L. D., 284
Dornbusch, S. M., 311
Dörner, J., 463
Dorner, L. M., 147
Dosoky, M. El, 280, 281
Dougherty, L. R., 190
Douglass, S., 264
Dounskaia, N. V., 451
Dowden, A., 120
Dowshen, S., 219
Doyle, A. B., 264
Doyle, R., 223
Draper, T. W., 187
Dreher, G. F., 379
Drew, C. J., 241
Dreyer, P. H., 285
Drummond, J. A., 227
Drusnecov, A. W., 406
Drutz, J. E., 108
Dubas, J. S., 322
Dubois, D. L., 308
Dubois, M., 314
Dubow, E. F., 192
Dubowitz, H., 153
Dudek, R. W., 48
Duffy, G. G., 230
Duffy, S. N., 267
Dukes, C., 172
Dunbar, M. D., 261

Duncan, G. J., 146, 163
Duncan, L. E., 406, 407
Duncan, R. M., 171
Dunn, E. C., 323
Dunn, J., 57, 201, 202, 209
DuPaul, G. J., 244
Dupre, J., 37
Durkin, K., 373, 374
Durston, S., 290, 324
Duwe, K. N., 91
Dweck, C. S., 229, 238, 239, 253, 457
Dyches, K. D., 261
Dykas, M. J., 316
Dykens, E. M., 47
Dyson, L. L., 244

E

Eaglesfield, G. D., 109
Eagly, A. H., 203, 204, 238
Earls, F., 284
Easterbrooks, M. A., 142, 143
Eaton, W., 417, 437
Ebersole, P., 446
Ebner, N. C., 478
Eccles, J. S., 252, 279, 322
Eckert, J. K., 491
Eddy, D. M., 319
Eddy, K. T., 282
Edgerton, J., 363
Edwards, A., 256
Edwards, C. P., 199
Edwards, E. P., 147
Edwards, J. M., 434
Edwards, M., 74
Egeland, B., 212
Egelund, B., 153
Eggum, N. D., 188, 195, 256
Eichler, J., 386
Eimas, P. D., 123, 126
Einspieler, C., 160
Einstein, G. O., 459
Eisenberg, M. E., 282
Eisenberg, N., 146, 188, 194, 195, 196, 200, 208, 256, 259, 297
Eisenstat, S. A., 397
Ejei, J., 208
Ekehammer, B., 52
Ekman, P., 131
El Sarraj, E., 7
El Tom, S., 194
Elden, R. D., 147
Elder, G. H., 60
Elder, G. H. Jr., 284, 324
Elfers, T., 254, 259
Elias, G., 122
Elieff, C., 345
Elizabeth Glaser Pediatric AIDS Foundation, The, 77
Elkind, D., 296, 326
Ellicott, A., 354
Elliot, A. J., 239
Elliott, D., 161
Ellis, A. B., 203
Ellis, B. J., 281
Ellis, S., 170
Elster, N., 91
Emery, C. R., 289
Emery, R. E., 269
Engels, R., 314
Engeser, S., 363
Engle, P. L., 74
English and Romanian Adoptees (ERA) Study Team, the, 243
English, T., 474
Enns, L. N., 116
Enoch, M., 51
Ensor, R., 178
Epstein, I., 6
Erath, S. A., 316
Erber, J. T., 396
Erickson, M., 212
Erikson, E. H., 142, 196, 197, 305, 353, 472, 473
Erikson, J. M., 472, 473
Ernst, M., 290
Eron, L. D., 194
Erskine, J., 242
Eschen, A., 459
Espelage, D. L., 261, 346
Espinosa, L., 176
Espinoza, G., 315
Espy, K. A., 79, 88
Essink-Bot, M., 399
Euwema, M. C., 436
Evans, C. A., 421
Evans, G. W., 25, 43

F

Fabes, R. A., 194, 195
Fabiano, G. A., 245
Fabre, J. M., 447
Fadiga, L., 113
Fagen, J., 120
Faith, M. S., 226
Fan, X., 286
Fang, F., 166
Farfan, E. B., 81
Farmer, T. W., 261
Farooqi, S., 226
Farr, R. H., 370
Farrant, B. M., 143
Farrell, M. P., 295, 394, 419
Farroni, T., 113
Fass, P. S., 6, 7
Feaganes, J. R., 438
Fearon, R. P., 137
Featherstone, M., 400
Federal Interagency Forum on Aging Related Statistics, 450, 453, 456, 464, 477, 481, 485, 486, 488, 489
Federal Interagency Forum on Child and Family Statistics, 72, 225
Feeney, J. A., 95
Feeney, S., 237
Fehr, B., 365
Feigenbaum, P., 174
Feigenbaum, R., 343
Feinberg, M. E., 374
Feinglass, J., 396
Feldman, R., 90, 374
Felmlee, D., 426
Femia, E. E., 483
Femyhough, C., 174
Fenwick, K. D., 116
Fergus, S., 328
Ferguson, C. J., 193
Ferguson, T. J., 254
Fergusson, D. M., 323
Fernandez, F. S., 73
Fernandez, M., 102
Fernyhough, C., 18, 199
Ferrari, P., 114
Ferrer, A., 447
Ferrer-Wreder, L., 306, 307
Ferretti, P., 75
Ferri, M., 449
Fiatarone, M. A., 448
Fiatarone-Singh, M. A., 449
Fiddler, M., 69
Fidler, D. J., 47
Field, D., 482
Field, T., 102
Fields, J., 376
Fields, M., 230
Fields, R. D., 221
Fierson, W. M., 242
Figueroa De Calume, Z., 90
Fikke, L., 132
Filippi, M., 452
Finch, C., 399
Finch, C. E., 404
Fincham, F. D., 370
Fine, M. A., 428, 430, 431
Finer, L. B., 66
Fingerman, K. L., 152, 424
Finkelhor, D., 213, 214, 322
Finkelson, L., 322
Finn, S. C., 398
Fiorentino, D. D., 451
Fisanick, C., 81, 84, 89, 92
Fischel, J. E., 175
Fischer, W., 159
Fischman, M. W., 29
Fishbein, M., 315
Fisher, D. A., 286
Fisher, S. E., 125
Fisher, S. J., 79
Fisk, A. D., 410, 411, 452, 459
Fiske, M., 426
Fitzmaurice, G., 109
Fitzmaurice, G. M., 244
Flanagan, K. S., 316
Flavell, E. R., 180
Flavell, J. H., 167, 180, 229, 230
Fleer, M., 180, 199
Flegal, K. M., 405
Fleishman, J. A., 424, 425
Fletcher, A. C., 207
Fletcher, J., 143
Fletcher, P., 123
Flint, M., 398
Floccia, C., 102, 122
Flook, L., 311
Flores, R., 109
Flouri, E., 265
Flynn, J., 235, 408
Flynn, J. R., 53
Foehr, U. G., 351
Fogassi, L., 113
Fogel, A., 18
Folkman, S., 29, 30, 406
Fonagy, P., 138
Fonda, S. J., 491
Fontes, L. A., 212
Forbes, D., 132
Forgac, T., 398
Forgatch, M. S., 430
Formiga, F., 447
Foroud, A., 105
Forrester, M. B., 80
Forssell, S. L., 370
Fortenberry, J., 344
Fortenberry, J. D., 344
Fortuna, K., 345
Fosco, G. M., 311, 313
Foster, H., 284
Fowler, C. A., 242
Fox, N. A., 133
Foxon, M. J., 379
Fozard, J. L., 396, 450
Fracasso, M. P., 265
Frala, J. L., 284
Fraley, R. C., 136
Franco, A., 120
Frank, L. R., 318
Frankenberger, K. D., 296
Franklin, A., 113
Franklin, C. A., 192
Frankman, E. A., 82
Franks, J. S., 491
Franks, M. M., 486
Fraser, J., 244
Fratiglioni, L., 467
Fredstrom, B., 259
Freeman, E. C., 309
Freeman, G., 224
Freeman, G. P., 335
Freeman, H., 145
French, D. C., 262
Freund, A. M., 394, 472, 474, 477, 478
Fried, P. A., 80
Friedlander, Y., 69
Friedler, G., 69
Friedman, E. M., 476
Friedman, H. S., 23, 395
Friedman, S. L., 226
Friedmann, T., 50
Frisard, M. I., 447
Frisch, R. E., 280
Frisoni, G. B., 449, 452
Frith, C. D., 254
Frith, U., 254
Frost, M. H., 267
Fudge, J. L., 290
Fujimura, J. H., 38
Fukuda, H., 24
Fukunaga, A., 450
Fuligni, A., 263, 264, 312, 422
Fuligni, A. J., 311, 312, 317, 422
Fuligni, A. S., 24, 25
Fulker, D. W., 345
Fuller, E., 349
FullerRowell, T. E., 483
Fung, H., 474
Furman, R., 175
Furman, W., 316, 317, 366
Furrer, C. J., 24

Furstenberg, F. F., Jr., 289
Furukawa, E., 190

G

Gabbard, C., 336, 337, 338, 396, 448
Gabora, L., 234
Gabriel, S. W., 200
Gaertner, B. M., 146, 200
Gaffin, D., 38
Gafni, A., 87
Gagnon, J. H., 343, 400, 401
Gahr, J. L., 284
Galand, B., 237
Galatzer-Levy, R. M., 345
Galinsky, E., 267
Gallagher, W., 394
Galler, J., 109
Galler, J. R., 109
Gallese, V., 113, 114
Galli, R. L., 457
Galluzzi, S., 452
Galotti, K. M., 294
Galst, J., 91
Galupo, M. P., 349
Galvan, A., 11
Galván, A., 318
Galvin, K. B., 257
Ganiban, J., 138
Ganong, L., 430, 431, 432, 433
Ganong, L. H., 428, 431, 432, 433
Gans, D., 457
Gantz, W., 315
Gao, Y., 143
Garbarino, J., 267
Garcia Coll, C., 263
Garcia, E., 208
Garcia, E. E., 176, 177, 179
Garcia, F., 208
Garcia, J. F., 208
Garcia, O., 177, 208
Garcia-Sierra, A., 176
Gardner, H., 233
Gardner, M., 24
Garland, A. F., 326
Garner, M., 474
Garrido, F., 79
Garside, D. B., 396
Garzarolli, B., 160
Gaskins, I. W., 237
Gathercole, S. E., 177, 459
Gatz, M., 467
Gaugler, J. E., 465, 491
Gavidia-Payne, S., 152
Gazelle, H., 187
Gazzaniga, M. S., 99, 100, 171
Ge, X., 284, 324
Geary, D. C., 280
Geddes, J. F., 106
Geddes, L., 457
Gellhaar, T., 378
Gelman, R., 178
Gelman, S. A., 117, 124, 178, 204, 205
Genbacev, O., 79
Genesoni, L., 91
Genro, J. P., 244
Gentile, D. A., 193
Gentner, D., 230
Gentzler, A. L., 265
Geoffreoy, M., 262
Georgas, J., 5
George, C., 137
Gerard, J. M., 311
Gerberding, J. L., 337, 338
Gergely, C., 114
Gergely, G., 114
Gernsbacher, M. A., 114
Gerow, L., 199
Gerris, J. R. M., 322
Gershoff, E. T., 6
Gerstorf, D., 409
Gertner, Y., 119
Gervain, J., 122, 123
Gesell, A., 103
Gest, S. D., 267
Getchell, N., 220
Gettman, D. C., 313
Getz, S., 11
Giannetta, J. M., 318
Gibbons, F. X., 209
Gibbons, J., 187
Gibbs, J., 256
Gibson, C. L., 79
Gibson, E. J., 115, 120
Giedd, J. N., 11, 220, 221, 290, 291, 324
Gil, E., 153
Gilca, M., 457
Gilet, A., 474
Gilger, J. W., 244
Gillam, R. B., 122
Gilligan, C., 256
Gillis, J. J., 244
Gillis, J. R., 346
Gilman, E., 120
Gilman, S. E., 323
Gilmore, R. O., 159
Gingo, M., 256
Gini, M., 135
Giorgio, A., 290
Giron, M., 90
Giuliano, F., 399
Glass, R. M., 79
Gleason, R. R., 199
Gleaves, D. H., 22
Glenberg, A. M., 114
Glewwe, P., 108
Glick, B. R., 50
Glick, G. C., 257, 259
Gliga, T., 117
Gluck, J., 463
Gluth, S., 474
Gnagy, E. M., 245
Goble, M., 222
Goddard, S., 93, 94
Godinho, M., 451
Goeleven, E., 474
Goetestam-Skorpen, C., 474
Goh, J. O., 452
Golant, S. M., 491
Gold, E. B., 397
Goldberg, A. E., 370, 385, 386, 387
Goldberg, W. A., 268
Goldin-Meadow, S., 125, 175, 230
Goldman, B. D., 202, 262
Goldman, L., 281
Goldman, S., 325
Goldrick-Rab, S., 58
Goldschmidt, A. B., 80, 283
Goldschmidt, L., 80
Goldstein, I., 399
Goldstein, M. H., 122, 126
Goldstein, S., 244
Goldstein, S. E., 322
Goldstein, T. R., 325
Goleman, D., 350
Golinkoff, R. M., 122, 123
Gomes, L., 200
Gomez, G., 336
Gomez, V., 437
Goncu, A., 142
Gonzalez, C., 254
Gonzalez, Z., 140
Good, C., 457
Good, M., 309
Goodman, G. S., 213
Goodvin, R., 133
Goodwin, R. D., 395
Goodyer, I. M., 324
Gooren, E. M. J., 199
Goossens, L., 309
Gopinath, B., 450
Gopnik, A., 100, 104
Gopnik. A., 107, 120
Gorchoff, S. M., 421, 423
Gordon, A. J., 237
Gordon, B. N., 172
Gordon, R. A., 58
Gordon-Salant, S., 396, 450
Gorman, E., 423
Gorman, K. S., 74
Goslin, J., 122
Gosselin, J., 432
Goswami, U., 244
Gotlib, I., 374
Goto, R., 24
Gottesman, I. I., 51
Gottfredson, G. D., 380
Gottlieb, G., 43, 51, 66
Gottman, J., 208
Gottman, J. M., 208, 431
Goubet, N., 105, 115
Graber, J. A., 208, 283, 284, 307
Grabill, C. M., 265
Graf, S. C., 306
Graham, J., 238
Graham, M., 296
Graham, S., 297
Gramzow, E., 172
Granic, I., 310
Granier-Deferre, C., 115
Granrud, C. E., 115
Grant, K. E., 267
Grantham-McGregor, S., 73, 108
Graves, N., 260
Gray, J. H., 480, 482
Gray, S. L., 455
Graziano, W. G., 259
Gredeback, G., 132
Greeff, A. P., 500, 514
Green, B. L., 24
Green, C. L., 122
Green, C. S., 452
Green, F. L., 180
Greenberg, J., 498, 499
Greene, A. L., 293
Greene, S., 79
Greene, S. M., 430
Greenfield, P. M., 336
Greenman, P. S., 137, 262
Greenspan, S., 131
Greenstein, D. K., 221, 291
Greenwood, P. M., 409
Greif, G. L., 365, 426
Greitmeyer, T., 193
Greven, C. U., 244
Greving, K. A., 146
Griffin, M., 444
Griffin, P., 231
Griffin, T. M., 231
Grigorenko, E. L., 37, 234, 240
Grimes, T., 193
Grimm, K. J., 163
Grimm-Thomas, K., 361
Grinyer, A., 513
Grissmer, D., 163
Grisson, J. A., 80
Grodstein, F., 399
Groebel, J., 193
Groen-Blokhuis, M. M., 88
Groeschel, S., 11, 159, 220
Grohl, A. M., 136
Grom, R. M., 244
Groningen, G., 130
Gross, J., 296
Gross, J. J., 474
Grossman, L. S., 347
Groth, L. A., 230
Grube, J. W., 286
Gruber-Baldini, A. L., 491
Gruenewald, T. L., 335
Gruhn, D., 474
Gruman, C., 491
Grusec, J. E., 208
Guay, F., 237
Guerra, N. G., 260
Guidice, S., 221
Guilliano, S., 172
Gungor, I., 75
Guo, G., 315
Gupta, R., 244
Gur-Yaish, N., 423
Gurian, M., 238
Gussekloo, J., 476
Gutman, D. L., 477
Guttman, L., 279
Gutwinski, S., 160
Gwiazda, J., 112
Gwyther, L. P., 467, 483

H

Ha, J., 486
Ha, T., 286
Haas, A. P., 346
Hagerman, R. J., 45
Haight, W., 126
Hakim-Larson, 349
Hakvoort, E. M., 324

Halberstadt, A. G., 135
Hale, W. W. III, 306
Haley, W. E., 465
Halford, G. S., 171
Halim, M. L., 252, 263, 264
Hall, G. B., 11
Hall, P., 91
Halliday, G., 409
Halpern, D. F., 203, 235, 408
Halter, S., 213
Hamberger, L., 68, 70, 89, 92
Hamilton, B. E., 68, 91, 287, 288
Hamilton-West, K., 406
Hammack, P. L., 309, 345
Hammond, A. J., 171
Hamon, R. R., 369
Hampton, D., 309
Hampton, M., 286
Han, G., 212
Handler, S. M., 242
Hane, A., 133
Hanif, R., 208
Hannah, M. E., 87
Hannah, W. J., 87
Hans, J., 431, 432
Hanscombe, K. B., 265
Hansen-Tift, A. M., 113
Hanson, L. K., 172
Hanson, R., 138
Hardesty, J. L., 308
Hardman, M. L., 241
Harkins, S., 448
Harkins, S. W., 396
Harkness, S., 56, 140
Harlap, S., 69
Harley, T. A., 174
Harlow, H. F., 138
Harlow, M. K., 138
Harms, R. W., 67, 74
Harringer, J. A., 131
Harrington, M., 424
Harrington, R., 406
Harris-Britt, A., 308
Harris, C., 442
Harris, L. S., 213
Harris, R., 354
Harrison, R., 109
Hart, B., 126
Hart, D., 253
Hart, H. M., 421
Hart, S. N., 212
Harter, S., 202, 253, 308
Hartl, D. L., 42
Hartup, W. W., 56, 199, 259
Harty, L., 189
Harvey, J. H., 428, 430, 431
Harwood, K., 373, 374
Harwood, R. L., 140
Haryu, E., 123
Hasher, L., 458
Hashimoto, T., 368
Hasselhorn, M., 172
Hasting, P. D., 187
Hatcher, R., 80
Hathaway, A., 212
Hathaway, J., 84
Hathaway, M., 84
Hattori, K., 51
Hauer, J., 512, 513
Hauser, S. T., 280
Havighurst, R. J., 377
Haviland-Jones, J. M., 144
Havusha-Morgenstern, H., 370
Hawes, C., 455
Hawley, P. H., 261
Haworth, C., 265
Hawver, T. H., 350
Hay, D. F., 153
Hayden, M., 349
Haydon, J., 45, 46
Hayes, S. J., 161
Hayflick, L., 457
Hayne, H., 120, 296
Haynes, O. M., 139
Häyry, M., 52
Hays, R. D., 397
Hayslip, B. Jr., 511
Hayward, C., 284
Hayward, M. D., 453
Haywood, K., 220
Hazen, N., 143
Head, D., 409, 452
Head, M. R., 312
Heard, K. V., 285
Heath, A. C., 269
Hebebrand, J., 226
Hebel, J. R., 491
Heckhausen, J., 239
Hedeker, D., 477
Hedlund, L., 52
Heigel, C., 189
Heilbron, N., 261
Heimann, M., 120
Heinz, A., 160
Helmert, U., 480
Helms, H. M., 317
Helsen, M., 307
Helson, R., 355, 392, 393, 421, 423
Helwig, C. C., 294
Henderson, H. A., 133
Henderson, V. W., 399
Hendriks, A. A., 437
Hendry, J., 77
Henkens, K., 445
Hennekens, C. H., 399
Hennessy, M., 315
Hennon, C. B., 431
Henrich, J., 144
Henry, D. B., 318
Henry, N. J., 482
Hepper, P. G., 160
Hepworth, M., 400
Herbenick, D., 344
Herbenick, D. C., 344
Herbert, J. S., 113
Herbiest, T., 500, 514
Herbst, J. H., 438
Herek, G. M., 346
Herman, C., 283
Herman, C. P., 282
Herman, S., 400
Hermanns, J., 207
Hernandez, M. D., 257
Hernandez-Reif, M., 102
Hernandez, S., 77
Herr, E. L., 380
Herrera, M. G., 109
Hersen, M., 225
Hershberger, P. J., 434
Hershow, R. C., 453
Hertwig, R., 425
Hertzog, C., 411, 476
Herzog, C., 459
Herzog, D. B., 282
Heslegrave, R. J., 451
Hespos, S. J., 126
Hess, E. H., 138
Hess, R., 397
Hess, T. M., 335, 409
Hetherington, E. M., 267, 268, 269, 270, 430, 431, 433
Hetzner, N. M., 24
Hevek, G. M., 346
Hewitt, B., 428
Hewitt, B. G., 77
Hewitt, J. K., 51
Hewson, S., 87
Heyes, C., 114
Heyman, R. E., 374
Heywood, C., 6
Hickey, M., 397
Hickok, G., 114
Higgs, P. F., 334
Hildenbrand, M., 166
Hill, E. D., 346
Hill, M. S., 146
Hill, N. E., 263
Hill, R., 434
Hill, W. G., 51
Hills, A., 345
Himes, J. H., 281
Himsel, A., 268
Hines, M., 238, 345
Hinney, A., 226
Hinshaw, S. R., 245
Hiris, J., 455
Hirsch, B. J., 421
Hirsh-Pasek, K., 122, 123
Hirshinger, N., 80
Ho, M. J., 317
Hoare, C., 353
Hobart, C. J., 172
Hochschild, A. R., 385
Hock, E., 145
Hock, R. R., 400
Hoddinott, J., 109
Hodge, R., 52
Hodnett, E. D., 87
Hoefnagels, M., 38
Hoehn, K., 67, 68, 73
Hoeve, M., 322
Hofer, M. A., 11
Hoff, E., 102, 175, 177
Hoff, E. V., 199
Hofferth, S., 146
Hofferth, S. L., 146
Hoffman, B. J., 309
Hoffman, C., 424
Hoffman, C. L., 457
Hoffman, J. H., 295
Hogan, M. J., 452
Hogart, A., 47
Högnäs, R. S., 25
Holahan, C. K., 24, 474
Holbrook, M., 152
Holden, G. W., 142
Holding, A., 180
Holditch-Davis, D., 90
Holland, A., 345
Holland, J. L., 379, 384
Holland, J. M., 477
Hollenstein, T., 310
Hollich, G., 116, 122
Hollingsworth, C., 491
Hollingsworth, H., 202, 262
Holmes, F. B., 187
Holmes, T. H., 405
Holsen, I., 281
Holt, M. K., 261
Holter, A., 255
Holtz, P., 315
Homma, A., 462
Hommel, B., 408
Hommes, D., 354
Honein, M. A., 91
Hong, J. S., 346
Hood, K. E., 51
Hood, M., 175, 231
Hooper, C. J., 290
Hoorens, T., 91
Hooven, C., 208
Hoover, J. R., 173
Hopkins, B., 103
Hoppin, A. G., 108
Hoppmann, C., 409
Horiuchi, S., 404
Horn, J. L., 408
Horowitz, J., 91
Horowitz, S. M., 325
Horton-Ikard, R., 126
Horwitz, B. N., 412
Horwood, J. L., 323
Hospice Association of America, 504
Houser, J. J., 261
Houts, R. M., 226
Howard, K., 304
Howe, N., 207
Howe, T. R., 430
Howell, K. K., 79
Howes, C., 198, 202
Howieson, N., 137
Hoyer, W. J., 446, 459
Hruschka, D. J., 426
Hsia, J. F., 365
Hsiu-Hsin, T., 442
Hsu, A. Y. C., 474
Hsu, H., 135
Hu, F. B., 399
Hu, S., 345
Hua, F., 79
Hudley, C., 263
Hudson, J. A., 172
Huesmann, L. R., 193, 194
Huesmann, R. L., 192
Huettel, S. A., 297
Hugdahl, K., 459
Hughes, C., 178, 202, 209

Hughes, C. S., 417
Hughes, D., 263, 264
Hughes, J. P., 280, 281
Hughes, M., 170
Huizink, A. C., 80
Hull, R. H., 450
Hulme, C., 244
Hulshoff Pol, H. E., 290, 324
Hummert, M. L., 442
Humphrey, G. K., 114
Humphrey, R. H., 350
Hund, A. M., 172
Hung, K., 113, 117
Hunt, L. A., 451
Hur, Y., 52
Hurlbert, A., 113
Hurley, K. M., 108
Hurry, J., 308
Hurst, J. A., 125
Hurt, H., 318
Huston, A., 268
Huston, A. C., 158
Hutchinson, J., 74
Hutchison, B., 378
Hutman, T., 143
Huttenlocher, J., 126
Hutton, M., 467
Hutz, M. H., 244
Huyck, M. H., 435, 436
Hwang, P. C., 265
Hyde, J., 238, 345
Hyde, J. D., 370, 400
Hyde, J. S., 203, 297, 383

I

Iacoboni, M., 113, 114
Ibraheem, A. N., 7
Ickovics, J., 387
Icoboni, M., 292
Iedema, J., 307
Ihsen, E., 151
Imai, M., 123
Imhof, A. E., 336
Impett, E. A., 193
Ince, P., 409
Indurkhya, A., 244
Ingoldsby, B. B., 369
Inhelder, B., 293
Insel, T. R., 283
Institute for Behavioral Genetics, 51
International Human Genome Sequencing Consortium, 35, 38
International Monetary Fund, 488
Iqbal, M. M., 80
Irving, M., 263
Isaacowitz, D. M., 418
Isaacs, L. D., 104, 219
Isaacs, S., 226
Ishizuka, T., 175
Isingrini, M., 452
Israel, S. E., 230
Itakura, S., 166, 177
Iverson, J. M., 126
Iverson, P., 122
Ivry, R. B., 99, 100

J

Jacklin, C. N., 238
Jackson, C., 315
Jackson, J. J., 437
Jackson, J. S., 376
Jackson-Newsom, J., 311
Jacob, C. J., 434
Jacobus, J., 318
Jacobvitz, D., 143
Jacoby, A. P., 285
Jacoby, L. L., 459
Jacquez, F. M., 324, 325
Jadack, R. A., 297
Jaffe, S. R., 265
Jaffee, S. R., 5
James, J., 226
James, R. S., 187
James, W., 101
Jameson, H., 198
Jamison, T., 432
Jankowiak, W. R., 369
Jarrett, O., 178
Jarvin, L., 234, 461, 463
Jaswal, V. K., 174
Jay, J., 396
Jayson, S., 405
Jedlicka, D., 285
Jedrychowski, W., 80
Jeffery, B., 286
Jekel, J. F., 325
Jenike, B. R., 442
Jenkins, W. J., 345
Jensen, A. C., 147, 209
Jensen, L. A., 7
Jenvey, V., 180, 198, 200
Jenvey, V. B., 194
Jeong, S., 420
Jersild, A. T., 187
Jessor, R., 318
Jeune, B., 447
Jewkes, A. M., 237
Jin, K. M., 143
Jing, O., 125
Jobin, J., 478
Joe, S., 326
Joffe, M., 399
Johansson, B., 467
John, O. P., 421, 423
Johnson, A. M., 451
Johnson, B. T., 443
Johnson, C., 79, 152
Johnson, D. W., 237
Johnson-Glenberg, M. C., 47
Johnson, L., 455
Johnson, L. C., 102
Johnson, M., 399
Johnson, M. H., 10, 113, 117, 159, 161, 163, 220
Johnson, M. W., 90
Johnson, R. T., 237
Johnson, R. W., 481
Johnson, S. P., 112
Johnson, W., 51
Johnston, L. D., 320, 321
Johnston, T. D., 18, 19
Johnstun, M. L., 380
Joint United Nations Programme on HIV/AIDS (UNAIDS), 75, 341
Jolley, R. P., 167
Jones, B. L., 286
Jones, C. M., 457
Jones, D. C., 202
Jones, E., 113
Jones, G. V., 160
Jones, I. R., 334
Jones, K. L., 79
Jones, L., 213, 214
Jones, L. M., 213
Jones, S. S., 113
Jordan, A., 315
Jordan, J. R., 503, 510
Joseph, D. L., 351
Joseph, J. A., 457
Judd, F. K., 397
Juffer, F., 94
Jun, H., 418
Juncosa, B., 465
Jung, S. H., 143
Junn, E., 209
Just, M. A., 120, 247
Juvonen, J., 284

K

Kaciroti, N., 109, 123
Kaffashi, F., 90
Kagan, J., 187
Kâgitçibasi, C., 5, 180
Kahana, B., 396
Kahana, E., 396
Kai, I. K., 80
Kaiser Family Foundation, 456
Kajanne, A., 409
Kakar, S., 317
Kakihara, F., 313
Kalb, S., 197, 200
Kalbitzer, J., 160
Kaloustian, G., 136
Kan, M. L., 374
Kana, R. K., 247
Kandler, C., 437
Kane, R. L., 491
Kaneshiro, N. K., 437
Kaniskan, R., 267
Kante, S., 343
Kaplan, B. H., 396
Kaplan, N., 235
Kapoor, W. N., 397
Karasik, L. B., 103, 105
Karen, R., 141
Karlsen, M., 307
Karr, B. R., 244
Karraker, A., 401
Kärtner, J., 144
Kastenbaum, R., 497, 500, 506
Katz, D. L., 226
Katz, I., 474
Katz, L., 208
Katz, L. F., 208
Katz, L. G., 200
Katz, R., 423
Katzel, L. I., 403
Kaufman, J., 113
Kaufman, J. C., 234
Kaufman, W. E., 159
Kauh, T. J., 261
Kavanaugh, R. D., 120, 180
Kavšek, M., 102
Kawas, C. H., 447
Kawashima, R., 24
Kay, M. A., 50
Kaye, S. D., 481
Kearns, K. T., 257
Keating, D. P., 99, 293
Keefer, C. H., 102
Keekeren, H. R., 459
Keesee, N. J., 214
Kehrer-Sawatzki, H., 37
Keijsers, L., 306
Keller, M. L., 297
Keller, T. A., 120, 247
Kelley, M. M., 500
Kelly, D. J., 113
Kelly, J., 268, 431
Kelly, S. J., 79
Kenneavy, K., 315
Kennedy, E. A., 152
Kennedy, G., 238
Kennedy, K. M., 409, 410, 452, 460
Ker, H., 144
Kermoian, R., 115
Kern, L., 244
Kern, M. L., 23, 24
Kerns, K. A., 265
Kerpelman, J. L., 369
Kerr, D., 226
Kerr, M., 313, 314, 322
Kerr, M. E., 209
Kerrick, S., 421
Kersebaum, S., 160
Kerzner, B., 138
Kesebir, P., 498, 499
Kesselring, T., 165
Kessler, E., 463
Kessler, R. C., 324, 392, 393, 394, 407, 417, 476
Kestler, L., 80
Ketcham, C. J., 448, 451
Ketterlinus, R. D., 265
Ketterman, A., 122
Keyes, C. L. M., 423
Khan, F. A., 50
Khan, K., 267
Kherzi, H., 208
Kiang, L., 312, 317, 396, 422
Kibbe, M. M., 119
Kidd, K. K., 37, 234
Kieling, C., 244
Kilburn, J., 193
Kildea, D., 399
Kilgore, W. D., 292
Killen, M., 256, 298
Killgore, W., 292
Killian, T. S., 424
Kilner, L. A., 280
Kim-Cohen, J., 5
Kim, H. J., 435
Kim, J., 212
Kim, P., 25, 43

Kim, P. Y., 345
Kim, T., 421
Kim, T. E., 260
Kim, Y. J., 419
Kindermann, T. A., 261
King, B. J., 18
King, B. M., 343
King, C. M., 447
King, M. D., 11, 159, 220
King, S. V., 491
Kinicki, A. J., 434
Kinnon, J. B., 84
Kinnunen, M., 226
Kinomura, S., 24
Kins, E., 421
Kinsbourne, M., 160
Kirby, R. S., 73
Kirkels, W. J., 399
Kirkham, N. Z., 107
Kirsh, S. J., 193
Kistner, J., 262
Kit, B. K., 405
Kita, S., 175
Kite, M. E., 443
Kitzinger, C., 345
Kivnick, H. Q., 472, 473
Klamen, D. L., 347
Klare, M. T., 7
Klarman, L., 176
Klass, D., 511
Klausen, E., 198
Klavora, P., 451
Kleban, M. H., 424
Klebanov, P., 58
Klein, R. G., 244
Kleinhaus, K., 69
Klemmack, D. L., 478
Klerman, L. V., 325
Klevens, J., 478
Kliegel, M., 187, 459
Klimstra, T. A., 306
Klump, K. L., 283
Knee, D. O., 505
Knight, G. P., 264
Knight, J. A., 45, 46
Kochanek, K. D., 403, 404, 405, 512
Koehler, K., 514
Koenig, H. G., 478
Koepke, S., 309, 363, 421
Kohlberg, L., 255, 256, 298
Kohn, A., 253
Kohn, M. L., 410
Kolata, G., 400
Konarski, R., 316
Kong, S., 477
Konigsberg, R. D., 500
Konner, M., 5, 142
Konopka, G., 125
Koopman, C., 88
Koot, H. M., 199, 200
Kopacz, D. R., 347
Kopp, C. B., 188
Korb, R., 237
Koren, G., 76
Korfage, I. J., 399
Korner-Bitensky, N., 451
Korrick, S. A., 81
Kosloff, S., 499
Kost, K., 66
Kostelny, K., 267
Kovelman, I., 176
Kozma, A., 396
Kral, M. J., 346
Krampe, R., 410
Kravitz, H. M., 397
Kreider, R. M., 369, 370
Kreppner, J., 243
Krettenauer, T., 297
Kril, J. J., 409
Krishnakumar, A., 153
Kristiansson, R., 147
Kroger, J., 305, 306, 307, 308, 309, 364
Krombholz, H., 209
Kron-Sperl, V., 172
Krucoff, C., 448
Krüger, A., 459
Kruger, A. C., 142
Kua, A., 451
Kuebli, J. E., 152
Kuhl, E. S., 226
Kuhl, P., 122
Kuhl, P. K., 100, 116, 122, 176, 231
Kuhn, D., 165, 230, 293
Kulik, L., 370
Kulin, H. E., 281
Kuller, L. H., 397
Kung, H., 405
Kung, R., 87
Kunzmann, U., 461, 463, 467
Kurtz-Costas, B., 308
Kutner, L., 193
Kwan, M. L., 476

L

Labouvie-Vief, G., 349, 474
Lachman, M. E., 393, 395, 412, 437, 475, 476
Ladd, G. W., 262
Ladd, L. D., 260
LaFontana, K. M., 261, 262
LaFreniére, P., 11
Lagaay, A. M., 476
Lagasse, L. L., 80, 115, 297
Lagattuta, K., 189
Lagrasse, L., 80
Lahikainen, A. R., 187
Lai, C. S. L., 125
Lai, M., 170
Laird, R. D., 192, 265
Lally, M., 281
Lam, R. C., 442
Lamanna, M. A., 370, 428
Lamaze, F., 84
Lamb, M. E., 141, 145, 146, 147, 205, 265, 270, 361
Lamb, S., 193
Lambert, B. L., 477
Lamborn, S. D., 311
Land, K. C., 222
Landau, M., 499
Lander, R., 198
Langelaan, S., 435
Lansford, J. E., 192, 213, 261, 269
Lantos, J. D., 84
Lapsley, A., 137
Lapsley, D. K., 363
Larkby, C., 79
Larose, S., 237
Larouche, M., 237
Larson, N. I., 282
Larson, R., 295
Larson, R. W., 295, 313
LaSalle, J., 47
Last, C. G., 188
Lauderdale, D. S., 84
Lauer, J. C., 423, 430
Lauer, R. H., 423, 430
Laumann, E. O., 343, 400, 401
Laursen, B., 257, 310, 311
Lautenschlager, G. J., 259
Lavassani, M. G., 208
Lavelli, M., 135
Lawrence, E., 374
Lawrence-Jacobson, A. R., 490
Lawrence, K., 256
Lawson, D. W., 209
Lawton, M. P., 459, 474, 483
Layden, J., 453
Lazarus, R. S., 406
Le Grange, D., 80, 283
Leafstedt, J. M., 244
Leaper, C., 203, 204, 238, 252
Learmonth, A. E., 120
Learner, S., 84
Lecanuet, J., 115
Lecanuet, J. P., 115
Ledingham, J., 192
Lee, C. S., 235
Lee, G. R., 486
Lee, J., 419
Lee, J. H., 194
Lee, J. S. Y., 436
Lee, K., 113, 208
Lee, P. A., 281
Lee, S., 324
Lee, S. J., 192
Lee, S. M., 222
Leech, S. L., 79
Leeder, S. R., 450
Leen-Feldner, E. W., 284
Leerkes, E., 374
Leerkes, E. M., 58, 146, 147
Legacy, 425
Legate, N., 346
Lehalle, H., 346
Lehman, C., 244
Leibowitz, H. W., 449
Leicht, K., 380
Leinonen, J., 265
Leiter, M. P., 435, 436
L'Engle, K. L., 315
Lenhardt, M., 448
Lenhardt, M. L., 396
Lenroot, R. K., 220, 221, 291
Leo, I., 113
Leo, J., 285
Leon, K., 430
Leonard, K. E., 147
Leone, C., 259
Lequien, P., 115
Lerner, A C., 462
Lerner, A. W., 462
Lerner, R. M., 9, 19
Lesaux, N. K., 177
Leslie, A. M., 119
Lester, B., 80
Lester, B. M., 102
Let's Move, 80
Leung, J. L. Y., 84
Levay, S., 89
Levenson, M. R., 406
Leventhal, E. A., 448
Leventhal, H., 448
Leventhal, T., 24, 234
Levin, D. E., 193
Levine, J. A., 289
Levine, R., 368
Levine, R. A., 89, 209
Levinson, D., 353, 354, 393, 474
Levitas, J., 190, 197, 200
Levrini, A., 244
Levy, T. M., 138
Lewin-Bizan, S., 9
Lewin-Epstein, N., 387
Lewinsohn, P. M., 283, 284
Lewis, C., 145, 205
Lewis, D. C., 442
Lewis, L., 423
Lewis, L. J., 40
Lewis, M., 11, 80, 138, 144
Lewis, R., 38, 48
Lewkowicz, D. J., 113, 116
Li, J., 119
Li, L., 123, 345
Li, Q., 244
Li, S., 172, 459
Li, S.-C., 408
Li, V., 106
Liang, W., 123
Liben, L. S., 204, 252
Lichtenwalner, R. J., 452
Lickliter, R., 51, 66, 116
Lieberman, J. D., 499
Lieberman, M., 256
Lieberman, M. A., 473
Lillard, A., 166, 170, 178, 202
Lillycrop, K. A., 226
Lin, G., 486
Lin, S., 477
Lindberg, S. M., 203
Lindenberger, U., 2, 19, 172, 408, 437, 459, 460, 467
Line, N., 90
Ling, Y., 113
Linke, D. B., 160
Linn, M. C., 203
Linsenmeier, J. A. W., 345
Liotti, G., 137
Lippa, R., 345
Lister, K. M., 227
Little, T. D., 261
Litvin, S. J., 424
Litwack, S. D., 261
Liu, D., 166
Liu, G., 244
Liu, L., 166
Liu, Y., 73
Livesey, D., 200

Llanos, M. N., 79
Llop, S., 80
Lloyd, B., 205
Lo-Castro, A., 45
Lobo, R. A., 398, 399
Lock, J., 345
Lock, M., 398
Löckenhoff, C. E., 443
Lohaus, A. G., 103
Lohman, B. J., 286
Lonca, M., 77
Lonigan, C. J., 175
Loparo, K. A., 90
Lopez, L. S., 314
Lopez, M., 77
Lord, M., 481
Loscher, A., 160
Loth, K., 282
Loth, K. A., 80, 283
Lövdén, M., 459
Lovegreen, L. D., 423
Low, S. M., 317
Lowder, J. L., 82
Lowe, E. D., 268
Lowenstein, A., 423
Lowenstein, S. R., 451
Lowenthal, B., 212
Lozada, F. T., 135
Lozoff, B., 109
Lucas, R. E., 437
Lucas-Thompson, R., 268
Lucassen, P. J., 324
Luciana, M., 290, 291
Lucock, M., 73
Ludden, A., 281
Ludington-Hoe, S., 90
Luetters, C., 399
Lui, J., 260
Lui, L., 464, 467
Luk, G., 177
Lumpkin, J. R., 425
Luna, B., 292
Luo, S. W., 236
Lurquin, P. F., 41
Lustgarten, M., 457
Lustig, C., 452
Lutjens, S. L., 6
Lutz, A., 474
Lutz, W., 145
Luyckx, K., 307, 309
Lwayama, M., 69
Lykken, D. T., 457
Lynam, D., 191
Lynch, C., 160
Lynch, M. E., 79
Lynm, C., 79
Lynn, R., 51
Lyons, T., 126
Lysle, D. T., 406
Lytel, L., 307
Lyytinen, H., 242

M

Ma-Kellams, C., 498
Maas, L. C., 450
Macchi, C., 113
Maccoby, E. E., 206, 238, 259, 265
MacDermid, S. M., 265
MacDorman, M. F., 83
Mace, R., 209
MacEacheron, A. E., 323
MacFarlane, A., 113
Machung, A., 385
Mack, W. J., 399
Mackin, R. S., 406
Mackler, J. S., 200
Macnee, C. L., 267
MacPhee, A. R., 324
Madden, D. J., 451, 458
Madden, P. A., 269
Madden, T., 308
Maddox, G. L., 491
Madison, K. J., 207
Madole, K. L., 117
Madsen, M. C., 195
Maestripieri, D., 457
Magai, C., 477
Mageau, G. A., 142
Magen, R. H., 417
Mahler, L., 160
Mahoney, D. H., 108
Main, M., 136, 138
Mainstream Science on Intelligence, 234
Maital, S., 123
Majors, K., 202, 257
Maki, P. M., 399
Makin, J. W., 116
Malahmadi, E., 208
Malamuth, N. M., 193
Malaspina, D., 69
Malave, V. L., 247
Malone, L. M., 24
Malone, P. S., 261
Malouff, J. M., 51, 53
Maluccio, J. A., 109
Man-Son-Hing, M., 451
Mancilla-Martinez, J., 177
Mandler, J., 119, 120
Mandler, J. M., 117, 119, 120
Manganello, J. A., 192
Mangun, G. R., 99, 100
Manis, J., 383
Manly, J., 212
Mann, T. D., 120
Mannarino, A. P., 212
Manning, K. J., 451
Manning, W. D., 370
Manson, J. E., 399
March of Dimes, 90, 109
Marchman, V. A., 123, 124
Marcia, J., 306
Marcia, J. E., 308, 309, 364
Marcus, G. F., 174
Mares, M., 193
Mareschal, D., 117
Margett, T. E., 131
Marieb, E., 67, 68, 73
Maring, B. L., 199
Mark, D. B., 396
Markovic, N., 80
Marks, J. S., 337, 338
Marks, N. F., 418, 424
Markus, H., 383
Markus, H. S., 460
Marmeleira, J. F., 451
Marmor, R., 91
Marschark, M., 203
Marschik, P. B., 160
Marshal, M. P., 324, 346
Marshall, S., 451
Martin, A., 58
Martin, A. C., 193
Martin, C., 204, 205
Martin, C. L., 204
Martin, J., 254, 259
Martin, J. A., 68, 87, 91, 206, 287, 288
Martin, M., 160, 393, 394
Martin-Storey, A., 192
Martin, T. A., 437
Martin, T. L., 510
Martinez, C., 73
Martinez, G., 287, 288
Martínez, I., 208
Martins, A., 350
Martinussen, M., 364
Martorell, R., 74, 109
Marzano, J. S., 237
Marzano, R. J., 237
Marzolf, D. P., 167
Mashek, D. J., 190
Maslach, C., 435, 436
Maslow, A. H., 362
Mason, M. A., 431
Mason, M. G., 426
Masoro, E. J., 457
Massad, S., 7
Mast, B. T., 452
Masten, C. L., 312
Master, A., 239, 253
Mata, R., 409
Mather, M., 474
Mathias, J. L., 459
Mathieson, K., 178
Maton, K., 7
Matsumoto, D., 308
Matthews, F. E., 409
Matthews, G., 351
Matthews, K., 397
Matthews, K. A., 397
Mattingley, J. B., 114
Mattock, K., 115, 126
Matzo, M., 508
Mauer, M., 166
Maughan, A., 138
Maybery, M. T., 143
Mayer, J. D., 350
Mayer, R. E., 171
Mayer, V., 376, 377
Mayeux, L., 261
Mayhew, E. M. Y., 172
Maynard, A. M., 296
Mayo Clinic, 74, 86, 87
Mazor, K., 79
Mazur, P., 106
Mazziotta, J. C., 292
McAdams, D. P., 417, 420, 421
McAdoo, H. P., 376
McAllister, C. L., 24
McBean, L. D., 398
McBride-Chang, C., 231
McCabe, L., 25
McCabe, S. F., 267
McCarthy, B. W., 323
McCartney, K., 150
McClellan, D. E., 200
McClelland, D. C., 237
McCloskey, L., 189
McCormick, M. C., 58, 244
McCormick, W. C., 455
McCoshen, J. A., 90
McCrae, R. R., 436, 437, 438, 475, 476
McCredie, J., 437
McCurdy, K. P., 154
McDaniel, A., 162
McDaniel, B., 297
McDaniel, M. A., 459
McDonald, K. L., 200, 202, 257, 259
McDonald, L., 170
McDowell, M. A., 280, 281
McFadden, K. E., 377
McGoldrick, M., 374, 419
McGue, M., 447
McHale, S. M., 261, 265, 311, 312
McIlvane, J. M., 423
McIntosh, J. L., 503
McIntosh, T., 82
Mcintosh, W. D., 442
McIsaac, C., 316
McKee, A., 350
McKee-Ryan, F., 434
McKenna, M., 222
McKercher, D. A., 174
McLanahan, S., 25
McLaughlin, A. E., 483
McLean, N., 373, 374
McLoyd, V., 265, 268, 269
McLoyd, V. C., 268, 269
McMahon, C. A., 138
McMahon, C. M., 450
McMahon, M., 378
McMahon, R. J., 265
McMahon, S. D., 267
McMaster, M. T., 79
McNeil, D. W., 187
McVary, K. T., 399
McWatters, B., 286
Meade, C. S., 286
Meador, K. G., 478
Meadows, D., 122
Meaney, M., 10, 43, 44, 47
Mebert, C. J., 192
Medford, G., 109
Medin, D., 256
MedlinePlus, 85, 91
Medvedev, K., 442
Meeks, S., 485
Meeus, W., 306, 307, 308, 309, 311
Meeus, W. H. J., 306
Meglin, D. E., 483
Mehler, J., 122, 123
Mehta, C. M., 426
Mehta, M., 243
Mei-Hui, C., 442
Meijer, L., 103
Meilahn, E. N., 397
Meins, E., 199
Meisami, E., 336

Meisner, B. A., 474
Meji, L., 513
Mejía-Arauz, R., 195
Melbye, M., 73
Melinder, A., 132
Melkevik, O., 281
Mello, N. K., 450
Melquist, S., 467
Meltzoff, A. N., 100, 104, 113, 116, 119, 120
Menacker, F., 83
Menacker, P. H., 91
Mendelson, J. H., 450
Meng, X., 126
Menon, E., 113
Merali, N., 367
Mermin, G. B., 481
Merrick, M. T., 322, 323
Merrifield, M., 234
Merrill, S. S., 396, 403
Merten, M. J., 315
Merz, R. D., 80
Mesch, G. S., 315
Mesle, F., 404
Meyer, F., 365
Meyer, I. H., 345
Michael, R. T., 343, 400, 401
Michaels, S., 343, 400, 401
Middleton, L. E., 464, 467
MIDUS, 407
Mijovic, A., 46
Mikhai, L., 336
Mikulincer, M., 503
Milano, K., 477
Miles, T. P., 453
Milevsky, A., 147
Milkie, M. A., 386
Miller, B. C., 286
Miller, B. D., 317
Miller, D. N., 293
Miller-Johnson, S., 213
Miller, L. S., 193
Miller, M., 245
Miller, M. A., 405
Miller, M. L., 423
Miller, P. H., 9, 15, 165, 167, 169, 293, 326
Miller-Perrin, C. L., 213
Miller, R. A., 449
Miller, S. A., 167
Mills, J. L., 80
Mills, J. S., 282
Mills-Koonce, W. R., 146
Min, D., 146
Mincic, M., 197, 200
Minear, S., 102
Miniño, A. M., 405
Minnesota Center for Twin & Family Research, 51
Minshew, N. J., 120
Mir, M., 368
Mirwald, R. L., 281
Misago, C., 83
Missotten, L. C., 309
Mistry, J., 135, 142
Mistry, R., 268
Mistry, R. S., 268
Mitchell, B. A., 423
Mitchell, D., 410
Mitchell, E., 401
Mitchell, K., 322
Mitchell, P., 450
Mitnick, D. M., 374
Mittelman, M. S., 465
Mitteness, L. S., 419
Mix, K. S., 170
Moas, O., 133
Moen, P., 434
Moerk, E. L., 124
Mohammed, S. A., 406, 407
Mohay, H., 88
Moilanen, K. L., 286
Moinar, B. E., 323
Moise-Titus, J., 194
Mokdad, A. H., 337, 338
Molenberghs, P., 114
Monaco, A. P., 125
Mond, J., 283
Monea, H. E., 446
Monga, M., 399
Mongeau, C., 195
Monsour, M., 365
Monteiro, L., 138
Moody, H. R., 457
Moore, C. F., 297
Moore, D. R., 115
Moore III, W. E., 292
Moore, M., 437
Moore, M. K., 113, 119
Moore, S., 315
Moore, T. M., 400
Moos, R. H., 477
Mor, N., 56
Mor, V., 455
Mora, J. O., 109
Moradi, B., 309, 347
Moravcik, E., 237
Morgan, K., 449
Morgan, L. A., 491
Morgan, M., 193
Morgan, S., 377
Mori, T., 83
Moriguchi, Y., 177
Morin, E., 350
Morris, A., 297
Morris, L. A., 323
Morris, P. A., 19
Morris, R., 244
Morris, R. G., 460
Morrison, A. B., 459
Morrison, F. J., 237
Morrongiello, B. A., 116
Morrow, J., 372
Moses, A. M., 194
Moshman, D., 292, 293, 297, 305
Mosier, C., 142
Moss, E., 195
Motil, K. J., 108
Motzoi, C., 365
Moulin, C. J., 171, 172, 459
Moynihan, J., 406
Moynihan, J. A., 406
Mroczek, D. K., 335
Muir, D., 114
Mulatu, M. S., 410
Mulder, E., 80
Muller, F. L., 457
Müller, R., 480
Muller, U., 169
Mullineaux, P. Y., 57
Mullis, A. K., 307
Mullis, R. L., 307
Mulvaney, M. K., 192
Munafò, M. R., 160
Munakata, Y., 159
Munn, Z., 412
Murachver, T., 167
Muraco, A., 426
Muramatsu, N., 477
Muris, P., 186, 187, 188
Murphy, C., 144
Murphy, D. P., 481
Murphy, M. P., 457
Murphy, S. L., 403, 404, 405, 512
Murrah, W. M., 163
Murray, A. D., 452
Murray-Close, D., 212, 260
Murray, J. P., 193
Murray, V., 209
Murstein, B. I., 285, 367
Musa, D., 337
Musser, L. M., 259
Mustanski, B. S., 345
Myers, J., 172
Mylander, C., 125

N

Nadel, L., 47
Nader, P. R., 226
Nagle, K. J., 175
Nagoshi, C. T., 346
Nagoshi, J. L., 346
Nagriff, S., 153
Nagy, E., 132
Nagy, T. F., 29, 30
Nair, S. N., 411
Najafi, B., 195
Najman, J. M., 79
Nakamura, J., 363
Nakazawa, J., 7
Nanez, J. E. Sr., 176, 177, 179
Naninck, E. F. G., 324
Napier, A. Y., 421
Naroleski, A. R., 172
Narvaez, D., 254
Nathani, S., 122
Nathanson, C. A., 419
National Alliance on Mental Illness (NAMI), 225, 324
National Association of Anorexia Nervosa, 282, 286
National Center for Biotechnology Information (NCBI), 39
National Center for Health Statistics, 68, 70, 222, 223, 224, 285, 319, 337, 338, 339, 402, 403, 452, 453, 455, 502
National Heart and Lung Institute, 223–224
National Hospice and Palliative Care Organization (NHPCO), 504
National Institute of Child Health & Human Development, 149
National Institute of Mental Health, 326
National Institute of Neurological Disorders and Stroke, 106, 246
National Institute on Drug Abuse (NIDA), 321
National Institute on Mental Health (NIMH), 244, 326
National Institutes of Health, 42, 45, 398, 448
Natsuaki, M., 284
Navarro, R. L., 309
Nave-Herz, R., 422
Nawaz, H., 226
Nayak, L., 411
Neal, A. R., 122
Neikrug, A. B., 449
Neil, A., 396
Neil, P. A., 116
Neimeyer, R. A., 214
Nelson, C. A., 100, 113, 116, 117, 120, 160
Nelson, D. L., 37
Nelson, J. K., 141
Nelson, L. J., 311, 421
Nelson, M. E., 448
Nelson, T. D., 442, 443
Neppl, T. K., 289
Ness, R. B., 80, 397
Nesse, R., 486
Nesselroade, J., 474
Nettelbeck, T., 459
Netting, N. S., 368
Neugarten, B. L., 334, 394
Neugarten, D. L., 334
Neulinger, K., 88
Neumark-Sztainer, D., 80, 282, 283
Neuner, J. M., 397
Nevill, D., 283
New, R. S., 135
Newberry, J., 448
Newell, K. M., 396, 448
Newland, L. A., 145
Newman, B. M., 396
Newman, D. A., 351
Newman, E., 80, 297
Newman, K., 407
Newman, K. S., 407
Newman, L. S., 172
Newton, E., 180, 198, 200
Newton, N. J., 418
Nguyen, S. P., 205
Nichols, B., 159, 220
Nichols, L. M., 434
Nichols, T., 138
Nicholson, J. M., 226
Nicoladis, E., 176
Nicolas, D. B., 513
Nicolopoulou, A., 199
Nieto, F. J., 7
Nihiser, A. J., 222
Nijmegen, N., 286
Nikitin, J., 472
Niles, S. G., 378, 380, 434
Nilsson, L., 68, 70, 89, 92
Nisbett, R. E., 235, 408
Njike, V. Y., 226
Noguchi, M., 83
Noll, J., 408

Nolte, S., 237
Norbis, S. S., 179
North American Menopause Society (NAMS), 399
Northern, J. J., 227
Northridge, M. E., 345
Norton, M. C., 286
Norton, M. I., 264
Norton, R. D., 325
Nottebohm, F., 452
Nowak, M., 123
Nucci, L. P., 256
Nugent, J. K., 7, 56, 79, 92, 102, 103, 116
Nugent, K. J., 103
Nunner-Winkler, G., 298
Nurmi, J. E., 257
Nurse, A. D., 220
Nurse-Family Partnership, 83
Nuselovici, J. N., 187
Ny, P., 91
Nydegger, C. N., 419

O

Oak Ridge National Laboratory, 37
Oakes, L. M., 102, 117, 120
Oates, G., 410
Oates, J., 126
Obeidallah, D., 284
Oberklaid, F., 147
O'Boyle, E. H., 350
O'Brien, M., 175, 226
O'Brien, M. A., 153
O'Brien, W. H., 227
O'Callaghan, F. V., 79
O'Callaghan, M., 79, 88
Ocampo, K. A., 264
Ochs, A., 448
Ochsner, K., 474
O'Connell, M., 226
O'Conner, T. G., 243
O'Connor, P. G., 320
O'Connor, T. G., 406
Odden, H., 166
Odom, E., 222
O'Dougherty Wright, M., 213
Oetinger, M., 421
Offer, D., 304
Offer, S., 385
Offerhaus, L., 455
Ogan, A. T., 120
Ogden, C. L., 405
Okada, H., 123
Okamura, H., 112
Okanda, M., 177
Oki, M., 292
Oldham, M., 125
Olds, D. L., 83
Oleson, T., 346
Olgiati, P., 465
Oller, D. K., 122
Olmedo, C., 447
Olsen, J., 73
Olshansky, S. J., 453
Olsho, L. W., 396
Olson, B., 420
Olson, B. D., 417
Olson, C., 193
Olson, H., 80
Olson, I. R., 459
Olson, L. N., 430
Olukoya, A. A., 91
O'Malley, P. M., 320, 321
Omoto, C. K., 41
O'Neill-Arana, M. R., 212
O'Neill, E. F., 448
Ong, A., 308
Ong, A. D., 483
Ono, K., 52
Ontai, L. L., 289
Orellana, M. F., 147
Ornstein, P. A., 172
Orom, H., 56
Orr, R., 449
Ortega, S., 267
Orth, U., 474
Ortiz, S., 176
Oryol, V. E., 437
Osgood, D., 311
Osofsky, J. D., 188
Ossa, K. L., 457
Ossorio, P. N., 38, 235
Ostendorf, F., 437
Oster, H., 115
Osterman, M. J. K., 68, 288
Ostrov, E., 304
Ostrov, J. M., 193
Oswalt, R., 322
Overton, Willis, F., 2
Owen, M., 150
Owen, M. T., 150
Owens, A., 400
Owens, J. F., 397
Owens, R. E., 173
Ownby, R. L., 411
Ozcan, I., 81
Özyürek, A., 175

P

Paas, F., 411
Pace, C. S., 94
Padavic, I., 381
Padilla-Walker, L. M., 142, 143, 311, 421
Padma-Nathan, H., 399
Paduch, D. A., 399
Paez, L., 138
Pagani, L., 322
Painter, K., 123
Pak, R., 410
Pal, S., 51
Palencia, R., 87
Palladino Schultheiss, D. E., 378
Palmer, E., 193
Palmon, R., 410
Palmore, E., 443
Palomo-Gonzalez, S. A., 152
Palta, M., 7
Paltiel, O., 69
Pang, S. M. C., 84
Panneton, R., 122
Paoloni-Giacobino, A., 47
Papadatou-Pastou, M., 160
Papousek, H., 102
Paquette, J. A., 316
Parade, S. H., 317
Pardun, C. J., 315
Paris, S. G., 236
Park, A., 35
Park, C. C., 264
Park, C. L., 457
Park, D. C., 452, 458, 460
Park, H., 210
Park, S., 123
Parke, R. D., 146
Parker, B., 38
Parker, J. G., 200
Parker, M. W., 478
Parkhurst, J. T., 261
Parmelee, P. A., 474
Parra, M., 177
Parrat, P., 455
Partnership for Maternal, Newborn & Child Health, The, 90
Partridge, L., 457
Pascalis, O., 113, 116, 120
Pascual, L., 123
Pasley, K., 431
Passaro, D. J., 453
Passman, R. H., 198
Passmore, N. L., 95
Passow, S., 459
Pasternak, C., 52
Pasternak, J. J., 50
Pasupathi, M., 474
Patrinos, A., 38
Pattatucci, A. M. L., 345
Patten, C. L., 50
Patterson, C., 345
Patterson, C. J., 347, 370
Patterson, M. M., 252
Patton, W., 378
Patzel, K., 47
Pauker, K., 264
Paulsen, D. J., 297
Paulussen-Hoogeboom, M., 207
Paunonen, S. V., 437
Paus, T., 115
Paxton, S. J., 283
Payne, V. G., 104, 219
Pearce, G., 482
Pearl, R., 261
Pearlin, L. I., 483
Pease, M., 230
Peay, H., 48
Peck, R. C., 417, 418
Pedersen, N. L., 467
Pedersen, S., 261, 422
Peelen, L. M., 88
Peets, K., 260
Peets, K. F., 177
Peetsma, T., 207
Pelegrini, A. D., 261
Pelham, B. W., 207
Pelhan, W. E., Jr., 245
Pellegrino, J. W., 237
Pelletz, L., 283
Peltonen, K., 7
Peltz, C. B., 447
Penn, R., 367
Peplau, L. A., 370
Percaccio, C. R., 176
Perez-Castejon, J., 447
Pergament, E., 69
Perkins, D. F., 318, 326, 328
Perkins, M. M., 491
Perner, J., 166
Perrewe, P. L., 436
Perrin, M., 69
Perrin, R. D., 213
Perry-Jenkins, M., 265, 361, 385, 386, 387
Perry, W. G. Jr., 348
Pertea, M., 38
Peter, J., 315
Peters, J., 474
Peters, R. M., 406, 407
Petersen, I., 447
Peterson, B. E., 406, 407
Peterson, C. C., 95, 166, 167
Petitto, L., 176
Petkov, B., 374
Petot, D., 304
Petrauskas, B. J., 56, 92, 103
Petrill, S. A., 57
Pettie, G. S., 265
Pettit, G. S., 192, 201, 213, 261
Peveto, C. A., 511
Pew Research Center, 421, 422
Pew Social Trends, 365
Pfeifer, J. H., 292
Pharo, H., 296
Philipsen, N., 194, 226
Phillips, A. T., 105
Phillips, M. G., 379
Phinney, J. S., 308
Piaget, J., 16, 17, 293
Pianta, R., 153
Picano, J., 355
Pichora-Fuller, M. K., 450
Pick, A. D., 116
Pickard, J. D., 225
Picton, T. W., 115
Pierce, C. P., 385, 386
Pierrat, V., 115
Pierson, R., 221, 291
Pietilainen, K., 226
Pietromonaco, P. R., 383
Pillemer, K., 486
Pine, D. S., 324
Pinkham, A. M., 178
Pinn, V. W., 398
Pinquart, M., 445
Pioli, L., 120
Pioli, M. F., 483
Pirttila-Backman, A. M., 409
Pirzada, A., 396
Pixley, J. E., 392, 393, 394, 417
Place, S., 177
Plantin, L., 91
Platt, M. L., 297
Platzman, K. A., 79
Pleck, J. H., 146
Pleger, B., 194
Plomin, R., 51, 209, 244, 265
Plotnick, R. D., 386
Plunkett, J., 106
Podolski, C. L., 194
Polivy, J., 282, 283
Polka, L., 126

Pollack, H., 289
Pollack, J. M., 350
Pollatsek, A., 244
Pollitt, E., 74, 108
Poorting, Y. H., 5
Popenoe, D., 429
Porter, C. A., 187
Porter, R. H., 116
Posada, G., 136, 143
Posada, R., 143
Posner, M. I., 133, 188
Posthuma, D., 51
Potts, M. K., 486
Poulsen, C., 115
Powell, C., 73
Powell, C. A., 73
Powell, M. D., 260
Powers, S. I., 280
Pranjic, N., 324
Prause, J., 268
Prechtl, H., 160
Prescott, C. A., 51
Presser, H. B., 386
Pressley, M., 237
Preston, S. D., 114
Prevatt, F., 244
Price, T. S., 5
Priddis, L., 137
Priest, L., 411
Prigot, J., 120
Prince, C. G., 116
Principe, G. F., 172
Prinstein, M., 261
Prinstein, M. J., 286
Prinz, W., 408
Pritchard, M., 200
Pruett, K., 374
Pruett, K. D., 91
Pruett, M., 374
Pruett, M. K., 431
Pudrovska, T., 419
Pujol, R., 447
Puka, B., 255
Pulverman, R. B., 126
Punamäki, R., 7, 265
Putney, N. M., 419, 422, 424, 425, 457, 483
Putnick, D. L., 135
Pyszcynski, T., 419, 422, 425, 483, 498

Q

Qouta, S., 7
Quackenbush, J., 41
Qui, M., 244
Quick, J. C., 436
Quinn, P. C., 113, 117, 126
Quintana, S. M., 263

R

Rabago-Smith, M., 41
Rabin, C., 448
Racine, S. E., 283
Racz, S. J., 265
Radcliffe, F., 120
Radke-Yarrow, M., 143
Radvansky, G. A., 171
Raffaelli, M., 286
Ragert, P., 194
Raglioni, S. S., 116
Rahe, R. H., 405
Rainie, L., 336
Rajagopalan, R., 38
Rakison, D., 104
Rakison, D. H., 120
Ram, N., 409
Ramalho, N., 350
Ramaswami, A., 379
Ramsey, F., 109
Ramus, F., 242
Randolph, J., 397
Randolph, L. A., 80
Rao, U., 324
Raphael-Leff, J., 89
Rasmussen, S. A., 91
Ratner, H. H., 172
Rattan, A., 457
Rattan, S., 457
Rattaz, C., 115
Rauste-Von Wright, M., 283
Rawson, N. E., 336
Ray, K., 237
Raymond, J., 449
Rayner, K., 244
Raynor, R., 16
Raz, N., 409, 410, 452, 460
Raznahan, A., 220
Reardon, L. E., 284
Reddy, L. A., 180
Reddy, M., 231
Reeb-Sutherland, B. C., 133
Reece, J. B., 68
Reece, M., 344
Reed, I., 491
Reefhuis, J., 91
Reese, E., 199
Reeve, P., 443
Regan, P., 365
Reich, S. M., 315
Reidmann, A. C., 370, 428
Reinhard, S., 455
Reinikainen, K., 122
Reinke, B. J., 419
Reinold, C., 222
Reis, O., 311
Reitman, D., 225
Renk, K., 322
Renkert, L. E., 147
Renner, M. J., 406
Renshaw, P. F., 450
Repetti, R., 435
Rescorla, L., 304
Reskin, B. F., 381
Resnick, B., 467
Resnik, D. B., 52
Respass, J., 79
Restrepo, D., 336
Reuben, D. B., 491
Reuter-Lorenz, P. A., 161, 460
Reynolds, B. M., 284
Reynolds, C. A., 24
Reynolds, J. F., 147
Reznick, J. S., 187
Rhee, S. H., 51
Rhoades, G. K., 370
Rhodes, M., 204
Rhymer, P. M., 230
Rice, D. P., 489
Rice, J. C., 192
Rice, V. H., 267
Richards, C., 244
Richards, F. A., 349
Richardson, D. C., 107
Richardson, G. A., 79, 80
Richardson, R. A., 265
Richardson, S. O., 244
Richardson, U., 242
Richardson, V. E., 480
Richmond, L. L., 459
Richter, L., 108
Rickman, A., 295
Riddle, D. R., 452
Rideout, V., 315
Rideout, V. J., 194
Riediger, M., 474
Riegel, K. F., 348
Riemann, R., 437
Rieskamp, J., 409
Rigato, S., 113
Rigby, K., 260, 261
Riggio, R. E., 364
Rijsdijk, F. V., 244
Rinaldi, C. M., 207
Rinne, T., 122
Risley, T. R., 126
Rissanen, A., 226
Ritter, J. O., 394, 472
Ritter, M., 194
Rittle-Johnson, B., 172
Rivera-Gaxiola, M., 122, 176
Rivera, J., 74
Rizzo, M., 451
Rizzolatti, G., 113, 114
Roberson, K. C., 95
Roberto, K. A., 467, 486
Roberts, D. F., 351
Roberts, J. E., 123
Roberts, R. D., 351
Robertson, J., 396
Robin, D. J., 115
Robins, G., 229
Robins, R. W., 474
Robinso, J., 491
Robinson, C. W., 116
Robinson, G., 398
Robinson, I. E., 285
Robinson, J., 145, 146
Robinson, J. P., 386
Robles, M., 90
Robles, N., 79
Rochat, P., 105, 115, 143, 144, 166
Roche, A. F., 281
Rocke, C., 393, 394, 395
Rocke, C. U., 412
Rodin, J., 387
Rodkin, P. C., 261, 262, 264
Rodrigue, K. M., 452
Rodriguez, J. L., 176
Rodriguez, M. A., 179
Rodrique, K. M., 409
Roesle, H., 365
Roff, L. L., 478
Rogers, C., 362
Rogers, L., 263, 264
Rogers, P., 346
Rogers, W. A., 410, 411, 452, 459
Rogerson, P. A., 486
Rogoff, B., 18, 142, 180, 195, 336
Rogosch, F., 138
Rogosch, F. A., 153, 212, 213
Rohde, L. A., 244
Roisman, G. I., 136, 137, 261, 262, 345
Romani, G. B., 143
Rombouts, S. A., 290
Romer, D., 318
Romig, C., 307
Romo, H., 176
Ronco, A. M., 79
Roobol, M., 399
Roodin, P., 446
Roof, E., 47
Rooke, S. E., 51, 53
Root, C., 172
Root, T. L., 283
Rose, A. J., 200, 257, 259
Rose, J. S., 324, 325
Rose-Krasnor, L., 200
Rose, S. M., 426
Rosen, D. S., 278
Rosen, L. H., 252
Rosenberg, H. J., 394, 419
Rosenberg, S. D., 394, 419
Rosenberger, K., 374
Rosenfeld, R. M., 123
Rosenstein, D., 115
Rosenthal, E., 226
Rosenzweig, M. R., 100
Roseth, C. J., 261
Roskos, K. A., 180, 198
Rösler, F., 161
Rosnick, C. B., 412
Ross, C. A., 22
Ross, D. A., 449
Ross, M. H., 450
Ross, S., 87
Rossi, A., 436
Rossi, A. S., 397, 398
Rossi, G., 422
Roth, D. L., 465
Roth-Hanania, R., 143
Roth, J., 24, 25
Rothbart, M. K., 133, 134, 188, 190
Rothblum, E. D., 347
Rothman, A. D., 374
Rothman, M. T., 374
Rovee-Collier, C., 120
Rovine, M. J., 419
Rowe, S. V., 452
Rowley, S. J., 308
Roze, E., 103
Rozzini, R., 449
Rubin, K., 187, 200, 202, 257, 259
Rubin, K. H., 208
Rubini, M., 307
Ruble, D., 252, 263, 264
Ruble, D. N., 204, 205, 312
Rudisill, J. R., 434
Rudy, D., 208
Rueda, M. R., 188

Ruiter, S. A. J., 103
Ruiz-Palaez, J. G., 90
Ruiz, S. A., 148, 424, 425
Rukavishnikov, A. A., 437
Rumiche, R., 177
Runswick-Cole, K., 512
Rushton, J. P., 52
Russell, R. D., 447
Rutter, M., 5, 243, 262
Ruttle, P. L., 116
Rvachew, S., 122, 123, 126
Ryan, C. L., 346
Ryan, J., 399
Ryan, N. D., 448
Ryan, R. M., 346
Ryff, C. D., 335, 392, 393, 407, 419, 423, 475, 476
Ryzin, M. J., 261

S

Sabatini, T., 449
Sabbagh, M. A., 166
Sabo, D., 261
Sachdeva, S., 256
Sadek, S., 260
Safron, M., 226
Sagiv, S. K., 81
Sahin, N. H., 75
Sainio, K., 122
Salaway, J. L., 244
Salerno-Kennedy, R., 453
Sales, B. D., 29, 30
Salihu, H. M., 73
Salkind, S. J., 122
Salmivalli, C., 260
Salovey, P., 350
Salthouse, T., 337, 409, 410, 459
Salthouse, T. A., 408, 409, 458, 459, 460
Saltvedt, I., 467
Salzberg, S., 38
Sampson, P. D., 80
Samter, W., 365
Samuels, B., 211
Sandberg, J. F., 146
Sanders, S., 483
Sanders, S. A., 344
Sanderson, S. C., 226
Sandfort, T., 324
Sando, S., 467
Sandstrom, M., 259
Santiago, C., 268
Santos, A. J., 138
Santos, O., 138
Saperstein, A., 483
Saracho, O. N., 145
Saraswathi, T. S., 135
Saribay, S., 254
Sarkadi, A., 147
Sarrazin, J., 430
Sata, K., 24
Sato, S., 368
Saucier, G., 437
Saunders, B. E., 138
Savage, L. S., 349
Savin-Williams, R. C., 309, 347
Savoy, H., 309
Sawyer, K., 190, 197, 200
Sawyer, P., 478
Sayer, A. G., 385, 386
Sayer, L. C., 386
Sayfan, L., 187
Saylor, M., 172
Sazawal, S., 109
Scararnella, L. V., 289
Scarr, S., 234
Schaie, K., 409
Schaie, K. W., 351, 408, 409, 446, 458, 459, 460, 461
Scharff, C., 452
Schaufeli, W. B., 435, 436
Schedle, A., 431
Scheibe, S., 461, 463, 467
Scheier, C., 116
Schellenbach, M., 459
Schemer, J., 437
Scher, M. S., 90
Schibli, K., 120
Schibli, S. E., 120
Schick, V., 344
Schieber, F., 450
Schiefelbein, V. L., 284
Schiepe-Tiska, A., 363
Schieve, L. A., 91
Schiffman, S. S., 450
Schindler, I., 445
Schlotz, W., 243
Schmidt, L. A., 11, 187
Schmidt, M. E., 252, 257, 313
Schmitt, M., 187
Schneider, B., 385
Schneider, B. A., 450
Schneider, B. H., 138, 262
Schneider, J. M., 450
Schneider, M., 76
Schneider, W., 171, 172, 457
Schneiderman, G., 513
Schoelmerich, A., 140
Schoeny, M. E., 318
Schooler, C., 410, 412
Schooler, L. J., 409
Schott, L. L., 397
Schottenfeld, R. S., 320
Schröder, F. H., 399
Schubert, C. M., 281
Schulenberg, J. E., 320
Schulkin, J., 11
Schultheis, M. T., 451
Schulz, R., 337
Schulze, P. A., 140
Schurman, D. L., 510
Schusterbauer, E., 325
Schut, H., 509, 513
Schutte, K. K., 477
Schutte, N. S., 51, 53
Schvaneveldt, J. D., 369
Schvaneveldt, P. L., 369
Schwade, J. A., 122, 126
Schwartz, N., 315
Schwartz, P. D., 296
Schwartz, S. J., 306, 307, 392, 394
Schwartzman, A. E., 192
Schwarzer, G., 113
Schweinle, W. E., 365
Schwenkreis, P., 194
Scott, L. S., 116
Scott, W. D., 56
Scottham, K. M., 307
Sears, R. R., 24
Seaton, E., 268
Seaton, E. K., 307
Sebanc, A. M., 199, 257
Sebastian, C., 291
Sedikides, C., 253
Sedlacek, W. E., 285
Seeley, J. R., 283, 284
Seeman, R., 448
Segal, N. J., 281
Segal, N. L., 51, 52
Segal, Y., 197, 200
Segerstrom, S. C., 406
Seider, S., 233
Seidman, S. M., 399
Seiffge-Krenke, I., 281, 378
Selin, H., 82
Sellers, R. M., 307
Seltzer, M., 126
Seltzer, M. M., 419
Senders, S. J., 105
Senin, I. G., 437
Senor, M., 177
Seponski, D. M., 442
Serbin, L. A., 116, 192
Seroczynski, A. D., 324, 325
Serretti, A., 465
Sesardic, N., 51
Shadel, W. G., 56
Shaffer, M. L., 106
Shahaeian, A., 166, 167
Shakib, S., 261
Shamoo, A. E., 52
Shanahan, L., 311
Shanker, S. G., 18
Shannon, J. D., 147
Shapiro, A., 187
Shapka, J., 289
Sharifzadeh, V., 369
Sharit, J., 410
Sharma, D., 336
Shatz, M., 175, 178
Shaver, P. R., 136, 137, 138, 503
Shaw, D. S., 192
Shaw, L. M., 80
Shaywitz, B. A., 244
Shaywitz, S. E., 244
Sheaks, C., 482
Shearer, C. L., 311
Shears, J., 145, 146
Sheely, A., 386
Sheese, B. E., 133, 188, 190
Sherar, L. B., 281
Sherman, C. W., 482
Sherman, D., 508
Sherrid, P., 481
Shiffrin, R. M., 171
Shigematsu, J., 123
Shigeta, M., 462
Shimojo, S., 116
Shin, K. H., 435
Shing, Y. L., 172
Shinskey, J. L., 119
Shipley, T. F., 112
Shirley, C., 384, 386
Shirom, A., 435
Shivram, R., 7
Shiyko, M. P., 284
Shoelmerich, A., 143
Short, E. L., 235
Shugrue, N., 491
Shukitt-Hale, B., 457
Shulman, E. P., 297
Shum, D., 88
Shwalb, B. J., 7, 145
Shwalb, D. W., 7, 145
Shweder, R. A., 7
Shyam, R., 51
Siddique, J., 84
Siebens, J., 346
Sieber, R. T., 237
Siebert, C., 122
Siegler, I. C., 396, 438
Siegler, R. S., 170, 337
Sikma, S. K., 455
Silbereisen, R. K., 275, 286
Silva, K. G., 180
Silverstein, M., 148, 424, 425, 457
Sim, C., 296
Simard, M., 314
Simion, F., 113
Simkin, P., 84, 92
Simon, T., 232
Simoneau, G. G., 449
Simonoff, E., 73
Simons, R. L., 209
Simpson, J. A., 138
Singer, B., 335, 476
Singer, B. H., 335, 419, 475, 476
Singer, D. G., 193
Singer, J. L., 193
Singh, J., 106
Singh, M., 449
Singh, M. A., 448, 449
Singh, N. A., 449
Singh, P., 256
Singh, R., 51
Sinigaglia, C., 114
Sinnott, J., 349
Sinnott, J. D., 349
Skaff, M. M., 475
Skovronek, E., 410
Slater, A., 112
Slater, A. M., 113
Slaughter, V., 166, 167, 200
Slavin, R. E., 237
Slawinski, E. B., 122
Sletvold, O., 467
Sloane, P. D., 491
Slobin, D. I., 124, 125
Slopen, N. B., 323
Sloutsky, V. M., 116
Slowinski, J., 399
Sluss, D., 178
Slutske, W. S., 269
Smahel, D., 314
Small, G. W., 194
Smeenk, W., 322
Smeets, F., 452

Smetana, J., 298, 304
Smetana, J. G., 294, 304, 310, 313
Smith, B. S., 172
Smith, C., 205
Smith, C. D., 316
Smith, C. J., 188, 208, 259
Smith, D. G., 80, 297
Smith, D. M., 487
Smith, E., 178
Smith, G. H., 79
Smith, J., 59, 488
Smith, J. M., 81
Smith, K., 106
Smith, L., 120
Smith, L. B., 114, 158
Smith, L. M., 80, 297
Smith, M., 7
Smith, M. C., 237
Smith, P., 286, 491
Smith, P. K., 199, 260, 261
Smith, R. L., 257, 259
Smith, S. D., 244
Smith, S. G., 322, 323
Smith, S. M., 442
Smith, S. W., 506
Smith Slep, A. M., 374
Smith, T. W., 482
Smolak, L., 281
Sneed, J. R., 353, 392, 394, 472, 474
Snow, C. E., 230, 231
Snowling, M. J., 244
So, K., 112
Soberanes, B., 73
Society for Research in Child Development, 29
Soenens, B., 421
Soken, N. H., 116
Sokol, B., 254, 259
Sokol, B. W., 11
Solantaus, T., 265
Solares, G. R., 448
Solberg, D. W., 261
Solheim, B., 307
Solic, K., 237
Solomon, J., 136, 137
Solomon, S., 499
Solomon, S. E., 347
Solomontes-Kountouri, O., 308
Solway, A., 52
Sommer, I. E. C., 160, 238
Sommers, S. R., 264
Sommerville, J. A., 171
Song, H., 119
Song, Z., 434
Sonuga-Barke, E., 243
Sorensen, K., 58
Sorenson, R. C., 285
Sosnoff, J. J., 396, 448
Soto, C. J., 392
Southgate, V., 113, 114
Sowers, M., 397
Spangler, K., 230
Sparrow, J. D., 102
Spear, L., 290
Spear, L. P., 11
Spector, W. D., 424, 425
Spelke, E. S., 126, 203
Spencer, P. E., 203
Spencer-Rodgers, J., 253
Spencer, S. J., 253
Spinard, T. L., 188
Spinath, F. M., 437
Spinrad, T. L., 143, 146, 188, 194, 195, 196, 200, 208, 259, 297
Spiro, A., 403, 457
Spiteri, E., 125
Spitze, G., 486
Spivak, A. L., 198
Spodek, B., 145
Spore, D. L., 455
Springer, S. P., 160
Srinivasan, N., 244
Sroufe, L. A., 188
St-Laurent, D., 195
Stack, D. M., 116, 160, 192
Stack, S., 326
Staff, R. T., 452
Stallings, M. C., 51
Stampfer, M. J., 399
Stams, G., 207
Stanczyk, F. Z., 399
Stange, A., 463
Stanley, J. T., 418
Stanley, S. M., 370
Stark, L. J., 226
Starr, J. M., 478
Starr, R. H., 153
Staszewski, J., 337
Stattin, H., 313, 314
Staudinger, U. M., 2, 19, 437, 463, 467
Stavrinos, T. M., 449
Steca, P., 437, 475
Steele, J. S., 163
Stegarud, L., 307
Steggall, M. J., 399
Stegge, H., 199
Stein, A., 120
Stein, J. A., 281
Stein, J. F., 244
Steinberg, L., 9, 150, 290, 296, 297, 311, 318
Steinbock, B., 52
Steinbrenner, G. M., 403
Stelmach, G. E., 448
Stelmach, G. W., 451
Stemler, S. E., 234
Stemmer, B., 160
Stenson, H., 80
Stephens, M. A. P., 486
Sterling, A. M., 173
Stern, C., 412
Sternberg, G., 141
Sternberg, R. J., 37, 234, 365, 461, 462, 463
Sternberg, R. L., 234
Sterns, H. L., 435, 436, 480, 482
Stevens-Graham, B., 221
Stevens, M. R., 322, 323
Stevens, S. Y., 406
Stewart, A. J., 383, 387, 418
Stewart, S. H., 187
Stickland, A. L., 496, 500, 505, 511
Stier, H., 387
Stifter, C. A., 143
Stine-Morrow, E., 412
Stine-Morrow, E. A. L., 459, 467
Stockdale, G. D., 443
Stohs, J., 281
Stoian, I., 457
Stoltz, K. B., 436
Stone, P., 82
Stoneman, Z., 152
Stones, J. J., 396
Stoodley, C. J., 244
Stopp, C., 79
Stoppard, M., 84
Storck, S., 69
Storkel, H. L., 173
Stormshak, E. A., 294, 311, 313
Story, P. A., 350
Story, T. N., 482
Strauch, B., 291
Strauss, J. L., 400
Strauss, J. R., 397
Streissguth, A. P., 79, 80
Strid, K., 120
Stroebe, M., 509, 513
Stroebe, M. S., 509
Stroebe, W., 513
Strohmeier, A., 160
Strong, B., 509
Stroud, L. R., 79
Strough, J., 426
Stroup, D. F., 337, 338
Strupp, B., 108
Stuart-Hamilton, I., 170, 411
Studer, J., 474
Stuewig, J., 189, 190
Sturman, E., 348
Stutaro, C., 200
Subbotsky, E., 167
Subrahmanyam, K., 314, 315
Substance Abuse and Mental Health Services Administration, 320, 337
Sugimoto, K., 450
Suicide Prevention Resource Center, 325
Suitor, J. J., 486
Sulik, M. J., 188
Sullivan, T., 193
Sungkuo, H., 325
Suomi, S. J., 139
Super, C. M., 56, 109, 139
Supple, A. J., 317
Surles, J., 138
Sussman, A. L., 374
Sussman, E. J., 284
Sutin, A. R., 417, 437
Sutton, P. D., 91
Suwalsky, J. T. D., 135
Suy, A., 77
Suzuki, L. A., 235, 368
Sved, A., 406
Swami, V., 366
Swanger, N., 435
Swanson, M. W., 80
Swartz, A., 226
Sweden.se, 151
Sweet, S., 434
Swendsen, J., 324, 325
Swenson, L. P., 308
Swerdlik, M. E., 234, 348
Swingley, D., 123
Swinson, R. P., 11
Swygert, K. E., 172
Szaflarski, J. P., 160
Szalacha, L., 263
Szenkovits, G., 242
Szinovacz, M. E., 425
Szoeke, C., 399

T

Tabbers, H. K., 411
Taimalu, M., 187
Taki, Y., 24
Tallandini, M. A., 91
Talmud, I., 315
Tamis-LeMonda, C. S., 103, 105, 139, 145, 146, 147, 377
Tangney, J., 190
Tangney, J. P., 189
Tanner, J. M., 278, 280
Tanzi, R. E., 465
Tapert, S. F., 318
Tappan, M., 193
Tardif, G., 137
Tardif, T., 124, 126, 166
Tardif, W., 123
Tardiff, C., 138
Target, M., 138
Tariq, N., 208
Tarr, M. J., 126
Tarulli, D., 171
Tascon, M., 143
Tasopoulos-Chan, M., 313
Tavernise, S., 483
Taylor, C. A., 192
Taylor, H. G., 88
Taylor, J., 109
Taylor, J. J., 267
Taylor, M., 199
Taylor, M. G., 204, 205
Taylor, R. D., 268
Tegenthoff, M., 194
Tejada-Vera, B., 403, 404
Teller, D. Y., 113
Temcheff, C. E., 192
Tennen, H., 207
Tepper, M., 400
Terracciano, A., 437, 475
Terrell, H. K., 346
Terwilliger, R., 292
Terwogt, M. M., 199
Tessier, R., 90
Tevendale, H. D., 308
Thabet, A., 7
Thabet, A. A., 7
Thal, D. J., 124
Thapar, A., 324
Thapar, A. K., 324
Thatcher, R. W., 221
Thayer, R. E., 318
Thelen, E., 158
Theuring, C., 107
Thomas, A., 133
Thomas, J. D., 77
Thomas, K. M., 160, 220
Thomas, M., 163
Thomas, P., 226
Thompson, L. A., 57

Thompson, N., 491
Thompson, R. A., 133, 142, 143, 189
Thomson, N. R., 152
Thorne, B., 376
Thorne, C., 77
Thurston, S. W., 81
Tiemcani, M., 451
Tiemeier, H., 221, 291
Tikalsky, F. D., 187
Tilton-Weaver, L., 313
Tisher, R., 238
Tither, J. M., 281
Tivnan, T., 231
Tjus, T., 120
Tobin, S. S., 473
Tohkura, Y., 122
Tolar, M. H., 379
Tolbert, P. E., 81
Tomada, G., 262
Tomasello, M., 125, 173, 175
Tonidandel, S., 379
Topham, G., 154
Torpy, J. M., 79
Torres, N., 138
Toth, S., 138, 212
Toth, S. L., 153, 154, 212, 213
Toydemir, P. B., 69
Trabucchi, M., 449
Trainor, C. D., 284
Tran, L., 221, 291
Traphagan, J. W., 442
Trapolini, T., 138
Tremblay, R. E., 192, 261, 262, 322
Trickett, P. K., 153
Trim, R. S., 318
Trinh, S., 482
Trionfi, G., 199
Troester, H., 151
Troll, L. E., 424, 475
Tronick, E., 132
Tronick, E. Z., 131
Troop, W., 262
Troseth, G. L., 167
Trzesniewski, K. H., 309
Tsai, J., 474
Tse, H., 201
Tseng, V., 364
Tu, K. M., 316
Tucker-Drob, E. M., 408, 409
Turati, C., 113
Turiel, E., 256
Turk, J., 46
Turkheimer, E., 51, 209, 235, 269, 408
Turnbull, A., 152
Turnbull, R., 152
Twenge, J. M., 309

U

Uc, E. Y., 451
Uematsu, H., 450
Uleman, J. S., 254
Umenai, T., 83
UNAIDS, 341
Underwood, M. K., 191
Undewood, M., 365
Ungerer, J. A., 138
Uniken Venema, M. M. A., 88
United Nations Children's Fund (UNICEF), 7, 108, 109, 110, 236, 340
United Nations High Commissioner for Refugees, 7
Urry, S. A., 311
U.S. Bureau of Labor Statistics, 148, 266, 382
U.S. Census Bureau, 148, 149, 266, 268, 334, 368, 369, 370, 371, 372, 375, 376, 385, 402, 403, 411, 423, 428, 429, 443, 445, 446, 487
U.S. Department of Education, 240
U.S. Department of Health and Human Services (USD-HHS), 79
U.S. Department of Health and Human Services, Administration for Children and Families, Administration on Children, Youth, and Families, Children's Bureau, 211, 212
U.S. Department of Labor, 146, 266, 382, 384
U.S. Food and Drug Administration, 52, 399
U.S. Surgeon General, 398
Usmiani, S., 283
Ustun, T. B., 324
Uszyriska-Jarmoc, J., 253
Utz, R. L., 486
Uzelac, S. M., 296

V

Vaillancourt, D. E., 396, 448
Vaillant, G. E., 477
Vaillant-Molina, M., 141
Valenza, E., 113
Valenzuela, M., 138
Valenzuela, M. J., 409
Valkenburg, P. M., 315
Valla, J. M., 11
Vallantine, A. D., 396
Vallin, J., 404
Valrie, C. R., 308
Valtin, R., 257
Van Acker, R., 261
van Aken, M., 190
van Beijsterveldt, C. E. M., 88
Van Braeckel, K. N., 103
van de Vijver, F. J. R., 5
Van Den Bout, J., 513
Van Den Wittenboer, G., 207
van der Dries, L., 94
Van Der Heijden, P. G. M., 513
van der Laan, P. H., 322
Van Doom, M. D., 311
van Doornen, L., 435
Van Engeland, H., 290, 324
Van Exel, E., 476
Van Gerven, P., 411
van Haastert, I. C., 88
van Hooff, J. H., 385–386
van IJzendoorn, M. H., 94, 137
Van Leijenhorst, L., 290
van Lier, P. A. C., 199, 200
Van Remmen, H., 457
van Solinge, H., 445
Van Vorst, R. F., 115
Vandell, D., 150
Vandell, D. L., 150
Vandenberg, K. A., 90
Vanderborght, M., 174
Vandergrift, N., 150
VanderWeele, T. J., 84
Vandewater, E., 268
Vandewater, E. A., 194, 383, 387
VanFleet, R., 154
Vanhalst, J., 309
Vanmanen, K.-J., 364
VanMeel, C. S., 290
Vansteenkiste, M., 421
Vansteenwegen, A., 500, 514
Vargha-Khadem, F., 125
Varki, A., 37
Varma, S., 247
Vaughn, B. E., 138
Vaupel, J. W., 447
Vaydich, J. L., 255
Velasquez, K., 474
Velez, S., 90
Veliz, P., 261
Ventura, S. J., 91, 287, 288
Venuti, P., 135
Verbrugge, L. M., 396, 403
Verhaeghen, P., 459
Verissimo, M., 138
Verkuyten, M., 264
Verma, J., 368
Verma, S., 295
Vernon, P. A., 437
Veronneau, M., 261, 286, 313
Veysey, M., 73
Vickerstaff, S., 482
Vida, M. N., 252
Vigil, J. M., 280
Vihman, M., 123
Villalobos, M., 294, 313
Virgolici, B., 457
Visher, E. B., 431, 433
Visher, J. S., 431, 433
Visscher, P. M., 51
Vitaro, F., 261, 322
Vitiello, B., 30
Vogt, Y., 283
Vollebergh, W., 307
Vollmer, B., 11, 159, 220
Von Dras, D. D., 396
Von Faber, M., 476
Vorvick, L. J., 69
Vostanis, P., 7
Votruba-Drzal, E., 268
Vukman, K. B., 348
Vygotsky, L. S., 18, 174
Vyse, S. A., 285

W

Waber, D. P., 109
Wachs, T. D., 133
Wadsworth, M. E., 268
Wagner, L., 172
Wahlsten, D., 51, 66
Wahlstrom, D., 291
Wainright, J. L., 347
Wais, P., 474
Waismeyer, A., 104
Waizenhofer, R. N., 311
Waldenstroem, U., 87
Waldfogel, J., 25, 58, 80
Waldman, I. D., 234
Waldron, M., 209
Walk, R. D., 115
Walker-Andrews, A. S., 116
Walker, D., 160
Walker, R. A., 221
Walker, R. F., 167
Walker, S., 286
Walker, S. P., 73
Wall, M., 80, 282, 283
Wall, S., 136
Wallace, B. A., 174
Wallace, M., 384, 386
Wallace, P., 374
Wallace, S. D., 187
Walls, J. K., 207
Walsh, R., 463
Walter, C., 510
Walter, T., 511
Walters, M. L., 322, 323
Wanberg, C. R., 434
Wang-Cheng, R., 397
Wang, H., 406
Wang, J., 244
Wang, J. J., 450
Wang, L., 82, 201
Wang, M., 188, 294, 311
Wang, S., 435
Ward, J. T., 79
Ward, R., 486
Wardjiman, E., 483
Warr, P. B., 434
Warren, A. E., 9
Warren, K. R., 77
Warren, S. L., 188
Warshauer-Baker, E., 38
Wartella, E. A., 194
Wartenburger, I., 459
Warzinik, K., 428
Waterhouse, L., 214
Waterman, A. S., 308, 349
Waterman, S., 349
Waters, E., 136
Watson, A. J., 257
Watson, J. B., 16
Watson, J. D., 35
Watts, S. D., 399
Wauterickx, N., 425
Way, E., 197, 200
Wechsler, D., 232
Wechsler, H., 222
Weiffenbach, J. M., 396
Weigt, J., 377
Weinbaum, E., 170
Weinberg, R. A., 234
Weinstein, N., 346
Weir, J. M., 324
Weir, P. L., 474
Weismer, S. E., 126
Weisner, T. S., 135
Weiss, D., 477
Weitz, R., 347, 442
Wellman, H. M., 105, 166, 167
Wells, D. L., 160

Welte, J. W., 295
Wenar, C., 186
Werkle-Bergner, M., 172
Werner, E. E., 267
Werner, J. S., 267
Wertheim, E. H., 283
Wertsch, J. V., 18
West, D. J., 345
West, R. L., 452
West, T., 202, 262
Westenberg, P., 290, 291
Westerhausen, R., 459
Westerhof, G. J., 335
Westerlund, A., 113, 117
Westermeyer, J. F., 417
Western, M., 428
Wethington, E., 392, 393, 394, 417, 437
Whalley, L. J., 452, 478
Wheeler, H. B., 282
Wheeler, P. L., 106
Wheeler-Scruggs, K. S., 354
Whipple, N., 142
Whishaw, I. Q., 105
Whitaker, D. J., 478
Whitaker, H. A., 160
Whitbourne, S., 335
Whitbourne, S. B., 356, 383, 393, 396, 398, 445, 473, 478, 482, 488, 501, 509
Whitbourne, S. K., 335, 353, 356, 364, 383, 392, 393, 394, 396, 398, 445, 472, 473, 474, 478, 482, 485, 488, 501, 509
White, C. S., 174
White, D., 41
White, K. J., 262
White, K. R., 152
White, R., 322
White, T., 291
Whitebread, D., 198
Whitefield, S., 474
Whiteley, L. B., 289
Whiteman, S. D., 147, 209
Whitley, B. E., 443
Whitman, B. Y., 152
Whitmore, J. K., 235
Whittington, F. J., 491
Wick, M., 74
Widaman, K. F., 474
Widman, S., 180
Wiebe, S. A., 79
Willan, A., 87
Willard, B., 244
Willett, J. B., 294, 311, 323
Willett, W. C., 399
Willford, J. A., 80
Williams, A. L., 315
Williams, C. C., 203
Williams, D. L., 120
Williams, D. R., 406, 407
Williams, G. M., 79
Williams, J. D., 285
Williams, K. R., 260
Williams, M., 122
Williams, M. N., 148
Williams, W. M., 11
Williamson, R. A., 113
Willis, S. L., 393, 394, 408, 409, 460
Willms. J., 289
Willoughby, M., 146
Willoughby, T., 309
Wilson, B. J., 193
Wilson, M., 370
Wilson-Quayle, A., 174
Wilson, R. E., 73
Wilson, T., 264
Wilt, J., 420
Winberg, J., 116
Winer, A. C., 133
Winer, G. A., 170
Wing, R. R., 397
Winkles, J. K., 366
Winsler, A., 174, 176
Winter, C. E., 313
Winter, E. A., 7
Wiseman, D. G., 428
Witherington, D. C., 131
Witherspoon, D. P., 263
Witkow, M., 312
Witkow, M. R., 312
Wohlfahrt, P. C., 73
Wolak, J., 322
Wold, B., 281
Wolf, J. H., 83, 84
Wolfe, D. A., 212
Wolfe, V. V., 212
Wolff, P. H., 101
Wolraich, M. L., 244
Wong, F. Y., 106
Wong, H. M., 236
Woo, J., 292
Wood, R. H., 447
Wood, W., 203, 204, 238
Woods, N., 401
Woodward, A., 104
Woolard, J., 297
World Health Organization (WHO), 71, 88, 108, 110, 211, 341, 454, 490
Worthington, R. L., 309, 347
Wortmann, J. H., 500
Wray, N. R., 51
Wright, K., 138
Wrosch, C., 478
Wu, D., 119
WU, F., 143
Wu, P., 348, 349
Wu, R., 107
Wyatt, T., 197, 200
Wyman, P. A., 406

X

Xiao, L., 80, 297
Xiaowei, M., 73
Xie, B., 244
Xinyin, C., 262
Xu, F., 124
Xu, H., 397
Xu, J., 512
Xu, JQ, 403, 404, 405
Xu, Y., 198, 199

Y

Yaffe, K., 464, 467
Yamagata, S., 52
Yamaguchi, M. K., 112
Yamamoto, S. L., 87
Yan, L. L., 396
Yang, S., 177, 463
Yang, W., 318
Yang, Y., 453
Yarger, R. S., 290
Ybarra, M. L., 322
Ye, Z., 244
Yeh, M. C., 226
Yeung, A. S., 236
Yeung, W. J., 146
Yin Bun, C., 108
Yin, H., 477
Yip, T., 264, 317
Yolton, K., 81
Yonas, A., 102, 115
Yoo, J. J., 52
Yoshimura, K., 52
Youdim, K. A., 457
Young, A., 152
Young, A. M., 379
Young, H. M., 455
Young, K. M., 227
Young, S. E., 51
Young-Wolff, K. C., 51
Youniss, J., 311
Yu, J. W., 244
Yubero, S., 208
Yun-Fang, T., 442
Yurgelun-Todd, D. A., 292, 450

Z

Zaborski, L. B., 396
Zacks, J. M., 112
Zacks, R. T., 458
Zahn-Waxler, C., 143
Zakama, A., 324
Zamsky, E. S., 268
Zander, L., 83
Zang, Z., 123
Zanjani, F. A. K., 351
Zanolie, K., 290
Zarit, S. H., 419, 483
Zavattini, G. C., 94
Zdravkovic, T., 79
Zeanah, C., 138
Zeidner, M., 351
Zeintl, M., 459
Zeisel, S. A., 123
Zembar, M. J., 219, 257
Zerwas, S., 143
Zezza, M., 488
Zhang, J., 396
Zhao, J., 188
Zhu, L., 126, 166
Ziebland, S., 396
Zigler, E., 120, 326, 374
Zimmer-Gembeck, M. J., 201
Zimmerman, J., 452
Zimmerman, M. A., 328
Zimmerman, S., 491
Zimprich, D., 437, 475, 476
Zinke, K., 459
Ziporyn, T. D., 397
Zoe, Y., 73
Zosuls, K. M., 263, 264
Zucker, M. S., 115
Zucker, N. L., 282
Zvolensky, M. J., 187

SUBJECT INDEX

A

AAIDD. *See* American Association on Intellectual and Development Disabilities (AAIDD)
ABA. *See* Applied behavior analysis (ABA)
Abusive head trauma, 106
Accommodation, 17, 117
Acetylcholine, 466
Achievement motivation, 237
Acquired immune deficiency syndrome (AIDS), 75–77, 340
Active euthanasia, 505–506
Activities of daily living, 491
Adaptation, 16, 117
Adenine (A), 36
ADHD. *See* Attention-deficit/hyperactivity disorder (ADHD)
Adolescence
  body image and adjustments, 281, 283–284
  characteristics of emerging adulthood, 278
  cognitive changes, 290–294, 296–298
  decision making in, 296–297
  and delinquency, 322
  depression in, 324–326
  development in cultural and historical context, 275–278
  developmental tasks, 304–309
  drug usage, 318–322
  and eating disorders, 282–283
  and family dynamics, 310–311, 313
  gender identity and sexual practices, 284–289
  high-risk behaviors in, 326
  identity formation, 305–309
  intergenerational communication, 310–311, 313
  moral development, 297–298
  mother–son conflict patterns during, 310
  and parental interactions, 317
  peer relations, 313–317
  periods of, 276
  physical development and adaptation, 278–281, 283–284
  psychological disorders in, 326
  risks and resilience in, 318–323
  scope and content of thoughts, 294, 296–298
  sexual abuse in, 322–323
  sexual behavior, consequences of, 286–289
  social comparison, 313–315
  stress, depression, and coping, 323–328
  suicide, risk factors, 325
  in United States, 276–278
Adolescent growth spurt, 278
Adolescents, launching of, 420
Adult children, relationships with, 420–423
Adult development, Peck's Issues of, 418
Adult life cycle, 373
Affordable Care Act, 407
Afterbirth, 82
Age-adjusted death rates, 402, 403
Age clocks, 334
Age cohort, 59
Age of viability, 70
Age segregation, 276
Ageism, 442
Ageist stereotypes, 442–445
Aggression, 191–194
Aggressive behavior, 262
  due to prenatal exposure to cocaine, 80
  and TV violence, 26, 27
Aging
  biological clock theories of, 457
  causes of, 456–457
  cognitive changes, 458–468
  demographics of, 487–489
  health, disease, and nutrition, 452–456
  life expectancy, 445–447
  modern times, 442–445
  pathological factors, 448
  and personality, 472–478
  physical aspects of, 447–452
  successful, 477–478
Aging parents, relationships with, 423–425
AIDS. *See* Acquired immune deficiency syndrome (AIDS)
Ainsworth's strange-situation test, 136
Alcohol consumption, by young people, 320–321
Alcohol, effect on pregnancy, 77, 79
Alleles, 40
Alzheimer's disease, 464–468
American Association on Intellectual and Development Disabilities (AAIDD), 241
American Society for Aesthetic Plastic Surgery (ASAPS), 444
Amniocentesis, 85, 86
Amniotic fluid, 68
Amniotic sac, 68
Amphetamine, 78
Anal fixation, 143
Anal stage, 12
Androgens, 279
Androgynous personality, 203
Angelman syndrome (AS), 46, 47
Animism, 165, 168
Anorexia nervosa, 281
Anoxia, 80
Anticipatory grief, 509–510
Apgar scale, 88
Apgar scoring system, 88
Applied behavior analysis (ABA), 55–56
Apprenticeship, 18
Arousal states, 101
Arranged marriages, 367–368
ART. *See* Assisted reproductive technologies (ART)
Artificial insemination, 92
AS. *See* Angelman syndrome (AS)
ASPAS. *See* American Society for Aesthetic Plastic Surgery (ASAPS)
Asperger's disorder, 246
Assertiveness, 191
Assimilation, 17, 117, 165
Assisted reproductive technologies (ART), 91, 92
Assisted suicide, 506
Associative play, 198
Asthma, 223–224
Atherosclerosis, 453
Attachment relationships, 94–95
  avoidant, 136
  and behavioral problems, 138
  culture, role of, 140–141
  disorganized/disoriented, 137
  effects of, 137–138
  infant and toddler, 136–137
  insecure, 136
  parent–child interaction, nature of, 140
  reciprocal nature of, 139–140
  relationship with trust, 140
  resistant, 136
  secure, 136, 142
  and separation, 144–145
Attention-deficit/hyperactivity disorder (ADHD), 225, 244–245
Attitudinal independence, 363
Auditory perception, 115
Authoritarian parents, 206, 207
Authoritative parents, 206–207
Autism, 114, 225, 245
Autism spectrum disorder, 225, 245–247
Automaticity, 162
Autonomy versus shame and doubt, 142
Autosomal disorders, 44, 45–47
Autosomes, 39
Avoidant attachment, 136

B

Babbling, 122
Baby biographies, 21
Baby boomers, 59, 309
Base, 36
Base pair, 36
Basic emotions, 131
Bear walking, 105
Behavior genetics, 50–53
Behavior, shaping of, 55
Behavioral inhibition, 187
Behavioral views, 20
Behaviorism, 13
Bereavement, 508–509
Bereavement overload, 510
Beta-endorphin, 92
Bilingual education, 179
Bilingualism, 176–177
Binge drinking, by young adults, 318–319
Bioecological model, 18–20
Biological age, 335
Biological clock theories of aging, 457
Biological factors, influencing development, 4
Biological views, 20, 125–126
Birth order, 209–210
Birthing centers, 84
Bisexual persons, 345
Blastula, 67–68
Blended family, 431–433
Blood-clotting disorder, 44
Bobo doll experiment, 27
Bodily–kinesthetic intelligence, 234
Body mass index, 222–223
"Boomerang generation," 422
Botox injections, 445
Bottle-feeding, 109–110
Bowlby's stages of attachment, 139
Brain development
  for adolescence, 290, 291–292
  for early childhood, 159–161
  for middle childhood, 220–222
Brain growth spurt, 100, 159
Brain lateralization, 221
Braxton–Hicks contractions, 82
Brazelton Neonatal Behavioral Assessment Scale, 88
Breast milk, 110
Breastfeeding, 109–110, 111
Breech presentation, 87
Bulimia nervosa, 281

C

C-section, 87–88
Caffeine, 78
Calorie deficiency, 109
Career counseling, 379
Careers
  adjustment process in workplace, 378
  choices, 379–380
  gender discrimination, 380
  Holland's theory, 379–380
  midcareer, 379
  occupational choice and preparation, 380
  role of mentors, 379
  stages of occupational life, 377–378
  women and, 381–387
CAs. See Chronological ages (CAs)
Cataract, 450
Categories, 117
Causation, 26
Cell division, 39–40
Cell membrane, 35
Cells, 35
  replication of, 39
Centration, 168
Cephalocaudal trend, 71
Cesarean section surgery, 87–88
Child abuse, 153
Child care, cross-cultural perspectives of, 148, 151
Child maltreatment, 153, 210–214
Child neglect, 153
Child rearing, 6
Childbirth
  approaches to, 82–84
  complications in, 87–89
  practices of, 84

stages of, 81–82
technology, advances in, 84–86
traditional, 84. *See also* Pregnancy
Childhood
in ancient Western civilizations, 6
cultural influences on, 6–8
historical views of, 5–6
in modern times, 6
poverty and environmental stress on children, impact of, 25
and punishment, 6
social and political factors affecting, 8
Children and war, 7
Chlamydia, 343
Cholinesterase inhibitor drugs, 466
Chorionic villus sampling (CVS), 84, 85–86
Chromosomal breakage, 45
Chromosomal disorders, 44
Chromosomes, 39
Chronic grief, 511
Chronological ages (CAs), 232
Chronological approach, study of development, 2, 3
Classical conditioning, 13–14, 16, 54
Climacteric, 397–399
Clique members, 316
Cocaine, 78
effect on pregnancy, 80
Codominance, 41
Cognitive development
early childhood, 164, 177–181
of infants, 116–121
middle childhood
control processes, 230
individual differences in intelligence, 231–236
language and literacy development, 230–231
memory and metacognition, 229–230
preoperational and concrete operational thinking, 227–228
Piaget's theory of, 16–17
play and, 177–181
Cognitive-developmental theories, 16, 185, 251
Cognitive domain development, 8
Cognitive mechanics, 408
Cognitive pragmatics, 408
Cognitive views, 20
Cohabiting couples, 370
Cohort effects, 24
Cold decision process, 296–297
Collective monologues, 174
Collectivist cultures, 7
Color blindness, 44
Color discrimination, 112
Colorado Adoption Project, 51
Colostrum, 94
Command generation, 392
Commitment, 305
Competition, 7
Componential intelligence, 234
Conception, 66
Concordance rates, 51
Concrete operational period, 227
Concrete operational thinking, 227–229
Conditioning principles, 55–56
Conditions of worth, 362
Confidentiality, 30
Conflictual independence, 363
Confounding, 24
Congenital anomalies, 44, 73
Conservation problems, 168–169
Context, 5
development in, 30
Contextual intelligence, 234
Contextual paradigms, 335
Control group, 30
Control processes, 229–230
Cooperative play, 198
Coping, Kübler-Ross's stage theory of, 500
Coregulation, 265
Corporal punishment, 6
Correlation, 24, 28
coefficients, 26
Counseling, genetic, 48, 50
Crisis model, 393
Cross-sectional designs, 24
Crowd, 315
Crystallized intelligence, fluid versus, 408–410
Culture, 3, 5, 135
CVS. *See* Chorionic villus sampling (CVS)
Cystic fibrosis, 46
Cytoplasm, 35, 36

D

Data, 10
Dating, 316–317
Day mothers, 151
Death and dying
of a child, 512
adjustments, 500
completion of life cycle, 514–515
confronting with death, 499–503
coping with terminal illness, 500–501
due to illness, 500–501
grief and bereavement, 508–514
hospice concept, 504–505
humane end-of-life care for children and their families, 513
right to die, 505–508
rituals and customs, 511–512
society's general attitude toward, 503
suicide, 502–503
thoughts and fears of, 496–499
Decision/commitment, 366
Declarative knowledge, 410
Defense mechanism, 188, 189
Deferred imitation, 119
Delinquency, 322
Dementia, 451, 462
Deoxyribonucleic acid (DNA), 35–38, 43
Dependent variable, 27
Depth perception, of infants, 114–115
Descriptive methods, 21–23
Development, 2
Developmental neuroscience, 10–11
Developmental niche, 56
Developmental periods, or stages, 2, 3, 8
Developmental psychologists, 2, 10, 22
Developmental research, ethics in, 29–30
Developmental trends, 71
Deviation IQ approach, 232
Dia de los Muertos, 511
Diabetes, 76
Dialectical thought, 348
Differentiation process, 67
Diffusion status, 306, 307
Discrepancy hypothesis, 141
Discrimination, 262
Disorganized/disoriented attachment, 136
Distance perception, of infants, 114–115
Dizygotic (fraternal) twins, 68
DNA. *See* Deoxyribonucleic acid (DNA)
Dominant, 40
Double helix, 36
Down Syndrome, 39, 45–46
Dramatic play, 179
Dual-earner couple, 383
Dyslexia, 242, 244

E

Early amniocentesis, 85
Early childhood
aggression and prosocial behavior, 191–196
child abuse and neglect, impact, 211–212
cognitive development, 164
coping behavior
emotional regulation, 188–189
fear and anxiety, 186–188
developmental conflicts, 196–197
family dynamics
discipline, rules of, 208–209
parenting styles, 205–208
siblings, role of, 209–210
imaginary companions, 198–199
language development, 173–177
motor skills development, 161–164
peer relations and playing, 198–201
physical development, 158–161
play and learning, 177–181
social competence, 199–201
social concepts and rules, 201–202
Early-onset Alzheimer's disease, 465
Early parenthood, effects of, 288–289
Eclampsia, 76
Economic downturn, 382
Economic factors, influencing development, 8
Ectoderm, 69
Ectopic (tubal) pregnancy, 84
Ego, 12
Ego identity, 13
Egocentrism
adolescence, 294, 296
early childhood, 165, 168, 178
Electronic media, 194
Embryo, 69
Embryonic disk, 68
Embryonic period, 68–69
Emergent literacy, 230
Emerging adulthood, 3, 276
Emotional development, 131–132
Emotional independence, 363
Emotional intelligence (EQ), 349, 350–351
Emotional regulation, 188–189
Emotional responses, 54
Empathy, 114, 143
Empty nest, 422
Enculturation, 8
End-of-life care, 508
Endocrine glands, 278
Endoderm, 69
Endoplasmic reticulum, 35, 36
Environmental factors, influencing development, 4
Environmental pollutants and radiation, 80–81
Epigenetics, 10
principle of, 13
study of, 43–44
Episiotomy, 82
EQ. *See* Emotional intelligence (EQ)
Erikson, Erik, 12–13
generativity versus self-absorption, 417
identity versus identity confusion, 305
industry versus inferiority, 252
initiative versus guilt, 197
integrity versus despair, 472–473
intimacy versus isolation, 353
psychosocial theory, 12–13, 14
stages of development autonomy versus shame and doubt, 142
theory of development, 12–13, 353
trust versus mistrust, 140
Escherichia coli, 37
Estrogen, 279
Ethical dilemmas, in gene testing, 49
Ethnicity, 38
and adolescence, 308
development, 263–264
middle adulthood, 406–407
young adulthood, 380
Ethnocentrism, 57
Euthanasia, 505
Evolutionary theory, 11, 20
Experiential intelligence, 234
Experimental research methods, 28
Explaining attachment, 138–140
Extrinsic factors, 364
Extrinsically motivated behavior, 164
Extroversion, 134

F

Failure-to-thrive syndrome, 153
Fallopian tubes, 67
False labor, 82
Family
as a transmitter of culture, 57–58
and childbirth, 92–95
and infancy and early childhood, 145–151
systems, 56–57
extended, 58
transition to parenthood, 89, 91
Family alliances, 310–311
Family and Medical Leave Act (FMLA) of 1993, 387
Family leave, 387
Family life cycle, 373
FAS. *See* Fetal alcohol syndrome (FAS)
FASD. *See* Fetal alcohol spectrum disorder (FASD)
Fear and anxiety
causes of, 186
coping with, 188
historical, cultural, and developmental influences, 187–188
individual differences in, 186–187

Fertility drugs, 92
Fertilization, 67
Fetal alcohol spectrum disorder (FASD), 79, 96
Fetal alcohol syndrome (FAS), 79
Fetal monitors, 86
Fetal period, 69–71
Fetoscopy, 86
Fetus, 70
Filial piety, 442
Fine motor skills, 105, 162–163
  in middle childhood, 220
Five-factor model, 436–437
"Five Wishes" method, 503, 504, 507
Fluid versus crystallized intelligence, 408–410
FMLA of 1993. *See* Family and Medical Leave Act (FMLA) of 1993
fMRI. *See* Functional magnetic resonance imaging (fMRI)
Fontanels, 92
Footedness, 160
Foreclosure status, 305, 307
Formal operational thinking, 292–293
FOXP2 gene mutation, 125
Fragile Families and Child Well-Being Study, 25
Fragile X syndrome, 45
Freud, Sigmund, 11–13
Freud's psychoanalytic theory, 12
Freud's psychosexual stages, 12
Friendship development, Selman's stages of, 258
Friendships, 426
  adult, 365
  children's concepts of, 257
  and dating, 316–317
  developmental patterns in, 257–259
  in-groups and out-groups, 262–264
  peer groups, 259, 261–262
Frustration, 191
Functional independence, 363
Functional magnetic resonance imaging (fMRI), 114
Functional subordination, 162

G

Gametes, 40
Gardner's eight types of intelligence, 234, 235
Gay and lesbian, 345, 370
Gender, 203
Gender constancy, 204
"Gender gap," 382
Gender identity, 203–205
Gender-role stereotypes, 204
Gender roles, 203
Gender schemes, 204
Gene imprinting, 47
Gene testing, ethical dilemmas in, 49
Gene therapies, 50
Gene–environment Interactions, 43–44
Genes, 38
  combination of, 41
Genetic disorders, 44
Genetics, 10
  adoption studies, 51–53
  anomalies, 44
  behavior, 50–53
  cell division and reproduction, 39–40
  counseling, 48, 50
  disorders, 44–50
  DNA, 35–38
  engineering and cloning, 52
  environmental influences and contexts, 53–56
  genes, 38
  genotypes and phenotypes, 40–41
  human cells, 35
  inheritance of traits, 41
  molecular, 35–38
  protein synthesis, 38
  recessiveness in, 40
  research and treatment, advances in, 50
  twin studies, 51–53
Genital stage, 12
Genotypes, 40
Germinal period, conception and, 66–68
Gesell Scales, 103
Gestational diabetes testing, 86
Glaucoma, 450
Glial cells, 99
Golgi apparatus, 35
Golgi complex, 36
Gonorrhea, 76, 343
Grammar, 122
Grammar acquisition, stages of, 173
Grandparents, 425–426
"Gray matter," 221
Grief work, 509
Gross motor skills, 105, 161–162
  in middle childhood, 220
Gross-to-specific trend, 71
Groups, experiments focusing on, 26–28
Growth trends, 104
Guided participation, 18
Guidelines, for research with human participants
  beneficial treatments, 30
  informed consent, 29–30
  knowledge of results, 30
  privacy and confidentiality, 30
  protection from harm, 29

H

HAART. *See* Highly active antiretroviral therapies (HAART)
Habituation method, of learning, 54, 101–102, 120
Handedness, 160
Havighurst's developmental model, of traditional one-career work cycle, 378
hcg. *See* Human chorionic gonadotropin (hcg)
Head-to-body proportion
  early childhood, 159
  during infancy, 104
Health
  accidents and injuries, 224
  asthma, 223–224
  obesity, 222–223
  physical fitness, 222
  psychological disorders and mental illness, 224–225, 227
Health habits, cumulative effects of, 403–405
Hearing perception, 115
Hemophilia A and B, 45
Heritability, 51
Herpes, 343
Herpes simplex, 76
Heterozygous allele, 41
High-risk pregnancies, 86
Highly active antiretroviral therapies (HAART), 77
HIV. *See* Human immunodeficiency virus (HIV)
HIV/AIDS infections, 340–343
Holophrastic speech, 123
Home birthing, 82–83
Homophobia, 346–347
Homosexuality. *See* Same-sex orientation; Sexual orientation
Homozygous allele, 41
Hormone replacement therapy (HRT), 398–399
Hormone therapy, 92
Hormones
  changes in lifetime, 278–279
  influence on brain, 291–292
  raging, 279
Hospice, 504–505
Hostile aggression, 191
HRT. *See* Hormone replacement therapy (HRT)
Human cells, 35
Human chorionic gonadotropin (hcg), 68
Human development, 161
  behavioral views of, 13–16
  biological and environmental influences, 4–5
  domains of, 8
  guiding themes in, 4
  lifespan theory, 19–20
  nature of, 4–8
  scientific approach to the study of
    correlational study, 24, 26
    cross-sectional method, 24
    descriptive methods, 21–23
    ethics in, 29–30
    experimental methods, 26
    longitudinal studies, 23, 24
    sequential-cohort design, 24
  significance of sociocultural context in, 4–8
  theoretical frameworks
    behaviorist approach, 13–16
    biological views of, 10–11
    cognitive views, 16–18
    integrating theoretical approaches, 18–20
    psychodynamic approach, 11–13
    role of theories, 9–10
    systems approach, 18–19
Human genome, 10
Human immunodeficiency virus (HIV), 76, 340
Human karyotypes, 39
Human lifespan, developmental periods in, 3
Huntington's disease, 46
Hypertension, 450
Hypothalamus, 279

I

Id, 12
IDEA. *See* Individuals with Disabilities Education Act (IDEA)
IDEIA. *See* Individuals with Disabilities Education Improvement Act (IDEIA)
Identity achievement, 306, 307
Identity crisis, 305
Identity formation, modes of, 305
Identity status, 305
Idiosyncratic events, 333
IEP. *See* Individual education plan (IEP)
IGT. *See* Iowa Gambling Task (IGT)
IHDP. *See* Infant Health and Development Program (IHDP)
Imaginary audience, 296
Imaginary companions, 198–199
Imitation, 114, 120, 124–125
Imprinting, 138
Incomplete dominance, 41
Independent assortment, 42
Independent variable, 27
Indifferent parents, 206, 207
Individual development, factors influencing, 59
Individual education plan (IEP), 240
Individualist cultures, 7–8
Individuals with Disabilities Education Act (IDEA), 240
Individuals with Disabilities Education Improvement Act (IDEIA), 240, 244
Industry versus inferiority, 252
Infancy and early childhood
  arousal states, 101
  attachment, 136–141, 144–145
  autonomy, development of, 142–143
  brain's plasticity in, 100
  child abuse and neglect, 153–154
  child care, 148, 151
  children with special needs
    hearing impairments, 152
    severe disabilities, 152
    visual impairments, 151–152
  cognitive development, 116–121
  competence of the newborn, 102
  cultural differences in motor development, 103
  developing brain, 99–100
  disciplining, 142–143
  emotional development, 131–132
  and family system, 145–151
  feeding and comforting, 134–135
  grandparents' roles, 147–148
  gross motor skills, 105
  habituation method of learning, 101–102
  hearing and auditory perception, 115
  language development, 121–127
  linguistic rules, 124
  malnutrition, impact of, 108
  motor milestones, 104
  neonatal period, 100–103

physical and motor development
first four months, 104–105
five to eight months, 105
nine to twelve months, 105, 107
nineteen to twenty four months, 107
thirteen to eighteen months, 107
prosocial behavior, development of, 143
self, development of, 143–144
senses of taste and smell, 115–116
sensory and perceptual development, 112–116
sensory integration, 116
and social referencing, 141–142
stranger anxiety or separation anxiety, 141, 143
temperament, 133
toilet training, 143
trust, development of, 134–136
vision and visual perception, 112–115
weaning, 110–111
Infant Health and Development Program (IHDP), 58
Infant health care, 70
Infant mortality rates, 70, 71
Infant reflexes, 93–95
Infertility treatment, common approaches to, 92
Influenza, 76
Information-processing functions, 293
Informed consent, 29–30
Initial labor, 82
Initiative versus guilt, 197
Insecure attachment, 136, 138
Institutional Review Boards (IRBs), 29
Instrumental activities of daily living, 491
Instrumental aggression, 191
Integrating theoretical approaches, 18–20
Intellectual disability, 240–242
Intelligence, 231–236
Intelligence quotient (IQ), 232
Interactive approach, to study of development, 3–4
Interdependence, 304
Intergenerational communication, 310–311, 313
Internalization, 201
Interpersonal intelligence, 234
Interviews, 22
Intimacy, 365
in adolescent friendship, 314
Intrapersonal intelligence, 234
Intrauterine insemination (IUI), 92
Intrinsic factors, 364
Intrinsically motivated behavior, 164
Intuitive/transitional period, 165
Iodine deficiency, 109
Iowa Gambling Task (IGT), 297
IQ. *See* Intelligence quotient (IQ)
IRBs. *See* Institutional Review Boards (IRBs)
Iron deficiency, 109
IUI. *See* Intrauterine insemination (IUI)

J

Job burnout, 435–436
Justice, 257

K

Kangaroo care, 89, 90
Karyotypes, 39
Kibbutz, 57
Kinkeeper, 420
Klinefelter syndrome, 45
Kohlberg's six-stage model of moral development, 255, 256
Kübler-Ross's stage theory, 500
Kung-San culture, 82, 142
Kwashiorkor, 108

L

Laboratory observation, 22
LAD. *See* Language acquisition device (LAD)
Language acquisition device (LAD), 125
Language development
early childhood
expanding grammar, 173–174
influence of parent's language use, 175–176
multicultural aspects, 176–177
subtleties of speech, 174–175
words and concepts, 173
infants, 121–127
middle childhood, 230–231
schooling and, 230
Language explosion, 123–124
Language, structure and function of, 121
Late-maturing boys, 283–284
Latency stage, 12
Lateralization, 159–160
LBW. *See* Low birth weight (LBW)
Learning, 5
during early childhood, 163–164, 177–181
habituation method of, 101–102
during middle childhood, 236–239
Learning disorders, 242, 244
Learning motor skills, 163–164
Learning/habituation-based methods, 112
Lesbian, 345
Life structure, 353
Lifespan
brain development, 160–161
developmental periods in human lifespan, 2–4
developmental stages throughout, 14
fertility, patterns of, 342
human development theory of, 19–20
profile on influences, 60
and sexuality, 279
sociocultural influences on development across, 58–61
Linguistic intelligence, 234
Linguistic terminology, 122
Liver spots, 448
Living will, 506
Logical–mathematical intelligence, 234
Loners, 316
Longitudinal designs, 23–24
Longitudinal studies, 58
Love theory, 365–367
Low birth weight (LBW), 88
Lung cancer, 404

M

MA. *See* Mental age (MA)
Macromolecule, 36
MADD. *See* Mothers Against Drunk Driving (MADD)
Malnutrition, 73–74, 107–111, 161
and brain development, 161
during infancy and early childhood, 107–111
protein, 109
Marasmus, 108
Marginal group, 281
Marijuana, 78, 321
effect on pregnancy, 80
Marriage, 368–370
and divorce, 428–431
Maslow's hierarchy of needs, 362
Maternal age, 73
Maternal blood analysis, 86
Maternal diseases, 75–77
Maternal health and nutrition, 73–74
Maternal high blood pressure, 76
Maturation, 5
cultural influences on, 103–104
Mediating factors, 59–60
Medical power of attorney, 506
Medicare, 488
Meiosis, 41–42
Memory processes, 120
early childhood, 171–173
Men
changing body proportions in girls and boys from birth to maturity, 159
fathering styles, 145–147
father's role, 91
hormonal changes, 278–279
and moral development, 256
phenotypes, 44
physical changes in adolescence, 280
and school success, 238–239
sex chromosomes in, 39
sex-linked traits in, 41
sexual maturation, 280
Menarche, 280–281
Menopause, 5, 397–398
Menstruation, onset of, 281
Mental age (MA), 232
Mental health, environmental influences on, 434
Mental retardation. *See* Intellectual disability
Mesoderm, 69
Meta-analysis technique, 52
Metacognition, 230
Methamphetamine-exposed infants, 80
Microcephaly, 84
Microtubules, 36
MID. *See* Multi-infarct dementia (MID)
Midcareer reassessment, 436
Middle adulthood
changes in capabilities, 396
cognitive development, 408–412
conceptions of midlife, 393–394
development in, 392–394
disease and health, 402–407
family dynamics, 427–433
interpersonal interactions, 420–426
occupational continuity and change, 433–436
personal reactions, 418–420
personality changes, 436–438
physical continuity and change, 395–401
tasks of, 417–418
Middle childhood
cognitive development
control processes, 230
individual differences in intelligence, 231–236
language and literacy development, 230–231
memory and metacognition, 229–230
preoperational and concrete operational thinking, 227–229
crisis of industry versus inferiority, 252
divorce, impact of, 270
family influences in, 264–271
intellectual and developmental disabilities, 240–242, 244–247
learning and thinking, in school, 236–239
major theoretical perspectives on, 251
peer relations, 257–264
personality development, 251–253
physical and motor development, 219
health, 222–226, 227
motor skills development, 220
physical growth and change, 219–220
skeletal changes, 219–220
social knowledge and reasoning, 253–257
Midlife
crisis model, 393–394
perceptions and realities at, 394
"MIDUS refresher" component, 407
Midwife, 83
Milestones, in language development, 122
Mirror neurons, 113–114
Mistrust, 135, 140
Mitochondria, 35, 36
disorders, 47–48
Mitosis, 39
Molding, 92
Molecular genetics
DNA, 35–38
genes, 38
human cells, 35
protein synthesis, 38
Monozygotic (identical) twins, 68
Moral absolutism, 256
Moral development
in adolescence, 297–298
Freud's view of, 10
Kohlberg's six-stage model, 256
men and, 256
Moral dilemmas, 255
Moral realism, 255
Moral relativism, 255
Morality development
in middle childhood, 254–257
Piaget's view of, 255
Moratorium status, 306, 307
Morphemes, 122
Mothers Against Drunk Driving (MADD), 514
Motor milestones, 104

Motor skills development, 8, 220
  fine motor skills, 162–163
  gross motor skills, 161–162
  learning and motor skills, 163–164
Multi-infarct dementia (MID), 464
Musical intelligence, 234
Mutation, 42
Myelin, 99, 221
Myelination, 99, 159

N

Narcotics, 78
Natural selection theory, 11
Naturalist intelligence, 234
Naturalistic observation, 22
Natural/prepared childbirth, 84
NBAS. *See* Neonatal Behavioral Assessment Scale (NBAS)
NBO system. *See* Newborn Behavioral Observation (NBO) system
Negative correlations, 26
Neo-Freudian, 12
Neonatal assessment, 102–103
Neonatal Behavioral Assessment Scale (NBAS), 102
Neonatal period, 100–103
Neonate, 92
Neural tube, 69
Neurons, 99
Neuroticism, 436
Newborn Behavioral Observation (NBO) system, 102
Nitrogen–carbon–hydrogen bases, 36
No Child Left Behind Act, 240
Nonagenarians, 446
Nonnormative influences, 59
Normative age-graded influences, 59
Normative events, 333
Normative history-graded influences, 59
North American Menopause Society 2012, 399
Novelty paradigm, 112
Nucleotides, 36
Nucleus, 36
Nurse–Family Partnerships, 81, 83
Nursing homes, 489–490
Nutrient deficiencies, 109
Nutrition, 73–74, 107–111

O

Obesity, childhood, 222–223
Object permanence, 118–119
Object play, 118–119
Observational studies, 22
Occupational cycle, 377–380
Octogenarians, 446
Older adulthood. *See* also Aging
  continuity and change, 474–477
  developmental tasks, 472–474
  emotional development, 474
  family and friends, 482–487
  retirement, 478–482
  U.S. social policy for, 487–492
    day-care centers, older adults, 490
    nursing homes, older adults, 489–490
    social security and Medicare programs, 488
  widowers/widows, 483–487
Onlooker play, 198
Operant conditioning, 14–15, 54–55
Oral fixation, 12
Oral stage, 12
Ossification, 158
Osteoporosis, 398, 413
OTC drugs. *See* Over-the-counter (OTC) drugs
"Other-race" effect, 113
Over-the-counter (OTC) drugs, 77, 78
Overextensions, 123, 124
Overregularize, 174
Ovulation, 67
Oxytocin, 94

P

Palliative care, 507–508
Palmar grasp, 93
Parallel play, 178, 180, 198
Parental conditions, 48
Parental control, 206
Parental discipline, 145
Parental warmth, 206
Parent–child, interactions and relationships, 265
Parenthood, stages of, 374
Parenting styles, impact on childhood development, 205–208
Partial schedules, 55
Passion, love, 366
Passive euthanasia, 506–507
Pathological aging factors, 448
PCBs. *See* Polychlorinated biphenyl compounds (PCBs)
Peer acceptance, 262
Peer group conformity, 259, 261
Peers, role of, 180–181
Perception, 112
Perceptual organization, 117
Perceptual skill, 8
Permissive parents, 206, 207
Personal fable, 296
Personality, 131
  five factors of, 437, 438
Personality domain development, 8
Phallic stage, 12
Phenotypes, 40
Phenylketonuria (PKU), 44, 46
Phobias, 54
Phonemes, 121, 122
Physical domain development, 8
Physical fitness, 222
  during young adulthood, 337–338
Piaget, Jean, 16
  concept of schemes, 117
  education, 228–229
  matchstick problem, 228
  period of formal operations, 292–293
  preoperational and concrete operational thinking, 227–228
  sensorimotor period, 117–120
  theory of cognitive development, 16–17
Pincer grasp, 107
Pituitary gland, 279
PKU. *See* Phenylketonuria (PKU)
Placenta, 68
Plasticity, of brain, 100
Play
  cognitive development, 177–181
  cultural variations in, 199
  development of, 198
Pneumonia, 46
Polar bodies, 40
Polychlorinated biphenyl compounds (PCBs), 78
Polygenic inheritance, 41
Positive correlations, 26
Postformal thinking, 349
Posttraumatic stress disorder (PTSD), in children, 7, 267
Posttraumatic stress syndrome, 267
Practice, 163
Prader–Willi syndrome (PWS), 46, 47
Pragmatics, 174–175
Preconceptual period, 165
Preference paradigm, 112
Pregnancy
  childbirth
    approaches to, 82–84
    complications, 87–89
    contemporary practices, 84
    prenatal screening, 84–86
    stages of, 81–82
  prenatal environmental influences
    critical periods in prenatal development, 74–75
    maternal age, 73
    maternal health and nutrition, 73–74
    prenatal health care, 74
    teratogens, effect of, 75–81
  prenatal growth and development
    conception and germinal period, 66–68
    development of twins, 68
    developmental trends, 71–72
    effects of selected drugs and chemicals on, 78
    embryonic period, 68–69
    fetal period, 69–71
    trimesters and periods, 66
  teenage, 287–288
Preimplantation genetic diagnosis, 86
Preimplantion screening, 86
Prejudice, 262
Premature birth, 88–89
Premature infants, 88–89
Prenatal assessment methods, 86
Prenatal development
  critical periods of, 74–75
  maternal age and, 73
Prenatal health care, 74
Prenatal mercury exposure, 80
Prenatal PCB exposure, 81
Prenatal screening, 84–86
Preoperational period, 165
Preoperational thinking, 164–165
  conservation, 168–169
  early childhood
    limitations, 167–168
    substages, 165, 167
  memory, role of, 171–173
  middle childhood, 227–229
  Piaget's perspective, 170–171
  Piaget's theory evaluation, 169–170
  substages and thought, 165, 167
Preoperational thought, characteristics of, 168
Preoperational versus concrete operational thought, in children, 227
Prepared childbirth, 84
Preterm status, 88
Primitive reflexes, 93
Privacy, 30
Private speech, 174
Procedural knowledge, 410
Productive language, 121
Progesterone, 279
Prolactin, 94
Prosocial behavior, 143, 194–196
Protein deficiency, 109
Protein malnutrition, 109
Protein synthesis, 38
Proteins, 38
Proximal development, zone of, 170–171
Proximodistal trend, 71
Psychoanalytic approach, 11–12
Psychoanalytic theory, 12
Psychoanalytic view, 185
Psychodynamic approach, 11
Psychodynamic theories, 11–13
Psychodynamic views, 20, 251
Psychological abuse, 212
Psychological age, 335
Psychological cues, 392
Psychological harm, 29
Psychological tests, 23
Psychosexual stages, 12
Psychosocial stages, 14
Psychosocial theory, 13
PTSD. *See* Posttraumatic stress disorder (PTSD)
Puberty, 279–281
Public Law 94-142 (PL 94-142), 240
Punishments, 54
PWS. *See* Prader–Willi syndrome (PWS)

Q

Quad screen, 86
Quasi-experimental method, 28
Questionnaires, 22–23

R

Radiation, 78
  environmental pollutants and, 80–81
Raging hormones, 279
Random assignment, 26, 27
Rationalization, 188, 189
Readiness, 163
Realistic play, 118
Recall, 171–172
Receptive language, 121
Recessive, 40
Recessiveness, in genetics, 40
Recognition, 171–172
Recombinant alleles, 41
Recombinant DNA techniques, 50
Reconstituted family. *See* Blended family
Reflexes, 93, 118

Reification, 165, 168
Reinforcement views, 54, 124–125
Relationships, cause-and-effect of, 26
Replication/replicate, 27–28
of cells, 39
Representative sampling, 23
Reproductive technologies, 91
Resilient children, 267
Resistant attachment, 136
Retirement, 478–482
Retirement maturity index, 482
Retroviruses, 50
Rh factor, 76
Rh incompatibility, 76
Ribosomes, 36
Right to die, 505–508
Rite of passage, 275
Robert Sternberg's triarchic (three-part) theory of intelligence, 234
Rogers, Carl, 362–363
Role conflict, 419
Role strain, 419
Rosenzweig's results, 100
Rothbart's broad dimensions of temperament, 134
Rubella (German measles), 75, 76

S

Same-sex orientation, 285
Scaffolding, 171, 265
Schaie's stages of adult thinking, 351
sex and sexuality, 342–347
single parenthood, 375–377
transition to parenthood, 373–374
understanding the developmental changes in
Erikson's theory of development, 353
Gould's transformations in early adulthood, 355–356
Havighurst's developmental tasks, 352–353
Levinson's seasons of a man's life, 353–354
Schemas, 17, 117
Schemes. *See* Schemas
Schizophrenia, 324
Sebaceous (oil-producing) glands, 278
Secular trend, 280
Secure attachment, 136
Self-actualization, 362
Self-concept, 56, 143, 145, 202, 252, 362–363
Self-discovery, 105
Self-efficacy, 56
Self-esteem, 252–253
Self-regulated behavior, 265
Self-regulation, 304
Self-socialization, 204
Selman's stages of friendship development, 258
Semantics, 122
Senescence, 456
Senility, 462
Sensation, 112, 396
Sensorimotor development, overview of, 121
Sensorimotor period, 117–120
Sensorimotor stages, 117
Sensory and perceptual development, 112–116
Sensory integration, 116, 119
Sensuality, 190–191, 401
Separation anxiety, 141
Septuagenarians, 446
Sequential-cohort design, 24
Sex, 203
Sex chromosomes, 39
Sex-linked disorders, 44
Sex-linked genetic disorders, 44–45
Sex-linked traits, 40, 41
Sexual curiosity, 190–191
Sexual double standard, 285
Sexual identity formation, 344
Sexual maturity. *See* Puberty
Sexual orientation, 344–347
Sexual prejudice, 346
Sexual relationships, influencing factors of, 286
Sexual revolution, 285
Sexually transmitted diseases (STDs), 286, 342–353
Shaken baby syndrome, 104–105, 106
Shaping of behavior, 55
Shared goals, 209
Shared meanings, 18
Sibling dynamics, 209–210
Sibling rivalry, 147
Sickle-cell anemia, 41, 46, 48
Sickle-cell trait, 46
SIDS. *See* Sudden infant death syndrome (SIDS)
Silent killer, 454
Single-neuron recording technique, 114
Single parenthood, 375–377
Skeletal maturation, 219–220
Skinner, B. F., 14
Small-for-date indication, 88
Social age, 335
Social cognition, 253–254
Social-cognitive theory, 17–18
Social competence, 199–201
Social concepts, 202
Social ecology, of child care, 148, 151
Social inference, 254
Social isolation, 213
Social learning theory, 15, 56
Social-learning view, 185, 251
Social perspective taking, 254
Social reference groups, 305
Social referencing, 141–142, 145
Social regulations, 254
Social responsibility, 254
Social Security, 480, 481, 488, 489
Social skills, 8
Socialization, 8, 57–58
Society, 5
Sociocentric thinking, 167
Sociocultural context, 4–8
Sociocultural domain development, 8
Solitary play, 198
Somatic (bodily) cells, 35
Sonograms, 84
Spatial intelligence, 234
Special needs children, caring of, 151–154
Sperm cells, 40
Spontaneous abortions, 69
relation with maternal age, 73
Standard amniocentesis, 85
Stanford-Binet Intelligence Scale, 232, 234
Status passages, 472
STDs. *See* Sexually transmitted diseases (STDs)
Step family. *See* Blended family
Sternberg's triangular theory of love, 366
Stochastic theories of aging, 457
Strange-situation test, 136, 137
Stranger and separation anxiety, 141
Stress and coping, dual-process model of, 508–509
Stress and single parent, 268
Stress scale, 405
Strokes, 464
Stunting, 108
Submissive death, 502
Success in school, 238–239
Successive approximations, 55
Sudden infant death syndrome (SIDS), 106
Suicidal erosion, 502
Suicide prevention, American psychological association guidelines for, 326
Superego functions, 12
Superfemale syndrome, 45
Supermale syndrome, 45
Surgery, 92
Surprise paradigm, 112
Surrogacy, 92
Surveys, 22–23, 28
Survival reflexes, 93
Symbolic representation, 120, 167, 168
Synapses, 99
Synchrony, 139
Syntax, 122
Syphilis, 76, 343
Systematic observation, 22
Systems views, 20

T

Tay-Sachs disease, 46
Telegraphic speech, 124
Telomeres, 457
Temperament, 133, 145, 187
Teratogens, 74
Terrible twos, 196
Testosterone, 279
Theories, 9
Theory of mind, early childhood, 166–167
TIAs. *See* Transient ischemic attacks (TIAs)
Tobacco smoking
effect on pregnancy, 79–80
by young adults, 319–320
Toddlers, 99, 105, 123
Toilet training, 143
Toxemia, 76
Toxoplasmosis, 76
Traditional childbirth, 83
Traditional one-career work cycle, Havighurst's developmental model of, 378
Tranquilizers and sleeping pills, 78
Transient ischemic attacks (TIAs), 464
Transition model, 393
Treatment conditions, 27
Trimesters and periods, 66
Trisomy-21, 45–46
Trust, 134–136
development of, 134–136
relationship with attachment, 140
Trust versus mistrust, 140
Turner syndrome, 45
Twin studies, 51–53
Type 1 diabetes, 454
Type 2 diabetes, 454

U

Ultrasound, 84–85, 86
Umbilical cord, 68
Unconscious processes, 12
UNICEF, 109–110
U.S. Civilian Labor Force (1960–2007), percentages of women in, 266
Uterus, 67

V

Vacuum extractor, 82
Vision and visual perception, of infants, 112–115
Visual acuity, 112, 450
Visual cliff apparatus, 115
Visually guided reach, 105
Vitamin A deficiency, 109
Vygotsky, Lev, 17–18, 170–171

W

WAIS. *See* Wechsler Adult Intelligence Scale (WAIS)
War, psychological impacts of, 7
Weaning, 110–111
Wear-and-tear theories, 457
Wechsler Adult Intelligence Scale (WAIS), 232
Wechsler Intelligence Scale for Children (WISC), 232
Wechsler Preschool and Primary Scale of Intelligence (WPPSI), 232
"White matter," 221
WISC. *See* Wechsler Intelligence Scale for Children (WISC)
Wisdom, 461–462
Women. *See also* Pregnancy
hormonal changes, 278–279
and infertility, 46
meiosis in, 40
and menopause, 397–398
and moral development, 256–257
phenotypes, 44
physical changes in adolescence, 280
sex chromosomes in, 39–40
sexual maturation, 280–281
and sexual practices, 285–286
work patterns, 381–382
WPPSI. *See* Wechsler Preschool and Primary Scale of Intelligence (WPPSI)

X

X-chromosome genes, 40, 44

Y

Y-chromosome genes, 40, 44
Young adulthood
age clocks and social norms, 334–335
children's developmental stages, coping with, 374–375
cognitive development, 348–351
contextual paradigms, 335
development of close relationships
cohabitation, 370
couple formation and development, 365–368
friendships, 365
gay and lesbian couples, 370
marriage, 368–370
staying single, 371
family life cycle and, 373
occupational cycle, 377–380
physical development
death rates, 338–339
disease, disability, and physical limitations, 339, 341
fitness and health, 337–339, 341
strength and stamina, 335–337
self conceptualizations, 361–363
Youth literacy rates, 236

Z

Zone of proximal development, 170–171
Zygote, 67